T0189190

Lecture Notes in Computer Science

Lecture Notes in Artificial Intelligence   **14169**

Founding Editor

Jörg Siekmann

Series Editors

Randy Goebel, *University of Alberta, Edmonton, Canada*
Wolfgang Wahlster, *DFKI, Berlin, Germany*
Zhi-Hua Zhou, *Nanjing University, Nanjing, China*

The series Lecture Notes in Artificial Intelligence (LNAI) was established in 1988 as a topical subseries of LNCS devoted to artificial intelligence.

The series publishes state-of-the-art research results at a high level. As with the LNCS mother series, the mission of the series is to serve the international R & D community by providing an invaluable service, mainly focused on the publication of conference and workshop proceedings and postproceedings.

Danai Koutra · Claudia Plant ·
Manuel Gomez Rodriguez · Elena Baralis ·
Francesco Bonchi
Editors

Machine Learning and Knowledge Discovery in Databases

Research Track

European Conference, ECML PKDD 2023
Turin, Italy, September 18–22, 2023
Proceedings, Part I

 Springer

Editors
Danai Koutra ⓘ
University of Michigan
Ann Arbor, MI, USA

Claudia Plant ⓘ
University of Vienna
Vienna, Austria

Manuel Gomez Rodriguez ⓘ
Max Planck Institute for Software Systems
Kaiserslautern, Germany

Elena Baralis ⓘ
Politecnico di Torino
Turin, Italy

Francesco Bonchi ⓘ
CENTAI
Turin, Italy

ISSN 0302-9743   ISSN 1611-3349 (electronic)
Lecture Notes in Artificial Intelligence
ISBN 978-3-031-43411-2   ISBN 978-3-031-43412-9 (eBook)
https://doi.org/10.1007/978-3-031-43412-9

LNCS Sublibrary: SL7 – Artificial Intelligence

Preface

The 2023 edition of the European Conference on Machine Learning and Principles and Practice of Knowledge Discovery in Databases (ECML PKDD 2023) was held in Turin, Italy, from September 18 to 22, 2023.

The ECML PKDD conference, held annually, acts as a worldwide platform showcasing the latest advancements in machine learning and knowledge discovery in databases, encompassing groundbreaking applications. With a history of successful editions, ECML PKDD has established itself as the leading European machine learning and data mining conference, offering researchers and practitioners an unparalleled opportunity to exchange knowledge and ideas.

The main conference program consisted of presentations of 255 accepted papers and three keynote talks (in order of appearance):

- Max Welling (University of Amsterdam): Neural Wave Representations
- Michael Bronstein (University of Oxford): Physics-Inspired Graph Neural Networks
- Kate Crawford (USC Annenberg): Mapping Generative AI

In addition, there were 30 workshops, 9 combined workshop-tutorials, 5 tutorials, 3 discovery challenges, and 16 demonstrations. Moreover, the PhD Forum provided a friendly environment for junior PhD students to exchange ideas and experiences with peers in an interactive atmosphere and to get constructive feedback from senior researchers. The conference included a Special Day on Artificial Intelligence for Financial Crime Fight to discuss, share, and present recent developments in AI-based financial crime detection.

In recognition of the paramount significance of ethics in machine learning and data mining, we invited the authors to include an ethical statement in their submissions. We encouraged the authors to discuss the ethical implications of their submission, such as those related to the collection and processing of personal data, the inference of personal information, or the potential risks. We are pleased to report that our call for ethical statements was met with an overwhelmingly positive response from the authors.

The ECML PKDD 2023 Organizing Committee supported Diversity and Inclusion by awarding some grants that enable early career researchers to attend the conference, present their research activities, and become part of the ECML PKDD community. A total of 8 grants covering all or part of the registration fee (4 free registrations and 4 with 50% discount) were awarded to individuals who belong to underrepresented communities, based on gender and role/position, to attend the conference and present their research activities. The goal of the grants was to provide financial support to early-career (women) scientists and Master and Ph.D. students from developing countries. The Diversity and Inclusion action also includes the SoBigData Award, fully sponsored by the SoBigData++ Horizon2020 project, which aims to encourage more diverse participation in computer science and machine learning events. The award is intended to cover expenses for transportation and accommodation.

The papers presented during the three main conference days were organized in four different tracks:

- Research Track: research or methodology papers from all areas in machine learning, knowledge discovery, and data mining;
- Applied Data Science Track: papers on novel applications of machine learning, data mining, and knowledge discovery to solve real-world use cases, thereby bridging the gap between practice and current theory;
- Journal Track: papers published in special issues of the journals Machine Learning and Data Mining and Knowledge Discovery;
- Demo Track: short papers introducing new prototypes or fully operational systems that exploit data science techniques and are presented via working demonstrations.

We received 829 submissions for the Research track and 239 for the Applied Data Science Track.

We accepted 196 papers (24%) in the Research Track and 58 (24%) in the Applied Data Science Track. In addition, there were 44 papers from the Journal Track and 16 demo papers (out of 28 submissions).

We want to thank all participants, authors, all chairs, all Program Committee members, area chairs, session chairs, volunteers, co-organizers, and organizers of workshops and tutorials for making ECML PKDD 2023 an outstanding success. Thanks to Springer for their continuous support and Microsoft for allowing us to use their CMT software for conference management and providing support throughout. Special thanks to our sponsors and the ECML PKDD Steering Committee for their support. Finally, we thank the organizing institutions: CENTAI (Italy) and Politecnico di Torino (Italy).

September 2023

Elena Baralis
Francesco Bonchi
Manuel Gomez Rodriguez
Danai Koutra
Claudia Plant
Gianmarco De Francisci Morales
Claudia Perlich

Organization

General Chairs

Elena Baralis — Politecnico di Torino, Italy
Francesco Bonchi — CENTAI, Italy and Eurecat, Spain

Research Track Program Chairs

Manuel Gomez Rodriguez — Max Planck Institute for Software Systems, Germany
Danai Koutra — University of Michigan, USA
Claudia Plant — University of Vienna, Austria

Applied Data Science Track Program Chairs

Gianmarco De Francisci Morales — CENTAI, Italy
Claudia Perlich — NYU and TwoSigma, USA

Journal Track Chairs

Tania Cerquitelli — Politecnico di Torino, Italy
Marcello Restelli — Politecnico di Milano, Italy
Charalampos E. Tsourakakis — Boston University, USA and ISI Foundation, Italy
Fabio Vitale — CENTAI, Italy

Workshop and Tutorial Chairs

Rosa Meo — University of Turin, Italy
Fabrizio Silvestri — Sapienza University of Rome, Italy

Demo Chairs

Nicolas Kourtellis   Telefonica, Spain
Natali Ruchansky   Netflix, USA

Local Chairs

Daniele Apiletti   Politecnico di Torino, Italy
Paolo Bajardi   CENTAI, Italy
Eliana Pastor   Politecnico di Torino, Italy

Discovery Challenge Chairs

Danilo Giordano   Politecnico di Torino, Italy
André Panisson   CENTAI, Italy

PhD Forum Chairs

Yllka Velaj   University of Vienna, Austria
Matteo Riondato   Amherst College, USA

Diversity and Inclusion Chair

Tania Cerquitelli   Politecnico di Torino, Italy

Proceedings Chairs

Eliana Pastor   Politecnico di Torino, Italy
Giulia Preti   CENTAI, Italy

Sponsorship Chairs

Daniele Apiletti   Politecnico di Torino, Italy
Paolo Bajardi   CENTAI, Italy

Web Chair

Alessandro Fiori   Flowygo, Italy

Social Media and Publicity Chair

Flavio Giobergia   Politecnico di Torino, Italy

Online Chairs

Alkis Koudounas   Politecnico di Torino, Italy
Simone Monaco   Politecnico di Torino, Italy

Best Paper Awards Chairs

Peter Flach   University of Bristol, UK
Katharina Morik   TU Dortmund, Germany
Arno Siebes   Utrecht University, The Netherlands

ECML PKDD Steering Committee

Massih-Reza Amini   Université Grenoble Alpes, France
Annalisa Appice   University of Bari, Aldo Moro, Italy
Ira Assent   Aarhus University, Denmark
Tania Cerquitelli   Politecnico di Torino, Italy
Albert Bifet   University of Waikato, New Zealand
Francesco Bonchi   CENTAI, Italy and Eurecat, Spain
Peggy Cellier   INSA Rennes, France
Saso Dzeroski   Jožef Stefan Institute, Slovenia
Tias Guns   KU Leuven, Belgium
Alípio M. G. Jorge   University of Porto, Portugal
Kristian Kersting   TU Darmstadt, Germany
Jefrey Lijffijt   Ghent University, Belgium
Luís Moreira-Matias   Sennder GmbH, Germany
Katharina Morik   TU Dortmund, Germany
Siegfried Nijssen   Université catholique de Louvain, Belgium
Andrea Passerini   University of Trento, Italy

Program Committee

Guest Editorial Board, Journal Track

Helge Langseth	Norwegian University of Science and Technology, Norway
Thien Le	MIT, USA
Hsuan-Tien Lin	National Taiwan University, Taiwan
Marco Lippi	University of Modena and Reggio Emilia, Italy
Corrado Loglisci	University of Bari, Aldo Moro, Italy
Manuel López-ibáñez	University of Manchester, UK
Nuno Lourenço	CISUC, Portugal
Claudio Lucchese	Ca' Foscari University of Venice, Italy
Brian Mac Namee	University College Dublin, Ireland
Gjorgji Madjarov	Ss. Cyril and Methodius University in Skopje, North Macedonia
Luigi Malagò	Transylvanian Institute of Neuroscience, Romania
Sagar Malhotra	Fondazione Bruno Kessler, Italy
Fragkiskos Malliaros	CentraleSupélec, Université Paris-Saclay, France
Giuseppe Manco	ICAR-CNR, Italy
Basarab Matei	Sorbonne Université Paris Nord, France
Michael Mathioudakis	University of Helsinki, Finland
Rosa Meo	University of Turin, Italy
Mohamed-Lamine Messai	Université Lumière Lyon 2, France
Sara Migliorini	University of Verona, Italy
Alex Mircoli	Università Politecnica delle Marche, Italy
Atsushi Miyauchi	University of Tokyo, Japan
Simone Monaco	Politecnico di Torino, Italy
Anna Monreale	University of Pisa, Italy
Corrado Monti	CENTAI, Italy
Katharina Morik	TU Dortmund, Germany
Lia Morra	Politecnico di Torino, Italy
Arsenii Mustafin	Boston University, USA
Mirco Mutti	Politecnico di Milano/University of Bologna, Italy
Amedeo Napoli	University of Lorraine, CNRS, LORIA, France
Kleber Oliveira	CENTAI, Italy
Gabriella Olmo	Politecnico di Torino, Italy
Marios Papachristou	Cornell University, USA
Panagiotis Papapetrou	Stockholm University, Sweden
Matteo Papini	Universitat Pompeu Fabra, Spain
Vincenzo Pasquadibisceglie	University of Bari, Aldo Moro, Italy
Eliana Pastor	Politecnico di Torino, Italy
Andrea Paudice	University of Milan, Italy
Charlotte Pelletier	IRISA - Université Bretagne-Sud, France
Ruggero G. Pensa	University of Turin, Italy
Simone Piaggesi	University of Bologna/ISI Foundation, Italy

Matteo Pirotta	Meta, France
Marc Plantevit	EPITA, France
Konstantinos Pliakos	KU Leuven, Belgium
Kai Puolamäki	University of Helsinki, Finland
Jan Ramon	Inria, France
Rita P. Ribeiro	INESC TEC/University of Porto, Portugal
Matteo Riondato	Amherst College, USA
Antonio Riva	Politecnico di Milano, Italy
Shota Saito	University College London, UK
Flora Salim	University of New South Wales, Australia
Roberto Santana	University of the Basque Country, Spain
Lars Schmidt-Thieme	University of Hildesheim, Germany
Thomas Seidl	LMU Munich, Germany
Kijung Shin	KAIST, South Korea
Shinichi Shirakawa	Yokohama National University, Japan
Konstantinos Sotiropoulos	Boston University, USA
Fabian Spaeh	Boston University, USA
Gerasimos Spanakis	Maastricht University, The Netherlands
Myra Spiliopoulou	Otto-von-Guericke-University Magdeburg, Germany
Jerzy Stefanowski	Poznan University of Technology, Poland
Mahito Sugiyama	National Institute of Informatics, Japan
Nikolaj Tatti	University of Helsinki, Finland
Maximilian Thiessen	TU Vienna, Austria
Josephine Thomas	University of Kassel, Germany
Kiran Tomlinson	Cornell University, USA
Leonardo Trujillo	Tecnológico Nacional de México, Mexico
Grigorios Tsoumakas	Aristotle University of Thessaloniki, Greece
Genoveva Vargas-Solar	CNRS, LIRIS Lab, France
Edoardo Vittori	Politecnico di Milano/Intesa Sanpaolo, Italy
Christel Vrain	University of Orléans, France
Willem Waegeman	Ghent University, Belgium
Yanbang Wang	Cornell University, USA
Pascal Welke	University of Bonn, Germany
Marcel Wever	LMU Munich, Germany
Stefan Wrobel	University of Bonn/Fraunhofer IAIS, Germany
Guoxian Yu	Shandong University, China
Ilias Zavitsanos	National Center for Scientific Research Demokritos, Greece
Ye Zhu	Deakin University, Australia
Albrecht Zimmermann	Université de Caen Normandie, France

Area Chairs, Research Track

Fabrizio Angiulli	University of Calabria, Italy
Annalisa Appice	University of Bari, Aldo Moro, Italy
Antonio Artés	Universidad Carlos III de Madrid, Spain
Martin Atzmueller	Osnabrück University, Germany
Christian Böhm	University of Vienna, Austria
Michael R. Berthold	KNIME, Switzerland
Albert Bifet	Université Paris-Saclay, France
Hendrik Blockeel	KU Leuven, Belgium
Ulf Brefeld	Leuphana University, Germany
Paula Brito	INESC TEC - LIAAD/University of Porto, Portugal
Wolfram Burgard	University of Technology Nuremberg, Germany
Seshadhri C.	UCSC, USA
Michelangelo Ceci	University of Bari, Aldo Moro, Italy
Peggy Cellier	IRISA - INSA Rennes, France
Duen Horng Chau	Georgia Institute of Technology, USA
Nicolas Courty	IRISA - Université Bretagne-Sud, France
Bruno Cremilleux	Université de Caen Normandie, France
Jesse Davis	KU Leuven, Belgium
Abir De	IIT Bombay, India
Tom Diethe	AstraZeneca, UK
Yuxiao Dong	Tsinghua University, China
Kurt Driessens	Maastricht University, The Netherlands
Tapio Elomaa	Tampere University, Finland
Johannes Fürnkranz	JKU Linz, Austria
Sophie Fellenz	RPTU Kaiserslautern-Landau, Germany
Elisa Fromont	IRISA/Inria rba - Université de Rennes 1, France
Thomas Gärtner	TU Vienna, Austria
Patrick Gallinari	Criteo AI Lab - Sorbonne Université, France
Joao Gama	INESC TEC - LIAAD, Portugal
Rayid Ghani	Carnegie Mellon University, USA
Aristides Gionis	KTH Royal Institute of Technology, Sweden
Chen Gong	Nanjing University of Science and Technology, China
Francesco Gullo	UniCredit, Italy
Eyke Hüllermeier	LMU Munich, Germany
Junheng Hao	University of California, Los Angeles, USA
José Hernández-Orallo	Universitat Politècnica de Valencia, Spain
Daniel Hernández-Lobato	Universidad Autonoma de Madrid, Spain
Sibylle Hess	TU Eindhoven, The Netherlands

Jaakko Hollmén	Aalto University, Finland
Andreas Hotho	University of Würzburg, Germany
Georgiana Ifrim	University College Dublin, Ireland
Jayaraman J. Thiagarajan	Lawrence Livermore, USA
Alipio M. G. Jorge	INESC TEC/University of Porto, Portugal
Ross King	Chalmers University of Technology, Sweden
Yun Sing Koh	University of Auckland, New Zealand
Lars Kotthoff	University of Wyoming, USA
Peer Kröger	Christian-Albrecht University of Kiel, Germany
Stefan Kramer	JGU Mainz, Germany
Jörg Lücke	University of Oldenburg, Germany
Niklas Lavesson	Blekinge Institute of Technology, Sweden
Bruno Lepri	Fondazione Bruno Kessler, Italy
Jefrey Lijffijt	Ghent University, Belgium
Marius Lindauer	Leibniz University Hannover, Germany
Patrick Loiseau	Inria, France
Jose A. Lozano	UPV/EHU, Spain
Emmanuel Müller	TU Dortmund, Germany
Donato Malerba	University of Bari, Aldo Moro, Italy
Fragkiskos Malliaros	CentraleSupelec, France
Giuseppe Manco	ICAR-CNR, Italy
Pauli Miettinen	University of Eastern Finland, Finland
Dunja Mladenic	Jožef Stefan Institute, Slovenia
Anna Monreale	University of Pisa, Italy
Luis Moreira-Matias	Sennder GmbH, Germany
Katharina J. Morik	TU Dortmund, Germany
Siegfried Nijssen	Université catholique de Louvain, Belgium
Evangelos Papalexakis	UC, Riverside, USA
Panagiotis Papapetrou	Stockholm University, Sweden
Andrea Passerini	University of Trento, Italy
Mykola Pechenizkiy	TU Eindhoven, The Netherlands
Jaakko Peltonen	Tampere University, Finland
Franz Pernkopf	TU Graz, Austria
Bernhard Pfahringer	University of Waikato, New Zealand
Fabio Pinelli	IMT Lucca, Italy
Goran Radanovic	Max Planck Institute for Software Systems, Germany
Jesse Read	École Polytechnique, France
Matthias Renz	Christian-Albrecht University of Kiel, Germany
Marian-Andrei Rizoiu	University of Technology, Sydney, Australia
Celine Robardet	INSA Lyon, France
Juho Rousu	Aalto University, Finland

Sriparna Saha	IIT Patna, India
Ute Schmid	University of Bamberg, Germany
Lars Schmidt-Thieme	University of Hildesheim, Germany
Michele Sebag	LISN CNRS, France
Thomas Seidl	LMU Munich, Germany
Junming Shao	University of Electronic Science and Technology of China, China
Arno Siebes	Utrecht University, The Netherlands
Fabrizio Silvestri	Sapienza University of Rome, Italy
Carlos Soares	University of Porto, Portugal
Christian Sohler	University of Cologne, Germany
Myra Spiliopoulou	Otto-von-Guericke-University Magdeburg, Germany
Jie Tang	Tsinghua University, China
Nikolaj Tatti	University of Helsinki, Finland
Evimaria Terzi	Boston University, USA
Marc Tommasi	Lille University, France
Heike Trautmann	University of Münster, Germany
Herke van Hoof	University of Amsterdam, The Netherlands
Celine Vens	KU Leuven, Belgium
Christel Vrain	University of Orleans, France
Jilles Vreeken	CISPA Helmholtz Center for Information Security, Germany
Wei Ye	Tongji University, China
Jing Zhang	Renmin University of China, China
Min-Ling Zhang	Southeast University, China

Area Chairs, Applied Data Science Track

Annalisa Appice	University of Bari, Aldo Moro, Italy
Ira Assent	Aarhus University, Denmark
Martin Atzmueller	Osnabrück University, Germany
Michael R. Berthold	KNIME, Switzerland
Hendrik Blockeel	KU Leuven, Belgium
Michelangelo Ceci	University of Bari, Aldo Moro, Italy
Peggy Cellier	IRISA - INSA Rennes, France
Yi Chang	Jilin University, China
Nicolas Courty	IRISA - UBS, France
Bruno Cremilleux	Université de Caen Normandie, France
Peng Cui	Tsinghua University, China
Anirban Dasgupta	IIT Gandhinagar, India

Tom Diethe	AstraZeneca, UK
Carlotta Domeniconi	George Mason University, USA
Dejing Dou	BCG, USA
Kurt Driessens	Maastricht University, The Netherlands
Johannes Fürnkranz	JKU Linz, Austria
Faisal Farooq	Qatar Computing Research Institute, Qatar
Paolo Frasconi	University of Florence, Italy
Elisa Fromont	IRISA/Inria rba - Université de Rennes 1, France
Glenn Fung	Liberty Mutual, USA
Joao Gama	INESC TEC - LIAAD, Portugal
Jose A. Gamez	Universidad de Castilla-La Mancha, Spain
Rayid Ghani	Carnegie Mellon University, USA
Aristides Gionis	KTH Royal Institute of Technology, Sweden
Sreenivas Gollapudi	Google, USA
Francesco Gullo	UniCredit, Italy
Eyke Hüllermeier	LMU Munich, Germany
Jingrui He	University of Illinois at Urbana-Champaign, USA
Jaakko Hollmén	Aalto University, Finland
Andreas Hotho	University of Würzburg, Germany
Daxin Jiang	Microsoft, Beijing, China
Alipio M. G. Jorge	INESC TEC/University of Porto, Portugal
George Karypis	University of Minnesota, USA
Eamonn Keogh	UC, Riverside, USA
Yun Sing Koh	University of Auckland, New Zealand
Parisa Kordjamshidi	Michigan State University, USA
Lars Kotthoff	University of Wyoming, USA
Nicolas Kourtellis	Telefonica Research, Spain
Stefan Kramer	JGU Mainz, Germany
Balaji Krishnapuram	Pinterest, USA
Niklas Lavesson	Blekinge Institute of Technology, Sweden
Chuan Lei	Amazon Web Services, USA
Marius Lindauer	Leibniz University Hannover, Germany
Patrick Loiseau	Inria, France
Giuseppe Manco	ICAR-CNR, Italy
Gabor Melli	PredictionWorks, USA
Anna Monreale	University of Pisa, Italy
Luis Moreira-Matias	Sennder GmbH, Germany
Nuria Oliver	ELLIS Alicante, Spain
Panagiotis Papapetrou	Stockholm University, Sweden
Mykola Pechenizkiy	TU Eindhoven, The Netherlands
Jian Pei	Simon Fraser University, Canada
Julien Perez	Naver Labs Europe, France

Fabio Pinelli	IMT Lucca, Italy
Zhiwei (Tony) Qin	Lyft, USA
Visvanathan Ramesh	Goethe University, Germany
Zhaochun Ren	Shandong University, China
Sriparna Saha	IIT Patna, India
Ute Schmid	University of Bamberg, Germany
Lars Schmidt-Thieme	University of Hildesheim, Germany
Thomas Seidl	LMU Munich, Germany
Fabrizio Silvestri	Sapienza University of Rome, Italy
Myra Spiliopoulou	Otto-von-Guericke-University Magdeburg, Germany
Karthik Subbian	Amazon, USA
Liang Sun	Alibaba Group, China
Jie Tang	Tsinghua University, China
Jiliang Tang	Michigan State University, USA
Sandeep Tata	Google, USA
Nikolaj Tatti	University of Helsinki, Finland
Marc Tommasi	Lille University, France
Yongxin Tong	Beihang University, China
Vincent S. Tseng	National Yang Ming Chiao Tung University, Taiwan
Antti Ukkonen	University of Helsinki, Finland
Willem Waegeman	Ghent University, Belgium
Fei Wang	Cornell University, USA
Jie Wang	University of Science and Technology of China, China
Sinong Wang	Meta AI, USA
Zheng Wang	Alibaba DAMO Academy, China
Lingfei Wu	Pinterest, USA
Yinglong Xia	Meta, USA
Hui Xiong	Rutgers University, USA
Hongxia Yang	Alibaba Group, China
Min-Ling Zhang	Southeast University, China
Jiayu Zhou	Michigan State University, USA
Xingquan Zhu	Florida Atlantic University, USA
Fuzhen Zhuang	Institute of Artificial Intelligence, China
Albrecht Zimmermann	Université de Caen Normandie, France

Program Committee, Research Track

Matthias Aßenmacher	LMU Munich, Germany
Sara Abdali	Microsoft, USA
Evrim Acar	Simula Metropolitan Center for Digital Engineering, Norway
Homayun Afrabandpey	Nokia Technologies, Finland
Reza Akbarinia	Inria, France
Cuneyt G. Akcora	University of Manitoba, Canada
Ranya Almohsen	West Virginia University, USA
Thiago Andrade	INESC TEC/University of Porto, Portugal
Jean-Marc Andreoli	Naverlabs Europe, France
Giuseppina Andresini	University of Bari, Aldo Moro, Italy
Alessandro Antonucci	IDSIA, Switzerland
Xiang Ao	Institute of Computing Technology, CAS, China
Héber H. Arcolezi	Inria/École Polytechnique, France
Jerónimo Arenas-García	Universidad Carlos III de Madrid, Spain
Yusuf Arslan	University of Luxembourg, Luxemburg
Ali Ayadi	University of Strasbourg, France
Steve Azzolin	University of Trento, Italy
Pierre-Luc Bacon	Mila, Canada
Bunil K. Balabantaray	NIT Meghalaya, India
Mitra Baratchi	LIACS/Leiden University, The Netherlands
Christian Bauckhage	Fraunhofer IAIS, Germany
Anna Beer	Aarhus University, Denmark
Michael Beigl	Karlsruhe Institute of Technology, Germany
Khalid Benabdeslem	Université de Lyon, Lyon 1, France
Idir Benouaret	Epita Research Laboratory, France
Paul Berg	IRISA, France
Christoph Bergmeir	Monash University, Australia
Gilberto Bernardes	INESC TEC/University of Porto, Portugal
Eva Besada-Portas	Universidad Complutense de Madrid, Spain
Jalaj Bhandari	Columbia University, USA
Asmita Bhat	TU Kaiserslautern, Germany
Monowar Bhuyan	Umeå University, Sweden
Adrien Bibal	University of Colorado Anschutz Medical Campus, USA
Manuele Bicego	University of Verona, Italy
Przemyslaw Biecek	Warsaw University of Technology, Poland
Alexander Binder	University of Oslo, Norway
Livio Bioglio	University of Turin, Italy
Patrick Blöbaum	Amazon Web Services, USA

Thomas Bonald	Télécom Paris, France
Ludovico Boratto	University of Cagliari, Italy
Stefano Bortoli	Huawei Research Center, Germany
Tassadit Bouadi	Université de Rennes 1, France
Ahcène Boubekki	UiT, Arctic University of Norway, Norway
Luc Brogat-Motte	Télécom Paris, France
Jannis Brugger	TU Darmstadt, Germany
Nhat-Tan Bui	University of Science - VNUHCM, Vietnam
Mirko Bunse	TU Dortmund, Germany
John Burden	University of Cambridge, UK
Wolfram Burgard	University of Technology, Germany
Julian Busch	Siemens Technology, Germany
Sebastian Buschjäger	TU Dortmund, Germany
Oswald C.	NIT Trichy, India
Seshadhri C.	UCSC, USA
Xin-Qiang Cai	University of Tokyo, Japan
Zekun Cai	University of Tokyo, Japan
Xiaofeng Cao	University of Technology, Sydney, Australia
Giuseppe Casalicchio	LMU Munich, Germany
Guilherme Cassales	University of Waikato, New Zealand
Oded Cats	TU Delft, The Netherlands
Remy Cazabet	Université de Lyon, Lyon 1, France
Mattia Cerrato	JGU Mainz, Germany
Ricardo Cerri	Federal University of Sao Carlos, Brazil
Prithwish Chakraborty	IBM Research, USA
Harry Kai-Ho Chan	University of Sheffield, UK
Joydeep Chandra	IIT Patna, India
Vaggos Chatziafratis	Stanford University, USA
Zaineb Chelly Dagdia	UVSQ - Université Paris-Saclay, France
Hongyang Chen	Zhejiang Lab, China
Huaming Chen	University of Sydney, Australia
Hung-Hsuan Chen	National Central University, Taiwan
Jin Chen	University of Electronic Science and Technology of China, China
Kuan-Hsun Chen	University of Twente, The Netherlands
Ling Chen	University of Technology, Australia
Lingwei Chen	Wright State University, USA
Minyu Chen	Shanghai Jiaotong University, China
Xi Chen	Ghent University, Belgium
Xiaojun Chen	Institute of Information Engineering, CAS, China
Xuefeng Chen	Chongqing University, China
Ying Chen	RMIT University, Australia

Yueguo Chen	Renmin University of China, China
Yuzhou Chen	Temple University, USA
Zheng Chen	Osaka University, Japan
Ziheng Chen	Walmart, USA
Lu Cheng	University of Illinois, Chicago, USA
Xu Cheng	Shanghai Jiao Tong University, China
Zhiyong Cheng	Shandong Academy of Sciences, China
Yann Chevaleyre	Université Paris Dauphine, France
Chun Wai Chiu	Keele University, UK
Silvia Chiusano	Politecnico di Torino, Italy
Satyendra Singh Chouhan	MNIT Jaipur, India
Hua Chu	Xidian University, China
Sarel Cohen	Academic College of Tel Aviv-Yaffo, Israel
J. Alberto Conejero	Universitat Politècnica de València, Spain
Lidia Contreras-Ochando	Universitat Politècnica de València, Spain
Giorgio Corani	IDSIA, Switzerland
Luca Corbucci	University of Pisa, Italy
Roberto Corizzo	American University, USA
Baris Coskunuzer	University of Texas at Dallas, USA
Fabrizio Costa	Exeter University, UK
Gustavo de Assis Costa	Instituto Federal de Goiás, Brazil
Evan Crothers	University of Ottawa, Canada
Pádraig Cunningham	University College Dublin, Ireland
Jacek Cyranka	University of Warsaw, Poland
Tianxiang Dai	Huawei European Research Institute, Germany
Xuan-Hong Dang	IBM T.J. Watson Research Center, USA
Thi-Bich-Hanh Dao	University of Orleans, France
Debasis Das	Indian Institute of Technology Jodhpur, India
Paul Davidsson	Malmö University, Sweden
Marcilio de Souto	LIFO, University of Orleans, France
Klest Dedja	KU Leuven, Belgium
Elena Demidova	University of Bonn, Germany
Caglar Demir	Paderborn University, Germany
Difan Deng	Leibniz University Hannover, Germany
Laurens Devos	KU Leuven, Belgium
Nicola Di Mauro	University of Bari, Aldo Moro, Italy
Jingtao Ding	Tsinghua University, China
Yao-Xiang Ding	Nanjing University, China
Lamine Diop	EPITA, France
Gillian Dobbie	University of Auckland, New Zealand
Stephan Doerfel	Kiel University of Applied Sciences, Germany
Carola Doerr	Sorbonne Université, France

Nanqing Dong	University of Oxford, UK
Haizhou Du	Shanghai University of Electric Power, China
Qihan Du	Renmin University of China, China
Songlin Du	Southeast University, China
Xin Du	University of Edinburgh, UK
Wouter Duivesteijn	TU Eindhoven, The Netherlands
Inês Dutra	University of Porto, Portugal
Sourav Dutta	Huawei Research Centre, Ireland
Saso Dzeroski	Jožef Stefan Institute, Slovenia
Nabil El Malki	IRIT, France
Mohab Elkaref	IBM Research Europe, UK
Tapio Elomaa	Tampere University, Finland
Dominik M. Endres	University of Marburg, Germany
Georgios Exarchakis	University of Bath, UK
Lukas Faber	ETH Zurich, Switzerland
Samuel G. Fadel	Leuphana University, Germany
Haoyi Fan	Zhengzhou University, China
Zipei Fan	University of Tokyo, Japan
Hadi Fanaee-T	Halmstad University, Sweden
Elaine Ribeiro Faria	UFU, Brazil
Fabio Fassetti	University of Calabria, Italy
Anthony Faustine	ITI/LARSyS - Técnico Lisboa, Portugal
Sophie Fellenz	RPTU Kaiserslautern-Landau, Germany
Wenjie Feng	National University of Singapore, Singapore
Zunlei Feng	Zhejiang University, China
Daniel Fernández-Sánchez	Universidad Autónoma de Madrid, Spain
Luca Ferragina	University of Calabria, Italy
Emilio Ferrara	USC ISI, USA
Cèsar Ferri	Universitat Politècnica València, Spain
Flavio Figueiredo	Universidade Federal de Minas Gerais, Brazil
Lucie Flek	University of Marburg, Germany
Michele Fontana	University of Pisa, Italy
Germain Forestier	University of Haute-Alsace, France
Raphaël Fournier-S'niehotta	CNAM, France
Benoît Frénay	University of Namur, Belgium
Kary Främling	Umeå University, Sweden
Holger Froening	University of Heidelberg, Germany
Fabio Fumarola	Prometeia, Italy
María José Gómez-Silva	Universidad Complutense de Madrid, Spain
Vanessa Gómez-Verdejo	Universidad Carlos III de Madrid, Spain
Pratik Gajane	TU Eindhoven, The Netherlands
Esther Galbrun	University of Eastern Finland, Finland

Claudio Gallicchio   University of Pisa, Italy
Chen Gao   Tsinghua University, China
Shengxiang Gao   Kunming University of Science and Technology,
                              China
Yifeng Gao   University of Texas Rio Grande Valley, USA
Luis Garcia   University of Brasilia, Brazil
Dominique Gay   Université de La Réunion, France
Suyu Ge   University of Illinois at Urbana-Champaign, USA
Zhaocheng Ge   Huazhong University of Science and Technology,
                              China
Alborz Geramifard   Facebook AI, USA
Ahana Ghosh   Max Planck Institute for Software Systems,
                              Germany
Shreya Ghosh   Penn State University, USA
Flavio Giobergia   Politecnico di Torino, Italy
Sarunas Girdzijauskas   KTH Royal Institute of Technology, Sweden
Heitor Murilo Gomes   University of Waikato, Sweden
Wenwen Gong   Tsinghua University, China
Bedartha Goswami   University of Tübingen, Germany
Anastasios Gounaris   Aristotle University of Thessaloniki, Greece
Michael Granitzer   University of Passau, Germany
Derek Greene   University College Dublin, Ireland
Moritz Grosse-Wentrup   University of Vienna, Austria
Marek Grzes   University of Kent, UK
Xinyu Guan   Xian Jiaotong University, China
Massimo Guarascio   ICAR-CNR, Italy
Riccardo Guidotti   University of Pisa, Italy
Lan-Zhe Guo   Nanjing University, China
Lingbing Guo   Zhejiang University, China
Shanqing Guo   Shandong University, China
Karthik S. Gurumoorthy   Walmart, USA
Thomas Guyet   Inria, France
Huong Ha   RMIT University, Australia
Benjamin Halstead   University of Auckland, New Zealand
Massinissa Hamidi   LIPN-UMR CNRS 7030, France
Donghong Han   Northeastern University, USA
Marwan Hassani   TU Eindhoven, The Netherlands
Rima Hazra   Indian Institute of Technology, Kharagpur, India
Mark Heimann   Lawrence Livermore, USA
Cesar Hidalgo   University of Toulouse, France
Martin Holena   Institute of Computer Science, Czech Republic
Mike Holenderski   TU Eindhoven, The Netherlands

Adrian Horzyk	AGH University of Science and Technology, Poland
Shifu Hou	Case Western Reserve University, USA
Hongsheng Hu	CSIRO, Australia
Yaowei Hu	University of Arkansas, USA
Yang Hua	Queen's University Belfast, UK
Chao Huang	University of Hong Kong, China
Guanjie Huang	Penn State University, USA
Hong Huang	Huazhong University of Science and Technology, China
Nina C. Hubig	Clemson University, USA
Dino Ienco	Irstea Institute, France
Angelo Impedovo	Niuma, Italy
Roberto Interdonato	CIRAD, France
Stratis Ioannidis	Northeastern University, USA
Nevo Itzhak	Ben-Gurion University, Israel
Raghav Jain	IIT Patna, India
Kuk Jin Jang	University of Pennsylvania, USA
Szymon Jaroszewicz	Polish Academy of Sciences, Poland
Shaoxiong Ji	University of Helsinki, Finland
Bin-Bin Jia	Lanzhou University of Technology, China
Caiyan Jia	School of Computer and Information Technology, China
Xiuyi Jia	Nanjing University of Science and Technology, China
Nan Jiang	Purdue University, USA
Renhe Jiang	University of Tokyo, Japan
Song Jiang	University of California, Los Angeles, USA
Pengfei Jiao	Hangzhou Dianzi University, China
Di Jin	Amazon, USA
Guangyin Jin	National University of Defense Technology, China
Jiahui Jin	Southeast University, China
Ruoming Jin	Kent State University, USA
Yilun Jin	The Hong Kong University of Science and Technology, Hong Kong
Hugo Jonker	Open University of the Netherlands, The Netherlands
Adan Jose-Garcia	Lille University, France
Marius Köppel	JGU Mainz, Germany
Vana Kalogeraki	Athens University of Economics and Business, Greece
Konstantinos Kalpakis	University of Maryland Baltimore County, USA

Andreas Kaltenbrunner	ISI Foundation, Italy
Shivaram Kalyanakrishnan	IIT Bombay, India
Toshihiro Kamishima	National Institute of Advanced Industrial Science and Technology, Japan
Bo Kang	Ghent University, Belgium
Murat Kantarcioglu	UT Dallas
Thommen Karimpanal George	Deakin University, Australia
Saurav Karmakar	University of Galway, Ireland
Panagiotis Karras	Aarhus University, Denmark
Dimitrios Katsaros	University of Thessaly, Greece
Eamonn Keogh	UC, Riverside, USA
Jaleed Khan	University of Galway, Ireland
Irwin King	Chinese University of Hong Kong, China
Mauritius Klein	LMU Munich, Germany
Tomas Kliegr	Prague University of Economics and Business, Czech Republic
Dmitry Kobak	University of Tübingen, Germany
Dragi Kocev	Jožef Stefan Institute, Slovenia
Lars Kotthoff	University of Wyoming, USA
Anna Krause	University of Würzburg, Germany
Amer Krivosija	TU Dortmund, Germany
Daniel Kudenko	L3S Research Center, Germany
Meelis Kull	University of Tartu, Estonia
Sergey O. Kuznetsov	HSE, Russia
Beatriz López	University of Girona, Spain
Jörg Lücke	University of Oldenburg, Germany
Firas Laakom	Tampere University, Finland
Mateusz Lango	Poznan University of Technology, Poland
Hady Lauw	Singapore Management University, Singapore
Tuan Le	New Mexico State University, USA
Erwan Le Merrer	Inria, France
Thach Le Nguyen	Insight Centre, Ireland
Tai Le Quy	L3S Research Center, Germany
Mustapha Lebbah	UVSQ - Université Paris-Saclay, France
Dongman Lee	KAIST, South Korea
Yeon-Chang Lee	Georgia Institute of Technology, USA
Zed Lee	Stockholm University, Sweden
Mathieu Lefort	Université de Lyon, France
Yunwen Lei	University of Birmingham, UK
Vincent Lemaire	Orange Innovation, France
Daniel Lemire	TÉLUQ University, Canada
Florian Lemmerich	RWTH Aachen University, Germany

Youfang Leng   Renmin University of China, China
Carson K. Leung   University of Manitoba, Canada
Dan Li   Sun Yat-Sen University, China
Gang Li   Deakin University, Australia
Jiaming Li   Huazhong University of Science and Technology,
                                China
Mark Junjie Li   Shenzhen University, China
Nian Li   Tsinghua University, China
Shuai Li   University of Cambridge, UK
Tong Li   Hong Kong University of Science and
                                Technology, China
Xiang Li   East China Normal University, China
Yang Li   University of North Carolina at Chapel Hill, USA
Yingming Li   Zhejiang University, China
Yinsheng Li   Fudan University, China
Yong Li   Huawei European Research Center, Germany
Zhihui Li   University of New South Wales, Australia
Zhixin Li   Guangxi Normal University, China
Defu Lian   University of Science and Technology of China,
                                China
Yuxuan Liang   National University of Singapore, Singapore
Angelica Liguori   University of Calabria, Italy
Nick Lim   University of Waikato, Sweden
Baijiong Lin   The Hong Kong University of Science and
                                Technology, Hong Kong
Piotr Lipinski   University of Wrocław, Poland
Marco Lippi   University of Modena and Reggio Emilia, Italy
Bowen Liu   Stanford University, USA
Chien-Liang Liu   National Chiao Tung University, Taiwan
Fenglin Liu   University of Oxford, UK
Junze Liu   University of California, Irvine, USA
Li Liu   Chongqing University, China
Ninghao Liu   University of Georgia, USA
Shenghua Liu   Institute of Computing Technology, CAS, China
Xiao Fan Liu   City University of Hong Kong, Hong Kong
Xu Liu   National University of Singapore, Singapore
Yang Liu   Institute of Computing Technology, CAS, China
Zihan Liu   Zhejiang University/Westlake University, China
Robert Loftin   TU Delft, The Netherlands
Corrado Loglisci   University of Bari, Aldo Moro, Italy
Mingsheng Long   Tsinghua University, China
Antonio Longa   Fondazione Bruno Kessler, Italy

Grigorios Loukides | King's College London, UK
Tsai-Ching Lu | HRL Laboratories, USA
Zhiwu Lu | Renmin University of China, China
Pedro Henrique Luz de Araujo | University of Vienna, Austria
Marcos M. Raimundo | University of Campinas, Brazil
Maximilian Münch | University of Applied Sciences
Würzburg-Schweinfurt, Germany
Fenglong Ma | Pennsylvania State University, USA
Pingchuan Ma | The Hong Kong University of Science and
Technology, Hong Kong
Yao Ma | New Jersey Institute of Technology, USA
Brian Mac Namee | University College Dublin, Ireland
Henryk Maciejewski | Wrocław University of Science and Technology,
Poland
Ayush Maheshwari | IIT Bombay, India
Ajay A. Mahimkar | AT&T, USA
Ayan Majumdar | Max Planck Institute for Software Systems,
Germany
Donato Malerba | University of Bari, Aldo Moro, Italy
Aakarsh Malhotra | IIIT-Delhi, India
Fragkiskos Malliaros | CentraleSupelec, France
Pekka Malo | Aalto University, Finland
Hiroshi Mamitsuka | Kyoto University, Japan/Aalto University, Finland
Domenico Mandaglio | University of Calabria, Italy
Robin Manhaeve | KU Leuven, Belgium
Silviu Maniu | Université Paris-Saclay, France
Cinmayii G. Manliguez | National Sun Yat-Sen University, Taiwan
Naresh Manwani | IIIT Hyderabad, India
Giovanni Luca Marchetti | KTH Royal Institute of Technology, Sweden
Koji Maruhashi | Fujitsu Research, Fujitsu Limited, Japan
Florent Masseglia | Inria, France
Sarah Masud | IIIT-Delhi, India
Timothée Mathieu | Inria, France
Amir Mehrpanah | KTH Royal Institute of Technology, Sweden
Wagner Meira Jr. | Universidade Federal de Minas Gerais, Brazil
Joao Mendes-Moreira | INESC TEC, Portugal
Rui Meng | BNU-HKBU United International College, China
Fabio Mercorio | University of Milan-Bicocca, Italy
Alberto Maria Metelli | Politecnico di Milano, Italy
Carlo Metta | CNR-ISTI, Italy
Paolo Mignone | University of Bari, Aldo Moro, Italy
Tsunenori Mine | Kyushu University, Japan

Nuno Moniz	INESC TEC, Portugal
Pierre Monnin	Université Côte d'Azur, Inria, CNRS, I3S, France
Carlos Monserrat-Aranda	Universitat Politècnica de València, Spain
Raha Moraffah	Arizona State University, USA
Davide Mottin	Aarhus University, Denmark
Hamid Mousavi	University of Oldenburg, Germany
Abdullah Mueen	University of New Mexico, USA
Shamsuddeen Hassan Muhamamd	University of Porto, Portugal
Koyel Mukherjee	Adobe Research, India
Yusuke Mukuta	University of Tokyo, Japan
Pranava Mummoju	University of Vienna, Austria
Taichi Murayama	NAIST, Japan
Ankur Nahar	IIT Jodhpur, India
Felipe Kenji Nakano	KU Leuven, Belgium
Hideki Nakayama	University of Tokyo, Japan
Géraldin Nanfack	University of Namur, Belgium
Mirco Nanni	CNR-ISTI, Italy
Franco Maria Nardini	CNR-ISTI, Italy
Usman Naseem	University of Sydney, Australia
Reza Nasirigerdeh	TU Munich, Germany
Rajashree Nayak	MIT ADT University, India
Benjamin Negrevergne	Université Paris Dauphine, France
Stefan Neumann	KTH Royal Institute of Technology, Sweden
Anna Nguyen	IBM, USA
Shiwen Ni	SIAT, CAS, China
Siegfried Nijssen	Université catholique de Louvain, Belgium
Iasonas Nikolaou	Boston University, USA
Simona Nisticò	University of Calabria, Italy
Hao Niu	KDDI Research, Japan
Mehdi Nourelahi	University of Wyoming, USA
Slawomir Nowaczyk	Halmstad University, Sweden
Eirini Ntoutsi	Bundeswehr University Munich, Germany
Barry O'Sullivan	University College Cork, Ireland
Nastaran Okati	Max Planck Institute for Software Systems, Germany
Tsuyoshi Okita	Kyushu Institute of Technology, Japan
Pablo Olmos	Universidad Carlos III de Madrid, Spain
Luis Antonio Ortega Andrés	Autonomous University of Madrid, Spain
Abdelkader Ouali	Université de Caen Normandie, France
Latifa Oukhellou	IFSTTAR, France
Chun Ouyang	Queensland University of Technology, Australia
Andrei Paleyes	University of Cambridge, UK

Menghai Pan	Visa Research, USA
Shirui Pan	Griffith University, Australia
Apostolos N. Papadopoulos	Aristotle University of Thessaloniki, Greece
Chanyoung Park	KAIST, South Korea
Emilio Parrado-Hernandez	Universidad Carlos III de Madrid, Spain
Vincenzo Pasquadibisceglie	University of Bari, Aldo Moro, Italy
Eliana Pastor	Politecnico di Torino, Italy
Anand Paul	Kyungpook National University, South Korea
Shichao Pei	University of Notre Dame, USA
Yulong Pei	TU Eindhoven, The Netherlands
Leonardo Pellegrina	University of Padua, Italy
Ruggero Pensa	University of Turin, Italy
Fabiola Pereira	UFU, Brazil
Lucas Pereira	ITI/LARSyS - Técnico Lisboa, Portugal
Miquel Perello-Nieto	University of Bristol, UK
Lorenzo Perini	KU Leuven, Belgium
Matej Petkovifá	University of Ljubljana, Slovenia
Lukas Pfahler	TU Dortmund, Germany
Ninh Pham	University of Auckland, New Zealand
Guangyuan Piao	Maynooth University, Ireland
Francesco Piccialli	University of Naples Federico II, Italy
Martin Pilát	Charles University, Czech Republic
Gianvito Pio	University of Bari, Aldo Moro, Italy
Giuseppe Pirrò	Sapienza University of Rome, Italy
Francesco S. Pisani	ICAR-CNR, Italy
Srijith P. K.	IIIT Hyderabad, India
Marc Plantevit	EPITA, France
Mirko Polato	University of Turin, Italy
Axel Polleres	Vienna University of Economics and Business, Austria
Giovanni Ponti	ENEA, Italy
Paul Prasse	University of Potsdam, Germany
Mahardhika Pratama	University of South Australia, Australia
Philippe Preux	Inria, France
Ricardo B. Prudencio	Universidade Federal de Pernambuco, Brazil
Chiara Pugliese	CNR-ISTI, Italy
Erasmo Purificato	Otto-von-Guericke-University Magdeburg, Germany
Abdulhakim Qahtan	Utrecht University, The Netherlands
Lianyong Qi	China University of Petroleum, China
Kun Qian	Amazon Web Services, USA
Tieyun Qian	Wuhan University, China

Chuan Qin	BOSS Zhipin, China
Yumou Qiu	Iowa State University, USA
Dimitrios Rafailidis	University of Thessaly, Greece
Edward Raff	Booz Allen Hamilton, USA
Chang Rajani	University of Helsinki, Finland
Herilalaina Rakotoarison	Inria, France
M. José Ramírez-Quintana	Universitat Politècnica de Valencia, Spain
Jan Ramon	Inria, France
Rajeev Rastogi	Amazon, India
Domenico Redavid	University of Bari, Aldo Moro, Italy
Qianqian Ren	Heilongjiang University, China
Salvatore Rinzivillo	CNR-ISTI, Italy
Matteo Riondato	Amherst College, USA
Giuseppe Rizzo	Niuma, Italy
Marko Robnik-Sikonja	University of Ljubljana, Slovenia
Christophe Rodrigues	Pôle Universitaire Léonard de Vinci, France
Federica Rollo	University of Modena and Reggio Emilia, Italy
Luca Romeo	University of Macerata, Italy
Benjamin Roth	University of Vienna, Austria
Céline Rouveirol	LIPN - Université Sorbonne Paris Nord, France
Salvatore Ruggieri	University of Pisa, Italy
Pietro Sabatino	ICAR-CNR, Italy
Luca Sabbioni	Politecnico di Milano, Italy
Tulika Saha	University of Manchester, UK
Pablo Sanchez Martin	Max Planck Institute for Intelligent Systems, Germany
Parinya Sanguansat	Panyapiwat Institute of Management, Thailand
Shreya Saxena	Quantiphi, India
Yücel Saygin	Sabanci Universitesi, Turkey
Patrick Schäfer	Humboldt-Universität zu Berlin, Germany
Kevin Schewior	University of Southern Denmark, Denmark
Rainer Schlosser	Hasso Plattner Institute, Germany
Johannes Schneider	University of Liechtenstein, Liechtenstein
Matthias Schubert	LMU Munich, Germany
Alexander Schulz	CITEC - Bielefeld University, Germany
Andreas Schwung	Fachhoschschule Südwestfalen, Germany
Raquel Sebastião	IEETA/DETI-UA, Portugal
Pierre Senellart	ENS, PSL University, France
Edoardo Serra	Boise State University, USA
Mattia Setzu	University of Pisa, Italy
Ammar Shaker	NEC Laboratories Europe, Germany
Shubhranshu Shekhar	Carnegie Mellon University, USA

Jiaming Shen   Google Research, USA
Qiang Sheng   Institute of Computing Technology, CAS, China
Bin Shi   Xi'an Jiaotong University, China
Jimeng Shi   Florida International University, USA
Laixi Shi   Carnegie Mellon University, USA
Rongye Shi   Columbia University, USA
Harsh Shrivastava   Microsoft Research, USA
Jonathan A. Silva   Universidade Federal de Mato Grosso do Sul,
                                  Brazil
Esther-Lydia Silva-Ramírez   Universidad de Cádiz, Spain
Kuldeep Singh   Cerence, Germany
Moshe Sipper   Ben-Gurion University of the Negev, Israel
Andrzej Skowron   University of Warsaw, Poland
Krzysztof Slot   Lodz University of Technology, Poland
Marek Smieja   Jagiellonian University, Poland
Gavin Smith   University of Nottingham, UK
Carlos Soares   University of Porto, Portugal
Cláudia Soares   NOVA LINCS, Portugal
Andy Song   RMIT University, Australia
Dongjin Song   University of Connecticut, USA
Hao Song   Seldon, UK
Jie Song   Zhejiang University, China
Linxin Song   Waseda University, Japan
Liyan Song   Southern University of Science and Technology,
                                  China
Zixing Song   Chinese University of Hong Kong, China
Arnaud Soulet   University of Tours, France
Sucheta Soundarajan   Syracuse University, USA
Francesca Spezzano   Boise State University, USA
Myra Spiliopoulou   Otto-von-Guericke-University Magdeburg,
                                  Germany
Janusz Starzyk   WSIZ, Poland
Jerzy Stefanowski   Poznan University of Technology, Poland
Julian Stier   University of Passau, Germany
Michiel Stock   Ghent University, Belgium
Eleni Straitouri   Max Planck Institute for Software Systems,
                                  Germany
Łukasz Struski   Jagiellonian University, Poland
Jinyan Su   University of Electronic Science and Technology
                                  of China, China
David Q. Sun   Apple, USA
Guangzhong Sun   University of Science and Technology of China,
                                  China

Mingxuan Sun	Louisiana State University, USA
Peijie Sun	Tsinghua University, China
Weiwei Sun	Shandong University, China
Xin Sun	TU Munich, Germany
Maryam Tabar	Pennsylvania State University, USA
Anika Tabassum	Virginia Tech, USA
Shazia Tabassum	INESC TEC, Portugal
Andrea Tagarelli	University of Calabria, Italy
Acar Tamersoy	NortonLifeLock Research Group, USA
Chang Wei Tan	Monash University, Australia
Cheng Tan	Zhejiang University/Westlake University, China
Garth Tarr	University of Sydney, Australia
Romain Tavenard	LETG-Rennes/IRISA, France
Maguelonne Teisseire	INRAE - UMR Tetis, France
Evimaria Terzi	Boston University, USA
Stefano Teso	University of Trento, Italy
Surendrabikram Thapa	Virginia Tech, USA
Maximilian Thiessen	TU Vienna, Austria
Steffen Thoma	FZI Research Center for Information Technology, Germany
Simon Tihon	Euranova, Belgium
Kai Ming Ting	Nanjing University, China
Abhisek Tiwari	IIT Patna, India
Gabriele Tolomei	Sapienza University of Rome, Italy
Guangmo Tong	University of Delaware, USA
Sunna Torge	TU Dresden, Germany
Giovanni Trappolini	Sapienza University of Rome, Italy
Volker Tresp	Siemens AG/LMU Munich, Germany
Sofia Triantafillou	University of Crete, Greece
Sebastian Trimpe	RWTH Aachen University, Germany
Sebastian Tschiatschek	University of Vienna, Austria
Athena Vakal	Aristotle University of Thessaloniki, Greece
Peter van der Putten	Leiden University, The Netherlands
Fabio Vandin	University of Padua, Italy
Aparna S. Varde	Montclair State University, USA
Julien Velcin	Université Lumière Lyon 2, France
Bruno Veloso	INESC TEC/University of Porto, Portugal
Rosana Veroneze	LBiC, Brazil
Gennaro Vessio	University of Bari, Aldo Moro, Italy
Tiphaine Viard	Télécom Paris, France
Herna L. Viktor	University of Ottawa, Canada

Joao Vinagre	Joint Research Centre - European Commission, Belgium
Jordi Vitria	Universitat de Barcelona, Spain
Jean-Noël Vittaut	LIP6 - CNRS - Sorbonne Université, France
Marco Viviani	University of Milan-Bicocca, Italy
Paola Vocca	Tor Vergata University of Rome, Italy
Tomasz Walkowiak	Wrocław University of Science and Technology, Poland
Ziwen Wan	University of California, Irvine, USA
Beilun Wang	Southeast University, China
Chuan-Ju Wang	Academia Sinica, Taiwan
Deng-Bao Wang	Southeast University, China
Di Wang	KAUST, Saudi Arabia
Dianhui Wang	La Trobe University, Australia
Hongwei Wang	University of Illinois at Urbana-Champaign, USA
Huandong Wang	Tsinghua University, China
Hui (Wendy) Wang	Stevens Institute of Technology, USA
Jiaqi Wang	Penn State University, USA
Puyu Wang	City University of Hong Kong, China
Qing Wang	Australian National University, Australia
Ruijie Wang	University of Illinois at Urbana-Champaign, USA
Senzhang Wang	Central South University, China
Shuo Wang	University of Birmingham, UK
Suhang Wang	Pennsylvania State University, USA
Wei Wang	Fudan University, China
Wenjie Wang	Shanghai Tech University, China
Yanhao Wang	East China Normal University, China
Yimu Wang	University of Waterloo, Canada
Yue Wang	Microsoft Research, USA
Yue Wang	Waymo, USA
Zhaonan Wang	University of Tokyo, Japan
Zhi Wang	Southwest University, China
Zijie J. Wang	Georgia Tech, USA
Roger Wattenhofer	ETH Zurich, Switzerland
Pascal Weber	University of Vienna, Austria
Jörg Wicker	University of Auckland, New Zealand
Michael Wilbur	Vanderbilt University, USA
Weng-Fai Wong	National University of Singapore, Singapore
Bin Wu	Zhengzhou University, China
Chenwang Wu	University of Science and Technology of China, China

Di Wu	Chongqing Institute of Green and Intelligent Technology, CAS, China
Guoqiang Wu	Shandong University, China
Peng Wu	Shanghai Jiao Tong University, China
Xiaotong Wu	Nanjing Normal University, China
Yongkai Wu	Clemson University, USA
Danyang Xiao	Sun Yat-Sen University, China
Zhiwen Xiao	Southwest Jiaotong University, China
Cheng Xie	Yunnan University, China
Hong Xie	Chongqing Institute of Green and Intelligent Technology, CAS, China
Yaqi Xie	Carnegie Mellon University, USA
Huanlai Xing	Southwest Jiaotong University, China
Ning Xu	Southeast University, China
Xiaolong Xu	Nanjing University of Information Science and Technology, China
Hao Xue	University of New South Wales, Australia
Yexiang Xue	Purdue University, USA
Sangeeta Yadav	Indian Institute of Science, India
Qiao Yan	Shenzhen University, China
Yan Yan	Carleton University, Canada
Yu Yan	People's Public Security University of China, China
Yujun Yan	Dartmouth College, USA
Jie Yang	University of Wollongong, Australia
Shaofu Yang	Southeast University, China
Yang Yang	Nanjing University of Science and Technology, China
Liang Yao	Tencent, China
Muchao Ye	Pennsylvania State University, USA
Michael Yeh	Visa Research, USA
Kalidas Yeturu	Indian Institute of Technology Tirupati, India
Hang Yin	University of Copenhagen, Denmark
Hongwei Yong	Hong Kong Polytechnic University, China
Jaemin Yoo	KAIST, South Korea
Mengbo You	Iwate University, Japan
Hang Yu	Shanghai University, China
Weiren Yu	University of Warwick, UK
Wenjian Yu	Tsinghua University, China
Jidong Yuan	Beijing Jiaotong University, China
Aras Yurtman	KU Leuven, Belgium
Claudius Zelenka	Christian-Albrechts University of Kiel, Germany

Akka Zemmari	University of Bordeaux, France
Bonan Zhang	Princeton University, USA
Chao Zhang	Zhejiang University, China
Chuang Zhang	Nanjing University of Science and Technology, China
Danqing Zhang	Amazon, USA
Guoqiang Zhang	University of Technology, Sydney, Australia
Guoxi Zhang	Kyoto University, Japan
Hao Zhang	Fudan University, China
Junbo Zhang	JD Intelligent Cities Research, China
Le Zhang	Baidu Research, China
Ming Zhang	National Key Laboratory of Science and Technology on Information System Security, China
Qiannan Zhang	KAUST, Saudi Arabia
Tianlin Zhang	University of Manchester, UK
Wenbin Zhang	Michigan Tech, USA
Xiang Zhang	National University of Defense Technology, China
Xiao Zhang	Shandong University, China
Xiaoming Zhang	Beihang University, China
Xinyang Zhang	University of Illinois at Urbana-Champaign, USA
Yaying Zhang	Tongji University, China
Yin Zhang	University of Electronic Science and Technology of China, China
Yongqi Zhang	4Paradigm, China
Zhiwen Zhang	University of Tokyo, Japan
Mia Zhao	Airbnb, USA
Sichen Zhao	RMIT University, Australia
Xiaoting Zhao	Etsy, USA
Tongya Zheng	Zhejiang University, China
Wenhao Zheng	Shopee, Singapore
Yu Zheng	Tsinghua University, China
Yujia Zheng	Carnegie Mellon University, USA
Jiang Zhong	Chongqing University, China
Wei Zhou	School of Cyber Security, CAS, China
Zhengyang Zhou	University of Science and Technology of China, China
Chuang Zhu	Beijing University of Posts and Telecommunications, China
Jing Zhu	University of Michigan, USA
Jinjing Zhu	Hong Kong University of Science and Technology, China

Junxing Zhu	National University of Defense Technology, China
Yanmin Zhu	Shanghai Jiao Tong University, China
Ye Zhu	Deakin University, Australia
Yichen Zhu	Midea Group, China
Zirui Zhuang	Beijing University of Posts and Telecommunications, China
Tommaso Zoppi	University of Florence, Italy
Meiyun Zuo	Renmin University of China, China

Program Committee, Applied Data Science Track

Jussara Almeida	Universidade Federal de Minas Gerais, Brazil
Mozhdeh Ariannezhad	University of Amsterdam, The Netherlands
Renato M. Assuncao	ESRI, USA
Hajer Ayadi	York University, Canada
Ashraf Bah Rabiou	University of Delaware, USA
Amey Barapatre	Microsoft, USA
Patrice Bellot	Aix-Marseille Université - CNRS LSIS, France
Ludovico Boratto	University of Cagliari, Italy
Claudio Borile	CENTAI, Italy
Yi Cai	South China University of Technology, China
Lei Cao	University of Arizona/MIT, USA
Shilei Cao	Tencent, China
Yang Cao	Hokkaido University, Japan
Aniket Chakrabarti	Amazon, USA
Chaochao Chen	Zhejiang University, China
Chung-Chi Chen	National Taiwan University, Taiwan
Meng Chen	Shandong University, China
Ruey-Cheng Chen	Canva, Australia
Tong Chen	University of Queensland, Australia
Yi Chen	NJIT, USA
Zhiyu Chen	Amazon, USA
Wei Cheng	NEC Laboratories America, USA
Lingyang Chu	McMaster University, Canada
Xiaokai Chu	Tencent, China
Zhendong Chu	University of Virginia, USA
Federico Cinus	Sapienza University of Rome/CENTAI, Italy
Francisco Claude-Faust	LinkedIn, USA
Gabriele D'Acunto	Sapienza University of Rome, Italy
Ariyam Das	Google, USA

Jingtao Ding	Tsinghua University, China
Kaize Ding	Arizona State University, USA
Manqing Dong	eBay, Australia
Yushun Dong	University of Virginia, USA
Yingtong Dou	University of Illinois, Chicago, USA
Yixiang Fang	Chinese University of Hong Kong, China
Kaiyu Feng	Beijing Institute of Technology, China
Dayne Freitag	SRI International, USA
Yanjie Fu	University of Central Florida, USA
Matteo Gabburo	University of Trento, Italy
Sabrina Gaito	University of Milan, Italy
Chen Gao	Tsinghua University, China
Liangcai Gao	Peking University, China
Yunjun Gao	Zhejiang University, China
Lluis Garcia-Pueyo	Meta, USA
Mariana-Iuliana Georgescu	University of Bucharest, Romania
Aakash Goel	Amazon, USA
Marcos Goncalves	Universidade Federal de Minas Gerais, Brazil
Francesco Guerra	University of Modena e Reggio Emilia, Italy
Huifeng Guo	Huawei Noah's Ark Lab, China
Ruocheng Guo	ByteDance, China
Zhen Hai	Alibaba DAMO Academy, China
Eui-Hong (Sam) Han	The Washington Post, USA
Jinyoung Han	Sungkyunkwan University, South Korea
Shuchu Han	Stellar Cyber, USA
Dongxiao He	Tianjin University, China
Junyuan Hong	Michigan State University, USA
Yupeng Hou	UC San Diego, USA
Binbin Hu	Ant Group, China
Jun Hu	National University of Singapore, Singapore
Hong Huang	Huazhong University of Science and Technology, China
Xin Huang	Hong Kong Baptist University, China
Yizheng Huang	York University, Canada
Yu Huang	University of Florida, USA
Stratis Ioannidis	Northeastern University, USA
Radu Tudor Ionescu	University of Bucharest, Romania
Murium Iqbal	Etsy, USA
Shoaib Jameel	University of Southampton, UK
Jian Kang	University of Rochester, USA
Pinar Karagoz	METU, Turkey
Praveen C. Kolli	Carnegie Mellon University, USA

Manos Papagelis	York University, Canada
Leonardo Pellegrina	University of Padua, Italy
Claudia Perlich	TwoSigma, USA
Fabio Pinelli	IMT Lucca, Italy
Giulia Preti	CENTAI, Italy
Buyue Qian	Xi'an Jiaotong University, China
Chuan Qin	BOSS Zhipin, China
Xiao Qin	Amazon Web Services AI/ML, USA
Yanghui Rao	Sun Yat-Sen University, China
Yusuf Sale	LMU Munich, Germany
Eric Sanjuan	Avignon University, France
Maria Luisa Sapino	University of Turin, Italy
Emmanouil Schinas	CERTH/ITI, Greece
Nasrullah Sheikh	IBM Research, USA
Yue Shi	Meta, USA
Gianmaria Silvello	University of Padua, Italy
Yang Song	Apple, USA
Francesca Spezzano	Boise State University, USA
Efstathios Stamatatos	University of the Aegean, Greece
Kostas Stefanidis	Tampere University, Finland
Ting Su	Imperial College London, UK
Munira Syed	Procter & Gamble, USA
Liang Tang	Google, USA
Ruiming Tang	Huawei Noah's Ark Lab, China
Junichi Tatemura	Google, USA
Mingfei Teng	Amazon, USA
Sofia Tolmach	Amazon, Israel
Ismail Hakki Toroslu	METU, Turkey
Kazutoshi Umemoto	University of Tokyo, Japan
Yao Wan	Huazhong University of Science and Technology, China
Chang-Dong Wang	Sun Yat-Sen University, China
Chong Wang	Amazon, USA
Chuan-Ju Wang	Academia Sinica, Taiwan
Hongzhi Wang	Harbin Institute of Technology, China
Kai Wang	Shanghai Jiao Tong University, China
Ning Wang	Beijing Jiaotong University, China
Pengyuan Wang	University of Georgia, USA
Senzhang Wang	Central South University, China
Sheng Wang	Wuhan University, China
Shoujin Wang	Macquarie University, Australia
Wentao Wang	Michigan State University, USA

Yang Wang   University of Science and Technology of China,
                                    China
Zhihong Wang   Tsinghua University, China
Zihan Wang   Shandong University, China
Shi-ting Wen   Ningbo Tech University, China
Song Wen   Rutgers University, USA
Zeyi Wen   Hong Kong University of Science and
                                    Technology, China
Fangzhao Wu   Microsoft Research Asia, China
Jun Wu   University of Illinois at Urbana-Champaign, USA
Wentao Wu   Microsoft Research, USA
Yanghua Xiao   Fudan University, China
Haoyi Xiong   Baidu, China
Dongkuan Xu   North Carolina State University, USA
Guandong Xu   University of Technology, Sydney, Australia
Shan Xue   Macquarie University, Australia
Le Yan   Google, USA
De-Nian Yang   Academia Sinica, Taiwan
Fan Yang   Rice University, USA
Yu Yang   City University of Hong Kong, China
Fanghua Ye   University College London, UK
Jianhua Yin   Shandong University, China
Yifang Yin   A*STAR-I2R, Singapore
Changlong Yu   Hong Kong University of Science and
                                    Technology, China
Dongxiao Yu   Shandong University, China
Ye Yuan   Beijing Institute of Technology, China
Daochen Zha   Rice University, USA
Feng Zhang   Renmin University of China, China
Mengxuan Zhang   University of North Texas, USA
Xianli Zhang   Xi'an Jiaotong University, China
Xuyun Zhang   Macquarie University, Australia
Chen Zhao   Baylor University, USA
Di Zhao   University of Auckland, New Zealand
Yanchang Zhao   CSIRO, Australia
Kaiping Zheng   National University of Singapore, Singapore
Yong Zheng   Illinois Institute of Technology, USA
Jingbo Zhou   Baidu, China
Ming Zhou   University of Technology, Sydney, Australia
Qinghai Zhou   University of Illinois at Urbana-Champaign, USA
Tian Zhou   Alibaba DAMO Academy, China
Xinyi Zhou   University of Washington, USA

Yucheng Zhou	University of Macau, China
Jiangang Zhu	ByteDance, China
Yongchun Zhu	CAS, China
Ziwei Zhu	George Mason University, USA
Jia Zou	Arizona State University, USA

Program Committee, Demo Track

Ferran Diego	Telefonica Research, Spain
Jan Florjanczyk	Netflix, USA
Mikko Heikkila	Telefonica Research, Spain
Jesus Omaña Iglesias	Telefonica Research, Spain
Nicolas Kourtellis	Telefonica Research, Spain
Eduard Marin	Telefonica Research, Spain
Souneil Park	Telefonica Research, Spain
Aravindh Raman	Telefonica Research, Spain
Ashish Rastogi	Netflix, USA
Natali Ruchansky	Netflix, USA
David Solans	Telefonica Research, Spain

Sponsors

Platinum

Gold

Silver

Bronze

PhD Forum Sponsor

Publishing Partner

Invited Talks Abstracts

Neural Wave Representations

Max Welling

University of Amsterdam, The Netherlands

Abstract. Good neural architectures are rooted in good inductive biases (a.k.a. priors). Equivariance under symmetries is a prime example of a successful physics-inspired prior which sometimes dramatically reduces the number of examples needed to learn predictive models. In this work, we tried to extend this thinking to more flexible priors in the hidden variables of a neural network. In particular, we imposed wavelike dynamics in hidden variables under transformations of the inputs, which relaxes the stricter notion of equivariance. We find that under certain conditions, wavelike dynamics naturally arises in these hidden representations. We formalize this idea in a VAE-over-time architecture where the hidden dynamics is described by a Fokker-Planck (a.k.a. drift-diffusion) equation. This in turn leads to a new definition of a disentangled hidden representation of input states that can easily be manipulated to undergo transformations. I also discussed very preliminary work on how the Schrödinger equation can also be used to move information in the hidden representations.

Biography. Prof. Dr. Max Welling is a research chair in Machine Learning at the University of Amsterdam and a Distinguished Scientist at MSR. He is a fellow at the Canadian Institute for Advanced Research (CIFAR) and the European Lab for Learning and Intelligent Systems (ELLIS) where he also serves on the founding board. His previous appointments include VP at Qualcomm Technologies, professor at UC Irvine, postdoc at the University of Toronto and UCL under the supervision of Prof. Geoffrey Hinton, and postdoc at Caltech under the supervision of Prof. Pietro Perona. He finished his PhD in theoretical high energy physics under the supervision of Nobel laureate Prof. Gerard 't Hooft. Max Welling served as associate editor-in-chief of IEEE TPAMI from 2011–2015, he has served on the advisory board of the NeurIPS Foundation since 2015 and was program chair and general chair of NeurIPS in 2013 and 2014 respectively. He was also program chair of AISTATS in 2009 and ECCV in 2016 and general chair of MIDL in 2018. Max Welling was a recipient of the ECCV Koenderink Prize in 2010 and the ICML Test of Time Award in 2021. He directs the Amsterdam Machine Learning Lab (AMLAB) and co-directs the Qualcomm-UvA deep learning lab (QUVA) and the Bosch-UvA Deep Learning lab (DELTA).

Physics-Inspired Graph Neural Networks

Michael Bronstein

University of Oxford, UK

Abstract. The message-passing paradigm has been the "battle horse" of deep learning on graphs for several years, making graph neural networks a big success in a wide range of applications, from particle physics to protein design. From a theoretical viewpoint, it established the link to the Weisfeiler-Lehman hierarchy, allowing us to analyse the expressive power of GNNs. We argue that the very "node-and-edge"-centric mindset of current graph deep learning schemes may hinder future progress in the field. As an alternative, we propose physics-inspired "continuous" learning models that open up a new trove of tools from the fields of differential geometry, algebraic topology, and differential equations so far largely unexplored in graph ML.

Biography. Michael Bronstein is the DeepMind Professor of AI at the University of Oxford. He was previously a professor at Imperial College London and held visiting appointments at Stanford, MIT, and Harvard, and has also been affiliated with three Institutes for Advanced Study (at TUM as a Rudolf Diesel Fellow (2017–2019), at Harvard as a Radcliffe fellow (2017–2018), and at Princeton as a short-time scholar (2020)). Michael received his PhD from the Technion in 2007. He is the recipient of the Royal Society Wolfson Research Merit Award, Royal Academy of Engineering Silver Medal, five ERC grants, two Google Faculty Research Awards, and two Amazon AWS ML Research Awards. He is a Member of the Academia Europaea, Fellow of the IEEE, IAPR, BCS, and ELLIS, ACM Distinguished Speaker, and World Economic Forum Young Scientist. In addition to his academic career, Michael is a serial entrepreneur and founder of multiple startup companies, including Novafora, Invision (acquired by Intel in 2012), Videocites, and Fabula AI (acquired by Twitter in 2019).

Mapping Generative AI

Kate Crawford

USC Annenberg, USA

Abstract. Training data is foundational to generative AI systems. From Common Crawl's 3.1 billion web pages to LAION-5B's corpus of almost 6 billion image-text pairs, these vast collections – scraped from the internet and treated as "ground truth" – play a critical role in shaping the epistemic boundaries that govern generative AI models. Yet training data is beset with complex social, political, and epistemological challenges. What happens when data is stripped of context, meaning, and provenance? How does training data limit what and how machine learning systems interpret the world? What are the copyright implications of these datasets? And most importantly, what forms of power do these approaches enhance and enable? This keynote is an invitation to reflect on the epistemic foundations of generative AI, and to consider the wide-ranging impacts of the current generative turn.

Biography. Professor Kate Crawford is a leading international scholar of the social implications of artificial intelligence. She is a Research Professor at USC Annenberg in Los Angeles, a Senior Principal Researcher at MSR in New York, an Honorary Professor at the University of Sydney, and the inaugural Visiting Chair for AI and Justice at the École Normale Supérieure in Paris. Her latest book, *Atlas of AI* (Yale, 2021) won the Sally Hacker Prize from the Society for the History of Technology, the ASIS&T Best Information Science Book Award, and was named one of the best books in 2021 by *New Scientist* and the *Financial Times*. Over her twenty-year research career, she has also produced groundbreaking creative collaborations and visual investigations. Her project *Anatomy of an AI System* with Vladan Joler is in the permanent collection of the Museum of Modern Art in New York and the V&A in London, and was awarded with the Design of the Year Award in 2019 and included in the Design of the Decades by the Design Museum of London. Her collaboration with the artist Trevor Paglen, *Excavating AI*, won the Ayrton Prize from the British Society for the History of Science. She has advised policymakers in the United Nations, the White House, and the European Parliament, and she currently leads the Knowing Machines Project, an international research collaboration that investigates the foundations of machine learning.

Contents – Part I

Bayesian Methods

Active Learning

Learning Objective-Specific Active Learning Strategies with Attentive Neural Processes

Tim Bakker[1]([✉]), Herke van Hoof[1], and Max Welling[1,2,3,4]

[1] AMLab, University of Amsterdam (UvA), Amsterdam, The Netherlands
{t.b.bakker,h.c.vanhoof,m.welling}@uva.nl
[2] Canadian Institute for Advanced Research (CIFAR), Toronto, Canada
[3] European Lab for Learning and Intelligent Systems (ELLIS), Amsterdam, The Netherlands
[4] Microsoft Research (MSR), Amsterdam, The Netherlands

Abstract. Pool-based active learning (AL) is a promising technology for increasing data-efficiency of machine learning models. However, surveys show that performance of recent AL methods is very sensitive to the choice of dataset and training setting, making them unsuitable for general application. In order to tackle this problem, the field Learning Active Learning (LAL) suggests to learn the active learning strategy itself, allowing it to adapt to the given setting. In this work, we propose a novel LAL method for classification that exploits symmetry and independence properties of the active learning problem with an Attentive Conditional Neural Process model. Our approach is based on learning from a myopic oracle, which gives our model the ability to adapt to nonstandard objectives, such as those that do not equally weight the error on all data points. We experimentally verify that our Neural Process model outperforms a variety of baselines in these settings. Finally, our experiments show that our model exhibits a tendency towards improved stability to changing datasets. However, performance is sensitive to choice of classifier and more work is necessary to reduce the performance the gap with the myopic oracle and to improve scalability. We present our work as a proof-of-concept for LAL on nonstandard objectives and hope our analysis and modelling considerations inspire future LAL work.

Keywords: Active Learning · Deep Learning · Neural Process

1 Introduction

Supervised machine learning models rely on large amounts of representative annotated data and the cost of gathering sufficient data can quickly become prohibitive. Active learning (AL) attempts to mitigate this problem through clever selection of data points to be annotated, thereby reducing total data requirements. To achieve this, AL exploits available information about the dataset and/or supervised task model (e.g. an image classifier) to select data points whose labels are expected to

© The Author(s), under exclusive license to Springer Nature Switzerland AG 2023
D. Koutra et al. (Eds.): ECML PKDD 2023, LNAI 14169, pp. 3–19, 2023.
https://doi.org/10.1007/978-3-031-43412-9_1

lead to the greatest increase in task model performance. Most classical AL strategies are hand-designed heuristics, based on researcher intuition or theoretical arguments [49]. Recently, much work has been focused on scaling AL to deep learning (DL) settings, which are even more data-hungry [47]. Such works for instance combine heuristics with representations learned by neural networks [8,9,20,51]), focus specifically on batch acquisition [2,7,44,48,50], or adapt Bayesian Active Learning by Disagreement (BALD) [17,26,28,32,33,40,52]. Despite these developments, it has been observed that modern AL strategies can vary wildly in performance depending on data setting and that there is no single strategy that consistently performs best [3,12,15,45,47,55]. This observation has spurred the development of Learning Active Learning (LAL) methods, which attempt to directly learn an active learning strategy on some data. The goal is to either learn a method that is specifically adapted to the data setting at hand [23,27,34], or to learn a strategy that performs well for various data settings [21,35,38,41]. Such methods have the potential of adapting to additional properties of the task as well, such as nonstandard objectives. A prominent real-life example of such objectives appears in imbalanced data settings, where rare classes are typically more important than their standard contribution to the loss or accuracy suggests. Current active learning surveys generally focus on balanced data settings; few large-scale empirical studies exist for alternative objectives, such as imbalanced data and AL methods designed to work with imbalanced data. In this paper, we propose a novel Learning Active Learning (LAL) method for pool-based active learning. The model learns from a myopic oracle, which gives it the ability to adapt to objectives besides standard classification accuracy. We validate our model in imbalanced data settings, where we show that 1) existing AL methods underperform, and 2) the myopic oracle provides a strong signal for learning. Our contributions are as follows:[1]

1. We show that a wide range of current pool-based AL methods do not outperform uniformly random acquisition on average across multiple deep learning image classification benchmarks. The tested methods generally perform worse on imbalanced data settings than on balanced data settings, suggesting that current AL methods may be under-optimised for the former.
2. We present experiments with a myopic oracle that show large performance gains over standard AL methods on simple benchmarks. We observe that these gains are larger for imbalanced data settings, suggesting the oracle exploits specific highly-informative samples during acquisition.
3. We propose a novel LAL method based on Attentive Conditional Neural Processes that learn from the myopic oracle. The model naturally exploits symmetries and independence properties of the active learning problem. In contrast to many existing LAL methods, it is not restricted to heuristics and requires no additional data and/or feature engineering.

---

[1] Experiment code can be found at: https://github.com/Timsey/npal.

2   Related Work

The field of active learning has a rich history going back decades, with the current taxonomy of methods founded on the extensive survey by [49]. In this work, we focus on *pool-based* active learning, where a 'pool' of unlabelled data points is available, and the goal is to select one or more of these to label (i.e. 'acquire' the label). Here we focus on some relevant works, and refer to the supplementary material[2], for additional discussion.

The aforementioned survey discusses a number of classical pool-based active learning methods, the most notable among which is Uncertainty Sampling. Here label acquisition is determined by the uncertainty of the classifier. How this uncertainty is measured determines the flavour of Uncertainty Sampling: Entropy selects the points that have maximum predictive entropy, Least Confident acquires the sample on which the task model is least confident in its prediction, and Margin selects the data point with the smallest difference in predicted probability for the first and second most likely class. CoreSet [48] instead take a fully geometric approach to active learning by formulating it as a Core-Set selection problem. Acquisition proceeds through optimising annotated data coverage in some representation space. The authors provide a greedy approximation to their algorithm, called k-Center Greedy, which shows competitive performance while being cheaper to compute. Learning Loss [54] adds a loss prediction module to the base task model, motivated by the idea that difficult-to-classify samples are promising acquisition candidates. This module has the goal of predicting the task model's loss on any given data point and is jointly trained with the task model. Unlabelled samples with the highest predicted loss are then acquired after training.

One potential goal in doing active learning is to select an annotated dataset that represents the true data distribution as well as possible. Based on this idea, Discriminative Active Learning (DAL) [20] learns a classifier (discriminator) to distinguish labelled and unlabelled data based on a representation learned by the task model. Acquisition proceeds by annotating the points that the classifier predicts are most likely to be part of the current unlabelled data pool. Variational Adversarial Active Learning (VAAL) [51] builds on this idea by setting up a two-play mini-max game where a Discriminator network classifies data points as belonging to the labelled or unlabelled set, based on a representation learned by a Variational AutoEncoder (VAE). The VAE is incentivised to fool the discriminator, such that the resulting discriminator probabilities encode similarity between any data point and the currently annotated set. Acquisition then occurs by choosing the least similar points. [8] is a recent Convolutional Graph Neural Network (GCN) method that represents data points as nodes in a graph instead. It too is trained to distinguish labelled and unlabelled datapoints; after training the point with the highest uncertainty according to the GCN is selected for labelling. By representing the full dataset as a graph, this method can encode

---

[2] Supplementary material can be found at: https://github.com/Timsey/npal/blob/main/full_paper.pdf.

relevant correlations between data points explicitly. [9] extend this method by using Visual Transformers to learn the graph representation. Although research into active learning methods continues, it has been widely observed that AL strategies performance varies heavily depending on data setting and that there is no single strategy that consistently performs best. Such studies typically focus on balanced data settings [3, 12, 15, 45, 47, 55].

Active Learning for Imbalanced Data: Compared to the wealth of research on active learning, little work has been done on AL for imbalanced datasets specifically. This further motivates imbalanced data settings as relevant nonstandard objectives for active learning. Existing work in this area typically incorporates explicit class-balancing strategies or additional exploration towards difficult examples. Hybrid Active Learning (HAL) [30] is built on the idea that rare samples may differentiate themselves in feature space. HAL trades off geometry-based exploration (e.g. some average distance to the currently annotated data) with informativeness-based exploitation (e.g. as in Uncertainty Sampling). Class-Balanced Active Learning (CBAL) [5] combines entropy sampling with a regulariser that assigns high values to rare points. This regulariser is the difference between a desired class-histogram (i.e. fully balanced classes) and the sum of softmax values of currently sampled points. This intuitively will have the effect of selecting rare points more often. [10] derives an active learning strategy based on selecting the example with the highest estimated probability of misclassification through Bayes' theorem and various approximate distributions learned by VAE. [1] describe a two-step approach that uses the data's class imbalance profile to switch from classical AL to a class-balancing acquisition function that favours pool points close (in embedding space) to the rarest class in the annotated data. [4] suggests that doing active learning using the variation ratio of a model ensemble may help counteract imbalance in the data.

Learning Active Learning: With the observation that existing AL methods do not consistently perform well across data settings, interest in learning pool-based active learning has risen. The seminal paper by [27] formulates Active Learning By Learning (ALBL) as a multi-armed bandit problem, where the arms are different AL heuristics. The goal is to learn to select the best heuristic for each acquisition round. [23] learns to fine-tune existing AL heuristics using a Bayesian acquisition net trained with the REINFORCE algorithm. [38] instead learn to imitate actions performed by an approximate oracle. Relatedly, [21] reduce the imitation learning goal to a learning-to-rank problem. They meta-train on synthetic data and show this generalises to other datasets. [34] formulates learning active learning as a regression problem. Similarly to our proposed method, they train a model to predict the reduction in generalisation error expected upon adding a label to the dataset. However, their method requires handcrafted global features representing the classification state and annotated dataset as input to their regressor. In contrast, our method implicitly learns the required features from the raw data, allowing for more complex relationships and simplifying engineering choices. Finally, both [41] and [35] perform meta-learning over various binary classification datasets. The former employs a meta-network that encodes dataset and classifier states into parameters for a policy, which is reinforcement learned by the REINFORCE algorithm. The latter employs reinforcement learning with a Deep Q-Network and eschews the meta-network. These methods are either still restricted to heuristics [23,27], or require gathering additional representative or synthetic datasets for training [21,35,38,41,46], as well as dataset-independent features.

3   A Study on Existing Active Learning Methods

In pool-based active learning, we are given a labeled (classification) dataset $\mathcal{D}_{annot} = \{(\boldsymbol{x}_i, \boldsymbol{y}_i)\}_{i=0}^M$ of size M, where i indexes the data points, $\boldsymbol{x}_i \in \mathbb{R}^K$ are feature vectors of size K, and $\boldsymbol{y}_i \in \{0,1\}^C$ is a (one-hot) label on C total classes. We are further given an unlabelled dataset $\mathcal{D}_{pool} = \{\boldsymbol{x}_j\}_{j=0}^N$ of size N and are tasked with selecting candidates $\boldsymbol{x}_j$ from $\mathcal{D}_{pool}$ to annotate: i.e. select the index j, obtain the label $\boldsymbol{y}_j$, and subsequently add $(\boldsymbol{x}_j, \boldsymbol{y}_j)$ to $\mathcal{D}_{annot}$. The goal of this procedure is to iteratively improve a task model, e.g. a classifier, trained on the annotated data $\mathcal{D}_{annot}$. Improvement is typically measured by some performance metric, e.g. the accuracy on some test dataset $\mathcal{D}_{test}$. Most existing AL methods depend on combinations of heuristics and representation learning for selecting the index j. The implicit expectation is that the selections such heuristics make are also highly performant according to the chosen performance metric. Here we explore whether this assumption holds in modern deep active learning.

Data: To explore the performance of existing heuristic-based AL strategies, we perform active learning on four standard ten-class image classification benchmark datasets: MNIST [11], FashionMNIST [53], SVHN [39], and CIFAR-10 [37]. We use a standard ResNet18 convolutional neural network [24] as the base classifier. We consider three objective settings for each benchmark: Balanced, Imbalanced, and Imbalanced weighted. In imbalanced settings, half the classes are undersampled by a factor 10. Evaluation is performed with a balanced accuracy metric, where instances from undersampled classes are upweighted such that all classes have the same importance. Imbalance weighted additionally takes these weights into account during training. This mimics objectives in typical imbalanced data applications, where rare class instances are often considered more important than common ones [29]. Following [8], we initialise active learning with an annotated dataset $\mathcal{D}_{annot}$ of 1000 data points that follow the specified class ratios; the remaining point also follow these class ratios and are left as the pool dataset $\mathcal{D}_{pool}$. Every acquisition step we batch annotate 1000 points using the specified AL strategy, for a total of ten steps. After each step, we retrain the classifier from scratch. See the supplementary material for further implementation details.

AL Strategies: First, we consider the three classical uncertainty sampling strategies [49]: ENTROPY, MARGIN and LstConf (least-confident). Second, we include the purely geometric approach of [48]: KCGRDY (K-center greedy). Third, active learning through Learning Loss Module: LLOSS [54]. Fourth, Variational Adversarial Active Learning VAAL [51]; a discriminator method based on VAE-learned representations. Fifth, two variations on the same convolutional graph neural network method – UNCGCN and COREGCN [8] – that employ a jointly learned discriminator and graph embedding; unlike VAAL, this approach can explicitly model inter-datapoint correlations. Sixth, we employ HAL [30] and CBAL [5] as baselines specifically developed for active learning in imbalanced data settings. HAL is further split into HALUNI and HALGAU, depending on the exploration scheme (uniform or Gaussian). Finally, RANDOM is the uniformly random sampling baseline, corresponding to no active learning.

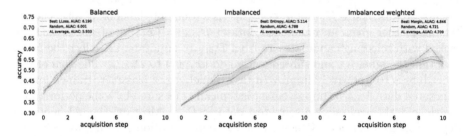

Fig. 1. Random vs. best and average of remaining AL strategies for CIFAR-10 dataset and ResNet18 classifier, 1000 acquisitions per step, and 1000 initial labels. Shaded region represents standard deviation over three seeds.

Results: In Fig. 1 we plot CIFAR-10 test accuracy as a function of acquisition step for RANDOM, the best performing AL method, and the average of all AL methods (excluding RANDOM). AUAC is the Area Under the Acquisition Curve, which is computed as the area under the curves of Fig. 1. It measures performance of the whole AL trajectory. We observe that the average active learning strategy does not perform significantly better than RANDOM in any setting. The best performing AL strategy (by AUAC) does outperform RANDOM. These results suggest that AL can be useful, but only if an appropriate strategy is found for the data at hand; a mismatched strategy can lead to performance worse than uniformly random labelling. Note that there is no consistent best performer among the AL methods. This variation in (relative) performance across benchmarks has been previously observed in the literature [3,12,15,45,47,55]. We refer to the supplementary material for implementation details and additional results. We further argue in the supplementary that the tested AL methods generally perform worse on the imbalanced objective settings than on the balanced settings, suggesting that current AL methods may be under-optimised for the former.

4   Myopic Oracle Active Learning

Given the results of the previous section, we may wonder if stronger AL strategies can be found. In particular, it would be valuable to develop strategies that perform well out of the box on many different settings. To this end, the field of Learning Active Learning (LAL) has emerged. The motivating idea is that information about the problem setting should be used for constructing the AL strategy: LAL-methods attempt to do this through learning. What is learned can vary from a choice between existing heuristics [27], to a fine-tuning of such heuristics [23], to a labelling policy that tries to generalise over datasets [21,35,38,41], to the direct improvement to the underlying classifier upon annotating a data point in the given dataset [34]. Ideally, the learned AL strategy should not be constrained to be close to human heuristics, as there is no guarantee that optimal strategies can be represented as such. Additionally, we will only require the availability of a single dataset to train an AL strategy, since finding additional datasets representative of the problem setting at hand is often not feasible in real-world applications. That leaves us with strategies similar to those in e.g. [34], where the AL strategy tries to learn a function mapping the features of an unlabelled datapoint to the expected improvement of the classifier after retraining with that datapoint labelled. Before attempting to train such a strategy, we should quantify whether such a method – if properly learned – actually improves much over existing methods. To this end, we introduce the myopic oracle strategy – denoted ORACLE in the below – which computes the actual classifier improvement on the test data for an unlabelled datapoint x_j in $\mathcal{D}_{pool}$, by treating the corresponding label y_j as known and retraining the classifier with this additional label. This improvement is stored, the classifier is reset, and the process is repeated for every datapoint in $\mathcal{D}_{pool}$. Pseudocode for obtaining improvement scores with the ORACLE is presented in the supplementary. ORACLE then selects the datapoint (x^*, y^*) corresponding to the largest classifier improvement and this point is added to the annotated dataset $\mathcal{D}_{annot}$. This oracle uses information that is typically unavailable during the AL process, namely the true labels y_j and the exact classifier improvements on the test set. The oracle is myopic, as it greedily acquires the best datapoint every acquisition step, rather than planning ahead: looking ahead t acquisition steps requires retraining the classifier $\binom{|\mathcal{D}_{pool}|}{t}$ times, which is infeasible.

Classifiers: Even for $t = 1$, the myopic oracle strategy requires retraining the underlying classifier $|\mathcal{D}_{pool}|$ times every acquisition step, which is computationally intractable for neural network classifiers. For this reason, our experiments in this setting use simpler classification models. We run experiments with logistic regression classifiers and provide additional experiments with support vector machine (SVM) classifiers in the supplementary material. These are both quick-to-train models that have a long history of being used in AL research [16,36,49,55], including within the subfield of LAL [27,34,35,46]. For both classifiers, we employ the default scikit-learn implementations [43], with class-weighting when specified.

Table 1. AL strategy AUAC and final-step test accuracy on UCI waveform dataset with logistic regression classifier, 1 acquisition per step, and 100 initial labels. Averages and standard deviations are computed over nine seeds.

Strategy	Balanced		Imbalanced		Imbalanced weighted	
	AUAC	Test acc.	AUAC	Test acc.	AUAC	Test acc.
ORACLE	**9.14 ± 0.12**	**0.93 ± 0.01**	**8.84 ± 0.39**	**0.89 ± 0.04**	**9.22 ± 0.18**	**0.93 ± 0.02**
UNCSAMP	8.67 ± 0.17	0.87 ± 0.01	8.40 ± 0.49	0.85 ± 0.04	8.55 ± 0.33	0.86 ± 0.02
KCGRDY	8.68 ± 0.28	0.87 ± 0.03	8.29 ± 0.49	0.84 ± 0.04	8.58 ± 0.37	0.86 ± 0.03
HALUNI	8.66 ± 0.26	0.87 ± 0.03	8.11 ± 0.55	0.81 ± 0.06	8.45 ± 0.46	0.85 ± 0.05
HALGAU	8.68 ± 0.23	0.87 ± 0.02	8.16 ± 0.54	0.82 ± 0.05	8.48 ± 0.45	0.85 ± 0.04
CBAL	8.67 ± 0.15	0.87 ± 0.02	8.30 ± 0.45	0.84 ± 0.04	8.65 ± 0.34	0.87 ± 0.03
RANDOM	8.65 ± 0.23	0.87 ± 0.02	8.17 ± 0.54	0.82 ± 0.05	8.42 ± 0.48	0.85 ± 0.05
NP	8.69 ± 0.19	0.87 ± 0.02	8.25 ± 0.53	0.83 ± 0.05	8.61 ± 0.33	0.87 ± 0.03

Data: These simpler classifiers do not perform well on the image datasets of Sect. 3. In order to properly study the effects acquisition has on model performance, we instead use simpler datasets. A popular choice in the field of learning active learning [35,38,46] are binary classification datasets from the UCI data repository [13]. We use the 'waveform', 'mushrooms' and 'adult' datasets, since these contain sufficient samples for our experiments post-imbalancing. Data is imbalanced by a factor of ten, as in the previous experiments. In all experiments we initialise the runs with 100 annotated examples and acquire one additional label in each of ten acquisition steps. We set aside 200 datapoints as test data $\mathcal{D}_{test}$ for evaluating the classifiers; oracle scores are also computed on this test data.

AL Strategies: We first compare ORACLE with a logistic regression classifier to the same set of AL strategies we compared to in Sect. 3. However, we skip the comparisons to LLOSS, VAAL, UNCGCN, and COREGCN, since these all require neural network classifiers as their base. Additionally, the three uncertainty sampling methods ENTROPY, MARGIN, and LSTCONF reduce to the same algorithm for binary classification: we henceforth denote this method as UNCSAMP. Our goal is to work towards a general-purpose AL method that can be trained using only available data. Therefore, we do not include the discussed LAL methods in our baselines, as these methods either adapt existing heuristics or require heavy feature engineering and/or additional datasets to train.

Results: Table 1 compares the performance of the ORACLE to pre-existing AL methods on the waveform dataset for the logistic regression classifier. The NP method will be introduced and discussed in the next section. It is clear that ORACLE dominates all other AL strategies in all settings. Note that AL is only responsible for a small fraction of the total datapoints in the final step here (10 of 110), whereas in the experiments of the previous section, it was responsible for the majority of datapoints (10000 of 11000). As may be observed in the table, such a small number of points is enough to obtain meaningful differences in scores between AL strategies. This indicates that this benchmark contains sufficient variability between strategies to observe meaningful differences in AL quality, making it an appropriate environment for learning active learning. These results suggest that the function represented by ORACLE is a strong active learner that adapts to the given objective. Moreover, we note that the performance gap between ORACLE and RANDOM – and more generally between the various AL strategies – is larger in the imbalanced settings, providing evidence that acquisition choice is more important in these settings; something ORACLE can directly exploit. We refer to the supplementary material for implementation details and additional results. In the next section, we turn our attention to an attempt at learning an approximation to the ORACLE using a Neural Process model.

5   Learning Active Learning with a Neural Process

Our approach will be to learn an approximation to ORACLE, by training a model to predict classifier improvement values for every point in $\mathcal{D}_{pool}$, given a context of annotated datapoints and classifier state. However, we cannot train on the true myopic oracle values, as this requires pool data labels and test data that we do not have access to at training time. Instead, we opt to simulate active learning scenarios by subsampling $\mathcal{D}_{annot}$. For these simulated settings we can compute the improvement values that provide the training signal. Our approach will perform the following procedure at every step of the acquisition process:

1. Simulate many active learning scenarios by subsampling $\mathcal{D}_{annot}$ into N_{sim} pairs of annotated and pool data $\left(\mathcal{S}_{annot}^{(i)}, \mathcal{S}_{pool}^{(i)}\right)$, with $i \in [1, N_{sim}]$.
2. Use the myopic oracle to compute – for each point in all the $\mathcal{S}_{pool}^{(i)}$ – the classifier improvement observed after retraining with that point and its label to the current dataset $\mathcal{S}_{annot}^{(i)}$.
3. Train a model to predict these improvements from the input $\left(\mathcal{S}_{annot}^{(i)}, \mathcal{S}_{pool}^{(i)}\right)$.

The challenge is now to design a model and training setup that can generalise strategies learned in the simulated settings to the full test-time AL setting represented by $\mathcal{D}_{annot}$ and $\mathcal{D}_{pool}$. Here we describe our considerations and resulting approach to this challenge. First, the classifier improvements used for training should not be computed using test data, as this data is not available during training. Instead, we compute these scores on a held-out 'reward' dataset $\mathcal{D}_{val}$. In practice, this reward set was used instead of a validation set, so the usual train-val-test split suffices for training our active learner. Second, our problem setup contains permutation symmetries that can be exploited: the (simulated) annotated dataset forms the context that informs the predictions (improvement scores) of our model, but the order of these points does not matter for the prediction: the context representation should be permutation invariant. Additionally, if our model predicts scores for every (simulated) pool datapoint, then these scores should be permutation equivariant: exchanging the index of two pool points should simply exchange the scores. Third, in the myopic setting, the score of any pool point is independent of any other pool point, so all point points should be treated individually (i.e., not exchange information). This imposes that the model should be invariant to the number of points in $\mathcal{D}_{pool}$. Note that the independence condition is broken in the non-myopic setting, as combinations of pool points can lead to stronger improvements than the individual myopic scores would suggest. The combination of the second and third conditions/inductive biases heavily restrict the choice of model. A natural choice is to use Neural Process (NP) models [14,18,19,31] to learn the approximate ORACLE.

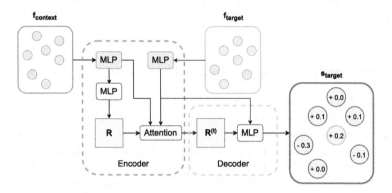

Fig. 2. Computational graph for the Attentive Conditional Neural Process model. The model takes sets of datapoints as input and predicts improvement values for the target points. Context points correspond to annotated data and target points to pool data. All MLPs are applied pointwise. The top two MLPs (in purple) share weights. (Color figure online)

The Neural Process: The Neural Process comprises a class of models for meta-learning context-conditional predictors and is a natural choice for our approximator. Given a context $\mathcal{C}$ and target input features $\boldsymbol{f}_\tau$, the Neural Process outputs a distribution $p(\boldsymbol{s}_\tau|\boldsymbol{f}_\tau;\mathcal{C})$ over target predictions $\boldsymbol{s}_\tau$. To apply this model to our problem, we identify the context $\mathcal{C}$ with the information stored in the annotated data and the classifier state, the target input features $\boldsymbol{f}_\tau$ with the features of pool datapoints, and the target predictions $\boldsymbol{s}_\tau$ with the predicted classifier improvements associated to those pool points. We can then train the NP by performing supervised learning – maximising the log likelihood of target improvements $\boldsymbol{y}_\tau$ – on simulated AL scenarios. At test time we apply the trained model with the full $\mathcal{D}_{annot}$ as context and $\mathcal{D}_{pool}$ as target input. In particular, we utilise an Attentive Conditional NP (AttnCNP) [18,31], with cross-attention between the pool and annotated points. The CNP factorises the predictive distribution conditioned on the context set, as

$$p(\boldsymbol{s}_\tau|\boldsymbol{f}_\tau;\mathcal{C}) = \prod_{t=1}^{T} p(s^{(t)}|f_\tau^{(t)};\mathcal{C}), \tag{1}$$

where T is the number of target datapoints. This modelling choice satisfies the independence of pool point predictions. The context $\mathcal{C}$ should be permutation invariant and is typically encoded into a global representation R. The NP is parameterised by a neural network with parameters $\{\theta, \phi\}$ and each factor is typically set to be a Gaussian density [14], as:

$$
p_{\theta,\phi}(\boldsymbol{s}_\tau|\boldsymbol{f}_\tau;\mathcal{C}) = p_{\theta,\phi}(\boldsymbol{s}_\tau|\boldsymbol{f}_\tau;R) = \prod_{t=1}^{T} p_{\theta,\phi}(s^{(t)}|f_\tau^{(t)};R) = \prod_{t=1}^{T} \mathcal{N}(s^{(t)}; \mu^{(t)}, \sigma^{2(t)}),
$$
(2)

where $R = \mathrm{Enc}_\theta(\mathcal{C})$ encodes the context and $(\mu^{(t)}, \sigma^{2(t)}) = \mathrm{Dec}_\phi(R, \boldsymbol{f}_\tau^{(t)})$ decodes the context encoding and the target features into target predictive parameters. The AttnCNP extends this model by replacing the global representation R with a target-specific representation $R^{(t)}$ through the use of an attention mechanism. In particular, we use the attention mechanism taken from the Image Transformer [42] to perform cross-attention between context and target features, constructing $R^{(t)}$. Here context features $\boldsymbol{f}_\mathcal{C}$ are treated as keys and target features $\boldsymbol{f}_\tau$ as queries. Values are constructed from $\boldsymbol{f}_\mathcal{C}$ by applying a pointwise MLP with 2 hidden layers of size 32 and ReLU activations. Our implementation does not use self-attention on the context or target features, as applying self-attention to the target features violates the independence of the pool point scores. In preliminary experimentation, we found that omitting the attention mechanism – e.g. $R^{(t)} = R$ – resulted in performance drops due to underfitting the target function, as has been observed in the Neural Process literature [31]. A computational graph of our model is presented in Fig. 2. This model satisfies the required permutation symmetries while allowing scores of pool points to be given by expressive functions that depend on the context and pool point. In this proof-of-concept study we do not explore the use of uncertainty information for acquisition, rather opting to acquire the datapoint for which $\mu^{(t)}$ – the predicted mean score – is maximal, as $j = \arg\max_{t\in[1,T]} \mu^{(t)}$. We then acquire the pool datapoint with index j, completing a single step in the Active Learning process. The Neural Process is then initialised from scratch, in preparation for the next acquisition step.

Data: The experiments for our Neural Process model (NP) are performed on the datasets described in the previous section. In order to train the NP model, we simulate active learning scenarios by sampling from the existing annotated dataset $\mathcal{D}_{annot}$. We define a set of fractions Q and uniformly sample from these a total of N_{sim} times, leading to a set of annotation fractions $\{q_i\}_{i=1}^{N_{sim}}$. For each value of i, we then assign the corresponding fraction q_i of datapoints from $\mathcal{D}_{annot}$ to a *simulated* annotated dataset $\mathcal{S}_{annot}^{(i)}$; the remaining points are assigned to a *simulated* pool dataset $\mathcal{S}_{pool}^{(i)}$. This procedure results in a set of N_{sim} simulated/sampled active learning problems of various sizes. We then compute oracle scores of all pool points in each of the resulting AL problems $(\mathcal{S}_{annot}^{(i)}, \mathcal{S}_{pool}^{(i)})$. Since we do not have access to test data at train time, the oracle scores are instead computed on the held-out $\mathcal{D}_{val}$. We present pseudocode in Algorithm 1.

Algorithm 1: Training the NP model.

Data: Annotated dataset $\mathcal{D}_{annot}$, Neural Process model NP_θ, number of simulations N_{sim}, set of fractions Q, oracle ORACLE, base classifier model C, scoring function SCORE evaluated on $\mathcal{D}_{val}$.

Result: Trained parameters θ^* for NP.

for $i = 1, 2, ..., N_{sim}$ **do**

    $q_i \leftarrow$ sample(Q) ;   /* Uniformly sample an 'annotation fraction' */

    $S_{annot}^{(i)} \leftarrow \varnothing$;   /* Initialise a simulated annotated set */

    $S_{pool}^{(i)} \leftarrow \mathcal{D}_{annot}$;   /* Initialise a simulated pool set */

    while $|S_{annot}^{(i)}| < round(q_i \cdot |\mathcal{D}_{annot}|)$ **do**

        Sample index j of datapoints in $\mathcal{D}_{annot}$ uniformly without replacement ;

        $S_{annot}^{(i)} \leftarrow S_{annot}^{(i)} \cup (\boldsymbol{x}_j, \boldsymbol{y}_j)$;

        $S_{pool}^{(i)} \leftarrow S_{pool}^{(i)} \setminus (\boldsymbol{x}_j, \boldsymbol{y}_j)$;

    end

    $V_i \leftarrow$ ORACLE $\left(S_{annot}^{(i)}, S_{pool}^{(i)}, C, \text{SCORE} \right)$;   /* Obtain improvement scores with Oracle (pseudocode in supplementary) */

end

$\theta^* \leftarrow NP_\theta.\text{FIT} \left(\{ S_{annot}^{(i)}, S_{pool}^{(i)}, V_i \}_{i=1}^{N_{sim}} \right)$;   /* Train the NP on the simulated AL settings */

return θ^*

Experimentally we find that simulating with a variety of fractions in Q improves generalisation to the target problem over using a fixed single fraction. Our experiments use $Q = \{0.1, 0.2, ..., 0.8, 0.9\}$ and $N_{sim} = 300$. Preliminary experimentation showed no performance increase for larger values of N_{sim}, while using $N_{sim} = 100$ led to slight performance decreases. The held-out dataset $\mathcal{D}_{val}$ consists of the same 100 datapoints for all i.

Results: Table 1 shows the performance of our method – NP – on the UCI waveform dataset with logistic regression classifier. Ignoring ORACLE, the Neural Process ranks best of all active learning methods in AUAC on the Balanced setting, second on Imbalanced weighted, and fourth on Imbalanced. In Fig. 3 we show the performance difference between our method and a chosen baseline. Here we choose the average of AL strategies – AL AVERAGE – as the baseline, where we exclude ORACLE, RANDOM, and NP from the average. This choice of baseline allows us to clearly see whether any particular method is expected to improve over a naive application of active learning. We also show the performance of the best AL strategy – BEST – again excluding ORACLE, RANDOM, and NP from the selection. This represents the relative performance of choosing the best AL strategy post-hoc. We observe that NP performs on par with BEST for Balanced and Imbalanced weighted, and performs similarly to AL AVERAGE for the Imbalanced setting. In all cases, the gap with ORACLE remains large, indicating potential room for improvement. Shaded regions correspond to twice

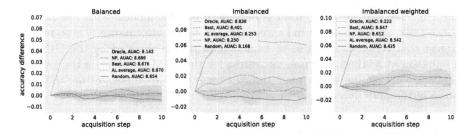

Fig. 3. Relative performance of acquisition strategies for waveform dataset and logistic regression classifier, 1 acquisition per step, and 100 initial labels. Accuracy differences of RANDOM, ORACLE, NP and the best remaining AL strategy (BEST) are computed w.r.t. the average of remaining AL strategies (AL AVERAGE). The shaded region represents twice the standard error of the mean over nine seeds.

the standard error of the mean, i.e., $2 \cdot \frac{\sigma}{\sqrt{n}}$, where σ is the standard deviation and n the number of runs. Peformance tables and figures for the mushrooms and adult dataset are provided in the supplementary material. NP at least slightly outperforms AL AVERAGE on Imbalanced and Imbalanced weighted for these datasets and in half those cases achieves near-BEST performance. However, NP ranks near the bottom in the Balanced setting here. Interestingly, RANDOM outperforms almost all methods on Balanced, possibly indicating increased difficulty in active learning, although ORACLE does still demonstrate a large performance gap.

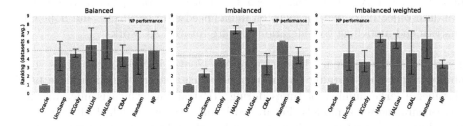

Fig. 4. Relative AUAC rank of AL strategies averaged over the three UCI datasets for logistic regression. The standard deviation of this rank is denoted by the error bars.

Our method is partially motivated by the need for AL algorithms that perform more stably across different data settings. To this end, Fig. 4 shows the average AUAC ranking of every AL method across the three UCI datasets. We observe that NP is the best performing AL method on average for the Imbalanced weighted setting and has more middling performance for the other two settings, with Balanced being the worst for our model. Inspecting the ranking standard deviation, we further see that our model achieves a relatively stable ranking across the three datasets in the Imbalanced weighted setting. This stability again degrades for Imbalanced and even further for Balanced. However, note that low standard deviation is only desirable for models with low performance rank, as it otherwise indicates a stable underperformance. These results suggest that NP is better able to exploit information encoded by the ORACLE in imbalanced settings. We present results for the SVM classifier in the supplementary. This setting seems more difficult for NP to learn, suggesting that the choice of the underlying classifier is important.

6   Conclusion and Discussion

It has been observed in the literature that a wide range of current pool-based active learning methods do not perform better than uniform acquisition on average across standard deep learning benchmarks. We have experimentally verified these results and extended them to imbalanced data settings, which are relevant alternative objectives for many real-world applications. We have explored the validity of using a myopic oracle as a target function for learning active learning (LAL) and have shown its dominating performance on simple active learning tasks. Finally, we have identified symmetry and independence properties of such active learning problems and have modelled these using an Attentive Conditional Neural Process. Unlike existing LAL methods, our model (NP) is not based on existing heuristics, and requires no feature engineering and/or additional datasets to train. Our model generally outperforms the average of the competing AL methods in imbalanced data settings, and occasionally all of them individually. However, future work is needed to evaluate performance on additional datasets, reduce the performance gap with the myopic oracle, and improve scalability. We present our work as a proof-of-concept for LAL on non-standard objectives – with a focus on imbalanced data settings – and hope our analysis and modelling considerations inspire future LAL work.

Limitations: The primary limitation of our Neural Process approach is scalability. Supervised learning on the myopic oracle requires retraining the base classifier a large number of times during NP training, which is infeasible for large neural network models. Future work may explore to which degree functions learned on simple classifiers can be transferred to more powerful models. Next, the acquisition procedure may be improved through the use of uncertainty information present in the NP. Finally, the NP input may be augmented with additional features – e.g., predicted class probabilities of pool points – to potentially improve learning. Preliminary experimentation showed little effect on performance: we leave further exploring the use of extra features for future work.

Ethical Considerations. In recent years, machine learning has had a large impact on society by enabling the development of a variety of new, widely-deployed technologies. Opinions on the value of such technologies vary, but it is clear that they have had both positive and negative impacts. Our research topic of active learning is a promising technology for increasing the efficiency of machine learning model training. Developments in active learning may reduce barrier-to-entry for training and deploying high-performing predictive models, which potentially has both positive and negative downstream consequences. On the positive side, wider access to strong models may increase the adoption of life-saving or simply quality-of-life-improving technologies. Additionally, it may allow relatively less powerful interest groups to not fall behind larger or more powerful institutions in capabilities, thus supporting democratisation of AI. On the negative side, improved active learning has the potential to exacerbate the negative effects of machine learning applications as well. Such exacerbation may happen through widening the aforementioned capability gap between less and more powerful institutions (e.g., by potentially easing model scaling), or through reinforcing existing model biases during training. Additionally, training large-scale models consumes a large amount of energy, potentially worsening the current energy and climate crises. Finally, any machine learning capabilities research potentially exacerbates the future risks of AI misalignment; risks that are worrying to an increasing share of the research community [22, 25].

Acknowledgments. This work is supported by the 'Efficient Deep Learning' (EDL, https://efficientdeeplearning.nl) research programme, which is financed by the Dutch Research Council (NWO) domain Applied and Engineering Sciences (TTW). We are have used Weights & Biases [6] for experiment tracking.

References

1. Aggarwal, U., Popescu, A., Hudelot, C.: Active learning for imbalanced datasets. In: WACV (2020)
2. Ash, J.T., Zhang, C., Krishnamurthy, A., Langford, J., Agarwal, A.: Deep batch active learning by diverse, uncertain gradient lower bounds. In: ICLR (2020)
3. Baram, Y., El-Yaniv, R., Luz, K.: Online choice of active learning algorithms. JMLR **5**, 255–291 (2004)
4. Beluch, W.H., Genewein, T., Nurnberger, A., Kohler, J.M.: The power of ensembles for active learning in image classification. In: CVPR (2018)
5. Bengar, J., van de Weijer, J., Fuentes, L., Raducanu, B.: Class-balanced active learning for image classification. In: WACV (2022)
6. Biewald, L.: Experiment tracking with Weights and Biases (2020). https://www.wandb.com/
7. Bıyık, E., Wang, K., Anari, N., Sadigh, D.: Batch active learning using determinantal point processes. arXiv e-prints (2019)
8. Caramalau, R., Bhattarai, B., Kim, T.K.: Sequential graph convolutional network for active learning. In: CVPR (2021)
9. Caramalau, R., Bhattarai, B., Kim, T.K.: Visual transformer for task-aware active learning. arXiv e-prints (2021)
10. Choi, J., et al.: VaB-AL: incorporating class imbalance and difficulty with variational Bayes for active learning. In: CVPR (2020)
11. Deng, L.: The MNIST database of handwritten digit images for machine learning research. IEEE-SPM **26**, 141–142 (2012)
12. Desreumaux, L., Lemaire, V.: Learning active learning at the crossroads? Evaluation and discussion. arXiv e-prints (2020)

13. Dua, D., Graff, C.: UCI machine learning repository (2017). http://archive.ics.uci.edu/ml

14. Dubois, Y., Gordon, J., Foong, A.Y.: Neural process family (2020). http://yanndubs.github.io/Neural-Process-Family/

15. Ebert, S., Fritz, M., Schiele, B.: RALF: a reinforced active learning formulation for object class recognition. In: CVPR (2012)

16. Ertekin, S., Huang, J., Bottou, L., Giles, L.: Learning on the border: active learning in imbalanced data classification. In: CIKM (2007)

17. Gal, Y., Islam, R., Ghahramani, Z.: Deep Bayesian active learning with image data. In: ICML (2017)

18. Garnelo, M., et al.: Conditional neural processes. In: ICML (2018)

19. Garnelo, M., et al.: Neural Processes. arXiv e-prints (2018)

20. Gissin, D., Shalev-Shwartz, S.: Discriminative active learning. arXiv e-prints (2019)

21. Gonsior, J., Thiele, M., Lehner, W.: ImitAL: learning active learning strategies from synthetic data. arXiv e-prints (2021)

22. Grace, K.: What do ML researchers think about AI in 2022? https://aiimpacts.org/what-do-ml-researchers-think-about-ai-in-2022/

23. Haussmann, M., Hamprecht, F., Kandemir, M.: Deep active learning with adaptive acquisition. In: IJCAI (2019)

24. He, K., Zhang, X., Ren, S., Sun, J.: Deep residual learning for image recognition. In: CVPR (2016)

25. Hendrycs, D.: Statement on AI Risk. http://www.safe.ai/statement-on-ai-risk

26. Houlsby, N., Huszár, F., Ghahramani, Z., Lengyel, M.: Bayesian active learning for classification and preference learning. arXiv e-prints (2011)

27. Hsu, W.N., Lin, H.T.: Active learning by learning. In: AAAI (2015)

28. Jesson, A., Tigas, P., van Amersfoort, J., Kirsch, A., Shalit, U., Gal, Y.: Causal-BALD: deep Bayesian active learning of outcomes to infer treatment-effects from observational data. In: NeurIPS (2021)

29. Johnson, J.M., Khoshgoftaar, T.M.: Survey on deep learning with class imbalance. J. Big Data **6**, 27 (2019). https://doi.org/10.1186/s40537-019-0192-5

30. Kazerouni, A., Zhao, Q., Xie, J., Tata, S., Najork, M.: Active learning for skewed data sets. arXiv e-prints (2020)

31. Kim, H., et al.: Attentive neural processes. In: ICLR (2019)

32. Kirsch, A., Gal, Y.: PowerEvaluationBALD: efficient evaluation-oriented deep (Bayesian) active learning with stochastic acquisition functions. arXiv e-prints (2021)

33. Kirsch, A., Rainforth, T., Gal, Y.: Test distribution-aware active learning: a principled approach against distribution shift and outliers. arXiv e-prints (2021)

34. Konyushkova, K., Sznitman, R., Fua, P.: Learning active learning from data. In: NeurIPS (2017)

35. Konyushkova, K., Sznitman, R., Fua, P.: Discovering general-purpose active learning strategies. arXiv e-prints (2018)

36. Kremer, J., Steenstrup Pedersen, K., Igel, C.: Active learning with support vector machines. DMKD **4**, 313–326 (2014)

37. Krizhevsky, A.: Learning multiple layers of features from tiny images. University of Toronto, Technical report (2009)

38. Liu, M., Buntine, W., Haffari, G.: Learning how to actively learn: a deep imitation learning approach. In: ACL (2018)

39. Netzer, Y., Wang, T., Coates, A., Bissacco, A., Wu, B., Ng, A.Y.: Reading digits in natural images with unsupervised feature learning. In: NeurIPS Workshop (2011)

40. Nikoloska, I., Simeone, O.: BAMLD: Bayesian active meta-learning by disagreement. arXiv e-prints (2021)
41. Pang, K., Dong, M., Wu, Y., Hospedales, T.: Meta-learning transferable active learning policies by deep reinforcement learning. arXiv e-prints (2018)
42. Parmar, N., et al.: Image transformer. In: ICML (2018)
43. Pedregosa, F., et al.: Scikit-learn: machine learning in Python. In: JMLR (2011)
44. Pinsler, R., Gordon, J., Nalisnick, E.T., Hernández-Lobato, J.M.: Bayesian batch active learning as sparse subset approximation. In: NeurIPS (2019)
45. Ramirez-Loaiza, M.E., Sharma, M., Kumar, G., Bilgic, M.: Active learning: an empirical study of common baselines. DMKD **31**, 287–313 (2017). https://doi.org/10.1007/s10618-016-0469-7
46. Ravi, S., Larochelle, H.: Meta-learning for batch mode active learning. In: ICLR Workshop (2018)
47. Ren, P., et al.: A survey of deep active learning. arXiv e-prints (2020)
48. Sener, O., Savarese, S.: Active learning for convolutional neural networks: a core-set approach. In: ICLR (2018)
49. Settles, B.: Active learning literature survey. University of Wisconsin-Madison, Technical report (2009)
50. Shui, C., Zhou, F., Gagn'e, C., Wang, B.: Deep active learning: unified and principled method for query and training. In: AISTATS (2020)
51. Sinha, S., Ebrahimi, S., Darrell, T.: Variational adversarial active learning. In: ICCV (2019)
52. Woo, J.O.: BABA: beta approximation for Bayesian active learning. arXiv e-prints (2021)
53. Xiao, H., Rasul, K., Vollgraf, R.: Fashion-MNIST: a novel image dataset for benchmarking machine learning algorithms. arXiv e-prints (2017)
54. Yoo, D., Kweon, I.S.: Learning loss for active learning. In: CVPR (2019)
55. Zhan, X., Chan, A.B.: ALdataset: a benchmark for pool-based active learning. arXiv e-prints (2020)

Real: A Representative Error-Driven Approach for Active Learning

Cheng Chen[1], Yong Wang[2]([⊠]), Lizi Liao[2], Yueguo Chen[1],
and Xiaoyong Du[1]

[1] Renmin University of China, Beijing, China
{chchen,chenyueguo,duyong}@ruc.edu.cn
[2] Singapore Management University, Singapore, Singapore
{yongwang,lzliao}@smu.edu.sg

Abstract. Given a limited labeling budget, active learning (AL) aims to sample the most informative instances from an unlabeled pool to acquire labels for subsequent model training. To achieve this, AL typically measures the informativeness of unlabeled instances based on uncertainty and diversity. However, it does not consider erroneous instances with their neighborhood error density, which have great potential to improve the model performance. To address this limitation, we propose REAL, a novel approach to select data instances with Representative Errors for Active Learning. It identifies minority predictions as *pseudo errors* within a cluster and allocates an adaptive sampling budget for the cluster based on estimated error density. Extensive experiments on five text classification datasets demonstrate that REAL consistently outperforms all best-performing baselines regarding accuracy and F1-macro scores across a wide range of hyperparameter settings. Our analysis also shows that REAL selects the most representative pseudo errors that match the distribution of ground-truth errors along the decision boundary. Our code is publicly available at https://github.com/withchencheng/ECML_PKDD_23_Real.

Keywords: Active learning · Text classification · Error-driven

1 Introduction

Labeling data for machine learning is costly, and the budget on the amount of labels we can gather is often limited. Therefore, it is crucial to make the training process of machine learning models more label-efficient, especially for applications where labels are expensive to acquire. Active learning (AL) is to select a small amount of the most informative instances from an unlabeled pool, aiming to maximize the model performance gain when using the selected instances (labeled) for further training. Identification of the most informative instances from the unlabeled data pool is critical to the success of AL.

The AL techniques can be classified into three groups: uncertainty-based, diversity-based, and hybrid methods. Uncertainty-based methods select

D. Koutra et al. (Eds.): ECML PKDD 2023, LNAI 14169, pp. 20–37, 2023.
https://doi.org/10.1007/978-3-031-43412-9_2

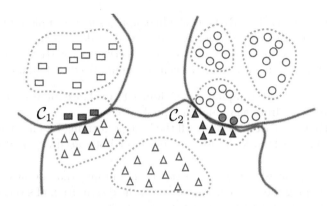

Fig. 1. An illustrative example of REAL. The solid thick lines denote the model decision boundaries, separating data points into three predicted classes (rectangles, circles, and triangles). The dashed irregular circles are clusters of data points. REAL samples the minority predictions as *pseudo errors* (■ ▲) in cluster C_1 and C_2 for labeling. If our budget exceeds the number of pseudo errors, REAL will pick blue instances (▲ ●) where the model has the least confidence in its predictions. (Color figure online)

instances whose prediction probability is more evenly distributed over classes [27, 28], instances with a larger expected loss/gradient [3,44], or those closer to decision boundaries [13,37]. However, solely relying on instance-level uncertainty metrics may cause redundancy in samples [45]. Hence, diversity-based methods try to mitigate the redundancy problem by selecting a small but diverse set of data instances to represent *the whole unlabeled pool* [23]. However, they ignore the fact that training on errors is more label-efficient [7]. Hybrid methods try to select instances that are both uncertain and diverse [45,46]. Our proposed method belongs to the hybrid category. Our novelty is to seek representativeness for the *errors* rather than the *whole unlabeled pool*, by selecting instances with a larger error probability and higher neighborhood error density. Figure 1 shows an illustrative example of our method. Specially, we first cluster the unlabeled instances by their representations. The majority prediction in a cluster is expected to be correct even with limited labeled training data [1,6,39], owing to the strong representation power of the pretrained models for images [18] or texts [31]. Also, it is common for AL to achieve a decent test accuracy after the warm-up training on the initial limited labeled data [33,45]. Consequently, we treat the majority prediction in a cluster as the *pseudo label* for all the instances in the cluster. We call instances in a cluster whose predictions disagree with the cluster *pseudo label* as *pseudo errors*. More pseudo errors with a lower prediction probability (larger disagreement) on the pseudo label will bring a larger sampling budget to its affiliated cluster. In this way, we emphasize dense areas of errors, and thus adaptively select more representative errors.

To our best knowledge, REAL is the first approach to sample representative errors to achieve label-efficient active learning. By taking text classification as an example application, we demonstrate the effectiveness of REAL. In summary, the major contributions of this paper can be summarized as follows:

- We propose a new AL sampling algorithm, REAL, that explores selecting representative errors from the unlabeled pool.
- We show REAL consistently beats all the best-performing baselines on five text classification benchmark datasets in terms of both accuracy and F1-macro scores.
- We empirically investigate error distribution and find that 1) most errors are distributed along the decision boundary; 2) the distribution of selections made by REAL align well with that of ground-truth errors.

2   Preliminaries

2.1   Related Work

Uncertainty-Based. Uncertainty-based sampling is to sample the most uncertain instances for model training. Three classical metrics for the uncertainty of model prediction probabilities are: entropy [27,28], least confidence [27,29], and smallest margin [36]. Recent research studies take the expected loss [44], expected generalization error reduction [24], or distance to the decision boundary [37] as surrogates for uncertainty. CAL [33] selects contrastive examples that are similar in the feature space of pre-trained language model (PLM) and maximally different in the output probabilities. Unlike CAL which ignores the correctness of sampled instances, our method aims to mine the yet-to-be errors. OPAL [25] computes the expected misclassification loss reduction, but is limited to binary classification using the outdated Parzen window classifier.

Diversity-Based. Diversity-based sampling aims to maximize the diversity of sampled instances. Cluster-Margin [9] selects a diverse of instances with the smallest margin using hierarchical agglomerate clustering. Sener and Savarese [38] proposed a coreset approach to find a representative subset from the unlabeled pool. Kim et al. [23] assessed the density of unlabeled pool and selected diverse samples mainly from regions of low density. Meanwhile, generative adversarial learning [17] is applied in AL as a binary classification task. They trained an adversarial classifier to confuse data from the training set and that from the pool. However, our method cares about the density of errors rather than the whole unlabeled pool.

Hybrid. Hybrid AL methods try to combine uncertainty and diversity sampling. Such a combination can be achieved by meta learning [5,19] and reinforcement learning [14,30], which automatically learn a sampling strategy in each AL round instead of using a fixed heuristic. BADGE [3] and ALPS [46] both compute uncertainty representations of instances and then cluster them. BADGE transforms data into gradient embeddings that encode the model confidence and then apply

K-Means++ [2]. ALPS first utilizes the self-supervision loss of PLM as uncertainty representation. ACTUNE [45] uses weighted K-Means clustering to find highly uncertain regions. The K-Means clustering in ACTUNE is weighted by some uncertainty measure, e.g., entropy or CAL [33]. ACTUNE deliberately tries to separate the uncertain regions from the confident regions via weighted clustering, with an implicit assumption that the two kinds of regions are separable.

2.2 Problem Definition

We take text classification as an example to illustrate the core idea of our approach. Given a small labeled set $\mathcal{D}_l = \{(x_i, y_i)\}_{i=1}^{L}$ (warm-up dataset) for initial model training and a large unlabeled data pool $\mathcal{D}_u = \{(x_i,)\}_{i=1}^{U}$, where x_i is the i−th input instance (e.g., the token sequence for text classification), $y_i \in \{1, \dots, Y\}$ is the target label, and $\mathcal{D}_l \ll \mathcal{D}_u$, we want to select and obtain the labels of the most informative instances in $\mathcal{D}_u$ for training model $\mathcal{M}$, so that the performance of $\mathcal{M}$ can be maximized given a fixed labeling budget B^1. $\mathcal{M}$ is trained iteratively. Suppose there are T AL rounds in total, then the budget for each round is $b = B/T$. In each AL round, a sampling function $\alpha(\mathcal{D}_u, \mathcal{M})$ selects b samples from $\mathcal{D}_u$ based on the previously learned model $\mathcal{M}$, and then moves the labeled b samples into $\mathcal{D}_l$. Model $\mathcal{M}$ is trained on the updated $\mathcal{D}_l$ and then evaluated on a hold-out test set. The AL process terminates when the total budget B is exhausted or the model performance is good enough. The core of an AL method is to study the sampling function α.

3 Representative Pseudo Errors

3.1 Overview of Representative Error-Driven Active Learning

We aim to explore one critical research question for active learning: how will *learning from errors* improve the active learning accuracy for models? Intuitively, sampling more errors for model training will prevent the model from making the same mistakes on the test set, thus improving the test accuracy. Errors bring larger loss values, making them more informative for model training [44]. Though one existing work [7] tries to directly calculate the erroneous probability for some image using the Bayesian theorem, it ignores the density of errors. Other than computing a single unlabeled instance's erroneous probability, we develop a sense of representativeness for the selected errors into our approach.

The AL process starts from training the model $\mathcal{M}$ on the initial labeled data set $\mathcal{D}_l^{(0)}$. Formally, we minimize the average cross entropy loss ℓ for all the

---

1 Following the convention in machine learning community [9,24,28,30], we ignore the cognitive difference for labeling different instances studied in the HCI community[8, 34], and assume the labeling cost is 1 for every instance. For example, if our total labeling budget is $B = 800$ and we have $T = 8$ rounds of AL, then $b = 100$ is the budget per round.

instances in $\mathcal{D}_l^{(0)}$:

$$\min_{\theta} \frac{1}{|\mathcal{D}_l^{(0)}|} \sum_{(x_i, y_i) \in \mathcal{D}_l} \ell(\mathcal{M}(x_i, \theta^{(0)}), y_i). \tag{1}$$

In each of the following AL rounds, REAL (Algorithm 1) selects a set of representative errors Q consisting of b instances from $\mathcal{D}_u$, obtains their labels, and then adds Q into $\mathcal{D}_l$ for subsequent model training. Algorithm 1 consists of two components: *pseudo error identification* and *adaptive sampling of representative errors*.

3.2   Pseudo Error Identification

The first challenge is to select instances from $\mathcal{D}_u$ where the model $\mathcal{M}$ makes mistakes, which is non-trivial since we do not have access to the ground truth labels before selection. However, prior studies [1,39,49] have shown that PLM can effectively learn the sentence representations and support accurate classifications very well by simply clustering the embedded representations of sentences [39]. Also, it is commonly-seen that active learning will be employed after the machine learning models have achieved a reasonable performance [33,45]. Building upon these facts, it is safe to expect the majority prediction in a cluster by the PLM has a high probability to be the ground truth label, even with a small amount of training data. Thus, we assume that the majority prediction is the correct label for all the instances in the cluster. Our preliminary experiments also show a relatively high and stable accuracy of our pseudo-label assignment strategy, i.e., over 0.80 for all the chosen datasets. Since the majority prediction is treated as the pseudo label to each cluster, pseudo errors are defined as those instances whose predictions disagree with the majority prediction in each cluster. As will be shown in Sect. 5, the sampled pseudo errors usually have higher error rates when compared with ground truths, indicating that such a way of defining pseudo labels and pseudo errors is effective.

In round t ($1 \le t \le T$) of active learning, we first obtain the representations of instances in $\mathcal{D}_u$ by feeding them into model $\mathcal{M}$'s encoder $\Phi(.)$. Specifically, we only take the [CLS] token embedding from the output in the last layer of encoder $\Phi(.)$. Then K-Means++ [2] is employed as an initialization of the seeding scheme for the following clustering process. We denote the k-th cluster as $\mathcal{C}_k^{(t)} = \{x_i | c_i^{(t)} = k\}, k \in \{1, \ldots, K\}$, where $c_i^{(t)}$ is the cluster id for the instance x_i at AL round t. After obtaining K clusters with the corresponding data $\mathcal{C}_k^{(t)}$, we assign a pseudo label for each cluster. First, the pseudo label for an individual instance x_i at round t of AL is computed as:

$$\tilde{y}_i = \underset{j \in \{1, \ldots, Y\}}{\mathrm{argmax}} \; [\mathcal{M}(x_i; \theta^{(t)})]_j, \tag{2}$$

where $\mathcal{M}(x_i; \theta^{(t)}) \in \mathbb{R}^Y$ is the probability distribution for instance x_i over the Y target classes, and $[\mathcal{M}(x_i; \theta^{(t)})]_j$ is the j-th entry denoting the probability of

x_i belonging to the target class j, inferenced by the current model. Then the majority vote (the pseudo label of cluster $\mathcal{C}_k^{(t)}$) is derived as:

$$y_{maj} = \underset{j}{\arg\max}(\sum_{i \in \mathcal{C}_k^{(t)}} \mathbb{1}\{\widetilde{y}_i = j\})/|\mathcal{C}_k^{(t)}|. \tag{3}$$

The instances that are not predicted as y_{maj} are defined as pseudo errors in the corresponding cluster $\mathcal{C}_k^{(t)}$.

3.3   Adaptive Sampling of Representative Errors

For each round of active learning, assuming that the labeling budget is b, we need to decide how we should select the b samples from the unlabeled pseudo errors. To ensure the representativeness of selected samples, we allocate the sampling budget b to each cluster according to the density of pseudo errors in the cluster, i.e., the percentage of the pseudo errors within a cluster over the total number of pseudo errors in the whole unlabeled data pool. A larger sampling budget will be allocated to the cluster with a higher pseudo error density. The density of pseudo errors ϵ_k for cluster $\mathcal{C}_k^{(t)}$ is defined as:

$$\epsilon_k = \sum_{x_e \in \widetilde{E}_k} \epsilon(x_e), \tag{4}$$

Algorithm 1. Round t of REAL
***

Input: unlabeled pool $\mathcal{D}_u$, budget for one iteration b, classification model $\mathcal{M}$, number
of clusters K, model's encoding part $\Phi(.)$
Output: sampled set Q

1 $\mathcal{C}_k^{(t)} = \text{KMeans}(\Phi(\mathcal{D}_u)), (k \in \{1, \ldots, K\})$ ▷ Clustering $\mathcal{D}_u$
2 **for** $k \in \{1, \ldots, K\}$ **do**   ▷ Process cluster $\mathcal{C}_k$
3 $\quad$ Run Eq. 2 for cluster $\mathcal{C}_k$ to get the instance-level pseudo labels
4 $\quad$ Run Eq. 3 to find the cluster-level pseudo label y_{maj} for $\mathcal{C}_k$
5 $\quad$ Init pseudo error set $\widetilde{E}_k$ in Eq. 4
6 $\quad$ Compute the error density ϵ_k for cluster $\mathcal{C}_k$ by Eq. 4
7 **end**
8 Get the sampling budget b_k based on error density for each cluster using Eq. 6
9 **if** $\sum_k b_k < b$ **then**
10 $\quad$ $\Delta = b - \sum_k b_k$ ▷ Budget residual
11 **end**
12 $b_k \mathrel{+}= 1, \forall k \in \Delta\text{-}\arg\max_k(b_k)$ and $b_k > 0$ ▷ Allocate residual to top-Δ largest b_k
13 $Q = \emptyset$ ▷ Init the sample set
14 **for** $k \in \{1, \ldots, K\}$ **do**
15 $\quad$ Random sample $\min(|\widetilde{E}_k|, b_k)$ instances from $\widetilde{E}_k$ into Q
16 **end**
17 **if** $|Q| < b$ **then**
18 $\quad$ $Q = Q \cup \{(b - |Q|)$ instances from $\mathcal{D}_u$ with top $\epsilon(.)$ scores (Eq. 5) and not in $Q\}$
19 **end**

where $\widetilde{E}_k = \{\mathrm{x}_e | \mathrm{x}_e \in \mathcal{C}_k^{(t)} \text{ and } \widetilde{y}_e \neq y_{maj}\}$ is the pseudo error set in the k-th cluster, and $\epsilon(\mathrm{x}_e)$ is one pseudo error x_e's contribution to the cluster-level error density:

$$\epsilon(\mathrm{x}_e) = 1 - [\mathcal{M}(\mathrm{x}_e; \theta^{(t)})]_{maj}. \tag{5}$$

The sampling budget b_k for the k-th cluster is then normalized as:

$$b_k = \left\lfloor b \frac{\epsilon_k}{\sum_i \epsilon_i} \right\rfloor, \forall k \in \{1 \ldots K\}. \tag{6}$$

Apart from selecting pseudo errors, we also try to select errors near the classification decision boundary by emphasizing clusters with denser pseudo errors. The empirical evidences in Sect. 5 also show that our adaptive budget allocation is able to pick more *representative* pseudo errors along the decision boundary.

In real-world applications of AL, it is possible that there may not be enough pseudo errors to be sampled in a cluster (i.e., $|E_k| < b_k$). For instance, when the model is already well-trained via active learning, most of the data instances will be correctly classified. In those cases, we complement the sampled set Q by instances with a higher erroneous probability within all the unlabeled pool $\mathcal{D}_u$ (Line 18 in Algorithm 1), which are illustrated as blue instances (▲ ●) in Fig. 1.

The complexity of REAL consists of two parts: the inference time $O(|\mathcal{D}_u|)$ and the time for K-Means clustering $O(dK|\mathcal{D}_u|)$, where d is the encoder feature dimension $|\Phi(.)|$. K-Means implemented in faiss [22] costs only 2 or 3 s even for large datasets such as AGNEWS and PUBMED in Sect. 4.

4   Experimental Setup

4.1   Datasets

Following prior research [33,45,46], We conduct experiments on five text classification datasets from different application domains, i.e., SST-2 [40], AGNEWS [48], PUBMED [11], SNIPS [10], and STOV [43]. Table 1 shows their detailed statistics. Due to the limited computational resources, we follow the prior study [45] and take a subset of the original training set and validation set if they are too large. Specifically, we randomly sample 20K×Y instances form each training set if its size exceeds 20K×Y, where Y is the number of target classes. We also keep the size of validation set no more than 3K to speed up the validation process.

Table 1. Dataset statistics.

DATASET	LABEL TYPE	#TRAIN	#VAL	#TEST	#CLASSES
SST-2	Sentiment	40K	3K	1.8K	2
AGNEWS	News Topic	80K	3K	7.6K	4
PUBMED	Medical Abstract	100K	3K	30.1K	5
SNIPS	Intent	13K	0.7K	0.7K	7
STOV	Question	8.0K	1K	1K	10

4.2   Baselines and Implementation Details

We compare REAL against 8 baselines: (1) ENTROPY selects instances with the most even distribution of prediction probability [27]; (2) PLM-KM [46] is a diversity-based baseline which selects b instances closest to K-Means centers of the [CLS] token embeddings; (3) BADGE [3] transforms data into gradient embeddings that encode the model confidence and then use K-Means++ to select; (4) BALD [16] defines uncertainty as the mutual information among different versions (via multiple MC dropouts [15]) of the model's predictions; (5) ALPS [46] selects by masked language modeling loss in PLM; (6) CAL [33] tries to sample the most contrastive instances along the classification decision boundary; (7) ACTUNE [45] selects the unlabeled samples with high uncertainty for active annotation and those with low uncertainty for semi-supervised self-training by weighted K-Means; Since semi-supervised self-training is out of the scope of our current work, we remove the self training part from ACTUNE for a fair comparison. (8) RANDOM uniformly samples data from the unlabeled pool $\mathcal{D}_u$.

For the text classification model $\mathcal{M}$, we follow the prior study [45] and use ROBERTA-BASE [31] implemented in the HuggingFace library [42] for our experiments. We train the model on the initial warm-up labeled set for 10 epochs, and continually train the model for 4 epochs after each round of active sampling to avoid overfitting. We evaluate the model 4 times per training epoch on the validation set and keep the best version. At the end of training, we test the previously-saved best model on the hold-out test set. We choose the best hyperparameters for baselines as indicated in their original papers. We set the AL rounds to be 8 for all the 9 AL methods. Following [33,46], all of our methods and baselines are run with 4 different random seed and the result is based on the average performance on them. This creates 5 (datasets) × 4 (random seeds) × 13 (8 baselines + 1 REAL + 4 REAL variants) × 8 (rounds) = 2080 experiments, which is almost the limit of our computational resources. More details on the experiment setup can be found in our code repository.

5   Results

In the experimental study, we try to answer the following research questions:

- **RQ1.** *Classification Performance*: How is the classification performance of REAL compared to baselines? (Sect. 5.1)
- **RQ2.** *Representative errors*: What are the characteristics of the samples, e.g., error rate and representativeness? (Sect. 5.2)
- **RQ3.** *Ablation & hyperparameter*: What is the performance of different design variants of REAL? How robust is REAL under different hyperparameter settings? (Sect. 5.3)

5.1   Classification Performance

For **RQ1**, we compare the classification performance of REAL against state-of-the-art baselines. Following the existing work of text classification [26], we use two criteria: accuracy and F1-macro to measure the model performances. Accuracy is the fraction of predictions our model got right. F1-macro is the average of accuracy independently measured for each class (i.e., treating different classes equally).

Table 2. Mean accuracy (top half) and mean F1-macro (bottom half).

DATASET	ENTROPY	PLM-KM	BALD	BADGE	ALPS	CAL	AcTUNE	RANDOM	REAL
SST-2	91.95	90.74	90.23	90.90	90.88	91.49	91.82	89.91	**92.41**
AGNEWS	90.34	90.19	89.73	90.11	89.70	90.65	90.57	89.23	**91.08**
PUBMED	80.99	80.90	79.06	81.28	79.93	81.26	81.53	80.60	**82.17**
SNIPS	95.99	95.51	95.26	95.52	94.93	96.07	96.16	94.81	**96.63**
STOV	86.56	85.83	85.40	86.39	85.62	86.67	86.27	84.82	**87.37**
SST-2	91.94	90.47	90.22	90.90	90.95	91.48	91.82	89.90	**92.41**
AGNEWS	90.35	89.84	89.66	90.12	89.60	90.26	90.66	89.31	**90.96**
PUBMED	73.92	74.21	71.54	74.82	73.48	74.99	75.30	73.90	**75.78**
SNIPS	96.06	95.60	95.35	95.58	94.82	96.13	96.22	94.86	**96.69**
STOV	86.76	85.96	85.46	86.53	85.72	86.83	86.41	84.99	**87.53**

Table 2 shows the average accuracy and F1-macro scores of different AL strategies on all the datasets. The detailed accuracy for each AL round is shown in Fig. 2. REAL outperforms all the baselines by 0.43%–0.70% performance gain w.r.t. the mean accuracy of all the eight AL rounds. The two most recent baselines, CAL and AcTUNE rank in the second or third places in most cases, which is consistent with the reports in their original papers. ENTROPY is also a strong baseline and performs better than PLM-KM and ALPS. The relatively good performance of ENTROPY can be explained by pretrained language model's good uncertainty estimations [12]. It stands out in SST-2 dataset, probably because it is relatively easy to pick samples around the decision boundary for the binary classification task. As shown in Fig. 2, PUBMED is a difficult dataset to learn. The model's test accuracy on it is less than 85% even with the full training set. It is probably because the professional medical text is rarely seen in RoBERTA and the label distribution of PUBMED is a skewed. ENTROPY and BALD perform very badly on PUBMED, since they heavily rely on the distribution of the prediction probability. Compared to other baseline methods, REAL has a clear advantage on PUBMED.

5.2   Representative Errors

We address **RQ2** by investigating whether REAL can sample *representative errors* and comparing it with those baselines. Specifically, we evaluate the capability of REAL in selecting representative error samples from the following two perspectives:

- The error rate and initial training loss of samples (Table 3 and Fig. 4);
- The distribution divergence between samples and boundary errors (Fig. 4).

Error Rate and Initial Training Loss of Samples. Table 3 shows the mean error rates and initial training loss (for all AL rounds) of samples Q for different AL strategies across all the datasets. The error rate $\varepsilon(Q)$ is the proportion of wrongly-predicted instances in Q by comparing the model prediction with the ground truth label for each instance. It is inappropriate to directly compare the error rates $\varepsilon(Q)$ of different AL strategies, because the error rates $\varepsilon(\mathcal{D}_u)$ in the whole unlabeled pool $\mathcal{D}_u$ are different. It is more easier to achieve a high sampling error rate $\varepsilon(Q)$ given a high background error rate $\varepsilon(\mathcal{D}_u)$. Therefore, we compares the `lift` of sampling error rate, which is defined as $\varepsilon(Q)/\varepsilon(\mathcal{D}_u)$, which implies how effective does an AL strategy select errors, compared with random selection. Another metric is the average cross entropy loss ℓ_0 of samples Q in the first training step , which is a more fine-grained version of error rate. Many previous research work [20,32,41,47] have already validated that samples with higher loss are usually more informative to the model.

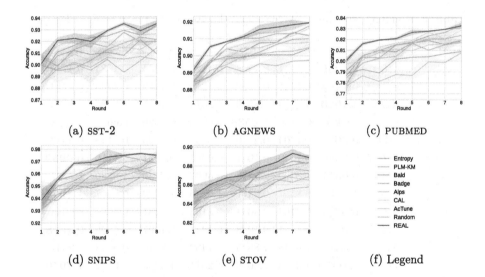

(a) SST-2   (b) AGNEWS   (c) PUBMED

(d) SNIPS   (e) STOV   (f) Legend

Fig. 2. The accuracy of different active learning rounds on each dataset. The height of the shadow area denotes the std of accuracy.

Table 3 shows REAL usually has a large `lift` of sampling error rate, second only to ENTROPY, despite the fact that the unlabeled pool error rate $\varepsilon(\mathcal{D}_u)$ of REAL is the lowest. The large `lift` of sampling error rate implies REAL successfully identifies the errors in $\mathcal{D}_u$. It is worth mentioning that $\varepsilon(\mathcal{D}_u)$ can serve as test set because we don't use $\mathcal{D}_u$ in the previous AL rounds for training or validation. REAL has the lowest error rate on 4 out of 5 datasets, which means the highest accuracy when testing on $\mathcal{D}_u$. The initial training loss of REAL's samples is also the largest in the last four datasets. Figure 4 shows more detailed loss distribution for each AL round.

Representativeness. We investigate how REAL's samples align with ground-truth errors on decision boundary compared to baselines. Based on theoretical studies on margin theory for active learning [4], selecting instances close to the decision boundary can significantly reduce the number of annotations required [21,33,37,50]. Though identifying the precise decision boundaries for deep neural networks is intractable [13], we use the basic grid statistics on t-SNE embeddings as an empirical solution. Specifically, we apply t-SNE to the [CLS] token embeddings of $\Phi(\mathcal{D}_u)$ and project the original token embeddings of 768 dimensions to 2D plane, as shown in Fig. 3. Then, we split the bounding box of $\mathcal{D}_u$ on 2-D plane into 50×50 uniform grids, where g_i denotes the number of instances that fall into the i-th grid.

We keep only the ground-truth errors within the decision boundaries. Our intuition of decision boundary is where instances have similar representations

Table 3. Sampling error rate $\varepsilon(.)$, lift, and the average first step training loss ℓ_0.

DATASET	METRIC	ENTROPY	PLM-KM	BADGE	CAL	ACTUNE	RANDOM	REAL
SST-2	$\varepsilon(Q)$	**0.4959**	0.1841	0.2308	0.4821	0.4334	0.1284	0.4739
	$\varepsilon(\mathcal{D}_u)$	**0.1194**	0.1251	0.1259	0.1215	0.1170	0.1338	0.1212
	lift	**4.1530**	1.4713	1.8325	3.9670	3.7055	0.9596	3.9113
	ℓ_0	0.6984	0.8100	**1.0538**	0.6915	0.8526	0.6660	0.9938
AGNEWS	$\varepsilon(Q)$	**0.6092**	0.1904	0.2246	0.5637	0.5325	0.1142	0.5537
	$\varepsilon(\mathcal{D}_u)$	0.1009	0.1039	0.1041	0.0995	0.0991	0.1115	**0.0959**
	lift	**6.0377**	1.8320	2.1576	5.6667	5.3730	1.0239	5.7737
	ℓ_0	1.2504	0.8597	0.9477	1.0926	1.3009	0.5707	**1.3636**
PUBMED	$\varepsilon(Q)$	**0.6701**	0.3164	0.3634	0.6103	0.6231	0.1987	0.6046
	$\varepsilon(\mathcal{D}_u)$	0.1943	0.1971	0.1928	0.1941	0.1907	0.1998	**0.1858**
	lift	**3.4487**	1.6048	1.8845	3.1452	3.2670	0.9943	3.2531
	ℓ_0	1.5117	1.3533	1.6009	1.2871	1.4494	1.0222	**1.7040**
SNIPS	$\varepsilon(Q)$	0.4107	0.1226	0.1120	**0.4237**	0.2963	0.0276	0.4002
	$\varepsilon(\mathcal{D}_u)$	0.0268	0.0337	0.0308	0.0280	0.0265	0.0393	**0.0231**
	lift	15.3183	3.6410	3.6338	15.1568	11.1895	0.7023	**17.2902**
	ℓ_0	**1.0176**	0.5209	0.5080	1.0470	0.9491	0.1842	0.9356
STOV	$\varepsilon(Q)$	**0.7328**	0.2536	0.3506	0.6904	0.6659	0.1307	0.7162
	$\varepsilon(\mathcal{D}_u)$	0.1048	0.1263	0.1209	0.1094	0.1101	0.1386	**0.1045**
	lift	**6.9934**	2.0079	2.8994	6.3114	6.0509	0.9435	6.8548
	ℓ_0	**2.1434**	1.0260	1.3874	2.0255	2.0062	0.6331	2.1131

but different predictions [4]. We hypothesize that the pseudo errors selected by REAL is near to the model's decision boundary because 1) instances in the same cluster have similar representations; and 2) pseudo errors have different predictions than the majority in a cluster. To verify this hypothesis, we compute the distribution entropy of ground-truth labels for each grid, and reserve only the top 0.15 grids with high entropy values. We call grids with top 15% high entropy values as boundary grids. g_i^ε denotes the number of ground-truth errors fall into i-th boundary grid.

We compare the Jensen-Shannon divergence (JSD) between boundary grids set $\{g_i^\varepsilon\}_{i=1}^m$ (m is the number of boundary grids) and $\{s_i\}_{i=1}^m$, where s_i is the number of sampled instances in the i-th grid. Together with previously introduced sampling loss, we plot the divergence in Fig. 4 for the two largest datasets AGNEWS and PUBMED. REAL clearly has the lowest divergence, which means our samples' distribution aligns well with the ground-truth errors on the boundary.

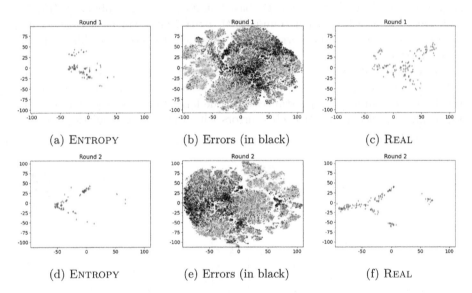

(a) ENTROPY	(b) Errors (in black)	(c) REAL
(d) ENTROPY	(e) Errors (in black)	(f) REAL

Fig. 3. The t-SNE based visualization for the sample/error distribution. Visualizations in the first row are from the first round active selection on AGNEWS and the second row from the second round. Two subfigures in the middle (b and e) are all instances in $\mathcal{D}_u$. The four colors in b and e indicate different correctly predicted categories, except black. Black dots indicate the ground truth errors. Purple dots in the left side two visualizations are ENTROPY's selections and the right side are REAL's selections. (Color figure online)

Besides the lowest divergence, REAL also has the largest sampling loss. As shown in Fig. 4, REAL's samples clearly distribute in the upper left corner. In contrast, RANDOM's samples lie in the lower right corner. The least sampling loss and largest divergence from boundary errors may be the reason why RANDOM fails. To our surprise, darker dots usually appear in higher positions, in Fig. 4, which means samples in later AL rounds provide larger loss. The reason may be that the model in later AL rounds is stable and confident in its predictions, thus introducing new samples will cause a larger loss.

Figure 3 provides the case studies of our samples against ENTROPY on AGNEWS. We can see that most errors distribute near the decision boundaries. ENTROPY tends to miss some decision boundary areas and is lack of diversity. REAL matches the boundary errors better.

5.3   Ablation and Hyperparameter Study

In this section, we address **RQ3** by extensive ablation (Fig. 5) and hyperparameter studies (Fig. 6) to understand the important components in REAL.

A. Ablation Study. (1) We test REAL with different budget allocation strategies (Eq. 6) per cluster. (1.1) Ignore the idea of "allocation by cluster". Specifically, we rank all the instances in $\mathcal{D}_u$ based on its erroneous probability (Eq. 5), and select top-b instances per round (`REAL pool`). (1.2) For each cluster, uniformly sample B/K pseudo errors, i.e., ignore cluster error weights in Eq. 6. (`REAL uniform`)

(2) REAL randomly samples within each cluster's pseudo errors (line 15 in Algorithm 1) based on the adaptive budget. Given the adaptive budget in each cluster, we also try to sample: (2.1) Instances with the largest erroneous probabilities in Eq. 5 (`REAL cluster`); (2.2) Pseudo errors with the largest prediction entropy (`REAL entropy`).

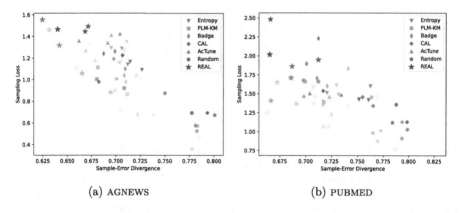

(a) AGNEWS   (b) PUBMED

Fig. 4. Loss v.s. sample-error divergence. Each dot represents a sample set Q from one AL round. The dot shape and color hue indicate AL strategy. The dot transparency indicates different AL rounds. More transparent dot comes from earlier AL round, and darker dot comes from later AL round. REAL clearly shows a lower divergence to the ground truth errors on the decision boundary, and a larger sampling loss.

Figure 5 show that most of REAL's variants still perform better than the best baseline ACTUNE on large datasets AGNEWS and PUBMED. However, the results on SST-2 are unstable. The reason may be that the decision boundary of binary classification is too simple so that dedicated methods are not necessary. REAL cluster fails only on SST-2. REAL uniform is slightly worse than AcTune in later rounds, which indicates the importance of weighted budget allocation for REAL. REAL pool is very close to AcTune on PUBMED, possibly because lacking diversity hurts it on the most difficult dataset.

B. Hyperparameter Study. We study the impact of varying the number of clusters K. Experiment results in Fig. 6 shows our method stably beats the best baseline across a wide range of K (on a scale of tens to hundreds).

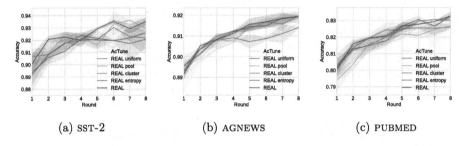

(a) SST-2   (b) AGNEWS   (c) PUBMED

Fig. 5. Ablation study on different variants of REAL.

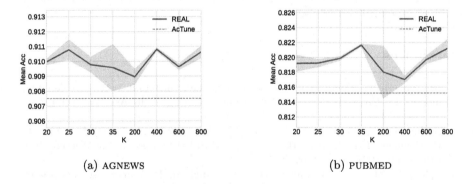

(a) AGNEWS   (b) PUBMED

Fig. 6. Mean acc under a wide range of #clusters K for REAL against the best baseline AcTune on our largest two datasets.

6 Conclusion and Future Work

We present REAL, a novel AL sampling strategy that selects *representative pseudo errors* for efficient model training. We define pseudo errors as minority predictions within each cluster. The sampling budget per cluster is adaptive to the cluster's total estimated error density. Experiments on five datasets demonstrate that REAL performs better than other AL sampling strategies consistently. By analyzing the actively sampled instances, we find that REAL improves over all the best-performing baselines by guiding uncertainty sampling in errors near the decision boundary. The ablation study shows most alternative designs of REAL still beat the state-of-the-art baseline.

Future work will investigate the theoretical effectiveness of selecting errors near decision boundary for AL and the diversity within pseudo errors. Currently we only take text classification as an example to illustrate the effectiveness of REAL. But the framework of REAL can be easily adapted to other tasks such as image classification implemented in neural classification architectures.

Acknowledgments. This work was done during Cheng Chen's internship at Singapore Management University (SMU) under the supervision of Dr. Yong Wang. This work was supported by the National Key Research and Development Program of China (2020YFB1710004), Lee Kong Chian Fellowship awarded to Dr. Yong Wang by SMU, and the National Science Foundation of China under the grant 62272466. We would like to thank all the anonymous reviewers for their valuable feedback.

Ethical Statement. All the datasets are widely-used benchmark text classification datasets and are publicly-available online, which do not have any privacy issues. Also, our approach can benefit data labeling workers and bring welfare to them. Data labeling is very costly and labour-intensive. For example, labeling toxic content is reported to be a "mental torture" [35]. Our approach aims to make active learning more label-efficient and can reduce the workload of data labeling workers, which is beneficial to the mental health of data labeling workers.

References

1. Aharoni, R., Goldberg, Y.: Unsupervised domain clusters in pretrained language models. In: Proceedings of the 58th Annual Meeting of the Association for Computational Linguistics, pp. 7747–7763 (2020)
2. Arthur, D., Vassilvitskii, S.: K-means++: the advantages of careful seeding. In: Proceedings of the Eighteenth Annual ACM-SIAM Symposium on Discrete Algorithms, pp. 1027–1035 (2007)
3. Ash, J.T., Zhang, C., Krishnamurthy, A., Langford, J., Agarwal, A.: Deep batch active learning by diverse, uncertain gradient lower bounds. In: Proceedings of the International Conference on Learning Representations (2020)
4. Balcan, M.F., Broder, A., Zhang, T.: Margin based active learning. In: 20th Annual Conference on Learning Theory, pp. 35–50 (2007)
5. Baram, Y., Yaniv, R.E., Luz, K.: Online choice of active learning algorithms. J. Mach. Learn. Res. **5**, 255–291 (2004)
6. Chen, T., Kornblith, S., Norouzi, M., Hinton, G.: A simple framework for contrastive learning of visual representations. In: International Conference on Machine Learning, pp. 1597–1607 (2020)

7. Choi, J., et al.: VaB-AL: incorporating class imbalance and difficulty with variational Bayes for active learning. In: Proceedings of the IEEE/CVF Conference on Computer Vision and Pattern Recognition, pp. 6749–6758 (2021)
8. Chung, C., et al.: Understanding human-side impact of sampling image batches in subjective attribute labeling. Proc. ACM Hum. Comput. Interact. **5**, 1–26 (2021)
9. Citovsky, G., et al.: Batch active learning at scale. Adv. Neural. Inf. Process. Syst. **34**, 11933–11944 (2021)
10. Coucke, A., et al.: SNIPS voice platform: an embedded spoken language understanding system for private-by-design voice interfaces. arXiv preprint arXiv:1805.10190 (2018)
11. Dernoncourt, F., Lee, J.Y.: PubMed 200k RCT: a dataset for sequential sentence classification in medical abstracts. In: Proceedings of the Eighth International Joint Conference on Natural Language Processing (Volume 2: Short Papers), pp. 308–313 (2017)
12. Desai, S., Durrett, G.: Calibration of pre-trained transformers. In: Proceedings of the 2020 Conference on Empirical Methods in Natural Language Processing, pp. 295–302 (2020)
13. Ducoffe, M., Precioso, F.: Adversarial active learning for deep networks: a margin based approach. arXiv preprint arXiv:1802.09841 (2018)
14. Fang, M., Li, Y., Cohn, T.: Learning how to active learn: a deep reinforcement learning approach. In: Proceedings of the 2017 Conference on Empirical Methods in Natural Language Processing, pp. 595–605 (2017)
15. Gal, Y., Ghahramani, Z.: Bayesian convolutional neural networks with Bernoulli approximate variational inference. arXiv preprint arXiv:1506.02158 (2015)
16. Gal, Y., Islam, R., Ghahramani, Z.: Deep Bayesian active learning with image data. In: Proceedings of the 34th International Conference on Machine Learning, vol. 70, pp. 1183–1192 (2017)
17. Gissin, D., Shalev-Shwartz, S.: Discriminative active learning. arXiv preprint arXiv:1907.06347 (2019)
18. He, K., Fan, H., Wu, Y., Xie, S., Girshick, R.: Momentum contrast for unsupervised visual representation learning. In: Proceedings of the IEEE/CVF Conference on Computer Vision and Pattern Recognition, pp. 9729–9738 (2020)
19. Hsu, W.N., Lin, H.T.: Active learning by learning. In: Proceedings of the AAAI Conference on Artificial Intelligence (2015)
20. Huang, S., Wang, T., Xiong, H., Huan, J., Dou, D.: Semi-supervised active learning with temporal output discrepancy. In: Proceedings of the IEEE/CVF International Conference on Computer Vision, pp. 3447–3456 (2021)
21. Huijser, M., van Gemert, J.C.: Active decision boundary annotation with deep generative models. In: Proceedings of the IEEE International Conference on Computer Vision, pp. 5286–5295 (2017)
22. Johnson, J., Douze, M., Jégou, H.: Billion-scale similarity search with GPUs. IEEE Trans. Big Data **7**(3), 535–547 (2019)
23. Kim, Y., Shin, B.: In defense of core-set: a density-aware core-set selection for active learning. In: Proceedings of the 28th ACM SIGKDD Conference on Knowledge Discovery and Data Mining, pp. 804–812 (2022)
24. Konyushkova, K., Sznitman, R., Fua, P.: Learning active learning from data. In: Advances in Neural Information Processing Systems, vol. 30 (2017)
25. Krempl, G., Kottke, D., Lemaire, V.: Optimised probabilistic active learning (OPAL) for fast, non-myopic, cost-sensitive active classification. Mach. Learn. **100**, 449–476 (2015)

26. Lai, S., Xu, L., Liu, K., Zhao, J.: Recurrent convolutional neural networks for text classification. In: Proceedings of the AAAI Conference on Artificial Intelligence (2015)
27. Lewis, D.D.: A sequential algorithm for training text classifiers. In: ACM SIGIR Forum, vol. 29, pp. 13–19 (1995)
28. Lewis, D.D., Catlett, J.: Heterogeneous uncertainty sampling for supervised learning. In: Machine Learning Proceedings, pp. 148–156 (1994)
29. Li, M., Sethi, I.K.: Confidence-based active learning. IEEE Trans. Pattern Anal. Mach. Intell. **28**(8), 1251–1261 (2006)
30. Liu, M., Buntine, W., Haffari, G.: Learning how to actively learn: a deep imitation learning approach. In: Proceedings of the 56th Annual Meeting of the Association for Computational Linguistics (Volume 1: Long Papers), pp. 1874–1883 (2018)
31. Liu, Y., et al.: RoBERTa: a robustly optimized BERT pretraining approach. arXiv preprint arXiv:1907.11692 (2019)
32. Luo, J., Wang, J., Cheng, N., Xiao, J.: Loss prediction: end-to-end active learning approach for speech recognition. In: 2021 International Joint Conference on Neural Networks, pp. 1–7 (2021)
33. Margatina, K., Vernikos, G., Barrault, L., Aletras, N.: Active learning by acquiring contrastive examples. In: Proceedings of the 2021 Conference on Empirical Methods in Natural Language Processing, pp. 650–663 (2021)
34. Muller, M., et al.: Designing ground truth and the social life of labels. In: Proceedings of the 2021 CHI Conference on Human Factors in Computing Systems, pp. 1–16 (2021)
35. Perrigo, B.: Inside Facebook's African sweatshop. Time https://time.com/6147458/facebook-africa-content-moderation-employee-treatment/. Accessed 28 Mar 2023
36. Roth, D., Small, K.: Margin-based active learning for structured output spaces. In: Proceedings of the 17th European Conference on Machine Learning, pp. 413–424 (2006)
37. Ru, D., et al.: Active sentence learning by adversarial uncertainty sampling in discrete space. In: Findings of the Association for Computational Linguistics, EMNLP 2020, pp. 4908–4917 (2020)
38. Sener, O., Savarese, S.: Active learning for convolutional neural networks: a core-set approach. In: International Conference on Learning Representations (2018)
39. Sia, S., Dalmia, A., Mielke, S.J.: Tired of topic models? Clusters of pretrained word embeddings make for fast and good topics too! In: Proceedings of the 2020 Conference on Empirical Methods in Natural Language Processing, pp. 1728–1736 (2020)
40. Socher, R., et al.: Recursive deep models for semantic compositionality over a sentiment treebank. In: Proceedings of the 2013 Conference on Empirical Methods in Natural Language Processing, pp. 1631–1642 (2013)
41. Wan, C., Jin, F., Qiao, Z., Zhang, W., Yuan, Y.: Unsupervised active learning with loss prediction. Neural Computing and Applications, pp. 1–9 (2021)
42. Wolf, T., et al.: Transformers: state-of-the-art natural language processing. In: Proceedings of the 2020 Conference on Empirical Methods in Natural Language Processing: System Demonstrations, pp. 38–45 (2020)
43. Xu, J., Wang, P., Tian, G., Xu, B., Zhao, J., Wang, F., Hao, H.: Short text clustering via convolutional neural networks. In: Proceedings of the 1st Workshop on Vector Space Modeling for Natural Language Processing, pp. 62–69 (2015)

44. Yoo, D., Kweon, I.S.: Learning loss for active learning. In: Proceedings of the IEEE/CVF Conference on Computer Vision and Pattern Recognition, pp. 93–102 (2019)
45. Yu, Y., Kong, L., Zhang, J., Zhang, R., Zhang, C.: AcTune: uncertainty-based active self-training for active fine-tuning of pretrained language models. In: Proceedings of the 2022 Conference of the North American Chapter of the Association for Computational Linguistics: Human Language Technologies, pp. 1422–1436 (2022)
46. Yuan, M., Lin, H.T., Boyd-Graber, J.: Cold-start active learning through self-supervised language modeling. In: Proceedings of the 2020 Conference on Empirical Methods in Natural Language Processing, pp. 7935–7948 (2020)
47. Yuan, T., et al.: Multiple instance active learning for object detection. In: Proceedings of the IEEE/CVF Conference on Computer Vision and Pattern Recognition, pp. 5330–5339 (2021)
48. Zhang, X., Zhao, J., LeCun, Y.: Character-level convolutional networks for text classification. In: Advances in Neural Information Processing Systems, vol. 28 (2015)
49. Zhang, Z., Fang, M., Chen, L., Namazi Rad, M.R.: Is neural topic modelling better than clustering? An empirical study on clustering with contextual embeddings for topics. In: Proceedings of the 2022 Conference of the North American Chapter of the Association for Computational Linguistics: Human Language Technologies, pp. 3886–3893 (2022)
50. Zhu, J.J., Bento, J.: Generative adversarial active learning. arXiv preprint arXiv:1702.07956 (2017)

Knowledge-Driven Active Learning

Gabriele Ciravegna[1,2(✉)] [ID], Frédéric Precioso[2] [ID], Alessandro Betti[2] [ID],
Kevin Mottin[2] [ID], and Marco Gori[2,3] [ID]

[1] DAUIN, Politecnico di Torino, Torino, Italy
gabriele.ciravegna@polito.it
[2] Université Côte d'Azur, Inria, CNRS, I3S, Maasai, Nice, France
[3] DIISM, Università di Siena, Siena, Italy

Abstract. The deployment of Deep Learning (DL) models is still precluded in those contexts where the amount of supervised data is limited. To answer this issue, active learning strategies aim at minimizing the amount of labelled data required to train a DL model. Most active strategies are based on uncertain sample selection, and even often restricted to samples lying close to the decision boundary. These techniques are theoretically sound, but an understanding of the selected samples based on their content is not straightforward, further driving non-experts to consider DL as a black-box. For the first time, here we propose to take into consideration common domain-knowledge and enable non-expert users to train a model with fewer samples. In our Knowledge-driven Active Learning (KAL) framework, rule-based knowledge is converted into logic constraints and their violation is checked as a natural guide for sample selection. We show that even simple relationships among data and output classes offer a way to spot predictions for which the model need supervision. We empirically show that KAL (i) outperforms many active learning strategies, particularly in those contexts where domain knowledge is rich, (ii) it discovers data distribution lying far from the initial training data, (iii) it ensures domain experts that the provided knowledge is acquired by the model, (iv) it is suitable for regression and object recognition tasks unlike uncertainty-based strategies, and (v) its computational demand is low.

Keywords: Active Learning · Knowledge-aided Learning · Neurosymbolic Learning

1 Introduction

Deep Learning (DL) methods have achieved impressive results over the past decade in fields ranging from computer vision to text generation [29]. However, most of these contributions relied on overly data-intensive models (e.g. Transformers), trained on huge amounts of data [31]. With the advent of Big Data, sample collection does not represent an issue any more, but, nonetheless, in some contexts the number of *supervised* data is limited, and manual labelling can be

© The Author(s), under exclusive license to Springer Nature Switzerland AG 2023
D. Koutra et al. (Eds.): ECML PKDD 2023, LNAI 14169, pp. 38–54, 2023.
https://doi.org/10.1007/978-3-031-43412-9_3

expensive [51]. Therefore, a common situation is the unlabelled pool scenario [33], where many data are available, but only some are annotated. Historically, two strategies have been devised to tackle this situation: semi-supervised learning which exploits the unlabelled data to enrich feature representations [55], and active learning which selects the smallest set of data to annotate to improve the most model performances [43].

The main assumption behind active learning strategies is that there exists a subset of samples that allows to train a model with a similar accuracy as when fed with all training data. Iteratively, the strategy indicates the optimal samples to be annotated from the unlabelled pool. This is generally done by ranking the unlabelled samples w.r.t. a given measure, usually on the model predictions [35,43,48], or on the input data distribution [39,54] and by selecting the samples associated to the highest rankings [37,52]. While being theoretically sound, an understanding of the selected samples based on their content is not straightforward, in particular to non-ML experts. This issue becomes particularly relevant when considering that Deep Neural Networks are already seen as black box models [11,19] On the contrary, we believe that neural models must be linked to Commonsense knowledge related to a given learning problem. Therefore, in this paper, we propose for the first time to exploit this symbolic knowledge in the selection process of an active learning strategy. This not only lower the amount of supervised data, but it also enables domain experts to train a model leveraging their knowledge. More precisely, we propose to compare the predictions over the unsupervised data with the available knowledge and to exploit the inconsistencies as a criterion for selecting the data to be annotated. Domain knowledge, indeed, can be expressed as First-Order Logic (FOL) clauses and translated into real-valued logic constraints (among other choices) by means of T-Norms [27] to assess its satisfaction [14,21,34].

In the experiments, we show that the proposed Knowledge-driven Active Learning (KAL) strategy (i) performs better (on average) than several standard active learning methods, particularly in those contexts where domain-knowledge is rich. We empirically demonstrate (ii) that this is mainly due to the fact that the proposed strategy allows discovering data distributions lying far from the initial training data, unlike uncertainty-based approaches. Furthermore, we show that (iii) the KAL strategy can be easily employed also in regression and object-detection contexts, where standard uncertainty-based strategies are not-straightforward to apply [24], (iv) the provided knowledge is acquired by the trained model, (iv) KAL can also work on domains where no knowledge is available if combined with a XAI technique, and, finally, (vi) KAL is not computationally expensive unlike many recent methods.

The paper is organized as follows: in Sect. 2 the proposed method is explained in details, with first an example on inferring the XOR operation and then contextualized in more realistic active learning domains; the aforementioned experimental results on different datasets are reported in Sect. 3, comparing the proposed technique with several active learning strategies; in Sect. 4 the related work about active learning and about integrating reasoning with machine learning is briefly resumed; finally, in Sect. 5 we conclude the paper by considering possible future work.

2 Knowledge-Driven Active Learning

In this paper, we focus on a variety of learning problems, ranging from classification to regression and also object-detection. Therefore, we consider the problem $f\colon X \to Y$, where $X \subseteq \mathbb{R}^d$ represents the feature space which may also comprehend non-structured data (e.g., images) and d represents the input dimensionality and Y the output space. More precisely, in classification problems we consider a vector function $f = [f_1, \ldots, f_c]$, where each function f_i predicts the probability that x belongs to the i-th class. When considering an object-detection problem, instead, for a given class i and a given image $x \in X$, we consider as class membership probability f_i the maximum score value among all predicted bounding boxes around the objects belonging to the i-th class. Formally, $f_i(x) = \max_{s \in \mathcal{S}^i(x)} s(x)$ where $\mathcal{S}^i(x_j)$ is the set of the confidence scores of the bounding boxes predicting the i-th class for sample x. Finally, in regression problems the learning function f_i represents the predicted value for the i-th class and takes values outside the unit interval, i.e. $f_i(x) \in \mathbb{R}$.

In the Active Learning context, we also define $X_s \subset X$ as the portion of input data already associated to an annotation $y_i \in Y_s \subset Y$ and n the dimensionality of the starting set of labelled data. At each iteration, a set of p samples $X_p \subset X_u \subset X$ is selected by the active learning strategy to be annotated from X_u, the unlabelled data pool, and be added to X_s. This process is repeated for q iterations, after which the training terminates. The maximum budget of annotations b therefore amounts to $b = n + q \cdot p$.

Let us also consider the case in which additional *domain knowledge* is available for the problem at hand, involving relationships between data and classes. By considering the logic predicate $\mathbf{f}$ associated to each function f, First-Order Logic (FOL) becomes the natural way of describing these relationships. For example, $\forall x \in X,\ \mathbf{x_1}(x) \wedge \mathbf{x_2}(x) \Rightarrow \mathbf{f}(x)$, meaning that when both predicates are true also the output function $f(x)$ needs to be true and where $\mathbf{x_1}(x), \mathbf{x_2}(x)$ respectively represent the logic predicates associated to the first and the second input features. Also, we can consider relations among classes, such as $\forall x \in X,\ \mathbf{f_v}(\mathbf{x}) \wedge \mathbf{f_z}(\mathbf{x}) \Rightarrow \mathbf{f_u}(\mathbf{x})$, meaning that the intersection between the v-th class and the z-th class is always included in the u-th one. Finally, we can consider predicates defined over open $\mathbf{f}(x) > k$ or closed intervals, $k_1 < \mathbf{f}(x) < k_2$.

2.1 Converting Domain-Knowledge into Loss Functions

Among different approaches that allow to inject domain knowledge into a learning problem (see [20] for a complete review of approaches), in this work we employ the Learning from Constraints framework [14,21] which converts domain knowledge into numerical constraints. Among a variety of other type of constraints (see, e.g., Table 2 in [21]), it studies the process of handling FOL formulas so that they can be either injected into the learning problem (in semi-supervised learning [32]) or used as a knowledge verification measure (as in [34] and in the proposed method). Going into more details, the FOL formulas representing the

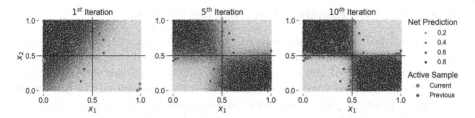

Fig. 1. A visual example of KAL working principles on the *XOR-like* problem. We depict network predictions with different colour degrees. Also, we depict in orange the samples selected by the active strategy in the current iteration and in blue those selected in previous iterations (or initially randomly annotated). Notive how the proposed method immediately discovers the data distribution not covered by the initial random sampling (right-bottom quadrant).

domain knowledge are converted into numerical constraints using the Triangular Norms (T-Norms, [27]). These binary functions generalize the conjunction operator $\wedge$ and offer a way to mathematically compute the satisfaction level of a given rule.

Following the previous example, $\mathbf{x_1}(x) \wedge \mathbf{x_2}(x) \Rightarrow \mathbf{f}(x)$[1] is converted into a bilateral constraint $\phi(f(x)) = 1$. By first rewriting the rule as a conjunction of terms $\neg((\mathbf{x_1} \wedge \mathbf{x_2}) \wedge \neg\mathbf{f})$[2] and by employing the product T-Norm which replaces the $\wedge$ with the product operators and $\neg\mathbf{x}$ with $1 - \mathbf{x}$, the bilateral constraint becomes $1 - (\mathbf{x_1}\mathbf{x_2}(1 - \mathbf{f})) = 1$. With $\varphi(f(x)) = 1 - \phi(f(x))$ we indicate the loss function associated to the bilateral constraints, which measures the level of satisfaction of the given constraints and has its minimum value in zero. Again, recalling the previous example, the associated loss function would be $\varphi(f(x)) = \mathbf{x_1}\mathbf{x_2}(1 - \mathbf{f})$, which indeed is satisfied when either $\mathbf{x_1}$ or $\mathbf{x_2}$ is zero or $\mathbf{f}$ is approximately one. For further detail on how to convert FOL formulas into numerical constraints check the supplementary material and [32] which also proposed an automatic computation of the loss function φ associated to a rule.

Based on this assumption, we can detect whether the predictions made by the model on unlabelled data are coherent with the domain knowledge, and we select the data associated to the highest violations as those to be annotated. More precisely, considering the set $\mathcal{K}$ of all available FOL formulas for the given problem, we select the points $x^\star$ which violate the most the constraints as follows:

$$KAL: \qquad x^\star = \arg\max_{x \in X_u} \sum_{\varphi \in \mathcal{K}} \varphi(f(x)) \qquad (1)$$

At each iteration, the KAL strategy selects p samples $x^\star$ to annotate from the unlabelled pool X_u.

---

[1] Practically, the predicate $\mathbf{x_i}(x)$ is obtained applying a steep logistic function over the i-th input feature: $\mathbf{x_i} = \sigma(x_i) = 1/(1 + e^{-\tau(x_i - h)})$, where τ is a temperature parameter and h represents the midpoint of the logistic function ($h = 0.5$). For predicates expressing inequalities, e.g., $\mathbf{f}(x) > k$ we simply need to set $h = k$.

[2] For the sake of simplicity, we drop the argument (x) of the logic predicates.

2.2   An Intuitive Example: The *XOR-like* Problem

A well-known problem in machine learning is the inference of the eXclusive OR (XOR) operation. To show the working principles of the proposed approach, we propose a variant of this experiment, in which a neural network learns the *XOR-like* operation from a distribution of non-boolean samples. Specifically, we sampled 10^5 points $x \in [0,1]^2$, and we assigned a label $y(x)$ as following: $y(x) = 1$ if $(x_1 > 0.5 \wedge x_2 \le 0.5) \vee (x_1 \le 0.5 \wedge x_2 > 0.5)$ else $y(x) = 0$. Also, we express the XOR operation through a FOL formula $(\mathbf{x_1} \wedge \neg\mathbf{x_2}) \vee (\neg\mathbf{x_1} \wedge \mathbf{x_2}) \Leftrightarrow \mathbf{f}$. As seen before, through the T-Norm operation we can convert the logic rule into a numerical constraint, compute its violation as:

$$\begin{aligned}
\varphi_{\mathbf{x_1} \oplus \mathbf{x_2} \to \mathbf{f}} &= (\mathbf{x_1} + \mathbf{x_2} - 2\mathbf{x_1}\mathbf{x_2})(1 - \mathbf{f}), \\
\varphi_{\mathbf{f} \to \mathbf{x_1} \oplus \mathbf{x_1}} &= \mathbf{f}(1 - (\mathbf{x_1} + \mathbf{x_2} - 2\mathbf{x_1}\mathbf{x_2}))
\end{aligned} \tag{2}$$

In Fig. 1, we reported an example of the proposed strategy starting from $n = 10$ randomly selected labelled data and by selecting $p = 5$ samples at each iteration violating the most Eq. 2, and for $q = 100$ iterations. We can appreciate how, as is often the case, the initial random sampling (blue points-figure on the left) does not well represent the whole data distribution: no samples drawn from the bottom-right quadrant. Nonetheless, the proposed method immediately discovers the data distribution not represented by the initial sampling (orange points-figure on the left), by selecting the samples violating $\mathbf{x_1} \oplus \mathbf{x_2} \to \mathbf{f}$. After 5 iterations (figure at the centre) the network has mostly learnt the correct data distribution. Later, the proposed strategy refines network predictions by sampling along the decision boundaries (blue points-figure on the right), allowing the network to almost already solve the learning problem (accuracy $\sim$100%) in just 10 iterations. As it will be seen in the next section, standard random selection (but also uncertainty-based ones) will require many more iterations.

2.3   Real-Life Scenario: Partial Knowledge and Different Type of Rules

It is clear that, in the case of the *XOR-like* problem, the knowledge is complete: if we compute the predictions directly through the rule, we already solve the learning problem. However, the purpose of this simple experiment is to show the potentiality of the proposed approach in integrating the available symbolic knowledge into a learning problem. In real-life scenarios, such a situation is unrealistic, but still we might have access to some partial knowledge that may allow solving more quickly a given learning problem. Also, it may facilitate domain experts to accept and understand the active learning labelling process, since here the samples to label are the ones violating the knowledge they provided.

More precisely, when we consider structured data (e.g., tabular data), a domain expert may know some simple relations taking into consideration few features and the output classes. This knowledge may not be sufficient to solve the learning problem, but a KAL strategy can still exploit it to drive the network to a fast convergence, as we will see in Sect. 3. On the opposite, when we consider unstructured data (e.g., images or audio signals) the employed knowledge cannot directly rely on the input features. Nonetheless, in multi-label learning problems, a user may know in advance some relations between the output classes. Let us consider, as an example, a Dog-vs-Person classification: we might know that a main a dog is composed of several parts (e.g., a muzzle, a body, a tail). A straightforward translation of this compositional property into a FOL rule is **Dog** $\Rightarrow$ **Muzzle** $\vee$ **Body** $\vee$ **Tail**. Formulating the composition in the opposite way is correct as well i.e., **Muzzle** $\Rightarrow$ **Dog**. Also, in all classification problems, at least one of the main classes needs to be predicted, i.e., **Dog** $\vee$ **Person**, with main classes being mutually exclusive in standard multi-class problems, i.e., **Dog** $\oplus$ **Man**. Finally, we can always incorporate an uncertainty-like rule requiring each predicate to be either true or false, i.e., **Dog** $\oplus$ ¬**Dog**.

3   Experiments

In this work, we considered six different learning scenarios, comparing the proposed technique with several standard active strategies. We evaluated the proposed method on two standard classification problems [4], the inference of the *XOR-like* problem (already introduced in Sect. 2.2), and the classification of *IRIS* plants given their characteristics. To assess the validity of the proposed method on regression tasks, we experimented on the Insurance dataset[3], which requires to model insurance charges based on insured persons features. We also considered two standard image-classification tasks: the *ANIMALS* dataset, representing 7 classes of animals extracted from ImageNet [13], and the Caltech-UCSD Birds-200-2011 dataset (*CUB200*, [47]), a fine-grained classification dataset representing 200 bird species. At last, as a proof of concept, we analysed the performances of the KAL in the simple *DOGvsPERSON* object recognition task, a novel publicly available dataset that we extracted from *PASCAL-Part* [7]. For more details regarding the latter, please refer to supplementary material. For each dataset, n, p, q, as well as the number of training epochs and the network structure are arbitrarily fixed in advance according to the number of classes, the dataset size and the task complexity. Reported average results are computed on the test sets of a k-fold Cross Validation (with $k = 10$ in the first three tasks and $k = 5$ in the computer vision ones). More details regarding each experimental problem, as well as the tables reporting all the rules employed, are available in the supplementary material. The code to run all the experiments is published on a public GitHub repository[4]. A simple code example is also reported in the supplementary material, showing how to solve the *XOR-like* problem with the KAL strategy. All experiments were run on an Intel i7-9750H CPU machine with an NVIDIA 2080 RTX GPU and 64 GB of RAM.

---

[3] Available from Kaggle https://www.kaggle.com/datasets/teertha/ushealthinsurance dataset.

[4] KAL repository: github.com/gabrieleciravegna/Knowledge-driven-Active-Learning.

Compared Methods. We compared KAL with 12 active learning strategies commonly considered in literature [37,53]. As representatives of uncertainty-based strategies, we considered **Entropy** [43] selecting samples associated to predictions having maximum entropy, **Margin** [35] predictions with minimum margin between the top-two classes, and **LeastConf** [48] predictions with the lowest confidences, together with their Monte Carlo Dropout versions [3] (respectively **Entropy**$_D$, **Margin**$_D$, **LeastConf**$_D$), which, by applying dropout a test time, compare the predictions of Monte Carlo sampled networks to better asses uncertain predictions. As more recent uncertainty-based strategies, we compared with Bayesian Active Learning by Disagreements **BALD** [17], with two strategies computing the margin by means of adversarial attacks **ADV**$_{DEEPFOOL}$ [16], **ADV**$_{BIM}$ [53] and with **SupLoss** a simplified upper bound of the method proposed in [50] employing the actual labels (available only on benchmarks). As Diversity-based methods, we selected **KMeans** [54] and **KCenter** a greedy version of the CoreSet method [42]. More details are reported in the supplementary material, together with a table resuming the associated losses.

3.1   KAL Provides Better Performance Than Many Active Strategies

For a quantitative comparison of the different methods, we evaluated the network accuracy when equipped with the different active learning strategies. In Fig. 2 we reported the average F1 scores (R score for regression) budget curves when increasing the number of selected labelled data. In Table 1 we also report the Area Under the Budget Curves (AUBC), as defined in [52].

XOR-like, IRIS. In both standard machine learning problems, we can observe how KAL and KAL$_D$ (the corresponding Monte-Carlo Dropout version) reach the highest performance with a 4–10% higher AUC over standard uncertainty-based strategies in both cases. The only competitive methods in both cases are the CoreSet-based approach KCenter and the SupLoss method. This behaviour will be better analysed in Sect. 3.3. Interestingly, when analysing the corresponding plots in Fig. 2 we can appreciate how the proposed methods not only allows to reach a higher overall accuracy, but it also enables the network to learn more quickly the given tasks w.r.t. the other ones. While this was an expected behaviour on the *XOR-like* task since the provided rules completely explain the learning problem, on the *IRIS* classification task it is surprising since only 3 simple rules are given, considering a maximum of 2 features each (e.g., ¬**Long_Petal** ⇒ **Setosa**).

Insurance (R). Also in the regression scenario, KAL results to be the most effective active learning strategy, with only the CoreSet-based approach KCenter reaching similar performance (top-right plot in Fig. 2). Other methods, instead, report average performance at least 10% lower than KAL. Furthermore, also in this case, KAL employs simple relations like ¬**Smoker** ∧ **Age** < 40 ⇔

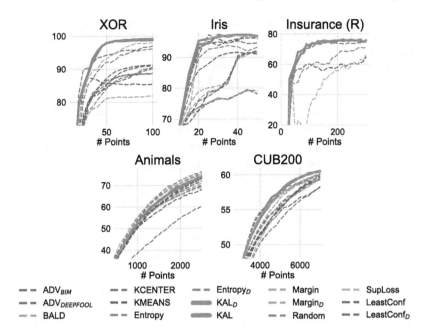

Fig. 2. Average test performance growth when increasing the number of labelled samples in terms of F1 or R score (%) in the regression task. Confidence intervals are not reported for better readability. Method variants (e.g., the Monte-Carlo Dropout versions) are displayed with the same colour.

Charge < 7500. Uncertainty-based strategies are not reported in this case, as they cannot be applied in regression problems (unless using auxiliary models to estimate confidence over open intervals as in [10]).

ANIMAL, CUB200. A slightly-different situation can be observed in the image classification tasks (bottom plots in Fig. 2). Here we notice the importance of employing well-structured knowledge. In the *ANIMALS* task, indeed, only 17 rules are provided relating animal species and their characteristics (e.g., **Fly** $\Rightarrow$ **¬Penguin**). In this case, the results with KAL are only on average w.r.t. uncertainty-based approaches (better than LeastConf, BALD and ADV but worse than Margin and Entropy). On the contrary, KAL performs much better than KCENTER and KMEANS which are unable to correctly represents data distributions in complex scenarios even though being applied in the network latent space. In the *CUB200* task instead, where 311 rules are employed in the KAL strategy considering bird species and their attributes (e.g., **WhitePelican** $\Rightarrow$ **BlackEye** $\vee$ **SolidBellyPattern** $\vee$ **SolidWingPattern**), the proposed approaches are once again the best two strategies. SupLoss, instead, provide low performances in the computer vision problems. We believe that selecting samples with high supervision loss is not an optimal active strategy in this scenario, as it might mostly select outliers.

Table 1. Comparison of the methods in terms of the mean F1 score (R score on the regression dataset) AUBC and standard deviation when increasing the number of labelled points. On top, starting and ending labelling budget for each dataset. The two best results are reported in bold. Uncertainty strategies are reported with – in the regression task, since they cannot be applied in this context.

Dataset	XOR	IRIS	Insurance (R)	Animals	CUB200
Strategy Budget	10-100	10-50	10-300	100-2500	2000-7000
KAL	**93.44** $\pm$3.39	**92.05** $\pm$4.19	**67.52** $\pm$7.28	55.57 $\pm$1.55	**51.98** $\pm$0.29
KAL$_D$	**93.38** $\pm$3.31	**91.47** $\pm$4.51	**66.54** $\pm$9.04	55.52 $\pm$1.68	**52.10** $\pm$0.24
ADV$_{BIM}$	82.77 $\pm$11.06	90.60 $\pm$3.92	–	53.93 $\pm$0.42	50.77 $\pm$0.50
ADV$_{DEEPFOOL}$	83.79 $\pm$9.49	90.45 $\pm$4.59	–	54.35 $\pm$1.02	50.41 $\pm$0.29
BALD	78.13 $\pm$9.75	75.21 $\pm$10.18	–	53.87 $\pm$1.36	51.17 $\pm$0.62
KCENTER	91.84 $\pm$1.73	90.55 $\pm$4.76	66.04 $\pm$6.04	43.37 $\pm$3.29	48.90 $\pm$0.39
KMEANS	83.53 $\pm$3.89	86.49 $\pm$9.80	53.63 $\pm$12.99	52.87 $\pm$1.18	49.90 $\pm$0.33
Entropy	81.98 $\pm$10.77	75.04 $\pm$10.05	–	56.85 $\pm$0.92	51.91 $\pm$0.12
Entropy$_D$	83.21 $\pm$10.98	75.07 $\pm$9.88	–	**57.68** $\pm$0.95	51.92 $\pm$0.39
LeastConf	83.12 $\pm$11.31	80.21 $\pm$15.74	–	53.95 $\pm$1.99	50.17 $\pm$0.28
LeastConf$_D$	84.77 $\pm$10.95	80.50 $\pm$15.91	–	54.31 $\pm$2.17	50.07 $\pm$0.45
Margin	83.12 $\pm$11.31	81.85 $\pm$16.90	–	**57.59**$\pm$1.24	51.64 $\pm$0.30
Margin$_D$	84.77 $\pm$10.95	80.88 $\pm$16.24	–	56.88 $\pm$1.33	51.54 $\pm$0.48
Random	88.96 $\pm$2.90	88.08 $\pm$6.39	56.66 $\pm$12.87	54.22 $\pm$1.11	50.63 $\pm$0.25
SupLoss	90.81 $\pm$2.13	90.24 $\pm$3.60	42.44 $\pm$5.65	54.14 $\pm$1.48	49.42 $\pm$0.23

These results prove that KAL is a very effective active learning strategy when the provided knowledge sufficiently represents the given task, both in standard and in computer vision problems. In the *ANIMALS* task, instead, where the provided knowledge is scarce, KAL performance are only on average w.r.t. uncertainty strategies.

3.2   Ablation Studies

Amount of Knowledge Directly Proportional to Performance Improvement. To further show the importance of having a diverse and rich set of rules as introduced in Sect. 3.1, we performed here an ablation study. Table 2 reports the performance of the network when equipped with a KAL strategy considering only 0%, 25%, 50%, 75% or 100% of the available knowledge. The results show evidently that the amount of knowledge is directly proportional to the performance improvement, up to +1.8%. In the 0% scenario, the only rule employed is the uncertainty-like rule, which was always retained. Notice how 50.13 is similar to the LeastConf result (50.20), suggesting that KAL without any further knowledge results in an uncertainty-based strategy. In the supplementary material, we report the complete table showing that this result is valid for all experimented scenarios.

Table 2. Ablation study on the quantity of knowledge employed to support the KAL strategy on the *CUB200* dataset. The amount of knowledge is directly proportional to the increase of performance.

KAL$_{0\%}$	KAL25%	KAL50%	KAL75%	KAL100%
50.13	50.19	50.22	51.28	**51.98**

Selecting Diverse Constraint Violations and Employing Uncertainty-Like Rule Improves the Performance Given a set of rules $\mathcal{K}$, the proposed method might in theory select p samples all violating the same rule $\phi_k(f(x))$. To avoid this issue, we select a maximum number r of samples violating a certain rule k, similarly to [5] introducing diversity in margin-based approaches. Specifically, we group samples $x \in X_u$ according to the rule they violate the most, and we allow a maximum number of $p/2$ samples from each group (still following the ranking given by Eq. 1). In the supplementary material, we report a table showing how requiring samples violating diverse constraints improves the overall quality of the KAL selection process. Also, we show the importance of adding the uncertainty-like rule $\bigwedge_i \mathbf{f_i} \oplus \neg\mathbf{f_i}$ introduced at the end of Sect. 2.3. Together, these two features allow improving the average performances of the network up to 2%.

3.3 KAL Discovers Novel Data Distributions, Unlike Uncertainty Strategies

To further analyse the results obtained, in Fig. 3 we report the samples selected by some compared strategies at the last iteration on the *XOR-like* task (100 labelled data), starting from the same randomly selected samples of Fig. 1. As introduced in Sect. 2.2, the KAL strategy enables to discover novel data distribution (leftmost figure) even when they are not represented by the initial random sampling. On the contrary, uncertainty-based strategies (like Margin but also BALD, central figures) are unable to discover new data distributions. Indeed, all the data required to label is selected along the decision boundaries of already

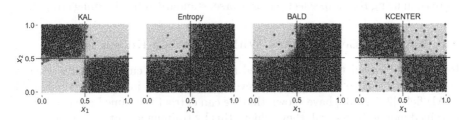

Fig. 3. Comparison of the sample selection process on the *XOR-like* task after 100 labelled samples (starting from the same points as in Fig. 1). Notice how uncertainty-based strategies (BALD, Margin) have not discovered the novel data distribution (right-bottom quadrant).

Table 3. Violation of the $\mathcal{K}_{CUB-S}$ knowledge computed as the increased percentage over the violation of a model actively trained to respect this knowledge (KAL$_{small}$). The lower, the better. The proposed method ensures domain experts that their knowledge is acquired by the model.

KAL$_{small}$	Random	BALD	Entropy	LeastConf
+0.00%	+483.10%	+720.25	+861.74%	+1334.50%

known distributions. For this reason, they provide mediocre results on average on the *XOR-like* and *IRIS* tasks and very high variance (>10–15% on *IRIS*). The CoreSet representative strategy, instead, has covered the four quadrants. However, by only working on input features statistics and without notion on the predictions, this strategy does not choose points along the decision boundaries, preventing the network from reaching high accuracy performances. More figures are reported in the supplementary material.

3.4   KAL Ensures Domain Experts that Their Knowledge is Acquired

It may be the case that domain experts are provided with a small corpus of rules which is crucial to be respected by the trained model, e.g., because it has to be deployed in a sensitive context. By always selecting the data that violate this corpus of rules, KAL ensures them that their knowledge is aquired by the model. To simulate this scenario, we computed the argument of Eq. 1 over a small part of the CUB knowledge $\mathcal{K}_{CUB-S}$ (where $-S$ stands for small) on the test data X_T for the f^b model trained with all the budget: $\varphi(\mathcal{K}_{CUB-S}, f^b, X_T) = \sum_{x \in X_T} \sum_{k \in \mathcal{K}_{CUB-S}} \varphi_k(f^b(x))$. In Table 3 we report the increased percentage of the violation by models trained following a few compared methods w.r.t. the violation of a model trained following the KAL strategy and equipped with the small corpus of rules (KAL$_{small}$). The complete table together with more experimental detail is reported in the supplementary material. For the sake of completeness, this model reaches a lower test F1 AUBC (49.04). Nonetheless, it ensures domain experts that the provided knowledge is respected significantly more than using Random selection, or, worse, standard active learning strategies.

3.5   KAL Can Be Used Even Without Domain-Knowledge

It might be argued that the proposed strategy can be employed only when a domain knowledge is available. However, recent works in the eXplainable AI (XAI) field [2,9,23,38] have shown that we can extract the same knowledge from a trained model. In general, they achieve this by training a white-box model (e.g. a decision tree) to globally explain the behaviour of a neural network. Here, we propose to employ these FOL-based explanations ($\mathcal{K}_{XAI}$) as the base knowledge of the proposed strategy when no other knowledge is available (KAL_{XAI}). More precisely, after each iteration, we employ a simple decision tree as proposed in [23]

Table 4. Accuracy of the KAL strategy coupled with a XAI method, extracting the knowledge from the same network. Notice how the AUCB reduction of performance is always smaller than 1–2%.

	XOR	IRIS	Animals	CUB
KAL	93.44 ±3.39	92.05 ±4.19	55.57 ±1.55	51.98 ±0.29
KAL$_{XAI}$	92.18 ±2.64	90.00 ±5.99	54.07 ±2.21	50.33 ±0.47

to extract the knowledge. More details on how we trained the XAI method are reported in the supplementary material. However, the knowledge may be partial, particularly during the first iterations, since it is extracted on the training distribution only. Therefore, we use Eq. 1 to select only 60% of the samples, with the remaining randomly selected. This allows to eventually recover the complete knowledge. In Table 4, we report the performance of the network when equipped with this strategy (KAL$_{XAI}$), together with the performance of the standard strategy. Notice how the reduction of performance is less than 1–2%, confirming the validity of the proposed approach even in this scenario. The amount of randomly chosen samples has not been cross-validated, therefore we expect to get even higher results by fine-tuning this parameter.

3.6   KAL Can Be Employed in Object Recognition Tasks

To test the proposed method in an object recognition context, as a proof of concept, we experimented on the simple *DOGvsPERSON* dataset. On this task, we compute the AUBC of the mean Average Precision curves. Also in this case, the network increases more its performances when equipped with the KAL strategy (55.90 ±0.39) with respect to standard random sampling (51.41 ±1.25) but also compared to the SupLoss method (55.30 ±0.54), proving the efficacy of the KAL strategy also in this context. A figure showing the three budget curves is reported in the supplementary material. Reported results are averaged over 3 initialization seeds. We only compared with Random selection and the simplified version of [50], since uncertainty-based strategies are not straightforward to apply in this context [24]. Finally, we wamt to highlight that the SupLoss performance reported here is an upper bound of the performance of the method proposed in [50]. Particularly in this context, we believe that the object recognition loss might not be easily learnt by an external model, thus reducing the performance of the SupLoss method (Table. 5).

3.7   KAL Is Not Computationally Expensive

When devising novel active learning techniques, of crucial importance is also the computational effort. Indeed, since re-training a deep neural network already requires a substantial amount of resources, the associated active strategy should be as light as possible. In [53], authors used as a term of comparison the average

Table 5. Comparison of the methods in terms of the test mAP (%) AUBC [52] when increasing the number of labelled points on the object recognition task.

Dataset	Random	SupLoss	KAL
Dog vs Person	51.27 ±1.41	55.30 ±0.54	**55.90** ±0.39

Table 6. Computational demand of some of the compared methods computed as the proportional increase over the time required for random sampling as defined in [53]. The lower, the better. Notice how the proposed method is less computationally expensive than many recent methods. Standard deviation is not reported for better readability.

Strategy	XOR	Iris	Insurance (R)	Animals	CUB200
KAL	**5.22**	**16.92**	**20.52**	41.34	180.22
KAL$_D$	15.79	23.80	31.43	53.41	197.05
ADV$_{BIM}$	36.93	657.37	–	5600.65	7440.67
ADV$_{DEEPFOOL}$	401.73	6451.91	–	57950.46	188435.28
BALD	20.70	21.50	–	157.47	613.48
KCENTER	31.82	42.89	158.28	2379.57	8713.37
KMEANS	7.90	142.36	**28.75**	718.70	4724.60
Entropy	**4.00**	**13.07**	–	**14.58**	**39.02**
Entropy$_D$	14.51	18.79	–	**22.83**	**52.77**

time needed to randomly sample a novel batch of data. In Table 6, we report the proportional increased computational time w.r.t. random sampling. KAL strategies are not computationally expensive (5–180 times slower than random sampling). On the contrary, BALD (20-613) and, more importantly, KMEANS (8-4724), KCENTER (30-8713) and ADV-based (37-188435) strategies demand considerable amounts of computational resources, strongly reducing the usability of the same methods. Standard uncertainty-based techniques like Entropy, instead, are not computationally demanding, with only the Dropout versions increasing 14–52 times the computational demand of random sampling (similarly to KAL$_D$). The complete table is reported in the supplementary material.

4   Related Work

Active Learning. In the literature, two main approaches have been followed: uncertainty sampling which selects the data on which the model is the least confident; curriculum learning which focuses first on easy samples and then extends the training set to incorporate more difficult ones while also targeting more diversity. Standard uncertainty-based strategies choose samples associated to maximal prediction entropy [25] or at minimum distance from the hyperplane in SVM [40] or with the highest variation ratio in Query-by-committee with ensemble methods [3,15]. Establishing prediction uncertainty is more difficult with DL models. Indeed, they tend to be over-confident, particularly when employing softmax activation functions [46]. Furthermore, as there is no easy access to the distance to the decision boundary, it needs to be computed. This problem has been tackled by devising different uncertain strategies, such as employing Bayesian Neural Network with Monte Carlo Dropout [17], by calculating the minimum distance required to create an adversarial example [16], or even predicting the loss associated to unlabelled sample [50]. As pointed out by [36], however, uncertain strategy may choose the same categories many times and create unbalanced datasets. To solve this, uncertain sample selection can be coupled with diversity sampling strategies. Diversity can be obtained by preferring batches of data maximizing the mutual information between model parameters and predictions [26], or selecting core-set points [41], samples nearest to k-means cluster centroids [54], or even by learning sample dissimilarities in the latent space of a VAE with an adversarial strategy [44] or by means of a GCN [6].

Hybrid Models. It has been pondered that human cognition mainly consists in two different tasks: perceiving the world and reasoning over it [45]. While these two tasks in humans take place at the same times, in artificial intelligence they are separately conducted by machine learning and logic programming. It has been argued that joining these tasks (to create a so-called hybrid model) may overcome some of the most important limits of deep learning, among which the *"data hungry"* issue [31]. In the literature, there exists a variety of proposals aiming to create hybrid models, ranging from Statistical Relational Learning (SRL) [28] and Probabilistic Logic Programming [12] which focuses on integrating learning with logic reasoning, to enhanced networks focusing on relations or with external memories [22,39]. Recently, several approaches have been devised to computes and enforce the satisfaction of a given domain knowledge within DL models [1,30,49], (see survey [20] for a complete list of works in this domain). Among these options, in this work we chose to employ the learning from constraints framework [14,21] since it provides the great logical expressivity (both universal and existential quantifier) and a straightforward implementation.

5   Conclusions

In this paper, we proposed an active learning strategy leveraging available domain knowledge to select the data to label. The performance of a model equipped with such a strategy outperforms standard uncertainty-based approaches in context where the domain knowledge is sufficiently rich, without being computationally demanding. Furthermore, we think that KAL could induce more trust in DL, since it enables non-expert users to train models leveraging their domain knowledge and ensuring them that it will be acquired by the model. A main limitation of the proposed approach is in computer vision contexts, if no attributes about main classes are known. A possible solution could be to automatically extract such concepts from the latent space of the network, as proposed in [8,18]. Also, if the domain knowledge is highly complex, FOL may not be able to fully express it and higher-order logic may be required.

Acknowledgments. This work was supported by the EU Horizon 2020 project AI4Media, under contract no. 951911 and by the French government, through the 3IA Côte d'Azur, Investment in the Future, project managed by the National Research Agency (ANR) with the reference number ANR-19-P3IA-0002.

References

1. Badreddine, S., d'Avila Garcez, A., Serafini, L., Spranger, M.: Logic tensor networks. Artif. Intell. **303**, 103649 (2022)
2. Barbiero, P., Ciravegna, G., Giannini, F., Lió, P., Gori, M., Melacci, S.: Entropy-based logic explanations of neural networks. In: Proceedings of the AAAI Conference on Artificial Intelligence, vol. 36, pp. 6046–6054 (2022)
3. Beluch, W.H., Genewein, T., Nürnberger, A., Köhler, J.M.: The power of ensembles for active learning in image classification. In: Proceedings of the IEEE Conference on Computer Vision and Pattern Recognition, pp. 9368–9377 (2018)
4. Bishop, C.M.: Pattern Recognition and Machine Learning, vol. 4. Springer, New York (2006)
5. Brinker, K.: Incorporating diversity in active learning with support vector machines. In: ICML, pp. 59–66 (2003)
6. Caramalau, R., Bhattarai, B., Kim, T.K.: Sequential graph convolutional network for active learning. In: Proceedings of the IEEE/CVF Conference on Computer Vision and Pattern Recognition, pp. 9583–9592 (2021)
7. Chen, X., Mottaghi, R., Liu, X., Fidler, S., Urtasun, R., Yuille, A.: Detect what you can: detecting and representing objects using holistic models and body parts. In: CVPR, pp. 1971–1978 (2014)
8. Chen, Z., Bei, Y., Rudin, C.: Concept whitening for interpretable image recognition. Nat. Mach. Intell. **2**(12), 772–782 (2020). https://doi.org/10.1038/s42256-020-00265-z
9. Ciravegna, G., et al.: Logic explained networks. Artif. Intell. **314** (2023). https://doi.org/10.1016/j.artint.2022.103822. https://www.sciencedirect.com/science/article/abs/pii/S000437022200162X
10. Corbiere, C., Thome, N., Saporta, A., Vu, T.H., Cord, M., Perez, P.: Confidence estimation via auxiliary models. IEEE Trans. Pattern Anal. Mach. Intell. **44**, 6043–6055 (2022)
11. Das, A., Rad, P.: Opportunities and challenges in explainable artificial intelligence (XAI): a survey. arXiv preprint arXiv:2006.11371 (2020)
12. De Raedt, L., Kimmig, A.: Probabilistic (logic) programming concepts. Mach. Learn. **100**(1), 5–47 (2015)
13. Deng, J., Dong, W., Socher, R., Li, L.J., Li, K., Fei-Fei, L.: ImageNet: a large-scale hierarchical image database. In: 2009 IEEE Conference on Computer Vision and Pattern Recognition, pp. 248–255. IEEE (2009)
14. Diligenti, M., Gori, M., Sacca, C.: Semantic-based regularization for learning and inference. Artif. Intell. **244**, 143–165 (2017)
15. Ducoffe, M., Precioso, F.: Active learning strategy for CNN combining batchwise dropout and query-by-committee. In: ESANN (2017)
16. Ducoffe, M., Precioso, F.: Adversarial active learning for deep networks: a margin based approach. arXiv:1802.09841 (2018)
17. Gal, Y., Islam, R., Ghahramani, Z.: Deep Bayesian active learning with image data. In: International Conference on Machine Learning, pp. 1183–1192. PMLR (2017)

18. Ghorbani, A., Wexler, J., Zou, J.Y., Kim, B.: Towards automatic concept-based explanations. In: Advances in Neural Information Processing Systems, vol. 32 (2019)
19. Gilpin, L.H., Bau, D., Yuan, B.Z., Bajwa, A., Specter, M., Kagal, L.: Explaining explanations: an overview of interpretability of machine learning. In: 2018 IEEE 5th International Conference on Data Science and Advanced Analytics (DSAA), pp. 80–89. IEEE (2018)
20. Giunchiglia, E., Stoian, M.C., Lukasiewicz, T.: Deep learning with logical constraints. arXiv preprint arXiv:2205.00523 (2022)
21. Gnecco, G., Gori, M., Melacci, S., Sanguineti, M.: Foundations of support constraint machines. Neural Comput. **27**(2), 388–480 (2015)
22. Graves, A., et al.: Hybrid computing using a neural network with dynamic external memory. Nature **538**, 471–476 (2016)
23. Guidotti, R., Monreale, A., Ruggieri, S., Pedreschi, D., Turini, F., Giannotti, F.: Local rule-based explanations of black box decision systems. arXiv preprint arXiv:1805.10820 (2018)
24. Haussmann, E., et al.: Scalable active learning for object detection. In: IEEE IV Symposium, pp. 1430–1435. IEEE (2020)
25. Houlsby, N., Huszár, F., Ghahramani, Z., Lengyel, M.: Bayesian active learning for classification and preference learning (2011)
26. Kirsch, A., Van Amersfoort, J., Gal, Y.: BatchBALD: efficient and diverse batch acquisition for deep Bayesian active learning. NeurIPS **32**, 7026–7037 (2019)
27. Klement, E., Mesiar, R., Pap, E.: Triangular Norms, vol. 8. Springer, Dordrecht (2013). https://doi.org/10.1007/978-94-015-9540-7
28. Koller, D., et al.: Introduction to Statistical Relational Learning. MIT Press, Cambridge (2007)
29. LeCun, Y., Bengio, Y., Hinton, G.: Deep learning. Nature **521**(7553), 436–444 (2015)
30. Manhaeve, R., Dumancic, S., Kimmig, A., Demeester, T., De Raedt, L.: DeepProbLog: neural probabilistic logic programming. In: Advances in Neural Information Processing Systems, vol. 31 (2018)
31. Marcus, G.: Deep learning: a critical appraisal. arXiv:1801.00631 (2018)
32. Marra, G., Giannini, F., Diligenti, M., Gori, M.: Lyrics: a general interface layer to integrate logic inference and deep learning. In: ECML/PKDD (2019)
33. McCallumzy, A.K., Nigamy, K.: Employing EM and pool-based active learning for text classification. In: ICML, pp. 359–367. Citeseer (1998)
34. Melacci, S., et al.: Domain knowledge alleviates adversarial attacks in multi-label classifiers. IEEE PAMI **44**, 9944–9959 (2021). https://doi.org/10.1109/TPAMI.2021.3137564
35. Netzer, Y., Wang, T., Coates, A., Bissacco, A., Wu, B., Ng, A.Y.: Reading digits in natural images with unsupervised feature learning. In: NIPS Workshop on Deep Learning and Unsupervised Feature Learning 2011 (2011). http://ufldl.stanford.edu/housenumbers/nips2011_housenumbers.pdf
36. Pop, R., Fulop, P.: Deep ensemble Bayesian active learning: addressing the mode collapse issue in Monte Carlo dropout via ensembles. arXiv:1811.03897 (2018)
37. Ren, P., et al.: A survey of deep active learning. ACM Comput. Surv. (CSUR) **54**(9), 1–40 (2021)
38. Ribeiro, M.T., Singh, S., Guestrin, C.: Anchors: high-precision model-agnostic explanations. In: Proceedings of the AAAI Conference on Artificial Intelligence, vol. 32 (2018)

39. Santoro, A., et al.: A simple neural network module for relational reasoning. In: NeurIPS, vol. 30 (2017)
40. Schohn, G., Cohn, D.: Less is more: active learning with support vector machines. In: ICML, October 2000
41. Sener, O., Savarese, S.: Active learning for convolutional neural networks: a core-set approach. In: ICLR (2018)
42. Sener, O., Savarese, S.: Active learning for convolutional neural networks: a core-set approach. arXiv preprint arXiv:1708.00489 (2017)
43. Settles, B.: Active learning literature survey (2009)
44. Sinha, S., Ebrahimi, S., Darrell, T.: Variational adversarial active learning. In: Proceedings of the IEEE/CVF International Conference on Computer Vision, pp. 5972–5981 (2019)
45. Solso, R., MacLin, M., MacLin, O.: Cognitive Psychology. Pearson Education, New Zealand (2005)
46. Thulasidasan, S., Chennupati, G., Bilmes, J., Bhattacharya, T., Michalak, S.: On mixup training: improved calibration and predictive uncertainty for deep neural networks. In: NeurIPS, vol. 32 (2019)
47. Wah, C., Branson, S., Welinder, P., Perona, P., Belongie, S.: The Caltech-UCSD Birds-200-2011 Dataset. Technical report, CNS-TR-2011-001, CalTech (2011)
48. Wang, D., Shang, Y.: A new active labeling method for deep learning. In: 2014 International Joint Conference on Neural Networks (IJCNN), pp. 112–119. IEEE (2014)
49. Xu, J., Zhang, Z., Friedman, T., Liang, Y., Broeck, G.: A semantic loss function for deep learning with symbolic knowledge. In: International Conference on Machine Learning, pp. 5502–5511. PMLR (2018)
50. Yoo, D., Kweon, I.: Learning loss for active learning. In: IEEE CVPR, pp. 93–102 (2019)
51. Yu, F., Seff, A., Zhang, Y., Song, S., Funkhouser, T., Xiao, J.: LSUN: construction of a large-scale image dataset using deep learning with humans in the loop. arXiv:1506.03365 (2015)
52. Zhan, X., Liu, H., Li, Q., Chan, A.B.: A comparative survey: benchmarking for pool-based active learning. In: Zhou, Z.H. (ed.) Proceedings of the Thirtieth International Joint Conference on Artificial Intelligence, IJCAI-21, pp. 4679–4686. International Joint Conferences on Artificial Intelligence Organization, August 2021. https://doi.org/10.24963/ijcai.2021/634
53. Zhan, X., Wang, Q., Huang, K., Xiong, H., Dou, D., Chan, A.B.: A comparative survey of deep active learning (2022). https://doi.org/10.48550/ARXIV.2203.13450. https://arxiv.org/abs/2203.13450
54. Zhdanov, F.: Diverse mini-batch active learning. arXiv:1901.05954 (2019)
55. Zhu, X., Goldberg, A.: Introduction to Semi-supervised Learning. Synthesis Lectures on Artificial Intelligence and Machine Learning, vol. 3, no. 1, pp. 1–130 (2009). https://doi.org/10.1007/978-3-031-01548-9

ActiveGLAE: A Benchmark for Deep Active Learning with Transformers

Lukas Rauch[1]([✉]), Matthias Aßenmacher[2,3], Denis Huseljic[1], Moritz Wirth[1], Bernd Bischl[2,3], and Bernhard Sick[1]

[1] University of Kassel, Wilhelmshöher Allee 73, 34121 Kassel, Germany
{lukas.rauch,dhuseljic,moritz.wirth,bsick}@uni-kassel.de
[2] Department of Statistics, LMU Munich, Ludwigstr. 33, 80539 Munich, Germany
[3] Munich Center for Machine Learning (MCML), LMU Munich, Munich, Germany
{matthias,bernd.bischl}@stat.uni-muenchen.de

Abstract. Deep active learning (DAL) seeks to reduce annotation costs by enabling the model to actively query instance annotations from which it expects to learn the most. Despite extensive research, there is currently no standardized evaluation protocol for transformer-based language models in the field of DAL. Diverse experimental settings lead to difficulties in comparing research and deriving recommendations for practitioners. To tackle this challenge, we propose the ACTIVEGLAE benchmark, a comprehensive collection of data sets and evaluation guidelines for assessing DAL. Our benchmark aims to facilitate and streamline the evaluation process of novel DAL strategies. Additionally, we provide an extensive overview of current practice in DAL with transformer-based language models. We identify three key challenges - data set selection, model training, and DAL settings - that pose difficulties in comparing query strategies. We establish baseline results through an extensive set of experiments as a reference point for evaluating future work. Based on our findings, we provide guidelines for researchers and practitioners.

Keywords: Deep Active Learning · Transformer · NLP · Benchmarking

1 Introduction

Transformer-based pre-trained language models (PLMs) have exhibited state-of-the-art (SOTA) performance in various natural language processing (NLP) applications, including supervised fine-tuning [9] and few-shot learning [6,36]. The commonality of these deep neural networks (DNNs) is their ability of general language understanding acquired through self-supervised pre-training [12,40,41]. While pre-training reduces the need for annotated data for a downstream task, obtaining annotations (e.g., class labels) from humans is still time-intensive and costly in practice [10,42]. Additionally, real-world applications require reliable models that can quickly adapt to new data and learn efficiently with few annotated instances [54]. Active Learning aims to minimize annotation cost by allowing the model to query annotations for instances which it expects to yield the highest performance gains [16,51].

© The Author(s), under exclusive license to Springer Nature Switzerland AG 2023
D. Koutra et al. (Eds.): ECML PKDD 2023, LNAI 14169, pp. 55–74, 2023.
https://doi.org/10.1007/978-3-031-43412-9_4

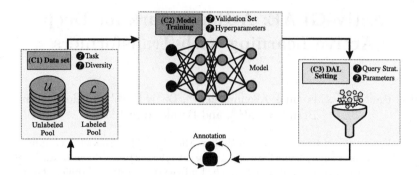

Fig. 1. DAL cycle with three essential challenges that influence the evaluation protocol.

However, in the context of deep learning, evaluating deep active learning (DAL) is challenging due to several reasons [18,43]. First, to ensure the practical applicability of query strategies, it is essential to have a wide range of diverse data sets (i.e., tasks). Second, the iterative fine-tuning of PLMs in each cycle iteration with multiple influential factors (i.e., model hyperparameters and DAL settings) results in substantial runtime overhead. Third, in a realistic scenario, DAL poses a one-time learning problem with no validation set for hyperparameter optimization, requiring careful consideration during evaluation [20]. These challenges lead to researchers simplifying their experimental design, compromising the comparability of results and practical recommendations [18]. Thus, the benefits of applying DAL in a realistic scenario are still ambiguous [30]. For example, it remains unclear whether employing DAL query strategies yields any benefits compared to randomly querying instances. Despite current efforts to enhance comparability of DAL research in the vision domain [3,18,22,26,30], a standardized evaluation protocol or a widely-accepted benchmark for DAL in the NLP domain with PLMs is lacking.

To overcome these challenges, we propose the **Active General Language Adaption Evaluation** (ACTIVEGLAE) benchmark. ACTIVEGLAE comprises a wide range of NLP classification tasks, along with guidelines for a realistic and comparative evaluation of DAL. We aim to encourage research to employ a more comparable experimental design of DAL with PLMs, hopefully enabling the identification of best practices for real-world scenarios. Following our guidelines, we provide an extensive experimental study, which yields baseline results for three SOTA PLMs utilizing various popular DAL strategies. Our main **contributions** can be summarized as follows:

1. We highlight current practice and limitations in existing research in DAL with transformer-based PLMs through an extensive literature analysis revealing three critical challenges for a comparative and realistic evaluation. More specifically, the evaluation of a DAL process is heavily influenced by the selection of data sets (C1), the model training (C2), and the DAL setting (C3). Figure 1 illustrates these challenges along with their influential underlying factors.

2. We propose the ACTIVEGLAE benchmark comprising ten NLP classification tasks that cover a diverse range of genres, sizes, class cardinalities, and degrees of difficulty. Additionally, we provide guidelines to enable a standardized evaluation protocol. To streamline the evaluation process in DAL, we will contribute ACTIVEGLAE to Huggingface Datasets [24].

3. We conduct an extensive empirical study that provides baseline results for the ACTIVEGLAE benchmark. These serve as a reference for assessing novel DAL processes and establish a minimum level of performance query strategies must exceed to be considered effective. Moreover, analyzing these baseline results and additional ablations regarding the identified challenges allows us to derive best practices for researchers and guidelines for practitioners.

4. We provide the code[1] for all experiments to facilitate further research. The implementations are based on Huggingface [58] to improve reusability. By providing each experiment's queried instances, we offer insights into the underlying DAL process to ensure reproducibility. Additionally, all experimental results are publicly available[2] through Weights and Biases [4].

2   Problem Setting

We consider text classification problems where a D-dimensional instance is mapped to a feature vector $\mathbf{x} \in \mathcal{X}$ with the feature space $\mathcal{X} = \mathbb{R}^D$. An instance $\mathbf{x}$ is linked to a ground truth class label $y \in \mathcal{Y}$ with $\mathcal{Y} = \{1, ..., C\}$ as the space of C classes. We denote a model at cycle iteration t through its parameters θ_t, equipped with a pre-trained encoder backbone and a sequence classification head. The model $f^{\theta_t} : \mathcal{X} \rightarrow \mathbb{R}^C$ maps an instance $\mathbf{x}$ to a vector of class probabilities $\hat{\mathbf{p}} = f^{\theta_t}(\mathbf{x})$ corresponding to a prediction of the categorical class distribution. We investigate a pool-based DAL scenario with an unlabeled pool data set $\mathcal{U}(t) \subseteq \mathcal{X}$ and a labeled pool data set $\mathcal{L}(t) \subseteq \mathcal{X} \times \mathcal{Y}$. We initialize the DAL process at $t = 0$ with a randomly sampled set of annotated instances. At each cycle iteration t, the DAL query strategy aggregates the most-useful instances in a batch $\mathcal{B}(t) \subset \mathcal{U}(t)$ with the size b. We denote an annotated batch as $\mathcal{B}^*(t) \in \mathcal{X} \times \mathcal{Y}$. We update the unlabeled pool $\mathcal{U}(t+1) = \mathcal{U}(t) \setminus \mathcal{B}(t)$ and the labeled pool $\mathcal{L}(t+1) = \mathcal{L}(t) \cup \mathcal{B}^*(t)$ with the annotated batch. At each cycle iteration t, the model θ_t can be retrained from scratch (model cold-stat) or initialized with model parameters from the previous iteration (model warm-start). This leads to an update of the model parameters θ_{t+1}. The DAL process ends upon depletion of the budget B, representing the maximum number of queries.

---

[1] Github repository.
[2] Weights and Biases project.

3   Current Practice in Evaluating Deep Active Learning

The current trend towards data-centric methods [64] and the adaptive capabilities of DNNs [54] has led to numerous studies on DAL with transformer-based PLMs. However, comparing DAL results is a complex challenge [35], as indicated by varying evaluation protocols in current work. This lack of standardization makes it difficult to determine a given task's most effective query strategy. We identified three challenges that researchers need to address when designing a DAL process (cf. Fig. 1). In the following, we analyze the current practice concerning these challenges and briefly describe our suggested benchmark approach. While we focus on the NLP domain, we also include insights from (CV) where we observe a trend towards unified evaluation protocols [3,18,22,26,30,35].

Table 1. Data sets employed in current work with transformers in DAL.

	AGN	B77	DBP	CR	COLA	FNC1	IMDB	MNLI	MR	PUBM	QNLI	QQP	SUBJ	SST2	SST5	TREC6	WIK	YELP5
[11]	✓	✗	✗	✓	✗	✗	✗	✗	✓	✗	✗	✗	✓	✗	✗	✓	✓	✗
[31]	✓	✗	✓	✗	✗	✗	✗	✗	✗	✓	✗	✗	✓	✗	✗	✗	✗	✗
[67]	✓	✗	✗	✗	✗	✗	✓	✗	✗	✗	✗	✗	✗	✓	✗	✗	✗	✗
[47]	✓	✗	✗	✗	✗	✗	✗	✗	✗	✗	✗	✗	✗	✓	✗	✗	✗	✗
[41]	✓	✗	✗	✗	✗	✗	✗	✗	✗	✗	✗	✗	✗	✗	✗	✓	✗	✗
[33]	✓	✗	✓	✗	✗	✗	✓	✗	✗	✗	✗	✗	✗	✓	✗	✓	✗	✗
[35]	✓	✗	✗	✗	✗	✗	✓	✗	✗	✓	✓	✓	✗	✓	✗	✗	✗	✗
[57]	✓	✗	✗	✗	✗	✗	✓	✗	✗	✓	✗	✗	✗	✗	✗	✗	✗	✗
[9]	✓	✗	✓	✗	✗	✗	✗	✗	✓	✗	✗	✗	✓	✗	✗	✗	✗	✗
[51]	✓	✗	✗	✓	✗	✗	✗	✗	✓	✗	✗	✗	✓	✗	✗	✓	✗	✗
[15]	✓	✗	✗	✗	✓	✗	✓	✗	✓	✗	✗	✗	✓	✓	✗	✓	✗	✗
[53]	✓	✗	✗	✗	✗	✗	✗	✗	✗	✓	✗	✗	✗	✗	✗	✗	✗	✗
[65]	✓	✗	✓	✗	✗	✗	✗	✗	✗	✓	✗	✗	✗	✓	✗	✓	✗	✗
[69]	✓	✗	✗	✗	✗	✗	✓	✗	✗	✗	✓	✓	✗	✗	✗	✓	✗	✗
[20]	✓	✗	✗	✗	✗	✗	✗	✗	✗	✗	✗	✗	✓	✗	✗	✓	✗	✗
[22]	✗	✗	✗	✗	✗	✗	✗	✗	✓	✗	✗	✗	✗	✗	✗	✓	✗	✗
[34]	✓	✗	✓	✗	✗	✗	✓	✗	✗	✗	✗	✗	✗	✗	✗	✓	✗	✗
[66]	✓	✗	✓	✗	✗	✗	✓	✗	✗	✗	✗	✗	✗	✗	✗	✓	✗	✗
glae	✓	✓	✓	✗	✗	✓	✓	✓	✓	✗	✗	✗	✗	✓	✗	✓	✓	✓

3.1   (C1) Data Set Selection

Developing robust DAL processes that can be applied out-of-the-box (or at least task-specifically) is critical since they cannot be tested beforehand, and models only have one attempt to learn in a practical setting [20]. Additionally, a lack of variation in the selection of data sets may lead to biased and non-generalizable results. Thus, to ensure generalizable results, a DAL process needs to be evaluated on data sets covering a diverse range of text genres, pool sizes, class cardinalities, task difficulties, and label distributions. At the same time, a diverse data set selection across publications leads to difficulties in comparing results.

Current Practice. There is an abundance of benchmark classification data sets in NLP leading to a disjoint selection between publications [44]. Table 1 provides an overview of data sets employed in related work. While some specific data sets (e.g., AGN, SST2, TREC6) are used more frequently, the research landscape needs to be more cohesive. This lack of consensus reduces the comparability of results [2]. Current work reports diverse and contradictory findings across data sets, stressing the importance of further investigating the benefits of applying query strategies compared to randomly selecting instances. Additionally, we found that related studies often employ data sets covering similar tasks, training data volumes, and task difficulties. We assume data sets are often bypassed due to a large unlabeled pool, which can result in high query times.

Our Study. We propose ACTIVEGLAE, a selection of data sets as a benchmark suite similar to (Super)GLUE [55,56]. We consider a wide variety of real-world tasks, aiming at spurring the applicability of DAL. This diverse set of tasks allows us to highlight task-specific challenges and derive evaluation guidelines. We intend to improve the generalizability and comparability of DAL research.

3.2 (C2) Model Training

Conventional hyperparameter-tuning cannot be performed when simulating a real-world setting in a DAL process for several reasons [20]: First, a validation data set contradicts the purpose of DAL to reduce annotation effort (i.e., validation paradox [30]). Second, model hyperparameters (e.g., number of learning steps and learning rate) can only be determined once at the beginning of the cycle. Third, the iterative nature of DAL would necessitate hyperparameter optimization at each cycle iteration, leading to runtime overhead. Overcoming these challenges is crucial for successfully employing DAL in practice [35].

Current Practice. Table 4 in Appendix[3] A depicts the adjustable model hyperparameters and the current practice in related work. In general, we identify three validation settings: (1) assuming the availability of all or parts of the validation data [33,49], (2) (dynamically) sample a validation set from the labeled pool [53], or (3) omitting the validation set entirely [19,29]. All approaches with a validation set employ early stopping (or selecting the model with the best validation results) and consider the number of epochs as an optimizable hyperparameter. Ji et al. [18] report that while early stopping can speed up the training process, it introduces randomness and decreases comparability. They recommend a fixed number of epochs suitable for the model architecture and data set. Recent studies suggest that model training is more important than the choice of a query strategy [19,31], as fine-tuning PLMs on small data sets can suffer from training instability [13,47,48]. A real-world setting without a validation set is similar to few-shot learning, particularly at the beginning of a DAL process with a small labeled pool. [47] and [48] omit the validation set entirely and deploy fixed hyperparameters in a practical few-shot learning setting. [37] find out that the presence of a validation set led to a significant overestimation of the few-shot ability of language models. In parallel, we consider this a major problem of deploying DAL in practice. Jukić and Šnajder [19] address this by introducing an early stopping technique utilizing the representation smoothness of PLMs layers from training. Training strategies usually follow the standard training procedure from [9], employing a fixed number of training epochs (3 to 15), the AdamW

---

[3] The appendix can be accessed at ArXiv.

[28] optimizer with a learning rate between 2e−5 and 5e−5 and a learning rate scheduler with warmup (5–10% of the steps). Researchers apply a fixed and well-established training strategy to a particular model to focus on the results of query strategies. However, the lack of established benchmarks in DAL and partly incomplete hyperparameter specifications result in diverse training approaches (cf. Table 4), that decrease comparability across publications.

Our Study. Our benchmark study adopts a similar approach to previous work on few-shot learning [37,47,48]. We simulate a real-world DAL process by entirely omitting the validation set without early stopping [30]. We employ various fixed model hyperparameters (e.g., epochs and learning rates) that are data set-agnostic with different PLMs as baselines to highlight their impact on resulting model performance. Therefore, our study provides reference points for further research by presenting results for various hyperparameter configurations.

3.3   (C3) Deep Active Learning Setting

Evaluating DAL requires determining a DAL setting which includes key factors such as the choice of query strategy, query size, and budget. These factors are often set as fixed without having established default values from comparable benchmark studies or meaningful baselines serving as reference points. Query strategies can be sorted into uncertainty, diversity, and hybrid sampling. Uncertainty sampling identifies the most-uncertain instances in the hypothesis space, while diversity sampling focuses on diversity in the feature space [63]. Hybrid approaches combine uncertainty and diversity sampling.

Current Practice. In Appendix A, Table 5 presents an overview of DAL settings and query strategies used in related work. Our benchmark study analyzes factors that influence the resulting model performance of query strategies in a DAL process. These factors include:

– *Initialization and update*: All prior studies use a model cold-start approach, where the model parameters are initialized from scratch at each cycle iteration (cf. Table 5). In contrast, a model warm-start initializes the model with parameters from the previous iteration. While a model warm-start may lead to faster convergence, it could likewise cause performance degradation due to potential bias towards the initial labeled pool [1,17]. In contrast, Lang et al. [22] and Ji et al. [18] find that a model warm-start stabilizes the learning curve in CV. Uncertainty-based query strategies rely on the model's predictive uncertainty, which may require prior model training with task-specific information [62,63]. We refer to this as a data warm-start. Alternatively, if no initial labeled pool is available for model training, we refer to it as data cold-start. While related work commonly employs a data warm-start with a fixed initial pool size, Yuan et al. [63] and Yu et al. [62] aim to leverage the pre-trained knowledge of a transformer-based PLMs focusing on data cold-start in a DAL process.

- *Stopping criterion*: To ensure comparability, current studies usually use a fixed budget with a maximum limit of 2000 annotations as the stopping criterion. Alternatively, the budget may be data set-specific (e.g., 15% of the available unlabeled pool) [32,65]. Tran et al. [54] and Hacohen et al. [15] determine the budget based on the complexity of the learning task (e.g., with the number of classes). Once the budget depletes, the DAL process stops. Recent work in CV differentiates between budget sizes to simulate a diverse set of real-world scenarios. Hacohen et al. report that uncertainty-based strategies perform better with higher budgets. Note that [15] use the terms budget and warm-start interchangeably and refer to a high-data regime when a sizeable initial set is available (i.e., data warm-start) and vice versa. At the current state, there are no detailed investigations concerning the budget in NLP with transformer-based PLMs.
- *Query size*: The query size is crucial since it affects the number of cycle iterations given a specific annotation budget. For example, a larger query size leads to fewer model updates and may affect model performance and runtime. While Lüth et al. [30] and Lang et al. [22] report better results with smaller query sizes in the CV domain, D'Arcy and Downey [8] demonstrate no difference between a query size of 12 and 25 with transformer-based PLMs. Current work mostly uses a fixed query size of 100 annotations or less [10,62], with some studies also applying a relative size, such as 2% of the unlabeled pool [31,32].
- *Pool subset*: Since the size of the unlabeled pool significantly impacts query time, researchers often avoid large data sets or introduce an unlabeled subset from which they query annotations [49]. For instance, [31] subsamples DBPedia [23] via stratified sampling once at the beginning of the DAL process to maintain the initial label distribution. However, [18] suggest avoiding sub-sampling as it can potentially alter the ranking of DAL query strategies.

Our Study. We present baseline results for low and high-budget settings alongside two query sizes on ACTIVEGLAE. We concentrate on a fixed number of initial instances (i.e., data warm-start) and use the term budget size independent of the initial pool. We contend that the number of classes cannot easily determine the task complexity since other factors like class imbalance or pool size play a crucial role. Therefore, to ensure comparability across experiments and draw conclusions on the influence of the data set complexity, we employ a fixed DAL setting that is independent of the data set. We also explore the influence of model warm-start and model cold-start. While iteratively subsampling at each cycle iteration may introduce randomness [18], it significantly reduces experiment runtime. Thus, we examine the effect of employing a pool subset on model performance across query strategies.

4   ActiveGLAE - Data Sets and Tasks

We aim at creating a benchmark collection of real-world tasks enabling a standardized and realistic evaluation of DAL strategies. Thus, we carefully select data sets (cf. Table 2) exhibiting different characteristics relevant to practical applications. Our selection covers balanced as well as imbalanced data sets and binary as well as multi-class settings. We choose sets of low (3 to 6 classes), medium (14 classes), and high (77 classes) class cardinality. Since class imbalance is a common practical problem, we consider naturally imbalanced data sets, rather than artificially introducing imbalance. The data sets differ in size (10k–650k examples) and encompass various classification tasks.

Table 2. Overview of ActiveGLAE data sets and tasks. When no test set is available (MNLI, QNLI, SST2), we use the validation set.

Corpus	|Train|	|Test|	Task	#classes	Balanced
AG's News	120k	7600	news classification	4	✓
Banking77	10k	3000	conversational language	77	✓
DBPedia	560k	5000	ontology classification	14	✓
FNC-1	40k	4998	stance detection	4	✗
MNLI	390k	9815	textual entailment	3	✓
QNLI	104k	5463	question answering	2	✓
SST-2	67k	872	sentiment classification	2	✓
TREC-6	5452	500	question classification	6	✓
Wiki Talk	159k	64k	toxic comment detection	2	✗
Yelp-5	650k	50k	sentiment classification	5	✓

AG's News [66] is a large multi-class news data set, with four target classes and a pool of 120k training instances. Further, it is currently the most popular one for DAL with transformers (cf. Table 1). **Banking77** [7] focuses on conversational language understanding and intent detection. We include it due to its high class cardinality and small training pool, making it challenging for DAL. **DBPedia** [23] is representative of medium class cardinality (14 classes). It poses a rather easy multi-class problem indicated by a high passive baseline performance, leaving room for DAL strategies to prove their effectiveness. **FNC-1** [38] was derived from the Emergent data set [11] for the 2017 Fake News Challenge. Instances consist of news headlines and articles, with a stance detection task. It contains long texts and has a strongly imbalanced class distribution (>70% unrelated stance), posing a challenging task for DAL. **MNLI** [57], **QNLI** [56] **and SST-2** [52] are part of the GLUE benchmark. While the former two are sentence-pair inference tasks for textual entailment (MNLI) and question answering (QNLI), the latter is a single-sentence sentiment classification task (SST-2). Both question answering and sentiment classification represent important practical challenges, while entailment is a linguistically meaningful task. **TREC-6** [25] presents a multi-class classification task requiring question language understanding. It is a valuable addition to ActiveGLAE due to its short average text length ($\sim$10 words) and the small training pool of 5.5k questions. **Wikipedia Talk** [59] is a large-scale data set of Wikipedia discussion comments, potentially containing toxic content. The binary classification task to detect toxicity is imbalanced (only $\sim$10% toxic) and has a rather large training pool ($\sim$159k samples). **Yelp-5** [66] was introduced for multi-class sentiment detection and constitutes a valuable counterpart to the binary sentiment classification task (SST-2).

5   Experimental Setup

Baselines. To obtain the baseline results, we follow our insights from Sect. 3.2 and simulate a real-world DAL scenario without a validation set. We employ BERT [9], DistilBERT [46], and RoBERTa [27] as they are among the most popular contemporary models. We resort to a model for sequence classification from the Huggingface Transformers code base [58] to ensure reproducibility. We adopt the model hyperparameters from [19]: a short training (ST) with 5 epochs [9] and a long training (LT) with 15 epochs [62]. We use AdamW [28] with a learning rate of 5e$-$5 and a linear scheduler with a warmup of 5% [62]. To establish baseline performance values, we implement popular query strategies that cover uncertainty-based (ENTROPY), diversity-based (CORESET), and hybrid approaches (BADGE, CAL). We employ random sampling as the baseline query strategy. The model's [CLS] token embedding corresponds to the embedding of an instance $\mathbf{x}$. For ENTROPY, and CAL, we aggregate a batch $\mathcal{B}(t)$ by greedily selecting the most-useful instances until we reach the desired query size b. For BADGE and CORESET, b instances are selected in a batch $\mathcal{B}(t)$ (cf. Appendix C for further details). We focus on a data warm-start and begin each DAL experiment by initializing 100 randomly selected instances (fixed per seed) from the unlabeled pool. We assess the impact of low and high budgets by setting them to 500 and 1600, respectively (c.f. Table 5, A). For each cycle iteration t, we select a query size b of 100 and randomly query a subset of 10,000 instances from the entire unlabeled pool $\mathcal{U}(t)$. This enables us to reduce the query times and substantially increase the number of experiments. To ensure a fair comparison, we maintain fixed hyperparameters and DAL settings across all tasks. For a comprehensive overview, please refer to Table 6 in Appendix B.

Ablations. In ablation studies, we only investigate BERT with ST and LT to reduce runtime. More specifically, we examine the impact on model performance across query strategies by (1) using a model warm-start instead of a model cold-start in each cycle iteration, (2) querying the entire unlabeled pool without a subset, and (3) reducing the query size to 25 with the same budget resulting in 60 cycle iterations. Additionally, we adopt the learning strategy from [34], who recommend a lower learning rate (2e$-$5), an increased number of epochs (20) warmup ratio of 10% (LT$^+$) to increase training stability on small data sets.

Evaluation. Following related work, we visualize the performance of DAL query strategies with learning curves for all experiments [49,62]. For balanced data sets, we use accuracy, while for imbalanced data sets (FNC-1, WikiTalk), we report the balanced accuracy [5] as metrics to report test performance after each cycle iteration. To facilitate comparability, we additionally present a single metric for each query strategy's model performance on the test set - the final (balanced) accuracy (FAC) and the area under the learning curve (AUC). The AUC score is normalized to ensure comparability [49]. In addition to reporting the results for each data set individually, we compute an aggregate performance score by taking the average across the entire ACTIVEGLAE benchmark, with equal weighting for each data set, following the methodology of GLUE. We repeat each experiment with five random seeds.

6 Results

In this section, we present our main results as well as the ablations based on the three challenges - data set selection (C1), model training (C2), and DAL settings (C3) - we identified in the design of a DAL process in Sect. 3. For each challenge, we provide a takeaway summarizing our key findings. Table 3 reports the AUC

Table 3. Baseline **BERT AUC results** on ACTIVEGLAE with ST, LT, LT$^+$, budget sizes (500, 1600) and 5 repetitions (±sd). **Best** and <u>second</u> best results are highlighted for each data set and the highest Average result. ↑ and ↓ demonstrate improvements over RANDOM. Ranking indicates the placement of a query strategy.

		AGN	B77	DBP	FNC1	MNLI	QNLI	SST2	TREC6	WIKI	YELP5	Average	R
		Low Data Budget: 100 + 400											
random	ST	85.4±1.8	11.0±3.1	79.5±4.2	31.7±4.6	41.2±0.9	63.6±2.0	81.9±1.9	84.2±3.8	68.1±1.4	43.5±2.0	59.24←	2
random	LT	87.7±0.3	**34.5±1.6**	<u>96.6±0.4</u>	43.92±4.8	46.1±1.6	67.6±1.9	82.1±2.3	90.7±0.9	72.2±3.6	**48.8±1.6**	67.02←	4
random	LT$^+$	87.1±0.7	24.3±2.3	93.6±1.2	42.6±4.3	45.0±2.3	66.5±2.0	82.2±2.3	89.8±2.4	71.2±4.2	46.9±2.2	64.93←	2
entropy	ST	82.8±3.6	8.3±1.4	74.2±6.7	32.7±2.5	42.0±1.8	62.9±2.7	82.2±1.6	80.3±5.3	73.5±1.7	42.6±2.9	58.18 ↓0.83	5
entropy	LT	<u>88.3±0.3</u>	32.3±1.4	94.9±2.2	<u>46.9±3.1</u>	45.5±0.8	**67.81±2.1**	82.3±2.1	90.5±2.2	77.6±2.6	46.5±1.5	67.28 ↑0.26	3
entropy	LT$^+$	87.0±1.5	21.3±2.8	92.7±2.5	38.8±1.9	45.7±1.2	65.0±2.9	<u>83.1±1.2</u>	89.0±2.3	75.6±2.5	45.0±2.2	64.34 ↓0.59	4
badge	ST	86.4±1.2	11.7±3.6	84.4±1.8	33.1±3.7	42.1±2.9	65.6±2.1	81.9±1.6	85.5±3.4	73.3±2.1	45.4±1.1	60.96 ↑1.95	1
badge	LT	**88.5±0.2**	<u>34.1±2.6</u>	**96.9±0.6**	46.0±4.5	44.9±1.7	66.5±2.6	**83.2±0.8**	**92.3±1.0**	**78.7±1.3**	<u>48.4±1.6</u>	**67.97** ↑0.95	1
badge	LT$^+$	87.8±0.6	25.4±2.0	94.9±1.0	42.6±3.6	44.6±1.3	66.5±2.7	82.7±2.1	91±2.1	74.9±2.4	46.7±2.4	65.73 ↑0.80	1
coreset	ST	84.0±1.8	9.3±1.1	74.6±4.2	34.2±3.3	40.1±2.1	62.9±0.6	78.6±5.1	82.7±3.5	70.7±2.6	43.7±1.3	58.12 ↓0.89	4
coreset	LT	88.2±0.4	32.3±3.9	96.3±1.1	**49.2±4.0**	43.8±1.0	66.6±1.8	82.3±2.1	91.5±1.8	77.0±1.3	47.0±1.0	<u>67.42</u> ↑0.40	2
coreset	LT$^+$	87.5±0.3	21.6±2.5	94.7±0.7	44.4±3.0	45.9±1.5	64.8±2.9	80.4±2.4	90.9±1.8	71.7±1.4	44.8±2.0	64.71 ↓0.22	3
cal	ST	84.5±3.7	7.9±1.6	71.3±4.4	32.9±3.3	42.1±1.9	64.7±1.6	81.9±2.8	80.9±5.2	72.3±4.5	40.0±2.9	57.86 ↓1.15	5
cal	LT	88.2±0.3	30.0±1.5	94.5±1.6	43.2±4.0	**46.0±2.1**	<u>67.7±2.1</u>	82.4±2.4	<u>91.7±1.1</u>	<u>78.2±1.6</u>	47.5±1.2	66.94 ↓0.08	5
cal	LT$^+$	87.4±0.8	19.6±1.3	91.9±1.9	40.7±2.9	45.2±2.9	65.9±3.2	82.2±2.1	90.4±1.8	74.7±1.9	44.5±1.5	64.28 ↓0.65	5
		High Data Budget: 100 + 1500											
random	ST	88.5±0.5	39.8±3.2	93.6±1.1	43.8±5.6	52.6±0.8	72.8±1.2	85.6±0.6	92.1±0.8	78.4±1.4	52.5±0.5	70.03←	3
random	LT	89.0±0.2	<u>65.3±0.7</u>	98.1±0.1	54.9±2.2	**54.2±1.0**	74.3±0.8	85.6±0.6	94.3±0.4	79.2±1.6	53.4±0.6	74.83←	5
random	LT$^+$	88.9±0.2	56.9±1.3	97.3±0.3	53.9±1.9	<u>53.8±1.3</u>	73.7±1.4	85.9±0.7	94.0±0.8	77.7±2.2	53.1±0.7	73.56←	5
entropy	ST	88.2±1.4	36.8±2.5	92.2±1.8	49.5±1.2	51.4±1.5	72.2±1.5	86.2±0.8	92.2±1.4	82.5±0.6	51.0±0.6	70.22 ↑0.23	2
entropy	LT	**90.0±0.1**	62.2±3.7	97.9±0.6	61.2±1.8	52.7±0.9	<u>74.6±1.2</u>	86.1±0.5	95.1±0.6	83.5±0.5	51.1±1.0	75.44 ↑0.61	4
entropy	LT$^+$	89.8±0.4	56.6±3.4	97.3±0.7	58.0±1.0	53.1±0.7	73.7±1.5	**86.7±0.7**	94.6±0.7	83.1±0.5	51.4±1.1	74.24 ↑0.68	2
badge	ST	89.5±0.3	41.3±7.2	95.1±0.5	50.1±3.9	52.7±1.2	73.2±2.2	86.1±0.6	93.6±1.0	82.9±0.6	53.1±0.6	71.76 ↑1.77	1
badge	LT	**90.1±0.1**	**67.8±0.9**	**98.5±0.2**	<u>61.3±2.1</u>	52.93±0.6	74.1±0.9	86.4±0.5	**95.7±0.4**	**84.1±0.7**	53.1±0.7	**76.41** ↑1.58	1
badge	LT$^+$	**90.1±0.1**	59.3±1.6	97.9±0.3	58.6±1.2	53.3±0.9	74.2±1.4	<u>86.6±0.6</u>	<u>95.5±0.5</u>	82.3±1.0	<u>53.3±0.8</u>	75.11 ↑1.55	1
coreset	ST	88.1±0.8	35.6±1.9	92.3±1.2	49.6±2.5	52.5±2.0	72.0±0.7	83.9±1.8	92.7±0.9	81.8±1.2	51.2±0.3	69.79 ↓0.20	4
coreset	LT	89.6±0.3	64.6±1.8	<u>98.3±0.6</u>	**62.4±1.3**	52.3±0.9	73.8±0.9	85.6±0.9	95.4±0.5	83.5±0.4	50.0±0.5	75.57 ↑0.74	3
coreset	LT$^+$	89.5±0.1	53.3±1.9	97.9±0.2	60.3±1.4	53.1±0.7	72.9±1.6	85.0±0.9	95.1±0.5	81.4±0.5	50.7±0.5	73.92 ↑0.36	3
cal	ST	89.0±1.1	32.9±3.7	91.3±1.1	47.7±3.3	51.8±1.4	73.4±1.0	86.3±0.8	92.4±1.4	82.2±1.3	49.9±1.0	69.71 ↓0.28	5
cal	LT	**90.0±0.1**	62.8±1.1	97.4±0.6	59.8±1.7	53.6±1.4	**74.6±1.0**	86.2±1.0	**95.7±0.4**	<u>83.8±0.8</u>	52.3±0.8	<u>75.63</u> ↑0.80	2
cal	LT$^+$	89.9±0.3	50.6±1.2	97.0±0.5	58.1±0.8	53.2±1.4	74.1±1.6	86.6±0.8	95.2±0.6	82.4±0.6	51.9±1.1	73.90 ↑0.34	4

results of our extensive benchmark study on ACTIVEGLAE with BERT. Figure 2 shows a selection of learning curves with ST, LT, and LT$^+$ that supply the first two challenges (C1, C2). Additionally, we depict selected learning curves for our ablations to address the third challenge (C3) in Figs. 5, 4, and 3. For additional details and the complete set of results, refer to Appendix D and E.

(C1) Data Sets. Our results suggest that the effectiveness of a DAL query strategy crucially depends on the data set and the accompanying task, as the results vary notably (cf. Table 9 in Appendix D). We see in Table 3 that model performance across query strategies hinges on data set characteristics, including task difficulty, task type, class cardinality, and class balance. For instance, we observe in Fig. 2 that the performance differences are most noticeable in the imbalanced task (Wikitalk), and the query strategies' effectiveness vary across tasks. In fact, we record the highest model performance gains of DAL imbalanced data sets (Banks77 and Wikitalk) across all models. This parallels results shown in related work [10,30,60].

(C1) Takeaway. The results of query strategies vary notably across data sets in our benchmark suite. We observe the greatest gains in model performance with DAL in class-imbalance scenarios. To evaluate the robustness of query strategies and model training, using a diverse collection of data sets with varying tasks, difficulties, and class imbalances is crucial.

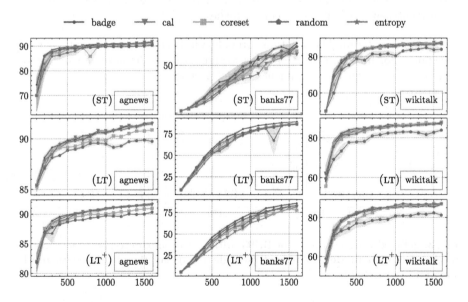

Fig. 2. Selected learning curves for BERT reporting test accuracy with ST (5 epochs), LT (15 epochs) and LT$^+$ (20 epochs and a lower learning rate).

(C2) Model Training. Our benchmark study emphasizes model training in DAL [31] and highlights the importance of the number of epochs as a hyperparameter when no validation set is available. Employing a short training ST with only five epochs leads to consistently worse model performance regardless of the query strategy or task. Especially when applying DAL with a low budget, we observe substantial disparities between ST and LT in the overall AUC (Table 3) and FAC (Tables 7, 8, Appendix D) benchmark scores. This is prominently shown on Banks77 in Table 3, where the differences are as high as 22%. Although the differences diminish with a higher budget, extensive training time still leads to better model performance across all query strategies. We report similar results for DistilBERT and RoBERTa in Tables 9 and 11 in Appendix D. Table 3 also illustrates that the ranking of query strategies is heavily influenced by model training, except for BADGE, which consistently outperforms the other strategies. Additionally, the ablation LT$^+$ with a lower learning rate (2e−5) and more epochs (20) performs better than ST but generally worse than LT. However, we see in Fig. 2 that LT$^+$ further stabilizes the learning curves with a lower learning rate and more epochs, which follows the findings of [34].

(C2) Takeaway. Increasing the number of epochs leads to improved model performance regardless of the budget and query strategy. While the performance gains with a lower budget are larger, higher budget sizes also profit from longer training times (15–20 epochs). Model hyperparameters impact the overall performance more than the query strategy. The rankings of query strategies depend on the model hyperparameters, except for BADGE, which consistently outperforms all other strategies.

(C3) DAL Setting. The ablations provide additional baseline results as reference points for future work. We further examine the results based on key factors of a DAL setting that may influence model performance.

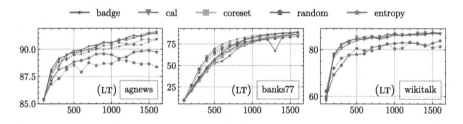

Fig. 3. Selected learning curves for BERT with LT to compare test accuracy between the baseline with **model cold-start** (straight lines) and the ablation with **model warm-start** (dotted lines).

– *Model initialization and update.* Surprisingly, the results in Table 17 in Appendix E reveal that model warm-start improves overall model performance compared to model-cold-start regardless of the query strategy. The

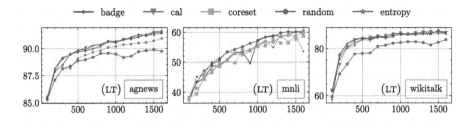

Fig. 4. Learning curves for BERT with LT to compare test accuracy between the baseline with a **pool subset** (straight lines) and the ablation with no subset (dotted lines).

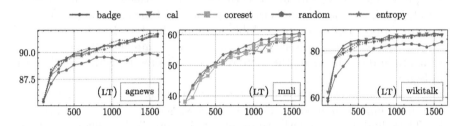

Fig. 5. Learning curves for BERT with LT to compare test accuracy between the baseline with an **query size** of 100 (straight lines) and the ablation with 25 (dotted lines).

difference is especially pronounced when using a low budget with ST and for more complicated tasks like Banks77 or FNC-1. Although less pronounced, we also observe improvements for LT and in a high-budget setting. Interestingly, the performance disparities between ST and LT are drastically reduced across query strategies when employing a model warm-start. This is further illustrated in Fig. 3, where we can see that using ST for model warm-start can achieve even higher model performance than with LT in Banks77.

- *Stopping criterion:* We consider the budget an essential parameter governing the resulting model performance of a query strategy. In the low-budget setting, only BADGE and CORESET can outperform RANDOM while CAL performs worse and ENTROPY has only a minimal improvement (cf. Table 3). This is in line with the findings of [15], who report RANDOM outperforming most DAL query strategies in low-budget settings. With a higher budget, the differences become more prevalent, and all query strategies outperform RANDOM. Interestingly, when considering the FAC in Table 8 in Appendix D, almost all query strategies outperform RANDOM in the lower budget. While we report similar results for DistilBERT (cf. Table 9, D), the overall model performance for RoBERTa diminishes with a query strategy in a high-budget setting (cf. Table 11, D). Additionally, we see in Table 3 that the ranking of query strategies changes with different budgets, except for BADGE.
- *Query strategy:* While no query strategy clearly outperforms all other strategies by a large margin, BADGE a exhibits consistently better performance across a variety of tasks. The AUC and the FAC are often higher for the

low and the high budgets. Figure 9 in Appendix D further highlights this by showing nearly constant positive improvements upon RANDOM performance on our ACTIVEGLAE benchmark. These results emphasize the variability in the results across tasks and hyperparameter configurations since BADGE not always outperforms other query strategies. Additionally, there is no clear second place.

- *Pool subset:* Interestingly, we can see no meaningful drawback in the effectiveness of a query strategy when employing a dynamic pool subset (cf. Table 15, E). Note that the pool is redrawn in each cycle iteration rather than fixed once, increasing the diversity of the queried pool. By reducing the pool size, the query time per cycle iteration is heavily reduced, which allows an extensive set of experiments and reduces the computational time accordingly. Without a subset, our baseline results exhibit an approximately 10-fold increase in average query time. Notably, uncertainty-based sampling (ENTROPY) even seems to improve by using the more diverse pool subsets, which can be seen in Fig. 4.

- *Query size:* Comparing the ablation results with the baseline results, we notice a minimal impact on model performance across query strategies (cf. Table 13, E). These findings align with the results of [3] from CV but differ from those of [30] in the CV domain. However, the investigated query sizes in CV are much larger (>1000), while we investigate in a smaller setting between 25 and 100. Additionally, in Fig. 5, we observe that more re-trainings (60 instead of 25) also increase the noise in the learning curve.

(C3) Takeaway. Despite modest performance differences, BADGE consistently excels across tasks. The budget size influences query strategy efficacy, with BADGE and CORESET surpassing random sampling at lower budgets, while all strategies outperform random only with a high budget. Model warm-start improves performance while mitigating the impact of model hyperparameters. Dynamically sampling a pool subset improves query time without compromising performance. Minor adjustments to the query size do not have a notable influence on the performance.

---

7   Conclusion

In this paper, we introduced the ACTIVEGLAE benchmark comprising various NLP classification tasks and a robust evaluation protocol to foster comparability of DAL with PLMs. By analyzing the scientific environment, we identified three crucial challenges in DAL evaluation protocols: data set selection, model training, and DAL setting. Our extensive set of experiments provides baseline results for future work and practical guidelines. Our findings highlighted the task-dependent effectiveness of query strategies, emphasizing to ensure their robustness to diverse NLP classification tasks to enable a real-world deployment. We confirmed the importance of model training in DAL and recommend an extended training period to improve overall model performance across query strategies. Additionally, we observed that model warm-start improves and stabilizes performance, and employing a pool subset reduces query time with minimal impact on model performance. We reported BADGE to perform consistently better than other query strategies on ACTIVEGLAE.

Acknowledgments. This work received partial funding from the WIBank Hessen (EFRE) for the project INFINA, and the Deutsche Forschungsgemeinschaft (DFG, German Research Foundation), as part of BERD@NFDI - grant number 460037581.

Ethics Statement. *Limitations.* This work represents a snapshot of the current practice of applying DAL to the NLP domain. This comes with the limitation that we do not explicitly go into detail about other fields, like e.g. Computer Vision or Speech Processing. Especially in the former of these two fields, an active research community is working on evaluating DAL [3,18,22,26,30], and the difference in modalities make a comparison across fields highly intriguing. Further, the experimental outcome of our work is not exhaustive. We tested a limited number of models and query strategies on a given number of data sets, which we considered representative, controlling for as much exogenous influence as possible. This should be seen as a blueprint for the experimental setup rather than a definite statement about the SOTA.

Ethical Considerations. To the best of our knowledge, no ethical considerations are implied by our work. There are only two aspects that are affected in a broader sense. First, the environmental impact of the computationally expensive experiments that come with evaluating deep active learning (DAL) strategies. Given the ever-increasing model sizes and the already controversial debate around this topic, this is a crucial aspect to consider. The second point to be addressed is substituting human labor for labeling data sets by DAL. Especially when it comes to labeling toxic or explicit content, suitable DAL strategies might be one way to limit human exposure to such data.

References

1. Ash, J.T., Adams, R.P.: On warm-starting neural network training. CoRR (2020). https://doi.org/10.48550/arXiv.1910.08475
2. Aßenmacher, M., Heumann, C.: On the comparability of pre-trained language models. In: Proceedings of the 5th Swiss Text Analytics Conference and 16th Conference on Natural Language Processing. CEUR Workshop Proceedings, Zurich, Switzerland, June 2020 (2020, Online). http://ceur-ws.org/Vol-2624/paper2.pdf
3. Beck, N., Sivasubramanian, D., Dani, A., Ramakrishnan, G., Iyer, R.: Effective evaluation of deep active learning on image classification tasks (2021). https://doi.org/10.48550/arXiv.2106.15324
4. Biewald, L.: Experiment tracking with weights and biases (2020). Software available from wandb.com. https://www.wandb.com/
5. Brodersen, K.H., Ong, C.S., Stephan, K.E., Buhmann, J.M.: The balanced accuracy and its posterior distribution. In: 2010 20th International Conference on Pattern Recognition, August 2010, pp. 3121–3124 (2010). https://doi.org/10.1109/ICPR.2010.764

6. Brown, T., et al.: Language models are few-shot learners. In: Larochelle, H., Ranzato, M., Hadsell, R., Balcan, M., Lin, H. (eds.) Advances in Neural Information Processing Systems. vol. 33, pp. 1877–1901. Curran Associates, Inc. (2020). https://proceedings.neurips.cc/paper_files/paper/2020/file/1457c0d6bfcb4967418bfb8ac142f64a-Paper.pdf

7. Casanueva, I., Temčinas, T., Gerz, D., Henderson, M., Vulić, I.: Efficient intent detection with dual sentence encoders. In: Proceedings of the 2nd Workshop on Natural Language Processing for Conversational AI, Online, July 2020, pp. 38–45. Association for Computational Linguistics (2020). https://doi.org/10.18653/v1/2020.nlp4convai-1.5. https://aclanthology.org/2020.nlp4convai-1.5

8. D'Arcy, M., Downey, D.: Limitations of active learning with deep transformer language models (2022). https://openreview.net/forum?id=Q8OjAGkxwP5

9. Devlin, J., Chang, M.W., Lee, K., Toutanova, K.: BERT: pre-training of deep bidirectional transformers for language understanding. In: Proceedings of the 2019 Conference of the North American Chapter of the Association for Computational Linguistics: Human Language Technologies, Volume 1 (Long and Short Papers), Minneapolis, Minnesota, pp. 4171–4186. Association for Computational Linguistics (2019). https://doi.org/10.18653/v1/N19-1423. https://aclanthology.org/N19-1423

10. Ein-Dor, L., et al.: Active learning for BERT: an empirical study. In: Proceedings of the 2020 Conference on Empirical Methods in Natural Language Processing (EMNLP), pp. 7949–7962. Association for Computational Linguistics (2020, Online). https://doi.org/10.18653/v1/2020.emnlp-main.638

11. Ferreira, W., Vlachos, A.: Emergent: a novel data-set for stance classification. In: Proceedings of the 2016 Conference of the North American Chapter of the Association for Computational Linguistics: Human Language Technologies, San Diego, California, June 2016, pp. 1163–1168. Association for Computational Linguistics (2016). https://doi.org/10.18653/v1/N16-1138. https://aclanthology.org/N16-1138

12. Gao, L., et al.: The pile: an 800 GB dataset of diverse text for language modeling. CoRR (2020). https://doi.org/10.48550/arXiv.2101.00027

13. Gao, T., Fisch, A., Chen, D.: Making pre-trained language models better few-shot learners. In: Proceedings of the 59th Annual Meeting of the Association for Computational Linguistics and the 11th International Joint Conference on Natural Language Processing (Volume 1: Long Papers), Online, August 2021, pp. 3816–3830. Association for Computational Linguistics (2021). https://doi.org/10.18653/v1/2021.acl-long.295. https://aclanthology.org/2021.acl-long.295

14. Gonsior, J., Falkenberg, C., Magino, S., Reusch, A., Thiele, M., Lehner, W.: To Softmax, or not to Softmax: that is the question when applying active learning for transformer models. CoRR (2022). https://doi.org/10.48550/arXiv.2210.03005

15. Hacohen, G., Dekel, A., Weinshall, D.: Active learning on a budget: opposite strategies suit high and low budgets (2022). https://doi.org/10.48550/arXiv.2202.02794

16. Herde, M., Huseljic, D., Sick, B., Calma, A.: A survey on cost types, interaction schemes, and annotator performance models in selection algorithms for active learning in classification. CoRR (2021). https://doi.org/10.48550/arXiv.2109.11301

17. Hu, P., Lipton, Z.C., Anandkumar, A., Ramanan, D.: Active learning with partial feedback. CoRR (2019). https://doi.org/10.48550/arXiv.1802.07427

18. Ji, Y., Kaestner, D., Wirth, O., Wressnegger, C.: Randomness is the root of all evil: more reliable evaluation of deep active learning. In: 2023 IEEE/CVF Winter Conference on Applications of Computer Vision (WACV), Waikoloa, HI, USA, pp. 3932–3941. IEEE (2023). https://doi.org/10.1109/WACV56688.2023.00393

19. Jukić, J., Šnajder, J.: Smooth sailing: improving active learning for pre-trained language models with representation smoothness analysis (2022). https://doi.org/10.48550/arXiv.2212.11680

20. Kottke, D., Calma, A., Huseljic, D., Krempl, G., Sick, B., et al.: Challenges of reliable, realistic and comparable active learning evaluation. In: Proceedings of the Workshop and Tutorial on Interactive Adaptive Learning, pp. 2–14 (2017)

21. Kwak, B., Kim, Y., Kim, Y.J., Hwang, S., Yeo, J.: TrustAL: trustworthy active learning using knowledge distillation (2022). https://doi.org/10.48550/arXiv.2201.11661

22. Lang, A., Mayer, C., Timofte, R.: Best practices in pool-based active learning for image classification (2022). https://openreview.net/forum?id=7Rnf1F7rQhR

23. Lehmann, J., et al.: DBpedia – a large-scale, multilingual knowledge base extracted from Wikipedia. Semant. Web 6(2), 167–195 (2015). https://doi.org/10.3233/SW-140134

24. Lhoest, Q., et al.: Datasets: a community library for natural language processing. In: Proceedings of the 2021 Conference on Empirical Methods in Natural Language Processing: System Demonstrations, Online and Punta Cana, Dominican Republic, pp. 175–184. Association for Computational Linguistics (2021). https://aclanthology.org/2021.emnlp-demo.21

25. Li, X., Roth, D.: Learning question classifiers. In: Proceedings of the 19th International Conference on Computational Linguistics, Taipei, Taiwan, vol. 1, pp. 1–7. Association for Computational Linguistics (2002). https://doi.org/10.3115/1072228.1072378

26. Li, Y., Chen, M., Liu, Y., He, D., Xu, Q.: An empirical study on the efficacy of deep active learning for image classification (November 2022)

27. Liu, Y., et al.: RoBERTa: a robustly optimized BERT pretraining approach. CoRR (2019). https://doi.org/10.48550/arXiv.1907.11692

28. Loshchilov, I., Hutter, F.: Decoupled weight decay regularization. CoRR (2017). https://doi.org/10.48550/arXiv.1711.05101

29. Lu, J., MacNamee, B.: Investigating the effectiveness of representations based on pretrained transformer-based language models in active learning for labelling text datasets (2020). https://doi.org/10.48550/arXiv.2004.13138

30. Lüth, C.T., Bungert, T.J., Klein, L., Jaeger, P.F.: Toward realistic evaluation of deep active learning algorithms in image classification. CoRR (2023). https://doi.org/10.48550/arXiv.2301.10625

31. Margatina, K., Barrault, L., Aletras, N.: Bayesian active learning with pretrained language models. CoRR (2021). https://doi.org/10.48550/arXiv.2104.08320

32. Margatina, K., Barrault, L., Aletras, N.: On the importance of effectively adapting pretrained language models for active learning. In: Proceedings of the 60th Annual Meeting of the Association for Computational Linguistics (Volume 2: Short Papers), Dublin, Ireland, May 2022, pp. 825–836. Association for Computational Linguistics (2022). https://doi.org/10.18653/v1/2022.acl-short.93. https://aclanthology.org/2022.acl-short.93

33. Margatina, K., Vernikos, G., Barrault, L., Aletras, N.: Active learning by acquiring contrastive examples. In: Proceedings of the 2021 Conference on Empirical Methods in Natural Language Processing, Online and Punta Cana, Dominican Republic, pp. 650–663. Association for Computational Linguistics (2021). https://doi.org/10.18653/v1/2021.emnlp-main.51

34. Mosbach, M., Andriushchenko, M., Klakow, D.: On the stability of fine-tuning BERT: misconceptions, explanations, and strong baselines (2021). https://doi.org/10.48550/arXiv.2006.04884

35. Munjal, P., Hayat, N., Hayat, M., Sourati, J., Khan, S.: Towards robust and reproducible active learning using neural networks (2022). https://doi.org/10.48550/arXiv.2002.09564
36. OpenAI: ChatGPT: optimizing language models for dialogue (2022). https://openai.com/blog/chatgpt/. Accessed 10 Jan 2023
37. Perez, E., Kiela, D., Cho, K.: True few-shot learning with language models. CoRR (2021). https://doi.org/10.48550/arXiv.2105.11447
38. Pomerleau, D., Rao, D.: Fake news challenge (2017). http://www.fakenewschallenge.org/
39. Prabhu, S., Mohamed, M., Misra, H.: Multi-class text classification using BERT-based active learning. CoRR (2021). https://doi.org/10.48550/arXiv.2104.14289
40. Radford, A., Wu, J., Child, R., Luan, D., Amodei, D., Sutskever, I.: Language models are unsupervised multitask learners. OpenAi Blog (2019)
41. Raffel, C., et al.: Exploring the limits of transfer learning with a unified text-to-text transformer. J. Mach. Learn. Res. **21**(1), 5485–5551 (2020)
42. Rauch, L., Huseljic, D., Sick, B.: Enhancing active learning with weak supervision and transfer learning by leveraging information and knowledge sources. In: IAL@PKDD/ECML (2022)
43. Ren, P., Xiao, Y., Chang, X., Huang, P.Y., Li, Z., Gupta, B.B., Chen, X., Wang, X.: A survey of deep active learning. ACM Comput. Surv. **54**(9) (2021). https://doi.org/10.1145/3472291
44. Ren, P., et al.: A survey of deep active learning. ACM Comput. Surv. **54**(9) (2021). https://doi.org/10.1145/3472291
45. Ru, D., et al.: Active sentence learning by adversarial uncertainty sampling in discrete space. In: Findings of the Association for Computational Linguistics, EMNLP 2020, Online, November 2020, pp. 4908–4917. Association for Computational Linguistics (2020). https://doi.org/10.18653/v1/2020.findings-emnlp.441. https://aclanthology.org/2020.findings-emnlp.441
46. Sanh, V., Debut, L., Chaumond, J., Wolf, T.: DistilBERT, a distilled version of BERT: smaller, faster, cheaper and lighter. CoRR (2020). https://doi.org/10.48550/arXiv.1910.01108
47. Schick, T., Schütze, H.: Exploiting cloze-questions for few-shot text classification and natural language inference. In: Proceedings of the 16th Conference of the European Chapter of the Association for Computational Linguistics: Main Volume, pp. 255–269. Association for Computational Linguistics (2021, Online). https://doi.org/10.18653/v1/2021.eacl-main.20. https://aclanthology.org/2021.eacl-main.20
48. Schick, T., Schütze, H.: It's not just size that matters: small language models are also few-shot learners. In: Proceedings of the 2021 Conference of the North American Chapter of the Association for Computational Linguistics: Human Language Technologies, pp. 2339–2352. Association for Computational Linguistics (2021, Online). https://doi.org/10.18653/v1/2021.naacl-main.185. https://aclanthology.org/2021.naacl-main.185
49. Schröder, C., Niekler, A., Potthast, M.: Revisiting uncertainty-based query strategies for active learning with transformers. In: Findings of the Association for Computational Linguistics, ACL 2022, Dublin, Ireland, pp. 2194–2203. Association for Computational Linguistics (2022). https://doi.org/10.18653/v1/2022.findings-acl.172. https://aclanthology.org/2022.findings-acl.172
50. Seo, S., Kim, D., Ahn, Y., Lee, K.H.: Active learning on pre-trained language model with task-independent triplet loss. Proc. AAAI Conf. Artif. Intell. **36**(10), 11276–11284 (2022). https://doi.org/10.1609/aaai.v36i10.21378

51. Settles, B.: Active learning literature survey. Computer Sciences, Technical report, 1648, University of Wisconsin-Madison (2010)
52. Socher, R., et al.: Recursive deep models for semantic compositionality over a sentiment treebank. In: Proceedings of the 2013 Conference on Empirical Methods in Natural Language Processing, Seattle, Washington, USA, October 2013, pp. 1631–1642. Association for Computational Linguistics (2013). https://aclanthology.org/D13-1170
53. Tan, W., Du, L., Buntine, W.: Diversity enhanced active learning with strictly proper scoring rules. In: Advances in Neural Information Processing Systems (NeurIPS), vol. 35 (2021)
54. Tran, D., et al.: Plex: towards Reliability using Pretrained Large Model Extensions. CoRR (2022). https://doi.org/10.48550/arXiv.2207.07411
55. Wang, A., et al.: SuperGLUE: a stickier benchmark for general-purpose language understanding systems. CoRR (2020). https://doi.org/10.48550/arXiv.1905.00537
56. Wang, A., Singh, A., Michael, J., Hill, F., Levy, O., Bowman, S.R.: GLUE: a multi-task benchmark and analysis platform for natural language understanding. CoRR (2018). https://doi.org/10.48550/arXiv.1804.07461
57. Williams, A., Nangia, N., Bowman, S.: A broad-coverage challenge corpus for sentence understanding through inference, June 2018. https://doi.org/10.18653/v1/N18-1101. https://aclanthology.org/N18-1101
58. Wolf, T., et al.: Transformers: state-of-the-art natural language processing. In: Proceedings of the 2020 Conference on Empirical Methods in Natural Language Processing: System Demonstrations, Online, pp. 38–45. Association for Computational Linguistics (2020). https://doi.org/10.18653/v1/2020.emnlp-demos.6. https://aclanthology.org/2020.emnlp-demos.6
59. Wulczyn, E., Thain, N., Dixon, L.: Ex Machina: personal attacks seen at scale. In: Proceedings of the 26th International Conference on World Wide Web, Republic and Canton of Geneva, CHE, pp. 1391–1399. International World Wide Web Conferences Steering Committee (2017). https://doi.org/10.1145/3038912.3052591. https://doi.org/10.1145/3038912.3052591
60. Yi, J.S.K., Seo, M., Park, J., Choi, D.G.: PT4AL: using self-supervised pretext tasks for active learning, July 2022
61. Yu, Y., Kong, L., Zhang, J., Zhang, R., Zhang, C.: AcTune: uncertainty-based active self-training for active fine-tuning of pretrained language models. In: Proceedings of the 2022 Conference of the North American Chapter of the Association for Computational Linguistics: Human Language Technologies, Seattle, United States, pp. 1422–1436. Association for Computational Linguistics (2022). https://doi.org/10.18653/v1/2022.naacl-main.102
62. Yu, Y., Zhang, R., Xu, R., Zhang, J., Shen, J., Zhang, C.: Cold-start data selection for few-shot language model fine-tuning: a prompt-based uncertainty propagation approach (2022). https://doi.org/10.48550/arXiv.2209.06995
63. Yuan, M., Lin, H.T., Boyd-Graber, J.: Cold-start active learning through self-supervised language modeling. In: Proceedings of the 2020 Conference on Empirical Methods in Natural Language Processing (EMNLP), Online, pp. 7935–7948. Association for Computational Linguistics (2020). https://doi.org/10.18653/v1/2020.emnlp-main.637
64. Zha, D., Bhat, Z.P., Lai, K.H., Yang, F., Hu, X.: Data-centric AI: perspectives and Challenges (2023). https://doi.org/10.48550/arXiv.2301.04819

65. Zhang, S., Gong, C., Liu, X., He, P., Chen, W., Zhou, M.: ALLSH: active learning guided by local sensitivity and hardness. In: Findings of the Association for Computational Linguistics, NAACL 2022, Seattle, United States, July 2022, pp. 1328–1342. Association for Computational Linguistics (2022). https://doi.org/10.18653/v1/2022.findings-naacl.99. https://aclanthology.org/2022.findings-naacl.99

66. Zhang, X., Zhao, J., LeCun, Y.: Character-level convolutional networks for text classification. In: Cortes, C., Lawrence, N., Lee, D., Sugiyama, M., Garnett, R. (eds.) Advances in Neural Information Processing Systems, vol. 28. Curran Associates, Inc. (2015)

DiffusAL: Coupling Active Learning with Graph Diffusion for Label-Efficient Node Classification

Sandra Gilhuber[1,2(✉)], Julian Busch[1,3], Daniel Rotthues[1],
Christian M. M. Frey[4], and Thomas Seidl[1,2,4]

[1] LMU Munich, Munich, Germany
{gilhuber,seidl}@dbs.ifi.lmu.de
[2] Munich Center for Machine Learning (MCML), Munich, Germany
[3] Siemens Technology, Princeton, NJ, USA
busch.julian@siemens.com
[4] Fraunhofer IIS, Erlangen, Germany
christian.maximilian.michael.frey@iis.fraunhofer.de

Abstract. Node classification is one of the core tasks on attributed graphs, but successful graph learning solutions require sufficiently labeled data. To keep annotation costs low, active graph learning focuses on selecting the most qualitative subset of nodes that maximizes label efficiency. However, deciding which heuristic is best suited for an unlabeled graph to increase label efficiency is a persistent challenge. Existing solutions either neglect aligning the learned model and the sampling method or focus only on limited selection aspects. They are thus sometimes worse or only equally good as random sampling. In this work, we introduce a novel active graph learning approach called *DiffusAL*, showing significant robustness in diverse settings. Toward better transferability between different graph structures, we combine three independent scoring functions to identify the most informative node samples for labeling in a parameter-free way: i) *Model Uncertainty*, ii) *Diversity Component*, and iii) *Node Importance* computed via graph diffusion heuristics. Most of our calculations for acquisition and training can be pre-processed, making DiffusAL more efficient compared to approaches combining diverse selection criteria and similarly fast as simpler heuristics. Our experiments on various benchmark datasets show that, unlike previous methods, our approach significantly outperforms random selection in 100% of all datasets and labeling budgets tested.

Keywords: active learning · node classification · graph neural networks

1 Introduction

Graph representation learning [17] and, especially, *Graph Neural Networks* (GNNs) [2,5,16] have been adopted as a primary approach for solving machine

---

S. Gilhuber and J. Busch—Equal contribution

© The Author(s), under exclusive license to Springer Nature Switzerland AG 2023
D. Koutra et al. (Eds.): ECML PKDD 2023, LNAI 14169, pp. 75–91, 2023.
https://doi.org/10.1007/978-3-031-43412-9_5

learning tasks on graph-structured data, including node classification [18], graph classification [21], and link prediction [41]. Applications range from quantum chemistry [16] over traffic forecasting [44] to cyber-security [6].

However, supervised GNN models require sufficient training labels and usually assume that such labels are freely available. But, in reality, while unlabeled data is usually abundant, it is laborious and costly to provide annotations. Graph active learning has emerged as a promising direction to reduce labeling costs by carefully deciding which data should be labeled to increase label efficiency. Under a limited budget, e.g., a fixed number of data samples to be labeled or time spent labeling by a domain expert, active learning aims to annotate an optimized set of training data iteratively. Hence, a key aspect of graph active learning is identifying the most informative instances in the abundance of unlabeled data for labeling. In particular, the goal is to be consistently more label-efficient than random labeling. Since random sampling is arguably the fastest and least complex method, active learning methods that are not significantly better than random sampling are not worthwhile.

However, since graphs can vary widely, it is very difficult to design an approach significantly better than random sampling across different labeling budgets and graph structures. Existing graph-active learning approaches reach their limits for various reasons: Some approaches focus only on limited selection aspects [23,28] and outperform random selection only on certain graphs. Others focus on one-shot selection without iterative re-training and active selection and can therefore not exploit model-related uncertainty scores [37,43]. Other methods try to include various criteria in the selection but are sensitive to user-defined hyper-parameters or are not deliberately aligned with the used model architecture [8,15]. Moreover, many methods use a GCN [18] for training and acquisition. However, GCNs learn latent node features and perform neighborhood aggregation in a coupled fashion, which can negatively influence the time needed for the active learning procedure. In contrast, *Graph diffusion* is a promising direction tackling limitations such as restriction to k-hop neighborhoods [7] or over-smoothing, where neighborhood aggregation and learning are decoupled.

In this work, we use diffusion-based heuristics to combine graph learning with active learning. In particular, we propose *DiffusAL*, a novel graph active learning method that leverages graph diffusion for highly accurate node classification and efficiently re-uses the computed diffusion matrix and diffused node feature vectors in the learning procedure.

We introduce a new scoring function for identifying a node's utility which consists of three factors: i) *Model Uncertainty*, ii) *Diversity Component*, and iii) *Node Importance*. DiffusAL combines these scores in a parameter-free scoring function that naturally adapts to consecutively learning iterations.

Specifically, for i) *Model Uncertainty*, we exploit a state-of-the-art scoring that has shown an improving impact on the selection of nodes [32]. Next, the ii) *Diversity Component* refers to the variability of node features and, therefore, their respective labels. For that, we apply a clustering method on the precomputed diffusion matrix where diversity is reached by picking samples from underrepresented communities. Finally, for computing iii) *Node Importance*, we exploit the information given by diffusion matrix based on the Personalized

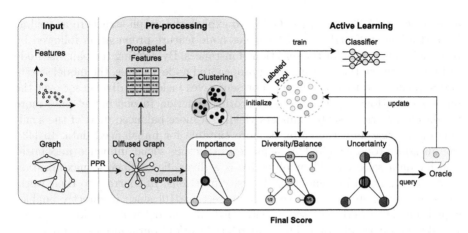

Fig. 1. DiffusAL pipeline consisting of the original input graph and corresponding node features (grey box), pre-computed static model-independent scores, such as the propagated feature matrix and derived node importance (green box), a dynamic, model-independent score based on the composition of the labeled pool (Diversity/Balance), as well as a dynamic, model-dependent informativeness score (Uncertainty). These scores are combined into a final node rating (white box) to select the most useful instances for annotation. (Color figure online)

PageRank (PPR), which provides information about the relative importance of nodes in a graph w.r.t. a particular seed node. The high-level key concepts of DiffusAL are illustrated in Fig. 1.

We evaluate DiffusAL on five real-world benchmark datasets, demonstrating its superiority over a variety of competitors. Notably, DiffusAL is the only competitor to outperform random selection with statistical significance in 100% of the evaluated datasets and labeling budgets. In a series of ablation studies, we show that DiffusAL works consistently well on all benchmark datasets, analyze which components contribute to its performance, and investigate its efficiency.

In summary, our contributions are as follows:

- Enhancing the selection of influential nodes by using *diffusion-based node importance* and utilizing pre-computed *clustering on diffused features* to prevent oversampling a particular region.
- Combining three complementary node scoring components in a parameter-free way.
- Achieving high efficiency by propagating statically pre-computed features stored in a diffusion matrix.

2   Related Work

Early works on graph active learning [3,24] exploit the graph structure for selecting nodes for querying without graph representation learning. More recent approaches [8, 15, 23, 28, 38] use GCNs to exploit the graph structure as well as learned features. FeatProp [38] leverages node feature propagation followed by K-Medoids clustering for the selection of instances. By defining the pairwise node distances between the corresponding propagated node features, the model selects nodes being closest to the cluster representatives yielding a diverse set over the input space. However, the diversity scoring function in our model puts more weight on underrepresented clusters yielding a more balanced view of the available data space and, therefore, is more suitable for imbalanced data. In [43], the authors proposed *GRAIN*, a model inspecting social influence maximization for data selection. Their objective is a diversified influence maximization by exploiting novel influence and diversity functions. In contrast to their work, we focus on an iterative active learning setting [10] since it directly enables exploiting the uncertainty scores entangled to a model which is known to be valuable for query selection. The most related work to our approach is presented in [8] where the authors propose *Active Graph Embedding* (AGE) using as selection heuristic a weighted sum of information entropy, information density, and graph centrality defined on direct neighborhoods. For the latter, they propose to use PageRank centrality. The time-sensitive coefficients of the weighted sum are chosen from a beta distribution using the number of training iterations as input. We overcome these limitations related the restriction on direct neighborhoods aggregations used in standard GNNs [2, 5, 16] by leveraging continuous relationships via graph diffusion [7, 20]. In [15], *ANRMAB* is proposed. It uses a multi-armed bandit mechanism for adaptive decision-making by assigning different weights to different criteria when constructing the score to select the most informative nodes for labeling. The model *LSCALE* [23] exploits clustering-based (K-Medoids) active learning on a designed latent space leveraging two properties: low label requirements and informative distances. For the latter, the authors integrate *Deep Graph Infomax* [36] as an unsupervised model. Therefore, in contrast to our approach, the model utilizes a purely distance-based selection heuristic. The method *GEEM* [29] maximizes the expected error reduction to select informative nodes to label.

To the best of our knowledge, we are the first to leverage the power of diffusion-based heuristics for the computation of node importance, being an integral part of our scoring function, combining three complementary components to compute the nodes yielding the highest utility scores. Moreover, our novel scoring function uncouples from any parameter presets, being a critical choice without any a priori knowledge about the input data.

3   DiffusAL

3.1   Preliminaries

Notation. We consider the problem of active learning for node classification. We are given a graph $G = (V, E)$ represented by an adjacency matrix $A \in \{0, 1\}^{n \times n}$ along with a node feature matrix $X \in \mathbb{R}^{n \times d}$. Each node $v \in V$ belongs to exactly one class $c_v \in \{1, \ldots, C\}$, where C is the number of classes present in the dataset. A budget constraint B denotes the maximum number of nodes for which the active learning algorithm may request the correct labels from the oracle. The main goal is to select a subset of nodes $S \subset V$ such that $|S| = B$ and the accuracy of a classification model trained on these nodes is maximized. In a batch setting, b denotes the number of nodes selected within each acquisition round.

Recap: Feature Diffusion. In contrast to conventional GNN architectures [18,35,39] that learn latent node features and perform neighborhood aggregation in a coupled fashion, *graph diffusion* effectively decouples the two steps to address certain shortcomings of conventional GNN architectures, including the restriction to k-hop neighborhoods [7] and issues related to over-smoothing[14,22,26,40]. The general effectiveness of diffusion, when paired with conventional GNN architectures, was shown in [20]. In general, a parametric diffusion matrix can be defined as

$$P = \sum_{k=0}^{\infty} \theta_k T^k, \tag{1}$$

where T is a transition matrix and θ are weighting parameters. A popular choice is *Personalized PageRank (PPR)* [4,7,11,12,19], where $T = AD^{-1}$ is the random walk matrix, D is the diagonal degree matrix, and $\theta_k = \alpha(1 - \alpha)^k$. Intuitively, P_{ij} corresponds to the probability that a random walk starting at node i will stop at node j and can be interpreted as the importance of node j for node i. The restart probability $\alpha \in [0,1]$ controls the effective size of a node's PPR-neighborhood. An approximation of the PPR matrix can be pre-computed in time $O(n)$ using push-based algorithms [7]. This approximation requires a second hyper-parameter $\varepsilon > 0$ that thresholds small entries and, thus, has a sparsification and noise reduction effect. Once computed, the PPR matrix can replace the adjacency matrix used by conventional message-passing networks for neighborhood aggregation [7,19].

3.2   Model Architecture

For DiffusAL, we propagate the original node features such that the propagated node features don't depend on any learned transformations and can be pre-computed as well. We propose a query-by-committee (QBC) approach [33], where the propagated node features are connected to an ensemble of MLP classifiers to robustify uncertainty estimation during the sample selection process compared to a commonly used single MLP. Additionally, features are diffused over multiple scales by varying the hyper-parameter α controlling the effective neighborhood size over which features are aggregated. In particular, the model predictions are given as

$$Y = predict \left(\sum_{j \in \{1,\ldots,M\}} transform_j \left(\sum_{i \in \{1,\ldots,K\}} P^{(\alpha_i)} X \right) \right), \tag{2}$$

where K denotes the number of scales, and M denotes the number of MLPs in the classification ensemble. The pre-computed diffused features are aggregated over multiple scales using the *sum* function and fed to the hidden layer of each MLP. The learned representations are then aggregated using the *sum* function and passed to the shared prediction layer. All ensemble members share the same architecture and only differ in the random initialization of their weights and biases. The QBC can be trained very efficiently with gradient descent, and, in particular, the expensive diffusion step needs to be performed only once as a pre-processing step.

3.3   Node Ranking and Selection

In addition to facilitating highly effective and efficient prediction, the previously computed diffusion matrix $P = \sum_{i \in \{1,...,K\}} P^{(\alpha_i)}$ and diffused features PX are reused to calculate expressive ranking scores for active node selection.

Model Uncertainty. For measuring model uncertainty, we utilize the QBC defined above. In particular, we compute the Shannon entropy over the softmax-ed output distribution to determine the **uncertainty score** for node i:

$$s_{\text{unc}}(i) = - \sum_{j \in \{1,...,C\}} y_{ij} \log y_{ij}. \tag{3}$$

The scores are L1-normalized over all unlabeled nodes to $[0,1]$, so all scoring functions share the same scale and can be sensibly combined.

While this score is inspired by the classical query-by-committee [33] approach, it differs in the sense that it doesn't average the softmax outputs of the individual committee members but rather considers the softmax output of a single shared prediction layer applied to aggregated latent representations. Thereby, differing predictions become more distinct in the softmax output.

Diversity Component. For the diversity component, we perform k-Means clustering on the *diffused features* with $k = b$ and assign each node a pseudo-label based on the clustering result. Note that we pre-compute these cluster assignments such that no re-computations are necessary at query time, in contrast to other approaches (e.g., based on GCNs), where updated node features would change the clustering.

The cluster-based pseudo labels are used to ensure decent coverage of the feature space. At each iteration, each node i receives a **diversity score**

$$s_{\text{div}}(i) = 1 - \frac{|c_{train}|}{|V_{train}|}, \tag{4}$$

where $c \in C$ denotes the cluster node i was assigned to, $|c_{train}|$ denotes the number of nodes in the currently labeled training set belonging to cluster c, and $|V_{train}|$ is the number of currently labeled training nodes. In short, each node in the unlabeled pool is weighted by the relative size of its cluster in the training set, such that nodes from currently underrepresented clusters receive a higher score. In contrast to only focusing on avoiding redundancy in the current batch [1], our diversity score can also be interpreted as a balancing score ensuring that no region is over-sampled within the labeled pool.

Some existing works on graph active learning [8,15] ignore the limitations of a randomly initialized labeled pool and ensure class balance. However, this simplification is rather unrealistic in a real-world active learning setting. To overcome this limitation, we again exploit the k-Means clustering used for the diversity score and select nodes closest to centroids for the initial pool, inspired by clustering-based sampling approaches [23,37] and existing work on initial pool selection [9].

Node Importance. Graph diffusion allows for a natural way to quantify node importance. Since the weights P_{ij} used for neighborhood aggregation can be interpreted as importance scores, summing up the importance of a node i for all other nodes j yields a measure of the general importance of node i, measuring its total influence on the predictions for other nodes. Since the columns of S are stochastic, this procedure yields consistently scaled overall importance scores. In particular, the **importance score** of node i is given by the row-wise sum

$$s_{\text{imp}}(i) = \sum_{j \in V} P_{ij}. \tag{5}$$

Since the importance scores for all nodes can be computed directly from the PPR matrix, they can be pre-computed before the active learning cycle starts. Our node importance score is a proxy for how much influence a node has on other nodes, where nodes with higher scores are assumed to carry more valuable information about many other nodes as well. Node importance could be interpreted as a novel representativeness measure, which has been quantified via density- or center-based selection within previous (graph) active learning approaches [8,15,42]. However, we do not need to recompute a clustering on learned representations after each selected sample, nor do we require good representations since we can extract the information directly from the graph topology. Further, our importance score of a node directly reflects the influence of that node on the model's predictions, since the weights from which we compute the scores are directly used for neighborhood aggregation. This is not the case for alternative existing measures.

Score Combination and Node Selection. In summary, the uncertainty score assigns higher weights to nodes about which the committee is most uncertain, the diversity score assigns higher weights to nodes belonging to underrepresented clusters, and the node importance score assigns higher weights to nodes with a higher influence on the predictions for other nodes. The individual scores for a node are combined in a multiplicative fashion to determine the node's utility:

$$s(i) = s_{\text{unc}}(i) \cdot s_{\text{div}}(i) \cdot s_{\text{imp}}(i). \tag{6}$$

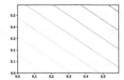 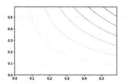

(a) **Sum aggregation**: Isolines are straight due to fixed weighting.

(b) **Multiplicative aggregation**: Isolines are curved, favoring similar values over diverging ones.

Fig. 2. Score aggregation: for two arbitrary scores on the x and y axes (e.g. uncertainty and representativeness), the corresponding aggregated score is depicted as an isoline, i.e., each point on the line corresponds to the same final value.

As illustrated in Fig. 2, the intuition behind the multiplicative combination is to slightly favor nodes displaying a well-rounded distribution of scores over those with a strong imbalance when the sum of the scores is identical while still allowing extraordinarily important or uncertain nodes to be selected. Existing works use slightly different variations of time-sensitive weighted sums, thereby gradually shifting the focus from representativeness to uncertainty [8,42]. A disadvantage of time-sensitive weighting is that the performance of the selection algorithm depends on the choice of good hyper-parameters, which is difficult in a real-world active learning setting. In contrast, our multiplicative approach is parameter-free and naturally time-sensitive. In the early stages of training, the classifiers essentially guess predictions more or less uniformly, leading to roughly similar uncertainty scores for most nodes. Consequently, the uncertainty score is close to a constant factor applied equally to all nodes, thus naturally making the model-free scores the deciding ones in the final score. However, uncertainty scores become increasingly important once the classifiers become more confident in their predictions. The combined utility score is determined for each unlabeled node in each active learning cycle. Afterward, the unlabeled nodes are ranked according to their utility, and the nodes with the highest utility scores are labeled.

4   Experiments

To demonstrate the effectiveness and efficiency of DiffusAL, we conduct a series of experiments. In particular, we investigate three research questions:

R1 - How does DiffusAL perform compared to state-of-the-art methods?
R2 - How does each of DiffusAL's components contribute?
R3 - How is the training and acquisition efficiency?

4.1   Experimental Setup

Datasets. We evaluate DiffusAL on several well-established benchmark datasets for node classification, namely the citation networks Citeseer [30], Cora [30] and

Table 1. Dataset statistics (only considering the largest connected component).

Dataset	#Nodes	#Edges	#Features	#Classes
Citeseer	2120	3679	3703	6
Cora	2485	5069	1433	5
Pubmed	19717	44324	500	3
Co-author CS	18333	81894	6805	15
Co-author Physics	34493	247962	8415	5

Pubmed [25], as well as the co-author networks Computer Science (CS) [34] and Physics [34], summarized in Table 1. For each dataset, only the largest connected component is used, and features are L1-normalized.

Implementation Details. All experiments were implemented using PyTorch [27] and PyTorch Geometric [13] and run on a single Nvidia Quadro RTX 8000 GPU. For more details, we refer to our publicly available codebase[1].

Competitors. We compare DiffusAL with *random* sampling, *entropy* sampling [32], and *coreset* [31] as graph-independent uncertainty-aware and diversity-aware active learning strategies, respectively. Furthermore, we include *degree* sampling as a graph-based representativeness-based baseline, selecting the highest degree nodes, as well as the state-of-the-art graph-specific active learning methods *AGE* [8], *FeatProp* [37], *LSCALE* [23] and *GRAIN* [43].

As proposed in [8,23,37,43], all baselines use GCNs as classifiers, except LSCALE, which uses the proposed distance-based classifier. Our proposed method DiffusAL uses the introduced QBC as a classifier, and we provide comprehensive experiments showing the influence of the prediction model.

Hyperparameters. We use the same hyper-parameters having a hidden layer size of 16, a dropout rate of 0.5, a learning rate of 0.01, and L2-regularization of 5×10^{-4} as proposed in [37]. For DiffusAL, we select α and ϵ as suggested in [7]. We follow a batch selection and retrain from scratch after each acquisition round. However, to ensure more diverse uncertainties (and because the other two scores are static), we follow the setting of [8] and also incrementally train the model for one epoch between instance selection within one acquisition round. The evaluation in Sect. 4.4 shows that this does not impair our efficiency. To provide a meaningful evaluation without the effects of an under-trained model or randomness factors, we report test accuracy for all approaches using a validation set of size 500 and early stopping. However, the validation set is only part of the evaluation, not the procedure itself. We set the size of the initial pool to 2C (cf. 3.1) and report results up to a budget of 20C with step sizes also twice the number of classes. To simulate a fairly realistic active learning scenario, the initial pool is sampled randomly without guaranteeing class balance for the baseline approaches without a specific initialization method. All experiments report an average of ten random seeds.

---

[1] https://github.com/lmu-dbs/diffusal.

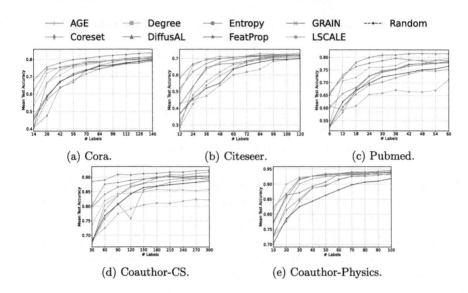

Fig. 3. Active learning curves with the number of labeled nodes on the x-axis and average accuracy (over 10 random seeds) on the y-axis.

4.2   R1 - Performance Comparison

Figure 3 depicts the active learning curves for all budgets and datasets. DiffusAL (blue) is among the best-performing methods on all datasets. Especially on Cora and Coauthor-CS, we reach the highest mean accuracy for all labeling budgets and are the only competitor to reach a final accuracy of 83.6% and 92.4%, respectively. On Pubmed, GRAIN is similarly strong for the first two iterations. However, afterward, DiffusAL outperforms all methods for the remaining budgets and reaches a final average accuracy of 81.4%. In comparison, LSCALE, the second-best performing method with respect to the final budget, only reaches 79.9%.

On Citeseer and Physics[2], GRAIN and LSCALE are similarly strong as DiffusAL. For both datasets, the learning curves converge to similar accuracies above a certain labeling budget for some methods such that a clear winner can no longer be pronounced. Therefore, Fig. 4 provides a comprehensive dueling matrix indicating how often each strategy has won and lost against the other strategy in a similar fashion as was proposed in [1]. We apply a two-sided t-test with a p-value of 0.05 to the classification accuracies over 10 random seeds to count whether one method outperformed another with statistical significance.

---

[2] On Physics, Degree underperformed considerably and is therefore omitted for better presentation.

In total, we evaluated 50 experimental settings for each strategy (5 different datasets, 10 different labeling budgets from 2C to 20C). The values in a column and row of a method denote the percentage of losses and wins against another method, respectively. The bottom row indicates the average losses of each strategy over all experiments, and the right-most column indicates the average wins of a strategy over all experiments. The losses and wins in the cells c_{ij} and c_{ji} do not necessarily add up to 100%. The margin between the wins in cell ij and the losses in cell ji indicates how often the strategy i has performed equally well as competitor j. Both numbers, the average losses *and* the average wins, are particularly interesting when evaluating the success of an active learning method.

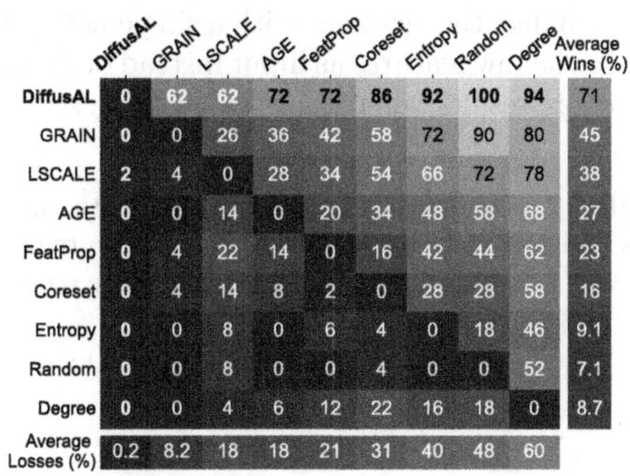

Fig. 4. Pairwise dueling matrix. Cell ij indicates how often competitor i won against competitor j **with statistical significance** over all datasets and labeling budgets (in %). The bottom-most row and right-most column denote each method's average losses and wins, respectively (in %).

In summary, the dueling matrix reveals the following insights:

- DiffusAL has the **fewest losses (0.2%, see first column)** and the **most wins (71%, see first row)**.
- DiffusAL **wins over random sampling most often (100%)**.
- Concerning wins over random sampling, GRAIN is the second-best method (90%). However, DiffusAL statistically never loses against GRAIN.
- The only strategy that can outperform DiffusAL is LSCALE. However, we beat LSCALE in 62% of experiments and lost only 2% of experiments.

4.3   R2 - Analysis of Contributing Factors

The selected datasets vary widely in terms of the number of nodes, edges, features, classes, and class distribution, making it difficult to develop an approach that can perform well across the spectrum. In the following, we analyze which components contribute most to DiffusAL's success and why it is so strong over a broad range of datasets. Table 2 shows the performance of DiffusAL (bottom row) and DiffusAL when switching off individual parts of the acquisition function, i.e., the diversity component (D), the uncertainty score (U) and the importance score (I) and exchanging the model architecture (middle rows) for 2C, 6C, and 12C labeling budgets on all datasets where C is the number of classes. Red, bold numbers indicate the smallest accuracy, indicating the largest influence of a switched-off component, and blue, bold numbers indicate the highest accuracy.

We exchange the classifier with a single network variant (MLP) and with a GCN taking the raw features as input instead of diffused features (GCN). Furthermore, we report results when using an additive score instead of a multiplicative score.

Table 2. Comparison of DiffusAL with ablated variants. **Blue, bold** numbers indicate the **highest, i.e. best,** accuracy. Red, bold numbers indicate the lowest, i.e. worst, accuracy and hence the component with largest influence.

D	U	I	Cora 2C	6C	12C	Citeseer 2C	6C	12C	Pubmed 2C	6C	12C	CS 2C	6C	12C	Physics 2C	6C	12C
		✓	45.5	77.8	80.6	43.3	63.8	69.7	56.3	68.0	69.8	71.9	81.7	82.2	71.9	89.8	93.8
	✓		45.5	76.1	80.1	43.3	65.5	70.0	56.3	70.6	75.4	71.9	83.3	90.8	71.9	89.6	93.1
	✓	✓	45.5	78.5	81.7	43.3	69.8	71.3	56.3	75.3	80.0	71.9	89.3	91.4	71.9	92.4	93.9
✓			-	74.5	76.0	-	67.6	71.1	-	64.6	76.5	-	89.4	90.4	-	86.4	87.1
✓		✓	-	76.4	80.5	-	67.7	71.0	-	77.2	79.9	-	87.5	87.3	-	91.5	92.4
✓	✓		-	78.6	81.9	-	69.1	71.0	-	74.9	77.1	-	90.5	91.6	-	88.3	90.9
Additive			-	78.8	81.3	-	70.8	71.3	-	79.1	80.2	-	91.0	92.1	-	91.7	92.7
MLP			62.0	78.8	81.8	52.7	70.6	71.8	64.1	78.8	79.9	87.8	90.4	91.2	80.4	91.4	93.6
GCN			61.8	77.5	80.7	49.8	69.3	71.3	64.5	76.5	78.5	83.3	89.6	91.2	82.7	91.6	93.1
DiffusAL			68.0	79.9	82.3	58.2	69.9	71.8	65.9	80.0	81.4	88.5	90.8	91.8	82.3	92.6	94.1

The importance, uncertainty, and additive scoring have no influence on the initial pool selection, so we leave out numbers there. Our QBC robustifies the accuracy, especially in the first iteration, compared to the other two variants (MLP, GCN). The performance difference between the models gets smaller with increasing label information. In particular, when label information is sparse, the committee stabilizes the prediction. However, the diversity component has the largest impact on the initial set for all datasets. When switching off diversity (first three rows), the accuracy drops between 9.6% (Pubmed) and 22.5% (Cora). Other approaches, such as FeatProp or LSCALE, also use clustering in the first iteration. However, our sampling directly operates on the diffused features, which subsequently directly influence the training and thus results in a very strong initial performance.

In general, switching off two scores yields worse results than only switching off one score, which indicates that the other two scores stabilize the results. But there is not one most important score over all datasets, supporting our claim that a robust selection benefits from diverse criteria. For instance, the accuracy drops the most when switching off *uncertainty* and *diversity* on Citeseer (by 2.1%) and especially on Coauthor-CS (by 9.6%). However, the performance on Cora and Physics primarily needs *uncertainty* and *importance*. In contrast, Pubmed benefits most from *diversity* and *importance*. Interestingly, some of our findings might give an indication of the performance of other methods. For instance, we found that importance, i.e., representativeness, is not beneficial on Coauthor-CS. LSCALE, which mainly focuses on representativeness sampling, yields the worst performance on this dataset. On Pubmed, however, uncertainty seems not to work well. Entropy and AGE both include uncertainty sampling and

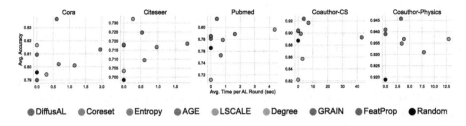

Fig. 5. Average time in seconds (x-axis) required for one active learning round compared to the average final accuracy (y-axis) for all methods (color). (Color figure online)

Table 3. Average time in seconds required for acquisition (acq), training (train), and in total ($\sum$) within one active learning iteration. Bold and underlined numbers indicate the fastest and second fastest methods, respectively. In total, DiffusAL is the fastest method on Physics and Pubmed, and the second fastest method on Cora and Citeseer.

	CS			Citeseer			Cora			Physics			Pubmed		
	acq	train	$\sum$	acq	train	$\sum$	acq	train	$\sum$	acq	train	$\sum$	acq	train	$\sum$
AGE	41.271	1.849	43.120	1.177	0.665	1.842	1.409	0.544	1.953	4.506	3.366	7.873	0.952	0.679	1.631
Coreset	5.191	1.797	6.988	0.344	0.615	0.960	0.537	0.616	1.154	0.572	3.258	3.830	0.138	0.675	0.813
Entropy	**0.005**	1.831	**1.836**	**0.002**	0.605	0.607	**0.002**	0.665	0.667	**0.011**	3.358	<u>3.369</u>	**0.002**	0.674	<u>0.676</u>
LSCALE	2.649	**0.317**	<u>2.966</u>	<u>0.019</u>	**0.249**	**0.269**	**0.042**	**0.250**	**0.292**	12.722	**0.258**	12.980	4.121	**0.247**	4.368
DiffusAL	<u>2.567</u>	<u>1.282</u>	3.849	0.183	<u>0.356</u>	<u>0.539</u>	0.268	<u>0.339</u>	<u>0.608</u>	<u>0.357</u>	<u>2.863</u>	**3.220**	<u>0.043</u>	<u>0.361</u>	**0.404**

yield worse results. On Cora, where uncertainty and representativeness seem effective, Coreset and FeatProp, which mainly focus on diversity, are among the worst-performing methods.

Using an *additive* score instead of a multiplicative score yields slightly worse results in general. From 10 comparisons, summing up the scores only yields three times slightly better results. However, the maximum difference is 0.9% (Citeseer 6C), whereas using the multiplicative in DiffusAL, the additive score is up to 1.4% (Physics 12C) better.

4.4   R3-Acquisition and Training Efficiency

Figure 5 shows the total average time (in seconds) for one active learning step on the x-axis (smaller is better) and the final accuracy after all 20C labels are selected on the y-axis (larger is better) for all methods (color).

We focus on an iterative AL selection where re-training between acquisition steps is necessary to get new uncertainty scores. In contrast, GRAIN, FeatProp, degree sampling, and random sampling select all instances for labeling at once and do not require re-training. Therefore, their average time is set to zero, and their accuracy is plotted for comparison. However, these methods are generally less label-efficient since they are not directly coupled to the current learning model. Except for Citeseer, DiffusAL is always on the Pareto-front, yielding the best final average accuracy while still being fairly time-efficient. In Table 3, we split the total time into the acquisition and the training time for the iterative methods. All GCN-based methods (Coreset, AGE, Entropy) denote fairly similar training times. Despite using an ensemble, DiffusAL is slightly faster than the GCN-based methods since the features are pre-computed. AGE and Coreset both require a longer time for acquisition. AGE can exploit pre-calculated centrality scores. However, the uncertainty score and especially the density score must be freshly calculated in each round. Especially for the very large graph data CS, AGE requires over 40 s for one active learning iteration. Coreset extracts the latent representations from the current model and requires the computation of a pairwise distance matrix. Compared to that, DiffusAL only needs to calculate the uncertainty scores derived from the QBC model since the other scores are pre-computed. Only the entropy-based selection scheme has a faster acquisition time since it only needs one forward pass through the network.

LSCALE, which also defined a dedicated network towards a unified learning and selection framework, has the fastest training times out of all methods. However, depending on the dataset, the acquisition time is much larger than DiffusAL's acquisition time. As such, the overall time needed for one active learning round varies considerably between datasets. For instance, on Citeseer and Cora, LSCALE is the fastest method out of all iterative methods. Still, on the much larger graphs Pubmed and Physics, it is the slowest method due to larger acquisition times (4.4 s and 12.7 s, respectively). Overall, even though we use an ensemble method, our training and acquisition times are fairly stable across datasets and, in total, comparably good as plain uncertainty sampling with a GCN.

5   Conclusion

The annotation of unlabeled nodes in graphs is a time-consuming and costly task and, accordingly, it is of great interest to advance label-efficient methods. Motivated by the success of diffusion-based graph learning approaches, we propose DiffusAL, a novel active learning strategy for node classification. DiffusAL uses diffusion to predict node labels accurately and compute meaningful utility scores consisting of *model uncertainty, diffused feature diversity,* and *node importance* for active node selection, such that training and data selection cooperate toward label-efficient node classification. DiffusAL is significantly better generalizable over a wide range of datasets and is, in terms of statistical significance, not beaten by any other method in 99.8% of all experiments. Moreover, it is the only method that significantly outperforms random selection in 100% of the evaluated settings. Due to pre-computed features stored in a diffusion matrix, our model can efficiently compute a node's utility for training and acquisition. Our extensive ablation study shows that each component of DiffusAL contributes to different datasets and active learning stages, making it robust in diverse graph settings.

References

1. Ash, J.T., Zhang, C., Krishnamurthy, A., Langford, J., Agarwal, A.: Deep batch active learning by diverse, uncertain gradient lower bounds. In: ICLR (2020)
2. Battaglia, P.W., et al.: Relational inductive biases, deep learning, and graph networks. arXiv preprint arXiv:1806.01261 (2018)
3. Bilgic, M., Mihalkova, L., Getoor, L.: Active learning for networked data. In: Proceedings of the 27th International Conference on Machine Learning (ICML 2010), pp. 79–86 (2010)
4. Borutta, F., Busch, J., Faerman, E., Klink, A., Schubert, M.: Structural graph representations based on multiscale local network topologies. In: WI-IAT (2019)
5. Bronstein, M.M., Bruna, J., LeCun, Y., Szlam, A., Vandergheynst, P.: Geometric deep learning: going beyond euclidean data. IEEE SPM **34**(4), 18–42 (2017)
6. Busch, J., Kocheturov, A., Tresp, V., Seidl, T.: Nf-gnn: network flow graph neural networks for malware detection and classification. In: SSDBM (2021)
7. Busch, J., Pi, J., Seidl, T.: Pushnet: efficient and adaptive neural message passing. In: ECAI (2020)
8. Cai, H., Zheng, V.W., Chang, K.C.C.: Active learning for graph embedding. arXiv preprint arXiv:1705.05085 (2017)
9. Chandra, A.L., Desai, S.V., Devaguptapu, C., Balasubramanian, V.N.: On initial pools for deep active learning. In: NeurIPS 2020 Workshop on Pre-registration in Machine Learning, pp. 14–32. PMLR (2021)
10. Contardo, G., Denoyer, L., Artières, T.: A meta-learning approach to one-step active-learning. In: AutoML@PKDD/ECML (2017)
11. Faerman, E., Borutta, F., Busch, J., Schubert, M.: Semi-supervised learning on graphs based on local label distributions. In: MLG (2018)
12. Faerman, E., Borutta, F., Busch, J., Schubert, M.: Ada-lld: adaptive node similarity using multi-scale local label distributions. In: WI-IAT (2020)
13. Fey, M., Lenssen, J.E.: Fast graph representation learning with PyTorch Geometric. In: ICLR Workshop on Representation Learning on Graphs and Manifolds (2019)
14. Frey, C.M.M., Ma, Y., Schubert, M.: Sea: graph shell attention in graph neural networks. In: European Conference on Machine Learning and Principles and Practice of Knowledge Discovery in Databases (2022)
15. Gao, L., Yang, H., Zhou, C., Wu, J., Pan, S., Hu, Y.: Active discriminative network representation learning. In: IJCAI (2018)
16. Gilmer, J., Schoenholz, S.S., Riley, P.F., Vinyals, O., Dahl, G.E.: Neural message passing for quantum chemistry. In: ICML, pp. 1263–1272. PMLR (2017)
17. Hamilton, W.L.: Graph representation learning. Synth. Lect. Artifi. Intell. Mach. Learn. **14**(3), 1–159 (2020)
18. Kipf, T.N., Welling, M.: Semi-supervised classification with graph convolutional networks. In: ICLR (2017)
19. Klicpera, J., Bojchevski, A., Günnemann, S.: Predict then propagate: graph neural networks meet personalized pagerank. In: ICLR (2019)
20. Klicpera, J., Weißenberger, S., Günnemann, S.: Diffusion improves graph learning. Adv. Neural. Inf. Process. Syst. **32**, 13354–13366 (2019)
21. Lee, J.B., Rossi, R., Kong, X.: Graph classification using structural attention. In: KDD, pp. 1666–1674 (2018)
22. Li, Q., Han, Z., Wu, X.M.: Deeper insights into graph convolutional networks for semi-supervised learning. In: AAAI (2018)

23. Liu, J., Wang, Y., Hooi, B., Yang, R., Xiao, X.: Lscale: latent space clustering-based active learning for node classification. In: Machine Learning and Knowledge Discovery in Databases: European Conference, ECML PKDD 2022, Grenoble, France, 19–23 September 2022, Proceedings, Part I, pp. 55–70. Springer (2023). https://doi.org/10.1007/978-3-031-26387-3_4
24. Moore, C., Yan, X., Zhu, Y., Rouquier, J.B., Lane, T.: Active learning for node classification in assortative and disassortative networks. In: Proceedings of the 17th ACM SIGKDD international Conference on Knowledge Discovery and Data Mining, pp. 841–849 (2011)
25. Namata, G.M., London, B., Getoor, L., Huang, B.: Query-driven active surveying for collective classification. In: MLG (2012)
26. Ogawa, Y., Maekawa, S., Sasaki, Y., Fujiwara, Y., Onizuka, M.: Adaptive node embedding propagation for semi-supervised classification. In: Oliver, N., Pérez-Cruz, F., Kramer, S., Read, J., Lozano, J.A. (eds.) ECML PKDD 2021. LNCS (LNAI), vol. 12976, pp. 417–433. Springer, Cham (2021). https://doi.org/10.1007/978-3-030-86520-7_26
27. Paszke, A., et al.: Pytorch: an imperative style, high-performance deep learning library. In: Wallach, H., Larochelle, H., Beygelzimer, A., d'Alché-Buc, F., Fox, E., Garnett, R. (eds.) Advances in Neural Information Processing Systems 32, pp. 8024–8035. Curran Associates, Inc. (2019)
28. Regol, F., Pal, S., Zhang, Y., Coates, M.: Active learning on attributed graphs via graph cognizant logistic regression and preemptive query generation. In: ICML, pp. 8041–8050. PMLR (2020)
29. Regol, F., Pal, S., Zhang, Y., Coates, M.: Active learning on attributed graphs via graph cognizant logistic regression and preemptive query generation. In: Proceedings of the 37th International Conference on Machine Learning, ICML 2020, JMLR.org (2020)
30. Sen, P., Namata, G., Bilgic, M., Getoor, L., Galligher, B., Eliassi-Rad, T.: Collective classification in network data. AI Mag. 29(3), 93 (2008)
31. Sener, O., Savarese, S.: Active learning for convolutional neural networks: a core-set approach. In: ICLR (2018)
32. Settles, B.: Active learning literature survey. Computer Sciences Technical Report 1648, University of Wisconsin-Madison (2009)
33. Seung, H.S., Opper, M., Sompolinsky, H.: Query by committee. In: Proceedings of the Fifth Annual Workshop on Computational Learning Theory, COLT 1992, pp. 287–294. Association for Computing Machinery, New York (1992)
34. Shchur, O., Mumme, M., Bojchevski, A., Günnemann, S.: Pitfalls of graph neural network evaluation. In: NeurIPS Relational Representation Learning Workshop (2018)
35. Veličković, P., Cucurull, G., Casanova, A., Romero, A., Lio, P., Bengio, Y.: Graph attention networks. In: ICLR (2018)
36. Veličković, P., Fedus, W., Hamilton, W.L., Lió, P., Bengio, Y., Hjelm, R.D.: Deep graph infomax. In: ICLR (2018)
37. Wu, Y., Xu, Y., Singh, A., Yang, Y., Dubrawski, A.: Active learning for graph neural networks via node feature propagation. arXiv preprint arXiv:1910.07567 (2019)
38. Wu, Y., Xu, Y., Singh, A., Yang, Y., Dubrawski, A.: Active learning for graph neural networks via node feature propagation. CoRR abs/ arXiv: 1910.07567 (2019)
39. Xu, K., Hu, W., Leskovec, J., Jegelka, S.: How powerful are graph neural networks?. In: ICLR (2019)

40. Xu, K., Li, C., Tian, Y., Sonobe, T., Kawarabayashi, K.i., Jegelka, S.: Representation learning on graphs with jumping knowledge networks. In: ICML, pp. 5453–5462. PMLR (2018)
41. Zhang, M., Chen, Y.: Link prediction based on graph neural networks. In: Advances in Neural Information Processing Systems 31 (2018)
42. Zhang, W., Shen, Y., Li, Y., Chen, L., Yang, Z., Cui, B.: Alg: fast and accurate active learning framework for graph convolutional networks. In: SIGMOD, pp. 2366–2374 (2021)
43. Zhang, W., et al.: Grain: Improving data efficiency of graph neural networks via diversified influence maximization. Proc. VLDB Endow. 14(11), 2473–2482 (2021)
44. Zhao, L., et al.: T-gcn: a temporal graph convolutional network for traffic prediction. IEEE Trans. Intell. Transp. Syst. 21(9), 3848–3858 (2019)

Adversarial Machine Learning

Adversarial Machine Learning

Quantifying Robustness to Adversarial Word Substitutions

Yuting Yang[1,2], Pei Huang[3], Juao Cao[1,2], Feifei Ma[2,4,5(✉)], Jian Zhang[2,4(✉)], and Jintao Li[1]

[1] Key Lab of Intelligent Information Processing, Institute of Computing Technology, Chinese Academy of Sciences, Beijing, China
[2] University of Chinese Academy of Sciences, Beijing, China
[3] Department of Computer Science, Stanford University, Stanford, California, USA
[4] State Key Laboratory of Computer Science, Institute of Software, Chinese Academy of Sciences, Beijing, China
`maff@ios.ac.cn, yangyuting@ict.ac.cn`
[5] Laboratory of Parallel Software and Computational Science, Institute of Software, Chinese Academy of Sciences, Beijing, China

Abstract. Deep-learning-based NLP models are found to be vulnerable to word substitution perturbations. Before they are widely adopted, the fundamental issues of robustness need to be addressed. Along this line, we propose a formal framework to evaluate word-level robustness. First, to study safe regions for a model, we introduce robustness radius which is the boundary where the model can resist any perturbation. As calculating the maximum robustness radius is computationally hard, we estimate its upper and lower bound. We repurpose attack methods as ways of seeking an upper bound and design a pseudo-dynamic programming algorithm for a tighter upper bound. Then verification method is utilized for a lower bound. Further, for evaluating the robustness of regions outside a safe radius, we reexamine robustness from another view: quantification. A robustness metric with a rigorous statistical guarantee is introduced to measure the quantification of adversarial examples, which indicates the model's susceptibility to perturbations outside the safe radius. The metric helps us figure out why state-of-the-art models like BERT can be easily fooled by a few word substitutions, but generalize well in the presence of real-world noises.

Keywords: Adversarial example · robustness · natural language processing

1 Introduction

Deep learning models have achieved impressive improvements on various NLP tasks [32]. However, they are found to be vulnerable to input perturbations, such as paraphrasing [26], inserting character [3] and replacing words with similar ones [25,31]. In this paper, we focus on word substitution perturbation [14,22,34] as

© The Author(s), under exclusive license to Springer Nature Switzerland AG 2023
D. Koutra et al. (Eds.): ECML PKDD 2023, LNAI 14169, pp. 95–112, 2023.
https://doi.org/10.1007/978-3-031-43412-9_6

shown in Fig. 1, in which the output of a model can be altered by replacing some words in the input sentence while maintaining the semantics. Before deep learning models are widely adopted in practice, understanding their robustness to word substitution is critical.

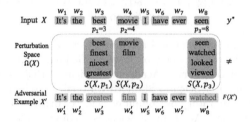

Fig. 1. An example of word substitution perturbation.

In recent years, several studies focus on generating adversarial examples [10, 14, 30] or certifying the absence of adversarial examples in the whole perturbation space [11, 13, 33]. However, almost all current deep learning models are unable to be regarded as absolutely robust under such a yes-or-no binary judgment. Along this line, some deeper questions can be asked. Where is the safe boundary of a model to resist perturbation? Why can a well-trained NLP model be fooled by small perturbations but generalize well to real-world inputs with noises? Does the existence of an adversarial example in the exponential input space completely destroy the defense capability of the model?

To answer these questions more comprehensively, we propose a formal framework for evaluating models' robustness to word substitution from the view of quantification. We quantify the magnitude of the perturbation (or the number of substitutions) a model can resist. Figure 2 visualizes the problems we study in this paper. Robustness radius (safe radius) r, which is defined as the magnitude of the perturbation space where no adversarial examples exist, is useful for studying the safe regions of models. In particular, the maximum robustness radius R depicts the boundary of perturbations a model can resist. Apart from safe regions, the vulnerability outside safe regions also needs to be evaluated as it can influence the model's performance in practice. A natural idea is to quantify the number of adversarial examples for a given radius as a metric for robustness.

The main challenge of the evaluation framework is that the perturbation space can be exponentially large, so solving these problems exactly is not feasible in many cases. To overcome this problem, we retreat from the exact computation of R to estimate its upper and lower bounds. An adversarial example with fewer substitutions can provide a tighter upper bound for R. Therefore, we repurpose attack methods for evaluating the upper bound and design an algorithm called pseudo-dynamic programming (PDP) to craft adversarial examples with as few substitutions as possible. Then, for the lower bound, we find that certifying word-level robustness with a fixed radius can be solved in polynomial time.

So we use verification methods to give a lower bound. Finally, we introduce a robustness metric PR which denotes the number of adversarial examples for a given radius. It can provide a quantitative indicator for the models' robustness outside the absolute safe radius. As it is a more difficult problem than calculating the maximum safe radius, we estimate the value of PR with a rigorous statistical guarantee.

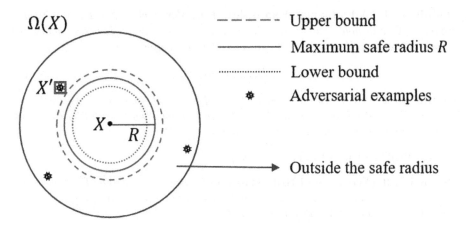

Fig. 2. Diagram of our methods for evaluating robustness: (1) evaluating maximum safe radius R via obtaining its upper and lower bound; (2) measuring the model's vulnerability outside the safe radius via a robustness metric PR.

We design experiments on two important NLP tasks (text classification and textual entailment) and two models (BiLSTM and BERT) to study our methods empirically. Experiments show that PDP algorithm has a stronger search capability to provide a tighter upper bound for the maximum robustness radius. The robustness metric PR results present an interesting phenomenon: although most well-trained models can be attacked by a few word substitutions with a high success rate, the word-substitution-based adversarial examples distribute widely in perturbation space but just occupy a small proportion. For example, BERT can be successfully (>89.7%) attacked by manipulating 4.5 words on average on IMDB. However, more than 90.66% regions can resist random word perturbations with a high probability (>0.9). We conclude that some adversarial examples may be essentially on-manifold generalization errors, which can explain the reason why these "vulnerable" models can generalize well in practice.

-

2   Preliminary

Given a natural language classifier $F : \mathcal{X} \rightarrow \mathcal{Y}$, which is a mapping from an input space to an output label space. The input space $\mathcal{X}$ contains all possible texts $X =$

$w_1, w_2, ..., w_n$ and output space $\mathcal{Y} = \{y_1, y_2, ..., y_c\}$ contains c possible predictions of an input. w_i is usually a word embedding or one-hot vector. $F_y(\cdot)$ is the prediction score for the y label. Let $P = \{p_1, p_2, ..., p_m\}$ be the set of perturbable positions. For each perturbable position $p \in P$, there is a set $S(X, p)$ which contains all candidate words for substitution without changing the semantics (the original word w_p is also in $S(X, p)$). Figure 2 is a schematic diagram and contains explanations of some notations.

Definition 1 (Adversarial Example). *Consider a classifier $F(x)$. Given a sequence X with gold label y^* and $X' = w_1', w_2', ..., w_n'$ which is a text generated by perturbing X, X' is said to be an adversarial example if:*

$$F(X') \neq y^* \tag{1}$$

Definition 2. *A perturbation space $\Omega(X)$ of an input sequence X is a set containing all perturbations generated by substituting the original word by candidate words in $S(X, p)$ for each perturbable position $p \in \mathcal{P}$.*

The cardinality of $\Omega(X)$ is $\prod_{p \in \mathcal{P}} |S(X, p)|$.

Definition 3 (Word-level Robustness). *Consider a classifier $F(x)$. Given a sequence X with gold label y^*, classifier F is said to be robust in the perturbation space $\Omega(X)$ if the following formula holds:*

$$\forall X'. \ X' \in \Omega(X) \Rightarrow F(X') = y^* \tag{2}$$

If a classifier is not robust in $\Omega(X)$, we also want to know what maximum perturbation it can resist. We use L_0 distance r to describe the degree of perturbation, which is also called **robustness radius** or **safe radius**. The maximum robustness radius is denoted as R.

Definition 4 (Word-level L_0-Robustness). *Consider a classifier $F(x)$. Given an L_0 distance r and a sequence X with gold label y^*. Let $\Omega_r(X) := \{X' : X' \in \Omega(X) \wedge \|X' - X\|_0 \leq r\}$ and $\|\cdot\|_0$ denote the number of substituted words. The classifier F is said to be robust with respect to $\Omega_r(X)$ if the following formula holds true:*

$$\forall X'. \ X' \in \Omega_r(X) \Rightarrow F(X') = y^* \tag{3}$$

If formula (3) is true, that the means neural network can resist any substitutions in $\Omega_r(X)$. For the point-wise robustness metric, substitution length and ratio can be easily converted to each other.

2.1 Problems

From a high-level perspective, there are four types of relevant problems:

- **Type-1 (Satisfaction problem).** Find an adversarial example in the perturbation space. It helps to prove that a neural network is unsafe in certain input space.

- **Type-2** (`Optimization problem`). Find the adversarial example with minimal perturbation. This can help us figure out the boundary of safe regions.
- **Type-3** (`Proving problem`). Certify the absence of adversarial examples in the perturbation space. In other words, prove that the formulas like (2) or (3) is true. This problem can prove that the network is absolutely safe in certain input spaces.
- **Type-4** (`Counting problem`). Give the number of adversarial examples in the perturbation space. It further investigates the model's susceptibility outside the absolutely safe radius.

In recent years, most relevant works focused on developing effective attacking algorithms for generating adversarial examples [11,13,33], which can be viewed as "**Type-1 problem**": finding an adversarial example in the perturbation space. However, finding an adversarial example or not can not reflect the model's defense ability in the whole perturbation space. Type-2–4 problems are more informative and remain to be studied, which are our focuses in this work.

These four problems present different levels of difficulty. In more details, Type-1 problem is in $\mathcal{NP}$; Type-2 problem is $\mathcal{NP}$-hard; Type-3 problem is in $\mathcal{CoNP}$ [15]; and Type-4 problem is $\#\mathcal{P}$-hard ($\mathcal{NP} \subseteq \#\mathcal{P}$) [2]. Type-3 problem is the complement of Type-1 problem. Sometimes, Type-1 and Type-3 problems are not strictly distinguished, so certifying robustness is sometimes said to be in $\mathcal{NP}$ as well. These conclusions are drawn when the tasks and neural networks have no restrictions.

3   Methods

In this section, we propose a formal framework for evaluating robustness of word substitution perturbation. We first study the upper and the lower bound for the safe boundary which belongs to Type 2 and Type 3 problem respectively. Then we use a statistical inference method to quantify the adversarial examples outside a safe region with a rigorous guarantee, which is a Type 4 problem. For a more clear state, we organize the following sections according to the three problems.

3.1   Type-2 Problem: Pseudo-Dynamic Programming for Crafting Adversarial Examples

As shown in Fig. 1, if an adversarial example is found in $\Omega_r(X)$, it means $\Omega_r(X)$ is not L_0-Robust according to Definition 4 or the maximum robustness radius of the model must be lower than r. An adversarial example offers an upper bound for the maximum robustness radius. Naturally, we wonder about a tighter upper bound for estimating safe boundaries. So, we design an efficient algorithm to find adversarial examples with fewer substituted words in $\Omega(X)$. The algorithm can not only find high-quality adversarial examples, but also provide a tighter upper bound for robustness radius in $\Omega_r(X)$. The basic idea of our method is inspired by dynamic programming.

Methodology. Finding the optimal adversarial example X' can be seen as a combinatorial optimization problem with two goals:

i) Optimize the output confidence score of $F(X')$ to fool the classifier.
ii) Minimize the number of substituted words (i.e. Minimize $\|X' - X\|_0$).

Algorithm 1 PDP (Pseudo-Dynamic Programming)

Require:
    F: A classifier
    X: An input text with n words
    τ: the maximum percentage of words for modification.
Ensure: An adversarial example X' *or* Failed.
1: $A(X,0) \leftarrow \{X\}$;
2: $P_1 \leftarrow \emptyset, P_2 \leftarrow \{p_1, p_2, ...p_m\}$;
3: **for all** $t \leftarrow 1$ **to** m **do**
4:     $A(X, t-1) \leftarrow \mathrm{TopK}(A(X, t-1))$;
5:     $p* \leftarrow \arg\max_{p \in P_2} \{I_p(A(X, t-1), p)\}$;
6:     $A(X, t) \leftarrow A(X, t-1) \times S(X, p^*)$;
7:     $P_1 \leftarrow P_1 \cup \{p*\}, P_2 \leftarrow P_2 \setminus \{p*\}$;
8:     **if** $\exists X' \in A(X, t), F(X') \neq y*$ **and** $\|X' - X\|_0 \leq \tau \cdot n$ **then**
9:         $X' \leftarrow$ the best adversarial example in $A(X, t)$
10:         **return** X'
11:     **end if**
12: **end for**
13: **return** Failed

We consider the optimizing procedure is in correlation with a time variable t. Let $A(X, t)$ denote the text set containing all combinations of word substitutions for first t perturbed positions $\{p_1, p_2, ...p_t\}$. $\mathrm{Opt}[(A(X, t))]$ denotes the operation to get the optimal adversarial example from $A(X, t)$. Operation $A(X, t-1) \times S(X, p_t)$ means substitute the p_t-th position with candidate words in $S(X, p_t)$ for all texts in $A(X, t-1)$. Then we get the optimal adversarial example from $A(X, m)$ in m steps:

$$\mathrm{Opt}[A(X, t)] := \mathrm{Opt}[A(X, t-1) \times S(X, p_t)] \qquad (4)$$

where $|P|=m$, $t \in \{1, ..., m\}$ and $A(X, 0)=\{X\}$. This procedure can guarantee finding the optimal adversarial example. However, it has exponential time complexity as the size of $A(X, t)$ increases exponentially with t.

We make some relaxations for this procedure to ensure it can be executed in polynomial time. At step t, we only keep top K texts in $A(X, t-1)$ which are considered to be more promising in generating adversarial examples. The others will be forgotten at this step. In this context, we have:

$$A(X, t) := \mathrm{TopK}(A(X, t-1)) \times S(X, p_t) \qquad (5)$$

This relaxation comes at the cost of the guarantee of finding the optimal adversarial example. Due to that, the recurrence relation in Eq. 5 is similar to the dynamic programming equation, we call it **pseudo-dynamic programming (PDP)**.

Notice that the number of substituted words of all texts in $A(X, t)$ is less than t. So, when an adversarial example is found at an earlier time t, it has greater chances to achieve the goal (ii) better. So, we make use of the future information to help the procedure encounter an adversarial example at an earlier time t. At time $t - 1$, the position set P can be divided into two sets $P_1 = \{p_i\}_{i=1}^{t-1}$ and $P_2 = \{p_i\}_{i=t}^m$. P_1 is the set of positions that have been considered and P_2 is the set of positions to be considered in the future. Then we look ahead and pick the best position p^* in P_2 to increase the chance of finding an adversarial example in the next time t. So the recurrence relation 5 can be optimized as:

$$A(X, t) := \text{TopK}(A(X, t - 1)) \times S(X, p^*) \tag{6}$$

This pseudo dynamic programming procedure is designed for GPU computing. It can make good use of the characteristics of parallel computing. For each step, the texts in $A(X, t)$ can be fed into classifier F simultaneously as a batch to find adversarial examples and calculate evaluation scores.

Score Functions. Next, we explain how to realize $TopK(\cdot)$ for remembering **history** information and how to look ahead for the **future** in finding $p*$, which is the key to the PDP.

TopK(·.) We use the score $I_s(X')$ to measure the importance of a text $X' \in A(X, t)$. It can be:

- $I_s(X') := 1 - F_{y*}(X')$ Untargeted attack
- $I_s(X') := F_{\hat{y}}(X')$ Targeted ($\hat{y}$) attack

Operation TopK($\cdot$) will preserve K texts with highest score I_s. For an untargeted attack, it will preserve K texts with the lowest confidence score for the gold label; For a targeted attack, it will preserve K texts with the highest confidence score for the expected output label $\hat{y}$.

Looking Ahead. We call $A(X, t)$ as a **configuration** at time t. Let $X_{w_p \leftarrow w}$ denote the text after replacing the word w_p in position p of X by w. The importance score of the perturbed position p under the current configuration $A(X, t)$ is $I_p(A(X, t), p)$. It can be:

- Untargeted attack:
  $$I_p(A(X, t), p) := 1 - \min_{X' \sim A, w \in S(X, p)} \{F_{y*}(X'_{w_p \leftarrow w})\}$$
- Targeted attack:
  $$I_p(A(X, t), p) := \max_{X' \sim A, w \in S(X, p)} \{F_{\hat{y}}(X'_{w_p \leftarrow w})\}$$

where $X' \sim A$ means drawing some texts from $A(X, t)$ with probability proportional to $I_s(X')$. Then we have the position $p*$, which has the highest score I_p, for the next step t to consider:

$$p* := \arg\max_{p \in P_2}\{I_p(A(X, t-1), p)\} \tag{7}$$

Under the white-box setting, gradient information also can be used to measure the importance of position p.

The overall PDP algorithm is shown in Algorithm 1. It is a polynomial-time algorithm ($\mathcal{O}(n^2 \cdot poly(|F|, n))$) in the worst case, and the proof is in the supplementary material). $poly(|F|, n)$ represents prediction time of classifier F for an input with length n. It is a polynomial function.

3.2   Type-3 Problem: Robustness Verification

Verification is a method to prove the correctness of a system with respect to a certain property via formal methods of mathematics. If we can prove formula 3 is true for a certain radius r (Type-3 problem), that means r is a lower bound of maximum safe radius. Via combining the upper and lower bound, we can figure out the boundary of the safe regions. Generally speaking, proving is much more difficult than finding an adversarial example (Type-1 problem), which needs to enumerate the exponential space or design a theorem proving algorithm. Several over-approximate verification methods like Interval Bound Propagation (IBP) [12,13] have recently been introduced from image to NLP. Limited by time cost, scaling to large neural networks is a challenge for these methods. In this section, we introduce a property of L_0-robustness, which is helpful for certifying robustness when radius r is fixed. It can also be used to improve the efficiency of other verification methods.

Theorem 1. *For any fixed r, Type-3 problem is in time complexity class $\mathcal{P}$.*

Proof. Suppose that a classifier F can output a prediction for an input X with length n in $poly(|F|, n)$ time and X has m perturbable positions. For a given r, we have:

$$|\Omega_r(X)| \leq mr \cdot v^r \leq nr \cdot v^r \tag{8}$$

where $v = \max_{p \in P}\{|S(X, p)|\}$. We know that the size of $\Omega_r(X)$ is bounded by $\mathcal{O}((nv)^r)$. So, one can test all the possible substitutions in $\Omega_r(X)$ in $\mathcal{O}((nv)^r) \cdot poly(|F|, n)$ time to answer problems of Type-3.

Such conclusions are specific for NLP area owing to its discrete nature. In many cases, the upper bound of r can be given by our PDP algorithm. In such a situation, we can directly enumerate all the possible substitutions to prove the absence of adversarial examples within r (or formula 3 holds) in polynomial time. The enumeration procedure accomplished by a simple prover (SP), returns "Certified Robustness" or "Found an adversarial example". After the absence of adversarial examples in $\Omega_r(X)$ is proved, r is a lower bound for the maximum L_0-robustness radius.

All the possible substitutions compose a polynomial-time verifiable formal proof for the absence of adversarial examples. A checkable proof can make the result more convincing. If an algorithm finds an adversarial example, we can check the result easily. However, if an algorithm reports no adversarial examples, it is difficult to figure out whether there are indeed no adversarial samples or the verification algorithm has some bugs.

Under the white-box setting, the gradient information can be used to accelerate the verification algorithm. The basic idea is to test more sensitive positions first. Once an adversarial example occurs, the program can be terminated. Let $\|\partial F_{y^*}(X)/\partial w_p\|_1$ denote sensitivity score of perturbable position p, we can pre-sort the perturbable positions in P based on the sensitivity score.

3.3 Type-4 Problem: Robustness Metric

Why are neural networks often fooled by small crafted perturbations, but have good generalization to noisy inputs in the real environment? How about the ability of a model to resist perturbation outside the robust radius? These questions promote us to analyze robustness from another perspective: the quantity of adversarial examples. Sometimes, it is difficult to enumerate all the adversarial examples in the perturbation space.

We relax the universal quantifier "$\forall$" in formula 2 to a quantitative version as word-level robustness metric PR:

$$PR := \frac{|\{X' : X' \in \Omega_r(X) \wedge F(X') = y^*\}|}{|\Omega_r(X)|}, \tag{9}$$

where we can see that 1-PR is the proportion of adversarial examples. Therefore, the higher the PR value is, the less vulnerable the classifier F is to be fooled by random perturbations around the point X. When $PR = 1$, it is equivalent to formula 2.

Apparently, the exact computation of PR is essentially a **Type-4 problem**. For a long input sequence, calculating the value of PR is infeasible at the moment due to the limitation of computational power. As an alternative, we estimate PR via a statistical method. Suppose that $X_1, X_2, ..., X_N$ are taken from $\Omega_r(X)$ with uniform sampling, then an estimator $\hat{PR}$ for PR is:

$$\hat{PR} := \frac{1}{N} \sum_{i=1}^{N} \mathbb{I}(F(X_i) = y^*) \tag{10}$$

The satisfaction of $(F(X_i) = y^*)$ can be seen as Bernoulli random variable Y_i, i.e., $Y_i \sim Bernoulli(PR)$. So, if we want estimator $\hat{PR}$ to satisfy a prior guarantee such as the probability of producing an estimation which deviates from its real value PR by a certain amount ϵ is less than δ, the following must hold:

$$Pr(|\hat{PR} - PR| < \epsilon) > 1 - \delta \tag{11}$$

Based on Hoeffding's inequality:

$$Pr(|\frac{1}{N}\sum_{i=1}^{N}Y_i - PR| \geq \epsilon) \leq 2e^{-2N\epsilon^2} \tag{12}$$

For given parameters ϵ and δ, the estimator $\hat{PR}$ satisfies formula (11) if:

$$N > \frac{1}{2\epsilon^2}\ln\frac{2}{\delta} \tag{13}$$

$\hat{PR}$ is a metric for a model's susceptibility to random perturbations with rigorous statistical guarantees. As the error bound is **P**robably **A**pproximate **C**orrect, we also call it PAC-style robustness metric. Reexamining robustness in a quantitative perspective can be helpful for constructing weak robustness notion and designing robustness enhancement methods [9].

4   Experiments

In this section, we design three sets of experiments to study the three problems and methods we proposed. Code is available at https://github.com/YANG-Yuting/pdp.

4.1   General Experiment Setup

Tasks. We conduct experiments on two important NLP tasks: text classification and textual entailment. MR [23] and IMDB [19] are sentence-level and document-level sentiment classifications respectively on positive and negative movie reviews. SNLI [4] is used to learn to judge the relationship between two sentences: whether the second sentence can be derived from entailment, contradiction, or neutral relationship with the first sentence.

Target Models. For each task, we choose two widely used models, bidirectional LSTM (BiLSTM) [5] and BERT [6] as the attacking target models. For BiLSTM, we used a 1-layer bidirectional LSTM with 150 hidden units, and 300-dimensional pre-trained GloVe [24] word embeddings. We used the 12-layer-based version of BERT model with 768 hidden units and 12 heads, with 110M parameters.

4.2   Type-2 Problem: Attack Evaluation

Baselines. We use three state-of-the-art adversarial crafting methods (TextFooler [14], SemPSO [34] and BertAttack [16]) as references to compare the search capability of PDP. TextFooler is a greedy algorithm and SemPSO is a particle-swarm-based algorithm. BertAttack [16] uses the masked language model (BERT) as a perturbation generator and finds perturbations that maximize the risk of making wrong predictions. They all focus on Type 1 problem while PDP focuses on Type 2 problem.

Metrics. We evaluate the performance of these attack methods including the rate of successful attacks and the percentage of word substitution. A smaller percentage (or number) of word substitution means a tighter upper bound for the maximum L_0-robustness radius.

Table 1. The attack results of different methods. #Attacks is the number of texts to be attacked. #Succ is the number of successful attacks. #Win is the number of successful attacks crafted with the least substitutions for the same texts among various attack methods. %S is the average percentage of substituted words.

Dataset	Model	#Attacks	SemPSO			TextFooler			BertAttack			PDP		
			#Succ	#Win	%S	#Succ	#Win	%S	#Succ	#Win	%S	#Succ	#Win	%S
MR	BiLSTM	880	636(72.27%)	0	10.64	484(55.00%)	0	12.09	502(57.05%)	0	12.73	**655(74.43%)**	**33**	**10.44**
	BERT	956	580(60.67%)	0	12.10	323(33.79%)	0	13.96	390(40.79%)	0	13.84	**621(64.96%)**	**30**	**11.80**
IMDB	BiLSTM	1000	947(94.7%)	0	4.58	854(85.4%)	0	6.78	936(93.6%)	0	7.2	**989(98.9%)**	**599**	**3.11**
	BERT	1000	871(87.1%)	0	4.31	714(71.4%)	0	8.47	813(81.3%)	0	8.63	**899(89.9%)**	**498**	**2.87**
SNLI	BiLSTM	1000	505(50.5%)	0	15.99	592(59.2%)	0	15.76	713(71.3%)	0	16.32	**764(76.4%)**	**31**	**14.91**
	BERT	1000	587(58.7%)	0	16.10	636(63.6%)	0	15.83	755(75.5%)	0	16.27	**845(84.5%)**	**30**	**15.09**

Settings. For a fair comparison, we set the same candidate set and constraints for different attack methods. The candidate is generated by HowNet [7] and similarities of word embeddings. HowNet is arranged by the sememe and can find the potential semantic-preserving words. Word embeddings can further help to select the most similar candidate words. So, we generate $S(X, p)$ via cleaning the synonyms obtained by HowNet with cosine similarity of word embeddings. We reserve top η ($\eta = 5$) synonyms as candidates for each position.

For MR, we experiment on all the test texts classified correctly. For IMDB and SNLI, we randomly sample 1000 texts classified correctly from the test set. Following [1,34], only the hypotheses are perturbed for SNLI. The adversarial examples with modification rates less than 25% are considered valid.

Attack Results. We present the average percentage of substitutions (%S) in Table 1 and the number of times each method "wins" the others in terms of substitution length (#Win). The experimental results show that PDP always gives adversarial examples with fewer substitutions. Especially for the long-text dataset, IMDB, 599 (59.9%) adversarial examples found by PDP contains the least word substitutions for BiLSTM (the remaining 40.1% holds the same number of substitutions as others). The examples crafted by PDP contain very few substitutions, such as average **4.52** word substitution for BERT on IMDB whose average number of words is 215. The comparison of the substitution length on IMDB is shown in Fig. 3. Besides, PDP achieves the highest attack success rates on all three datasets and two target models. These experimental results indicate PDP has stronger search capabilities. Then, we repurpose PDP attack to evaluate the robustness, and Fig. 4 shows that PDP can provide a tighter bound for the maximum robustness radii compared with other attacking methods. More experimental results are shown in the supplementary.

4.3   Type-3 Problem: Robustness Verification

For a given L_0 distance r ($r = 1$ to 4), the certified results on 200 randomly sampled test instances are shown in Table 2. We find that: (1) The percentage of certified robustness is decreasing with the increase of radius r. (2) For many short-text tasks (MR and SNLI), considering $r \leq 4$ is sufficient because most regions cannot resist 4-word substitutions. For example, only 6.42% regions of BERT can resist any 4-word substitutions adversarial attack on SNLI. (3) For the long-text task IMDB, BERT has more regions (61.52%) that can resist any 3-word substitutions attack compared with BiLSTM. It takes a long time to certify robustness when $r = 4$, so we don't show the results. Experimental results also show that this simple verification method is effective for many NLP tasks.

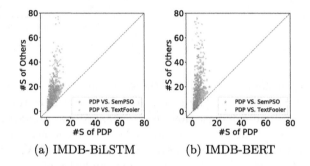

(a) IMDB-BiLSTM   (b) IMDB-BERT

Fig. 3. Comparison of the number of substituted words of different methods on IMDB. Each point represents a text (x-axis is the number of substituted (#S) words of PDP and y-axis is that of other attack methods). Points over the diagonal are where PDP finds an adversarial example with fewer substitutions.

Table 2. Certified robustness. "Found" and "Certified" are the abbreviations for "an adversarial example found" and "certified to be robust" respectively. %F and %C are the percentage of "Found" and "Certified". "T" is the average time.

Dataset	Model	$r = 1$				$r = 2$				$r = 3$				$r = 4$			
		Found		Certified		Found		Certified		Found		Certified		Found		Certified	
		%F	T(s)	%C	T(s)	%F	T(s)	%C	T(s)	%F	T(s)	%C	T(s)	%F	T(s)	%C	T(s)
MR	BiLSTM	36.00	0.01	64.00	0.02	58.00	0.04	42.00	0.05	72.00	0.30	28.00	0.27	78.00	3.62	22.00	2.26
	BERT	20.00	0.12	80.00	0.24	40.00	1.95	60.00	2.49	56.50	28.86	43.50	20.95	67.50	256.78	32.50	46.23
IMDB	BiLSTM	15.59	0.04	84.41	0.13	31.99	1.93	68.01	2.89	45.50	2.47	54.50	953.19	-	-	-	-
	BERT	12.66	2.89	87.34	3.11	25.91	3.40	74.09	246.54	38.48	7.97	61.52	6448.39	-	-	-	-
SNLI	BiLSTM	56.90	0.04	43.10	0.01	76.87	0.03	23.13	0.07	82.52	0.14	17.48	0.11	84.63	0.66	15.37	0.23
	BERT	71.43	0.03	28.57	0.01	88.01	0.07	11.99	0.06	92.37	0.47	7.63	0.07	93.58	3.17	6.42	0.04

4.4   Type-4 Problem: Robustness Metric

We evaluate the robustness score (Eq. 9) of different models on different tasks. The evaluation is performed on the randomly sampled 1000 test data and the sample size N is 5000 ($\epsilon = 0.025$, $\delta = 0.005$). The violin plots of $\hat{PR}$ are shown in Fig. 5. As most attacking algorithms limit the maximum perturbation ratio to smaller than 25%, we set r to 25% of the length of the sentence.

Most of the shadows in all sub-figures are close to the top horizontal line (maximum $\hat{PR}$), which means that most regions have high robustness scores $\hat{PR}$. Take BERT model on IMDB task as an example, 89.9% regions are found with adversarial examples as shown in Table 1, which indicates the "vulnerability" of the model. However, via robustness metric, we find that 90.66% regions achieve $\hat{PR}$ larger than 0.9. It means, most regions (90.66%) can resist random word perturbations with high probability (>0.9). A conclusion can be drawn: these well-trained models are usually robust to word substitutions in a non-adversarial environment.

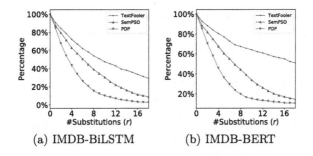

Fig. 4. The percentage of regions ($\Omega_r(X)$) that do not yield to different attacking methods in each perturbation radius. x-axis can be seen as the upper bounds given by different attacking methods.

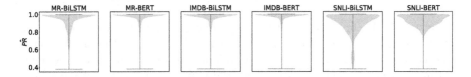

Fig. 5. Violin plots of robustness score on the test set when r is 25% of the length of sentence. The width of x-axis represents the frequency of corresponding $\hat{PR}$ in y-axis. Top and bottom horizontal lines are the maximum and minimum value of $\hat{PR}$.

For a well-trained model, the adversarial examples crafted by word substitution are almost everywhere and close to the normal point in the perturbation space, but their proportion is very low. In 2019, Stutz et al. pointed out that on-manifold robustness is essentially generalization and on-manifold adversarial examples are generalization errors [29]. Suppose users' selection from a synonym candidate is similar to the process of rolling a die, which means the usage of a word for position p in $S(X,p)$ is conditional on a latent variable z_p, i.e. $Pr(w_p|z_p)$

corresponding to the underlying, low dimensional manifold. All possible substitutions in $\Omega(X)$ can be seen as on the manifold corresponding to a latent variable $Z = (z_{p_1}, z_{p_2}, ..., z_{p_k})$. Thus, the adversarial examples found by attacking algorithms are essentially on-manifold generalization errors. From this perspective, we can explain why a well-trained model like BERT has a good generalization but can be easily attacked by word substitutions.

For all three tasks, BERT always presents better robustness performance. For instance, on MR task, the proportion of regions with $\hat{PR}$ larger than 0.9 is 79.22% and 90.97% for BiLSTM and BERT respectively. It means BERT is always more robust outside the safe regions.

5 Related Work

Various attack algorithms are developed for generating adversarial examples via substitutions including gradient descent methods [18,27,30], genetic algorithm [1], particle-swarm-based method [34], greedy-based methods [14,25] and BERT-based methods [8,17]. They focus on how to generate adversarial examples and simply regard robustness as the opposite of attack success rate.

Existing work [11,13,28] migrates the over-approximate method IBP from the image field to certify the robustness in the continuous space based on word embedding. Although they can give a provably robust to all possible perturbations within the constraints, the limitation is that a model which is not robust in continuous space can be robust in discrete space, as the vectors that can fool the model may not correspond to any real words. Randomized smoothing-based method is introduced to certify the robustness of a smoothed classifier [33]. An MCTS-based method is designed to assess the maximum safe radius of CNNs and LSTM [21]. Existing robustness evaluation works focus on robustness verification which aims to verify the absolute safe for a given model in the whole perturbation space. They ignore the safe sub-regions and unsafe regions.

Naturally, the final goal is to defend against attacking and improve the robustness. Adversarial data augmentation (ADA) is one of the most effective empirical methods [8,14,17,25,30]. ADA adopts the adversarial examples generated by their attack methods for adversarial training and achieve some robustness improvement. Adversarial training is another similar method, which incorporates a min-max optimization between adversarial perturbations and the models by adding norm-bounded perturbations to word embeddings [20,35]. They depend on search algorithms for adversarial examples, so our PDP with better search ability can provide support for these robustness enhancement methods.

6 Conclusion

Overall, we build a formal framework to study the word-level robustness of the deep-learning-based NLP systems. We repurpose the attack method for robustness evaluation and design a pseudo-dynamic programming framework to provide a tighter upper bound. Besides, we notice that the absence of adversarial examples within any fixed radius can be verified in polynomial time, and give a simple prover to certify the lower bound. Experimental results show that our methods can provide tighter bounds for robustness evaluation, and most state-of-the-art models like BERT cannot resist a few word substitutions. Further, we discuss the robustness from the view of quantification and introduce a PAC-style metric to show they are robust to random perturbations, as well as explain why they generalize well but are poor in resisting adversarial attacks. It can be helpful in studying defense and interpretability of NLP models.

Acknowledgments. This work has been supported by the Project of Chinese Academy of Sciences (E141020), the Zhejiang Provincial Key Research and Development Program of China (No. 2021C01164), the National Natural Science Foundation of China (62203425), the Innovation Funding from the Institute of Computing Technology, the Chinese Academy of Sciences (E161020) and the National Science Foundation of China (No. 61972384 and No. 62132020).

Ethics. Our work does not arise ethical issues directly and all used datasets are publicly available with no privacy violation. With the emergence of more and more adversarial scenarios, few perturbations, e.g., modifying some words with their synonyms, can mislead a well-trained DNN's prediction. It arises society's concern about the safety and applicability of DNNs in piratical scenarios. This paper has an important significance and role in building a trustworthy AI system.

References

1. Alzantot, M., Sharma, Y., Elgohary, A., Ho, B., Srivastava, M.B., Chang, K.: Generating natural language adversarial examples. In: Proceedings of the 2018 Conference on Empirical Methods in Natural Language Processing, Brussels, Belgium, 31 October–4 November 2018, pp. 2890–2896 (2018)
2. Baluta, T., Shen, S., Shinde, S., Meel, K.S., Saxena, P.: Quantitative verification of neural networks and its security applications. In: Proceedings of the 2019 ACM SIGSAC Conference on Computer and Communications Security, CCS 2019, London, UK, 11–15 November 2019, pp. 1249–1264 (2019)
3. Belinkov, Y., Bisk, Y.: Synthetic and natural noise both break neural machine translation. In: 6th International Conference on Learning Representations, ICLR 2018, Conference Track Proceedings, Vancouver, BC, Canada, 30 April–3 May 2018 (2018)
4. Bowman, S.R., Angeli, G., Potts, C., Manning, C.D.: A large annotated corpus for learning natural language inference. In: Proceedings of the 2015 Conference on Empirical Methods in Natural Language Processing, EMNLP 2015, Lisbon, Portugal, 17–21 September 2015, pp. 632–642 (2015)
5. Conneau, A., Kiela, D., Schwenk, H., Barrault, L., Bordes, A.: Supervised learning of universal sentence representations from natural language inference data. In: Proceedings of the 2017 Conference on Empirical Methods in Natural Language Processing, EMNLP 2017, Copenhagen, Denmark, 9–11 September 2017, pp. 670–680 (2017)

6. Devlin, J., Chang, M., Lee, K., Toutanova, K.: BERT: pre-training of deep bidirectional transformers for language understanding. In: Proceedings of the 2019 Conference of the North American Chapter of the Association for Computational Linguistics: Human Language Technologies, NAACL-HLT 2019, Minneapolis, MN, USA, 2–7 June 2019, Volume 1 (Long and Short Papers), pp. 4171–4186 (2019)

7. Dong, Z., Dong, Q.: Hownet and the Computation of Meaning. World Scientific (2006)

8. Garg, S., Ramakrishnan, G.: BAE: BERT-based adversarial examples for text classification. In: Proceedings of the 2020 Conference on Empirical Methods in Natural Language Processing, EMNLP 2020, Online, 16–20 November 2020, pp. 6174–6181 (2020)

9. Huang, P., Yang, Y., Jia, F., Liu, M., Ma, F., Zhang, J.: Word level robustness enhancement: Fight perturbation with perturbation. In: Thirty-Sixth AAAI Conference on Artificial Intelligence, AAAI 2022 Virtual Event, 22 February–1 March 2022, pp. 10785–10793 (2022)

10. Huang, P., Yang, Y., Liu, M., Jia, F., Ma, F., Zhang, J.: ϵ-weakened robustness of deep neural networks. In: Ryu, S., Smaragdakis, Y. (eds.) 31st ACM SIGSOFT International Symposium on Software Testing and Analysis, ISSTA 2022, Virtual Event, South Korea, 18–22 July 2022, pp. 126–138. ACM (2022)

11. Huang, P., et al.: Achieving verified robustness to symbol substitutions via interval bound propagation. In: Proceedings of the 2019 Conference on Empirical Methods in Natural Language Processing and the 9th International Joint Conference on Natural Language Processing, EMNLP-IJCNLP 2019, Hong Kong, China, 3–7 November 2019, pp. 4081–4091 (2019)

12. Huang, P., et al.: Achieving verified robustness to symbol substitutions via interval bound propagation. In: Inui, K., Jiang, J., Ng, V., Wan, X. (eds.) Proceedings of the 2019 Conference on Empirical Methods in Natural Language Processing and the 9th International Joint Conference on Natural Language Processing, EMNLP-IJCNLP 2019, Hong Kong, China, 3–7 November 2019, pp. 4081–4091. Association for Computational Linguistics (2019)

13. Jia, R., Raghunathan, A., Göksel, K., Liang, P.: Certified robustness to adversarial word substitutions. In: Proceedings of the 2019 Conference on Empirical Methods in Natural Language Processing and the 9th International Joint Conference on Natural Language Processing, EMNLP-IJCNLP 2019, Hong Kong, China, 3–7 November 2019, pp. 4127–4140 (2019)

14. Jin, D., Jin, Z., Zhou, J.T., Szolovits, P.: Is BERT really robust? A strong baseline for natural language attack on text classification and entailment. In: The Thirty-Fourth AAAI Conference on Artificial Intelligence, AAAI 2020, New York, NY, USA, 7–12 February 2020, pp. 8018–8025 (2020)

15. Katz, G., Barrett, C., Dill, D.L., Julian, K., Kochenderfer, M.J.: Reluplex: an efficient SMT solver for verifying deep neural networks. In: Majumdar, R., Kunčak, V. (eds.) CAV 2017. LNCS, vol. 10426, pp. 97–117. Springer, Cham (2017). https://doi.org/10.1007/978-3-319-63387-9_5

16. Li, L., Ma, R., Guo, Q., Xue, X., Qiu, X.: BERT-ATTACK: adversarial attack against BERT using BERT. In: Webber, B., Cohn, T., He, Y., Liu, Y. (eds.) Proceedings of the 2020 Conference on Empirical Methods in Natural Language Processing, EMNLP 2020, Online, 16–20 November 2020, pp. 6193–6202. Association for Computational Linguistics (2020). https://doi.org/10.18653/v1/2020.emnlp-main.500. https://doi.org/10.18653/v1/2020.emnlp-main.500

17. Li, L., Ma, R., Guo, Q., Xue, X., Qiu, X.: BERT-ATTACK: adversarial attack against BERT using BERT. In: Proceedings of the 2020 Conference on Empirical Methods in Natural Language Processing, EMNLP 2020, Online, 16–20 November 2020, pp. 6193–6202 (2020)
18. Liang, B., Li, H., Su, M., Bian, P., Li, X., Shi, W.: Deep text classification can be fooled. In: Proceedings of the Twenty-Seventh International Joint Conference on Artificial Intelligence, IJCAI 2018, 13–19 July 2018, Stockholm, Sweden, pp. 4208–4215 (2018)
19. Maas, A.L., Daly, R.E., Pham, P.T., Huang, D., Ng, A.Y., Potts, C.: Learning word vectors for sentiment analysis. In: The 49th Annual Meeting of the Association for Computational Linguistics: Human Language Technologies, Proceedings of the Conference, 19–24 June, 2011, Portland, Oregon, USA, pp. 142–150 (2011)
20. Madry, A., Makelov, A., Schmidt, L., Tsipras, D., Vladu, A.: Towards deep learning models resistant to adversarial attacks. In: 6th International Conference on Learning Representations, ICLR 2018, Conference Track Proceedings, Vancouver, BC, Canada, 30 April–3 May 2018 (2018)
21. Malfa, E.L., Wu, M., Laurenti, L., Wang, B., Hartshorn, A., Kwiatkowska, M.: Assessing robustness of text classification through maximal safe radius computation. In: Findings of the Association for Computational Linguistics: EMNLP 2020, Online Event, 16–20 November 2020, pp. 2949–2968 (2020)
22. Neekhara, P., Hussain, S., Dubnov, S., Koushanfar, F.: Adversarial reprogramming of text classification neural networks. In: Proceedings of the 2019 Conference on Empirical Methods in Natural Language Processing and the 9th International Joint Conference on Natural Language Processing, EMNLP-IJCNLP 2019, Hong Kong, China, 3–7 November 2019, pp. 5215–5224 (2019)
23. Pang, B., Lee, L.: Seeing stars: exploiting class relationships for sentiment categorization with respect to rating scales. In: Proceedings of the Conference on 43rd Annual Meeting of the Association for Computational Linguistics, ACL 2005, University of Michigan, USA, 25–30 June 2005, pp. 115–124 (2005)
24. Pennington, J., Socher, R., Manning, C.D.: GloVe: global vectors for word representation. In: Proceedings of the 2014 Conference on Empirical Methods in Natural Language Processing, EMNLP 2014, Doha, Qatar, A meeting of SIGDAT, a Special Interest Group of the ACL, 25–29 October 2014, pp. 1532–1543 (2014)
25. Ren, S., Deng, Y., He, K., Che, W.: Generating natural language adversarial examples through probability weighted word saliency. In: Proceedings of the 57th Conference of the Association for Computational Linguistics, ACL 2019, Florence, Italy, 28 July–2 August 2019, Volume 1: Long Papers, pp. 1085–1097 (2019)
26. Ribeiro, M.T., Singh, S., Guestrin, C.: Semantically equivalent adversarial rules for debugging NLP models. In: Proceedings of the 56th Annual Meeting of the Association for Computational Linguistics, ACL 2018, Melbourne, Australia, 15–20 July 2018, Volume 1: Long Papers, pp. 856–865 (2018)
27. Sato, M., Suzuki, J., Shindo, H., Matsumoto, Y.: Interpretable adversarial perturbation in input embedding space for text. In: Proceedings of the Twenty-Seventh International Joint Conference on Artificial Intelligence, IJCAI 2018, Stockholm, Sweden, 13–19 July 2018, pp. 4323–4330 (2018)
28. Shi, Z., Zhang, H., Chang, K., Huang, M., Hsieh, C.: Robustness verification for transformers. In: 8th International Conference on Learning Representations, ICLR 2020, Addis Ababa, Ethiopia, 26–30 April 2020 (2020)
29. Stutz, D., Hein, M., Schiele, B.: Disentangling adversarial robustness and generalization. In: IEEE Conference on Computer Vision and Pattern Recognition, CVPR 2019, Long Beach, CA, USA, 16–20 June 2019, pp. 6976–6987 (2019)

30. Wang, X., Yang, Y., Deng, Y., He, K.: Adversarial training with fast gradient projection method against synonym substitution based text attacks. In: Thirty-Fifth AAAI Conference on Artificial Intelligence, AAAI 2021, Thirty-Third Conference on Innovative Applications of Artificial Intelligence, IAAI 2021, The Eleventh Symposium on Educational Advances in Artificial Intelligence, EAAI 2021, Virtual Event, 2–9 February 2021, pp. 13997–14005. AAAI Press (2021)

31. Yang, Y., Huang, P., Cao, J., Jintao Li, Y.L., Ma, F.: A prompt-based approach to adversarial example generation and robustness enhancement. Front. Comput. Sci. **18**(4), 184318 (2024)

32. Yang, Y., Lei, W., Huang, P., Cao, J., Li, J., Chua, T.: A dual prompt learning framework for few-shot dialogue state tracking. In: Proceedings of the ACM Web Conference 2023, WWW 2023, Austin, TX, USA, 30 April 2023–4 May 2023, pp. 1468–1477. ACM (2023)

33. Ye, M., Gong, C., Liu, Q.: SAFER: A structure-free approach for certified robustness to adversarial word substitutions. In: Proceedings of the 58th Annual Meeting of the Association for Computational Linguistics, ACL 2020, Online, 5–10 July 2020, pp. 3465–3475 (2020)

34. Zang, Y., et al.: Word-level textual adversarial attacking as combinatorial optimization. In: Proceedings of the 58th Annual Meeting of the Association for Computational Linguistics, ACL 2020, Online, 5–10 July 2020, pp. 6066–6080 (2020)

35. Zhu, C., Cheng, Y., Gan, Z., Sun, S., Goldstein, T., Liu, J.: FreeLB: enhanced adversarial training for natural language understanding. In: 8th International Conference on Learning Representations, ICLR 2020, Addis Ababa, Ethiopia, 26–30 April 2020 (2020)

Enhancing Adversarial Training
via Reweighting Optimization Trajectory

Tianjin Huang[1]([✉]), Shiwei Liu[2], Tianlong Chen[2], Meng Fang[1,3], Li Shen[4],
Vlado Menkovski[1], Lu Yin[1], Yulong Pei[1], and Mykola Pechenizkiy[1]

[1] Eindhoven University of Technology, Eindhoven, The Netherlands
{t.huang,v.menkovski,l.yin,y.pei.1,m.penchenizkiy}@tue.nl
[2] University of Texas at Austin, Austin, USA
shiwei.liu@austin.utexas.edu, tianlong.chen@utexas.edu
[3] University of Liverpool, Liverpool, UK
mfang@liverpool.ac.uk
[4] JD Explore Academy, Beijing, China

Abstract. Despite the fact that adversarial training has become the de facto method for improving the robustness of deep neural networks, it is well-known that vanilla adversarial training suffers from daunting robust overfitting, resulting in unsatisfactory robust generalization. A number of approaches have been proposed to address these drawbacks such as extra regularization, adversarial weights perturbation, and training with more data over the last few years. However, the robust generalization improvement is yet far from satisfactory. In this paper, we approach this challenge with a brand new perspective – refining historical optimization trajectories. We propose a new method named **Weighted Optimization Trajectories (WOT)** that leverages the optimization trajectories of adversarial training in time. We have conducted extensive experiments to demonstrate the effectiveness of WOT under various state-of-the-art adversarial attacks. Our results show that WOT integrates seamlessly with the existing adversarial training methods and consistently overcomes the robust overfitting issue, resulting in better adversarial robustness. For example, WOT boosts the robust accuracy of AT-PGD under AA-L_∞ attack by 1.53%–6.11% and meanwhile increases the clean accuracy by 0.55%–5.47% across SVHN, CIFAR-10, CIFAR-100, and Tiny-ImageNet datasets.

Keywords: Adversarial training · Optimization trajectories

1 Introduction

Deep neural networks (DNNs) have achieved enormous breakthroughs in various fields, e.g., image classification [22,23], speech recognition [23], object detection [19] and etc. However, it has been shown that they are vulnerable to adversarial examples, i.e., carefully crafted imperceptible perturbations on

---

T. Huang, S, Liu and T. Chen—These authors contributed equally to this research.

D. Koutra et al. (Eds.): ECML PKDD 2023, LNAI 14169, pp. 113–130, 2023.
https://doi.org/10.1007/978-3-031-43412-9_7

inputs can easily change the prediction of the model [20,44]. The vulnerability of DNNs hinders their applications in risk-sensitive tasks such as face recognition, autonomous driving, and medical diagnostics. While various methods have been proposed to obtain robustness against adversarial perturbations, adversarial training [29] is the leading approach to achieve adversarial robustness.

However, the vanilla adversarial training usually suffers from daunting robust overfitting, resulting in poor robust generalization[1] [37]. To tackle this issue, a number of methods from different perspectives have been proposed including but not limited to training with more data [1,6,36,39,40], adversarial weights perturbation [48,50], and knowledge distillation and stochastic weights averaging (SWA) [7]. Recently, [43] empirically show that the improved adversarial robustness can be attributed to the flatter loss landscape at the minima.

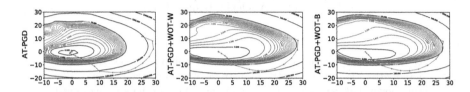

Fig. 1. Visualization of loss contours and optimization trajectories for AT-PGD, AT-PGD+WOT-W, and AT-PGD+WOT-B, respectively. The experiments are conducted on CIFAR-10 with PreRN-18.

Although the generalization properties of SGD-based optimizer under standard training setting have been well studied [16,21,52,56], the corresponding robust generalization property under adversarial setting has not been fully explored. Among previous studies, [7] heuristically adopts stochastic weight averaging (SWA) and average model weights along the optimization trajectory, which potentially mitigates robust overfitting. However, it has been shown that naive weight averaging is not general enough to fundamentally address this problem, still prone to robust overfitting [36]. Instead of simply averaging weights, we propose a new approach - **Weighted Optimization Trajectories** (briefly **WOT**) for the first time showing that we can largely improve the flatness of solutions of existing adversarial training variants by periodically refining a set of historical optimization trajectories. Compared with the existing approaches, our method has three unique design contributions: ❶ our refinement is obtained by maximizing the robust accuracy on the <u>unseen hold-out set</u>, which is naturally advantageous to address the overfitting issue; ❷ our refinement is performed on a set of previous optimization trajectories rather than solely on previous weights; ❸ we further propose a block-wise trajectory refinement, which significantly enlarges the optimization space of refinement, leading to better robust performance. We conduct rigorous experiments to demonstrate the effectiveness

---

[1] Robust generalization refers to the gap between the adversarial accuracy of the training set and test set, following previous work [7,43,48].

of these design novelties in Sect. 4.1 as well as the ablation study in Sect. 4.3. Simple as it looks in Fig. 1, the optimization trajectories after refining converge to a flatter loss valley compared to the vanilla AT-PGD, indicating the improved robust generalization [43,47,48].

Extensive experiments on different architectures and datasets show that WOT seamlessly mingles with the existing adversarial training methods with consistent robust accuracy improvement. For example, WOT-B directly boosts the robust accuracy over AT-PGD (early stops) under AA-L_∞ attack by 6.11%, 1.53%, 1.57%, and 4.38% on SVHN, CIFAR-10, CIFAR-100, and Tiny ImageNet, respectively; meanwhile improves the corresponding clean accuracy by 0.55% $\sim$ 5.47%. Moreover, we show that WOT can completely prevent robust overfitting across different attack approaches, including the strongest one off-the-shelf - AA-L_∞ attack.

2   Related Work

Adversarial Attacks. Adversarial examples were first illustrated in [44]. Following [44], many adversarial attacks have been proposed and can be categorized into white-box and black-box attacks. White-box attacks have full access to the model when crafting adversarial examples. Popular white-box attacks are FGSM attack [20], PGD attack [30], Deepfool [31] and C&W [5]. Black-box attacks generate adversarial examples without any knowledge of the model. They are query-based attacks, e.g., SPSA attack [45], Square attack [2], and transferability-based attacks, e.g., DIM [49], TIM [13] and DA attack [26]. Recently, [11] proposed Autoattack (AA) for reliable adversarial robustness evaluation which is an ensembled adversarial attack containing white-box and black-box attacks. AA attack has been recognized as the most reliable method for evaluating the model's adversarial robustness [11] and will be used as the main evaluation method in this paper.

Adversarial Robustness. Many methods have been proposed to improve the model's robustness such as gradient regularization [38], curvature regularization [24,32], randomized smoothing [9], local linearization [35], adversarial training methods [4,20,25,30,34,46,48,53–55], and etc. Among all these methods, adversarial training has been the de facto method for achieving adversarial robustness. We briefly introduce four commonly used adversarial training methods that we use as baselines in this study.

Given a C-class dataset $S = \{(x_i, y_i)|x_i \in \mathbb{R}^d, y_i \in \mathbb{R}\}_{i=1}^n$, the cross-entropy loss $L(\cdot)$ and the DNN function $f_w : \mathbb{R}^d \to \mathbb{R}^C$.

AT-PGD [30] is formalized as *min-max* optimization problem.

$$\min_w \rho^{AT}(w), \quad \rho^{AT}(w) = \mathbb{E}_{(x,y) \sim S}\{\max_{\|\Delta x\| \le \epsilon} L(f_w(x_i + \Delta x), y_i)\},$$

where the *inner maximization* finds the adversarial examples and ϵ is the allowed perturbation magnitude. We use by default AT to denote AT-PGD in the following sections.

Trades [53] separates training loss into a cross-entropy loss (CE) and Kullback-Leibler (**KL**) divergence loss to control clean accuracy and adversarial robustness respectively.

$$\rho^{TRADES}(w) = \mathbb{E}_{(x,y)\sim S}\{CE(f_w(x_i, y_i) + \beta \cdot \max_{\|\Delta x\|\leq\epsilon} \mathbf{KL}(f_w(x_i)\|f_w(x_i + \Delta x))\}$$

MART [46] designs the training loss as the binary cross-entropy loss (BCE) and an explicit regularization for misclassified examples.

$$\rho^{MART}(w) = \mathbb{E}_{(x,y)\sim S}\{BCE(f_w(x_i + \Delta x), y_i)$$
$$+\lambda \cdot \mathbf{KL}(f_w(x_i)\|f_w(x_i + \Delta x)) \cdot (1 - [f_w(x_i)]_{y_i})\} \tag{1}$$

Adversarial Weights Perturbation (AWP) [48] explicitly flattens the loss landscape by injecting the worst weight perturbations.

$$\rho^{AWP}(w) = \max_{v\in\mathcal{V}} \mathbb{E}_{(x,y)\sim S} \max_{\|\Delta x\|\leq\epsilon} CE(f_{w+v}(x_i + \Delta x), y_i)$$

Robust Overfitting and its Mitigation. [37] first identified the robust overfitting issue in AT that robust accuracy in test set degrades severely after the first learning rate decay and found that early stop is an effective strategy for mitigating the robust overfitting issue. Following [37], several studies have been proposed to explain and mitigate the robust overfitting issue [7,8,14,42,43,48]. [7] showed that stochastic weight averaging (SWA) and knowledge distillation can mitigate the robust overfitting issue decently and [42] found that low curvature activation function helps to mitigate the robust overfitting problem. [14] took a step further to explain that the robust overfitting issue may be caused by the memorization of hard samples in the final phase of training. [43,48,50] demonstrated that a flat loss landscape improves robust generalization and reduces the robust overfitting problem, which is in line with the sharpness studies in standard training setting [15,18,27].

3   Methodology

In this section, we will introduce **weighted optimization trajectories (WOT)**, a carefully designed method that refines the optimization trajectory of adversarial training towards a flatter region in the training loss landscape, to avoid robust overfitting. Specifically, WOT collects a set of historical optimization trajectories and further learns a weighted combination of them explicitly on the unseen set. The sketch map of WOT is shown in Fig. 2. Concretely, WOT contains two steps: (1) collect optimization trajectories of adversarial training. (2) re-weight collected optimization trajectories and optimize weights according to the robust loss on an unseen set. Two unanswered problems of this process are how to collect optimization trajectories and how to construct the objective function of optimizing weights. We give detailed solutions as follows.

3.1 WOT: Optimization Trajectories

We denote optimization trajectories as the consecutively series status of weights in weight space after n steps optimization. Formally, given a deep neural network f with the parameter $w \in \mathcal{W}$. n steps of optimization trajectories of adversarial training are denoted as $\{w^1, w^2...w^i, ..., w^n\}$ where w^i is the weight after the i-th optimization step. This process can also be simplified as follows: $\{w^1, \Delta w^1...\Delta w^i, ..., \Delta w^{n-1}\}$ where $\Delta w^i = w^{i+1} - w^i$. In practice, it is time-consuming and space-consuming to collect the weights of

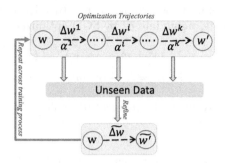

Fig. 2. Sketch map of WOT.

each batch optimization step and it is also not necessary to collect the weights at a high frequency (see details in Fig. 5). Therefore, we propose to collect weights for every m batch optimization step and the collected trajectories with n optimization steps are re-denoted as follows:

$$\Delta W = \{w^1, \Delta w^1, ..., \Delta w^i, ..., \Delta w^k\}, \tag{2}$$

where $k = \frac{n}{m}$. For brevity, we call m the Gaps that control the length between two consecutive collections and k the number of Gaps that controls the number of weights that are collected.

3.2 WOT: Objective Function

We design the objective function based on historical optimization trajectories of model training. From the description of optimization trajectories introduced above, the weights w' with n batch optimization steps from w can be written as $w' = w + \Delta w^1 + ... + \Delta w^i + .. + \Delta w^k$. Since WOT refines the optimization trajectories by re-weighting them, the new model weights $\widetilde{w'}$ after refining optimization trajectories can be expressed as follows:

$$\widetilde{w'} = w + \widetilde{\Delta w}, \quad \widetilde{\Delta w} = \alpha^1 \Delta w^1 + ... + \alpha^i \Delta w^i + ... + \alpha^k \Delta w^k, \tag{3}$$

where $\alpha^1, ..., \alpha^i, ..., \alpha^k$ are optimizable variables. Considering that we expect to find the model with better robust generalization via optimizing α, a straightforward idea is to optimize α^i with respect to improving its robust performance on a small unseen set. The philosophy for this idea is that if a model can generalize robustness better to an unseen set, it would probably generalize robustness well to the target unseen set.

Formally, the **objective function** of optimizing α^i is defined as follows:

$$\min_{0 \leq \alpha^i \leq 1} \max_{\|\Delta x_{uns}\| \leq \epsilon} L(f_{w+\widetilde{\Delta w}}(x_{uns} + \Delta x_{uns}), y_{uns}), \tag{4}$$

where (x_{uns}, y_{uns}) is from an unseen set and Δx_{uns} is the corresponding adversarial perturbations. We constrain α^i to [0,1] (see Appendix F[2] for the results of other constraints for α^i). **Update** α^i. α^i can be optimized by any SGD-based optimizers according to the objective function (Eq. 4) described above. In this study, we update α^i by SGD optimizer with momentum buffer.

$$m^t = m^{t-1} \cdot \gamma + \nabla_{\alpha^i} L(f_{w^{i-1}+\widetilde{\Delta w}}(x_{uns} + \Delta x_{uns}), y_{uns}) \qquad (5)$$

$$\alpha^i = \alpha^i - lr \cdot m^t, \qquad (6)$$

where m^t is the momentum buffer of α^i at the t-th step and lr is the learning rate.

Table 1. Robust accuracy of WOT under multiple adversarial attacks with various adversarial training variants. The experiments are conducted on CIFAR-10 with the PreRN-18 architecture. The best results are marked in bold.

MODELS	FGSM	PGD-20	PGD-100	CW$_\infty$	AA-L_∞
AT+EARLY STOP	57.30	52.90	51.90	50.90	47.43
AT+SWA	58.89	53.02	51.86	52.32	48.61
AT+WOT-W (OURS)	58.50	53.19	51.90	51.74	48.36
AT+WOT-B (OURS)	**59.67**	**54.85**	**53.77**	**52.56**	**48.96**
TRADES	58.16	53.14	52.17	51.24	48.90
TRADES+SWA	58.07	53.17	52.22	50.91	49.07
TRADES+WOT-W (OURS)	**58.95**	**54.07**	**53.29**	51.74	49.95
TRADES+WOT-B (OURS)	58.50	53.73	52.95	**52.12**	**50.19**
MART	59.93	54.07	52.30	50.16	47.01
MART+SWA	58.19	54.21	53.56	49.39	46.86
MART+WOT-W (OURS)	58.13	53.79	52.66	50.24	47.43
MART+WOT-B (OURS)	**59.95**	**55.13**	**54.09**	**50.56**	**47.49**
AT+AWP	59.11	55.45	54.88	52.50	49.65
AT+AWP+SWA	58.23	55.54	54.91	51.88	49.39
AT+AWP+WOT-W (OURS)	59.05	**55.95**	54.96	52.70	49.84
AT+AWP+WOT-B (OURS)	**59.26**	55.69	**55.09**	**52.82**	**50.00**

3.3   WOT: In-Time Refining Optimization Trajectories

WOT reconstructs a set of historical optimization trajectories in time during the course of training on an unseen set to avoid overfitting. A naive strategy is treating each optimization trajectory w^i as a whole and learning an individual

---

[2] Appendix can be found in https://arxiv.org/pdf/2306.14275v2.pdf.

weight for each trajectory shown as Eq. 3. This simple method naturally has limited learning space for refinement especially when we only have a few historical trajectories. To improve the learning space of WOT, we further propose blockwise WOT which breaks down each trajectory into multiple blocks based on the original block design of the model itself. For convenience, we dot these two methods WOT-W and WOT-B, respectively.

WOT-W takes one trajectory as whole and assigns a single α for each trajectory. Hence the number of α that need to be learned exactly equals to the number of Gaps:k.

WOT-B in contrast learns a vector of α whose length is determined by the number of the model's block. Therefore, Eq. 3 can be reformulated as:

$$\widetilde{\Delta w} = \begin{bmatrix} \widetilde{\Delta w_1} \\ ... \\ \widetilde{\Delta w_j} \\ ... \\ \widetilde{\Delta w_t} \end{bmatrix}, \quad \widetilde{\Delta w_j} = \alpha_j^1 \Delta w_j^1 + \alpha_j^2 \Delta w_j^2 + ... + \alpha_j^k \Delta w_j^k \tag{7}$$

where j denotes the j-th block. Optimizing α for blockwise WOT is exactly the same as the description in Eq. 5 and Eq. 6.

The main difference between WOT-W and WOT-B is that WOT-W learns one α for each cached Δw (the difference of parameters in two checkpoints) whereas WOT-B further breakdowns each cached Δw into several blocks (each block contains several layers depending on the specific architectures as explained in detail in Appendix B) and learns an individual α value for each block. Therefore, the learning space of WOT-B is larger than WOT-W, leading to better performance in general. The pseudocode of WOT can be found in Appendix C.

4 Experiments

We perform extensive experiments to show the effectiveness of our method in improving adversarial robustness as well as addressing the robust overfitting issue.

Datasets. Four datasets are considered in our experiments: CIFAR-10, CIFAR-100 [28], Tiny-ImageNet [12] and SVHN [33]. For experiments of WOT, we randomly split 1000 samples from the original CIFAR-10 training set, 10000 samples from Tiny-ImageNet, and 2000 samples from the original CIFAR-100 and SVHN training set as the unseen hold-out sets.

Baselines. Five baselines are included: AT [37], Trades [53], AWP+AT [48], MART [46] and SWA [7]. Three architectures including VGG-16 [41], PreActResNet-18 (PreRN-18) [22], WideResNet-34-10 (WRN-34-10) [51].

Experimental Setting. For WOT, we adopt an SGD optimizer with a momentum of 0.9, weight decay of 5e-4, and a total epoch of 200 with a batch size of 128 following [37]. By default, we start to refine optimization trajectories after 100 epochs. For WOT-B, we set each block in PreRN-18 and WRN-34-10 architectures as the independent weight space. We set the layers with the same width

Table 2. Test robustness under multiple adversarial attacks based on VGG-16/WRN-34-10 architectures. The experiments are conducted on CIFAR-10 with AT and Trades. The bold denotes the best performance.

Architecture	Method	CW_∞	PGD-20	PGD-100	AA-L_∞
VGG16	AT+EARLY STOP	46.87	49.95	46.87	43.63
VGG16	AT+SWA	47.01	49.58	49.13	43.89
VGG16	AT+WOT-W(OURS)	47.42	49.96	49.36	44.01
VGG16	AT+WOT-B(OURS)	**47.52**	**50.28**	**49.58**	**44.10**
VGG16	TRADES	45.47	48.24	47.54	43.64
VGG16	TRADES+SWA	45.92	48.64	47.86	44.12
VGG16	TRADES+WOT-W(OURS)	**46.75**	**49.19**	**48.28**	**44.82**
VGG16	TRADES+WOT-B(OURS)	46.21	48.81	47.85	44.17
WRN-34-10	AT+EARLY STOP	53.82	55.06	53.96	51.77
WRN-34-10	AT+SWA	56.04	55.34	53.61	52.25
WRN-34-10	AT+WOT-W(OURS)	56.05	58.21	57.11	52.88
WRN-34-10	AT+WOT-B(OURS)	**57.13**	**60.15**	**59.38**	**53.89**
WRN-34-10	TRADES	54.20	56.33	56.07	53.08
WRN-34-10	TRADES+SWA	54.55	54.95	53.08	51.43
WRN-34-10	TRADES+WOT-W(OURS)	56.10	57.56	56.20	53.68
WRN-34-10	TRADES+WOT-B(OURS)	**56.62**	**57.92**	**56.80**	**54.33**

as a group and set each group as an independent block for VGG-16 (see details in Appendix B). We by default set the gaps m to 400, the number of gaps k to 4 and initialize α as zero. For all baselines, we use the training setups and hyperparameters exactly the same as their papers (see details in Appendix A).

Evaluation Setting. We use AA attack [11] as our main adversarial robustness evaluation method. AA attack is a parameter-free ensembled adversarial attack that contains three white-box attacks: APGD-CE [11], APGD-T [11], FAB-T [10] and one black-box attack: Square attack [2]. To the best of our knowledge, AA attack is currently the most reliable adversarial attack for evaluating adversarial robustness. We also adopt three other commonly used white-box adversarial attacks: FGSM [20], PGD-20/100 [29] and C&W$_\infty$ attack [5]. Besides, we also report the performance of query-based SPSA black-box attack [45] (100 iterations with a learning rate of 0.01 and 256 samples for each gradient estimation). By default, we report the mean of three random runs for all experiments of our method and omit the standard deviation since it is very small ($\leq 0.3\%$). We by default set $\epsilon = 8/255$ for L_∞ version adversarial attack and $\epsilon = 64/255$ for L_2 version adversarial attack.

4.1 Superior Performance in Improving Adversarial Robustness

We evaluate the effectiveness of WOT in improving adversarial robustness across AT and three of its variants, four popular used datasets, i.e., SVHN, CIFAR-10,

Table 3. Test robustness under AA-L_2 and AA-L_∞ attacks across various datasets. The experiments are based on PreRN-18 and AT. The bold denotes the best performance.

ATTACK	METHOD	SVHN	CIFAR-10	CIFAR-100	TINY-IMAGENET
L_∞	AT+EARLY STOP	45.72	47.43	23.69	14.39
L_∞	AT+SWA	40.24	48.61	23.90	17.94
L_∞	AT+WOT-W(OURS)	50.42	48.36	24.41	17.10
L_∞	AT+WOT-B(OURS)	**51.83**	**48.96**	**25.26**	**18.77**
L_2	AT+EARLY STOP	72.13	71.30	42.75	36.61
L_2	AT+SWA	67.76	73.28	43.10	42.40
L_2	AT+WOT-W(OURS)	72.75	73.20	**43.88**	42.43
L_2	AT+WOT-B(OURS)	**72.80**	**73.39**	43.32	**42.54**

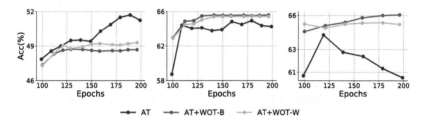

Fig. 3. Robust accuracy under black-box attack over epochs. **(Left)** Robust accuracy on the unseen robust model transfer attacked from checkpoints of AT, AT+WOT-W/B. **(Middle)** Robust accuracy on checkpoints of AT, AT+WOT-W/B transfer attacked from the unseen model. **(Right)** Robust accuracy on checkpoints of AT, AT+WOT-W/B under SPSA black-box attack. The experiments are conducted on PreRN-18 and CIFAR-10. The unseen robust model is WRN-34-10 trained by AT.

CIFAR-100 and Tiny-ImageNet, and three architectures, i.e., VGG16, PreRN-18, and WRN-34-10.

WOT Consistently Improves the Adversarial Robustness of All Adversarial Training Variants. In Table 1, we applied WOT-B and WOT-W to AT+early stop, Trades, MART, and AWP variants and compare them with their counterpart baselines. Besides, we add the combination of SWA and these adversarial training variants as one of the baselines. The results show ① WOT consistently improves adversarial robustness among the four adversarial training variants under both weak attacks, e.g. FGSM, PGD-20, and strong attacks, e.g., C&W$_\infty$, AA-L_∞ attacks. ② WOT-B as the WOT variant confirms our hypothesis and consistently performs better than WOT-W. WOT-B improves the robust accuracy over their counterpart baselines by 0.35% ~ 1.53% under AA-L_∞ attack. ③ WOT boosts robust accuracy with a larger margin on AT and Trades than MART and AWP under AA-L_∞ attack. One reason might be that MART and AWP themselves enjoy good ability in mitigating robust over-fitting [43,48], leading to less space for WOT to further boost the performance.

WOT Can Generalize to Different Architectures and Datasets. Table 2 and Table 3 show that WOT consistently outperforms the counterpart base-line under AA-L_∞ attack, which indicates that the effectiveness of WOT generalizes well to different architectures and datasets. In Table 2, WOT boosts robust accuracy by 0.47% ~ 2.12% on VGG16 and WRN-34-10 architectures. In Table 3, WOT improves robust accuracy with 1.53% ~ 6.11% among SVHN, CIFAR-10, CIFAR-100 and Tiny-ImageNet under AA-L_∞ attack. Besides, the success of WOT can also be extended to AA-L_2 attack with the improvement by 0.67% ~ 5.93%.

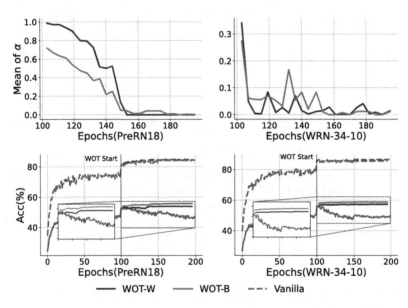

Fig. 4. Mean value of α and results of test robust/clean accuracy over epochs. The experiments are conducted on CIFAR-10 with PreRN-18 based on AT.

Excluding Obfuscated Gradients. [3] claims that obfuscated gradients can also lead to the "counterfeit" of improved robust accuracy under gradients-based white-box attacks. To exclude this possibility, we report the performance of different checkpoints under transfer attack and SPSA black-box attack over epochs. In Fig. 3, the left figure shows robust accuracy of the unseen robust model on the adversarial examples generated by the PreRN-18 model trained by AT, AT+WOT-B, AT+WOT-W respectively with PGD-10 attack on CIFAR-10. A higher robust accuracy on the unseen robust model corresponds to a weaker attack. It can be seen that both AT+WOT-B and AT+WOT-W generate more transferable adversarial examples than AT. Similarly, the middle figure

Table 4. Test robustness under AA-L_∞ attack to show the robust overfitting issue in AT and the effectiveness of WOT in overcoming it. The difference between the best and final checkpoints indicates performance degradation during training and the best checkpoint is chosen by PGD-10 attack on the validation set. The experiments are conducted on CIFAR-10 with PreRN-18/WRN-34-10 architectures.

Architectures	Method	Robust Accuracy(RA)			Standard Accuracy(SA)		
		Best	Final	Diff	Best	Final	Diff
PreRN-18	AT	48.02	42.48	−5.54	81.33	84.40	+3.07
PreRN-18	AT+SWA	48.93	48.61	-0.32	84.19	85.23	+1.04
PreRN-18	AT+WOT-W(Ours)	48.04	48.36	+0.32	84.05	84.47	−0.42
PreRN-18	AT+WOT-B(Ours)	48.90	48.96	+0.06	83.84	83.83	-0.01
WRN-34-10	AT	51.77	46.78	−4.99	85.74	86.34	+0.6
WRN-34-10	AT+SWA	53.38	52.25	−1.13	87.14	88.45	+1.31
WRN-34-10	AT+WOT-W(Ours)	52.84	52.88	+0.04	84.83	84.88	+0.05
WRN-34-10	AT+WOT-B(Ours)	52.23	53.89	+1.66	83.46	85.50	+2.04

shows the robust accuracy of the PreRN-18 model trained by AT, AT+WOT-B, AT+WOT-W on the adversarial examples generated by the unseen robust model. It can be seen that AT+WOT-B and AT+WOT-W can better defend the adversarial examples from the unseen model. What's more, in the right figure, we observe again that both AT+WOT-B and AT+WOT-W outperform AT under SPSA black-box attack over different checkpoints during training. All these empirical results sufficiently suggest that the improved robust accuracy of WOT is not caused by obfuscated gradients.

4.2 Ability to Prevent Robust Overfitting

We report the robust accuracy under AA-L_∞ attack for the best checkpoint and the last checkpoint based on PreRN-18 and WRN-34-10 architectures on CIFAR-10 (Table 4). Besides, we show the robust accuracy curve under PGD-10 attack on different checkpoints over epochs (Fig. 4).

In Fig. 4, the third and fourth figures show that after the first learning rate decay (at 100 epoch), there is a large robust accuracy drop for AT between the best checkpoint and the last checkpoint on both PreRN-18 and WRN-34-10 architectures. In comparison, there is completely no robust accuracy drop for AT+WOT-W/B between the best checkpoint and the last checkpoint on both PreRN-18 and WRN-34-10 architectures. In Table 4, we further show the evidence that there is no robust accuracy drop for AT+WOT-B/W under stronger attack, i.e., AA-L_∞ attack. From the first and second figures of Fig. 4, we observe that the mean of α decreases to a very small value after 150,100 epochs for PreRN-18 and WRN-34-10 respectively. The small mean of α indicates that WOT stops the model's weights from updating with unexpected magnitudes, which prevents the occurrence of robust overfitting.

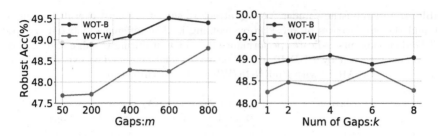

Fig. 5. The impact of gaps m and the number of gaps k on robust accuracy under AA-L_∞ attack. The experiments are conducted on CIFAR-10 with PreRN-18 based on AT. k is fixed to 4 for the left figure and m is fixed to 400 for the right figure.

Table 5. Robust Accuracy of ablation experiments on CIFAR-10 with PreRN-18.

METHODS	PGD-20	PGD-100	CW$_\infty$	AA-L$_\infty$
AT+B1	49.68	47.44	49.04	45.26
AT+B2	52.74	51.28	51.31	48.22
AT+WOT-B+B3 (m=400,k=4)	47.14	44.23	43.87	41.02
AT+WOT-W (m=400,k=4)	53.19	51.90	51.74	48.36
AT+WOT-B (m=400,k=4)	54.85	53.77	52.56	48.96

4.3 Ablations and Visualizations

In this section, we first conduct ablation studies to show the effectiveness of the designed optimization trajectories and the unseen hold-out set in WOT. Then we investigate the impact of gaps:m and the number of gaps:k, the effect of WOT on the loss landscapes w.r.t weight space, and the visualization of α for blocks. The results are shown in Table 5, Fig. 5, and Fig. 6. All experiments in the two figures are conducted on CIFAR-10 with PreRN-18 based on AT except for Fig. 6 where Trades is also included. The robust accuracy is evaluated under AA-L_∞ attack for all three figures.

Ablation Studies. To demonstrate the effectiveness of the designed optimization trajectories and the unseen hold-out set in boosting adversarial robustness, we designed the following baselines: 1) Keep the same unseen hold-out set and training strategy with WOT but optimize model weights instead of α on the unseen hold-out set (Abbreviated as "B1"); 2) Keep the same unseen hold-out set and optimize the hyperparameter of SWA by the hold-out set (Abbreviated as "B2"); 3) Replace the unseen hold-out set with a seen set, i.e. keep the same number of samples from the training set (Abbreviated as "B3"). Results in Table 5 show that ① AT+WOT-W/B outperforms AT+B1 and AT+B2, indicating the designed optimization trajectories play key roles in WOT. ② AT+WOT-W/B outperforms AT+B3 with a large margin, indicating the unseen hold-out set is crucial for WOT.

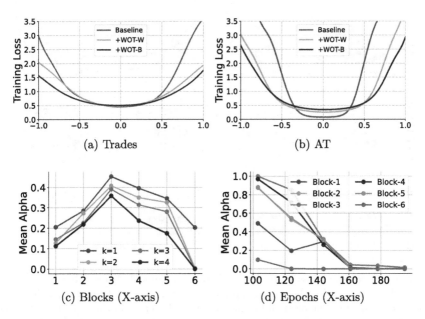

Fig. 6. Loss landscape w.r.t weight space (Fig. 6a and Fig. 6b). z-axis denotes the loss value. We plot the loss landscape following the setting in [48]. The averaged α by averaging along training process (Fig. 6c). The k-averaged α during the training process. (Figure 6d). The experiments are conducted on CIFAR-10 with PreRN-18.

Impact of m and k. Figure 5 shows the impact of gaps m and number of gaps k on robust accuracy under AA-L_∞ attack. In the left figure, we observe that robust accuracy increases with an increase of m. Besides, we find that WOT-W is more sensitive to m than WOT-B. The right figure shows that both WOT-W and WOT-B are not sensitive to the number of gaps k.

Averaged α for Blocks. To shed insights on why WOT-B outperforms WOT-W, we plot the learned α for each block. Experiments are conducted on CIFAR-10 with PreRN-18 based on WOT-B (K=4, m=400). Results in Fig. 6c and Fig. 6d show that the magnitude of learned α are different among blocks. Specifically, WOT-B assigns a large value of α for middle blocks, i.e., Block-2,3,4,5, and a small value of α for the bottom and top blocks, i.e., Block-1,6. This indicates that assigning different weights for different blocks may play a crucial role in boosting adversarial robustness.

Visualizing Loss Landscape. We expect WOT to search flatter minima for adversarial training to boost its robust generalization. We demonstrate that it indeed happens via visualizing the loss landscape with respect to weight space (Fig. 6a and Fig. 6b) and input space (Fig. 7). Figure 6a and Fig. 6b show that WOT+baseline obtains flatter minima than baseline, which indicates an improved robust generalization [43,48]. Figure 7 demonstrates that, compared to AT, WOT achieves a lower loss value as the x-axis and y-axis values increase,

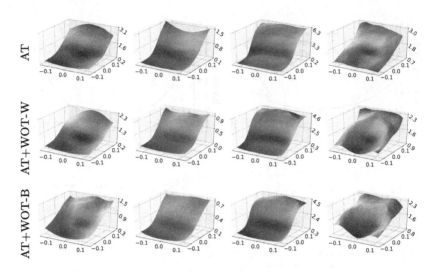

Fig. 7. Comparison of loss landscapes of PreRN-18 models trained by AT (the first row) and our methods (the second and third row). Loss plots in each column are generated from the same original image randomly chosen from the CIFAR-10 test set. z-axis denotes the loss value. Following the setting in [17], we plot the loss landscape function: $z = loss(x \cdot r_1 + y \cdot r_2)$ where $r_1 = sign(\nabla_x f(x))$ and $r_2 \sim Rademacher(0.5)$.

indicating a lower curvature. This finding is consistent with the robust generalization claim presented in [32].

5   Conclusion

In this paper, we propose a new method named weighted optimization trajectories (WOT) for improving adversarial robustness and avoiding robust overfitting. We re-weight the optimization trajectories in time by maximizing the robust performance on an unseen hold-out set during the training process. The comprehensive experiments demonstrate: (1) WOT can effectively improve adversarial robustness across various adversarial training variants, model architectures, and benchmark datasets. (2) WOT enjoys superior performance in mitigating robust overfitting. Moreover, visualizing analysis validates that WOT flattens the loss landscape with respect to input and weight space, showing an improved robust generalization.

Acknowledgement. This work is partially supported by NWO EDIC and EDF KOIOS projects. Part of this work used the Dutch national e-infrastructure with the support of the SURF Cooperative using grant no. NWO2021.060, EINF-5587 and EINF-5587/L1. We would like to express our deepest gratitude to the anonymous reviewers whose insightful comments and suggestions significantly improved the quality of this paper.

Ethical statement. Our proposed method, Weighted Optimization Trajectories (WOT), enhances the robustness of deep neural networks against adversarial attacks. While the primary goal is to improve AI system security, it is crucial to consider the ethical implications of our work:

— Personal Data Protection: Researchers and practitioners must ensure proper data handling, privacy, and compliance with data protection laws when working with personal data

— Privacy Preservation: Improved robustness could inadvertently increase the capacity to infer personal information from data. Privacy-preserving techniques, like differential privacy, should be employed to mitigate these risks.

References

1. Alayrac, J.B., Uesato, J., Huang, P.S., Fawzi, A., Stanforth, R., Kohli, P.: Are labels required for improving adversarial robustness?. In: Advances in Neural Information Processing Systems 32 (2019)
2. Andriushchenko, M., Croce, F., Flammarion, N., Hein, M.: Square attack: a query-efficient black-box adversarial attack via random search. In: Vedaldi, A., Bischof, H., Brox, T., Frahm, J.-M. (eds.) ECCV 2020. LNCS, vol. 12368, pp. 484–501. Springer, Cham (2020). https://doi.org/10.1007/978-3-030-58592-1_29
3. Athalye, A., Carlini, N., Wagner, D.: Obfuscated gradients give a false sense of security: Circumventing defenses to adversarial examples. arXiv preprint arXiv:1802.00420 (2018)
4. Balaji, Y., Goldstein, T., Hoffman, J.: Instance adaptive adversarial training: Improved accuracy tradeoffs in neural nets. arXiv preprint arXiv:1910.08051 (2019)
5. Carlini, N., Wagner, D.: Towards evaluating the robustness of neural networks. In: 2017 IEEE Symposium on Security and Privacy (SP), pp. 39–57. IEEE (2017)
6. Carmon, Y., Raghunathan, A., Schmidt, L., Duchi, J.C., Liang, P.S.: Unlabeled data improves adversarial robustness. In: Advances in Neural Information Processing Systems 32 (2019)
7. Chen, T., Zhang, Z., Liu, S., Chang, S., Wang, Z.: Robust overfitting may be mitigated by properly learned smoothening. In: International Conference on Learning Representations (2020)
8. Chen, T., et al.: Sparsity winning twice: Better robust generaliztion from more efficient training. arXiv preprint arXiv:2202.09844 (2022)
9. Cohen, J.M., Rosenfeld, E., Kolter, J.Z.: Certified adversarial robustness via randomized smoothing. arXiv preprint arXiv:1902.02918 (2019)
10. Croce, F., Hein, M.: Minimally distorted adversarial examples with a fast adaptive boundary attack. In: International Conference on Machine Learning, pp. 2196–2205. PMLR (2020)
11. Croce, F., Hein, M.: Reliable evaluation of adversarial robustness with an ensemble of diverse parameter-free attacks. In: International Conference on Machine Learning, pp. 2206–2216. PMLR (2020)
12. Deng, J., Dong, W., Socher, R., Li, L.J., Li, K., Fei-Fei, L.: Imagenet: a large-scale hierarchical image database. In: 2009 IEEE Conference on Computer Vision and Pattern Recognition, pp. 248–255. IEEE (2009)
13. Dong, Y., Pang, T., Su, H., Zhu, J.: Evading defenses to transferable adversarial examples by translation-invariant attacks. In: Proceedings of the IEEE/CVF Conference on Computer Vision and Pattern Recognition, pp. 4312–4321 (2019)

14. Dong, Y., et al.: Exploring memorization in adversarial training. arXiv preprint arXiv:2106.01606 (2021)
15. Dziugaite, G.K., Roy, D.M.: Computing nonvacuous generalization bounds for deep (stochastic) neural networks with many more parameters than training data. arXiv preprint arXiv:1703.11008 (2017)
16. Elisseeff, A., Evgeniou, T., Pontil, M., Kaelbing, L.P.: Stability of randomized learning algorithms. J. Mach. Learn. Res. 6(1) (2005)
17. Engstrom, L., Ilyas, A., Athalye, A.: Evaluating and understanding the robustness of adversarial logit pairing. arXiv preprint arXiv:1807.10272 (2018)
18. Foret, P., Kleiner, A., Mobahi, H., Neyshabur, B.: Sharpness-aware minimization for efficiently improving generalization. arXiv preprint arXiv:2010.01412 (2020)
19. Girshick, R., Donahue, J., Darrell, T., Malik, J.: Rich feature hierarchies for accurate object detection and semantic segmentation. In: Proceedings of the IEEE Computer Society Conference on Computer Vision and Pattern Recognition (2014). https://doi.org/10.1109/CVPR.2014.81
20. Goodfellow, I.J., Shlens, J., Szegedy, C.: Explaining and Harnessing Adversarial Examples (Dec 2014). arxiv.org/abs/1412.6572
21. Hardt, M., Recht, B., Singer, Y.: Train faster, generalize better: Stability of stochastic gradient descent. In: International Conference on Machine Learning, pp. 1225–1234. PMLR (2016)
22. He, K., Zhang, X., Ren, S., Sun, J.: Deep residual learning for image recognition. In: Proceedings of the IEEE Conference on Computer Vision and Pattern Recognition, pp. 770–778 (2016)
23. Hinton, G., et al.: Deep neural networks for acoustic modeling in speech recognition. IEEE Signal Process. Mag. (2012). https://doi.org/10.1109/MSP.2012.2205597
24. Huang, T., Menkovski, V., Pei, Y., Pechenizkiy, M.: Bridging the performance gap between fgsm and pgd adversarial training. arXiv preprint arXiv:2011.05157 (2020)
25. Huang, T., Menkovski, V., Pei, Y., Pechenizkiy, M.: Calibrated adversarial training. In: Asian Conference on Machine Learning, pp. 626–641. PMLR (2021)
26. Huang, T., Menkovski, V., Pei, Y., Wang, Y., Pechenizkiy, M.: Direction-aggregated attack for transferable adversarial examples. ACM J. Emerging Technol. Comput. Syst. (JETC) 18(3), 1–22 (2022)
27. Jiang, Y., Neyshabur, B., Mobahi, H., Krishnan, D., Bengio, S.: Fantastic generalization measures and where to find them. arXiv preprint arXiv:1912.02178 (2019)
28. Krizhevsky, A., Nair, V., Hinton, G.: Cifar-10 (canadian institute for advanced research). https://www.cs.toronto.edu/~kriz/cifar.html (2010)
29. Madry, A., Makelov, A., Schmidt, L., Tsipras, D., Vladu, A.: Towards deep learning models resistant to adversarial attacks. arXiv preprint arXiv:1706.06083 (2017)
30. Madry, A., Makelov, A., Schmidt, L., Tsipras, D., Vladu, A.: Towards Deep Learning Models Resistant to Adversarial Attacks, arxiv.org/abs/1706.06083 (Jun 2017)
31. Moosavi-Dezfooli, S.M., Fawzi, A., Frossard, P.: DeepFool: a simple and accurate method to fool deep neural networks. In: Proceedings of the IEEE Computer Society Conference on Computer Vision and Pattern Recognition, vol. 2016-Decem, pp. 2574–2582. IEEE Computer Society (Dec 2016). https://doi.org/10.1109/CVPR.2016.282
32. Moosavi-Dezfooli, S.M., Fawzi, A., Uesato, J., Frossard, P.: Robustness via curvature regularization, and vice versa, arXiv: 1811.09716 (Nov 2018)
33. Netzer, Y., Wang, T., Coates, A., Bissacco, A., Wu, B., Ng, A.Y.: Reading digits in natural images with unsupervised feature learning (2011)
34. Pang, T., Lin, M., Yang, X., Zhu, J., Yan, S.: Robustness and accuracy could be reconcilable by (proper) definition. arXiv preprint arXiv:2202.10103 (2022)

35. Qin, C., et al.: Adversarial Robustness through Local Linearization, arXiv: 1907.02610 (Jul 2019) '
36. Rebuffi, S.A., Gowal, S., Calian, D.A., Stimberg, F., Wiles, O., Mann, T.: Fixing data augmentation to improve adversarial robustness. arXiv preprint arXiv:2103.01946 (2021)
37. Rice, L., Wong, E., Kolter, Z.: Overfitting in adversarially robust deep learning. In: International Conference on Machine Learning, pp. 8093–8104. PMLR (2020)
38. Ross, A., Doshi-Velez, F.: Improving the adversarial robustness and interpretability of deep neural networks by regularizing their input gradients. In: Proceedings of the AAAI Conference on Artificial Intelligence, vol. 32 (2018)
39. Schmidt, L., Santurkar, S., Tsipras, D., Talwar, K., Madry, A.: Adversarially robust generalization requires more data. In: Advances in Neural Information Processing Systems, pp. 5014–5026 (2018)
40. Sehwag, V., et al.: Robust learning meets generative models: Can proxy distributions improve adversarial robustness? arXiv preprint arXiv:2104.09425 (2021)
41. Simonyan, K., Zisserman, A.: Very deep convolutional networks for large-scale image recognition. arXiv preprint arXiv:1409.1556 (2014)
42. Singla, V., Singla, S., Feizi, S., Jacobs, D.: Low curvature activations reduce overfitting in adversarial training. In: Proceedings of the IEEE/CVF International Conference on Computer Vision, pp. 16423–16433 (2021)
43. Stutz, D., Hein, M., Schiele, B.: Relating adversarially robust generalization to flat minima. In: Proceedings of the IEEE/CVF International Conference on Computer Vision, pp. 7807–7817 (2021)
44. Szegedy, C., et al.: Intriguing properties of neural networks, arXiv: 1312.6199 (dec 2013)
45. Uesato, J., O'donoghue, B., Kohli, P., Oord, A.: Adversarial risk and the dangers of evaluating against weak attacks. In: International Conference on Machine Learning, pp. 5025–5034. PMLR (2018)
46. Wang, Y., Zou, D., Yi, J., Bailey, J., Ma, X., Gu, Q.: Improving adversarial robustness requires revisiting misclassified examples. In: International Conference on Learning Representations (2020)
47. Wu, D., Wang, Y., Xia, S.T.: Revisiting loss landscape for adversarial robustness. arXiv preprint arXiv:2004.05884 (2020)
48. Wu, D., Xia, S.T., Wang, Y.: Adversarial weight perturbation helps robust generalization. In: Advances in Neural Information Processing Systems 33 (2020)
49. Xie, C., et al.: Improving transferability of adversarial examples with input diversity. In: Proceedings of the IEEE/CVF Conference on Computer Vision and Pattern Recognition, pp. 2730–2739 (2019)
50. Yu, C., et al.: Robust weight perturbation for adversarial training (2021)
51. Zagoruyko, S., Komodakis, N.: Wide residual networks. arXiv preprint arXiv:1605.07146 (2016)
52. Zhang, C., et al.: Musings on deep learning: Properties of sgd. Tech. rep, Center for Brains, Minds and Machines (CBMM) (2017)
53. Zhang, H., Yu, Y., Jiao, J., Xing, E., El Ghaoui, L., Jordan, M.: Theoretically principled trade-off between robustness and accuracy. In: International Conference on Machine Learning, pp. 7472–7482. PMLR (2019)
54. Zhang, J., et a;.: Attacks which do not kill training make adversarial learning stronger. In: International Conference on Machine Learning, pp. 11278–11287. PMLR (2020)

55. Zhang, J., Zhu, J., Niu, G., Han, B., Sugiyama, M., Kankanhalli, M.: Geometry-aware instance-reweighted adversarial training. arXiv preprint arXiv:2010.01736 (2020)
56. Zhou, Y., Liang, Y., Zhang, H.: Generalization error bounds with probabilistic guarantee for sgd in nonconvex optimization. arXiv preprint arXiv:1802.06903 (2018)

Adversarial Imitation Learning with Controllable Rewards for Text Generation

Keizaburo Nishikino[✉] and Kenichi Kobayashi

Fujitsu Research, Fujitsu Limited, Kanagawa, Japan
{nishikino,kenichi}@fujitsu.com

Abstract. Supervised fine-tuning of large language models (LMs) does not always provide good text-generation performance in terms of quality and diversity. This is because such models maximize the likelihood of correct subsequent words based on previous contexts encountered in the training phase, instead of evaluating the entire structure of the generated texts. In this context, fine-tuning methods for LMs using adversarial imitation learning (AIL) have been proposed to improve the trade-off relationship between quality and diversity. This method leverages the evaluations of the discriminators without requiring manually designed metrics. Previously proposed AIL methods cannot control the shapes of the reward functions and constrain updates of LMs using fixed ranges, independent of the quality, e.g., proximal policy optimization. This study proposes a combination of an AIL method and an approximation of mixture distributions (AMDAIL), synergizing with LMs for text generation. AMDAIL exhibits two features: (1) controlling the distribution of the bounded reward values by varying the shape of the bounded reward function, and (2) a variable constraint to promote updates using the confidence of the discriminator as the quality of the texts. The proposed method exhibits stable behavior in the training phases and improves the trade-off relationship between the quality and diversity in the inference phases.

Keywords: Text generation · Adversarial imitation learning · Reinforcement learning

1 Introduction

Large language models (LMs) yield better text generation performance as their total numbers of weight parameters are increased exponentially [1]. The generative pretrained transformer (GPT) series of pre-trained autoregressive LMs [2,3] is widely utilized in the field of natural language processing because it can considerably fine-tune new tasks even when the datasets are small. However, supervised fine-tuning (SFT) of LMs may deteriorate the trade-off relationship

---

The source code is available at https://github.com/zabu-nishiki/amdail.

© The Author(s), under exclusive license to Springer Nature Switzerland AG 2023
D. Koutra et al. (Eds.): ECML PKDD 2023, LNAI 14169, pp. 131–146, 2023.
https://doi.org/10.1007/978-3-031-43412-9_8

between the quality and diversity of the generated text, e.g., repeated and frequently occurring words [4]. This is because SFT maximizes the likelihood of correct subsequent words based on previous contexts in the training phases instead of evaluating the entire structure of the text generated by LMs.

Therefore, several methods [5] have been proposed to bridge the gap between the training phase involving correct text and the inference phase involving text generation. In direct assimilation methods used for training and text generation with LMs, leveraging the advantages of reinforcement learning (RL) is generally successful; e.g., InstructGPT [6], which is an LM of RL based on human feedback (RLHF) [7]. However, RLHF approaches require considerable annotation for reward models because they require human feedback and numerous pairs of generated texts to ensure adequate accuracy of reward models. To improve the quality and diversity of LMs without human feedback, adversarial imitation learning (AIL) has been utilized in numerous applications [8]. AIL methods for LMs with text generation, such as self-adversarial learning (SAL) [9], TextGAIL [10], and Generative Cooperative Networks (GCN) [11], outperform previous generative adversarial network (GAN) methods [12–14]. An advantage of AIL methods is that they consider total structures using discriminators without requiring human feedback or manually designed metrics.

However, AIL methods for text generation suffer from certain shortcomings. The distributions of the reward values are not always stable, and their linear normalization in each dataset does not always stabilize the LMs' updates practically. Hence, controlling the reward functions nonlinearly is effective in practical applications; however, AIL methods may not enable such control. In this paper, we contribute to overcoming this problem in two ways. (1) We propose a controllable reward function for the stable distribution of reward values. Besides enabling the capacity to reshape the distribution of reward values, this also enables the quantitative generation of the optimal LMs.

Proximal policy optimization (PPO) [15], which is utilized as an update method in InstructGPT and TextGAIL, suffers from another problem related to the constraints of fixed ranges—the fixed clipping of the probability ratios handles high- and low-quality text similarly. The constraints of updates should also be dependent on the quality of the text to encourage updates among high-quality texts and suppress that among low-quality texts. Further, the fixed clipping constraints of the PPO reduce the probability ratios rapidly and make their distributions non-smooth. The second contribution of this paper is related to this problem: (2) We provide a variable constraint based on the quality of the texts, which avoids the rapidly fixed clipping of the PPO ratios and makes their distributions smooth.

The proposed method is named after AIL combined with the approximation of the mixture distribution (AMDAIL). AMDAIL exhibits two beneficial properties: (1) bounded reward and (2) clipped surrogate objective of the mixture distribution. For simple implementation of these properties, AMDAIL uses an approximation of the mixture distribution of the generator and an expert policy based on the confidence of the discriminator. In this study, AMDAIL exhibits stable behavior during the training phase and improves the trade-off relationship between quality and diversity during the inference phase.

2 Adversarial Imitation Learning for Text Generation

Text generation using a simple GAN framework is challenging because LMs sample discrete words from the distributions of their vocabularies, and may not backpropagate gradients along the paths of the discriminators. To utilize adversarial learning approaches for text generation, several methods (e.g., SAL, TextGAIL, and DCN) have been proposed to overcome the unstable behavior of LMs in AIL methods and considerably improve the trade-off relationship between quality and diversity relative to those of LMs with SFT. An AIL method involves a type of reinforcement learning that imitates the behavior of experts via adversarial learning approaches without requiring the manual design of metrics. In this section, we discuss TextGAIL, which is a simple implementation of AIL methods upon which the proposed method is based, and provide general insights into SFT and AIL methods.

2.1 TextGAIL

TextGAIL is based on generative AIL (GAIL) [16], which involves contrastive discriminators and utilizes PPO for text generation. Contrastive discriminators prevent saturated confidence in adversarial learning caused by standard discriminators, which identify the differences between the correct and generated texts rapidly. This is because they learn the relative realities, instead of the differences between the correct and generated texts. The confidences of the contrastive discriminators $D(x, y_\pi)$ and $D(x, y_e)$, for the generated text y_π and correct text y_e based on the context x are described using the logits z of the standard discriminators, as follows:

$$[D(x, y_\pi), D(x, y_e)] = \mathrm{softmax}\left([z(x, y_\pi), z(x, y_e)]\right). \tag{1}$$

The discriminators and generators are optimized to determine the saddle points of the following equation sampling from the probabilistic densities, $\rho_\pi(x, y)$ and $\rho_e(x, y)$, of the generator and expert policies, respectively:

$$\min_\pi \max_D \mathbb{E}_{(x,y)\sim\rho_e}[\log D(x, y)] + \mathbb{E}_{(x,y)\sim\rho_\pi}[\log(1 - D(x, y))]. \tag{2}$$

TextGAIL recognizes this min-max problem as an AIL problem—the generator policy $\pi(y|x)$ and confidence $D(x, y)$ of the discriminator are recognized as the agent policy and reward function, respectively. The generator policy attempts to maximize the expected reward using PPO as a policy update method, ensuring that the current policy is not drastically updated based on the old policy. The generator policy of TextGAIL encodes the t-th word based on the context x and the t-1 subsequent words $y^{1:t-1}$ as the states, and the subsequent word y^t is sampled from the policy distribution as the action. In our implementations,

Table 1. Reward functions and optimized objectives of the AIL methods.

Method	Reward Function	Optimized Objective
GAIL	$-\log(1 - D(x,y))$	$\mathrm{JS}(\rho_\pi(x,y)\|\rho_e(x,y))$
AIRL	$\log \frac{D(x,y)}{1-D(x,y)}$	$\mathrm{KL}(\rho_\pi(x,y)\|\rho_e(x,y))$

the generator policy $\pi(y|x)$ is the geometric mean of the joint probabilities of all words in the text y and the context x, based on the temporal distributions of the generator policy $\pi(y^t|x, y^{1:t-1})$ and text length T, as given below:

$$\pi(y|x) = \left(\prod_{t=1}^{T} \pi(y^t|x, y^{1:t-1}) \right)^{1/T}.$$ (3)

Hence, the policy maximizes the expected rewards by optimizing the following clipped surrogate objective of PPO, using importance sampling [17] of the geometric mean of the joint probabilities with the new and old generator policies, $\pi_{\mathrm{new}}(y|x)$ and $\pi_{\mathrm{old}}(y|x)$, respectively:

$$L(x,y) = -\min \begin{cases} \frac{\pi_{\mathrm{new}}(y|x)}{\pi_{\mathrm{old}}(y|x)} R(x,y) \\ \mathrm{clip}\left(\frac{\pi_{\mathrm{new}}(y|x)}{\pi_{\mathrm{old}}(y|x)}, 1 - \epsilon, 1 + \epsilon \right) R(x,y). \end{cases}$$ (4)

2.2 Divergence Minimization of Adversarial Imitation Learning

Understanding AIL methods, such as GAIL and adversarial inverse reinforcement learning (AIRL) [18], is essential for quantitative recognition. We may regard reward maximizations in several AIL methods as divergence minimizations between the generator and expert policies [19]. The primary differences between GAIL and AIRL are the reward functions and optimized objectives, as listed in Table 1. The reward functions of GAIL and AIRL are similar; however, the optimal generator policies of these methods are not equal owing to the differences in their optimized objectives led by their reward functions. We demonstrate the transformation from reward maximization to divergence minimization.

Generative Adversarial Imitation Learning. The confidence of the optimal discriminator $D^*(x,y)$ in (2) can be described as $\frac{\rho_e(x,y)}{\rho_\pi(x,y)+\rho_e(x,y)}$ with the probability densities, $\rho_\pi(x,y)$ and $\rho_e(x,y)$, of the context x and the subsequent text y pairs, respectively, obtained via the generator and expert policies, respectively. Hence, the generator policy $\pi(y|x)$ is optimized to minimize the Jensen-Shannon

(JS) divergence between the probability densities $\rho_\pi(x, y)$ and $\rho_e(x, y)$ as follows:

$$\max_\pi \mathbb{E}_{(x,y)\sim\rho_e}\left[-\log D^*(x, y)\right] + \mathbb{E}_{(x,y)\sim\rho_\pi}\left[-\log(1 - D^*(x, y))\right] \tag{5}$$

$$= -\min_\pi \mathbb{E}_{(x,y)\sim\rho_e}\left[\log \frac{\rho_e(x, y)}{\rho_\pi(s, a) + \rho_e(x, y)}\right] + \mathbb{E}_{(x,y)\sim\rho_\pi}\left[\log \frac{\rho_\pi(x, y)}{\rho_\pi(s, a) + \rho_e(x, y)}\right]$$

$$= -\min_\pi \mathrm{JS}\left(\rho_\pi(x, y)\|\rho_e(x, y)\right) + 2\log 2$$

Adversarial Inverse Reinforcement Learning. The reward function of AIRL is described as $\log \frac{D(x,y)}{1-D(x,y)}$, and the optimized objective with the optimized discriminator D^* is the Kullback-Leibler (KL) divergence between the probability densities, $\rho_\pi(x, y)$ and $\rho_e(x, y)$, which is obtained in the same manner as GAIL, as follows:

$$\max_\pi \mathbb{E}_{(x,y)\sim\rho_\pi}\left[\log \frac{D^*(x, y)}{1 - D^*(x, y)}\right] = -\min_\pi \mathbb{E}_{(x,y)\sim\rho_\pi}\left[\log \frac{\rho_\pi(x, y)}{\rho_e(x, y)}\right]$$

$$= -\min_\pi \mathrm{KL}(\rho_\pi(x, y)\|\rho_e(x, y)). \tag{6}$$

2.3 Relationship Between Maximum Likelihood Estimation and Adversarial Imitation Learning

The different optimized objectives of AIL methods are crucial for fine-tuning them based on LMs with SFT. In terms of the maximum likelihood estimation, SFT may be considered to minimize the forward KL divergence $\mathrm{KL}(\rho_e(x, y)\|\rho_\pi(x, y))$ as follows:

$$\arg\min_\pi \mathbb{E}_{(x,y)\sim\rho_e}\left[-\log \rho_\pi(x, y)\right] = \arg\min_\pi \mathbb{E}_{(x,y)\sim\rho_e}\left[-\log \rho_\pi(x, y) + \log \rho_e(x, y)\right]$$

$$= \arg\min_\pi \mathrm{KL}\left(\rho_e(x, y)\|\rho_\pi(x, y)\right). \tag{7}$$

This is the inverse of the reverse KL divergence $\mathrm{KL}(\rho_\pi(x, y)\|\rho_e(x, y))$ in AIRL. They exhibit different properties of mass expression based on the probabilistic density of the generator policy $\rho_\pi(x, y)$ compared to that based on the probabilistic density of the expert policy $\rho_e(x, y)$. The generator policy with the forward KL divergence attempts to cover all expert modes, and that with the reverse KL divergence seeks partial expert modes to avoid non-existing modes in the expert policy. The generator policy with SFT in mode covering exhibits a synergistic effect with fine-tuning by AIL in mode seeking. This is because the generator policy can be refined to fit the complex distribution of the expert policy, based on the distribution of the generator policy acquired by SFT [20]. Owing to their synergistic combination, adapting AIL methods for reverse KL divergence results in good performance. However, mode seeking via AIL methods may deteriorate the mode covering of SFT and the performance of LMs, owing to over-encouraging them to expand the zero-probabilistic densities of the generator policies relative to those of the expert policies [21]. Hence, the mitigation of this zero-forcing mode seeking behavior is key to stabilizing fine-tuning using AIL methods.

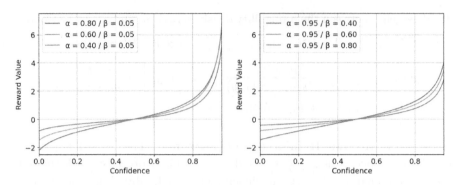

(a) Shape of bounded reward function with respect to varying β.

(b) Shape of bounded reward function with respect to varying α.

Fig. 1. Behavior of bounded reward function respect to varying hyperparameters, α and β.

3   Adversarial Imitation Learning with Approximation of Mixture Distribution

Utilizing the performance of LMs with AIL methods for forward KL divergence is challenging owing to the zero-forcing behavior of mode seeking; for example, the reward value of AIRL can approach negative infinity when the confidence of the discriminator approaches zero. To overcome this problem, we propose AMDAIL, which is an AIL method combined with approximation of mixture distribution using two properties—a lower bounded reward and a clipped surrogate objective depending on the confidence of the discriminator.

3.1   Lower Bounded Reward Function

The lower bounded reward function of AMDAIL is derived from that of AIRL and can be described by the hyperparameters $\alpha \in [0.0, 1.0]$ and $\beta \in [0.0, 1.0]$ depending on the reward shape, as follows:

$$R(x, y) = \frac{\alpha(1 - D(x,y)) + (1 - \alpha)D(x,y)}{1 - D(x,y)} \log \frac{\beta(1 - D(x,y)) + (1 - \beta)D(x,y)}{\alpha(1 - D(x,y)) + (1 - \alpha)D(x,y)}. \quad (8)$$

The lower bound of this reward function is given by $\alpha \log(\beta/\alpha) \leq R(x, y)$. Hence, infinite reward values are avoided when the confidence of the discriminator is almost zero. Based on Fig. 1, it may be intuitively concluded that α and β are related to the lower bound and slope of the reward function, respectively. Similar to GAIL and AIRL, the maximization of the expected reward value may be considered as divergence minimization between the mixture distributions, $\rho_\alpha(x, y) := \alpha\rho_\pi(x, y) + (1 - \alpha)\rho_e(x, y)$ and $\rho_\beta(x, y) := \beta\rho_\pi(x, y) + (1 - \beta)\rho_e(x, y)$, as follows:

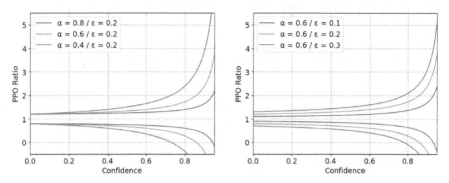

(a) Shape of variable clipping with respect to varying α.

(b) Shape of variable clipping with respect to varying ϵ.

Fig. 2. Variable clipping with respect to varying hyperparameters, α, β, and ϵ.

$$\max_{\pi} \mathbb{E}_{(x,y)\sim\rho_\pi} \left[\frac{\alpha(1 - D^*(x,y)) + (1-\alpha)D^*(x,y)}{1 - D^*(x,y)} \log \frac{\beta(1 - D^*(x,y)) + (1-\beta)D^*(x,y)}{\alpha(1 - D^*(x,y)) + (1-\alpha)D^*(x,y)} \right]$$

$$= \max_{\pi} \mathbb{E}_{(x,y)\sim\rho_\pi} \left[\frac{\rho_\alpha(x,y)}{\rho_\pi(x,y)} \log \frac{\rho_\beta(x,y)}{\rho_\alpha(x,y)} \right] = \max_{\pi} \mathbb{E}_{(x,y)\sim\rho_\alpha} \left[\log \frac{\rho_\beta(x,y)}{\rho_\alpha(x,y)} \right]$$

$$= -\min_{\pi} \mathrm{KL}(\rho_\alpha(x,y)||\rho_\beta(x,y)). \tag{9}$$

When α is larger than β, $\mathrm{KL}(\rho_\alpha(x,y)||\rho_\beta(x,y))$ is the reverse KL divergence seeking partial expert modes. On the other hand, when α is smaller than β, $\mathrm{KL}(\rho_\alpha(x,y)||\rho_\beta(x,y))$ is the forward KL divergence covering all expert modes. Hence, AMDAIL can modify the direction of the optimized objective between the mixture probabilistic densities of the generator and expert policies, $\rho_\alpha(x,y)$ and $\rho_\beta(x,y)$. In the experiment, we assume α to be larger than β for the reverse KL divergence to refine the generator modes from those of SFT. To ensure robustness in RL, the clipping of the reward functions can be considered with a constant C_R, as follows:

$$R_{\mathrm{clip}}(x,y) = \mathrm{clip}\left(R(x,y), -C_R, C_R\right). \tag{10}$$

However, the reward gradients are diminished when the reward values lie in the range $(-\infty, -C_R]$ or $[C_R, \infty)$, and reward maximization becomes challenging. Conversely, the reward values of all samples with AMDAIL can be ordered owing to the slopes of the reward functions in all the ranges.

3.2 Clipped Surrogate Objective with Approximation of Mixture Distribution

The surrogate objective subjected to the constraint is proposed as a robust policy update for RL. The trust region method (TRPO) [22] proposes a penalty

---

Algorithm 1. AMDAIL

1: **Initialize:**
   Collect expert texts y_e.
   Supervised fine-tuning LM $\pi(y|x)$ based on expert texts y_e and context x.
   Buffer B_π and B_e.
2: **for** $i = 1, 2, 3, \ldots$ **do**
3:    Buffer pairs of generated texts y_π and contexts x into B_π.
4:    Buffer pairs of expert texts y_e and contexts x into B_e.
5:    Sample pairs of (x, y_π) and (x, y_e) based on B_π and B_e.
6:    Buffer confidences $D(x, y_\pi)$ and robust scaling rewards for (x, y_π).
7:    Buffer constant rewards for (x, y_e).
8:    Update discriminator $D(x, y)$ with (2).
9:    Update LMs based on (x, y_π) with (14) and (x, y_e) with (4).
10:   Clear Buffer B_π and B_e
11: **end for**

---

term for KL divergence between the old and new policies. TRPO estimates the expected reward obtained via importance sampling [17] based on the old and new policies, as follows:

$$\mathbb{E}_{(x,y)\sim\rho_{\pi^{\text{old}}}} \left[\frac{\pi^{\text{new}}(y|x)}{\pi^{\text{old}}(y|x)} R(x,y) - \beta \text{KL}(\pi^{\text{new}}(y|x)||\pi^{\text{old}}(y|x)) \right]. \tag{11}$$

However, the calculation of KL divergence with LMs between the old and new generator policies is computationally complicated, involving numerous outputs as the vocabulary. To implement a simpler approach, PPO proposes a clipped surrogate objective, clipping the ratio of the old and new policies, as described in 4. Ratio clipping suppresses radical updates of the policy without penalizing a surplus. PPO has been successfully implemented in broad applications in RL models because of the simplicity of its implementation and its effectiveness. However, fine-tuning LMs via AIL suffers from difficulties owing to degrading the policies for text generation. This is caused by penalizing the generated texts, which can lead to initialized LMs instead of improving the generator policy. Consequently, enhancing updates among high-quality generated texts is essential for AIL methods to improve LMs. To implement this concept, the proposed lower bounded reward emphasizes the updates among high-quality generated texts and suppresses updates among low-quality generated texts. However, products with a large ratio and low reward and those with a small ratio and high reward may exhibit values similar to those of the objective. Hence, we propose the clipping of mixture distributions using a variable range depending on the quality of the generated text—constraint strict for low-quality text and liberal for high-quality text. The proposed clipping range is expressed as follows:

Table 2. Hyperparameters of model implementation

Hyper Parameters	CommonGEN	ROCStory
SFT Epoch	2	2
AIL Epoch	1	1
Batch Size	64	32
Buffer Size	512	256
Learning Rate of GPT2	4e-5	4e-5
Learning Rate of OPT	1e-5	1e-5
Learning Rate of DeBERTa	5e-7	1e-6

$$\text{LB} := \frac{(\alpha(1 - D(x,y)) + (1 - \alpha)D(x,y))(1 - \epsilon) - (1 - \alpha)D(x,y)}{\alpha(1 - D(x,y))} \leq \frac{\pi^{\text{new}}(x,y)}{\pi^{\text{old}}}$$

$$\leq \text{UB} := \frac{(\alpha(1 - D(x,y)) + (1 - \alpha)D(x,y))(1 + \epsilon) - (1 - \alpha)D(x,y)}{\alpha(1 - D(x,y))}. \tag{12}$$

This clipping range extends through the confidence of the discriminator, interpreting the quality of the generated text to prioritize tricking them, as depicted in Fig. (2). It is derived from the constraint on the ratio of the mixture probabilistic densities $\pi_\alpha^{new}/\pi_\alpha^{old}$, instead of the PPO constraint on the ratio π^{old}/π^{new}, as described below:

$$1 - \epsilon \leq \frac{\pi_\alpha^{\text{new}}(y|x)}{\pi_\alpha^{\text{old}}(y|x)} \leq 1 + \epsilon.$$

We approximate the expert policy using the old policy and the confidence of the discriminator, as follows: $\pi_e(y|x) \approx \frac{\rho_e(x,y)}{\rho_\pi(x,y)}\pi^{\text{old}}(y|x) = \frac{D^*(x,y)}{1-D^*(x,y)}\pi^{\text{old}}(y|x)$. This is because the policy is proportional to the probability density, i.e., $\pi(y|x) \propto \frac{\rho_\pi(x,y)}{\rho(x)}$, when the probabilistic density of the context $\rho(x)$ is fixed as the dataset. We may then use the following inequality as the constraint on the mixture distributions and Eq. (12):

$$1 - \epsilon \leq \frac{\frac{\pi^{\text{new}}(y|x)}{\pi^{\text{old}}(y|x)}\alpha(1 - D(x,y)) + (1 - \alpha)D(x,y)}{\alpha(1 - D(x,y)) + (1 - \alpha)D(x,y)} \leq 1 + \epsilon \tag{13}$$

Accordingly, the surrogate objective of AMDAIL can be described as follows:

$$L(x,y) = -\min \begin{cases} \frac{\pi^{\text{new}}(y|x)}{\pi^{\text{old}}(y|x)}R(x,y) \\ \\ \text{clip}\left(\frac{\pi^{\text{new}}(y|x)}{\pi^{\text{old}}(y|x)}, \text{LB}, \text{UB}\right)R(x,y). \end{cases} \tag{14}$$

Then, the algorithm of AMDAIL is summarized in Algorithm 1.

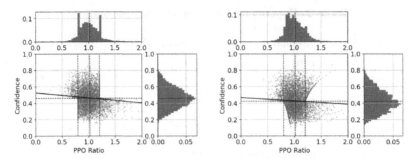

(a) Ratios and confidence in TextGAIL (b) Ratios and confidence in AMDAIL

Fig. 3. Relationships between the policy ratios and confidences of the text and AIL methods. The x- and y-axes describe the policy ratios and the confidences of the discriminator, respectively. The histograms depict the discrete sample distributions of the axes, and the black lines represent their linear regressions.

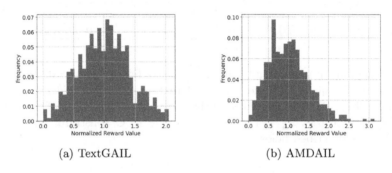

(a) TextGAIL   (b) AMDAIL

Fig. 4. Histograms of the reward values of the AIL methods.

4 Study and Result

We conducted experiments on the trade-off relationship between quality and diversity, and analyzed the behavior of each AIL method. This section describes the details of the experimental implementation, including the dataset, models, and evaluation metrics, and presents the experimental results.

4.1 Dataset and Models

We tested the text generation performance of each AIL method using the following datasets:

1. The CommonGEN data set [23]: Evaluate the reasoning performances of relationships based on common-sense knowledge and the generalization performance of text generation based on unseen combinations of concepts.

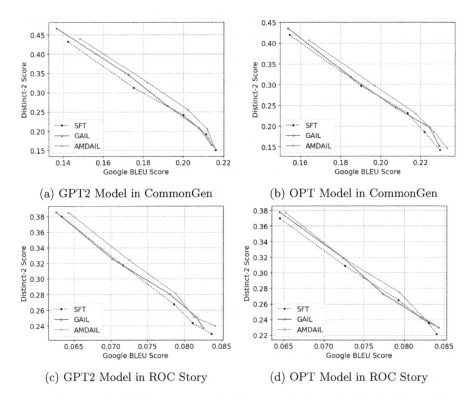

(a) GPT2 Model in CommonGen   (b) OPT Model in CommonGen

(c) GPT2 Model in ROC Story   (d) OPT Model in ROC Story

Fig. 5. Relationships between the qualities and diversities of the generated texts. The x- and y-axes represent the Google BLEU scores as the qualities and distinct-N scores as the diversities, respectively. We utilized top-p sampling to decode the texts from the contexts.

2. The ROC Story data set [24]: Evaluate the capturing performances of the causal and temporal common-sense knowledge of daily events and the generalization performance of text generation in daily life.

We utilized the GPT-2, OPT[27], and DeBERTa[28] models as the two generators and discriminator, respectively—the hyperparameters used for model implementation are listed in Table 2. The generator policy decodes the text via nucleus (a.k.a. top-p) sampling from the top-p distribution of the vocabulary. This decoding method exhibits good performance in text generation with various patterns based on similar contexts and reduces the repetition of words.

4.2 Evaluation Metrics

We evaluated the qualities and diversity of the generated sentences. We used the google bilingual evaluation understudy (Google BLEU) score [25] as the n-gram metric of the matching ratio of sub-sequences of 1, 2, 3, or 4 tokens to evaluate the quality of the generated text. GoogleBLEU can evaluate the qualities of

Table 3. Comparison Experiments for methods on GPT2. We utilized top-p sampling to decode the texts at temperature = 1.0 in the comparison experiments with 3 seeds.

Methods	CommonGen	
	Google Bleu	Distinct-2
SFT	0.1413 ± 0.0007	0.4330 ± 0.0021
TextGAIL	0.1359 ± 0.0005	0.4645 ± 0.0015
AMDAIL (Ours)	0.1470 ± 0.0010	0.4409 ± 0.0014
Methods	ROC Story	
	Google Bleu	Distinct-2
SFT	0.0634 ± 0.0002	0.3796 ± 0.0005
TextGAIL	0.0625 ± 6.6e-5	0.3858 ± 0.0007
AMDAIL (Ours)	0.0642 ± 2.4e-5	0.3845 ± 0.0009

single sentences effectively, such as the entries in the ROC Story dataset. To evaluate the diversity of the generated text, we utilized the Distinct-n score [26] as the n-gram uniqueness metric in the dataset.

4.3   PPO Ratio and Confidence

Figure 3 depicts the relationships between the ratio $\frac{L(x,y)}{\lceil R(x,y) \rceil}$ of the clipped surrogate objective and abstract reward values, and the confidences of the discriminator $D(x,y)$. As is evident from Fig. 3a, PPO clipping handles all samples larger than the thresholds equally, and the histogram of the ratio is not smooth because of multiple clipped PPO ratios. Conversely, Fig. 3b depicts the smooth histogram of the ratios in AMDAIL via clipping with the various ranges depending on the confidence. Additionally, samples with low confidences are clipped strictly, and those with high confidences are clipped lightly in AMDAIL. Therefore, AMDAIL promotes considerable updates to high-quality texts and suppresses updates among low-quality texts to suppress the effect of zero-forcing induced by reverse KL divergences, which may deteriorate the performance of LMs with SFT.

4.4   Comparison Distributions of the Reward Values

We evaluated the dependence of distributions of the reward values based on the confidences of the discriminator on the proposed lower bounded reward, as depicted in Fig. 4. TextGAIL exhibits symmetric distributions of reward values, as depicted in Fig. 4a. Therefore, it corresponds to nearly identical degrees of penalization of low-quality texts and promotion of high-quality texts. On the other hand, Fig. 4b depicts the asymmetric distribution of the reward values in AMDAIL. Hence AMDAIL is confirmed to suppress over-penalizing by lower bounds and promote high-quality texts more than AIL methods (Table 5).

Table 4. Examples of ground truth and texts generated using different methods via top-p sampling at temperature = 1.0 by each AIL method with GPT2 in CommonGEN.

Method	Example 1
Context	table beat music sit tap
Ground Truth	The girl sits at the table and the girl taps her feet to the beat of the music
SFT	this table has four taps on it that sit on the table.
TextGAIL	dancing men sit at tables and tap music
AMDAIL	Two women sit on chairs in the dining room. One has a glass of beer and a smile. The other has a teabag

Table 5. Examples of ground truth and texts generated using different methods via top-p sampling at temperature = 1.0 by each AIL method with GPT2 in ROC Story.

Method	Example 1
Context	Kate started playing the Xbox with her nephew. But a year later she was hooked and played alone. One day she found a new version of the game she always played. They released a new game every year
Ground Truth	Kate was shocked to realized she had been playing the Xbox a year
SFT	Now she can play any game with her nephew.
TextGAIL	Kate bought a new console every year for her nephew.
AMDAIL	Kate liked playing with her nephew but was worried about her privacy

4.5 Quality and Diversity

We evaluated the trade-off relationship between quality and diversity based on the plots of the Google BLEU and Distinct-n scores, as depicted in Fig. 5. We can observe greater improvement in AMDAIL compared to TextGAIL and SFT models. On the other hand, some scores of TextGAIL exhibit lesser deterioration than those of SFT, demonstrating that TextGAIL sometimes fails to fine-tune and its learning behaviors are not stable. AMDAIL improved text generation corresponding to all combinations of datasets and models, demonstrating the robustness of learning behaviors in AMDAIL. This is attributed to the effective suppression of zero-forcing induced by reverse KL divergences in AMDAIL and the consequent quality preservation and improvement of the performances of LMs with SFT. Table 4 lists samples of generated texts corresponding to each method.

5 Conclusions

Text generation using AIL methods is difficult as they also promote updating policy among low-quality texts. To address this problem, we propose AMDAIL that promotes the updating policy among high-quality texts with high reward values and suppresses updating policy among low-quality texts. We demonstrate that AMDAIL minimizes the divergence between the generator policy and expert policy. Experimental results indicate that AMDAIL improves the trade-off relationship between quality and diversity, and its properties solve the problems of AIL related to smoothing and controlling the distributions of the reward values to a greater degree than those of other AIL methods with PPO. It also mitigates the deterioration in performance caused by zero-forcing induced by reverse KL divergence.

Ethical Statement. In this study, we utilized pretrained LMs for text generation. Pretrained LMs, e.g., GPTs, may contain personal data in the weight parameters. Thus, LMs should be tested in advance and the personal information should be removed from both datasets and models. In this study, we utilized public datasets and models to avoid the misuse of personal information. We confirm that the models did not generate any texts, including any personal information. However, this study can be utilized in deception involving fake documents, news, etc., even though we only intend to improve the quality and diversity of LMs for text generation. Hence, we intend to manage and survey the utilization of this study, to ensure that its negative influences are monitored and constrained.

References

1. Kaplan, J., et al.: Scaling Laws for Neural Language Models (2020), arXiv:2001.08361
2. I. Solaiman, M. Brundage, J. Clark, A. Askell, A. Herbert-Voss, J. Wu, A. Radford, G. Krueger, J. W. Kim, S. Kreps, M. McCain, A. Newhouse, J. Blazakis, K. McGuffie, and J. Wang, "Release Strategies and the Social Impacts of Language Models," 2019, arXiv:1908.09203
3. Brown, T.B., et al.: Language Models are Few-Shot Learners (2020), arXiv:2005.14165
4. Holtzman, A., Buys, J., Du, L., Forbes, M., Choi, Y.: The curious case of neural text degeneration. Presented at the International Conference on Learning Representations (2020)
5. Welleck, S., Kulikov, I., Roller, S., Dinan, E., Cho, K., Weston, J.: Neural Text Generation With Unlikelihood Training. Presented at the International Conference on Learning Representations (2020)
6. Ouyang, L.: Training language models to follow instructions with human feedback. In: Advances in Neural Information Processing Systems (2022)
7. Stiennon, N., et al.: Learning to summarize with human feedback. In Advances in Neural Information Processing Systems 33, pp. 3008–3021 (2020)
8. Torabi, F., Warnell, G., Stone, P.: Recent Advances in Imitation Learning from Observation In: Proceedings of 28th International Joint Conference on Artificial Intelligence, pp. 6325–6331 (2019)

9. Zhou, W., Ge, T., Xu, K., Wei, F., Zhou, M.: Self-Adversarial Learning with Comparative Discrimination for Text Generation. In: International Conference on Learning Representations (2020)
10. Wu, Q., Li, L., Yu, Z.: TextGAIL: generative adversarial imitation learning for text generation. In: Proceedings of AAAI Conference on Artificial Intelligence, vol. 35(16), pp. 14067–14075 (2021)
11. Lamprier, S., et al.: Generative cooperative networks for natural language generation. In: Proceedings of 39th International Conference on Machine Learning, vol. 162, pp. 11891–11905. PMLR (2022)
12. Goodfellow, I., et al.: Generative adversarial nets. In: Advances in Neural Information Processing Systems, vol. 27 (2014)
13. Lin, K., Li, D., He, X., Zhang, Z., Sun, M.: Adversarial Ranking for Language Generation. In Advances in Neural Information Processing Systems, vol. 30 (2017)
14. Guo, J., Lu, S., Cai, H., Zhang, W., Yu, Y., Wang, J.: Long text generation via adversarial training with leaked information. In: Proceedings of AAAI Conference on Artificial Intelligence, vol. 32(1) (2018)
15. Schulman, J., Wolski, F., Dhariwal, P., Radford, A., Klimov, O.: Proximal Policy Optimization Algorithms, arXiv:1707.06347 (2017)
16. Ho, J., Ermon, S.: Generative Adversarial Imitation Learning. In: Advances in Neural Information Processing Systems, vol. 29 (2016)
17. Kloek, T., van Dijk, H.K.: Bayesian estimates of equation system parameters: an application of integration by Monte Carlo. Econometrica $46(1)$, 1–19 (1978)
18. Fu, J., Luo, K., Levine, S.: Learning robust rewards with adverserial inverse reinforcement learning. In: International Conference on Learning Representations (2018)
19. Ghasemipour, S.K.S., Zemel, R.S., Gu, S.: A divergence minimization perspective on imitation learning methods, In: 3rd Annual Conference on Robot Learning, Proceedings of Machine Learning Research, vol. 100, pp. 1259–1277. PMLR (2019)
20. Zhao, M., Cong, Y., Dai, S., Carin, L.: Bridging maximum likelihood and adversarial learning via α-divergence. In: Proceedings of AAAI Conference on Artificial Intelligence, vol. 34(04), pp. 6901–6908 (2020)
21. Kirkpatrick, J., et al.: Overcoming catastrophic forgetting in neural networks. Proc. Nat. Academy Sci. $114(13)$, 3521–3526 (2017)
22. Schulman, J., Levine, S., Abbeel, P., Jordan, M., Moritz, P.: Trust region policy optimization. In: The 32nd International Conference on Machine Learning, In Proc. Machine Learning Research, vol. 37, pp. 1889–1897. PMLR (2015)
23. Lin, B.Y., et al.: CommonGen: a constrained text generation challenge for generative commonsense reasoning. In: Findings of the Association for Computational Linguistics: EMNLP 2020, pp. 1823–1840. Association for Computational Linguistics (2020)
24. Mostafazadeh, N., et al.: A corpus and cloze evaluation for deeper understanding of commonsense stories. In: Proceedings of 2016 Conference of the North American Chapter of the Association for Computational Linguistics: Human Language Technologies, pp. 839–849. Association for Computational Linguistics (2016)
25. Wu, Y., et al.: Google's Neural Machine Translation System: Bridging the Gap between Human and Machine Translation, arXiv:1609.08144 (2016)
26. Li, J., Galley, M., Brockett, C., Gao, J., Dolan, B.: A diversity-promoting objective function for neural conversation models. In: Proceedings of 2016 Conference of the North American Chapter of the Association for Computational Linguistics: Human Language Technologies, pp. 110–119. Association for Computational Linguistics (2016)

27. Zhang, S.,et al.: OPT: Open Pre-trained Transformer Language Models, arxiv:2205.01068 (2022)
28. He, P., Liu, X., Gao, J., Chen, W.: DeBERTa: Decoding-enhanced BERT with Disentangled Attention, arxiv:2006.03654 (2021)

Towards Minimising Perturbation Rate for Adversarial Machine Learning with Pruning

Zhiyu Zhu[1] , Jiayu Zhang[2] , Zhibo Jin[1] , Xinyi Wang[3] , Minhui Xue[4] ,
Jun Shen[5] , Kim-Kwang Raymond Choo[6] , and Huaming Chen[1(✉)]

[1] The University of Sydney, Sydney, Australia
{zzhu2018,zjin0915}@uni.sydney.edu.au, huaming.chen@sydney.edu.au
[2] Suzhou Yierqi, Zhenjiang, China
[3] Jiangsu University, Zhenjiang, China
[4] CSIRO's Datat61, Eveleigh, Australia
[5] University of Wollongong, Wollongong, Australia
[6] University of Texas at San Antonio, San Antonio, USA

Abstract. Deep neural networks can be potentially vulnerable to adversarial samples. For example, by introducing tiny perturbations in the data sample, the model behaviour may be significantly altered. While the adversarial samples can be leveraged to enhance the model robustness and performance with adversarial training, one critical attribute of the adversarial samples is the perturbation rate. A lower perturbation rate means a smaller difference between the adversarial and the original sample. It results in closer features learnt from the model for the adversarial and original samples, resulting in higher-quality adversarial samples. How to design a successful attacking algorithm with a minimum perturbation rate remains challenging. In this work, we consider pruning algorithms to dynamically minimise the perturbation rate for adversarial attacks. In particularly, we propose, for the first time, an attribution based perturbation reduction method named Min-PR for white-box adversarial attacks. The comprehensive experiment results demonstrate Min-PR can achieve minimal perturbation rates of adversarial samples while providing guarantee to train robust models. The code in this paper is available at: https://github.com/LMBTough/Min-PR.

Keywords: Adversarial learning · adversarial sample · model pruning · white-box attacks

1 Introduction

Recent years have witnessed significant progress with deep learning (DL) in various fields, such as image classification [21], voice recognition [23], and sentiment analysis [1]. Though DL technique can be a powerful tool [5,9], it raises new security-related requirements [32] and a successful attack can impact on the performance of the system and lead to fatalities, say in autonomous driving [26].

D. Koutra et al. (Eds.): ECML PKDD 2023, LNAI 14169, pp. 147–163, 2023.
https://doi.org/10.1007/978-3-031-43412-9_9

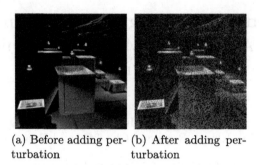

(a) Before adding per-   (b) After adding perturbation   turbation

Fig. 1. ImageNet example with and without sample perturbation

DL systems are vulnerable to attacks from well crafted adversarial examples [8,25], which means that adversarial attacks may be an inherent weakness
of deep neural networks (DNNs) [15]. One popular way is by designing adversarial samples for the targeting model, which adds imperceptible perturbations to
the original sample to manipulate the model behaviour [7]. For example, Fig. 1 is
one of the hard-to-attack images for ImageNet dataset, in which the perturbation
is added by FGSM method [16]. The trained model will thus output different
labels. Different outputs indicate manipulated behaviour via adversarial samples,
posing a significant threat to the model security. It also lead to many researches
leveraging adversarial samples for training, which can largely enhance the model
robustness to adversarial interference [27], such as adversarial training [2,14].

Adversarial attacks can be classified as white-box attacks [18] and black-
box attacks [20] based on the knowledge level of the target model. In white-
box attacks, the attackers have access to various information about the target model, such as model parameters, network structure, training dataset, and
defense mechanisms. For black-box attacks, they are more challenging since no
relevant information about the model will be available. It is widely agreed that,
for white-box attacks, the adversarial samples are easier to be constructed for
highest success rates with minimal perturbations [19]. How to obtain adversarial samples with a small perturbation rate to avoid detection is the main goal.
Some recent methods for generating adversarial samples include FGSM [6,7],
FTGSM [31], PGD [16], AdvGan [29] and so on.

In general, there are two measurements for the adversarial samples: (1) the
adversarial sample and the original sample should have as little difference as
possible (within a certain range); (2) the adversarial sample should have a high
probability to cause misclassification in the model. Lower perturbation rates
of the sample result in smaller differences between the adversarial and original
sample, making it less detectable to the model's defense mechanisms. The feature
learnt by the model from the adversarial sample will be closer to original sample,
indicating a higher likelihood of successful attacks. Therefore, there is a research
trend of minimising the perturbation rate of adversarial sample.

In the meantime, the parameter number for the state-of-the-art DNN models
ranges from millions to billions. However, not all of them are of same importance

for the model [3]. Pruning algorithms are one popular way to discard some parameters, and improve the model efficiency while maintaining the performance [22]. Thus, we propose a novel optimization algorithm to minimise the perturbation rate for adversarial samples, which is the first time to the best of our knowledge. Particularly, the algorithm to *Min*imising the *P*erturbation *R*ate (Min-PR) is designed with the attribution method to evaluate importance of the perturbation and remove perturbations that are not important for the attack.

The key idea of this paper is to minimize the perturbation rate in constructing adversarial samples to the white-box attacks, while maintaining a certain degree of generalization and improving the model's robustness and accuracy. We identify Min-PR supported by the following contributions:

- We propose Min-PR to innovatively utilise the pruning algorithms to minimise perturbation rate for gradient-based adversarial attack algorithms.
- In line with two different goals, which aim to attack as few parameters as possible and allow manipulation to all sample points, we develop Min-PR in two different implementations, namely Min-PRv1 and Min-PRv2 algorithms.
- Both theoretical and empirical investigation details for the attribution algorithm, which is a core part of Min-PR, are included in Sect. 3.
- A comprehensive statistical analysis is performed based on our benchmarking experiments on various datasets and various adversarial attacks. The results in Sect. 4 demonstrates the state-of-the-art performance of Min-PR.

2 Related Works

2.1 Adversarial Attack Algorithms

Adversarial attack algorithms have been extensively studied, which are mostly based on either gradient [10,28] or GAN [29]. As an important category, gradient-based adversarial attacks was firstly identified in the work of fast gradient sign method (FGSM) by Goodfellow et al [7]. FGSM is a gradient-based method generating adversarial examples for non-targeted attacks (i.e., the generated adversarial examples do not need to be predicted as a specific target class, as long as they are different from the original prediction). Unlike traditional gradient descent, FGSM uses one-step gradient ascent to train the adversarial examples.

I-FGSM is proposed to apply a single transformation to all the pixels of the original image [6], while the projected gradient descent method (PGD) [16] is presented aiming to eliminate the sign function and instead uses the F-norm as the scale for not only linear models but also nonlinear models. C&W algorithm (Carlini&Wagner) is proposed to reduce the perturbations by several constraints considering gradient descent [4]. Another group of studies is to use the generative adversarial network (GAN) for adversarial sample generation, such as AdvGAN [29], since GAN is effective for data generation.

2.2 Pruning Algorithm

When referring to the parameters of DNN, it generally means the learnable parameters of the network including the weight matrix and bias. The purpose of pruning is to remove the unimportant weight matrices while not impacting the model performance. Traditional pruning methods include optimization-based pruning, magnitude-based pruning, importance-based structured pruning, and reconstruction error-based structured pruning. However, pruning algorithm has some limitations: 1) Most of the pruning algorithms require data validation, and they need to be adapted to scenarios where only one sample is attacked for adversarial attacks; 2)Most of the pruning algorithms will modify the original parameters, and the pure application to adversarial attacks cannot guarantee an optimised perturbation rate. To address these issues, Min-PR is proposed in this paper to minimise the ideal perturbation rate we need. Additionally, a comprehensive experimental evaluation is presented to demonstrate the performance of the algorithm following the works from [12,17].

3 Method

A lower perturbation rate can help the attack method find more similar samples compared to original examples. Many adversarial attack algorithms opt for limiting the perturbation's norm to minimise the final perturbation rate, such as projected gradient descent on negative loss function [11], or designing a specific optimization formula [4]. However, we observe that the perturbation rate can be further optimised. In particular, we propose the Min-PRv1 and Min-PRv2 algorithm in following sections. As shown in Fig. 2, Fig. 2a is the figure after attacking as few parameter positions as possible using Min-PRv1, and Fig. 2b is the figure after modifying the attack position using Min-PRv2.

(a) Using Min-PRv1 (D1)   (b) Using Min-PRv2 (D2)

Fig. 2. Comparison images using Min-PRv1 and Min-PRv2 (ImageNet)

3.1   Problem Definition

Formally, suppose we have a deep neural network $N : \mathbb{R}^n \rightarrow \mathbb{R}^c$ and original sample $x \in R^n$. The adversarial attack methods aim to find Δx to construct a manipulated input sample $x' = x + \Delta x$, where the optimization goal is

$$\min_{x'} D(x, x') \quad \text{subject to} \quad N(x) \neq N(x') \tag{1}$$

D can be considered as the distance function, i.e., L2norm. For classification task, $N(x) \neq N(x')$ while for regression tasks, the constraint can be defined as $N(x) - N(x') \geq \epsilon$ depending on the application. Considering the different definitions of minimum distance, we extend the optimization goal to two conditions of D1 and D2 in Eq. (2), resulting in Sect. 3.2 and 3.3. $\odot$ means element-wise product.

$$x' = M \odot \Delta x + x, \quad \text{with } M = [m_1, m_2, \ldots, m_n] \tag{2}$$

D1. Minimise the required number of input features to be manipulated by the adversarial attack method, which is equivalent to finding M as sparse as possible in Eq. (2) while satisfying $N(x) \neq N(x')$. In this case, $m_i \in \{0, 1\}$.
D2. Minimise the overall distance between the original input x and adversarial example x', considering all input features, which is equivalent to finding M as small as possible to minimum $(x')^2$ in Eq. (2). In this case, $m_i \in [0, 1]$.

3.2   Min-PRv1 for D1

To address D1 goal, the perturbation rate is optimised by removing insignificant changes while retaining salient attack features. In this way, the optimisation objective of D1 becomes to remove as many unimportant Δx as possible while retaining the attacking success rate. Thus, we implement Min-PRv1 by applying attribution based neural network pruning method to selectively remove unimportant deviations between original and adversarial samples. The attribution method applied in Min-PRv1 can trace the individual relationship between the input and output, corresponding to Δx and the attacking result of the sample.

We firstly discuss two axioms, as the fundamental definition in [24], for one-to-one relationship between output changes and inputs in attribution method:

Sensitivity: An attribution method satisfies Sensitivity if it assigns a non-zero attribution to any feature that differs between an input and its baseline and results in different predictions. This implies that any changes in outputs can be traced back to corresponding inputs.
Implementation Invariance: The attributions are always identical for two functionally equivalent networks. This axiom is easy to understand.

Fundamental of Min-PRv1. Equation (3) provides the fundamental attribution formula to trace the contribution of changes in Δx:

$$
\begin{aligned}
L(N(x + \Delta x), c) &- L\left(N\left(x + \Delta x^F\right), c\right) \\
&= \sum_{i=1}^{T} \Delta x_i \cdot \frac{\partial L\left(N\left(x + \Delta x + \sum_{j=1}^{i} \Delta x_j\right), c\right)}{\partial(\Delta x + \sum_{j=1}^{i} \Delta x_j)} \\
&= \sum_{k=1}^{n} \sum_{i=1}^{T} \Delta x_i^{(k)} \cdot \frac{\partial L\left(N\left(x + \Delta x + \sum_{j=1}^{i} \Delta x_j\right), c\right)}{\partial(\Delta x + \sum_{j=1}^{i} \Delta x_j)^{(k)}}
\end{aligned}
\tag{3}
$$

where $L(N(x + \Delta x), c)$ denotes the obtained loss function value, the input is $x + \Delta x$ and target label is c. The perturbation $\Delta x \in \mathbf{R}^n$ consists of $\Delta x^{(k)}$ with $k = 1, 2, \ldots, n$. The path between $x + \Delta x$ and $x + \Delta x^F$ is illustrated in Fig. 3. We will use $\Delta x^t = \Delta x + \sum_{j=1}^{t} \Delta x_j$ in the following statement for simplification.

$$
A\left(\Delta x^{(k)}\right) = \sum_{i=1}^{T} \Delta x_i^{(k)} \cdot \frac{\partial L\left(N\left(x + \Delta x^t\right), c\right)}{\partial \Delta x^{t(k)}}
\tag{4}
$$

$$
L(N(x + \Delta x), c) - L\left(N\left(x + \Delta x^F\right), c\right) = \sum_{k=1}^{n} A\left(\Delta x^{(k)}\right)
\tag{5}
$$

Here, $A\left(\Delta x^{(k)}\right)$ in (4) can be considered as the attribution result of $\Delta x^{(k)}$. As $\Delta x^{(k)}$ is a component of Δx, the sum of the attribution results equals the loss function changes. Given Eq. (5), any changes in loss function can be attributed by the attribution result, which satisfies the Sensitivity axioms. Thus, $A\left(\Delta x^{(k)}\right)$ can be considered as a reliable method for calculating the attribution result.

Poof of equation (3):

$$
f(x_t) = f(x_{t-1}) + \frac{\partial f(x_{t-1})}{\partial x_{t-1}}(x_t - x_{t-1}) + \varepsilon
$$

$$
\sum_{t=1}^{T} f(x_t) = \sum_{t=0}^{T-1} f(x_t) + \sum_{t=0}^{T-1} \frac{\partial f(x_t)}{\partial x_t}(x_{t+1} - x_t)
$$

$$
f(x_T) - f(x_0) = \sum_{t=0}^{T-1} \frac{\partial f(x_t)}{\partial x_t}(x_{t+1} - x_t)
$$

$$
= \sum_{k=0}^{n} \sum_{t=0}^{T-1} \frac{\partial f(x_t)}{\partial x_t^k}\left(x_{t+1}^k - x_t^T\right)
$$

$$
\tag{6}
$$

where $f(x_t) = L(N(x + \Delta x^t), c)$. We use the first-order Taylor approximation to expand the loss function and combine the information for the path from Δx to Δx^F. Here ϵ is omitted due to the principle of higher-order Taylor expansions.

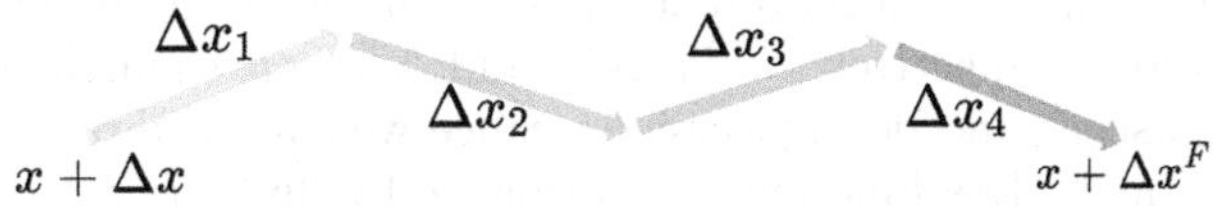

Fig. 3. Illustrating of the path between $x + \Delta x$ and $x + \Delta x^F$

Further Steps of Min-PRv1. We consider two scenarios for loss function in attribution: one is when the loss function increases and the other is when it decreases. Before obtaining the optimization result of the attribution formula, we firstly need to understand that the loss function value represents the network's attacking ability given a correct specific target output. For example, if we choose the adversarial label as the target, a lower loss function value implies a stronger attack ability of the sample. Thus, when the loss function value increases, changes in Δx with higher attribution values will be critical. These changes will be firstly preserved. In another way, when the loss function value decreases, Δx changes with lower attribution values become critical, which will be kept.

Moreover, the role of attribution is to trace the changes. Therefore, it is crucial to determine which changes for tracing. When we refer to D1 in 3.1, removing changes means pushing $\Delta x^{(k)}$ towards zero. We, hereby, apply adversarial attacking progress from FGSM to search the changes for Δx.

$$\Delta x_i' = \alpha * \text{sign} \left(\frac{\partial L \left(N \left(x + \Delta x^i \right), c \right)}{\partial \left(x + \Delta x^i \right)} \right) \tag{7}$$

$$d = sign(\Delta x_i) \oplus sign(x + \Delta x^i)$$
$$\Delta x_i = d \odot \Delta x_i' \tag{8}$$

Equations (7) and (8) describe the update rule for the j-th step of Δx using gradient ascent. Using the sign function in these equations ensures that all input features are updated equally. The symbol $\odot$ denotes the element-wise product, while $\oplus$ represents the XOR operation and α represents learning rate. The use of d in Eq. (8) enables control over the direction of updates for Δx. Additionally, the attribution value is only calculated when the value of Δx is close to zero, as per the condition in the same equation. This is particularly useful when removing irrelevant changes, as it restricts the search space to areas closer to zero. The only difference between the gradient descent version and the gradient ascent version is the sign of $\Delta x_i'$. This indicates that the directions of the updates are opposite. Using both ascent and descent versions can help explore most features, as the total number of updated features in the first step is equal to n.

$$A \left(\Delta x^{(k)} \right) = \left(\frac{A_a}{\Delta L_a} - \frac{A_d}{\Delta L_b} \right)^{(k)} \tag{9}$$

$$\text{Score} \left(\Delta x^{(k)} \right) = abs \left(\Delta x^{(k)} \right) \cdot A \left(\Delta x^{(k)} \right) \tag{10}$$

In the final step, A_a and A_d represent the attribution results under the ascent and decent versions respectively, while ΔL_a and ΔL_b represent the loss function bias under the ascent and decent versions. Since we cannot directly control the level of change in the loss function, we normalize by dividing ΔL such that the attribution values for both the ascent and descent during the evaluation point sum up to 1. To determine the score of $\Delta x^{(k)}$, we use Eq. (10). After computing, we get Min-PRv1(score) by sorting the changes in descending order and removing those with lower scores, retaining only the ones with higher scores. Following, we provide the pseudocode for Min-PRv1.

Algorithm 1. Min-PRv1

Input: Original image x, attack perturbation Δ x, label o, adversarial label c, learning rate lr, interactive step T
Output: Mask m
1: $A_a = [0, 0, ..., 0] \in R^k$, k=dim(x)
2: $A_d = [0, 0, ..., 0] \in R^k$
3: **for** $i = 0, 1..., T$ **do**
4:     $\Delta x_i = d \odot \Delta x_i$
5:     $A_a += \Delta x_i \cdot \frac{\partial L(N(x + \Delta x^t, c))}{\partial \Delta x^t}$
6:     $A_a = \frac{A_a}{\Delta L_a}$, $\Delta L_a = L(N(x + \Delta x)) - L(N(x + \Delta x^F))$
7: **end for**
8: **for** $i = 0, 1..., T$ **do**
9:     $\Delta x_i' = -\Delta x_i'$
10:     A_d is the same calculate progress as A_a
11: **end for**
12: A_d calculated by the same step of A_a
13: Score $= abs(\Delta x) \cdot (A_a - A_d)$
14: m removes the charges in Δx according to the sort of score until $x + m \odot \Delta x$ is just the category not equal to c (dichotomous lookup optimization)

3.3   Min-PRv2 for D2

This section presents the Min-PRv2 algorithm for the optimization problem D2 in Sect. 3.1. The main architecture of Min-PRv2 is shown in Fig. 4.

Details of Min-PRv2. From Fig. 4, a Feed-Forward Network (FFN) is applied for the purpose of acquiring a mask $m \in [0, 1]$, which can be utilised to project Δx to a lower level via $m \odot \Delta x$.

$$m = \text{sigmoid}(FFN([x, \Delta x]))$$
$$L = \text{CrossEntropy } (N(x + m \odot \Delta x), c) + \lambda \cdot \| m \|^2 \tag{11}$$

In Eq. (11), L is the optimising objective for Min-PRv2, while λ is a scalar used to balance the attack capability and the total value of m. Our objective is to

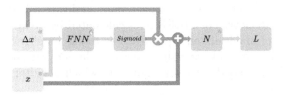

Fig. 4. Architecture of Min-PRv2

minimize changes while still preserving the ability to attack. The FFN shown in Eq. (11) can take on various forms such as MLP, Convolutional Neural Network, or any other structure that allows for back-propagation to optimize. It should be noted that the Min-PRv2 method only uses $\triangle$x to reduce the perturbation rate, while the Min-PRv2 (concat) method uses x and $\triangle$x for splicing to reduce the perturbation rate. Following, we provide the pseudocode for Min-PRv2.

Algorithm 2. Min-PRv2

Input: Original image x, attack perturbation $\triangle$ x, label o, adversarial label c, learning rate lr, interative step T, regularization rate λ, optimizer
Output: Mask m
1: Initialize FFN, optimizer
2: **for** $i = 0, 1..., T$ **do**
3:     $m = FFN(concat(x + \triangle x)$
4:     $L = CE(N(x + m \odot \triangle x), c) + \lambda \left\| m \right\|^2$
5:     Use optimizer to update parameters in FFN
6: **end for**

---

4   Experiments

For the experiment, we aim to provide a thorough evaluation, covering three popular datasets (CIFAR10, CIFAR100 and ImageNet) and different types of attacking algorithms (FGSM [7], LinfPGD, l2PGD [16], and AdvGan [29]). Following, we evaluate the proposed methods of Min-PRv1, Min-PRv1(score), Min-PRv2 and Min-PRv2(concat), together with the Taylor [17] and OBD [13] methods as the baseline, to reduce the perturbation rate of adversarial samples. The learning rate is 0.01 for original labels and a learning rate of 0.2 for the adversarial labels. The difference between these labels is whether they are under attack or not.

Upon the agreements of achieving same level of adversarial attacking success rate, two statistical measurements are applied in the evaluation, which are the *reduced perturbation rate* (RPR) and *minimum required feature rate* (MRFR).

For RPR, it is calculated by dividing the perturbation rate after our algorithm to the original perturbation rate. A higher value indicates a better performance of perturbation reduction. For MRFR, it is calculated by dividing the minimum required number of manipulated input features to the number of input features in the original operation. A lower value indicates a larger portion of manipulating input feature is not needed with our algorithm, which is better.

Table 1. Experiment results for FGSM attack

Dataset	Perturbation reduction method	RPR	MRFR
CIFAR10	Taylor(adversarial label)	0.0198	0.9025
	OBD(adversarial label)	0.6402	0.1428
	Min-PRv1 (original label)	0.6438	0.1473
	Min-PRv1 (adversarial label)	0.6348	0.1533
	Min-PRv1(score) (original label)	**0.6441**	**0.1386**
	Min-PRv1(score) (adversarial label)	0.6236	0.1552
	Min-PRv2 (adversarial label)	0.3311	–
	Min-PRv2(concat) (adversarial label)	0.3219	–
CIFAR100	Taylor(adversarial label)	0.5267	0.2685
	OBD(adversarial label)	0.8197	0.0436
	Min-PRv1 (original label)	**0.8235**	0.0439
	Min-PRv1 (adversarial label)	0.8181	0.0485
	Min-PRv1(score) (original label)	0.8227	**0.0406**
	Min-PRv1(score) (adversarial label)	0.8163	0.0450
	Min-PRv2 (adversarial label)	0.0673	–
	Min-PRv2(concat) (adversarial label)	0.0806	–
ImageNet	Taylor(adversarial label)	0.5206	0.2530
	OBD(adversarial label)	0.7659	0.0942
	Min-PRv1 (original label)	**0.7798**	**0.0866**
	Min-PRv1 (adversarial label)	0.7647	0.0977
	Min-PRv1(score) (original label)	0.7776	0.0868
	Min-PRv1(score) (adversarial label)	0.7654	0.0958
	Min-PRv2 (adversarial label)	0.5521	–
	Min-PRv2(concat) (adversarial label)	0.4107	–

4.1 Experiments for FGSM

Adversarial samples are generated using the same parameters (steps = 1, relative stepsize = 1.0, $\epsilon = 0.3$) on the datasets by FGSM method for the successfully attacked samples. A sample of 1000 images is taken for each dataset to test [30].

Firstly, we use the Min-PRv2 and Min-PRv2(concat) methods with the adversarial labels to reduce the perturbation rate of the adversarial samples. The results in Table 1 show that, the Min-PRv2 and Min-PRv2(concat) methods successfully reduce the perturbation rate by 0.3311 and 0.3219 on the CIFAR10. The results are 0.0673 and 0.0806 for CIFAR100 dataset, respectively. For ImageNet dataset, Min-PRv2 and Min-PRv2(concat) methods reduced the perturbation rate by 0.5521 and 0.4107. For Taylor method, it can reduce the perturbation rates of 0.0198, 0.5267, and 0.5206 on each dataset, while the MRFR of the post-perturbation samples are 0.9025, 0.2685, and 0.2530. OBD method reduces the perturbation rates of 0.6402, 0.8197, and 0.7659 on the three datasets, while the results for MRFRs are 0.1428, 0.0436, and 0.0941.

We can see that, Min-PRv1 has successfully reduced the perturbation rates by 0.6438, 0.8235, and 0.7798 on each dataset by using the original label, while the MRFR for the reduced perturbed samples are 0.1472, 0.0438, and 0.0866. However, with the adversarial labels, the perturbation rates drop at 0.6348, 0.8181, and 0.7647 for each dataset, while MRFR with the adversarial labels are 0.1533, 0.0485, and 0.0977. The Min-PRv1 (score) method reduces the perturbation rates of 0.6441, 0.8227, and 0.7776 on each dataset before the attack, and MRFR results of the post-perturbation samples are 0.1386, 0.0406, and 0.0867. After the attack, the perturbation rates become 0.6236, 0.8163, and 0.7654, and the MRFR on post-perturbation samples are 0.1552, 0.0450, and 0.0958. Overall, Min-PRv1 method using the original labels achieves the best performance.

4.2 Experiments for LinfPGD

As shown in Table 2, the results on the three datasets are collected with a same experimental setting for the linfPGD attack approach, which is steps = 40, relative stepsize = 0.033, ϵ = 0.3. Similar to Sect. 4.1, Min-PRv2 and Min-PRv2(concat) methods successfully reduced the perturbation rate by 0.5453 and 0.4239 on the CIFAR10 dataset, and by 0.5367 and 0.5211 on the CIFAR100 dataset. On ImageNet dataset, Min-PRv2 and Min-PRv2(concat) methods reduced the perturbation rate by 0.7992 and 0.4755. The Taylor method reduced the perturbation rates of 0.4494, 0.6068, and 0.5846 on each dataset, while MRFR of the post-perturbation samples are 0.1046, 0.0522, and 0.0642. The OBD method reduced the perturbation rates of 0.4968, 0.6987, and 0.6325 on three datasets, and the corresponding MRFRs are 0.1553, 0.0579, and 0.0959.

Min-PRv1 method reduced the perturbation rates of 0.4957, 0.7073, and 0.6425 on each dataset before the attack, while the MRFR of the reduced perturbed samples were 0.2892, 0.1141, and 0.1432. After the attack, the perturbation rates of 0.5631, 0.7061, and 0.6159 were reduced on each dataset, while the MRFR of the post-perturbation samples were 0.1581, 0.0653, and 0.0684.

The Min-PRv1(score) method reduces the perturbation rates of 0.502, 0.7013, and 0.6651 on each dataset before the attack, and the MRFR of the post-perturbation samples were 0.1474, 0.0552, and 0.0655. After the attack, the perturbation rates of 0.5618, 0.7118, and 0.7304 were reduced on each dataset, and the MRFR of the post-perturbation samples were 0.1148, 0.0494, and 0.0474.

Table 2. Experiment results for LinfPGD attack

Dataset	Perturbation reduction method	RPR	MRFR
CIFAR10	Taylor (adversarial label)	0.4494	**0.1046**
	OBD (adversarial label)	0.4968	0.1553
	Min-PRv1 (original label)	0.4957	0.2893
	Min-PRv1 (adversarial label)	**0.5631**	0.1581
	Min-PRv1(Score) (original label)	0.502	0.1475
	Min-PRv1(Score) (adversarial label)	0.5618	0.1148
	Min-PRv2 (adversarial label)	0.5453	–
	Min-PRv2(Concat) (adversarial label)	0.4239	–
CIFAR100	Taylor (adversarial label)	0.6068	0.0522
	OBD (adversarial label)	0.6987	0.0580
	Min-PRv1 (original label)	0.7073	0.1141
	Min-PRv1 (adversarial label)	0.7061	0.0653
	Min-PRv1(Score) (original label)	0.7013	0.0552
	Min-PRv1(Score) (adversarial label)	**0.7118**	**0.0494**
	Min-PRv2 (adversarial label)	0.5367	–
	Min-PRv2(Concat) (adversarial label)	0.5211	–
ImageNet	Taylor (adversarial label)	0.5846	0.0642
	OBD (adversarial label)	0.6325	0.0959
	Min-PRv1 (original label)	0.6425	0.1433
	Min-PRv1 (adversarial label)	0.6159	0.0684
	Min-PRv1(Score) (original label)	0.6651	0.0655
	Min-PRv1(Score) (adversarial label)	0.7304	**0.0474**
	Min-PRv2 (adversarial label)	**0.7992**	–
	Min-PRv2(Concat) (adversarial label)	0.4755	–

4.3   Experiments for L2PGD

In Table 3, we use the same parameters (steps = 50, relative stepsize= 0.025, ϵ = 0.3) for the l2PGD attack approach on three datasets. Min-PRv2 and Min-PRv2(concat) methods successfully reduce the perturbation rate by 0.1873 and 0.1980 on the CIFAR10, and by 0.3111 and 0.3334 on the CIFAR100. For ImageNet, the Min-PRv2 and Min-PRv2(concat) methods reduced the perturbation rate by 0.9760 and 0.5899. Taylor method reduces the perturbation rates of 0.3489, 0.4932, and 0.5206 on each dataset, while the MRFR of the post-perturbation samples are 0.1058, 0.0493, and 0.1052. The OBD method reduces the perturbation rates of 0.3727, 0.4912, and 0.3809 on the three datasets, and the MRFR of the reduced perturbation samples are 0.0998, 0.0693, and 0.1128.

The Min-PRv1 method reduced the perturbation rates of 0.3859, 0.5291, and 0.3921 on each dataset before the attack, while the MRFR of the reduced

Table 3. Experiment results for l2PGD attack

Dataset	Perturbation reduction method	RFR	MRFR
CIFAR10	Taylor (adversarial label)	0.3489	0.1058
	OBD (adversarial label)	0.3727	0.0999
	Min-PRv1 (original label)	**0.3859**	0.1317
	Min-PRv1 (adversarial label)	0.3437	0.3092
	Min-PRv1(Score) (original label)	0.3775	**0.0919**
	Min-PRv1(Score) (adversarial label)	0.3589	0.1215
	Min-PRv2 (adversarial label)	0.1873	–
	Min-PRv2(Concat) (adversarial label)	0.1980	–
CIFAR100	Taylor (adversarial label)	0.4932	0.0493
	OBD (adversarial label)	0.4912	0.0694
	Min-PRv1 (original label)	**0.5291**	0.0948
	Min-PRv1 (adversarial label)	0.4732	0.2303
	Min-PRv1(Score) (original label)	0.5215	**0.0487**
	Min-PRv1(Score) (adversarial label)	0.4942	0.0726
	Min-PRv2 (adversarial label)	0.3111	–
	Min-PRv2(Concat) (adversarial label)	0.3334	–
ImageNet	Taylor (adversarial label)	0.3608	0.1052
	OBD (adversarial label)	0.3809	0.1128
	Min-PRv1 (original label)	0.3921	0.1300
	Min-PRv1 (adversarial label)	0.3883	0.1951
	Min-PRv1(Score) (original label)	0.3820	**0.0932**
	Min-PRv1(Score) (adversarial label)	0.3807	0.1069
	Min-PRv2 (adversarial label)	**0.9760**	–
	Min-PRv2(Concat) (adversarial label)	0.5899	–

perturbed samples were 0.1317, 0.0948, and 0.1299. After the attack, the perturbation rates of 0.3437, 0.4732, and 0.3883 were reduced on each dataset, while MRFR of the post-perturbation samples were 0.3092, 0.2303, and 0.1951.

The Min-PRv1(score) method reduces the perturbation rates of 0.3775, 0.5215, and 0.382 on each dataset before the attack, and the MRFR of the post-perturbation samples were 0.0918, 0.0486, and 0.0931. After the attack, the perturbation rates of 0.3589, 0.4942, and 0.3807 were reduced on each dataset, and MRFR of the post-perturbation samples were 0.1215, 0.0726, and 0.1069.

4.4 Experiments for AdvGAN

In Table 4, we use the same parameters (steps = 50, optimizer_G learning rate = 0.001, optimizer_D learning rate = 0.001) for AdvGAN attack on three datasets. Min-PRv2 and Min-PRv2(concat) methods reduce the perturbation rate by

Table 4. Experiment results for AdvGAN attacks

Dataset	Perturbation reduction method and loss target	RPR	MRFR
CIFAR10	Taylor (adversarial label)	0.4975	**0.0682**
	OBD (adversarial label)	0.5798	0.0821
	Min-PRv1 (original label)	**0.5931**	0.2139
	Min-PRv1 (adversarial label)	0.5769	0.1998
	Min-PRv1(Score) (original label)	0.5866	0.0788
	Min-PRv1(Score) (adversarial label)	0.5441	0.0934
	Min-PRv2 (adversarial label)	0.3336	–
	Min-PRv2(Concat) (adversarial label)	0.3065	–
CIFAR100	Taylor (adversarial label)	0.8152	**0.0120**
	OBD (adversarial label)	0.8351	0.0133
	Min-PRv1 (original label)	0.8401	0.0453
	Min-PRv1 (adversarial label)	**0.8424**	0.0396
	Min-PRv1(Score) (original label)	0.8358	0.0131
	Min-PRv1(Score) (adversarial label)	0.8328	0.0132
	Min-PRv2 (adversarial label)	0.4215	–
	Min-PRv2(Concat) (adversarial label)	0.2850	–
ImageNet	Taylor (adversarial label)	0.4047	0.1636
	OBD (adversarial label)	0.5423	0.1619
	Min-PRv1 (original label)	**0.5904**	0.2312
	Min-PRv1 (adversarial label)	0.5528	0.2717
	Min-PRv1(Score) (original label)	0.5721	**0.1313**
	Min-PRv1(Score) (adversarial label)	0.5328	0.1516
	Min-PRv2 (adversarial label)	0.5367	–
	Min-PRv2(Concat) (adversarial label)	0.3812	–

0.3336 and 0.3065 on CIFAR10, and by 0.4215 and 0.2850 on CIFAR100. For ImageNet, the Min-PRv2 and Min-PRv2(concat) methods reduce the perturbation rate by 0.5367 and 0.3812. The perturbation rates of Taylor method are 0.4975, 0.8152, and 0.4047 on each dataset, while MRFR for the adversarial labels are 0.0682, 0.0120, and 0.1636. OBD method reduces the perturbation rates of 0.5798, 0.8351, and 0.5423 on the three datasets, and the MRFR results of adversarial labels are 0.0821, 0.0133, and 0.1619. Min-PRv1 method reduced the perturbation rates of 0.5931, 0.8401, and 0.5904 on each dataset before the attack, while the MRFR of the reduced perturbed samples are 0.2139, 0.0452, and 0.2312. With the post-perturbation samples, the perturbation rates are 0.5769, 0.8424, and 0.5528, and the MRFR results are 0.1998, 0.0396, and 0.2717.

For Min-PRv1 (score) method, it initially reduces the perturbation rates of 0.5866, 0.8358, and 0.5721 on each dataset, and the MRFR of the post-perturbation samples are 0.0788, 0.0130, and 0.1313. With the perturbed samples, the perturbation rates become 0.5441, 0.8328, and 0.5328, and the MRFR of the post-perturbation samples are 0.0934, 0.0131, and 0.1516.

Since the learning rate is the only hyperparameter for Min-PR, the ablation study result is included in Fig. 5. While Min-PRv2 algorithm performs more stable than others, we can see it is stable for all Min-PR algorithms. In general, as the learning rate increases, the Min-PRv1 algorithm may becomes slightly worse, while the Min-PRv2 algorithm performs smoothly, indicating that a high utility and performance of Min-PR algorithm.

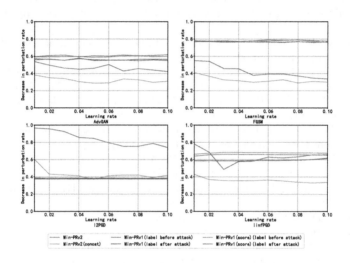

Fig. 5. Line chart of algorithm performance

5   Conclusion

In this paper, we propose the Min-PR algorithm to minimise the adversarial attack perturbation rate. We are the first to introduce the attribution based pruning technique for the topic, and consequently we have implemented two different forms of Min-PR to address different types of requirements and constraints. Min-PRv1 is capable of reducing as many adversarial features as possible, while Min-PRv2 is to reduce as much holistic perturbation as possible. Finally, we have benchmarked our algorithms to different adversarial attack methods on different datasets. The comprehensive experimental results highlight the possibility of further minimising the perturbation rate for adversarial samples, and demonstrate the effectiveness of our algorithms.

References

1. Ain, Q.T., et al.: Sentiment analysis using deep learning techniques: a review. Int. J. Adv. Comput. Sci. Appl. **8**(6) (2017)
2. Bai, T., Luo, J., Zhao, J., Wen, B., Wang, Q.: Recent advances in adversarial training for adversarial robustness. arXiv preprint arXiv:2102.01356 (2021)
3. Cao, W., Wang, X., Ming, Z., Gao, J.: A review on neural networks with random weights. Neurocomputing **275**, 278–287 (2018)
4. Carlini, N., Wagner, D.: Towards evaluating the robustness of neural networks. In: 2017 IEEE Symposium on Security and Privacy (SP), pp. 39–57. IEEE (2017)
5. Dong, S., Wang, P., Abbas, K.: A survey on deep learning and its applications. Comput. Sci. Rev. **40**, 100379 (2021)
6. Dong, Y., et al.: Boosting adversarial attacks with momentum. In: Proceedings of the IEEE Conference on Computer Vision and Pattern Recognition, pp. 9185–9193 (2018)
7. Goodfellow, I.J., Shlens, J., Szegedy, C.: Explaining and harnessing adversarial examples. arXiv preprint arXiv:1412.6572 (2014)
8. He, Y., Meng, G., Chen, K., Hu, X., He, J.: Towards security threats of deep learning systems: a survey. IEEE Trans. Softw. Eng. **48**(5), 1743–1770 (2020)
9. Janiesch, C., Zschech, P., Heinrich, K.: Machine learning and deep learning. Electron. Markets **31**(3), 685–695 (2021)
10. Kim, H., Park, J., Lee, J.: Generating transferable adversarial examples for speech classification. Pattern Recognit. **137**, 109286 (2023)
11. Kurakin, A., Goodfellow, I.J., Bengio, S.: Adversarial machine learning at scale. In: International Conference on Learning Representations
12. LeCun, Y., Denker, J., Solla, S.: Optimal brain damage. Adv. Neural Inf. Process. Syst. **2** (1989)
13. LeCun, Y., Denker, J., Solla, S.: Optimal brain damage. Adv. Neural Inf. Process. Syst. **2** (1989)
14. Liao, F., Liang, M., Dong, Y., Pang, T., Hu, X., Zhu, J.: Defense against adversarial attacks using high-level representation guided denoiser. In: Proceedings of the IEEE Conference on Computer Vision and Pattern Recognition, pp. 1778–1787 (2018)
15. Lin, Y., Zhao, H., Tu, Y., Mao, S., Dou, Z.: Threats of adversarial attacks in DNN-based modulation recognition. In: IEEE INFOCOM 2020-IEEE Conference on Computer Communications, pp. 2469–2478. IEEE (2020)
16. Madry, A., Makelov, A., Schmidt, L., Tsipras, D., Vladu, A.: Towards deep learning models resistant to adversarial attacks. arXiv preprint arXiv:1706.06083 (2017)
17. Molchanov, P., Mallya, A., Tyree, S., Frosio, I., Kautz, J.: Importance estimation for neural network pruning. In: Proceedings of the IEEE/CVF Conference on Computer Vision and Pattern Recognition, pp. 11264–11272 (2019)
18. Nasr, M., Shokri, R., Houmansadr, A.: Comprehensive privacy analysis of deep learning: passive and active white-box inference attacks against centralized and federated learning. In: 2019 IEEE Symposium on Security and Privacy (SP), pp. 739–753. IEEE (2019)
19. Nazemi, A., Fieguth, P.: Potential adversarial samples for white-box attacks. arXiv preprint arXiv:1912.06409 (2019)
20. Papernot, N., McDaniel, P., Goodfellow, I., Jha, S., Celik, Z.B., Swami, A.: Practical black-box attacks against machine learning. In: Proceedings of the 2017 ACM on Asia Conference on Computer and Communications Security, pp. 506–519 (2017)

21. Perez, L., Wang, J.: The effectiveness of data augmentation in image classification using deep learning. arXiv preprint arXiv:1712.04621 (2017)
22. Reed, R.: Pruning algorithms-a survey. IEEE Trans. Neural Netw. **4**(5), 740–747 (1993)
23. Song, Z.: English speech recognition based on deep learning with multiple features. Computing **102**(3), 663–682 (2020)
24. Sundararajan, M., Taly, A., Yan, Q.: Axiomatic attribution for deep networks. In: International Conference on Machine Learning, pp. 3319–3328. PMLR (2017)
25. Szegedy, C., et al.: Intriguing properties of neural networks. arXiv preprint arXiv:1312.6199 (2013)
26. Wang, K., Li, F., Chen, C.M., Hassan, M.M., Long, J., Kumar, N.: Interpreting adversarial examples and robustness for deep learning-based auto-driving systems. IEEE Trans. Intell. Transport. Syst. **23**(7), 9755–9764 (2021)
27. Wang, Y., Ma, X., Bailey, J., Yi, J., Zhou, B., Gu, Q.: On the convergence and robustness of adversarial training. arXiv preprint arXiv:2112.08304 (2021)
28. Wong, E., Kolter, Z.: Provable defenses against adversarial examples via the convex outer adversarial polytope. In: International Conference on Machine Learning, pp. 5286–5295. PMLR (2018)
29. Xiao, C., Li, B., Zhu, J.Y., He, W., Liu, M., Song, D.: Generating adversarial examples with adversarial networks. arXiv preprint arXiv:1801.02610 (2018)
30. Zhang, J., et al.: Improving adversarial transferability via neuron attribution-based attacks. In: Proceedings of the IEEE/CVF Conference on Computer Vision and Pattern Recognition, pp. 14993–15002 (2022)
31. Zhong, Y., Deng, W.: Towards transferable adversarial attack against deep face recognition. IEEE Trans. Inform. Forens. Secur. **16**, 1452–1466 (2020)
32. Zhou, S., Liu, C., Ye, D., Zhu, T., Zhou, W., Yu, P.S.: Adversarial attacks and defenses in deep learning: from a perspective of cybersecurity. ACM Comput. Surv. **55**(8), 1–39 (2022)

Adversarial Sample Detection Through Neural Network Transport Dynamics

Skander Karkar[1,2(✉)], Patrick Gallinari[1,2], and Alain Rakotomamonjy[1]

[1] Criteo AI Lab, Criteo, Paris, France
{as.karkar,p.gallinari,a.rakotomamonjy}@criteo.com
[2] MLIA, ISIR, Sorbonne Université, Paris, France

Abstract. We propose a detector of adversarial samples that is based on the view of neural networks as discrete dynamic systems. The detector tells clean inputs from abnormal ones by comparing the discrete vector fields they follow through the layers. We also show that regularizing this vector field during training makes the network more regular on the data distribution's support, thus making the activations of clean inputs more distinguishable from those of abnormal ones. Experimentally, we compare our detector favorably to other detectors on seen and unseen attacks, and show that the regularization of the network's dynamics improves the performance of adversarial detectors that use the internal embeddings as inputs, while also improving test accuracy.

Keywords: Deep learning · Adversarial detection · Optimal transport

1 Introduction

Neural networks have improved performances on many tasks, including image classification. They are however vulnerable to adversarial attacks which modify an image in a way that is imperceptible to a human but that fools the network into wrongly classifying the image [41]. These adversarial images transfer between networks [33], can be carried out physically (e.g. causing autonomous cars to misclassify road signs [12]), and can be generated without access to the network [28]. Developing networks that are robust to adversarial samples or accompanied by detectors that can detect them is indispensable to deploying them safely [3].

We focus on detecting adversarial samples. Networks trained with a softmax classifier produce overconfident predictions even for out-of-distribution inputs [35]. This makes it difficult to detect such inputs via the softmax outputs. A detector is a system capable of predicting if an input at test time has been adversarially modified. Detectors are trained on a dataset made up of clean and adversarial inputs, after the network training. While simply training the detector on the inputs has been tried, using their intermediate embeddings works better [7]. Detectors vary by which activations to use and how to process them to extract the features that the classifier uses to tell clean samples from adversarial ones.

We make two contributions. First, we propose an adversarial detector that is based on the view of neural networks as dynamical systems that move inputs

D. Koutra et al. (Eds.): ECML PKDD 2023, LNAI 14169, pp. 164–181, 2023.
https://doi.org/10.1007/978-3-031-43412-9_10

in space, time represented by depth, to separate them before applying a linear classifier [45]. Our detector follows the trajectory of samples in space, through time, to differentiate clean and adversarial images. The statistics that we extract are the positions of the internal embeddings in space approximated by their norms and cosines to a fixed vector. Given their resemblance to the Euler scheme for differential equations, residual networks [17,18,45] are particularly amenable to this analysis. Skip connections and residuals are basic building blocks in many architectures such as EfficientNet [42] and MobileNetV2 [39], and ResNets and their variants such as WideResNet [50] and ResNeXt [49] remain competitive [47]. Visions Transformers [11,29] are also mainly made up of residual stages. Besides, [48] show an increased vulnerability of residual-type architectures to transferable attacks, precisely because of the skip connections. This motivates the need for a detector that is well adapted to residual-type architectures. But the analysis and implementation can extend immediately to any network where most layers have the same input and output dimensions.

Our second contribution is to use the transport regularization during training proposed in [21] to make the activations of adversarial samples more distinguishable from those of clean samples, thus making adversarial detectors perform better, while also improving generalization. We prove that the regularization achieves this by making the network more regular on the support of the data distribution. This does not necessarily make it more robust, but it will make the activations of the clean samples closer to each other and further from those of out-of-distribution samples, thus making adversarial detection easier. This is illustrated on a 2-dimension example in Fig. 1.

2   Related Work

Given a classifier f in a classification task and $\epsilon > 0$, an adversarial sample y constructed from a clean sample x is $y = x + \delta$, such that $f(y) \neq f(x)$ and $\|\delta\|_p \leq \epsilon$ for a certain L_p norm. The maximal perturbation size ϵ has to be so small as to be almost imperceptible to a human. Adversarial attacks are algorithms that find such adversarial samples, and they have been particularly successful against neural networks [6,41]. We present the adversarial attacks we use in our experiments in Appendix D.1. The main defense mechanisms are robustness, i.e. training a network that is not easily fooled by adversarial samples, and having a detector of these samples.

An early idea for detection was to use a second network [32]. However, this network can also be adversarially attacked. More recent statistical approaches include LID [30], which trains the detector on the local intrinsic dimensionality of activations approximated over a batch, and the Mahalanobis detector [27], which trains the detector on the Mahalanobis distances between the activations and a Gaussian fitted to them during training, assuming they are normally distributed. Our detector is not a statistical approach and does not need batch-level statistics, nor statistics from the training data. Detectors trained in the Fourier domain of activations have also been proposed in [16]. See [1] for a review.

Our second contribution is to regularize the network in a way that makes it Hölder-continuous, but only on the data distribution's support. Estimations of the Lipschitz constant of a network have been used as estimates of its robustness to adversarial samples in [19,41,44,46], and making the network more Lipschitz (e.g. by penalizing an upper bound on its Lipschitz constant) has been used to make it more robust (i.e. less likely to be fooled) in [9,19]. These regularizations often work directly on the weights of the network, therefore making it more regular on all the input space. The difference with our method is that we only endue the network with regularity on the support of the clean data. This won't make it more robust to adversarial samples, but it makes its behavior on them more distinguishable, since they tend to lie outside the data manifold.

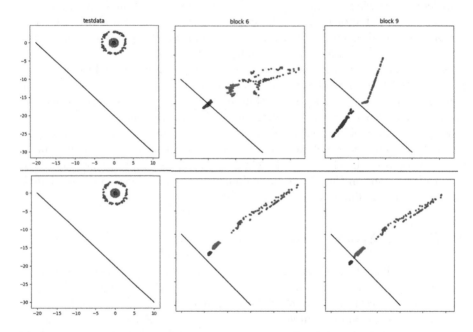

Fig. 1. Transformed circles test set from scikit-learn (red and blue) and out-of-distribution points (green) after blocks 6 and 9 of a small ResNet with 9 blocks. In the second row, we add our proposed regularization during training, which makes the movements of the clean points (red and blue) more similar to each other and more different from the movements of the green out-of-distribution points than when using the vanilla network in the first row. In particular, without the regularization, the green points are closer to the clean red points after blocks 6 and 9 which is undesirable. (Color figure online)

That adversarial samples lie outside the data manifold, particularly in its co-dimensions, is a common observation and explanation for why adversarial samples are easy to find in high dimensions [2,13,14,24,30,38,40,43]. To the best of our knowledge, [37] is the only other method that attempts to improve detection by encouraging the network during training to learn representations that are more different between clean and adversarial samples. They do this by replacing cross-entropy by a reverse cross-entropy that encourages uniform softmax outputs among the non-predicted classes. We find that our regularization leads to better classification accuracy and adversarial detection than this method.

3   Background

Our detector is based on the dynamic viewpoint of neural networks that followed from the analogy between ResNets and the Euler scheme made in [45]. We present this analogy in Sect. 3.2. The regularization we use was proposed in [21] to improve generalization and we also present it in Sect. 3.2. The regularity results that follow from this regularization require the use of optimal transport theory, which we present in Sect. 3.1.

3.1   Optimal Transport

Let α and β be absolutely continuous densities on a compact set $\Omega \subset \mathbb{R}^d$. The Monge problem is to look for $T : \mathbb{R}^d \to \mathbb{R}^d$ moving α to β, i.e. $T_\sharp \alpha = \beta$, with minimal transport cost:

$$\min_{T \text{ s.t. } T_\sharp \alpha = \beta} \int_\Omega \|T(x) - x\|_2^2 \, d\alpha(x) \tag{1}$$

and this problem has a unique solution $T^\star$. An equivalent formulation of the Monge problem in this setting is the dynamical formulation. Here, instead of directly pushing points from α to β through T, we continuously displace mass from time 0 to 1 according to velocity field $v_t : \mathbb{R}^d \to \mathbb{R}^d$. We denote ϕ_t^x the position at time t of the particle that was at $x \sim \alpha$ at time 0. This position evolves according to $\partial_t \phi_t^x = v_t(\phi_t^x)$. Rewriting the constraint, Problem (1) is equivalent to the dynamical formulation:

$$\min_v \int_0^1 \|v_t\|_{L^2((\phi_t)_\sharp \alpha)}^2 \, dt \tag{2}$$
$$\text{s.t. } \partial_t \phi_t^x = v_t(\phi_t^x) \text{ for } x \in \text{support}(\alpha) \text{ and } t \in [0, 1[$$
$$\phi_0 = \text{id}, (\phi_1)_\sharp \alpha = \beta$$

3.2   Least Action Principle Residual Networks

A residual stage made up of M residual blocks applies $x_{m+1} = x_m + h r_m(x_m)$ for $0 \le m < M$, with x_0 being the input and $h=1$ in practice. The final point x_M is then classified by a linear layer F. The dynamic view considers a residual network as an Euler discretization of a differential equation:

$$x_{m+1} = x_m + h r_m(x_m) \longleftrightarrow \partial_t x_t = v_t(x_t) \tag{3}$$

where r_m approximates the vector field v_t at time $t = m/M$. The dynamic view allows to consider that ResNets are transporting their inputs in space by following a vector field to separate them, the depth representing time, before classification by a linear layer. [21] look for a network $F \circ T$ that solves the task while having minimal transport cost:

$$
\inf_{T,F} \quad \int_\Omega \|T(x) - x\|_2^2 \, d\alpha(x) \tag{4}
$$
$$
\text{s.t.} \quad \mathcal{L}(F, T_\sharp \alpha) = 0
$$

where T is made up of the M residual blocks, α is the data distribution, F is the classification head and $\mathcal{L}(F, T_\sharp \alpha)$ is the (cross-entropy) loss obtained from classifying the transformed data distribution $T_\sharp \alpha$ through F. Given Sect. 3.1, the corresponding dynamical version of (4) is

$$
\inf_{v,F} \quad \int_0^1 \|v_t\|_{L^2((\phi_t)_\sharp \alpha)}^2 \, dt \tag{5}
$$
$$
\text{s.t.} \quad \partial_t \phi_t^x = v_t(\phi_t^x) \text{ for } x \in \text{support}(\alpha) \text{ and } t \in [0,1[
$$
$$
\phi_0 = \text{id}, \quad \mathcal{L}(F, (\phi_1)_\sharp \alpha) = 0
$$

[21] show that (4) and (5) are equivalent and have a solution such that T is an optimal transport map. In practice, (5) is discretized using a sample $\mathcal{D}$ from α and an Euler scheme, which gives a residual architecture with residual blocks r_m (parametrized along with the classifier by θ) that approximate v. This gives the following problem

$$
\min_\theta \quad \mathcal{C}(\theta) = \sum_{x \in \mathcal{D}} \sum_{m=0}^{M-1} \|r_m(\varphi_m^x)\|_2^2 \tag{6}
$$
$$
\text{s.t} \quad \varphi_{m+1}^x = \varphi_m^x + h r_m(\varphi_m^x), \quad \varphi_0^x = x \ \ \forall \, x \in \mathcal{D}
$$
$$
\mathcal{L}(\theta) = 0
$$

In practice, we solve Problem (6) using a method of multipliers (see Sect. 4.2). Our contribution is to show, theoretically and experimentally, that this makes adversarial examples easier to detect.

4   Method

We take the view that a ResNet moves its inputs through a discrete vector field to separate them, points in the same class having similar trajectories. Heuristically, for a successful adversarial sample that is close to clean samples, the vector field it follows has to be different at some step from that of the clean samples, so that it joins the trajectory of the points in another class. In Sect. 4.1, we present how we detect adversarial samples by considering these trajectories. In Sect. 4.2, we apply the transport regularization by solving (6) to improve detectability of adversarial samples.

4.1 Detection

Given a network that applies $x_{m+1} = x_m + h r_m(x_m)$ to an input x_0 for $0 \leq m < M$, we consider the embeddings x_m for $0 < m \leq M$, or the residues $r_m(x_m)$ for $0 \leq m < M$. To describe their positions in space, we take their norms and their cosine similarities with a fixed vector as features to train our adversarial detector on. Using only the norms already gave good detection accuracy. Cosines to other orthogonal vectors can be added to better locate the points at the price of increasing the number of features. We found that using only one vector already gives state-of-the-art detection, so we only use the norms and cosines to a fixed vector of ones. We train the detector (a random forest in practice, see Sect. 5.2) on these features. The embeddings x_m and the residues $r_m(x_m)$ can equivalently describe the trajectory of x_0 in space through the blocks. In practice, we use the residues $r_m(x_m)$, with their norms squared and averaged. So the feature vector given to the random forest for each input x_0 that goes through a network that applies $x_{m+1} = x_m + h\, r_m(x_m)$ is

$$\left(\frac{1}{d_m} \|r_m(x_m)\|_2^2, \ \cos\Big(r_m(x_m), \mathbf{1}_m\Big) \right)_{0 \leq m < M} \tag{7}$$

and the label is 0 if x_0 is clean and 1 if it is adversarial. Here cos is the cosine similarity between two vectors and $\mathbf{1}_m$ is a vector of ones of size d_m where d_m is the size of $r_m(x_m)$. For any non-residual architecture $x_{m+1} = g_m(x_m)$, the vector $x_{m+1} - x_m$ can be used instead of $r_m(x_m)$ on layers that have the same input and output dimension, allowing to apply the method to any network with many such layers. And we do test the detector on a ResNeXt, which does not fully satisfy the dynamic view, as the activation is applied after the skip-connection, i.e. $x_{m+1} = \mathrm{ReLU}(x_m + h\, r_m(x_m))$.

The number of features is twice that of residual blocks (a norm and a cosine per block). This is of the same order as for other popular detectors such as Mahalanobis [27] and LID [30] that extract one feature per residual stage (a residual stage is a group of blocks that keep the same dimension). Even for common large architectures, twice the number of residual blocks is still a small number of features for training a binary classifier (ResNet152 has 50 blocks). More importantly, the features we extract (norms and cosines) are quick to calculate, whereas those of other methods require involved statistical computations on the activations. We include in Appendix D.10 a favorable time comparison of our detector to the Mahalanobis detector. Another advantage is that our detector does not have a hyper-parameter to tune unlike the Mahalanobis and LID detectors.

4.2 Regularization

Regularity of neural networks (typically Lipschitz continuity) has been used as a measure of their robustness to adversarial samples [9, 19, 41, 44, 46]. Indeed, the smaller the Lipschitz constant L of a function f satisfying $\|f(x) - f(y)\| \leq$

$L\|x - y\|$, the less f changes its output $f(y)$ for a perturbation (adversarial or not) y of x. Regularizing a network to make it more Lipschitz and more robust has therefore been tried in [9,19]. For this to work, the regularization has to apply to adversarial points, i.e. outside the support of the clean data distribution. Indeed, the Lipschitz continuity obtained though most of these methods and analyses apply on the entire input space $\mathbb{R}^d$ as they penalize the network's weights directly. Likewise, a small step size h as in [51] will have the same effect on all inputs, clean or not.

We propose here an alternative approach where we regularize the network only on the support of the input distribution, making it η-Hölder on this support (a function f is η-Hölder on X if $\forall\, a, b \in X$, we have $\|f(a) - f(b)\| \leq C\|a - b\|^{\eta}$ for some constants $C{>}0$ and $0{<}\eta{\leq}1$, and we denote this $f \in \mathcal{C}^{0,\eta}(X)$). Since this result does not apply outside the input distribution's support, particularly in the adversarial spaces, then this regularity that only applies to clean samples can serve to make adversarial samples more distinguishable from clean ones, and therefore easier to detect. We show experimentally that the behavior of the network will be more distinguishable between clean and adversarial samples in practice in Sect. 5.1. We discuss the implementation of the regularization in Sect. 4.2 and prove the regularity it endues the network with in Sect. 4.2.

Implementation. We regularize the trajectory of the samples by solving Problem (6). This means finding, among the networks that solve the task (condition $\mathcal{L}(\theta) = 0$ in (6)), the network that moves the points the least, that is the one with minimal kinetic energy $\mathcal{C}$. The residual functions r_m we find are then our approximation of the vector field v that solves the continuous version (5) of Problem (6).

We solve Problem (6) via a method of multipliers: since $\mathcal{L} \geq 0$, Problem (6) is equivalent to the min-max problem $\min_\theta \max_{\lambda>0}\ \mathcal{C}(\theta) + \lambda\, \mathcal{L}(\theta)$, which we solve, given growth factor $\tau > 0$, and starting from initial weight given to the loss λ_0 and initial parameters θ_0, through

$$\begin{cases} \theta_{i+1} = \arg\min_{\theta}\ \mathcal{C}(\theta) + \lambda_i\, \mathcal{L}(\theta) \\ \lambda_{i+1} = \lambda_i + \tau\, \mathcal{L}(\theta_{i+1}) \end{cases} \tag{8}$$

We use SGD for $s{>}0$ steps (i.e. batches) for the minimization in the first line of (8), starting from the previous θ_i. When using a ResNeXt, where a residual block applies $x_{m+1} = \mathrm{ReLU}(x_m + r_m(x_m))$, we regularize the norms of the true residues $x_{m+1}{-}x_m$ instead of $r_m(x_m)$.

Theoretical Analysis. We take $\Omega{\subset}\mathbb{R}^d$ convex and compact and the data distribution $\alpha{\in}\mathcal{P}(\Omega)$ absolutely continuous such that $\delta\Omega$ is α-negligible. We suppose that there exists an open bounded convex set $X{\subset}\Omega$ such that α is bounded away from zero and infinity on X and is zero on X^{C}. From [21], Problems (4) and (5) are equivalent and have solutions (T, F) and (v, F) such that T is an optimal transport map between α and $\beta{:=}T_{\sharp}\alpha$. We suppose that β is absolutely continuous and that there exists an open bounded convex set $Y \subset \Omega$ such that β is bounded away from zero and infinity on Y and is zero on $Y^{\complement}$. In the rest of this section, v solves (5) and we suppose that we find a solution to the discretized problem (6) that is an $\varepsilon/2$-approximation of v, i.e. $\|r_m - v_{t_m}\|_\infty \leq \varepsilon/2$ for all $0 \leq m < M$, with $t_m = m/M$.

Definition 1. *A function f is η-Hölder on X if $\forall\, a, b \in X$, we have $\|f(a) - f(b)\| \leq C\|a - b\|^\eta$ for some constants $C > 0$ and $0 < \eta \leq 1$. We denote this $f \in \mathcal{C}^{0,\eta}(X)$.*

In Theorem 1, we show that the regularization makes the residual blocks of the network η-Hölder (with an error of ε) on the support of the input distribution as it moves according to the theoretical vector field solution v. The results hold for all norms on $\mathbb{R}^d$.

Theorem 1. *For $a, b \in support(\alpha_{t_m})$, $\alpha_t := (\phi_t)_\sharp \alpha$ where ϕ solves (5) along with v, we have*

$$\|r_m(a) - r_m(b)\| \leq \varepsilon + K\|a - b\|^{\zeta_1} \text{ if } \|a - b\| \leq 1$$
$$\|r_m(a) - r_m(b)\| \leq \varepsilon + K\|a - b\|^{\zeta_2} \text{ if } \|a - b\| > 1$$

for constants $K > 0$ and $0 < \zeta_1 \leq \zeta_2 \leq 1$.

Proof. The detailed proof is in Appendix C.1. First, we have that $v_t = (T - \text{id}) \circ T_t^{-1}$ where $T_t := (1 - t)\text{id} + tT$ and T solves (4). Being an optimal transport map, T is η-Hölder. So for all $a, b \in support(\alpha_t)$ and $t \in [0, 1[$, where $\alpha_t = (\phi_t)_\sharp \alpha = (T_t)_\sharp \alpha$ with ϕ solving (5) with v, we have

$$\|v_t(a) - v_t(b)\| \leq \|T_t^{-1}(a) - T_t^{-1}(b)\| + C\|T_t^{-1}(a) - T_t^{-1}(b)\|^\eta \qquad (9)$$

We then show that T_t^{-1} is an optimal transport map and so is η_t-Hölder with $0 < \eta_t \leq 1$. Using the hypothesis on r and the triangle inequality, we get, for all $a, b \in support(\alpha_{t_m})$

$$\|r_m(a) - r_m(b)\| \leq \varepsilon + C_{t_m}\|a - b\|^{\eta_{t_m}} + CC_{t_m}^\eta\|a - b\|^{\eta\eta_{t_m}} \qquad (10)$$

Then set the constants K, ζ_1 and ζ_2 as necessary. $\qquad \square$

We use Theorem 1 to now bound the distance between the residues at depth m as a function of the distance between the network's inputs. For inputs a_0 and b_0 to the network, the intermediate embeddings are $a_{m+1} = a_m + hr_m(a_m)$ and $b_{m+1} = b_m + hr_m(b_m)$, and the residues used to compute features for adversarial detection are $r_m(a_m)$ and $r_m(b_m)$. So we want to bound $\|r_m(a_m) - r_m(b_m)\|$ as a function of $\|a_0 - b_0\|$. This is usually done by multiplying the Lipschitz constants of each block up to depth m, which leads to an overestimation [20], or through more complex estimation algorithms [4,26,44]. Bound (9) allows through T_t^{-1} to avoid multiplying the Hölder constants of the blocks. If a_0 and b_0 are on the clean data support X, we get Theorem 2 below with proof in Appendix C.2.

Theorem 2. *For* $a_0, b_0 \in X$ *and constants* $C, L > 0$,

$$\|r_m(a_m) - r_m(b_m)\| \leq \varepsilon + \|a_0 - b_0\| + C\|a_0 - b_0\|^\eta +$$
$$+ L(\|a_m - \phi_{t_m}^{a_0}\| + \|b_m - \phi_{t_m}^{b_0}\|)$$

Term $\mu(a_0) := \|a_m - \phi_{t_m}^{a_0}\|$ (and $\mu(b_0) := \|b_m - \phi_{t_m}^{b_0}\|$) is the distance between the point a_m after m residual blocks and the point $\phi_{t_m}^{a_0}$ we get by following the theoretical solution vector field v up to time t_m starting from a_0. If a_0 and b_0 are not on the data support X, an extra term has to be introduced to use bound (9). Bounding the terms $\mu(a_0)$ and $\mu(b_0)$ is possible under more regularity assumptions on v. We assume then that v is $\mathcal{C}^1$ and Lipschitz in x, which is not stronger than the regularity we get on v through our regularization, as it does not give a similar result to bound (9). We have for all inputs a_0 and b_0, whether they are clean or not, Theorem 3 below with proof in Appendix C.2.

Theorem 3. *For* $a_0, b_0 \in \mathbb{R}^d$ *and constants* $R, S > 0$,

$$\|r_m(a_m) - r_m(b_m)\| \leq \varepsilon + LS\varepsilon + LSRh + \|a_0 - b_0\| + C\|a_0 - b_0\|^\eta +$$
$$+ LS(dist(a_0, X) + dist(b_0, X))$$

Terms $dist(a_0, X)$ and $dist(b_0, X)$ show that the regularity guarantee is increased for inputs in X. The trajectories of clean points are then closer to each other and more different from those of abnormal samples outside X.

5   Experiments

We evaluate our method on adversarial samples found by 8 attacks. The threat model is as follows. We use 6 white-box attacks that can access the network and its weights and architecture but not its training data: FGM [15], BIM [25], DF [34], CW [6], AutoAttack (AA) [10] and the Auto-PGD-CE (APGD) variant of PGD [31], and 2 black-box attacks that only query the network: HSJ [8] and BA [5]. We assume the attacker has no knowledge of the detector and use the untargeted (i.e. not trying to direct the mistake towards a particular class) versions of the attacks. We use a maximal perturbation of $\epsilon = 0.03$ for FGM, APGD, BIM and AA. We use the L_2 norm for CW and HSJ and L_∞ for the other attacks. We compare our detector (which we call the Transport detector or TR) to the Mahalanobis detector (MH in the tables below) of [27] and to the detector of [22,23] that uses natural scene statistics (NS in the tables below), and our regularization to reverse cross entropy training of [37], which is also meant to improve detection of adversarial samples. We use ART [36] and its default hyper-parameter values (except those specified) to generate the adversarial samples, except for AA for which we use the authors' original code. The code and Appendix are at github.com/skander-karkar/adv. See Appendix D.1 for more details.

We use 3 networks and datasets: ResNeXt50 on CIFAR100, ResNet110 on CIFAR10 and WideResNet on TinyImageNet. Each network is trained normally with cross entropy, with the transport regularization added to cross entropy (called a LAP-network for Least Action Principle), and with reverse cross entropy instead of cross entropy (called an RCE-network). For LAP training, we use (8) with $\tau=1$, $s=1$ and $\lambda_0=1$ for all networks. These hyper-parameters are chosen to improve validation accuracy during training not adversarial detection. Training details are in Appendix D.2.

In Sect. 5.1, we conduct preliminary experiments to show that LAP training improves generalization and stability, and increases the difference between the transport costs of clean and adversarial samples. In Sect. 5.2, we test our detector when it is trained and tested on samples generated by the same attack. In Sect. 5.3, we test our detector when it is trained on samples generated by FGM and tested on samples from the other attacks. We then consider OOD detection and adaptive attacks on the detector.

5.1 Preliminary Experiments

Our results confirm those in [21] that show that LAP training improves test accuracy. Vanilla ResNeXt50 has an accuracy of 74.38% on CIFAR100, while LAP-ResNeXt50 has an accuracy of 77.2%. Vanilla ResNet110 has an accuracy of 92.52% on CIFAR10, while LAP-ResNet110 has an accuracy of 93.52% and the RCE-ResNet110 of 93.1%. Vanilla WideResNet has an accuracy of 65.14% on TinyImageNet, while LAP-WideResNet has an accuracy of 65.34%. LAP training is also more stable by allowing to train deep networks without batch-normalization in Fig. 4 in Appendix D.4.

We see in Fig. 2 that LAP training makes the transport cost $\mathcal{C}$ more different between clean and adversarial points. Using its empirical quantiles on clean points allows then to detect samples from some attacks with high recall and a fixed false positive rate, without seeing adversarial samples.

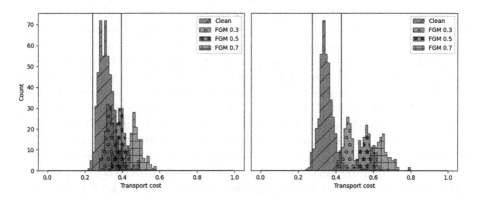

Fig. 2. Histogram of transport cost $\mathcal{C}$ for clean and FGM-attacked test samples with different values of ϵ on CIFAR100. The vertical lines represent the 0.02 and 0.98 empirical quantiles of the transport cost of the clean samples. Left: ResNeXt50. Right: LAP-ResNeXt50.

5.2   Detection of Seen Attacks

For detection training, the test set is split in 0.9/0.1 proportions into two datasets, B1 and B2. For each image in B1 (respectively B2), an adversarial sample is generated and a balanced detection training set (respectively a detection test set) is created. Since adversarial samples are created for a specific network, this is done for the vanilla version of the network and its LAP and RCE versions. We tried augmenting the detection training dataset with a randomly perturbed version of each image, to be considered clean during detection training, as in [27], but we found that this does not improve detection accuracy. This dataset creation protocol is standard and is depicted in Fig. 3 in Appendix D.3. We did not limit the datasets to successfully attacked images only as in [27], as we consider the setting of detecting all adversarial samples, whether or not they fool the network, more challenging (which is seen in the results). It also allows to detect any attempted interference with the network, even if it fails at fooling it.

Samples in the detection training set are fed through the network and the features for each detector are extracted. We tried three classifiers (logistic regression, random forest and SVM) trained on these features for all detectors, and kept the random forest as it always performs best. We tried two methods to improve the accuracy of all detectors: class-conditioning and ensembling. In class-conditioning, the features are grouped by the class predicted by the network, and a detector is trained for every class. At test time, the detector trained on the features of the predicted class is used. A detector is also trained on all samples regardless of the predicted class and is used in case a certain class is never targeted by the attack. We also tried ensembling the class-conditional detector with the general all-class detector: an input is considered an attack if at least one detector says so. This ensemble of the class-conditional detector and the general detector performs best for all detectors, and is the one we use.

We report the accuracy of each detector on the detection test set for both the vanilla and the LAP network in Table 1. In each cell, the first number corresponds to the vanilla network and the second to the regularized LAP-network. Since the NS detector takes the image and not its embeddings as input, the impact of LAP and RCE training on its performance is minimal and we report its performance on the vanilla network only. These results are averaged over 5 runs and the standard deviations (which are tight) are in Tables 3 to 7 in Appendix D.5, along with results on RCE-networks. Since some attacks are slow, we don't test them on all network-dataset pairs in this experiment. Results in Table 1 show two things. First, our detector performs better than both other detectors, with or without the regularization. Second, both the TR and MH detectors work better on the LAP-networks most times. The MH detector benefits more from the regularization, but on all attacks, the best detector is always the Transport detector. In the tables in Appendix D.5, RCE often improves detection accuracy in this experiment, but clearly less than LAP training. On CIFAR10, our detector outperforms the MH detector by 9 to 16% points on the vanilla ResNet110, and the NS detector by up to 5 points. LAP training improves the accuracy of our detector by an average 1.5 points and that of the MH detector by a substantial 8.3 points on average. On CIFAR100, our detector outperforms the MH detector by 1 to 5 points on the vanilla ResNeXt50, and the NS detector by up to 3 points. LAP training improves the accuracy of both detectors by an average 1 point. On TinyImageNet, our detector greatly outperforms the MH detector by 3 to 15 points on the vanilla WideResNet, and the NS detector slightly. LAP training does not change the accuracy of our detector and improves that of the MH detector by 0.85 points on average. Detection rates of successful adversarial samples (i.e. those that fool the network) are in Table 14 in Appendix D.7 and are higher than 95% on our detector. False positive rates (positive meaning adversarial) are in Table 16 in Appendix D.8 and are always less than 5% on our detector. The AUROC is in Table 18 in Appendix D.9. On all these metrics, our detector outperforms the other detectors largely, and LAP-training greatly improves the performance of the Mahalanobis detector.

Table 1. Average accuracy of detectors on adversarial samples from seen attacks on Network/LAP-Network over 5 runs.

Attack	Detector	ResNet110 CIFAR10	ResNeXt50 CIFAR100	WideResNet TinyImageNet
FGM	TR	97.14/**98.70**	97.26/**98.32**	**95.36**/95.14
	MH	87.78/95.64	95.82/96.82	81.06/85.26
	NS	94.56	94.70	94.90
APGD	TR	94.10/**97.50**	96.04/**97.84**	**95.22**/95.20
	MH	82.08/90.70	93.94/94.60	79.66/85.10
	NS	94.28	94.18	94.86
BIM	TR	97.54/**99.28**	98.02/**98.92**	**95.26**/95.12
	MH	86.78/95.38	96.06/97.76	81.20/82.46
	NS	95.04	94.72	95.00
AA	TR	88.88/**94.08**	84.90/**87.56**	**81.38**/81.24
	MH	80.46/89.96	83.90/86.58	78.40/78.40
	NS	88.78	84.82	81.32
DF	TR	**99.98**/99.84	**99.80**/99.58	
	MH	91.50/96.70	97.30/97.12	
	NS	99.78	99.6	
CW	TR	**98.04**/97.96	97.04/**97.80**	
	MH	85.58/93.36	95.38/96.42	
	NS	93.86	90.7	
HSJ	TR	**99.94**/99.92		
	MH	85.50/94.56		
	NS	99.68		
BA	TR	96.56/**97.02**		
	MH	80.20/89.62		
	NS	92.10		

5.3   Detection of Unseen Attacks

An important setting is when we don't know which attack might be used or only have time to train detectors on samples from one attack. We still want our detector to generalize well to unseen attacks. To test this, we use the same vanilla networks as above but the detectors are now trained on the detection training set created by the simplest and quickest attack (FGM) and tested on the detection test sets created by the other attacks. Results are in Table 2. We see that our detector has very good generalization to unseen attacks, even those very different from FGM, comfortably better than the MH detector, by up to 19% points, while the NS detector only generalizes to variants of FGM (APGD and BIM), and fails on the other attacks. These results are averaged over 5 runs and the standard deviations are in Tables 8 to 13 in Appendix D.6. On our detector, the detection rate of successful adversarial samples remains higher than 90% in most cases (Table 15 in Appendix D.7) and the FPR is always lower than 10% (Table 17 in Appendix D.8). The AUROC is in Table 19 in Appendix D.9. Our detector almost always outperforms the other detectors on all these metrics.

Table 2. Average accuracy of detectors on samples from unseen attacks after training on FGM over 5 runs.

Attack	Detector	ResNet110 CIFAR10	ResNeXt50 CIFAR100	WideResNet TinyImageNet
APGD	TR	89.32	91.94	93.26
	MH	77.34	90.86	76.96
	NS	**92.08**	**92.16**	**94.06**
BIM	TR	**96.02**	**95.02**	**94.66**
	MH	77.24	93.16	77.02
	NS	93.88	93.88	94.62
AA	TR	**85.10**	**73.32**	**77.04**
	MH	72.12	73.08	60.36
	NS	51.82	51.32	65.60
DF	TR	**91.02**	**85.16**	**90.62**
	MH	80.12	82.72	73.18
	NS	51.40	51.62	72.82
CW	TR	**93.18**	**78.18**	**91.42**
	MH	79.92	76.44	75.52
	NS	50.84	51.02	71.96
HSJ	TR	**93.00**	**85.04**	
	MH	79.70	82.82	
	NS	52.12	52.04	
BA	TR	**90.92**	**92.14**	
	MH	79.32	84.46	
	NS	59.88	57.90	

However, this experiment shows that our regularization has some limitations. We see in Tables 8 to 13 in Appendix D.6 that LAP training does not improve detection accuracy as much, and sometimes reduces it. It still improves it for the MH detector on all attacks on ResNet110 and WideResNet by up to 10 points, and LAP training still always does better than RCE training. We claim this is because these methods reduce the variance of features extracted on the seen attack, harming generalization to unseen attacks. This explains why detection of APGD and BIM, variants of FGM, improves.

5.4 Detection of Out-of-Distribution Samples

Since our analysis applies to all out-of-distribution (OOD) samples, we test detection of OOD samples in a similar setting to [27]. We train a model on a first dataset (ResNet110 on CIFAR10 and ResNeXt50 on CIFAR100), then train detectors to tell this first dataset from a second dataset (which can be an adversarially attacked version of the first dataset), then test their ability to tell the first dataset from a third unseen dataset (SVHN). Our detector does very well and better than the MH detector on both experiments, and detection accuracy of samples from the unseen distribution is higher than 90% when using the CW attack to create the second dataset. Details are in Appendix D.11.

5.5 Attacking the Detector

We consider the case where the detector is also attacked (adaptive attacks). We try 2 attacks on the TR and MH detectors. Both are white-box with respect to the network. The first is black-box with respect to the detector and only knows if a sample has been detected or not. The second has some knowledge about the detector. It knows what features it uses and can attack it directly to find adversarial features. We test these attacks by looking at the percentage of detected successful adversarial samples that they turn into undetected successful adversarial samples. For the first attack, this is 6.8% for our detector and 12.9% for the MH detector on the LAP-ResNet110, and is lowered by LAP training. For the second attack it is 14% on our detector. Given that detection rates of successful adversarial samples are almost 100% (see Appendix D.7), this shows that an adaptive attack does not circumvent the detector, as detection rates drop to 85% at worst. Details are in Appendix D.12.

6 Conclusion

We proposed a method for detecting adversarial samples, based on the dynamical view of neural networks. The method examines the discrete vector field moving the inputs to distinguish clean and abnormal samples. The detector requires minimal computation to extract the features it uses for detection and achieves state-of-the-art detection accuracy on seen and unseen attacks. We also use a transport regularization that both improves test classification accuracy and the accuracy of adversarial detectors.

Ethical Statement. Adversarial detection and robustness are essential to safely deploy neural networks that attackers might target for nefarious purposes. But adversarial attacks can be used to evade neural networks that are deployed for nefarious purposes.

References

1. Aldahdooh, A., Hamidouche, W., Fezza, S.A., Déforges, O.: Adversarial example detection for DNN models: a review and experimental comparison. Artif. Intell. Rev. (2022)
2. Alemany, S., Pissinou, N.: The dilemma between data transformations and adversarial robustness for time series application systems. In: Proceedings of the Workshop on Artificial Intelligence Safety 2022 (SafeAI 2022) Co-located with the Thirty-Sixth AAAI Conference on Artificial Intelligence (AAAI2022), Virtual, February 2022. CEUR Workshop Proceedings, vol. 3087. CEUR-WS.org (2022)
3. Amodei, D., Olah, C., Steinhardt, J., Christiano, P., Schulman, J., Mané, D.: Concrete problems in AI safety. arXiv preprint arXiv:1606.06565 (2016)
4. Bhowmick, A., D'Souza, M., Raghavan, G.S.: Lipbab: Computing exact lipschitz constant of relu networks. arXiv preprint arXiv:2105.05495 (2021)
5. Brendel, W., Rauber, J., Bethge, M.: Decision-based adversarial attacks: reliable attacks against black-box machine learning models. In: International Conference on Learning Representations (2018). https://openreview.net/forum?id=SyZI0GWCZ
6. Carlini, N., Wagner, D.: Towards evaluating the robustness of neural networks. In: 2017 IEEE Symposium on Security and Privacy (SP), pp. 39–57. IEEE Computer Society, Los Alamitos (2017). https://doi.org/10.1109/SP.2017.49
7. Carlini, N., Wagner, D.: Adversarial Examples Are Not Easily Detected: Bypassing Ten Detection Methods, pp. 3–14. Association for Computing Machinery, New York (2017). https://doi.org/10.1145/3128572.3140444
8. Chen, J., Jordan, M.I., Wainwright, M.J.: Hopskipjumpattack: a query-efficient decision-based attack. In: 2020 IEEE Symposium on Security and Privacy, pp. 1277–1294. IEEE (2020). https://doi.org/10.1109/SP40000.2020.00045
9. Cisse, M., Bojanowski, P., Grave, E., Dauphin, Y., Usunier, N.: Parseval networks: improving robustness to adversarial examples. In: Proceedings of the 34th International Conference on Machine Learning, pp. 854–863. PMLR (2017)
10. Croce, F., Hein, M.: Reliable evaluation of adversarial robustness with an ensemble of diverse parameter-free attacks. In: Proceedings of the 37th International Conference on Machine Learning. PMLR (2020)
11. Dosovitskiy, A., et al.: An image is worth 16x16 words: transformers for image recognition at scale. In: International Conference on Learning Representations (2021). https://openreview.net/forum?id=YicbFdNTTy
12. Eykholt, K., et al.: Robust physical-world attacks on deep learning visual classification. In: 2018 IEEE/CVF Conference on Computer Vision and Pattern Recognition (CVPR), pp. 1625–1634. IEEE Computer Society, Los Alamitos (2018). https://doi.org/10.1109/CVPR.2018.00175
13. Feinman, R., Curtin, R.R., Shintre, S., Gardner, A.B.: Detecting adversarial samples from artifacts (2017)

14. Gilmer, J., et al.: Adversarial spheres: the relationship between high-dimensional geometry and adversarial examples (2018). arXiv preprint arXiv:1801.02774
15. Goodfellow, I.J., Shlens, J., Szegedy, C.: Explaining and harnessing adversarial examples. In: ICLR (2015)
16. Harder, P., Pfreundt, F.J., Keuper, M., Keuper, J.: Spectraldefense: detecting adversarial attacks on CNNs in the fourier domain (2021). arXiv preprint arXiv:2103.03000
17. He, K., Zhang, X., Ren, S., Sun, J.: Deep residual learning for image recognition. In: CVPR (2016)
18. He, K., Zhang, X., Ren, S., Sun, J.: Identity mappings in deep residual networks. In: ECCV (2016)
19. Hein, M., Andriushchenko, M.: Formal guarantees on the robustness of a classifier against adversarial manipulation. In: Advances in Neural Information Processing Systems, pp. 2263–2273. Curran Associates Inc., Red Hook (2017)
20. Huster, T., Chiang, C.-Y.J., Chadha, R.: Limitations of the lipschitz constant as a defense against adversarial examples. In: Alzate, C., et al. (eds.) ECML PKDD 2018. LNCS (LNAI), vol. 11329, pp. 16–29. Springer, Cham (2019). https://doi.org/10.1007/978-3-030-13453-2_2
21. Karkar, S., Ayed, I., de Bézenac, E., Gallinari, P.: A principle of least action for the training of neural networks. In: ECML-PKDD (2020)
22. Kherchouche, A., Fezza, S.A., Hamidouche, W.: Detect and defense against adversarial examples in deep learning using natural scene statistics and adaptive denoising. Neural Comput. Appl. **34**(24), 21567–21582 (2022). https://doi.org/10.1007/s00521-021-06330-x
23. Kherchouche, A., Fezza, S.A., Hamidouche, W., Déforges, O.: Detection of adversarial examples in deep neural networks with natural scene statistics. In: 2020 International Joint Conference on Neural Networks (IJCNN), pp. 1–7 (2020). https://doi.org/10.1109/IJCNN48605.2020.9206959
24. Khoury, M., Hadfield-Menell, D.: On the geometry of adversarial examples (2018). arXiv preprint arXiv:1811.00525
25. Kurakin, A., Goodfellow, I., Bengio, S.: Adversarial examples in the physical world. In: ICLR (Workshop) (2017)
26. Latorre, F., Rolland, P., Cevher, V.: Lipschitz constant estimation of neural networks via sparse polynomial optimization. In: International Conference on Learning Representations (2020). https://openreview.net/forum?id=rJe4_xSFDB
27. Lee, K., Lee, K., Lee, H., Shin, J.: A simple unified framework for detecting out-of-distribution samples and adversarial attacks. In: Bengio, S., Wallach, H., Larochelle, H., Grauman, K., Cesa-Bianchi, N., Garnett, R. (eds.) Advances in Neural Information Processing Systems, vol. 31. Curran Associates, Inc. (2018). https://proceedings.neurips.cc/paper/2018/file/abdeb6f575ac5c6676b747bca8d09cc2-Paper.pdf
28. Liu, Y., Chen, X., Liu, C., Song, D.: Delving into transferable adversarial examples and black-box attacks. In: International Conference on Learning Representations. OpenReview.net (2017). https://openreview.net/forum?id=Sys6GJqxl
29. Liu, Z., et al.: Swin transformer: hierarchical vision transformer using shifted windows. In: Proceedings of the IEEE/CVF International Conference on Computer Vision (ICCV) (2021)
30. Ma, X., et al.: Characterizing adversarial subspaces using local intrinsic dimensionality. In: ICLR (2018)

31. Madry, A., Makelov, A., Schmidt, L., Tsipras, D., Vladu, A.: Towards deep learning models resistant to adversarial attacks. In: ICLR (2018). https://openreview.net/forum?id=rJzIBfZAb
32. Metzen, J.H., Genewein, T., Fischer, V., Bischoff, B.: On detecting adversarial perturbations. In: ICLR (2017)
33. Moosavi-Dezfooli, S., Fawzi, A., Fawzi, O., Frossard, P.: Universal adversarial perturbations. In: 2017 IEEE Conference on Computer Vision and Pattern Recognition (CVPR), pp. 86–94. IEEE Computer Society, Los Alamitos (2017). https://doi.org/10.1109/CVPR.2017.17
34. Moosavi-Dezfooli, S.M., Fawzi, A., Frossard, P.: Deepfool: A simple and accurate method to fool deep neural networks. In: 2016 IEEE Conference on Computer Vision and Pattern Recognition (CVPR), pp. 2574–2582 (2016)
35. Nguyen, A., Yosinski, J., Clune, J.: Deep neural networks are easily fooled: high confidence predictions for unrecognizable images. In: 2015 IEEE Conference on Computer Vision and Pattern Recognition (CVPR), pp. 427–436 (2015). https://doi.org/10.1109/CVPR.2015.7298640
36. Nicolae, M.I., et al.: Adversarial robustness toolbox v1.0.0 (2018). arXiv preprint arXiv:1807.01069
37. Pang, T., Du, C., Dong, Y., Zhu, J.: Towards robust detection of adversarial examples. In: Bengio, S., Wallach, H., Larochelle, H., Grauman, K., Cesa-Bianchi, N., Garnett, R. (eds.) Advances in Neural Information Processing Systems, vol. 31. Curran Associates, Inc. (2018)
38. Samangouei, P., Kabkab, M., Chellappa, R.: Defense-GAN: protecting classifiers against adversarial attacks using generative models. In: International Conference on Learning Representations (2018). https://openreview.net/forum?id=BkJ3ibb0-
39. Sandler, M., Howard, A.G., Zhu, M., Zhmoginov, A., Chen, L.: Mobilenetv 2: inverted residuals and linear bottlenecks. In: 2018 IEEE Conference on Computer Vision and Pattern Recognition, CVPR 2018, Salt Lake City, 18–22 June 2018, pp. 4510–4520. Computer Vision Foundation/IEEE Computer Society (2018)
40. Song, Y., Kim, T., Nowozin, S., Ermon, S., Kushman, N.: Pixeldefend: leveraging generative models to understand and defend against adversarial examples. In: International Conference on Learning Representations (2018). https://openreview.net/forum?id=rJUYGxbCW
41. Szegedy, C., et al.: Intriguing properties of neural networks (2013). arXiv preprint arXiv:1312.6199
42. Tan, M., Le, Q.: EfficientNet: rethinking model scaling for convolutional neural networks. In: Chaudhuri, K., Salakhutdinov, R. (eds.) Proceedings of the 36th International Conference on Machine Learning. Proceedings of Machine Learning Research, vol. 97, pp. 6105–6114. PMLR (2019). https://proceedings.mlr.press/v97/tan19a.html
43. Tanay, T., Griffin, L.: A boundary tilting persepective on the phenomenon of adversarial examples (2016)
44. Virmaux, A., Scaman, K.: Lipschitz regularity of deep neural networks: analysis and efficient estimation. In: Bengio, S., Wallach, H., Larochelle, H., Grauman, K., Cesa-Bianchi, N., Garnett, R. (eds.) Advances in Neural Information Processing Systems, vol. 31. Curran Associates, Inc. (2018). https://proceedings.neurips.cc/paper/2018/file/d54e99a6c03704e95e6965532dec148b-Paper.pdf
45. Weinan, E.: A proposal on machine learning via dynamical systems. Commun. Math. Stat. (2017)
46. Weng, T.W., et al.: Evaluating the robustness of neural networks: an extreme value theory approach. In: International Conference on Learning Representations (2018)

47. Wightman, R., Touvron, H., Jégou, H.: Resnet strikes back: an improved training procedure in TIMM. arXiv (2021)
48. Wu, D., Wang, Y., Xia, S.T., Bailey, J., Ma, X.: Skip connections matter: On the transferability of adversarial examples generated with resnets. In: International Conference on Learning Representations (2020)
49. Xie, S., et al.: Aggregated residual transformations for deep neural networks. In: CVPR (2017)
50. Zagoruyko, S., Komodakis, N.: Wide residual networks. In: BMVC (2016)
51. Zhang, J., et al.: Towards robust resnet: a small step but a giant leap. In: Proceedings of the Twenty-Eight International Joint Conference on Artificial Intelligence (IJCAI-19) (2019)

Anomaly Detection

CVTGAD: Simplified Transformer with Cross-View Attention for Unsupervised Graph-Level Anomaly Detection

Jindong Li, Qianli Xing, Qi Wang$^{(\boxtimes)}$, and Yi Chang

School of Artificial Intelligence, Jilin University, Changchun 130012, China
jdli21@mails.jlu.edu.cn, {qianlixing,qiwang,yichang}@jlu.edu.cn

Abstract. Unsupervised graph-level anomaly detection (UGAD) has received remarkable performance in various critical disciplines, such as chemistry analysis and bioinformatics. Existing UGAD paradigms often adopt data augmentation techniques to construct multiple views, and then employ different strategies to obtain representations from different views for jointly conducting UGAD. However, most previous works only considered the relationship between nodes/graphs from a limited receptive field, resulting in some key structure patterns and feature information being neglected. In addition, most existing methods consider different views separately in a parallel manner, which is not able to explore the inter-relationship across different views directly. Thus, a method with a larger receptive field that can explore the inter-relationship across different views directly is in need. In this paper, we propose a novel Simplified Transformer with Cross-View Attention for Unsupervised Graph-level Anomaly Detection, namely, CVTGAD. To increase the receptive field, we construct a simplified transformer-based module, exploiting the relationship between nodes/graphs from both intra-graph and inter-graph perspectives. Furthermore, we design a cross-view attention mechanism to directly exploit the view co-occurrence between different views, bridging the inter-view gap at node level and graph level. To the best of our knowledge, this is the first work to apply transformer and cross attention to UGAD, which realizes graph neural network and transformer working collaboratively. Extensive experiments on 15 real-world datasets of 3 fields demonstrate the superiority of CVTGAD on the UGAD task. The code is available at https://github.com/jindongli-Ai/CVTGAD.

Keywords: Transformer · Cross-View Attention · Graph-level Anomaly Detection · Unsupervised Learning · Graph Neural Network

1 Introduction

Graph data has drawn extensive attention in a variety of domains due to its ubiquity in the real world, such as small molecules, bioinformatics, and social

D. Koutra et al. (Eds.): ECML PKDD 2023, LNAI 14169, pp. 185–200, 2023.
https://doi.org/10.1007/978-3-031-43412-9_11

networks [23]. Graph-level anomaly detection, which is one of the vital research problems in dealing with graph data, aims to identify graphs with anomalous information. Usually, anomalous graphs deviate significantly from the normal graphs in the sample [20]. It has received increasing attention due to its power in various practical applications, such as identifying toxic molecules in chemical compounds analysis, and spotting the molecules with anti-cancer activity in cancer drug discovery [14,18–20,34]. Despite the remarkable performance achieved by advanced methods and learning paradigms [14,18,19,34], there are still some issues that need to be further discussed and addressed in graph-level anomaly detection task.

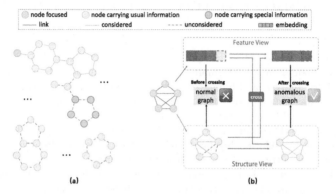

Fig. 1. Toy examples to show two major issues: (a) if obtaining the embedding of the current node or graph with a limited receptive field, some nodes or patterns that carry key information would be ignored (e.g., grey in figure); (b) if ignoring the view co-occurrence across different views, some anomalous graphs would not be distinguished accurately. (Color figure online)

Firstly, existing methods mainly rely on the GNN encoder to obtain the representation of the node/graph [14,19]. However, due to its limited receptive field, GNNs only consider the local neighbors or sub-graphs (own nodes) of the current node (graph), missing the key anomalous information from the global perspective. For instance, as shown in Fig. 1 (a), the subgraph composed of grey nodes is difficult to be considered in the existing GNN-based methods with rather limited layers, but this subgraph carries the key information to determine whether the chemical molecular graph is an anomalous graph or not. In addition, the relationship between the current graph and other graphs in the whole dataset (e.g., as shown in the lower part of Fig. 1(a)) should also be considered with a larger receptive field. It is because each graph is associated latently and inseparable in the target dataset, which is particularly evident in fields such as chemistry analysis and bioinformatics [18,34]. Existing technologies that simply increase the number of layers for the GNN encoder may cause the over-smoothing problem [4]. Therefore, it is necessary to design a specific module that increases the considered receptive field of the current node/graph, which can exploit the relationship between nodes/graphs from both intra-graph and inter-graph perspectives, preventing ignoring key information.

Secondly, some existing methods employ data augmentation techniques to get multiple graph views to enrich the graph information. The latent mutual agreement between different views is then maximized in the form of a loss item (e.g., InfoNCE-like Loss [14]) [7,33,37,38]. Nevertheless, these works consider different views separately in a parallel manner and simply consider the latent influence between different views via a loss function at the final training step, which is not able to capture the complicated view co-occurrence across different views. In fact, the features of nodes and the structure between nodes influence and entangle each other in the anomalous graph forming process. Specifically, nodes with certain characteristics are more likely to form abnormal links. Similarly, the characteristics of nodes connected by abnormal links may also change accordingly [5]. Information from different views reflects different characteristics of an anomalous graph, which are consistent in nature and own view co-occurrence instinctively [1]. For example, as shown in Fig. 1(b), it is hard to determine whether the current graph is an anomalous graph or not from any single view alone. Only by comprehensively considering the cross-view information can a more accurate judgment be made. Therefore, there is an urgent need for a novel mechanism to capture such co-occurrence across different views in an explicit way to bridge the inter-view gap of graph-level anomalies.

In this paper, to address the aforementioned issues, we propose a novel Simplified Transformer with Cross-View Attention for Unsupervised Graph-level Anomaly Detection (CVTGAD in short). In concrete, **for the first issue,** we design a simplified transformer module including projection network, residual network, and transformer to exploit the relationship between nodes/graphs from not only intra-graph but also inter-graph perspectives for increasing the receptive field. **For the second issue,** we design a cross-view attention mechanism to directly exploit the view co-occurrence between different views (i.e., feature view and structure view), bridging the inter-view gap at node level and graph level. Finally, the anomaly score is obtained by an adaptive anomaly scoring module. **Our major contributions are summarized as follows:**

- We propose a novel simplified transformer framework with cross-view attention for unsupervised graph-level anomaly detection task (CVTGAD). To the best of our knowledge, this is the first work to introduce transformer and cross-attention to unsupervised graph-level anomaly detection, realizing graph neural network and transformer working collaboratively.
- We design a simplified transformer with its attention mechanism to capture the relationship between nodes/graphs in both intra-graph and inter-graph perspectives, preventing ignoring key information. In addition, a cross-view attention module is introduced to directly exploit the view co-occurrence across different views, bridging the inter-view gap at both node level and graph level.

- We conduct comprehensive experiments against 15 real-world datasets of different fields to demonstrate the effectiveness and superiority of CVTGAD on unsupervised graph-level anomaly detection task.

2 Related Work

2.1 Graph-Level Anomaly Detection

Given a graph dataset, graph-level anomaly detection aims to distinguish anomalous graphs from normal graphs [20], where the anomalous graphs usually represent very few but essential patterns. Most traditional methods contain two modules: firstly, a graph kernel, such as Weisfeiler-Leman kernel (WL) [26] and propagation kernel (PK) [24], is used to learn node representations. And secondly, an anomaly detector, such as isolation forest (iF) [12], one-class support vector machine (OCSVM) [22], and local outlier factor (LOF) [3], is applied to detect anomalous graphs based on the acquired graph representations.

In addition, graph neural networks (GNNs) have attracted significant attention due to their remarkable performance in dealing with graph data [6,10,14,30,32]. Thus, various types of GNN are employed as the backbone to conduct graph-level anomaly detection [18,19,35]. For example, LocalKD [19] employs GNN as encoder and achieves random knowledge distillation (KD) [2,8]. The method is achieved by predicting one GNN via training another GNN, where the network weights are all initialized in a random way [19]. GOOD-D [14] designs a novel graph data augmentation method and employs GIN [32] as encoder to conduct graph-level anomaly detection. However, according to our investigation, graph-level anomaly detection is still under-explored and there are only several research works.

2.2 Graph Contrastive Learning

Graph contrastive learning utilizes the mutual information maximization mechanism to obtain a rich representation by maximizing instances with similar semantic information [13,16]. It has been widely employed for achieving remarkable graph representation learning performance in an unsupervised manner [7,15,17,25,27,31,33,36,38]. For instance, GraphCL [33] proposes four general data augmentations for graph-structured data to generate pairs for contrastive learning. For graph classification tasks, InfoGraph [27] is proposed by maximizing the mutual information between graph-level representations and the substructures-level representations. The substructures-level representations are calculated at different scales.

Some recent works have employed graph contrastive learning to conduct graph-level anomaly detection. For instance, by developing a dual-graph encoder module, GLADC [18] captures node-level and graph-level representations of graphs with graph contrastive learning techniques. GOOD-D [14] detects anomalous graphs based on semantic inconsistencies at different granularities according to the designed hierarchical contrastive learning framework.

3   Problem Definition

A graph is denoted as $G = (\mathcal{V}, \mathcal{E})$, where $\mathcal{V}$ is the set of nodes and $\mathcal{E}$ is the set of edges. The topology information of G is represented by an adjacent matrix $\mathbf{A} \in \mathbb{R}^{n \times n}$, where n is the number of nodes. $\mathbf{A}_{i,j} = 1$ if there is an edge between node v_i and node v_j, otherwise, $\mathbf{A}_{i,j} = 0$. An attributed graph is denoted as $G = (\mathcal{V}, \mathcal{E}, \mathbf{X})$, where $\mathbf{X} \in \mathbb{R}^{n \times d_f}$ represents the feature matrix of node features. Each row of $\mathbf{X}$ represents a node's feature vector with d_f dimensions. The graph set is denoted as $\mathcal{G} = \{G_1, G_2, ..., G_m\}$, where m is the total number of graphs.

In this paper, we focus on the unsupervised graph-level anomaly detection problem. Given a graph set $\mathcal{G}$ containing normal graphs and anomalous graphs, CVTGAD aims to distinguish the anomalous graphs which are different from the normal graphs.

4   Methodology

In this section, we introduce the proposed method named Simplified Transformer with Cross-View Attention for Unsupervised Graph-level Anomaly Detection (CVTGAD). The overall framework of CVTGAD is illustrated in Fig. 2, which contains three modules: a graph pre-processing module, a simplified transformer-based embedding module, and an adaptive anomaly scoring module. In the graph pre-processing module, we create two views of each graph by data augmentation. Then, the preliminary node/graph embeddings are calculated by GNN encoders. After that, we exploit the view co-occurrence in the simplified transformer-based embedding module. In this module, we design a simplified transformer structure with a cross-view attention mechanism to obtain the node/graph embedding with cross-view information. Finally, an adaptive anomaly scoring module is employed to estimate the anomaly detection score.

4.1   Graph Pre-processing Module

In this module, we first generate the feature view and the structure view of each graph. Then, the preliminary node/graph embeddings of two views are calculated, which are used as the input for the simplified transformer-based embedding module. To generate the feature view and structure view of each graph, we adopt the perturbation-free graph augmentation strategy [14,28].

To calculate the preliminary node embedding, we adopt a GNN encoder. Specifically, we employ GIN [32] and GCN [10] as GNN encoder in this work. Through the GNN encoder, two preliminary node embeddings of feature view and structure view are obtained. As the calculating process of the two kinds of representation is the same, we only show the calculating process of feature view representation obtained from GIN and GCN. The propagation rule in the l-th layer on the feature view of GIN ($\epsilon = 0$ for simplicity) can be expressed as [32]:

$$\mathbf{h}_i^{(f,l)} = MLP^{(f,l)} \left(\mathbf{h}_i^{(f,l-1)} + \sum_{v_j \in \mathcal{N}(v_i)} \mathbf{h}_j^{(f,l-1)} \right), \tag{1}$$

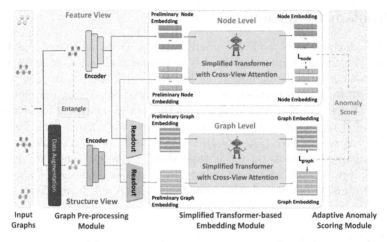

(a) The overall framework of CVTGAD.

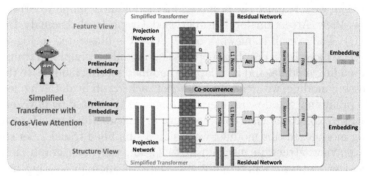

(b) The Simplified Transformer with Cross-View Attention.

Fig. 2. (a) The overview of CVTGAD. The proposed method contains three modules: graph pre-processing module, simplified transformer-based embedding module, and adaptive anomaly scoring module. (b) Specially, we extend the receptive field through a simplified transformer structure and design a cross-view attention mechanism by crossing the matrix K.

where f is the indicator for the feature view. MLP is a multi-layer perception network. $\mathbf{h}_i^{(f,l-1)}$ is the preliminary embedding of node v_i in the $l-1$-th layer of feature view, and $\mathcal{N}(v_i)$ is the set of first-order neighbor nodes of node v_i.

And the propagation rule in the l-th layer on the feature view of GCN can be expressed as [10]:

$$\mathbf{H}^{(f,l)} = \sigma\left(\hat{\mathbf{D}}^{-\frac{1}{2}}\hat{\mathbf{A}}\hat{\mathbf{D}}^{-\frac{1}{2}}\mathbf{H}^{(f,l-1)}\mathbf{W}^{(l-1)}\right), \tag{2}$$

where $\hat{\mathbf{A}} = \mathbf{A} + \mathbf{I}_N$ is the adjacency matrix of the input graph G with added self-connections, and $\mathbf{I}_N$ is the identity matrix. $\hat{\mathbf{D}}$ is the degree matrix, $\mathbf{H}^{(f,l-1)}$

is node embedding matrix in the $l-1$-th layer of feature view, $\mathbf{W}^{(l-1)}$ is a layer-specific trainable weight matrix, and $\sigma(\cdot)$ is a non-linear activation function. $\mathbf{h}_i^{(f,l)}$ is the i-th row of $\mathbf{H}^{(f,l)}$. And the preliminary node embedding of structure view $\mathbf{h}_i^{(s,l)}$ can be calculated in the same way, where s is the indicator for the structure view.

After getting the preliminary embeddings of nodes, a readout function is needed to acquire the preliminary graph embeddings. In this work, we employ global mean pooling as the readout function, which can be represented by:

$$\mathbf{h}_G^{(f)} = \frac{1}{|\mathcal{V}_G|} \sum_{v_i \in \mathcal{V}_G} \mathbf{h}_i^{(f)}, \quad \mathbf{h}_G^{(s)} = \frac{1}{|\mathcal{V}_G|} \sum_{v_i \in \mathcal{V}_G} \mathbf{h}_i^{(s)}, \tag{3}$$

where $\mathcal{V}_G$ is the node set of input graph G. $\mathbf{h}_G^{(f)}$ and $\mathbf{h}_G^{(s)}$ are the feature view and structure view preliminary graph embedding of input graph G, respectively.

4.2 Simplified Transformer-Based Embedding Module

In this module, we design a novel and simple transformer to adapt to the current graph datasets and unsupervised graph-level anomaly detection task. The proposed simplified transformer architecture comprises a projection network, a residual network, and a transformer (including an attention mechanism, a feed-forward layer, and a norm layer). After we get the preliminary embeddings of nodes/graphs from different views through graph pre-processing module, we feed them into the projection network, which is achieved by a multi-layer perceptron (MLP) to project them into latent space. The output of it is the input of the residual network and the transformer. The residual network is achieved by a MLP and makes a shortcut between the output of the projection network and the output of the attention layer.

We achieve feed-forward layer and norm layer with MLP and LayerNorm, respectively [29]. The attention mechanism comprises three parametric matrices: the query matrix $\mathbf{Q} \in \mathbb{R}^{m \times d_k}$, the key matrix $\mathbf{K} \in \mathbb{R}^{m \times d_k}$, and the value matrix $\mathbf{V} \in \mathbb{R}^{m \times d_k}$. m is the number of embedding fed into the transformer and d_k is the dimension of embedding. For each embedding, the attention matrix $\mathbf{Att} \in \mathbb{R}^{m \times m}$ represents how much it attends to other embeddings, and then transforms the embedding into contextual one [9]. $\mathbf{Att}$ is computed as follows:

$$\mathbf{Att}_{|\mathcal{B}|} = softmax\left(\frac{\mathbf{Q}\mathbf{K}^T}{\sqrt{d_k}}\right). \tag{4}$$

Each input embedding attends to all other embeddings through the attention mechanism, which could be computed as:

$$Attention(\mathbf{Q}, \mathbf{K}, \mathbf{V})_{|\mathcal{B}|} = softmax\left(\frac{\mathbf{Q}\mathbf{K}^T}{\sqrt{d_k}}\right)\mathbf{V}. \tag{5}$$

Note that $\mathcal{B}$ reflects the receptive field. For each node/graph, we calculate the attention of all the nodes/graphs in $\mathcal{B}$. And such a number of nodes/graphs is extremely larger than the existing works. Through this module, the receptive field is extended, which leads to a better representation of nodes/graphs.

Furthermore, we propose a cross-view attention mechanism that aims to directly exploit the view co-occurrence between different views. Specifically, the output of cross-view attention mechanism on the feature view is computed as follows:

$$Attention(\mathbf{Q}^{(f)}, \mathbf{K}^{(s)}, \mathbf{V}^{(f)})_{|\mathcal{B}|}^{(f)} = softmax - L1 \; norm \left(\frac{\mathbf{Q}^{(f)}\mathbf{K}^{(s)^T}}{\sqrt{d_k}} \right) \mathbf{V}^{(f)}, \quad (6)$$

where $\mathcal{B}$ is the training/testing batch. Following [11], $softmax - L1 \; norm$ means we adopt $softmax$ and $L1 \; norm$ to normalize the two dimensions of the attention matrix, respectively. The output of cross-view attention mechanism on the structure view is computed as follows:

$$Attention(\mathbf{Q}^{(s)}, \mathbf{K}^{(f)}, \mathbf{V}^{(s)})_{|\mathcal{B}|}^{(s)} = softmax - L1 \; norm \left(\frac{\mathbf{Q}^{(s)}\mathbf{K}^{(f)^T}}{\sqrt{d_k}} \right) \mathbf{V}^{(s)}. \quad (7)$$

Through the cross-view attention mechanism, we could directly exploit the view co-occurrence between different views, which bridges the inter-view gap at both node level and graph level.

4.3   Adaptive Anomaly Scoring Module

Following [14], we design an adaptive strategy considering both node-level loss and graph-level loss to calculate the anomaly score.

Node-Level Cross-View Contrastive Loss. For an input graph G, we construct node-level contrastive loss to maximize the agreement between the embedding belonging to different views on the node level:

$$\mathcal{L}_{node} = \frac{1}{|\mathcal{B}|} \sum_{G_j \in \mathcal{B}} \frac{1}{2|\mathcal{V}_{G_j}|} \sum_{v_i \in \mathcal{V}_{G_j}} \left[l(\mathbf{h}_i^{(f)}, \mathbf{h}_i^{(s)}) + l(\mathbf{h}_i^{(s)}, \mathbf{h}_i^{(f)}) \right], \quad (8)$$

$$l(\mathbf{h}_i^{(f)}, \mathbf{h}_i^{(s)}) = -log \frac{e^{(sim(\mathbf{h}_i^{(f)}, \mathbf{h}_i^{(s)})/\tau)}}{\sum_{v_k \in \mathcal{V}_{G_j} \backslash v_i} e^{(sim(\mathbf{h}_i^{(f)}, \mathbf{h}_k^{(s)})/\tau)}}. \quad (9)$$

In Eq. 8, $\mathcal{B}$ is the training/testing batch and $\mathcal{V}_{G_j}$ is the node set of graph G_j. The calculation of $l(\mathbf{h}_i^{(s)}, \mathbf{h}_i^{(f)})$ and $l(\mathbf{h}_i^{(f)}, \mathbf{h}_i^{(s)})$ are the same, and we show the calculation of $l(\mathbf{h}_i^{(f)}, \mathbf{h}_i^{(s)})$ in Eq. 9 for briefly. In Eq. 9, the $sim(.,.)$ is the function to measure the similarity between different views. In this work, we compute the cosine similarity.

Graph-Level Cross-View Contrastive Loss. Similar to node-level loss, we construct a graph-level loss for mutual agreement maximization on graph level:

$$\mathcal{L}_{graph} = \frac{1}{2|\mathcal{B}|} \sum_{G_i \in \mathcal{B}} \left[l(\mathbf{h}_{G_i}^{(f)}, \mathbf{h}_{G_i}^s) + l(\mathbf{h}_{G_i}^{(s)}, \mathbf{h}_{G_i}^{(f)}) \right], \tag{10}$$

$$l(\mathbf{h}_{G_i}^{(f)}, \mathbf{h}_{G_i}^{(s)}) = -log \frac{e^{(sim(\mathbf{h}_{G_i}^{(f)}, \mathbf{h}_{G_i}^{(s)})/\tau)}}{\sum_{G_j \in \mathcal{B} \backslash G_i} e^{(sim(\mathbf{h}_{G_i}^{(f)}, \mathbf{h}_{G_j}^{(s)})/\tau)}}, \tag{11}$$

where notations are similar to node-level loss, and $l(\mathbf{h}_{G_i}^{(s)}, \mathbf{h}_{G_i}^{(f)})$ is calculated in the same way as $l(\mathbf{h}_{G_i}^{(f)}, \mathbf{h}_{G_i}^{(s)})$.

In the training phase, we employ the adaptive loss function:

$$\mathcal{L} = \lambda_1 \mathcal{L}_{node} + \lambda_2 \mathcal{L}_{graph}, \tag{12}$$

where $\lambda_1 = (\sigma_{node})^\alpha$, and $\lambda_2 = (\sigma_{graph})^\alpha$. $\sigma_{node}/\sigma_{graph}$ is the standard deviations(std) of predicted errors of the node-level/graph-level, where $\alpha \geq 0$ is a hyper-parameter.

In the inference phase, we employ the normalization method *norm* to get the final anomaly score:

$$score_{G_i} = norm(\mathcal{L}_{node\,G_i}) + norm(\mathcal{L}_{graph\,G_i}), \tag{13}$$

where $norm(\mathcal{L}_{node\,G_i}) = (\mathcal{L}_{node\,G_i} - \mu_{node})/\sigma_{node}$ and $norm(\mathcal{L}_{graph\,G_i}) = (\mathcal{L}_{graph\,G_i} - \mu_{graph})/\sigma_{graph}$. μ_{node}/μ_{graph} is the mean values of predicted errors of training samples of node-level/graph-level.

5 Experiment

In this section, we conduct extensive experiments to validate the effectiveness of our proposed CVTGAD method against 9 baselines on 15 real-world datasets.

Table 1. The statistics of the 15 datasets [23].

Dataset	PROTEINS_full	ENZYMES	AIDS	DHFR	BZR	COX2	DD	NCI1	IMDB-B	REDDIT-B	COLLAB	HSE	MMP	p53	PPAR-gamma
Graphs	1113	600	2000	467	405	467	1178	4110	1000	2000	5000	8417	7558	8903	8451
Avg. Nodes	39.06	32.63	15.69	42.43	35.75	41.22	284.32	29.87	19.77	429.63	74.49	16.89	17.62	17.92	17.38
Avg. Edges	72.82	62.14	16.20	44.54	38.36	43.45	715.66	32.30	96.53	497.75	2457.78	17.23	17.98	18.34	17.72
Node Attr.	29	18	4	3	3	3	-	-	-	-	-	-	-	-	-

5.1 Experimental Setting

Datasets. We conduct experiments on 15 public real-world datasets from [23], which involved small molecules, bioinformatics, and social networks. Following the setting in [14,19], the samples in the minority class or real anomalous class are viewed as anomalies, while the rest are viewed as normal data. Similar to [14,19,35], only normal data are used for training. The statistics of the datasets are presented in Table 1.

Baselines. To illustrate the effectiveness of our proposed model, we compare CVTGAD with 9 competitive baselines, which can be classified into two groups according to whether contrastive learning is utilized: (1) For non-contrastive learning-based methods, we select 6 baselines, including PK-OCSVM, PK-iF, WL-OCSVM, WL-iF, OCGIN, and GLocalKD. The PK and WL represent the propagation kernel [24] and the Weisfeiler-Lehman kernel [26] separately, which are used to learn the graph embedding. The OCSVM and the iF represent one-class SVM [22] and isolation forest [12] separately, which are used as detectors. OCGIN [35] and GLocalKD [19] are the two latest methods that realize graph anomaly detection in an end-to-end manner; (2) For contrastive learning-based methods, we select 3 baselines named InfoGraph+iF, GraphCL+iF, and GOOD-D. InfoGraph [27] and GraphCL [33] are two graph embedding methods that use contrastive learning. GOOD-D [14] is the latest work that realizes graph anomaly detection in an end-to-end manner using contrastive learning.

Table 2. The performance comparison in terms of AUC (in percent, mean value ± standard deviation). The best performance is highlighted in bold, and the second-best performance is underlined. †: we report the result from [14].

Method	PK-OCSVM†	PK-iF†	WL-OCSVM†	WL-iF†	InfoGraph-iF†	GraphCL-iF†	OCGIN†	GLocalKD†	GOOD-D†	CVTGAD
PROTEINS-full	50.49 ± 4.92	60.70 ± 2.55	51.35 ± 4.35	61.36 ± 2.54	57.47 ± 3.03	60.18 ± 2.53	70.89 ± 2.44	**77.30 ± 5.15**	71.97 ± 3.86	75.73 ± 2.79
ENZYMES	53.67 ± 2.66	51.30 ± 2.01	55.24 ± 2.66	51.60 ± 3.81	53.80 ± 4.50	53.60 ± 4.88	58.75 ± 5.98	61.39 ± 8.81	63.90 ± 3.69	**67.79 ± 5.43**
AIDS	50.79 ± 4.30	51.84 ± 2.87	50.12 ± 3.43	61.13 ± 0.71	70.19 ± 5.03	79.72 ± 3.98	78.16 ± 3.05	93.27 ± 4.19	97.28 ± 0.69	**99.39 ± 0.55**
DHFR	47.91 ± 3.76	52.11 ± 3.96	50.24 ± 3.13	50.29 ± 2.77	52.68 ± 3.21	51.10 ± 2.35	49.23 ± 3.05	56.71 ± 3.57	62.67 ± 3.11	**62.95 ± 3.03**
BZR	46.85 ± 5.31	55.32 ± 6.18	50.56 ± 5.87	52.46 ± 3.30	63.31 ± 8.52	60.24 ± 5.37	65.91 ± 1.47	69.42 ± 7.78	75.16 ± 5.15	**75.92 ± 7.09**
COX2	50.27 ± 7.91	50.05 ± 2.06	49.86 ± 7.43	50.27 ± 0.34	53.36 ± 8.86	52.01 ± 3.17	53.58 ± 5.05	59.37 ± 12.67	62.65 ± 8.14	**64.11 ± 3.22**
DD	48.30 ± 3.98	71.32 ± 2.41	47.99 ± 4.09	70.31 ± 1.09	55.80 ± 1.77	59.32 ± 3.92	72.27 ± 1.83	**80.12 ± 5.24**	73.25 ± 3.19	77.82 ± 1.60
NCI1	49.90 ± 1.18	50.58 ± 1.38	50.63 ± 1.22	50.74 ± 1.70	50.10 ± 0.87	49.88 ± 0.53	**71.98 ± 1.21**	68.48 ± 2.39	61.12 ± 2.21	69.07 ± 1.15
IMDB-B	50.75 ± 3.10	50.80 ± 3.17	54.08 ± 5.19	50.20 ± 0.40	56.50 ± 3.58	56.50 ± 4.90	60.19 ± 8.90	52.09 ± 3.41	65.88 ± 0.75	**70.97 ± 1.35**
REDDIT-B	45.68 ± 2.24	46.72 ± 3.42	49.31 ± 2.33	48.26 ± 0.32	68.50 ± 5.56	71.80 ± 4.38	75.93 ± 8.65	77.85 ± 2.62	**88.67 ± 1.24**	84.97 ± 2.41
COLLAB	49.59 ± 2.24	50.49 ± 1.72	52.60 ± 2.56	50.69 ± 0.32	46.27 ± 0.73	47.61 ± 1.29	60.70 ± 2.97	52.94 ± 0.85	72.08 ± 0.90	**72.92 ± 1.44**
HSE	57.02 ± 8.42	56.87 ± 10.51	62.72 ± 10.13	53.02 ± 5.12	53.56 ± 3.98	51.18 ± 2.71	64.84 ± 4.70	59.48 ± 1.44	69.65 ± 2.14	**70.30 ± 2.90**
MMP	46.65 ± 6.31	50.06 ± 3.73	55.24 ± 3.26	52.68 ± 3.34	54.59 ± 2.01	54.54 ± 1.86	**71.23 ± 0.16**	67.84 ± 0.59	70.51 ± 1.56	70.96 ± 1.01
p53	46.74 ± 4.88	50.69 ± 2.02	54.59 ± 4.46	50.85 ± 2.16	52.66 ± 1.95	53.29 ± 2.32	58.50 ± 0.37	64.20 ± 0.81	62.99 ± 1.55	**67.58 ± 3.31**
PPAR-gamma	53.94 ± 6.94	45.51 ± 2.58	57.91 ± 6.13	49.60 ± 0.22	51.40 ± 2.53	50.30 ± 1.56	**71.19 ± 4.28**	64.59 ± 0.67	67.34 ± 1.71	68.25 ± 4.66
Avg.Rank	8.73	7.73	6.93	7.47	6.53	6.93	3.60	3.27	2.40	1.40

Evaluation Metrics. We evaluate methods using a popular graph-level anomaly detection metric, i.e., the area under the receiver operating characteristic curve (AUC) following [14,18,19]. Higher AUC values indicate better anomaly detection performance.

Implementation Details. In practice, we implement CVTGAD with Pytorch[1] In order to reduce the uncertainty of this process and ensure reproducibility, we set random seeds explicitly as much as possible following [14]. We achieve the projection networks and residual networks with two-layer MLP.

5.2 Overall Performance Comparison

The overall performance of all methods w.r.t AUC against 15 datasets is shown in Table 2. As shown in Table 2, our proposed CVTGAD outperforms all baselines on 9 datasets and achieves the second-best performance on 6 datasets.

---

[1] https://pytorch.org/.

And CVTGAD achieves the first place in average rank among all comparative methods against 15 datasets as shown in the last row in Table 2. The graph kernel-based methods achieve the worst performance. It may be because they fail to capture regular patterns and key information. The GCL-based methods achieve a modest performance, indicating that GCL-based methods are competitive on this task. These results demonstrate the superiority and effectiveness of CVTGAD on graph-level anomaly detection in different fields.

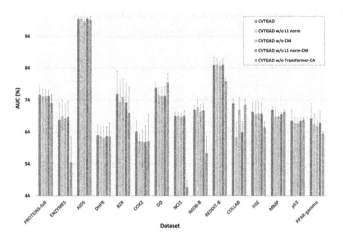

Fig. 3. The comparison of ablating different key components in terms of AUC.

Table 3. Ablation study results of key components in terms of average rank.

	CVTGAD	CVTGAD w/o L1 norm	CVTGAD w/o CM	CVTGAD w/o L1 norm-CM	CVTGAD w/o Transformer-CA
Avg.Rank	1.40	1.87	1.80	1.80	2.80

5.3   Ablation Study–Effects of Key Components

To get a better understanding of the proposed model CVTGAD, we conduct ablation study experiments on 15 datasets to investigate the effects of the three key components: simplified transformer, crossing matrix, and L1 norm. For convenience, let CVTGAD w/o L1 norm, CVTGAD w/o CM, CVTGAD w/o L1 norm-CM, CVTGAD w/o Transformer-CA denote the customized variants of CVTGAD without L1 norm, crossing matrix operation, L1 norm and crossing matrix operation, and simplified transformer module with cross-view attention module, respectively. The experimental results are illustrated in Fig. 3 and Table 3. We can observe that CVTGAD consistently achieves the best performance against other variants, demonstrating that the simplified transformer with cross-view attention is necessary to yield the best detection results. Compared with CVTGAD, the poor performance of CVTGAD w/o CM proves the significance of directly exploiting view co-occurrence between different views. And the poor performance of CVTGAD w/o Transformer-CA proves the importance of directly exploiting the relationship between nodes/graphs in both intra-graph and inter-graph perspectives. By observing CVTGAD w/o L1 norm, CVTGAD w/o CM, and CVTGAD w/o L1 norm-CM simultaneously, we can draw a preliminary conclusion: L1 norm and crossing operation are both important for implementing the cross-view attention mechanism. L1 norm has little significance for the self-attention mechanism and is even harmful to it.

5.4   Hyper Parameter Analysis and Visualization

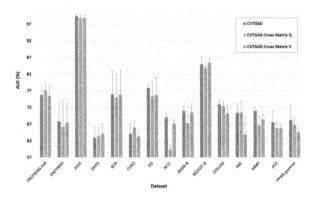

Fig. 4. The comparison of crossing different matrices in cross-view attention mechanism in terms of AUC.

Table 4. The comparison of crossing different matrices in cross-view attention mechanism in terms of average rank.

Model	CVTGAD	CVTGAD-Cross Matrix Q	CVTGAD-Cross Matrix V
Avg. Rank	1.40	1.80	1.87

The Effect of Different Matrices in Cross-View Attention. In cross-view attention, there are three parametric matrices that can cross. We conduct experiments on 15 datasets to investigate the impact of crossing different matrices on detection performance. For convenience, let CVTGAD-Cross Matrix Q and CVTGAD-Cross Matrix V denote the customized variants of CVTGAD by crossing matrix Q and crossing matrix V in cross-view attention, respectively. The experimental results are illustrated in Fig. 4 and Table 4. We find that: 1) the performance of crossing matrix K is better than the other two operations; 2) the performance of crossing matrix K on attribute graphs is more pronounced than on plain graphs. We think it may be that attribute graphs tend to rely on explicit information, while plain graphs can only rely on implicit information, and crossing operation is better at capturing implicit information.

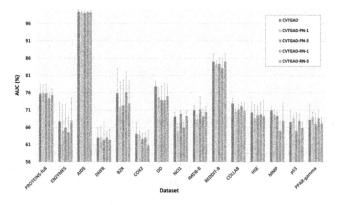

Fig. 5. The comparison of different numbers of layers for projection network and residual network in terms of AUC.

Table 5. performance of different numbers of layers for the projection network and residual network in terms of average rank.

Model	CVTGAD	CVTGAD-PN-1	CVTGAD-PN-3	CVTGAD-RN-1	CVTGAD-RN-3
Avg. Rank	1.40	1.73	1.87	1.60	1.87

Number of Layers for Projection Network and Residual Network. We conduct experiments on 15 datasets to investigate the impact of layer number on the projection network and residual network. For convenience, let CVTGAD-PN-1 and CVTGAD-PN-3 denote the customized variants of CVTGAD by achieving the projection network with 1 layer- and 3 layers- MLP, respectively. Let CVTGAD-RN-1, and CVTGAD-RN-3 denote the customized variants of CVTGAD by achieving the residual network with 1 layer- and 3 layers- MLP, respectively. The experimental results are illustrated in Fig. 5 and Table 5. Based on the performance of different variants of CVTGAD, we can conclude that setting the number of layers for the projection network and residual network to 2 is the best choice. We think that the poor performance obtained when the number of layers is 1 is due to insufficient expression ability of the network, and the poor performance when the number of layers is 3 is due to overfitting caused by too deep layers.

Visualization. We use t-SNE [21] to visualize the embeddings learned by CVTGAD. We can observe that it is difficult to directly distinguish anomalous graphs from normal graphs by relying solely on feature space or structure space. But there is a clear scoring boundary (anomaly score=18), which results in a good performance on anomaly detection. This shows the effectiveness of CVTGAD.

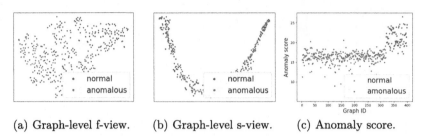

(a) Graph-level f-view.   (b) Graph-level s-view.   (c) Anomaly score.

Fig. 6. Visualization on AIDS dataset (a) and (b): visualization of testing sample embeddings of feature view (f-view) and structure view (s-view) on graph-level by t-SNE. (c): anomaly score on testing samples.

6   Conclusion

In this paper, we propose a novel framework named CVTGAD, which mainly employs a simplified transformer with a proper receptive field to capture key information and employs a cross-view attention mechanism to directly exploit the view co-occurrence across different views. To the best of our knowledge, we are the first to introduce a transformer and cross attention to the UGAD task, achieving graph neural network and transformer working collaboratively. Extensive experiments demonstrate the superiority of CVTGAD against 15 real-world datasets of different fields.

Acknowledgements. This work is supported by the Youth Fund of the National Natural Science Foundation of China (No. 62206107).

Ethical Statement. The following statement outlines the ethical considerations that were taken into account during the research process.

    Data Collection. In the experimental part, we used a publicly available dataset. And the public dataset has preprocessed the information involved in the data, so there are no issues of confidentiality and privacy.

    Protection of Participants. Throughout the research process, there were no additional participants except the authors. The personal information of all personnel is not related to the experiment. The experiment only used information from public dataset.

    Data Analysis. Our data analysis is only from the perspective of algorithmic metrics, without any discrimination or illegal tendencies.

    Conflict of Interest. We declare that they have no conflicts of interest that may have influenced the research.

    Research Involving Animals. This study does not involve the use of animals.

    Cultural Sensitivity. The research team was aware of the potential cultural biases that could have an impact on the study results. To ensure cultural sensitivity, the research team worked with participants from diverse cultural backgrounds and used culturally appropriate language in the consent form and data collection procedures.

    Beneficence. The research team considered the potential benefits and harms of the study. The research team made efforts to minimize any potential harms to participants while maximizing the potential benefits to both individuals and society.

References

1. Baltrušaitis, T., Ahuja, C., Morency, L.P.: Multimodal machine learning: a survey and taxonomy. IEEE Trans. Pattern Anal. Mach. Intell. **41**(2), 423–443 (2018)
2. Bergmann, P., Fauser, M., Sattlegger, D., Steger, C.: Uninformed students: student-teacher anomaly detection with discriminative latent embeddings. In: Proceedings of the IEEE/CVF Conference on Computer Vision and Pattern Recognition, pp. 4183–4192 (2020)
3. Breunig, M.M., Kriegel, H.P., Ng, R.T., Sander, J.: Lof: identifying density-based local outliers. In: Proceedings of the 2000 ACM SIGMOD International Conference on Management of Data, pp. 93–104 (2000)
4. Chen, D., Lin, Y., Li, W., Li, P., Zhou, J., Sun, X.: Measuring and relieving the over-smoothing problem for graph neural networks from the topological view. In: Proceedings of the AAAI Conference on Artificial Intelligence, pp. 3438–3445 (2020)
5. Ding, K., Li, J., Bhanushali, R., Liu, H.: Deep anomaly detection on attributed networks. In: Proceedings of the 2019 SIAM International Conference on Data Mining, pp. 594–602. SIAM (2019)
6. Hamilton, W., Ying, Z., Leskovec, J.: Inductive representation learning on large graphs. Adv. Neural Inf. Process. Syst. **30** (2017)
7. Hassani, K., Khasahmadi, A.H.: Contrastive multi-view representation learning on graphs. In: International Conference on Machine Learning, pp. 4116–4126. PMLR (2020)
8. Hinton, G., Vinyals, O., Dean, J.: Distilling the knowledge in a neural network. arXiv preprint arXiv:1503.02531 (2015)
9. Huang, X., Khetan, A., Cvitkovic, M., Karnin, Z.: Tabtransformer: tabular data modeling using contextual embeddings. arXiv preprint arXiv:2012.06678 (2020)
10. Kipf, T.N., Welling, M.: Semi-supervised classification with graph convolutional networks. arXiv preprint arXiv:1609.02907 (2016)
11. Lee, K.H., Chen, X., Hua, G., Hu, H., He, X.: Stacked cross attention for image-text matching. In: Proceedings of the European Conference on Computer Vision (ECCV), pp. 201–216 (2018)
12. Liu, F.T., Ting, K.M., Zhou, Z.H.: Isolation forest. In: 2008 Eighth IEEE International Conference on Data Mining, pp. 413–422. IEEE (2008)
13. Liu, X., et al.: Self-supervised learning: generative or contrastive. IEEE Trans. Knowl. Data Eng. **35**(1), 857–876 (2021)
14. Liu, Y., Ding, K., Liu, H., Pan, S.: Good-d: on unsupervised graph out-of-distribution detection. In: Proceedings of the Sixteenth ACM International Conference on Web Search and Data Mining, pp. 339–347 (2023)
15. Liu, Y., Ding, K., Wang, J., Lee, V., Liu, H., Pan, S.: Learning strong graph neural networks with weak information. In: Proceedings of the 29th ACM SIGKDD International Conference on Knowledge Discovery & Data Mining (2023)
16. Liu, Y., et al.: Graph self-supervised learning: a survey. IEEE Trans. Knowl. Data Eng. (2022)
17. Liu, Y., Zheng, Y., Zhang, D., Lee, V., Pan, S.: Beyond smoothing: unsupervised graph representation learning with edge heterophily discriminating. In: Proceedings of the AAAI Conference on Artificial Intelligence (2023)

18. Luo, X., et al.: Deep graph level anomaly detection with contrastive learning. Sci. Rep. **12**(1), 19867 (2022)
19. Ma, R., Pang, G., Chen, L., van den Hengel, A.: Deep graph-level anomaly detection by glocal knowledge distillation. In: Proceedings of the Fifteenth ACM International Conference on Web Search and Data Mining, pp. 704–714 (2022)
20. Ma, X., et al.: A comprehensive survey on graph anomaly detection with deep learning. IEEE Trans. Knowl. Data Eng. (2021)
21. Van der Maaten, L., Hinton, G.: Visualizing data using t-sne. J. Mach. Learn. Res. **9**(11) (2008)
22. Manevitz, L.M., Yousef, M.: One-class SVMS for document classification. J. Mach. Learn. Res. **2**, 139–154 (2001)
23. Morris, C., Kriege, N.M., Bause, F., Kersting, K., Mutzel, P., Neumann, M.: Tudataset: a collection of benchmark datasets for learning with graphs. arXiv preprint arXiv:2007.08663 (2020)
24. Neumann, M., Garnett, R., Bauckhage, C., Kersting, K.: Propagation kernels: efficient graph kernels from propagated information. Mach. Learn. **102**, 209–245 (2016)
25. Qiu, J., et al.: GCC: graph contrastive coding for graph neural network pre-training. In: Proceedings of the 26th ACM SIGKDD International Conference on Knowledge Discovery & Data Mining, pp. 1150–1160 (2020)
26. Shervashidze, N., Schweitzer, P., Van Leeuwen, E.J., Mehlhorn, K., Borgwardt, K.M.: Weisfeiler-lehman graph kernels. J. Mach. Learn. Res. **12**(9) (2011)
27. Sun, F.Y., Hoffman, J., Verma, V., Tang, J.: Infograph: Unsupervised and semi-supervised graph-level representation learning via mutual information maximization. In: International Conference on Learning Representations (2020)
28. Tan, Y., Liu, Y., Long, G., Jiang, J., Lu, Q., Zhang, C.: Federated learning on non-IID graphs via structural knowledge sharing. In: Proceedings of the AAAI Conference on Artificial Intelligence (2023)
29. Vaswani, A., et al.: Attention is all you need. Adv. Neural Inf. Process. Syst. **30** (2017)
30. Veličković, P., Cucurull, G., Casanova, A., Romero, A., Lio, P., Bengio, Y.: Graph attention networks. arXiv preprint arXiv:1710.10903 (2017)
31. Velickovic, P., Fedus, W., Hamilton, W.L., Liò, P., Bengio, Y., Hjelm, R.D.: Deep graph infomax. ICLR (Poster) **2**(3), 4 (2019)
32. Xu, K., Hu, W., Leskovec, J., Jegelka, S.: How powerful are graph neural networks? arXiv preprint arXiv:1810.00826 (2018)
33. You, Y., Chen, T., Sui, Y., Chen, T., Wang, Z., Shen, Y.: Graph contrastive learning with augmentations. Adv. Neural Inf. Process. Syst. **33**, 5812–5823 (2020)
34. Zhang, G., et al.: Dual-discriminative graph neural network for imbalanced graph-level anomaly detection. Adv. Neural Inf. Process. Syst. (2022)
35. Zhao, L., Akoglu, L.: On using classification datasets to evaluate graph outlier detection: peculiar observations and new insights. Big Data (2021)
36. Zheng, Y., Pan, S., Lee, V., Zheng, Y., Yu, P.S.: Rethinking and scaling up graph contrastive learning: an extremely efficient approach with group discrimination. Adv. Neural Inf. Process. Syst. **35**, 10809–10820 (2022)
37. Zheng, Y., Zheng, Y., Zhou, X., Gong, C., Lee, V.C., Pan, S.: Unifying graph contrastive learning with flexible contextual scopes. In: 2022 IEEE International Conference on Data Mining (ICDM), pp. 793–802. IEEE (2022)
38. Zhu, Y., Xu, Y., Yu, F., Liu, Q., Wu, S., Wang, L.: Graph contrastive learning with adaptive augmentation. In: Proceedings of the Web Conference 2021, pp. 2069–2080 (2021)

Graph-Level Anomaly Detection via Hierarchical Memory Networks

Chaoxi Niu[1], Guansong Pang[2]([✉]), and Ling Chen[1]

[1] AAII, University of Technology Sydney, Sydney, Australia
`Chaoxi.Niu@student.uts.edu.au`, `Ling.Chen@uts.edu.au`
[2] Singapore Management University, Singapore, Singapore
`pangguansong@gmail.com`

Abstract. Graph-level anomaly detection aims to identify abnormal graphs that exhibit deviant structures and node attributes compared to the majority in a graph set. One primary challenge is to learn normal patterns manifested in both fine-grained and holistic views of graphs for identifying graphs that are abnormal in part or in whole. To tackle this challenge, we propose a novel approach called Hierarchical Memory Networks (HimNet), which learns hierarchical memory modules—node and graph memory modules—via a graph autoencoder network architecture. The node-level memory module is trained to model fine-grained, internal graph interactions among nodes for detecting locally abnormal graphs, while the graph-level memory module is dedicated to the learning of holistic normal patterns for detecting globally abnormal graphs. The two modules are jointly optimized to detect both locally- and globally-anomalous graphs. Extensive empirical results on 16 real-world graph datasets from various domains show that i) HimNet significantly outperforms the state-of-art methods and ii) it is robust to anomaly contamination. Codes are available at: https://github.com/Niuchx/HimNet.

Keywords: Graph-level Anomaly Detection · Memory Networks · Graph Neural Networks · Autoencoder

1 Introduction

Graphs are widely used to model complex relationships between data instances in various fields, such as social networks, bioinformatics, chemistry, etc. Graph neural networks (GNNs) have become the predominant approach to learning effective node/graph representations and have achieved impressive performance in many graph-related tasks, such as node classification [13], link prediction [42] and graph classification [40]. Despite the remarkable success achieved by GNNs, it is still challenging for GNNs to tackle some notoriously difficult tasks. Graph-level anomaly detection (GLAD), which aims to identify abnormal graphs that exhibit deviant structures and node attributes in comparison to the majority in a set of graphs, is one of such tasks.

© The Author(s), under exclusive license to Springer Nature Switzerland AG 2023
D. Koutra et al. (Eds.): ECML PKDD 2023, LNAI 14169, pp. 201–218, 2023.
https://doi.org/10.1007/978-3-031-43412-9_12

In recent years, a number of graph anomaly detection methods have been proposed. However, a majority of them focus on the detection of abnormal nodes or edges in a single graph [7,9,14,19,28,35]. In contrast, graph-level anomaly detection is significantly less explored, despite its great importance and broad application [1,15,21]. In general, anomalous graphs can be any graphs that are abnormal in part or in whole, which are referred to as locally-anomalous or globally-anomalous graphs [20,21]. The local abnormality requires a fine-grained inspection of the graphs, as it is primarily due to the presence of unusual local graph structures, e.g., nodes and their associated local neighborhoods, compared to the corresponding structures in the other graphs. The global abnormality, on the other hand, requires a holistic treatment of the graphs, as it is manifested only at the graph-level representations. Thus, the main challenge in GLAD is to learn normal patterns from both fine-grained and holistic views of graphs for identifying both locally- and globally-anomalous graphs.

A few GLAD methods have been introduced, e.g., [20,21]. They employ knowledge distillation [21] or contrastive learning [20] on the node and graph representations to capture the local/global normal patterns. The key intuition of these methods is that the model trained to fit exclusively normal training graphs learns normality representations, on which abnormal test graphs would be discriminative from the normal graphs. Despite their effectiveness, the learned normality representations may not preserve the primary semantics of graph structures and attributes, since their learning objectives ignore these semantics and focus on enlarging the relative difference between normal and abnormal graphs in the representation space. Consequently, they become ineffective in detecting abnormal graphs in which semantic-rich graph representations are required.

This paper introduces a novel approach, namely hierarchical memory networks (**HimNet**), via a graph autoencoder architecture to learn hierarchical node and graph memory modules for GLAD, which not only help effectively differentiate normal and abnormal graphs but also preserve rich primary semantics. Autoencoder (AE) [3,11], which utilizes a decoder to reconstruct the original input based on the representations learned by an encoder, is a widely-used approach to preserve the rich semantics of the input data in the new representation space. AE is also commonly used for anomaly detection in various domains [6,8,27,41,46,47] since anomalies are generally difficult to reconstruct, and thus, they have a higher reconstruction error than normal samples. However, reconstructing graphs is difficult since it involves the reconstruction of diverse graph structures and attributes. Our hierarchical memory learning is designed to address this issue. Specifically, the node-level memory module captures the local normal patterns that describe the fine-grained, internal graph interactions among nodes, and it is optimized by minimizing *a graph reconstruction error* between original input graphs and the graphs reconstructed from the node memory module. On the other hand, the graph-level memory module is dedicated to the learning of holistic normal patterns of graph-level representations, and it is optimized by minimizing *a graph approximation error* between graph-level representations and their approximated representations based on the graph memory. The two modules are jointly optimized to detect both locally and globally anomalous graphs. Memory-augmented AEs [8,27] have been introduced to add a memory module for anomaly detection in image and video data. The memory module has shown promise in enabling improved detection performance. However, their memory module is not applicable to graph data. HimNet addresses this problem by learning hierarchical node and graph memory modules to capture the local and global normal patterns of those non-Euclidean graph data.

In summary, our main contributions include: i) we introduce a hierarchical node-to-graph memory network HimNet for GLAD, which is the first work of memory-based GLAD; ii) we introduce a three-dimensional node memory module that consists of multiple two-dimensional memory blocks (with each block capturing one type of normal pattern on the representations of all nodes), as well as a graph memory module with each memory block capturing graph-level normal patterns; and iii) we further propose to learn these two memory modules by jointly minimizing a graph reconstruction error and a graph approximation error. We evaluate the effectiveness of HimNet via extensive experiments on 16 GLAD datasets from different domains, which show that HimNet significantly outperforms several state-of-art models and it also demonstrates remarkable robustness to anomaly-contaminated training data.

2 Related Work

2.1 Graph-Level Anomaly Detection

Graph anomaly detection has attracted increasing research interest in recent years and various methods have been proposed [2,24]. However, most of them focus on detecting anomalous nodes or edges in a single graph [7,9,14,19,28,35]; significantly fewer studies are conducted on GLAD. Recently, a few GLAD methods have been proposed. These works can be divided into two categories: two-step methods and end-to-end methods. The first category typically obtains graph representations using graph kernels (e.g., Weisfeiler-Leman Kernel [32] and propagation kernels [23]), or advanced GNNs (such as Graph2Vec [22] and InfoGraph [33]). An off-the-shelf anomaly detector is then applied to the learned graph representations to detect abnormal graphs, such as k-nearest-neighbor distance [26], isolation forest [17], local outlier factor [4], and one-class support vector machine [31]. However, the two-step methods may achieve suboptimal performance since the anomaly detectors are independent of the graph representation learning. To address this issue, end-to-end methods unify graph representation learning and anomaly detection. Typically, they utilize powerful GNNs as the backbone and learn graph representations tailored for graph anomaly detection. For example, [45] applied the Deep SVDD objective [30] on top of the GNN-based graph representations for anomalous graph detection. [21] utilized random knowledge distillation on both node and graph representations to capture graph regularity information. Some works also employed contrastive learning strategy for detecting anomalous graphs [18,20,29]. These methods show better performance than the two-step methods, but they focus on learning discriminative representations only, which may fail to preserve the primary graph semantics. Our method addresses this issue by learning hierarchical memory modules with the objective of preserving as much semantic as possible in the representation space.

2.2   Memory Networks

Due to the ability to store and retrieve important information, memory networks have been proposed and successfully applied to a wide range of domains [8,10,16,27,36,38]. For generative models, external memory is exploited to store local detail information [16] and prevent the model collapsing problem [10]. Considering that memory can be used to record prototypical patterns of normal data, a number of studies [8,27] proposed to augment AEs with a memory module for image or video anomaly detection. Despite the success of these methods, their memory networks are not applicable to GLAD as graph data is non-Euclidean and contains diverse graph structures and attributes where graph abnormality may exist. Our hierarchical node-to-graph memory modules are specifically designed to address this problem.

3   Methodology

3.1   The GLAD Problem

Let $\mathcal{G} = (\mathcal{V}, \mathcal{E})$ denote a graph, where $\mathcal{V}$ is the set of N nodes and $\mathcal{E}$ is the set of edges. $\mathcal{E}$ is commonly represented by an adjacency matrix $\mathbf{A} \in [0,1]^{N \times N}$ where $\mathbf{A}_{ij} = 1$ if node i and j are connected with an edge and $\mathbf{A}_{ij} = 0$ otherwise. If $\mathcal{G}$ is an attributed graph, the node features can be represented as $\mathbf{X} \in \mathbb{R}^{N \times d}$ where d is the feature dimension. Therefore, a graph can also be denoted as $\mathcal{G} = (\mathbf{A}, \mathbf{X})$. This work targets graph-level anomaly detection. Specifically, given a set of K normal training graphs $\{\mathcal{G}_i = (\mathbf{A}_i, \mathbf{X}_i)\}_{i=1}^{K}$, we aim to learn an anomaly scoring function that assigns a high anomaly score to a test graph $\mathcal{G}$ if it significantly deviates from the majority in a set of graphs.

3.2   Overview of the Proposed Hierarchical Memory Networks

We introduce HimNet to learn hierarchical node and graph memory blocks that respectively capture local and global normal patterns for GLAD. HimNet consists of four key components, namely graph encoder, graph decoder, node and graph memory modules, as shown in Fig. 1. The node memory module is designed as a three-dimensional tensor that consists of multiple two-dimensional memory blocks, with each block capturing one type of normal pattern on all nodes. On the other hand, the graph memory is designed as a two-dimensional matrix, with each memory block capturing normal patterns on graph-level representations. These two memory modules are trained to capture hierarchical normal patterns of graph data, enabling the detection of locally- and globally-anomalous graphs.

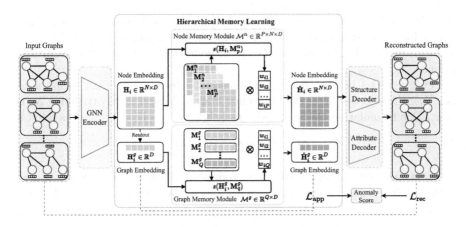

Fig. 1. Overview of the proposed HimNet. It learns a three-dimensional node memory module $\mathcal{M}^n \in \mathbb{R}^{P \times N \times D}$ and a two-dimensional graph memory module $\mathcal{M}^g \in \mathbb{R}^{Q \times D}$, where P and Q denotes the number of node and graph memory blocks respectively, D is the dimensionality of learned node representations, and N is the number of nodes.

Given an input graph, the graph encoder learns the node-level representation, and graph-level representation is obtained by applying a readout function on it. Traditionally, the graph decoder takes the node-level representation as input to reconstruct the input graph. However, this would increase the probability of the graph autoencoder reconstructing the abnormal graphs well. To tackle this issue, HimNet decouples the decoder from the encoder by replacing the encoded node-level representation with a combination of local patterns in the node memory module. Moreover, the graph-level representation is approximated by global patterns in the graph memory module. Then, the proposed model is optimized by minimizing graph reconstruction error and graph approximation error. This not only optimizes the parameters of the encoder and decoder but also forces the two memory modules to learn prime patterns of normal training graphs at both node and graph levels. After model optimization, given a test graph, the decoder takes the local normal patterns in the node memory module as input and the graph-level representation is approximated by global normal patterns in the graph memory module. In this way, the graph reconstruction error together with the graph approximation error can be used as an effective anomaly score.

3.3 Graph Autoencoder

In this paper, we build HimNet using a graph autoencoder (GAE) [12] architecture to learn hierarchical memory modules. Before delving into the details of HimNet, we give an introduction to graph autoencoder which consists of a GNN-based encoder and decoder.

Encoder. GNNs have recently emerged as a powerful class of deep-learning models for graph-structured data [13,34,40]. In this work, we employ GCN [13] as the graph encoder to generate the latent node-level and graph-level representations.

Let $\phi_e(\cdot : \Theta_e)$ be the encoder parameterized by Θ_e. For every graph $\mathcal{G}_i = (\mathbf{A}_i, \mathbf{X}_i)$, the encoder takes the adjacency matrix $\mathbf{A}_i$ and node attributes $\mathbf{X}_i$ as input. The formulation of the encoder at l-th layer can be expressed as follows:

$$\mathbf{H}_i^l = \text{ReLU}(\hat{\mathbf{A}}_i \mathbf{H}_i^{(l-1)} \Theta_e^l), \tag{1}$$

where $\mathbf{H}_i^l$ and Θ_e^l represent the node representations and weight parameters of the GCN encoder at the l-th layer respectively, and $\text{ReLU}(\cdot)$ is the non-linear activation function. $\hat{\mathbf{A}}_i = \tilde{\mathbf{D}}_i^{-\frac{1}{2}} \tilde{\mathbf{A}}_i \tilde{\mathbf{D}}_i^{-\frac{1}{2}}$, where $\tilde{\mathbf{A}}_i = \mathbf{A}_i + \mathbf{I}$ ($\mathbf{I}$ is an identity matrix) and $\tilde{\mathbf{D}}_i$ is the degree matrix of $\tilde{\mathbf{A}}_i$. $\mathbf{H}_i^{(l-1)}$ represents the node representation at the $(l-1)$-th layer and $\mathbf{H}_i^{(0)} = \mathbf{X}_i$. If the input graph $\mathcal{G}_i$ is a plain graph, the node degree is typically used as the attribute [43]. Assuming the output dimension of the encoder is D, the learned node representation can be formulated as $\mathbf{H}_i \in \mathbb{R}^{N \times D}$ where N is the number of nodes in the graph.

To obtain the graph-level representation, a readout function is commonly applied to the learned node representation $\mathbf{H}_i$. There are many readout functions, such as maxing, averaging, summation, and concatenation [39,44]. In this paper, we adopt the averaging function which calculates the mean of node representations along the node dimension to get the graph-level representation $\mathbf{H}_i^g \in \mathbb{R}^D$. The resulting representation $\mathbf{H}_i^g$ captures the overall structural and semantic information of the graph $\mathcal{G}_i$.

Decoder. To accurately reconstruct the original graph $\mathcal{G}_i$, two decoders $\phi_d^s(\mathbf{H}_i)$ and $\phi_d^a(\mathbf{H}_i)$, which take node representation $\mathbf{H}_i$ as input, are employed to reconstruct the graph structure and node attribute respectively.

For the graph structure decoder $\phi_d^s(\mathbf{H}_i)$, we implement it as the inner product of the latent node representation $\mathbf{H}_i$ as follows:

$$\mathbf{A}_i' = \sigma(\mathbf{H}_i \mathbf{H}_i^T), \tag{2}$$

where $\mathbf{A}_i'$ denotes the reconstructed graph structure, $\mathbf{H}_i^T$ is the transpose of $\mathbf{H}_i$, and $\sigma(\cdot)$ represents the activation function.

To reconstruct the node attribute, we use the GCN [13] as the attribute decoder $\phi_d^a(\mathbf{H}_i)$ and the formulation at the l-th layer can be expressed as:

$$\tilde{\mathbf{H}}_i^l = \text{ReLU}(\hat{\mathbf{A}}_i \tilde{\mathbf{H}}_i^{(l-1)} \Theta_d^l), \tag{3}$$

where $\tilde{\mathbf{H}}_i^l$ and Θ_d^l represent the latent node representations and weight parameters at l-th layer of the decoder respectively, with $\tilde{\mathbf{H}}_i^{(0)} = \mathbf{H}_i$. We denote the reconstructed node attribute as $\mathbf{X}_i'$, which is the output of the decoder $\phi_d^a(\mathbf{H}_i)$.

For each input graph $\mathcal{G}_i = (\mathbf{A}_i, \mathbf{X}_i)$, GAE is optimized to minimize the reconstruction errors on the graph structure and node attributes:

$$\mathcal{L}_{\text{GAE}} = \|\mathbf{A}_i - \mathbf{A}_i'\|_F^2 + \|\mathbf{X}_i - \mathbf{X}_i'\|_F^2, \tag{4}$$

where $\|\cdot\|_F$ represents Frobenius norm.

By minimizing Eq. (4), GAE is driven to fit the patterns of normal training graph data and preserve the semantics of them. During inference, GAE would produce higher reconstruction errors for anomalous graphs than normal graphs, as abnormal graphs are distinctive from normal graphs and are not accessible to GAE during the training process. Therefore, the reconstruction error $\mathcal{L}_{GAE}$ can be directly used as the criterion for anomaly detection. However, solely relying on $\mathcal{L}_{GAE}$ often cannot yield satisfactory anomaly detection performance, as demonstrated in the experiments section. This is primarily because graph is difficult to reconstruct, leading to less discriminative power in differentiating normal and abnormal graphs. Moreover, such a GAE cannot model graph-level patterns well, as graph representations are not explored in GAE. In this work, we propose to learn hierarchical memory modules to address this problem.

3.4 Hierarchical Memory Learning

Hierarchical memory learning consists of two memory modules: node and graph memory modules, which are designed to capture hierarchical node-to-graph patterns of the normal training graphs and facilitate the detection of graphs that are abnormal in part or in whole.

Graph Memory Module. The graph memory module aims to capture the prototypical patterns inherent in the graph representations $\{\mathbf{H}_i^g\}_{i=1}^K$ (K is the number of training graphs) through a set of graph memory blocks, denoted as $\mathcal{M}^g = \{\mathbf{M}_q^g \in \mathbb{R}^D\}_{q=1}^Q$, where Q is the total number of memory blocks and each block $\mathbf{M}_q^g$ is of the same dimensionality size as the graph representation $\mathbf{H}_i^g$.

Since the graph memory blocks capture prototypical patterns of graph representations, a graph representation $\mathbf{H}_i^g$ can be approximated using the following equation:

$$\hat{\mathbf{H}}_i^g = \sum_{q=1}^Q w_{iq} \mathbf{M}_q^g, \quad \text{s.t.} \quad \sum_{q=1}^Q w_{iq} = 1, \tag{5}$$

where $\hat{\mathbf{H}}_i^g$ is the approximated representation of $\mathbf{H}_i^g$ from the memory blocks, and w_{iq} is the weight of the memory block $\mathbf{M}_q^g$ for $\mathbf{H}_i^g$, with the summation of the weights constrained to be one. The weight w_{iq} reflects the correlation between each graph memory block and the graph representation, i.e., a higher correlation induces a larger weight. Therefore, to calculate w_{iq}, we first employ a cosine similarity function $s(\cdot)$ to measure the similarity between $\mathbf{M}_q^g$ and $\mathbf{H}_i^g$:

$$s(\mathbf{H}_i^g, \mathbf{M}_q^g) = \frac{\mathbf{H}_i^g (\mathbf{M}_q^g)^T}{\|\mathbf{H}_i^g\| \|\mathbf{M}_q^g\|}. \tag{6}$$

To impose the summation constraint, we further normalize the similarities via the following softmax operation to obtain the final weight:

$$w_{iq} = \frac{\exp(s(\mathbf{H}_i^g, \mathbf{M}_q^g))}{\sum_{q=1}^{Q} \exp(s(\mathbf{H}_i^g, \mathbf{M}_q^g))}. \tag{7}$$

After obtaining the approximated graph representation $\hat{\mathbf{H}}_i^g$, we calculate the approximation error via the following $\mathcal{L}_{\mathrm{app}}$ loss:

$$\mathcal{L}_{\mathrm{app}} = \|\mathbf{H}_i^g - \hat{\mathbf{H}}_i^g\|_F^2. \tag{8}$$

In the training phase, the optimization of Eq. (8) not only minimizes the approximation error through an efficient combination of the graph memory blocks but also forces the graph memory blocks to learn the most crucial patterns of the graph representations. In this way, during the test phase, the approximation errors for normal and abnormal graphs would become distinct. This occurs because the approximated graph representation is constructed solely through the weighted combination of the learned normal patterns of graph representations.

Node Memory Module. Different from the graph memory module that captures the normal patterns at the graph-level representations, the node memory module is designed to capture the fine-grained, normal patterns on the node representations $\{\mathbf{H}_i \in \mathbb{R}^{N \times D}\}_{i=1}^K$. Specifically, the node memory module is designed as a three-dimensional tensor, consisting of P two-dimensional memory matrices, $\mathcal{M}^n = \{\mathbf{M}_p^n \in \mathbb{R}^{N \times D}\}_{p=1}^P$, with each memory block $\mathbf{M}_p^n$ having the same dimensionality size as the representations of all nodes. This way helps effectively capture interactions across all nodes and their local neighborhood.

To reduce the probability of the decoder reconstructing the abnormal graph unexpectedly, for a node representation $\mathbf{H}_i$, the node memory module approximates it with $\hat{\mathbf{H}}_i$ and feeds $\hat{\mathbf{H}}_i$ to the decoder. Formally, $\hat{\mathbf{H}}_i$ is obtained by:

$$\hat{\mathbf{H}}_i = \sum_{p=1}^P w_{ip}\mathbf{M}_p^n, \quad \text{s.t.} \quad \sum_{p=1}^P w_{ip} = 1, \tag{9}$$

where w_{ip} is the weight of the memory block $\mathbf{M}_p^n$ for $\mathbf{H}_i$ and the summation of w_{ip} is constrained to 1. To compute the value of w_{ip}, we adopt the same approach used in the graph memory block. Specifically, we first calculate the similarity between the node representation $\mathbf{H}_i$ and each node memory block $\mathbf{M}_p^n$. Then, we normalize the similarities through the softmax function to obtain the final weight value w_{ip}.

The approximated node representation $\hat{\mathbf{H}}_i$ is fed as the input to the graph structure decoder $\phi_d^s(\cdot)$ and node attribute decoder $\phi_d^a(\cdot)$. In this way, the reconstruction error based on $\hat{\mathbf{H}}_i$ can be reformulated as:

$$\mathcal{L}_{\mathrm{rec}} = \|\mathbf{A}_i - \phi_d^s(\hat{\mathbf{H}}_i)\|_F^2 + \|\mathbf{X}_i - \phi_d^a(\hat{\mathbf{H}}_i)\|_F^2. \tag{10}$$

Compared to GAE which reconstructs the original graph depending on the encoded node representation, the node memory module performs graph construction solely based on the weighted combination of the node memory blocks. During training, the graph memory blocks are driven to learn the most representative patterns in the encoded node representations by minimizing the reconstruction error in Eq. (10). While in the testing phase, regardless of whether the input graph is normal or not, the decoder only takes different combinations of the learned normal patterns as input and outputs the normal-like graphs. Consequently, the reconstruction errors between normal and abnormal graphs would become significantly different. Overall, the node memory module decouples the decoder from the encoder, resulting in the graph reconstruction being more sensitive to the anomaly.

3.5   Training and Inference

Training Objective. By jointly employing the graph and node memory modules, HimNet aims to capture the hierarchical normal patterns of graphs. To achieve this goal, for each graph, our model is optimized by minimizing the combined objective of Eq. (8) and Eq. (10):

$$\mathcal{L}'_{\text{rec}} = \|\mathbf{A}_i - \phi_d^s(\hat{\mathbf{H}}_i)\|_F^2 + \|\mathbf{X}_i - \phi_d^a(\hat{\mathbf{H}}_i)\|_F^2 + \|\mathbf{H}_i^g - \hat{\mathbf{H}}_i^g\|_F^2. \tag{11}$$

To further enhance the discrimination of HimNet for normal and abnormal graphs, we adopt the hard shrinkage strategy [8] to promote the sparsity of weight parameters w_{ip} and w_{iq}. Besides, the entropy of w_{ip} and w_{iq} are calculated and minimized during the training, which can be formulated as follows:

$$\mathcal{L}_{\text{entropy}} = \sum_{i=1}^{P} -w_{ip} \log w_{ip} + \sum_{i=1}^{Q} -w_{iq} \log w_{iq}. \tag{12}$$

By employing the hard shrinkage and the entropy term, the weight parameters would become more sparse, i.e., the encoded node and graph representations are approximated with fewer memory blocks. This requires the chosen memory blocks to be more relevant to the encoded representations and also forces the memory blocks to learn more informative patterns.

The final training objective is obtained by combining Eq. (11) and Eq. (12):

$$\mathcal{L}_{\text{train}} = \mathcal{L}'_{\text{rec}} + \alpha \mathcal{L}_{\text{entropy}}, \tag{13}$$

where α is a hyperparameter controlling the importance of the entropy term.

Inference. By optimizing Eq. (13), HimNet can capture the hierarchical normal patterns of graphs. As a result, for a normal graph, HimNet is capable of reconstructing it effectively with the memory blocks learned in both node and graph memory modules. However, for an abnormal graph, the value in Eq. (11) tends to be high. Therefore, we adopt the loss term Eq. (11) as the anomaly score, where a higher value indicates a larger probability of being an abnormal graph.

4 Experiments

4.1 Experimental Setups

Datasets. To verify the effectiveness of HimNet, we conduct experiments on 16 publicly available graph datasets from two popular application domains: i) biochemical molecules (PROTEINS_full, ENZYMES, AIDS, DHFR, BZR, COX2, DD, NCI1, HSE, MMP, p53, PPAR-gamma, and hERG) and ii) social networks (IMDB, REDDIT, and COLLAB). The statistics of these graph datasets[1] are summarized in Table 1. Specifically, the first six datasets in Table 1 are attributed graphs and the other datasets consist of plain graphs. Moreover, HSE, MMP, p53, and PPAR-gamma contain real anomalies while the other graph datasets are originally constructed for graph classification. Following [5,17,21,25], these datasets are converted for GLAD by treating the minority class in these datasets as anomalies.

Table 1. Key Statistics of Graph Datasets.

Dataset	Category	# Graphs	# Avg.Nodes	# Avg.Edges	# Anomaly Rate
PROTEINS_full	Biochemical Molecules	1,113	39.06	72.82	0.60
ENZYMES	Biochemical Molecules	600	32.63	62.14	0.17
AIDS	Biochemical Molecules	2,000	15.69	16.2	0.20
DHFR	Biochemical Molecules	467	42.43	44.54	0.61
BZR	Biochemical Molecules	405	35.75	38.36	0.79
COX2	Biochemical Molecules	467	41.22	43.45	0.78
DD	Biochemical Molecules	1,178	284.32	715.66	0.58
NCI1	Biochemical Molecules	4,110	29.87	32.3	0.50
HSE	Biochemical Molecules	8,417	16.89	17.23	0.04
MMP	Biochemical Molecules	7,558	17.62	17.98	0.16
p53	Biochemical Molecules	8,903	17.92	18.34	0.10
PPAR-gamma	Biochemical Molecules	8,451	17.38	17.72	0.06
hERG	Biochemical Molecules	655	26.48	28.79	0.31
IMDB	Social Networks	1,000	19.77	96.53	0.50
REDDIT	Social Networks	2,000	429.63	497.75	0.50
COLLAB	Social Networks	5,000	74.49	2,457.78	0.52

Competing Methods. Several competing methods from two categories are used for comparison to the proposed method. The first category consists of two-step methods that use state-of-art graph representation learning methods

---

[1] All the graph datasets are available on https://chrsmrrs.github.io/datasets/docs/datasets/ except hERG which is obtained from https://tdcommons.ai/single_pred_tasks/tox/.

to extract graph representations and then apply an advanced anomaly detector on the learned representations to identify anomalous graphs. Specifically, we employ InfoGraph [33], Weisfeiler-Lehamn (WL) [32], and propagation kernel (PK) [23] as the graph encoder respectively and utilize isolation forest as the anomaly detector following [21]. The second category of baselines includes OCGCN [45], GLocalKD [21], and GAE [12] that are trained in an end-to-end manner. OCGCN [45] applied an SVDD objective on top of GCN-based representation for graph anomaly detection. GLocalKD [21] utilized random knowledge distillation to identify anomalies. GAE [12] used the graph reconstruction error to detect anomalous graphs.

Implementation Details. To ensure fair comparisons, we utilize a three-layer GCN [13] as the graph encoder following [21]. The dimensions of the latent layer and output feature are set to 512 and 256 respectively. The node attribute decoder is a two-layer GCN with the dimension of the latent layer set as 256. The batch size is 300 for all datasets except for HSE, MMP, p53, and PPAR-gamma whose bath size is 2000 since these datasets contain more graphs. The hyperparameter α is set to 0.01 for all datasets. This work targets detecting anomalous graphs within multiple graphs. However, the number of nodes varies across graphs which hinders the parallel processing of graph data. To address this issue, we augment the adjacency and the attribute matrices with zero padding to match the same size of the largest graph.

Evaluation. We employ the commonly used metric, area under receiver operating characteristic curve (AUC), to evaluate the anomaly detection performance. A higher AUC value indicates better performance. The mean and standard deviation of AUC results are reported by performing 5-fold cross-validation for all datasets except for HSE, MMP, p53 and PPAR-gamma which have widely used predefined train and test splits. For these datasets, we report the results by running the experiments five times with different random seeds.

4.2 Comparison to State-of-the-Art Methods

The AUC results of the proposed method and the competing methods are reported in Table 2. From the average rank results in the table, we can see end-to-end methods generally perform better than two-step methods, which highlights the significance of learning tailored representations for graph-level anomaly detection. Further, our method outperforms all the methods on 13 out of 16 datasets and achieves highly competitive performance in the remaining three datasets. In comparison to GAE [12], our method incorporates two memory modules to learn hierarchical normal patterns. The performance improvements over GAE [12] and other counterparts demonstrate the effectiveness of exploiting memory modules to capture hierarchical normal patterns for anomalous graph detection. Note that GAE performs poorly on NCI1 and REDDIT while our method achieves very promising results. This demonstrates that the rich semantics learned in HimNet allow significantly better performance than GAE in distinguishing abnormal and normal graphs, especially when the graphs are large and difficult to reconstruct, e.g., those in REDDIT.

We also perform a paired Wilcoxon signed rank test [37] to verify the statistical significance of HimNet against the baselines across all 16 datasets and the results are shown in the bottom line of Table 2. We can see that our method surpasses all baseline approaches with a confidence level greater than 98%.

Table 2. AUC results (in percent, mean±std) on 16 real-world graph datasets. The best and second performances in each row are boldfaced and underlined respectively.

Dataset	InfoGraph-iF	WL-iF	PK-iF	OCGCN	GLocalKD	GAE	Our
PROTEINS_full	46.4±1.9	63.9 ± 1.8	62.7 ± 0.9	71.8 ± 3.6	**78.5 ± 3.4**	76.6 ± 2.2	<u>77.2 ± 1.5</u>
ENZYMES	48.3 ± 2.7	49.8 ± 2.9	49.3 ± 1.3	61.3 ± 8.7	<u>63.6 ± 6.1</u>	51.6 ± 2.7	**58.9 ± 7.6**
AIDS	70.3 ± 3.6	63.2 ± 5.0	47.6 ± 1.4	66.4 ± 8.0	<u>99.2 ± 0.4</u>	99.0 ± 0.5	**99.7 ± 0.3**
DHFR	48.9 ± 1.5	46.6 ± 1.3	46.7 ± 1.3	49.5 ± 8.0	<u>55.8 ± 3.0</u>	51.4 ± 3.6	**70.1 ± 1.7**
BZR	52.8 ± 6.0	53.3 ± 3.2	52.5 ± 5.2	65.8 ± 7.1	<u>67.9 ± 6.5</u>	65.5 ± 8.3	**70.3 ± 5.4**
COX2	58.0 ± 5.2	53.2 ± 2.7	51.5 ± 3.6	<u>62.8 ± 7.2</u>	58.9 ± 4.5	58.7 ± 4.9	**63.7 ± 7.6**
DD	47.5 ± 1.2	69.9 ± 0.6	70.6 ± 1.0	60.5 ± 8.6	<u>80.5 ± 1.7</u>	80.4 ± 1.7	**80.6 ± 2.1**
NCI1	49.4 ± 0.9	54.5 ± 0.8	53.2 ± 0.6	62.7 ± 1.5	<u>68.3 ± 1.5</u>	35.0 ± 1.9	**68.6 ± 1.9**
HSE	48.4 ± 2.6	47.7 ± 0.0	48.9 ± 0.3	38.8 ± 4.1	<u>59.1 ± 0.1</u>	59.0 ± 0.5	**61.3 ± 3.9**
MMP	53.9 ± 2.2	47.5 ± 0.0	48.8 ± 0.2	45.7 ± 3.8	<u>67.6 ± 0.1</u>	67.3 ± 0.4	**70.3 ± 2.9**
p53	51.1 ± 1.4	47.3 ± 0.0	48.6 ± 0.4	48.3 ± 1.7	63.9 ± 0.2	<u>64.0 ± 0.1</u>	**64.6 ± 0.2**
PPAR-gamma	52.1 ± 2.3	51.0 ± 0.0	49.9 ± 1.7	43.1 ± 4.3	64.4 ± 0.1	<u>65.8 ± 1.6</u>	**71.1 ± 3.4**
hERG	60.7 ± 3.3	66.5 ± 4.2	67.9 ± 3.4	56.9 ± 4.9	<u>70.4 ± 4.9</u>	68.1 ± 8.7	**75.4 ± 3.2**
IMDB	52.0 ± 2.8	44.2 ± 3.2	44.2 ± 3.5	53.6 ± 14.8	51.4 ± 3.9	<u>65.2 ± 4.4</u>	**68.3 ± 3.2**
REDDIT	45.7 ± 0.3	45.0 ± 1.3	45.0 ± 1.2	75.9 ± 5.6	**78.2 ± 1.6**	21.8 ± 1.9	<u>78.0 ± 2.5</u>
COLLAB	45.3 ± 0.3	50.6 ± 2.0	52.9 ± 2.3	40.1 ± 18.3	<u>52.5 ± 1.4</u>	52.8 ± 1.4	**55.3 ± 3.2**
Avg. Rank	5.25	5.63	5.31	4.75	2.31	3.50	1.25
p-value	0.0004	0.0004	0.0004	0.0008	0.0113	0.0004	–

4.3   Robustness w.r.t Anomaly Contamination

This subsection evaluates the robustness of HimNet under different levels of anomaly contamination in training data. This scenario is generally very realistic since the graph data collected in the world may be contaminated by anomalies and noises. To simulate this setting, given the original training data that contain normal and abnormal data, instead of discarding abnormal data, we combine $\tau\%$ of the abnormal data with the normal training data to form the contaminated training data. Specifically, we vary the anomaly contamination rate τ from 0% to 16% and compare the performance of HimNet, with the two best competing methods—GLocalKD [21] and GAE [12]—as the baselines. Without loss of generality and due to the page limits, we perform experiments on four datasets, including three from biochemical molecules (AIDS, BZR, and DHFR) and one from social networks (IMDB).

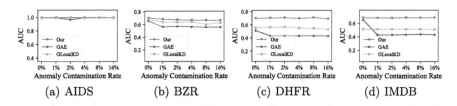

Fig. 2. Results of GAE, GLocalKD, and HimNet under various contamination rates.

Figure 2 shows the AUC results of GAE, GLocalKD, and HimNet w.r.t. different anomaly contamination rates. Compared to the two baselines, our method achieves the best anomaly detection performance in all settings, particularly on DHFR and IMDB. We can also see that both GLocalKD and our method demonstrate consistent performance on all datasets for different anomaly contamination rates, while GAE experiences a significant performance drop with a slight increase in the number of anomalous training instances, except for the AIDS dataset. The reason for the superior and stable performance of our method is its ability to learn and store hierarchical patterns of the majority of training data. As a result, anomalous graphs can be readily detected since they cannot be reconstructed effectively using the learned hierarchical memory blocks. Note that all three methods perform similarly on the AIDS dataset, which could be due to the distinguishability between normality and abnormality being more apparent compared to the other datasets.

4.4 Ablation Study

We use the GAE as our base model to evaluate the importance of our proposed node and graph memory modules, which are the key driving components in HimNet. To verify the importance of each component, we conduct experiments on two variants of the proposed method, i.e., HimNet$_{w/o\ node}$ and HimNet$_{w/o\ graph}$ that respectively discard the node and graph memory module.

The results of HimNet, its two variants, and GAE are reported in Table 3. From the table, we can derive the following observations. First, by incorporating node or graph memory module into GAE, the anomaly detection performance is significantly enhanced on nearly all datasets, which verifies the effectiveness of each of our proposed memory modules. Using GAE without memory modules is ineffective on some challenging datasets with large graphs and/or complex node attributes, such as DHFR and REDDIT. Second, HimNet$_{w/o\ node}$ and HimNet$_{w/o\ graph}$ perform differently across graph datasets, which indicates that the dominance of locally or globally anomalous graphs varies across the graph datasets. For example, HimNet$_{w/o\ graph}$ outperforms HimNet$_{w/o\ node}$ on NCI1, indicating the anomalous graphs are more dominated by locally anomalous graphs in NCI1. Third, the performance improvement over GAE is further boosted by the utilization of both node and graph memory modules. This demonstrates the importance of capturing the hierarchical normal patterns that enable the simultaneous detection of locally and globally anomalous graphs.

Table 3. AUC performance of the proposed method and its variants.

Dataset	GAE	HimNet w/o node	HimNet w/o graph	HimNet
PROTEINS_full	76.6 ± 2.2	76.4 ± 2.5	76.3 ± 3.1	$\mathbf{77.2 \pm 1.5}$
ENZYMES	51.6 ± 2.7	52.0 ± 4.3	55.7 ± 5.4	$\mathbf{58.9 \pm 7.6}$
AIDS	99.0 ± 0.5	99.3 ± 0.4	99.6 ± 0.3	$\mathbf{99.7 \pm 0.3}$
DHFR	51.4 ± 3.6	51.9 ± 3.5	68.3 ± 6.7	$\mathbf{70.1 \pm 1.7}$
BZR	65.5 ± 8.3	69.9 ± 4.9	67.4 ± 4.8	$\mathbf{70.3 \pm 5.4}$
COX2	58.7 ± 4.9	59.7 ± 7.0	$\mathbf{64.7 \pm 5.9}$	63.7 ± 7.6
DD	80.4 ± 1.7	80.2 ± 1.8	80.4 ± 2.0	$\mathbf{80.6 \pm 2.1}$
NCI1	35.0 ± 1.9	33.9 ± 5.7	62.2 ± 2.4	$\mathbf{68.6 \pm 1.9}$
HSE	59.0 ± 0.5	59.4 ± 0.4	61.6 ± 4.3	$\mathbf{61.3 \pm 3.9}$
MMP	67.3 ± 0.4	68.7 ± 0.8	69.1 ± 0.2	$\mathbf{70.3 \pm 2.9}$
p53	64.0 ± 0.1	64.4 ± 0.1	$\mathbf{64.9 \pm 0.8}$	64.6 ± 0.1
PPAR-gamma	65.8 ± 1.6	67.6 ± 0.1	67.5 ± 3.9	$\mathbf{71.1 \pm 3.4}$
hERG	68.1 ± 8.7	68.7 ± 0.8	73.2 ± 3.2	$\mathbf{75.4 \pm 3.2}$
IMDB	65.2 ± 4.4	65.2 ± 4.4	66.0 ± 3.0	$\mathbf{68.3 \pm 3.2}$
REDDIT	21.8 ± 1.9	21.9 ± 2.4	31.1 ± 8.9	$\mathbf{78.0 \pm 2.5}$
COLLAB	52.8 ± 1.4	52.2 ± 1.6	51.7 ± 1.6	$\mathbf{55.3 \pm 3.2}$

4.5   Analysis of Hyperparameters

We examine the sensitivity of HimNet w.r.t the number of memory blocks in node and graph memory modules. Specifically, for one memory module, we fix the number of memory blocks to one and vary the number of memory blocks in the other memory module across $\{1, 2, 3, 4, 5, 6\}$. The results of all graph datasets are reported in Fig. 3. The results show that even using one memory block in each memory module, the proposed method can still achieve promising performance on some datasets, such as DD, DHFR, REDDIT, and hERG. This may be because the normal graphs in these datasets are more homogeneous and deviate from the abnormal graphs distinctly. HimNet is generally more robust to the number of graph memory blocks than the number of node memory blocks except on the AIDS, BZR, NCI1, and REDDIT. Also, increasing the number of memory blocks does not always bring better results. In some cases, it can even degrade the detection performance. This is mainly because the larger memory modules may boost the expressiveness of memory modules, leading to the failure cases that the abnormal graphs can also be well reconstructed.

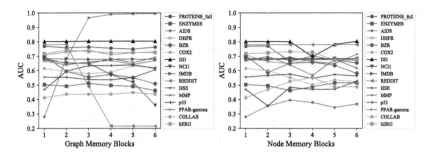

Fig. 3. Results of HimNet w.r.t different numbers of graph and node memory blocks.

5 Conclusion

This paper proposes hierarchical memory networks (HimNet) to learn hierarchical node and graph memory modules. These memory modules explicitly capture hierarchical normal patterns of graphs by jointly minimizing graph reconstruction and graph approximation errors, enabling effective detection of both locally- and globally-anomalous graphs. Extensive experiments demonstrate the superiority of HimNet in detecting anomalous graphs compared to state-of-the-art methods. Furthermore, HimNet achieves promising performance even when the training data is largely contaminated by abnormal graphs, which shows its applicability in real-world applications with unclean training data.

Acknowledgment. This work is partially supported by Australian Research Council under Grant DP210101347.

Ethical Statement. In this work, we study the problem of graph-level anomaly detection which aims to identify abnormal graphs that exhibit unusual patterns in comparison to the majority in a graph set. Since graphs are widely used in various domains, anomaly detection on graphs has broad applications, such as identifying toxic molecules from chemical compound graphs and recognizing abnormal internet activity graphs. To capture the hierarchical normal patterns of graph data, we propose hierarchical memory networks to learn node and graph memory modules. The proposed method enables the detection of both locally and globally anomalous graphs. For all the used data sets in this paper, there is no private personally identifiable information or offensive content. However, when using the proposed method for solving realistic problems, it is essential to ensure that appropriate measures are taken to protect the privacy of individuals. This may include anonymizing data, limiting access to sensitive information, or obtaining informed consent from individuals before collecting their data.

References

1. Aggarwal, C.C., Wang, H.: Graph data management and mining: a survey of algorithms and applications. In: Managing and Mining Graph Data, pp. 13–68. Springer, Boston (2010). https://doi.org/10.1007/978-1-4419-6045-0_2
2. Akoglu, L., Tong, H., Koutra, D.: Graph based anomaly detection and description: a survey. Data Mining Knowl. Discov. **29**, 626–688 (2015)
3. Bengio, Y., Lamblin, P., Popovici, D., Larochelle, H.: Greedy layer-wise training of deep networks. Adv. Neural Inf. Process. Syst. **19** (2006)
4. Breunig, M.M., Kriegel, H.P., Ng, R.T., Sander, J.: Lof: identifying density-based local outliers. In: Proceedings of the 2000 ACM SIGMOD International Conference on Management of Data, pp. 93–104 (2000)
5. Campos, G.O., et al.: On the evaluation of unsupervised outlier detection: measures, datasets, and an empirical study. Data Mining Knowl. Discov. **30**, 891–927 (2016)
6. Chen, J., Sathe, S., Aggarwal, C., Turaga, D.: Outlier detection with autoencoder ensembles. In: Proceedings of the 2017 SIAM International Conference on Data Mining, pp. 90–98. SIAM (2017)
7. Ding, K., Li, J., Agarwal, N., Liu, H.: Inductive anomaly detection on attributed networks. In: Proceedings of the Twenty-Ninth International Conference on International Joint Conferences on Artificial Intelligence, pp. 1288–1294 (2021)
8. Gong, D., et al.: Memorizing normality to detect anomaly: memory-augmented deep autoencoder for unsupervised anomaly detection. In: Proceedings of the IEEE/CVF International Conference on Computer Vision, pp. 1705–1714 (2019)
9. Jin, M., Liu, Y., Zheng, Y., Chi, L., Li, Y.F., Pan, S.: Anemone: graph anomaly detection with multi-scale contrastive learning. In: Proceedings of the 30th ACM International Conference on Information & Knowledge Management, pp. 3122–3126 (2021)
10. Kim, Y., Kim, M., Kim, G.: Memorization precedes generation: learning unsupervised GANs with memory networks. In: International Conference on Learning Representations (2018)
11. Kingma, D.P., Welling, M.: Auto-encoding variational bayes. arXiv preprint arXiv:1312.6114 (2013)
12. Kipf, T.N., Welling, M.: Variational graph auto-encoders. arXiv preprint arXiv:1611.07308 (2016)
13. Kipf, T.N., Welling, M.: Semi-supervised classification with graph convolutional networks. In: International Conference on Learning Representations (2017)
14. Kumagai, A., Iwata, T., Fujiwara, Y.: Semi-supervised anomaly detection on attributed graphs. In: 2021 International Joint Conference on Neural Networks (IJCNN), pp. 1–8. IEEE (2021)
15. Lee, C.Y., Chen, Y.P.P.: Descriptive prediction of drug side-effects using a hybrid deep learning model. Int. J. Intell. Syst. **36**(6), 2491–2510 (2021)
16. Li, C., Zhu, J., Zhang, B.: Learning to generate with memory. In: International Conference on Machine Learning, pp. 1177–1186. PMLR (2016)
17. Liu, F.T., Ting, K.M., Zhou, Z.H.: Isolation forest. In: 2008 Eighth IEEE International Conference on Data Mining, pp. 413–422. IEEE (2008)
18. Liu, Y., Ding, K., Liu, H., Pan, S.: Good-d: on unsupervised graph out-of-distribution detection. In: Proceedings of the Sixteenth ACM International Conference on Web Search and Data Mining, pp. 339–347 (2023)

19. Liu, Y., Li, Z., Pan, S., Gong, C., Zhou, C., Karypis, G.: Anomaly detection on attributed networks via contrastive self-supervised learning. IEEE Trans. Neural Netw. Learn. Syst. **33**(6), 2378–2392 (2021)
20. Luo, X., et al.: Deep graph level anomaly detection with contrastive learning. Sci. Rep. **12**(1), 19867 (2022)
21. Ma, R., Pang, G., Chen, L., van den Hengel, A.: Deep graph-level anomaly detection by glocal knowledge distillation. In: The Fifteenth ACM International Conference on Web Search and Data Mining (WSDM 2022) (2022)
22. Narayanan, A., Chandramohan, M., Venkatesan, R., Chen, L., Liu, Y., Jaiswal, S.: graph2vec: learning distributed representations of graphs. arXiv preprint arXiv:1707.05005 (2017)
23. Neumann, M., Garnett, R., Bauckhage, C., Kersting, K.: Propagation kernels: efficient graph kernels from propagated information. Mach. Learn. **102**, 209–245 (2016)
24. Pang, G., Shen, C., Cao, L., Hengel, A.V.D.: Deep learning for anomaly detection: a review. ACM Comput. Surv. **54**(2), 1–38 (2021)
25. Pang, G., Shen, C., van den Hengel, A.: Deep anomaly detection with deviation networks. In: Proceedings of the 25th ACM SIGKDD International Conference on Knowledge Discovery & Data Mining, pp. 353–362 (2019)
26. Pang, G., Ting, K.M., Albrecht, D.: Lesinn: detecting anomalies by identifying least similar nearest neighbours. In: 2015 IEEE International Conference on Data Mining Workshop (ICDMW), pp. 623–630. IEEE (2015)
27. Park, H., Noh, J., Ham, B.: Learning memory-guided normality for anomaly detection. In: Proceedings of the IEEE/CVF Conference on Computer Vision and Pattern Recognition, pp. 14372–14381 (2020)
28. Qiao, H., Pang, G.: Truncated affinity maximization: one-class homophily modeling for graph anomaly detection. arXiv preprint arXiv:2306.00006 (2023)
29. Qiu, C., Kloft, M., Mandt, S., Rudolph, M.: Raising the bar in graph-level anomaly detection. arXiv preprint arXiv:2205.13845 (2022)
30. Ruff, L., et al.: Deep one-class classification. In: International Conference on Machine Learning, pp. 4393–4402. PMLR (2018)
31. Schölkopf, B., Williamson, R.C., Smola, A., Shawe-Taylor, J., Platt, J.: Support vector method for novelty detection. Adv. Neural Inf. Process. Syst. **12** (1999)
32. Shervashidze, N., Schweitzer, P., Van Leeuwen, E.J., Mehlhorn, K., Borgwardt, K.M.: Weisfeiler-lehman graph kernels. J. Mach. Learn. Res. **12**(9) (2011)
33. Sun, F.Y., Hoffman, J., Verma, V., Tang, J.: Infograph: unsupervised and semi-supervised graph-level representation learning via mutual information maximization. In: International Conference on Learning Representations (2020)
34. Veličković, P., Cucurull, G., Casanova, A., Romero, A., Lió, P., Bengio, Y.: Graph attention networks. In: International Conference on Learning Representations (2018)
35. Wang, Q., Pang, G., Salehi, M., Buntine, W., Leckie, C.: Cross-domain graph anomaly detection via anomaly-aware contrastive alignment. arXiv preprint arXiv:2212.01096 (2022)
36. Weston, J., Chopra, S., Bordes, A.: Memory networks. In: International Conference on Learning Representations (2015)
37. Woolson, R.F.: Wilcoxon signed-rank test. In: Wiley Encyclopedia of Clinical Trials, pp. 1–3 (2007)
38. Wu, Z., Xiong, Y., Yu, S.X., Lin, D.: Unsupervised feature learning via non-parametric instance discrimination. In: Proceedings of the IEEE Conference on Computer Vision and Pattern Recognition, pp. 3733–3742 (2018)

39. Wu, Z., Pan, S., Chen, F., Long, G., Zhang, C., Philip, S.Y.: A comprehensive survey on graph neural networks. IEEE Trans. Neural Netw. Learn. Syst. **32**(1), 4–24 (2020)
40. Xu, K., Hu, W., Leskovec, J., Jegelka, S.: How powerful are graph neural networks? In: International Conference on Learning Representations (2019)
41. Zhai, S., Cheng, Y., Lu, W., Zhang, Z.: Deep structured energy based models for anomaly detection. In: International Conference on Machine Learning, pp. 1100–1109. PMLR (2016)
42. Zhang, M., Chen, Y.: Link prediction based on graph neural networks. Adv. Neural Inf. Process. Syst. **31** (2018)
43. Zhang, M., Cui, Z., Neumann, M., Chen, Y.: An end-to-end deep learning architecture for graph classification. In: Proceedings of the AAAI Conference on Artificial Intelligence, vol. 32 (2018)
44. Zhang, Z., Cui, P., Zhu, W.: Deep learning on graphs: a survey. IEEE Trans. Knowl. Data Eng. **34**(1), 249–270 (2020)
45. Zhao, L., Akoglu, L.: On using classification datasets to evaluate graph outlier detection: peculiar observations and new insights. Big Data (2021)
46. Zhou, C., Paffenroth, R.C.: Anomaly detection with robust deep autoencoders. In: Proceedings of the 23rd ACM SIGKDD International Conference on Knowledge Discovery and Data Mining, pp. 665–674 (2017)
47. Zong, B., et al.: Deep autoencoding gaussian mixture model for unsupervised anomaly detection. In: International Conference on Learning Representations (2018)

Semi-supervised Learning from Active Noisy Soft Labels for Anomaly Detection

Timo Martens$^{(\boxtimes)}$, Lorenzo Perini , and Jesse Davis

DTAI Research Group and Leuven.AI, KULeuven, Leuven, Belgium
{timo.martens,lorenzo.perini,jesse.davis}@kuleuven.be

Abstract. Anomaly detection aims at detecting examples that do not conform to normal behavior. Increasingly, anomaly detection is being approached from a semi-supervised perspective where active learning is employed to acquire a small number of strategically selected labels. However, because anomalies are not always well-understood events, the user may be uncertain about how to label certain instances. Thus, one can relax this request and allow the user to provide soft labels (i.e., probabilistic labels) that represent their belief that a queried example is anomalous. These labels are naturally noisy due to the user's inherent uncertainty in the label and the fact that people are known to be bad at providing well-calibrated probability instances. To cope with these challenges, we propose to exploit a Gaussian Process to learn from actively acquired soft labels in the context of anomaly detection. This enables leveraging information about nearby examples to smooth out possible noise. Empirically, we compare our proposed approach to several baselines on 21 datasets and show that it outperforms them in the majority of experiments.

Keywords: Anomaly Detection · Probabilistic Labels · Noisy Labels

1 Introduction

Anomaly detection is the task of detecting abnormal behaviour in the data. These unexpected occurrences are usually related to critical events, such as machine failure [8], intrusion detection [19] or medical applications [31]. Thus, detecting anomalies in time allows us to save money, preserve privacy and save lives.

Because anomalies are, by definition, rare events, obtaining labels (especially anomalous ones) is often expensive, unethical, or simply time-consuming. Hence, anomaly detection is usually tackled from an unsupervised perspective [10,12]. However, it has been shown in the literature that providing limited, but specific labels to the model can have a large impact on its performance [35,45]. Therefore, one can implement active learning strategies to collect labels strategically, such as those in regions where the model has high uncertainty [1,11,24].

However, sometimes it can be challenging to provide a correct label for a given instance. For example, when labeling abnormal water usage, it may happen

D. Koutra et al. (Eds.): ECML PKDD 2023, LNAI 14169, pp. 219–236, 2023.
https://doi.org/10.1007/978-3-031-43412-9_13

that some normal behaviour (e.g., system maintenance) is infrequent and the user presumes it is anomalous and labels it as such [44]. More generally, an instance's label may be ambiguous, and different annotators may label it in different ways (e.g., crowdsourcing). When reconciling these inconsistencies to get a hard decision, selecting the correct label may be a difficult task [21,39]. A solution to this problem is to relax our request by allowing the user to provide a soft label (i.e., a probability). Thus, one asks how likely it is that an instance is anomalous. Previous work has shown that this relaxation increases performance, especially in highly imbalanced data sets [26,43].

Unfortunately, soft labels that reflect the inherent label probability are hard to collect [9,15]. For example, a user may be overly confident and annotate a slightly excessive usage of water as having a very high probability of being anomalous. Similarly, in crowdsourcing, a group of users may be affected by a biased selection of instances that ends up producing inaccurate probabilities for some specific instances [25]. Thus, asking for a user to provide soft labels often results in examples that are annotated with noisy probabilities. This can have a negative effect on the detector's performance as using incorrect soft labels at training time affects its ability to make accurate predictions at test time. For example, overly high (low) probabilities would make the model sensitive to producing false positives (negatives). Therefore, accounting for the (possible) noise both during training and inference is an important problem.

Additionally, we require a method that has both an unsupervised and supervised component. Many, but not all, anomalies are non-repetitive events. These anomalies are best detected by unsupervised anomaly detectors. However, these unsupervised detectors have difficulties detecting anomalies that look similar to normal instances or might detect some normal behavior as anomalous. Labels can help distinguish these last two cases. Thus, we want to make predictions such that (1) we fall back to unsupervised scores if instances are distant from labeled training data and (2) the instances that are closer to the labeled data receive a score that is mostly based on the soft labels.

Therefore, we fill this gap in the literature by proposing SLADE (Soft Label Anomaly DEtector), the first semi-supervised anomaly detector that learns from noisy soft labels using active learning. Initially, it uses an unsupervised anomaly detector as an indication of how anomalous instances are (prior knowledge). Then, it sets up an active learning loop that (1) measures the uncertainty inherent to dealing with noisy soft labels, (2) uses the uncertainty metric to collect noisy soft labels, and (3) learns from such labels by training a Gaussian Process to model the deviation between the given soft labels and the unsupervised scores. Finally, at inference time, SLADE removes the noise from the soft labels by averaging out the GP's prediction over a Gaussian surface. By summing this average with the unsupervised score, SLADE computes the probability that a test instance is anomalous.

2 Background and Notation

We assume a d-dimensional instance space $\mathcal{X} \subseteq \mathbb{R}^d$ and a binary output space $\mathcal{Y} = \{0, 1\}$ where 1 denotes the anomaly class. Moreover, we assume that we are given an unlabeled dataset $U = \{x_i | x_i \in \mathcal{X}\}_{i=1}^N$ of size N, an initially empty (soft) labeled dataset L, and a label budget $B \in \mathbb{N}$ that indicates how many (soft) labels the user is willing to provide. We now review the necessary background on anomaly detection and Gaussian processes.

2.1 Anomaly Detection

In unsupervised anomaly detection, the goal is to learn a function $s : \mathcal{X} \to \mathbb{R}$ that assigns real-valued anomaly scores to any instance in $\mathcal{X}$ where, without loss of generality, we assume that higher scores represent more anomalous instances. Unsupervised detectors are trained by making assumptions about what constitutes an anomaly, which typically results in defining how anomalies are dissimilar to normal instances. For example, Isolation Forest (IFOREST) [22] assumes that anomalies can be easily isolated when randomly splitting the instance space, and assigns anomaly scores inversely proportional to the number of splits needed to isolate an instance. The k-NN outlier detector (KNNO) [2] assumes that anomalies are far away from normals with respect to some notion of distance, and uses the distance to the k-th nearest neighbor as the anomaly score.

A practical issue is how to convert an anomaly score into a hard prediction [32]. One way to do this is to use the contamination factor $\gamma \in [0, 1]$, which is the fraction of anomalies in a dataset [33,34]. Using γ one can define a threshold λ so that a fraction γ of the training data receives an anomaly score greater than λ. For an unseen test instance x_t,

$$y(x_t) = \begin{cases} 0 & s(x_t) \leq \lambda \\ 1 & s(x_t) > \lambda. \end{cases} \tag{1}$$

Recently, there is increasing recognition that incorporating strategically chosen labeled instances is important for improving the performance of anomaly detectors [35,45]. Active learning (AL) is commonly used to select which instances to label [17,41]. At a high level, it is possible to distinguish among three approaches to AL [24]: *uncertainty-based* strategies aim to select the unlabeled data samples with the highest uncertainty [11], *diversity-based* strategies aim to maximize the diversity among the labeled training data [1] and *combined* strategies integrate the advantages of these two [6]. The first category is widely used due to its simplicity and strong performance. Starting with an unlabeled dataset U and an empty (soft) labeled dataset L, a detector is learned in an unsupervised manner. Then, the following steps are repeated until a given label budget is exhausted. First, query a human annotator to provide a (soft) label for the strategically chosen instances. In uncertainty sampling, one approach is to use the probabilistic gap $|P(Y = 1|x) - P(Y = 0|x)|$ where smaller gaps indicate higher uncertainty. Second, the queried instances and their (soft) labels are added to L and the model is retrained using this newly expanded dataset.

2.2   Gaussian Processes

A Gaussian process (GP) is a collection of random variables over the instance space, such that any finite subset of them have a joint Gaussian distribution [37]. Roughly speaking, a GP can be seen as a distribution over functions $f \colon \mathcal{X} \to \mathbb{R}$ such that for any $x, x' \in \mathcal{X}$

$$f(x) \sim \mathcal{GP}(m(x), \mathcal{K}(x, x')),$$

where $m \colon \mathcal{X} \to \mathbb{R}$ is called the mean function, and $\mathcal{K} \colon \mathcal{X} \times \mathcal{X} \to \mathbb{R}$ is the covariance function (otherwise known as the kernel). The Gaussian process is completely characterized by these two functions m and $\mathcal{K}$, which define

$$\mathbb{E}[f(x)] = m(x) \quad \text{and} \quad \text{Cov}[f(x), f(x')] = \mathcal{K}(x, x').$$

Picking an appropriate prior mean and kernel enables encoding prior beliefs of the data-generating process into the model. More importantly, the GP fully relies on these prior beliefs to make predictions for an unseen instance that falls in a region far from any training instance. Given a training set of pairs $\mathcal{R} = \{(x_i, r_i)\}_{i=1}^{|\mathcal{R}|}$, where $r_i \in \mathbb{R}$, the posterior distribution of a GP for any $x, x' \in \mathcal{X}$ is

$$f|\mathcal{R} \sim \mathcal{GP}(m_{\mathcal{R}}, \mathcal{K}_{\mathcal{R}})$$
$$m_{\mathcal{R}}(x) = m(x) + \Sigma_{x,X} \left(\Sigma_{X,X}\right)^{-1} \left(\mathbf{r} - m(X)\right) \qquad (2)$$
$$\mathcal{K}_{\mathcal{R}}(x, x') = \mathcal{K}(x, x') - \Sigma_{x,X} \left(\Sigma_{X,X}\right)^{-1} \Sigma_{X,x'},$$

where the elements of $\Sigma_{a,b}$ depend on the kernel $(\Sigma_{a,b})_{i,j} = \mathcal{K}(a_i, b_j)$, which makes $\Sigma_{X,X}$ the training-training covariance matrix, and $\Sigma_{x,X}$, $\Sigma_{X,x'}$, respectively, $1 \times |\mathcal{R}|$ and $|\mathcal{R}| \times 1$ covariance vectors. Note that the posterior covariance is always lower than the prior due to the subtraction of a strictly positive term.

   Given a test set $T = \{x_t\}_{t=1}^{|T|}$, the GP predicts a posterior multivariate normal distribution ($|T|$-dimensional) $\mathcal{N}(m_{\mathcal{R}}(T), \mathcal{K}_{\mathcal{R}}(T, T))$. Note, that each individual instance has a Gaussian marginal distribution that can be used for instance-wise predictions. In practice, one can derive the final prediction from the given distribution by either taking a sample (Bayesian perspective) or extracting the mean (frequentist perspective). In this work, we use the latter.

3   SLADE

Our goal is to learn a model to estimate the probability that an instance is anomalous in an active learning setting where a user provides soft labels. Starting from an unlabeled dataset $U = \{x_n | x_n \in \mathcal{X}\}_{n=1}^{N}$, an empty soft labeled dataset L, and a label budget B, the algorithm can iteratively query instance $x \in U$. However, instead of receiving its exact label, the user provides a real value $p \in [0, 1]$ indicating the probability that the instance belongs to the anomaly class.

Designing an approach to learn in this setting has three key challenges. First, we need an informative unsupervised score about what is and is not likely to be anomalous. This allows the model to output probabilities even in regions where no soft labels are given. Second, we need a way to combine the weak supervision provided by the soft labels with this unsupervised score such that (1) we fall back to the initial scores if instances are distant from labeled training data and (2) the instances that are closer to the soft labeled data in L receive a score that is mostly based on those labels. Third, we need to explicitly model the uncertainty that is inherent when working with soft labels.

We address these challenges by combining unsupervised anomaly detection with a Gaussian process. Intuitively, the anomaly detector will provide an informative prior for the GP. A key question is what the GP should model. One choice would be to have it directly model the soft labels. However, because the labels are uncertain and noisy, we want to decouple the noise arising from the soft labels and the uncertainty of unsupervised scores. Therefore, we model the deviation of the soft labels from the unsupervised prior. When making a prediction, we propose a novel way to combine the estimated deviation and the unsupervised score in a noise-robust way. Next, we describe our training and inference procedures in more detail.

3.1 Training

SLADE constructs the informative prior by taking a completely unsupervised approach. First, SLADE trains an unsupervised anomaly detector on U that can compute an anomaly score for any instance $x \in \mathcal{X}$, which is denoted as $s(x)$. SLADE is detector agnostic and we will discuss possible choices in the experimental evaluation. Second, we want to learn the deviation of the soft labels from these scores. However, working with the raw scores is not possible because scores provided by different unsupervised models have different meanings. Moreover, anomaly scores often cannot be interpreted as probabilities (e.g., kNNo assigns a distance) and thus, in this form they can not be compared with soft labels (i.e., probabilities). Therefore, we apply the linear unification transformation (i.e., min-max normalisation) [18]

$$\tilde{s}(x) = \frac{s(x) - min(\mathbf{s})}{max(\mathbf{s}) - min(\mathbf{s})}$$

to map anomaly scores into $[0, 1]$, where $\mathbf{s} = \{s_1, \ldots, s_N\}$ are the anomaly scores for U. We opt for linear unification because we do not want to introduce strong assumptions on the unsupervised scores (which, working as a prior, is supposed to be flexible [46]).

Our GP models the deviation between the user-provided soft labels and these prior probabilities and it is initialized as $g_0 \sim \mathcal{GP}(0, \mathcal{K})$. The posterior GP is then defined as

$$g_0 | L_0 \sim \mathcal{GP}(m_{L_0}, \mathcal{K}_{L_0}),$$

where $L_0 = \{(x_j, p_j - \tilde{s}(x_j)) : (x_j, p_j) \in L\}$ denotes a dataset containing the difference between the soft labels (i.e., p_j) and the unified unsupervised scores of the training data in L. To gather soft labeled training data and train the GP, we run an active learning loop. Given a label budget B, we repeat the following steps until our label budget is exhausted. (1) We query the instance $x_* \in U$ where the model is the most uncertain. Quantifying uncertainty requires assigning a prediction to each instance in U. By combining the unsupervised prior $\tilde{s}$ with the GP's mean m_{L_0}, we obtain a first probability estimate:

$$P_1(Y = 1 | x, L) = \tilde{s}(x) + m_{L_0}(x). \tag{3}$$

Model uncertainty can arise for two reasons: making weak predictions (≈ 0.5) and a lack of labeled instances in certain regions of the instance space. To capture both types of uncertainty, we use Kapoor et al. [16]'s strategy to query labels for

$$\underset{x_* \in U}{argmin} \frac{|0.5 - P_1(Y = 1 | x_*, L)|}{\sqrt{\mathcal{K}_{L_0}(x_*, x_*)}}.$$

This formula assigns low scores if (a) the posterior probability is close to 0.5 (small numerator), or (b) if the instance is far from the labeled instances and hence has high prediction variance (big denominator). (2) Finally, SLADE updates $L = L \cup \{(x_*, p_*)\}$ and $U = U \setminus \{x_*\}$. Subsequently, $g_0 | L_0$ is updated with the newly obtained soft labels.

3.2   Inference

Given an unseen test instance x_t and a set of soft labels L, computing the posterior probability $P(Y = 1 | x_t, L)$ is challenging for the following reason. An initial estimate of the posterior probability can be obtained via Eq. 3. However, this probability is heavily affected by noisy soft labels. Per definition, the GP predicts the exact soft labels for each soft-labeled training instance. Consequently, if x_t is in close proximity to a noisy soft label, the predicted posterior probability would be affected by this noise.

We propose to mitigate the effect of noisy labels as follows. We distinguish between two types of test instances: (1) those that are far from the training data and (2) those that have many training instances nearby. Since the unsupervised anomaly scores model the proximity to other data points, we can use this as a measure without introducing any new assumptions (i.e. high anomaly scores represent distant instances). For the first type of test instances, there is no reason to try and fix the noise. They are far from the training data and will thus not be influenced by noise. The second type, on the other hand, is influenced by label noise. We cope with this problem by smoothing out the estimated deviation over a Gaussian surface that has x_t as the center and a given variance σ_t^2. Formally,

$$P_2(Y = 1 | x_t, L) = \tilde{s}(x_t) + \mathbb{E}_{V \sim \mathcal{N}(x_t, \sigma_t^2)}[m_{L_0}(V)], \tag{4}$$

where V is a normally distributed random variable. Using the surrounding instances forces the model to use more soft labels when computing the posterior probability, which clearly averages out the negative effects that the presence of noise has on the model. σ_t is dependent on x_t and we define it as one-third of the radius of a hypersphere with center x_t that captures $q\%$ of the instances in U. Thus, for every test instance, we average out over the same number of training data. We then formalize our final probability estimate as

$$\hat{P}(Y = 1|x_t, L) = \begin{cases} P_1(Y = 1|x_t, L) & s(x_t) > \lambda \\ P_2(Y = 1|x_t, L) & s(x_t) \leq \lambda, \end{cases} \quad (5)$$

where λ denotes the anomaly score threshold as defined in Eq. 1. A hard prediction is obtained by setting a threshold, typically 0.5, on the probability estimates.

4   Experiments

We address the following two research questions: **Q1:** How do the methods compare under various noise regimes? **Q2:** How sensititive is SLADE to the choice of its hyperparameters?

4.1   Experimental Setup

Methods. We compare SLADE[1] against four baselines. Conceptually, these can be divided into two groups. The first group learns directly from probabilistic labels: GP [31] simply uses a Gaussian Process to model the soft labels without including the unsupervised prior, while P-SVM [20] uses a Support Vector Machine (SVM) with class labels that are weighted by the given soft labels. The second group cannot operate directly on the soft labels. Therefore, we convert them to hard labels by flipping a weighted coin. Then we apply traditional semi-supervised models. SSDO [44] is a propagation-based detector that uses the distance to hard labels to assign anomaly scores. HIF [23] is a semi-supervised variant of the widely used unsupervised Isolation Forest [22] that improves its anomaly scores by adding the distance to the anomalous hard labels.

Data. We evaluate our method and the baselines on 21 benchmark datasets that are widely used in the anomaly detection literature [4,12]. These datasets vary in size, number of features, and proportion of anomalies. To limit the computational cost of the experiments, we subsample each dataset to at most 5000 instances keeping the same proportion between normals and anomalies. See Table 1 for the characteristics of the datasets.

---

[1] The code and Supplement are available via https://github.com/TimoM99/SLADe.

Table 1. Characteristics (full size, subsampled size, number of features d, contamination factor γ) of the 21 benchmark datasets used for the experiments.

Dataset	Full size	Size	d	γ	Dataset	Full size	Size	d	γ
ALOI	50,000	5000	27	0.030	PEN	9,868	5000	16	0.002
ANNTHY	7,200	5000	21	0.075	PIMA	555	555	8	0.099
ARRHY	271	271	259	0.100	SHUTTLE	1,013	1013	9	0.013
CARDIO	2,112	2112	21	0.221	SPAM	2,661	2661	57	0.050
GLASS	213	213	7	0.042	STAMPS	340	340	9	0.091
HEART	166	166	13	0.096	WAVE	3,443	3443	21	0.029
HEPA	80	80	19	0.163	WBC	223	223	9	0.045
IONO	350	350	32	0.357	WDBC	367	367	30	0.027
KDD	48,113	5000	40	0.040	WILT	4,819	4819	5	0.053
PAGE	5,393	5000	10	0.095	WPBC	198	198	33	0.237
PARKIN	60	60	22	0.200					

Setup. Our setup can be divided into three parts: (1) generating the ground-truth soft labels, (2) introducing the noise, and (3) evaluating the methods.

The first part requires modeling the human annotator: given an instance x, a soft label p indicates the proportion of anomalous labels that we would obtain if we queried x multiple times. Moreover, similar instances are likely to obtain similar probabilities. We model this aspect by training a Random Forest with low depth ($= 4$) on the original dataset and use it to compute the soft labels as class probabilities. The low depth guarantees that Random Forest does not push all probabilities to the extremes (0 or 1) but assigns smooth values over $[0, 1]$.

In the second part, we introduce noise into the soft labels. We use a standard transformation [7] that changes the label p into $1 - p$ for a fixed percentage of the soft labels. The noisy instances are picked uniformly at random. The percentage of swapped labels is the noise level of the dataset.

Finally, for each of the 21 datasets, we run the following experiment: (i) We randomly split the dataset into 80% training and 20% test set; (ii) We compute the ground-truth soft labels and add the given level of noise to the training soft labels; (iii) We run the active learning loop with a label budget $B = 60\%$ of the training set size N, which we split into 12 rounds of 5% each. We choose a label budget of 60% for completeness reasons. All baseline methods also employ uncertainty sampling. (iv) We evaluate the Area Under the Receiving Operating Curve (AUROC) [14] of each method at every iteration of the loop. As the test set also has soft labels, we sample a hard label to make the evaluation consistent within our probabilistic setting. To average out the randomness introduced by sampling labels, we repeat the active learning loop 20 times. All four steps are then repeated five times. We carry out a total of $5 \times 20 \times 21 = 2100$ experiments.

Hyperparameters. SLADE has three hyperparameters. We choose IFOR-EST [22] as the unsupervised method. We use the Matèrn kernel with $\nu = \frac{1}{2}$

in the GP as it is widely used in the literature [36]. Moreover, we optimize the length scale hyperparameter of the Gaussian Process by maximizing the log marginal likelihood [37]. Finally, we set $q = 2$. SSDO uses the same prior model as SLADE and the default values for α and k. HIF has two hyperparameters: α_1 and α_2. Since the paper does not suggest any values, we set both to 0.5, which makes a fair weighting between the different parts of the score. P-SVM utilizes an RBF kernel with the default parameters [20]. Finally, GP relies on a Gaussian Process that has the same hyperparameters as for SLADE.

4.2 Experimental Results

Q1. Comparing the Methods. We want to evaluate SLADE on two aspects: (1) its robustness against noise and (2) its ability to rank anomalies. Therefore, we compare SLADE against the baselines on three different noise levels and compare both their noise-robustness and performance at different label percentages.

First, we compare SLADE against the baselines for each label frequency of the active learning loop under the three noise levels (0%, 10%, 20%). For this task, we plot the learning curve, which has on the x-axis the label percentage as a proportion of the dataset's size, and, on the y-axis, the methods' AUROC. Figure 1 shows the results on five representative datasets, while the Supplement includes the plots for all the remaining datasets. Regardless of the noise, SLADE clearly outperforms all the baselines on SHUTTLE (left plot), while it performs similarly to the baselines on PIMA and HEART (second and third plots). On the other hand, on PAGE and IONO (right plots), SLADE obtains competitive AUROC values with no noise present while outperforming all the baselines at higher noise levels (10% and 20%). Overall, the major strength of SLADE is the ability to improve its performance when acquiring (possibly noisy) soft labels: on SHUTTLE, SLADE's learning curve is steeper than all the baselines' for all noise levels. On the other hand, looking at PAGE and IONO, all methods' learning curves are flat, but SLADE's does not deteriorate as hard as the baselines when introducing higher noise levels.

Second, we dive deeper into the noise-robustness of the methods. Therefore, we aggregate the results on a per-dataset basis and measure how their performance decreases when moving from a setting with no noise to a setting with (a) 10% and (b) 20% of noise. Figure 2 reports the methods' mean AUROC drop aggregated over all of the label percentages for the two scenarios. The star (cross) markers indicate the mean AUROC with no noise (the given level of noise), while the length of the segment is indicative of how robust each model is against noise: the shorter the segment, the smaller the change of AUROC, and the more robust the model. The results show that SLADE obtains the lowest/similar (i.e., within a gap of 0.01) drop in performance in 13 out of 21 datasets when the noise goes from 0% to 10%, while it does so on six datasets when increasing the noise to 20%. Unsurprisingly, the second-best baseline is HIF, which is naturally noise-robust because it only leverages anomalous labels to assign scores, which hides the negative effect of noisy negative labels provided by the user. In fact, HIF obtains the lowest drop in performance on six datasets under 10% noise, and

Table 2. Wins (W), Draws (D), and Losses (L) of **SLADe against each baseline** in terms of average AUROC per dataset, for each label percentage, under 20% of noise. A draw means that the absolute difference in AUROC is ≤ 0.01.

Labels	SSDO			P-SVM			HIF			GP		
	W	D	L	W	D	L	W	D	L	W	D	L
5%	13	5	3	16	1	4	10	5	6	17	2	2
10%	15	3	3	16	1	4	12	5	4	16	2	3
15%	17	3	1	17	0	4	12	8	1	15	2	4
20%	16	5	0	17	0	4	17	4	0	15	0	6
25%	17	4	0	18	0	3	15	6	0	15	0	6
30%	14	6	1	18	0	3	18	3	0	14	2	5
35%	13	5	3	17	1	3	17	3	1	15	1	5
40%	13	6	2	17	1	3	17	2	2	15	1	5
45%	12	6	3	17	1	3	17	2	2	14	3	4
50%	12	4	5	17	0	4	17	2	2	14	2	5
55%	12	3	6	17	1	3	17	2	2	14	2	5
60%	12	3	6	16	2	3	16	2	3	11	6	4

nine datasets under 20% noise. Furthermore, GP is the most affected by the noise: because it only learns from the given soft labels, incorrect probabilities have a strong impact on the surrounding test instances.

Finally, because our task is to develop a noise-resistant model, we zoom in on the high noise scenario (20%) and analyze how often SLADe outperforms each baseline.[2] Table 2 shows the number of times (out of 21) SLADe's average AUROC is higher (Win), within a margin of 0.01 (Draw) or lower (Loss) than that of the baselines at every label percentage. For any label percentage SLADe never loses more than six times against any baseline. As expected, SLADe outperforms HIF more often at higher label percentages because HIF only uses positive labels. Moreover, against GP, SLADe wins more in the lower label percentage settings (which are more realistic in Active Learning) because SLADe needs less data to learn effectively.

Q2. Sensitivity Analysis. We evaluate the effect of varying SLADe's three hyperparameters: the unsupervised anomaly detector, the GP's kernel, and the percentage of training instances inside the hypersphere, q, used to fix the noise at inference time. We assume a default level of noise equal to 10% and vary one hyperparameter at a time while keeping the other two as specified in Sect. 4.1. We subsample the datasets to at most 500 instances for computational reasons.

Table 3 shows SLADe's AUROC averaged over all datasets for different label percentages when using Isolation Forest (IForest) [22], One-Class SVM

---

[2] Results for 0% and 10% noise are, for completeness, in the Supplement.

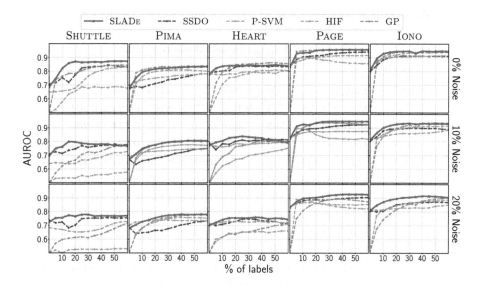

Fig. 1. Learning curves for all methods on five representative datasets for three different noise levels (0%, 10%, 20%). On the x-axis we vary the label percentage, while on the y-axis we report the average AUROC (higher is better).

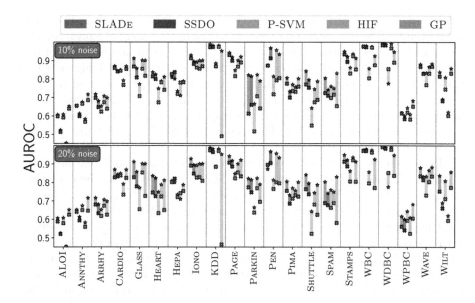

Fig. 2. Comparison on all 21 datasets between the methods' mean AUROC when moving from a clean setting to 10% (top) and 20% (bottom) of noise. The AUROC is aggregated over all percentages of labels. For every dataset and method, the star/cross marker indicates the AUROC with no noise/given level of noise. The length of the segment quantifies the drop in AUROC when introducing noise (shorter is more resistant).

Table 3. AUROC (avg ± std) of SLADE for different unsupervised detectors.

Labels	Unsupervised detector			
	IFOREST	LOF	KNNO	OCSVM
0%	0.730 ± 0.181	0.669 ± 0.180	0.707 ± 0.173	0.664 ± 0.223
5%	0.745 ± 0.178	0.724 ± 0.175	0.750 ± 0.167	0.725 ± 0.204
10%	0.776 ± 0.174	0.763 ± 0.180	0.787 ± 0.165	0.744 ± 0.201
15%	0.800 ± 0.168	0.780 ± 0.177	0.798 ± 0.166	0.776 ± 0.183
20%	0.817 ± 0.163	0.791 ± 0.174	0.808 ± 0.160	0.794 ± 0.179
25%	0.826 ± 0.160	0.793 ± 0.179	0.816 ± 0.155	0.800 ± 0.173
30%	0.833 ± 0.154	0.805 ± 0.169	0.818 ± 0.153	0.816 ± 0.163
35%	0.839 ± 0.150	0.807 ± 0.161	0.825 ± 0.145	0.821 ± 0.159
40%	0.841 ± 0.148	0.816 ± 0.158	0.830 ± 0.137	0.822 ± 0.159
45%	0.843 ± 0.146	0.817 ± 0.156	0.832 ± 0.136	0.823 ± 0.158
50%	0.843 ± 0.143	0.821 ± 0.148	0.834 ± 0.133	0.828 ± 0.154
55%	0.844 ± 0.141	0.819 ± 0.148	0.835 ± 0.131	0.827 ± 0.152
60%	0.844 ± 0.140	0.819 ± 0.146	0.833 ± 0.134	0.826 ± 0.152

(OCSVM) [42], Local Outlier Factor (LOF) [13] and the k-NN outlier detector (KNNO) [2] as unsupervised detectors to assign the anomaly scores. SLADE seems to be robust to the selected anomaly detector as all approaches perform similarly. There are small differences for the three lowest label budgets, where using IFOREST offers some performance gains. This happens because IFOREST assigns better rankings to the anomalies, as confirmed by [12] as well. A bad unsupervised model will thus require a certain number of labels before it is able to accurately detect anomalies. Therefore, selecting the correct unsupervised model is an important decision.

Table 4 shows the AUROC averaged over all datasets for different label percentages when using four variants of the Matérn kernel [36] as the covariance function of the GP. We vary its hyperparameter $\nu \in \{\frac{1}{2}, \frac{3}{2}, \frac{5}{2}, +\infty\}$, where $\nu = +\infty$ represents the Radial Basis Function (RBF) kernel [3]. The results illustrate that SLADE has the highest performance for $\nu = \frac{1}{2}$, in agreement with the existing literature on Gaussian Processes [36]. Unsurprisingly, results show that SLADE's performance deteriorates when increasing the hyperparameter ν: because ν indicates the smoothness of the GP's kernel (i.e., high differentiability), high values of ν underpin the assumption that the class probability function is smooth, which is not true in several real-world datasets. Moreover, the effect of changing ν increases with the number of soft labels, which ends up being > 0.06 against $\nu = +\infty$ with 60% of soft labels.

Table 5 shows the AUROC averaged over all datasets for varying label budgets for $q \in [0.5, 1, 2, 5, 10]$. The results show that the value of this hyperparameter has a negligible impact on SLADE's performance. Therefore, we set

q's default value to 2, as it is an in-between value that avoids averaging over too many instances, which might slightly decrease the performance with little noise, and averaging over almost no instance, which would make the model too sensitive to noise.

Table 4. AUROC (avg $\pm$ std) of SLADE for different values of the Matérn kernel's hyperparameter ν.

Labels	Matérn Kernel			
	$\nu = 0.5$	$\nu = 1.5$	$\nu = 2.5$	$\nu = +\infty$
0%	0.728 ± 0.183	0.728 ± 0.183	0.728 ± 0.183	0.728 ± 0.183
5%	0.742 ± 0.182	0.733 ± 0.182	0.727 ± 0.184	0.719 ± 0.186
10%	0.770 ± 0.180	0.758 ± 0.180	0.753 ± 0.179	0.745 ± 0.177
15%	0.794 ± 0.176	0.779 ± 0.175	0.771 ± 0.177	0.759 ± 0.178
20%	0.809 ± 0.175	0.791 ± 0.174	0.783 ± 0.175	0.765 ± 0.178
25%	0.820 ± 0.167	0.798 ± 0.171	0.789 ± 0.174	0.770 ± 0.178
30%	0.827 ± 0.162	0.804 ± 0.168	0.795 ± 0.170	0.774 ± 0.174
35%	0.832 ± 0.157	0.808 ± 0.165	0.798 ± 0.166	0.776 ± 0.174
40%	0.836 ± 0.152	0.812 ± 0.160	0.798 ± 0.166	0.776 ± 0.174
45%	0.837 ± 0.151	0.812 ± 0.159	0.799 ± 0.164	0.776 ± 0.173
50%	0.839 ± 0.147	0.814 ± 0.156	0.799 ± 0.161	0.778 ± 0.171
55%	0.839 ± 0.145	0.813 ± 0.154	0.799 ± 0.159	0.775 ± 0.169
60%	0.841 ± 0.143	0.813 ± 0.152	0.798 ± 0.158	0.775 ± 0.168

5   Related Work

There is, to our knowledge, no work that tackles learning from active noisy soft labels in anomaly detection. However, three related research lines exist that are of interest, of which the first two relate to traditional binary classification tasks.

Learning from Soft Labels. The literature on learning from soft labels consists of three common approaches: ranking methods, regression methods and traditional methods adapted for soft labels. (1) Ranking methods solve a constrained optimization problem where the constraints are pairwise rankings between the soft labels [26,27,38]. (2) Regression methods use soft labels as target values in their learning mechanism [31]. (3) Probabilistic Support Vector Machines (P-SVM) use soft labels to micro-steer the obtained margin [20,28]. Empirical evaluation [26] shows that this third category performs best. However, in Sect. 4.2 we showed that SLADE outperforms P-SVM.

Learning from Noisy Hard Labels. The existing work on models that are designed to be noise-robust mostly takes a supervised approach [5,7,48]. These make strong assumptions that do not hold in our setting. For instance, there is no correctly labeled subset of data available [48]. A strictly weaker assumption is the availability of a large set of noisy data [5]. It is non-trivial how to adapt these methods for small sets of noisy labels.

Weakly Supervised Models. Some existing literature in anomaly detection deals with weak supervision. For example, some semi-supervised methods need access only to a small set of clean labels [29,30,40,47]. However, it is unclear how to extend them to deal with soft labels.

Table 5. AUROC (avg $\pm$ std) of SLADE for different values of q (% of training instances inside the hypersphere).

Labels	q				
	0.5	1	2	5	10
5%	0.739 ± 0.183	0.740 ± 0.183	0.740 ± 0.184	0.740 ± 0.184	0.741 ± 0.184
10%	0.769 ± 0.183	0.768 ± 0.184	0.768 ± 0.185	0.767 ± 0.185	0.768 ± 0.185
15%	0.794 ± 0.175	0.793 ± 0.176	0.792 ± 0.177	0.791 ± 0.177	0.790 ± 0.178
20%	0.810 ± 0.169	0.810 ± 0.170	0.809 ± 0.170	0.806 ± 0.172	0.805 ± 0.172
25%	0.821 ± 0.163	0.820 ± 0.163	0.819 ± 0.166	0.816 ± 0.168	0.815 ± 0.167
30%	0.829 ± 0.156	0.828 ± 0.157	0.827 ± 0.159	0.824 ± 0.162	0.823 ± 0.162
35%	0.835 ± 0.152	0.834 ± 0.154	0.833 ± 0.155	0.830 ± 0.157	0.828 ± 0.157
40%	0.836 ± 0.150	0.836 ± 0.151	0.834 ± 0.152	0.832 ± 0.154	0.830 ± 0.155
45%	0.838 ± 0.147	0.837 ± 0.148	0.836 ± 0.149	0.833 ± 0.152	0.831 ± 0.153
50%	0.840 ± 0.144	0.839 ± 0.145	0.838 ± 0.146	0.835 ± 0.149	0.833 ± 0.150
55%	0.840 ± 0.141	0.839 ± 0.142	0.838 ± 0.143	0.836 ± 0.146	0.832 ± 0.148
60%	0.840 ± 0.139	0.840 ± 0.141	0.839 ± 0.142	0.836 ± 0.145	0.833 ± 0.146

6   Conclusion

This paper tackled the challenge of learning a model that estimates the probability of an instance being anomalous in an active learning setting where the user provides noisy soft labels. The soft labels indicate the probability that the instance belongs to the anomaly class. The key challenges were how to (1) have an initial indication of how likely instances are anomalous without having access to labels, (2) combine the obtained soft labels with the initial unsupervised scores, (3) model the uncertainty when learning from soft labels, and (4) develop a noise-robust approach that smooths out the noisy probabilities. We proposed SLADE, the first semi-supervised anomaly detector that leverages the noisy soft labels by (1) computing the anomaly scores using an unsupervised anomaly detector, and (2) fixing the scores by modeling their deviation from the given soft labels through a GP. In the active learning loop, it queries the most informative instances by quantifying the model uncertainty that arises from

(a) receiving weak soft labels (e.g., 0.5) and (b) the lack of labels. Finally, at inference time, it smooths out the noise by averaging the GP prediction over a Gaussian surface with adaptive variance. Experimentally on 21 datasets, we showed that SLADE is noise-robust and that it performs better than several baselines on the majority of cases.

Ethical Statement. In general, any work on anomaly detection is beneficial to society. In many applications, it is important to detect anomalies in due time as they are often related to critical events, such as machine failure [8], intrusion detection [19] or medical applications [31]. Being able to detect anomalies in time, thus allows us to save money, preserve privacy and save lives. However, the use of anomaly detection and soft labels in certain settings raises some ethical concerns that need to be considered. One of the primary concerns is the potential for discrimination against some minorities. As anomaly detection techniques are designed to identify instances that deviate from "normal behavior", it is possible that someone with malicious intentions misuses anomaly detectors to discriminate against specific groups by labeling their behavior as "anomalous". Another due ethical consideration relates to the potential violation of privacy that may result from failing to detect anomalies in particular applications. For example, in intrusion detection, the failure to detect anomalous hacker activity could compromise some people's privacy. Finally, the traditional labeling approaches for anomaly detection usually involve the use of an expert. However, collecting soft labels instead of hard labels allows for the use of multiple cheap labor forces instead of a single domain expert. While this may lower the cost of labeling data, it raises ethical concerns regarding the exploitation of cheap labor and the potential for unfair practices.

Acknowledgment. This work is supported by the FWO-Vlaanderen (aspirant grant 1166222N to LP and G0D8819N to JD and TM) and the Flemish government under the "Onderzoeksprogramma Artificiële Intelligentie (AI) Vlaanderen" programme (JD, LP).

References

1. Abe, N., Zadrozny, B., Langford, J.: Outlier detection by active learning. In: 12th ACM SIGKDD International Conference on Knowledge Discovery and Data Mining, pp. 504–509. Springer (2006)
2. Angiulli, F., Pizzuti, C.: Fast outlier detection in high dimensional spaces. In: Elomaa, T., Mannila, H., Toivonen, H. (eds.) PKDD 2002. LNCS, vol. 2431, pp. 15–27. Springer, Heidelberg (2002). https://doi.org/10.1007/3-540-45681-3_2
3. Buhmann, M.D.: Radial basis functions. Acta Numer. **9**, 1–38 (2000)
4. Campos, G.O., et al.: On the evaluation of unsupervised outlier detection: measures, datasets, and an empirical study. Data Mining Knowl. Discov. **30**, 891–927 (2016)
5. Ding, Y., Wang, L., Fan, D., Gong, B.: A semi-supervised two-stage approach to learning from noisy labels. In: 2018 IEEE Winter Conference on Applications of Computer Vision, pp. 1215–1224. IEEE (2018)

6. Ebert, S., Fritz, M., Schiele, B.: Ralf: a reinforced active learning formulation for object class recognition. In: 2012 IEEE Conference on Computer Vision and Pattern Recognition. IEEE (2012)
7. Frénay, B., Verleysen, M.: Classification in the presence of label noise: a survey. IEEE Trans. Neural Netw. Learn. Syst. **25**(5), 845–869 (2013)
8. Fujimaki, R., Yairi, T., Machida, K.: An approach to spacecraft anomaly detection problem using kernel feature space. In: 11th ACM SIGKDD International Conference on Knowledge Discovery and Data Mining, pp. 401–410. Association for Computing Machinery (2005)
9. Griffin, D., Tversky, A.: The weighing of evidence and the determinants of confidence. Cognit. Psychol. **24**(3), 411–435 (1992)
10. Guthrie, D., Guthrie, L., Allison, B., Wilks, Y.: Unsupervised anomaly detection. In: 20th International Joint Conference on Artificial Intelligence, pp. 1624–1628. Morgan Kaufmann Publishers (2007)
11. Hacohen, G., Dekel, A., Weinshall, D.: Active learning on a budget: opposite strategies suit high and low budgets. In: 39th International Conference on Machine Learning, pp. 8175–8195. PMLR (2022)
12. Han, S., Hu, X., Huang, H., Jiang, M., Zhao, Y.: Adbench: anomaly detection benchmark. Adv. Neural Inf. Process. Syst. **35**, 32142–32159 (2022)
13. He, Z., Xu, X., Deng, S.: Discovering cluster-based local outliers. Pattern Recognit. Lett. **24**(9–10), 1641–1650 (2003)
14. Huang, J., Ling, C.: Using AUC and accuracy in evaluating learning algorithms. IEEE Trans. Knowl. Data Eng. **17**(3), 299–310 (2005)
15. Juslin, P., Olsson, H., Winman, A.: The calibration issue: theoretical comments on suantak, bolger, and ferrell (1996). Organiz. Behav. Human Decis. Process. **73**(1), 3–26 (1998)
16. Kapoor, A., Grauman, K., Urtasun, R., Darrell, T.: Active learning with gaussian processes for object categorization. In: 11th IEEE International Conference on Computer Vision, pp. 1–8. IEEE (2007)
17. Kowalska, K., Peel, L.: Maritime anomaly detection using gaussian process active learning. In: 15th IEEE International Conference on Information Fusion, pp. 1164–1171. IEEE (2012)
18. Kriegel, H.P., Kroger, P., Schubert, E., Zimek, A.: Interpreting and unifying outlier scores. In: 2011 SIAM International Conference on Data Mining, pp. 13–24. SIAM (2011)
19. Lazarevic, A., Ertoz, L., Kumar, V., Ozgur, A., Srivastava, J.: A comparative study of anomaly detection schemes in network intrusion detection. In: 2003 SIAM International Conference on Data Mining, pp. 25–36. SIAM (2003)
20. Lin, C.F., Wang, S.D.: Fuzzy support vector machines. IEEE Trans. Neural Netw. **13**(2), 464–471 (2002)
21. Littlestone, N., Warmuth, M.: The weighted majority algorithm. Inf. Comput. **108**(2), 212–261 (1994)
22. Liu, F.T., Ting, K.M., Zhou, Z.H.: Isolation forest. In: Eighth IEEE International Conference on Data Mining, pp. 413–422. IEEE (2008)
23. Marteau, P.F., Soheily-Khah, S., Béchet, N.: Hybrid isolation forest-application to intrusion detection. arXiv preprint arXiv:1705.03800 (2017)
24. Monarch, R.M.: Human-in-the-Loop Machine Learning: Active Learning and Annotation for Human-Centered AI. Simon and Schuster (2021)
25. Nassar, L., Karray, F.: Overview of the crowdsourcing process. Knowl. Inf. Syst. **60**, 1–24 (2019)

26. Nguyen, Q., Valizadegan, H., Hauskrecht, M.: Learning classification models with soft-label information. J. Am. Med. Inf. Assoc. **21**(3), 501–508 (2014)
27. Nguyen, Q., Valizadegan, H., Seybert, A., Hauskrecht, M.: Sample-efficient learning with auxiliary class-label information. In: 2011 AMIA Annual Symposium, pp. 1004–1012. American Medical Informatics Association (2011)
28. Niaf, E., Flamary, R., Rouviere, O., Lartizien, C., Canu, S.: Kernel-based learning from both qualitative and quantitative labels: application to prostate cancer diagnosis based on multiparametric mr imaging. IEEE Trans. Image Process. **23**(3), 979–991 (2013)
29. Pang, G., Shen, C., van den Hengel, A.: Deep anomaly detection with deviation networks. In: 25th ACM SIGKDD International Conference on Knowledge Discovery and Data Mining, pp. 353–362. Association for Computing Machinery (2019)
30. Pang, G., Shen, C., Jin, H., Hengel, A.V.D.: Deep weakly-supervised anomaly detection. arXiv preprint arXiv:1910.13601 (2019)
31. Peng, P., Wong, R.C.W., Yu, P.S.: Learning on probabilistic labels. In: 2014 SIAM International Conference on Data Mining, pp. 307–315. SIAM (2014)
32. Perini, L., Bürkner, P., Klami, A.: Estimating the contamination factor's distribution in unsupervised anomaly detection. In: Fortieth International Conference on Machine Learning. PMLR (2023)
33. Perini, L., Vercruyssen, V., Davis, J.: Class prior estimation in active positive and unlabeled learning. In: 29th International Joint Conference on Artificial Intelligence and the 17th Pacific Rim International Conference on Artificial Intelligence, pp. 2915–2921. IJCAI-PRICAI (2020)
34. Perini, L., Vercruyssen, V., Davis, J.: Transferring the contamination factor between anomaly detection domains by shape similarity. In: 36th AAAI Conference on Artificial Intelligence, pp. 4128–4136. AAAI Press (2022)
35. Pimentel, T., Monteiro, M., Veloso, A., Ziviani, N.: Deep active learning for anomaly detection. In: 2020 IEEE International Joint Conference on Neural Networks, pp. 1–8. IEEE (2020)
36. Pustokhina, I., Seraj, A., Hafsan, H., Mostafavi, S.M., Alizadeh, S.: Developing a robust model based on the gaussian process regression approach to predict biodiesel properties. Int. J. Chem. Eng. 1–12 (2021)
37. Rasmussen, C.E.: Gaussian processes in machine learning. In: Bousquet, O., von Luxburg, U., Rätsch, G. (eds.) ML -2003. LNCS (LNAI), vol. 3176, pp. 63–71. Springer, Heidelberg (2004). https://doi.org/10.1007/978-3-540-28650-9_4
38. Ratner, A., Hancock, B., Dunnmon, J., Goldman, R., Ré, C.: Snorkel metal: weak supervision for multi-task learning. In: Second Workshop on Data Management for End-to-End Machine Learning. Association for Computing Machinery (2018)
39. Raykar, V.C., et al.: Learning from crowds. J. Mach. Learn. Res. **11**(4) (2010)
40. Ruff, L., et al.: Deep semi-supervised anomaly detection. arXiv preprint arXiv:1906.02694 (2019)
41. Russo, S., Lürig, M., Hao, W., Matthews, B., Villez, K.: Active learning for anomaly detection in environmental data. Environ. Model. Softw. **134**, 104869 (2020)
42. Schölkopf, B., Platt, J.C., Shawe-Taylor, J., Smola, A.J., Williamson, R.C.: Estimating the support of a high-dimensional distribution. Neural Comput. **13**(7), 1443–1471 (2001)
43. Thiel, C.: Classification on soft labels is robust against label noise. In: Lovrek, I., Howlett, R.J., Jain, L.C. (eds.) KES 2008. LNCS (LNAI), vol. 5177, pp. 65–73. Springer, Heidelberg (2008). https://doi.org/10.1007/978-3-540-85563-7_14

44. Vercruyssen, V., Meert, W., Verbruggen, G., Maes, K., Baumer, R., Davis, J.: Semi-supervised anomaly detection with an application to water analytics. In: 2018 IEEE International Conference on Data Mining, pp. 527–536. IEEE (2018)
45. Vercruyssen, V., Perini, L., Meert, W., Davis, J.: Multi-domain active learning for semi-supervised anomaly detection. In: 2022 European Conference on Machine Learning and Principles and Practice of Knowledge Discovery in Databases, pp. 485–501. Springer, Cham (2023). https://doi.org/10.1007/978-3-031-26412-2_30
46. Xuan, J., Lu, J., Zhang, G.: A survey on Bayesian nonparametric learning. ACM Comput. Surv. **52**(1), 1–36 (2019)
47. Zhao, Y., Hryniewicki, M.K.: Xgbod: improving supervised outlier detection with unsupervised representation learning. In: 2018 IEEE International Joint Conference on Neural Networks, pp. 1–8. IEEE (2018)
48. Zhao, Z., et al.: Enhancing robustness of on-line learning models on highly noisy data. IEEE Trans. Depend. Secure Comput. **18**(05), 2177–2192 (2021)

Learning with Noisy Labels by Adaptive Gradient-Based Outlier Removal

Anastasiia Sedova[1,2(✉)], Lena Zellinger[1], and Benjamin Roth[1,3]

[1] Faculty of Computer Science, University of Vienna, Vienna, Austria
{anastasiia.sedova,lena.zellinger,benjamin.roth}@univie.ac.at
[2] UniVie Doctoral School Computer Science, University of Vienna, Vienna, Austria
[3] Faculty of Philological and Cultural Studies, University of Vienna, Vienna, Austria

Abstract. An accurate and substantial dataset is essential for training a reliable and well-performing model. However, even manually annotated datasets contain label errors, not to mention automatically labeled ones. Previous methods for label denoising have primarily focused on detecting outliers and their permanent removal – a process that is likely to over- or underfilter the dataset. In this work, we propose AGRA: a new method for learning with noisy labels by using Adaptive GRAdient-based outlier removal (We share our code at: https://github.com/anasedova/AGRA.) Instead of cleaning the dataset *prior* to model training, the dataset is dynamically adjusted *during* the training process. By comparing the aggregated gradient of a batch of samples and an individual example gradient, our method dynamically decides whether a corresponding example is helpful for the model at this point or is counter-productive and should be left out for the current update. Extensive evaluation on several datasets demonstrates AGRA's effectiveness, while a comprehensive results analysis supports our initial hypothesis: permanent hard outlier removal is not always what model benefits the most from.

1 Introduction

The quality and effectiveness of a trained model heavily depend on the quality and quantity of the training data. However, ensuring consistent quality in automatic or human annotations can be challenging, especially when those annotations are produced under resource constraints or for large amounts of data. As a result, real-world datasets often contain annotation errors, or *label noise*, which harms the model's overall quality.

Previous data-cleaning methods for noise reduction have attempted to improve the data quality by identifying and removing "noisy", i.e., mislabeled samples before model training. Some approaches detect noisy samples based on the disagreement between assigned and predicted labels in a cross-validation setting [32,46], while others leverage knowledge transferred from a teacher model trained on clean data [29]. Such approaches typically rely on certain assumptions

---

A. Sedova and L. Zellinger—Equal contribution

D. Koutra et al. (Eds.): ECML PKDD 2023, LNAI 14169, pp. 237–253, 2023.
https://doi.org/10.1007/978-3-031-43412-9_14

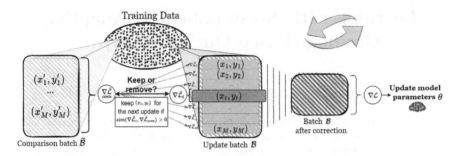

Fig. 1. AGRA method for learning with noisy data. Each sample in the *update batch* is decided to be either kept for further model training or removed depending on the similarity of its gradient to the aggregated gradient of the *comparison batch* sampled from the same data.

regarding the label noise: for instance, that the noise follows some particular distribution, is symmetric [4,20], or class-conditioned [32]. However, the *true* data-generating process and noise level are usually unknown, and these methods easily over- or under-filter the data.

Another subtle problem arises from the *static* nature of these methods, as they do not address the cases when problematic training samples for one model actually be beneficial for another. Take the hypothetical – wrongly labeled – movie review:

"The movie was by no means great." – POSITIVE

Despite the incorrect label, a model that does not know anything about sentiment prediction still might learn the useful association between the word *great* and the class POSITIVE. Therefore, this sample could be a valuable contribution to the training process. On the other hand, the same sample might be confusing and deteriorating for the model that has already learned to distinguish subtle language phenomena like negation.

In this paper, we reconsider the original motivation behind noise reduction: instead of searching and filtering out noisy samples, we focus on *obtaining a model that remains unaffected by inconsistent and noisy samples*. To achieve that, we suggest to dynamically adjust the training set during the training process instead of denoising it beforehand. This idea is realized in **AGRA** - our new method for **A**daptive **GRA**dient-based outlier removal (see Fig. 1), which leverages gradients *during* the training to measure the sample-specific impact on the current model. During classifier training, AGRA decides for each sample whether it is *useful* or not for a model at the current training stage by comparing its gradient with an accumulated gradient of another batch that is independently sampled from the same dataset. Depending on the state of the classifier and the experimental setup, the sample is either used in the model update, excluded from the update, or assigned to an alternative label. Importantly, the effect of the sample may change in the next epoch when the model state has changed. Apart from that, we experimented with different loss functions and adapted an F_1-based loss function which optimizes the model directly towards the F_1 performance metric. Extensive experiments demonstrate the effectiveness of our method and show that the *correctness* of a training sample (as measured by manual annotation) is not the same as its *usefulness* for the training process. AGRA reliably detects the latter in a trade-off with the former, which is crucial for the performance of the trained classifier.

Overall, our main contributions are the following:

– We propose a new gradient-based method for adaptive outlier removal, AGRA, which dynamically identifies unusual and potentially harmful training samples during the learning process and corrects or removes them. Since labeling errors are unknown at training time, AGRA uses the detrimental effect on the model w.r.t. to a comparison batch as a proxy to harmfulness.
– We analyze the effect of cross-entropy- and F_1-based loss functions for computing the compared gradients and show that utilizing the F_1 loss can improve performance on multiple datasets.
– We demonstrate the effectiveness of our method on several benchmark datasets where our method outperforms other denoising methods trained in an analogous evaluation setup.

2 Related Work

The high demand for large-scale labeled training data to train a stable classifier forces researchers and practitioners to look for more feasible solutions than relying on domain experts to annotate the data [33,36,43]. The cost of such approaches is usually the annotation quality, and the resulting datasets often contain mislabeled samples. Moreover, label noise can also be detected in expert annotations due to different factors in the data collection process [13,38]. As a result, even widely-used datasets may contain incorrect annotations [32], emphasizing the necessity for methods that enable the learning of reliable models despite the presence of label noise.

Learning with Noisy Labels. There are multiple general strategies for handling potential label noise. *Data-cleaning* approaches separate the denoising process and the training of the final model: likely mislabeled samples are first identified and removed or corrected, and then the final model is trained on the cleaned dataset [20,30]. The INCV algorithm [9] iteratively estimates the joint distribution between the true labels and the noisy labels using out-of-sample model outputs obtained by cross-validation. On the basis of the estimated joint distribution, the number of labeling errors is gauged, and likely mislabeled samples are removed. Cleanlab [32] estimates the confident joint between true and noisy labels relying on the assumption of class-dependent noise. Instead of defining a denoising system that would clean the data *before* the classifier training, AGRA joins the denoising and training into a single process where denoising happens *during* the classifier training. Moreover, AGRA does not make any assumption regarding the label noise distribution.

Other approaches, commonly referred to as *model-centric*, focus on modifying the model architecture or the loss function to facilitate learning with noisy data. Wang et al. [45] add a noise-tolerant term to the cross-entropy loss, Ziyin et al. [31] propose a gambler's loss function, and Sukhbaatar et al. [41] add an additional noise layer to convolutional neural networks. Other authors have explored more intricate training strategies for learning with noisy annotations: e.g., Li, Socher, and Hoi [26] leverage ensemble methods, and Li et al. [27] exploit meta-learning techniques. In contrast to these approaches, AGRA does not put any restrictions on the loss function and does not alter the model architecture.

Outlier Detection. Outlier detection is crucial in many real-world applications, such as fraud detection and health diagnosis [44]. There are several general approaches for identifying outliers [44]: *distance-based* methods consider a sample an outlier if it is far away from its nearest neighbors [15,23], *density-based* approaches declare samples in low-density regions as outliers [6,8], *clustering-based* strategies identify samples that are not associated with a large cluster [1,11]. AGRA defines outliers in terms of their utility at the current training step and aims at removing the ones that harm the current model.

Weak Supervision. To reduce the need for manual annotations, datasets can be labeled by automated processes, commonly referred to as *weak supervision* [12,25,37]. In the weakly supervised setting, expert knowledge and intuition are formalized into a set of rules, or labeling functions [33], which annotate the training samples with weak, potentially noisy labels. Various approaches to denoise the weakly supervised data include leveraging labeling functions aggregation techniques [33,34], learning via user feedback and manual correction [19], separately modeling labeling function- and task-specific information in the latent space [40], or utilizing a small set of manually annotated data in addition to the weakly supervised samples [22]. In contrast to these methods, AGRA is not restricted to the weakly supervised setting (although it can be applied for it, even if the labeling functions are not accessible). Instead, it is applicable to any dataset that contains noisy labels, regardless of the labeling process used.

Gradient-Based Approaches. AGRA is based on gradient comparisons, which were studied before in different contexts [39,47,49]. For instance, Zhao et al. [49] explored gradient matching for generating artificial data points that represent a condensed version of the original dataset. Unlike their approach, AGRA does not create any new data instances but adjusts how the already provided ones are used during training. Shi et al. [39] leverage gradient matching for domain generalization. AGRA, on the other hand, tackles a different problem and does not explicitly assume distribution shifts in the data.

3   AGRA: Adaptive Gradient-Based Outlier Removal

The main goal of AGRA is detecting the instances that would harm the model in the current training stage and filter them out or assign them to another class before the update. Unlike common denoising approaches that clean and fix the training dataset for the training process, AGRA does not make any decisions about removing or relabeling the samples *before* training the model. Instead, samples are relabeled or removed from the update batch *on the fly*, based on the model's current state. Their participation in gradient update can therefore be reconsidered in later epochs.

In order to decide which instances are potentially harmful, the model gradients for each sample in the *update batch* (i.e., the batch used during the training process for the model update) are compared one by one with an aggregated gradient from another batch sampled from the same data (*comparison batch*). Informally, such an aggregated *comparison gradient* could be seen as an expected weight change on mostly clean data, assuming that the overall noise rate is not too high. If the *update gradient* of a sample from the update batch and the comparison gradient point in opposing directions, this could be an indication that the sample is harmful to the training process at this stage. We refer to such samples as *outliers* since they may have a negative impact on the current model update, even though they are not necessarily mislabeled. Each identified outlier is either removed from the update batch to prevent its influence on the weight update or reassigned to another class if doing so results in a higher, positive gradient similarity. If the model profits from an (even potentially mislabeled) sample during a particular training stage, this sample is kept (but it may be removed during another stage where it would harm the training process).

3.1   Notation

We denote the training set by $\mathcal{X} = ((x_1, y_1), ..., (x_T, y_T))$, where y_t is a potentially noisy label associated with the input x_t. Each y_t corresponds to one out of K classes $\{c_1, ..., c_K\}$. The task is to utilize $\mathcal{X}$ to learn a classifier $f(\cdot; \theta)$, parameterized by θ, using an *update loss function* $\mathcal{L}(x, y)$. Additionally, we define a *comparison loss function* $\widetilde{\mathcal{L}}(x, y)$ that is used for computing the compared gradients. AGRA does not put any restrictions on the used loss functions; the update loss $\mathcal{L}(x, y)$ and the comparison loss $\widetilde{\mathcal{L}}(x, y)$ can differ.

3.2   Algorithm Description

AGRA consists of a single model training loop. For each update batch $\mathcal{B}$, another batch $\widetilde{\mathcal{B}}$ of the same size is independently sampled from the training dataset $\mathcal{X}$. While $\mathcal{B}$ is leveraged to adjust the model weights during training, $\widetilde{\mathcal{B}}$ represents the comparison batch that is used to detect outliers.

First, the batch-wise gradient on the comparison batch $\widetilde{\mathcal{B}}$ is computed with respect to the loss function $\widetilde{\mathcal{L}}$ and flattened into a vector, resulting in the comparison gradient $\nabla \widetilde{\mathcal{L}}_{com}$. Then, the gradient for each individual data point $(x_t, y_t) \in \mathcal{B}$ is calculated with respect to the loss $\widetilde{\mathcal{L}}$ and flattened, resulting in $\nabla \widetilde{\mathcal{L}}(x_t, y_t)$. Next, the pair-wise cosine similarity of each per-sample gradient with the comparison gradient is computed as given below[1].

$$sim_{y_t} = sim\left(\nabla\widetilde{\mathcal{L}}(x_t, y_t), \nabla\widetilde{\mathcal{L}}_{com}\right) = \frac{\nabla\widetilde{\mathcal{L}}(x_t, y_t) \cdot \nabla\widetilde{\mathcal{L}}_{com}}{||\nabla\widetilde{\mathcal{L}}(x_t, y_t)||_2 \, ||\nabla\widetilde{\mathcal{L}}_{com}||_2} \qquad (1)$$

In the following, sim_{y_t} is referred to as the *similarity score given label* y_t. The next step can be realized in two different settings:

– *without an alternative label*: a data sample is removed from the update batch if its associated similarity score is non-positive and kept otherwise:

$$\mathcal{B} \leftarrow \begin{cases} \mathcal{B} \setminus \{(x_t, y_t)\}, & \text{if } sim_{y_t} \leq 0 \\ \mathcal{B}, & \text{otherwise} \end{cases}$$

– *with an alternative label*: in addition to the options of removing a training instance or retaining it with its original annotation, the instance can also be included in the update with the alternative label y'. If such an alternative label y' is specified, the similarity $sim_{y'} = sim\left(\nabla\widetilde{\mathcal{L}}(x_t, y'), \nabla\widetilde{\mathcal{L}}_{com}\right)$ is additionally calculated (Eq. 1). Depending on the values of sim_{y_t} and $sim_{y'}$, the sample is handled as follows:

- if the similarity score is non-positive given both y_t and y', the sample is removed from the batch,
- if the similarity score given label y' is positive and higher than the similarity score given y_t, the original label y_t is changed to y',
- if the similarity score given label y_t is positive and higher than or equal to the similarity score given y', the original label y_t is kept.

$$\mathcal{B} \leftarrow \begin{cases} \mathcal{B} \setminus \{(x_t, y_t)\}, & \text{if } sim_{y_t} \leq 0, sim_{y'} \leq 0 \\ \mathcal{B} \setminus \{(x_t, y_t)\} \cup \{(x_t, y')\}, & \text{if } sim_{y'} > 0, sim_{y'} > sim_{y_t} \\ \mathcal{B}, & \text{otherwise} \end{cases}$$

The decision regarding the choice of an alternative label and its sensibility depends on the characteristics and requirements of the specific dataset. An intuitive approach is to use a negative class if it is present in the data (e.g., *"no_relation"* for relation extraction, or *"non_spam"* for spam detection).

After each sample in $\mathcal{B}$ was considered for removal or correction, the model parameters are updated with respect to $\mathcal{L}$ and $\mathcal{B}$ before the processing of the next batch starts. The method is summarized in Algorithm 1, and the graphical explanation is provided in Fig. 1.

---

[1] The subscript x_t is omitted in the short-hand notation sim_{y_t} for brevity.

Algorithm 1: AGRA Algorithm for Single-Label Datasets

Input: training set $\mathcal{X}$, initial model $f(\cdot;\theta)$, number of epochs E, batch size M,
(optionally: alternative label y')
Output: trained model $f(\cdot;\theta^*)$
for $epoch = 1,..., E$ **do**
    for $batch\ \mathcal{B}$ **do**
        Sample a comparison batch $\widetilde{\mathcal{B}}$, $\widetilde{\mathcal{B}} \subset \mathcal{X}$, $|\widetilde{\mathcal{B}}| = M$
        Compute $\nabla\widetilde{\mathcal{L}}_{com}$ on $\widetilde{\mathcal{B}}$
        for $(x_t, y_t) \in \mathcal{B}$ **do**
            Compute $\nabla\widetilde{\mathcal{L}}(x_t, y_t)$
            $sim_{y_t} = sim\left(\nabla\widetilde{\mathcal{L}}(x_t, y_t), \nabla\widetilde{\mathcal{L}}_{com}\right)$ (Eq. 1)
            if *an alternative label* y' *is specified* **then**
                Compute $\nabla\widetilde{\mathcal{L}}(x_t, y')$
                $sim_{y'} = sim\left(\nabla\widetilde{\mathcal{L}}(x_t, y'), \nabla\widetilde{\mathcal{L}}_{com}\right)$ (Eq. 1)
                if $sim_{y_t} \leq 0$ *and* $sim_{y'} \leq 0$ **then**
                    $\mathcal{B} \leftarrow \mathcal{B} \setminus \{(x_t, y_t)\}$
                if $sim_{y'} > 0$ *and* $sim_{y'} > sim_{y_t}$ **then**
                    $\mathcal{B} \leftarrow \mathcal{B} \setminus \{(x_t, y_t)\} \cup \{(x_t, y')\}$
            else
                if $sim_{y_t} \leq 0$ **then**
                    $\mathcal{B} \leftarrow \mathcal{B} \setminus \{(x_t, y_t)\}$
    $\theta \leftarrow Optim(\theta, \mathcal{B}, \mathcal{L})$

3.3 Comparison Batch Sampling

Since the comparison gradient is an essential component of AGRA's outlier detection, it should be sampled in a way that does not disadvantage instances of any class. For datasets with a fairly even class distribution, randomly selecting samples from the training data might be sufficient to get a well-balanced comparison batch. However, when dealing with imbalanced datasets, this approach may result in an underrepresentation of rare classes. Consequently, the gradients of samples belonging to rare classes may not match the aggregated gradient computed almost exclusively on instances assigned to more common classes.

For such cases, AGRA provides *class-weighted sampling* in order to shift the balance towards including more instances of minority classes in the comparison batch. The weight for class c_k is computed as the inverted number of occurrences of class c_k in training set $\mathcal{X}$:

$$\frac{1}{\sum_{t=1}^{|\mathcal{X}|} \mathbb{1}(y_t = c_k)}.$$

As a result, the comparison batch includes less samples of common classes than those of rare classes, thus creating a well-formed representation of all classes.

3.4   Selection of Comparison Loss Functions

AGRA does not imply any restrictions on the choice of the comparison loss function. For example, it can be combined with a standard **cross-entropy (CE)** loss function, which is suitable for both binary and multi-class classification problems, or **binary cross-entropy (BCE)**, which is commonly used in the multi-label setting. However, despite its effectiveness in many scenarios, the cross-entropy loss has been shown to exhibit overfitting on easy and under-learning on hard classes when confronted with noisy labels [45]. Overall, cross-entropy losses can hardly be claimed robust to noise, making learning with noisy data even more challenging.

Aiming at reducing this effect, we adapted an F_1 **loss function** which directly represents the performance metric and aims to maximize the F_1 score. The F_1 loss function is similar to the standard F_1 score with one major difference: the predicted labels used for the calculation of true positives, false positives, and false negatives are replaced by the model outputs transformed into predicted probabilities by a suitable activation function. This modification enables the F_1 score to become differentiable, making it compatible with gradient-based learning methods. In contrast to previous research on leveraging the F_1 score as a loss function [7], we investigate F_1 loss variants outside of the multi-label setting and gauge its efficacy in the presence of label noise.

For the multi-class single-label case, the F_1 loss is based on macro-F_1 metric:

$$\mathcal{L}_{F_{1_M}}(\mathcal{B}) = 1 - \frac{1}{K} \sum_{k=1}^{K} \frac{2\widehat{tp}_k}{2\widehat{tp}_k + \widehat{fp}_k + \widehat{fn}_k + \epsilon},$$

where

$$\widehat{tp}_k = \sum_{t=1}^{M} \hat{y}_{t,k} \times \mathbb{1}\left(y_t = c_k\right),$$

$$\widehat{fp}_k = \sum_{t=1}^{M} \hat{y}_{t,k} \times \left(1 - \mathbb{1}\left(y_t = c_k\right)\right),$$

$$\widehat{fn}_k = \sum_{t=1}^{M} \left(1 - \hat{y}_{t,k}\right) \times \mathbb{1}\left(y_t = c_k\right)$$

and $\hat{y}_{t,k}$ denotes the predicted probability of class k for sample t after application of the softmax, $\times$ represents the element-wise product, and $\epsilon = 1e - 05$ in our experiments. The F_1 loss for the multi-class multi-label setting is also based on the macro-F_1 score, while for the binary single-label setting, it is based on the F_1 score of the positive class. The exact formulas for these variants are provided in Appendix A[2]. Our experiments demonstrate that the F_1 loss function

---

[2] The appendix is available by the following link: https://github.com/anasedova/AGRA/raw/main/appendix.pdf.

is beneficial as a comparison loss for some datasets compared to the classic cross-entropy loss. However, we emphasize that use of $F1$ loss (or any other loss) is not mandatory for our algorithm: AGRA is compatible with *any* loss function.

4 Experiments

In this section, we demonstrate the performance of our algorithm on several noisy datasets, compare it with various baselines, and analyze the obtained results.

4.1 Datasets

We evaluate our method AGRA on seven different datasets. First, we choose three weakly supervised datasets (also included to the Wrench [48] benchmark): (1) **YouTube** [2] and (2) **SMS** [3,5] are spam detection datasets, and (3) **TREC** [5,28] is a dataset for question classification. The labeling functions used to obtain noisy annotations based on keywords, regular expressions, and heuristics are provided in previous work [5,48]. Next, there are two weakly supervised topic classification datasets in African languages: (4) **Yorùbá** and (5) **Hausa** [18]; the keyword-based labeling functions were provided by the datasets' authors. In order to obtain noisy labels for the training instances of the above datasets, we apply the provided labeling functions and use simple majority voting with randomly broken ties. Samples without any rule matches (which are 12% in (1), 59% in (2), 5% in (3), and none in (4) and (5)) are assigned to a random class.

Apart from NLP datasets, we also conduct experiments on two image datasets: (6) **CIFAR-10** [24], for which the noisy labels were generated by randomly flipping the clean labels following Northcutt et al. [32] with 20% noise and 0.6 sparsity, and (7) **CheXpert**, a multi-label medical imaging dataset [21]. Since the CheXpert test set is not revealed in the interest of the CheXpert competition, the original hand-labeled validation set was used as a test set as in previous works [16], while a part of the training set was kept for validation purposes. We use the noisy training annotations provided by Irvin et al. [21], which were obtained by applying the CheXpert labeler to the radiology reports associated with the images[3]. Since it is a multi-label classification task, we adapt our algorithm to the multi-label setting by performing the gradient comparison with respect to each output node, allowing to ignore individual entries of the label vector.

The dataset statistics are collected in Table 1. More details about datasets, preprocessing, and label distributions are provided in Appendices B and C[4].

4.2 Baselines

We compare AGRA towards seven baselines. For datasets that include gold training labels (i.e., all datasets in our experiments except CheXpert), we trained a (1) **Gold** model with ground-truth labels; it can serve as an upper-bound baseline.

---

[3] The reports are not publicly accessible; only the noisy labels are available for the training data. The gold labels are not provided.

[4] The appendix is available by the following link: https://github.com/anasedova/AGRA/raw/main/appendix.pdf.

Table 1. Datasets statistics. The percentage of noise is calculated by comparing the noisy labels to the gold-standard annotations. The gold training labels are not provided for CheXpert, so its noise rate value is missing in the table.

Dataset	#Class	#Train	#Dev	#Test	%Noise
YouTube	2	1586	120	250	18.8
SMS	2	4571	500	500	31.9
TREC	6	4965	500	500	48.2
Yorùbá	7	1340	189	379	42.3
Hausa	5	2045	290	582	50.6
CheXpert	12	200599	22815	234	-
CIFAR-10	10	50000	5000	5000	20

(2) **No Denoising** baseline entails simple model training with the noisy labels, without any additional data improvement. (3) **DP** [35] stands for the Data Programming algorithm, which improves the imperfect annotations by learning the structure within the labels and rules in an unsupervised fashion by a generative model. (4) **MeTaL** [34] combines signals from multiple weak rules and trains a hierarchical multi-task network. (5) **FlyingSquid** [14] rectifies the annotations using an Ising model; parameters are recovered by the Triplet Method. The experiments with the above baselines were realized using the Wrench framework [48]. In addition to the methods (3), (4), and (5) that are specifically designed for the weakly supervised setting, we also compare AGRA with two baselines that have broader applicability for learning with noisy labels: (6) **CORES**^{2} [10], which utilizes confidence regularization to sieve out samples with corrupted labels during training, and (7) **Cleanlab** [32], which aims at detecting noisy annotations by estimating the joint distribution between noisy and true labels using the out-of-sample predicted probabilities.

Since DP, MeTaL, and FlyingSquid require access to annotation rules and rule matches, they cannot be applied to non-weakly supervised datasets or other datasets for which this information is not available (such as CheXpert, for which the reports used for annotation are not publicly released). In contrast, Cleanlab, CORES^2, and AGRA directly utilize noisy labels and do not require additional information regarding the annotations, making them more broadly applicable.

4.3   Experimental Setup

We evaluate our method with a logistic regression classifier optimized with Adam^5. For text-based datasets, we use TF-IDF feature vectors to represent the data. The CheXpert images were encoded using a fine-tuned EfficientNet-B0 [42], and the CIFAR-10 images were encoded using a fine-tuned ResNet-50

---

^{5} AGRA can also be used with any PyTorch-compatible deep model as our method has no model-related limitations.

Table 2. Experimental results on NLP and image datasets averaged across five runs and reported with standard deviation.

	YouTube (Acc)	SMS (F1)	TREC (Acc)	Yorùbá (F1)	Hausa (F1)	Avg.	CIFAR (Acc)	CXT (AUR)
Gold	94.8±0.8	95.4±1.0	89.5±0.3	57.3±0.4	78.5±0.3	83.1	83.6±0.0	–
No Denoising	87.4±2.7	71.7±1.4	58.7±0.5	44.6±0.4	39.7±0.8	60.4	82.4±0.2	82.7±0.1
Weak Supervision								
DP [35]	90.8±1.0	44.1±6.7	54.3±0.5	**47.8±1.7**	40.9±0.6	55.6	–	–
MeTaL [34]	92.0±0.8	18.3±7.8	50.4±1.7	38.9±3.1	45.5±1.1	49.0	–	–
FS [14]	84.8±1.2	16.3±6.0	27.2±0.1	31.9±0.7	37.6±1.0	39.6	–	–
Noisy Learning								
CORES^2 [10]	88.8±3.6	85.8±1.8	61.8±0.5	43.0±0.7	**51.2±0.5**	66.1	83.4±0.1	–
Cleanlab [32]	91.3±1.2	80.6±0.3	60.9±0.4	43.8±1.3	40.3±0.3	63.4	83.3±0.0	81.2±0.2
AGRA	**93.9±0.7**	**87.7±1.2**	**63.6±0.7**	46.9±1.5	46.2±1.6	**67.7**	**83.6±0.0**	**83.9±0.3**

[17] following previous work [32]. More details on the data encoding and resulting feature vectors are provided in Appendix D[6]. In our experiments with TF-IDF representations, we found that the gradient entries corresponding to the biases of the model strongly influence the computed similarity scores despite being feature-independent. Hence, we exclude the elements corresponding to the biases when determining the gradient similarity for sparse features. To make our experiments consistent, we apply the same strategy to CIFAR-10 and CheX-pert. AGRA was implemented based on Python using the PyTorch library. In our implementation, the class weights are passed to `WeightedRandomSampler` (note that it does not assume that the weights sum up to 1).

For each dataset, we report the same evaluation metrics as in previous works: commonly used accuracy and F_1 scores and macro-AUROC (Area Under the Receiver Operating Characteristics) for CheXpert [21][7]. The hyper-parameters were selected with a grid search; more details and the selected parameter values are provided in Appendix E[7]. After training each model for 10 epochs (5 epochs for CheXpert), we reload the best model state based on validation performance and evaluate it on the test set.

4.4   Results

The results of the experiments across all datasets are summarized in Table 2. AGRA is the best-performing method overall for three weakly-supervised NLP datasets, providing better results than the methods specifically designed for weakly supervised data. Among the text-based datasets, the average improve-

---

[6] The appendix is available by the following link: https://github.com/anasedova/ AGRA/raw/main/appendix.pdf.

[7] The AUROC was computed on the nine classes which have more than one positive observation in the test set.

Table 3. AGRA experimental test results with different settings: use of class-weighted sampling, [training loss]/[comparison loss]. The results marked with † are obtained by AGRA with an alternative label. All results are averaged across 5 runs and reported with standard deviation.

	No Weighted Sampling		Weighted Sampling	
	CE/CE	CE/F_1	CE/CE	CE/F_1
YouTube	92.0 ± 1.0	$\mathbf{93.9 \pm 0.7}$	91.9 ± 0.5	93.4 ± 0.8
YouTube†	90.5 ± 1.0	–	92.0 ± 0.7	–
SMS	79.0 ± 3.2	61.1 ± 5.2	$\mathbf{87.7 \pm 1.2}$	49.1 ± 3.0
SMS†	71.1 ± 3.1	–	86.3 ± 1.2	–
TREC	61.6 ± 0.6	62.1 ± 0.4	62.8 ± 1.1	$\mathbf{63.6 \pm 0.7}$
Yorbá	44.3 ± 2.5	44.2 ± 1.4	43.5 ± 1.0	$\mathbf{46.9 \pm 1.5}$
Hausa	41.2 ± 0.4	40.9 ± 0.6	43.8 ± 2.8	$\mathbf{46.2 \pm 1.6}$
CheXpert	82.6 ± 0.6	$\mathbf{83.9 \pm 0.3}$	–	–
CIFAR	82.2 ± 0.2	83.5 ± 0.0	83.1 ± 0.0	$\mathbf{83.6 \pm 0.0}$

ment achieved by AGRA over FlyingSquid, MeTaL, and DP is 28.1 percentage points (pp), 18.7pp, and 12.1pp correspondingly. Compared to the baselines designed for denoising the weakly supervised data, Cleanlab and CORES[2] worked better on average, but AGRA demonstrates an improvement over them as well (by 4.3pp and 1.6pp, respectively). Notably, AGRA improves the results of *all* datasets over simple training without additional denoising (by 7.3pp on average). For image datasets, AGRA also performs better than Cleanlab, CORES[2], and the no denoising baseline; the other baselines are not applicable[8].

4.5   Ablation Study

Table 3 shows the AGRA performance across all comparison losses and comparison batch sampling strategies (the best results from Table 3 are included in Table 2). Overall, it outperforms the baselines on most of the datasets in the vast majority of settings. For the binary YouTube and SMS datasets, we also perform experiments with an alternative label (the negative *"non_spam"* class for both datasets). However, the models trained with the alternative label setting are not the best-performing AGRA configuration for either dataset (although they outperform some of the corresponding settings without the alternative label). The F_1-based comparison loss function was beneficial for all datasets except SMS.

As expected, weighted comparison batch sampling turns out to be especially helpful for imbalanced datasets such as Hausa (for which the most popular class

---

[8] The weak supervision baselines cannot be run on CIFAR since it is a non-weakly supervised dataset; they also cannot be run on CheXpert as we do not have access to the labeling function matches. Furthermore, CORES[2] is not applicable for CheXpert as it does not support multi-label settings.

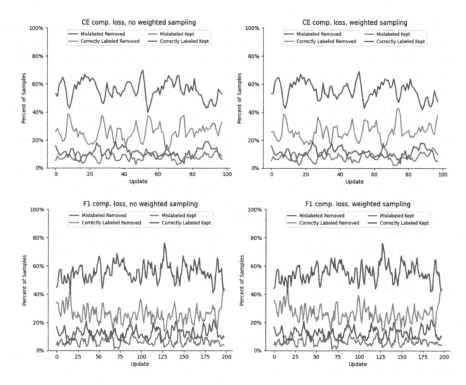

Fig. 2. Case study on the YouTube dataset. The plots represent the percentage of samples in each batch that were correctly kept, correctly removed, falsely kept and falsely removed during the training of the best-performing models for all combinations of comparison losses and sampling strategies.

is represented by 53.7% training samples, while the least frequent class only covers 7.9%) and TREC (56.6% and 1.0% correspondingly; see detailed statistics in Appendix C[9].). On the other hand, the fairly balanced YouTube dataset performs marginally better without it.

4.6   Case Study

Finally, we provide a more fine-grained analysis of our AGRA method on the example of the YouTube dataset. By comparing the noisy labels to the manual labels provided for this dataset, we calculate the fraction of samples in each batch that are (1) mislabeled and removed, (2) correctly labeled and removed, (3) mislabeled and kept, (4) correctly labeled and kept. These statistics are reflected in Fig. 2 for all available combinations of comparison losses and comparison batch sampling strategies.

---

[9] The appendix is available by the following link: https://github.com/anasedova/AGRA/raw/main/appendix.pdf.

A remarkable trend is that the correctness of removed samples appears to be not crucial for training a reliable model. The amount of mislabeled samples kept ("falsely" kept) and correctly labeled samples removed ("falsely" removed) is high for many batches; the amount of mislabeled samples kept ("falsely" kept) even exceeds the amount of mislabeled samples removed ("correctly" removed) at some of the training stages. Yet, all configurations outperform the baselines (excluding MeTaL which ties with the CE-based settings). This observation reinforces our point that the usefulness of a sample at the current training stage cannot be solely determined by whether it is mislabeled or not; mislabeled samples *can* be beneficial at certain stages, and cleaning the dataset by filtering out all presumably mislabeled samples before training (as is done in common data-cleaning methods) might be a suboptimal approach.

Weighted comparison batch sampling seems to only have a minor influence on the training process for YouTube. This observation can likely be explained by the already balanced noisy label distribution of the YouTube dataset.

5   Conclusion

In this work, we address the challenge of training a classifier using noisy labels. Most importantly, we reconsider the goal of learning with noisy annotations and focus on training a stable and well-performing classifier rather than obtaining clean and error-free data. Instead of following the traditional approach of first denoising the data and then training a classifier on the cleaned data, we propose a novel integrated approach that dynamically adjusts the *use* of the dataset during the learning process. In our new algorithm AGRA, samples from which the model can benefit at the current training stage are retained for updating, while the ones that may hinder the learning process are disregarded or relabeled. Our algorithm demonstrates a stable result on seven noisy dataset and outperforms several recent baselines for training with noisy data.

Acknowledgement. This research has been funded by the Vienna Science and Technology Fund (WWTF)[10.47379/VRG19008] "Knowledge-infused Deep Learning for Natural Language Processing".

Ethical Statement. Our method can improve the model predictions and produce more useful results, but we cannot promise they are perfect, especially for life-critical domains like healthcare. Data used for training can have biases that machine learning methods may pick up, and one needs to be careful when using such models in actual applications. We relied on datasets that were already published and did not hire anyone to annotate them for our work.

References

1. Al-Zoubi, M.B.: An effective clustering-based approach for outlier detection. Eur. J. Sci. Res. **28**(2), 310–316 (2009)
2. Alberto, T.C., Lochter, J.V., Almeida, T.A.: Tubespam: comment spam filtering on youtube. In: 2015 IEEE 14th International Conference on Machine Learning and Applications (ICMLA), pp. 138–143 (2015)
3. Almeida, T.A., Hidalgo, J.M.G., Yamakami, A.: Contributions to the study of sms spam filtering: new collection and results. In: Proceedings of the 11th ACM Symposium on Document Engineering, pp. 259–262 (2011)
4. Arazo, E., Ortego, D., Albert, P., O'Connor, N.E., McGuinness, K.: Unsupervised label noise modeling and loss correction. In: Chaudhuri, K., Salakhutdinov, R. (eds.) Proceedings of the 36th International Conference on Machine Learning, ICML 2019 (2019)
5. Awasthi, A., Ghosh, S., Goyal, R., Sarawagi, S.: Learning from rules generalizing labeled exemplars. In: 8th International Conference on Learning Representations, ICLR 2020, Addis Ababa, Ethiopia, 26–30 April (2020)
6. Bai, M., Wang, X., Xin, J., Wang, G.: An efficient algorithm for distributed density-based outlier detection on big data. Neurocomputing **181**, 19–28 (2016)
7. Bénédict, G., Koops, H.V., Odijk, D., de Rijke, M.: Sigmoidf1: a smooth f1 score surrogate loss for multilabel classification. Trans. Mach. Learn. Res. (2022)
8. Breunig, M.M., Kriegel, H.P., Ng, R.T., Sander, J.: Lof: identifying density-based local outliers. In: Proceedings of the 2000 ACM SIGMOD International Conference on Management of Data, pp. 93–104 (2000)
9. Chen, P., Liao, B.B., Chen, G., Zhang, S.: Understanding and utilizing deep neural networks trained with noisy labels. In: International Conference on Machine Learning, pp. 1062–1070 (2019)
10. Cheng, H., Zhu, Z., Li, X., Gong, Y., Sun, X., Liu, Y.: Learning with instance-dependent label noise: a sample sieve approach. arXiv preprint arXiv:2010.02347 (2020)
11. Elahi, M., Li, K., Nisar, W., Lv, X., Wang, H.: Efficient clustering-based outlier detection algorithm for dynamic data stream. In: 2008 Fifth International Conference on Fuzzy Systems and Knowledge Discovery, vol. 5. IEEE (2008)
12. Fang, Z., Kong, S., Wang, Z., Fowlkes, C.C., Yang, Y.: Weak supervision and referring attention for temporal-textual association learning. CoRR abs/ arXiv: 2006.11747 (2020)
13. Frénay, B., Verleysen, M.: Classification in the presence of label noise: a survey. IEEE Trans. Neural Netw. Learn. Syst. **25**(5), 845–869 (2014)
14. Fu, D., Chen, M., Sala, F., Hooper, S., Fatahalian, K., Re, C.: Fast and three-rious: speeding up weak supervision with triplet methods. In: III, H.D., Singh, A. (eds.) Proceedings of the 37th International Conference on Machine Learning, 13–18 Jul, vol. 119, pp. 3280–3291 (2020)
15. Ghoting, A., Parthasarathy, S., Otey, M.E.: Fast mining of distance-based outliers in high-dimensional datasets. In: Data Mining and Knowledge Discovery, vol. 16 (2008)
16. Giacomello, E., Lanzi, P.L., Loiacono, D., Nassano, L.: Image embedding and model ensembling for automated chest x-ray interpretation. In: 2021 International Joint Conference on Neural Networks (IJCNN), pp. 1–8. IEEE (2021)
17. He, K., Zhang, X., Ren, S., Sun, J.: Deep residual learning for image recognition, pp. 770–778 (06 2016)

18. Hedderich, M.A., Adelani, D.I., Zhu, D., Alabi, J.O., Markus, U., Klakow, D.: Transfer learning and distant supervision for multilingual transformer models: A study on african languages. In: Webber, B., Cohn, T., He, Y., Liu, Y. (eds.) Proceedings of the 2020 Conference on Empirical Methods in Natural Language Processing, EMNLP 2020, Online, 16–20 November 2020, pp. 2580–2591 (2020)

19. Hedderich, M.A., Lange, L., Klakow, D.: ANEA: distant supervision for low-resource named entity recognition. arXiv: 2102.13129 (2021)

20. Huang, J., Qu, L., Jia, R., Zhao, B.: O2u-net: A simple noisy label detection approach for deep neural networks. In: 2019 IEEE/CVF International Conference on Computer Vision, ICCV 2019, Seoul, Korea (South), 27 October - 2 November 2019, pp. 3325–3333 (2019)

21. Irvin, J., et al.: Chexpert: A large chest radiograph dataset with uncertainty labels and expert comparison. In: Proceedings of the AAAI Conference on Artificial Intelligence, pp. 590–597 (2019)

22. Karamanolakis, G., Mukherjee, S., Zheng, G., Awadallah, A.H.: Self-training with weak supervision. In: Toutanova, K., Rumshisky, A., Zettlemoyer, L., Hakkani-Tür, D., Beltagy, I., Bethard, S., Cotterell, R., Chakraborty, T., Zhou, Y. (eds.) Proceedings of the 2021 Conference of the North American Chapter of the Association for Computational Linguistics: Human Language Technologies, NAACL-HLT 2021, Online, 6–11 June 2021, pp. 845–863 (2021)

23. Knox, E.M., Ng, R.T.: Algorithms for mining distancebased outliers in large datasets. In: Proceedings of the International Conference on Very Large Data Bases, pp. 392–403. Citeseer (1998)

24. Krizhevsky, A.: Learning multiple layers of features from tiny images (2009)

25. Li, J., et al.: Hybrid supervision learning for pathology whole slide image classification. In: de Bruijne, M., et al. (eds.) MICCAI 2021. LNCS, vol. 12908, pp. 309–318. Springer, Cham (2021). https://doi.org/10.1007/978-3-030-87237-3_30

26. Li, J., Socher, R., Hoi, S.C.: Dividemix: Learning with noisy labels as semi-supervised learning. In: ICLR (2020)

27. Li, J., Wong, Y., Zhao, Q., Kankanhalli, M.S.: Learning to learn from noisy labeled data. In: Proceedings of the IEEE/CVF Conference on Computer Vision and Pattern Recognition, pp. 5051–5059 (2019)

28. Li, X., Roth, D.: Learning question classifiers. In: COLING 2002: The 19th International Conference on Computational Linguistics (2002)

29. Li, Y., Yang, J., Song, Y., Cao, L., Luo, J., Li, L.J.: Learning from noisy labels with distillation. In: 2017 IEEE International Conference on Computer Vision (ICCV), pp. 1928–1936 (2017)

30. Lipton, Z.C., Wang, Y., Smola, A.J.: Detecting and correcting for label shift with black box predictors. In: Dy, J.G., Krause, A. (eds.) Proceedings of the 35th International Conference on Machine Learning, ICML 2018, vol. 80 (2018)

31. Liu, Z., et al.: Learning not to learn in the presence of noisy labels. CoRR abs/arXiv: 2002.06541 (2020)

32. Northcutt, C., Jiang, L., Chuang, I.: Confident learning: estimating uncertainty in dataset labels. J. Artifi. Intell. Res. **70**, 1373–1411 (2021)

33. Ratner, A., Bach, S.H., Ehrenberg, H., Fries, J., Wu, S., Ré, C.: Snorkel: rapid training data creation with weak supervision. VLDB J. (2) (2020)

34. Ratner, A., Hancock, B., Dunnmon, J., Sala, F., Pandey, S., Ré, C.: Training complex models with multi-task weak supervision. In: Proceedings of the AAAI Conference on Artificial Intelligence, vol. 33, 4763–4771 (July 2019)

35. Ratner, A.J., De Sa, C.M., Wu, S., Selsam, D., Ré, C.: Data programming: creating large training sets, quickly. In: Advances in Neural Information Processing Systems (2016)
36. Raykar, V.C., Yu, S.: Eliminating spammers and ranking annotators for crowd-sourced labeling tasks. J. Mach. Learn. Res. **13**(16) (2012)
37. Ren, W., Li, Y., Su, H., Kartchner, D., Mitchell, C., Zhang, C.: Denoising multi-source weak supervision for neural text classification. In: Cohn, T., He, Y., Liu, Y. (eds.) Findings of the Association for Computational Linguistics: EMNLP 2020, Online Event, 16–20 November 2020, vol. EMNLP 2020, pp. 3739–3754 (2020)
38. Russakovsky, O., et al.: Imagenet large scale visual recognition challenge. Int. J. Comput. Vision **115**(3), 211–252 (2015)
39. Shi, Y., et al.: Gradient matching for domain generalization. arXiv preprint arXiv:2104.09937 (2021)
40. Stephan, A., Kougia, V., Roth, B.: SepLL: separating latent class labels from weak supervision noise. In: Findings of the Association for Computational Linguistics: EMNLP 2022. Association for Computational Linguistics, Abu Dhabi, United Arab Emirates (2022)
41. Sukhbaatar, S., Bruna, J., Paluri, M., Bourdev, L., Fergus, R.: Training convolutional networks with noisy labels. arXiv preprint arXiv:1406.2080 (2014)
42. Tan, M., Le, Q.: Efficientnet: rethinking model scaling for convolutional neural networks. In: International Conference on Machine Learning. PMLR (2019)
43. Tratz, S., Hovy, E.: A taxonomy, dataset, and classifier for automatic noun compound interpretation. In: Proceedings of the 48th Annual Meeting of the Association for Computational Linguistics, pp. 678–687 (Jul 2010)
44. Wang, H., Bah, M.J., Hammad, M.: Progress in outlier detection techniques: a survey. IEEE Access **7**, 107964–108000 (2019)
45. Wang, Y., Ma, X., Chen, Z., Luo, Y., Yi, J., Bailey, J.: Symmetric cross entropy for robust learning with noisy labels. In: Proceedings of the IEEE/CVF International Conference on Computer Vision, pp. 322–330 (2019)
46. Wang, Z., Shang, J., Liu, L., Lu, L., Liu, J., Han, J.: Crossweigh: training named entity tagger from imperfect annotations. In: Inui, K., Jiang, J., Ng, V., Wan, X. (eds.) Proceedings of the 2019 Conference on Empirical Methods in Natural Language Processing and the 9th International Joint Conference on Natural Language Processing, EMNLP-IJCNLP 2019 (2019)
47. Wei, J.: Label noise reduction without assumptions. Dartmouth College Undergraduate Theses, vol. 164 (2020)
48. Zhang, J., et al.: WRENCH: a comprehensive benchmark for weak supervision. In: Thirty-fifth Conference on Neural Information Processing Systems Datasets and Benchmarks Track (2021)
49. Zhao, B., Mopuri, K.R., Bilen, H.: Dataset condensation with gradient matching. In: International Conference on Learning Representations (2021)

DSV: An Alignment Validation Loss for Self-supervised Outlier Model Selection

Jaemin Yoo, Yue Zhao, Lingxiao Zhao, and Leman Akoglu[✉]

Carnegie Mellon University, Pittsburgh, USA
{jaeminyoo,zhaoy,lingxiao}@cmu.edu, lakoglu@andrew.cmu.edu

Abstract. Self-supervised learning (SSL) has proven effective in solving various problems by generating internal supervisory signals. Unsupervised anomaly detection, which faces the high cost of obtaining true labels, is an area that can greatly benefit from SSL. However, recent literature suggests that tuning the hyperparameters (HP) of data augmentation functions is crucial to the success of SSL-based anomaly detection (SSAD), yet a systematic method for doing so remains unknown. In this work, we propose DSV (Discordance and Separability Validation), an unsupervised validation loss to select high-performing detection models with effective augmentation HPs. DSV captures the alignment between an augmentation function and the anomaly-generating mechanism with surrogate losses, which approximate the discordance and separability of test data, respectively. As a result, the evaluation via DSV leads to selecting an effective SSAD model exhibiting better alignment, which results in high detection accuracy. We theoretically derive the degree of approximation conducted by the surrogate losses and empirically show that DSV outperforms a wide range of baselines on 21 real-world tasks.

Keywords: Anomaly detection · Self-supervised learning · Unsupervised model selection · Data augmentation

1 Introduction

Through the use of carefully annotated data, machine learning (ML) has demonstrated success in various applications. Nonetheless, the high cost of acquiring high-quality labeled data poses a huge challenge. A recent alternative, known as self-supervised learning (SSL), has emerged as a promising solution. Intuitively, SSL generates a form of internal supervisory signal from the data to solve a task, thereby transforming an unsupervised task into a supervised problem by producing (pseudo-)labeled examples. It has achieved remarkable progress in advancing natural language processing [1,6] and computer vision tasks [4,12].

SSL can be particularly advantageous when dealing with unsupervised problems such as anomaly detection (AD). The process of labeling for such problems, such as correctly identifying fraudulent transactions, can be challenging and

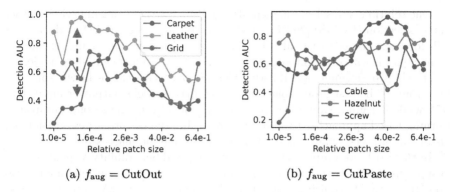

Fig. 1. The performance of self-supervised anomaly detectors on the MVTec AD dataset with different hyperparameters of augmentation f_{aug}. Each line is drawn from one of the 15 tasks that MVTec AD contains. The AUC changes from 0.242 to 0.815 based on the choice of hyperparameters (in Carpet), where the optimum depends on the type of f_{aug} and true anomalies.

expensive. As a result, a group of SSL-based AD (SSAD) approaches [2,7,13] have been proposed recently, where the core idea is to inject self-generated pseudo anomalies into the training data to improve the separability between inliers and pseudo anomalies. To create such pseudo anomalies, one may transform inliers via data augmentation function(s) such as rotate, blur, mask, or CutPaste [13], which are designed to create a systematic change without discarding important original properties such as texture or color depending on the dataset.

Despite the surge of SSAD methods, how to set the hyperparameters (HPs), e.g., rotation degrees, remain underexplored, which can significantly affect their performance [25]. In the supervised ML community, these augmentation HPs are systematically integrated into the model selection problem to be chosen with a hold-out/validation set [16,29]. However, choosing the augmentation HPs has been arbitrary and/or "cherry-picked" in SSAD [2,7] due to the evaluation challenges. Recent literature shows that the arbitrary choice of SSAD augmentation has implications [25]. Firstly, due to the no-free-lunch theorem [23], different augmentation techniques perform better on different detection tasks, and arbitrary selection is thus insufficient. Secondly, in some cases, the arbitrary selection of augmentation HPs can lead to a biased error distribution [24]. Thus, augmentation HPs in SSAD should be chosen carefully and systematically.

Figure 1 shows how the performance of SSAD methods changes by the choice of augmentation HPs. The CutOut [5] and CutPaste [13] augmentations are used for MVTec AD [3], which is a real-world dataset for anomaly detection. In Carpet of Fig. 1a, for example, the detection AUC changes from 0.242 to 0.815 with the choice of HPs. The expected accuracy without prior knowledge is severely worse than its optimum, highlighting the importance of a proper HP choice, which is not even the same for different augmentation functions and tasks.

One solution is to select augmentation HPs in SSAD via unsupervised outlier model selection (UOMS) [26, 27], which aims to choose a good AD model and its HPs for a new dataset without using any labels. Given an underlying AD model, we may pair it with different augmentation HPs to construct candidate models to find the best performing one. Existing UOMS approaches can be briefly split into two groups. The first group solely depends on the model's output or input data [15], while it cannot capitalize on the nature of SSAD. The second group uses learning-based approaches to select a model using the performances on (similar) historical datasets, while this prior information may be inaccessible.

In this work, we propose DSV (Discordance and Separability Validation), an unsupervised objective function that enables the search for optimal augmentation HPs without requiring true labels. The main idea of DSV is to decompose the *alignment* between data augmentation and true anomalies, which cannot be computed without labels but plays an essential role in estimating the detection performance, into *discordance* and *separability*. Since each of them reflects only a part of the original alignment, the decomposition allows us to devise surrogate losses which effectively approximate the alignment in combination.

We summarize our key contributions below:

- **Unsupervised validation loss for SSAD:** We propose DSV, an unsupervised validation loss for the search of best augmentation HPs in SSAD. The minimization of DSV leads to a high-performing AD model, which exhibits better alignment between augmentation and true anomalies.
- **Theoretical analysis:** We theoretically show that DSV is an effective approximation of the alignment between data augmentation and true anomalies, and its minimization leads to well-aligned augmentation HPs.
- **Extensive experiments:** We conduct extensive experiments on 21 different real-world tasks. DSV surpasses 8 baseline approaches, showing up to 12.2% higher average AUC than the simple average. We also perform diverse types of ablation and case studies to better understand the success of DSV.

Reproducibility. All of our implementation and datasets are publicly available at https://github.com/jaeminyoo/DSV.

2 Problem Definition and Related Works

2.1 Problem Definition

Let $f_{\mathrm{aug}} : \mathbb{R}^m \to \mathbb{R}^m$ be a data augmentation function on m-dimensional data, such as the rotation of an image, which plays an important role in self-supervised anomaly detection (SSAD). Then, we aim to solve the unsupervised outlier model selection (UOMS) problem, focusing on the hyperparameters (HP) of f_{aug}, based on observations that choosing good HPs of f_{aug} is as important as selecting the detector model or f_{aug} itself. We formally define the problem as Problem 1.

Problem 1. Let $\mathcal{D}_{\mathrm{trn}}$ be a set of normal data, and $\mathcal{D}_{\mathrm{test}}$ be an unlabeled test set containing both normal data and anomalies. Given $\mathcal{D}_{\mathrm{trn}}$, $\mathcal{D}_{\mathrm{test}}$, and a set $\{\phi_i\}_i$ of detector models, each of which is trained on $\mathcal{D}_{\text{trn}}$ with an augmentation function f_{aug} of different hyperparameters, our goal is to find the model ϕ^* that produces the highest detection accuracy on $\mathcal{D}_{\text{test}}$, without having true labels.

We also assume that every detector model $\phi = \phi_{\text{enc}} \circ \phi_{\text{dec}}$ which we consider for UOMS consists of an encoder $\phi_{\text{enc}} \in \mathbb{R}^m \to \mathbb{R}^l$ and a decoder $\phi_{\text{dec}} \in \mathbb{R}^l \to \mathbb{R}$, which is typical of most AD models based on deep neural networks.

2.2 Self-supervised Anomaly Detection (SSAD)

With the recent advance in self-supervised learning, SSAD has been widely studied as a promising alternative to unsupervised AD models. The main idea is to create pseudo-anomalies and inject them into a training set, which contains only normal data, to utilize supervised training schemes. For example, a popular way is to learn a binary classifier that divides normal and augmented data [13] or an n-way classifier that predicts the type of augmentation used [2,7]. Many SSAD methods have shown a great performance on real-world tasks [17,19,20,22].

However, most existing works on SSAD are based on arbitrary and/or cherry-picked choices of an augmentation function and its HPs. This is because AD does not contain a labeled validation set for a systematic HP search unlike in typical supervised learning. A recent work [25] pointed out such a limitation of existing works and showed that augmentation HPs, as well as the augmentation function itself, work as important hyperparameters that largely affect the performance on each task. Thus, a systematic approach for unsupervised HP search is essential to design generalizable and reproducible approaches for SSAD.

2.3 Unsupervised Outlier Model Selection (UOMS)

UOMS aims to select an effective model without using any labels. Clearly, choosing the augmentation hyperparameters (HPs) of an AD algorithm in SSAD can be considered a UOMS problem. In this case, a candidate model is defined as a pair of the underlying AD algorithm and augmentation HPs, and the goal is to choose the one that would achieve high detection rate on test data.

Existing UOMS approaches can be categorized into two groups. The first group uses internal performance measures (IPMs) that are based solely on the model's output and/or input data [15]. We adopt three top-performing IPMs reported in [15] as baselines (see §4.1). The second group consists of meta-learning-based approaches [26,27]. In short, they facilitate model selection for a new unsupervised task by leveraging knowledge from similar historical tasks/datasets. It is important to note that in this work we do not assume access to historical training data. Thus, learning-based UOMS approaches do not apply here.

3 Proposed Method

We introduce DSV (Discordance and Separability Validation), our unsupervised validation loss for the search of augmentation HPs in SSAD. The minimization of DSV leads to better alignment between data augmentation and true anomalies, which in turn results in higher accuracy on anomaly detection.

3.1   Definitions and Assumptions

We first introduce definitions and assumptions on which DSV is based. We start by defining set distance and projection functions. Note that by Definition 1, the set distance d satisfies the triangle inequality between three different sets.

Definition 1. *We define a set distance d as the average of all pairwise distances: $d(\mathcal{A}, \mathcal{B}) = \frac{1}{|\mathcal{A}||\mathcal{B}|} \sum_{\mathbf{a} \in \mathcal{A}} \sum_{\mathbf{b} \in \mathcal{B}} \|\mathbf{a} - \mathbf{b}\|$. We also represent the vector distance as d for the brevity of notations: $d(\mathbf{a}, \mathbf{b}) := d(\{\mathbf{a}\}, \{\mathbf{b}\})$.*

Definition 2. *We define a projected norm as $\mathrm{proj}(\mathbf{a}, \mathbf{b}, \mathbf{c}) = \frac{(\mathbf{c}-\mathbf{a})^\top (\mathbf{b}-\mathbf{a})}{\|(\mathbf{b}-\mathbf{a})\|}$. The meaning of proj is the norm of $\mathbf{c} - \mathbf{a}$ projected onto the direction of $\mathbf{b} - \mathbf{a}$, using $\mathbf{a}$ as the anchor point. Note that $\mathrm{proj}(\mathbf{a}, \mathbf{b}, \mathbf{c}) \leq \|\mathbf{c} - \mathbf{a}\|$.*

Then, we introduce an assumption on data embeddings. Recall that our detector $\phi = \phi_{\mathrm{enc}} \circ \phi_{\mathrm{dec}}$ contains an encoder function $\phi_{\mathrm{enc}} \in \mathbb{R}^m \rightarrow \mathbb{R}^l$. Let $\mathcal{Z}_{\mathrm{trn}}$ and $\mathcal{Z}_{\mathrm{test}}$ be sets of embeddings for training and test samples, respectively, such that $\mathcal{Z}_{\mathrm{trn}} = \{\phi_{\mathrm{enc}}(\mathbf{x}) \mid \mathbf{x} \in \mathcal{D}_{\mathrm{trn}}\}$ and $\mathcal{Z}_{\mathrm{test}} = \{\phi_{\mathrm{enc}}(\mathbf{x}) \mid \mathbf{x} \in \mathcal{D}_{\mathrm{test}}\}$. Let $\mathcal{Z}_{\mathrm{test}}^{(n)}$ and $\mathcal{Z}_{\mathrm{test}}^{(a)}$ be the normal and anomalous data in $\mathcal{Z}_{\mathrm{test}}$, respectively. We also define $\mathcal{Z}_{\mathrm{aug}} = \{\phi_{\mathrm{enc}}(f_{\mathrm{aug}}(\mathbf{x})) \mid \mathbf{x} \in \mathcal{D}_{\mathrm{trn}}\}$ as a set of augmented embeddings.

Assumption 1. *By convention, we assume that training normal and test normal data are generated from the same underlying distribution. Let $d(\mathcal{Z}_{\mathrm{trn}}, \mathcal{Z}_{\mathrm{trn}}) = \sigma$. Then, $d(\mathcal{Z}_{\mathrm{test}}^{(n)}, \mathcal{Z}_{\mathrm{test}}^{(n)}) = \sigma$ and $d(\mathcal{Z}_{\mathrm{trn}}, \mathcal{Z}_{\mathrm{test}}^{(n)}) = \sigma + \epsilon$, where $\epsilon < \sigma$.*

3.2   Main Ideas: Discordance and Separability

Let $f_{\mathrm{gen}} \in \mathbb{R}^m \rightarrow \mathbb{R}^m$ be the underlying (unknown) anomaly-generating function in $\mathcal{D}_{\mathrm{test}}$, which transforms a normal data into an anomaly. We aim to find f_{aug} that maximizes the functional similarity between f_{aug} and f_{gen}, which we refer to *alignment* in this work. There are various ways to measure the alignment, but we focus on the embedding space, as it allows us to avoid the high dimensionality of real-world data. We informally define the extent of alignment as follows.

Proposition 1. *Data augmentation function f_{aug} is aligned with the anomaly-generating function f_{gen} if $\mathcal{L}_{\mathrm{ali}} = d(\mathcal{Z}_{\mathrm{aug}}, \mathcal{Z}_{\mathrm{test}}^{(a)})$ is small.*

The problem is $\mathcal{L}_{\mathrm{ali}}$ cannot be computed without test labels. To extract $\mathcal{Z}_{\mathrm{test}}^{(a)}$ from $\mathcal{Z}_{\mathrm{test}}$ is as difficult as solving the anomaly detection problem itself. Then, *how can we approximate $\mathcal{L}_{\mathrm{ali}}$ without test labels?* We propose to decompose the alignment geometrically into *discordance* h_d and *separability* h_s as shown in Fig. 2. For an intuitive illustration, we assume that only one data exists in each set, e.g., $\mathcal{Z}_{\mathrm{trn}} = \{\mathbf{z}_{\mathrm{trn}}\}$. Then, the simplified definitions of h_d and h_s are given as

$$h_d(\mathbf{z}_{\mathrm{trn}}, \mathbf{z}_{\mathrm{aug}}, \mathbf{z}_{\mathrm{test}}^{(a)}) = \frac{d(\mathbf{z}_{\mathrm{trn}}, \mathbf{z}_{\mathrm{test}}^{(a)}) + d(\mathbf{z}_{\mathrm{aug}}, \mathbf{z}_{\mathrm{test}}^{(a)})}{d(\mathbf{z}_{\mathrm{trn}}, \mathbf{z}_{\mathrm{aug}})} - 1 \tag{1}$$

$$h_s(\mathbf{z}_{\mathrm{trn}}, \mathbf{z}_{\mathrm{aug}}, \mathbf{z}_{\mathrm{test}}^{(a)}) = \frac{\mathrm{proj}(\mathbf{z}_{\mathrm{trn}}, \mathbf{z}_{\mathrm{aug}}, \mathbf{z}_{\mathrm{test}}^{(a)})}{d(\mathbf{z}_{\mathrm{trn}}, \mathbf{z}_{\mathrm{aug}})}. \tag{2}$$

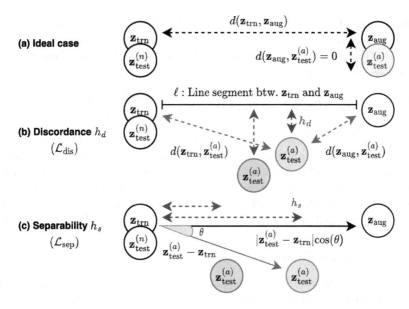

Fig. 2. Simplified illustrations of *discordance* and *separability*. We assume that all sets are of size one, e.g., $\mathcal{Z}_{\mathrm{trn}} = \{\mathbf{z}_{\mathrm{trn}}\}$. Blue is better than red in (b) and (c). To minimize $\mathcal{L}_{\mathrm{ali}} = d(\mathbf{z}_{\mathrm{aug}}, \mathbf{z}_{\mathrm{test}}^{(a)})$ as in (a), we propose the (b) discordance h_d, which is the distance between $\mathbf{z}_{\mathrm{test}}^{(a)}$ and the line segment ℓ, and the (c) separability h_s, which is the distance between $\mathbf{z}_{\mathrm{trn}}$ and $\mathbf{z}_{\mathrm{test}}^{(a)}$ projected onto ℓ. (Color figure online)

In combination, h_d and h_s allow us to minimize $\mathcal{L}_{\mathrm{ali}} = d(\mathbf{z}_{\mathrm{aug}}, \mathbf{z}_{\mathrm{test}}^{(a)})$ without actually computing it. Let $\ell = \mathbf{z}_{\mathrm{trn}} + t(\mathbf{z}_{\mathrm{aug}} - \mathbf{z}_{\mathrm{trn}})$ be a line segment between $\mathbf{z}_{\mathrm{trn}}$ and $\mathbf{z}_{\mathrm{aug}}$, where t ranges over $[0, 1]$. Then, h_d represents a distance between $\mathbf{z}_{\mathrm{test}}^{(a)}$ and ℓ, which is minimized when $\mathbf{z}_{\mathrm{test}}^{(a)}$ is exactly on ℓ. On the other hand, h_s means the distance between $\mathbf{z}_{\mathrm{test}}^{(a)}$ and $\mathbf{z}_{\mathrm{trn}}$ when $\mathbf{z}_{\mathrm{test}}^{(a)}$ is projected onto ℓ. Thus, $\mathcal{L}_{\mathrm{ali}}$ is minimized as zero if $h_d = 0$ and $h_s = 1$.

A difference between h_d and h_s is that h_d becomes a more accurate approximation of $\mathcal{L}_{\mathrm{ali}}$ if $\mathbf{z}_{\mathrm{test}}^{(a)}$ is far from both $\mathbf{z}_{\mathrm{trn}}$ and $\mathbf{z}_{\mathrm{aug}}$. Thus, we consider h_d as a coarse-grained measure, while we bound the range of h_s into $[0, 1]$ and consider it as a fine-grained measure to address the incapability of h_d to locate $\mathbf{z}_{\mathrm{test}}^{(a)}$ on ℓ. Then, h_d is lower the better (alignment), while h_s is higher the better.

The exact definitions of h_d and h_s are direct generalization of Eq. (1) and (2) from vectors to sets. The idea is to compute the average of all possible distances by replacing the vector distance with the set distance in Definition 1:

$$h_d(\mathcal{Z}_{\mathrm{trn}}, \mathcal{Z}_{\mathrm{aug}}, \mathcal{Z}_{\mathrm{test}}^{(a)}) = \frac{d(\mathcal{Z}_{\mathrm{trn}}, \mathcal{Z}_{\mathrm{test}}^{(a)}) + d(\mathcal{Z}_{\mathrm{aug}}, \mathcal{Z}_{\mathrm{test}}^{(a)})}{d(\mathcal{Z}_{\mathrm{trn}}, \mathcal{Z}_{\mathrm{aug}})} - 1 \tag{3}$$

$$h_s(\mathcal{Z}_{\mathrm{trn}}, \mathcal{Z}_{\mathrm{aug}}, \mathcal{Z}_{\mathrm{test}}^{(a)}) = \frac{\sum_{\mathbf{z}_{\mathrm{trn}}, \mathbf{z}_{\mathrm{aug}}, \mathbf{z}_{\mathrm{test}}^{(a)} \in \mathcal{Z}_{\mathrm{trn}}, \mathcal{Z}_{\mathrm{aug}}, \mathcal{Z}_{\mathrm{test}}^{(a)}} \mathrm{proj}(\mathbf{z}_{\mathrm{trn}}, \mathbf{z}_{\mathrm{aug}}, \mathbf{z}_{\mathrm{test}}^{(a)})}{d(\mathcal{Z}_{\mathrm{trn}}, \mathcal{Z}_{\mathrm{aug}})|\mathcal{Z}_{\mathrm{trn}}||\mathcal{Z}_{\mathrm{aug}}||\mathcal{Z}_{\mathrm{test}}^{(a)}|}. \tag{4}$$

Surrogate Losses. Based on our decomposition of the alignment, we propose surrogate losses $\mathcal{L}_{\text{dis}}$ and $\mathcal{L}_{\text{sep}}$ to approximate h_d and h_s, respectively, which have the term $\mathcal{Z}_{\text{test}}^{(a)}$ (unknown at test time) in their definitions. Our final validation loss $\mathcal{L}_{\text{DSV}}$ is given as

$$\mathcal{L}_{\text{DSV}}(\mathcal{Z}_{\text{trn}}, \mathcal{Z}_{\text{aug}}, \mathcal{Z}_{\text{test}}) = \mathcal{L}_{\text{dis}}(\cdot) - \frac{\max(\mathcal{L}_{\text{sep}}(\cdot), 1/2)}{\mathcal{L}_{\text{dis}}(\cdot)}, \tag{5}$$

where $\mathcal{Z}_{\text{trn}}$, $\mathcal{Z}_{\text{aug}}$, and $\mathcal{Z}_{\text{test}}$ are inputs also to the right-hand side terms. The minus sign is used since higher $\mathcal{L}_{\text{sep}}$ means better alignment until it reaches the optimum, which is $1/2$ in $\mathcal{L}_{\text{sep}}$, while it is 1 for h_s. We divide $\mathcal{L}_{\text{sep}}$ by $\mathcal{L}_{\text{dis}}$, since we want $\mathcal{L}_{\text{sep}}$ to have an effect especially when $\mathcal{L}_{\text{sep}}$ is small. Then, we use $\mathcal{L}_{\text{DSV}}$ to perform unsupervised model selection by choosing the hyperparameters of f_{aug} that yields the smallest $\mathcal{L}_{\text{DSV}}$, which indicates the model with best alignment.

3.3   Discordance Surrogate Loss

We now describe how our surrogate losses $\mathcal{L}_{\text{dis}}$ and $\mathcal{L}_{\text{sep}}$ effectively approximate the discordance h_d and separability h_s, respectively. $\mathcal{L}_{\text{dis}}$ is defined as

$$\mathcal{L}_{\text{dis}}(\mathcal{Z}_{\text{trn}}, \mathcal{Z}_{\text{aug}}, \mathcal{Z}_{\text{test}}) = \frac{d(\mathcal{Z}_{\text{trn}} \cup \mathcal{Z}_{\text{aug}}, \mathcal{Z}_{\text{test}})}{d(\mathcal{Z}_{\text{trn}}, \mathcal{Z}_{\text{aug}})}. \tag{6}$$

The idea is that $d(\mathcal{Z}_{\text{trn}} \cup \mathcal{Z}_{\text{aug}}, \mathcal{Z}_{\text{test}})$ can approximate h_d based on the triangle inequality. To show the exact relation between $\mathcal{L}_{\text{dis}}$ and h_d, we first derive the lower and upper bounds of $\mathcal{L}_{\text{dis}}$ with respect to h_d in Lemma 1. Then, we show in Corollary 1 that $\mathcal{L}_{\text{dis}}$ is represented as a linear function of h_d if some constraints are met, which makes $\mathcal{L}_{\text{dis}}$ an effective approximation of h_d.

Lemma 1. *If* $|\mathcal{Z}_{\text{trn}}| = |\mathcal{Z}_{\text{aug}}|$, *then the lower and upper bounds of* $\mathcal{L}_{\text{dis}}$ *are given as functions of* h_d *and* $d(\mathcal{Z}_{\text{trn}}, \mathcal{Z}_{\text{aug}})$:

$$c_2 h_d + c_2 + c_3 \le \mathcal{L}_{\text{dis}}(\cdot) \le c_2 h_d + c_2 + c_3 + \frac{(c_1 + c_3)(\sigma + \epsilon)}{d(\mathcal{Z}_{\text{trn}}, \mathcal{Z}_{\text{aug}})},$$

where $c_i = \hat{c}_i / \sum_{k=1}^{4} \hat{c}_k$ *are data size-based constants such that* $\hat{c}_1 = |\mathcal{Z}_{\text{trn}}| \cdot |\mathcal{Z}_{\text{test}}^{(n)}|$, $\hat{c}_2 = |\mathcal{Z}_{\text{trn}}| \cdot |\mathcal{Z}_{\text{test}}^{(a)}|$, $\hat{c}_3 = |\mathcal{Z}_{\text{aug}}| \cdot |\mathcal{Z}_{\text{test}}^{(n)}|$, *and* $\hat{c}_4 = |\mathcal{Z}_{\text{aug}}| \cdot |\mathcal{Z}_{\text{test}}^{(a)}|$.

Proof. The proof is in Appendix A.1.   □

Corollary 1. *If* $|\mathcal{Z}_{\text{trn}}| = |\mathcal{Z}_{\text{aug}}|$, $\sigma \ll d(\mathcal{Z}_{\text{trn}}, \mathcal{Z}_{\text{aug}})$, *and* $\epsilon \ll d(\mathcal{Z}_{\text{trn}}, \mathcal{Z}_{\text{aug}})$, *then* $\mathcal{L}_{\text{dis}}$ *is a linear function of* h_d: $\mathcal{L}_{\text{dis}}(\mathcal{Z}_{\text{trn}}, \mathcal{Z}_{\text{aug}}, \mathcal{Z}_{\text{test}}) \approx c_2 h_d + c_2 + c_3$.

3.4   Separability Surrogate Loss

The separability surrogate loss $\mathcal{L}_{\text{sep}}$ for approximating h_s is defined as follows:

$$\mathcal{L}_{\text{sep}}(\cdot) = \frac{\text{std}(\{\text{proj}(\mu_{\text{trn}}, \mathbf{z}_{\text{aug}}, \mathbf{z}_{\text{test}}) \mid \mathbf{z}_{\text{aug}}, \mathbf{z}_{\text{test}} \in \mathcal{Z}_{\text{aug}}, \mathcal{Z}_{\text{test}}\})}{d(\mathcal{Z}_{\text{trn}}, \mathcal{Z}_{\text{aug}})}, \tag{7}$$

Table 1. Average AUC (top) and rank (bottom) across 21 different tasks in the two datasets. The best is in bold, and the second best is underlined. Our DSV achieves the best in six, and the second-best in two out of the 8 cases.

f_{aug}	Avg.	Rand.	Base	MMD	STD	MC	SEL	HITS	DSV
CutOut	0.739	<u>0.776</u>	0.741	0.735	0.739	0.749	0.727	0.757	**0.813**
CutAvg	0.739	**0.817**	0.721	0.692	0.745	0.751	0.744	0.742	<u>0.806</u>
CutDiff	0.743	0.711	0.739	0.730	0.744	0.747	0.741	<u>0.777</u>	**0.811**
CutPaste	0.788	0.841	0.694	0.756	0.818	<u>0.862</u>	0.830	0.850	**0.884**
f_{aug}	Avg	Rand	Base	MMD	STD	MC	SEL	HITS	DSV
CutOut	7.33	6.10	6.62	6.93	6.29	6.50	7.10	<u>5.43</u>	**3.79**
CutAvg	7.00	<u>5.02</u>	7.64	8.36	5.52	5.48	5.98	5.60	**4.19**
CutDiff	6.43	7.24	6.45	7.38	6.00	<u>5.64</u>	6.24	6.21	**3.60**
CutPaste	7.67	6.29	8.67	7.21	5.60	**4.33**	5.17	4.64	<u>4.57</u>

where $\text{std}(\mathcal{A}) = \sqrt{|\mathcal{A}|^{-1}\sum_{a\in\mathcal{A}}(a - \text{mean}(\mathcal{A}))}$ is the standard variation of a set, and μ_{trn} is the mean vector of $\mathcal{Z}_{\text{trn}}$. One notable difference from Eq. (4) is that only the mean μ_{trn} is used in the numerator, instead of whole $\mathcal{Z}_{\text{trn}}$, based on the observation that $\mathcal{Z}_{\text{trn}}$ is usually densely clustered as a result of training.

Intuitively, $\mathcal{L}_{\text{sep}}$ measures how much $\mathcal{Z}_{\text{test}}$ is scattered along the direction of $\mathbf{z}_{\text{aug}} - \mu_{\text{trn}}$. The amount of scatteredness is directly related to the value of h_s, since we assume by convention that $\mathcal{Z}_{\text{test}}^{(n)}$ is close to $\mathcal{Z}_{\text{trn}}$. In Lemma 2, we show that $\mathcal{L}_{\text{sep}}$ is a linear function of h_s if some constraints are met, and its optimum is $1/2$ in the ideal case, which corresponds to $h_s = 1$, if $\bar{\sigma}_{\text{test}} \ll \|\mathbf{z}_{\text{aug}} - \mathbf{z}_{\text{trn}}\|$.

Lemma 2. *We assume that $\mathcal{Z}_{\text{trn}} = \{\mathbf{z}_{\text{trn}}\}$, $\mathcal{Z}_{\text{aug}} = \{\mathbf{z}_{\text{aug}}\}$, and $\mathbf{z}_{\text{test}}^{(n)} = \mathbf{z}_{\text{trn}}$ for all $\mathbf{z}_{\text{test}}^{(n)} \in \mathcal{Z}_{\text{test}}^{(n)}$. Let $\gamma = |\mathcal{Z}_{\text{test}}^{(a)}|/|\mathcal{Z}_{\text{test}}|$, and $\bar{\sigma}_{\text{test}}$ be the standard deviation of the projected norms $\mathcal{Z}_{\text{test}}^{(p)} = \{\text{proj}(\mathbf{z}_{\text{trn}}, \mathbf{z}_{\text{aug}}, \mathbf{z}) \mid \mathbf{z} \in \mathcal{Z}_{\text{test}}^{(a)}\}$. Then, the separability surrogate loss $\mathcal{L}_{\text{sep}}$ is rewritten as a function of h_s as follows:*

$$\mathcal{L}_{\text{sep}}(\mathcal{Z}_{\text{trn}}, \mathcal{Z}_{\text{aug}}, \mathcal{Z}_{\text{test}}) = \sqrt{\gamma(1-\gamma)}h_s + \frac{\sqrt{\gamma}\bar{\sigma}_{\text{test}}}{\|\mathbf{z}_{\text{aug}} - \mathbf{z}_{\text{trn}}\|}.$$

Proof. The proof is in Appendix A.2. □

4   Experiments

We answer the following questions through experiments on real datasets:

Q1. **Performance.** Are the models selected by DSV better than those selected by baseline measures for unsupervised model selection? Is the improvement statistically significant across different tasks and datasets?

Q2. **Ablation study.** Are the two main components of DSV for the discordance and separability, respectively, meaningful to performance? How do they complement each other across different augmentation functions and tasks?

Q3. **Case studies.** How does DSV work on individual cases with respect to the distribution of embedding vectors or anomaly scores?

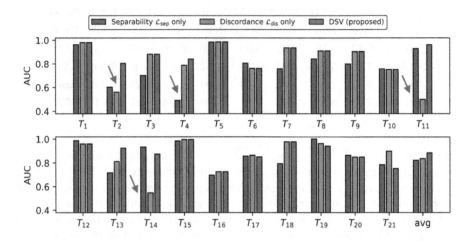

Fig. 3. Ablation study to compare $\mathcal{L}_{\mathrm{dis}}$, $\mathcal{L}_{\mathrm{sep}}$, and $\mathcal{L}_{\mathrm{DSV}}$ on 21 different tasks and on average when $f_{\mathrm{aug}} = \mathrm{CutPaste}$. DSV shows a dramatic improvement in a few cases, such as tasks T_2 (both fail), T_4 ($\mathcal{L}_{\mathrm{sep}}$ fails), T_{11} and T_{14} ($\mathcal{L}_{\mathrm{dis}}$ fails).

4.1 Experimental Settings

Datasets. We include two datasets for anomaly detection in natural images: MVTec AD [3] and MPDD [10], which contain 21 different tasks in total. MVTec AD mimics real-world industrial inspection scenarios and contains 15 different tasks: five unique textures and ten unique objects from different domains. MPDD focuses on defect detection during painted metal parts fabrication and contains 6 different object types with a non-homogeneous background. The evaluation is done by AUC (the area under the ROC curve) scores on test data.

Detector Models. We use a classifier-based anomaly detector model used in a previous work [13], which first learns data embeddings and then computes anomaly scores on the space. The model structure is based on ResNet18 [9]. All model hyperparameters are set to the default setting, except for the number of training updates, which we changed for MPDD since the model converged much faster due to the smaller data size; we set the number of updates to 10,000 in MVTec AD, while to 1,000 in MPDD.

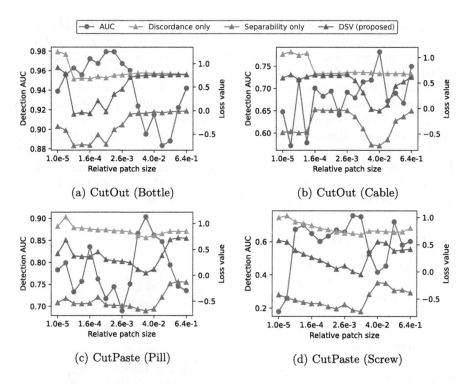

Fig. 4. The AUC and loss values $\mathcal{L}_{\mathrm{dis}}$, $\mathcal{L}_{\mathrm{sep}}$, and $\mathcal{L}_{\mathrm{DSV}}$ with CutOut or CutPaste as f_{aug}. We preprocessed $\mathcal{L}_{\mathrm{sep}}$ so that it can be directly added to $\mathcal{L}_{\mathrm{dis}}$ for creating $\mathcal{L}_{\mathrm{DSV}}$. We have two main observations from the figures. First, $\mathcal{L}_{\mathrm{DSV}}$ is negatively correlated with the actual AUC. Second, $\mathcal{L}_{\mathrm{sep}}$ and $\mathcal{L}_{\mathrm{dis}}$ work in a complementary way, which is shown especially well on (a) and (b).

Augmentation Functions. We use four different augmentation functions in experiments: CutOut [5], CutAvg, CutDiff, and CutPaste [13]. CutOut replaces a random patch from an image with black pixels. CutAvg is similar to CutOut, but it replaces a patch with the average color of the patch, instead of the black. CutDiff is a smooth version of CutOut, and it makes a smooth boundary when selecting a patch. The resulting image has the black at the center of the original position of the patch, and it becomes brighter as it goes close to the boundary. CutPaste copies a patch and pastes it into a random location of the image.

We use the patch size as the target augmentation hyperparameter to search for all these functions, since it directly controls the amount of modification by f_{aug}. We consider 17 settings in the range from 10^{-5} to 0.64 in the log scale. For example, 0.1 represents we select a patch whose size is 10% of the image.

Baselines. We compare our DSV with eight baseline methods for unsupervised model selection. *Average* is the simplest one, which is to take the average performance of all settings we consider. *Random* means we change the hyperparameter for each inference during training and test. *Base* is to use the distance

$\mathcal{L}_{\text{dis}}(\mathcal{Z}_{\text{trn}}, \mathcal{Z}_{\text{aug}}, \mathcal{Z}_{\text{test}})$ as the simplest approximation of $\mathcal{L}_{\text{ali}}$. *MMD* replaces the distance function in Base with the maximum mean discrepancy [21]. *STD* measures standard deviation of the all-pair distances between $\mathcal{Z}_{\text{trn}}$ and $\mathcal{Z}_{\text{test}}$.

MC, SEL, and HITS were proposed in a previous work [15] for unsupervised outlier model selection (see §2.3). They are top-performing baselines based on internal performance measures. MC [14,15] combines different models based on outlier score similarities, assuming that good models have similar outputs as the optimal model, and thus are close to each other. HITS uses the HITS algorithm originally designed for web graphs [11] to compute the importance of each model. SELECT (SEL in short) originates from model ensembles [18,28], and calculates the similarity between the output of each model and the "pseudo ground truth" which is initialized to the average of all candidate models.

4.2   Detection Performance (Q1)

Table 1 shows the average AUC and rank of various methods on 21 different tasks. Due to the lack of space, we include the full results on individual tasks in the supplementary material. DSV shows the best performance on 6 out of the 8 cases, and the second-best on the remaining two cases. MC and HITS perform well compared to the other baselines, but their performances are not consistent across different augmentation functions and tasks.

In Fig. 5, we perform the Wilcoxon signed rank test [8] to check if the differences between models are statistically significant. Each number in the (i, j)-th cell represents the p-value comparing models i and j, and it represents model i is significantly better than model j if

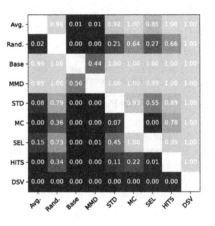

Fig. 5. Wilcoxon signed rank test for all pairs of approaches. DSV is superior to all other approaches with p-values smaller than 0.001.

the p-value is smaller than 0.05. DSV is significantly better than all of the other approaches in the figure, demonstrating its superiority in unsupervised model selection.

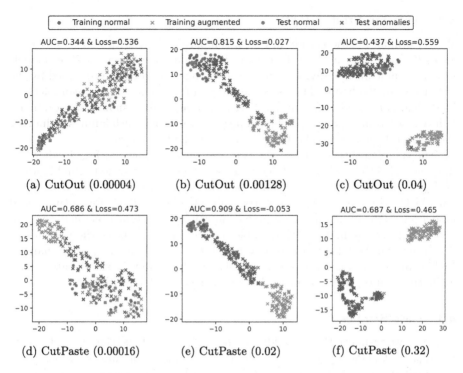

Fig. 6. t-SNE visualizations of embeddings in (top) $f_{\text{aug}} = $ CutOut and (bottom) $f_{\text{aug}} = $ CutPaste, where values in parentheses represent different HPs. $\mathcal{L}_{\text{DSV}}$ is the smallest in (b) and (e), where the anomalies are in between $\mathcal{Z}_{\text{trn}}$ and $\mathcal{Z}_{\text{aug}}$. Detection fails in (a), (c) & (d), (f), showing larger $\mathcal{L}_{\text{DSV}}$ than in (b) & (e), resp.

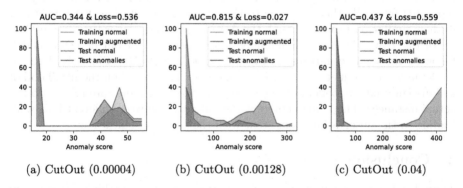

Fig. 7. Anomaly scores for the three different HPs of $f_{\text{aug}} = $ CutOut in Fig. 6. The distributions of embeddings are clearly observed also in the scores: (a) No separation in test data, (b) reasonable separation with as high AUC as 0.815, and (c) drastic separation between augmented points and all other sets.

4.3 Ablation Studies (Q2)

We perform an ablation study in Fig. 3, comparing $\mathcal{L}_{\text{DSV}}$ with its two surrogate losses $\mathcal{L}_{\text{dis}}$ and $\mathcal{L}_{\text{sep}}$ on $f_{\text{aug}} = \text{CutPaste}$. The difference between the three models is more significant in individual cases, rather than on average, as denoted by the red arrows in the figure. This is because each of $\mathcal{L}_{\text{dis}}$ and $\mathcal{L}_{\text{sep}}$ is incomplete by its design. For example, h_d surpasses h_s on average, but it shows some dramatic failure cases as in T_{11} and T_{14}. Our proposed $\mathcal{L}_{\text{DSV}}$ avoids such failures, achieving the best performance by effectively combining the two terms.

The complementary roles of the two losses is also shown in Fig. 4, where we draw actual AUC and three different losses together for various combinations of f_{aug} and tasks. Overall, the value of $\mathcal{L}_{\text{DSV}}$ is negatively correlated with the true AUC, which is exactly the purpose of introducing $\mathcal{L}_{\text{DSV}}$ for unsupervised model selection. In detail, we observe complementary interactions between $\mathcal{L}_{\text{dis}}$ and $\mathcal{L}_{\text{sep}}$ from the figures; for example, in Fig. 4a, $\mathcal{L}_{\text{sep}}$ makes the overall loss decrease when AUC peaks the top, although $\mathcal{L}_{\text{dis}}$ makes only negligible changes. In Fig. 4b, in contrast, the two losses change drastically in small patch sizes, while their sums remain similar, allowing us to avoid HPs with low AUC.

4.4 Case Studies (Q3)

In Fig. 6, we visualize the embeddings when $f_{\text{aug}} = \text{CutOut}$ (the task is Carpet) and $f_{\text{aug}} = \text{CutPaste}$ (the task is Metal Nut). In Figs. 6b and 6e, which show the smallest $\mathcal{L}_{\text{DSV}}$, test anomalies $\mathcal{Z}_{\text{test}}^{(a)}$ are scattered in between $\mathcal{Z}_{\text{trn}}$ and $\mathcal{Z}_{\text{aug}}$. Although some of $\mathcal{Z}_{\text{test}}^{(a)}$ are mixed with $\mathcal{Z}_{\text{test}}^{(n)}$ in Fig. 6b, the AUC is as high as 0.815. On the other hand, in Figs. 6a and 6c, the AUC is lower than even 0.5, while $\mathcal{L}_{\text{DSV}}$ is large. In Fig. 6a, $\mathcal{Z}_{\text{test}}^{(n)}$ and $\mathcal{Z}_{\text{test}}^{(a)}$ are mixed completely, since the amount of modification through augmentation is too small. In Fig. 6c, $\mathcal{Z}_{\text{aug}}$ are separated from all other sets, due to the drastic augmentation. Figures 6d and 6f show similar patterns, although the AUC is generally higher than in CutOut.

In Fig. 7, we visualize the anomaly scores generated by our detector model, following the same scenarios as in Fig. 6 when $f_{\text{aug}} = \text{CutOut}$. Since the detector model in our experiments computes an anomaly score based on the likelihood of a Gaussian mixture model in the embedding space, the scores are related to the actual distances. The scores represent the difference between different HPs well, leading to the observations consistent with the t-SNE visualization.

5 Conclusion

There has been a recent surge of self-supervised learning methods for anomaly detection (SSAD), but how to systematically choose the augmentation hyperparameters here remains vastly understudied. To address this, we introduce DSV, an unsupervised validation loss for selecting optimal SSAD models with effective augmentation hyperparameters. The main idea is to maximize the alignment between augmentation and unknown anomalies with surrogate losses that estimate the discordance and separability of test data. Our experiments demonstrate that DSV outperforms a broad range of baselines. Future work involves extending it to incorporate other distance measures such as the Chebyshev distance.

Acknowledgments. This work is partially sponsored by PwC Risk and Regulatory Services Innovation Center at Carnegie Mellon University. Any conclusions expressed in this material are those of the author and do not necessarily reflect the views, expressed or implied, of the funding parties.

A   Proofs of Lemmas

A.1   Proof of Lemma 1

Proof. Let $\hat{\sigma} = \sigma + \epsilon$. We rewrite the numerator of $\mathcal{L}_{\mathrm{dis}}$ based on the definition of h and Assumption 1.

$$d(\mathcal{Z}_{\mathrm{trn}} \cup \mathcal{Z}_{\mathrm{aug}}, \mathcal{Z}_{\mathrm{test}}) = c_1\hat{\sigma} + c_2((1+h)d(\mathcal{Z}_{\mathrm{trn}}, \mathcal{Z}_{\mathrm{aug}}) - d(\mathcal{Z}_{\mathrm{aug}}, \mathcal{Z}_{\mathrm{test}}^{(a)}))$$
$$+ c_3 d(\mathcal{Z}_{\mathrm{aug}}, \mathcal{Z}_{\mathrm{test}}^{(n)}) + c_4 d(\mathcal{Z}_{\mathrm{aug}}, \mathcal{Z}_{\mathrm{test}}^{(a)})$$

Then, we derive the lower bound as follows:

$$d(\mathcal{Z}_{\mathrm{trn}} \cup \mathcal{Z}_{\mathrm{aug}}, \mathcal{Z}_{\mathrm{test}})$$
$$\geq c_2((1+h)d(\mathcal{Z}_{\mathrm{trn}}, \mathcal{Z}_{\mathrm{aug}}) - d(\mathcal{Z}_{\mathrm{aug}}, \mathcal{Z}_{\mathrm{test}}^{(a)}))$$
$$+ c_3 d(\mathcal{Z}_{\mathrm{trn}}, \mathcal{Z}_{\mathrm{aug}}) + c_4 d(\mathcal{Z}_{\mathrm{aug}}, \mathcal{Z}_{\mathrm{test}}^{(a)}) + (c_1 - c_3)\hat{\sigma}$$
$$= (c_4 - c_2)d(\mathcal{Z}_{\mathrm{aug}}, \mathcal{Z}_{\mathrm{test}}^{(a)}) + (c_2 + c_2 h + c_3)d(\mathcal{Z}_{\mathrm{trn}}, \mathcal{Z}_{\mathrm{aug}}) + (c_1 - c_3)\hat{\sigma}$$

Similarly, the upper bound is given as follows:

$$d(\mathcal{Z}_{\mathrm{trn}} \cup \mathcal{Z}_{\mathrm{aug}}, \mathcal{Z}_{\mathrm{test}})$$
$$\leq c_2((1+h)d(\mathcal{Z}_{\mathrm{trn}}, \mathcal{Z}_{\mathrm{aug}}) - d(\mathcal{Z}_{\mathrm{aug}}, \mathcal{Z}_{\mathrm{test}}^{(a)}))$$
$$+ c_3 d(\mathcal{Z}_{\mathrm{trn}}, \mathcal{Z}_{\mathrm{aug}}) + c_4 d(\mathcal{Z}_{\mathrm{aug}}, \mathcal{Z}_{\mathrm{test}}^{(a)}) + (c_1 + c_3)\hat{\sigma}$$
$$= (c_4 - c_2)d(\mathcal{Z}_{\mathrm{aug}}, \mathcal{Z}_{\mathrm{test}}^{(a)}) + (c_2 + c_2 h + c_3)d(\mathcal{Z}_{\mathrm{trn}}, \mathcal{Z}_{\mathrm{aug}}) + (c_1 + c_3)\hat{\sigma}$$

If we apply the assumption $|\mathcal{Z}_{\mathrm{trn}}| = |\mathcal{Z}_{\mathrm{aug}}|$, which results in $c_2 = c_4$, the first term from both bounds disappears. We get the inequalities in the lemma by dividing both bounds by $d(\mathcal{Z}_{\mathrm{trn}}, \mathcal{Z}_{\mathrm{aug}})$. $\qquad\square$

A.2   Proof of Lemma 2

Proof. Let $\mu_{\mathrm{test}} = \mathrm{mean}(\{\mathrm{proj}(\mathbf{z}_{\mathrm{trn}}, \mathbf{z}_{\mathrm{aug}}, \mathbf{z}) \mid \mathbf{z} \in \mathcal{Z}_{\mathrm{test}}^{(a)}\})$ be the average of projected norms. We first rewrite h_s as follows:

$$h_s = \frac{\sum_{\mathbf{z}_{\mathrm{trn}}, \mathbf{z}_{\mathrm{aug}}, \mathbf{z}_{\mathrm{test}}^{(a)} \in \mathcal{Z}_{\mathrm{trn}}, \mathcal{Z}_{\mathrm{aug}}, \mathcal{Z}_{\mathrm{test}}^{(a)}} \mathrm{proj}(\mathbf{z}_{\mathrm{trn}}, \mathbf{z}_{\mathrm{aug}}, \mathbf{z}_{\mathrm{test}}^{(a)})}{d(\mathcal{Z}_{\mathrm{trn}}, \mathcal{Z}_{\mathrm{aug}})|\mathcal{Z}_{\mathrm{trn}}||\mathcal{Z}_{\mathrm{aug}}||\mathcal{Z}_{\mathrm{test}}^{(a)}|}$$
$$= \frac{\sum_{\mathbf{z}_{\mathrm{test}}^{(a)} \in \mathcal{Z}_{\mathrm{test}}^{(a)}} \mathrm{proj}(\mathbf{z}_{\mathrm{trn}}, \mathbf{z}_{\mathrm{aug}}, \mathbf{z}_{\mathrm{test}}^{(a)})}{\|\mathbf{z}_{\mathrm{aug}} - \mathbf{z}_{\mathrm{trn}}\| |\mathcal{Z}_{\mathrm{test}}^{(a)}|}$$
$$= \frac{|\mathcal{Z}_{\mathrm{test}}^{(a)}|\mu_{\mathrm{test}}}{\|\mathbf{z}_{\mathrm{aug}} - \mathbf{z}_{\mathrm{trn}}\| |\mathcal{Z}_{\mathrm{test}}^{(a)}|} = \frac{\mu_{\mathrm{test}}}{\|\mathbf{z}_{\mathrm{aug}} - \mathbf{z}_{\mathrm{trn}}\|}$$

We rewrite the *squared* numerator of $\mathcal{L}_{\text{sep}}$:

$$
\text{std}^2(\{\text{proj}(\mu_{\text{trn}}, \mathbf{z}_{\text{aug}}, \mathbf{z}_{\text{test}}) \mid \mathbf{z}_{\text{aug}}, \mathbf{z}_{\text{test}} \in \mathcal{Z}_{\text{aug}}, \mathcal{Z}_{\text{test}}\})
$$
$$
= \text{std}^2(\{\text{proj}(\mu_{\text{trn}}, \mathbf{z}_{\text{aug}}, \mathbf{z}_{\text{test}}) \mid \mathbf{z}_{\text{test}} \in \mathcal{Z}_{\text{test}}\})
$$
$$
= \frac{1}{|\mathcal{Z}_{\text{test}}|} \sum_{\mathbf{z}_{\text{test}}} (\text{proj}(\mu_{\text{trn}}, \mathbf{z}_{\text{aug}}, \mathbf{z}_{\text{test}}) - \gamma\mu_{\text{test}})^2
$$
$$
= \frac{1}{|\mathcal{Z}_{\text{test}}|} \left(|\mathcal{Z}_{\text{test}}^{(n)}| \gamma^2 \mu_{\text{test}}^2 + |\mathcal{Z}_{\text{test}}^{(a)}| (\bar{\sigma}_{\text{test}}^2 + (1-\gamma)^2 \mu_{\text{test}}^2) \right)
$$
$$
= (1-\gamma)\gamma^2\mu_{\text{test}}^2 + \gamma(\bar{\sigma}_{\text{test}}^2 + (1-\gamma)^2\mu_{\text{test}}^2)
$$
$$
= \gamma(1-\gamma)\mu_{\text{test}}^2 + \gamma\bar{\sigma}_{\text{test}}^2.
$$

Then, $\mathcal{L}_{\text{sep}}$ is rewritten as follows:

$$
\mathcal{L}_{\text{sep}} = \frac{\sqrt{\gamma(1-\gamma)\mu_{\text{test}}^2 + \gamma\bar{\sigma}_{\text{test}}^2}}{d(\mathcal{Z}_{\text{trn}}, \mathcal{Z}_{\text{aug}})} = \sqrt{\gamma(1-\gamma)}h_s + \frac{\sqrt{\gamma}\bar{\sigma}_{\text{test}}}{\|\mathbf{z}_{\text{aug}} - \mathbf{z}_{\text{trn}}\|},
$$

which is the equation in the lemma. □

References

1. Baevski, A., Hsu, W.N., Xu, Q., Babu, A., Gu, J., Auli, M.: Data2vec: a general framework for self-supervised learning in speech, vision and language. In: International Conference on Machine Learning, pp. 1298–1312. PMLR (2022)
2. Bergman, L., Hoshen, Y.: Classification-based anomaly detection for general data. In: ICLR (2020)
3. Bergmann, P., Fauser, M., Sattlegger, D., Steger, C.: Mvtec AD - A comprehensive real-world dataset for unsupervised anomaly detection. In: CVPR (2019)
4. Chen, X., Xie, S., He, K.: An empirical study of training self-supervised vision transformers. In: ICCV (2021)
5. Devries, T., Taylor, G.W.: Improved regularization of convolutional neural networks with cutout. CoRR abs/1708.04552 (2017)
6. Elnaggar, A.: Prottrans: toward understanding the language of life through self-supervised learning. IEEE Trans. Pattern Anal. Mach. Intell. **44**(10), 7112–7127 (2021)
7. Golan, I., El-Yaniv, R.: Deep anomaly detection using geometric transformations. In: NeurIPS (2018)
8. Groggel, D.J.: Practical nonparametric statistics. Technometrics **42**(3), 317–318 (2000)
9. He, K., Zhang, X., Ren, S., Sun, J.: Deep residual learning for image recognition. In: CVPR (2016)
10. Jezek, S., Jonak, M., Burget, R., Dvorak, P., Skotak, M.: Deep learning-based defect detection of metal parts: evaluating current methods in complex conditions. In: ICUMT (2021)
11. Kleinberg, J.M.: Authoritative sources in a hyperlinked environment. J. ACM **46**(5), 604–632 (1999)
12. Kolesnikov, A., Zhai, X., Beyer, L.: Revisiting self-supervised visual representation learning. In: CVPR (2019)

13. Li, C., Sohn, K., Yoon, J., Pfister, T.: Cutpaste: Self-supervised learning for anomaly detection and localization. In: CVPR (2021)
14. Lin, Z., Thekumparampil, K.K., Fanti, G., Oh, S.: InfoGAN-CR and modelcentrality: Self-supervised model training and selection for disentangling GANs. In: ICML (2020)
15. Ma, M.Q., Zhao, Y., Zhang, X., Akoglu, L.: The need for unsupervised outlier model selection: a review and evaluation of internal evaluation strategies. ACM SIGKDD Explor. Newslett. **25**(1) (2023)
16. MacKay, M., Vicol, P., Lorraine, J., Duvenaud, D., Grosse, R.: Self-tuning networks: Bilevel optimization of hyperparameters using structured best-response functions. arXiv preprint arXiv:1903.03088 (2019)
17. Qiu, C., Pfrommer, T., Kloft, M., Mandt, S., Rudolph, M.: Neural transformation learning for deep anomaly detection beyond images. In: ICML (2021)
18. Rayana, S., Akoglu, L.: Less is more: Building selective anomaly ensembles. ACM Trans. Knowl. Discov. Data **10**(4), 42:1–42:33 (2016)
19. Sehwag, V., Chiang, M., Mittal, P.: SSD: A unified framework for self-supervised outlier detection. In: ICLR (2021)
20. Shenkar, T., Wolf, L.: Anomaly detection for tabular data with internal contrastive learning. In: ICLR (2022)
21. Smola, A.J., Gretton, A., Borgwardt, K.: Maximum mean discrepancy. In: 13th International Conference, ICONIP, pp. 3–6 (2006)
22. Sohn, K., Li, C., Yoon, J., Jin, M., Pfister, T.: Learning and evaluating representations for deep one-class classification. In: ICLR (2021)
23. Wolpert, D.H., Macready, W.G.: No free lunch theorems for optimization. IEEE Trans. Evol. Comput. **1**(1), 67–82 (1997)
24. Ye, Z., Chen, Y., Zheng, H.: Understanding the effect of bias in deep anomaly detection. In: IJCAI (2021)
25. Yoo, J., Zhao, T., Akoglu, L.: Self-supervision is not magic: Understanding data augmentation in image anomaly detection. arXiv (2022)
26. Zhao, Y., Rossi, R., Akoglu, L.: Automatic unsupervised outlier model selection. Adv. Neural. Inf. Process. Syst. **34**, 4489–4502 (2021)
27. Zhao, Y., Zhang, S., Akoglu, L.: Toward unsupervised outlier model selection. In: ICDM, pp. 773–782. IEEE (2022)
28. Zimek, A., Campello, R.J.G.B., Sander, J.: Ensembles for unsupervised outlier detection: challenges and research questions a position paper. SIGKDD Explor. **15**(1), 11–22 (2013)
29. Zoph, B., Cubuk, E.D., Ghiasi, G., Lin, T.Y., Shlens, J., Le, Q.V.: Learning data augmentation strategies for object detection. In: ECCV (2020)

Marvolo: Programmatic Data Augmentation for Deep Malware Detection

Mike Wong[1], Edward Raff[2(✉)], James Holt[3], and Ravi Netravali[1]

[1] Princeton University, Princeton, NJ, USA
{mikedwong,rnetravali}@cs.princeton.edu
[2] Booz Allen Hamilton, Annapolis Junction, MD, USA
Raff_Edward@bah.com
[3] Laboratory for Physical Sciences, College Park, MD, USA
holt@lps.umd.edu

Abstract. Data acquisition for ML-driven malware detection is challenging. While large commercial datasets exist, they are prohibitively expensive. On the other hand, an entity (e.g., a bank or government), may be targeted with unique malware, but the data samples available will never be sufficient to train a bespoke ML-based detector. While data augmentation has been a key component in improving deep learning models by providing requisite diversity for generalization, it has proven far more challenging for malware detection. The main challenges are that (1) determining the augmentations to make is not straightforward, (2) operations are on binaries rather than source code (which is not available), complicating correctness and understanding, and (3) labeling new files mandates expensive binary reverse engineering. We present MARVOLO for creating realistic, semantics preserving transformations that mimic the code alterations made by malware authors in practice, allowing us to generate augmented data on raw binary files. This also enables MARVOLO to safely propagate labels to newly-generated data. Across several malware datasets and recent ML-based detectors, MARVOLO improves accuracy and AUC by up to 5% and 10% respectively, while boosting efficiency by 79x by avoiding redundant computation.

1 Introduction

Malware detection is a problem with real-world ramifications, and machine learning has been used in building malware detectors for decades which can be trained with large commercial datasets [6,12] of malicious and benign binaries. Unfortunately, detection in the wild continues to fall short of expectations, with attacks regularly occurring [2]. The core issue is cost: large and comprehensive datasets generally require licensing costs that can reach $400 k/year. Thus, it is often impractical to obtain sufficiently general and representative training datasets, and yet, these datasets govern the efficacy of these models. As a result, a victim may only be able to discover 1–50 samples of a malware family [15]. Worse, targeted malware, such as banking and nation-state malware, which are designed for a specific target for which data samples are limited makes detection even more difficult due to the lack of available training samples.

Data augmentation techniques have been proposed to mitigate these issues [14,18], but they face several challenges that limit their utility. The main issue is that augmentation strategies are typically decoupled from the behavior of malware authors in the wild, and instead focus on random alterations to boost dataset heterogeneity. Further, they directly modify feature representations of raw binaries (since source code is unavailable), which further convolute the semantic understanding of the effects of those perturbations. This, in turn, also precludes correctness-preserving labeling of the newly created samples. Lastly, despite the focus on coarse alterations, the programmatic processing of binaries is costly, both resource- and time-wise.

Analysis of malware over the years has revealed that malware authors typically use semantics preserving transformations [1,28] to sidestep malware detectors and deter reverse engineering efforts. Our key insight is that the same observation can be used to enhance the efficacy of malware datasets through data augmentation. We introduce MARVOLO, a data augmentation engine for malware datasets. The key insight underlying MARVOLO is the use of semantics-preserving code transformations inspired by a study of real-world datasets we conducted in Sect. 3 that highlight the nature with which malware authors use code transformations. Building on this, MARVOLO embeds several key ideas. First, we use a 'lifter' to convert the files into a higher level representation, allowing us to perform code transformations on binaries and check for correctness. Second, we embed two complementary optimizations to collectively maximize the utility (i.e., number of realistic and diverse data samples) of the transformations within a time budget. Third, MARVOLO automatically labels newly-generated samples without mandating expensive binary reverse engineering.

We test MARVOLO using the state of the art MalConv2 [22] malware detector and multiple commercially-available large/small-scale datasets, i.e., the large-scale Ember [6] dataset, as well as a small-scale Brazilian dataset [9]. Overall, MARVOLO boosts detection accuracy by up to 5% and AUC by up to 10%, with most wins coming from detecting previously unseen novel families, which are intuitively more difficult to catch. MARVOLO also yields 2.35–3.8% higher accuracy and 8.4–9% higher AUC over prior augmentation approaches, which modify feature representations. Our optimizations provide a 79× speedup in contrast to the naive binary rewriting approach, making our approach tenable for generating large amounts of data samples. Further, we show that MARVOLO also yields accuracy and AUC improvements with non-deep baselines for detection.

We have open sourced MARVOLO at https://github.com/michaeldwong/marvolo. Appendices can be found at https://michaeldwong.github.io/papers/marvolo.pdf.

2   Background and Related Work

Though prior attempts have been made in data augmentation for malware detection, they do not yet perform meaningful data augmentation. In [14,18],

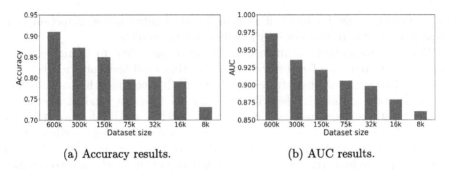

(a) Accuracy results.   (b) AUC results.

Fig. 1. Performance of MalConv2 [22] when training on different subsets of the Ember dataset [6]. All accuracy results were attained using a fixed threshold.

programs are represented as sequences of opcodes and augmentation is performed by replacing one opcode with another without necessarily preserving semantics. Further, [19] augments "images" generated from malware, which are known to be flawed representation [20]. These unrealistic augmentations exacerbate a common problem in malware research that labels are not always accurate [7]. In contrast to these efforts, MARVOLO's contributions lie in (1) a deep-dive analysis of large-scale malware datasets to uncover the usage patterns of semantics-preserving code transformations in malware, and (2) a system that leverages those insights to efficiently grow small datasets into larger ones with improved heterogeneity and realism that aid ML-based malware detection.

There exists a wide array of malware detection approaches with varying trade-offs, ranging in amount of pre-processing done at prediction time from none (fast, less accurate) [4,20] to full dynamic analysis (slow, more accurate) [13]. In this work we are focusing on small and incomprehensive datasets, where there is a need to triage files proactively especially when there is targeted malware. For this reason, signature-based methods are separate tools that capture what is known [25], where we still want a method to triage potential risk that are not known. In these situations it is common to use the probability of a classifier as a ranking for triage [17], meaning we often care about Area Under the Curve (AUC) as it corresponds to the quality of the detector at ranking correctly [21]. Put differently, the probability score from the classifier to rank is important for characterizing and ranking the files by maliciousness so that the most malicious files are identified and quarantined sooner rather than later. The goal of our modeling is thus to be good enough to triage for more expensive analysis (automated or human), as building an accurate detector standalone is not realistic given limited data.

We note that high quality labeled data is extraordinarily difficult to obtain for research purposes. The seminal EMBER [6] and SOREL-20M [12] require a Virus-Total license to obtain the original files, which can cost up to $400k/year. Consequently, groups must resort to far smaller datasets [26]. To show the importance of large datasets, we show the accuracy and AUC degradation of using progressively smaller Ember datasets in 1. To contextualize these results, we note that

Zenpak   **Sivis**

```
inc eax        dec eax        nop                    inc eax
inc ecx        dec ecx        nop                    push edx
inc edx        dec edx        nop                    xor edx, edx
inc ebx        dec ebx        xor eax, eax           pop edx
inc esp        dec esp        inc ebx                inc eax
inc ebp        dec ebp        dec ebx                dec eax
inc esi        dec esi        inc ecx                cmp 0x17b8ef93, eax
inc edi        dec edi        dec ecx                jne 0x407033
```

Fig. 2. Code snippets from two malware families in the Ember dataset that exhibit semantics-preserving code transformations.

the implications of detecting even a single additional malicious binary in the wild can be substantial, and that single-digit accuracy improvements are celebrated by malware analysts. For this reason our work uses only a subset of Ember with only several malware families as well as a Brazilian dataset [9], which will let us test the effectiveness of MARVOLO. This maintains relevance to our target use case as defenders can run honeypots to collect malware targeted at themselves [8]. Further background and related work is provided in Appendix A.

3 Approach

Our results from Sect. 2 highlight the inadequacies of small malware datasets relative to the large (commercial) datasets that have supported high accuracies for ML-driven malware detectors in practical settings. However, given the superior attainability of small datasets, our main goal is to determine whether they can be altered to more closely mimic the properties of their larger counterparts and deliver similar efficacy when used to train malware detectors. To do so, we programmatically analyzed the binaries in the large Ember dataset to identify their defining characteristics. We start with several representative case studies that illustrate our findings, before describing more general takeaways.

Case Study I. Figure 2 shows code snippets from the Zenpak and Sivis malware families.[1] The Zenpak binary uses a code obfuscation technique called junk code insertion [28]. As its name suggests, junk code is comprised of instructions that are executed but do not affect the externalized output(s) of the program. Here, junk code manifests as a series of inc instructions (line 1-8) that each increment a register's value, immediately followed by a series of dec instructions (lines 9-16) that decrement them.

The Sivis binary also uses multiple forms of junk code insertion: (1) the nop instructions (lines 1-3) which do not trigger any computation or data movement, (2) the interleaved inc and dec that sequentially alter the same registers (lines 5-8, 13-14), and (3) lines 10-12 which push the value of edx onto the stack, set the value of edx to 0 using xor, and then pop the old value of edx from the stack and store it back into edx (rendering the xor operation useless). The Sivis

---

[1] x86 assembly code samples are written in Intel syntax.

Binary 1

```
push ebx
push esi
mov esi,DWORD PTR [ebp+0x8]
push edi
mov eax,ds:0x470208
push 0x7
pop ecx
lea edi,DWORD PTR [ebp-0x2c]
```

Binary 2

```
mov eax,ds:0x423e88
push ebx
push esi
mov esi,DWORD PTR [ebp+0x8]
push edi
push 0x7
pop ecx
lea edi,DWORD PTR [ebp-0x28]
```

Fig. 3. Snippets from two binaries in the same "InstallMonster" family that exhibit minor differences due to code obfuscations.

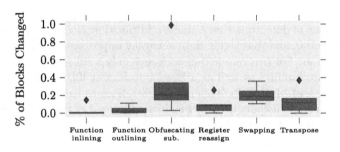

Fig. 4. Percentages of code blocks in Ember's binaries that are affected by different code transformations.

binary embeds another code obfuscation technique called opaque predicates [28], which are (typically) known a priori by a programmer to always evaluate to true or false. This manifests in relation to `eax`. At the start of the snippet, `eax` is definitively set to 0 after the `xor` instruction (line 4). However, at the point of the `cmp` instruction in line 15, the value stored in `eax` is definitively 1 due to the series of `inc` and `dec` operations in the preceding statements. In line 15, since `eax` $\neq$ `0x17b8ef93`, the jump in the following `jne` instruction is always taken.

Case Study II. Figure 3 depicts snippets from two sample binaries from the Ember dataset that belong to the same family. Unsurprisingly, the two code snippets are similar at first glance. However, there exist minor differences due to two code obfuscation techniques that they embed. First, each binary uses a `mov` instruction to write data from the data segment into `eax`. However, the data is located in different memory locations across the two version; the two binaries retrieve the value from `ds:0x470208` and `ds:0x324e88`, respectively. This pattern is also seen in the `lea` instructions where the two binaries use different offsets from the stack base pointer, `ebp`, to retrieve their values. In addition, the two binaries use instruction swapping to reorder instructions (in this case, the `mov` instruction) in a manner that preserves overall semantics.

Takeaways. Our case studies highlight two main points (which we repeatedly observed across the Ember dataset):

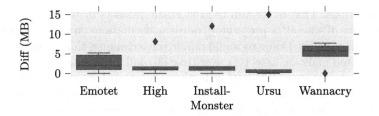

Fig. 5. Pairwise byte diffs between binaries in five representative malware families.

(1) *Semantics-preserving code transformations.* Malware authors routinely alter prior versions of malicious programs using code obfuscation techniques that preserve program behavior. The reason is intuitive: generating malware involves a lot of manual labor and sophisticated code alteration. As malware detectors discern already-deployed malware by recognizing patterns in their code composition or execution regimes (Sect. 2), a far less challenging way for malware authors to continue deploying their malicious code is to perform semantics-preserving code transformations. These transformations alter that code minimally, to preserve its malicious behavior while deviating from the patterns used to detect its predecessor. Unsurprisingly, we did not observe any remnants of semantics-preserving code transformations in the benign samples that we analyzed.

(2) *Combinations of Transformations.* To ensure sufficient differences from detected malware versions, malware authors often resort to performing semantics-preserving transformations, e.g., as in case study II above. This approach is fruitful as such transformations are often (logically) complementary, and the effect of each transformation depends on subtle interactions between the transformation logic and binary code (ranges shown in Fig. 4). Additionally, we find that, to further boost diversity with multiple transformations, each obfuscation is not necessarily applied to all possible blocks in a binary, i.e., some binaries exhibited the effects of an obfuscation in all code blocks that it applied to, while others demonstrated the effects in only a fraction of those blocks.

Taking a step back, these observations lead to two implications about the large datasets that have been successfully used for ML-driven malware detection. First, there exist far fewer families of malicious binaries than malicious binaries themselves; the Ember dataset includes 300 K malicious binary samples spread across only 332 families. There exist many binary versions per family: there are 287 and 13,951 binaries in the median and 99th percentile families, respectively. Second, the binaries within each family can differ quite substantially depending on the specific transformations that are applied across versions. Figure 5 highlights this property, showing that for subsets of five representative families, the constituent binaries exhibit median pairwise percent differences of 38-99% (which equates to raw differences of 0.8–5.4 MB).

Our Approach. The results above motivate a new approach to bolstering the efficacy of the small datasets: data augmentation via semantics-preserving transformations. That is, we aim to grow small datasets by performing different combinations of semantics-preserving code transformations on varying numbers of blocks in the binaries. Doing so would mimic the techniques that malware authors use to sidestep malware detectors over time [3], and yield data similar to that in (proven) large datasets. We employ further code transformations done by optimizing compilers to generate new benign binaries. More importantly, semantics-preserving transformations provide a direct path to accurately labeling newly generated data without manual effort since pre- and post-transformation binaries will exhibit the same behavior (and thus can safely share labels). In Sect. 4, we describe our system, MARVOLO, that realizes this approach in a practical manner.

4   MARVOLO

4.1   Binary Rewriting Overview

Figure 6 illustrates MARVOLO's binary mutation process for performing semantics-preserving transformations on a single (malicious) binary. To begin mutation, MARVOLO decompiles existing PE32 binaries using Ddisasm [11] and internally represents the binary as a series of basic instruction (or code) *blocks*.

To operate on (i.e., mutate) instruction blocks, MARVOLO first disassembles each block. The resulting blocks are then passed into the MARVOLO code transformation engine, which (1) selects a set of

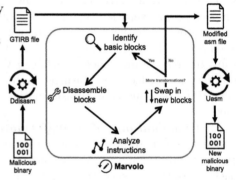

Fig. 6. MARVOLO workflow for mutating a malicious binary.

semantics-preserving code transformations to apply to the binary during a given iteration, (2) analyzes all blocks to determine which blocks each considered transformation is applicable to, (3) selects the fraction of potential blocks to apply each transformation to, and (4) sequentially carries out the transformations on the selected blocks; Sect. 4.2 details this process. After code transformations are complete for a given iteration, MARVOLO then directly swaps out the corresponding (unmodified) blocks with their transformed counterparts and invokes an assembler to get the output binary. This binary is then added to the original dataset and tagged with the same label (i.e., malicious or benign) as the one used during its generation. This end-to-end process repeats multiple times for each binary in the dataset in accordance with a user-specified time or resource budget.

4.2   Code Transformations

MARVOLO currently supports a wide range of different semantics-preserving code transformations that cover the set of mutations we observed in our analysis of the popular Ember dataset (Sect. 3). To ensure that a modified code block is semantically equivalent to the original block, static analysis is performed after the code transformation is applied. This analysis tracks program reads and writes and determines whether the reads from the registers and memory locations in that basic block would still return the same values after the modification. If a violation occurs from the code transformation, it is reverted and a new transformation is attempted. Appendix B provides an overview of the transformations supported.

MARVOLO's goal is to generate new versions of input binaries that differ in diverse ways from their originals while adhering to a user-specified time and/or resource budget (which dictates potential parallelism across mutation iterations). The main challenge is that it is difficult to determine, a priori, how a given transformation will alter a given binary. It depends on subtle interactions between the transformation logic and the binary instructions, which collectively dictate how many blocks are applicable for a transformation, and how many instructions will be modified, added, or deleted. Thus, during each mutation iteration, MARVOLO instead opts to randomly select multiple transformations for each mutation iteration and stochastically order them. This follows from our finding that malware authors typically employ multiple transformations together, and that binaries in the same family can differ by (largely) varying amounts (Sect. 3).

To further bolster variance across the transformed binaries, MARVOLO varies two parameters across the mutation iterations for each input binary. m specifies the number of transformation iterations to perform on each binary, and c governs the fraction of blocks to mutate in each iteration. MARVOLO maintains a running list of parameter values used for a given binary and selects subsequent values to maximize diversity, i.e., maximizing the distance from all previously used values. Note that the overarching time budget takes precedence over per-binary parameter values; to enforce this, MARVOLO round robins through the input binaries, performing one mutation iteration on each one, and circling back to fulfill the selected m per binary only if time permits. In practice, we find that 1–6 mutation iterations for each binary suffices in providing diversity in the amount of code that is perturbed while still being computationally feasible (keeping mutation times within several minutes).

4.3 Optimizations for Practicality

Sources of Inefficiency. Binary mutation of a single executable with MARVOLO can be broken down into 3 stages: (1) invoking Ddisasm on the binary (*decompilation*), (2) carrying out semantics-preserving code transformations (*mutation*), and (3) generating the output binary (*reasssembly*). We profiled the runtime of each stage by passing 3K random binaries from Ember through MARVOLO. As shown in Fig. 7, all three stages consume substantial time: median values for the three stages across binary sizes are 0.6–33, 0.1–585, and 0.1–34 s, respectively. We additionally observed that per-stage delays grow as binary sizes grow and span upwards of 460, 961, and 44 s. Accordingly, aiming to even perform a single mutation iteration on each binary in existing small datasets (which

Algorithm 1. MARVOLO data augmentation

Input: dataset S, number of new binaries k, set of supported transformations T
Output: augmented dataset S^*
$S^* \leftarrow \{\}$
for $i = 1$ **to** k **do**
  $\hat{x} \leftarrow SampleBinary(S)$
  for $j = 1$ **to** m **do**
    $t \leftarrow SelectNextTransformation(T)$
    $\hat{x} \leftarrow t(\hat{x})$
  end for
  $S^* \leftarrow S^* \cup \{\hat{x}\}$
end for
return S^*

---

would not fully bridge the size gap with large datasets) could take up to several thousand hours! The associated resource costs would forego the savings that practitioners reap by not purchasing existing large datasets. Instead, MARVOLO embeds the following two optimizations to boost MARVOLO's utility for a given time budget; we evaluate their effectiveness Sect. 5, and provide more details in Appendix C.

(1) **Code similarity clustering.** A clustering strategy to group binaries based on their compositions. We make the key observation that many binaries within a malware family have equivalent code sections (i.e., the instructions are the same) and differ in other sections of the binary and leverage this insight to cluster binaries together with the same code section. Only a single binary per cluster is operated on, and the resulting code blocks are rapidly (but safely, from a semantics perspective) dropped into the other binaries in the same cluster. This approach circumvents costly operations for all-but-one binary per cluster, while preserving diverse interactions between code alterations and other sections in each binary.

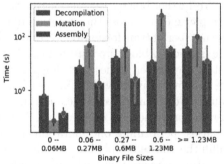

Fig. 7. Breakdown of time spent on each stage in MARVOLO's pipeline (Fig. 6) for (a single run on) binaries in different size groups. Bars list medians, with error bars for 25-75th percentiles.

(2) **Intermediate binary generation.** A technique to increase the number of diverse binaries output from each pass through the pipeline. The main difficulty is that it is difficult to (efficiently) determine, a priori, the effects that a transformation will have on a given binary's code blocks. Thus, MARVOLO opts for a dynamic approach, whereby a lightweight runtime check determines the efficacy of outputting a binary – based on code discrepancies from the original

and previously output versions – after each transformation that is performed in a pipeline pass.

5 Evaluation

5.1 Methodology

We focus on byte-based detectors that require no feature engineering and extraction to deploy. First, such methods are the fastest to run (naturally, they require no feature extractor to run) making them realistic for triage use. Second, manual human effort to understand a file can take days or weeks of work [27] and the needed features will change over time [3]. Byte-based models allow immediate adaption to new content. Thus, we use the state-of-the-art MalConv2 deep malware detector as our primary model [22]. We also include two non-deep approaches based on compression algorithms that are commonly used for malware detection, the Lempel Ziv Jaccard Distance (LZJD) [23] and Burrows Wheeler Markov Distance (BWMD) [24].

Our experiments consider two main datasets: (1) the commercial Ember dataset with 1.1M samples, and (2) the smaller-scale Brazilian malware dataset [9] with 50K samples. Given the realism of Ember observed by researchers and practitioners, we use its test set, which consists of 200K benign and malicious samples, to reflect malware detection scenarios in the wild. For training, we use a subset of the 600K-sample Ember training dataset, as well as the Brazilian dataset; we train a separate MalConv2 model for each case. In contrast to the Ember subsets in Fig. 1, we constrain the number of families to realistically mimic the dataset compositions commonly used in smaller datasets [5,26].

5.2 Overall Accuracy Improvements

For each dataset, we train MalConv2 to convergence. Training involves first collecting (converged) "pre-trained" weights on the original training dataset, and then running an additional training round (5 epochs) with the augmented dataset that MARVOLO generates. For all baselines, we use the default hyperparameters provided. Accuracy is reported as the percentage of correct labels (i.e., benign

Table 1. Accuracy and AUC percentage improvements for opcode sequence augmentation and MARVOLO augmentation

Approach	Accuracy	AUC
Random Insertion	1.09	0.53
Dropout	0.27	0.69
Random Replacement	1.72	−0.10
Synonym Replacement	0.99	−3.90
MARVOLO	**4.07**	**9.06**

or malicious) output by MalConv2. We also measure AUC, which is an especially important metric for malware analysts because of the need to characterize and rank binaries to determine which ones should be analyzed, identified, and quarantined sooner rather than later [5,20]. Thus, A high AUC is crucial since it corresponds to a successful ranking of most malicious files above benign files.

A discussion on using MARVOLO following our experiments can be found in Appendix D.

We first compare how MARVOLO performs in contrast to prior malware augmentation approaches. We first compared MARVOLO using all code transformations across both benign and malicious files against prior approaches that modify the opcode sequence representations of programs [14,18]. We mimic the experimental setup used in [18] by using the Continuous Bag of Words (CBOW) word2vec algorithm [16] trained on opcode sequences from the binaries in our dataset to construct an embedding matrix with information that represents the semantic similarity (e.g., add and adc) between opcodes. Opcodes with similar embedding vectors tend to be semantically similar. Each opcode in the sequence is then replaced with its corresponding word2vec embedding vector and converted to a binary file to be ingested by MalConv2. We implement four core strategies featured in opcode sequence augmentation: (1) random insertion, (2) random deletion, (3) random replacement, and (4) synonym replacement. For each experiment, we generated 6K mutated binaries. Table 1 contains the results, with MARVOLO yielding 2.35–3.8% higher accuracy and 8.4% – 9% higher AUC over the opcode sequence augmentation strategies. Since MARVOLO performs *meaningful* data augmentation by mimicking the code alterations made in practice, we generate more realistic data samples. We also applied image-based augmentation [19] to our dataset by converting our binaries to RGB images and augmenting them with Gaussian, Poisson, and Laplace noise. Across multiple experiments, performance improvements did not exceed 1%, and thus significantly trails the wins delivered by MARVOLO and even led to occasional accuracy degradations.

We also evaluated MARVOLO using the subset of the Brazilian malware dataset which yielded accuracy gains of 1–2%. Unlike the Ember dataset, the Brazilian dataset does not contain family labels for its malware so we could not constrain the training set to several families of interest. Thus, the original training dataset exhibited more heterogeneity so adding addi-

Table 2. Accuracy and AUC percentage improvements for non-deep baselines yielded by MARVOLO augmentation

Model	Accuracy	AUC
LZJD + Logistic Regression	0.87	1.01
LZJD + XGBoost	1.14	1.14
BWMD + Logistic Regression	1.18	1.61
BWMD + XGBoost	1.01	−0.23

tional augmented samples had a weaker effect. Table 2 shows our results for evaluating BWMD [24] and LZJD [23]. For each of these algorithms, we use both logistic regression and XGBoost [10] for malware classification. Overall, MARVOLO achieves up to a 1.18% improvement in accuracy and 1.61% improvement in AUC. Some of the effects of the mutations are lost after compression so the difference between the new embeddings and the embeddings from the unmodified binaries is less pronounced than the difference between the binaries without compression. Nonetheless, we note that even a 1% increase in accuracy is significant because of the sheer size and heterogeneity of our test dataset as well as the potential catastrophic consequences of misclassifying just a single file.

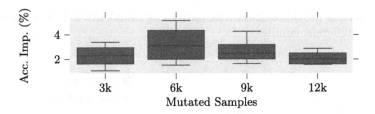

Fig. 8. Accuracy improvements (y-axis) when training MalConv2 on the Ember dataset augmented with different numbers of mutated samples (from MARVOLO).

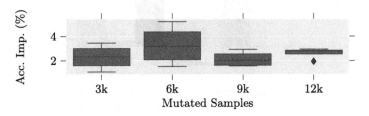

Fig. 9. MARVOLO's accuracy improvements (y-axis) when testing on only unseen (in the training data) malware families in the Ember test dataset. 8.

5.3   Analyzing MARVOLO

Figore 8 shows the accuracy improvements that MARVOLO brings to MalConv2 when augmenting the Ember training dataset with different numbers of mutated samples (ranging from 3-12K). We run each experiment four times and report on the distributions. Accuracy improvements range from 1–5% atop the baseline accuracy of 61.3% and AUC improvements range from 5–10% atop the baseline AUC of 65.2% achieved when considering the unmodified Ember dataset alone. These results highlight that accuracy improvements typically come quickly, while operating on only a small number of binaries, e.g., adding only 3 K and 6 K mutated samples to the dataset delivers 3.5% and 5% of accuracy boosts, respectively. The reason is that MARVOLO's efficiency-centric optimizations promote rapid diversity amongst the generated samples, which in turn enable MalConv2 to quickly strike a desirable balance between (1) learning to detect obfuscation patterns, while (2) not overfitting to mutated samples. Results on the smaller Brazilian malware dataset [9] were comparable: adding 2K mutated files delivered median accuracy improvements of 2% (atop the 61% without MARVOLO).

Further analysis reveals that a key driver of the overall accuracy wins delivered by MARVOLO are improvements on test samples from *previously unseen* malware families, i.e., families that did not appear in the training dataset. Recall from Sect. 2 that such samples are the ones which static analysis and small-scale ML approaches typically struggle to generalize to. Figure 9 illustrates this, showing that MARVOLO's accuracy boosts on only the subset of test binaries that were not seen during training are on par with the wins on the complete test set (1–5%). The underlying reason for these improvements is that code transformations provide a discernible pattern for MalConv2 to link across diverse binaries in different families.

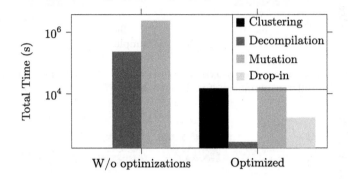

Fig. 10. Time spent on various stages of the mutation pipeline for two versions of MARVOLO: one with both optimizations, and one without. Mutation and reassembly are combined into a single bar for ease of disposition. Results are aggregate times when generating 3K mutated samples.

Importance of Number of Binaries Mutated. Figures 8 and 9 show MARVOLO's performance as the number of added mutated binaries changes. As discussed, the benefits from MARVOLO's mutations come early as most accuracy wins can be realized by using only a small fraction of the overall dataset as input. More generally, however, MARVOLO's performance with regards to input size is collectively governed by two factors - (1) the overall dataset size, and (2) the number of input samples - that influence the relationship between the utility of malware detection insights from newly added (mutated) samples and the risk of overfitting. Intuitively, larger datasets require more mutated samples to reap benefits because they already exhibit a sufficient amount of heterogeneity (as shown in Fig. 1), and they are also far less susceptible to overfitting (as the weight of each added sample is relatively smaller).

Table 3. MARVOLO's accuracy improvements when using a version of MARVOLO that only performs a single type of semantics-preserving code transformation during mutation.

Code transformation	Type	Accuracy
Junk code	Malware	2.62
Swapping	Malware	1.41
Obfuscating sub	Malware	3.18
Register reassignment	Malware	1.80
Code transposition	Malware	2.47
Opaque predicates	Malware	1.00
Optimizing sub	Benign	2.83
Function outlining	Benign	1.23
Function inlining	Benign	2.60
Function reordering	Benign	0.04

Importance of Different Transformations. Table 3 shows the effect that each transformation has on accuracy improvement. In summary, we find that we generally reap more accuracy improvements when mutating malicious files over benign files. Intuitively, many datasets only consist of malicious files from several families that do not employ a diverse set of obfuscations. Delving further, we find that obfuscating instruction substitution (replacing an instruction with an abstruse sequence of different instructions) yields the highest accuracy wins followed by junk code insertion and code transposition (reordering code blocks). These are commonly obfuscations that significantly change the file's appearance. Further, we attain significant improvements for mutations on benign files with optimizing instruction substitution and function inlining being the most prominent. These transformations improve the model by mimicking common types of optimizations that compilers employ in practice (which are not as widely used by malware authors, who opt to use their own toolchains and have fewer incentives to deploy optimized code). Function reordering, which changes the positions of functions in the file, shows that simply making arbitrary modifications that do not represent the transformations made in practice provide little benefit.

Importance of MARVOLO***'s Optimizations.*** Recall from Sect. 4 that MAR-VOLO embeds two optimizations to tackle the overheads in the mutation process. To uncover the effects of these optimizations, we profiled two runs of MARVOLO's mutation pipeline, one with the two optimizations enabled, and one without them. Each pipeline was used to generate 3K mutated samples, and we note that the MalConv2 models trained on these mutated samples (atop the Ember dataset) delivered accuracy within 1% of one another.

Figure 10 shows the aggregate time spent in each pipeline stage across these two variants. The optimized version runs $79\times$ faster to generate mutated samples of similar efficacy (given the near-identical MalConv2 performance across the two cases noted above). Speedups are primarily from the lower decompilation and mutation/reassembly costs, which in turn are due to running only a single binary per cluster through the pipeline (85% fewer binaries), with each run yielding a larger number of mutated samples. These drops dwarf the drop-in overheads used to mix (altered) code and data blocks, and the slight (blocking) overhead of performing clustering prior to mutation; note that clustering overheads are paid once, and will thus steadily decrease in relative importance as the number of mutated samples grows.

6   Conclusion

MARVOLO is a data augmentation engine that boosts the efficacy of the malware datasets that practitioners commonly are restricted to by performing semantics-preserving code transformations on the constituent binaries. To the best of our knowledge, we are the first to leverage insights from a deep-dive analysis of existing malware datasets to apply meaningful data augmentation to the domain of malware detection. Key to MARVOLO's practicality are its ability to (safely) propagate labels across input and output binary samples, and its optimizations to boost the number of fruitful (i.e., diverse and representative) data samples generated within a fixed time budget. Experiments using commercial malware datasets and a recent ML-driven malware detector show that MARVOLO boosts accuracies by up to 5%, while operating on only 15% of the available binaries (mutation speedups of $79\times$).

References

1. Code obfuscation (2021). https://en.wikibooks.org/wiki/X86_Disassembly/ Code_Obfuscation (Accessed 12 June 2023)
2. Global Ransomware Damage Costs Predicted To Reach $20 Billion (USD) By (2021). https://bit.ly/3j3bTEB (2021), (Accessed 6 Oct 2021)
3. Labs Report at RSA: Evasive Malware's Gone Mainstream. https://bit.ly/ 3p2lH5G (2021), (Accessed 6 Oct 2021)
4. Yara: The pattern matching swiss knife for malware researchers (and everyone else) (2021). https://virustotal.github.io/yara/, (Accessed 7 Aug 2021)
5. Abedelaziz Mohaisen, O.A.: Unveiling zeus: automated classification of malware samples. In: WWW Companion (2013)
6. Anderson, H.S., Roth, P.: EMBER: An Open Dataset for Training Static PE Malware Machine Learning Models. arXiv: 1804.04637 (2018)
7. Arp, D., et al.: Dos and don'ts of machine learning in computer security. In: USENIX Security Symposium (2022)
8. Bhagat, N., Arora, B.: Intrusion detection using honeypots. In: PDGC (2018)
9. Ceschin, F., Pinagé, F., Castilho, M., Menotti, D., Oliveira, L.S., Grégio, A.: The need for speed: an analysis of brazilian malware classifiers. In: IEEE Security & Privacy (2018)
10. Chen, T., Guestrin, C.: Xgboost: a scalable tree boosting system. In: Proceedings of the 22nd ACM SIGKDD International Conference on Knowledge Discovery and Data Mining, KDD 2016, pp. 785–794. Association for Computing Machinery, New York (2016). https://doi.org/10.1145/2939672.2939785
11. Flores-Montoya, A., Schulte, E.: Datalog disassembly. In: 29th USENIX Security Symposium (2020)
12. Harang, R., Rudd, E.M.: Sorel-20m: A large scale benchmark dataset for malicious pe detection (2020)
13. Jamalpur, S., Sai Navya, Y., Raja, P., Tagore, G., Rama Koteswara Rao, G.: Dynamic malware analysis using cuckoo sandbox. In: IEEE (ICICCT) (2018)
14. Jason Wei, K.Z.: Eda: Easy data augmentation techniques for boosting performance on text classification tasks. In: IJCNLP (2020)
15. Joyce, R.J., Amlani, D., Nicholas, C., Raff, E.: MOTIF: a large malware reference dataset with ground truth family labels. In: The AAAI-22 Workshop on Artificial Intelligence for Cyber Security (AICS) (2022). 10.48550, https://github.com/ boozallen/MOTIF, arXiv: 2111.15031
16. Mikolov, T., Chen, K., Corrado, G., Dean, J.: Efficient Estimation of Word Representations in Vector Space. arXiv:1301.3781v3
17. Nguyen, A.T., Raff, E., Sant-Miller, A.: Would a file by any other name seem as malicious? In: IEEE Big Data (2019)
18. Niall McLaughlin, J.M.d.R.: Data augmentation for opcode sequence based malware detection. arXiv: 2106.11821 (2021)
19. Ozgur, F., Catak, Ahmed, J., Sahinbas, K., Hussain Khand, Z.: Data augmentation based malware detection using convolutional neural networks. In: PeerJ Computer Science (2021)
20. Raff, E., Barker, J., Sylvester, J., Brandon, R., Catanzaro, B., Nicholas, C.: Malware Detection by Eating a Whole EXE. arXiv:1710.09435 (Oct 2017)
21. Raff, E., Filar, B., Holt, J.: Getting passive aggressive about false positives: patching deployed malware detectors. In: 2020 International Conference on Data Mining Workshops (ICDMW), pp. 506–515. IEEE (Nov 2020). https://doi.org/10.1109/ ICDMW51313.2020.00074, https://ieeexplore.ieee.org/document/9346444/

22. Raff, E., Fleshman, W., Zak, R., Anderson, H.S., Filar, B., McLean, M.: Classifying sequences of extreme length with constant memory applied to malware detection. In: AAAI (2021)
23. Raff, E., Nicholas, C.: An Alternative to NCD for Large Sequences, Lempel-Ziv Jaccard Distance. In: ACM SIGKDD, pp. 1007–1015 (2017)
24. Raff, E., Nicholas, C., McLean, M.: A new burrows wheeler transform markov distance. In: The Thirty-Fourth AAAI Conference on Artificial Intelligence (2020). https://arxiv.org/abs/1912.13046
25. Raff, E., et al.: Automatic yara rule generation using biclustering. In: ACM CCS AISec (2020)
26. Smith, M.R., et al.: Mind the gap: on bridging the semantic gap between machine learning and malware analysis. In: ACM CCS AISec (2020)
27. Votipka, D., Rabin, S.M., Micinski, K., Foster, J.S., Mazurek, M.M.: An observational investigation of reverse engineers ' processes. In: USENIX Security Symposium (2019)
28. You, I., Yim, K.: Malware obfuscation techniques: a brief survey. In: BWCCA (2010)

A Transductive Forest for Anomaly Detection with Few Labels

Jingrui Zhang, Ninh Pham$^{(\boxtimes)}$ ⓘ, and Gillian Dobbie

School of Computer Science, University of Auckland, Auckland, New Zealand
{jzha968,ninh.pham,g.dobbie}@auckland.ac.nz

Abstract. Extensive labeled training data for anomaly detection is enormously expensive and often unavailable in data-sensitive applications due to privacy constraints. We propose TransForest, a transductive forest for anomaly detection, in the semi-supervised setting where few labels are available. Guided by little label information, TransForest pushes classification boundaries toward sensitive areas where abnormal and normal points are located, increasing learning capacity. Empirically, TransForest is competitive with other unsupervised and semi-supervised representative detectors given a small number of labeled points. TransForest also offers a feature importance ranking consistent with the rankings provided by popular supervised forests on low-dimensional data sets. Our code is available at https://github.com/jzha968/transForest.

1 Introduction

Anomaly detection is a fundamental data mining task with many applications in several domains, such as banking fraud detection, system health monitoring, medical diagnosis, and law enforcement [1]. In these applications, the data features are represented as a high-dimensional vector, and anomalous behaviors tend to be masked by the noise effects of irrelevant features. More importantly, the label information is often limited due to privacy constraints and significant human effort. For instance, labeling medical images is very expensive, and releasing their label information can be against the privacy rights [2,7]. Therefore, it is challenging to detect anomalies effectively and efficiently, given a limited amount of labeled points, and provide explanations regarding detected anomalous patterns to support end-users decisions.

Due to the difficulty of accessing the ground truth, unsupervised methods are popular techniques to detect anomalies in the last decades [1,25]. These approaches are based on a common assumption that anomalies are likely located in relatively sparse regions while normal points are often distributed in dense neighborhoods. Unsupervised methods proposed different notions to measure the sparsity of a point, for example, distance/density-based models [4,24,28], isolation-based models [10,11,17], histogram-based models [9,23,27], and distribution-based models [15,16]. Since anomaly detection is performed in high-dimensional space and anomalies are masked by multiple irrelevant dimensions, anomaly detectors in relevant subspaces show superiority over

D. Koutra et al. (Eds.): ECML PKDD 2023, LNAI 14169, pp. 286–301, 2023.
https://doi.org/10.1007/978-3-031-43412-9_17

full space counterpart solutions [13,14,17]. However, the exponential complexity of the number of subspaces is the main bottleneck in detecting anomalous patterns accurately and efficiently.

Instead of finding relevant subspaces, recent semi-supervised models [21,26, 30] use a little label information to extract rich feature representations for the data points. These features preserve discriminative information of abnormal and normal points and are helpful for anomaly detection. XGBOD [30], a boosting-based approach, combines unsupervised feature representations with the original features to enrich the augmented feature space. Deep learning models [20,26] couple rich feature representation learning with some specific anomaly score. These methods significantly improve unsupervised models by leveraging advances in boosting and deep neural networks. A recent benchmark [12] shows that the strongest baseline XGBOD [30] can improve up to 10% of the average detection accuracy over unsupervised competitors with just 5% labeled anomalies. However, we find that these semi-supervised methods require many labeled points for training to achieve reasonable accuracy.

This work studies tree-based semi-supervised ensembles for anomaly detection. We propose TransForest, a novel transductive semi-supervised forest, that requires few labeled points to select relevant subspaces for constructing the forest. Unlike the conventional transductive decision forest [6] that maximizes the *mixed* information gain derived from the unlabeled and labeled points, TransForest estimates the information gain by spreading the known label information to the other unlabeled points during the feature selection process. In particular, at each tree level, we construct a histogram on each of the randomly selected features. Then, we pseudo-label unlabeled points based on the data distribution of the histogram and labeled points. Both labeled and pseudo-labeled points are used to estimate the information gain for the selected feature and its corresponding splitting value.

Given few labeled abnormal and normal points, TransForest can not only discriminate the sparse subspace areas that contain normal points or anomalies, but also push the classification boundaries toward dense subspace areas where points from both classes constitute. Empirically, TransForest is fast and outperforms other unsupervised tree-based forests with just 10 labeled points. Given the same amount of label information, TransForest achieves competitive accuracy compared with current advanced semi-supervised methods. Especially, TransForest offers a feature importance ranking consistent with the rankings provided by well-known supervised methods, including Random Forest [3] and Extra Trees [8] trained on fully labeled data.

2   Related Work

We briefly review popular unsupervised and semi-supervised anomaly detectors.

Unsupervised Models. Due to the difficulty of accessing the ground truth, traditional unsupervised models compute an anomaly score for each data point such that anomalies are likely scored larger than normal points. The anomaly score of a point $\mathbf{q}$ is derived from the sparsity of the local area around $\mathbf{q}$. Different approaches use different notions to measure the sparsity of q in high-dimensional space; for example, distance-based methods [24] using the k-nearest neighbor distance and density-based methods [4] using the difference ratio between the sparsity of q and the average sparsity of its local neighborhood.

Subspace Methods. Since proximity-based methods suffer the "curse of dimensionality" and detected anomalies tend to be uninteresting noise instances, their subspace variants [13,14] compute anomaly scores on specific subsets of dimensions where interesting anomalies tend to appear. Histogram-based approaches construct a histogram on each dimension or random subsets of dimensions [9,27], and use the bin size of the histogram where q locates to estimate the sparsity of q. iForest [17] and its variants [10,11] are tree-based solutions that measure the subspace sparsity of a point via the isolation concept. Since anomalies are few and different on a specific subset of dimensions, they will be likely isolated on the leaf node of a decision tree built on randomly selected features and random splitting values. Combined with subsampling, tree-based ensembles are the most efficient and accurate unsupervised anomaly detectors [12].

Semi-supervised Models. Semi-supervised models combine a small amount of labeled data with unlabeled data to learn better classification boundaries or extract rich representations to distinguish abnormal and normal points.

Tree-Based Methods. Popular supervised tree-based ensembles such as Random Forest [3] and Extra Trees [8] build the tree via the information gain derived from labeled points. Given the limit of label information, their transductive semi-supervised variants [6] select the feature and its splitting value that maximizes the *mixed* information gain derived from both unlabeled and labeled points. The unlabeled information gain component is derived from the Gaussian density estimation learned by the maximum likelihood over many samples. This step suffers substantial computational overheads, significantly increasing the training time. A semi-supervised variant Hybrid iForest [19] incorporates a new distance-based score from the test point to the labeled points into the iForest's anomaly score to improve the accuracy. Given little label information, its performance is unstable due to the high dependence on the data distribution.

Boosting-Based Methods. XGBOD [30] is a recent semi-supervised approach that leverages XGBoost [5], a fast and accurate gradient boosting library, to improve detection performance. XGBOD first constructs a new set of features based on unsupervised anomaly scores. This new set of features augmented with the original ones forms a new rich feature space where XGBoost is used to learn a binary classification. Though XGBOD achieves good performance, it does not provide any explanation for detected anomalies.

Deep Learning Methods. Different from XGBOD, several deep learning-based approaches [20,22,26] couple the learning representations and anomaly scores to improve the detection accuracy. For example, REPEN [20] learns low-dimensional representations that separate normal and abnormal distance-based behaviors. DeepSAD [26] maps data points into the sphere of minimum volume and learns a hyperplane that separates the sphere center and the projected data points.

Algorithm 1. An ExtraTree Construction

1: **procedure** BUILDTREE(A subset of points S, h_{max}, n_{min}, the current depth $h = 0$)
2:     If $h \geq h_{max}$ or $|S| \leq n_{min}$, create a leaf node and return
3:     Generate k pairs (f_i, v_{f_i}) where f_i is the feature and v_{f_i} is a random splitting value uniformly within the empirical range of f_i
4:     $(f_*, v_{f_*}) = \arg\max_i I(S, f_i, v_{f_i})$ using Eq. (1)
5:     Split S into S^l and S^r using (f_*, v_{f_*})
6:     BuildTree($S^l, h + 1$)
7:     BuildTree($S^r, h + 1$)

Although semi-supervised deep learning approaches require a significant number of labeled points, their learned representations are often difficult to interpret.

3   Preliminary

We present the preliminary tree-based ensemble methods, including Extra Trees (ET) [8], Random Forest (RF) [3], and iForest [17]. Since these forest variants build an ensemble of t trees, each over a random sample of s points, for simplicity, we will discuss the generic tree construction and point out their key differences.

Tree construction. Both RF and ET grow a tree by computing the feature and its splitting values that maximize the information gain for a given node. The information gain I measures the impurity gain of a node S after splitting S into two nodes S^l and S^r using the feature f_i and splitting value v_{f_i}. Let p_0 and p_1 be the empirical probability of the normal and abnormal classes in any node A, the impurity of A is derived from its entropy value $H(A) = -p_0 \log_2 (p_0) - p_1 \log_2 (p_1)$. The information gain of S for the feature f_i and splitting value v_{f_i} is as follows.

$$I(S, f_i, v_{f_i}) = H(S) - \frac{|S^l|}{|S|} H(S^l) - \frac{|S^r|}{|S|} H(S^r). \tag{1}$$

Denote by n_{min} and h_{max} the maximum number of points on leaf nodes and the maximum tree depth. These parameters are used to control the over-fitting in the forests. Algorithm 1 shows how to build an ET tree using information gain.

Difference between ET and RF. While both ET and RF build a tree on a *subset* of features, their primary difference is on generating the splitting values. ET picks the splitting value uniformly within the empirical range. RF computes the local optimal splitting value from randomly selected features. Since ET uses more randomness than RF, ET offers slightly lower classification accuracy but runs significantly faster than RF.

Difference between ET and iForest. In the unsupervised setting, building a tree of iForest is identical to the ET process without Step 4. Since there is no label information, Step 3 just needs $k = 1$ to reduce the training time. The key difference between iForest and ET is that iForest sets $n_{min} = 1$, $h_{max} = \log_2 (s)$

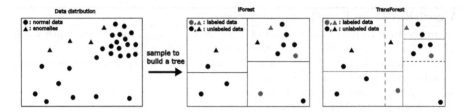

Fig. 1. An illustration of the tree constructions. Without label information, iForest's splits tend to separate dense/sparse regions. Guided by few labeled points and pseudo-labeled points via constructed histograms (dashed black lines), TransForest tends to split the node (blue lines) on sensitive regions where labeled points of two classes appear (Rule 3). (Color figure online)

and uses the path length from the leaf node to the root as an anomaly score. Since anomalies tend to differ from the other points on a specific subspace, they are likely isolated at shallow leaf nodes while normal points are likely located on deeper leaves. Building a forest will boost the performance since each tree deals with a random subspace derived from randomly selected features.

4   TransForest: A Transductive Forest

We observe that the unsupervised isolation-based mechanism tends to detect anomalies in sparse subspace areas. When two anomalies in a dense anomalous cluster are sampled to build trees, this cluster of anomalies receives similar anomaly scores as normal points. Since high-dimensional data sets contain multiple irrelevant features caused by measurement noise, sparse regions in randomly selected subspaces consist of both abnormal and normal points. In this case, normal points will be flagged as anomalies by the isolation-based mechanism.

We present TransForest to overcome these drawbacks by leveraging few labeled abnormal and normal points. TransForest is a novel transductive tree-based ensemble that spreads the little known label information to the other unlabeled points. Guided by pseudo-labeled and labeled points, each tree of TransForest selects more relevant subspaces and splitting values to investigate, providing higher performance with negligible computational overheads.

We denote the unlabeled and labeled sets by X_u and X_l, respectively. These two sets of sizes $|X_u| = n_u, |X_l| = n_l$ form the data set X of $n = n_u + n_l$ points in d dimensions. Since the number of labeled points is tiny, i.e. $n_l \ll n_u$, we *always* use X_l to build every tree of TransForest to learn more discriminate subspaces via the feature selection and its corresponding splitting value.

Overview. Providing the class probability is essential for enabling information gain-based splitting criterion. Given few labeled points, the information gain guides the feature selection on just a few shallow nodes in supervised tree-based methods. After a certain level, supervised models switch to unsupervised learning which unfortunately limits the use of label information. To maximize the

---

Algorithm 2. Compute Information Gain $I(S, f_i, v_{f_i})$

1: **function** COMPUTEGAIN(The node S, X_l, f_i, v_{f_i})
2:     Create a fixed bin width histogram for S on f_i using $\log_2(|S|) + 1$ bins
3:     Split the bin containing v_{f_i} into two new bins
4:     Compute the density threshold $\Delta = 0.1|S|$
5:     **for each** bin B in the histogram **do**
6:         Count pseudo-labeled abnormal and normal points in B using PSEUDO-LABEL COUNTING(B, Δ, X_l) in Algorithm 3
7:         Given the number of abnormal and normal points in each bin, compute the entropy $H(S)$, $H(S^l)$, $H(S^r)$ for the pair (f_i, v_{f_i})
8:     **return** $I(S, f_i, v_{f_i})$ using Eq.(1)

Algorithm 3. Counting # pseudo-labels of each class

1: **function** PSEUDO-LABEL COUNTING(Bin B, Δ, X_l)
Ensure: # normal points, # anomalies in bin B
2:     **if** B does not contain labeled points **then**
3:         **if** $|B| \geq \Delta$ **then return** $(|B|, 0)$ ▷ Dense area: label all points as normal
4:         **else return** $(0, |B|)$ ▷ Sparse area: label all points as anomalies
5:     **if** $|B| \geq \Delta$ and B contains only anomalies **then return** $(0.9|B|, 0.1|B|)$
6:     **if** B has $m_0 \geq 0$ normal points and $m_1 \geq 0$ anomalies **then return** $\left(\frac{m_0}{m_0+m_1}|B|, \frac{m_1}{m_0+m_1}|B| \right)$

---

use of labeled points, we propose a label propagation that spreads label information to their local regions to improve the tree construction. We implement the spreading mechanism via a histogram built from the empirical range of each feature. The constructed histograms will be used to *pseudo-label* unlabeled points based on their distribution and labeled points. Given labeled and pseudo-labeled points, we can compute the information gain and resort to standard supervised learning Extra Trees to build learning trees. We also output approximate feature importance ranking as an interpretation effort for TransForest. Figure 1 shows how TransForest leverages few labels to learn better splitting values than iForest.

Training Phase. TransForest uses Algorithm 1 to build trees. Each tree uses *all* labeled points, and the information gain in Step 4 is derived from a histogram-based label propagation. On the tree node S, for a randomly selected feature f_i and random splitting value v_{f_i}, TransForest constructs a histogram and pseudo-labels *all* unlabeled points by propagating labeled points to the other points in every histogram bin, as shown in Algorithm 2. In particular, we count the number of pseudo-labeled normal and abnormal points in each bin and use them to compute the information gain for the pair (f_i, v_{f_i}).

Counting Pseudo-Labels of each Class. We construct a fixed bin width histogram on the empirical range of random feature f_i to pseudo-label unlabeled points due to the fact that many histogram-based unsupervised methods [9,23,27] are efficient and effective on detecting anomalies in high-dimensional space. For a node S, we construct a histogram using $\log_2 (|S|) + 1$ bins. If there are no labeled points in the bin, we resort to the commonly assumed prior of unsupervised learning, which is anomalies tend to be located in sparse local regions whereas dense local regions tend to contain normal points. We use the threshold $\Delta = 0.1|S|$ to determine a dense/sparse bin. For a bin B of size $|B|$, Algorithm 3 shows how to count the number of pseudo-labels for each class using the following rules.

1. **Rule 1:** If B does not have labeled points, we resort to the common unsupervised prior. That is, if B is dense, i.e. $|B| \geq \Delta$, all points in B are labeled as normal points; otherwise, they are all anomalies (Lines 2 – 4).
2. **Rule 2:** If B is dense but contains only anomalies, B will have $0.9|B|$ normal points and $0.1|B|$ anomalies (Line 5) (e.g. normal points dominate anomalies).
3. **Rule 3:** Otherwise, we use the ratio between labeled abnormal and normal points to compute the number of pseudo-labels for each class (Line 6).

Rule 1 reflects the unsupervised prior; hence, TransForest can run in the unsupervised setting. Rules 2 and 3 push the classification boundaries toward sensitive areas where abnormal and normal points appear. Since normal points dominate anomalies, pushing the learning boundary toward sensitive areas increases the chance of finding discriminate local sparse areas to isolate anomalies in shallow nodes, as shown in Fig. 1.

Testing Phase. Since few labeled points of both classes are available in every tree, we will adjust the anomaly scores on isolated leaves where labeled points locate. In particular, for the leaves that contain only labeled anomalies, we set $anomalyScore = 1$. We set $anomalyScore = h_{max}$ for the leaves containing only labeled normal points. In other words, the local areas with only one-side labeled points are classified as this one-sided class. For most leaves without labeled points, we set $anomalyScore$ as the path length from the leaf to the root, similar to iForest. This adjustment leverages the labeled points to significantly improve the accuracy of TransForest on real-world data sets where local areas tend to contain the same class information.

Hyperparameter Setting. Since TransForest is a semi-supervised variant of iForest, we use $t = 100$ trees, each built on a subset of random points of size s. For each tree node, we select the best (f_i, v_{f_i}) among $k = 10$ random choices.

Since each tree of TransForest uses all labeled points X_l, and we need a sufficient unlabeled point to execute the spreading mechanism, we set $s = \max(256, 2n_l)$ to use additional $s - n_l$ unlabeled points. Since X_l is often tiny, this setting will not affect the training time complexity of TransForest.

We heuristically use $\Delta = 0.1|S|$ as a density threshold for the node S in the training phase to determine dense/sparse regions. We observe that the fixed bin width histogram constructed on the empirical range of a feature has a very skew distribution. Most of the sampled points are distributed in a few bins, while the rest of the bins are almost empty. Hence, the performance is similar for any density threshold $\Delta \in \{0.05, 0.1, 0.2, 0.3\}|S|$, as shown in the experiment.

The last hyperparameter is the heuristic setting used for the dense area with only anomalies (Rule 2). Without the class imbalance ratio, we set the ratio of

90% normal points and 10% anomalies to illustrate the domination of the normal class. Otherwise, this ratio can be set as the known class imbalance ratio. We observe that the case of dense regions with only anomalies is very rare due to the imbalanced property, changing the anomaly ratio from 10% to 30% would not affect the performance, as shown in the experiment.

Computational Complexity. Given the same settings of t trees, each tree uses s samples, $n_{min} = 1$, and $h_{max} = \log_2(s)$, TransForest and iForest share the same asymptotically linear running time. Though both have $O(ts\log_2(s))$ training time, TransForest runs slower than iForest due to the additional $O(ks)$ cost of constructing the histogram and pseudo-labeling for feature selection. In the testing phase, their empirical running time is similar to $O(nt\log_2(s))$ time.

Feature Importance Ranking of TransForest. Given pseudo-labeled and labeled points and the information gain computed in each node while constructing each tree, TransForest computes an important feature ranking similar to supervised tree-based RF and ET. Note that TransForest can compute the feature importance ranking without any labeled points by applying the common unsupervised prior. The feature important ranking will facilitate decision-marking on detected anomalies and identify irrelevant features from the data set. Empirically, TransForest with few labeled points can offer the feature important ranking consistent with supervised RF and ET on low-dimensional data sets.

5 Experiments

We implement our TransForest in Python and compare its performance with other unsupervised models, including iForest [17], OCSVM [18] and HBOS [9], and with recent semi-supervised models, including XGBOD [30], DevNet [22], DeepSAD [26] and Hybrid iForest [19]. Regarding the recent benchmark ADBench [12], these approaches are the strongest competitors in unsupervised and semi-supervised anomaly detection. We conduct experiments on a 2.90 GHz core i7-10700 16GB of RAM with a single CPU.

We use the standard AUC score (i.e. area under the ROC curve) to evaluate the accuracy of unsupervised and semi-supervised ensemble detectors since they output the outlier rankings. All results of each algorithm are the average over 5 runs. Semi-supervised models take labeled points randomly for each run. We present empirical evaluations on real-world data sets, including tabular and continuous data sets from computer vision and natural language processing domains, with a variety of differences in sizes and dimensions from ADBench[1] (see Table 1) to verify our claims, including:

1. Given limited label information, TransForest outperforms XGBOD, Hybrid iForest, and recent deep learning approaches, including DevNet and Deep-SAD, regarding detection accuracy.

---

[1] https://github.com/Minqi824/ADBench/tree/main/datasets.

2. Given just 20 labeled points, TransForest improves up to 10% AUC score compared to strong unsupervised baselines, including iForest and HBOS.
3. TransForest offers a feature importance ranking consistent with supervised RF and ET. TransForest is also robust to noisy and corrupted data sets while other deep learning-based approaches are not.

5.1   Semi-supervised Comparisons

We compare the AUC scores provided by TransForest and other semi-supervised approaches, including XGBOD, DeepSAD, DevNet, and Hybrid iForest.

Parameter Settings. TransForest uses $t = 100$ trees, $s = \max(256, 2n_l)$ samples, $n_{min} = 1$, $h_{max} = \log_2(s)$, $k = 10$. We train Hybrid iForest with $t = 128, s = 128$. The hyperparameters in score aggregation, the coefficient of unsupervised and supervised scores $\alpha_1 = 0.2, \alpha_2 = 0.7$ are set as suggested in [19]. We use the DevNet implementation [22] with the setting $n_{epochs} = 50$, batch size $b = 512$, $\alpha = 5$, and 20 steps. Keras's RMSprop optimization has a learning rate of 0.001 and $\rho = 0.95$. The pre-trained AutoEncoder uses $n_{epochs} = 100$, $b = 128$. Adam optimization with a learning rate of 0.001 and weight decay $L^2 = 10^{-6}$ is applied in both training and pre-training stages. For XGBOD and DeepSAD, we

Table 1. Dataset descriptions: 15 tabular and 20 continuous data sets.

Dataset	Size	Dimension	Anomalies
ALOI	50000	27	1508 (3.02%)
Annthyroid	7200	6	534 (7.42%)
Breastw	683	9	239 (35%)
Cardio	1831	21	176 (9.6%)
Letter	1600	32	100 (6.25%)
Mammography	11183	6	260 (2.32%)
Mnist	7603	100	700 (9.2%)
Optdigits	5216	64	150 (3%)
Pendigits	6870	16	156 (2.27%)
Pima	768	8	268 (35%)
Satellite	6435	36	2036 (32%)
Satimage-2	5803	36	71 (1.2%)
Shuttle	49097	9	3511 (7%)
Speech	3686	400	61 (1.65%)
Thyroid	3772	6	93 (2.5%)
20news (5 versions)	3090	768	154 (5%)
agnews (5 versions)	10000	768	500 (5%)
FashionMNIST (10 versions)	6315	512	315 (5%)

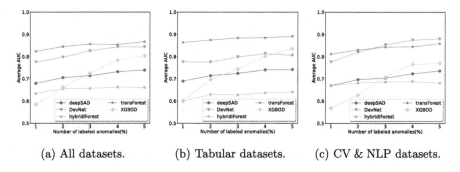

(a) All datasets.   (b) Tabular datasets.   (c) CV & NLP datasets.

Fig. 2. Average AUC over different types of data with various percentages of labeled anomalies. We use the same amount of labeled points for both classes.

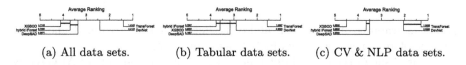

(a) All data sets.   (b) Tabular data sets.   (c) CV & NLP data sets.

Fig. 3. Critical difference in average ranking of AUC scores over different types of data using 1% labeled anomalies. We use the same amount of labeled points for both classes.

follow the parameter settings from ADBench [12]. XGBOD uses default parameters with unsupervised estimators, including KNN, LOF, HBOS, OCSVM and iForest, and XGBoost, with a learning rate of 0.1. DeepSAD uses $n_{epochs} = 50$ with batch size $b = 128$.

Limited Label Information. Due to the difficulty of labeling training data, we limit the availability of labeled anomalies to $\{1\%, 2\%, \ldots, 10\%\}$ and use the same number of labeled normal points. In other words, we have $n_l/2$ labeled points from each class. We select labeled points randomly, train semi-supervised detectors on labeled and unlabeled points, and test on *all* unlabeled points.

Very Limited Labeled Points on Both Classes. Figure 2 shows the average AUC scores provided by DevNet, DeepSAD, XGBOD, Hybrid iForest, and TransForest over a wide range of numbers of known anomalies. Overall, TransForest provides higher accuracy than other competitors, especially on tabular data sets. The advantage of TransForest is significant when using less label information. While DevNet performs best in continuous data sets, TransForest offers a competitive performance by achieving a better accuracy with up to 3% labeled anomalies.

Compared to XGBOD, the advantage of TransForest is significant when using less label information and on continuous data sets. Since XGBOD uses unsupervised outlier scores to enrich feature learning during training, it requires more labeled points to achieve reasonable accuracy. Similarly, deep learning approaches require significant labeled data on tabular data sets. Hybrid iForest shows inferior performance. Although it incorporates labeled and unlabeled

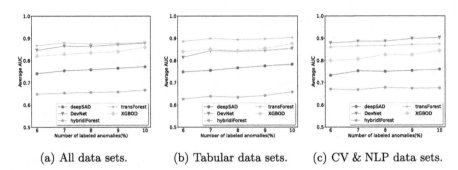

(a) All data sets.   (b) Tabular data sets.   (c) CV & NLP data sets.

Fig. 4. Average AUC over different types of data with various numbers of labeled anomalies. We use the same amount of labeled points for both classes.

points in training, its detection ability is emphasized for clustered anomalies, and therefore benefits less from little label information.

Figure 3 shows the critical difference diagram in average rank of AUC scores of the 5 semi-supervised approaches. While XGBOD, DeepSAD, and Hybrid iForest perform similarly, TransForest and DevNet are statistically better over all data sets when the label information is limited. Compared to DevNet, Trans-Forest's ranking is significant on tabular data sets but is marginal on continuous ones.

More Available Labeled Points. Fig. 4 shows the increase in accuracy of all semi-supervised methods when using more labeled points. Though TransForest still offers superior performance over all (15 tabular + 20 continuous) data sets, its gap with DevNet is marginal since DevNet is well-designed for continuous data sets. Nevertheless, TransForest is still competitive with DeepSAD, XGBOD, and Hybric iForest on both tabular and continuous data sets.

5.2 Effects of Pseudo-Labeling of TransForest

This subsection evaluates the effects of pseudo-labeling by comparing TransForest to several representative unsupervised methods, including iForest, OCSVM, and HBOS. To demonstrate the effectiveness of TransForest on utilizing label information, we vary both numbers of abnormal and normal points from 1 to 10. For other parameter settings of TransForest, we use the same as described above. For unsupervised methods, we use the default parameter setting provided in PyOD [31], and the whole data set as the training and testing sets.

Figure 5 presents the average AUC provided by iForest, OCSVM, HBOS and TransForest on tabular data sets. It is clear that TransForest significantly improves the unsupervised approach while leveraging limited label information. Given only 3 abnormal and 3 normal points, TransForest improves nearly 7% detection accuracy over iForest and HBOS, and 20% over OCSVM.

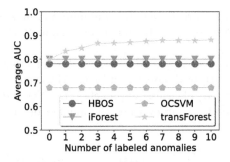

Fig. 5. Average AUC compared with unsupervised methods. We use the same amount of labeled points for both classes.

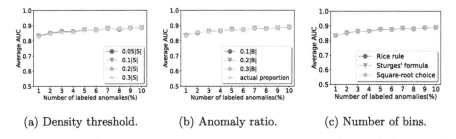

(a) Density threshold.   (b) Anomaly ratio.   (c) Number of bins.

Fig. 6. Average AUC over all data sets with different parameter configurations.

5.3 Parameter Sensitivity of TransForest

We examine the sensitivity of core hyperparameters of TransForest, including the density threshold Δ, anomaly ratio in Rule 2, and the number of bins for constructing the histogram. We examine $\Delta = \{0.05, 0.1, 0.2, 0.3\}|S|$, the ratio of anomalies in dense areas with only labeled anomalies $\{0.1, 0.2, 0.3\}|B|$, and the actual class imbalance ratio of the data sets. For the number of bins, we use 3 popular recommendations, including square-root choice $\sqrt{|S|}$, Sturges' formula $\log_2 (|S|) + 1$, and Rice rule $2 \sqrt[3]{|S|}$ [29].

Figure 6 shows the stable performance by TransForest with different settings of hyperparameters over all data sets for a wide range of labeled points. In other words, TransForest does not need heavy parameter tuning.

5.4 Robustness Against Irrelevant Features

This subsection evaluates the robustness of semi-supervised approaches with noisy features. Following ADBench [12], we add irrelevant features up to 50% of the original features. We select a few representative data sets from a wide range of dimensions, including Satellite, Mnist and 20news_0 to test the impact of irrelevant features. Similar to the previous setting, we use 10% labeled anomalies and use the same labeled points for each class. We vary the percentage of additional irrelevant features from 10% up to 50%. To generate an additional noisy feature, we randomly select a feature f_i, get the minimum and maximum values of f_i to generate the uniform noise from this range, and augment this noise feature into the original data.

Figure 7 shows the decrease in AUC scores of 5 detectors, including DevNet, TransForest, XGBOD, Hybrid iForest and DeepSAD when increasing the number of irrelevant features. Deep learning approaches, DevNet and DeepSAD, suffer a substantial downgrade in accuracy when the number of irrelevant features rises.

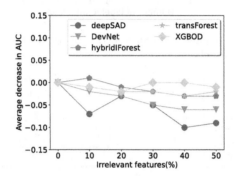

Fig. 7. Average decrease in AUC score with additional irrelevant features. We use 10% labeled anomalies and the same amount of labeled points for both classes.

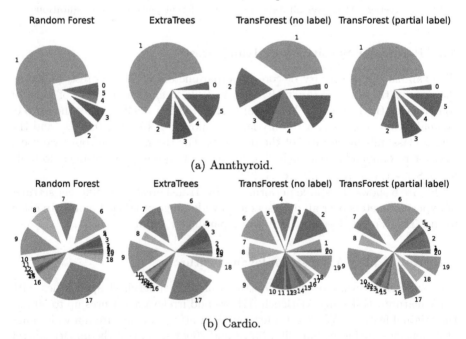

(a) Annthyroid.

(b) Cardio.

Fig. 8. Feature importance ranking on Annthyroid and Cardio. The number is the dimension index, and the wedge size reflects the feature's importance.

With augmented 50% irrelevant features, their AUC scores are reduced by 5% and 8%, respectively. XGBOD performs superior due to its built-in feature selection to select the best splitting value, while semi-supervised forest variants show less but reasonable robustness against irrelevant features. TransForest selects the local-optimal feature and its splitting value among $k = 10$ random features to compute the information gain. We note that increasing k will improve the robustness of TransForest. In contrast, Hybrid iForest randomly selects a feature and a splitting value. Nonetheless, Hybrid iForest combines the ratio between a testing point to the centroid of labeled anomaly and normal points with iForest's anomaly score. By setting $\alpha_2 = 0.7$, the supervised score dominates, and the use of ratio reduces the impact of irrelevant features.

5.5   Feature Importance Ranking

This subsection evaluates the feature importance ranking provided by TransForest and popular supervised RF and ET on the 2 medical data sets, Annthyroid and Cardio. Note that this utility is not available in XGBOD and deep learning approaches. For RF and ET, we use the whole data sets to train.

Figure 8 shows the feature importance ranking provided by RF, ET, unsupervised TransForest, TransForest with 10 anomalies and 100 normal points on Annthyroid and Cardio. On these 2 data sets, TransForest shows consistent feature importance rankings to that of RF and ET. On Annthyroid, the feature rankings provided by ET and TransForest are almost identical though TransForest uses just 2% labeled anomalies. On the higher dimensional Cardio, TransForest with 5% labeled anomalies shares similar top-4 important features with ET and RF (features 6, 7, 9, 17).

5.6   Running Time

Table 2 shows the total running time of DevNet, DeepSAD, TransForest, Hybrid iForest and XGBOD on the large 3 data sets using the same settings described above. Though our Python implementation of TransForest is not well-optimized, it still runs faster than Hybrid iForest and deep learning, and slightly slower than XGBOD.

Table 2. Average running time (s).

Dataset	Mammography	Mnist	agnews_0
DevNet	16.93	17.33	27.04
DeepSAD	35.86	28.88	52.18
TransForest	11.59	16.25	28.78
XGBOD	10.22	8.82	29.21
Hybrid iForest	52.1	55.28	81.6

6   Conclusion

We study the semi-supervised anomaly detection with the limit of label information. This setting suits many practical applications due to the high cost of accessing the ground truth. We propose TransForest, a transductive forest, that can learn feature selection from little label information. Empirically, TransForest with 1% labeled anomalies provides 5% improvement in AUC score compared with DevNet, and up to 20% compared to other semi-supervised learning approaches. Given 10 labeled anomalies and 100 normal points, the semi-supervised TransForest offers a feature importance ranking consistent with popular supervised models on several low-dimensional data sets.

Ethical Statement. Since we propose a new learning model for anomaly detection, there are no ethical issues.

References

1. Aggarwal, C.C.: Outlier Analysis. Springer (2013). https://doi.org/10.1007/978-3-319-47578-3
2. Bercea, C.I., Wiestler, B., Rueckert, D., Albarqouni, S.: Federated disentangled representation learning for unsupervised brain anomaly detection. Nat. Mach. Intell. **4**(8), 685–695 (2022)
3. Breiman, L.: Random forests. Mach. Learn. **45**(1), 5–32 (2001)
4. Breunig, M.M., Kriegel, H.P., Ng, R.T., Sander, J.: LOF: identifying density-based local outliers. In: SIGMOD, pp. 93–104 (2000)
5. Chen, T., Guestrin, C.: XGBoost: a scalable tree boosting system. In: KDD, pp. 785–794 (2016)
6. Criminisi, A., Shotton, J., Konukoglu, E.: Decision forests: a unified framework for classification, regression, density estimation, manifold learning and semi-supervised learning. Found. Trends Comput. Graph. Vis. **7**(2–3), 81–227 (2012)
7. Dou, Q., et al.: Federated deep learning for detecting COVID-19 lung abnormalities in CT: a privacy-preserving multinational validation study. npj Digit. Med. **4**(60) (2021)
8. Geurts, P., Ernst, D., Wehenkel, L.: Extremely randomized trees. Machine Learn. **63**(1), 3–42 (2006)
9. Goldstein, M., Dengel, A.: Histogram-based outlier score (HBOS): A fast unsupervised anomaly detection algorithm. In: KI-2012: Poster And Demo Track, vol. 9 (2012)
10. Gopalan, P., Sharan, V., Wieder, U.: PIDForest: anomaly detection via partial identification. In: NeurIPS, pp. 15783–15793 (2019)
11. Guha, S., Mishra, N., Roy, G., Schrijvers, O.: Robust random cut forest based anomaly detection on streams. In: ICML, pp. 2712–2721 (2016)
12. Han, S., Hu, X., Huang, H., Jiang, M., Zhao, Y.: ADBench: anomaly detection benchmark. In: NeurIPS (2022)
13. Keller, F., Müller, E., Böhm, K.: HiCS: high contrast subspaces for density-based outlier ranking. In: ICDE, pp. 1037–1048 (2012)
14. Kriegel, H.P., Kröger, P., Schubert, E., Zimek, A.: Outlier detection in axis-parallel subspaces of high dimensional data. In: PAKDD, pp. 831–838 (2009)

15. Li, Z., Zhao, Y., Botta, N., Ionescu, C., Hu, X.: COPOD: copula-based outlier detection. In: ICDM, pp. 1118–1123 (2020)
16. Li, Z., Zhao, Y., Hu, X., Botta, N., Ionescu, C., Chen, G.: ECOD: unsupervised outlier detection using empirical cumulative distribution functions. In: TKDE, pp. 1–1 (2022)
17. Liu, F.T., Ting, K.M., Zhou, Z.H.: Isolation forest. In: ICDM, pp. 413–422 (2008)
18. Manevitz, L.M., Yousef, M.: One-class svms for document classification. J. Mach. Learn. Res. **2**, 139–154 (2001)
19. Marteau, P.F., Soheily-Khah, S., Béchet, N.: Hybrid isolation forest-application to intrusion detection. arXiv preprint arXiv:1705.03800 (2017)
20. Pang, G., Cao, L., Chen, L., Liu, H.: Learning representations of ultrahigh-dimensional data for random distance-based outlier detection. In: KDD, pp. 2041–2050 (2018)
21. Pang, G., Shen, C., Cao, L., Hengel, A.V.D.: Deep learning for anomaly detection: a review. ACM Comput. Surv. (CSUR) **54**(2), 1–38 (2021)
22. Pang, G., Shen, C., van den Hengel, A.: Deep anomaly detection with deviation networks. In: KDD, pp. 353–362 (2019)
23. Pevný, T.: LODA: lightweight on-line detector of anomalies. Mach. Learn. **102**(2), 275–304 (2016)
24. Ramaswamy, S., Rastogi, R., Shim, K.: Efficient algorithms for mining outliers from large data sets. In: SIGMOD, pp. 427–438 (2000)
25. Ruff, L., et al.: A unifying review of deep and shallow anomaly detection. In: Proceedings of the IEEE (2021)
26. Ruff, L., et al.: Deep semi-supervised anomaly detection. In: ICLR (2020)
27. Sathe, S., Aggarwal, C.C.: Subspace histograms for outlier detection in linear time. Knowl. Inf. Syst. **56**(3), 691–715 (2018)
28. Schubert, E., Zimek, A., Kriegel, H.: Generalized outlier detection with flexible kernel density estimates. In: SDM, pp. 542–550 (2014)
29. Scott, D.W.: Multivariate Density Estimation: Theory, Practice, and Visualization. Wiley Series in Probability and Statistics. Wiley (1992)
30. Zhao, Y., Hryniewicki, M.K.: XGBOD: improving supervised outlier detection with unsupervised representation learning. In: IJCNN, pp. 1–8 (2018)
31. Zhao, Y., Nasrullah, Z., Li, Z.: PyOD: a python toolbox for scalable outlier detection. JMLR **20**, 1–7 (2019)

Applications

Co-Evolving Graph Reasoning Network for Emotion-Cause Pair Extraction

Bowen Xing[1,2,3] and Ivor W. Tsang[1,2,3(✉)]

[1] AAII, University of Technology Sydney, Sydney, Australia
ivor_tsang@cfar.a-star.edu.sg
[2] CFAR, Agency for Science, Technology and Research, Singapore, Singapore
[3] IHPC, Agency for Science, Technology and Research, Singapore, Singapore

Abstract. Emotion-Cause Pair Extraction (ECPE) aims to extract all emotion clauses and their corresponding cause clauses from a document. Existing approaches tackle this task through multi-task learning (MTL) framework in which the two subtasks provide indicative clues for ECPE. However, the previous MTL framework considers only one round of multi-task reasoning and ignores the reverse feedbacks from ECPE to the subtasks. Besides, its multi-task reasoning only relies on semantics-level interactions, which cannot capture the explicit dependencies, and both the encoder sharing and multi-task hidden states concatenations can hardly capture the causalities. To solve these issues, we first put forward a new MTL framework based on Co-evolving Reasoning. It (1) models the bidirectional feedbacks between ECPE and its subtasks; (2) allows the three tasks to evolve together and prompt each other recurrently; (3) integrates prediction-level interactions to capture explicit dependencies. Then we propose a novel multi-task relational graph (MRG) to sufficiently exploit the causal relations. Finally, we propose a Co-evolving Graph Reasoning Network (CGR-Net) that implements our MTL framework and conducts Co-evolving Reasoning on MRG. Experimental results show that our model achieves new state-of-the-art performance, and further analysis confirms the advantages of our method.

Keywords: Multi-Task Learning · Relational Graph Reasoning · Emotion-Cause Extraction · Natural Language Processing

1 Introduction

Emotion-Cause Pair Extraction (ECPE) is a new while challenging task in the field of natural language processing/artificial intelligence. It aims to automatically extract all emotion clauses and the corresponding cause clauses from a raw document, which is of great value for real-world application [26]. Consider a document "*[In the memory of the students]*$_1$, *[he often paid the tuition fees for them]*$_2$, *[which is respectable and touching]*$_3$.", the third clause expresses an emotion, which is triggered by the second clause, so these two clauses form an emotion-cause pair. Intuitively, detecting the clauses that express causes and

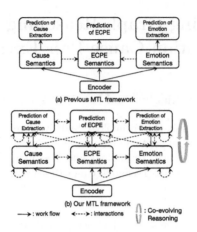

Fig. 1. Comparison of the previous MTL framework and our MTL framework for ECPE.

emotions, namely cause extraction (CE) and emotion extraction (EE), are two subtasks of ECPE. Accordingly, recent models [1, 10, 13, 37] implement the multi-task learning framework in Fig. 1(a), introducing CE and EE to provide indicative clues for ECPE.

Although the previous multi-task learning (MTL) framework has made promising progress, based on our observation, it still suffers from several issues which hinder the multi-task reasoning between ECPE and CE/EE. First, previous works only consider one-way messages from CE/EE to ECPE. The predictions of CE/EE may be incorrect due to their unreliable semantics. In this case, the false information from CE/EE may mislead ECPE. Second, the single-round multi-task reasoning process in previous works is not competent, considering that it is hard for machines to understand emotions, causes, and their causalities like humans due to the inherent ambiguity and subtlety of emotions and causes [12]. Third, in previous works, the multi-task reasoning between ECPE and CE/EE is only achieved by implicit semantics-level interactions such as shared encoders. For one thing, this is inconsistent with human intuition and the causal relations between ECPE and CE/EE, both of which are based on predictions or labels; for another, the indicative information conveyed in semantics is implicit and relatively insufficient compared with prediction information.

On account of the above issues, we propose a new MTL framework based on Co-evolving Reasoning as shown in Fig. 1(b). Firstly, in addition to the one-way message from CE/EE to ECPE, our MTL framework also models the reverse feedbacks from ECPE to CE/EE. If ECPE predicts correctly, the indicative information transferred to CE/EE can improve them. And the two improved subtasks can further promote ECPE reversely. If ECPE predicts incorrectly, the defective information transferred to CE/EE can act as their feedback and make them rethink to provide better information for ECPE, which thus can further prompt CE/EE reversely. Secondly, to achieve this virtuous cycle, we design the recurrent multi-task reasoning mechanism. In this way, the knowledge of the three tasks can gradually evolve together and mutually prompt each other. Thirdly, we propose to exploit the correlations in predictions via introducing two kinds of prediction-level interactions: prediction-prediction and prediction-semantics interactions. In this way, explicit correlative information conveyed by predictions (estimated label distributions) can flow in our MTL framework then facilitate *Co-evolving Reasoning*. And the semantics can get straightforward feedback at each step from the predictions then rethink to improve.

Furthermore, the MTL sequence structures employed in previous works are simply based on shared encoder and multi-task hidden states concatenations, which can hardly capture the causal relations. This motivates us to seek a more effective method to sufficiently exploit the causalities among ECPE and CE/EE. To this end, we design a novel multi-task relational graph (MRG), in which there are three groups of nodes derived from the clauses in the document and corresponding to ECPE, CE, and EE, respectively. Moreover, we design different relation types which correspond to the causal relations between ECPE and CE/EE.

To implement our MTL framework and conduct Co-evolving Reasoning on MRG, we propose a Co-evolving Graph Reasoning Network (CGR-Net), whose core is a multi-task relational graph transformation (MRGT) cell. CGR-Net first generates the task-specific hidden states and produces the initial estimated label distributions. Then the MRGT cell recurrently takes the hidden states and label distributions of the three tasks as input and then updates them in three steps: projection of label distributions, relational local graph transformation, and non-local self-transformation. Finally, the predictions of ECPE at the final step are used to extract the potential emotion-cause pairs. And we design a harness loss based on logical constraints to force the three tasks to gradually promote each other in the virtuous cycle of Co-evolving Reasoning.

In summary, our contributions are three-fold:

(1) We propose a new MTL framework based on Co-evolving Reasoning and an MRG to exploit the correlations and causal relations sufficiently. To the best of our knowledge, our MTL framework is the first one allowing ECPE and CE/EE to promote each other recurrently, and MRG is the first MTL graph structure for ECPE.
(2) To implement our MTL framework and conduct Co-evolving Reasoning on MRG, we propose a novel CGR-Net, whose core is a multi-task relational graph transformation cell.
(3) Experimental results on the benchmark dataset show that our CGR-Net significantly outperforms existing state-of-the-art models. And further analysis proves the effectiveness of different components of CGR-Net and the superiority of MRG.

2   Related Works

Emotion cause extractions (ECE) [4,9,14–16,18,20,21,36] is a long-standing task whose objective is to extract the causes of given emotion expressions in the document. However, it requires that the emotions must be annotated manually, which constrains the practical application. Therefore, recently [26] propose the ECPE task and a two-step solution while the error propagation may occur from the first step to the second. To this end, recent works propose unified end-to-end models [2,5,6,10,11,13,23,25] to tackle ECPE in the MTL framework.

[10] propose a model integrating the 2D representation of emotion-cause pair, the interactions, and predictions. [23] tackle ECPE from a ranking perspective and adopt kernel-based relative position embedding for ranking. [38] propose a tagging scheme coding the distance between the emotion clause and cause clause in an emotion-cause pair. Based on this, [13] propose a tag distribution refinement method that adjusts the output label distribution of ECPE using the ones of CE and EE according to a pre-defined rule. However, the refinement method does not participate in model training, only working on the output of evaluation.

More recently, Multi-Granularity Semantic Aware Graph model (MGSAG) [1] incorporates fine-grained and coarse-grained semantic features jointly, aiming to resolve the distance limitation of clause semantics. And the Matrix Capsule-based multi-granularity framework (MaCa) [37] introduces the matrix capsule to obtain more fine-grained features of clause pairs, clustering the relationship of each clause pair.

Different from previous works, we (1) propose Co-evolving Reasoning, which allows the three tasks gradually and sufficiently promote each other; (2) introduce prediction-prediction and prediction-semantics interactions to model the explicit correlations and provide feedback for semantics which can rethink to improve; (3) effectively exploit the casual relations via designing a novel MRG.

3 Methodology

Before delving into MRG and CGR-Net, we first introduce the task formulation in our work.

We cast ECPE as a *tag* classification task and use the cause-centric tagging scheme [38]. Each clause x_i has a two-tuples tag $y_i^t = (y_i^{t,c}, y_i^{t,d}) \in \mathcal{C}_t$, where $y_i^{t,c} \in \{C, O\}$ denotes whether x_i is a cause clause, and $y_i^{t,d} \in \{-\gamma, ..., -1, 0, 1, ..., \gamma, \perp\}$ denotes the distance between x_i and its triggered emotion clause, while '$\perp$' always associates with 'O', denoting that x_i is a non-cause clause. And γ is a hyperparameter controlling the max span of emotion-cause pairs. Thus ECPE (*tag*) totally has $|\mathcal{C}_t| = 2(\gamma+1)$ classes.

As for CE (*cause*) and EE (*emotion*), they are both formulated as binary classification tasks: $y_i^c \in \mathcal{C}_c = \{1, 0\}$ and $y_i^e \in \mathcal{C}_e = \{1, 0\}$.

3.1 Constructing a MRG from a Document

In this paper, we design a multi-task relational graph (MRG) $\mathcal{G} = (\mathcal{V}, \mathcal{E}, \mathcal{R})$ to exploit the causalities via modeling the self- and mutual-interactions of the three tasks (*cause, tag* and *emotion*). Each clause x_i in document $\mathcal{D}$ derives

Table 1. Relation types in MRG, w.l.o.g. $\gamma = 2$. $I_t(i)$ indicates node i is a cause (c) node, tag (t) node or emotion (e) node. '-' denotes the set of [-2, -1, 0, 1, 2].

r_{ij}	cc	tt	ee	ct	tc	te:-2	te:-1	te:0	te:1	te:2	et:-2	et:-1	et:0	et:1	et:2
$I_t(i)$	c	t	e	c	t	t	t	t	t	t	e	e	e	e	e
$I_t(j)$	c	t	e	t	c	e	e	e	e	e	t	t	t	t	e
rdis(i,j)	-	-	-	0	0	-2	-1	0	1	2	-2	-1	0	1	2

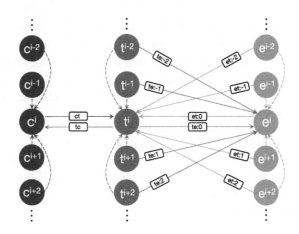

Fig. 2. An example of MRG ($\gamma = 2$). W.L.O.G, only the edges directed into c_i, t_i and e_i are illustrated. And self-loops are not shown for simplification.

three nodes c_i, t_i and e_i, respectively for *cause*, *tag* and *emotion*, thus $|\mathcal{V}| = 3n$. The edge $(i, j, r_{ij}) \in \mathcal{E}$ denotes the information propagation from node i to node j, and $r_{ij} \in \mathcal{R}$ is the relation type of the edge. Note that node i and node j may correspond to different tasks. We define three kinds of rules to determine the connection between two nodes in MRG:

Direction: $(j, i, r_{ji}) \in \mathcal{E}$ if $(i, j, r_{ij}) \in \mathcal{E}$. In MRG, the information propagation between two nodes is bidirectional. This guarantees the bidirectional correlations between *tag* and *cause*/*emotion*. **Local Connection:** $\forall (i, j, r_{ij}), |\text{rdis}(i, j)| \leq \gamma$, where rdis$(i, j)$ denotes the relative distance between the clauses of node i and node j in $\mathcal{D}$. In general, the probability of two distant clauses having causal relation is relatively small regarding the cohesion and coherence of discourse [7]. Therefore, the edges in MRG are based on local connections, and in this work, we constrain that the relative distance of two connected nodes' clauses in $\mathcal{D}$ ranges from $-\gamma$ to γ, consistent with the span range of the ECPE tag.

Relation Type for Causality: Table 1 lists the relation types in MRG. And an example of MRG is shown in Fig. 2. To capture the self-task local contextual dependencies, we define $r_{ij} = cc$, $r_{ij} = tt$ and $r_{ij} = ee$ to model the local self-transformation of *cause*, *tag* and *emotion*, respectively. As for inter-task interactions, first of all, regarding the scheme of *tag* task, there are two explicit causal relations between *cause* and *tag* tasks: (1) if $y_i^c = 1$, then $y_i^{t,c} = C$, and vice versa; (2) if $y_i^c = 0$, then $y_i^{t,c} = O$, and vice versa. To model these causalities in MRG, we define $r_{ij} = ct$ and $r_{ij} = tc$ to achieve the mutual transformations between *cause* and *tag*. Besides, there are four kinds of causal relations between *tag* and *emotion* tasks. First, if $y_i^{t,c} = C$, there is at least one emotion clause among $x_{i-\gamma} \sim x_{i+\gamma}$: $y_{i-\gamma}^e = 1$ or $y_{i-\gamma+1}^e = 1$ or ... or $y_{i+\gamma-1}^e = 1$ or $y_{i+\gamma}^e = 1$. Second, if there is no emotion clause among $x_{i-\gamma} \sim x_{i+\gamma}$: $y_{i-\gamma}^e = 0$ and $y_{i-\gamma+1}^e = 0$ and ... and $y_{i+\gamma-1}^e = 0$ and $y_{i+\gamma}^e = 0$, then $y_i^{t,c} = O$ and $y_i^{t,d} = \perp$. Third, if $y_i^{t,d} = m$, then $y_{i+m}^e = 1$. Reversely, $y_{i+m}^e = 1$ cannot deduce $y_i^{t,d} = m$, but intuitively if $p(y_{i+m}^e = 1)$ increases, $p(y_i^{t,d} = m)$ should also increase. Forth, if $y_{i+m}^e = 0$, then $y_i^{t,d} \neq m$. Reversely, although $y_i^{t,d} \neq m$ cannot deduce $y_{i+m}^e = 0$, intuitively if $p(y_i^{t,d} = m)$ decreases, $p(y_{i+m}^e = 0)$ should increase. To model these *tag-emotion* causal relations in MRG, we define a set of relations represented by $r_{ij} = I_t(i)I_t(j) : rdis(ij)$, and some instances are shown in Fig. 2. For example, $r_{ij} = et : -2$ denotes the relation from node i (an *emotion* node) to node j (a *tag* node) and the relative distance between node i and node j.

In MRG, each inter-task relation corresponds to a fine-grained relative distance, consistent with the definition of the tagging scheme. Therefore, the inter-task graph transformations along these relations can achieve more sufficient and explicit multi-task reasoning.

3.2   CGR-Net

The overall architecture of our Co-evolving Graph Reasoning Network (CGR-Net) is shown in Fig. 3 (1). It consists of three components: Hierarchical Encoding, Initial Estimation, and Co-evolving Reasoning. Next, we depict the procedures of these three components.

Hierarchical Encoding.

Word-level Clause Encoding. The objective of clause encoding is to generate a representation containing the word-level dependencies for each clause. Following previous works, each clause is fed into BERT [8] encoder, then the last hidden state of [CLS] token is taken as the clause representation. Now we obtain the sequence of clause representation for $\mathcal{D}$: $H = (h_0, ..., h_n)$.

Multi-task Clause-level Document Encoding. In this paper, we utilize BiLSTM [17] to generate the context-sensitive clause hidden states via modeling the inter-clause dependencies. To obtain task-specific clause hidden states for the three tasks, we separately apply three BiLSTMs over H to obtain the initial clause hidden states for *cause*, *tag* and *emotion*, respectively: $H_c^0 = (h_{c,1}^0, ..., h_{c,n}^0)$, $H_t^0 = (h_{t,1}^0, ..., h_{t,n}^0)$ and $H_e^0 = (h_{e,1}^0, ..., h_{e,n}^0)$.

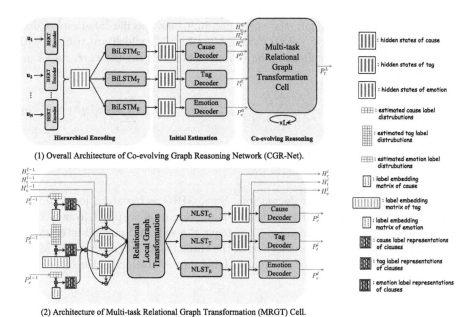

(1) Overall Architecture of Co-evolving Graph Reasoning Network (CGR-Net).

(2) Architecture of Multi-task Relational Graph Transformation (MRGT) Cell.

Fig. 3. The architectures of CGR-Net and MRGT cell. NLST denotes Non-Local Self-Transformation.

Initial Estimation. Since MRGT cell takes the three tasks' label distributions predicted in previous step as input, H_c^0, H_t^0 and H_e^0 are separately fed into Cause Decoder, Tag Decoder and Emotion Decoder to produce the initial estimated label distributions:

$$
\begin{aligned}
P_c^0 &= \{P_{c,i}^0\}_{i=1}^n, P_t^0 = \{P_{t,i}^0\}_{i=1}^n, P_e^0 = \{P_{e,i}^0\}_{i=1}^n \\
P_{c,i}^0 &= \mathrm{softmax}(\mathrm{MLP}_c(h_{c,i}^0)) = [p_{c,i}^0[1], p_{c,i}^0[2]] \\
P_{t,i}^0 &= \mathrm{softmax}(\mathrm{MLP}_t(h_{t,i}^0)) = [p_{t,i}^0[1], ..., p_{c,i}^0[|\mathcal{C}_t|]] \\
P_{e,i}^0 &= \mathrm{softmax}(\mathrm{MLP}_e(h_{e,i}^0)) = [p_{e,i}^0[1], p_{e,i}^0[2]]
\end{aligned}
\tag{1}
$$

Co-evolving Reasoning. Co-evolving Reasoning is achieved by the recurrent MRGT cell, whose details are shown in Fig. 3 (2). At step l, MRGT cell takes two streams of inputs: 1) hidden states of the three tasks: $H_c^{l-1} \in \mathbb{R}^{n \times d}$, $H_t^{l-1} \in \mathbb{R}^{n \times d}$ and $H_e^{l-1} \in \mathbb{R}^{n \times d}$; 2) label distributions of the three tasks: P_c^{l-1}, P_t^{l-1} and P_e^{l-1}. The procedure of an MRGT cell consists of three steps (1) projecting the input label distributions into vectors; (2) Relational Local Graph Transformation on MRG; (3) Non-local Self-Transformation.

Projection of Label Distribution. To achieve the prediction-level interactions, the input label distributions should be projected into vector form, and thus they can participate in representation learning. Accordingly, we ues P_c^{l-1}, P_t^{l-1} and

P_e^{l-1} to respectively multiply the corresponding task-specific label embedding matrices $M_c^e \in \mathbb{R}^{|\mathcal{C}_c| \times d}$, $M_t^e \in \mathbb{R}^{|\mathcal{C}_t| \times d}$ and $M_e^e \in \mathbb{R}^{|\mathcal{C}_e| \times d}$, which are trained with the whole model. Specifically, x_i's label representations for the three tasks are obtained as:

$$e_{t,i}^l = \sum_{k=1}^{|\mathcal{C}_t|} p_{t,i}^{l-1}[k] \cdot v_t^k; \quad e_{c,i}^l = \sum_{k'=1}^{|\mathcal{C}_c|} p_{c,i}^{l-1}[k'] \cdot v_c^{k'}; \quad e_{e,i}^l = \sum_{k''=1}^{|\mathcal{C}_e|} p_{e,i}^{l-1}[k''] \cdot v_e^{k''} \quad (2)$$

where v_t^k, $v_c^{k'}$ and $v_e^{k''}$ denotes the label embeddings of *tag*, *cau* and *emo*, respectively.

Relational Local Graph Transformation. Since MRG is based on local connections, we conduct relational local graph transformation inspired from [22, 28–31, 33–35] for multi-task reasoning. To achieve the self- and mutual-interactions between the semantics and predictions of the three tasks, for each node in MRG, we superimpose its corresponding clause's label representations of the three tasks on its hidden state:

$$\begin{aligned} e_i^l &= e_{c,i}^l + e_{t,i}^l + e_{e,i}^l, \\ \hat{h}_{c,i}^l = h_{c,i}^{l-1} + e_i^l; \quad \hat{h}_{t,i}^l &= h_{t,i}^{l-1} + e_i^l; \quad \hat{h}_{e,i}^l = h_{e,i}^{l-1} + e_i^l \end{aligned} \quad (3)$$

Thus each node representation contains the task-specific semantic features as well as the explicit correlative information conveyed by label representations, which are then integrated together into the relational local graph transformation to achieve semantics-level and prediction-level interactions.

Specifically, the relational local graph transformation updates the nodes on MRG as follows:

$$\overline{h}_i^l = W_1 \hat{h}_i^t + \sum_{r \in \mathcal{R}} \sum_{j \in \mathcal{N}_i^r} \frac{1}{|\mathcal{N}_i^r|} W_2^r \hat{h}_j^l \quad (4)$$

where W_1 is the self-message matrix and W_2^r is the relation-specific matrix. $\mathcal{N}_i^r$ denotes the neighbors set of node i along corresponding to the relation r. Now we obtain the updated hidden states: $\overline{H}_c^l$, $\overline{H}_t^l$ and $\overline{H}_e^l$.

Non-Local Self-Transformation Despite the advantages of the relational local graph transformation, it has two potential issues: (1) due to the local self-transformation, some beneficial contextual dependencies between a node and its distant same-task nodes may be lost; (2) the information fusion weaken the task-specificity of the nodes to some extent, which is against predictions. To this end, inspired by [27, 32], we conduct non-local self-transformation (NLST) over the sequence of nodes of each task, and this is implemented by a task-specific BiLSTM which can capture long-range dependencies. The final hidden states of the three tasks at step l are obtained by:

$$H_c^l = \text{NLST}_C(\overline{H}_c^l); \quad H_t^l = \text{NLST}_T(\overline{H}_t^l); \quad H_e^l = \text{NLST}_E(\overline{H}_e^l) \quad (5)$$

Then H_c^l, H_t^l and H_e^l are fed to respective decoders to produce P_c^l, P_t^l and P_e^l.

Optimization with Logical Constraints. In CGR-Net, there are two vital logic rules. First, the label distributions estimated in the previous step should be relatively good to provide effective label representations for the current step. Otherwise, much incorrect and misleading explicit correlations would be introduced, harming multi-task reasoning. Second, ECPE and CE/EE are supposed to gradually promote each other via capturing more and more beneficial mutual knowledge and correlations in Co-evolving Reasoning. In other words, the estimated label distributions should be gradually improved along the steps. To satisfy these two rules, we propose a harness loss $\mathcal{L}_{harn}$ that includes two terms: estimate loss $\mathcal{L}_{est}$ and margin loss $\mathcal{L}_{marg}$, corresponding to the two rules, respectively.

Estimate Loss. Formally, $\mathcal{L}_{est}$ is the cross-entropy loss. For ECPE task, $\mathcal{L}_{est}^{tag,l}$ is defined as:

$$\mathcal{L}_{est}^{tag,l} = \frac{1}{n}\sum_{i=1}^{n}\sum_{k=1}^{|\mathcal{C}_t|} y_{t,i}^k \log\left(p_{t,i}^l[k]\right), \tag{6}$$

Margin Loss. $\mathcal{L}_{marg}$ works on the label distributions output in two adjacent steps, forcing CGR-Net to produce better predictions at step l than step $l-1$. For ECPE task, $\mathcal{L}_{marg}^{tag,l}$ is defined as:

$$\mathcal{L}_{marg}^{tag,(l,l-1)} = \frac{1}{n}\sum_{i=1}^{n}\sum_{k=1}^{|\mathcal{C}_t|} y_{t,i}^k \max(0, p_{t,i}^{l-1}[k] - p_{s,i}^l[k]) \tag{7}$$

Harness loss $\mathcal{L}_{harn}$ is the weighted sum of $\mathcal{L}_{est}$ and $\mathcal{L}_{marg}$. For ECPE task, $\mathcal{L}_{harn}^{tag}$ is defined as:

$$\mathcal{L}_{harn}^{tag} = \sum_{l=0}^{L-1}\mathcal{L}_{est}^{tag,l} + \beta * \sum_{l=1}^{L}\mathcal{L}_{marg}^{tag,(l,l-1)} \tag{8}$$

where β is a hyper-parameter balancing the impact of the two kinds of punishments.

Final Training Objective The total loss for ECPE task ($\mathcal{L}_{tag}$) is the sum of $\mathcal{L}_{harn}^{tag}$ and $\mathcal{L}_{pred}^{tag}$:

$$\mathcal{L}_{tag} = \mathcal{L}_{pred}^{tag} + \mathcal{L}_{harn}^{tag} \tag{9}$$

where $\mathcal{L}_{pred}^{tag}$ is the cross-entropy loss of the produced tag label distributions at the final step L:

$$\mathcal{L}_{pred}^{tag} = \frac{1}{n}\sum_{i=1}^{n}\sum_{k=1}^{|\mathcal{C}_t|} y_{t,i}^k \log\left(p_{t,i}^L[k]\right) \tag{10}$$

The total losses of CE ($\mathcal{L}_{cau}$) and EE ($\mathcal{L}_{emo}$) can be derivated like Eqs. (6) to (10).

The final training objective of CGR-Net is the weighted sum of the total losses of the three tasks:

$$\mathcal{L} = \alpha * \mathcal{L}_{tag} + \frac{1 - \alpha}{2} \mathcal{L}_{cau} + \frac{1 - \alpha}{2} \mathcal{L}_{emo} \qquad (11)$$

where α is a hyperparameter balancing the three tasks and it is intuitively set as 0.5 in this work.

4   Experiments

4.1   Datasets and Evaluation Metrics

The only benchmark dataset for ECPE task is released by [26] who construct it on an emotion-cause extraction corpus [16]. The dataset totally consists of 1,945 documents, among which 1,746 ones have one emotion-cause pair, 177 ones have two emotion-cause pairs, and 22 ones have more than two emotion-cause pairs. The average number of clauses per document is 14.77, and the max number is 73.

Following previous works, we adopt the 10-fold cross-validation for evaluations. And the averages of precision (P), recall (R), and F1-score over ten runs are adopted as metrics. Besides ECPE, we also report the results of EE and CE, which are evaluated based on the emotion clauses and cause clauses in the extracted emotion-cause pairs.

4.2   Implement Details

We adopt the $BERT_{Chinese}$ implemented in PyTorch [24] as the clause encoder. And the three decoders are implemented as three 2-layer MLPs whose hidden size is set as 256. The AdamW optimizer [19] is used for model training, and the learning rate is $1e^{-5}$ for BERT and $1e^{-4}$ for other modules. The dimension d is 512, the max span γ is 3 and the margin loss coefficient β is $1e^{-3}$. The step number of Co-evolving Reasoning is 3. The dropout rate is 0.1, and the batch size is 4. The epoch number is 10, and the early stopping strategy is adopted. All experiments are conducted on a DGX A100 server.

4.3   Compared Baselines

We compare our CGR-Net with the following two groups of baselines.

Group 1: M_1: ECPE-2D (BERT) [10]; M_2 :Hier-BiLSTM-BERT; M_3: PairGCN-BERT [3]; M_4: TransECPE [12]; M_5: RankCP+BERT [23]; M_6: UTOS+BERT [5]; M_7: ECPE-MLL(BERT) [11]; M_8: MGSAG(BERT) [1]; M_9: MaCa(BERT) [37];

Group 2: M_8: SLNT + BERT [38]; M_9: MTST + Refinement [13].

Our CGR-Net uses the same ECPE tagging scheme with the second group of baselines.

Table 2. Results comparison on ECPE task and the two subtasks. All scores are averages over 10 runs. All models adopt BERT for clause encoding. $^\natural$ denotes the results are reproduced by us. † and ‡ denote the results are retrieved from [13] and [5], respectively. * denotes our CGR-Net significantly overpasses M_{10} and M_{11} with $p < 0.05$ under t-test.

Models	Emotion-Cause Pair Ext.			Emotion Ext.			Cause Ext.		
	P (%)	R (%)	F1 (%)	P (%)	R (%)	F1 (%)	P (%)	R (%)	F1 (%)
M_1: ECPE-2D(BERT)	72.92	65.44	68.89	86.27	92.21	**89.10**	73.36	69.34	71.23
M_2: Hier-BiLSTM-BERT	75.37	64.34	69.26	88.80	74.70	81.00	78.03	65.35	70.96
M_3: PairGCN-BERT	76.92	67.91	72.02	88.57	79.58	83.75	79.07	69.28	73.75
M_4: TransECPE†	77.08	65.32	70.72	88.79	83.15	85.88	78.74	66.89	72.33
M_5: RankCP+BERT‡	68.21	74.83	71.21	86.79	89.26	87.97	72.62	76.46	74.37
M_6: UTOS+BERT	73.89	70.62	72.03	88.15	83.21	85.56	76.71	73.20	74.71
M_7: ECPE-MLL(BERT)	77.00	72.35	74.52	86.08	91.91	88.86	73.82	79.12	76.30
M_8: MGSAG(BERT)	77.43	73.21	75.21	92.08	92.11	87.17	79.79	74.68	77.12
M_9: MaCa(BERT)	80.47	72.15	73.87	88.19	89.55	87.04	78.41	72.60	74.35
M_{10}: SLNT+BERT$^\natural$	73.56	68.57	70.85	84.77	80.61	82.51	75.94	70.99	73.25
M_{11}: MTST+Refinement$^\natural$	77.14	67.81	72.11	88.25	79.01	83.31	79.18	69.79	74.12
CGR-Net (ours)	77.62	**75.49***	**76.48***	89.65	86.23*	87.75*	79.68	77.84*	**78.75***

4.4 Main Results

The overall results on ECPE and the two subtasks are shown in Table 2. We can observe that CE is much harder than EE, and CE determines the result of ECPE to a large extent. The reason is that CE plays a key role in identifying the causalities, which is difficult for machines. Our CGR-Net significantly outperforms the previous best-performing model M8 by 1.7%, 0.7%, and 2.1% in terms of F1 on ECPE, EE and CE, respectively. Using the same tagging scheme, our CGR-Net overpasses M_{10} and M_{11} by 6.1%, 5.3%, and 6.2% in F1 on the three tasks. In particular, we can find that the superior F1 of CGR-Net comes from the high recall and competitive precision. In contrast, previous models generally obtain low recalls because their single-round multi-task reasoning process and the one-way message only from CE/EE to ECPE are not competent enough to discover the emotion cause pairs sufficiently. Moreover, their implicit semantics interactions cannot effectively exploit the causal relations. We can find that our CGR-Net overpasses M_{10} and M_{11} by 10.1%, 7.0%, and 9.6% in terms of recall on the three tasks. This demonstrates that through Co-evolving Reasoning, CGR-Net can discover much more ground-truth emotion-cause pairs than baselines, while there are not many wrong-extracted pairs at the same time. CGR-Net's satisfying results come from the advantages of MRG, the well-designed supervision signals, and the advanced architecture of MRGT.

4.5 Variants of MRG Structure

In this section, we investigate how the structure of MRG would affect our CGR-Net's performance by applying different structures to MRG. Except for the orig-

Table 3. Results on different variants of MRG.

Variants	ECPE	EE	CE
	F1 (%)	F1 (%)	F1 (%)
MRG($\gamma = 3$)	76.48	87.75	78.75
MRG($\gamma = 1$)	75.15 ($\downarrow$ 1.33)	86.31 ($\downarrow$ 1.44)	77.32 ($\downarrow$ 1.43)
MRG($\gamma = 2$)	75.49 ($\downarrow$ 0.99)	87.55 ($\downarrow$ 0.20)	77.79 ($\downarrow$ 0.96)
MRG($\gamma = 4$)	74.87 ($\downarrow$ 1.61)	86.78 ($\downarrow$ 0.97)	77.21 ($\downarrow$ 1.54)
OWM	74.71 ($\downarrow$ 1.77)	86.30 ($\downarrow$ 1.45)	77.22($\downarrow$ 1.53))
NoRel	74.63 ($\downarrow$ 1.85)	85.33 ($\downarrow$ 2.42)	77.10 ($\downarrow$ 1.65)
FCG	73.65 ($\downarrow$ 2.83)	84.89 ($\downarrow$ 2.86)	76.56 ($\downarrow$ 2.19)

inal MRG($\gamma = 3$), we design four variants: (1) MRG($\gamma = 1$), MRG($\gamma = 2$) and MRG($\gamma = 4$), which have different span limitation; (2) OWM (one-way message), in which the edges from *tag* nodes to *emotion* nodes and *cause* nodes are deleted, thus there is only one-way message from EE/CE to ECPE, like previous works; (3) NoRel, in which there is no relation on edges; (4) FCG (fully-connected graph), in which all *tag* nodes are fully connected with all *emotion* nodes and all *cause* nodes, while there is no relation. The results over these variants are listed in Table 3.

Several instructive observations can be made from the results. **Firstly**, with γ varying from 1 to 4, the results first increase and then decrease. The reason is that too small γ cannot capture all emotion-pairs, while too large γ makes it much harder to predict correctly because $|\mathcal{C}_t|$ is directly proportional to γ. More than 95% emotion-cause pairs' spans in the dataset do not exceed 3, so intuitively $\gamma = 3$ performs best, and the results prove this. And this is consistent with the report of [13]. **Secondly**, compared with the original MRG, OWM's performances on all tasks drop significantly. This proves that the reverse feedbacks from ECPE to EE/CE is crucial, while previous works ignore them. In this paper, we propose a new MTL framework based on the novel Co-evolving Reasoning mechanism to solve this issue. **Thirdly**, without relations, NoRel performs much worse than the original MRG. The distinct decrease of results proves that our designed relations are indispensable for capturing the casualties between ECPE and EE/CE and significantly improve the performances. **Finally**, FCG performs even worse than NoRel. This is because causalities often exist between close clauses. In FCG, useless information from distant nodes is integrated into the current node, making the crucial information diluted and discarded, resulting in poor results. And this proves the validity of the local connection rule in MRG.

4.6 Investigation of Supervision Signals

To investigate the necessities of different supervision signals, we remove different loss terms, and the results are listed in Table 4. Firstly, we can observe that removing $\mathcal{L}_{emo}$ or $\mathcal{L}_{cau}$ both lead to obvious result decreases on all tasks. This

Table 4. Results of removing different loss terms.

Variants	EE	CE	ECPE
	F1 (%)	F1 (%)	F1 (%)
CGR-Net	76.48	87.75	78.75
$-\mathcal{L}_{emo}$	74.51 ($\downarrow$ 1.97)	86.21 ($\downarrow$ 1.54)	77.03 ($\downarrow$ 1.72)
$-\mathcal{L}_{cau}$	74.28 ($\downarrow$ 2.20)	86.25($\downarrow$ 1.50)	76.94 ($\downarrow$ 1.81)
$-\mathcal{L}_{emo} - \mathcal{L}_{cau}$	73.76 ($\downarrow$ 2.72)	85.05 ($\downarrow$ 2.70)	76.13 ($\downarrow$ 2.62)
$-\mathcal{L}_{est}$	75.43 ($\downarrow$ 1.05)	87.54 ($\downarrow$ 0.21)	77.97($\downarrow$ 0.78)
$-\mathcal{L}_{marg}$	74.22 ($\downarrow$ 2.26)	86.51($\downarrow$ 1.24)	76.64 ($\downarrow$ 2.11)
$-\mathcal{L}_{harn}$	74.89 ($\downarrow$ 1.59)	85.61 ($\downarrow$ 2.14)	77.60 ($\downarrow$ 1.15)

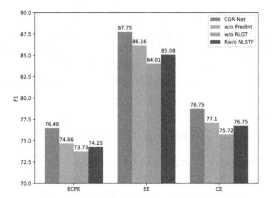

Fig. 4. Ablation results of MRGT cell.

is because our model exploits the beneficial mutual correlations between ECPE and the two subtasks. So removing the supervision signal of a subtask harms not only the performance of itself but also the performances of ECPE and another subtask. If both subtasks do not have supervision signals, the performances of all tasks drop dramatically. Then we can find that the performances decrease remarkably if $\mathcal{L}_{harn}$ or any of its two terms is removed. This is because without $\mathcal{L}_{harn}$ CGR-Net is hard to achieve the virtuous cycle of Co-evolving Reasoning.

4.7 Ablation Study of MRGT Cell

We conduct ablation experiments to study the efficacies of the components in MRGT cell, and the results are listed in Fig. 4. When removing prediction-level interactions (PredInt), the performances drop significantly. This proves that only relying on semantics-level interactions is insufficient for multi-task reasoning. An essential advantage of our model is achieving prediction-level interactions that convey explicit correlations and provide feedback for semantics that can then rethink to improve. Without RLGT, Co-evolving Reasoning cannot be achieved,

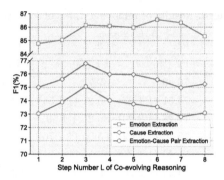

Fig. 5. CGR-Net's performances on different L.

causing the worst results. Removing NLST also leads to sharp decreases in results. This is because without NLST the hidden states cannot obtain long-range crucial contextual information, and the three streams of hidden states output at each step are not task-specific enough, which both harm the predictions.

4.8   Step Number of Co-evolving Reasoning

We plot the performance (F1) trends of CGR-Net on the three tasks over different Co-evolving Reasoning step numbers, as presented in Fig. 5. The best overall performances are achieved when $L = 3$, which justifies the step number setting in Sec. 4.2. Generally, the performances of ECPE and the two subtasks steadily increase until $L = 3$, while then having dropping trends or fluctuate in a relatively narrow range when L continues increasing. This indicates that ECPE and CE/EE can gradually promote each other in the process of Co-evolving Reasoning, whose advantage is validated. However, after the performance reaches its peak, more steps lead to decreasing. We speculate the possible reason is that too many Co-evolving Reasoning steps may cause redundant information and over-fitting.

5   Conclusion and Prospect

In this paper, we improve ECPE on three aspects. First, we propose a new MTL based on Co-evolving Reasoning, allowing ECPE and its two subtasks to promote each other gradually. Besides, prediction-level interactions are integrated to model the explicit correlations. Second, we design a novel multi-task relational graph (MRG) to sufficiently exploit the causal relations. Finally, we propose a Co-evolving Graph Reasoning Network (CGR-Net) to implement our framework and conduct Co-evolving Reasoning on MRG. Experiment results demonstrate the superiority of our method, and detailed analyses further validate the advantages.

This work contributes a new paradigm not only for ECPE but also for a group of scenarios in which different tasks share the same input sequence. Future works include improving our method on ECPE and applying our paradigm to other MTL tasks.

Acknowledgments. This work was supported by Australian Research Council Grant DP200101328. Authors were also supported by A*STAR Centre for Frontier AI Research.

References

1. Bao, Y., Ma, Q., Wei, L., Zhou, W., Hu, S.: Multi-granularity semantic aware graph model for reducing position bias in emotion cause pair extraction. In: Findings of the Association for Computational Linguistics: ACL 2022, pp. 1203–1213. Association for Computational Linguistics, Dublin, Ireland (May 2022)
2. Chen, X., Li, Q., Wang, J.: A unified sequence labeling model for emotion cause pair extraction. In: Proceedings of the 28th International Conference on Computational Linguistics, pp. 208–218. International Committee on Computational Linguistics, Barcelona, Spain (Online) (Dec 2020)
3. Chen, Y., Hou, W., Li, S., Wu, C., Zhang, X.: End-to-end emotion-cause pair extraction with graph convolutional network. In: Proceedings of the 28th International Conference on Computational Linguistics, pp. 198–207. International Committee on Computational Linguistics, Barcelona, Spain (Online) (Dec 2020)
4. Chen, Y., Lee, S.Y.M., Li, S., Huang, C.R.: Emotion cause detection with linguistic constructions. In: Proceedings of the 23rd International Conference on Computational Linguistics (Coling 2010), pp. 179–187. Coling 2010 Organizing Committee, Beijing, China (Aug 2010)
5. Cheng, Z., Jiang, Z., Yin, Y., Li, N., Gu, Q.: A unified target-oriented sequence-to-sequence model for emotion-cause pair extraction. IEEE/ACM Trans. Audio Speech Lang. Process. **29**, 2779–2791 (2021)
6. Cheng, Z., Jiang, Z., Yin, Y., Yu, H., Gu, Q.: A symmetric local search network for emotion-cause pair extraction. In: Proceedings of the 28th International Conference on Computational Linguistics, pp. 139–149. International Committee on Computational Linguistics, Barcelona, Spain (Online) (Dec 2020)
7. De Beaugrande, R., Dressler, W.U.: Introduction to Text Linguistics. Longmans, London (1981)
8. Devlin, J., Chang, M.W., Lee, K., Toutanova, K.: BERT: pre-training of deep bidirectional transformers for language understanding. In: Proceedings of the 2019 Conference of the North American Chapter of the Association for Computational Linguistics: Human Language Technologies, Volume 1 (Long and Short Papers), pp. 4171–4186. Association for Computational Linguistics, Minneapolis, Minnesota (2019)
9. Ding, Z., He, H., Zhang, M., Xia, R.: From independent prediction to reordered prediction: integrating relative position and global label information to emotion cause identification. In: AAAI, pp. 6343–6350. AAAI Press (2019)
10. Ding, Z., Xia, R., Yu, J.: ECPE-2D: emotion-cause pair extraction based on joint two-dimensional representation, interaction and prediction. In: Proceedings of the 58th Annual Meeting of the Association for Computational Linguistics, pp. 3161–3170. Association for Computational Linguistics (Online) (Jul 2020)

11. Ding, Z., Xia, R., Yu, J.: End-to-end emotion-cause pair extraction based on sliding window multi-label learning. In: Proceedings of the 2020 Conference on Empirical Methods in Natural Language Processing (EMNLP), pp. 3574–3583. Association for Computational Linguistics (Online) (Nov 2020)

12. Fan, C., Yuan, C., Du, J., Gui, L., Yang, M., Xu, R.: Transition-based directed graph construction for emotion-cause pair extraction. In: Proceedings of the 58th Annual Meeting of the Association for Computational Linguistics, pp. 3707–3717. Association for Computational Linguistics (Online) (Jul 2020)

13. Fan, C., Yuan, C., Gui, L., Zhang, Y., Xu, R.: Multi-task sequence tagging for emotion-cause pair extraction via tag distribution refinement. IEEE/ACM Trans. Audio Speech Lang. Process. **29**, 2339–2350 (2021)

14. Ghazi, D., Inkpen, D., Szpakowicz, S.: Detecting emotion stimuli in emotion-bearing sentences. In: Gelbukh, A. (ed.) CICLing 2015. LNCS, vol. 9042, pp. 152–165. Springer, Cham (2015). https://doi.org/10.1007/978-3-319-18117-2_12

15. Gui, L., Hu, J., He, Y., Xu, R., Lu, Q., Du, J.: A question answering approach for emotion cause extraction. In: Proceedings of the 2017 Conference on Empirical Methods in Natural Language Processing, pp. 1593–1602. Association for Computational Linguistics, Copenhagen, Denmark (Sep 2017)

16. Gui, L., Wu, D., Xu, R., Lu, Q., Zhou, Y.: Event-driven emotion cause extraction with corpus construction. In: Proceedings of the 2016 Conference on Empirical Methods in Natural Language Processing, pp. 1639–1649. Association for Computational Linguistics, Austin, Texas (Nov 2016)

17. Hochreiter, S., Schmidhuber, J.: Long short-term memory. Neural Comput. **9**(8), 1735–1780 (1997)

18. Lee, S.Y.M., Chen, Y., Huang, C.R.: A text-driven rule-based system for emotion cause detection. In: Proceedings of the NAACL HLT 2010 Workshop on Computational Approaches to Analysis and Generation of Emotion in Text, pp. 45–53. Association for Computational Linguistics, Los Angeles, CA (Jun 2010)

19. Loshchilov, I., Hutter, F.: Decoupled weight decay regularization. In: 7th International Conference on Learning Representations, ICLR 2019, New Orleans, LA, USA, 6–9 May 2019. OpenReview.net (2019)

20. Neviarouskaya, A., Aono, M.: Extracting causes of emotions from text. In: Proceedings of the Sixth International Joint Conference on Natural Language Processing, pp. 932–936. Asian Federation of Natural Language Processing, Nagoya, Japan (Oct 2013)

21. Russo, I., Caselli, T., Rubino, F., Boldrini, E., Martínez-Barco, P.: EMOCause: an easy-adaptable approach to extract emotion cause contexts. In: Proceedings of the 2nd Workshop on Computational Approaches to Subjectivity and Sentiment Analysis (WASSA 2011), pp. 153–160. Association for Computational Linguistics, Portland, Oregon (Jun 2011)

22. Schlichtkrull, M.S., Kipf, T.N., Bloem, P., van den Berg, R., Titov, I., Welling, M.: Modeling relational data with graph convolutional networks. In: ESWC, pp. 593–607 (2018)

23. Wei, P., Zhao, J., Mao, W.: Effective inter-clause modeling for end-to-end emotion-cause pair extraction. In: Proceedings of the 58th Annual Meeting of the Association for Computational Linguistics, pp. 3171–3181. Association for Computational Linguistics (Online) (Jul 2020)

24. Wolf, T., et al.: Transformers: State-of-the-art natural language processing. In: Proceedings of the 2020 Conference on Empirical Methods in Natural Language Processing: System Demonstrations, pp. 38–45. Association for Computational Linguistics (Online) (2020)

25. Wu, S., Chen, F., Wu, F., Huang, Y., Li, X.: A multi-task learning neural network for emotion-cause pair extraction. In: ECAI. Frontiers in Artificial Intelligence and Applications, vol. 325, pp. 2212–2219. IOS Press (2020)
26. Xia, R., Ding, Z.: Emotion-cause pair extraction: A new task to emotion analysis in texts. In: Proceedings of the 57th Annual Meeting of the Association for Computational Linguistics, pp. 1003–1012. Association for Computational Linguistics, Florence, Italy (Jul 2019)
27. Xing, B., et al.: Earlier attention? aspect-aware lstm for aspect-based sentiment analysis. In: Proceedings of the Twenty-Eighth International Joint Conference on Artificial Intelligence, IJCAI 2019, pp. 5313–5319. International Joint Conferences on Artificial Intelligence Organization (July 2019)
28. Xing, B., Tsang, I.: Co-guiding net: achieving mutual guidances between multiple intent detection and slot filling via heterogeneous semantics-label graphs. In: Proceedings of the 2022 Conference on Empirical Methods in Natural Language Processing, pp. 159–169. Association for Computational Linguistics, Abu Dhabi, United Arab Emirates (Dec 2022)
29. Xing, B., Tsang, I.: DARER: dual-task temporal relational recurrent reasoning network for joint dialog sentiment classification and act recognition. In: Findings of the Association for Computational Linguistics: ACL 2022, pp. 3611–3621. Association for Computational Linguistics, Dublin, Ireland (May 2022)
30. Xing, B., Tsang, I.: Dignet: digging clues from local-global interactive graph for aspect-level sentiment classification. arXiv preprint arXiv:2201.00989 (2022)
31. Xing, B., Tsang, I.: Group is better than individual: exploiting label topologies and label relations for joint multiple intent detection and slot filling. In: Proceedings of the 2022 Conference on Empirical Methods in Natural Language Processing, pp. 3964–3975. Association for Computational Linguistics, Abu Dhabi, United Arab Emirates (Dec 2022)
32. Xing, B., Tsang, I.: Neural subgraph explorer: reducing noisy information via target-oriented syntax graph pruning. In: Proceedings of the Thirty-First International Joint Conference on Artificial Intelligence, IJCAI 2022, pp. 4425–4431. International Joint Conferences on Artificial Intelligence Organization (July 2022), main Track
33. Xing, B., Tsang, I.: Relational temporal graph reasoning for dual-task dialogue language understanding. arXiv preprint arXiv:2306.09114 (2023)
34. Xing, B., Tsang, I.W.: Out of context: a new clue for context modeling of aspect-based sentiment analysis. J. Artifi. Intell. Res. **74**, 627–659 (2022)
35. Xing, B., Tsang, I.W.: Understand me, if you refer to aspect knowledge: Knowledge-aware gated recurrent memory network. IEEE Trans. Emerging Topics Comput. Intell. **6**(5), 1092–1102 (2022)
36. Yan, H., Gui, L., Pergola, G., He, Y.: Position bias mitigation: a knowledge-aware graph model for emotion cause extraction. In: Proceedings of the 59th Annual Meeting of the Association for Computational Linguistics and the 11th International Joint Conference on Natural Language Processing (Volume 1: Long Papers), pp. 3364–3375. Association for Computational Linguistics (Online) (Aug 2021)

37. Yang, C., Zhang, Z., Ding, J., Zheng, W., Jing, Z., Li, Y.: A multi-granularity network for emotion-cause pair extraction via matrix capsule. In: Proceedings of the 31st ACM International Conference on Information & Knowledge Management, pp. 4625–4629 (2022)
38. Yuan, C., Fan, C., Bao, J., Xu, R.: Emotion-cause pair extraction as sequence labeling based on a novel tagging scheme. In: Proceedings of the 2020 Conference on Empirical Methods in Natural Language Processing (EMNLP), pp. 3568–3573. Association for Computational Linguistics, Online (Nov 2020)

SpotGAN: A Reverse-Transformer GAN Generates Scaffold-Constrained Molecules with Property Optimization

Chen Li$^{(\boxtimes)}$ (ID) and Yoshihiro Yamanishi (ID)

Graduate School of Informatics, Nagoya University, Chikusa, Nagoya 464-8602, Japan
li.chen.z2@a.mail.nagoya-u.ac.jp, yamanishi@i.nagoya-u.ac.jp

Abstract. Generating molecules with a given scaffold is a challenging task in drug-discovery. Scaffolds impose strict constraints on the generation of molecules. Moreover, the order of the simplified molecular-input line-entry system (SMILES) strings changes substantially during sequence expansion. This study presents a scaffold-constrained, property-optimized transformer GAN (SpotGAN) to solve these issues. SpotGAN employs a decoration generator that fills decorations into a given scaffold using a transformer-decoder variant. The discriminator is a transformer-encoder variant with a global receptive field that improves the realism of the generated molecules. The chemical properties are optimized through reinforcement learning (RL), affording molecules with high property scores. Additionally, an extension of SpotGAN, called SpotWGAN, is proposed to optimize and stabilize the training process leveraging the Wasserstein distance and mini-batch discrimination. Experimental results show the usefulness of the proposed model on scaffold-constrained molecular-generation tasks in terms of the drug-likeness, solubility, synthesizability, and bioactivity of the generated molecules([1] Our code is available at: https://github.com/naruto7283/SpotGAN).

Keywords: Deep learning · Molecular generation · Scaffold-constrained

1 Introduction

In drug discovery, the postulated number of potential drug-like molecules is up to 10^{60}; however, only approximately 10^8 molecules have been synthesized [20]. Discovering molecules with the desired properties in such a vast and infinite chemical space is unrealistic. Deep generative models such as variational autoencoders (VAEs) [21] and generative adversarial networks (GANs) [13] inspired by text and image generation in natural language processing (NLP) [9] and image recognition [18] are promising directions for molecular generation. In *de novo* molecular generation [15], molecules in deep generative models are represented by graphs or the simplified molecular-input line-entry system (SMILES) [37]. Molecules in the SMILES notation are represented as strings and computed using deep learning models for NLP [23]. However, generating drug-like molecules with

© The Author(s), under exclusive license to Springer Nature Switzerland AG 2023
D. Koutra et al. (Eds.): ECML PKDD 2023, LNAI 14169, pp. 323–338, 2023.
https://doi.org/10.1007/978-3-031-43412-9_19

the desired chemical properties from SMILES strings is difficult in the framework of GANs. Within the limited discrete space of SMILES strings, the discriminator cannot effectively guide the training of the generator nor evaluate incomplete SMILES strings during the generation process [38]. Although reinforcement learning (RL) can alleviate the above problems and optimize the chemical properties of the generated molecules, discrete GANs are prone to severe mode collapse. Additionally, SMILES-based molecular representations are overly sensitive to syntax, leading to unsatisfactory generated molecules [14].

Furthermore, in processes such as lead optimization [6], molecular design often starts not from scratch but from a partially constructed molecule with explicit attachment points, called a *scaffold* [40]. The scaffold is a molecular core that preserves the underlying characteristic throughout the lead-optimization process. Only functional groups called *decorations* [17] can be designed, optimized, and ultimately combined with attachment points on the scaffold, forming a new molecule. Unfortunately, few studies on deep generative models for scaffold-constrained molecular generation have been conducted. It is imperative to consider scaffolds in molecular-generation tasks because several structural restrictions should be imposed on generated molecular structures [2,25]. For example, the GAN must remember the rules learned during training and the strict constraints imposed by the scaffold on the molecules. Moreover, the optimization of chemical properties is limited by the well-defined chemical composition of the given scaffold. Although SMILES representations of molecules are simple and faster than graph training, they change substantially during the sequential extension of decorations.

A transformer [36] is a suitable candidate for generating molecules from SMILES strings based on scaffolds. The self-attention mechanism has a global receptive field in which each atom in the SMILES string is accessible to all other atoms. However, the positional encoding poses two problems in scaffold-constrained molecular generation. First, it does not preserve the attachment-point location on the scaffold. This location is critical for the decoration because the chemical properties and structures of the decorations vary widely at different attachment points. Secondly, a decoration can contain an arbitrary number of atoms, whereas the transformer cannot encode strings of unknown length. This study proposes a scaffold-constrained property-optimized transformer GAN (SpotGAN) for addressing the above issues. In contrast to traditional transformers, the SpotGAN first uses the transformer decoder as the generator and subsequently applies the encoder as the discriminator. The decoration generator leverages a transformer-decoder variant to fill decorations into the given scaffold. The discriminator is a transformer-encoder variant with a global receptive field that guides the generator to produce drug-like molecules. RL is leveraged to generate molecules with high property scores in chemical-property optimization. In addition, an extension of SpotGAN, called SpotWGAN, is proposed to optimize and stabilize the training process using the Wasserstein distance [1] and mini-batch discrimination [33]. The main contributions are summarized as follows:

- **Novel transformer design:** The first discrete GAN for generating molecules on constrained scaffolds is proposed. In the reverse order of transformer-encoder-decoder, a transformer decoder and an encoder as the generator and discriminator of the GAN, are leveraged, respectively.

- **New training recipe:** GAN training is stabilized by techniques such as diversified SMILES data augmentation, Wasserstein distance, and mini-batch discrimination.
- **Superior performance:** Comparisons with state-of-the-art models, ablation studies, and case studies with five scaffolds for a therapeutic target demonstrate the effectiveness of the proposed models in practice.

2   Related Work

2.1   Structure-Unconstrained Molecular Generation

Structure-unconstrained models aim to generate molecules from scratch and represent the generated entities as graphs or SMILES strings. JTVAE [19] is a graph-based VAE that generates molecules using a tree-structured object representing the subgraphs and their rough relative arrangements. JTVAE constructs a molecular graph in two steps. First, the VAE encoder extracts the features of a molecular graph and junction tree into its latent embeddings. Secondly, the decoder reconstructs the junction tree and reassembles the atoms in the tree into molecules. GraphAF [34] is a flow-based molecular graph generation autoregressive model that generates atoms and bonds from existing molecular subgraphs. GraphAF examines the molecular graphs using chemical-domain knowledge at each generation step. MolGAN [5] uses RL to generate novel molecules from molecular graphs. However, it has a serious mode collapse problem whereby its uniqueness is less than 5%. MoFlow [39] generates atoms of given bonds through a graph conditional flow and finally assembles them into a valid molecular graph. GraphCNF [26] is a normalizing flow for graph generation, which is invariant to the order of atoms by generating all atoms and bonds at once.

The representation of molecules as strings in the SMILES notation is more concise than representing them on graphs. However, the generated molecules are fragile. Slight changes in the SMILES strings may lead to different or invalid molecules. CharVAE and GramVAE [23] are parse tree-based grammar VAEs that produce valid molecules from SMILES strings. Parse tree-based grammars can directly incorporate knowledge of the molecular structure from SMILES strings, whereas VAEs can encode and decode the trees. CharVAE is a character-based VAE that generates any possible atom for every token in the generated string, whereas GramVAE selects only the syntactically valid strings. Although CharVAE and GramVAE produce syntactically valid molecules, they ignore the semantic plausibility. ORGAN [14] is a SMILES-based GAN, where the generator is a recurrent neural network (RNN) that learns the features of SMILES strings and produces new molecules to deceive the discriminator. The discriminator is a convolutional neural network that distinguishes between the fake and real molecules. RL is used to improve the chemical properties of the generated molecules. RNNAttn and TransVAE [8] are an attention-based RNN and a transformer-based VAE that learn the semantics and syntax of SMILES strings.

2.2   Structure-Constrained Molecular Generation

Structure-constrained models generate molecules starting from a given molecular substructure. MoLeR [27] supports scaffolds as initial seeds of the generative procedure and generates molecules by adding entire molecule fragments in one step or generating atoms and bonds one by one. SCRNN [25] is a scaffold-constrained molecular generative model that uses a RNN to generate decorations. The scaffold-constraint algorithms of SCRNN are manually designed to constrain the decoration sampling of the RNN, which limits the model's capacity to learn complex SMILES strings. DecRNN [2] is a SMILES-based scaffold decorator that exploits a RNN to learn SMILES syntax and then generate decorations on specific scaffolds. However, using the RNN to learn SMILES syntax is quite limited. The generation is cost-intensive, and the validity of the generated molecules cannot be guaranteed since the RNN is sensitive to the SMILES strings of input scaffolds.

To satisfy the increasing demand, variants of the transformer have been employed recently [7,11]. Excluding the recurrent structure of RNN, transformers only use the self-attention that can be calculated in parallel, making them more suitable for a large chemical space. Additionally, self-attention has a global receptive field that captures the deep semantics and syntax of SMILES strings. This study aims to design a SpotGAN to produce molecules and optimize their chemical properties.

3   Models

3.1   Data Augmentation

To address the problem of the substantial changes in the SMILES representations of molecules generated during the sequential extension of decorations, a data-augmentation technique called *diversified SMILES* is proposed, which sufficiently learns the syntax and semantics from SMILES strings. Assuming that a molecule can obtain a scaffold and decoration by splitting its acyclic bond at an arbitrary position, then a molecule can be represented through different pairs of scaffolds and decorations. The order variation in the SMILES strings is mitigated by adequately learning the diversified SMILES. An example of diversified SMILES production is provided in Appendix A.1 [2]

3.2   SpotGAN

In a similar manner as an NLP task [41], the generator produces decorations from a scaffold. Formally, let $\boldsymbol{X}_{1:n} = [x_1, x_2, \cdots, x_n]$ and $\boldsymbol{Y}_{1:m} = [y_1, y_2, \cdots, y_m]$ denote the SMILES strings of the scaffold and the decoration of lengths n and m, respectively, where x_i ($i \in \mathbb{N}_{\leq n} = \{1, \cdots, n\}$) and y_j ($j \in \mathbb{N}_{\leq m} = \{1, \cdots, m\}$) represent the i-th and j-th atoms, respectively. The symbol, $*$, denotes an

---

[2] Appendices are available at https://yamanishi.cs.i.nagoya-u.ac.jp/spotgan/.

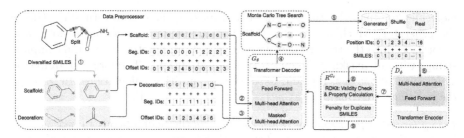

Fig. 1. Overview of SpotGAN. SpotGAN consists of four parts: the data preprocessor, generator (G_θ), discriminator (D_ϕ), and reward network (R^{G_θ}). During the data preprocessing, molecules are split into scaffolds and decorations, and assigned with segment (seg.) and offset IDs (①). The decoration generator is a variant of the transformer decoder. The scaffolds and decorations are input into the multi-head attention (②) and masked multi-head attention (③), respectively. The decorations are generated by the Monte Carlo (MC) search on the given scaffold (④). The generated strings and training SMILES strings are shuffled (⑤) and input into the discriminator (⑥). The discriminator is a transformer-encoder-based classifier that distinguishes the generated strings from the real SMILES strings (⑦). The chemical property scores and penalty scores of valid molecules are calculated by the RDKit tool and the count of occurrences in the training set, respectively (⑧). Finally, the outputs of the discriminator and reward network jointly guide the generator training (⑨).

attachment point for the decoration in the scaffold. For example, in $X_{1:n} = [x_1, \cdots, x_{i-1}, *, x_i, \cdots, x_n]$, the decoration is attached to the scaffold at the i-th position. The SMILES string expressed as $Z_{1:n+m} = [X_{1:i-1}, Y_{1:m}, X_{i:n}]$ replaces the attachment point in the scaffold with a decoration.

Transformer Decoder as the Generator. As different SMILES strings have different decorated positions and different numbers of decorated atoms, additional positional information must be injected into the SMILES strings. Let S denote the seg. IDs of a SMILES string, which are assigned according to the attachment points starting from 0. The seg. IDs distinguish the scaffold and decoration of a SMILES string. For example, depending on the attachment point, the SMILES string, $Z_{1:n+m}$, can be divided into three segments: $S_{X_{1:i-1}} = [0, \cdots, 0]$, $S_{Y_{1:m}} = [1, \cdots, 1]$, and $S_{X_{i:n}} = [2, \cdots, 2]$. The offset IDs locate the different atoms in each segment. They are denoted as O and assigned from 0. In the string, $Z_{1:n+m}$, the three offset IDs are $O_{X_{1:i-1}} = [0, 1, \cdots, i-2]$, $O_{Y_{1:m}} = [0, 1, \cdots, m-1]$, and $O_{X_{i:n}} = [0, 1, \cdots, n-i]$. Next, the positions are calculated by a linear function, such as $pos = a * S + O$, $a \in \mathbb{N}_{\leq |O_{max}|}$, where $|O_{max}|$ indicates the length of the longest decoration. Finally, the positions are input as a sinusoidal positional encoding function, summed with the embedding, and passed to the transformer decoder (see Appendix A.2 for details).

Transformer Encoder as the Discriminator. The local and global attention fields of the self-attention mechanism allow every atom in the SMILES string to access all other atoms. Here, the transformer encoder acts as a classifier, evaluating the molecules produced by the generator and making them more drug-like. Unlike the generator, which inputs the SMILES representations of the scaffolds and decorations into the transformer decoder, the discriminator inputs the complete strings without masking the multi-head self-attention. Therefore, it requires no assignment of the seg. IDs and offset IDs for position calculations. In $\boldsymbol{Z}_{1:n+m}$, the positions are computed as $pos = [0, 1, \cdots, n+m-1]$.

Policy Gradient for Property Optimization. As the scaffold-constrained molecular generation immobilizes parts of the SMILES strings, the generated decoration must fit the scaffold while also ensuring the desired chemical properties of the combined SMILES strings. RL, particularly the policy gradient [35], can not only update the policy (G_θ) but can also impart the training with the chemical properties as rewards. The objective function of the generator maximizes the expected reward score as

$$J(\theta) = \sum_{y_j \in \boldsymbol{Y}_{1:m}} G_\theta(y_j | \boldsymbol{X}_{1:n}, \boldsymbol{Y}_{1:j-1}) R^{G_\theta}(\boldsymbol{Y}_{1:j-1}, y_j), \tag{1}$$

where G_θ and R^{G_θ} denote the generator policy model parameterized by θ and the action-value function of the average reward of the chemical properties of state $\boldsymbol{Y}_{1:j-1}$ taking action y_j, following policy G_θ, respectively. For a complete decoration $\boldsymbol{Y}_{1:m}$, R^{G_θ} is calculated as

$$R^{G_\theta}(\boldsymbol{Y}_{1:m-1}, y_m) = \lambda D_\phi(\boldsymbol{Z}_{1:n+m}) + (1-\lambda)\left[R(\boldsymbol{Z}_{1:n+m})P(\boldsymbol{Z}_{1:n+m}) - b(\boldsymbol{Z}_{1:n+m})\right], \tag{2}$$

where $\lambda \in [0, 1]$ represents the trade-off between RL and GAN. R is the property score, which can be calculated using RDKit [24]. P is the penalty for producing duplicate SMILES strings, calculated as

$$P(\boldsymbol{Z}_{1:n+m}) = \frac{\# \text{ unique SMILES}}{(\# \text{ SMILES} \times \# \text{ repeated } \boldsymbol{Z}_{1:n+m})}. \tag{3}$$

Parameter b is the baseline below which molecules with low chemical-property scores are penalized. For simplicity, we apply the average property scores for R.

MC search for incomplete decorations. For incomplete decorations $\boldsymbol{Y}_{1:j}$ and $j < m$, the rewards are computed at intermediate time steps by K MC searches:

$$\boldsymbol{Z}_{1:n+m}^k = [\boldsymbol{X}_{1:i-1}, \boldsymbol{Y}_{1:m}^k, \boldsymbol{X}_{i:n}], \quad \boldsymbol{Y}_{1:m}^k \in \text{MC}^{G_\theta}(\boldsymbol{Y}_{1:j}, K), \text{ and } k \in [1, K], \tag{4}$$

where $\boldsymbol{Y}_{1:m}^k = [\boldsymbol{Y}_{1:j}^k, \boldsymbol{Y}_{j+1:m}^k]$ represents the complete decoration of the k-th MC search. $\boldsymbol{Y}_{1:j}^k = \boldsymbol{Y}_{1:j}$, and $\boldsymbol{Y}_{j+1:M}^k$ is sampled under policy G_θ. R^{G_θ} is calculated as

$$R^{G_\theta}(\boldsymbol{Y}_{1:j-1}, y_j) = \frac{1}{K}\sum_{k=1}^K \lambda D_\phi(\boldsymbol{Z}_{1:n+m}^k) + (1-\lambda)\left[R(\boldsymbol{Z}_{1:n+m}^k)P(\boldsymbol{Z}_{1:n+m}^k) - b(\boldsymbol{Z}_{1:n+m}^k)\right]. \tag{5}$$

Then, the gradient of the objective function is derived as

$$\nabla J(\theta) \simeq \frac{1}{m}\sum_{j=1}^m \sum_{y_j} R^{G_\theta}(\boldsymbol{Y}_{1:j-1}, y_j) \nabla \log G_\theta(y_j | \boldsymbol{X}_{1:n}, \boldsymbol{Y}_{1:j-1}). \tag{6}$$

Finally, the policy is updated by training the generator G_θ using $\theta \leftarrow \theta + \nabla J(\theta)$.

3.3 SpotWGAN

Although RL enables GANs to generate molecules from discrete SMILES strings, there remain the problems of unstable convergence and mode collapse. In addition, the diversity of the generated molecules decreases with training because the discriminator distinguishes each SMILES string independently without correlation between the gradients. Molecules that are discriminated to be true and structurally similar tend to get higher rewards, leading to a lack of diversity in the generated molecules.

Mini-Batch Discrimination for Stable Training. The above-mentioned problems are best avoided by mini-batch discrimination. To reduce the impact of the hyperparameters, nonparametric mini-batch discrimination is employed in the discriminator. Let $H \in \mathbb{R}^{B \times d_{model}}$ be the output before the last fully connected layer of the discriminator, where B denotes the mini-batch size. We compute the standard deviation of H on the d_{model} dimension of the SMILES strings of the mini-batch size. The average deviation is concatenated to H and fed into the fully connected layer. For simplicity, the mini-batch size is set to the batch size.

Wasserstein GAN (WGAN) for Mode-Collapse Mitigation. An extension of SpotGAN, called SpotWGAN, is also proposed to stabilize the training and mitigate the mode collapse caused by the discrete space of SMILES. The discriminator leverages the Wasserstein distance between the generated strings and SMILES strings. The objective function is based on the Kantorovich-Rubinstein duality, as follows:

$$W(\mathcal{D}_r, \mathcal{D}_z) = \sup_{||D_\phi||_L \leq 1} \mathbb{E}_{\boldsymbol{Z} \sim \mathcal{D}_r(\boldsymbol{Z})}\left[D_\phi(\boldsymbol{Z})\right] - \mathbb{E}_{\boldsymbol{Z} \sim \mathcal{D}_z}\left[D_\phi(G_\theta(\boldsymbol{Z}))\right], \quad (7)$$

where $\mathcal{D}_r$ and $\mathcal{D}_z$ denote the distributions of the real and generated SMILES strings, respectively. The parameters, sup and D_ϕ, denote the lowest upper bound and the 1-Lipschitz function satisfying this constraint, respectively.

Algorithm 1 in the section of Appendix A.3 shows an overview of the proposed models. First, the generator G_θ is pre-trained by maximum likelihood estimation on the real SMILES dataset $\mathcal{D}_r$. Next, the generator produces dataset $\mathcal{D}_z$ with the same number of SMILES strings as $\mathcal{D}_r$ to balance the two datasets. The two datasets are shuffled before pre-training the discriminator D_ϕ. Finally, the generator and the discriminator are alternately trained in adversarial training and parameters θ are updated with an MC search using the policy gradient.

4 Experiments

4.1 Experimental Setup

Datasets. All experiments were conducted on the QM9 [31] and ZINC [16] datasets. Each dataset contained 10,000 SMILES strings and was split into scaffold and decoration pairs during data-preprocessing stage. As the ZINC dataset contains more complex SMILES strings than the QM9 dataset, the average length of the decorations was around four times longer in ZINC than in QM9.

Table 1. Some average statistics for the QM9 and ZINC datasets.

Dataset	LEN	SLEN	DLEN	MW	QED	logP	SA
QM9	15	12	5	124	0.47	0.30	0.33
ZINC	38	21	19	321	0.79	0.63	0.76

⋆ LEN, SLEN, and DLEN indicate the average lengths of the SMILES strings, scaffolds, and decorations of the molecules. MW indicates the average molecular weights.

Implementation Details. The generator contained four decoder layers, each with four attention heads. The attention heads were 128-dimensional for the QM9 dataset and 256-dimensional for the ZINC dataset. The feedforward layer was 100-dimensional for both datasets. On both datasets, the generator was pre-trained for 100 and 200 epochs at learning rates of $1e-5$ and $1e-4$, respectively. In the sampling process, 10,000 molecules were generated per epoch, and the maximum lengths of the generated molecules were 20 and 50, respectively. The batch size and dropout probability were 64 and 0.1, respectively. The discriminator consists of four encoder layers, each with four attention heads and 128-dimensional. The size of the feedforward layer was 200. The learning rates of the SpotGAN and SpotWGAN were $1e-4$ and $1e-5$, respectively. The discriminator was pre-trained over 10 epochs. In the adversarial training, the learning rate of the generator was $2e-5$, and λ and K were set to 0.5 and 8, respectively (unless specified otherwise). Up to 100 and 50 training epochs were run on both datasets, respectively. All the experiments were implemented on an NVIDIA GV100GL GPU.

4.2   Metrics

Evaluation Measures. *Validity* is the proportion of chemically valid molecules among all generated molecules. In practice, the validity of the molecules was examined using the RDKit tool. *Uniqueness* (abbr. unique) is the proportion of nonduplicated molecules among all valid molecules. *Novelty* is the proportion of all unique molecules absent from the training set. *Total* is the total performance measure defined as the product of validity, uniqueness, and novelty. *Diversity* is the average Tanimoto distance [32] between the Morgan fingerprints [28] of novel molecules (see Appendix B.1 for details).

Optimized Properties. *Drug-likeness* indicates the likeness of a molecule to be a drug and is scored by the quantitative estimate of drug-likeness (QED) [3]. *Solubility* refers to the lipophilicity of a molecule and is quantified by the octanol-water partition coefficient (logP) [4]. *Synthesizability* indicates the ease of synthesizing a molecule and is called the synthetic accessibility (SA) score [10]. For consistency in rewards, the difference between "synthesizability knowledge" and synthesizability was used as the SA score. Note that the larger the SA score, the easier the synthesis of the molecule. *BIO* measures the bioactivity of a molecule

Table 2. Comparison with baselines using the ZINC dataset.

Method	Validity (%)	Unique (%)	Novelty (%)	Total (%)
ORGAN	67.96	98.20	98.39	65.66
RNNAttn	71.57	99.94	100.0	71.53
TransVAE	25.39	99.96	100.0	25.38
JTVAE	100.0	19.75	99.75	19.70
CharVAE	86.65	81.21	26.36	18.55
GramVAE	91.91	77.24	11.90	8.45
MolGAN	95.3	4.3	100.0	4.1
GraphCNF	63.56	100.0	100.0	63.56
MoFlow	27.12	99.97	100.0	27.11
GraphAF	100.0	83.19	100.0	83.19
Naïve RL	89.15	88.45	91.87	72.44
SCRNN	88.71	86.56	86.56	66.47
SCRNN-RL	79.27	93.71	94.69	70.34
MoLeR	94.53	88.22	88.22	73.57
Decorator	93.58	97.04	92.42	83.93
SpotGAN	93.26	92.78	92.75	80.25
SpotWGAN	96.21	93.63	92.37	83.21

⋆ The values in gray cells are the maximum values.

against a therapeutic target. For example, the dopamine receptor D2 (DRD2) [29] was used as a therapeutic target in this study. The calculations of these chemical properties are detailed in Appendix B.2. All of the above measures and properties range from 0 (the worst score) to 1 (the best score). We also calculated the execution times of all models in the GPU environment. Table 1 lists some average statistics for the QM9 and ZINC training datasets.

4.3 Evaluation of Molecular Generation

The performances of different models in both structure-unconstrained (upper panel of Table 2) and structure-constrained approaches (lower panel of Table 2) using the ZINC dataset were evaluated. Note that "Decorator" indicates the generator of SpotGAN. The validity, uniqueness, novelty, and total scores were assessed. Although ORGAN, RNNAttn, and TransVAE generated highly unique and novel molecules, the validity of these models was lower than those for the SpotGAN and SpotWGAN. The molecules generated by JTVAE scored nearly 100% on validity and novelty; however, the uniqueness score was the lowest among the models. CharVAE and GramVAE performed well on validity and uniqueness; however, their novelty scores were lower than those of our proposed models. MolGAN had severe mode collapse, with uniqueness being the lowest in the baselines at 4.3%. GraphCNF and MoFlow had lower validity, uniqueness,

Table 3. Evaluation results with the drug-likeness as the optimized property.

Dataset	Method	QED	Validity (%)	Unique (%)	Novelty (%)	Diversity	Time (h)
QM9	Decorator	0.47	97.13	93.72	64.61	0.92	0.32
	SpotGAN	0.53	93.25	94.23	91.29	0.92	3.07
	SpotWGAN	0.53	94.72	94.42	91.90	0.92	3.40
ZINC	Decorator	0.79	93.58	97.04	92.42	0.89	1.63
	SpotGAN	0.82	93.26	92.78	92.75	0.88	5.59
	SpotWGAN	0.82	96.21	93.63	92.37	0.88	5.65

Table 4. Evaluation results with the solubility as the optimized property.

Dataset	Method	logP	Validity (%)	Unique (%)	Novelty (%)	Diversity	Time (h)
QM9	Decorator	0.30	97.13	93.72	64.61	0.92	0.32
	SpotGAN	0.47	89.34	93.15	96.70	0.91	3.20
	SpotWGAN	0.48	84.64	91.65	95.80	0.90	3.63
ZINC	Decorator	0.63	93.58	97.04	92.42	0.89	1.63
	SpotGAN	0.71	90.30	95.86	94.22	0.88	6.21
	SpotWGAN	0.74	93.27	92.15	95.03	0.88	9.86

Table 5. Evaluation results with the synthesizability as the optimized property.

Dataset	Method	SA	Validity (%)	Unique (%)	Novelty (%)	Diversity	Time (h)
QM9	Decorator	0.33	97.13	93.72	64.61	0.92	0.32
	SpotGAN	0.43	96.10	90.68	90.14	0.91	3.89
	SpotWGAN	0.41	95.34	94.52	92.85	0.91	4.06
ZINC	Decorator	0.76	93.58	97.04	92.42	0.89	1.63
	SpotGAN	0.81	91.30	94.57	92.98	0.88	8.28
	SpotWGAN	0.82	94.32	92.21	93.33	0.88	10.44

and total scores. Although GraphAF achieved state-of-the-art performance in previous tasks, its uniqueness score was lower than those of our proposed models. SpotGAN and SpotWGAN outperformed Naïve RL (i.e., SpotGAN when $\lambda = 0$) and SCRNN for all evaluation metrics. Further, SpotGAN and SpotWGAN outperformed SCRNN-RL (i.e., SCRNN trained with RL) in terms of validity and novelty, and MoLeR on uniqueness and novelty. In summary, the Decorator, SpotGAN, and SpotWGAN achieved the top 1st, top 4th, and top 2nd spots in the structure-unconstrained evaluation, and the top three spots in the structure-constrained evaluation (Total).

4.4 Property Optimization

Drug-Likeness as the Optimized Property. Table 3 shows the evaluation results on the QM9 and ZINC datasets when the optimized property was the drug-likeness (calculated by the QED score). The proposed models delivered high

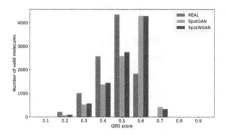

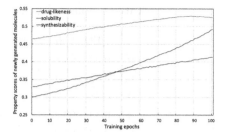

Fig. 2. QED Distributions on QM9 dataset.

Fig. 3. Property scores on QM9 dataset.

validity, uniqueness, and novelty. With the QM9 dataset, most of the SMILES representations of the decorations were simple (consisting only of C, N, and O), and their lengths were less than five. Only the validity and uniqueness scores of Decorator were high in this case. In contrast, since the molecules in the ZINC dataset contain more complex chemical rules, Decorator scored highly on all evaluation measures. Both the SpotGAN and SpotWGAN produced novel molecules and achieved high QED scores with only small costs in validity or uniqueness. Both models obtained the same QED scores because the fixed scaffolds restricted the generation of more molecules with high chemical-property scores. Unlike generative models, which design molecules from scratch under no scaffold constraints, the proposed models must remember not only the rules learned during the training but also the strict restriction on the generation of molecules imposed by scaffold fixation. Furthermore, as the QED score largely depends on the scaffold of a molecule, designing the decoration can only improve the QED score to a limited extent. Therefore, the evaluation results were reasonable.

Figures 2 and Appendix B.1 depict the QED distributions on the QM9 and ZINC datasets, respectively. Comparing the distributions of the proposed models with those of the training dataset (REAL), the QED distributions of the proposed SpotGAN and SpotWGAN models shifted toward relatively high ranges, suggesting the effectiveness of the proposed models in terms of the enhancement of the drug-likeness property. Additionally, the top-12 molecular structures are shown in Appendices B.2 and B.3. The generated molecules had higher QED scores than the original molecules in the training dataset.

Solubility as the Optimized Property. Table 4 shows the evaluation results when the optimized property was solubility (calculated by the logP score). The logP scores of the generated SMILES strings were significantly higher than those for the QM9 and ZINC datasets. On the QM9 dataset, the SpotGAN achieved the highest validity, uniqueness, and novelty scores, and the SpotWGAN achieved the best logP score. On the ZINC dataset, the SpotGAN achieved the highest uniqueness score, and the SpotWGAN performed best on the other scores. The logP distributions and the top-12 molecular structures generated on the QM9 and ZINC datasets are detailed in Appendices B.4, B.5, and B.6.

Table 6. Effect of λ on the drug-likeness of SpotGAN.

λ	QED	Validity (%)	Unique (%)	Novelty (%)
0	0.53	93.84	94.18	93.83
0.1	0.53	96.42	90.39	85.59
0.3	0.53	94.06	91.96	91.57
0.5	0.53	93.25	94.23	91.29
0.7	0.53	93.04	93.05	95.11
0.9	0.52	92.62	93.50	97.14
1.0	0.47	96.43	94.90	73.58

Table 7. Effect of K of SpotGAN on the QM9 dataset.

K	Validity (%)	Unique (%)	Novelty (%)	Time (h)
2	91.65	94.14	94.01	2.45
4	91.40	93.45	92.45	2.39
8	93.25	94.23	91.29	3.07
16	92.55	93.33	90.47	4.02
32	92.18	94.17	95.10	6.89

Table 8. Effect of diversified SMILES on the two datasets.

Dataset	Method	QED	Validity (%)	Unique (%)	Novelty (%)
QM9	Decorator w/o	0.47	52.21	94.79	76.88
	Decorator	0.47	97.13	93.72	64.61
	SpotGAN w/o	0.51	90.07	89.15	82.95
	SpotGAN	0.53	93.25	94.23	91.29
ZINC	Decorator w/o	0.75	41.61	95.65	98.17
	Decorator	0.79	93.58	97.04	92.42
	SpotGAN w/o	0.76	51.38	95.33	98.65
	SpotGAN	0.82	93.26	92.78	92.75

Synthesizability as the Optimized Property. Table 5 shows the evaluation results when the optimized property was synthesizability (calculated by the SA score). The SA scores of the molecules generated by the proposed models were highly enhanced. Additionally, the two models achieved high validity, uniqueness, and novelty scores ($> 90\%$) on both datasets. The SA distributions and top-12 molecules are provided in Appendices B.7, B.8, and B.9.

The property scores of SpotGAN on both datasets are plotted as functions of the epoch in Fig. 3 and Appendix B.6, respectively. All three property scores increased as the training epochs proceeded.

4.5   Ablation Studies

Effect of λ. The hyperparameter λ controls the trade-off between RL and the discriminator participating in the training. When $\lambda = 0$ and $\lambda = 1$, the decoration generator is learned under the total guidance of RL and the discriminator, respectively. Table 6 summarizes the effect of varying $\lambda \in \{0, 0.1, 0.3, 0.5, 0.7, 0.9, 1\}$. When λ was lower than 0.7, the QED score was mainly affected by the scaffold and the effect of λ was minimal. When the scaffold is fixed, the property optimization has a limited ability to improve the chemical properties of the generated molecules. In contrast, *de novo* molecular generation tasks can design an arbitrary molecule. Therefore, the constant QED scores in Table 6 can be explained by the limited ability of RL. When λ exceeded 0.7, the target task utilized the discriminator to generate molecules with higher validity rather than molecules with higher QED scores. Therefore, λ is influential on QED.

Effect of K. The hyperparameter K denotes the number of MC searches. A small K increases the sensitivity of the sampling, whereas a large K increases the computational load of the calculation. Therefore, a suitable K is critical to the model performance. Table 7 shows the effect of K on the molecules generated by SpotGAN on the QM9 dataset. When $K = 8$, the model achieved high validity and uniqueness at acceptable computational cost.

Effect of Diversified SMILES. Diversified SMILES was proposed for data augmentation and enhancement, making models sufficiently learn the semantics and syntax of SMILES strings. Table 8 shows the effect of diversified SMILES in Spot-GAN on the QM9 and ZINC datasets. The experimental results suggest that the proposed diversified SMILES trained the models more sufficiently and generated more valid and unique molecules.

4.6   Case Studies of Bioactivity Optimization for a Therapeutic Target

As case studies, we applied SpotGAN to generate new molecules with high bioactivity for a therapeutic target (DRD2 in this study) on the ZINC dataset. The evaluation results are detailed in Appendix B.7. We evaluated the improvement of the BIO scores of newly generated molecules and compared them with those obtained with the initial scaffolds. In the upper panel of Fig. 4, the five scaffolds, A, B, C, D, and E, were employed as the initial scaffolds to generate molecules, as they are known to be useful for the DRD2 ligands. The five scaffolds were decorated with 2, 3, 2, 4, and 2 decoration points, which are indicated by the asterisks in Fig. 4. The top five generated molecules and their BIO scores are shown in the bottom panel of Fig. 4. The BIO scores of newly generated molecules are considerably higher than those of the initial scaffolds, and this tendency was observed for all five scaffolds. Interestingly, all the generated molecules with the five scaffolds satisfied Hückel's rules [22], which are important for achieving the desired chemical properties of drugs. These results suggest that SpotGAN successfully generated new drug-like molecules with relatively high bioactivity.

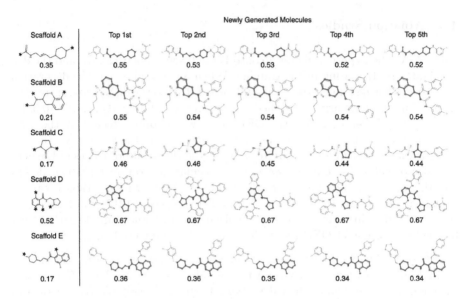

Fig. 4. Top-5 molecular structures on scaffolds A-E and their BIO scores using the ZINC dataset.

5   Conclusion

Here, SpotGAN and SpotWGAN were proposed for generating molecules with the desired chemical properties via a scaffold-constrained approach. The originality lies in the transformer-based GAN for generating molecules on constrained scaffolds and the training recipes for stabilizing the GAN through various techniques, including data augmentation with diversified SMILES, Wasserstein distance, and mini-batch discrimination. In the experiments, the usefulness of the proposed methods on scaffold-constrained molecular-generation tasks was evaluated in terms of the enhancement of the drug-likeness, solubility, synthesizability, and bioactivity of the generated molecules.

This work has two main limitations. First, the proposed models can only generate decorations sequentially according to the number of attachment points. The first decoration is generated based on the attachment points and attached to the scaffold before the next decoration is generated. The process repeats until all attachment points are decorated. Second, performing MC search to generate SMILES strings in the adversarial network requires significant computational time, which reduces the efficiency of the generation. These two issues will be considered in the future.

Acknowledgements. This research was supported by the International Research Fellow of Japan Society for the Promotion of Science (Postdoctoral Fellowships for Research in Japan [Standard]), AMED under Grant Number JP21nk0101111, and JSPS KAKENHI [grant number 20H05797]. The authors are grateful to Dr. Kazuma Kaitoh for fruitful discussion.

References

1. Arjovsky, M., Chintala, S., Bottou, L.: Wasserstein generative adversarial networks. In: International Conference on Machine Learning, pp. 214–223. PMLR (2017)
2. Arús-Pous, J., et al.: Smiles-based deep generative scaffold decorator for de-novo drug design. J. Cheminformatics **12**(1), 1–18 (2020)
3. Bickerton, G.R., Paolini, G.V., Besnard, J., Muresan, S., Hopkins, A.L.: Quantifying the chemical beauty of drugs. Nat. Chem. **4**(2), 90–98 (2012)
4. Comer, J., Tam, K.: Lipophilicity profiles: theory and measurement. Pharmacokinetic Optimization in Drug Research: Biological, Physicochemical and Computational Strategies, pp. 275–304 (2001)
5. De Cao, N., Kipf, T.: Molgan: an implicit generative model for small molecular graphs. arXiv preprint arXiv:1805.11973 (2018)
6. Deore, A.B., Dhumane, J.R., Wagh, R., Sonawane, R.: The stages of drug discovery and development process. Asian J. Pharmaceutical Res. Develom. **7**(6), 62–67 (2019)
7. Devlin, J., Chang, M.W., Lee, K., Toutanova, K.: Bert: pre-training of deep bidirectional transformers for language understanding. arXiv preprint arXiv:1810.04805 (2018)
8. Dollar, O., Joshi, N., Beck, D.A., Pfaendtner, J.: Giving attention to generative vae models for de novo molecular design. ChemRxiv (2021)
9. Donahue, C., Lee, M., Liang, P.: Enabling language models to fill in the blanks. In: Proceedings of the 58th Annual Meeting of the Association for Computational Linguistics, pp. 2492–2501 (2020)
10. Ertl, P., Schuffenhauer, A.: Estimation of synthetic accessibility score of drug-like molecules based on molecular complexity and fragment contributions. J. Cheminform. **1**(1), 1–11 (2009)
11. Floridi, L., Chiriatti, M.: Gpt-3: its nature, scope, limits, and consequences. Mind. Mach. **30**(4), 681–694 (2020)
12. Gaulton, A., et al.: Chembl: a large-scale bioactivity database for drug discovery. Nucleic Acids Res. **40**(D1), D1100–D1107 (2012)
13. Goodfellow, I., et al.: Generative adversarial nets. In: Advances in Neural Information Processing Systems 27 (2014)
14. Guimaraes, G.L., Sanchez-Lengeling, B., Outeiral, C., Farias, P.L.C., Aspuru-Guzik, A.: Objective-reinforced generative adversarial networks (organ) for sequence generation models. arXiv preprint arXiv:1705.10843 (2017)
15. Gupta, A., et al.: Generative recurrent networks for de novo drug design. Mol. Inf. **37**(1–2), 1700111 (2018)
16. Irwin, J.J., Sterling, T., Mysinger, M.M., Bolstad, E.S., Coleman, R.G.: Zinc: a free tool to discover chemistry for biology. J. Chem. Inf. Model. **52**(7), 1757–1768 (2012)
17. Jameel, A.G.A., et al.: A minimalist functional group (mfg) approach for surrogate fuel formulation. Combust. Flame **192**, 250–271 (2018)
18. Jiang, Y., Chang, S., Wang, Z.: Transgan: two pure transformers can make one strong gan, and that can scale up. In: Advances in Neural Information Processing Systems 34 (2021)
19. Jin, W., Barzilay, R., Jaakkola, T.: Junction tree variational autoencoder for molecular graph generation. In: International Conference on Machine Learning, pp. 2323–2332. PMLR (2018)

20. Kim, S., et al.: Pubchem substance and compound databases. Nucleic Acids Res. **44**(D1), D1202–D1213 (2016)
21. Kingma, D.P., Welling, M.: Auto-encoding variational bayes. arXiv preprint arXiv:1312.6114 (2013)
22. Klein, D., Trinajstic, N.: Hückel rules and electron correlation. J. Am. Chem. Soc. **106**(26), 8050–8056 (1984)
23. Kusner, M.J., Paige, B., Hernández-Lobato, J.M.: Grammar variational autoencoder. In: International Conference on Machine Learning, pp. 1945–1954. PMLR (2017)
24. Landrum, G.: Rdkit documentation. Release **1**(1–79), 4 (2013)
25. Langevin, M., Minoux, H., Levesque, M., Bianciotto, M.: Scaffold-constrained molecular generation. J. Chem. Inf. Model. **60**(12), 5637–5646 (2020)
26. Lippe, P., Gavves, E.: Categorical normalizing flows via continuous transformations. arXiv preprint arXiv:2006.09790 (2020)
27. Maziarz, K., et al.: Learning to extend molecular scaffolds with structural motifs. arXiv preprint arXiv:2103.03864 (2021)
28. Morgan, H.L.: The generation of a unique machine description for chemical structures-a technique developed at chemical abstracts service. J. Chem. Doc. **5**(2), 107–113 (1965)
29. Olivecrona, M., Blaschke, T., Engkvist, O., Chen, H.: Molecular de-novo design through deep reinforcement learning. J. Cheminform. **9**(1), 1–14 (2017)
30. Pedregosa, F., et al.: Scikit-learn: machine learning in python. J. Mach. Learn. Res. **12**, 2825–2830 (2011)
31. Ramakrishnan, R., Dral, P.O., Rupp, M., Von Lilienfeld, O.A.: Quantum chemistry structures and properties of 134 kilo molecules. Scientific Data **1**(1), 1–7 (2014)
32. Rogers, D.J., Tanimoto, T.T.: A computer program for classifying plants. Science **132**(3434), 1115–1118 (1960)
33. Salimans, T., Goodfellow, I., Zaremba, W., Cheung, V., Radford, A., Chen, X.: Improved techniques for training gans. In: Advances in Neural Information Processing Systems 29 (2016)
34. Shi, C., Xu, M., Zhu, Z., Zhang, W., Zhang, M., Tang, J.: Graphaf: a flow-based autoregressive model for molecular graph generation. arXiv preprint arXiv:2001.09382 (2020)
35. Sutton, R.S., McAllester, D., Singh, S., Mansour, Y.: Policy gradient methods for reinforcement learning with function approximation. In: Advances in Neural Information Processing Systems 12 (1999)
36. Vaswani, A., et al.: Attention is all you need. In: Advances in Neural Information Processing Systems 30 (2017)
37. Weininger, D.: Smiles, a chemical language and information system 1. introduction to methodology and encoding rules. J. Chem. Inform. Comput. Sci. **28**(1), 31–36 (1988)
38. Yu, L., Zhang, W., Wang, J., Yu, Y.: Seqgan: sequence generative adversarial nets with policy gradient. In: Proceedings of the Thirty-First AAAI Conference on Artificial Intelligence, pp. 2852–2858 (2017)
39. Zang, C., Wang, F.: Moflow: an invertible flow model for generating molecular graphs. In: Proceedings of the 26th ACM SIGKDD International Conference on Knowledge Discovery & Data Mining, pp. 617–626 (2020)
40. Zhao, H., Akritopoulou-Zanze, I.: When analoging is not enough: scaffold discovery in medicinal chemistry. Expert Opin. Drug Discov. **5**(2), 123–134 (2010)
41. Zhu, W., Hu, Z., Xing, E.: Text infilling. arXiv preprint arXiv:1901.00158 (2019)

Spatio-Temporal Pyramid Networks for Traffic Forecasting

Jia Hu, Chu Wang, and Xianghong Lin[✉]

College of Computer Science and Engineering, Northwest Normal University,
Lanzhou, China
linxh@nwnu.edu.cn

Abstract. Traffic flow forecasting is an important part of smart city construction. Accurate traffic flow forecasting helps traffic management agencies to make timely adjustments, thus improving pedestrian travel efficiency and road utilization. However, this work is challenging due to the dynamic stochastic factors affecting the variation of traffic data and the spatially hidden behavior. Existing approaches generally use attention mechanism or graph neural networks to model correlation in temporal and spatial terms, and despite some progress in performance, they still ignore a number of practical situations: (1) Anomalous data due to traffic accidents or traffic congestion can affect the accuracy of modeling in the current moment and further create potential optimization problems for model training. (2) According to the directedness of the road, the hiding behavior between nodes should also be unidirectional and dynamic. In this paper, we propose a dynamic graph network with a pyramid structure, named PYNet, and use it for traffic flow forecasting tasks. Specifically, first we propose the Pyramid Constructor for transforming multivariate time series into a pyramid network with a multilevel structure, where the higher the level, the larger the range of time scales represented. Second, we perform Trend-Aware Attention top-down in the pyramid network, which gradually enables the lower-level time series to learn their long-term dependence in multiples, and effectively reduces the impact of outliers. Furthermore, to fully capture the hidden behavior in the spatial dimension, we learn an adaptive unidirectional graph and perform forward and backward diffusion convolution on the graph. Experimental results on two types of datasets show that PYNet outperforms the state-of-the-art baseline.

Keywords: Traffic flow forecasting · Spatio-temporal data · Pyramid structure

1 Introduction

In recent years, many countries are focusing on the development of Intelligent Transportation Systems (ITS). Traffic flow forecasting, route planning and vehicle scheduling are important components of ITS, and they work together to

---

J. Hu and C. Wang—Equal contribution.

© The Author(s), under exclusive license to Springer Nature Switzerland AG 2023
D. Koutra et al. (Eds.): ECML PKDD 2023, LNAI 14169, pp. 339–354, 2023.
https://doi.org/10.1007/978-3-031-43412-9_20

improve the transportation service system of cities. In these applications, route planning and vehicle scheduling are based on the traffic conditions of roads, so traffic flow forecasting is the cornerstone of ITS. In this paper, we use the historical traffic data of roads to forecast the future traffic conditions. Traffic data is a time series data, collected by sensors deployed in the traffic network at a fixed continuous period of time. Early researchers applied the classical time series models Vector Auto-Regression (VAR) [15], Autoregressive Integrated Moving Average model (ARIMA) [8] to forecast future traffic conditions, they are limited by the assumption of linearity and smoothness of the data, and traffic data are usually unsteady and nonlinear, so these methods perform poorly. Deep learning methods based on Recurrent Neural Networks (RNN) [3,4,6] are not subject to these limitations, therefore they are widely used to extract long and short term dependencies in time series. A limitation of these methods is the inability to model spatial correlations in traffic networks, and with the deeper understanding of the problem and the development of graph neural networks (GNN) [7], researchers have proposed a spatial-temporal forecasting framework based on graph neural networks [14,23,26], which construct traffic graphs by taking sensors deployed in traffic networks as nodes and road networks or node distances as edges, updating node characteristics through information transfer effects between nodes. The advantage of these GNN-based methods is that they can handle data with a non Euclidean structure, which makes up for the fact that CNN-based methods [27] can only handle data with a grid structure. While having shown the effectiveness of introducing the graph structure of data into a model, but there is still a lack of satisfactory progress in accurate and long term traffic forecasting, which is mainly due to the following two challenges:

First, unexpected events in the road such as traffic accidents can cause transient anomalies in the traffic data, which may pose potential optimization problems in the training of the model if they are ignored. For instance, most current studies use attention mechanism or CNN to model temporal correlation. The attention mechanism obtains the similarity between node pairs in the form of point-to-point, which will incorrectly update the node features if there exists anomalous data and further cause error accumulation. CNN updates node features by aggregating local contextual information, which can weaken the effect brought by outliers. Considering the multi-scale nature of time series and the design of convolution kernel size, it is difficult to solve this problem with a single convolution layer.

Second, roads in the traffic network are unidirectional, which means that the impacts from traffic conditions on upstream roads are transmitted to downstream roads in the future and continue to spread dynamically over time. The distance-based adjacency matrix defines this diffusion relationship based on the distance of the road network, ignoring the hidden spatial correlation in the traffic network. Therefore, we propose to learn a dynamic directed graph to maintain the hidden property of state transfer between nodes, and in addition, if the dataset further provides information on the structure and distance between nodes, we expect the dynamic directed graph to easily incorporate this information to generate a more comprehensive representation of node embeddings and spatial matrices.

To solve the above challenges, we propose a new pyramid network for spatial-temporal forecasting, which we call PYNet, which mainly consists of three parts: Pyramid Constructor, Trend-Aware Attention and Diffusion Graph Convolution Network. Pyramid Constructor is based on CNN and is used to transform the input time series into a pyramid network with a multi-leveled structure, and can customize the time range of trend blocks in different levels (It means that the features of several consecutive time steps are aggregated). We then perform Trend-Aware Attention top-down, computing the similarity between trend blocks with different time scales in a local context, which allows not only the lower-level time series to receive several times the perceptual field, but also further attenuates the impact of outliers. In addition, we learn a dynamic directed graph that preserves the one way hidden relationship between nodes in the traffic network, and further, we describe this hidden relationship as a diffusion process of nodes over spatially and capture the potential spatial correlation by diffusion convolution. In summary, we summarize the contributions of this paper as follows:

- We propose a pyramid network for spatial-temporal forecasting tasks, named PYNet, which initializes the input time series into a pyramid network with a multi-leveled structure through the Pyramid Constructor. The trend blocks in the bottom-up levels of the pyramid represent progressively larger time ranges, and such time ranges are customizable.
- We perform Trend-Aware Attention and Diffusion Graph Convolution Network top-down in a pyramid network. The former computes the similarity between trend blocks in local context and gives several times the perceptual field to the lower-level trend blocks, which reduces the impact of outliers. The latter preserves the hidden spatial directed relations by performing diffusion GCN on the adaptive directed graph.
- We evaluate the performance of PYNet on four real-world datasets, and the experiments show that PYNet outperforms all the baseline.

2   Related Work

2.1   Traffic Forecasting

Traffic forecasting is an important component of intelligent transportation systems and has been widely studied in the last decades [10,14,23,26,27,29]. Earlier studies mainly used statistical methods, such as VAR [15], ARIMA [8], which rely on the assumption of linearity of the data and, without doubt, perform poorly when dealing with nonlinear traffic data. With the development of deep learning, recurrent neural networks [3,4,6], which ignore the smoothness assumption, have been successfully applied to time series modeling. To capture spatial correlations, [24,25,27,30] used CNNs to model spatial with regular grid structure, but were powerless for traffic networks with non-Euclidean spatial structure. With the evolution of graph neural networks, it has become the best method to model the spatial correlation of traffic data, for example, DCRNN [14] uses diffusion GCN to capture the diffusion phenomenon of traffic flow in spatial terms and applies GRU to capture the temporal correlation. Graph WaveNet [23] modeled spatial and temporal correlations using GCNs and temporal convolution networks (TCNs), respectively, and [10, 19, 22, 26] and other studies modeled spatial correlations based on GCNs. With the birth of Transformer [21], GMAN [29], ASTGCN [5], and ST-GRAT [17] introduced attention mechanisms into spatial-temporal modeling and further improved the forecasting accuracy.

If the spatial correlation of traffic networks is modeled using graph neural networks, then there is no doubt that the construction of the adjacency matrix is extremely important. DCRNN [14] computes the road network distance between sensors and uses it as a weight between nodes by means of a thresholded Gaussian kernel function. To react to hidden correlations in spatial, some works [16, 23] proposed adaptive adjacency matrix to describe such potential spatial correlations and can be learned by end-to-end. Further, DGCRN [10], MTGNN [22] set the adaptive adjacency matrix as a directed graph, which means that a change in the state of one node leads to a change in the state of other nodes, which brings the learning of adjacency matrix to a new level. In addition, some studies have proposed a data-driven spatial heterogeneity graph based on adding connections between functionally similar regions, [9, 12] proving its effectiveness, but it is static and still requires parameters to support training in the training of the model.

2.2   Graph Neural Network

The main idea of graph neural networks is to update node states through the information transfer effect between nodes, which has been a great success in dealing with spatial dependence between entities in a network and is now successfully applied to various tasks such as node classification [18] and link forecasting [31]. Various types of variants of GNN have been developed, such as GCN, Graph Attention Network (GAT), and there are two types of GCN, spatial GCN and spectral GCN. Spatial GCN on the neighboring nodes of the target node directly perform convolution filters, the spectral GCN defines the convolution in the spectral domain [13], which is firstly introduced in [1]. GAT introduces the attention mechanism into GNNs and uses node features to autonomously learn the weights between node pairs. Recently, spatial-temporal graph neural networks [2, 28] have been introduced to traffic forecasting for capturing spatial-temporal correlations in traffic data, such as the STGNN, DGCRN replacing the fully connected layer in recurrent neural networks with GCNs, and STJGCN [28] constructing joint graph convolution layers between any two time steps. In addition, some works [29] learn the spatial embedding representation of each node by graph embedding methods such as node2Vec and deepWalk to further improve the efficiency of information transfer between node pairs in spatial.

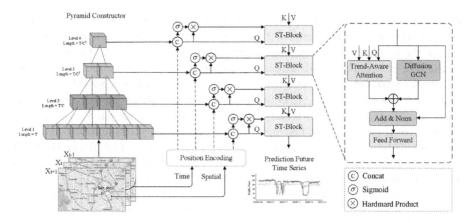

Fig. 1. The framework of PYNet.

3 Preliminary

We denote the traffic data recorded by N sensors at time t as traffic signals, C is the number of signals and the signals can be traffic volume, traffic speed, etc. The traffic forecasting problem aims to learn a function f that maps the traffic conditions at time step P of history to the next time step Q:

$$[\mathbf{X}_{t-P+1}, \mathbf{X}_{t-P+2}, \cdots, \mathbf{X}_t] \xrightarrow{f(\cdot)} [\mathbf{X}_{t+1}, \mathbf{X}_{t+2}, \cdots, \mathbf{X}_{t+Q}] \quad (1)$$

4 Methodology

In this section, we will introduce our proposed model in detail. The overall framework of our proposed model is shown in Fig. 1.

PYNet first takes multivariate time series and passes them through the Pyramid Constructor to obtain a pyramid network with a multi-level structure (the higher the level, the larger the range of time scales), and then adds learnable location codes to each level to facilitate labeling level structures with different scale information. Finally, the top-down stacked Spatial-Temporal Block (ST-Block), which consists of Trend-Aware Attention and Diffusion GCN, in the pyramid structure. Trend-Aware Attention uses both low level and high level features as common inputs, with the aim of enabling each trend block at the low level (aggregated by multiple time steps) to share the long term horizon represented at the high level. Diffusion GCN describes the behavior on spatial as a diffusion process of directed graphs and performs diffusion convolution operations on adaptive directed graphs.

4.1 Pyramid Constructor

Patterns in time series may evolve with time significantly due to various events, e.g. holidays and extreme weather, so whether an observed point is an anomaly, change point or part of the patterns is highly dependent on its surrounding context. Hence, the independent time steps in the original time series cannot reflect the anomalous information of the data. In order to make full use of the contextual information and reduce the loss caused by data anomalies, we use Pyramid Constructor to obtain a pyramid network with a multi-level structure, which has two advantages: (1) Different levels of time scales can be customized, such that, bottom-up each trend block (i.e., features aggregated over several consecutive time steps) can be considered as hourly, daily and monthly features. (2) There is better fault tolerance in the face of anomalies. The higher the level of the hierarchy, the larger the range of time scales of the trend blocks, then the impact caused by the anomalies is limited.

Given the length T multivariate time series and a set of convolution layers $F^{CNN}(\cdot)$, then each level of the pyramid structure can be defined as:

$$\mathrm{X}_L = F_L^{CNN}(\mathrm{X}_{L-1}, \Theta_L) \in \mathbb{R}^{T_{L-1}/C_L \times N \times D} \tag{2}$$

We take the time series $\mathrm{X}_{L-1} \in \mathbb{R}^{T_{L-1} \times N \times D}$ at the L-1 level and pass it through the standard convolution layer $F_L^{CNN}(\cdot)$ to obtain the time series representation $\mathrm{X}_L \in \mathbb{R}^{T_{L-1}/C_L \times N \times D}$ at the Lth level, where Θ_L corresponds to the parameters of the convolution layer and C_L is the size and step size of the convolution kernel.

4.2   Trend-Aware Attention

In the traditional attention mechanism, the similarities between queries and keys are computed based on their point-wise values without fully leveraging local context information. Query-key matching agnostic of local context may confuse the self-attention module in terms of whether the observed value is an anomaly, change point or part of patterns, and bring underlying optimization issues. Thus, we perform top-down attention mechanisms between adjacent levels of the pyramid, which has two advantages: (1) Compute the similarity between query and key in a local context, which reduces the impact caused by anomalies. (2) Key and value have longer time range information than query, and the top-down attention mechanism will gradually make the lower-level time series learn its own C_L-fold long term dependence until the update of the original time series is completed.

Given the time series of two adjacent levels $\mathrm{X}_L \in \mathbb{R}^{T_L \times N \times D}$ and $\mathrm{X}_{L+1} \in \mathbb{R}^{T_{L+1} \times N \times D}$, which $T_{L+1} = T_L/C_L$. The operation of Trend-Aware Attention can be expressed as follows:

$$Q_L^{(h)} = \mathrm{Softmax}(\frac{(\mathrm{X}_L^{(h)}\mathrm{W}_Q^{(h)})(\mathrm{X}_{L+1}^{(h)}\mathrm{W}_K^{(h)})^T}{\sqrt{d_h}} + \mathrm{W}_{adp})(\mathrm{X}_{L+1}^{(h)}\mathrm{W}_V^{(h)}) \tag{3}$$

$$Q_L = \mathrm{MLP}(\mathrm{Concat}(Q_L^{(1)}, Q_L^{(2)}, \dots, Q_L^{(H)})) \tag{4}$$

where $\mathrm{W}_Q^{(h)}, \mathrm{W}_K^{(h)}, \mathrm{W}_V^{(h)} \in \mathbb{R}^{d_h \times d_h}$ are learnable parameters. H is the number of attention heads. In addition, we adjust the inter level attention scores by a trainable parameter $\mathrm{W}_{adp} \in \mathbb{R}^{T_L \times T_{L-1}}$.

Trend-Aware Attention updates the lower level time series representation by the higher level time series, which helps to make the lower level time series learn longer time dependence. One drawback, however, is that time series at lower levels lose their inherent characteristics, which can make short term forecasting perform less well. To solve this problem, we compute Trend-Aware Attention and the self-attention of the current hierarchical time series synchronously in a parallel manner. The preference of self-attention for global information can impair the performance of short term forecasting, so we control the proportion of information flowing to the self-attention module at each time step by means of a selection gate:

$$V_L = \text{sigmoid}(\text{MLP}(\text{Concat}(X_L, \text{PE}_L))) \tag{5}$$

$$X_L^S = V_L \odot X_L \tag{6}$$

We take the time series representation of layer L, X_L and the spatial-temporal position encoding PE_L (see Sect. 4.4 for details) of the concatenation as the input to the selection gate, and automatically learn the gate value of $(0, 1)$ $V_L \in \mathbb{R}^{T_L \times N \times D}$ by the sigmoid activation function. The symbol $\odot$ denotes the element-wise product, the attention module takes X_L^S as input and its operation can be expressed as:

$$S_L^{(h)} = \text{Softmax}(\frac{(X_L^{S,(h)} U_Q^{(h)})(X_L^{S,(h)} U_K^{(h)})^T}{\sqrt{d_h}})(X_L^{S,(h)} U_V^{(h)}) \tag{7}$$

$$S_L = \text{Concat}(S_L^{(1)}, S_L^{(2)}, \ldots, S_L^{(H)}) \tag{8}$$

which $U_Q^{(h)}, U_K^{(h)}, U_V^{(h)} \in \mathbb{R}^{d_h \times d_h}$ denotes learnable parameters. Finally, we model jointly the long-short-term temporal dependence by using the output of the Self-Attention module as a complement to Trend-Aware Attention:

$$B_L = \text{MLP}(\text{Concat}(Q_L, S_L)) \tag{9}$$

where the MLP is a two-layer fully connected layer that weights and aggregates the feature representation of all attention heads. $B_L \in \mathbb{R}^{T_L \times N \times D}$ is the final output representation of Trend-Aware Attention in the corresponding ST-Block. In the process of forward calculation, in order to avoid high computational cost, we can set the vector dimension of each of the two parts to $D/2$, and finally recover to D by performing concat operation on the channel by Eq. (9).

4.3   Diffusion Graph Convolution Network

In multivariate time series forecasting, the relationships between node pairs are not negligible, for example, traffic conditions on roads upstream of the traffic network produce impacts that are transmitted to downstream roads in the future, and weather conditions in adjacent regions are usually similar. Therefore, it is necessary to consider these hidden spatial relationships. Existing studies usually construct the hidden relationships between node pairs through graphs, for instance, DCRNN computes the road network distance between pairs of nodes in the adjacency matrix using a threshold Gaussian kernel function. DSTAGNN calculates the similarity between different time series as the weights among node pairs by Wasserstein Distance. However, these approaches construct static or bi-directional graph-based structures, and we propose to learn a directed graph to preserve the property of state transfer between nodes (that is, a change in the state of one node leads to a change in the state of other nodes). It should be noted that the spatial structure in the traffic network includes both static and dynamic attributes, and for static attributes, it mainly refers to the inherent apriori knowledge of different correlations due to different road distances.

For dynamic attributes, let's take an example to help understand: due to the different attributes of different areas (apartment, school or industrial park), at 7 a.m., the correlation (A,B) between apartment A and school B is much greater than (B,A) due to students going to school, and at 6 p.m., (B,A) is much greater than (A,B) due to students leaving school. Therefore, in real traffic networks, there are hidden and uncertain relationships between different roads. If feature information is used to participate in the construction of the graph structure, the accuracy will be degraded during the testing process due to the different data and the accuracy deviation will be greater with time. Hence, we propose to learn the hidden graph structure in an adaptive manner and incorporate static attributes in an efficient way. It does not depend on the feature information at any moment and the graph structure is determined once the training of the model is completed.

First, we use thresholded Gaussian kernel function to measuring the proximity between different road pairs:

$$\mathrm{H}_{i,j} = \exp(-\frac{dist(v_i, v_j)^2}{\sigma^2}) \tag{10}$$

where $dist(v_i, v_j)$ represents the road network distance from node v_i to node v_j, σ is the standard deviation of distances, $\mathrm{H}_{i,j}$ denotes the edge weight between node v_i and node v_j.

Then, we obtain the embedding representation of each node by node2Vec:

$$\mathrm{N} = \mathrm{node2Vec}(\mathrm{H}) \tag{11}$$

$\mathrm{N} \in \mathbb{R}^{N \times D}$ is the embedding representation of the nodes in the spatial, taking the distance-based adjacency matrix H as input. The node2Vec algorithm makes nodes within the same region or nodes that have similar structural features represent similar. In particular, we randomly initialize two learnable node embedding matrices $\mathrm{E}_1, \mathrm{E}_2 \in \mathbb{R}^{N \times D}$ and concate them with N on the channel:

$$\mathrm{M}_1 = \tanh(\alpha(\mathrm{linear}(\mathrm{Concat}(\mathrm{E}_1, \mathrm{N})))) \tag{12}$$

$$\mathrm{M}_2 = \tanh(\alpha(\mathrm{linear}(\mathrm{Concat}(\mathrm{E}_2, \mathrm{N})))) \tag{13}$$

M_1 and M_2 are the new node embedding representation containing learnable and static spatial information. Then, we regularize the adjacency matrix by subtraction terms and the ReLU activation function:

$$A = \text{ReLU}(\tanh(\alpha(M_1 M_2^{\mathsf{T}} - M_2 M_1^{\mathsf{T}}))) \tag{14}$$

which $\Theta_1, \Theta_2 \in \mathbb{R}^{D \times D}$ are learnable parameters, α is a hyper-parameter for controlling the saturation rate of the activation function, Eq. (14) implements the asymmetric nature of the adjacency matrix.

We characterize the state transfer between nodes as a spatial diffusion process of nodes, and this Markovian stochastic process converges to a smooth distribution after K time steps by performing a random wander on the graph. Given the graph signal $X_L \in \mathbb{R}^{T_L \times N \times D}$ and adjacency matrix $A \in \mathbb{R}^{N \times N}$ at the Lth level, we describe the diffusion graph convolution as:

$$Z_L = \sum_{k=0}^{K} (D_O^{-1} A)^k X_L W_{Ok} + (D_I^{-1} A^{\mathsf{T}})^k X_L W_{Ik} \tag{15}$$

In the case of directed graphs, the diffusion process has two directions, outflow and inflow, and the corresponding state transfer matrix for both are $D_O^{-1} A$ and $D_I^{-1} A^{\mathsf{T}}$, respectively. Where D_O and D_I are the degree matrix of the corresponding matrix, $W_{Ok}, W_{Ik} \in \mathbb{R}^{D \times D}$ are the learnable parameter, and $Z_L \in \mathbb{R}^{T_L \times N \times D}$ is the output of the diffusion graph convolution layer in the ST-Block corresponding to the Lth level.

Then, we aggregate the outputs of the Trend-Aware Attention and diffusion graph convolution layer, either by summing or concatting over the channels. We select $\text{SUM}(\cdot)$ as the aggregator function which is differentiable and maintains high representational capacity:

$$Y_L = \text{Agg}(Q_L, Z_L) = Q_L + Z_L \tag{16}$$

Finally, we add residual connectivity and BatchNorm to Y_L and obtain the output of ST-Block by an MLP containing two layers of fully connected neural networks:

$$Y_L^{out} = \text{MLP}(\text{BatchNorm}(\text{Agg}(Y_L, X_L))) \tag{17}$$

$Y_L^{out} \in \mathbb{R}^{T_L \times N \times D}$ is the output of the ST-Block corresponding to the Lth level.

4.4   Position Encoding

Considering that the pyramid performs Trend-Aware Attention between adjacent levels, and that the sequential relationships of adjacent levels lose their relevance to each other. To solve this problem, we add location codes for the different levels, which are aggregations of temporal and spatial codes (the aggregation function uses $\text{SUM}(\cdot)$). Temporal encoding is one-hot encoding and concat separately for day-of-week and time-of-day of each time step. In spatial, we randomly initialize a vector representation for each node, both of which have the same number of channels after passing through the fully connected neural network. For example, for node v_i on time step t_j, its position encoding is defined as:

$$PE^{v_i,t_j} = \text{Agg}(\text{MLP}(\text{onehot}(t_j)), \text{MLP}(\text{emb}(v_i)))\qquad(18)$$

For the Lth level in the pyramid, the position encoding is defined as:

$$PE_L^{v_i,L_j} = \text{Agg}(\text{MLP}(\sum_{u=j\times p_L}^{u=(j+1)\times p_L-1} \text{onehot}(t_u)), \text{MLP}(\text{emb}(v_i)))\qquad(19)$$

In the Lth ($L > 1$) level, each trend block (aggregated by multiple consecutive time steps) represents a time horizon, as exemplified by Eq. (12), L_j is the jth trend block in the Lth hierarchy, p_L is the length of time of each trend block in the Lth level. We sum the one-hot encoding corresponding to successive time steps and set the maximum value to 1.

The position encoding preserves the correlation between level, effectively modeling long term dependence while better preserving similar information when performing Trend-Aware Attention.

5 Experiment

5.1 Dataset

To evaluate the model performance, we conducted extensive experiments on four traffic flow datasets [18], namely PEMS03, PEMS04, PEMS07 and PEMS08 datasets, which were collected on California freeways.

5.2 Baseline Methods

(1) VAR [15] which is a traditional time series model that captures the pairwise relationship of time series; (2) ARIMA [8] which is a classical time series model; (3) STGCN that models spatial and temporal correlations using GCN and CNN, respectively; (4) DCRNN [14] that captures spatial-temporal correlation using GRU and diffusion graph convolution network, respectively; (5) Graph WaveNet [23] that combines adaptive graph convolution and dilated casual convolution to capture spatial-temporal correlations; (6) ASTGCN [5] that is based on spatial-temporal attention and model spatial and temporal correlations by GCN and CNN; (7) STSGCN [19] that constructs a local spatio-temporal graph and captures local spatio-temporal correlations by spatio-temporal synchronous graph convolution; (8) AGCRN [20] that uses adaptive graphs to describe spatial correlation and GRU to model temporal correlation; (9) Z-GCNETS [11] that models spatial and temporal correlation using graph convolution and GRU; (10) GMAN [29] that captures spatio-temporal correlations by attention and designs a transformation layer to reduce error propagation; (11) DSTAGNN [9] that was designed to describe regions with similar functions.

5.3   Experimental Settings

The dataset is divided into training, validation and test sets in the ratio of 6:2:2, and they are normalized with Z-Score. Following the standard benchmark setting for the domain, we use data from 12 consecutive historical time steps to forecast traffic data from 12 consecutive future time steps, with an interval of 5 min between two consecutive time steps. We use Adam optimizer as the models' optimizer with initial learning rate set to 0.01, BathSize to 128, attention head to 8, vector dimension to 64, and Pyramid Constructor with convolution kernel and three convolution layers with step size [2, 2, 3]. We use mean absolute error (MAE), root mean squared error (RMSE), and mean absolute percentage error (MAPE) as the evaluation metric and MAE as the loss function.

Table 1. .

Model	PEMS03			PEMS04			PEMS07			PEMS08		
	MAE	RMSE	MAPE	MAE	RMSE	MAPE	MAE	RMSE	MAPE	MAE	RMSE	MAPE
VAR	23.65	38.26	24.51%	24.54	38.61	17.24%	50.22	75.63	32.22%	19.19	29.81	13.10%
ARIMA	35.41	47.59	33.78%	33.73	48.80	24.18%	38.17	59.27	19.46%	31.09	44.32	22.73%
FC-LSTM	21.33	35.11	23.33%	26.77	40.65	18.23%	29.98	45.94	13.20%	23.09	35.17	14.99%
STGCN	17.55	30.42	17.34%	21.16	34.89	13.83%	25.33	39.34	11.21%	17.50	27.09	11.29%
DCRNN	17.99	30.31	18.34%	21.22	33.44	14.17%	25.22	38.61	11.82%	16.82	26.36	10.92%
GraphWaveNet	19.12	32.77	18.89%	24.89	39.66	17.29%	26.39	41.50	11.97%	18.28	30.05	12.15%
ASTGCN	17.34	29.56	17.21%	22.93	35.22	16.56%	24.01	37.87	10.73%	18.25	28.06	11.64%
STSGCN	17.48	29.21	16.78%	21.19	33.65	13.90%	24.26	39.03	10.21%	17.13	26.80	10.96%
AGCRN	15.98	28.25	15.23%	19.83	32.26	12.97%	22.37	36.55	9.12%	15.95	25.22	10.09%
STFGNN	16.77	28.34	16.30%	20.48	32.51	16.77%	23.46	36.60	9.21%	16.94	26.25	10.60%
Z-GCNETS	16.64	28.15	16.39%	19.50	31.61	12.78%	21.77	35.17	9.25%	15.76	25.11	10.01%
GMAN	15.52	26.53	15.19%	19.25	30.85	13.00%	20.68	33.56	9.31%	14.87	24.06	9.77%
DSTAGNN	15.57	27.21	**14.68%**	19.30	31.46	12.70%	21.42	34.51	9.01%	15.67	24.77	9.94%
PYNet	**14.94**	**25.27**	14.94%	**18.46**	**30.36**	**12.46%**	**19.61**	**32.85**	**8.36%**	**14.03**	**23.84**	**9.39%**
improve	**3.73%**	**3.62%**	-	**4.10%**	**1.59%**	**1.89%**	**5.17%**	**2.11%**	**7.21%**	**5.65%**	**0.91%**	**3.89%**

5.4   Experiment Results

Table 1 shows the performance of PYNet and the thirteen baselines on the four datasets, and we report the average error of the one-hour ahead forecasting. As can be seen, PYNet achieves state-of-the-art performance on four datasets, and in terms of MAE, PYNet improves the state-of-the-art results by 2.51%, 4.16%, 5.08% and 5.51%, respectively. In addition, we observed that: (1) The performance of VAR and ARIMA is poor; they rely on the assumption of linearity in the data, while traffic data has dynamic non-linear feature. (2) GNN-based deep learning methods (STGCN, DCRNN, AGCRN, Graph-WaveNet, DSTAGNN) take spatial correlation into account and usually have better forecasting performance. However, the semantic information contained in the graph structure may be imperfect or even biased, which limits the expressive power of the graph model. (3) The models based on the attention mechanism,

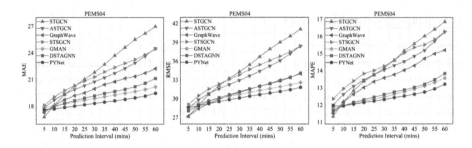

Fig. 2. Forecasting performance comparison at each horizon on the PEMS04 dataset.

ASTGCN and GMAN, perform better in long-term forecasting, but the insensitivity of attention to local information leads to poorer short-term forecasting performance.

Compared with the above methods, PYNet introduces a pyramid structure to learn the multi-scale representation of time series, which can effectively model long and short term dependence. In moreover, we add corresponding scale position encoding for each level in the pyramid to record the relative position relationship and retain the correlation between levels. We perform Trend-Aware Attention and diffusion GCN top-down in a pyramid network, where the former gradually causes the lower-level time series to learn several times their own long term dependence until the update of the initial time series is completed. The latter performs diffusion convolution operations on directed graphs to preserve the properties of state transfer between nodes. Considering these features, PYNet consistently outperforms other methods.

To investigate the specific performance of PYNet on short-medium term and medium-long term forecasting, we plot the error curves of the seven models on one-hour ahead forecasting in Fig. 2. We observe that STGCN and Graph WaveNet have the best short term (0min-10min) forecasting performance, and PYNet performs best when there is a medium-long term (>10 min) forecasting demand, and the error curve of PYNet grows the slowest with increasing time step, while the gap with other models gradually increases, which indicates that PYNet has strong stability while maintaining high performance.

5.5   Ablation Study

To verify the effectiveness of the individual components in PYNet, we made the following variants of PYNet: (1) PYNet-NC: We use the average pooling layer to construct the pyramid network. (2) PYNet-NT: We removed the Trend-Aware Attention from ST-Block. (3) PYNet-NS: We removed the self attention. (4) PYNet-ND: We remove the diffusion GCN from the ST-Block.

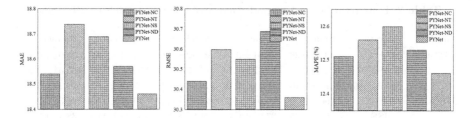

Fig. 3. Ablation study on PEMS04.

Figure 3 shows the average performance of PYNet and the four variants on the PEMS04 dataset. We observe that (1) The pyramid network constructed by CNN has better results compared to the average pooling layer because the convolution layer can weigh the importance of each time step in the window better than the pooling layer. (2) The performance of PYNet-NT decreases dramatically after removing the Trend-Aware Attention. This is because the Trend-Aware Attenion acts as a connection between two levels, and after removing it, the model cannot learn the correlation between the pyramid levels. (3) The self attention module complements the trend attention module with the aim of improving short term forecasting performance. When self attention is removed, PYNet-NS has the worst short term forecasting performance, which implies that self attention, as a complement to Trend-Aware Attenion, can effectively improve the performance of forecasting. (4) After removing the diffusion GCN, the model cannot capture the spatial correlation in the traffic network, and therefore the performance of PYNet-NS decreases.

5.6   Long Term Forecasting Performance

Long term (i.e., one hour or more) forecasting of traffic flow or traffic speed in a traffic network is challenging. The number of sensors deployed in a traffic network as nodes on a graph is usually huge, and if the model includes similarity calculation of nodes, the time complexity grows quadratically with the number of nodes, and secondly, the long term traffic conditions are difficult to forecast accurately due to the non-stationarity factor in the time series.

PYNet is based on a pyramid structure, which can effectively model correlations between time series with different time scales and has advantages in modeling long term temporal dependence. Therefore, to evaluate the performance of PYNet in long term forecasting, we forecast the future traffic data for 30, 60, 90 and 120 min on the PEMS04, and the results are shown in Table 2. We observe that PYNet improves the state-of-the-art baseline from 3.10% to 7.13% in MAE on the PEMS04 dataset, and as the time step, the gap further increases, which further demonstrates the performance of PYNet on long term traffic flow forecasting.

Table 2. Long term forecasting performance of different models on PEMS04.

Model	Metrics	30 min	60 min	90 min	120 min	Average
ASTGCN	MAE	22.08 ± 0.28	25.51 ± 0.69	29.32 ± 1.17	34.04 ± 1.42	26.01 ± 0.75
	RMSE	34.47 ± 0.42	39.35 ± 1.10	44.95 ± 1.87	51.60 ± 2.20	40.64 ± 1.28
	MAPE (%)	14.70 ± 0.10	16.84 ± 0.19	19.28 ± 0.28	22.49 ± 0.31	17.22 ± 0.19
STSGCN	MAE	21.66 ± 0.36	24.04 ± 0.41	26.70 ± 0.52	29.07 ± 0.64	24.35 ± 0.47
	RMSE	34.56 ± 0.75	37.98 ± 0.72	41.91 ± 0.75	45.45 ± 0.90	38.46 ± 0.79
	MAPE (%)	14.44 ± 0.13	15.76 ± 0.11	17.50 ± 0.18	18.92 ± 0.15	16.13 ± 0.20
GMAN	MAE	20.50 ± 0.01	21.02 ± 0.04	21.55 ± 0.08	22.29 ± 0.05	21.08 ± 0.05
	RMSE	33.21 ± 0.42	34.18 ± 0.48	35.09 ± 0.56	36.13 ± 0.54	34.24 ± 0.49
	MAPE (%)	15.06 ± 0.52	15.37 ± 0.57	15.78 ± 0.66	16.54 ± 0.76	15.48 ± 0.60
DSTAGNN	MAE	19.36 ± 0.04	20.69 ± 0.08	21.69 ± 0.03	22.91 ± 0.15	20.60 ± 0.02
	RMSE	31.36 ± 0.17	33.65 ± 0.27	35.29 ± 0.22	36.81 ± 0.04	33.47 ± 0.15
	MAPE (%)	12.88 ± 0.02	13.54 ± 0.03	14.22 ± 0.01	15.04 ± 0.05	13.58 ± 0.02
PYNet	MAE	**18.76 ± 0.02**	**19.35 ± 0.03**	**19.88 ± 0.03**	**20.70 ± 0.04**	**19.38 ± 0.02**
	RMSE	**30.72 ± 0.08**	**31.86 ± 0.07**	**32.79 ± 0.08**	**33.91 ± 0.07**	**31.84 ± 0.07**
	MAPE (%)	**12.46 ± 0.24**	**12.79 ± 0.29**	**13.15 ± 0.26**	**13.82 ± 0.31**	**12.86 ± 0.25**
Improve	MAE	**3.10%**	**6.48%**	**7.75%**	**7.13%**	**5.92%**
	RMSE	**2.04%**	**5.32%**	**6.55%**	**6.14%**	**4.87%**
	MAPE	**3.26%**	**5.54%**	**7.52%**	**8.11%**	**5.30%**

6   Conclusion

In this paper, we propose a pyramid network for traffic forecasting tasks, namely PYNet, where the Pyramid Constructor initialize a pyramid network with a multi-level structure through a set of convolution layers. Then we perform Trend-Aware Attention in the pyramid network top-down between adjacent levels to compute the attention matrix in local context, which not only reduces the impact of anomalies in the data, but also allows the trend blocks in the lower levels of the time series to benefit from their own multiplicity of perceptual fields. In spatial dimension, we learn an adaptive unidirection graph that maintains the properties of state transfer between nodes by a random walk process over spatially. Finally the effectiveness of PYNet was verified by experiments on four traffic flow datasets.

Acknowledgment. This research was supported by the National Natural Science Foundation of China (Grant no. 62266040), the Key Research and Development Project of Gansu Province (Grant no. 20YF8GA049), the Youth Science and Technology Fund Project of Gansu Province (Grant no. 20JR10RA097), the Industrial Support Plan Project for Colleges and Universities in Gansu Province (Grant no. 2022CYZC-13), and the Lanzhou Municipal Science and Technology Project (Grant no. 2019-1-34).

Ethical Considerations. The work studied in this paper can contribute not only towards more accurate predictions of traffic forecasts, but also to more efficient traffic scheduling. Our work also provides better planning methods for pedestrians, helping people to save time and, on an environmental level, to save energy. This research is primarily based on a Pyramid learning structure to more effectively and deeply mine the underlying features of traffic data. This prediction model also addresses to some extent the prediction problems of other spatio-temporal series, such as water quality prediction and weather prediction. There are no ethical implications for this work such as possible use in policing or military related applications.

References

1. Bruna, J., Zaremba, W., Szlam, A., LeCun, Y.: Spectral networks and locally connected networks on graphs. arXiv preprint arXiv:1312.6203 (2013)
2. Chen, W., Chen, L., Xie, Y., Cao, W., Gao, Y., Feng, X.: Multi-range attentive bicomponent graph convolutional network for traffic forecasting. In: Proceedings of the AAAI Conference on Artificial Intelligence, vol. 34, pp. 3529–3536 (2020)
3. Cho, K., et al.: Learning phrase representations using RNN encoder-decoder for statistical machine translation. arXiv preprint arXiv:1406.1078 (2014)
4. Connor, J.T., Martin, R.D., Atlas, L.E.: Recurrent neural networks and robust time series prediction. IEEE Trans. Neural Networks $5(2)$, 240–254 (1994)
5. Guo, S., Lin, Y., Wan, H., Li, X., Cong, G.: Learning dynamics and heterogeneity of spatial-temporal graph data for traffic forecasting. IEEE Trans. Knowl. Data Eng. $34(11)$, 5415–5428 (2021)
6. Hochreiter, S., Schmidhuber, J.: Long short-term memory. Neural Comput. $9(8)$, 1735–1780 (1997)
7. Kipf, T.N., Welling, M.: Semi-supervised classification with graph convolutional networks. arXiv preprint arXiv:1609.02907 (2016)
8. Kumar, S.V., Vanajakshi, L.: Short-term traffic flow prediction using seasonal ARIMA model with limited input data. Eur. Transp. Res. Rev. $7(3)$, 1–9 (2015)
9. Lan, S., Ma, Y., Huang, W., Wang, W., Yang, H., Li, P.: DSTAGNN: dynamic spatial-temporal aware graph neural network for traffic flow forecasting. In: International Conference on Machine Learning, pp. 11906–11917. PMLR (2022)
10. Li, F., et al.: Dynamic graph convolutional recurrent network for traffic prediction: benchmark and solution. ACM Trans. Knowl. Discov. Data $17(1)$, 1–21 (2023)
11. Li, M., Zhu, Z.: Spatial-temporal fusion graph neural networks for traffic flow forecasting. In: Proceedings of the AAAI Conference on Artificial Intelligence, vol. 35, pp. 4189–4196 (2021)
12. Li, P., Fang, J., Chao, P., Zhao, P., Liu, A., Zhao, L.: JS-STDGN: a spatial-temporal dynamic graph network using JS-Graph for traffic prediction. In: Bhattacharya, A., et al. (eds.) Database Systems for Advanced Applications: 27th International Conference, DASFAA 2022, Virtual Event, 11–14 April 2022, Proceedings, Part I, pp. 191–206. Springer, Cham (2022). https://doi.org/10.1007/978-3-031-00123-9_15
13. Li, Q., Han, Z., Wu, X.M.: Deeper insights into graph convolutional networks for semi-supervised learning. In: Proceedings of the AAAI Conference on Artificial Intelligence, vol. 32 (2018)
14. Li, Y., Yu, R., Shahabi, C., Liu, Y.: Diffusion convolutional recurrent neural network: data-driven traffic forecasting. arXiv preprint arXiv:1707.01926 (2017)
15. Lu, Z., Zhou, C., Wu, J., Jiang, H., Cui, S.: Integrating granger causality and vector auto-regression for traffic prediction of large-scale WLANs. KSII Trans. Internet Inf. Syst. $10(1)$, 136–151 (2016)

16. Oreshkin, B.N., Amini, A., Coyle, L., Coates, M.: FC-GAGA: fully connected gated graph architecture for spatio-temporal traffic forecasting. In: Proceedings of the AAAI Conference on Artificial Intelligence, vol. 35, pp. 9233–9241 (2021)

17. Park, C., et al.: ST-GRAT: a novel spatio-temporal graph attention networks for accurately forecasting dynamically changing road speed. In: Proceedings of the 29th ACM International Conference on Information & Knowledge Management, pp. 1215–1224 (2020)

18. Perozzi, B., Al-Rfou, R., Skiena, S.: DeepWalk: online learning of social representations. In: Proceedings of the 20th ACM SIGKDD International Conference on Knowledge Discovery and Data Mining, pp. 701–710 (2014)

19. Song, C., Lin, Y., Guo, S., Wan, H.: Spatial-temporal synchronous graph convolutional networks: a new framework for spatial-temporal network data forecasting. In: Proceedings of the AAAI Conference on Artificial Intelligence, vol. 34, pp. 914–921 (2020)

20. Sutskever, I., Vinyals, O., Le, Q.V.: Sequence to sequence learning with neural networks. In: Advances in Neural Information Processing Systems, vol. 27 (2014)

21. Vaswani, A., et al.: Attention is all you need. In: Advances in Neural Information Processing Systems, vol. 30 (2017)

22. Wu, Z., Pan, S., Long, G., Jiang, J., Chang, X., Zhang, C.: Connecting the dots: multivariate time series forecasting with graph neural networks. In: Proceedings of the 26th ACM SIGKDD International Conference on Knowledge Discovery & Data Mining, pp. 753–763 (2020)

23. Wu, Z., Pan, S., Long, G., Jiang, J., Zhang, C.: Graph WaveNet for deep spatial-temporal graph modeling. arXiv preprint arXiv:1906.00121 (2019)

24. Yao, H., Tang, X., Wei, H., Zheng, G., Li, Z.: Revisiting spatial-temporal similarity: a deep learning framework for traffic prediction. In: Proceedings of the AAAI Conference on Artificial Intelligence, vol. 33, pp. 5668–5675 (2019)

25. Yao, H., et al.: Deep multi-view spatial-temporal network for taxi demand prediction. In: Proceedings of the AAAI Conference on Artificial Intelligence, vol. 32 (2018)

26. Yu, B., Yin, H., Zhu, Z.: Spatio-temporal graph convolutional networks: a deep learning framework for traffic forecasting. arXiv preprint arXiv:1709.04875 (2017)

27. Zhang, J., Zheng, Y., Qi, D.: Deep spatio-temporal residual networks for citywide crowd flows prediction. In: Proceedings of the AAAI Conference on Artificial Intelligence, vol. 31 (2017)

28. Zheng, C., et al.: Spatio-temporal joint graph convolutional networks for traffic forecasting. IEEE Trans. Knowl. Data Eng. **17**, 691–703 (2023)

29. Zheng, C., Fan, X., Wang, C., Qi, J.: GMAN: a graph multi-attention network for traffic prediction. In: Proceedings of the AAAI Conference on Artificial Intelligence, vol. 34, pp. 1234–1241 (2020)

30. Zheng, C., Fan, X., Wen, C., Chen, L., Wang, C., Li, J.: DeepSTD: mining spatio-temporal disturbances of multiple context factors for citywide traffic flow prediction. IEEE Trans. Intell. Transp. Syst. **21**(9), 3744–3755 (2019)

31. Zhu, D., Cui, P., Wang, D., Zhu, W.: Deep variational network embedding in Wasserstein space. In: Proceedings of the 24th ACM SIGKDD International Conference on Knowledge Discovery & Data Mining, pp. 2827–2836 (2018)

A Passage Retrieval Transformer-Based Re-Ranking Model for Truthful Consumer Health Search

Rishabh Upadhyay[ID], Gabriella Pasi[ID], and Marco Viviani[✉][ID]

Department of Informatics, Systems, and Communication (DISCo), Information and
Knowledge Representation, Retrieval, and Reasoning (IKR3) Lab,
University of Milano-Bicocca, Milan, Italy
{rishabh.upadhyay,gabriella.pasi,marco.viviani}@unimib.it
https://ikr3.disco.unimib.it/

Abstract. Searching for online information is nowadays a critical task
in a scenario characterized by information overload and misinformation.
To address these issues, it is necessary to provide users with both topically relevant and truthful information. Re-ranking is a strategy often
used in Information Retrieval (IR) to consider multiple dimensions of
relevance. However, re-rankers often analyze the full text of documents
to obtain an overall relevance score at the re-ranking stage, which can
lead to sub-optimal results. Some recent Transformer-based re-rankers
actually consider text passages rather than the entire document, but
focus only on topical relevance. Transformers are also being used in non-
IR solutions to identify information truthfulness, but just to perform a
binary classification task. Therefore, in this article, we propose an IR
model based on re-ranking that focuses on suitably identified text passages from documents for retrieving both topically relevant and truthful
information. This approach significantly reduces the noise introduced by
query-unrelated content in long documents and allows us to evaluate the
document's truthfulness against it, enabling more effective retrieval. We
tested the effectiveness of the proposed solution in the context of the
Consumer Health Search task, considering publicly available datasets.
Our results show that the proposed approach statistically outperforms
full-text retrieval models in the context of multidimensional relevance,
such as those based on aggregation, and monodimensional relevance
Transformer-based re-rankers, such as BERT-based re-rankers.

1 Introduction

Retrieving online information that is useful to users concerning their information needs is an increasingly complex task in the development of *Information
Retrieval Systems* (IRSs) [9,11]. This is due to numerous reasons, including:
(*i*) the exponential increase in the amount of content generated online, which
leads to a situation of *information overload* [31,49]; (*ii*) the dissemination of

D. Koutra et al. (Eds.): ECML PKDD 2023, LNAI 14169, pp. 355–371, 2023.
https://doi.org/10.1007/978-3-031-43412-9_21

information whose level of truthfulness we cannot assess a priori, because of the phenomenon known as *disintermediation* [18], which leads to the problem of *misinformation* [15,38]; and (*iii*) the fact that the estimation of the *relevance* of information (i.e., the usefulness of retrieved documents to a user's information needs) depends on multiple aspects that are necessarily related to the *search task* and to the *domain* in which that search is carried out [12,22].

All these problems have an impact on the *decision-making* process of the user searching for useful information. With respect to (*i*), when a person is exposed to too much information, it can lead to feelings of stress, anxiety, confusion, and difficulty in making decisions, as the individual may find it challenging to focus on the most important information [48]. Problem (*ii*) also directly impacts personal choices; indeed, misinformation can have a significant impact on decision-making, as it can lead people to make choices that are not in their best interest, such as choosing to take a particular medication based on false information read online. Very important in this area is the fact that misinformation can also impact *group decision-making* processes [5,8]. This can be particularly problematic in contexts such as public health, where decisions have far-reaching consequences – just think of those related to the spread of misinformation during the COVID-19 period [4,17]. Regarding problem (*iii*), i.e., the fact that relevance in IR is a task- and domain-dependent concept, the IR solutions developed must be tailored to these aspects so as not to compromise users' decision-making. For example, the task of retrieving information about a particular disease has completely different characteristics than a task dedicated to identifying patients who are candidates for clinical trials. Furthermore, each domain of interest has its terminologies, concepts, and sources of information to account for. A medical researcher who needs to retrieve information from medical journals, for example, could need a solution able to synthesizing information from multiple sources; a different solution may not be effective for making decisions.

To take into consideration the issues enunciated above, a variety of IR models have been proposed in the literature, many of which are based on *re-ranking* to account from time to time for the peculiarities of the dimensions of relevance, task, and domain under consideration. An initial ranking phase is usually carried out with a standard IR model, followed by a second re-ranking phase that can further analyze the documents found in the first phase for the aspects listed above. One of the disadvantages of these solutions is that, during re-ranking, the *full text* of each document is considered for analysis, which may lead to suboptimal results as only certain parts of the document itself may be more relevant to a specific dimension or relevance, or a particular task, or a specific domain. Some recent solutions that have proposed the use of specific *text passages* to perform re-ranking, often based on the use of Transformer-based architectures, have only considered *topical relevance*. Such architectures have also been applied to the study of online *misinformation*, but, in this case, the problem has been addressed as a *binary classification* task aiming at identifying truthful documents with respect to non-truthful ones, and not as an IR task.

Therefore, in this article, we aim to overcome the limitations of current literature solutions by proposing a *Passage Retrieval* [30], *Transformer-based* model when performing re-ranking. We are especially concerned with identifying the most *topically relevant* text passages concerning a *query* to be used to assess the level of *truthfulness* of documents in the considered document collection. This model is applied in the *health domain*, and in particular for the task of *Consumer Health Search* (CHS), i.e., the search for health information by people without specific expertise in the medical field [57]. The results obtained show how the proposed solution enables results that outperform current re-ranking-based solutions that consider the entire document in scenarios involving multidimensional relevance, such as those that rely on aggregation, and monodimensional relevance Transformer-based re-rankers like BERT-based re-rankers.

2   Related Work

IR solutions accounting for *information truthfulness*, especially those based on re-ranking, never consider this concept (or one of the related concepts employed in the literature such as *credibility, veracity,* etc.),[1] as a single dimension of relevance. Instead, they act in a multidimensional context that takes into account at least the *topical relevance* of the documents to the query beyond truthfulness. Some approaches compute different *relevance scores* for the different dimensions of relevance considered and, subsequently, carry out an *aggregation* of the topicality score to other relevance dimension scores. For example, distinct solutions consider *credibility, correctness,* and *understandability* beyond topicality [12,22]. They use different solutions to calculate each relevance score, usually on the full text of documents, and employ either simple and compensative *linear aggregation* strategies [1,7,19,43,47,50,56], or *rank fusion* methods [47,56].

With respect to using text passages – instead of the entire document – to improve the effectiveness of IR models, there are some solutions that, however, consider just *topicality*, and have explored the use of Transformer-based architectures. In [39], the authors introduce a re-ranking method based on BERT and Passage Retrieval, specifically for truncated documents that exceed 512 tokens. One of their models, called *Contextualized Embeddings for Document Ranking* (CEDR), combines BERT with other neural IR models – such as *Position-Aware Convolutional Recurrent Relevance Matching* (PACRR) [27], *Kernelized Neural Ranking Model* (KNRM) [55], and *Deep Relevance Matching Model* (DRMM) [25] – to demonstrate its effectiveness. The work presented in [13] proposes an alternative approach by segmenting long documents into *overlapping passages* and defining the document's relevance score as the score of the first passage, of the best passage, or as the sum of all passage scores. In [34], the method just

---

[1] *Credibility* is a concept often identified with *believability*, and can be considered as a perception of the information receiver [46]. In this article, we refer to the *truthfulness* of health information as much as a factual concept. Hence, the proposed approach aims to limit the spread of *health misinformation* understood as "a health-related claim of fact that is currently false due to a lack of scientific evidence" [10].

described is extended by incorporating PARADE, i.e., *Passage Representation Aggregation for Document Reranking*, a hierarchical layer that uses max-pooling, attention mechanism, or complete Transformers to aggregate the passage representations for long documents. The model presented in [14] incorporates a *left-to-right recurrence window* between Transformers to prevent information from flowing in the opposite direction. Incorporating both *Convolutional* and *Recurrent Neural Networks* (CNNs and RNNs), the hierarchical model presented in [40] extracts *query-relevant blocks* and generates a combined representation of both queries and blocks. However, this method has a drawback in that it may overlook pertinent blocks that do not include query terms. To address this issue, the KeyBLD model described in [35] uses local *query-block pre-ranking* to select key blocks, which are segments of a lengthy document containing a maximum of 63 tokens. These selected blocks are then aggregated to create a condensed document that can be processed by the IR model.

Transformer-based architectures have also been used extensively to address the problem of spreading misinformation, but not necessarily in the context of IR solutions or the health domain. The self-ensemble SCIBERT model proposed in [32], and the FakeBERT model introduced in [28], combine BERT and CNNs to process textual content in a bidirectional manner. Other studies, such as [3, 24], have evaluated various Deep Learning models, including *Bidirectional Long Short-Term Memory* (BiLSTM) networks and CNNs, for detecting fake news and rumors in text data. Additionally, [51] fine-tuned Transformer models such as DistilBERT, COVID-BERT-Base, and COVID-Twitter-Base on a corpus of COVID-19 tweets for fake news detection tasks, while also exploring other models like parallel CNNs, single-layer LSTM, and hierarchical attention networks.

So as we can summarize, there are solutions in the health domain based on IR models that address the problem of the multidimensional nature of relevance but with approaches that focus on the analysis of the whole document. Other works use Transformer-based approaches and Passage Retrieval techniques but consider one single relevance dimension, i.e., topical relevance. Finally, there are other solutions based on the use of Transformers that aim to tackle the problem of (health) misinformation dissemination, but as a classification task and not as an IR one, and thus not considering the relationship between topicality and truthfulness of the information. The purpose of our model, as illustrated in the next section, is, therefore, to overcome the limits of current literature solutions by defining a re-ranking model based on Passage Retrieval and Transformers to the Consumer Health Search task, to increase the effectiveness of retrieval by identifying topically relevant textual passages, which will allow us to better assess information truthfulness by exploiting Transformer attention mechanisms.

3   The Passage Retrieval Transformer-Based Re-Ranking Model to Truthful Consumer Health Search

The proposed Passage Retrieval Transformer-based re-ranking model consists of four primary stages: (*i*) first-stage retrieval using BM25, (*ii*) passage segmentation, (iii) Passage Retrieval, and (iv) Transformer-based re-ranking of documents. These stages are described in detail in the next sections and illustrated visually in Fig. 1.

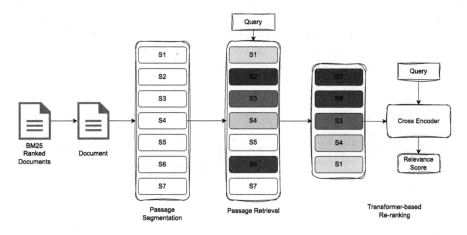

Fig. 1. The four stages of the Passage Retrieval Transformer-based re-ranking model.

3.1 First-Stage Retrieval: BM25

Our model's *first-stage retrieval* utilizes the BM25 retrieval model [45]. BM25 is particularly known for its effectiveness and efficiency, and is widely used as the first-stage ranker in Information Retrieval Systems [2, 21, 29].

This model calculates a *topicality score*, namely BM25(q, d), based on word frequency and distribution in both the query q and the document d, resulting in a ranked list of the most relevant documents. Formally:

$$BM25(q,d) = \sum_{t \in q,d} \log \frac{N - df(t) + 0.5}{df(t) + 0.5} \cdot \frac{tf(t,d) \cdot (k_1 + 1)}{tf(t,d) + k_1 \cdot (1 - b + b\frac{l_d}{L})} \quad (1)$$

In the equation, N represents the total number of documents in the collection, $df(t)$ represents the document frequency for the term t, i.e., the number of documents containing term t, $tf(t,d)$ refers to the term frequency, i.e., the number of times term t appears in document d.

To account for differences in document length, length normalization is applied. l_d refers to the length of document d, L represents the average length of documents in the collection, and k_1 and b are internal parameters used to adjust the scaling of term frequency and document length respectively.

3.2 Passage Segmentation

The second stage performed by the proposed model is *passage segmentation*, which involves breaking down lengthy relevant documents into smaller segments or passages. Unlike KeyBLD [35], which utilizes blocks, in this paper we opt to divide documents into *sentences* by using the NLTK sentence tokenizer,[2] as exemplified in Fig. 2. The tokenization process typically involves identifying boundaries between tokens based on certain rules or patterns, such as whitespaces, punctuation, or language-specific guidelines.

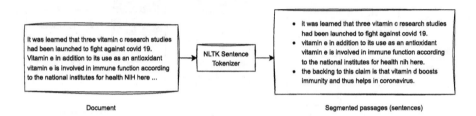

Fig. 2. An example of the subdivision of a document into sentences in the passage segmentation stage.

The primary rationale behind this decision is the assumption that sentences provide more punctual and interpretable information, especially concerning topical relevance and truthfulness. A block might contain details about several facts, which would make it difficult to relate it to a query (potentially related to a single fact); whereas individual sentences are more likely to talk about individual facts that can then be easily associated with user queries and evaluated concerning their truthfulness. To test this assumption, we performed a preliminary evaluation on publicly accessible datasets concerning the truthful health IR task using different passage segmentation, as explained in more detail in Sect. 4.3.

3.3 Passage Retrieval

Once the sentences have been extracted from the documents in the previous stage, in the *Passage Retrieval* phase the most (topically) relevant sentences from each document about a given query are retrieved. Both passage segmentation and Passage Retrieval are performed on the top-k documents returned by first-stage retrieval, discussed in Sect. 3.1, which were estimated to be "globally" relevant to a query. We use BioBERT [33] to represent both queries and sentences and *cosine similarity* to rank sentences. BioBERT is a leading-edge language model in the biomedical field. It has proven to be particularly effective in various *Natural Language Processing* (NLP) tasks related to medical texts, including *Named Entity Recognition* (NER) [6,36].

---

[2] https://www.nltk.org/api/nltk.tokenize.html.

NER is a process of identifying *Named Entities*, i.e., real-world entities, such as people, organizations, places, dates, and more, in unstructured text. It can enrich the sentences extracted in passage segmentation, discussed in Sect. 3.2, by providing context in the form of medical entities. For this reason, we incorporated NER to identify *disease* and *medication* entities in sentences before computing the similarity between the query and the document. In this way, if a query is about "vitamin D", we do not obtain sentences that contain "vitamin C," no matter how similar the two vector representations may be, as illustrated in Fig. 3.

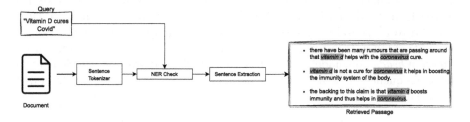

Fig. 3. Query-relevant Passage Retrieval with NER.

From a formal point of view, the similarity score $\sigma(q, s)$ for each query-sentence pair is computed as follows:

$$
\sigma(q, s) = \begin{cases} \cos(q, s), & \text{if } \mathrm{NER}_q(\mu, \delta) = \mathrm{NER}_s(\mu, \delta) \\ w_d \cdot \cos(q, s), & \text{otherwise} \end{cases}
\tag{2}
$$

In the equation, μ denotes the medication entity, δ the disease entity, $\cos(q, s)$ the cosine similarity, $\mathrm{NER}_x(\mu, \delta)$ the Named Entities extracted from x ($x \in \{q, s\}$), and w_d ($w_d \in [0, 1]$) is a discount weight,[3] employed to decrease the value of $\sigma(q, s)$ in the case of non-corresponding Named Entities in q and s.

3.4 Transformer-Based Re-Ranking

Once the similarity values have been computed for all query-sentence pairs, the most relevant top-h sentences need to be selected, which will form a *sentence-based document* on which the actual re-ranking phase will then be carried out. As it will be illustrated later, the choice of an appropriate number of sentences becomes critical to the effectiveness of the proposed model.

---

[3] For finding the optimal w_d value, we performed a *grid search* using 5 queries (randomly selected) and a document related to those queries. The grid search involved systematically testing different values of w_d within a predefined range, and evaluating the performance of the system for each value of w_d using the NDCG metric. This process identified the value of w_d that yielded the best performance in terms of the selected metric, and therefore the best overall performance for the system [54].

Sentence-Based Documents. From a formal point of view, a sentence-based document, denoted a $\tilde{d}$, is given by:

$$\tilde{d} = s_1 \oplus s_2 \oplus \cdots \oplus s_h \qquad (3)$$

where $\oplus$ denotes concatenation, and $s_1, s_2, \ldots, s_h$ are the sentences ranked in the first h positions based on $\sigma(q, s)$ values.

Cross-Encoder Re-Ranking. At this point, we propose the use of a *cross-encoder* re-ranker [16] to act on the newly obtained documents. This kind of approach, utilized in IR, involves combining two sequences, namely a *query* (referred to as q) and a *document candidate* (referred to as d), which are then passed through a Transformer model, such as BERT. By utilizing Transformer *attention heads*, the model can directly capture correlations between elements of the two sequences, enabling the calculation of *Retrieval Status Value* RSV(q, d). In formal terms:

$$\text{RSV}(q, d) = \text{CE}([\text{CLS}]\ q\ [\text{SEP}]\ d\ [\text{SEP}]) \cdot W \qquad (4)$$

where CE is the cross-encoder, CLS and SEP are special tokens to represent the *classifier token* and the *separator token*, and W is a learned weight matrix that represents the relationship between the query and document representations.

For our purposes, we fed the cross-encoder for the computation of the RSV not with the original full documents, but with the considered sentence-based documents, as exemplified at a high level in Fig. 4 and as formally defined as follows:

$$\text{RSV}(q, \tilde{d}) = \text{CE}([\text{CLS}]\ q\ [\text{SEP}]\ \tilde{d}\ [\text{SEP}]) \cdot W \qquad (5)$$

It is worth to be underlined that, since the labels used for *fine-tuning* the BERT model are based on both topicality and truthfulness, the proposed model is able to consider both relevance dimensions in the re-ranking phase. By reducing the document size by considering only query-relevant passages built as illustrated before, we provide the cross-encoder with a more focused and compact representation of the document, potentially improving the multidimensional retrieval scoring. This also reduces the computational complexity and time required for the cross-encoder to process the document, as it only needs to consider the relevant passages instead of the entire document.

4   Experimental Evaluation

We concentrated on the *ad-hoc retrieval* task of the TREC-2020 Health Misinformation Track [12] and CLEF-2020 eHealth Track [23] for evaluation purposes. Both tracks pertain to *Consumer Health Search* (CHS) and give weight

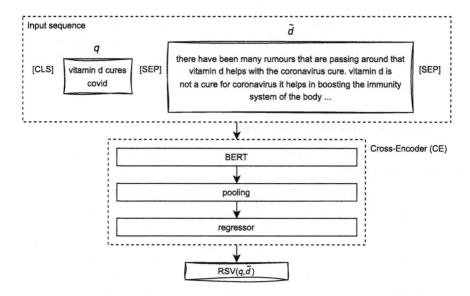

Fig. 4. An example of the CE architecture adopted in the proposed model.

to *credibility* as an essential factor of relevance, in addition to topicality.[4] We utilized a subset of 1 million documents from each track, with the TREC-2020 Track encompassing 46 topics linked to Coronavirus and the CLEF-2020 Track including 50 medical conditions. The TREC-2020 Health Misinformation Track categorizes documents into binary labels, with those that meet the criteria of being "topically relevant and credible" labeled as "1", and the remaining labeled as "0". The same binary labeling procedure applies to both topicality and credibility for the CLEF-2020 eHealth Track.

4.1 Implementation Details

For indexing purposes and to implement the BM25 model, we used *PyTerrier* [37]. We created two indexes: one for TREC-2020 and the other for CLEF-2020. For re-ranking, we used the top 500 documents retrieved from first-stage retrieval. Since the document set pertains to health-related topics, we utilized BioBERT [33] for cross-encoder re-ranking training and inference, in particular `dmis-lab/biobert-v1.1`.[5] As there was no provided split for TREC-2020 and CLEF-2020, we trained the cross-encoder on 80% of the queries from one dataset (e.g., TREC-2020) and employed the other query set as the test set. We selected all queries and documents from the other dataset (CLEF-2020) as the validation

---

[4] Given the current lack of datasets in Consumer Health Search that are labeled with respect to both topicality and truthfulness (understood as the factuality of the information, as previously introduced), in the experiments we approximate this concept with that of credibility used in datasets.

[5] https://huggingface.co/dmis-lab/biobert-v1.1.

set and vice versa. The BioBERT model was fine-tuned using a batch size of 4 and a maximum sequence length of 512 tokens for 10 epochs with the Adam optimizer and an initial learning rate of 2×10^{-5}. For training and inference, we used the *HuggingFace* library [53], the `cross-encoder` package of *Sentence-Transformers* library [44], and *PyTorch* [41].

4.2 Baselines and Evaluation Metrics

The baseline models that were considered for comparative evaluation of the proposed solution are:

- BM25: the BM25 model implemented by PyTerrier;
- WAM: the aggregation-based multidimensional relevance model presented in [50], based on a simple weighted average of distinct relevance scores. Specifically, weights associated with topicality and credibility are set as in the best model described in [50]. This model is tested with different percentages of relevant sentences, i.e., 5%, 10%, 15%, 20%, 25%, and Full Document;
- KeyBLD: the model for key-block detection that selects the most informative blocks from a document based on their topical relevance to the query;
- PARADE:[6] the Passage Retrieval model for document ranking that uses aggregation techniques to combine relevance signals from a document's passages;
- CE_{full} (512 tokens relevant passages): the cross-encoder model for re-ranking as proposed in [16], based on Equation (4), and with the maximum length obtainable for a BERT document, i.e., 512 tokens.

In the proposed solution, the last cross-encoder for re-ranking is employed in association with different percentages of relevant sentences constituting the sentence-based document, according to Equation (5). In this case, the model is denoted as CE_p, where p indicates a given percentage of sentences, i.e., 5%, 10%, 15%, 20%, 25%. The evaluation metrics considered for experiments are *Normalized Discounted Cumulative Gain* at 10 and 20 (NDCG@10, NDCG@20), *Precision* at 10 and 20 (P@10, P@20), *Mean Reciprocal Rank* at 10 (MRR@10), and *Mean Average Precision* (MAP). All results are statistically significant according to a paired t-test ($p < 0.05$) with Bonferroni correction for multiple testing, as described in [52].

4.3 Results

In this section we provide the results of the evaluation of the proposed solution against a couple of research questions, i.e., a preliminary research question that we estimated to be useful with respect to giving an indication about the usefulness of the sentences as text passages, and the actual research question about the effectiveness of the proposed solution. Specifically:

---

[6] https://github.com/canjiali/PARADE/.

- R1. *What is the impact of using sentence-level representations instead of block-level representations for document re-ranking based on topicality and truthfulness?*
- R2. *Is the use of Passage Retrieval and Transformer-based re-rankers actually more effective than current literature approaches?*

R1. Before testing our model against baselines, we actually wanted to verify that the choice of a single sentence as the length of the text passage was indeed the best one. To this aim, we tested the CE_{full} re-ranking model (the most effective at present in the literature) filling the 512 tokens with top-h passages constituted by 1 sentence, 2 sentences, and blocks. The results of this evaluation are shown in Table 1.

Table 1. Comparison of the CE_{full} cross-encoder re-ranker performance using different lengths of textual passages to fill the 512-token length of BERT documents on the CLEF and TREC datasets. In bold the best results.

	Passage Type	CLEF					
		NDCG@10	NDCG@20	P@10	P@20	MRR@10	MAP
CE_{full}	1 sentence	**0.2843**	**0.2848**	**0.2811**	**0.2818**	**0.4801**	**0.1474**
	2 sentences	0.2531	0.2511	0.2503	0.2495	0.4221	0.1023
	blocks	0.2632	0.2612	0.2661	0.2615	0.4434	0.1231
	Passage Type	TREC					
		NDCG@10	NDCG@20	P@10	P@20	MRR@10	MAP
CE_{full}	1 sentence	**0.6055**	**0.6023**	**0.6059**	**0.6011**	**0.6997**	**0.2986**
	2 sentences	0.5601	0.5578	0.5545	0.5396	0.6311	0.2589
	blocks	0.5691	0.5671	0.5631	0.5403	0.6324	0.2677

According to the findings, using one sentence as the passage type provides superior performance, as evidenced by its higher scores in all metrics for both datasets. This is most probably because sentences are more succinct compared to blocks or two-sentence passages, which can contain irrelevant or conflicting information. The results imply that employing one sentence as the passage type can enhance the cross-encoder model's effectiveness in document retrieval tasks. Nevertheless, determining the best approach may be contingent on the datasets and the task considered, and additional experimentation may be required.

R2. The results of the different literature models considered as a baseline and the proposed CE_p re-ranking model are shown below in Table 2 concerning both CLEF and TREC datasets.

Based on the results, the BM25 model, the baseline IR model, underperforms compared to the other models. When using Deep-Learning-based models, the

Table 2. Comparison of the performance of different models on CLEF and TREC datasets, with various percentages of relevant passages and Full Document (512 tokens in the cross-encoder model) as input. In bold the best results.

Model	Rel. Passage	CLEF					
		NDCG@10	NDCG@20	P@10	P@20	MRR@10	MAP
BM25		0.1054	0.1578	0.1081	0.1954	0.1578	0.0764
WAM	Full Document	0.0865	0.1591	0.1002	0.2034	0.1232	0.0632
	5%	0.0912	0.1699	0.1096	0.2156	0.1503	0.0694
	10%	0.0993	0.1643	0.1195	0.2213	0.1596	0.0701
	15%	0.1031	0.1694	0.1254	0.2284	0.1612	0.0744
	20%	0.1342	0.1864	0.1495	0.2443	0.1965	0.0985
	25%	0.1032	0.1703	0.1295	0.2294	0.1664	0.0792
KeyBLD		0.2635	0.261	0.2645	0.2645	0.4431	0.1233
PARADE		0.2512	0.2534	0.2551	0.2593	0.4342	0.1213
CE_{full}	512 tokens	0.2843	0.2848	0.2811	0.2818	0.4801	0.1474
CE_5	5%	0.2956	0.2958	0.2899	0.2931	0.5083	0.1499
CE_{10}	10%	0.3145	0.3058	0.3002	0.3012	0.5293	0.1552
CE_{15}	15%	0.3215	0.3198	0.3112	0.3098	0.5453	0.1659
CE_{20}	20%	**0.3475**	**0.3446**	**0.3423**	**0.3445**	**0.5923**	**0.1878**
CE_{25}	25%	0.3398	0.3223	0.3301	0.3311	0.5545	0.1599
Model	Relevant Passage	TREC					
		NDCG@10	NDCG@20	P@10	P@20	MRR@10	MAP
BM25		0.4166	0.4231	0.4177	0.4266	0.5107	0.2142
WAM	Full Document	0.5065	0.5164	0.4976	0.5001	0.5546	0.2453
	5%	0.5112	0.5199	0.4999	0.5051	0.6012	0.2579
	10%	0.5231	0.5221	0.5034	0.5093	0.6231	0.2734
	15%	0.5225	0.5223	0.5087	0.5102	0.6333	0.2788
	20%	0.5546	0.5533	0.5234	0.5212	0.6443	0.2945
	25%	0.5264	0.5288	0.5097	0.5143	0.6332	0.2834
KeyBLD		0.5432	0.5443	0.5342	0.5403	0.6324	0.2677
PARADE		0.5693	0.5664	0.5634	0.5669	0.6589	0.2785
CE_{full}	512 tokens	0.6055	0.6023	0.6059	0.6011	0.6997	0.2986
CE_5	5%	0.6194	0.6156	0.6012	0.6001	0.7211	0.3223
CE_{10}	10%	0.6534	0.6429	0.6267	0.6144	0.7345	0.3414
CE_{15}	15%	0.6623	0.6602	0.6322	0.6234	0.7541	0.3568
CE_{20}	20%	**0.6934**	**0.6801**	**0.6511**	**0.6311**	**0.7834**	**0.3784**
CE_{25}	25%	0.6634	0.6597	0.6374	0.6232	0.7431	0.3493

WAM model shows decent performance by utilizing query-relevant passages to reduce the document to 20% of its original size. Nevertheless, the CE model (in all its configurations) surpasses all other baseline models. This model utilizes a cross-encoder to compute relevance scores between the query and document, and its performance improves considerably when using query-relevant passages, as proposed in this work through the CE_p model. In particular, CE_p obtains the best results when the document is reduced to 20% of its original size using query-relevant passages. With higher percentages, performance begins to decline. This can be identified as demonstrating that after a certain number of sentences are taken into consideration, the effectiveness of identifying the truly most relevant ones is lost and we move back toward the introduction of noise that characterizes the scenario of taking full documents into consideration.

5 Conclusion

In the literature, various IR models have been proposed in the context of multidimensional relevance. Re-ranking models are often used in a two-phase approach where an initial ranking is performed with a standard IR model followed by a re-ranking phase that further analyzes the documents for specific dimensions of relevance, tasks, or domains. However, this approach has limitations as it considers the full text of each document during re-ranking, which may not be optimal for both effectiveness and efficiency. Many effective and efficient re-rankers nowadays are based on the use of Transformers, but they focus only on topical relevance. Transformers are also used for many misinformation identification solutions, but not in IR.

To overcome these issues, this paper proposed the usage of a Passage Retrieval solution during Transformer-based re-ranking to identify the most relevant portions of text for considering both topical relevance and information truthfulness in the health domain, for the task of Consumer Health Search. Results show that this proposed solution outperforms current re-ranking-based solutions that consider the entire document in scenarios involving multidimensional relevance, such as those that rely on aggregation, and monodimensional relevance Transformer-based re-rankers like BERT-based re-rankers.

As a future research direction, we aim to add an explainability layer to the model that details the contribution that individual text passages have with respect to the consideration of distinct dimensions of relevance in the re-ranking process. In addition, our aim is to employ and fine-tune this model in other domains too. However, it is important to note that the availability of comprehensive datasets with both topicality and truthfulness labels across other domains is still hard to find in the field of Information Retrieval, also with respect to the health domain itself. This is why it is important to continue the study and refinement of evaluation initiatives in the IR domain that can make such resources available [20, 26, 42].

Acknowledgements. This work was supported by the EU Horizon 2020 ITN/ETN on Domain-Specific Systems for Information Extraction and Retrieval (H2020-EU.1.3.1., ID: 860721). https://dossier-project.eu/

Data and Code Availability. The CLEF *eHealth* and TREC *Health Misinformation Track* datasets are publicly accessible upon request at the following URLs: https://

clefehealth.imag.fr/ and https://trec-health-misinfo.github.io/. In this paper, we used a subset of such datasets. Information and code for reconstructing this subset from the original datasets can be found at the following URL: https://github.com/ikr3-lab/TruthfulHealthSearchReranker/

References

1. Abualsaud, M., et al.: UWaterlooMDS at the TREC 2021 Health Misinformation Track. In: Proceedings of the Thirtieth Retrieval Conference Proceedings (TREC 2021), pp. 1–18. National Institute of Standards and Technology (NIST), Special Publication (2021)
2. Anand, M., Zhang, J., Ding, S., Xin, J., Lin, J.: Serverless bm25 search and BERT reranking. In: DESIRES, pp. 3–9 (2021)
3. Asghar, M.Z., Habib, A., Habib, A., Khan, A., Ali, R., Khattak, A.: Exploring deep neural networks for rumor detection. J. Ambient. Intell. Humaniz. Comput. **12**, 4315–4333 (2021)
4. Barua, Z., Barua, S., Aktar, S., Kabir, N., Li, M.: Effects of misinformation on Covid-19 individual responses and recommendations for resilience of disastrous consequences of misinformation. Prog. Disaster Sci. **8**, 100119 (2020)
5. Bavel, J.V., et al.: Using social and behavioural science to support Covid-19 pandemic response. Nat. Hum. Behav. **4**(5), 460–471 (2020)
6. Bhatia, P., Celikkaya, B., Khalilia, M., Senthivel, S.: Comprehend medical: a named entity recognition and relationship extraction web service. In: 2019 18th IEEE International Conference on Machine Learning and Applications (ICMLA), pp. 1844–1851. IEEE (2019)
7. Bondarenko, A., et al.: Webis at TREC 2021: Deep learning, health misinformation, and podcasts tracks. In: The Thirtieth Retrieval Conference Proceedings (TREC 2021), pp. 500–335 (2021)
8. Bryanov, K., Vziatysheva, V.: Determinants of individuals' belief in fake news: a scoping review determinants of belief in fake news. PLoS ONE **16**(6), e0253717 (2021)
9. Budd, J.M.: The complexity of information retrieval: a hypothetical example. J. Acad. Librariansh. **22**(2), 111–117 (1996)
10. Chou, W.Y.S., Oh, A., Klein, W.M.: Addressing health-related misinformation on social media. JAMA **320**(23), 2417–2418 (2018)
11. Chowdhury, G.G.: Introduction to modern information retrieval. Facet publishing (2010)
12. Clarke, C.L.A., Maistro, M., Rizvi, S., Smucker, M.D., Zuccon, G.: Overview of the TREC 2020 Health Misinformation Track (2020). https://trec.nist.gov/pubs/trec29/papers/OVERVIEW.HM.pdf
13. Dai, Z., Callan, J.: Deeper text understanding for ir with contextual neural language modeling. In: Proceedings of the 42nd International ACM SIGIR Conference on Research and Development in Information Retrieval, pp. 985–988 (2019)
14. Dai, Z., Yang, Z., Yang, Y., Carbonell, J., Le, Q., Salakhutdinov, R.: Transformer-XL: Attentive language models beyond a fixed-length context. In: Proceedings of the 57th Annual Meeting of the Association for Computational Linguistics (2019)
15. Del Vicario, M., et al.: The spreading of misinformation online. Proc. Natl. Acad. Sci. **113**(3), 554–559 (2016)

16. Devlin, J., Chang, M.W., Lee, K., Toutanova, K.: BERT: Pre-training of deep bidirectional transformers for language understanding. In: Proceedings of the 2019 Conference of the North American Chapter of the Association for Computational Linguistics: Human Language Technologies, Volume 1 (Long and Short Papers), pp. 4171–4186. Association for Computational Linguistics, Minneapolis, Minnesota (Jun 2019). https://aclanthology.org/N19-1423

17. Enders, A.M., Uscinski, J.E., Klofstad, C., Stoler, J.: The different forms of Covid-19 misinformation and their consequences. Harvard Kennedy School Misinformation Review (2020)

18. Eysenbach, G.: From intermediation to disintermediation and apomediation: new models for consumers to access and assess the credibility of health information in the age of web2. 0. Studies in health technology and informatics **129**(1), 162 (2007)

19. Fernández-Pichel, M., Losada, D.E., Pichel, J.C., Elsweiler, D.: CiTIUS at the TREC 2020 Health Misinformation Track. In: TREC (2020)

20. Fernández-Pichel, M., Meyer, S., Bink, M., Frummet, A., Losada, D.E., Elsweiler, D.: Improving the reliability of health information credibility assessments. In: Proceedings of ROMCIR 2023, European Conference on Information Retrieval (2023)

21. Gao, L., Dai, Z., Chen, T., Fan, Z., Van Durme, B., Callan, J.: Complement lexical retrieval model with semantic residual embeddings. In: Advances in Information Retrieval: 43rd European Conference on IR Research, ECIR 2021, Virtual Event, March 28 - April 1, 2021, Proceedings, Part I, pp. 146–160. Springer-Verlag, Berlin, Heidelberg (2021). https://doi.org/10.1007/978-3-030-72113-8_10

22. Goeuriot, L., et al.: CLEF eHealth Evaluation Lab 2021. In: Hiemstra, D., Moens, M.-F., Mothe, J., Perego, R., Potthast, M., Sebastiani, F. (eds.) ECIR 2021. LNCS, vol. 12657, pp. 593–600. Springer, Cham (2021). https://doi.org/10.1007/978-3-030-72240-1_69

23. Goeuriot, L., et al.: Overview of the clef ehealth evaluation lab 2020. In: Arampatzis, A., et al. (eds.) Exp. IR Meets Multilinguality, Multimodality, Interact., pp. 255–271. Springer International Publishing, Cham (2020)

24. Gundapu, S., Mamidi, R.: Transformer based automatic covid-19 fake news detection system. arXiv preprint arXiv:2101.00180 (2021)

25. Guo, J., Fan, Y., Ai, Q., Croft, W.B.: A deep relevance matching model for ad-hoc retrieval. In: Proceedings of the 25th ACM International on Conference on Information and Knowledge Management, pp. 55–64 (2016)

26. Hofstätter, S., Althammer, S., Schröder, M., Sertkan, M., Hanbury, A.: Improving efficient neural ranking models with cross-architecture knowledge distillation. arXiv preprint arXiv:2010.02666 (2020)

27. Hui, K., Yates, A., Berberich, K., de Melo, G.: PACRR: A position-aware neural IR model for relevance matching. In: Proceedings of the 2017 Conference on Empirical Methods in Natural Language Processing, pp. 1049–1058 (2017)

28. Kaliyar, R.K., Goswami, A., Narang, P.: Fakebert: fake news detection in social media with a BERT-based deep learning approach. Multimed. Tools Appl. **80**(8), 11765–11788 (2021)

29. Kamphuis, C., de Vries, A.P., Boytsov, L., Lin, J.: Which BM25 do you mean? a large-scale reproducibility study of scoring variants. In: Jose, J.M., et al. (eds.) ECIR 2020. LNCS, vol. 12036, pp. 28–34. Springer, Cham (2020). https://doi.org/10.1007/978-3-030-45442-5_4

30. Kaszkiel, M., Zobel, J.: Passage retrieval revisited. In: ACM SIGIR Forum. vol. 31, pp. 178–185. ACM New York, NY, USA (1997)

31. Klerings, I., Weinhandl, A.S., Thaler, K.J.: Information overload in healthcare: too much of a good thing? Z. Evid. Fortbild. Qual. Gesundhwes. **109**(4–5), 285–290 (2015)

32. Kumari, S., Reddy, H.K., Kulkarni, C.S., Gowthami, V.: Debunking health fake news with domain specific pre-trained model. Global Trans. Proc. **2**(2), 267–272 (2021)

33. Lee, J., et al.: Biobert: a pre-trained biomedical language representation model for biomedical text mining. Bioinformatics **36**(4), 1234–1240 (2020)

34. Li, C., Yates, A., MacAvaney, S., He, B., Sun, Y.: Parade: Passage representation aggregation for document reranking. arXiv preprint arXiv:2008.09093 (2020)

35. Li, M., Gaussier, E.: Keybld: Selecting key blocks with local pre-ranking for long document information retrieval. In: SIGIR '21: Proceedings of the 44th International ACM SIGIR Conference on Research and Development in Information Retrieval, pp. 2207–2211. Association for Computing Machinery, New York, NY, USA (2021)

36. Liu, N., Hu, Q., Xu, H., Xu, X., Chen, M.: Med-bert: a pretraining framework for medical records named entity recognition. IEEE Trans. Industr. Inf. **18**(8), 5600–5608 (2021)

37. Macdonald, C., Tonellotto, N., MacAvaney, S., Ounis, I.: Pyterrier: Declarative experimentation in python from bm25 to dense retrieval. In: Proceedings of the 30th ACM International Conference on Information Knowledge Management, pp. 4526–4533. CIKM '21, Association for Computing Machinery, New York, NY, USA (2021). https://doi.org/10.1145/3459637.3482013

38. Morahan-Martin, J., Anderson, C.D.: Information and misinformation online: recommendations for facilitating accurate mental health information retrieval and evaluation. CyberPsychol. Behav.r **3**(5), 731–746 (2000)

39. Nogueira, R., Cho, K.: Passage re-ranking with bert. arXiv preprint arXiv:1901.04085 (2019)

40. Pang, L., Lan, Y., Guo, J., Xu, J., Xu, J., Cheng, X.: Deeprank: A new deep architecture for relevance ranking in information retrieval. In: Proceedings of the 2017 ACM on Conference on Information and Knowledge Management, pp. 257–266 (2017)

41. Paszke, A., et al.: PyTorch: An Imperative Style, High-Performance Deep Learning Library, p. 12. Curran Associates Inc., Red Hook, NY, USA (2019)

42. Petrocchi, M., Viviani, M.: ROMCIR 2023: Overview of the 3rd Workshop on Reducing Online Misinformation Through Credible Information Retrieval. In: Proceedings of ROMCIR 2023, European Conference on Information Retrieval. pp. 405–411. Springer (2023). https://doi.org/10.1007/978-3-031-28241-6_45

43. Pradeep, R., et al.: H2oloo at TREC 2020: When all you got is a hammer... deep learning, health misinformation, and precision medicine. Corpus 5(d3), d2 (2020)

44. Reimers, N., Gurevych, I.: Sentence-BERT: Sentence embeddings using siamese bert-networks. In: Proceedings of the 2019 Conference on Empirical Methods in Natural Language Processing. Association for Computational Linguistics (2019). arXiv:arxiv.org/abs/1908.10084

45. Robertson, S., Zaragoza, H., et al.: The probabilistic relevance framework: Bm25 and beyond. Foundations and Trends® in Information Retrieval **3**(4), 333–389 (2009)

46. Robinson, M.J., Kohut, A.: Believability and the press. Public Opin. Q. **52**(2), 174–189 (1988)

47. Schlicht, I.B., de Paula, A.F.M., Rosso, P.: UPV at TREC Health Misinformation Track 2021 ranking with sBERT and quality estimators. arXiv preprint arXiv:2112.06080 (2021)
48. Schmitt, J.B., Debbelt, C.A., Schneider, F.M.: Too much information? predictors of information overload in the context of online news exposure. Inform., Commun. Society **21**(8), 1151–1167 (2018)
49. Swar, B., Hameed, T., Reychav, I.: Information overload, psychological ill-being, and behavioral intention to continue online healthcare information search. Comput. Hum. Behav. **70**, 416–425 (2017)
50. Upadhyay, R., Pasi, G., Viviani, M.: An unsupervised approach to genuine health information retrieval based on scientific evidence. In: Web Information Systems Engineering - WISE 2022: 23rd International Conference, Biarritz, France, November 1–3, 2022, Proceedings, pp. 119–135. Springer-Verlag, Berlin, Heidelberg (2022). https://doi.org/10.1007/978-3-031-20891-1_10
51. Wani, A., Joshi, I., Khandve, S., Wagh, V., Joshi, R.: Evaluating deep learning approaches for covid19 fake news detection. In: Combating Online Hostile Posts in Regional Languages during Emergency Situation: First International Workshop, CONSTRAINT 2021, Collocated with AAAI 2021, Virtual Event, February 8, 2021, Revised Selected Papers 1, pp. 153–163. Springer (2021)
52. Weisstein, E.W.: Bonferroni correction. https://mathworld.wolfram.com/ (2004)
53. Wolf, T., et al.: Huggingface's transformers: State-of-the-art natural language processing. arXiv preprint arXiv:1910.03771 (2019)
54. Wu, S., Bi, Y., Zeng, X., Han, L.: Assigning appropriate weights for the linear combination data fusion method in information retrieval. Inform. Process. Manage. **45**(4), 413–426 (2009)
55. Xiong, C., Dai, Z., Callan, J., Liu, Z., Power, R.: End-to-end neural ad-hoc ranking with kernel pooling. In: Proceedings of the 40th International ACM SIGIR Conference on Research and Development in Information Retrieval, pp. 55–64 (2017)
56. Zhang, B., Naderi, N., Jaume-Santero, F., Teodoro, D.: DS4DH at TREC Health Misinformation 2021: Multi-Dimensional Ranking Models with Transfer Learning and Rank Fusion. arXiv preprint arXiv:2202.06771 (2022)
57. Zuccon, G., Koopman, B.: Integrating understandability in the evaluation of consumer health search engines. In: MedIR@ SIGIR, pp. 32–35 (2014)

KESHEM: Knowledge Enabled Short Health Misinformation Detection Framework

Fei Liu[iD], Yibo Li[iD], and Meiyun Zuo[(✉)][iD]

Research Institute of Smart Senior Care, School of Information,
Renmin University of China, Beijing, China
{itliufei,yibo_li,zuomy}@ruc.edu.cn

Abstract. Health misinformation detection is a challenging but urgent problem in the field of information governance. In recent years, some studies have utilized long-form text detection models for this task, producing some promising early results. However, we found that most health information online is a short text, especially knowledge-based information. Meanwhile, the explainability of detection results is as important as the detection accuracy. There is no appropriate explainable short health misinformation detection model currently. To address these issues, we propose a novel **K**nowledge **E**nabled **S**hort **HE**alth **M**isinformation detection framework, called **KESHEM**. This method extracts abundant knowledge from multiple, multi-form, and dynamically updated knowledge graphs (KGs) as supplementary material and effectively represents semantic features of the information contents and the external knowledge by powerful language models. KG-attention is then applied to distinguish the effects of each external knowledge for the information credibility reasoning and enhance the model's explainability. We build a credible Chinese short text dataset for better evaluation and future research. Extensive experiments demonstrate that KESHEM significantly outperforms competing methods and accurately identifies important knowledge that explains the veracity of short health information.

Keywords: Short health misinformation · Knowledge graph · Explainable artificial intelligence · Attention mechanism

1 Introduction

With the popularity of various social media, the Internet has accumulated a wealth of information, data, and knowledge. Health information, referred to health-related statements, is an essential part of Internet information. According to [6], 81.5% of Americans retrieve health information online. However, due to the open nature of the Internet and ever-stronger text generators like GPT-4

This work is supported by the Fundamental Research Funds for the Central Universities and the Research Funds of Renmin University of China under grant No. 21XNL018.

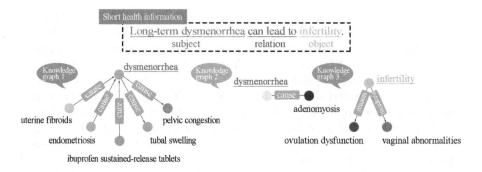

Fig. 1. An example of a piece of short health information and its related knowledge from knowledge graphs (KGs)

[19], there exists a lot of unrecognizable health misinformation on the Internet. Health misinformation can have serious implications for individuals and society, as it can harm health and increase the pressure on the medical system. For instance, a cancer patient mistakenly thought that a cancer treatment using ginger was reliable health information, which led to the death of the patient [3]. Thus, it is of great significance to effectively detect health misinformation online to deal with these problems.

Health misinformation has some unique characteristics that make its detection much more difficult than general information. *First*, health misinformation is usually a short statement presented in a relatively streamlined "subject-relation-object" form (see Fig. 1). Accordingly, health misinformation has fewer semantic features, thus text-CNN [11] and LSTM [7], which are typical text classification methods, are ineffective. *Second*, understanding health misinformation requires a high level of professional knowledge, which may result in fewer or incorrect comments and likes on social media. Thus, social context-based misinformation detection methods like CSI [24] and dEFEND [26] that use information propagation features, user group features, or comment contents are not always working out [2]. *Third*, most health misinformation is not hot news, that spreads without obvious periods of explosion or reduction, making it more difficult to discover and clarify [3]. However, there is no previous work to explore the detection of short health misinformation with these specific characteristics.

In this light, our research goal is to detect single-sentence health misinformation, without any other social and visual information, named the Short Health Misinformation Detection (SHMID) task. Considering external knowledge as a crucial factor for SHMID, we innovatively propose a novel **K**nowledge **E**nabled **S**hort **HE**alth **M**isinformation detection framework, called **KESHEM**. We facilitate the model with external knowledge for better detection performance.

Knowledge graphs (KGs) are adopted as the sources of external knowledge for our proposed KESHEM, which have stored a large amount of real-world knowledge. Accordingly, the model *first* extracts all the relevant external knowledge from multiple, multi-form, and dynamically updated KGs by the knowledge extraction layer. As seen in Fig. 1, given a piece of short health misinformation "long-term dysmenorrhea can lead to infertility", KESHEM obtains the knowledge about the real cause of infertility from KG3 and various dysmenorrhea-related diseases from KG1 and KG2. *Then*, the approach leverages the power of pre-trained language models to capture deep semantic features of information contents and external knowledge [4,18,22]. *Finally*, a KG-attention and a prediction layer are exploited to infer the credibility of the healthinformation with the external knowledge. Meanwhile, according to attention weights obtained by the KG-attention layer, KESHEM can present persuasive post-hoc explanations consisting of important knowledge pieces to enhance the model explainability, which significantly promotes public confidence in model results and helps experts to fact-check health misinformation manually [28]. Additionally, we use the focal loss to address dataset sample imbalances during training and decouple the knowledge extraction layer with the latter knowledge representation and classification layers for better adaptation to the dynamic update of the KGs. The main contributions of the paper include:

- We study a novel problem of short health misinformation detection (SHMID), and build a credible Chinese short health misinformation detection dataset, Jiaozhen, for better evaluation and future research;
- We propose a novel method KESHEM (**K**nowledge **E**nabled **S**hort **HE**alth **M**isinformation detection framework) that incorporates external knowledge from multiple KGs into information contents to boost SHMID accuracy performance, as well as capture explainable knowledge pieces as post-hoc explanations to enhance users' confidence in model results;
- KESHEM significantly outperforms several baselines based on extensive experiments. We further design a novel computable evaluation method named Cumulative Loss (CL) to prove the explainability of KESHEM quantitatively.

2   Related Work

2.1   Health Misinformation Detection

HMID is one of the most urgent and challenging parts of misinformation detection (MID), aiming to screen health, disease, care, and other related information. Most previous work just applies existing MID frameworks based on contents for HMID, without capturing unique characteristics of HMID tasks [14,18]. There have also been studies of integrating user interaction characteristics for HMID, but what they detected was misinformation about public health emergencies(e.g., Zika Fever, Ebola, and COVID-19) [12,15,25]. This type of health information is more similar to fake news, instead of knowledge-based information. Besides, some studies incorporate web structures, contexts, and other external information for better HMID performance [29,30]. However, health misinformation, as aforementioned, usually just contains short plain texts in many scenarios. How to screen health misinformation with textual features only remains obscure.

DETERRENT [2] firstly explores combining a medical KG for long-text HMID, creating a new research perspective for HMID. Moreover, due to the difficulties in obtaining credible HMID datasets, there is no benchmark HMID dataset in Chinese yet, which seriously hinders the development of research on HMID [34].

Hence, this study aims to design a practical detection framework focused on the characteristics of health misinformation, and construct a credible short-text dataset in Chinese for future research on SHMID.

2.2 Misinformation Detection with Knowledge Graphs

MID methods with knowledge graphs can be divided into three categories: **(1) knowledge graph-based methods** [5,9,20], which use scoring functions to calculate the correlation between subject embeddings, relation embeddings, and object embeddings; **(2) multimodal methods**, which applies multi-form features for MID. KMAGCN [21] integrates image information, external knowledge, and information contents together to represent the information, of which the accuracy in public dataset exceeds 0.8; **(3) Knowledge graph enabled models**, which integrates contents and KG information for MID.

DETERRENT [2] is the only one to apply the KG enabled architecture to MID tasks yet. The model verified on two disease datasets outperforms several baselines by a large margin, proving the effectiveness of the combination of information contents and external knowledge for SHMID. But it also has some limitations: *first*, the KG applied by it contains two kinds of relations, including "positive relations" (e.g.,<A, cure, B>) and "negative relations" (e.g., <A, can't cure B>). These normative knowledge structures, especially the "negative relations" are extremely beneficial for HMID. However, most of the KGs contain few "negative relations". *Second*, it uses GCN to learn entity representations, which cannot adapt to the dynamic updates of the KG, and it just integrates one single external KG. *Third*, positive and negative samples on their evaluation datasets are collected from different platforms. A classifier trained on such datasets is likely to be a platform classifier instead of a misinformation detector [3].

Compared with it, our model can simultaneously support multiple, multi-form, and dynamically updated public KGs to improve detection performance. Meanwhile, we collect true and false health information from the same platform, ensuring the consistency of information formats of positive and negative samples.

3 Preliminaries

3.1 Definitions and Notations

Definition 1. *Short health information. Let S be a piece of short health information, consisting of n words $\{w_i\}_{i=1}^n$. Each word in Chinese $w_{ci} = \{t_1, t_2, ..., t_m\}$ further contains m Chinese characters. In the following description, we will keep using token to denote a Chinese character or an English word.*

Definition 2. *External knowledge. Let $G = \{e, r\}$ be a KG, consisting of triples presented as $\{(e_i, r_l, e_j) \mid e_i, e_j \in e, r_l \in r\}$, where e_i and e_j are head entity and tail entity, respectively, and r_l is the relation between them. External knowledge of each short health information S, is a set of k knowledge triples extracted from multiple KGs G_s, denoted as $E = \{E_1, E_2, ..., E_k\}$.*

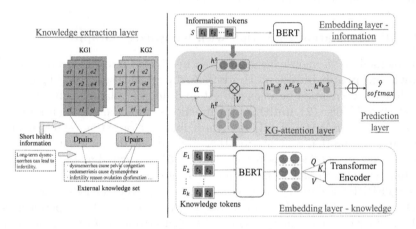

Fig. 2. The proposed framework KESHEM consists of four components: (1) a knowledge extraction layer, (2) an embedding layer, (3) a KG-attention layer, and (4) a prediction layer.

3.2   Problem Formulation

With the above definitions and notations, we formulate the knowledge enabled SHMID task as follows:

Knowledge Enabled SHMID: Given a piece of short health information S and multiple KGs G_s, extract external knowledge E of S from G_s, and learn a classification function $f : f(S, E) \rightarrow (\alpha, \hat{y})$, where α is a weight matrix indicating each knowledge's explainability for the information's credibility classification $\hat{y}$.

---

4   The Proposed Framework: KESHEM

As shown in Fig. 2, our proposed framework consists of 4 parts: **1) a knowledge extraction layer**, which extracts relevant triples of an input short health information from multiple KGs to form an external knowledge set; **2) an embedding layer**, representing deep semantic features of the short health information and the external knowledge set; **3) a KG-attention layer**, which distinguishes reference degrees of different triples in external knowledge set for the classification and obtains a renewed information-guided representation; and **4) a prediction layer**, which integrates the short health information representation and the renewed information-guided external knowledge set for the final classification.

4.1   Knowledge Extraction Layer

To extract external knowledge from multiple, multi-form, and dynamically updated KGs, we compile the general and decoupled knowledge extraction layer with the query construction (Q-Con) and knowledge construction (K-Con) processes. Specifically, given a dataset consisting of m pieces of short health information $S_{all} = \{\{w_{oi}\}_{i=1}^{n}\}_{o=1}^{m}$ and g KGs $G_s = \{\{(e_{pi}, r_{pl}, e_{pj})\}\}_{p=1}^{g}$, we first construct a downward query and an upward query based on all the words W in S_{all} in the Q-Con period. The downward query uses W to match all the head entities E_{head} in G_s to build a dictionary containing various key-value pairs $D_{pairs} = \{(w_i : \{(r_i, e_i)\}) \mid w_i \in W \cap E_{head}\}$, where the keys are the common entities between W and E_{head}, and the values are the corresponding relations and tail entities. Similarly, the upward query uses W to match all the tail entities E_{tail} in G_s to construct a dictionary as $U_{pairs} = \{(w_i : \{(r_i, e_i)\}) \mid w_i \in W \cap E_{tail}\}$. Q-Con can be formulated as (1),

$$D_{pairs}, U_{pairs} = Q\_Con(S_{all}, G_s). \tag{1}$$

Then, in K-Con, for each information S in S_{all}, we retrieve up to k pieces of related triples in G_s based on D_{pairs} and U_{pairs} to form an external knowledge set for S, denoted as $E = \{E_1, E_2, ..., E_k\}$. K-Con can be formulated as (2),

$$E = K\_Con(S, D_{pairs}, U_{pairs}). \tag{2}$$

In real applications, when the KGs have changed, KESHEM only needs to update D_{pairs} and U_{pairs} of the knowledge extraction layer, while the later model layers do not need to be retrained.

4.2   Embedding Layer

For the input short health information $S = \{t_1, t_2, ..., t_n\}$, we initial the token sequence as $X = \{x_{[CLS]}, x_1, x_2, ..., x_n, x_{[SEP]}\}$, where $X \in \mathbb{R}^{(n+2)*d}$, n represents the sequence length, and d represents the dimensionality of token vectors. [CLS] and [SEP] are special tokens, which respectively refer to a classification token and a sentence segmentation token. we denote the final hidden vector of the special [CLS] token after fine-tuning as the information representation $h^S \in \mathbb{R}^d$.

As for the external knowledge set $E = \{E_1, E_2, ..., E_k\}$, we first embed each external knowledge piece E_i following the above health information embedding approach, and obtain the basic external knowledge set representation as $h^{E'} \in \mathbb{R}^{k*d}$. To further enhance the holistic nature of the representation of E, we implement another Transformer encoder [31] to capture the correlation between knowledge pieces. Accordingly, the final representation of the external knowledge set is denoted as $h^E \in \mathbb{R}^{k*d}$. Given the fact that the Transformer encoder has been widely used in previous studies, we omit the exhaustive background descriptions of the model architectures and emphasize the KG-attention layer in the following section.

4.3   KG-Attention Layer

We have filtered various related external knowledge from multiple KGs through the former modules. However, the effects of different triples on the health misinformation detection task could have subtle differences. Thus, we introduce a novel KG-attention layer to capture external knowledge by assigning attention weights to all knowledge pieces, boosting the model's accuracy and explainability performance. The formula to calculate general attention is as follows:

$$Att(Q, K, V) = softmax(\frac{QK^T}{\sqrt{d_k}})V, \tag{3}$$

where queries, keys, and values are packed together into matrices Q, K, and V, d_k is the dimension of queries and keys.

Herein, queries come from the short health information representation h^S as seen in Fig. 2. Meanwhile, keys and values come from the external knowledge set representation h^E. By calculating the attention between health information and its corresponding external knowledge set, each piece of external knowledge in the knowledge set is assigned a weight α_i to represent its importance:

$$Q = W_Q h^S, K = W_K h^E, V = W_V h^E, \tag{4}$$

$$\alpha = softmax(\frac{QK^T}{\sqrt{d}}), \tag{5}$$

$$h^{E\_S} = \alpha \cdot V, \tag{6}$$

where W_Q, W_K, and W_V are parameter matrices, $\alpha \in \mathbb{R}^k$ refers to attention distribution between short health information and its external knowledge set, and $h^{E\_S} \in \mathbb{R}^d$ denotes the renewed information-guided knowledge representation.

4.4   Prediction Layer

The final representation of knowledge enabled short health information, i.e., H, can be obtained by concatenating h^S and h^{E_S}. Afterward, H is fed into a fully connected module followed by a *softmax* function to predict the credibility of the short health information with the following objective:

$$\hat{y} = softmax(W_f \cdot H + b_f), \tag{7}$$

$$H = Concat(h^S, h^E\text{-}^S), \tag{8}$$

where $\hat{y}$ is the predicted value which indicates the probability of the information being false. $y \in \{0, 1\}$ denotes the ground truth label. $b_f \in \mathbb{R}^{1*2}$ is bias term.

Additionally, we adopt the focal loss function [16] to alleviate the possible sample imbalance of SHMID datasets in this work. An unbalanced dataset can cause overfitting due to over-dependence on the smaller samples and lead to unsatisfactory model results. For a given piece of information, the goal is to minimize the focal loss as follows:

$$Loss(y, \hat{y}) = -[y^\gamma \cdot log(\hat{y}) + (1 - y)^\gamma \cdot log(1 - \hat{y})]. \tag{9}$$

Here, $(1 - \hat{y})$ is a modulation factor. When a sample is misclassified, if $\hat{y}$ is very small, the modulation factor is close to 1, which does not affect the original loss. In contrast, if $\hat{y}$ approaches 1, the modulation factor is close to 0, which reduces the weight of the loss of easy-to-classify samples. γ controls the rate of weight reduction.

5   Experiment

In this section, we present the experiments to evaluate the effectiveness of KESHEM. Specifically, we aim to answer the following evaluation questions:

Q1: Can KESHEM improve SHMID performance by coupling short health information contents and multiple external knowledge?

Q2: How effective are introducing multiple external knowledge and different model components in improving the SHMID performance of KESHEM?

Q3: Can KESHEM capture important external knowledge to provide reasonable explanations about SHMID results?

5.1   Datasets

To better evaluate the performance of KESHEM, we use two datasets, respectively, in Chinese and English.

Jiaozhen. Jiaozhen ("fact-checking" in Chinese) is one of the most influential Chinese rumor-refuting platforms, founded in 2015 by Tencent News. We crawled 5,352 pieces of misinformation and 1,369 pieces of verified true health information from the food safety and the medical health columns of its WeChat applet. Since there is no HMID benchmark dataset in Chinese so far, the constructed dataset and all our implement codes are publicly available for research purposes[1].

Diabetes [2]. It gathered 1,661 pieces of true diabetes-related information from seven reliable media outlets (e.g., Healthline and National Institutes of Health), and 608 pieces of false diabetes-related information from Snopes.com. We use all the titles which are short texts as our detection targets.

---

[1] https://github.com/fenella0401/KESHEM.

As the KGs, we employ three Chinese KGs, Cn-DBpedia [33], MedicalKG [17], and Web health concept KG², as well as three English KGs, ConceptNet [27], HealthKG [23], and SemMedDB [10]. CN-DBpedia and ConceptNet are two large-scale open-domain KGs, containing enormous entities and relations. To reduce the calculation amount, we refine the official CN-DBpedia by eliminating triples whose entity names are less than 2 in length or contain special characters, termed as CN-DBpedia\s. Since that ConceptNet is dynamically updated, we directly use its official API to obtain the required external knowledge. The other KGs are health domain KGs which contain more professional health-related knowledge. The detailed statistics of all the applied KGs are shown in Table 1.

5.2   Baselines

We compare KESHEM with representative and state-of-the-art text classification and MID algorithms, which are listed as follows:

Table 1. The statistics of KGs. ConceptNet is dynamically updated.

KG	# Entities	# Relations	# Triples
Cn-DBpedia\s	5,709,027	62,278	5,168,865
MedicalKG	13,558	1	13,864
Web health concept KG	7,387	3	13,046
ConceptNet	>8,000,000	36	>21,000,000
HealthKG	360	1	3,709
SemMedDB	214,572	1	214,590

(1) text-CNN: text-CNN [11] is a text classification model utilizing convolutional neural networks to model sentences.

(2) BERT: BERT [4] is developed by Google for pre-training language representation, which obtains state-of-the-art results on 11 NLP tasks when promoted.

(3) CSI\c: CSI [24] is a hybrid fake news detection model whose content representation is modeled via an LSTM model with the article embedding via Doc2Vec [13]. Due to the lack of user response, the corresponding part of the model is ignored, and termed as CSI\c.

(4) dEFEND\c: dEFEND [26] proposes a deep hierarchical co-attention network to learn information contents and user comments features for fake news detection. Due to the lack of user response, the corresponding part of the model is ignored, and termed as dEFEND\c.

---

² https://github.com/dagege/huadingkg.

(5) TransE: TransE [1] is a classic KG embedding method, embedding entities and relations into latent vectors. We first learn representations of Cn-DBpedia\s and diabetes-related KG. Then, we calculate the mean values of entity embeddings and relation embeddings in each information as the final health information embeddings for SHMID. Diabetes-related KG refers to a partial KG composed of diabetes-related triples extracted from ConceptNet.

(6) DETERRENT: DETERRENT [2] is an HMID model, that utilizes knowledge-guided information embeddings for detection. We employ DETERRENT with MedicalKG for Chinese SHMID and diabetes-related KG for English SHMID.

(7) K-BERT: K-BERT [17] is an improved knowledge enabled language representation model with KGs, in which triples are injected into the sentences as domain knowledge. We train K-BERT with the same KGs as our model.

(8) KPL: KPL [8] is a state-of-the-art fake news detection framework that leverages a pre-trained language model by prompt learning with external knowledge.

We choose the above contrasting methods that use features from the four aspects: (1) only information **contents**, such as text-CNN, BERT, CSI\c, and dEFEND\c; (2) only **KG**, such as TransE; (3) **contents with a single KG**, such as DETERRENT and (4) **contents** with **multiple KGs**, such as K-BERT and KPL.

To evaluate the performance of KESHEM and these baseline models, we use the following metrics, which are commonly used to evaluate classifiers in related areas: Accuracy, Precision, Recall, and F1 score.

5.3 Accuracy Performance (Q1)

To evaluate the effectiveness of coupling short health information contents and multiple external knowledge in improving SHMID performance (Q1), we compare KESHEM with the representative text classification and MID algorithms introduced in Sect. 5.2 when dealing with information in different languages. All competing methods' detection performance is summarized in Table 2. From the table, we make the following observations:

(1) Content-based methods: previous studies have proved that information content is the most important feature in MID tasks [2,26]. Similarly, it can be seen clearly that the F1 scores of the content-based methods are almost 10% higher than that of the knowledge graph-based method. For the Chinese dataset, text-CNN> BERT> dEFEND\c> CSI\c in F1 score. For the English dataset, BERT, CSI\c> text-CNN> dEFEND\c.

(2) Knowledge graph-based method: the performance of TransE is less satisfactory. Although the knowledge graph-based methods can better learn the feature representations of entities and relations of external knowledge, they do not obtain critical semantic features of information contents.

Table 2. Performance Comparison on Jiaozhen and Diabetes datasets. KESHEM outperforms all state-of-the-art baselines including all four types of methods.

Models	Jiaozhen				Diabetes			
	Accuracy	Precision	Recall	F1	Accuracy	Precision	Recall	F1
Content-based Methods								
text-CNN	0.8346	0.7563	0.6761	0.7013	0.8962	0.8709	0.8609	0.8657
BERT	0.8073	0.7016	0.6936	0.6974	0.8962	0.8647	0.8741	0.8692
CSI\c	0.7924	0.6304	0.5303	0.5143	0.8962	0.8647	0.8741	0.8692
dEFEND\c	0.8168	0.7384	0.5965	0.6136	0.8698	0.8341	0.8324	0.8332
Knowledge graph-based Method								
TransE	0.7917	0.6172	0.5212	0.4969	0.8411	0.8936	0.7077	0.7439
Single Knowledge graph enabled Methods								
DETERRENT	0.7989	0.6896	0.5225	0.4939	0.7395	0.7163	0.7495	0.7237
KESHEM\1	0.8566	0.8513	0.8566	0.8533	0.9029	0.9011	0.9029	0.9012
Multiple knowledge graphs enabled Methods								
K-BERT	0.8543	0.7759	0.7729	0.7744	0.7417	0.6643	0.6505	0.6561
KPL	0.8545	0.8511	0.8545	0.8524	0.9146	0.9160	0.9146	0.9143
KESHEM	**0.8673**	**0.8648**	**0.8673**	**0.8659**	**0.9338**	**0.9332**	**0.9338**	**0.9334**

(3) Single knowledge graph enabled method: the performance of DETERRENT on our datasets is not satisfactory. It mistakes "positive relations" as "negative relations" in the KG, which decreases the model detection effect. Actually, all the triples contained in the applied KGs are "positive relations". For a fair comparison, we also apply a single KG on KESHEM for an additional experiment, termed KESHEM\1. The result of KESHEM\1 surpasses DETERRENT and all the other baselines.

(4) Multiple knowledge graphs enabled methods: our model outperforms K-BERT and KPL when using the same three KGs for evaluation. Although K-BERT performs well on the Jiaozhen dataset, its classification performance is abysmal on the Diabetes dataset, indicating our model is more robust. As for KPL, its performance is better than all the other baseline models, proving the effectiveness and great potential of enriching prompt template representations with entity knowledge when applying prompt learning. However, more trials are needed to further optimize the design of prompt templates, which is relatively time-consuming.

(5) Generally, we see KESHEM with multiple KGs consistently outperforms all competing methods in all metrics. Specifically, it achieves a relative improvement of 1.50%, 1.58% on the Jiaozhen dataset and 2.10%, 2.09% on the Diabetes dataset, comparing against the best results of baselines in Accuracy and F1 score.

5.4   Ablation Analysis (Q2)

To investigate the influence of the KG number and each component of KESHEM for SHMID performance (Q2), we make extensive ablation analyses as follows.

Table 3. Effects of applying different numbers of KGs.

# of KGs	Jiaozhen				Diabetes			
	Accuracy	Precision	Recall	F1	Accuracy	Precision	Recall	F1
1	0.8566	0.8513	0.8566	0.8533	0.9029	0.9011	0.9029	0.9012
2	0.8578	0.8548	0.8578	0.8561	0.9316	0.9309	0.9316	0.9311
3	**0.8673**	**0.8648**	**0.8673**	**0.8659**	**0.9338**	**0.9332**	**0.9338**	**0.9334**

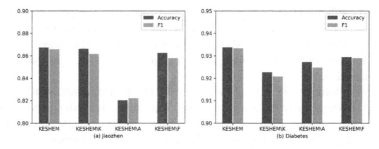

Fig. 3. Impact analysis of external knowledge, KG-attention, and focal loss function for SHMID.

Effects of Multiple KGs. We vary the number of KGs for KESHEM to investigate the efficiency of using multiple KGs. In particular, we search the number of KGs in the set of $\{1, 2, 3\}$. We select different KGs to conduct experiments and take the best results for the comparative analysis. The results are summarized in Table 3, from which we make the following observations:

- By analyzing Table 2 and 3, we can see that KESHEM with different numbers of KGs consistently outperforms all the content-based methods, which indicates the effectiveness of introducing external knowledge in SHMID.
- Increasing the number of KGs significantly improves the performance of KEHESM, demonstrating the effectiveness of modeling multiple KGs.
- Using a medical KG outperforms slightly than a general KG when only one KG is obtained. Besides, using a medical KG and a general KG outperforms using two medical KGs, proving that combining professional knowledge and general knowledge is necessary for SHMID.

Effects of Components of KESHEM. We investigate the effects of the main components in KESHEM by defining three variants:

(1) KESHEM\K: a variant of KESHEM without integrating external knowledge. It just embeds information contents with the information encoder and then feeds them into a softmax layer for classification.
(2) KESHEM\A: a variant of KESHEM that eliminates the KG-attention layer. Instead, it directly concatenates the short health information and external knowledge set representations for classification.
(3) KESHEM\F: a variant of KESHEM, where a cross-entropy loss function replaces the focal loss function for training.

The performances of all the variants are reported in Fig. 3, from which we make the following observations:

– When we eliminate the effect of external knowledge, the performance reduces. It further suggests the importance of introducing external knowledge from KGs to enable SHMID, especially when the volume of the training dataset is small (e.g., the Diabetes dataset). Besides, the quality and completeness of the KGs have a direct impact on the model's performance. Therefore, the impact of introducing external knowledge from different KGs for the two datasets varies significantly.
– When we eliminate the KG-attention layer, the performance is substantially reduced. It suggests that capturing important knowledge can sincerely benefit the performance of KESHEM. As the average number of external knowledge introduced per information in the Jiaozhen dataset is higher compared to the Diabetes dataset, the KG-attention layer is better equipped to perform knowledge distillation on the Jiaozhen dataset.
– Modifying the loss calculation method during the training of KESHEM can truly better adapt to the imbalanced SHMID task and improve the detection performance.

5.5 Explainability Evaluation (Q3)

Herein, we conduct a quantitative analysis and a case study to evaluate whether our model can capture important external knowledge to provide reasonable explanations about SHMID results and boost the model's explainability (Q3).

Firstly, to make a quantitative analysis, we propose a novel Cumulative Loss (CL) metric for evaluation, inspired by Normalized Cumulative Gain (NDCG) [32]. Given the short health information S and its external knowledge set $E = \{E_1, E_2, ..., E_k\}$. The importance sequence of E for identifying S obtained by KESHEM is $c = \{c_1, c_2, ..., c_k\}$, and the ideal importance sequence of E for identifying S labeled by an expert group is $z = \{z_1, z_2, ..., z_k\}$. Thus, the ability of the model to identify important knowledge can be calculated as follows:

$$CL = \sqrt{\frac{1}{k} \sum_{i=1}^{k} \left(\frac{c_i - z_i}{log_2(z_i + 1)}\right)^2}. \tag{10}$$

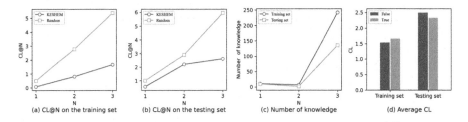

Fig. 4. Explainability analysis of KESHEM.

The smaller the CL, the better the explainability of the model.

We selected 408 pieces of information-external knowledge set pairs with knowledge number of $\{3, 5, 10\}$ in the training set and testing set of the Jiaozhen dataset for evaluation. To get the ideal ranking, we first invited two postgraduates of clinical medicine to label the pairs, and then asked two postgraduates of food safety to conduct a second review of the labeling results. Finally, the disagreement was decided through the four experts' discussion. All annotators were compensated 200 RMB/hour for however long it took them to complete the task. We have provided the ratings by the annotators along with our public codes. The evaluation results are shown in Fig. 4, where N denotes the number of KGs for experiments. From the figure, we can make the following observations:

- In general, we can see KESHEM> Random for the performance of capturing important knowledge for SHMID. It indicates that the KG-attention component in KESHEM can help to select important knowledge enabling SHMID.
- With the increase in the size of the external knowledge set, capturing important knowledge becomes more difficult for the model. This is consistent with the selection process of important knowledge by experts. The more knowledge the experts face, the greater the possibility of incorrect ranking.
- For the model, the difficulty of selecting important knowledge in the external knowledge set of misinformation is similar to that of true information.

Furthermore, we use an example with knowledge attention rankings in Fig. 5 to explain the explainability of KESHEM more vividly. The numbers on the brackets denote the knowledge rankings judged by models and experts. Given the information, the model digs out important knowledge triples for information credibility identification (the triples whose relation names are in red in Fig. 5), which is similar to the judgment of experts. Based on the important knowledge, we can reason that dysmenorrhea is usually a symptom of disease instead of the cause, and the cause of infertility should be ovulation dysfunction. Thus, we can judge the information as false. It should be noted that although our attention architecture can indeed identify important knowledge among all the external knowledge, its ability to distinguish the level of importance of the important knowledge needs to be further improved.

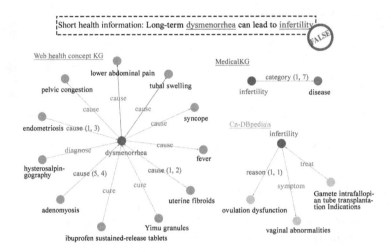

Fig. 5. The explainable knowledge captured by KESHEM.

6   Conclusion and Future Work

In this paper, we indicate a novel problem of short health misinformation detection (SHMID) and propose a knowledge enabled SHMID framework, named KESHEM. KESHEM extracts abundant external knowledge from multiple, multi-form, and dynamically updated KGs to enable the SHMID task. Moreover, we design a KG-attention layer to distinguish the importance of different external knowledge to boost the accuracy and explainability performance of KESHEM. Extensive experiments demonstrate that our method provides superior accuracy performance over state-of-the-art models. Meanwhile, the quantitative analysis and the case study have proved that the model achieves a certain degree of considerable explainability. For better evaluation and the promotion of SHMID research, we build a credible Chinese SHMID dataset. Future work could explore more high-quality KGs for SHMID, expand our collection of short health misinformation datasets in Chinese with richer structures, and further compare the explainability performance of our model with other baselines.

Ethical Considerations. The work is based solely on public data, with no privacy implications. Our data came from Chinese rumor-refuting platforms, where data is publicly available. Thus, we have no ethical violation in the collection data and experiment in our study. In addition, the detection results of health misinformation can only serve as a preliminary assessment and support, and for serious scenarios, experienced experts are required to make further assessments.

References

1. Bordes, A., Usunier, N., Garcia-Duran, A., Weston, J., Yakhnenko, O.: Translating embeddings for modeling multi-relational data. In: Neural Information Processing Systems (NIPS), pp. 1–9 (2013)
2. Cui, L., Seo, H., Tabar, M., Ma, F., Wang, S., Lee, D.: Deterrent: Knowledge guided graph attention network for detecting healthcare misinformation. In: Proceedings of the 26th ACM SIGKDD International Conference on Knowledge Discovery & Data Mining, pp. 492–502 (2020)
3. Dai, E., Sun, Y., Wang, S.: Ginger cannot cure cancer: battling fake health news with a comprehensive data repository. In: International Conference on Web and Social Media (2020)
4. Devlin, J., Chang, M.W., Lee, K., Toutanova, K.: BERT: Pre-training of deep bidirectional transformers for language understanding. In: Proceedings of the 2019 Conference of the North American Chapter of the Association for Computational Linguistics: Human Language Technologies, Volume 1 (Long and Short Papers), pp. 4171–4186 (Jun 2019)
5. Dun, Y., Tu, K., Chen, C., Hou, C., Yuan, X.: Kan: Knowledge-aware attention network for fake news detection. In: AAAI Conference on Artificial Intelligence (2021)
6. Finney Rutten, L.J., Blake, K.D., Greenberg-Worisek, A.J., Allen, S.V., Moser, R.P., Hesse, B.W.: Online Health Information Seeking Among US Adults: Measuring Progress Toward a Healthy People 2020 Objective. Public Health Reports **6**, 617–625 (2019)
7. Hochreiter, S., Schmidhuber, J.: Long Short-Term Memory. Neural Computation **9**(8), 1735–1780 (1997)
8. Jiang, G., Liu, S., Zhao, Y., Sun, Y., Zhang, M.: Fake news detection via knowledgeable prompt learning. Inf. Process. Manage. **59**, 103029 (2022)
9. Karagiannis, G., Trummer, I., Jo, S., Khandelwal, S., Wang, X., Yu, C.: Mining an "Anti-Knowledge Base" from Wikipedia Updates with Applications to Fact Checking and Beyond (2019)
10. Kilicoglu, H., Shin, D., Fiszman, M., Rosemblat, G., Rindflesch, T.C.: SemMedDB: A PubMed-scale repository of biomedical semantic predications. Bioinformatics **28**(23), 3158–3160 (2012)
11. Kim, Y.: Convolutional neural networks for sentence classification. In: Proceedings of the 2014 Conference on Empirical Methods in Natural Language Processing, pp. 1746–1751. Association for Computational Linguistics (2014)
12. Kolluri, N., Liu, Y., Murthy, D.: Covid-19 misinformation detection: Machine learned solutions to the infodemic (preprint). JMIR Infodemiology (2022)
13. Le, Q., Mikolov, T.: Distributed representations of sentences and documents. In: Proceedings of the 31st International Conference on International Conference on Machine Learning - Volume 32, p. II-1188-II-1196. ICML'14, JMLR.org (2014)
14. Li, J.: Detecting false information in medical and healthcare domains: a text mining approach. In: Chen, H., Zeng, D., Yan, X., Xing, C. (eds.) ICSH 2019. LNCS, vol. 11924, pp. 236–246. Springer, Cham (2019). https://doi.org/10.1007/978-3-030-34482-5_21
15. Li, Y., Marga, J.J., Cheung, C.M.K., Shen, X.L., Lee, M.K.O.: Health misinformation on social media: a systematic literature review and future research directions. AIS Trans. Human-Computer Interact. **14**(2), 116–149 (2022)

16. Lin, T.Y., Goyal, P., Girshick, R., He, K., Dollár, P.: Focal loss for dense object detection. In: Proceedings of the IEEE International Conference on Computer Vision, pp. 2980–2988 (2017)
17. Liu, W., et al.: K-BERT: Enabling language representation with knowledge graph. In: AAAI Conference on Artificial Intelligence (2019)
18. Liu, Y., Yu, K., Wu, X., Qing, L., Peng, Y.: Analysis and detection of health-related misinformation on Chinese social media. IEEE Access 7 (2019)
19. OpenAI: Gpt-4 technical report. arXiv:abs/2303.08774 (2023)
20. Pan, J.Z., Pavlova, S., Li, C., Li, N., Li, Y., Liu, J.: Content based fake news detection using knowledge graphs. Lecture Notes in Computer Science 11136 LNCS, pp. 669–683 (2018)
21. Qian, S., Hu, J., Fang, Q., Xu, C.: Knowledge-aware multi-modal adaptive graph convolutional networks for fake news detection. ACM Trans. Multimed. Comput., Commun. Appl. (TOMM) 17, 1–23 (2021)
22. Raffel, C., et al.: Exploring the limits of transfer learning with a unified text-to-text transformer. J. Mach. Learn. Res. 21(1), 5485–5551 (2019)
23. Rotmensch, M., Halpern, Y., Tlimat, A., Horng, S., Sontag, D.: Learning a health knowledge graph from electronic medical records. Sci. Reports 7(1) (2017)
24. Ruchansky, N., Seo, S., Liu, Y.: CSI: A Hybrid Deep Model for Fake News Detection. In: Proceedings of the 2017 ACM on Conference on Information and Knowledge Management. ACM (2017)
25. Saeed, F., Wael, Al-Sarem, M., Abdullah, E.: Detecting health-related rumors on twitter using machine learning methods. Int. J. Adv. Comput. Sci. Appl. 11(8) (2020)
26. Shu, K., Cui, L., Wang, S., Lee, D., Liu, H.: Defend: Explainable fake news detection. In:Proceedings of the ACM SIGKDD International Conference on Knowledge Discovery and Data Mining, pp. 395–405 (2019)
27. Speer, R., Chin, J., Havasi, C.: Conceptnet 5.5: An open multilingual graph of general knowledge. In: AAAI, pp. 4444–4451. AAAI Press (2017)
28. Sun, P., Wu, L., Zhang, K., Su, Y., Wang, M.: An unsupervised aspect-aware recommendation model with explanation text generation. ACM Trans. Inf. Syst. 40(3) (2021)
29. Upadhyay, R., Pasi, G., Viviani, M.: Health misinformation detection in web content: a structural-, content-based, and context-aware approach based on web2vec. In: Proceedings of the Conference on Information Technology for Social Good (2021)
30. Upadhyay, R., Pasi, G., Viviani, M.: Vec4cred: a model for health misinformation detection in web pages. Multimed. Tools Appl. 82, 1–20 (2022)
31. Vaswani, A., et al.: Attention is all you need. In: Advances in Neural Information Processing Systems. vol. 30. Curran Associates, Inc. (2017)
32. Wang, Y., Wang, L., Li, Y., He, D., Liu, T.Y., Chen, W.: A theoretical analysis of NDCG type ranking measures. J. Mach. Learn. Res. 30, 25–54 (2013)
33. Xu, B., et al.: CN-DBpedia: a never-ending Chinese knowledge extraction system. In: Benferhat, S., Tabia, K., Ali, M. (eds.) IEA/AIE 2017. LNCS (LNAI), vol. 10351, pp. 428–438. Springer, Cham (2017). https://doi.org/10.1007/978-3-319-60045-1_44
34. Zhang, Y., et al.: HKGB: An inclusive, extensible, intelligent, semi-auto-constructed knowledge graph framework for healthcare with clinicians' expertise incorporated. Inform. Process. Manage. 57(6), 102324 (2020)

Dynamic Thresholding for Accurate Crack Segmentation Using Multi-objective Optimization

Qin Lei[1], Jiang Zhong[1]([✉]), Chen Wang[1], Yang Xia[2], and Yangmei Zhou[3]

[1] School of Computer Science, Chongqing University, Chongqing 400044, China
{qinlei,zhongjiang,chenwang}@cqu.edu.cn
[2] Chongqing Academy of Big Data Co., Ltd., Chongqing 400000, China
yang.xia@cqdata.info
[3] Chongqing Academy of Science and Technology, Chongqing 401123, China

Abstract. To prevent damage caused by cracks, accurate segmentation of cracks is necessary. Deep learning models are commonly employed to achieve this goal, typically consisting of data-driven neural networks that are trained to determine classification probability for each pixel. However, these models often ignore the optimization of the binarization function, which maps the probability distribution of each pixel to a specific class. Typically, a fixed threshold of 0.5 is used, disregarding the sensitivity of crack data to the threshold. As a result, segmentation accuracy is compromised. To address this issue, we propose a multi-objective optimization method that incorporates both the conventional segmentation model's objective function and a dynamic threshold-based binarization objective function. By doing so, we aim to improve the accuracy of the segmentation results. Specifically, we introduce a dynamic thresholding branch (DTB) to our approach, which performs a regression task to determine the optimal threshold for each crack image at the image level. This optimal threshold is then utilized in the binarization function to optimize the dynamic thresholding-based binarization objective function. We have conducted experiments to validate the effectiveness of our multi-objective optimization approach with DTB on several well-known crack segmentation models. Additionally, we have evaluated its performance on various crack segmentation datasets. The results indicate that our approach can improve the accuracy of crack segmentation.

Keywords: Crack segmentation · Multi-objective optimization · Dynamic threshold

1 Introduction

Cracks are potential indicators of structural defects that can affect the structural health monitoring (SHM) and damage detection of various artifacts andstructures [13]. Surface cracks are prevalent in different materials, such as

D. Koutra et al. (Eds.): ECML PKDD 2023, LNAI 14169, pp. 389–404, 2023.
https://doi.org/10.1007/978-3-031-43412-9_23

pavement [10,20,21], concrete [8,15,24], brick and stone [5,12]. Crack repair is a crucial task to prevent hazard escalation and to ensure the safety of engineering structures and infrastructure. Moreover, repairing cracks before they worsen can substantially lower the maintenance costs [26]. Accurate assessment of cracks requires the results of crack segmentation. Crack segmentation is usually subdivided into semantic segmentation, which marks the pixels of a crack on a cracked image, and instance segmentation, which goes further to distinguish instances of cracks.

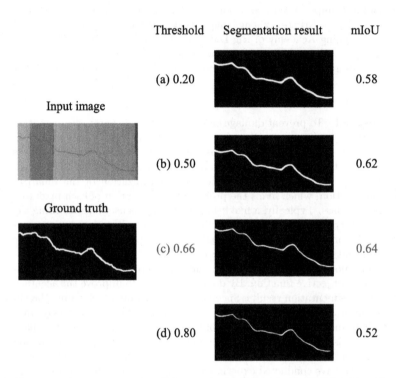

Fig. 1. Segmentation accuracy for different thresholds: (a) threshold 0.20 with mIoU 0.58, (b) threshold 0.50 with mIoU 0.62, (c) threshold 0.66 with mIoU 0.64 and (d) threshold 0.80 with mIoU 0.52. The optimal threshold is (c) 0.66.

The aim of crack segmentation is to generate a probability mask (classification probability for each pixel) of the crack image using the segmentation network and then to separate the crack from the background by applying a threshold (mapping the classification probability to a specific class). A common practice for binary image segmentation is to set the threshold to 0.5, which works well for common objects [7,16]. However, for crack segmentation with highly imbalanced class distribution, the threshold used in binarization can greatly affect the segmentation result due to its high sensitivity [13,17]. Figure 1 illustrates the impact of varying thresholds on crack segmentation, and 0.66 is the optimal threshold for this particular image because it produces the highest mIoU value (a common evaluation metric for image segmentation). We hypothesized that different crack images may require different thresholds for optimal segmentation. To test this hypothesis, we analyzed the distribution of optimal thresholds for U-Net [19] on the *Crack500* dataset [23] (Fig. 2). We found that the optimal threshold varied widely across images, and that the commonly used fixed threshold of 0.5 was not optimal.

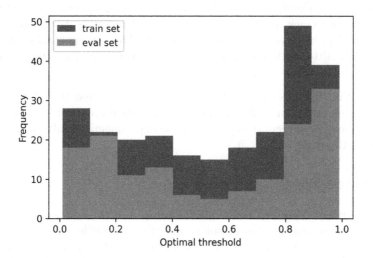

Fig. 2. Optimal threshold distribution for crack semantic segmentation with U-Net on the *Crack500* dataset.

We propose a novel crack segmentation method that adapts the threshold selection to each crack image. Our method consists of two branches: a conventional segmentation network that predicts crack probability masks, and a Dynamic Thresholding Branch (DTB) that predicts optimal thresholds for binarization. We formulate the crack segmentation problem as a multi-objective optimization problem that jointly optimizes both branches. This way, we can address the sensitivity of crack segmentation to threshold selection and improve the performance of our method.

By reusing the spatial features from the crack segmentation network and performing an extra regression task, DTB binarizes the probability mask with the optimal threshold and predict the optimal threshold on image-level. This significantly improves the test accuracy of crack segmentation. We evaluate our multi-objective optimization approach with DTB on various datasets for crack semantic segmentation and demonstrate its effectiveness.

The main contributions of this paper are as follows:

– We reformulate the crack segmentation problem as a multi-objective optimization problem that considers both the segmentation model's objective function and the binarization process that follows. By optimizing both processes simultaneously, we can achieve significant improvement in the model's inference performance than by optimizing only the segmentation model's objective function.

- To tackle the multi-objective optimization problem, we propose DTB to optimize the binarization process. DTB reuses the spatial features from the segmentation network to perform an extra regression task and predict the optimal threshold on image-level.
- We conducted experiments on various datasets with different sources and distributions for crack semantic segmentation tasks to evaluate the effectiveness of the multi-objective optimization approach. The experimental results show that the multi-objective optimization approach can improve the accuracy of crack segmentation.

The rest of this paper is structured as follows. We review the related work in Sect. 2. We describe our multi-objective optimization approach and the details of DTB in Sect. 3. We report and analyze the experimental results in Sect. 4. We summarize the paper in Sect. 5.

2   Related Work

Crack Segmentation is a technique that aims to accurately identify the location of cracks in images. This involves assigning a specific class label to each pixel in the image, which can be achieved through either semantic or instance segmentation. Semantic segmentation involves assigning all pixels in the image to a class without distinguishing between instances. For instance, all cracks in the image would be labeled as belonging to the "crack" class. On the other hand, instance segmentation differentiates between each individual instance, such that different cracks are assigned unique instance labels, but the same class label. Various methods have been proposed for crack semantic segmentation, including patch-based techniques [6,9], encoder-decoder methods [4,17,26], and hybrid approaches that combine both [11,14]. Among these, encoder-decoder methods, such as FCN [18], SegNet [2], and U-Net [19], have gained popularity. These methods do not use fully connected layers in the last layers to generate the segmentation output. An extension of U-Net is to incorporate an attention mechanism at the skip connection between the encoder and decoder [1,14,22]. Recent advancements in crack semantic segmentation have led to the development of improved architectures, such as deepcrack [26], which introduced a redesigned attention mechanism between the encoder-decoder.

3   Methodology

3.1   Problem Reformulation

We can use a model (CNN or transformer) f to solve the problem of crack semantic segmentation or instance segmentation with only two classes (class 0 and class 1). The model f takes an input image x with size (c, w, h) and network weights W, and outputs a probability mask p of class 1 with size $(1, w, h)$. Mathematically, this can be written as

$$p = f(x; W) \tag{1}$$

To find the optimal network weights W^*, we usually minimize the loss function L, which measures the difference between the probability mask p and the true label y with size $(1, w, h)$. The loss function L is often the cross-entropy loss. The optimization problem can be expressed as

$$W^* = \arg\min_W L(f(x; W), y) \tag{2}$$

To perform inference, we need to apply the function B to binarize the output of Eq. 1, as follows:

$$B(p_{i,j}) = \begin{cases} 1, p_{i,j} \geq 0.5 \\ 0, p_{i,j} < 0.5 \end{cases} \tag{3}$$

where $0 \leq i < w$ and $0 \leq j < h$. Here, B is a shorthand for a pixel-level binarization function $B_{i,j}$ that depends on the indices i, j (we omit them for brevity, and use the same notation for B_d later. Similarly $p_{i,j}$ is equivalent to p).

We do not directly plug Eq. 3 into Eq. 2 and optimize them together, because Eq. 3 is usually non-differentiable and the threshold 0.5 may change.

The results in Fig. 1 and Fig. 2 show that a fixed threshold may not be the best option. Hence, we propose a new binarization function B_d,

$$B_d(p_{i,j}) = \begin{cases} 1, p_{i,j} \geq thr_{opt}(x) \\ 0, p_{i,j} < thr_{opt}(x) \end{cases} \tag{4}$$

where $thr_{opt}(x)$ is the function that determines the optimal threshold from the input image. That is, $thr_{opt}(x)$ is an *image-level* threshold. Like Eq. 3, we do not jointly optimize Eq. 4 and Eq. 2 because they are non-differentiable.

We now reformulate the crack segmentation problem S.

$$\hat{Y} = S(x; W; B_d) \tag{5}$$

Specifically, Eq. 5 includes the following two processes,

$$p = f(x; W)$$
$$\hat{Y} = B_d(p) \tag{6}$$

where $\hat{Y} = B_d(p)$ is the mask containing the class labels by the binarization, and $p = f(x; W)$ is the mask containing the class probabilities predicted by the segmentation model.

To find S in Eq. 5, we need both W^* and $B_d(p)$. But $B_d(p)$ depends on W (P depends on W), so we have to optimize W^* before finding $B_d(p)$.

Moreover, to find $B_d(p)$, we need the optimal threshold $thr_{opt}(x)$. But $thr_{opt}(x)$ is an unknown distribution (as Fig. 2 shows, it is not a simple distribution) and a function of the input image x, so one possible way is to build another neural network that shares some weights with W.

Therefore, we split S into two tasks S_1 and S_2,

$$p = S_1(x, W_b + W_h) \tag{7}$$

$$\hat{thr}_{opt}(x) = S_2(x, W_b + W_t) \tag{8}$$

where W_b denotes the weights of backbone (encoder), W_h denotes the weights of output head (decoder), and W_t denotes the weights of the DTB (extra regression task branch), $\hat{thr}_{opt}(x)$ denotes the predicted optimal threshold. Note that $W = W_b + W_h$.

Thus only the following two optimization problems Eq. 9 and Eq. 10 need to be solved sequentially to solve S,

$$W^* = W_b^* + W_h^* = \underset{W_h, W_b}{\arg\min} L(S_1(x, W_b + W_h), y) \tag{9}$$

$$W_t^* = \underset{W_t}{\arg\min} L_{thr}(S_2(x, W_b + W_t), thr_{opt}(x)) \tag{10}$$

where W_b^*, W_h^* and W_t^* are the optimal weights for the backbone, output head and DTB, respectively. In Eq. 10, only the parameter W_t is optimized, and the parameter W_b is typically fixed during this process. The true optimal threshold of problem S is denoted as $thr_{opt}(x)$. For more information on how to obtain it, please refer to Sect. 3.3. L_{thr} refers to the loss function used in DTB, which is typically mean squared error (MSE).

In summary, we reformulate the crack segmentation problem in Eq. 5 by define it as a multi-objective optimization problem with two functions to solve (Eq. 6). To solve the new binarization function, we optimize the binarization process using the optimal threshold (Eq. 4) based on the analysis of the crack data (Fig. 1 and Fig. 2). To find the optimal threshold at the image level, we use another neural network that shares some weights with the segmentation network (Eq. 8), and its objective function is given by Eq. 10.

3.2   Dynamic Thresholding Branch

Figure 3 shows a schematic diagram of a DTB designed for semantic segmentation, which is marked with a gray background. The DTB consists of a global pooling layer (Pooling), two convolutional layers (conv) and two fully connected layers (fc). The input to the DTB is usually the spatial features of the convolutional layer from the segmentation network before the output head. For example, in the encoder-decoder structure of U-Net, the input to the DTB can be the spatial features of the convolutional layer between the last upsampling layer and the output probability mask. This allows the DTB to capture global information about the network structure. Another possible deployment option based on

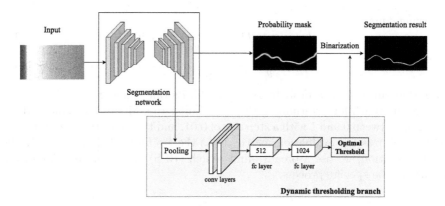

Fig. 3. Schematic diagram of DTB in semantic segmentation of cracks (gray background).

this idea is to use the output probability mask as the input to the DTB. This kind of input can also fit the structure of the DTB as described above, but it may cause the problem of data sparsity. The probability mask produced by the segmentation model is very sparse and thus needs a large amount of data for training to overcome this issue.

Since semantic segmentation does not impose any restriction on the image size, a global pooling layer is required in the DTB, whose parameters should be determined by the size of the input image. A common method to set the parameters of the global pooling layer is to make sure that the feature map after global pooling has half the size of the input image on average. After the global pooling layer, there are two convolutional layers. The reason for setting convolutional layers here is twofold: one is to extract spatial features, and the other is to reduce the number of DTB parameters. Therefore, the parameters of the convolutional layer here can be directly set with the parameters of the downsampling layer of U-Net. The function of adding the fully connected layers is to perform the regression task, and using fully connected layers instead of convolutional layers can achieve more accurate regression.

3.3   The Training of DTB

Obtaining Training Labels for DTB. The DTB is usually trained from scratch after a segmentation network $f(x; W)$ has been trained. Once $f(x; W)$ is ready, the next step is to get the training labels for the DTB that corresponds to $f(x; W)$. Since our model takes into account the different thresholds, we can express $f(x; W)$ as $f(x, thr; W)$. Suppose that $f(x; W)$ is trained using the training set $D = (x_0, y_0), (x_1, y_1), ..., (x_n, y_n)$, and the evaluation metric $M(y, \hat{y})$ is used in the test, where a higher value of $M(y, \hat{y})$ means a better segmentation performance. Then, the training labels thr_{opt} of DTB can be obtained by the following equation.

$$thr_{opt}(x, y, f) = \underset{thr \in [0,1]}{\arg\max} M(y, \hat{y}) \tag{11}$$

$$\hat{y} = F(x, thr; W)$$

Note that since thr is a probability threshold, its range is $[0, 1]$.

The approach for determining thr_{opt} is similar to a Monte Carlo method, by iterating between 0 and 1 with a step size of 0.01, and then selecting the threshold that maximizes the evaluation metric M as the training label. To simplify the implementation, we use a breadth-first search (BFS) approach, and Algorithm 1 outlines the specific process.

Algorithm 1. Finding optimal thresholds using BFS

1: **procedure** BFS(x, y)
2:      $Q \leftarrow \emptyset$
3:      $Q.push((1, 0.0))$
4:      **while** $Q \neq \emptyset$ **do**
5:          $(i, current\_m) \leftarrow Q.pop()$
6:          **if** $i = |thrs|$ **then**
7:              **if** $(x, y, thrs[i]) \notin best\_m$ or $current\_m > best\_m[(x, y, thrs[i])]$ **then**
8:                  $best\_m[(x, y, thrs[i])] \leftarrow current\_m$
9:              **end if**
10:         **else**
11:             $\hat{y} \leftarrow f(x, thrs[i])$
12:             $m \leftarrow M(\hat{y}, y)$
13:             $Q.push((i + 1, \max(current\_m, m)))$
14:             $Q.push((i + 1, current\_m))$
15:         **end if**
16:     **end while**
17: **end procedure**

18: **for** each $(x, y) \in D$ **do**
19:     BFS(x, y)
20: **end for**
21: $thr_{opt} \leftarrow best\_m$

By executing the first 20 lines of Algorithm 1, we get a dictionary $best\_m$ that stores the best evaluation metric value and the optimal threshold that achieved it for each image. To get the optimal threshold thr_{opt} for each image in the training set, we look up the corresponding dictionary entry and extract the threshold that has the highest evaluation metric. This process ensures that each image in the training set has a unique optimal threshold, which can be used to train the DTB model.

Loss Function of DTB. Usually, the loss function of DTB is defined as the Mean Square Error (MSE), which is expressed as Eq. 12.

$$L_{thr} = \frac{1}{n} \sum_{i=0}^{n} (\hat{thr}_{opt}(x) - thr_{opt}(x))^2 \qquad (12)$$

Here n denotes the number of images, $\hat{thr}_{opt}(x)$ and $thr_{opt}(x)$ denote the predicted threshold and the optimal threshold obtained from Algorithm 1, respectively.

4 Experiments

4.1 Dataset

We conducted our experiments on datasets *Crack500* [23] and *DeepCrack* [17], which are shown in Table 1.

Table 1. Overview of datasets

Set	Image size	Train/test split	Percentage of crack pixels
Crack500	2000×1500	247/148	0.523%
DeepCrack	544×384	300/237	3.54%

4.2 Comparison Methods

We compare our proposed method with the current mainstream crack semantic segmentation methods.

(a) FCN [18]: a fully convolutional network that performs pixel-level prediction in an end-to-end manner.
(b) U-Net [25]: a network with a U-shaped structure that fuses the features from each downsampling stage with the corresponding features from the upsampling stage.
(c) DeepLabV3 [3]: a deep learning model for image segmentation that uses atrous convolution, spatial pyramid pooling, and a decoder module with skip connections to achieve high accuracy.
(d) Deepcrack [17]: a deep hierarchical feature learning architecture that employs residual connections and dilated convolutions to capture multi-scale features for precise crack segmentation.

4.3   Implementation Details

We implemented our models using PyTorch, a popular deep learning framework. We conducted our experiments on an Nvidia A6000 GPU with 48 GB of memory. For optimization, we employed stochastic gradient descent (SGD) with a momentum of 0.9 and a weight decay of 1e−4. We set the initial learning rate to 0.01 and applied a piecewise linear learning rate schedule with warmup and decay phases, as proposed by DeepLabV3. During the warmup phase, the learning rate increased linearly from 0.001 to 1 in the first epoch. During the decay phase, the learning rate decreased according to a polynomial function of degree 0.9 until the end of training. We trained our models for 200 epochs or until convergence, whichever came first. We adjusted the batch size according to the resolution of the images in each dataset: for *Deepcrack*, which contains images with a resolution of 544 × 384 pixels, we used a batch size of 128; for *Crack500*, which contains images with a resolution of 2000 × 1500 pixels, we used a batch size of 16.

4.4   Experimental Results and Analysis

Table 2. Quantitative evaluation of various semantic segmentation methods on dataset *Crack500*.

Method	mIoU	mAcc	gAcc
FCN	73.2	94.8	81.4
FCN+DTB	**75.1**	**95.3**	**83.2**
U-Net	77.4	98.4	**86.8**
U-Net+DTB	**78.3**	**98.5**	87.6
DeepLabV3	74.2	95.1	81.1
DeepLabV3+DTB	**76.8**	**96.5**	**83.3**
Deepcrack	78.1	98.3	**86.7**
Deepcrack+DTB	**79.3**	**98.5**	86.6

As shown in Table 2 and Table 3, DTB improves the semantic segmentation performance of various models on *Crack500* and *Deepcrack* datasets. However, UNet benefits the least from DTB. This is because UNet already produces a probability distribution that is suitable for binary crack segmentation. In other words, pixels that belong to class 1 have a high output probability, leading to low entropy [13,26]. Thus, it is harder for DTB to enhance the segmentation performance by learning the optimal threshold and correcting misclassifications with high entropy for UNet. Figure 4 displays sample results of various semantic segmentation models on two datasets. As shown in (d) U-Net, DTB has limited improvement on the segmentation results, which is consistent with the findings in

Table 3. Quantitative evaluation of various semantic segmentation methods on dataset *Deepcrack*.

Method	mIoU	nmAcc	gAcc
FCN	81.2	88.6	93.3
FCN+DTB	**83.4**	**90.1**	**94.5**
U-Net	85.5	91.1	**98.6**
U-Net+DTB	**86.4**	**92.0**	98.4
DeepLabV3	78.5	82.3	95.8
DeepLabV3+DTB	**80.1**	**83.5**	**96.3**
Deepcrack	85.4	90.3	98.6
Deepcrack+DTB	**86.7**	**91.5**	**98.9**

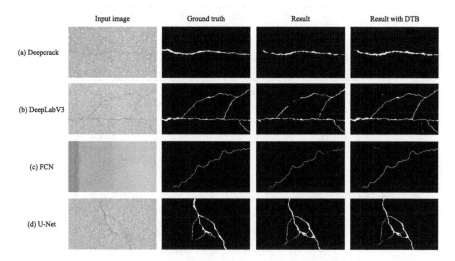

Fig. 4. Semantic segmentation samples for several models: (a) Deepcrack, (b) DeepLabV3, (c) FCN and (d) U-Net.

Table 2 and Table 3. However, DTB improves the segmentation results to varying degrees for all other models. Notably, DTB can introduce errors, as seen in (c) FCN, where image-level thresholds lead to misclassification of the background in the upper left corner. The use of pixel-level thresholds can significantly reduce such errors, and this is an area of future research.

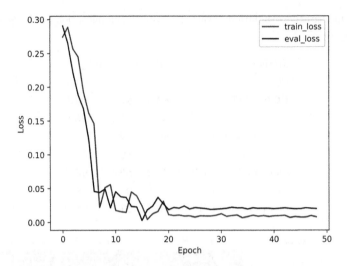

Fig. 5. MSE Loss curve of DTB on *Crack500* dataset.

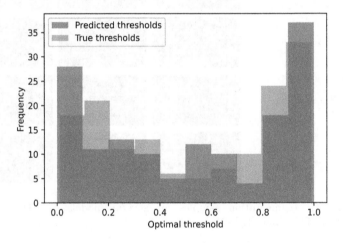

Fig. 6. Comparison of true and predicted optimal threshold distributions by DTB.

4.5   Validation of DTB

This section focuses on verifying the accuracy of the DTB. Since DTB involves a regression task, mean squared error (MSE) is used as an objective function during training and as an evaluation metric during testing. The plots in Fig. 5 depict the MSE loss of DTB on the *Crack500* dataset, which indicates that the model effectively learns the knowledge of the optimal threshold distribution. In addition, Fig. 6 shows a comparison of the optimal thresholds predicted by DTB with the true optimal thresholds obtained by Algorithm 1 on the *Crack500* dataset which shows that the difference between the two is acceptable.

Taken together, these two points serve as evidence that our proposed multi-objective approach with DTB is capable of successfully learning the optimal threshold distribution using the spatial features extracted from the crack images.

4.6 Time Consumption Analysis

Table 4. Inference Time Comparison

Set	Crack500 (FPS)	Deepcrack (FPS)
FCN	16.1	33.4
FCN+DTB	15.6	31.5
DeepLabV3	12.4	30.2
DeepLabV3+DTB	11.8	29.6
U-Net	16.7	33.8
U-Net+DTB	16.1	32.7
Deepcrack	14.4	31.5
Deepcrack+DTB	14.2	29.4

In crack segmentation, efficient computation is a crucial factor. In this paper, we evaluate the inference time of various segmentation models after integrating DTB and present the results in Table 4. The experiment was conducted using an AMD EPYC 7282 16-core processor on two crack segmentation datasets. The results show that all models with DTB achieve over 10 FPS at 2K resolution (*Crack500* dataset) and 30 FPS on average at 512 resolution (*Deepcrack* dataset), meeting the practical implementation requirement for vehicles with specialized image acquisition equipment.

The integration of DTB leads to improved accuracy of crack segmentation without sacrificing computational efficiency. Based on both quantitative and qualitative analyses, we conclude that our proposed multi-objective approach with DTB can serve as an optional, pluggable module for most crack segmentation tasks, enhancing the accuracy of the results.

5 Conclusion

Crack segmentation is a crucial task in structural health monitoring, but the visual characteristics of cracks have posed challenges for accurate segmentation. This paper proposes the Dynamic Thresholding Branch (DTB) for crack segmentation, which predicts an optimal threshold value for each crack image to improve segmentation accuracy. To achieve this, we adopt a multi-objective optimization approach and formulate the crack segmentation problem by combining crack probability mask prediction and threshold-based binarization into a complete optimization problem. We optimize the segmentation network to generate the crack probability mask, and DTB then determines the optimal threshold for binarization to optimize the overall segmentation process. DTB leverages the spatial features of crack images and can be easily integrated as a pluggable component for practical deployment. Our experiments, using various datasets with different distributions and sources, demonstrate the effectiveness of DTB in crack semantic and instance segmentation. Moreover, the multi-objective approach with DTB has potential for improving accuracy in similar binary classification image segmentation problems. Overall, our proposed method represents a significant advancement in the field of crack segmentation.

Acknowledgements. This work is funded in part by the National Natural Science Foundation of China under Grants No. 62176029. This work also is supported in part by the Chongqing Technology Innovation and Application Development Special under Grants CSTB2022TIAD-KPX0206. We express our sincere gratitude to the above funding agencies. We also acknowledge the computational support from the Chongqing Artificial Intelligence Innovation Center.

Ethical Statement. This study followed the ethical guidelines of the National Natural Science Foundation of China and the ethical review standards of the Chongqing Artificial Intelligence Innovation Center. This study did not involve any human or animal participants, nor did it use any sensitive or private data. The purpose of this study was to promote scientific advancement and social welfare in the field of artificial intelligence, and it did not cause any harm or adverse effects to any individual or group. All authors of this study are responsible for the content of this paper, and declare that they have no conflicts of interest or academic misconduct.

References

1. Augustauskas, R., Lipnickas, A.: Improved pixel-level pavement-defect segmentation using a deep autoencoder. Sensors **20**(9), 2557 (2020)
2. Badrinarayanan, V., Kendall, A., Cipolla, R.: SegNet: a deep convolutional encoder-decoder architecture for image segmentation. IEEE Trans. Pattern Anal. Mach. Intell. **39**(12), 2481–2495 (2017)
3. Chen, L.-C., Zhu, Y., Papandreou, G., Schroff, F., Adam, H.: Encoder-decoder with atrous separable convolution for semantic image segmentation. In: Ferrari, V., Hebert, M., Sminchisescu, C., Weiss, Y. (eds.) ECCV 2018. LNCS, vol. 11211, pp. 833–851. Springer, Cham (2018). https://doi.org/10.1007/978-3-030-01234-2_49
4. Cheng, J., Xiong, W., Chen, W., Gu, Y., Li, Y.: Pixel-level crack detection using U-Net. In: TENCON 2018–2018 IEEE Region 10 Conference, pp. 0462–0466. IEEE (2018)
5. Dung, C.V., et al.: Autonomous concrete crack detection using deep fully convolutional neural network. Autom. Constr. **99**, 52–58 (2019)
6. Fan, Z., Wu, Y., Lu, J., Li, W.: Automatic pavement crack detection based on structured prediction with the convolutional neural network. arXiv preprint arXiv:1802.02208 (2018)
7. He, K., Gkioxari, G., Dollár, P., Girshick, R.: Mask R-CNN. In: Proceedings of the IEEE International Conference on Computer Vision, pp. 2961–2969 (2017)

8. Huang, H., Zhao, S., Zhang, D., Chen, J.: Deep learning-based instance segmentation of cracks from shield tunnel lining images. Struct. Infrastruct. Eng. **18**(2), 183–196 (2022)
9. Inoue, Y., Nagayoshi, H.: Deployment conscious automatic surface crack detection. In: 2019 IEEE Winter Conference on Applications of Computer Vision (WACV), pp. 686–694. IEEE (2019)
10. Inoue, Y., Nagayoshi, H.: Crack detection as a weakly-supervised problem: towards achieving less annotation-intensive crack detectors. In: 2020 25th International Conference on Pattern Recognition (ICPR), pp. 65–72. IEEE (2021)
11. Jenkins, M.D., Carr, T.A., Iglesias, M.I., Buggy, T., Morison, G.: A deep convolutional neural network for semantic pixel-wise segmentation of road and pavement surface cracks. In: 2018 26th European Signal Processing Conference (EUSIPCO), pp. 2120–2124. IEEE (2018)
12. Kang, D., Benipal, S.S., Gopal, D.L., Cha, Y.J.: Hybrid pixel-level concrete crack segmentation and quantification across complex backgrounds using deep learning. Autom. Constr. **118**, 103291 (2020)
13. König, J., Jenkins, M., Mannion, M., Barrie, P., Morison, G.: What's cracking? A review and analysis of deep learning methods for structural crack segmentation, detection and quantification. arXiv preprint arXiv:2202.03714 (2022)
14. König, J., Jenkins, M.D., Barrie, P., Mannion, M., Morison, G.: A convolutional neural network for pavement surface crack segmentation using residual connections and attention gating. In: 2019 IEEE international conference on image processing (ICIP), pp. 1460–1464. IEEE (2019)
15. Li, Y., Wang, H., Dang, L.M., Piran, M.J., Moon, H.: A robust instance segmentation framework for underground sewer defect detection. Measurement **190**, 110727 (2022)
16. Lin, T.-Y., et al.: Microsoft COCO: common objects in context. In: Fleet, D., Pajdla, T., Schiele, B., Tuytelaars, T. (eds.) ECCV 2014. LNCS, vol. 8693, pp. 740–755. Springer, Cham (2014). https://doi.org/10.1007/978-3-319-10602-1_48
17. Liu, Y., Yao, J., Lu, X., Xie, R., Li, L.: DeepCrack: a deep hierarchical feature learning architecture for crack segmentation. Neurocomputing **338**, 139–153 (2019)
18. Long, J., Shelhamer, E., Darrell, T.: Fully convolutional networks for semantic segmentation. In: Proceedings of the IEEE Conference on Computer Vision and Pattern Recognition, pp. 3431–3440 (2015)
19. Ronneberger, O., Fischer, P., Brox, T.: U-Net: convolutional networks for biomedical image segmentation. In: Navab, N., Hornegger, J., Wells, W.M., Frangi, A.F. (eds.) MICCAI 2015. LNCS, vol. 9351, pp. 234–241. Springer, Cham (2015). https://doi.org/10.1007/978-3-319-24574-4_28
20. Safaei, N., Smadi, O., Masoud, A., Safaei, B.: An automatic image processing algorithm based on crack pixel density for pavement crack detection and classification. Int. J. Pavement Res. Technol. **15**(1), 159–172 (2022)
21. Tabernik, D., Šela, S., Skvarč, J., Skočaj, D.: Segmentation-based deep-learning approach for surface-defect detection. J. Intell. Manuf. **31**(3), 759–776 (2020)
22. Wu, Z., Lu, T., Zhang, Y., Wang, B., Zhao, X.: Crack detecting by recursive attention U-Net. In: 2020 3rd International Conference on Robotics, Control and Automation Engineering (RCAE), pp. 103–107. IEEE (2020)
23. Yang, F., Zhang, L., Yu, S., Prokhorov, D., Mei, X., Ling, H.: Feature pyramid and hierarchical boosting network for pavement crack detection. IEEE Trans. Intell. Transp. Syst. **21**(4), 1525–1535 (2019)

24. Zhao, S., Zhang, D., Xue, Y., Zhou, M., Huang, H.: A deep learning-based approach for refined crack evaluation from shield tunnel lining images. Autom. Constr. **132**, 103934 (2021)
25. Zhou, Z., Rahman Siddiquee, M.M., Tajbakhsh, N., Liang, J.: UNet++: a nested U-Net architecture for medical image segmentation. In: Stoyanov, D., et al. (eds.) DLMIA/ML-CDS-2018. LNCS, vol. 11045, pp. 3–11. Springer, Cham (2018). https://doi.org/10.1007/978-3-030-00889-5_1
26. Zou, Q., Zhang, Z., Li, Q., Qi, X., Wang, Q., Wang, S.: DeepCrack: learning hierarchical convolutional features for crack detection. IEEE Trans. Image Process. **28**(3), 1498–1512 (2018)

Co-supervised Pre-training of Pocket and Ligand

Zhangyang Gao, Cheng Tan, Jun Xia, and Stan Z. Li[✉]

Zhejiang University AI Lab, Research Center for Industries of the Future,
Westlake University, Hangzhou, China
{gaozhangyang,tancheng,xiajun,stan.zq.li}@westlake.edu.cn

Abstract. Can we inject the pocket-ligand complementarity knowledge into the pre-trained model and jointly learn their chemical space? Pre-training molecules and proteins have attracted considerable attention in recent years, while most of these approaches focus on learning one of the chemical spaces and lack the consideration of their complementarity. We propose a co-supervised pre-training (CoSP) framework to learn 3D pocket and ligand representations simultaneously. We use a gated geometric message passing layer to model 3D pockets and ligands, where each node's chemical features, geometric position, and direction are considered. To learn meaningful biological embeddings, we inject the pocket-ligand complementarity into the pre-training model via ChemInfoNCE loss, cooperating with a chemical similarity-enhanced negative sampling strategy to improve the representation learning. Through extensive experiments, we conclude that CoSP can achieve competitive results in pocket matching, molecule property prediction, and virtual screening.

Keywords: AI for Science · Bioinformatics · Molecular Representation Learning · Graph Neural Networks

1 Introduction

Is there a pre-trained model that explores the chemical space of pockets and ligands while considering their complementarity? Recently, many deep learning methods have been proposed to understand the chemical space of protein pockets or drug molecules (or called ligands) and facilitate drug design in many aspects, e.g., finding hits for a novel target [59], repurposing ancient drugs for new targets [25,57,67], and searching for similar pockets and molecules [35,46]. While these models have shown promising potential in learning separate pocket space or molecular space for specific tasks [17,21,31,47,71], jointly pre-training pockets and ligands considering their complementarity remains to be explored.

We propose **co-s**upervised **p**retraining (CoSP) framework for understanding the joint chemical space of pockets and ligands. Taking the ligand as an example,

---

Z. Gao and C. Tan—Equal Contribution.

contrastive self-supervised pre-training [17,49,56] has yielded significant achievements in recent years. By identifying well-defined positive and negative ligand pairs via contrastive loss, the model can learn the underlying knowledge to facilitate downstream tasks. However, these self-supervised methods only capture data dependencies in the "self" domain while ignoring additional information from other complementary fields, such as bindable pockets. Meanwhile, previous studies [1,5,11,37] have shown that pocket-ligand complementarity play a crucial role in determining molecular properties, since chemically similar ligands tend to bind to similar pockets. Inspired by this, we introduce cross-domain dependencies between pockets and ligands to improve molecular representation learning.

We propose **g**ated **g**eometric **m**assage **p**assing (GGMP) layer to extract expressive bio-representations for 3D pockets and ligands. All bio-objects are treated as 3D graphs [20,24] in that each node contains invariant chemical features (atomic number, etc.) and equivalent geometric features (position and direction). For each bio-object, we optimize the pairwise energy function [22], which considers both chemical features and geometric features via the gated operation. By minimizing the energy function, we derive the updating rules of position and direction vectors. Finally, we combine these rules with classical message passing, resulting in GGMP.

We introduce ChemInfoNCE loss to reduce the negative sampling bias [9,39]. When applying contrastive learning, the false negative pairs that are actually positive will lead to performance degradation, called negative sampling bias. Chuang [9] assumes that the label distribution of the classification task is uniform and propose DebiasedInfoNCE to alleviate this problem. Considering the specificity of the molecules and extending the situation to continuous properties prediction (regression task), we introduce chemical similarity-enhanced negative ligand sampling. Interestingly, improving the sampling strategy is equivalent to modifying sample weights; thus, we provide a systematic understanding from the view of loss functions and propose ChemInfoNCE.

We evaluates our model on several downstream tasks, from pocket matching, molecule property prediction to virtual screening. Numerous experiments show that our approach can achieve competitive results on these tasks, suggesting that the pocket-ligand complementarity could improve biorepresentation learning.

2   Related Work

Motivation. Protein and molecule achieve their biological functions by binding to each other [7], thus exploring the protein-ligand complex help to improve the understanding of both proteins, molecules, and their interactions. To improve generalization and reduce complexity, we further consider local patterns about the protein pocket x and the bindable ligand $\hat{x}$. Taking $(x, \hat{x})$ as the positive pair, while $(x, \hat{x}^-)$ as the negative pair, where $\hat{x}^-$ cannot bind to x, we aims to pre-train a pocket model $f : x \mapsto h$ and a ligand model $\hat{f} : \hat{x} \mapsto \hat{h}$, such that the mutual information between h and $\hat{h}$ are maximized.

Table 1. Protein and molecule pre-training methods

Protein				Molecule			
Method	Data	Code	Year	Method	Data	Code	Year
CPCProt [33]	sequence	PyTorch	2020	FragNet [44]	SMILEs	–	2021
Profile Prediction [48]	sequence	–	2020	MoCL [49]	graph	PyTorch	2021
ONTOPROTEIN [70]	sequence	PyTorch	2022	MPG [29]	graph	PyTorch	2021
CARP	sequence	–	2022	Grover [40]	graph	PyTorch	2020
GearNet	3D	–	2022	MICRO-Graph [71]	graph	–	2020
				CKGNN [17]	graph	–	2021
				MGSSL [73]	graph	PyTorch	2021
				MolCLR [56]	graph	PyTorch	2022
				3DInfomax [47]	graph+3D	PyTorch	2021
				GraphMVP [31]	graph+3D	–	2022
				GEM [16]	graph+3D	Paddle	2022

Equivalent 3D GNN. Extensive works have shown that 3D structural conformation can improve the quality of bio-representations with the help of equivalent massage passing layer [4,6,10,19,41,50]. Inspired by the energy analysis [20,22], we propose a new **g**ated **g**eometric **m**assage **p**assing (GGMP) layer that consider not only the node position but also its direction, where the latter could indicate the location of pocket cavities and the angle of molecular bonds.

InfoNCE. The original InfoNCE is proposed by [36] to contrast semantically similar (positive) and dissimilar (negative) pairs of data points, such that the representations of similar pairs $(x, \hat{x})$ to be close, and those of dissimilar pairs $(x, \hat{x}^-)$ to be more orthogonal. By default, the negative pairs are uniformly sampled from the data distribution. Therefore, false negative pairs will lead to significant performance drop. To address this issue, DebaisedInfoNCE [9] is proposed, which assumes that the label distribution of the classification task is uniform. Although DebaisedInfoNCE has achieved good results on image classification, it is not suitable for direct transfer to regression tasks, as the uniform distribution assumption is too strict. For bio-objects, we discard the above assumption, extend the situation to continuous attribute prediction, use fingerprint similarity to measure the probability of negative ligands, and propose ChemInfoNCE.

Self Bio Pre-training. Many pre-training methods have been proposed for a single protein or ligand domain, which can be classified as sequence-based, graph-based or structure-based. We summarize the **protein pre-training** models in Table.1. As for sequential models, CPCPort [33] maximizes the mutual information between predicted residues and context. Profile Prediction [48] suggests predicting MSA profile as a new pre-training task. OntoProtein [70] integrates GO (Gene Ontology) knowledge graphs into protein pre-training. While most of the sequence models rely on the transformer architecture, CARP [66] finds that CNNs can achieve competitive results with much fewer parameters and runtime costs. Recently, GearNet [74] explores the potential of 3D structural pre-training from the perspective of masked prediction and contrastive learning. We also summarize the **molecule pre-training** models in Table.1. As for sequential models, FragNet [44] combines masked language model and multi-view contrastive learning to maximize the inner mutual information of the same SMILEs and the agreement across augmented SMILEs. Beyond SMILEs, more approaches [17,29,40,49,56,71,73] tend to choose graph representation that can better model structural information. For example, Grover [40] integrates message passing and transformer architectures and pre-trains a super-large GNN using 10 million molecules. MICRO-Graph [71] and MGSSL [73] use motifs for contrastive learning. Considering the domain knowledge, MoCL [49] uses substructure substitution as a new data augmentation operation and predicts pairwise fingerprint similarities. Although these pre-training methods show promising results, they do not consider the 3D molecular conformations. To fill this gap, GraphMVP [31] and 3DInfomax [47] explore to maximize the mutual information between 3D and 2D views of the same molecule and achieve further performance improvements. Besides, GEM [16] proposes a geometry-enhanced graph neural network and pre-trains it via geometric tasks. For the pre-training of individual proteins or molecules, these methods demonstrate promising potential on various downstream tasks but ignore their complementarity.

Cross Bio Pre-training. In parallel with our study, Uni-Mol [76], probably the first pre-trained model that can handle both protein pockets and molecules, released the preprinted version. However, they pre-train the pockets and ligands separately without considering their interactions, whereas our approach differs in pre-training data, pre-training strategy, model structure and downstream tasks.

3 Methodology

3.1 Co-Supervised Pre-training Framework

We propose the **co-s**upervised **p**retraining (CoSP) framework, as shown in Figure.1, to explore the joint chemical space of protein pockets and ligands, where the methodological innovations include:

1. We propose the gated geometric message passing layer to model 3D pockets and ligands.
2. We establish a co-supervised pre-training framework to learn pocket and ligand representations.
3. We introduce ChemInfoNCE with improved negative sampling guided by chemical similarity.
4. We evaluate the model on pocket matching, molecule property prediction, and virtual-screening tasks.

3.2   Geometric Representation

We introduce the unified data representation and neural network for modeling 3D pockets and ligands. We use structures collected from the BioLip dataset [64] as pretraining data for developing $CoSP_{base}$ model. Further, we use augmente the pretraining data with CrossDock dataset [18], resulting in the $CoSP_{large}$ model. In downstream tasks where ligand conformations are not provided, we generate 3D conformations using MMFF [52] (if successful) or their 2D conformations (if failed).

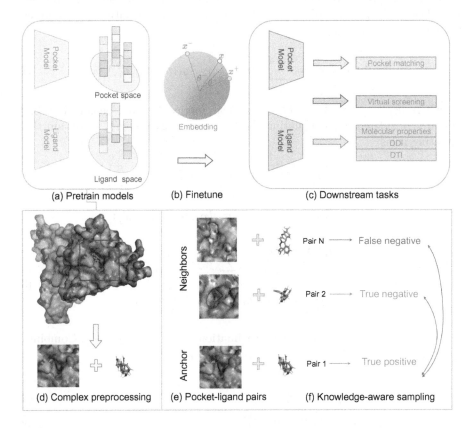

Fig. 1. Overview of CoSP. We contrast bound pocket-ligand pairs with unbound ones to learn the complementarity-aware chemical embeddings. We extract positive pocket-ligand pairs (e) from the protein-ligand complexes (d), and augment pos/neg relations of complexes via ligand similarity (f). We pretrain the model on BioLip dataset (a), followed by finetuning (b) and evaluation (c) on different tasks.

Pocket and Ligand Graph. We represent bio-object as graph $\mathcal{G}(X, \mathcal{V}, \mathcal{E})$, consisting of coordinate matrix $X \in \mathbb{R}^{n,3}$, node features $\mathcal{V} \in \mathbb{R}^{n,d_f}$, and edge features $\mathcal{E} \in \mathbb{R}^{n,d_e}$, where n, d_f and d_e represent the number of node, node features dimension and edge features dimension. For pockets, the graph nodes include amino acids within 10 Å to the ligand, X contrains the position of C_α of residues, on which we construct $\mathcal{E}$ via k-nn algorithm. For molecules, the graph nodes include all ligand atoms except Hs, X contrains the atom positions, and we use the molecular bonds as $\mathcal{E}$.

Gated Geometric Massage Passing. From layer t to $t+1$, we use the gated geometric massage passing (GGMP) layer to update 3D graph representations, i.e., $[v_i^{t+1}, x_i^{t+1}, n_i^{t+1}] = \text{GGMP}(v_i^t, x_i^t, n_i^t)$, where n_i is the direction vector. For molecules, n_i points to the negative neighborhood center of node i; for pockets, n_i indicates the position of protein caves. Given 3D conformations, we minimize the pairwise energy function E:

$$E(X, F, \mathcal{E}) = \sum_{(i,j)\in\mathcal{E}} u(v_i, v_j, e_{ij}) g(\langle n_i, n_j\rangle, d_{ij}^2) \tag{1}$$

where $d_{ij}^2 = ||x_i - x_j||^2$, both chemical energy $u(\cdot)$ and geometric energy $g(\cdot)$ are considered. By calculating the gradients of x_i and n_i, we obtain their updating rules:

$$\begin{aligned}
-\frac{\partial E(X, F, \mathcal{E})}{\partial x_i} &= -\sum_{j\in\mathcal{N}_i} 2u_{ij}\frac{\partial g_{ij}}{\partial d_{ij}^2}(x_i - x_j) \\
&\approx \sum_{j\in\mathcal{N}_i} u(v_i, v_j, e_{ij})\phi_x(d_{ij}^2, \langle n_i, n_j\rangle)(x_i - x_j)
\end{aligned} \tag{2}$$

$$\begin{aligned}
-\frac{\partial E(X, F, \mathcal{E})}{\partial n_i} &= -\sum_{j\in\mathcal{N}_i} u_{ij}\frac{\partial g_{ij}}{\partial\langle n_i, n_j\rangle}n_j \\
&\approx \sum_{j\in\mathcal{N}_i} u(v_i, v_j, e_{ij})\phi_n(d_{ij}^2, \langle n_i, n_j\rangle)n_j
\end{aligned} \tag{3}$$

Note that ϕ_x and ϕ_n are the approximation of $\frac{\partial g_{ij}}{\partial d_{ij}^2}$ and $\frac{\partial g_{ij}}{\partial\langle n_i, n_j\rangle}$. Combining graph message passing, we propose the GGMP layer:

$$m_{ij} = \phi_m(v_i^t, v_j^t, e_{ij}) \tag{4}$$

$$g_{ij} = \phi_g(d_{ij}^2, \langle n_i^t, n_j^t\rangle) \tag{5}$$

$$h_i^{t+1} = \phi_h(h_i^t, \sum_{j\in\mathcal{N}_i} m_{ij}g_{ij}) \tag{6}$$

$$x_i^{t+1} = x_i^t + \lambda\sum_{j\in\mathcal{N}_i} u(m_{ij})\phi_x(g_{ij})(x_i^t - x_j^t) \tag{7}$$

$$n_i^{t+1} = n_j^t + \lambda\sum_{j\in\mathcal{N}_i} u(m_{ij})\phi_n(g_{ij})n_j^t \tag{8}$$

where ϕ_* and u are approximated by neural networks, λ is a hyperparameter, and $n_i^0 = -\sum_{j\in\mathcal{N}(i)} x_j^0 / ||\sum_{j\in\mathcal{N}(i)} x_j^0||$.

3.3   Contrastive Loss

In contrastive learning, the biased negative sampling impairs model performance by sampling false negative data during training. Previous methods [9,39] address this problem with the assumption that false-negative samples are uniformly distributed under the classification setting. We propose chemical knowledge-based sampling to better address this issue, where fingerprint similarity is used to measure the probability of negative ligands. Interestingly, the change in sampling distribution is equivalent to the design of a weighted loss, and we provide a comprehensive understanding from the perspective of contrastive loss.

Uni-contrastive Loss. Given the pocket $x \sim p$, we draw positive ligands $\hat{x}^+$ from the distribution $\hat{p}_x^+$ of bindable molecules and negative ligands $\{\hat{x}_i^-\}_{i=1}^N$ from the distribution $\hat{q}$ of non-bindable ones. By default, the positive ligands are determined by the pocket-ligand complexes, while negative ones are uniformly sampled from the ligand sets. We use pocket model f and ligand model $\hat{f}$ to learn the latent representations $\boldsymbol{h}$, $\hat{\boldsymbol{h}}^+$ and $\{\hat{\boldsymbol{h}}_i^-\}_{i=1}^N$, where the proxy task is to maximize the positive similarity $s^+(\boldsymbol{h}, \hat{\boldsymbol{h}}^+)$ against the negative similarities $s_i^-(\boldsymbol{h}, \hat{\boldsymbol{h}}_i^-), i = 1, 2, \cdots$, resulting in:

$$L_{\text{Uni}} = \mathbb{E}_{\substack{x \sim p, \hat{x}^+ \sim \hat{p}_x^+, \\ \{\hat{x}_i^-\}_{i=1}^N \sim \hat{q}}} \left[\log \left(1 + \frac{Q}{N} \sum_{i=1}^N \frac{s_i^-(\boldsymbol{h}, \hat{\boldsymbol{h}}_i^-)}{s^+(\boldsymbol{h}, \hat{\boldsymbol{h}}^+)} \right) \right] \tag{9}$$

where Q and N are constants. For each data sample x, the gradients contributed to s^+ and s_i^- are:

$$\frac{\partial L}{\partial s^+} = \frac{1}{1 + \sum_{i=1}^N s_i^-/s^+} \sum_{i=1}^N \frac{\partial s_i^-/s^+}{\partial s^+} \tag{10}$$

$$\frac{\partial L}{\partial s_i^-} = \frac{1}{1 + \sum_{i=1}^N s_i^-/s^+} \frac{\partial s_i^-/s^+}{\partial s_i^-} \tag{11}$$

The L_{Uni} provides balanced gradient to positive and negative samples, i.e., $\frac{\partial L}{\partial s^+} = \sum_i \frac{\partial L}{\partial s_i^-}$. One can verify that InfoNCE is the special case of L_{Uni} by setting $s^+(\boldsymbol{h}, \hat{\boldsymbol{h}}^+) = e^{\gamma \boldsymbol{h}^T \boldsymbol{h}^+}$ and $s_i^-(\boldsymbol{h}, \hat{\boldsymbol{h}}_i^-) = e^{\gamma \boldsymbol{h}^T \boldsymbol{h}_i^-}$.

DebiasedInfoNCE. Uniformly sampling negative ligands from the data distribution $\hat{q}$ could mistaken positive samples as negative ones. Denote $h(\cdot)$ as the labeling function, [9] suggests to draw negative samples from the real negative distribution $\hat{q}_x^-(\hat{x}^-) = p(\hat{x}^-|h(\hat{x}^-) \neq h(x))$. To handle the $\{h(\hat{x}^-) \neq h(x)\}$ event, the joint distribution $p(\hat{x}, c) = p(\hat{x}|c)p(c)$ over data $\hat{x}$ and label c is considered. Assume the class probability $p(c) = \tau^+$ is uniform, and let $\tau^- = 1 - \tau^+$ be the probability of observing any different class, $\hat{q}$ could be decomposed as $\tau^- \hat{q}_x^-(\hat{x}^-) + \tau^+ \hat{q}_x^+(\hat{x}^-)$. Therefore, $\hat{q}_x^- = (\hat{q} - \tau^+ \hat{q}_x^+)/\tau^-$, and the DebiasedInfoNCE is:

$$L_{\text{Debiased}} = \mathbb{E}_{\substack{x \sim p, \hat{x}^+ \sim \hat{p}_x^+, \\ \{\hat{x}_i^-\}_{i=1}^N \sim \hat{q}_x^-}} \left[\log \left(1 + \frac{Q}{N} \sum_{i=1}^N \frac{s_i^-(\boldsymbol{h}, \hat{\boldsymbol{h}}_i^-)}{s^+(\boldsymbol{h}, \hat{\boldsymbol{h}}^+)}\right) \right] \tag{12}$$

where $s^+(\boldsymbol{h}, \hat{\boldsymbol{h}}^+) = e^{\boldsymbol{h}^T \hat{\boldsymbol{h}}^+}$, $s_i^-(\boldsymbol{h}, \hat{\boldsymbol{h}}_i^-) = e^{\boldsymbol{h}^T \hat{\boldsymbol{h}}_i^-}$. With mild assumptions, the approximated debaised InfoNCE can be written as:

$$\mathbb{E}_{\substack{x \sim p, \hat{x}^+ \sim \hat{p}_x^+, \\ \{\hat{x}_i^-\}_{i=1}^N \sim \hat{q}}} \left[\log \left(1 + \frac{Q}{\tau^-} \sum_{i=1}^N (e^{\boldsymbol{h}^T \boldsymbol{h}_i^- - \boldsymbol{h}^T \boldsymbol{h}^+} - \tau^+))\right) \right] \tag{13}$$

ChemInfoNCE. Although DebiasedInfoNCE solves the problem of sampling bias to some extent, it suffers from some shortcomings. Firstly, for classification with discrete labels, the assumption of uniform class probabilities may be too strong, especially for the unbalanced dataset. Secondly, when it comes to regression, molecules have continuous chemical properties and the event $\{h(\hat{x}) \neq h(\hat{x}^-)\}$ can not describe the validity of negative data. To address these issues, we introduce a new event $\{\text{sim}(\hat{x}, \hat{x}^-) < \tau\}$ to measure the validity of negative samples, where $\text{sim}(\cdot, \cdot)$ is the function of chemical similarity. The underlying assumption is that molecules with lower chemical similarity to the reference ligand are more likely to be negative samples.

$$\begin{aligned} q_x^-(\hat{x}^-) &:= q(\hat{x}^- | \text{sim}(x, \hat{x}^-) < \tau) \\ &\propto \max(1 - \text{sim}(x, \hat{x}^-) - \tau, 0) \cdot p(\hat{x}^-) \end{aligned} \tag{14}$$

By denoting $w_i = \max(1 - \text{sim}(x, \hat{x}^-) - \tau, 0)$, the final ChemInfoNCE can be simplfied as:

$$L_{\text{Chem}} \approx \mathbb{E}_{\substack{x \sim p, \hat{x}^+ \sim \hat{p}_x^+, \\ \{\hat{x}_i^-\}_{i=1}^N \sim \hat{q}}} \left[\log \left(1 + \sum_{i=1}^N (\rho_i e^{\boldsymbol{h}^T \hat{\boldsymbol{h}}_i^- - \boldsymbol{h}^T \hat{\boldsymbol{h}}^+}))\right) \right] \tag{15}$$

where $\rho_i = \frac{w_i}{\sum_{i=1}^N w_i}$.

4   Experiments

In this section, we conduct extensive experiments to verify the effectiveness of the proposed method from three perspectives:

1. **Ligand**: Could the ligand model provide competitive results in predicting molecular properties?
2. **Pocket**: How does the pre-trained pocket model perform on the pocket matching tasks?
3. **Pocket-ligand**: Could the joint model find potential binding pocket-ligand pairs, i.e., virtual screening?

Table 2. Molecule property prediction. We compare different methods across 9 benchmarks. The best and sub-optimum results are highlighted in **bold** and <u>underline</u>.

Methods	Classification (AUC-ROC % ↑)						Regression (RMSE ↓)		
Dataset	BBBP	BACE	ClinTox	Tox21	ToxCast	SIDER	ESOL	FreeSolv	Lipo
#Molecules	2039	1513	1478	7831	8575	1427	1128	642	4200
#Tasks	1	1	2	12	617	27	1	1	1
D-MPNN	71.0(0.3)	80.9(0.6)	90.6(0.6)	75.9(0.7)	65.5(0.3)	57.0(0.7)	1.050(0.008)	2.082(0.082)	0.683(0.016)
Attentive FP	64.3(1.8)	78.4(0.02)	84.7(0.3)	76.1(0.5)	63.7(0.2)	60.6(3.2)	0.877(0.029)	2.073(0.183)	0.721(0.001)
N-Gram$_{RF}$	69.7(0.6)	77.9(1.5)	77.5(4.0)	74.3(0.4)	–	66.8(0.7)	1.074(0.107)	2.688(0.085)	0.812(0.028)
N-Gram$_{XGB}$	69.1(0.8)	79.1(1.3)	87.5(2.7)	75.8(0.9)	–	65.5(0.7)	1.083(0.082)	5.061(0.744)	2.072(0.030)
MolCLR	72.2(2.1)	82.4(0.9)	91.2(3.5)	75.0(0.2)	–	58.9(1.4)	1.271(0.040)	2.594(0.249)	0.691(0.004)
PretrainGNN	68.7(1.3)	84.2(0.7)	72.6(1.5)	78.1(0.6)	65.7(0.6)	62.7(0.8)	1.100(0.006)	2.764(0.002)	0.739(0.003)
GraphMVP-G	70.8(0.5)	79.3(1.5)	79.1(2.8)	75.9(0.5)	63.1(0.2)	60.2(1.1)	–	–	–
GraphMVP-C	72.4(1.6)	81.2(0.9)	76.3(1.9)	74.4(0.2)	63.1(0.4)	63.9(1.2)	–	–	–
3DInfomax	69.1(1.1)	79.4(1.9)	59.4(3.2)	74.5(0.7)	64.4(0.9)	53.4(3.3)	0.894(0.028)	2.34(0.227)	0.695(0.012)
MICRO-graph	**77.2(2.0)**	84.4(1.1)	77.0(2.0)	77.0(0.8)	65.2(0.8)	56.7(1.1)	–	–	–
GROVER$_{base}$	70.0(0.1)	82.6(0.7)	81.2(3.0)	74.3(0.1)	65.4(0.4)	64.8(0.6)	0.983(0.090)	2.176(0.052)	0.817(0.008)
GROVER$_{large}$	69.5(0.1)	81.0(1.4)	76.2(3.7)	73.5(0.1)	65.3(0.5)	65.4(0.1)	0.895(0.017)	2.272(0.051)	0.823(0.010)
GEM	72.4(0.4)	85.6(1.1)	90.1(1.3)	78.1(0.1)	69.2(0.4)	**67.2(0.4)**	0.798(0.029)	1.877(0.094)	0.660(0.008)
Uni-Mol	72.9(0.6)	85.7(0.2)	**91.9(1.8)**	**79.6(0.5)**	69.6(0.1)	65.9(1.3)	0.788(0.029)	**1.620(0.035)**	0.603(0.010)
CoSP$_{base}$(w/o pre-train)	71.1(0.5)	82.2(1.4)	89.3(1.5)	73.8(0.4)	62.6(0.7)	61.7(1.2)	1.243(0.045)	2.135(0.045)	0.864(0.023)
CoSP$_{base}$(DebaisedInfoNCE)	72.3(0.4)	83.5(1.2)	90.2(1.3)	75.4(0.6)	64.7(0.4)	62.9(1.3)	0.843(0.038)	1.857(0.043)	0.748(0.029)
CoSP$_{base}$(ChemInfoNCE)	73.1(0.3)	84.3(1.1)	91.3(1.5)	78.5(0.1)	69.3(0.2)	64.7(1.5)	<u>0.785(0.029)</u>	1.752(0.042)	0.621(0.012)
CoSP$_{large}$	73.6(0.4)	**85.9(0.9)**	91.2(1.2)	79.3(0.1)	**70.0(0.2)**	66.4(1.2)	**0.783(0.023)**	1.715(0.017)	**0.598(0.011)**

4.1 Pre-training Setup

Pre-training Dataset. We adopt BioLip [64] dataset for pre-training CoSP$_{base}$, where the original BioLip contains 573,225 entries up to 2022.04.01. Compared to PDBBind [54] with 23,496 complexes, BioLip contains more complexes that lack binding affinity, thus could provide a more comprehensive view of binding mode analysis. To focus on the drug-like molecules and their binding pockets, we filtered out other unrelated complexes that contain peptides, DNA, RNA, single ions, etc. In addition, we augment the pretraining data with the CrossDock dataset [18] to develop CoSP$_{large}$.

Experimental Setting. We pre-train CoSP$_{base}$ with 6 layer GGMPs via ChemInfoNCE loss, where the hidden feature dimension is 128. We train the model for 50 epochs using Adam optimizer on NVIDIA A100s, where the initial learning rate is 0.01 and the batch size is 100. The chemical ligand similarity is calculated by RDKit [28]. To achieve better performance, CoSP$_{large}$ extends the 6-layer GNN to 12 layers, with hidden dimensions from 128 to 1024, and uses augmentated dataset (BioLip+CrossDock).

4.2 Downstream Task 1: Molecule Property Prediction

Experimental Setup. Could the model learn expressive features for molecule classification and regression tasks? We evaluate CoSP on 9 benchmarks collected by MoleculeNet [61]. Following previous researches, we use scaffold splitting to generate train/validation/test set with a ratio of 8:1:1. We report AUC-ROC and RMSE metrics for classification and regression tasks, respectively. The mean and standard deviations of results over three random seeds are provided by default. We finetune the model using the similar code of MGSSL [73].

Baselines. We evaluate CoSP against a broad of baselines, including D-MPNN [65], Attentive FP [63], N-Gram$_{RF}$, N-Gram$_{XGB}$ [30], MolCLR [56], PretrainGNN [23], GraphMVP-G, GraphMVP-C [32], 3DInfomax [47], MICRO-graph [71], GROVER$_{base}$, GROVER$_{large}$ [40], GEM [16], and Uni-Mol [76]. Most these baselines are pre-training methods, except for N-Gram$_{RF}$ and N-Gram$_{XGB}$. Some of the methods mentioned in the related works are not included because the experimental setup, e.g., data spliting, may be different.

Results and Analysis. We show results in Table.2. The main observations are: (1) CoSP$_{large}$ could achieve the best results on 4/9 downstream tasks, and top-3 results on 9/9 downstream tasks. (2) Pre-training techniques help improve the model's generalization ability, and the model could learn expressive molecular features via co-supervised pre-training. By extending the model size and pre-training data volumn, CoSP$_{large}$ achieves non-trivial performance gains compared to CoSP$_{base}$. (3) Through ablation studies, we further identified the superiority of ChemInfoNCE over DebaisedInfoNCE by achieving consistent performance gains on various datasets.

Table 3. Pocket matching results. We compare different methods across 10 benchmarks.

Category	Methods	Classification (AUC-ROC ↑)									
		D1	D1.2	D2	D3	D4	D5	D5.2	D6	D6.2	D7
Classical baselines	Cavbase	<u>0.98</u>	0.91	0.87	0.65	0.64	0.60	0.57	0.55	0.55	0.82
	FuzCav	0.94	<u>0.99</u>	<u>0.99</u>	0.69	0.58	0.55	0.54	0.67	0.73	0.77
	FuzCav (PDB)	0.94	<u>0.99</u>	0.98	0.69	0.58	0.56	0.54	0.65	0.72	0.77
	grim	0.69	0.97	0.92	0.55	0.56	0.69	0.61	0.45	0.65	0.70
	grim (PDB)	0.62	0.83	0.85	0.57	0.56	0.61	0.58	0.45	0.50	0.64
	IsoMIF	0.77	0.97	0.70	0.59	0.59	<u>0.75</u>	**0.81**	0.62	0.62	0.87
	KRIPO	0.91	1.00	0.96	0.60	0.61	**0.76**	<u>0.77</u>	**0.73**	<u>0.74</u>	0.85
	PocketMatch	0.82	0.98	0.96	0.59	0.57	0.66	0.60	0.51	0.51	0.82
	ProBiS	**1.00**	1.00	**1.00**	0.47	0.46	0.54	0.55	0.50	0.50	0.85
	RAPMAD	0.85	0.83	0.82	0.61	0.63	0.55	0.52	0.60	0.60	0.74
	shaper	0.96	0.93	0.93	0.71	0.76	0.65	0.65	0.54	0.65	0.75
	shaper (PDB)	0.96	0.93	0.93	0.71	0.76	0.66	0.64	0.54	0.65	0.75
	VolSite/shaper	0.93	<u>0.99</u>	0.78	0.68	0.76	0.56	0.58	0.71	**0.76**	0.77
	VolSite/shaper (PDB)	0.94	**1.00**	0.76	0.68	0.76	0.57	0.56	0.50	0.57	0.72
	SiteAlign	0.97	1.00	1.00	<u>0.85</u>	<u>0.80</u>	0.59	0.57	0.44	0.56	0.87
	SiteEngine	0.96	1.00	1.00	0.82	0.79	0.64	0.57	0.55	0.55	0.86
	SiteHopper	<u>0.98</u>	0.94	1.00	0.75	0.75	0.72	**0.81**	0.56	0.54	0.77
	SMAP	**1.00**	1.00	1.00	0.76	0.65	0.62	0.54	0.68	0.68	0.86
	TIFP	0.66	0.90	0.91	0.66	0.66	0.71	0.63	0.55	0.60	0.71
	TIFP (PDB)	0.55	0.74	0.78	0.56	0.57	0.54	0.53	0.56	0.61	0.66
	TM-align	**1.00**	1.00	1.00	0.49	0.49	0.66	0.62	0.59	0.59	<u>0.88</u>
Deeplearning baseline	DeeplyTough	0.95	0.98	0.90	0.76	0.75	0.67	0.63	0.54	0.54	0.83
Our methods	CoSP$_{base}$ (w/o direction)	0.95	0.95	0.92	0.55	0.58	0.56	0.56	0.53	0.54	0.76
	CoSP$_{base}$	**1.00**	**1.00**	<u>0.99</u>	0.79	<u>0.81</u>	0.62	0.63	0.61	0.62	0.81
	CoSP$_{large}$	**1.00**	**1.00**	**1.00**	**0.87**	**0.85**	<u>0.75</u>	0.74	<u>0.72</u>	<u>0.74</u>	**0.90**

4.3   Downstream Task 2: Pocket Matching

Experimental Setup. Could the pre-trained model identify chemically similar pockets? We explore the discriminative ability of the pocket model with the pocket matching tasks. To comprehensively understand the potential of the proposed method, we evaluated it on 10 benchmarks recently collected in the ProSPECCTs dataset [15]. For each sub-dataset, the positive and negative pairs of pockets are defined differently according to the research objectives. We summarize five research objectives as **O1**: Whether the model is robust to the pocket definition? **O2**: Whether the model is robust to the pocket flexibility? **O3**: Can the model distinguish between pockets with different properties? **O4**: Whether the model can distinguish dissimilar proteins binding to identical ligands and cofactors? **O5**: How about the performance on real applications? We report the AUC-ROC scores on all benchmarks.

Baselines. We compare CoSP with both classical and deeplearning baselines. The classical methods can be divided into profile-based, graph-based and grid-based ones. The profile-based methods encode topological, physicochemical and statistical properties in a unified way for comparing various pockets, e.g., SiteAlign [42], RAPMAD [27], TIFP [13], FuzCav [58], PocketMatch [69], SMAP [62], TM-align [72], KRIPO [60] and Grim [13]. The graph-based methods adopt isomorphism detection algorithm to find common motifs, e.g., Cavbase [43], IsoMIF [8], ProBiS [26]. Grid-based methods represent pockets by regularly spaced pharmacophoric grid points, e.g.,VolSite/Shaper [12]. Another tools include SiteEngines [45] and SiteHopper [3]. We also compare with the recent deeplearning model–DeeplyTough [46].

Results and Analysis. We present the pocket matching results in Table. 3, where the pre-trained model achieves competitive results in most cases. Specifically, CoSP is robust to pocket definition (**O1**) and achieves the highest AUC scores in D1 and D1.2. The robustness also remains when considering conformational variability (**O2**), where $CoSP_{large}$ achieves 1.00 AUC score in D2. It should be noted that robustness to homogeneous pockets does not mean that the model has poor discrimination; on the contrary, the model could identify pockets with different physicochemical and shape properties (**O3**) in D3 and D4. Compared with previous deep learning methods (DeeplyTough), $CoSP_{large}$ provides better performance in distinguishing different pockets bound to the same ligands and cofactors (**Q4**), refer to the results of D5, D5.2, D6 and D6.2. Last but not least, $CoSP_{large}$ showed good potential for practical applications (**O5**) with 0.90 AUC score. In addition, we found that pocket direction plays a key role in extracting pocket features, which is helpful to indicate the location of the pocket cavity. As shown in Table. 3, the performance of pocket matching will be degraded if the directional feature n is removed.

Table 4. Virtual screening results on DUD-E.

	DUD-E				
	AUC-ROC ↑	0.5% RE ↑	1.0% RE ↑	2.0% RE ↑	5.0% RE ↑
Vina	0.716	9.139	7.321	5.881	4.444
RF-score	0.622	5.628	4.274	3.499	2.678
NNScore	0.584	4.166	2.980	2.460	1.891
Graph CNN	0.886	44.406	29.748	19.408	10.735
3DCNN	0.868	42.559	29. 654	19.363	10.710
DrugVQA	0.972	88.17	58.71	35.06	17.39
GanDTi	**0.997**	71.13	68.78	49.40	19.79
AttentionSiteDTI	0.971	101.74	59.92	35.07	16.74
CoSP$_{large}$	0.996	**111.764**	**78.426**	**55.535**	**22.318**

4.4 Downstream Task 3: Virtual Screening

Experimental Setup. Could the model distinguish molecules most likely to bind to the given pocket? We evaluate CoSP on the DUD-E [34] dataset which consists of 102 targets across different protein families. For each target, DUD-E provides 224 actives (positive examples) and 10,000 decoy ligands (negative examples) in average. The decoys were calculated by choosing them to be physically similar but topologically different from the actives. During finetuning, we use the same data splitting as GraphCNN [51], and report the AUC-ROC and ROC enrichment (RE) scores. Note that x%RE indicates the ratio of the true positive rate (TPR) to the false positive rate (FPR) at x% FPR value.

Baselines. We compare CoSP$_{large}$ with AutoDock Vina [53], RF-score [2], NNScore [14], 3DCNN [38], GraphCNN [51], DrugVQA [75], GanDTi [55], and AttentionSiteDTI [68]. AutoDock Vina is an commonly used open-source program for doing molecular docking. RF-score use random forest capture protein-ligand binding effects. Other methods use deeplearning models to learn the protein-ligand binding.

Results and Analysis. We present results in Table.4, and observe that: (1) Random forest and MLP-based RF-score and NNScore achieve competitive results to Vina, indicating the potential of machine learning in virtual screening. (2) Deeplearning-based Graph CNN, 3DCNN, DrugVQA, GanDTi, and Attention-SiteDTI significantly outperforms both RF-score and NNScore. (3) CoSP$_{large}$ achieves competitive AUC score and outperforms all baselines in RE scores. The improvement of CoSP$_{large}$ suggests that the model can effectively learn protein-ligand interactions from the pre-training data. (4) In addition, we select Top 1% ligands identified by the model as actives for the given pocket and use AutoDock Vina to validate the docking results. In Fig. 2, the visual results show that our model can identify high-affinity ligands, which is helpful for drug discovery.

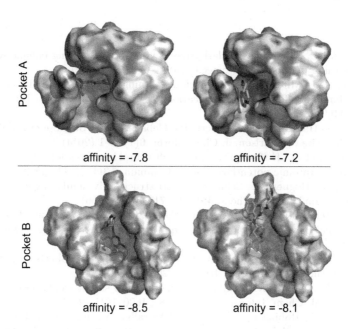

Fig. 2. Two examples of virtual screening. For each pocket, we choose two ligands that are Top 1% active molecules as identified by the model. We use AutoDock Vina to generate molecular binding pose and compute the affinity score.

5   Conclusion

This paper proposes a co-supervised pre-training framework to learn the joint pocket and ligand spaces via chemically inspired contrastive loss. The pre-trained model could achieve competitive results on molecule property predictions, pocket matching, and virtual screening. We hope the unified modeling framework could further advance the development of AI-guided drug discovery.

Acknowledgements. We thank the open-sourced codes of previous studies. This work was supported by the National Key R&D Program of China (Project 2022ZD0115100), the National Natural Science Foundation of China (Project U21A20427), the Research Center for Industries of the Future (Project WU2022C043).

Ethical Statement. Our submission does not involve any ethical issues, including but not limited to privacy, security, etc.

References

1. Altalib, M.K., Salim, N.: Similarity-based virtual screen using enhanced siamese deep learning methods. ACS omega **7**(6), 4769–4786 (2022)
2. Ballester, P.J., Mitchell, J.B.: A machine learning approach to predicting protein-ligand binding affinity with applications to molecular docking. Bioinformatics **26**(9), 1169–1175 (2010)
3. Batista, J., Hawkins, P.C., Tolbert, R., Geballe, M.T.: Sitehopper-a unique tool for binding site comparison. J. Cheminform. **6**(1), 1–1 (2014)
4. Batzner, S., et al.: E (3)-equivariant graph neural networks for data-efficient and accurate interatomic potentials. Nature Commun. **13**(1), 1–11 (2022)
5. Boström, J., Hogner, A., Schmitt, S.: Do structurally similar ligands bind in a similar fashion? J. Med. Chem. **49**(23), 6716–6725 (2006)
6. Brandstetter, J., Hesselink, R., van der Pol, E., Bekkers, E., Welling, M.: Geometric and physical quantities improve e (3) equivariant message passing. arXiv preprint arXiv:2110.02905 (2021)
7. Chaffey, N.: Alberts, B., Johnson, A., Lewis, J., Raff, M., Roberts, K., Walter, P. Molecular Biology of the Cell. 4th edn. (2003)
8. Chartier, M., Najmanovich, R.: Detection of binding site molecular interaction field similarities. J. Chem. Inform. Model. **55**(8), 1600–1615 (2015)
9. Chuang, C.Y., Robinson, J., Lin, Y.C., Torralba, A., Jegelka, S.: Debiased contrastive learning. Adv. Neural Inform. Process. Syst. **33**, 8765–8775 (2020)
10. Cohen, T., Welling, M.: Group equivariant convolutional networks. In: International conference on machine learning, pp. 2990–2999. PMLR (2016)
11. Dankwah, K.O., Mohl, J.E., Begum, K., Leung, M.Y.: Understanding the binding of the same ligand to gpcrs of different families. In: 2021 IEEE International Conference on Bioinformatics and Biomedicine (BIBM), pp. 2494–2501 (2021). https://doi.org/10.1109/BIBM52615.2021.9669761
12. Desaphy, J., Azdimousa, K., Kellenberger, E., Rognan, D.: Comparison and drugability prediction of protein-ligand binding sites from pharmacophore-annotated cavity shapes (2012)
13. Desaphy, J., Raimbaud, E., Ducrot, P., Rognan, D.: Encoding protein-ligand interaction patterns in fingerprints and graphs. J. Chem. Inform. Model. **53**(3), 623–637 (2013)
14. Durrant, J.D., McCammon, J.A.: Nnscore: a neural-network-based scoring function for the characterization of protein- ligand complexes. J. Chem. Inform. Model. **50**(10), 1865–1871 (2010)
15. Ehrt, C., Brinkjost, T., Koch, O.: A benchmark driven guide to binding site comparison: an exhaustive evaluation using tailor-made data sets (prospeccts). PLoS Comput. Biol. **14**(11), e1006483 (2018)
16. Fang, X.: Geometry-enhanced molecular representation learning for property prediction. Nature Mach. Intell. **4**(2), 127–134 (2022)
17. Fang, Y., Yang, H., Zhuang, X., Shao, X., Fan, X., Chen, H.: Knowledge-aware contrastive molecular graph learning. arXiv preprint arXiv:2103.13047 (2021)
18. Francoeur, P.G.: Three-dimensional convolutional neural networks and a cross-docked data set for structure-based drug design. J. Chem. Inform. Model. **60**(9), 4200–4215 (2020)
19. Fuchs, F., Worrall, D., Fischer, V., Welling, M.: Se (3)-transformers: 3d roto-translation equivariant attention networks. Adv. Neural Inform. Process. Syst. **33**, 1970–1981 (2020)

20. Ganea, O.E., et al.: Independent se (3)-equivariant models for end-to-end rigid protein docking. arXiv preprint arXiv:2111.07786 (2021)
21. Gao, Z., Tan, C., Li, S., et al.: Alphadesign: A graph protein design method and benchmark on alphafolddb. arXiv preprint arXiv:2202.01079 (2022)
22. Guan, J., Qian, W.W., Ma, W.Y., Ma, J., Peng, J., et al.: Energy-inspired molecular conformation optimization. In: International Conference on Learning Representations (2021)
23. Hu, W., et al.: Strategies for pre-training graph neural networks. arXiv preprint arXiv:1905.12265 (2019)
24. Jing, B., Eismann, S., Suriana, P., Townshend, R.J., Dror, R.: Learning from protein structure with geometric vector perceptrons. arXiv preprint arXiv:2009.01411 (2020)
25. Kinnings, S.L., Liu, N., Buchmeier, N., Tonge, P.J., Xie, L., Bourne, P.E.: Drug discovery using chemical systems biology: repositioning the safe medicine comtan to treat multi-drug and extensively drug resistant tuberculosis. PLoS Comput. Biol. **5**(7), e1000423 (2009)
26. Konc, J., Janežič, D.: Probis algorithm for detection of structurally similar protein binding sites by local structural alignment. Bioinformatics **26**(9), 1160–1168 (2010)
27. Krotzky, T., Grunwald, C., Egerland, U., Klebe, G.: Large-scale mining for similar protein binding pockets: with RAPMAD retrieval on the fly becomes real. J. Chem. Inform. Model. **55**(1), 165–179 (2015)
28. Landrum, G.: Rdkit: Open-source cheminformatics software (2016). https://github.com/rdkit/rdkit/releases/tag/Release_2016_09_4
29. Li, P., et al.: An effective self-supervised framework for learning expressive molecular global representations to drug discovery. Brief. Bioinform. **22**(6), bbab109 (2021)
30. Liu, S., Demirel, M.F., Liang, Y.: N-gram graph: simple unsupervised representation for graphs, with applications to molecules. Adv. Neural Inform. Process. Syst. **32** (2019)
31. Liu, S., Wang, H., Liu, W., Lasenby, J., Guo, H., Tang, J.: Pre-training molecular graph representation with 3D geometry-rethinking self-supervised learning on structured data
32. Liu, S., Wang, H., Liu, W., Lasenby, J., Guo, H., Tang, J.: Pre-training molecular graph representation with 3D geometry. arXiv preprint arXiv:2110.07728 (2021)
33. Lu, A.X., Zhang, H., Ghassemi, M., Moses, A.: Self-supervised contrastive learning of protein representations by mutual information maximization. BioRxiv (2020)
34. Mysinger, M.M., Carchia, M., Irwin, J.J., Shoichet, B.K.: Directory of useful decoys, enhanced (dud-e): better ligands and decoys for better benchmarking. J. Med. Chem. **55**(14), 6582–6594 (2012)
35. Nguyen, T., Le, H., Quinn, T.P., Nguyen, T., Le, T.D., Venkatesh, S.: Graphdta: predicting drug-target binding affinity with graph neural networks. Bioinformatics **37**(8), 1140–1147 (2021)
36. Oord, A.v.d., Li, Y., Vinyals, O.: Representation learning with contrastive predictive coding. arXiv preprint arXiv:1807.03748 (2018)
37. Pu, L., Govindaraj, R.G., Lemoine, J.M., Wu, H.C., Brylinski, M.: Deepdrug3d: classification of ligand-binding pockets in proteins with a convolutional neural network. PLoS Comput. Biol. **15**(2), e1006718 (2019)
38. Ragoza, M., Hochuli, J., Idrobo, E., Sunseri, J., Koes, D.R.: Protein-ligand scoring with convolutional neural networks. J. Chem. Inform. Model. **57**(4), 942–957 (2017)
39. Robinson, J., Chuang, C.Y., Sra, S., Jegelka, S.: Contrastive learning with hard negative samples. arXiv preprint arXiv:2010.04592 (2020)

40. Rong, Y.: Self-supervised graph transformer on large-scale molecular data. Adv. Neural Inform. Process. Syst. **33**, 12559–12571 (2020)
41. Satorras, V.G., Hoogeboom, E., Welling, M.: E (n) equivariant graph neural networks. In: International Conference on Machine Learning, pp. 9323–9332. PMLR (2021)
42. Schalon, C., Surgand, J.S., Kellenberger, E., Rognan, D.: A simple and fuzzy method to align and compare druggable ligand-binding sites. Proteins: Struct., Funct., Bioinform. **71**(4), 1755–1778 (2008)
43. Schmitt, S., Kuhn, D., Klebe, G.: A new method to detect related function among proteins independent of sequence and fold homology. J. Mol. Biol. **323**(2), 387–406 (2002)
44. Shrivastava, A.D., Kell, D.B.: Fragnet, a contrastive learning-based transformer model for clustering, interpreting, visualizing, and navigating chemical space. Molecules **26**(7), 2065 (2021)
45. Shulman-Peleg, A., Nussinov, R., Wolfson, H.J.: Siteengines: recognition and comparison of binding sites and protein-protein interfaces. Nucleic Acids Res. **33**(suppl_2), W337–W341 (2005)
46. Simonovsky, M., Meyers, J., Meyers, J.: Deeplytough: learning structural comparison of protein binding sites. J. Chem. Inform. Model. **60**(4), 2356–2366 (2020)
47. Stärk, H., et al.: 3d infomax improves GNNs for molecular property prediction. arXiv preprint arXiv:2110.04126 (2021)
48. Sturmfels, P., Vig, J., Madani, A., Rajani, N.F.: Profile prediction: An alignment-based pre-training task for protein sequence models. arXiv preprint arXiv:2012.00195 (2020)
49. Sun, M., Xing, J., Wang, H., Chen, B., Zhou, J.: Mocl: data-driven molecular fingerprint via knowledge-aware contrastive learning from molecular graph. In: Proceedings of the 27th ACM SIGKDD Conference on Knowledge Discovery & Data Mining, pp. 3585–3594 (2021)
50. Thomas, N., Smidt, T., Kearnes, S., Yang, L., Li, L., Kohlhoff, K., Riley, P.: Tensor field networks: Rotation-and translation-equivariant neural networks for 3D point clouds. arXiv preprint arXiv:1802.08219 (2018)
51. Torng, W., Altman, R.B.: Graph convolutional neural networks for predicting drug-target interactions. J. Chem. Inform. Model. **59**(10), 4131–4149 (2019)
52. Tosco, P., Stiefl, N., Landrum, G.: Bringing the MMFF force field to the RDKit: implementation and validation. J. Cheminform. **6**(1), 1–4 (2014)
53. Vina, A.: Improving the speed and accuracy of docking with a new scoring function, efficient optimization, and multithreading trott, oleg; olson, arthur j. J. Comput. Chem **31**(2), 455–461 (2010)
54. Wang, R., Fang, X., Lu, Y., Yang, C.Y., Wang, S.: The pdbbind database: methodologies and updates. J. Med. Chem. **48**(12), 4111–4119 (2005)
55. Wang, S., Shan, P., Zhao, Y., Zuo, L.: Gandti: a multi-task neural network for drug-target interaction prediction. Comput. Biol. Chem. **92**, 107476 (2021)
56. Wang, Y., Wang, J., Cao, Z., Barati Farimani, A.: Molecular contrastive learning of representations via graph neural networks. Nature Mach. Intell. **4**(3), 279–287 (2022)
57. Weber, A., et al.: Unexpected nanomolar inhibition of carbonic anhydrase by cox-2-selective celecoxib: new pharmacological opportunities due to related binding site recognition. J. Med. Chem. **47**(3), 550–557 (2004)
58. Weill, N., Rognan, D.: Alignment-free ultra-high-throughput comparison of druggable protein- ligand binding sites. J. Chem. Inform. Model. **50**(1), 123–135 (2010)

59. Willmann, D., et al.: Impairment of prostate cancer cell growth by a selective and reversible lysine-specific demethylase 1 inhibitor. Int. J. Cancer **131**(11), 2704–2709 (2012)
60. Wood, D.J., Vlieg, J.d., Wagener, M., Ritschel, T.: Pharmacophore fingerprint-based approach to binding site subpocket similarity and its application to bioisostere replacement. J. Chem. Inform. Model. **52**(8), 2031–2043 (2012)
61. Wu, Z., et al.: Moleculenet: a benchmark for molecular machine learning. Chem. Sci. **9**(2), 513–530 (2018)
62. Xie, L., Bourne, P.E.: Detecting evolutionary relationships across existing fold space, using sequence order-independent profile-profile alignments. Proc. National Acad. Sci. **105**(14), 5441–5446 (2008)
63. Xiong, Z., et al.: Pushing the boundaries of molecular representation for drug discovery with the graph attention mechanism. J. Med. Chem. **63**(16), 8749–8760 (2019)
64. Yang, J., Roy, A., Zhang, Y.: Biolip: a semi-manually curated database for biologically relevant ligand-protein interactions. Nucleic Acids Res. **41**(D1), D1096–D1103 (2012)
65. Yang, K., et al.: Analyzing learned molecular representations for property prediction. J. Chem. Inform. Model. **59**(8), 3370–3388 (2019)
66. Yang, K.K., Lu, A.X., Fusi, N.: Convolutions are competitive with transformers for protein sequence pretraining. In: ICLR2022 Machine Learning for Drug Discovery (2022)
67. Yang, Y., et al.: Computational discovery and experimental verification of tyrosine kinase inhibitor pazopanib for the reversal of memory and cognitive deficits in rat model neurodegeneration. Chem. Sci. **6**(5), 2812–2821 (2015)
68. Yazdani-Jahromi, M., et al.: Attentionsitedti: an interpretable graph-based model for drug-target interaction prediction using NLP sentence-level relation classification. Brief. Bioinform. **23**(4), bbac272 (2022)
69. Yeturu, K., Chandra, N.: Pocketmatch: a new algorithm to compare binding sites in protein structures. BMC Bioinform. **9**(1), 1–17 (2008)
70. Zhang, N., et al.: Ontoprotein: Protein pretraining with gene ontology embedding. arXiv preprint arXiv:2201.11147 (2022)
71. Zhang, S., Hu, Z., Subramonian, A., Sun, Y.: Motif-driven contrastive learning of graph representations. arXiv preprint arXiv:2012.12533 (2020)
72. Zhang, Y., Skolnick, J.: Tm-align: a protein structure alignment algorithm based on the TM-score. Nucleic Acids Res. **33**(7), 2302–2309 (2005)
73. Zhang, Z., Liu, Q., Wang, H., Lu, C., Lee, C.K.: Motif-based graph self-supervised learning for molecular property prediction. Adv. Neural Inform. Process. Syst. **34**, 15870–15882 (2021)
74. Zhang, Z., et al.: Protein representation learning by geometric structure pretraining. arXiv preprint arXiv:2203.06125 (2022)
75. Zheng, S., Li, Y., Chen, S., Xu, J., Yang, Y.: Predicting drug-protein interaction using quasi-visual question answering system. Nature Mach. Intell. **2**(2), 134–140 (2020)
76. Zhou, G., et al.: Uni-mol: A universal 3d molecular representation learning framework (2022)

Decompose, Then Reconstruct:
A Framework of Network Structures
for Click-Through Rate Prediction

Jiaming Li[1], Lang Lang[2], Zhenlong Zhu[3], Haozhao Wang[1(✉)], Ruixuan Li[1(✉)], and Wenchao Xu[4]

[1] School of Computer Science and Technology, Huazhong University of Science and Technology, Wuhan, China
{jiamingli,hz_wang,rxli}@hust.edu.cn
[2] Bytedance Inc, Beijing, China
[3] Microsoft, Beijing, China
zhenlongzhu@microsoft.com
[4] The Hong Kong Polytechnic University, Hong Kong, China
wenchao.xu@polyu.edu.hk

Abstract. Feature interaction networks are crucial for click-through rate (CTR) prediction in many applications. Extensive studies have been conducted to boost CTR accuracy by constructing effective structures of models. However, the performance of feature interaction networks is greatly influenced by the prior assumptions made by the model designer regarding its structure. Furthermore, the structures of models are highly interdependent, and launching models in different scenarios can be arduous and time-consuming. To address these limitations, we introduce a novel framework called DTR, which redefines the CTR feature interaction paradigm from a new perspective, allowing for the decoupling of its structure. Specifically, DTR first decomposes these models into individual structures and then reconstructs them within a unified model structure space, consisting of three stages: Mask, Kernel, and Compression. Each stage of DTR's exploration of a range of structures is guided by the characteristics of the dataset or the scenario. Theoretically, we prove that the structure space of DTR not only incorporates a wide range of state-of-the-art models but also provides potentials to identify better models. Experiments on two public real-world datasets demonstrate the superiority of DTR, which outperforms state-of-the-art models.

Keywords: Recommendation · CTR prediction · Feature interaction

1 Introduction

Click-through rate (CTR) prediction is critical for various applications, including recommender systems, online advertising, and product search. Mainstream CTR prediction models utilize an embedding table to map high-dimensional categorical features (e.g. *user_id* and *item_id*) to low-dimensional dense real-valued

© The Author(s), under exclusive license to Springer Nature Switzerland AG 2023
D. Koutra et al. (Eds.): ECML PKDD 2023, LNAI 14169, pp. 422–437, 2023.
https://doi.org/10.1007/978-3-031-43412-9_25

vectors, and a feature interaction network to model interactions and make predictions. Research has focused on optimizing the feature interaction network to capture beneficial interactions and improve accuracy in CTR prediction.

Existing methods for capturing feature interactions can be divided into two categories: inner product and outer product. The inner product or Hadamard product refers to interact on the same elements of pairwise feature embedding vectors [4,6,10,12,14,16,23], relying on a prior assumption that the embedding of different features is in the same vector space. The outer product refer to interact all elements of pairwise feature embedding vectors [14,22] without any prior assumption. AOANet [7] unifies feature interaction operations by designing generalized interaction network (GIN).

However, the performance of feature interaction networks is heavily impacted by the model designer's prior assumptions, resulting in potential bias in different scenarios. If a scenario arises that contradicts the prior assumptions, the model's performance will deteriorate significantly. For instance, if the embedding vectors of different features are not located in the same vector space, the inner product or Hadamard product will perform poorly. It is recommended to let the scenario or dataset guide the selection of appropriate structures, rather than relying solely on prior assumptions. Furthermore, the highly interdependent nature of existing model structures makes it difficult to identify specific components responsible for observed performance and the process of launching models in different scenarios can be arduous and time-consuming. One example of such challenges is when comparing the performance of models such as DCN [21] and FwFM [12], as it is unclear which aspect of the model contributes to the difference in performance. Additionally, it is typically necessary to implement DCN and FwFM separately for different scenarios due to the high coupling.

To effectively tackle these challenges, it is imperative to redefine the CTR feature interaction paradigm from a new perspective that enables decoupling of its structure. Therefore, we propose DTR, a novel framework that not only accommodates the knowledge of prior model structures but also allows better models to be explored and identified from it. Specifically, DTR first decomposes these models into individual structures and then reconstructs them within a unified model structure space, consisting of three stages: Mask, Kernel, and Compression. The mask stage masks feature interaction information to indicate which parts of the information model pay attention to. The kernel stage extracts masked feature interaction information to determine the model's capacity and degrees of freedom, such as which dimensions should share information. The compression stage aims to compress extracted feature interaction information to balance effectiveness and efficiency. Each stage of DTR's exploration of a range of structures, including existing and additional structures, is guided by the characteristics of the dataset or scenario. Theoretically, we prove that the structure space of DTR not only incorporates a wide range of state-of-the-art models but also provides potentials to identify better models. Furthermore, to inherit benefits from the mixture of experts (MOE) [3,15,17] and Transformer [5, 19], we extend DTR from single channel to multiple channels to explore better models in multiple channels. Overall, DTR represents a unified model structure space that enables efficient exploration and identification of superior models. The main contributions are summarized as follows.

- We propose a novel framework called DTR, which redefines the CTR feature interaction paradigm from a new perspective, consisting of three stages: Mask, Kernel, and Compression. DTR can accommodate knowledge from existing approaches and provide potential for discovering better models.
- Theoretically, we prove that the structure space of DTR not only incorporates a wide range of state-of-the-art models but also provides potentials to identify better models.
- Experiments on two public real-world datasets for CTR prediction tasks demonstrate the superiority of DTR over state-of-the-art algorithms in terms of CTR prediction performance. In addition, ablation studies provide a deeper insight into the workings of different stages of the model and their impact on performance and other stages.

2   Related Work

In this section, we provide an overview of the related work in the literature. Existing methods for capturing feature interactions can be divided into two categories: inner product and outer product. The inner product or Hadamard product refers to the interaction of pairwise feature embedding vectors on the same elements. FM [16] is an early work in the field of recommendation, which introduces second-order feature interaction to solve the problem that logistic regression [13] cannot automatically extract the feature interaction information. Since FM only considers the second-order feature interaction, a series of improved methods based on FM specify operations have been proposed to extract the feature interaction information, such as AFM [23], FwFM [12], NFM [6], DeepFM [4] and IPNN [14]. Some of these works, such as AFM and FwFM, focus on the importance of distinguishing feature interactions. On the other hand, the outer product refers to the interaction of all elements of pairwise feature embedding vectors without any prior assumption, as in OPNN [14], DCN-V2 [22]. DCN-V2 represents a remarkable improvement over the DCN, as it eschews prior assumptions regarding both feature interaction and weight learning, resulting in a significant performance boost. AOANet [7] proposed a generalized interaction network (GIN) to overcome the limitations of artificially specified operations in feature interaction. However, as discussed in Sect. 1, existing models are designed by model designers based on prior assumptions. For instance, DCN-V2 and AOANet remove certain hypotheses from the model structure based on prior assumptions, rather than specific scenarios or datasets. This means that models may introduce biases in different scenarios and adversely impact performance.

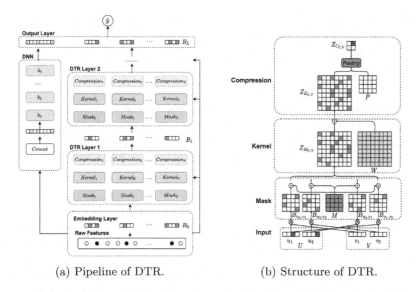

(a) Pipeline of DTR.   (b) Structure of DTR.

Fig. 1. Framework of DTR architecture. The left figure (a) shows the pipeline of DTR. Raw features are first fed into an embedding layer to compress them into low-dimensional feature vectors. Then, they are input in parallel to DNN and DTR to extract feature interaction information, which is finally used for prediction. The right figure (b) shows the structure of a single layer of DTR, consisting of the **Mask, Kernel**, and **Compression** stages. In the mask stage, the feature interaction matrix is first masked to retain only the relevant information. Next, the kernel stage interacts the masked feature interaction matrix with the weight matrix to extract feature interaction information. This is followed by the Compression stage which compresses the extracted feature information using pooling, for use as input to the next layer or for prediction.

3 Methodology

3.1 Framework of DTR Architecture

Overview. To establish a framework of existing model structures, we decompose the model architecture into three distinct stages, i.e., **Mask, Kernel**, and **Compression**, with an integrated DNN in parallel for extracting feature interaction information, as illustrated in Fig. 1(a). Specifically, as shown in Fig. 1(b), the mask stage first masks the matrix of the feature interaction information, and then the kernel stage extracts information from the masked feature interaction matrix, which is followed by the compression stage compressing the extracted feature information.

Embedding. Features of candidate items are usually sparse, discrete, and highly dimensional in industrial online recommendation scenarios, causing that the feature interaction information is hard to extract. To handle this challenge, existing model architectures usually adopt an embedding function $E(\cdot)$ to transform the input features x_i into continuous and low-dimensional vectors $a_i \in \mathbb{R}^d$:

$$a_i = E(x_i) = V_i \cdot x_i, \quad \forall i = 1, 2, \ldots, n, \tag{1}$$

where V_i denotes the embedding matrix. For clarity, we denote $X = \{x_1, x_2, ..., x_n\}$ by the integrated input features, and $A = \{a_1, a_2, ..., a_n\}$ by the matrix of embedding vectors of all input features. For simplicity, we use $A = E(X)$ to denote the embedding operation (1) in the following.

Mask. After obtaining the embedding vectors $A = \{a_1, a_2, ..., a_n\}$, the outer product is applied to any two vectors $a_i, a_j \in A$ to extract the feature interaction information $Z \in \mathbb{R}^{nd \times nd}$, as $Z_{(i-1)d+1:id,(j-1)d+1:jd} = a_i \otimes a_j$, where $\otimes$ denotes the outer product and $Z_{(i-1)d+1:id,(j-1)d+1:jd} \in \mathbb{R}^{d \times d}$ denotes the block in the i-th row and j-th column of Z. For clarity, we denote $Z_{(i-1)d+1:id,(j-1)d+1:jd}$ by B_{ij}. Considering that inappropriate interaction may even bring interventions between features, each block B of feature interaction matrix Z is further masked as

$$B_M = B \odot M, \tag{2}$$

where B_M denotes the masked result, and $\odot$ denotes the element-wise product of two matrixes. After the mask stage, Z is transformed into masked feature interaction matrix $Z_M \in \mathbb{R}^{nd \times nd}$.

Kernel. The kernel stage extracts information from the masked feature interaction matrix Z_M, indicating the capacity and degrees of freedom of the model. Inspired by the mixture of experts (MOE) [3,15,17] and Transformer [5,19], we build the framework of DTR with multiple channels to learn the extracted information in parallel. Specifically, we consider that there is C channels with kernel parameters matrix $W^c \in \mathbb{R}^{nd \times nd}$ to learn from the masked feature interaction matrix Z_M as

$$Z_k^c = Z_M \odot W^c, \quad \forall c = 1, 2, \cdots, C. \tag{3}$$

where $Z_k^c \in \mathbb{R}^{nd \times nd}$ denotes the result obtained from the c-th channel. Similarly, we use $Z_K = \{Z_k^1, Z_k^2, \ldots, Z_k^C\}$ to denote the result set consisting of Z_k^c from all channels.

Compression. Considering that the feature information obtained from the multi-channels kernel are highly-dimensional, we adopt the compression technology to reduce the size of the features for improving the efficiency of the model. Specifically, we leverage the pooling operation $\text{Pool}(\cdot)$ with the matrix P to make compression, as:

$$Z_C = \text{Pool}(Z_K, P), \tag{4}$$

where Z_C denotes the obtained matrix after the compression stage P denotes the shape of the submatrix of Z_K which is aggregated to one scalar element in Z_C. It is worthwhile to note that the size of P is adaptively determined in the learning process. Finally, the feature interaction compression matrix Z_C is flattened and delivered to the fully connected layer for CTR prediction.

Deep Network. Like previous studies, we adopt fully connected network to extract implicit interaction information:

$$H_l = \sigma(W_l H_{l-1} + b_l), \tag{5}$$

where H_l is output of lth layer, $\sigma(\cdot)$ is activation function which is RELU in our model, W_l and b_l are weights and bias of lth respectively.

Table 1. Connection between DTR and related models. n denotes the number of features, d denotes the size of the embedding vector. Mask matrix $M \in \mathbb{R}^{d\times d}$ is a zero-one matrix, where $m_{i,j}$ denotes the element in i-th row and j-th column, $\forall i \forall j \in [d]$. All models using $\sum$ (sum compression) in CM. **Note:** Kernel weight sharing description can be seen in Appendix.

Model	Mask matrix	Kernel weight sharing	Compression matrix
IPNN	$M = \{m_{ij} = 1 | \forall i \forall j, i = j\}$	Intra-block Sharing	$P \in \mathbb{R}^{d\times d}, Z_{C_{i,j}} = \sum_{p=i}^{i+d}\sum_{q=j}^{j+d} Z_{K_{p,q}}, \forall i \forall j \in [n]$
OPNN	$M = \{m_{ij} = 1 | \forall i \forall j\}$	Intra-block Sharing	$P \in \mathbb{R}^{d\times d}, Z_{C_{i,j}} = \sum_{p=i}^{i+d}\sum_{q=j}^{j+d} Z_{K_{p,q}}, \forall i \forall j \in [n]$
FwFM	$M = \{m_{ij} = 1 | \forall i \forall j, i = j\}$	Intra-block Sharing	$P \in \mathbb{R}^{d\times d}, Z_{C_{i,j}} = \sum_{p=i}^{i+d}\sum_{q=j}^{j+d} Z_{K_{p,q}}, \forall i \forall j \in [n]$
AFM	$M = \{m_{ij} = 1 | \forall i \forall j, i = j\}$	Non-linear Intra-block Sharing	$P \in \mathbb{R}^{d\times d}, Z_{C_{i,j}} = \sum_{p=i}^{i+d}\sum_{q=j}^{j+d} Z_{K_{p,q}}, \forall i \forall j \in [n]$
DCN	$M = \{m_{ij} = 1 | \forall i \forall j, i = j\}$	Row Sharing	$P \in \mathbb{R}^{1\times nd}, Z_{C_i} = \sum_{j=1}^{nd} Z_{K_{i,j}}, \forall i \in [nd]$
DCN-V2	$M = \{m_{ij} = 1 | \forall i \forall j\}$	No Sharing	$P \in \mathbb{R}^{1\times nd}, Z_{C_i} = \sum_{j=1}^{nd} Z_{K_{i,j}}, \forall i \in [nd]$
xDeepFM	$M = \{m_{ij} = 1 | \forall i \forall j\}$	Intra-block Sharing	$P \in \mathbb{R}^{n\times n}, Z_{C_{i,j}} = \sum_{p=1}^{n}\sum_{q=1}^{n} Z_{K_{i+pd,j+pd}}, \forall i \forall j \in [d]$
AOANet	$M = \{m_{ij} = 1 | \forall i \forall j\}$	Intra-block Sharing & Block Element Sharing	$P \in \mathbb{R}^{nn\times d}, Z_{C_i} = \sum_{p=1}^{n}\sum_{q=1}^{nd} Z_{K_{i+pd,q}}, \forall i \in [d]$

3.2 Model Analysis

We dive into connections between DTR and related models, as shown in Table 1. Theoretically, we show that DTR can be equal to extensive known CTR feature interaction networks. Due to space constraints, we analyze xDeepFM, IPNN&OPNN here, and defer other model analyses to the Appendix[1]. For Pool($\cdot$), all of the CTR feature interaction networks use $\sum$ (sum compression). Since multi-layer CTR feature interaction networks are constructed recursively with the same structure, for simplicity we propose analysis on the first layer.

---

[1] https://github.com/GeekRaw/Decompose-Then-Reconstruct-A-Framework-of-Network-Structures-for-Click-Through-Rate-Prediction.

xDeepFM. The first layer of xDeepFM is given by:

$$X^1 = \sum_{i,j} w_{i,j}^s (X_0^{j,*} \odot X_0^{i,*}) = \sum_{i,j} w_{i,j}^s (e^i \odot e^j), \tag{6}$$

where X^1 denotes the first layer output, s is a hyper-parameter that represents the number of feature vectors. w^s is the weight matrix for s-th feature vector. The main connection lies in the number of feature vectors, where one feature vector corresponds to one channel of DTR.

Theorem 1. *The structure of DTR is equivalent to xDeepFM when its mask matrix* $M = \{m_{ij} = 1 | \forall i \forall j, i = j\}$, *kernel weight matrix* $W = \{w_{ij} | \forall i \forall j, w_{i,j} = w_{\lfloor i/d \rfloor, \lfloor j/d \rfloor}\}$, *and compression matrix* $P \in \mathbb{R}^{n \times n}, Z_{C_{i,j}} = \sum_{p=1}^{n} \sum_{q=1}^{n} Z_{K_{i+pd,j+pd}}, \forall i,j \in [d]$.

Proof. Interaction of p-th and q-th feature vector in the first layer of DTR is given by $B^{p,q} = e^p \otimes e^q$. Give mask matrix $M = \{m_{ij} = 1 | \forall i \forall j, i = j\}$, we have

$$B_M^{p,q} = B^{p,q} \odot M = diag(e_1^p e_1^q, e_2^p e_2^q, \dots, e_d^p e_d^q). \tag{7}$$

Denote $W[p,q] \in \mathbb{R}^{d \times d}$ by a submatrix of W which equals to $B_M^{p,q}$. Considering that $\forall i, \forall j, w_{i,j} = w_{\lfloor i/d \rfloor, \lfloor j/d \rfloor}$, we conclude that each element in $W[p,q]$ shares the same value denoted as $w_{p,q}$. Thereby, we have

$$Z_K = W[p,q] \odot B_M^{p,q} = [W[p,q]]_{d \times d} \odot B_M^{p,q} = w_{p,q} B_M^{p,q}. \tag{8}$$

Given $P \in \mathbb{R}^{n \times n}, Z_{C_{i,j}} = \sum_{p=1}^{n} \sum_{q=1}^{n} Z_{K_{i+pd,j+pd}}, \forall i,j \in [d]$, combining with (7) and (8), we have

$$Z_C^1 = \sum_{p,q} w_{p,q} diag(e_1^p e_1^q, e_2^p e_2^q, \dots, e_d^p e_d^q). \tag{9}$$

Noting that

$$e^p \odot e^q = [e_1^p e_1^q, e_2^p e_2^q, \dots, e_d^p e_d^q], \tag{10}$$

we can derive that

$$X^1 = Z_C^1 [1, \dots, 1]^T, \tag{11}$$

which completes the proof.

IPNN & OPNN. The first layer of IPNN is given by:

$$X^1 = \boldsymbol{W}_p^n \odot \boldsymbol{p} = \sum_{i=1}^{n} \sum_{j=1}^{n} \langle \boldsymbol{\theta}_n^i, \boldsymbol{\theta}_n^j \rangle \langle \boldsymbol{f}_i, \boldsymbol{f}_j \rangle = \sum_{i=1}^{n} \sum_{j=1}^{n} (\theta_i^n \odot \theta_j^n)(e_i \odot e_j), \tag{12}$$

where n denotes the number of field feature, $\theta_n^i, \theta_n^j \in \mathbb{R}^n$, $f_i, f_j \in \mathbb{R}^d$.

Theorem 2. *The structure of DTR is equivalent to IPNN when its mask matrix* $M = \{m_{ij} = 1|\forall i \forall j, i = j\}$, *kernel weight matrix* $W = \{w_{ij}|\forall i \forall j, w_{i,j} = w_{\lfloor i/d \rfloor, \lfloor j/d \rfloor}\}$, *and compression matrix* $P \in \mathbb{R}^{d \times d}, Z_{C_{i,j}} = \sum\limits_{p=i}^{i+d} \sum\limits_{q=j}^{j+d} Z_{K_{p,q}}, \forall i \forall j \in [n]$.

Proof. For the first layer of IPNN, denote $\theta_n^i, \theta_n^j \in \mathbb{R}^n$ as $w_{ij} \in \mathbb{R}^{n \times n}$, we can derive that

$$X^1 = \sum_{i=1}^n \sum_{j=1}^n w_{ij}(e_i \odot e_j), \tag{13}$$

Interaction of p-th and q-th feature vector in the first layer of DTR is given by $B^{p,q} = e^p \otimes e^q$. Give mask matrix $M = \{m_{ij} = 1|\forall i \forall j, i = j\}$, we have

$$B_M^{p,q} = B^{p,q} \odot M = diag(e_1^p e_1^q, e_2^p e_2^q, \ldots, e_d^p e_d^q). \tag{14}$$

Denote $W[p,q] \in \mathbb{R}^{d \times d}$ by a submatrix of W which equals to $B_M^{p,q}$. Considering that $\forall i, \forall j, w_{i,j} = w_{\lfloor i/d \rfloor, \lfloor j/d \rfloor}$, we conclude that each element in $W[p,q]$ shares the same value denoted as $w_{p,q}$. Thereby, we have

$$Z_K = W[p,q] \odot B_M^{p,q} = [W[p,q]]_{d \times d} \odot B_M^{p,q} = w_{p,q} B_M^{p,q}. \tag{15}$$

Given $P \in \mathbb{R}^{d \times d}, Z_{C_{i,j}} = \sum\limits_{p=i}^{i+d} \sum\limits_{q=j}^{j+d} Z_{K_{p,q}}, \forall i \forall j \in [n]$, combining with (14) and (15), we have

$$Z_C^1 = \sum_{p,q} w_{p,q} diag(e_1^p e_1^q, e_2^p e_2^q, \ldots, e_d^p e_d^q). \tag{16}$$

Noting that

$$e^p \odot e^q = [e_1^p e_1^q, e_2^p e_2^q, \ldots, e_d^p e_d^q], \tag{17}$$

we can derive that

$$X^1 = Z_C^1[1, \ldots, 1]^T, \tag{18}$$

which completes the proof.

OPNN has the same kernel and compression structure as IPNN except that the mask structure is different from IPNN.

4 Evaluations

In this section, we conduct experiments on two public datasets to verify the effectiveness of the model in a real-world application environment. We aim to answer the following questions:

– RQ1: How does our proposed model perform as compared to the state-of-the-art methods?
– RQ2: How do different structures and settings influence the performance?

4.1   Evaluation Setup

Datasets. We conduct offline experiments on two real-world dataset: Criteo[2] and Avazu[3].

- **Criteo** dataset consists of user click data for displayed ads over a period of 7 d, which contains 13 numeric fields and 26 categorical fields. To process the numeric features, we apply a discretization function, which maps each value x to $\lfloor log^2(x) \rfloor$ if $x > 2$, and $x = 1$ otherwise. For the categorical features, we replace any feature that appears less than 10 times with a default "OOV" token.
- **Avazu** dataset contains mobile advertising data that spans a period of 10 d, and includes 22 feature fields that describe both user characteristics and advertisement attributes. We extract three new fields from the timestamp field: hour, weekday, and is_weekend. In addition, we handle categorical features that appear less than twice by replacing them with a default "OOV" token.

We randomly split each dataset into 80/10/10% train-test-validation splits. Criteo_x4 and Avazu_x4 dataset are used in experiments, and data preprocessing refers to FuxiCTR [25].

Table 2. Mask structure w.r.t. mask matrix. d denotes the size of the embedding vector. Mask $M \in \mathbb{R}^{d \times d}$ is a zero-one matrix, where $m_{i,j}$ denotes the element in i-th row and j-th column, $\forall i \forall j \in [d]$. M_5 denotes random mask according to r, which indicates the random mask ratio (RMR). $r = 0$ indicates all-one matrix, $r = 1$ indicates all-zero matrix.

Mask Structure	Mask Matrix	Mask Structure	Mask Matrix
M_0	$\{m_{ij} = 1\}$	M_1	$\{m_{ij} = 1 \mid i \leq j\}$
M_2	$\{m_{ij} = 1 \mid i \geq j\}$	M_3	$\{m_{ij} = 1 \mid i \neq j\}$
M_4	$\{m_{ij} = 1 \mid i + j - 1 \neq d\}$	M_6	$\{m_{ij} = 1 \mid i = j\}$

Baselines. We compared our model with eight feature interaction networks commonly used in the industry, including IPNN [14], OPNN [14], FwFM [12], AFM [23], DCN [21], DCN-V2 [22], xDeepFM [10], and AOANet [7]. Results of some models such as FmFM [18], AFN+ [2] and InterHAT [9] are not presented in this paper, because more recent models like xDeepFM [10] and DCN-V2 [22] have outperformed these methods significantly as experiments in BARS [24] shows.

Metrics. We use two widely-used metrics, Logloss and AUC, to evaluate the performance of all models. Notably, for CTR prediction task, a **0.001-level**

---

[2] https://www.kaggle.com/competitions/criteo-display-ad-challenge.
[3] https://www.kaggle.com/c/avazu-ctr-prediction.

Table 3. Kernel structure w.r.t. kernel weight sharing. Their constraints can be found in Appendix.

Kernel Struc	Sharing Type of Kernel Weight	Kernel Struc	Sharing Type of Kernel Weight
K_0	Full	K_1	No
K_2	Row	K_3	Intra-block
K_4	Block Row	K_5	Intra-block Element
K_6	Intra-block Dimension	K_7	Non-linear
K_8	Intra-block & Intra-block Element		

Table 4. Compression structure w.r.t. matrix. n denotes the number of features. d denotes the size of embedding vector.

Compression Struc	Compression Matrix
P_0	$P \in \mathbb{R}^{1 \times 1}, Z_C = \sum\limits_{p=1}^{nd} \sum\limits_{p=1}^{nd} Z_{K_{p,q}}$
P_1	$P \in \mathbb{R}^{nd \times nd}, Z_{C_{i,j}} = Z_{K_{i,j}}, \forall i \forall j \in [nd]$
P_2	$P \in \mathbb{R}^{1 \times nd}, Z_{C_i} = \sum\limits_{j=1}^{nd} Z_{K_{i,j}}, \forall i \in [nd]$
P_3	$P \in \mathbb{R}^{d \times d}, Z_{C_{i,j}} = \sum\limits_{p=i}^{i+d} \sum\limits_{q=j}^{j+d} Z_{K_{p,q}}, \forall i \forall j \in [n]$
P_4	$P \in \mathbb{R}^{nd \times d}, Z_{C_i} = \sum\limits_{p=1}^{nd} \sum\limits_{q=1}^{d} Z_{K_{p,q}}, \forall i \in [n]$
P_5	$P \in \mathbb{R}^{1 \times d}, Z_{C_i} = \sum\limits_{j=1}^{d} Z_{K_{i,j}}, \forall i \in [nd], \forall j \in [n]$
P_6	$P \in \mathbb{R}^{n \times n}, Z_{C_{i,j}} = \sum\limits_{p=1}^{n} \sum\limits_{q=1}^{n} Z_{K_{i+pd,j+pd}}, \forall i \forall j \in [d]$
P_7	$P \in \mathbb{R}^{nn \times d}, Z_{C_i} = \sum\limits_{p=1}^{n} \sum\limits_{q=1}^{nd} Z_{K_{i+pd,q}}, \forall i \in [d]$

improvement is considered significant, as has been pointed out in existing literature [4,21,22].

Model Settings. The structures of DTR are shown in Table 2, Table 3, Table 4. In addition, the compression method includes three types: S_0, S_1, and S_2. S_0 corresponds to the operation of maximum compression, S_1 corresponds to average compression, and S_2 adopts accumulation compression. It is worth noting that, in order to better explore the space of model architectures, we have developed novel structures that have not been previously identified by existing models. This approach enables us to more thoroughly investigate the design space and potentially discover more effective models that were previously undiscovered.

Parameter Setting. For fair comparison, we set the same embedding size, batch size, and optimizer for all models, which are 8, 8192, and Adam Optimizer respectively. Specifically, for each dataset of different scenarios, such as Criteo and Avazu, we utilize the Block Coordinate Descent (BCD) [1,20] method in

Table 5. Model structure settings. r denotes the random mask ratio. C denotes the number of channels.

Model	Mask structure	Kernel structure	Compression structure
IPNN	M_6	K_3	P_3, S_2
OPNN	M_0	K_3	P_3, S_2
FwFM	M_6	K_3	P_3, S_2
AFM	M_6	K_7	P_3, S_2
DCN	M_6	K_2	P_2, S_2
DCN-V2	M_0	K_1	P_2, S_2
xDeepFM	M_6	K_3	P_6, S_2
AOANet	M_0	K_8	P_7, S_2
DTR_{Criteo}	$M_5, r = 0.1$	$K_1, C = 1$	P_3, S_2
DTR_{Avazu}	$M_5, r = 0.4$	$K_1, C = 2$	P_3, S_2

combination with Beam Search [8,11] to search for the optimal structure of DTR in the scenario. Moreover, we use the DTR framework to reproduce each model, as Table 5 shows. The deep component also keeps the same for all models. The numbers of hidden units for each layer are $[400, 400, 400]$ from bottom to top respectively. For other models, we take the optimal settings from original papers. We conducted three rounds of repeated experiments for each model, and then recorded the average of metrics as the final results.

4.2   Performance Comparison (RQ1)

Table 6. Overall performance on Criteo and Avazu dataset. (Logloss $\times 10^{-2}$)

Dataset	Metrics	Model									Improv.
		IPNN	OPNN	FwFM	AFM	DCN	DCN-V2	xDeepFM	AOANet	DTR	
Criteo	LogLoss	44.59	45.09	44.60	44,59	44.69	<u>44.31</u>	44.51	44.45	**44.13**	−0.18
	AUC(%)	80.57	80.02	80.56	80.56	80.46	<u>80.83</u>	80.65	80.73	**81.07**	+0.24
Avazu	LogLoss	37.79	38.14	37.76	37.79	37.80	<u>37.68</u>	37.77	37.73	**37.54**	−0.14
	AUC(%)	78.33	77.73	78.38	78.32	78.30	<u>78.51</u>	78.35	78.41	**78.75**	+0.24

In this section, we discuss the experimental results demonstrated in Table 6. The results demonstrate that DTR outperforms all baselines on Criteo and Avazu two datasets. In particular, compared to the current SOTA model DCN-V2, DTR achieves a Logloss reduction of 0.18×10^{-2} and AUC improvement of 0.24% on the Criteo dataset, as well as a Logloss reduction of 0.14×10^{-2} and AUC improvement of 0.24% on the Avazu dataset. This demonstrates that DTR can not only implement extensive known CTR feature interaction networks, but also discover the optimal structure for different stages, which identifies some novel models that have not been proposed yet.

In addition, there are also some other interesting observations. We find that the mask, kernel, and compression structures are not independent, but rather exhibit a degree of coupling, and that a local optimal structure at any stage may not be optimal for the entire framework. OPNN has the worst performance among all models, and the mask structure uses M_0, but DCN-V2 and AOANet have good performance, which also use M_0. Another observation is that the performance of AFM ties with FwFM in both datasets. From the perspective of the DTR framework, the difference between FwFM and AFM lies in the difference in the kernel structure. FwFM adopts an intra-block weight sharing structure, while AFM learns the block importance through a shared MLP called attention network on this basis. It is not critical to establish the connection kennel between feature interaction terms and their significant coefficients. Furthermore, The model performance is closely related to the setting of the kernel structure. The sharing type of kernel weight greatly affects the performance of the model, such as DTR ($r = 0$) and OPNN. The biggest difference lies in the kernel structure. There is a huge gap in its performance, with an improvement of 1.05% on Criteo dataset and 1.02% on the Avazu dataset in terms of AUC.

4.3   Ablation Study (RQ2)

We conducted several ablation experiments to investigate the effectiveness of each stage in the DTR framework. During the ablation experiments, we set other parameters as initial settings to reduce interference and better explore the performance of each structure of DTR.

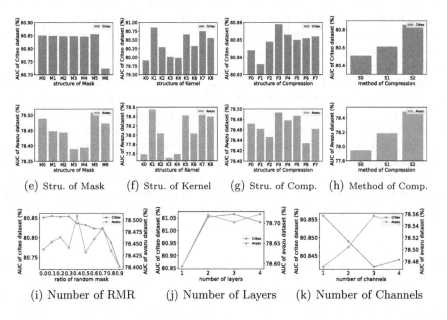

Fig. 2. Ablation study of model setting on the performance of AUC.

Structure of Mask. Table 2 presents the mask structures used in our experiments, and the results are shown in Fig. 2(e). For the random mask structure M_5, we experiment with different ratios and selected the final optimal result for M_5. The experimental results for various random mask ratios are shown in Fig. 2(i). The results indicate that, except M_0 and M_5 without any assumptions, have relatively good and stable performance on both datasets, while other mask structures vary significantly. Specifically, M_6 performs poorly in the Criteo dataset but performs well in Avazu. This reinforces our previous statement that prior assumptions regarding the model structure can significantly impact performance in different scenarios. Additionally, this further highlights the importance of the DTR framework, which can optimize the mask structure for each CTR prediction task to achieve optimal performance. Among all mask structures, M_5 performs the optimal in both datasets. Moreover, Fig. 2(i) indicates that the optimal random mask ratios are 10% and 40% for the Criteo and Avazu datasets, respectively. These results suggest that there exists some redundancy in the feature interaction information and that appropriate random mask can improve the performance. However, excessive masking can significantly affect the expression of feature interaction information, resulting in performance degradation.

Structure of Kernel. The descriptions of kernel structures are shown in Table 3, and the experimental results are presented in Fig. 2(f). Among all kernel structures, the optimal kernel structure is K_1, indicating that the interaction between any dimension of any feature embedding vector in the feature interaction matrix is different, and that the kernel structure achieves optimal performance without any assumptions. Furthermore, the size of the kernel weight matrix may also affect the performance. For K_0, the entire feature interaction matrix shares the same weight, resulting in the worst performance. On the other hand, K_1 does not share the weight of the feature interaction matrix, which leads to the most weight learned and optimal performance achieved. It is worth noting that different kernel weight sharing structures have a significant impact on performance. For instance, even though K_3 learns much more weight than K_5 and K_6, its performance is far worse than K_5 and K_6 due to the different weight sharing of structures. Specifically, K_3 uses the same weight for each block, while K_5 and K_6 adopt the same weight for all blocks of the same element and dimension, respectively. Consequently, different feature interaction information between different dimensions of feature embedding vectors and small interaction difference between different feature embedding vectors result. Overall, this experiment highlights the importance of selecting the appropriate kernel weight sharing structure for achieving optimal performance.

Structure of Compression. Table 4 describes the compression structures used in the experiment, while the experimental results are presented in Fig. 2(g).

The results demonstrate that P_3, which uses intra-block compression, achieves the optimal performance in both datasets. This suggests that information of the same feature interaction block can more effectively express the entire feature interaction matrix information. Furthermore, P_1 adopts full compression and has the worst performance, followed by P_0 which does not compress to any level and retains the entire matrix. Therefore, it is crucial to use an appropriate compression structure when compressing the feature interaction matrix.

Moreover, we explored a novel question that previous research has not addressed: which compression method works better. Figure 2(h) presents the experimental results. Interestingly, the sum compression method, which is commonly used, achieves the optimal performance. It is noteworthy that the sum compression method is a scalar multiple of the average compression method, with the scalar value equal to the length of the pairwise feature embedding vectors product. However, the average compression method performs much worse than the sum compression method, which may be due to the fact that it reduces the amount of feature interaction term information and the difference between different feature interaction terms, thus affecting the expression of the original feature interaction term information.

Number of Channels. Figure 2(k) shows that the optimal setting for C is 1 and 3 for Criteo and Avazu dataset, respectively. We can know that the large dataset contains more feature information, so the number of channels is relatively less important and does not necessarily boost performance. When working with a small dataset, increasing parallelism can lead to performance improvements.

Number of Layers. Figure 2(j) shows that the model performance promotes when L increases from 1 to 2. However, as L continues to increase, the performance improves slightly and even starts to decay. In addition, Table 5 shows the optimal setting of L does not exceed 3, which implies that feature interactions above third order may provide very little information for the sake that they are extremely sparse.

5   Conclusions

In this paper, we propose a unified framework called DTR that explores and optimizes the model structure for CTR prediction tasks. DTR decomposes these models into individual structures and then reconstructs them within a unified model structure space, consisting of three stages: Mask, Kernel, and Compression. Theoretically, we have demonstrated that the structure space of DTR not only incorporates a wide range of state-of-the-art models but also provides potentials to identify better models. Experimental results on two public real-world datasets confirm the superiority of DTR over state-of-the-art algorithms.

Acknowledgements. This work is supported by National Natural Science Foundation of China under grants 62206102, U1836204, U1936108, and Science and Technology Support Program of Hubei Province under grant 2022BAA046.

Ethical Statement. This research work on feature interaction networks and click-through rate (CTR) prediction was conducted with a focus on developing a novel framework for improving the accuracy of CTR prediction models. The research work was conducted with adherence to ethical principles and standards of research integrity. The research does not involve any human subjects or any sensitive data, and all the data are evaluated from the most mainstream public datasets in CTR prediction task, so no ethical approval is required. The research work was conducted with the aim of advancing the state-of-the-art in CTR prediction models, and the results of this study can have potential implications for businesses and industries that rely on CTR prediction models. The authors acknowledge the contributions of prior research in this area and have given appropriate credit to previous works. The authors have also disclosed any potential conflicts of interest related to this research work. The research work was conducted with transparency and openness, and has been peer-reviewed and vetted.

References

1. Birgin, E., Martínez, J.: Block coordinate descent for smooth nonconvex constrained minimization. Comput. Optim. Appl. **83**(1), 1–27 (2022)
2. Cheng, W., Shen, Y., Huang, L.: Adaptive factorization network: learning adaptive-order feature interactions. In: Proceedings of the AAAI Conference on Artificial Intelligence, vol. 34, pp. 3609–3616 (2020)
3. Du, N., et al.: GLaM: efficient scaling of language models with mixture-of-experts. In: International Conference on Machine Learning, pp. 5547–5569. PMLR (2022)
4. Guo, H., TANG, R., Ye, Y., Li, Z., He, X.: DeepFM: a factorization-machine based neural network for CTR prediction. In: Proceedings of the Twenty-Sixth International Joint Conference on Artificial Intelligence, IJCAI-17, pp. 1725–1731 (2017). https://doi.org/10.24963/ijcai.2017/239
5. Han, K., Xiao, A., Wu, E., Guo, J., Xu, C., Wang, Y.: Transformer in transformer. Adv. Neural. Inf. Process. Syst. **34**, 15908–15919 (2021)
6. He, X., Chua, T.S.: Neural factorization machines for sparse predictive analytics. In: Proceedings of the 40th International ACM SIGIR conference on Research and Development in Information Retrieval, pp. 355–364 (2017)
7. Lang, L., Zhu, Z., Liu, X., Zhao, J., Xu, J., Shan, M.: Architecture and operation adaptive network for online recommendations. In: Proceedings of the 27th ACM SIGKDD Conference on Knowledge Discovery & Data Mining, pp. 3139–3149 (2021)
8. Lemons, S., López, C.L., Holte, R.C., Ruml, W.: Beam search: faster and monotonic. In: Proceedings of the International Conference on Automated Planning and Scheduling, vol. 32, pp. 222–230 (2022)
9. Li, Z., Cheng, W., Chen, Y., Chen, H., Wang, W.: Interpretable click-through rate prediction through hierarchical attention. In: Proceedings of the 13th International Conference on Web Search and Data Mining, pp. 313–321 (2020)
10. Lian, J., Zhou, X., Zhang, F., Chen, Z., Xie, X., Sun, G.: xDeepFM: combining explicit and implicit feature interactions for recommender systems. In: Proceedings of the 24th ACM SIGKDD International Conference on Knowledge Discovery & Data Mining, pp. 1754–1763 (2018)

11. Libralesso, L., Focke, P.A., Secardin, A., Jost, V.: Iterative beam search algorithms for the permutation flowshop. Eur. J. Oper. Res. **301**(1), 217–234 (2022)
12. Pan, J., Xu, J., Ruiz, A.L., Zhao, W., Pan, S., Sun, Y., Lu, Q.: Field-weighted factorization machines for click-through rate prediction in display advertising. In: Proceedings of the 2018 World Wide Web Conference, pp. 1349–1357 (2018)
13. Peng, C.Y.J., Lee, K.L., Ingersoll, G.M.: An introduction to logistic regression analysis and reporting. J. Educ. Res. **96**(1), 3–14 (2002)
14. Qu, Y., Cai, H., Ren, K., Zhang, W., Yu, Y., Wen, Y., Wang, J.: Product-based neural networks for user response prediction. In: 2016 IEEE 16th International Conference on Data Mining (ICDM), pp. 1149–1154. IEEE (2016)
15. Rajbhandari, S., et al.: DeepSpeed-MoE: advancing mixture-of-experts inference and training to power next-generation AI scale. In: International Conference on Machine Learning, pp. 18332–18346. PMLR (2022)
16. Rendle, S., Gantner, Z., Freudenthaler, C., Schmidt-Thieme, L.: Fast context-aware recommendations with factorization machines. In: Proceedings of the 34th International ACM SIGIR Conference on Research and Development in Information Retrieval, pp. 635–644 (2011)
17. Riquelme, C., et al.: Scaling vision with sparse mixture of experts. Adv. Neural. Inf. Process. Syst. **34**, 8583–8595 (2021)
18. Sun, Y., Pan, J., Zhang, A., Flores, A.: FM2: field-matrixed factorization machines for recommender systems. In: Proceedings of the Web Conference 2021, pp. 2828–2837 (2021)
19. Tay, Y., Dehghani, M., Bahri, D., Metzler, D.: Efficient transformers: a survey. ACM Comput. Surv. **55**(6), 1–28 (2022)
20. Tseng, P.: Convergence of a block coordinate descent method for nondifferentiable minimization. J. Optim. Theory Appl. **109**(3), 475 (2001)
21. Wang, R., Fu, B., Fu, G., Wang, M.: Deep & cross network for ad click predictions. In: Proceedings of the ADKDD'17, pp. 1–7 (2017)
22. Wang, R., Shivanna, R., Cheng, D., Jain, S., Lin, D., Hong, L., Chi, E.: DCN V2: improved deep & cross network and practical lessons for web-scale learning to rank systems. In: Proceedings of the web conference 2021, pp. 1785–1797 (2021)
23. Xiao, J., Ye, H., He, X., Zhang, H., Wu, F., Chua, T.S.: Attentional factorization machines: learning the weight of feature interactions via attention networks. In: Proceedings of the Twenty-Sixth International Joint Conference on Artificial Intelligence, IJCAI-17, pp. 3119–3125 (2017). https://doi.org/10.24963/ijcai.2017/435
24. Zhu, J., et al.: BARS: towards open benchmarking for recommender systems. In: The 45th International ACM SIGIR Conference on Research and Development in Information Retrieval (SIGIR'22) (2022)
25. Zhu, J., Liu, J., Yang, S., Zhang, Q., He, X.: Open benchmarking for click-through rate prediction. In: The 30th ACM International Conference on Information and Knowledge Management (CIKM'21), pp. 2759–2769 (2021)

DynaBench: A Benchmark Dataset for Learning Dynamical Systems from Low-Resolution Data

Andrzej Dulny$^{(\boxtimes)}$, Andreas Hotho , and Anna Krause

University of Würzburg, Würzburg, Germany
{dulny,andreas.hotho,anna.krause}@uni-wuerzburg.de

Abstract. Previous work on learning physical systems from data has focused on high-resolution grid-structured measurements. However, real-world knowledge of such systems (e.g. weather data) relies on sparsely scattered measuring stations. In this paper, we introduce a novel simulated benchmark dataset, DynaBench, for learning dynamical systems directly from sparsely scattered data without prior knowledge of the equations. The dataset focuses on predicting the evolution of a dynamical system from low-resolution, unstructured measurements. We simulate six different partial differential equations covering a variety of physical systems commonly used in the literature and evaluate several machine learning models, including traditional graph neural networks and point cloud processing models, with the task of predicting the evolution of the system. The proposed benchmark dataset is expected to advance the state of art as an out-of-the-box easy-to-use tool for evaluating models in a setting where only unstructured low-resolution observations are available. The benchmark is available at https://professor-x.de/dynabench.

Keywords: neuralPDE · dynamical systems · benchmark · dataset

1 Introduction

Dynamical systems, which are systems described by partial differential equations (PDEs), are ubiquitous in the natural world and play a crucial role in many areas of science and engineering. They are used in a variety of applications, including weather prediction [5], climate modeling [7], fluid dynamics [22], electromagnetic field simulations [33] and many more. Traditionally, these systems are simulated by numerically solving a set of PDEs that are theorized to describe the behavior of the system based on physical knowledge. An accurate modelling technique is crucial for ensuring accurate predictions and simulations in these applications. However, the equations used are often just an approximation of a much more complex reality, either due to the sheer complexity of a more accurate model which would be computationally infeasible or because the true equations are not known [27].

D. Koutra et al. (Eds.): ECML PKDD 2023, LNAI 14169, pp. 438–455, 2023.
https://doi.org/10.1007/978-3-031-43412-9_26

In recent years, several models have been proposed in the deep learning community, which address the problem of simulating physical systems by learning to predict dynamical systems directly from data, without knowing the equations a priori [6,11,18,25,31]. These types of approaches have a distinct advantage over classical numerical simulations, as they do not require estimating the parameters of the equations, such as the permeability of a medium or the propagation speed of a wave. To ensure that the proposed models and architectures perform and generalize well and to be able to draw a fair comparison between them, it is necessary to compare them in a common experimental setting. As there are very few real-world datasets readily available for this purpose, it is common practice to employ simulated data as a simplified but easy-to-use and available alternative to evaluate novel machine learning methods [1,4,11,19,35].

While some progress has been made towards creating a standardized benchmark [17,29,35] dataset of physical simulations, the previous work in this area mainly focuses on the task of reconstructing the forward operator of the numerical solver, for which the full computed solution on a high-resolution grid of the differential equation is needed as training data. This makes it difficult to assess the applicability of any approach evaluated this way on real data, where measurements are typically neither high resolution nor grid-based, but instead rely on a sparse network of measuring stations (cf. Figure 1).

To achieve greater fidelity to real-world conditions, we propose a novel benchmark dataset, DynaBench, that focuses on the challenging task of predicting the evolution of a dynamical system using a limited number of measurements that are arbitrarily distributed within the simulation domain. This more closely resembles a real-world setting and allows for a more accurate assessment of the applicability of different models to real-world data. The benchmark consists of simulations of six physical systems with different properties that are commonly

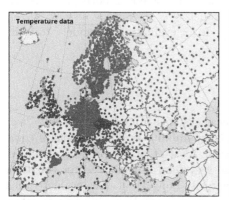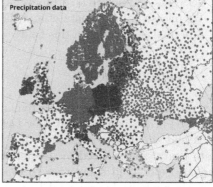

Fig. 1. Map of weather stations within the European Climate Assessment and Datasets (ECA&D) monitoring network for temperature and precipitation data [15]. Monitoring stations are not located on a grid but instead strategically placed based on a variety of factors such as topography, accessibility, and weather patterns.

used as synthetic data for learning dynamical systems. The simulations have been generated using a numerical solver. Our aim is not to cover all possible physical systems, parameters, and equations but rather to provide a good starting point to develop and compare machine learning models suited for this task. The selection we propose is a combination of typical equations used to evaluate deep learning models and equations with different properties (such as order of derivatives and number of variables) that complement them.

In addition, we present a detailed evaluation of various comparison models capable of learning functions on arbitrary geometries, including graph neural networks [14,18,21,37], point cloud neural networks [32,34,40], and continuous convolution models [36,39]. Our objective is to provide a set of strong baselines for further research, and thus facilitate the development and testing of new machine learning methods for predicting physical systems from unstructured low-resolution data. Our results show that the selected models are capable of providing accurate short-term predictions, but long-term forecasting remains an open challenge.

With the release of DynaBench, we hope to provide a valuable resource for the machine learning community, which will facilitate research and thus advance the state-of-the-art in learning dynamical systems from data on unstructured low-resolution observations.

The main contributions of our work can be summarized as follows.

1. We propose a new benchmark dataset for learning dynamical systems from data under the assumption that measurements are sparse and not structured on a grid.
2. We generate the dataset by simulating several differential equation systems typically used for the task of learning dynamical systems.
3. We thoroughly evaluate several models capable of learning functions on arbitrary geometries on the DynaBench dataset, including both graph neural networks and point-cloud processing models.
4. We release both the dataset and the code for evaluating all models, to facilitate further research in this field[1].

2   Related Work

Several approaches for learning dynamical systems from grid data have been proposed in recent years, but they lack comparability as different sets of equations and simulation parameters are used. Ayed et al. [4] propose a hidden-state neural solver-based model and use a system of shallow water equations and an Euler fluid simulation to evaluate it. Long et al. [26] evaluate their numeric-symbolic hybrid model on the Burgers' equation, diffusion equation and convection-diffusion equation with a reactive source. Dulny et al. [11] evaluate their neuralPDE Model based on neural solvers on several PDE systems, including advection-diffusion, Burgers' and wave equations. Li et al. [25] propose

---

[1] The benchmark is available at https://professor-x.de/dynabench.

a resolution invariant method based on the fourier transformation and test it on Burgers' equation, simplified Navier-Stokes system and steady-state darcy flow.

Similarly, authors proposing models for unstructured data (i.e. measurements not on a grid) also do not evaluate their models on a common set of systems. Karlbauer et al. [19] propose a graph-based recurrent model (Distana) to learn spatio-temporal processes and evaluate it on the wave propagation equation. Iakovlev et al. [18] use an advection-diffusion problem, as well as the heat equation and Burger's equation, to evaluate their graph message passing approach. Another approach proposed by Li et al. [24], the multipole graph neural operator, is evaluated on the steady state darcy flow, as well as the viscous variant of the Burgers' equation.

Recently, some progress has been made towards creating a standardized benchmark for learning PDEs from data. Huang et al. [17] proposed a dataset containing simulations of incompresible Navier-Stokes equations for fluid dynamics. While the main audience of the dataset is not the machine learning community, as its central purpose is to compare different discretization and solving schemes, the data could in theory still be used to train different models for learning the solutions from data. However, it remains limited in the choice of equations, as it only uses the Navier-Stokes equations, and furthermore is not suited for evaluating models in a low-resolution regime. Otness et al. [29] propose a benchmark specifically aimed at learning to simulate physical systems from data. However, the simulations are discrete systems (spring systems) rather than continuous spatiotemporal processes defined by partial differential equations. For this reason they cannot be used for the intended purpose of learning continuous systems from low-resolution measurements.

Takamoto et al. [35] propose a very extensive benchmark of eleven different equation systems called PDEBench, including fluid simulations, advection and diffusion equations, Burgers' equation and more. The authors also provide extensive experiments and evaluations for a variety of models. The benchmark is well suited for learning in a high-resolution framework, where the whole discretized grid used during numerical solving is also used for training the models. However, the selection of equations consisting mainly of fluid simulations is unsuitable for low-resolution predictions, as such systems show turbulent and chaotic behavior [9, 13] and therefore require a high-resolution discretization. As such PDEBench is neither suited nor easily usable in a low-resolution regime, where only limited number of scattered observation are available.

3 Dataset

In this section we describe the overall structure of the datasets, which equations were included in the benchmark, how the simulations were executed, and what postprocessing steps were performed.

3.1   Setting

A PDE is a equation in which an unknown function is to be found, based on the relations between itself and its partial derivatives in time and space. It can be summarized in the form:

$$F(u, \frac{\partial u}{\partial t}, \frac{\partial u}{\partial x}, \frac{\partial u}{\partial y}, ...) = 0 \tag{1}$$

As mentioned in Sect. 1 such equations can be used to model a variety of physical systems, by solving a previously known equation system using a measured initial state. In the context of scientific machine learning, a typically researched task is to reconstruct the parameters of the equation (i.e. the function F) from data obtained from a mixture of exact measurements and simulations. Reconstructing the differential equations requires high-resolution data (both in time and space), which is unavailable in a real world setting [11]. Our benchmark is focused on a different task, namely learning to predict the evolution of a dynamical system from data, under the assumption that only low-resolution measurements are available. Formally, a PDE solver seeks to approximate the true solution

$$u \colon \Omega \times T \longrightarrow \mathbb{R}$$

by some approximate

$$\hat{u}_h \colon \hat{\Omega}_h \times \hat{T}_h \longrightarrow \mathbb{R},$$

where $\hat{\Omega}_h$ is a high-resolution discretization of the solution domain $\Omega \subseteq \mathbb{R}^n$ (typically a grid) and $\hat{T}_h$ is a high-resolution time discretization of $T \subseteq \mathbb{R}$ (typically $\hat{T}_h = \{t_k^{(h)}, k \in \mathbb{N}\}$ for $t_k^{(h)} := t_0 + k\Delta_h t$ and some small $\Delta_h t > 0$).

For our task we assume that only low-resolution observations $\hat{u}_l$ at measurement locations $\hat{\Omega}_l$ of the physical process u are available (i.e. $|\hat{\Omega}_l| \ll |\hat{\Omega}_h|$), and the temporal resolution $\hat{T}_l = \{t_k^{(l)}, k \in \mathbb{N}\}$ for $t_k^{(l)} := t_0 + k\Delta_l t$ of the measurements is also low ($|\Delta_l t| \ll \Delta_h t$). The task is then to predict the evolution of the system $\hat{u}_l(\hat{\Omega}_l, t_{k+1}^{(l)}), \hat{u}_l(\hat{\Omega}_l, t_{k+2}^{(l)}), \ldots, \hat{u}_l(\hat{\Omega}_l, t_{k+R}^{(l)})$, from the past observations $\hat{u}_l(\hat{\Omega}_l, t_{k-H}^{(l)}), \ldots, \hat{u}_l(\hat{\Omega}_l, t_{k-1}^{(l)}), \hat{u}_l(\hat{\Omega}_l, t_k^{(l)})$.

3.2   Equations

Overall we curated a set of six different PDE equation systems, typically used in the context of learning dynamical systems from data, with various properties as summarized in Table 1. In the following we shortly describe each equation in more detail.

Advection. The advection equation

$$\frac{\partial u}{\partial t} = -\nabla \cdot (\mathbf{c}u) \tag{2}$$

describes the displacement of a quantity described by a scalar field u in a medium moving with the constant velocity $\mathbf{c}$. It is a widely used benchmark equation due to its simplicity and straightforward dynamics [11,26]

Table 1. Summary of the PDE systems used in our benchmark dataset

Equation	Components	Time Order	Spatial Order
Advection	1	1	1
Burgers	2	1	2
Gas Dynamics	4	1	2
Kuramoto-Sivashinsky	1	1	4
Reaction-Diffusion	2	1	2
Wave	1	2	2

Burgers' Equation. The Burgers' equation

$$\frac{\partial \mathbf{u}}{\partial t} = R(\nu \nabla^2 \mathbf{u} - \mathbf{u} \cdot \nabla \mathbf{u}) \tag{3}$$

is a non-linear second order PDE with respect to spatial derivatives

The equation describes the speed u of a fluid in space and time with ν representing the fluid's viscosity and R describing the rate of the simulation. It is one of the most often used equations in the context of deep learning for dynamical systems [11,18,24,35].

Gas Dynamics. In gas dynamics, the system of coupled non-linear PDEs

$$\frac{\partial \rho}{\partial t} = -\mathbf{v} \cdot \nabla \rho - \rho \nabla \cdot \mathbf{v}$$
$$\frac{\partial T}{\partial t} = -\mathbf{v} \cdot \nabla T - \gamma T \nabla \cdot \mathbf{v} + \gamma \frac{Mk}{\rho} \nabla^2 T \tag{4}$$
$$\frac{\partial \mathbf{v}}{\partial t} = -\mathbf{v} \cdot \nabla \mathbf{v} - \frac{\nabla P}{\rho} + \frac{\mu}{\rho} \nabla(\nabla \mathbf{v})$$

describes the evolution of temperature T, density ρ, pressure P and velocity $\mathbf{v}$ in a gaseous medium. The equations are derived from the physical laws of mass conservation, conservation of energy, and Newton's second law [3]. The parameters specify the physical properties of the system, γ being the heat capacity ratio, M the mass of a molecule of gas, and μ the coefficient of viscosity. This equation can be seen as a simplified weather system.

Kuramoto-Sivashinsky. The Kuramoto-Sivashinsky equation

$$\frac{\partial u}{\partial t} = -\frac{1}{2}|\nabla u|^2 - \nabla^2 u - \nabla^4 u \tag{5}$$

describes a model of the diffusive-thermal instabilities in a laminar flame front. Solutions of the Kuramoto-Sivashinsky equation possess rich dynamical characteristics [8] with solutions potentially including equilibria, relative equilibria, chaotic oscillations and travelling waves.

Table 2. Equation parameters used for the simulations

Equation	Parameters
Advection	$c_x = 1, c_y = 1$
Burgers	$\nu = 0.5, R = 25$
Gas Dynamics	$\mu = 0.01, k = 0.1, \gamma = 1, M = 1$
Kuramoto-Sivashinsky	-
Reaction-Diffusion	$D_u = 0.1, D_v = 0.001, k = 0.005, a_u = 1, a_v = 1$
Wave	$\omega = 1$

Reaction-Diffusion. The Reaction-Diffusion system

$$
\begin{aligned}
\frac{\partial u}{\partial t} &= D_u \nabla^2 u + a_u(u - u^3 - k - v) \\
\frac{\partial v}{\partial t} &= D_v \nabla^2 v + a_v(u - v)
\end{aligned}
\tag{6}
$$

describes the joint concentration distribution of a two component chemical reaction, where one of the components stimulates the reaction and the other inhibits it. The parameters D_u and D_v describe the diffusion speed of the activator and inhibitor respectively, k is the activation threshold, while a_u and a_v describe the reaction speed of the two components. The equation has applicability in describing biological pattern formation and forms rich and chaotic systems [12,35].

Wave. The wave equation

$$
\frac{\partial^2 u}{\partial t^2} = \omega^2 \nabla^2 u
\tag{7}
$$

describes the propagation of a wave in a homogeneous medium (e.g. water surface) where u describes the distance from equilibrium and ω represents the material-dependent speed of propagation. It is a linear, second-order PDE that has been widely used in scientific machine learning [11,19,20,28,30].

3.3   Simulation Parameters

The machine learning task for which our benchmark has been designed, is to learn predictions from observations of a physical system. The system is assumed to evolve according to a set of fixed physical laws that are have constant parameters such as thermal conductivity, diffusion coefficients etc. To create simulations of such systems, we specify the constant parameters with which the selected equations are solved, as shown Table 2. The parameters have been chosen to ensure a good balance between the complexity of the system and the numerical stability of the simulations.

The spatial domain of the simulation is set to $\Omega = [0, 1] \times [0, 1]$ and the temporal domain to $T = [0, 200]$. We initialize the state of each system using zeros, uniform (u) or normally (n) distributed noise, or a sum of Gaussian curves, individually for each field, similar to what has been used in related work [11,19,35]. The exact specification of which initial condition is used for each individual variable is summarized in Table 3. The sum of Gaussian curves has been calculated in the following manner:

$$I(x,y) = \sum_{i=1}^{K} A_i e^{-\frac{(x-\mu_{ix})^2 + (y-\mu_{iy})^2}{\sigma^2}} \qquad (8)$$

The positions (μ_{ix}, μ_{iy}) of each component i are sampled uniformly from the simulation domain Ω, while their contributions A_i are sampled uniformly from the interval $[-1, 1]$. The fixed parameters K and σ are set to 5 and 0.15 respectively (Fig. 2).

Table 3. Initial conditions used for each system

Equation	Field	Initial Cond
Advection	u	gaussian
Burgers	u	gaussian
	v	gaussian
Gas Dynamics	ρ	gaussian
	T	gaussian
	v_x	zero
	v_y	zero
Kuramoto-Sivashinsky	u	noise (u)
Reaction-Diffusion	u	noise (n)
	v	noise (n)
Wave	u	gaussian
	$\frac{\partial u}{\partial t}$	zero

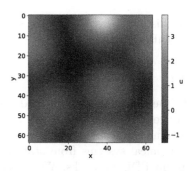

Fig. 2. Example of a gaussian initial condition as defined in Eq. (8)

To run the simulations, the domain Ω is discretized as a 64×64 grid, which yields a cell size of $\Delta x = \Delta y = 0.0156$. The equations are solved using the method of lines as numerical scheme [11]. We use the Explicit Runge-Kutta method of order 5(4) [10] as the numerical integrator.

3.4   Postprocessing

The simulation is saved with a temporal resolution of $\Delta t = 1$, producing exactly 201 observations per simulation. As some of the equations produce non-stationary physical processes, we normalize the data to ensure that range of values remains similar across different equations, simulations and times. Finally, we sample measurements to form the non-grid observation domain, by selecting uniformly K points from the simulation domain Ω and bilinearly interpolate the values from the grid measurements.

3.5 Data Availability

In total we generate 7000 different simulations for each equation, divided into 5000 training simulations and 1000 validation and test simulations each. For each simulation, we use a different initial seed to sample the initial condition. The benchmark is available in three different resolutions, where either $K = 225$, $K = 484$, or $K = 900$ measurements are recorded. Additionally we provide a low-resolution variant of the simulation measured on a grid with the same number of points in total - 15×15, 22×22, 30×30.

The full dataset (including the original high-resolution simulations) can be downloaded at https://professor-x.de/dynabench. Alternatively the same data can be generated from scratch using the provided source code and predefined seeds. Additionally more data can be generated

4 Experiments

In this section we describe a selection of experiments that we performed on the DynaBench dataset.

4.1 Models

In the following, we briefly describe the models used during the experiments. We select several graph neural network and point cloud network baselines as a comparison for available state-of-the-art architectures proposed for learning dynamical systems from scattered measurements - graph kernel networks and graph PDE networks. We do not include Distana [19] and Multipole Graph Operator [24] (cf. Section 2) as there is no code available for the former and the latter requires measurements obtained at different resolution levels and is unsuitable for our setting.

Additionally, to better understand how the change of structure affects the accuracy of the predictions, we evaluate three models that work on grid data trained on a version of the dataset using the same number of measurements but aligned on a grid, as described in Sect. 3.5. These include two variants of a simple convolutional neural network [23] - with and without residual connections [16] and neuralPDE, a model specifically designed to learn dynamical systems from gridded data [11].

Finally, we use the persistence baseline as a reference point for all deep learning models.

PointGNN is a graph neural network proposed by [34] to solve the task of object detection in a LiDAR point cloud. It uses MLP-based feature aggregation within a local neighborhood with an additional perturbation mechanism to offset the coordinates of the neighboring points. This increases the translation invariance of the calculated filters with respect to the center vertex coordinates.

Point Transformer (Point TF) is a model originally proposed by Zhao et al. [40] for object classification and segmentation on 3D point clouds. It uses self-attention, similar to transformer networks, to process features within a spatially local neighborhood. We modify the original segmentation architecture to use 2D point coordinates where the physical system has been measured.

Feature-Steered Graph Convolutions (FeaStNet) is a graph convolution operator developed by Verma at al. [38] for 3D object analysis. It uses the node features from the preceding layer to determine the correspondence between filter weights and nodes in a local neighborhood. Thus it is able to adjust the filters dynamically based on the final prediction task.

Graph Convolution Network (GCN) proposed by Kipf et al. [21] is a simple generalization of convolutions to graph structures where no ordering of the neighbors exists. It uses a first-order approximation of spectral graph convolutions to aggregate features from neighboring nodes.

Graph Attention Network (GAT) proposed by Veličković et al. [37] incorporates an attention mechanism into convolutions on graphs used as weights for aggregating the features from neighboring nodes in each layer. The attention mechanism is able to (implicitly) assign different weights to different nodes in a neighborhood.

Graph Kernel Network (KernelNN) is a deep learning approach proposed by Anandkumar et al. [2] for learning a mapping between two infinite-dimensional spaces. It uses kernel integration with a learnable Nyström kernel as an approximation of the true neural operator. In the original experiments Anandkumar et al. use a high-resolution grid on which the simulation is computed, but the model itself can be applied to non-grid measurements.

Graph PDE Networks (GraphPDE) proposed by Iakovlev et al. [18] use the neural network to parameterize the dynamics (rate of change) of the system rather than making predictions directly. Similar approaches been proposed for grid data [4,11], outperforming classical architectures for this type of task. All of these approaches, including graph PDE networks, use the parameterization learned by message passing graph neural networks together with an differentiable ODE solver to obtain predictions.

CNN originally developed by LeCun et al. [23] uses learnable convolutional filters to enforce translation invariance of the learned mapping with respect to the input position. While it was originally proposed for computer vision tasks it has since been used in the context of learning to predict dynamical systems from data. In our experiments we include a simple architecture with several stacked CNN layers, as well as ResNet variant with residual connections [16].

NeuralPDE is a model proposed by Dulny et al. [11] combing a convolutional neural network used to parametrize the dynamics (rate of change) of a physical system with differentiable ODE solvers to calculate predictions. The authors use convolutional layers to approximate partial differential operators, as they directly translate into a discretization using finite differences. This type of architecture has been shown to perform exceptionally well on a variety of physical data.

Persistence describes the baseline obtained by applying the rule "today's weath-er is tomorrow's weather". It suggests the last known input as the prediction of the next state. Any forecasting model should be able to outperform this baseline, to be counted as useful. The persistence baseline is a common method used in machine learning for time series forecasting tasks.

4.2   Setup

We trained and evaluated all selected models on the DynaBench dataset using 7000 simulations for each equation as training data, and 1000 for validation and testing each. The input for the models is a H-step lookback of the system state (the previous H states) measured at K locations that we merge along the feature dimension. Specifically, for an physical system describing D variables, the resulting input has the dimension $H \times D$.

We train all models on predicting the next step of the simulation by minimizing the mean squared error (MSE):

$$\min_{\phi} \mathbb{E}\big[m_\phi(X_t \parallel X_{t-1} \parallel \ldots \parallel X_{t-H+1}) - X_{t+1}\big]^2 \tag{9}$$

where $X_{t+1}, X_t, X_{t-1}, \ldots$ describes the state of the physical system at times $t+1, t, t-1, \ldots$; m_ϕ is the neural network model with learnable parameters ϕ; H is the lookback history; and $\parallel$ denotes the concatenation operator.

For evaluating the models we rollout R predictions steps in a closed-loop setting where the predictions of previous states are used as input for predicting the new state. Specifically:

$$\begin{aligned}
\hat{X}_{t+1} &= m_\phi(X_t \parallel X_{t-1} \parallel \ldots \parallel X_{t-H+1}) \\
\hat{X}_{t+2} &= m_\phi(\hat{X}_{t+1} \parallel X_t \parallel \ldots \parallel X_{t-H+2}) \\
\hat{X}_{t+3} &= m_\phi(\hat{X}_{t+2} \parallel \hat{X}_{t+1} \parallel \ldots \parallel X_{t-H+3}) \\
&\vdots \\
\hat{X}_{t+R} &= m_\phi(\hat{X}_{t+R-1} \parallel \hat{X}_{t+R-2} \parallel \ldots \parallel \hat{X}_{t-H+R})
\end{aligned} \tag{10}$$

In our experiments we use $H = 8$, $K = 900$ and $R = 16$.

4.3   Results

Table 4 shows the results of our experiments for single-step predictions on the test simulations. Our results show that non-grid models, such as kernel-based neural networks and graph-based neural networks, can perform similarly to grid-based models for short-term (1-step) predictions. Among the models trained

Table 4. MSE after 1 prediction step. The best perfoming model for each equation has been underlined. Additionally, the best non-grid model has been underwaved. A = Advection, B = Burgers', GD = Gas Dynamics, KS = Kuramoto-Sivashinsky, RD = Reaction-Diffusion, W = Wave

model	A	B	GD	KS	RD	W
FeaSt	$1.30 \cdot 10^{-4}$	$1.16 \cdot 10^{-2}$	$1.62 \cdot 10^{-2}$	$1.18 \cdot 10^{-2}$	$4.89 \cdot 10^{-4}$	$5.23 \cdot 10^{-3}$
GAT	$9.60 \cdot 10^{-3}$	$4.40 \cdot 10^{-2}$	$3.75 \cdot 10^{-2}$	$6.67 \cdot 10^{-2}$	$9.15 \cdot 10^{-3}$	$1.51 \cdot 10^{-2}$
GCN	$2.64 \cdot 10^{-2}$	$1.39 \cdot 10^{-1}$	$8.43 \cdot 10^{-2}$	$4.37 \cdot 10^{-1}$	$1.65 \cdot 10^{-1}$	$3.82 \cdot 10^{-2}$
GraphPDE	$1.37 \cdot 10^{-4}$	$1.07 \cdot 10^{-2}$	$1.95 \cdot 10^{-2}$	$7.20 \cdot 10^{-3}$	$1.42 \cdot 10^{-4}$	$2.07 \cdot 10^{-3}$
KernelNN	$6.31 \cdot 10^{-5}$	$1.06 \cdot 10^{-2}$	$1.34 \cdot 10^{-2}$	$6.69 \cdot 10^{-3}$	$1.87 \cdot 10^{-4}$	$5.43 \cdot 10^{-3}$
Point TF	$4.42 \cdot 10^{-5}$	$1.03 \cdot 10^{-2}$	$7.25 \cdot 10^{-3}$	$4.90 \cdot 10^{-3}$	$1.41 \cdot 10^{-4}$	$2.38 \cdot 10^{-3}$
PointGNN	$2.82 \cdot 10^{-5}$	$\underline{8.83 \cdot 10^{-3}}$	$9.02 \cdot 10^{-3}$	$6.73 \cdot 10^{-3}$	$\underline{1.36 \cdot 10^{-4}}$	$\underline{1.39 \cdot 10^{-3}}$
CNN	$5.31 \cdot 10^{-5}$	$1.11 \cdot 10^{-2}$	$4.20 \cdot 10^{-3}$	$6.70 \cdot 10^{-4}$	$3.69 \cdot 10^{-4}$	$1.43 \cdot 10^{-3}$
NeuralPDE	$\underline{8.24 \cdot 10^{-7}}$	$1.12 \cdot 10^{-2}$	$3.73 \cdot 10^{-3}$	$5.37 \cdot 10^{-4}$	$3.03 \cdot 10^{-4}$	$1.70 \cdot 10^{-3}$
ResNet	$2.16 \cdot 10^{-6}$	$1.48 \cdot 10^{-2}$	$\underline{3.21 \cdot 10^{-3}}$	$\underline{4.90 \cdot 10^{-4}}$	$1.57 \cdot 10^{-4}$	$1.46 \cdot 10^{-3}$
Persistence	$8.12 \cdot 10^{-2}$	$3.68 \cdot 10^{-2}$	$1.87 \cdot 10^{-1}$	$1.42 \cdot 10^{-1}$	$1.47 \cdot 10^{-1}$	$1.14 \cdot 10^{-1}$

on unstructured data, the PointGNN and Point Transformer show the best performance.

However, for longer-term predictions, the grid-based models outperform the non-grid models as shown in Table 5. For the grid-based models the underlying spatial structure is fixed and they do not need to additionally learn the dependencies between neighboring measurements. We hypothesize that because of the simpler spatial dependencies, grid-based models are able to generalize better and thus capture the long term evolution of the system more accurately.

Interestingly, we found that the models specifically designed to learn solving PDEs, such as KernelNN and GraphPDE, were not as good as the other models when the data was low-resolution as opposed to high-resolution data on which they were originally evaluated. This suggests that their underlying assumptions may be too strong to handle such data effectively.

Additionally, our study brings to light that long-term predictions are still an unsolved challenge for all models. The divergence in predictions, as illustrated in Fig. 3, occurs rapidly and is particularly prominent in systems such as Gas Dynamics and Kuramoto-Sivashinsky equations, where the prediction error exceeds 0.5 after only 16 prediction steps. This level of error, which is half of the standard deviation of the data (as explained in Sect. 3.4), renders it impossible to make use of these long-term predictions. Thus, our findings emphasize the need for further research and development in this field to address this issue.

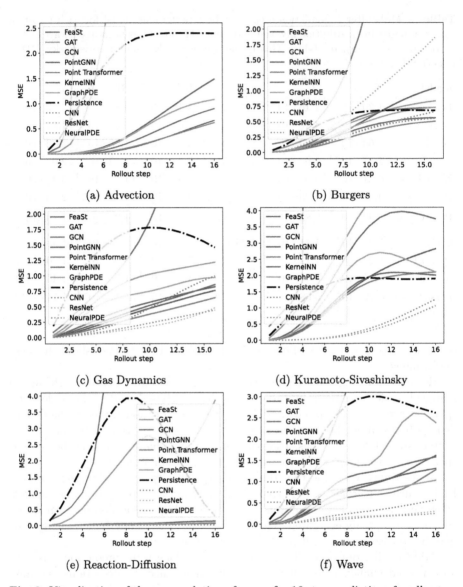

(a) Advection

(b) Burgers

(c) Gas Dynamics

(d) Kuramoto-Sivashinsky

(e) Reaction-Diffusion

(f) Wave

Fig. 3. Visualization of the accumulation of errors for 16 step predictions for all equations in DynaBench. For better readability, MSEs for diverging predictions are not fully displayed.

Table 5. MSE after 16 prediction steps, * - denotes that the system diverges ($MSE > 10$). The best perfoming model for each equation has been underlined. Additionally, the best non-grid model has been underwaved. A = Advection, B = Burgers', GD = Gas Dynamics, KS = Kuramoto-Sivashinsky, RD = Reaction-Diffusion, W = Wave

model	A	B	GD	KS	RD	W
FeaSt	$1.48 \cdot 10^0$	$5.61 \cdot 10^{-1}$	$8.20 \cdot 10^{-1}$	$3.74 \cdot 10^0$	$1.30 \cdot 10^{-1}$	$1.61 \cdot 10^0$
GAT	*	$8.33 \cdot 10^{-1}$	$1.21 \cdot 10^0$	$5.69 \cdot 10^0$	$3.86 \cdot 10^0$	$2.38 \cdot 10^0$
GCN	*	$1.31 \cdot 10^1$	$7.21 \cdot 10^0$	*	*	$7.89 \cdot 10^0$
GraphPDE	$1.08 \cdot 10^0$	$7.30 \cdot 10^{-1}$	$9.69 \cdot 10^{-1}$	$2.10 \cdot 10^0$	$8.00 \cdot 10^{-2}$	$1.03 \cdot 10^0$
KernelNN	$8.97 \cdot 10^{-1}$	$7.27 \cdot 10^{-1}$	$8.54 \cdot 10^{-1}$	$2.00 \cdot 10^0$	$6.35 \cdot 10^{-2}$	$1.58 \cdot 10^0$
Point TF	$6.17 \cdot 10^{-1}$	$5.04 \cdot 10^{-1}$	$6.43 \cdot 10^{-1}$	$2.10 \cdot 10^0$	$5.64 \cdot 10^{-2}$	$1.27 \cdot 10^0$
PointGNN	$6.61 \cdot 10^{-1}$	$1.04 \cdot 10^0$	$7.59 \cdot 10^{-1}$	$2.82 \cdot 10^0$	$5.82 \cdot 10^{-2}$	$1.31 \cdot 10^0$
CNN	$1.61 \cdot 10^{-3}$	$5.55 \cdot 10^{-1}$	$9.95 \cdot 10^{-1}$	$1.26 \cdot 10^0$	$1.83 \cdot 10^{-2}$	$5.61 \cdot 10^{-1}$
NeuralPDE	$2.70 \cdot 10^{-4}$	$6.60 \cdot 10^{-1}$	$4.43 \cdot 10^{-1}$	$1.06 \cdot 10^0$	$2.24 \cdot 10^{-2}$	$2.48 \cdot 10^{-1}$
ResNet	$8.65 \cdot 10^{-5}$	$1.86 \cdot 10^0$	$4.80 \cdot 10^{-1}$	$1.07 \cdot 10^0$	$7.05 \cdot 10^{-3}$	$2.99 \cdot 10^{-1}$
Persistence	$2.39 \cdot 10^0$	$6.79 \cdot 10^{-1}$	$1.46 \cdot 10^0$	$1.90 \cdot 10^0$	$2.76 \cdot 10^{-1}$	$2.61 \cdot 10^0$

5   Conclusion

We have proposed a new benchmark dataset for learning dynamical systems from data under the assumption that measurements are sparse and not structured on a grid. This is closer to real-world data than other resources available, as typically measurements are obtained from monitoring stations scattered withing the observation domain.

The DynaBench dataset covers a wide range of physical systems with different properties such as number of connected variables, degree of the differential operators etc. We have thoroughly evaluated several models capable of learning functions on arbitrary geometries on the DynaBench dataset, including graph neural networks, point-cloud processing models and several state-of-the-art approaches. Our results show that the selected models are on par with state-of-the-art grid models in providing accurate short-term predictions, but long-term forecasting remains an open challenge.

We hope that the release of DynaBench will facilitate and encourage research in this area, leading to advancements in the state-of-the-art and as a consequence more accurate models for real-world data, which our benchmark is mirroring.

Ethical statement. This research paper proposes a benchmark dataset and evaluates several machine learning models for learning dynamical systems from data. The use of benchmarking is a common practice in the machine learning community to compare different models in a standardized setting. Synthetic datasets are used because they allow for a controlled environment and can be generated easily. However, it should be noted that synthetic data can never perfectly represent real-world data, and as such, every model should also be evaluated on real-world data before being used in critical applications.

Potential risks associated with incorrect predictions of important systems such as weather and climate simulations or electromagnetic field simulations for safety assessment should be discussed thoroughly. Synthetic datasets can provide a useful starting point for model evaluation and the development of new approaches, but they need to be assessed on domain-specific data for real-world deployment. Particularly for safety-critical applications. While our proposed benchmark dataset and evaluated machine learning models provide useful insights into learning dynamical systems, they should not be used as the sole basis for making important political decisions, particularly concerning weather or climate data.

While data-driven approaches have again and again shown their superiority over classical methods in a variety of applications, they are also prone to overfitting and adversarial attacks, if not carefully designed and validated. The risks and benefits of replacing existing numerical simulations or expert knowledge with deep learning approaches should always be taken into account and thoroughly discussed when developing and applying new models. Any decision based on machine learning models should be made after considering the potential sources of errors the models introduce, as well as the lack of explainability of black-box approaches.

References

1. Anandkumar, A., et al.: Neural Operator: graph kernel network for partial differential equations. In: ICLR 2020 Workshop on Integration of Deep Neural Models and Differential Equations (2019). https://openreview.net/forum?id=fg2ZFmXFO3
2. Anandkumar, A., et al.: Neural operator: graph kernel network for partial differential equations. In: ICLR 2020 Workshop on Integration of Deep Neural Models and Differential Equations (2019). https://openreview.net/forum?id=fg2ZFmXFO3
3. Anderson, J.D.: Computational Fluid Dynamics. McGraw-Hill Education (1995). Google-Books-ID: dJceAQAAIAAJ
4. Ayed, I., de Bézenac, E., Pajot, A., Brajard, J., Gallinari, P.: Learning dynamical systems from partial observations. CoRR **abs/1902.11136** (2019). https://doi.org/10.48550/arXiv.1902.11136, http://arxiv.org/abs/1902.11136
5. Bauer, P., Thorpe, A., Brunet, G.: The quiet revolution of numerical weather prediction. Nature **525**(7567), 47–55 (2015). https://doi.org/10.1038/nature14956, https://www.nature.com/articles/nature14956
6. Berg, J., Nyström, K.: Data-driven discovery of PDEs in complex datasets. J. Comput. Phys. **384**, 239–252 (2019). https://doi.org/10.1016/j.jcp.2019.01.036, https://www.sciencedirect.com/science/article/pii/S0021999119300944
7. Cullen, M.J., Davies, T., Mawson, M.H., James, J.A., Coulter, S.C., Malcolm, A.: An overview of numerical methods for the next generation U.K. NWP and Climate Model. Atmosphere-Ocean **35**(sup1), 425–444 (1997). https://doi.org/10.1080/07055900.1997.9687359, https://doi.org/10.1080/07055900.1997.9687359
8. Cvitanović, P., Davidchack, R.L., Siminos, E.: On the state space geometry of the kuramoto–sivashinsky flow in a periodic domain. SIAM J. Appl. Dyn. Syst. **9**(1), 1–33 (2010). https://doi.org/10.1137/070705623

9. Deissler, R.G.: Is navier–stokes turbulence chaotic? Phys. Fluids **29**(5), 1453–1457 (1986). https://doi.org/10.1063/1.865663, https://aip.scitation.org/doi/abs/10.1063/1.865663

10. Dormand, J.R., Prince, P.J.: A family of embedded Runge-Kutta formulae. J. Comput. Appl. Math. **6**(1), 19–26 (1980). https://doi.org/10.1016/0771-050X(80)90013-3, https://www.sciencedirect.com/science/article/pii/0771050X80900133

11. Dulny, A., Hotho, A., Krause, A.: NeuralPDE: modelling dynamical systems from data. In: Bergmann, R., Malburg, L., Rodermund, S.C., Timm, I.J. (eds.) KI 2022: Advances in Artificial Intelligence, pp. 75–89. Lecture Notes in Computer Science, Springer International Publishing, Cham (2022). https://doi.org/10.1007/978-3-031-15791-2_8

12. FitzHugh, R.: Impulses and physiological states in theoretical models of nerve membrane. Biophys. J. **1**(6), 445–466 (1961). https://www.ncbi.nlm.nih.gov/pmc/articles/PMC1366333/

13. Foias, C., Manley, O., Rosa, R., Temam, R.: Navier-Stokes Equations and Turbulence. Encyclopedia of Mathematics and its Applications, Cambridge University Press (2001). https://doi.org/10.1017/CBO9780511546754

14. Gilmer, J., Schoenholz, S.S., Riley, P.F., Vinyals, O., Dahl, G.E.: Neural message passing for quantum chemistry. In: Proceedings of the 34th International Conference on Machine Learning, pp. 1263–1272. PMLR (2017). https://proceedings.mlr.press/v70/gilmer17a.html

15. Haylock, M.R., Hofstra, N., Klein Tank, A.M.G., Klok, E.J., Jones, P.D., New, M.: A european daily high-resolution gridded data set of surface temperature and precipitation for 1950–2006. J. Geophys. Res.: Atmos. **113**(D20) (2008). https://doi.org/10.1029/2008JD010201, https://agupubs.onlinelibrary.wiley.com/doi/abs/10.1029/2008JD010201

16. He, K., Zhang, X., Ren, S., Sun, J.: Deep residual learning for image recognition. In: 2016 IEEE Conference on Computer Vision and Pattern Recognition (CVPR), pp. 770–778 (2016). https://doi.org/10.1109/CVPR.2016.90, ISSN: 1063-6919

17. Huang, Z., Schneider, T., Li, M., Jiang, C., Zorin, D., Panozzo, D.: A large-scale benchmark for the incompressible navier-stokes equations. CoRR **abs/2112.05309** (2021). https://doi.org/10.48550/arXiv.2112.05309, https://arxiv.org/abs/2112.05309

18. Iakovlev, V., Heinonen, M., Lähdesmäki, H.: Learning continuous-time pdes from sparse data with graph neural networks. In: International Conference on Learning Representations (2021). https://openreview.net/forum?id=aUX5Plaq7Oy

19. Karlbauer, M., Otte, S., Lensch, H.P.A., Scholten, T., Wulfmeyer, V., Butz, M.V.: A distributed neural network architecture for robust non-linear spatio-temporal prediction. CoRR **abs/1912.11141** (2019). https://doi.org/10.48550/arXiv.1912.11141, http://arxiv.org/abs/1912.11141

20. Karlbauer, M., Otte, S., Lensch, H.P.A., Scholten, T., Wulfmeyer, V., Butz, M.V.: Inferring, predicting, and denoising causal wave dynamics. In: Farkaš, I., Masulli, P., Wermter, S. (eds.) Artificial Neural Networks and Machine Learning - ICANN 2020, pp. 566–577. Lecture Notes in Computer Science, Springer International Publishing, Cham (2020). https://doi.org/10.1007/978-3-030-61609-0_45

21. Kipf, T.N., Welling, M.: Semi-supervised classification with graph convolutional networks. In: International Conference on Learning Representations (2017). https://openreview.net/forum?id=SJU4ayYgl

22. Kleinstreuer, C.: Modern Fluid Dynamics: Basic Theory and Selected Applications in Macro- and Micro-Fluidics, Fluid Mechanics and Its Applications, vol. 87. Springer Netherlands (2010). https://doi.org/10.1007/978-1-4020-8670-0

23. LeCun, Y., Haffner, P., Bottou, L., Bengio, Y.: Object Recognition with Gradient-Based Learning, pp. 319–345. Springer Berlin Heidelberg, Berlin, Heidelberg (1999). https://doi.org/10.1007/3-540-46805-6_19

24. Li, Z., Kovachki, N., Azizzadenesheli, K., Liu, B., Stuart, A., Bhattacharya, K., Anandkumar, A.: Multipole graph neural operator for parametric partial differential equations. In: Advances in Neural Information Processing Systems, vol. 33, pp. 6755–6766. Curran Associates, Inc. (2020). https://proceedings.neurips.cc/paper/2020/hash/4b21cf96d4cf612f239a6c322b10c8fe-Abstract.html

25. Li, Z., Kovachki, N.B., Azizzadenesheli, K., liu, B., Bhattacharya, K., Stuart, A., Anandkumar, A.: Fourier neural operator for parametric partial differential equations. In: International Conference on Learning Representations (2021). https://openreview.net/forum?id=c8P9NQVtmnO

26. Long, Z., Lu, Y., Dong, B.: PDE-Net 2.0: Learning PDEs from data with a numeric-symbolic hybrid deep network. J. Comput. Phys. **399**(C) (2019). https://doi.org/10.1016/j.jcp.2019.108925

27. McGuffie, K., Henderson-Sellers, A.: Forty years of numerical climate modelling. Int. J. Climatol. **21**(9), 1067–1109 (2001). https://doi.org/10.1002/joc.632, https://onlinelibrary.wiley.com/doi/abs/10.1002/joc.632

28. Moseley, B., Markham, A., Nissen-Meyer, T.: Solving the wave equation with physics-informed deep learning (2020). https://doi.org/10.48550/arXiv.2006.11894, http://arxiv.org/abs/2006.11894, type: article

29. Otness, K., et al.: An extensible benchmark suite for learning to simulate physical systems. In: Thirty-fifth Conference on Neural Information Processing Systems Datasets and Benchmarks Track (Round 1) (2021). https://openreview.net/forum?id=pY9MHwmrymR

30. Otte, S., Karlbauer, M., Butz, M.V.: Active tuning (2020). https://doi.org/10.48550/arXiv.2010.03958, http://arxiv.org/abs/2010.03958, type: article

31. Praditia, T., Karlbauer, M., Otte, S., Oladyshkin, S., Butz, M.V., Nowak, W.: Finite volume neural network: Modeling subsurface contaminant transport. CoRR **abs/2104.06010** (2021). https://doi.org/10.48550/arXiv.2104.06010, https://arxiv.org/abs/2104.06010

32. Qi, C.R., Su, H., Mo, K., Guibas, L.J.: PointNet: deep learning on point sets for 3D classification and segmentation. In: Proceedings of the IEEE Conference on Computer Vision and Pattern Recognition (CVPR) (2017)

33. Sheikholeslami, M., Seyednezhad, M.: Simulation of nanofluid flow and natural convection in a porous media under the influence of electric field using CVFEM. Int. J. Heat Mass Transfer **120**, 772–781 (2018). https://doi.org/10.1016/j.ijheatmasstransfer.2017.12.087, https://www.sciencedirect.com/science/article/pii/S0017931017346124

34. Shi, W., Rajkumar, R.: Point-GNN: graph neural network for 3D object detection in a point cloud. In: Proceedings of the IEEE/CVF International Conference on Computer Vision (ICCV), pp. 1711–1719 (2020). https://openaccess.thecvf.com/content_CVPR_2020/html/Shi_Point-GNN_Graph_Neural_Network_for_3D_Object_Detection_in_a_CVPR_2020_paper.html

35. Takamoto, M., et al.: PDEBench: an extensive benchmark for scientific machine learning. In: Thirty-sixth Conference on Neural Information Processing Systems Datasets and Benchmarks Track (2022). https://arxiv.org/abs/2210.07182

36. Thomas, H., Qi, C.R., Deschaud, J.E., Marcotegui, B., Goulette, F., Guibas, L.: KPConv: Flexible and deformable convolution for point clouds. In: 2019 IEEE/CVF International Conference on Computer Vision (ICCV), pp. 6410–6419 (2019). https://doi.org/10.1109/ICCV.2019.00651, ISSN: 2380-7504

37. Veličković, P., Cucurull, G., Casanova, A., Romero, A., Liò, P., Bengio, Y.: Graph attention networks. In: International Conference on Learning Representations (2018). https://openreview.net/forum?id=rJXMpikCZ

38. Verma, N., Boyer, E., Verbeek, J.: FeastNet: feature-steered graph convolutions for 3D shape analysis. In: 2018 IEEE/CVF Conference on Computer Vision and Pattern Recognition (CVPR), pp. 2598–2606. IEEE Computer Society, Los Alamitos, CA, USA (2018). https://doi.org/10.1109/CVPR.2018.00275, https://doi.ieeecomputersociety.org/10.1109/CVPR.2018.00275

39. Wang, S., Suo, S., Ma, W., Pokrovsky, A., Urtasun, R.: Deep parametric continuous convolutional neural networks. In: 2018 IEEE/CVF Conference on Computer Vision and Pattern Recognition (CVPR), pp. 2589–2597. IEEE Computer Society, Los Alamitos, CA, USA (2018). https://doi.org/10.1109/CVPR.2018.00274, https://doi.ieeecomputersociety.org/10.1109/CVPR.2018.00274

40. Zhao, H., Jiang, L., Jia, J., Torr, P.H., Koltun, V.: Point transformer. In: Proceedings of the IEEE/CVF International Conference on Computer Vision (ICCV), pp. 16259–16268 (2021). https://openaccess.thecvf.com/content/ICCV2021/html/Zhao_Point_Transformer_ICCV_2021_paper.html

Bayesian Methods

Towards Efficient MCMC Sampling in Bayesian Neural Networks by Exploiting Symmetry

Jonas Gregor Wiese[1], Lisa Wimmer[2,3], Theodore Papamarkou[4],
Bernd Bischl[2,3], Stephan Günnemann[1,3], and David Rügamer[2,3(✉)]

[1] Technical University of Munich, Munich, Germany
[2] Department of Statistics, LMU Munich, Munich, Germany
[3] Munich Center for Machine Learning (MCML), Munich, Germany
`david@stat.uni-muenchen.de`
[4] Department of Mathematics, The University of Manchester, Manchester, UK

Abstract. Bayesian inference in deep neural networks is challenging due to the high-dimensional, strongly multi-modal parameter posterior density landscape. Markov chain Monte Carlo approaches asymptotically recover the true posterior but are considered prohibitively expensive for large modern architectures. Local methods, which have emerged as a popular alternative, focus on specific parameter regions that can be approximated by functions with tractable integrals. While these often yield satisfactory empirical results, they fail, by definition, to account for the multi-modality of the parameter posterior. Such coarse approximations can be detrimental in practical applications, notably safety-critical ones. In this work, we argue that the dilemma between exact-but-unaffordable and cheap-but-inexact approaches can be mitigated by exploiting symmetries in the posterior landscape. These symmetries, induced by neuron interchangeability and certain activation functions, manifest in different parameter values leading to the same functional output value. We show theoretically that the posterior predictive density in Bayesian neural networks can be restricted to a symmetry-free parameter reference set. By further deriving an upper bound on the number of Monte Carlo chains required to capture the functional diversity, we propose a straightforward approach for feasible Bayesian inference. Our experiments suggest that efficient sampling is indeed possible, opening up a promising path to accurate uncertainty quantification in deep learning.

Keywords: Uncertainty quantification · Predictive uncertainty · Bayesian inference · Monte Carlo sampling · Posterior symmetry

1 Introduction

Despite big data being the dominant paradigm in deep learning, the lack of infinitely many observations makes uncertainty quantification (UQ) an important problem in the field. Bayesian neural networks (BNNs) are a probabilistic

---

J. G. Wiese and L. Wimmer—Equal contribution.

© The Author(s), under exclusive license to Springer Nature Switzerland AG 2023
D. Koutra et al. (Eds.): ECML PKDD 2023, LNAI 14169, pp. 459–474, 2023.
https://doi.org/10.1007/978-3-031-43412-9_27

formulation of deep learning models and as such provide UQ in a principled manner. A key component of Bayesian learning is the parameter posterior density that assigns a posterior probability to each parameter value[1] [17]. Between the extreme cases of all posterior probability mass concentrating on a single value, indicating complete certainty about the model parameters, and being distributed uniformly over all possible values in a reflection of total ignorance, the shape of the parameter posterior density is central to the quantification of predictive uncertainty. However, the parameter posterior for BNNs is typically highly multi-modal and rarely available in closed form. The classical Markov chain Monte Carlo (MCMC) approach asymptotically recovers the true posterior but is considered prohibitively expensive for BNNs, as the large number of posterior modes prevents a reasonable mixing of chains [18]. Popular approximation techniques, such as Laplace approximation (LA; [7,22]) or deep ensembles (DE; [21]), therefore focus on local regions of the posterior landscape. While these methods are faster than traditional MCMC and perform well in many applications, they systematically omit regions of the parameter space that might be decisive for meaningful UQ [18] (also shown in Sect. 5.3).

In this work, we challenge the presumed infeasibility of MCMC for NNs and propose to exploit the – in this context, rarely considered – unidentifiability property of NNs, i.e., the existence of two or more equivalent parameter values that describe the same input-output mapping. We refer to these equivalent values as *equioutput parameter states*. Equioutput parameter states emerge from certain activation functions [6,20,29], as well as the free permutability of neuron parameters in hidden layers [15], and can be transformed into one another.

The functional redundancy arising from this phenomenon grows rapidly with the depth and width of a network (cf. Fig. 1) and induces symmetries in the posterior density. For exact inference (up to a Monte Carlo error), we need to incorporate all non-equioutput parameter states that lead to distinct input-output mappings. Considering only these *functionally diverse* mappings means, in turn, that our effective parameter space makes up a comparatively small fraction of the network's original parameter space. Since their numerous equioutput counterparts do not contribute any new information to predictive uncertainty, we need much fewer MCMC samples when approximating the posterior predictive density (PPD) via Monte Carlo integration. By explicitly removing symmetries from samples *post-hoc*, we can even expose the functionally relevant part of the posterior and provide an opportunity for interpretation and analytical approximation in the reduced effective parameter space.

Our Contributions. We analyze the role of posterior space redundancies in quantifying BNN uncertainty, making the following contributions: 1) We show that the full PPD can be obtained from a substantially smaller reference set containing uniquely identified parameter states in function space. 2) We propose an estimation procedure for the number of Monte Carlo chains required

---

[1] We assume the likelihood to be parameterized by a single parameter vector. In the case of neural networks (NNs), the parameter contains all weights and biases.

to discover functionally diverse modes, providing a practical guideline for sampling from the parameter space of multi-layer perceptrons (MLPs). 3) We supply experimental evidence that our approach yields superior predictive performance compared to standard MCMC and local approximation methods. 4) Lastly, we demonstrate the posterior interpretability and analytic approximation that can be obtained from explicitly removing symmetries *post-hoc*, for which we propose an algorithmic proof-of-concept.

2   Related Work

Existence of Parameter State Symmetries. Non-unique network parameter states have been considered in the literature before. [15] were among the first to note that equioutput states induce symmetries in the parameter space of MLPs. Focusing, within the general linear group of the parameter space, on the subgroup of transformations that leave the input-output mapping unchanged, they derived equivalence classes of equioutput parameter states and showed that, for every MLP, there exists a minimal and complete set of representatives covering all functionally different parameter states. [20,34] continued along this line of work to study single-hidden-layer MLPs with specific activation functions, advancing from tanh to more general self-affine activations. An extension to MLPs of arbitrary depth was studied by [6] in the context of tanh activations. More recently, [29] characterized equioutput parameter states for ReLU activations, again focusing on the case of a single hidden layer, and [1] classified all $\mathbb{G}$-invariant single-hidden-layer MLPs with ReLU activation for any finite orthogonal group $\mathbb{G}$. Lastly, [36] generalized much of the above in a framework addressing the identifiability of affine symmetries in arbitrary architectures.

Symmetry Removal. Symmetries in the parameter posterior density of Bayesian models can produce adverse effects that have been addressed in several research areas of statistics and machine learning. A prominent example is *label switching* in finite mixture models, where the permutability of label assignments to the mixture components induces symmetries similar to those in BNNs. To make mixture models identifiable, [3] introduced an adaptive Metropolis algorithm with online relabeling, effectively removing permutation symmetries by optimizing over discrete sets of permutation matrices. Such exhaustive-search approaches, however, scale poorly to modern NNs with many parameters, as the amount of equioutput states rises exponentially with the number of parameters.

In BNNs, symmetries have been known to slow down MCMC convergence to the stationary parameter posterior density due to budget wasted on visiting symmetric modes [24,27]. [18], reporting results from extensive and large-scale experiments, indeed find that MCMC chains tend to mix better in function space than in parameter space. Consequently, reducing the effect of symmetries by imposing parameter constraints and defining anchoring points for subsets of the latent variables has been shown to improve mixing [33]. A proposal for constrained sampling can be found, for example, in [31], with application to ReLU-activated MLPs.

Utilizing Symmetries. Symmetries in the parameter posterior density are not, however, necessarily a nuisance. Quite on the contrary, they can be useful to enhance generalization and make inference affordable. An increasing body of work has been exploring the use of symmetry removal in the context of *mode connectivity*, an approach to find more robust NN solutions by retrieving connected areas of near-constant loss rather than isolated local optima [8,12]. Focusing on equioutput permutations of hidden-layer neurons, [2,35], among others, propose to align the layer-wise embeddings of multiple networks and thus improve upon the performance of individual models. Following a similar idea, [30] apply a *post-hoc* standardization on parameter vectors in ReLU-activated NNs that draws from the notion of equioutput equivalence classes.

In the field of Bayesian deep learning, the idea of utilizing – exact or approximate – parameter symmetries, represented by permutation groups, has led to the development of *lifted MCMC* [5,26]. Orbital Markov chains have been introduced to leverage parameter symmetries in order to reduce mixing times [5,25]. Lifted MCMC has been considered mainly in the context of probabilistic graphical models. There is scope to harness lifted MCMC in the context of MLPs since these can be cast as graphical models [19,36].

We believe that equioutput symmetries have the potential to facilitate MCMC inference, despite the apparent complexity they introduce in the parameter posterior density. From the insight that a vast part of the sampling space is made up of symmetric copies of some minimal search set, we conclude that running multiple short MCMC chains in parallel, each of which can sample a functionally different mode, represents a more efficient use of the available budget than collecting a large number of samples from a single chain. In Sect. 4, we propose an upper bound for MCMC chains necessary to observe all functionally diverse posterior modes, which is a key criterion for successful inference. The perspective of parameter posterior symmetries thus lends a new theoretical justification to previous efforts in multi-chain MCMC that are motivated mainly by the exploitation of parallel computing resources [23,32]. Our experiments in Sect. 5 suggest that this approach is indeed more effective than single-chain MCMC in BNNs with many symmetries in their parameter posterior density. In agreement with [18], our findings advocate to focus on function-space instead of parameter-space mixing during MCMC sampling.

We thus view the existence of equioutput parameter states as a benign phenomenon. That said, there are still benefits to be gained from removing the symmetries: with a parameter posterior density reduced to the minimal parameter set sufficient to represent its full functional diversity, we get an opportunity for better interpretation, and possibly even analytical approximation. We demonstrate the potential of symmetry removal in Sect. 5.3 by means of a custom algorithm (Supplementary Material[2] B). In the following section, we provide the mathematical background and introduce the characterization and formal notation of equioutput transformations.

---

[2] https://github.com/jgwiese/mcmc_bnn_symmetry/.../sub_44_supplementary_material.pdf

3 Background and Notation

MLP Architectures. In this work, we consider NNs of the following form. Let $f : \mathcal{X} \to \mathcal{Y}$ represent an MLP with K layers, where layer $l \in \{1, \ldots, K\}$ consists of M_l neurons, mapping a feature vector $\boldsymbol{x} = (x_1, \ldots, x_n)^\top \in \mathcal{X} \subseteq \mathbb{R}^n, n \in \mathbb{N}$, to an outcome vector

$$f(\boldsymbol{x}) =: \hat{\boldsymbol{y}} = (\hat{y}_1, \ldots, \hat{y}_m)^\top \in \mathcal{Y} \subseteq \mathbb{R}^m, \quad m \in \mathbb{N},$$

to estimate $\boldsymbol{y} = (y_1, \ldots, y_m)^\top \in \mathcal{Y}$. The i-th neuron in the l-th layer of the MLP is associated with the weights $w_{lij}, j = 1, \ldots, M_{l-1}$, and the bias b_{li}. We summarize all the MLP parameters in the vector

$$\boldsymbol{\theta} := (w_{211}, \ldots, w_{K M_K M_{K-1}}, b_{21}, \ldots, b_{K M_K})^\top \in \Theta \subseteq \mathbb{R}^d$$

and write $f_{\boldsymbol{\theta}}$ to make clear that the MLP is parameterized by $\boldsymbol{\theta}$. For each hidden layer $l \in \{2, \ldots, K-1\}$, the inputs are linearly transformed and then activated by a function a. More specifically, we define the pre-activations of the i-th neuron in the l-th hidden layer as

$$o_{li} = \sum_{j=1}^{M_{l-1}} w_{lij} z_{(l-1)j} + b_{li}$$

with post-activations $z_{(l-1)i} = a(o_{(l-1)i})$ from the preceding layer. For the input layer, we have $z_{1i} = x_i, i = 1, \ldots, n$, and for the output layer, $z_{Ki} = \hat{y}_i, i = 1, \ldots, M_K$.

Predictive Uncertainty. In the Bayesian paradigm, a prior density $p(\boldsymbol{\theta})$ is imposed on the parameters, typically as part of a Bayesian model of the data. Using Bayes' rule, the parameter posterior density

$$p(\boldsymbol{\theta}|\mathcal{D}) = \frac{p(\mathcal{D}|\boldsymbol{\theta})p(\boldsymbol{\theta})}{p(\mathcal{D})}$$

updates this prior belief based on the information provided by the data $\mathcal{D}$ and encoded in the likelihood $p(\mathcal{D}|\boldsymbol{\theta})$. In supervised learning, the data are typically given by a set of N feature vectors $\boldsymbol{x} \in \mathcal{X}$ and outcome vectors $\boldsymbol{y} \in \mathcal{Y}$, forming the dataset $\mathcal{D} = \{(\boldsymbol{x}^{(1)}, \boldsymbol{y}^{(1)}), \ldots, (\boldsymbol{x}^{(N)}, \boldsymbol{y}^{(N)})\}$. The PPD $p(\boldsymbol{y}^*|\boldsymbol{x}^*, \mathcal{D})$ quantifies the predictive or functional uncertainty of the model for a new observation $(\boldsymbol{x}^*, \boldsymbol{y}^*) \in \mathcal{X} \times \mathcal{Y}$. Since

$$p(\boldsymbol{y}^*|\boldsymbol{x}^*, \mathcal{D}) = \int_\Theta p(\boldsymbol{y}^*|\boldsymbol{x}^*, \boldsymbol{\theta}) p(\boldsymbol{\theta}|\mathcal{D}) \, \mathrm{d}\boldsymbol{\theta},$$

deriving this uncertainty requires access to the posterior density $p(\boldsymbol{\theta}|\mathcal{D})$, which can be estimated from MCMC sampling.

Equioutput Transformations. Let us now characterize the notion of equioutput parameter states, and the transformations to convert between them, more formally. Two parameter states θ, θ' are considered *equioutput* if the maps $f_\theta, f_{\theta'}$ yield the same outputs for all possible inputs from $\mathcal{X}$. We denote this equivalence relation (see proof in Supplementary Material A.2) by $\sim$ and write:

$$\theta \sim \theta' \iff f_\theta(x) = f_{\theta'}(x) \, \forall x \in \mathcal{X}, \quad \theta, \theta' \in \Theta.$$

The equioutput relation is always defined with respect to a particular MLP f, which we omit in our notation when it is clear from the context.

All MLPs with more than one neuron in at least one hidden layer exhibit such equioutput parameter states that arise from permutation invariances of the input-output mapping [15,20]. Since the operations in the pre-activation of the i-th neuron in the l-th layer commute[3], the $M_l > 1$ neurons of a hidden layer l can be freely interchanged by permuting their associated parameters. In addition, equioutput transformations can arise from the use of certain activation functions with inherent symmetry properties. For example, in the case of tanh, the signs of corresponding parameters can be flipped using $\tanh(x) = -\tanh(-x)$. For ReLU activations, a scaling transformation can be applied such that the mapping of the network remains unchanged, i.e., $\text{ReLU}(x) = c^{-1} \cdot \text{ReLU}(c \cdot x)$ for $|c| > 0$ (see also Supplementary Material A.1).

We consider transformation maps that are linear in θ and induce a finite amount of equioutput transformation matrices, which includes, for example, the tanh activation function. The ReLU activation function allows for infinitely many possibilities of re-scaling the weights and is excluded from our findings. More specifically, let

$$\mathcal{F}_T : \Theta \to \Theta, \theta \mapsto T\theta, \quad T \in \mathbb{R}^{d \times d},$$

be an activation-related transformation of a parameter vector that might, for instance, encode an output-preserving sign flip. $\mathcal{F}_T$ constitutes an *equioutput* transformation if $f_\theta(\cdot) = f_{\mathcal{F}_T(\theta)}(\cdot)$. We collect all output-preserving transformation matrices T in the set $\mathcal{T}$, i.e.,

$$\mathcal{T} = \left\{ T \in \mathbb{R}^{d \times d} \mid f_\theta(\cdot) = f_{\mathcal{F}_T(\theta)}(\cdot) \right\}.$$

Similarly, let

$$\mathcal{F}_P : \Theta \to \Theta, \theta \mapsto P\theta, \quad P \in \{0, 1\}^{d \times d},$$

be a transformation that permutes elements in the parameter vector. We define the set of permutation matrices that yield equioutput parameter states as

$$\mathcal{P} = \left\{ P \in \mathbb{R}^{d \times d} \mid f_\theta(\cdot) = f_{\mathcal{F}_P(\theta)}(\cdot) \right\}.$$

---

[3] Recall that the pre-activation of neuron i in layer l is $o_{li} = \sum_{j=1}^{M_{l-1}} w_{lij} z_{(l-1)j} + b_{li}$. By the commutative property of sums, any permutation $\pi : J \to J$ of elements from the set $J = \{1, \ldots, M_{l-1}\}$ will lead to the same pre-activation: $o_{li} = \sum_{j \in J} w_{lij} z_{(l-1)j} + b_{li} = \sum_{j \in \pi(J)} w_{lij} z_{(l-1)j} + b_{li}.$.

The cardinality of $\mathcal{P}$ is at least $\prod_{l=2}^{K-1} M_l!$ [15] when traversing through the NN from the first layer in a sequential manner, applying to each layer permutations that compensate for permutations in its predecessor.

Since activation functions operate neuron-wise, activation- and permutation-related equioutput transformations do not interact (for instance, we could permute the associated weights of two neurons and later flip their sign). We can, therefore, define arbitrary combinations of activation and permutation transformations as

$$\mathcal{E} = \left\{ \boldsymbol{E} = \boldsymbol{T}\boldsymbol{P} \in \mathbb{R}^{d \times d}, \boldsymbol{T} \in \mathcal{T}, \boldsymbol{P} \in \mathcal{P} \mid f_{\boldsymbol{\theta}}(\cdot) = f_{\mathcal{F}_{\boldsymbol{E}}(\boldsymbol{\theta})}(\cdot) \right\}.$$

The transformation matrices in $\mathcal{E}$ will exhibit a block-diagonal structure with blocks corresponding to network layers. This is due to the permutations $\boldsymbol{P}$ affecting both incoming and outgoing weights, but only in the sense that two incoming and two outgoing weights swap places, never changing layers. The activation-related sign flips or re-scalings occur neuron-wise, making $\boldsymbol{T}$ a diagonal matrix that does not alter the block-diagonal structure of $\boldsymbol{P}$.

For the cardinality of the set $\mathcal{E}$ of equioutput transformations, we can establish a lower bound that builds upon the minimum cardinality of $\mathcal{P}$:

$$|\mathcal{E}| \geq \prod_{l=2}^{K-1} M_l! \cdot |\mathcal{T}_l|,$$

where $|\mathcal{T}_l|$ denotes the number of activation-related transformations applicable to neurons in layer l. From this, it becomes immediately clear that the amount of functional redundancy increases rapidly with the network size (see also Fig. 1). As a result of equioutput parameter states, the MLP parameter posterior density exhibits functional redundancy in the form of symmetries for commonly used priors (see Sect. 4; Supplementary Material A.3):

$$p(\boldsymbol{\theta}|\mathcal{D}) = \frac{p(\mathcal{D}|\boldsymbol{\theta})p(\boldsymbol{\theta})}{p(\mathcal{D})} = \frac{p(\mathcal{D}|\boldsymbol{E}\boldsymbol{\theta})p(\boldsymbol{E}\boldsymbol{\theta})}{p(\mathcal{D})} = p(\boldsymbol{E}\boldsymbol{\theta}|\mathcal{D}), \quad \boldsymbol{\theta} \in \Theta, \boldsymbol{E} \in \mathcal{E}. \quad (1)$$

4   Efficient Sampling

These symmetric structures in the parameter posterior density suggest that sampling can be made more efficient. In the following section, we show that the PPD can theoretically be obtained from a small reference set of non-equivalent parameter states and propose an upper bound on Markov chains that suffice to sample all non-symmetric posterior modes.

4.1   Posterior Reference Set

As introduced in Sect. 3, for each parameter state $\boldsymbol{\theta}$ of an NN, there are functionally redundant counterparts $\boldsymbol{\theta}'$ related to $\boldsymbol{\theta}$ by an equioutput transformation, such that $f_{\boldsymbol{\theta}}(\cdot) = f_{\boldsymbol{\theta}'}(\cdot)$. We can use this equivalence relation to dissect the

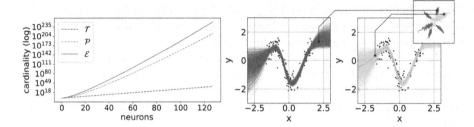

Fig. 1. Example of tanh-activated MLPs. *Left*: Cardinality lower bound of the equioutput transformation set for a single hidden layer with 1 to 128 neurons; the redundancy factor for 128 neurons is at $1.31 \cdot 10^{254}$. *Right*: A ten-dimensional MLP parameter posterior (top-right corner, depicted as bivariate marginal density) exhibits symmetries, such that all red sample clusters are equioutput-related to the green cluster. The associated function spaces are identical, i.e., many posterior modes are redundant. (Color figure online)

parameter space Θ into disjoint equivalence classes. For this, let the *reference set* $\mathcal{S}_1$ be a minimal set of representatives of each equivalence class (cf. *open minimal sufficient search sets* in [6]). All parameter states in $\mathcal{S}_1$ are functionally diverse, i.e., $\boldsymbol{\theta}, \tilde{\boldsymbol{\theta}} \in \mathcal{S}_1 \Rightarrow \boldsymbol{\theta} \not\sim \tilde{\boldsymbol{\theta}}$, and each element in Θ is equivalent to exactly one element in $\mathcal{S}_1$. For a finite amount of equioutput transformations, as in the case of tanh-activated MLPs (finite possibilities of sign-flip combinations of hidden neurons), the NN parameter space can then be dissected into $|\mathcal{E}|$ disjoint *representative sets*, which contain equioutput transformations of the elements of the reference set, in the following way.

Proposition 1 (Parameter space dissection). *Let $\mathcal{S}_1$ be the reference set of uniquely identified network parameter states. Then, for a finite number of equioutput transformations, it holds that the parameter space can be dissected into $|\mathcal{E}|$ disjoint, non-empty representative sets up to a set $\mathcal{S}^0 \subset \Theta$, i.e.,*

$$\Theta = \left(\dot{\bigcup}_{j=1}^{|\mathcal{E}|} \mathcal{S}_j \right) \dot{\cup} \mathcal{S}^0, \ where \ \mathcal{S}_j \cong \{ \boldsymbol{\theta} \mid \boldsymbol{\theta} = \boldsymbol{E}_j \boldsymbol{\theta}' \quad \forall \boldsymbol{\theta}' \in \mathcal{S}_1, \boldsymbol{E}_j \in \mathcal{E} \}, \quad (2)$$

where $\dot{\cup}$ denotes the union over disjoint sets. We use $\mathcal{S}^0$ as a residual quantity to account for cases that cannot be assigned unambiguously to one of the sets $\mathcal{S}_j$ because they remain unchanged even under a transformation with non-identity matrices $\boldsymbol{E}_j \in \mathcal{E}$.

The edge cases that make up $\mathcal{S}^0$ exist, e.g., on the boundary of two classes [6] or in degenerated cases such as the zero vector [34,36]. For a characterization of the involved sets, as well as a proof sketch, see Supplementary Material A.4.

Equioutput parameter states have the same posterior probabilities $p(\boldsymbol{\theta}|\mathcal{D}) = p(\boldsymbol{E\theta}|\mathcal{D})$ if the prior is transformation-invariant; see Supplementary Material A.3. Moreover, equioutput parameter states produce by definition the same predictions $p(\boldsymbol{y}^*|\boldsymbol{x}^*, \boldsymbol{\theta}) = p(\boldsymbol{y}^*|\boldsymbol{x}^*, \boldsymbol{E\theta})$ for any $\boldsymbol{E} \in \mathcal{E}$. Thus, the following corollary holds.

Corollary 1 (Reformulated posterior predictive density). *Let $\mathcal{E}$ be finite. As in Proposition 1, consider the disjoint non-empty sets $\mathcal{S}_j, j \in \{1, \ldots, |\mathcal{E}|\}$, and residual space $\mathcal{S}^0$. If the prior density $p(\boldsymbol{\theta})$ is transformation-invariant, then the posterior predictive density expresses as*

$$p(\boldsymbol{y}^*|\boldsymbol{x}^*, \mathcal{D}) = \int_{\Theta} p(\boldsymbol{y}^*|\boldsymbol{x}^*, \boldsymbol{\theta}) p(\boldsymbol{\theta}|\mathcal{D}) \, \mathrm{d}\boldsymbol{\theta} \tag{3}$$

$$= |\mathcal{E}| \int_{\mathcal{S}_j} p(\boldsymbol{y}^*|\boldsymbol{x}^*, \boldsymbol{\theta}) p(\boldsymbol{\theta}|\mathcal{D}) \, \mathrm{d}\boldsymbol{\theta} + \int_{\mathcal{S}^0} p(\boldsymbol{y}^*|\boldsymbol{x}^*, \boldsymbol{\theta}) p(\boldsymbol{\theta}|\mathcal{D}) \, \mathrm{d}\boldsymbol{\theta}$$

$$\approx |\mathcal{E}| \int_{\mathcal{S}_j} p(\boldsymbol{y}^*|\boldsymbol{x}^*, \boldsymbol{\theta}) p(\boldsymbol{\theta}|\mathcal{D}) \, \mathrm{d}\boldsymbol{\theta}. \tag{4}$$

The proof of Corollary 1 is given in Supplementary Material A.5. It follows from Proposition 1 and the assumption of transformation-invariant prior densities, which is often satisfied in practice (e.g., for widely-applied isotropic Gaussian priors). We can further approximate (3) by (4) as the set $\mathcal{S}^0 \subset \mathbb{R}^d$ is of negligible size (depending on Θ, potentially even with zero Lebesgue measure).

As a consequence of Corollary 1, the PPD can be obtained up to the residual set by only integrating over uniquely identified parameter states from one of the sets $\mathcal{S}_j$, with a multiplicative factor $|\mathcal{E}|$ that corrects the probability values by the amount of redundancy in the posterior. In other words, only a fraction $1/|\mathcal{E}|$ of the posterior must be sampled in order to infer a set of uniquely identified parameter states of the NN, and thus, to obtain the full PPD. This reduces the target sampling space drastically, as illustrated in Fig. 1. For example, it allows the posterior space of a single-layer, tanh-activated network with 128 neurons to be effectively reduced to a 10^{254}-th of its original size.

In the case of an infinite amount of equioutput transformations, such as in ReLU-activated MLPs (the scaling factor $|c| > 0$ can be chosen arbitrarily), we can use similar reasoning. Only one representative set of the posterior density needs to be observed in order to capture the full functional diversity of a network because the integrals over two representative sets are identical. For a more in-depth discussion of ReLU symmetries, see, for example, [4].

How to Obtain a Representative Set? In practice, when using Monte Carlo to approximate Equation (4), it is not necessary to actually constrain the sampling procedure to a specific set $\mathcal{S}_j$, which might indeed not be straightforward[4]. Since any equioutput transformation is known *a priori*, we just need to be aware of the fact that each sample can theoretically be mapped to different representative sets after running the sampling procedure. Hence, for the calculation of the PPD integral, the samples can remain scattered across the various representative sets as long as they cover all functionally diverse parameter states. For

---

[4] [10] demonstrate that finding invariant representations for groups acting on the input space is an NP-hard problem. While we are not aware of such a result for the parameter space, the NP-hardness in [10] for permutations of the inputs only suggests a similar property in our case.

the purpose of providing better interpretability and analytic approximation of the posterior, it may still be worthwhile to explicitly remove the symmetries. In Sect. 5.3, we demonstrate such symmetry removal using a custom algorithm for tanh-activated networks (Supplementary Material B).

4.2   An Upper Bound for Markov Chains

The question remains how many samples are needed to approximate a set of uniquely identified parameter states sufficiently well. Even in a symmetry-free setting, BNN posteriors can exhibit multiple functionally diverse modes representing structurally different hypotheses, depending on the network architecture and the underlying data-generating process. For example, in Sect. 5.3, we discuss the case of an under-parameterized network that preserves three distinctive modes caused by its restricted capacity.

In the following, we assume $\nu \in \mathbb{N}$ functionally diverse modes with the goal of visiting every mode or its local proximity at least once when running MCMC. As the ability to switch from one mode to another within a chain depends on various factors, such as the acceptance probability and the current state of other parameters, increasing the number of samples per chain does not necessarily correlate with the number of visited modes. We, therefore, propose to focus on the number of independent chains, rather than the number of samples per chain, to effectively control the number of visited modes.

This further allows us to derive an upper bound for the number of independent chains that are required to visit every mode at least once. The number of samples from each chain will then ultimately determine the approximation quality. In the computation of the PPD, we formulate the Monte Carlo integration over all samples from all chains simultaneously [23]. In practice, given a user-defined number of maximal resources ρ (e.g., CPU cores), the following proposition provides a lower bound on the probability that the number of chains $\mathcal{G}$ necessary to visit every mode remains below the resource limit of the user (i.e., $\mathcal{G} < \rho$).

Proposition 2 (Probabilistic bound for sufficient number of Markov chains).   *Let $\pi_1, \ldots, \pi_\nu$ be the respective probabilities of the ν functionally diverse modes to be visited by an independently started Markov chain and $\Pi_J := \sum_{j \in J} \pi_j$. Then, given ρ chains,*

$$\mathbb{P}(\mathcal{G} < \rho) \geq 1 - \rho^{-1} \left\{ \sum_{q=0}^{\nu-1} (-1)^{\nu-1-q} \sum_{J:|J|=q} (1 - \Pi_J)^{-1} \right\}. \tag{5}$$

The proof can be found in Supplementary Material A.6. Note that this bound is independent of the NN architecture and only depends on the assumptions about the number and probabilities of functionally diverse modes ν, disregarding symmetric copies. Proposition 2 can be used to calculate the number of MCMC chains given certain assumptions – for example, from domain knowledge, or in a worst-case scenario calculation – and thus provides practical guidance for MCMC sampling of MLPs. Judging by the comparably high predictive performance of local approximations such as LA and DE [21, 22], we conclude that a small amount of functional modes is reasonable to assume in practice. Our qualitative experiments in Sect. 5 support this supposition.

Table 1. Mean log pointwise predictive density (LPPD) values on test sets (larger is better; one standard error in parentheses). The highest performance per dataset and network is highlighted in bold.

	Smaller network f_1			Larger network f_2		
	MCMC (ours)	MCMC (s.c.)	DE	MCMC (ours)	MCMC (s.c.)	DE
$\mathcal{D}_S$	**−0.53** (± 0.09)	−0.56 (± 0.11)	−0.58 (± 0.11)	**−0.59** (± 0.12)	**−0.59** (± 0.12)	−2.13 (± 0.03)
$\mathcal{D}_I$	**0.79** (± 0.06)	0.65 (± 0.07)	0.56 (± 0.06)	**0.91** (± 0.09)	**0.91** (± 0.09)	−2.02 (± 0.02)
$\mathcal{D}_R$	0.64 (± 0.10)	**0.75** (± 0.11)	−1.46 (± 0.06)	**0.95** (± 0.08)	**0.95** (± 0.08)	−2.20 (± 0.02)
Airfoil	**−0.74** (± 0.04)	−0.80 (± 0.05)	−1.62 (± 0.03)	**0.92** (± 0.05)	0.72 (± 0.10)	−2.17 (± 0.01)
Concrete	**−0.41** (± 0.05)	−0.44 (± 0.06)	−1.59 (± 0.03)	**0.26** (± 0.07)	0.25 (± 0.07)	−2.03 (± 0.01)
Diabetes	**−1.20** (± 0.07)	**−1.20** (± 0.07)	−1.47 (± 0.07)	**−1.18** (± 0.08)	−1.22 (± 0.09)	−2.09 (± 0.04)
Energy	**0.92** (± 0.04)	0.69 (± 0.12)	−1.76 (± 0.02)	2.07 (± 0.46)	**2.38** (± 0.11)	−1.99 (± 0.02)
ForestF	**−1.37** (± 0.07)	**−1.37** (± 0.07)	−1.60 (± 0.06)	**−1.43** (± 0.45)	−1.69 (± 0.49)	−2.20 (± 0.02)
Yacht	**1.90** (± 0.16)	1.29 (± 0.56)	−1.14 (± 0.14)	**3.31** (± 0.21)	0.15 (± 0.09)	−2.18 (± 0.03)

As an example of applying Proposition 2, assume $\nu = 3$ functionally diverse modes in a reference set with $\pi_1 = 0.57, \pi_2 = 0.35, \pi_3 = 0.08$ (chosen to represent a rather diverse functional mode set). An upper bound of $\rho = 1274$ chains ensures that we observe all functionally diverse modes with probability $\mathbb{P}(\mathcal{G} < \rho) \geq 0.99$.

5 Experiments

We now investigate our theoretical findings and compare the resulting approach to single-chain MCMC and DE. In all experiments[5], we employ a Bayesian regression model with a normal likelihood function, standard normal prior for parameters $\boldsymbol{\theta}$, and a truncated standard normal prior restricted to the positive real line for the variance of the normal likelihood, which we treat as a nuisance parameter. Depending on the task, we either use a No-U-Turn sampler [16] with 2^{10} warmup steps to collect a single sample from the posterior or derive the maximum-a-posteriori estimator using a gradient-based method (details are given in Supplementary Material C.2, C.3).

5.1 Performance Comparison

In our first experiment, we demonstrate the predictive performance of BNNs, where the PPD is calculated based on MCMC sampling, using the derived upper bound for the number of chains (ours). In this case, we collect one sample per chain for G chains, and thus G samples in total. This is compared to

---

[5] https://github.com/jgwiese/mcmc_bnn_symmetry.

MCMC sampling collecting G samples from a single chain (s.c.), and DE with ten ensemble members on three synthetic datasets ($\mathcal{D}_S$, $\mathcal{D}_I$, and $\mathcal{D}_R$) as well as benchmark data from [9] (for dataset details and additional results on LA, see Supplementary Material C.1 and E.1, respectively). We use a smaller NN f_1 with a single hidden layer containing three neurons and a larger network f_2 with three hidden layers having 16 neurons each, both with tanh activation. As in Sect. 4.2, we assume three functionally diverse modes $\nu = 3$ and mode probabilities $\pi_1 = 0.57, \pi_2 = 0.35, \pi_3 = 0.08$ as in the given example. To demonstrate the performance of our MCMC-based PPD approximation, we measure the goodness-of-fit on the test data using the log point-wise predictive density (LPPD; [13])

$$\text{LPPD} = \log \int_\Theta p(\boldsymbol{y}^*|\boldsymbol{x}^*, \boldsymbol{\theta})p(\boldsymbol{\theta}|\mathcal{D})\, \mathrm{d}\boldsymbol{\theta} \approx \log \left(\tfrac{1}{G} \sum_{g=1}^G p(\boldsymbol{y}^*|\boldsymbol{x}^*, \boldsymbol{\theta}^{(g)}) \right), \quad (6)$$

where $\boldsymbol{\theta}^{(1)}, \ldots, \boldsymbol{\theta}^{(G)}$ are G samples obtained across all chains via MCMC sampling from the parameter posterior density $p(\boldsymbol{\theta}|\mathcal{D})$. Equation (6) is evaluated at each test point $(\boldsymbol{x}^*, \boldsymbol{y}^*)$. Table 1 reports the mean LPPD across N^* independent test points for each combination of dataset and sampling scheme (see Supplementary Material C.1 for details). Our results clearly indicate that using only a moderate amount of Markov chains, following our approach, yields equal or even better performance than single-chain MCMC and DE in all but two experiments.

5.2   Practical Evaluation of Corollary 1

Next, we investigate the property derived in Corollary 1 using our proposed upper bound of chains, again with the assumption from the example in Sect. 4.2. To this end, we analyze the PPD for dataset $\mathcal{D}_I$, using network f_2. For every newly collected sample in the MCMC run, the updated PPD is computed approximately on a two-dimensional (input/output) grid. Then, the Kullback-Leibler (KL) divergence between consecutive densities is averaged over the grid of input values of f_2 (details in Supplementary Material D.1). As shown in Fig. 2, despite the size of the network f_2 and the high amount of equioutput parameter states $|\mathcal{E}| = \left(16! \cdot 2^{16} \right)^3 \approx 2.58 \cdot 10^{54}$, the PPD converges after notably fewer than $|\mathcal{E}|$ samples and plots of the function space indicate the saturation of functional diversity already after 1274 samples from as many chains.

5.3   Posterior Symmetry Removal

So far we were mainly concerned with the predictive performance of MCMC sampling. Yet, mapping all samples to a joint representative set, as characterized in Sect. 4.1, has the potential to reduce the effective weight space enormously, facilitating interpretability and possibly even analytical approximation. For this, we propose a custom algorithm for tanh-activated MLPs as a proof-of-concept. Our algorithm removes symmetries in a data-dependent manner and thus minimizes the number of remaining modes in the representative set (details in Supplementary Material B).

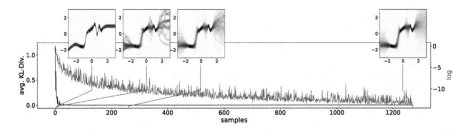

Fig. 2. Convergence of MCMC depicted as the change in KL-divergence on original (black) and log-scale (blue) when consecutively adding another sample from a new and independent chain and re-estimating the posterior density. Small overlaying plots: approximated PPD of the network after 2^0, 2^4, 2^8, and $G = 1274$ samples; darker colors correspond to higher probabilities. (Color figure online)

We demonstrate the efficacy of the approach for f_1 in two experiments A and B for datasets $\mathcal{D}_S$ and $\mathcal{D}_I$, respectively. For experiment A (Fig. 3, top) we visualize the neuron parameter space along the steps of the proposed algorithm (for details, see Algorithms 1–4 in Supplementary Material B). Different colors encode the current neuron index (i.e., one of $\{1, 2, 3\}$) in the hidden layer of the respective neuron parameter vector. Initially, symmetries of the posterior densities are clearly noticeable (Fig. 3a), and the neuron parameter vectors are distributed identically (Fig. 3d). Upon the first step of the algorithm (Fig. 3b), the parameter space is effectively halved as a consequence of removing the tanh-induced sign-flip symmetry, and three clusters remain. The second (clustering) step removes all permutation symmetries from the full posterior density by assigning areas of this parameter subspace to the neurons of the model. This is depicted in Fig. 3c and clearly shows the separation of states by different cluster colors. In Figs. 3d and 3e, the univariate marginal density of each neuron's incoming weight w_{2i1} reveals their reassignment to the parameter space. After running our algorithm, each neuron exhibits a distinct unimodal density, resulting in a unimodal density in the full parameter space (visualization in Supplementary Material E.3). We can conclude that only one functionally diverse mode exists in this case, which should also be recovered by local approximations like LA.

For experiment B (Fig. 3, bottom), we focus on the visualization of the full parameter posterior density obtained after the application of the symmetry removal algorithm (Fig. 3f). Three functionally diverse modes, represented by different colors, remain in the BNN posterior. We can now interpret these modes in function space by further clustering the transformed samples using a spectral clustering approach (details in Supplementary Material D.2). Figures 3g-j visualize the network parameter states in the function space, revealing three functionally diverse hypotheses the network can potentially learn from the given dataset. Such knowledge allows for a better-suited approximation by, e.g., a mixture of Laplace approximations (MoLA; [11]), as shown in Supplementary Material E.2. Note that approaches focusing on a single mode, such as standard

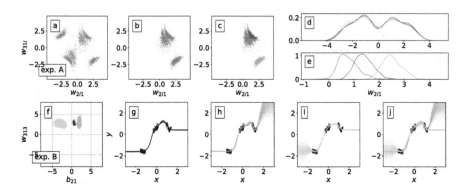

Fig. 3. For experiment A (top row), the parameter subspaces of hidden neurons are visualized in their initial state as obtained when running MCMC (a), and after their transformation and reassignment during the steps of Algorithm 4 (b, c). Different colors encode the current neuron index in the hidden layer. By reassigning neurons, Algorithm 4 effectively finds an optimal reference set and allows to separate the multimodal complex univariate marginal density (d) into three univariate densities. For experiment B (bottom row), the MLP parameter posterior density after symmetry removal results in a tri-modal system, here illustrated as a bivariate plot (f). Investigating these modes, we find that all are functionally diverse, i.e., represent a different hypothesis of the dataset (g-i). Combined, they form the full function space (j).

LA, would have captured only a third of the functional diversity. For meaningful UQ, it is thus imperative that all functionally diverse modes are accounted for.

6   Discussion

We showed that the PPD for Bayesian MLPs can be obtained from just a fraction of the parameter space due to the existence of equioutput parameter states. Together with an upper bound on the number of MCMC chains to guarantee the recovery of every functionally diverse mode, our approach paves the way towards exact uncertainty quantification (up to a Monte Carlo error) in deep learning. Furthermore, we demonstrate the use of symmetry removal and present a proof-of-concept approach to map samples of tanh-activated MLPs to a representative set. This *post-hoc* procedure improves the interpretability of the symmetry-free posterior density drastically and facilitates analytical approximations. As a future research direction, we plan to investigate whether our MCMC sampling approach can be improved by initializing the sampling states in an informative way via ensemble training, building upon insights in [14,28,37].

Acknowledgments. LW is supported by the DAAD programme Konrad Zuse Schools of Excellence in Artificial Intelligence, sponsored by the German Federal Ministry of Education and Research.

References

1. Agrawal, D., Ostrowski, J.: A classification of G-invariant shallow neural networks. In: Advances in Neural Information Processing Systems (2022)
2. Ainsworth, S., Hayase, J., Srinivasa, S.: Git Re-Basin: merging models modulo permutation symmetries. In: The Eleventh International Conference on Learning Representations (2023)
3. Bardenet, R., Kégl, B.: An adaptive Monte-Carlo Markov chain algorithm for inference from mixture signals. J. Phys. Conf. Ser. **368**, 012044 (2012)
4. Bona-Pellissier, J., Bachoc, F., Malgouyres, F.: Parameter identifiability of a deep feedforward ReLU neural network (2021)
5. Van den Broeck, G., Kersting, K., Natarajan, S., Poole, D.: An Introduction to Lifted Probabilistic Inference. MIT Press, Cambridge (2021)
6. Chen, A.M., Lu, H.M., Hecht-Nielsen, R.: On the geometry of feedforward neural network error surfaces. Neural Comput. **5**(6), 910–927 (1993)
7. Daxberger, E., Kristiadi, A., Immer, A., Eschenhagen, R., Bauer, M., Hennig, P.: Laplace redux - effortless Bayesian deep learning. In: 35th Conference on Neural Information Processing Systems (NeurIPS 2021) (2021)
8. Draxler, F., Veschgini, K., Salmhofer, M., Hamprecht, F.: Essentially no barriers in neural network energy landscape. In: Proceedings of the 35th International Conference on Machine Learning, pp. 1309–1318. PMLR (2018)
9. Dua, D., Graff, C.: UCI Machine Learning Repository (2017)
10. Ensign, D., Neville, S., Paul, A., Venkatasubramanian, S.: The complexity of explaining neural networks through (group) invariants. In: Proceedings of Machine Learning Research, vol. 76 (2017)
11. Eschenhagen, R., Daxberger, E., Hennig, P., Kristiadi, A.: Mixtures of Laplace approximations for improved post-Hoc uncertainty in deep learning. In: Bayesian Deep Learning Workshop, NeurIPS 2021 (2021)
12. Garipov, T., Izmailov, P., Podoprikhin, D., Vetrov, D.P., Wilson, A.G.: Loss surfaces, mode connectivity, and fast ensembling of DNNs. In: Proceedings of the 32nd Conference on Neural Information Processing Systems (NeurIPS 2018) (2018)
13. Gelman, A., Hwang, J., Vehtari, A.: Understanding predictive information criteria for Bayesian models. Stat. Comput. **24**(6), 997–1016 (2014)
14. Graf, S., Luschgy, H.: Foundations of Quantization for Probability Distributions. Springer, Heidelberg (2007). https://doi.org/10.1007/BFb0103945
15. Hecht-Nielsen, R.: On the algebraic structure of feedforward network weight spaces. In: Advanced Neural Computers, pp. 129–135. Elsevier, Amsterdam (1990)
16. Hoffman, M.D., Gelman, A.: The No-U-Turn sampler: adaptively setting path lengths in Hamiltonian Monte Carlo. J. Mach. Learn. Res. **15**(47), 1593–1623 (2014)
17. Hüllermeier, E., Waegeman, W.: Aleatoric and epistemic uncertainty in machine learning: an introduction to concepts and methods. Mach. Learn. **110** (2021)
18. Izmailov, P., Vikram, S., Hoffman, M.D., Wilson, A.G.: What are Bayesian neural network posteriors really like? In: Proceedings of the 38th International Conference on Machine Learning, vol. 139. PMLR (2021)
19. Kipf, T.N., Welling, M.: Semi-supervised classification with graph convolutional networks. In: ICLR 2017 (2017)
20. Kůrková, V., Kainen, P.C.: Functionally equivalent feedforward neural networks. Neural Comput. **6**(3), 543–558 (1994)

21. Lakshminarayanan, B., Pritzel, A., Blundell, C.: Simple and scalable predictive uncertainty estimation using deep ensembles. In: Proceedings of the 31st Conference on Neural Information Processing Systems (NIPS 2017) (2017)
22. MacKay, D.J.C.: Bayesian interpolation. Neural Comput. **4**, 415–447 (1992)
23. Margossian, C.C., Hoffman, M.D., Sountsov, P., Riou-Durand, L., Vehtari, A., Gelman, A.: Nested $\hat{R}$: assessing the convergence of Markov chain Monte Carlo when running many short chains (2022)
24. Nalisnick, E.T.: On priors for Bayesian neural networks. Ph.D. thesis, University of California, Irvine (2018)
25. Niepert, M.: Markov chains on orbits of permutation groups. In: Proceedings of the Twenty-Eighth Conference on Uncertainty in Artificial Intelligence, p. 624–633. UAI'12, AUAI Press, Arlington, Virginia, USA (2012)
26. Niepert, M.: Symmetry-aware marginal density estimation. In: Proceedings of the Twenty-Seventh AAAI Conference on Artificial Intelligence. AAAI'13, pp. 725–731. AAAI Press (2013)
27. Papamarkou, T., Hinkle, J., Young, M.T., Womble, D.: Challenges in Markov chain Monte Carlo for Bayesian neural networks. Stat. Sci. **37**(3) (2022)
28. Pearce, T., Leibfried, F., Brintrup, A.: Uncertainty in neural networks: approximately Bayesian ensembling. In: Proceedings of the Twenty Third International Conference on Artificial Intelligence and Statistics. Proceedings of Machine Learning Research, vol. 108, pp. 234–244. PMLR, 26–28 August 2020
29. Petzka, H., Trimmel, M., Sminchisescu, C.: Notes on the symmetries of 2-layer ReLU-networks. In: Northern Lights Deep Learning Workshop, vol. 1 (2020)
30. Pittorino, F., Ferraro, A., Perugini, G., Feinauer, C., Baldassi, C., Zecchina, R.: Deep networks on toroids: removing symmetries reveals the structure of flat regions in the landscape geometry. In: Proceedings of the 39th International Conference on Machine Learning, vol. 162. PMLR (2022)
31. Pourzanjani, A.A., Jiang, R.M., Petzold, L.R.: Improving the identifiability of neural networks for Bayesian inference. In: Second Workshop on Bayesian Deep Learning (NIPS) (2017)
32. Rosenthal, J.S.: Parallel computing and Monte Carlo algorithms. Far East J. Theor. Stat. **4**, 207–236 (2000)
33. Sen, D., Papamarkou, T., Dunson, D.: Bayesian neural networks and dimensionality reduction (2020). arXiv: 2008.08044
34. Sussmann, H.J.: Uniqueness of the weights for minimal feedforward nets with a given input-output map. Neural Netw. **5**(4), 589–593 (1992)
35. Tatro, N.J., Chen, P.Y., Das, P., Melnyk, I., Sattigeri, P., Lai, R.: Optimizing mode connectivity via neuron alignment. In: Proceedings of the 34th Conference on Neural Information Processing Systems (NeurIPS 2020) (2020)
36. Vlačić, V., Bölcskei, H.: Affine symmetries and neural network identifiability. Adv. Math. **376**, 107485 (2021)
37. Wilson, A.G., Izmailov, P.: Bayesian deep learning and a probabilistic perspective of generalization. In: Proceedings of the 34th International Conference on Neural Information Processing Systems. NIPS'20. Curran Associates Inc., Red Hook, NY, USA (2020)

Cooperative Bayesian Optimization
for Imperfect Agents

Ali Khoshvishkaie[1], Petrus Mikkola[1], Pierre-Alexandre Murena[1,2(✉)],
and Samuel Kaski[1,3]

[1] Department of Computer Science, Aalto University, Helsinki, Finland
{ali.khoshvishkaie,petrus.mikkola,pierre-Alexandre.murena,
samuel.kaski}@aalto.fi
[2] Hamburg University of Technology, Hamburg, Germany
[3] Department of Computer Science, University of Manchester, Manchester, UK

Abstract. We introduce a cooperative Bayesian optimization problem
for optimizing black-box functions of two variables where two agents
choose together at which points to query the function but have only
control over one variable each. This setting is inspired by human-AI
teamwork, where an AI-assistant helps its human user solve a problem, in
this simplest case, collaborative optimization. We formulate the solution
as sequential decision-making, where the agent we control models the
user as a computationally rational agent with prior knowledge about the
function. We show that strategic planning of the queries enables better
identification of the global maximum of the function as long as the user
avoids excessive exploration. This planning is made possible by using
Bayes Adaptive Monte Carlo planning and by endowing the agent with a
user model that accounts for conservative belief updates and exploratory
sampling of the points to query.

1 Introduction

Human-AI cooperation refers to the collaboration between human and artificial
intelligence (AI) driven agents to achieve a common goal [16]. In the *cooperative*
scenario, the agents work autonomously but interdependently, each leveraging
their unique skills and abilities to collectively reach the shared objective. The
cooperation between a human and an AI agent can be impaired by limitations
in their information processing abilities and various other factors such as biases,
heuristics, and incomplete knowledge [10]. It has already been established that
any cooperation is more effective when the involved agents have a *theory of mind*
of the others [7]. It would therefore be helpful if the AI agent could take into
account the human's information processing capabilities and biases and adapt
to the changing needs and preferences of the human user [19].

Supplementary Information The online version contains supplementary material
available at https://doi.org/10.1007/978-3-031-43412-9_28.

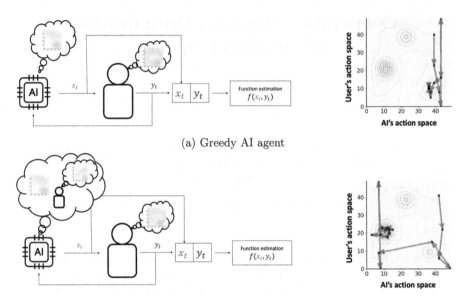

(a) Greedy AI agent

(b) Our proposed agent: Strategic planner with a user model.

Fig. 1. Interaction scenario between the user and the AI agent in the optimization task. Unlike a *greedy agent* (a), the AI agent we propose (b) has a *model* of the user and plans its actions by anticipating the user's behaviour. This results in a more efficient cooperative exploration of the domain, and therefore avoids getting stuck in a local optimum. This is visible in the right-hand side plots, showing the corresponding trajectories of queries to the function f.

A specific kind of human-AI cooperation is when the decision is jointly taken by two agents for a common goal, and each controls only their part of the decision. An illustrative example is Hand and Brain chess, a team chess variant in which two players (the Hand and the Brain) play on each side. Each move is jointly decided by the team, with the Brain calling out a piece and the Hand being responsible for moving it. In this game, the Brain should essentially consider a move that is understandable for the Hand. Otherwise, the Hand moves the piece to a strategically bad position, resulting in a disastrous move. If each player carries out their task without anticipating the other team member, the team will end up taking a sub-optimal action. The anticipation is done by building a *model* of the partner.

To study this setup in a controlled environment, we propose a cooperative Bayesian optimization task. The AI agent and human user aim to perform a sequential black-box optimization task in a 2D space. At each step, the human-AI team chooses a point to query the function. The choice is made by the AI agent opting for the first coordinate and then the human user selecting the other one. In this optimization task, the human user and the AI agent, both with partial information, cooperatively take part in data acquisition. We formulate this cooperative data acquisition as a repeated Bayesian game between the user and the agent played for a finite horizon. The contributions of this paper are:

- We propose a collaborative AI algorithm for settings where the AI agent plans its action by assessing the user's knowledge and decision process without any prior interaction with the user.
- We show empirically that the algorithm is able to learn the user's behaviour in an online setting and use it to anticipate the user's actions.
- We show empirically that the algorithm helps the team in the optimization task (measured as the team optimization score) compared to various baselines, such as a greedy algorithm that maximizes its own beliefs. This is done by helping a better exploration of the domain of the function.

2   Cooperative Bayesian Optimization

2.1   Problem Formulation

We consider a problem where a team of two agents, the *human user* and the *AI agent*, aims to maximize a black-box function $f : \mathcal{X} \times \mathcal{Y}$ of two parameters $(x, y) \in \mathcal{X} \times \mathcal{Y}$. Note here that the function is not necessarily 2-dimensional. The team explores the domain $\mathcal{X} \times \mathcal{Y}$ by acquiring new observations of f. The exploration consists of a sequence of queries of f at points $(x_t, y_t) \in \mathcal{X} \times \mathcal{Y}$. The outcomes of the query are noisy and we denote by $\bar{f}(x, y)$ the outcome of the query at point (x, y). In this respect, the task of the team is similar to a *Bayesian Optimization* (BO) task.

The team proceeds by sequentially querying T points. At each step t, the team adopts the following protocol for the choice of (x_t, y_t), presented in Fig. 1. The AI agent selects $x_t \in \mathcal{X}$ first. The human user observes the value of x_t picked by the AI agent and then selects $y_t \in \mathcal{Y}$. Finally, both agents observe the selected tuple (x_t, y_t) and the value of $f(x_t, y_t)$. In this paper, we adopt the point of view of the AI agent and therefore focus on how to optimally select the first coordinate x_t. It is important to mention that $\mathcal{X}$ and $\mathcal{Y}$ are not necessarily one-dimensional, but can describe any two sets of variables.

The final performance of the optimization process is measured by the *optimization score* (described in Sect. 4.2). We view this score as a more understandable alternative to the directly related measure of simple regret, defined as $f^* - f_T^*$.

2.2   Mathematical Formalization

We address the problem of the AI agent as a repeated Bayesian game, using the formalism of model-based reinforcement learning, considering the AI agent as a decision-making agent interacting with an environment made up of the function f and the human user. In this environment, the agent takes actions (choice of a coordinate x_t) and gets rewarded depending on the action x_t, the user's choice y_t and the value of the function $f(x_t, y_t)$.

We describe the agent's decision-making problem as Partially Observable Markov Decision Process (POMDP) $\mathcal{M} = \langle \mathcal{A}, \mathcal{S}, \mathcal{T}, \Omega, \mathcal{O}, \mathcal{R} \rangle$, where the notations are explained in what follows.

The space $\mathcal{A}$ is the space of the actions available to the agent. In our context, it corresponds to the set $\mathcal{X}$ of points available to the agent. For this reason, we will use x (instead of the standard notation a usually used in POMDPs) to designate the coordinate chosen by the agent. A state $s \in \mathcal{S}$ describes a state of the agent's environment, which is made up of the function f and the user. A state is then defined as a tuple $s = (f_{AI}, \theta)$, where $f_{AI} : \mathcal{X} \times \mathcal{Y} \to \mathbb{R}$ is agent's estimation of function f and θ is a parameters set characterizing the user. The transition $\mathcal{T}(s, x, s')$ measures the probability of a transition from state s to state s' after agent's action x. By definition, the function f is fixed, and consequently the transition probability $\mathcal{T}$ can be written as:

$$\mathcal{T}(s, x, s') = \mathbb{I}(f_{AI} = f'_{AI}) p(\theta'|s, x) \tag{1}$$

where $s = (f_{AI}, \theta)$, $s' = (f'_{AI}, \theta')$ and $\mathbb{I}$ is the identity function. An observation $\omega \in \Omega$ corresponds to the user's choice y and the value of f at point (x, y), i.e. $\Omega = \mathcal{Y} \times \mathbb{R}$. The observation prediction $\mathcal{O}(\omega|s, x) \in [0, 1]$ is the probability that $\omega \in \Omega$ is observed after action x has been played within environment state s. Unlike some other settings, the observation prediction $\mathcal{O}$ in our context does not depend on the new state, but only on the state before the action. This probability decomposes as

$$\mathcal{O}(\omega = (y, z)|s, x) = p(y|s, x) p(\bar{f}(x, y) = z|s, x, y) \tag{2}$$

where the probability $p(y|s, x)$ corresponds to user's decision-making and the probability $p(\bar{f}(x, y) = z|s, x, y)$ to function sampling. The reward $\mathcal{R}(x, s, \omega)$ measures the pay-off of agent's action x in state s after observing ω. The choice of the reward function in our implementation will be discussed in Sect. 3.4.

2.3   User Model

In Eqs. 1 and 2, the probabilities $p(\theta'|s, x)$ and $p(y|s, x)$ describe the user's behaviour, that is, how the user updates their beliefs and how they make decisions. We note that $p(\theta'|s, x)$ can be decomposed as

$$p(\theta'|s, x) = \int_z \sum_y p(\theta'|s, x, y, f(x, y) = z) p(f(x, y) = z|s, x, y) p(y|s, x) dz \tag{3}$$

where the term $p(f(x, y) = z|s, x, y)$ does not depend on the user. Therefore, the user's behaviour is fully defined by $p(\theta'|s, x, y, f(x, y))$ and $p(y|s, x)$.

In the following, we will call the tuple $(p(\theta'|s, x, y, f(x, y)), p(y|s, x))$ the *user model*. The user model describes the role played by the user within the environment of the agent. In practice, it will be used to simulate the behaviour of the user, which is useful in particular when planning for the action to play. The user model is not necessarily an accurate description of the user's behaviour, but is a model used by the agent for making decisions. The choice of this model will restrict the possibilities of behaviours that the agent will be able to consider. In the case where the user is human, a useful user model should be able to describe computationally rational behaviours [8].

3   Implementation

In this section, we introduce the practical solution to the Cooperative Bayesian Optimization problem, considering a minimal user model. This model describes a user with partial knowledge about the function, able to update their belief and select their actions in a way that balances exploitation and exploration.

3.1   Bayes Adaptive Monte Carlo Planning

In order to solve the POMDP introduced in Sect. 2.2 and plan the AI agent's actions, we rely on a Bayesian model-based Reinforcement learning method. This method is used to perform a *zero-shot* planning, where the agent has no initial information about the user's behaviour. At each iteration, the model is updated based on the previous user's actions, and a zero-shot planning method is employed to plan for the future.

In order to solve the POMDP, the posterior distribution of the parameters is estimated using the inference method described in Sect. 3.3 below. This posterior distribution is used to plan the actions x_t by enabling a Monte-Carlo estimation of the value of each action: At each iteration, we run several simulations with fixed state s_t sampled from the posterior distribution. In these conditions, having a fixed and known state transforms the POMDP into a simple MDP: This makes it possible to compute the value of the action for this state and, consequently, to get a Monte-Carlo estimation of the value of an action. Finally, the action that maximizes the estimated value is chosen. It has been proven that this process converges to the Bayes-optimal policy with infinite samples [9].

3.2   User Model Specification

We propose a simple user model describing a computationally rational user with partial knowledge about the function to be optimized. This user model is an instantiation of the general form of user models as introduced in Sect. 2.3.

User's Knowledge. We represent the user's partial knowledge of the function f using a Gaussian Process [18]. A Gaussian Process (GP) is a stochastic process over real-valued functions, such that every finite collection of these random variables has a multivariate normal distribution. We will denote this GP at step t as $f_{um}^{(t)}$. We emphasize that f_{um} is not a function, but a prior over functions $\mathcal{X} \times \mathcal{Y} \to \mathbb{R}$. This choice is motivated by the observation that Bayesian Optimization based on GPs provides a surprisingly good framework to explain active function learning and optimization in humans [2].

The user's GP is assumed to have been initialized based on the observation of a collection of N_u points $\mathcal{D}_u = \{(x_i^u, y_i^u, \bar{f}(x_i^u, y_i^u))\}_{i=1,\ldots,N_u}$, using GP regression. For any unseen function value $f(x, y)$, GP regression models this as a Gaussian random variable with closed-form mean and variance (see [18], Equations (2.23) and (2.24)). The equations require specifying the covariance (kernel) function, which in this paper is taken to be the squared exponential kernel [18, Eq. (2.16)]. The hyperparameters of the kernel function are optimized by maximizing the marginal likelihood.

Belief Update. The values of the function f sampled during the interaction are observed by the user and used to sequentially update their GP f_{um}. At time t, the user's GP $f_{um}^{(t)}$ is updated by observing $\mathcal{D}_t = \{(x_t, y_t), \bar{f}(x_t, y_t)\}$. We denote by $\mathcal{B}_{bayes}(f_{um}^{(t)}|\{(x_t, y_t), \bar{f}(x_t, y_t)\})$ the GP obtained after Bayes optimal belief updating, defined as the standard updates (Equations (2.23) and (2.24) in [18]).

However, it has been documented in behavioural studies [6] that humans deviate from the Bayesian optimal belief update, because of various cognitive biases [23]. Consequently, in our user model, we consider the *conservative belief updating* operator $\mathcal{B}$ introduced by Kovach [13]:

$$f_{um}^{(t+1)} = \alpha f_{um}^{(t)} + (1 - \alpha)\mathcal{B}_{bayes}(f_{um}^{(t)}|\{(x_t, y_t), \bar{f}(x_t, y_t)\}), \qquad (4)$$

where $\alpha \in [0, 1]$ represents the degree of *conservatism*. A low values of α corresponds to an almost Bayes-optimal behaviour, while the case $\alpha = 1$ corresponds to the user ignoring the new observations and not updating their belief.

Decision-Making. Motivated by the observation of Borji and Itti [2], we model the user's choice of an action y_t as the maximization of an acquisition function $y \mapsto A(x_t, y)$. We consider the UCB acquisition function based on the GP $f_{um}^{(t)}$:

$$A_t(y|x_t) = \mathbb{E}\left[f_{um}^{(t)}(x_t, y)\right] + \beta\sqrt{\mathbb{V}\left[f_{um}^{(t)}(x_t, y)\right]} \qquad (5)$$

where $\mathbb{E}[f_{um}^{(t)}(x_t, y)]$ and $\mathbb{V}[f_{um}^{(t)}(x_t, y)]$ are respectively the mean and the variance of the GP $f_{um}^{(t)}$ at point (x_t, y), and $\beta \in [0, 1]$ is an *exploration-exploitation trade-off* parameter. A low value of β corresponds to less explorative behaviour, exploiting the current belief over f, while a larger value corresponds to more explorative behaviour, evaluating f at points with larger uncertainty. Given the AI's action x_t, a sensible choice of an action y_t for the user would consist in maximizing the acquisition function $A_t(y|x_t)$.

This choice of y_t by a maximization can be interpreted as an event of many pairwise comparisons among different actions $y \in \mathcal{X}$: Choosing the action y_t means preferring it to all the others $y \neq y_t$. Inspired by [15], we build a probabilistic model of user preferences upon Thurstone's law of comparative judgment [22] by assuming that the user's action y_t given x_t is corrupted by Gaussian noise,

$$y_t = \arg\max_y \left(A_t(y|x_t) + W(y)\right), \qquad (6)$$

where W is a white Gaussian noise with mean $\mathbb{E}[W(y)] = 0$ and auto-correlation $\mathbb{E}[W(y)W(y')] = \sigma^2$ if $y = y'$ and 0 otherwise. The likelihood $p(y_t|s_t, x_t)$ of a single observation $y_t|x_t$ corresponding to this noise process takes the form

$$p(y_t|s_t, x_t) = \prod_{i=1}^{m} \left(1 - [\Phi * \phi]\left(\frac{A_t(y_i|x_t) - A_t(y_t|x_t)}{\sigma}\right)\right), \tag{7}$$

where Φ and ϕ are the cumulative and density function of the standard normal distribution, respectively, $*$ and is the convolution operator. To evaluate the likelihood, $f_{um}^{(t)}$ and $A_t(y|x_t)$ should be computed recursively by using the aforementioned equations. For fixed α and β, this is possible given the function sampling data $(\mathcal{D}_t)_{t=1}^{T}$. The joint likelihood $P\left((y_t|x_t)_{t=1}^{T}, (\mathcal{D}_t)_{t=1}^{T}|\alpha, \beta\right)$ is the product of the single events $y_t|x_t$ for $t = 1, ..., T$.

Summary: Definition of the User Model. The introduced user model is characterized by three parameters: the user's knowledge of the function f_{um}, the degree of conservatism α and the degree of explorativeness β. Using the notations of Sect. 2.2, we can write $\theta = (f_{um}, \alpha, \beta)$. We notice that these parameters are of different natures though: α and β are characteristics of the user, while f_{um} corresponds to a *mental state*, i.e. a description of what the user knows.

When defining the belief-updating probability $p(\theta'|s, a, y, f(a, y))$, we assume that the parameters α and β, as characteristics of the user, are stationary and therefore are not updated during the interaction. Only the user's GP is updated, following Eq. 4. With our definition of this user model, the user's decision-making $p(y|s, a)$ is defined in Eq. 7.

3.3   Inference of the User Model Parameters

The parameters $\theta = (f_{um}, \alpha, \beta)$ are not observed and need to be estimated online during the interaction, based on the user's actions. We adopt a Bayesian approach and the inference consists of estimating, at each time step t, the posterior distribution $p\left(\alpha, \beta, f_{um}\mid (y_\tau|x_\tau)_{\tau=1}^{t}, (\mathcal{D}_\tau)_{\tau=1}^{t}\right)$ given the interaction data $(y_\tau|x_\tau)_{\tau=1}^{t}$ and the function sampling data $(\mathcal{D}_\tau)_{\tau=1}^{t}$ with $\mathcal{D}_\tau = (x_\tau, y_\tau, \bar{f}(x_\tau, y_\tau))$. For this, we use the following decomposition:

$$p\left(\alpha, \beta, f_{um}\mid (y_\tau|x_\tau)_{\tau=1}^{t}, (\mathcal{D}_\tau)_{\tau=1}^{t}\right)$$
$$= p\left(\alpha, \beta\mid (y_\tau|x_\tau)_{\tau=1}^{t}, (\mathcal{D}_\tau)_{\tau=1}^{t}\right) p\left(f_{um}\mid (y_\tau|x_\tau)_{\tau=1}^{t}, (\mathcal{D}_\tau)_{\tau=1}^{t}, \alpha, \beta\right)$$

Estimation of (α, β). The estimation of (α, β) is done using Bayesian belief update. The initial prior is chosen to be the uniform distribution over the unit cube. The posterior distribution is approximated using the Laplace approximation, which consists in the following. The maximum a posteriori (MAP) estimate $(\alpha_{\text{MAP}}, \beta_{\text{MAP}})$ is computed by numerically maximizing the log posterior with the BFGS algorithm, which also approximates the Hessian. The posterior

$p\left(\alpha, \beta \mid (y_\tau | x_\tau)_{\tau=1}^t, (\mathcal{D}_\tau)_{\tau=1}^t\right)$ is approximated as a Gaussian distribution centered on $(\alpha_{\text{MAP}}, \beta_{\text{MAP}})$ with the covariance matrix corresponding to the inverse of the negative Hessian at the MAP estimate.

Estimation of f_{um}. The update of f_{um} as given in Equation (4) is deterministic when α is given. Consequently, the term $p\left(f_{um} \mid (y_\tau | x_\tau)_{\tau=1}^t, (\mathcal{D}_\tau)_{\tau=1}^t, \alpha, \beta\right)$ is trivial and does not need to be computed during the interaction. Since our planning algorithm (described in Sect. 3.1) relies on sampling from the parameters (α, β, f_{um}), f_{um} is computed from the whole trajectory $(\mathcal{D}_\tau)_{\tau=1}^t$ using the sampled value of α. For the initialization $f_{um}^{(0)}$, we consider that the user has a uniform prior over the function. This interprets as ignoring the fact that the user has prior knowledge.

3.4   Choice of the Reward Function

The reward for the agent, as introduced in Sect. 2.2, is designed to be a compromise of two parts, exposed in the following.

The first part is the expectation of the UCB score over the user's future action, calculated with f_{um} as estimated in the user model:

$$\mathcal{R}_1(x, s, \omega) = \mathbb{E}_{y \sim A_{usr}}\left[UCB(x, y)\right] \qquad (8)$$

Intuitively, this first part $\mathcal{R}_1$ shows how desirable the point (x, y) is for the user when the AI selects x. Therefore it values actions x for which the user is able to find a reasonably good y to query the function. Since $\mathcal{R}_1$ is based on the UCB score, it also guarantees a trade-off between the exploration and exploitation of the query point.

When the user's behaviour is almost uniform over actions (e.g. when the user is more explorative, because of having little knowledge of f or because of a high β), reward $\mathcal{R}_1$ is close to constant and is not enough to make good choices of x_t. We solve this problem by introducing a second part in the reward definition, that is based on the AI agent's knowledge of the function. This reward is defined as the average UCB score over the top K promising y values upon the AI's knowledge for a chosen action x:

$$\mathcal{R}_2(x, s, \omega) = \frac{1}{K} \sum_{y \in top_K(A_{ai})} UCB(x, y) \qquad (9)$$

This reduces the risk of relying too much on the user model, which is not prefect, especially at the beginning of the interaction.

We define the total reward as a linear combination of these two components:

$$\mathcal{R}(x, s, \omega) = \mathcal{R}_1(x, s, \omega) + C\,\mathcal{R}_2(x, s, \omega) \qquad (10)$$

where C is a compromising factor between the two terms, a hyperparameter of the proposed method.

4   Empirical Validation

In this section, we study the performance of our method in the proposed cooperative Bayesian game (Sect. 2). We examine scenarios where prior information is unevenly distributed among agents and when the human user characteristics vary. In particular, we are interested in how the user's degree of conservatism and explorativeness affect the outcome of the Bayesian game.[1]

4.1   Experimental Setup

Domain. We choose as a function f a 3-modal variant of the *Himmelblau function*. It is defined on $[0,1]^2$ and has 3 minima, located respectively at $(0.46, 0.8)$, $(0.22, 0.44)$ and $(0.74, 0.18)$. The amplitude of the maxima can be adjusted.

Experimental Protocol. We consider a synthetic user whose characteristics can be controlled. The agent follows the specification of a computationally rational user presented in Sect. 3.2: we assume a user who follows a Bayesian optimization routine based on the UCB acquisition function with an explorativeness parameter β, and a conservative GP-based belief updating with a conservatism parameter α. We create 2×2 configurations of the human user characteristics by considering the possible combinations of the values $\alpha \in \{0.1, 0.6\}$ and $\beta \in \{0.2, 0.7\}$. For example, the configuration $\alpha = 0.1$ and $\beta = 0.7$ refers to a human user who is conservative in belief updating but explorative in decision-making. These values have been chosen to reflect the extremes, with the user being almost completely conservative or almost perfectly Bayesian, and the user being almost exclusively exploitative or almost exclusively explorative.

We study the impact of this prior information by considering 3×3 configurations of prior information (see Sect. 2.2) as follows. We provide each of the two agents with either $N = 5$ points around local maxima or the global maximum, or no prior functions evaluations at all. We use the terms "Local", "Global", and "None" to refer to these configurations by considering possible permutations: (AI's prior, human's prior). The points are drawn from a multi-normal distribution centered on the position of the maximum (local or global). For example, (Global, Local) refers to the configuration, where the AI agent has $N = 5$ prior points around the global maximum, while the human user agent has $N = 5$ points around local maxima of the function.

For the experiments, we consider a discretization of the domain $\mathcal{X} \times \mathcal{Y}$ into a 50×50 grid. Given a simulated user, each experiment consists of 20 interaction steps. The results are averaged over a sample of 3 different functions f, generated as described above, and 10 different prior samples (initial points available to each agent before the interaction, see Sect. 2.3). For our agent, we use the reward defined in Eq. 10 with $C = 1$.

---

[1] Implementation of our method and source code for the experiments are available at https://github.com/ChessGeek95/AI-assisted-Bayesian-optimization/.

All experiments were run on a private cluster consisting of a mixture of Intel® Xeon® Gold 6248, Xeon® Gold 6148, Xeon® E5-2690 v3 and Xeon® E5-2680 v3 processors.

Baselines. To investigate the strengths of our method, we compare it to four baselines, two of which correspond to a single-agent Bayesian Optimization.

The single-agent BO baselines correspond to one single agent making the decision, i.e., opting for both coordinates of the point to query, and therefore correspond to the standard BO problem. The baselines illustrate empirical lower and upper bounds of the optimization performance:

- VanillaBO (random): Single-agent baseline, querying points (x, y) uniformly at random on the domain $\mathcal{X} \times \mathcal{Y}$. This is equivalent to two agents querying coordinates randomly, which is a lower bound on the performance that any team should at least achieve.
- VanillaBO (GP-UCB): Single-agent baseline, querying points (x, y) using an upper confidence bound [4] score upon a Gaussian processes pre-trained on the prior points. Since the agent has access to all prior data and absolute control over both coordinates, this is an upper bound on the performance. The value of β for this agent is chosen to be $\beta = 0.05$: it has been chosen because it gives optimal results compared to other β.

We also compare the performance of our method to two other comparable multi-agent BO algorithms, corresponding to different strategies for solving the Cooperative Bayesian Optimization task:

- RandomAI: The AI agent chooses x uniformly at random on the domain $\mathcal{X}$.
- GreedyAI: The AI chooses x by picking the first coordinate of the UCB score maximizer. It maximizes its own utility function (UCB score) without considering the other agent, hence the name. As for the GP-UCB agent, the value of β for this agent is also chosen to be $\beta = 0.05$,

4.2 Experiments

Experiment 1: Evolution of the Optimization Performance. We first study the efficiency of our algorithm in helping the team in the optimization task. To do so, we introduce, as a metric, the *optimization score*. We define this score as the maximum function value f_t^* queried during the cooperative game of t rounds. Since the objective function is normalized between 0 and 100, an optimization score of 100 denotes maximum performance (also note that simple regret $= 100 -$ optimization score).

The evolution of the optimization performance over the optimization rounds is presented in Fig. 2. It can be seen that our method indeed reaches better performance compared to the GreedyAI and RandomAI baselines. However, in the initial rounds, GreedyAI displays much better performances (even better than the VanillaBO (GP-UCB) agent): this is because GreedyAI exploits prior information and therefore is quickly able to guide the user toward finding a local

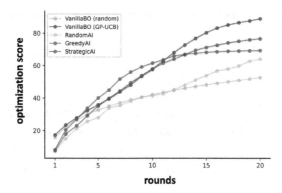

Fig. 2. Evolution of the optimization performance during the interaction. At the end of the interaction, our agent (`StragicAI`) gets better performance than other baselines. It performs slightly worse than the `VanillaBO` (`GP-UCB`), because, unlike this baseline, the `StrategicAI` does not have control over the full domain $\mathcal{X} \times \mathcal{Y}$.

maximum. However, once the optimum is found, it does not explore further and does not find any global optimum, unlike our method, which is more explorative from the beginning. We also notice that the `RandomAI` has initial performance close to the random VanillaBO baseline, but keeps improving: this is due to the fact that this agent keeps exploring, but in a sub-optimal way. Finally, we still notice that the `VanillaBO` (`GP-UCB`) baseline is indeed a valuable upper-bound in the long-term: even though our `StrategicAI` has similar performances on the first rounds, the AI not having total control over the exploration ends up making slightly less optimal decisions.

Experiment 2: Impact of the User's Parameters. The results presented in Fig. 2 are averaged over all user parameters. To study the impact of the user's conservatism and explorativeness on the optimization performance, we exploit the possibility offered by a controlled synthetic user to directly interpret the performance of our method in the case of various user profiles. The final optimization score for different (α, β) configurations is reported in Table 1. The scores are averaged over all combined prior knowledge configurations. These results confirm that the AI's strategic planning significantly improves optimization performance in all scenarios when compared to greedy or random strategies, but with the highest margin for conservative users. This suggests that strategic planning is more crucial when users update their beliefs conservatively. In contrast, the level of user exploration does not significantly affect the size of the margin.

As an addition to this experiment, we performed an ablation study to check the role played by the choice of the reward (Eq. 10), comparing the cases where $C = 1$ (used in all other reported experiments) and where $C = 0$ (which corresponds to reward $\mathcal{R}_1$ introduced in Eq. 8). The results reveal that the performance of strategic AI deteriorates with an explorative user, by using $\mathcal{R}_1$ instead of the full reward $\mathcal{R}$ (which corresponds to the case $C = 0$).

Table 1. Impact of the user's conservativeness (α) and explorativeness (β) onto the optimization score.

	$\beta = 0.2$		$\beta = 0.7$	
	$\alpha = 0.1$	$\alpha = 0.6$	$\alpha = 0.1$	$\alpha = 0.6$
GP-UCB	88.9 ± 21.4			
StrategicAI, $C = 1$ (ours)	77.5 ± 24.8	76.2 ± 23.6	$\mathbf{79.3 \pm 24.7}$	$\mathbf{73.5 \pm 23.2}$
StrategicAI, $C = 0$ (ours)	$\mathbf{79.6 \pm 24.3}$	$\mathbf{77.6 \pm 24.7}$	75.5 ± 25.2	66.6 ± 23.3
GreedyAI	71.0 ± 22.6	69.4 ± 22.5	69.5 ± 22.6	67.5 ± 21.6
RandomAI	71.0 ± 20.8	64.2 ± 20.3	62.0 ± 21.2	58.7 ± 20.0
Random	52.3 ± 9.1			

Experiment 3: Impact of the Prior Knowledge Allocation. Table 2 shows the impact of the prior knowledge allocation on the optimization score when all the (α, β) configurations are combined. The results reveal that the AI's strategic planning improves the optimization performance regardless of the agent and the quality of prior knowledge they possess about the function. The only exception occurs when both agents lack prior knowledge. This may harm the initialization of the AI's own Gaussian process belief. In such cases, early-round planning becomes ineffective. It is worth mentioning that the performance gap between the strategic AI agent and the greedy AI agent is usually most significant when the AI agent possesses high-quality prior information, as demonstrated by the results in rows 1-3 of Table 2.

Experiment 4: User Certainty About the Global Maximum. The optimization score alone may not provide a complete picture of the performance of collaboration, as the team may achieve a high function value but not "know" whether it is indeed close to the global maximum. Such certainty requires knowledge of the overall domain, which in turn necessitates exploration. To assess the

Table 2. Impact of the agents' prior knowledge onto the optimization score. The tested priors are: knowledge around the global optimum (G), knowledge around a local optimum (L) and no prior knowledge (N). Each prior condition is indicated with a subscript: AI for the AI agent, u for the user.

Prior	StrategicAI (ours)	GreedyAI
G_{AI} & G_u	$\mathbf{76.3 \pm 23.3}$	63.6 ± 18.6
G_{AI} & L_u	$\mathbf{75.4 \pm 23.7}$	67.4 ± 23.2
G_{AI} & N_u	$\mathbf{74.0 \pm 25.1}$	61.3 ± 18.6
L_{AI} & G_u	$\mathbf{79.0 \pm 23.0}$	75.8 ± 22.7
L_{AI} & L_u	$\mathbf{82.1 \pm 23.8}$	70.1 ± 25.5
L_{AI} & N_u	$\mathbf{80.0 \pm 23.5}$	75.1 ± 23.6
N_{AI} & N_u	69.5 ± 23.3	$\mathbf{72.1 \pm 20.4}$

level of exploration and knowledge, we examine the flatness of the distribution of the maximum based on the agent's belief over the function, represented as $p(z^*|f_{\text{belief}}) := p(z^* = \max_{(x,y)} f_{\text{belief}}(x,y))$. The degree of flatness is measured by differential entropy. Specifically, we are interested in how effectively the AI agent can increase the user's certainty about the maximum, which we refer to as the *user certainty*, $H(p(z^*|f_u))$, where H is the differential entropy and f_u is the human user's belief over the objective function. A higher user certainty value means that the human user has a better understanding of the global maximum.

Table 3 replicates Experiment 4.2, but instead of presenting the optimization score, it shows the user certainty about the global maximum. The results reveal that the AI using a random strategy is the most effective approach to reducing the user's uncertainty about the global maximum, and that there is a considerable amount of unexplored space left after $T = 20$ rounds when AI acts strategically or greedily. However, the results also indicate that with strategic planning, the user's understanding of the global maximum is slightly improved, regardless of whether they are conservative or Bayesian users and whether they are explorative or exploitative. In addition, the observation that strategic planning enables users to explore more space is also supported by a visual inspection of some of the experimental trials, which can be found in the appendix.

Table 3. User certainty about the global maximum at the end of the game.

	$\beta = 0.2$		$\beta = 0.7$	
	$\alpha = 0.1$	$\alpha = 0.6$	$\alpha = 0.1$	$\alpha = 0.6$
StrategicAI	1.54 ± 0.13	1.59 ± 0.15	1.56 ± 0.17	1.56 ± 0.19
GreedyAI	1.66 ± 0.05	1.67 ± 0.06	1.68 ± 0.06	1.68 ± 0.06
RandomAI	$\mathbf{1.27 \pm 0.17}$	$\mathbf{1.22 \pm 0.19}$	$\mathbf{1.16 \pm 0.22}$	$\mathbf{1.17 \pm 0.22}$

5   Related Work

Decomposition-based Optimization. The proposed cooperative BO game resembles a decomposition-based optimizer. Decomposed optimization partitions the dimensions of the optimized function into disjoint subsets and optimizes separately over these partitions [5]. Two popular families of decomposition-based optimizers are coordinate descent based methods [11] and cooperative co-evolutionary algorithms [17]. Recently, [12] proposed a decomposition-based optimization algorithm for large-scale optimization problems, which is based on Bayesian optimization. However, this literature is focused on algorithmic optimization and does not address the problem from the multi-agent learning perspective.

Multi-Agent Bayesian Optimization. The closest to our work is collaborative BO which considers multiple parties optimizing the same objective function. Still, the utility from evaluating the function is individual, as [20], where a trusted mediator selects an input query to be assigned to each party who then evaluates the objective function at the assigned input. The main difference with our work is the absence of this mediator. In other words, in our setting, the parties have autonomy over their own decisions.

Human-Agent Teaming. The autonomy mentioned above is a crucial characteristic of human-autonomy teams (HATs), where autonomous agents with a partial or high degree of self-governance work toward a common goal [14,16]. The HAT literature offers numerous testbeds that enable researchers to design algorithms and evaluate performance; a selection of these is presented in [16]. One such testbed is the game of Hanabi, which is a cooperative card game of imperfect information for two to five players [1]. Although the proposed cooperative BO game is similar to Hanabi, the crucial difference is that we do not allow direct communication, which would make collaboration easier and focus the solution on designing the communication aspects. By contrast, in Hanabi, players can exchange hints as a means of communication. This idea of communication is inherent to the whole field of Cooperative Game Theory [3], in which cooperation is made possible by using binding agreements. However, this domain mainly focuses on matrix games and not sequential repeated games in extensive form. Recently, Sundin et al. [21] considered a similar problem for an application to molecular design. In this work, the first agent's action corresponds to a restriction of a search space, and the second agent's action to picking within the restricted space. This differs from our work in that the function they optimize is known by the second agent but not observed by the first agent, while we consider a function unknown by both agents and the samples of which are observed.

6   Conclusion

We introduced a cooperative setup for Bayesian optimization of a function of two parameters, where a user and an AI agent sequentially select one coordinate each. The case where the AI agent chooses first is difficult because the agent cannot know the user's action. Therefore, we endow the AI agent with a model of the user, i.e. a probabilistic description of the user's behaviour and decision-making. We use this model within a Bayes Adaptive Monte Carlo Planning algorithm to simulate the user's behaviour. The AI agent's strategic planning of actions enables making choices adapted to the user's biases and current knowledge of the domain. We showed empirically that our method, based on a simple user model, leads to better optimization scores than a non-strategic planner. Even though our algorithm is, in principle, adapted to be used with human users, the current implementation is yet too computationally expensive to work in real-time (calculation time of the order of a minute per action). Alleviating this issue is an important future work to make our method usable in real-world applications with real users.

Acknowledgements. This research was supported by EU Horizon 2020 (HumanE AI NET, 952026) and UKRI Turing AI World-Leading Researcher Fellowship (EP/W002973/1). Computational resources were provided by the Aalto Science-IT project from Computer Science IT. The authors would like to thank Prof. Frans Oliehoek and Dr. Mert Celikok for their help in setting up the project and the reviewers for their insightful comments.

References

1. Bard, N., et al.: The hanabi challenge: a new frontier for AI research. Artif. Intell. **280**, 103216 (2020)
2. Borji, A., Itti, L.: Bayesian optimization explains human active search. In: Burges, C., Bottou, L., Welling, M., Ghahramani, Z., Weinberger, K. (eds.) Advances in Neural Information Processing Systems, vol. 26. Curran Associates, Inc. (2013)
3. Chalkiadakis, G., Elkind, E., Wooldridge, M.: Cooperative game theory: basic concepts and computational challenges. IEEE Intell. Syst. **27**(3), 86–90 (2012)
4. Cox, D.D., John, S.: A statistical method for global optimization. In: Proceedings of the 1992 IEEE International Conference on Systems, Man, and Cybernetics, pp. 1241–1246. IEEE (1992)
5. Duan, Q., Shao, C., Qu, L., Shi, Y., Niu, B.: When cooperative co-evolution meets coordinate descent: theoretically deeper understandings and practically better implementations. In: 2019 IEEE Congress on Evolutionary Computation (CEC), pp. 721–730. IEEE (2019)
6. El-Gamal, M.A., Grether, D.M.: Are people Bayesian? uncovering behavioral strategies. J. Am. Stat. Assoc. **90**(432), 1137–1145 (1995)
7. Etel, E., Slaughter, V.: Theory of mind and peer cooperation in two play contexts. J. Appl. Dev. Psychol. **60**, 87–95 (2019)
8. Gershman, S.J., Horvitz, E.J., Tenenbaum, J.B.: Computational rationality: a converging paradigm for intelligence in brains, minds, and machines. Science **349**(6245), 273–278 (2015)
9. Guez, A., Silver, D., Dayan, P.: Scalable and efficient bayes-adaptive reinforcement learning based on monte-carlo tree search. J. Artif. Intell. Res. **48**, 841–883 (2013)
10. Helander, M.G.: Handbook of human-computer interaction. Elsevier (2014)
11. Hildreth, C.: A quadratic programming procedure. Naval Res. Logistics Q. **4**(1), 79–85 (1957)
12. Jiang, P., Cheng, Y., Liu, J.: Cooperative Bayesian optimization with hybrid grouping strategy and sample transfer for expensive large-scale black-box problems. Knowl.-Based Syst. **254**, 109633 (2022)
13. Kovach, M.: Conservative updating. arXiv preprint arXiv:2102.00152 (2021)
14. Larson, L., DeChurch, L.A.: Leading teams in the digital age: four perspectives on technology and what they mean for leading teams. Leadersh. Q. **31**(1), 101377 (2020)
15. Mikkola, P., Todorović, M., Järvi, J., Rinke, P., Kaski, S.: Projective preferential bayesian optimization. In: Proceedings of the 37th International Conference on Machine Learning, pp. 6884–6892. PMLR (2020)
16. O'Neill, T., McNeese, N., Barron, A., Schelble, B.: Human-autonomy teaming: a review and analysis of the empirical literature. Hum. Factors **64**(5), 904–938 (2022)

17. Potter, M.A., De Jong, K.A.: A cooperative coevolutionary approach to function optimization. In: Davidor, Y., Schwefel, H.-P., Männer, R. (eds.) PPSN 1994. LNCS, vol. 866, pp. 249–257. Springer, Heidelberg (1994). https://doi.org/10.1007/3-540-58484-6_269
18. Rasmussen, C.E., Williams, C.K.I.: Gaussian processes for machine learning. MIT Press, Adaptive Computation and Machine Learning (2006)
19. Sears, A., Jacko, J.A.: Human-Computer Interaction Fundamentals. CRC Press (2009)
20. Sim, R.H.L., Zhang, Y., Low, B.K.H., Jaillet, P.: Collaborative Bayesian optimization with fair regret. In: Proceedings of the International Conference on Machine Learning, pp. 9691–9701. PMLR (2021)
21. Sundin, I., et al.: Human-in-the-loop assisted de novo molecular design. J. Cheminformatics **14**(1), 1–16 (2022)
22. Thurstone, L.L.: A law of comparative judgment. Psychol. Rev. **101**(2), 266 (1994)
23. Tversky, A., Kahneman, D.: Judgment under uncertainty: heuristics and biases: biases in judgments reveal some heuristics of thinking under uncertainty. Science **185**(4157), 1124–1131 (1974)

Leveraging Variational Autoencoders for Multiple Data Imputation

Breeshey Roskams-Hieter[1,2(✉)], Jude Wells[2,3], and Sara Wade[1]

[1] University of Edinburgh, Edinburgh, UK
b.j.roskams-hieter@sms.ed.ac.uk, sara.wade@ed.ac.uk
[2] Health Data Research UK, London, UK
[3] University College London, London, UK
jude.wells.21@ucl.ac.uk

Abstract. Missing data persists as a major barrier to data analysis across numerous applications. Recently, deep generative models have been used for imputation of missing data, motivated by their ability to learn complex and non-linear relationships. In this work, we investigate the ability of variational autoencoders (VAEs) to account for uncertainty in missing data through multiple imputation. We find that VAEs provide poor empirical coverage of missing data, with underestimation and overconfident imputations. To overcome this, we employ β-VAEs, which viewed from a generalized Bayes framework, provide robustness to model misspecification. Assigning a good value of β is critical for uncertainty calibration and we demonstrate how this can be achieved using cross-validation. We assess three alternative methods for sampling from the posterior distribution of missing values and apply the approach to transcriptomics datasets with various simulated missingness scenarios. Finally, we show that single imputation in transcriptomic data can cause false discoveries in downstream tasks and employing multiple imputation with β-VAEs can effectively mitigate these inaccuracies.

Keywords: VAEs · multiple imputation

1 Introduction

Missing data persists as a major barrier in analyses of multivariate data, due to issues like incomplete collection, data availability and low coverage. Early approaches for dealing with missing data tend to reduce the generalizability of results or skew the trends present in the data [38]. These include listwise deletion, where only complete observations are considered, or imputation methods, where the missing values are estimated. Some of these imputation strategies include substitution by the mean of observed values, stochastic regression techniques and hot deck imputation. Single imputation implicitly assumes that the imputation is perfect and thereby fails to account for the uncertainty introduced by the prediction. An attractive solution for this is multiple imputation, which

© The Author(s), under exclusive license to Springer Nature Switzerland AG 2023
D. Koutra et al. (Eds.): ECML PKDD 2023, LNAI 14169, pp. 491–506, 2023.
https://doi.org/10.1007/978-3-031-43412-9_29

models the uncertainty in the missing values by producing several plausible values for each imputed data point [30]. The imputed datasets are then combined and analyzed in downstream tasks to give estimates and standard errors that acknowledge uncertainty in the missing data.

Recently, deep generative models have emerged as a popular tool for imputing data, due to their ability to capture non-linear relationships and complex dependencies [3,7,10,12,17,21,23–26,29,31,32,34]. For example, Qiu et al. [34] use variational autoencoders (VAEs) for imputation of high-dimensional genomic data and find that it performs better than competing methods, such as singular value decomposition and K-nearest neighbours, but they focus solely on single imputation. In this work, we extend this approach to account for uncertainty through multiple imputation strategies. While expressive and powerful, deep models have been shown to be overconfident [39] and underestimate the variability of out-of-distribution test data [33]. In line with these results, we find that VAEs provide poor empirical coverage of the missing data, with underestimation and overconfident imputations for missing data values that are far from the mean.

To overcome this, we employ β-VAEs [14], which provide a framework for approximate Bayesian inference of deep generative models under the power likelihood. In statistics, inference based on the power likelihood has been shown to provide robustness against model misspecification [2], and thus, in our setting, it is crucial to avoid overfitting and achieve good coverage and well-calibrated uncertainty of the missing data. Assigning a good value of β is critical [15], and we employ cross-validation to tune β.

Lastly, we study the effects of imputation in downstream analyses. In the task of identifying discriminating gene sets in transcriptomic data from cancer cells, we show that single imputation can induce correlations that confound regression analyses. Further, we show that multiple imputation with β-VAEs yields fewer false positives in this task.

2   Background

2.1   Variational Autoencoders

Variational autoencoders [19] are probabilistic deep generative models comprised of two parts, the **encoder** and **decoder**. The encoder (also referred to as the inference model) takes an observed data point, $\mathbf{x} \in \mathbb{R}^D$, and computes the posterior distribution, $p_\theta(\mathbf{z}|\mathbf{x})$, of the latent variables, $\mathbf{z} \in \mathbb{R}^K$. As the true posterior is intractable in most cases, an approximate model, $q_\phi(\mathbf{z}|\mathbf{x})$, is used to approximate the true posterior, $p_\theta(\mathbf{z}|\mathbf{x})$, and encode the observed data into the latent variables. The second part is the decoder (also referred to as the generative model) where the latent variables, $\mathbf{z}$, are used to reconstruct data point, $\hat{\mathbf{x}}$, via the generative model, $p_\theta(\mathbf{x}|\mathbf{z})$. The standard choice of distribution for both the inference and generative model is a simple, factorized Gaussian, where the Gaussian mean and variance are parameterized by neural networks, with ϕ and θ containing the parameters of the encoder and decoder neural networks respectively. Based on a training data set $\mathbf{X} = (\mathbf{x}_1, \ldots, \mathbf{x}_N)$ containing N data points, the neural network parameters ϕ and θ are optimized during training of the VAE by minimizing the reconstruction loss (the negative log-likelihood of the data) and the latent loss (the Kullback-Leibler (KL) divergence between the variational posterior, $q_\phi(\mathbf{Z}|\mathbf{X})$, and the prior (which we set to a standard Gaussian), $p(\mathbf{Z})$, with $\mathbf{Z} = (\mathbf{z}_1, \ldots, \mathbf{z}_N)$).

From a Bayesian perspective, this is equivalent to approximate variational inference of deep latent variable models, under the generative model $\mathbf{x}_n \mid \mathbf{z}_n \sim p_\theta(\mathbf{x}_n \mid \mathbf{z}_n)$ with a Gaussian prior on latent variables $\mathbf{z}_n \sim N(\mathbf{0}, \mathbf{I})$. To overcome the intractability of the posterior, amortized variational inference [11] is employed, assuming the variational posterior $q_\phi(\mathbf{z}_n|\mathbf{x}_n)$ is parameterized by a neural network with ϕ containing the weights and biases. The variational parameters ϕ and generative model parameters θ are optimized by minimizing the KL divergence between the variational posterior $q_\phi(\mathbf{Z}|\mathbf{X})$ and the true posterior $p_\theta(\mathbf{Z}|\mathbf{X})$, or equivalently maximizing the evidence lower bound (ELBO):

$$\text{ELBO} = \sum_{n=1}^{N} \mathbb{E}_{\mathbf{z}_n \sim q_\phi(\mathbf{z}_n|\mathbf{x}_n)}[\log p_\theta(\mathbf{x}_n|\mathbf{z}_n)] - D_{\text{KL}}(q_\phi(\mathbf{z}_n|\mathbf{x}_n), p(\mathbf{z}_n)).$$

During training, the ELBO is maximized using stochastic gradient descent. To compute the required gradients, the re-parameterization trick [18,35] is used to obtain independence between the latent noise and ϕ.

β-**VAEs** An extension on the classic VAE is the β-VAE, which includes a hyperparameter β that adjusts the relative weight of the latent loss [14]:

$$\text{ELBO} = \sum_{n=1}^{N} \mathbb{E}_{\mathbf{z}_n \sim q_\phi(\mathbf{z}_n|\mathbf{x}_n)}[\log p_\theta(\mathbf{x}_n|\mathbf{z}_n)] - \beta \, D_{\text{KL}}(q_\phi(\mathbf{z}_n|\mathbf{x}_n), p(\mathbf{z}_n)). \tag{1}$$

While in the machine learning community, β-VAEs are motivated by their improvement in disentangling the latent variables [5], we provide an alternative motivation from a statistical perspective. In particular, maximizing the β-VAE bound in (1), is equivalent to maximizing:

$$\sum_{n=1}^{N} \mathbb{E}_{\mathbf{z}_n \sim q_\phi(\mathbf{z}_n|\mathbf{x}_n)}[\log p_\theta(\mathbf{x}_n|\mathbf{z}_n)^{1/\beta}] - D_{\text{KL}}(q_\phi(\mathbf{z}_n|\mathbf{x}_n), p(\mathbf{z}_n)),$$

or minimizing the KL divergence between the variational posterior $q_\phi(\mathbf{Z}|\mathbf{X})$ and the posterior under the power likelihood (see Appendix A.4 [36]):

$$p_{\theta,\beta}(\mathbf{Z}|\mathbf{X}) \propto \prod_{n=1}^{N} p_\theta(\mathbf{x}_n|\mathbf{z}_n)^{1/\beta} p(\mathbf{z}_n).$$

The use of the power likelihood in Bayesian statistics provides frequentist guarantees of posterior consistency in nonparametric models [40], while the Bayesian model under the standard updating with $\beta = 1$ may be inconsistent [1]. Moreover, the power likelihood provides robustness to model misspecification [2]. Given the complex, high-dimensional nature of the deep generative model $p_\theta(\mathbf{x}_n | \mathbf{z}_n)$, this acknowledges and allows for a mismatch between the generative model and the true data generating distribution.

2.2   Single Imputation with VAEs

VAEs are ideal for imputing missing transcriptomic data, as they can learn non-linear relationships and generate imputations over thousands of features. In this work, we develop the approach of Qiu et al. [34]. They first train the VAE using only the subset of complete data to optimize the parameters ϕ and θ. For each data point $n = 1, \ldots, N$, $\mathbf{x}_n$ can be split into two parts: $\mathbf{x}_{\text{obs},n}$ containing the observed features and $\mathbf{x}_{\text{mis},n}$ containing the missing features, where $\mathbf{X}_{\text{obs}} = (\mathbf{x}_{\text{obs},1}, \ldots, \mathbf{x}_{\text{obs},N})$ and $\mathbf{X}_{\text{mis}} = (\mathbf{x}_{\text{mis},1}, \ldots, \mathbf{x}_{\text{mis},N})$. For each data point with missing features, i.e. $\mathbf{x}_n \neq \mathbf{x}_{\text{obs},n}$, the optimal choice, under the squared error loss, is to impute with the mean under the generative model:

$$
\widehat{\mathbf{x}}_{\text{mis},n} = \mathbb{E}\left[\mathbf{x}_{\text{mis},n} \mid \mathbf{x}_{\text{obs},n}\right] = \int \mathbf{x}_{\text{mis},n} \, p_\theta(\mathbf{x}_{\text{mis},n} \mid \mathbf{x}_{\text{obs},n}) \, d\mathbf{x}_{\text{mis},n}
$$

$$
= \int \int \mathbf{x}_{\text{mis},n} \, p_\theta(\mathbf{x}_{\text{mis},n}, \mathbf{z}_n \mid \mathbf{x}_{\text{obs},n}) \, d\mathbf{z}_n d\mathbf{x}_{\text{mis},n}.
$$

This integral is intractable; thus in [34], it is approximated by iteratively computing: 1) the expectation of $\mathbf{z}_n$ (mean of the encoder) given $\widehat{\mathbf{x}}_{\text{mis},n}$ and $\mathbf{x}_{\text{obs},n}$:

$$
\widehat{\mathbf{z}}_n = \int \mathbf{z}_n \, q_\phi(\mathbf{z}_n \mid \widehat{\mathbf{x}}_{\text{mis},n}, \mathbf{x}_{\text{obs},n}) \, d\mathbf{z}_n,
$$

and 2) the expectation of $\widehat{\mathbf{x}}_{\text{mis},n}$ (mean of the decoder) given $\widehat{\mathbf{z}}_n$:

$$
\widehat{\mathbf{x}}_{\text{mis},n} = \int \mathbf{x}_{\text{mis},n} \, p_\theta(\mathbf{x}_{\text{mis},n} \mid \mathbf{x}_{\text{obs},n}, \widehat{\mathbf{z}}_n) \, d\mathbf{x}_{\text{mis},n}.
$$

Each missing value is initialized with the mean observed value for its respective feature, and subsequently re-estimated until convergence. Note that when the likelihood factorizes across features (e.g. factorized Gaussian), $p_\theta(\mathbf{x}_{\text{mis},n} \mid \mathbf{x}_{\text{obs},n}, \mathbf{z}_n) = p_\theta(\mathbf{x}_{\text{mis},n} \mid \mathbf{z}_n)$. In their paper, Qiu et al. [34] optimized the model and hyper-parameters through a grid search, claiming that the standard VAE ($\beta = 1$) and training for 250 epochs resulted in the lowest mean absolute error of the imputed values when compared to true values. However, the authors did not examine the uncertainty calibration nor did they consider multiple imputation.

2.3   Multiple Imputation

Multiple imputation (see e.g. [22, 30, 38]) improves upon single imputation by modelling the uncertainty associated with the imputed values. It does so by creating M plausible values for each missing data point. Combining the M datasets enables estimation of standard errors and confidence intervals for dataset derived statistics. Historically setting M between 3 and 5 was deemed adequate [37] others point to cases where it may be necessary to set M higher [13].

In multiple imputation we aim to obtain and simulate from the predictive distribution for the missing data given the observed data, i.e. $p(\mathbf{X}_{\mathrm{mis}}|\mathbf{X}_{\mathrm{obs}})$. In particular, we assume that $\mathbf{X}$ follows a distribution, $p(\mathbf{X}|\boldsymbol{\psi})$, where $\boldsymbol{\psi}$ is a collection of all parameters of the model. Then we can write our predictive distribution as:

$$p(\mathbf{X}_{\mathrm{mis}}|\mathbf{X}_{\mathrm{obs}}) = \int p(\mathbf{X}_{\mathrm{mis}}, \boldsymbol{\psi}|\mathbf{X}_{\mathrm{obs}})d\boldsymbol{\psi} = \int p(\mathbf{X}_{\mathrm{mis}}|\mathbf{X}_{\mathrm{obs}}, \boldsymbol{\psi})p(\boldsymbol{\psi}|\mathbf{X}_{\mathrm{obs}})d\boldsymbol{\psi}.$$

To impute the missing data, and thereby simulate one of M plausible datasets, data augmentation (DA) algorithms can be employed. Specifically, DA is a Markov chain method which iteratively samples 1) the parameters $\boldsymbol{\psi}$ from the posterior $p(\boldsymbol{\psi}|\mathbf{X}_{\mathrm{obs}}, \mathbf{X}_{\mathrm{mis}})$ and 2) missing data $\mathbf{X}_{\mathrm{mis}}$ given $\boldsymbol{\psi}$ from $p(\mathbf{X}_{\mathrm{mis}}|\mathbf{X}_{\mathrm{obs}}, \boldsymbol{\psi})$. This ultimately results in sampling from the predictive distribution $p(\mathbf{X}_{\mathrm{mis}}|\mathbf{X}_{\mathrm{obs}})$, producing one of the plausible datasets, denoted as $\mathbf{X}_{\mathrm{mis}}^m = (\mathbf{x}_{\mathrm{mis},1}^m, \ldots, \mathbf{x}_{\mathrm{mis},N}^m)$. This procedure is repeated M times to achieve M plausible datasets. Inferences based on these M imputed datasets can be combined via **Rubin's rules** to compute accurate inference about the entire dataset $\mathbf{X}$.

3   Methodology

In this work, we generalize single imputation with VAEs in two ways. First, we employ and compare three multiple imputation strategies to account for uncertainty in the missing data. Second, we extend using β-VAEs for improved robustness and uncertainty quantification. We propose an additional minor modification to the approach of Qiu et al., whereby we train the VAE by including both complete samples and those with some missingness. This requires that we apply mean imputation of missing values prior to training. We find this approach leads to modest improvements in imputation accuracy and allows the approach to be employed even in scenarios where the majority of samples contain some missingness.

3.1   Multiple Imputation with β-VAEs

In the case of multiple imputation (MI), the latent variables, $\mathbf{Z}$, of the β-VAE represent the parameters of our model, previously referred to as $\boldsymbol{\psi}$ in Sect. 2.3. To produce a sample from our target predictive distribution, $p_{\theta,\beta}(\mathbf{X}_{\mathrm{mis}}|\mathbf{X}_{\mathrm{obs}})$, we can iteratively sample from the joint distribution $p_{\theta,\beta}(\mathbf{X}_{\mathrm{mis}}, \mathbf{Z}|\mathbf{X}_{\mathrm{obs}})$ via a Markov chain Monte Carlo scheme. For β-VAEs, the predictive distribution is constructed from the power likelihood, that is the likelihood of our generative model is raised to the power $1/\beta$ (see Section 2.1):

$$
\begin{aligned}
p_{\theta,\beta}(\mathbf{X}_{\text{mis}}|\mathbf{X}_{\text{obs}}) &\propto \int p_{\theta}(\mathbf{X}_{\text{mis}}|\mathbf{X}_{\text{obs}}, \mathbf{Z})^{1/\beta} p_{\theta,\beta}(\mathbf{Z}|\mathbf{X}_{\text{obs}}) d\mathbf{Z} \\
&= \prod_{n=1}^{N} \int p_{\theta}(\mathbf{x}_{\text{mis},n}|\mathbf{x}_{\text{obs},n}, \mathbf{z}_n)^{1/\beta} p_{\theta,\beta}(\mathbf{z}_n|\mathbf{x}_{\text{obs},n}) d\mathbf{z}_n,
\end{aligned}
\tag{2}
$$

where standard VAEs correspond to $\beta = 1$. We note that in the case of the factored Gaussian generative model, the power likelihood $p_{\theta}(\mathbf{x}_{\text{mis},n}|\mathbf{x}_{\text{obs},n}, \mathbf{z}_n)^{1/\beta}$ is simply proportional to a Gaussian with variance rescaled by a factor of β. On the other hand, $p_{\theta,\beta}(\mathbf{Z}|\mathbf{X}_{\text{obs}})$ represents the intractable true posterior of the latent variables under the power likelihood given the observed data only.

In the following, we implement and compare three different approaches to sample from our target predictive distribution in (2): 1) pseudo-Gibbs (Sect. 3.1), 2) Metropolis-within-Gibbs (Sect. 3.1), and 3) sampling importance resampling (Sect. 3.1). These strategies are proposed in [28, 29, 35], respectively, for missing data imputation with deep generative models, and we describe a simple extension based on β-VAEs and the power likelihood. Prior to imputation, we first train the β-VAE, using mean imputation for the missing values, to obtain estimates of generative model parameters $\boldsymbol{\theta}$ and variational parameters $\boldsymbol{\phi}$, and thus also an approximation of the true posterior of the latent variables.

Pseudo-Gibbs. Pseudo-Gibbs sampling was the first strategy developed to generate approximate samples from the predictive distribution in deep generative models [35]. In particular, approximate samples from the joint $p_{\theta,\beta}(\mathbf{X}_{\text{mis}}, \mathbf{Z} \mid \mathbf{X}_{\text{obs}})$ are obtained by iteratively sampling from the encoder and decoder. More specifically, for $s = 1, \ldots, S$ iterations and every data point $n \in \{1, \ldots, N\}$ with missing features, the pseudo-Gibbs algorithm replaces the expectation steps in the single imputation of Sect. 2.2 with sampling, as follows: First, Sample $\mathbf{z}_n$ (sample of encoder) given $\mathbf{x}_{\text{mis},n}^{(s-1)}$:

$$
\mathbf{z}_n^{(s)} \sim q_{\phi}(\mathbf{z}_n \mid \mathbf{x}_{\text{mis},n}^{(s-1)}, \mathbf{x}_{\text{obs},n}).
\tag{3}
$$

Next, we sample $\mathbf{x}_{\text{mis},n}^{(s)}$ (sample of decoder) given $\mathbf{z}_n^{(s)}$ based on the power likelihood:

$$
\mathbf{x}_{\text{mis},n}^{(s)} \sim p_{\theta,\beta}(\mathbf{x}_{\text{mis},n} \mid \mathbf{x}_{\text{obs},n}, \mathbf{z}_n^{(s)}) \propto p_{\theta}(\mathbf{x}_{\text{mis},n} \mid \mathbf{x}_{\text{obs},n}, \mathbf{z}_n^{(s)})^{1/\beta}.
$$

Ideally, in the first step, we would aim to sample from the intractable true posterior of the latent variables. However, if the variational posterior provides a good approximation, the pseudo-Gibbs scheme will produce samples from a distribution close to our target.

Metropolis-Within-Gibbs. The pseudo-Gibbs algorithm was improved and extended by [28], who derived a Metropolis-within-Gibbs (MWG) sampler that is asymptotically guaranteed to produce samples from the target predictive distribution. This is a simple modification of pseudo-Gibbs that corrects the first step by using the variational posterior as a proposal within a Metropolis-Hastings algorithm. Specifically, in the first step, the sampled value from the encoder in (3) represents the proposed value for the latent variables, denoted by $\mathbf{z}_n^*$, which is then accepted according to the acceptance probability:

$$a\big(\mathbf{z}_n^{(s-1)} \rightarrow \mathbf{z}_n^*\big) = \min\left(1, \frac{p_\theta\big(\mathbf{x}_{\text{mis},n}^{(s-1)}, \mathbf{x}_{\text{obs},n} | \mathbf{z}_n^*\big)^{1/\beta} p(\mathbf{z}_n^*)}{p_\theta\big(\mathbf{x}_{\text{mis},n}^{(s-1)}, \mathbf{x}_{\text{obs},n} | \mathbf{z}_n^{(s-1)}\big)^{1/\beta} p(\mathbf{z}^{(s-1)})} \frac{q_\phi\big(\mathbf{z}_n^{(s-1)} | \mathbf{x}_{\text{mis},n}^{(s-1)}, \mathbf{x}_{\text{obs}}\big)}{q_\phi\big(\mathbf{z}_n^* | \mathbf{x}_{\text{mis},n}^{(s-1)}, \mathbf{x}_{\text{obs},n}\big)}\right)$$

Thus, we set:

$$\mathbf{z}_n^{(s)} = \begin{cases} \mathbf{z}_n^* & \text{with prob. } a\big(\mathbf{z}_n^{(s-1)} \rightarrow \mathbf{z}_n^*\big) \\ \mathbf{z}_n^{(s-1)} & \text{with prob. } 1 - a\big(\mathbf{z}_n^{(s-1)} \rightarrow \mathbf{z}_n^*\big) \end{cases}.$$

If the variational posterior is a perfect approximation of the true posterior, the acceptance probability will be one, and the algorithm reduces to pseudo-Gibbs. In general, MWG acknowledges and corrects for the approximation of the posterior; however, if the variational posterior is far from the true posterior, MWG will suffer from low acceptance rates and slow convergence.

Sampling Importance Resampling. An alternative to Gibbs is sampling importance resampling (SIR), proposed by [29]. First, we perform importance sampling using the variational posterior as the importance distribution. In this case, for every data point $n \in \{1, \dots, N\}$ with missing features, we take $s = 1, \dots, S$ samples of the latent variables from our importance distribution:

$$\mathbf{z}_n^{(s)} \sim q_\phi\big(\mathbf{z}_n \mid \mathbf{x}_{\text{mis},n}^{(0)}, \mathbf{x}_{\text{obs},n}\big),$$

where $\mathbf{x}_{\text{mis},n}^{(0)}$ denotes an initial mean imputation for the missing data (zero is the mean after feature standardization). These importance samples $(\mathbf{z}_n^{(s)})$, for $s = 1, \dots, S$, have weights $w_n^{(s)}$ proportional to:

$$\omega_n^{(s)} = \frac{p_\theta\big(\mathbf{x}_{\text{obs},n} | \mathbf{z}_n^{(s)}\big)^{1/\beta} p(\mathbf{z}_n^{(s)})}{q_\phi\big(\mathbf{z}_n^{(s)} | \mathbf{x}_{\text{mis},n}^{(0)}, \mathbf{x}_{\text{obs},n}\big)},$$

where $w_n^{(s)} = \omega_n^{(s)} / \sum_{s=1}^S \omega_n^{(s)}$ (for further details, see Appendix A.5 [36]). Then, for multiple imputation, we obtain M imputations by first sampling $(\mathbf{z}_n^m)$, for $m = 1, \dots M$, with replacement from the importance samples $(\mathbf{z}_n^{(s)})$ with probability $w_n^{(s)}$. Next, for each $\mathbf{z}_n^m$, we impute the missing data by sampling from

$$\mathbf{x}_{\text{mis},n}^m \sim p_{\theta,\beta}\big(\mathbf{x}_{\text{mis},n} \mid \mathbf{x}_{\text{obs},n}, \mathbf{z}_n^m\big).$$

In contrast to Gibbs sampling, an advantage of SIR is parallelizability. However, the discrepancy between the variational posterior and true posterior determines the efficiency of the algorithm, and a large discrepancy may result in degeneracy of the weights and require a large number of importance samples (which is required to be exponential in KL divergence between the importance distribution and the target [4]).

3.2 Cross-Validation Training Regime

When the generative model and θ match the true data generating distribution exactly, learning is achieved optimally with $\beta = 1$. However, in practice, we have a mismatch and assigning a good value of β becomes critical to achieve robustness and accurate uncertainty quantification. Indeed, if β is set too low, the posterior uncertainty can be underestimated, while if β is set too high, the posterior uncertainty is overestimated. Some directions for assigning a value of β from an information theoretic perspective are provided in [15]. Instead, we employ cross-validation (CV) to tune β for accurate multiple imputation and coverage of the missing data. A second consideration that affects uncertainty calibration in deep models is overfitting. We observe that training for too long leads to underestimated uncertainty on the held-out data (Supplementary Figure A.3 [36]). Therefore, selecting the correct number of epochs is critical for well-calibrated uncertainty. This motivates the CV approach to select β and the number of epochs jointly.

Specifically, the CV approach to tuning β and the number of epochs consists of creating k copies of the data and adding a small proportion of additional MCAR missingness in each copy. We then carry out a grid search over the number of epochs and values of β, training k models for each value of β. The final selection is the combination that has acceptable coverage while minimizing the mean absolute error (MAE) over the introduced missing values (averaged across the k models). Optimal values are selected by visual inspection of the MAE and coverage in the CV plots (Supplementary Figure A.3 [36]). Once the optimal hyper-parameters for β and epochs are selected, the model is retrained using all of the data. We observed that following this approach results in coverage and MAE on the test set being close to the values estimated through cross-validation.

3.3 Evaluating Imputation Performance

To evaluate the imputation performance, we consider two quantities: 1) the mean absolute error (MAE) to assess reconstruction accuracy and 2) the empirical coverage (EC) to quantify uncertainty. The MAE compares our imputed values to the ground truth that was originally masked in the complete dataset. Recall that $\widehat{\mathbf{X}}_{\text{mis}} = (\hat{\mathbf{x}}_{\text{mis},1}, \ldots, \hat{\mathbf{x}}_{\text{mis},N})$ represents the imputed values, while $\mathbf{X}_{\text{mis}}$ represents the true (masked) values. The MAE is defined as:

$$\text{MAE} = \frac{1}{N} \sum_{n=1}^{N} |\hat{\mathbf{x}}_{\text{mis},n} - \mathbf{x}_{\text{mis},n}|, \tag{4}$$

where $|\hat{\mathbf{x}}_{\text{mis},n} - \mathbf{x}_{\text{mis},n}|$ represents the average absolute difference across all missing features for the nth data point. For multiple imputation, the imputed values

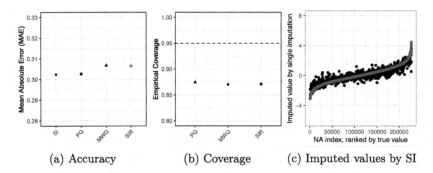

(a) Accuracy   (b) Coverage   (c) Imputed values by SI

Fig. 1. Standard VAE (β=1) underestimates the uncertainty in multiple imputation. Here we report **(a)** the accuracy at imputed missing values compared to the ground truth by MAE and **(b)** the fraction of true values that fall within the 95% CIs for the three multiple imputation approaches pseudo-Gibbs (PG), Metropolis-within-Gibbs (MWG) and sampling importance resampling (SIR). Dotted line represents the desired coverage at 0.95. Finally, **(c)** depicts the imputed values for the missing data by single imputation (SI), ranked by their true values (highlighted in red). (Color figure online)

in (4) are averaged across the M imputed datasets, $\widehat{x}_{\text{mis},n} = \frac{1}{M} \sum_{m=1}^{M} x_{\text{mis},n}^{m}$. To evaluate uncertainty in multiple imputation, we first compute $100(1 - \alpha)\%$ confidence intervals (CIs) for each missing value based on the M imputed values. The empirical coverage is then computed as the fraction of times where the true value falls within the predicted interval.

4   Results: Genomic Data Imputation

4.1   Limitations of Single Imputation and Standard VAEs

We compare single imputation with standard VAEs to multiple imputation using three methods to sample the posterior (MWG, PG, and SIR). In order to benchmark against [34] we employed the same RNA-sequencing dataset from the Cancer Genome Atlas (TCGA). This dataset contains $D = 17,175$ features (RNA-sequencing counts) for $N = 667$ glioma patients, comprised of two cancer subtypes, glioblastoma (GBM) and low-grade glioma (LGG). We first simulate missingness in this dataset by masking 10% of values completely at random (MCAR) in 20% of samples, scale the dataset and subsequently train the VAE with the zero imputation at missing value indices (see Sect. 3). In order to benchmark against their method, we use the same model and hyper-parameters that were found to be optimal in [34], specifically, the standard VAE (β=1) with 250 training epochs and a learning rate of 10^{-5}. Once our model is trained, we generate $M = 100$ plausible datasets for each multiple imputation approach and perform single imputation (as described in Sect. 2.2). We set M much higher than would typically be used in MI, in order to measure empirical coverage with a high degree of precision. We examine the effect of varying M as a hyper-parameter in our analysis (Supplementary Figure A.1 [36]).

To evaluate imputation of the original masked values, we consider imputation accuracy by MAE and find that the multiple imputation approaches have similar accuracy to single imputation (SI), with pseudo-Gibbs performing slightly better than the other MI approaches (Fig. 1a). Next, we consider the empirical coverage of the masked values based on the 95% CIs computed from the $M = 100$ imputed datasets for all three multiple imputation approaches, and find that the uncertainty is underestimated when $\beta = 1$ (Fig. 1b). Additionally, the values imputed at masked data points with single imputation are underestimated at more extreme true values (Fig. 1c). As [34] only used reconstruction accuracy with single imputation to optimize hyperparameters, they were unable to assess uncertainty calibration in the imputations. To overcome this, we explore regularization of the latent space through β-VAEs, optimizing the hyperparameters by considering both reconstruction accuracy and coverage.

4.2 Multiple Imputation with β-VAEs for Accurate Uncertainty Quantification

For improved robustness, we employ β-VAEs and the cross-validation scheme described in Sect. 3.2 to tune β and the number of training epochs, resulting in a value of $\beta = 2$ and 250 training epochs (Supplementary Figure A.3 [36]). We then train the β-VAE with these optimal parameters and impute values by SI and all three MI approaches PG, MWG and SIR. This results in good coverage at 95%, with a much lower deviation from the desired coverage than the standard VAE with $\beta = 1$ (Fig. 2, Supplementary Figure A.2, Supplementary Figure A.5, Supplementary Figure A.6 [36]). Even with regularization of the latent space, single imputation still results in underestimation at extreme values (Supplementary Figure A.2 [36]). Our multiple imputation by β-VAEs yields good coverage across all missing data, even extreme values, while still retaining comparable accuracy to single imputation (Fig. 2d).

4.3 Multiple Imputation Reduces False Positives in Downstream Tasks

We next investigate the impact of all imputation approaches on downstream tasks, namely in identifying discriminating gene sets through logistic regression with the LASSO penalty. In particular, we run LASSO regression on all imputed datasets to identify the genes which discriminate between the two cancer subtypes, GBM and LGG. This results in one gene set from our ground truth dataset with no missingness (GT), one from single imputation (SI), and 100 discriminating gene sets for each multiple imputation approach, PG, MWG and SIR. We propose that non-zero LASSO coefficients that arise in the imputed data but do not show up in the complete data LASSO model are false positives arising as artefacts of imputation.

We find that the union across all discriminating gene sets for each multiple imputation approach is much larger than the ground truth set, with the total number of possible non-zero coefficients ranging from 143 to 155, and only 31

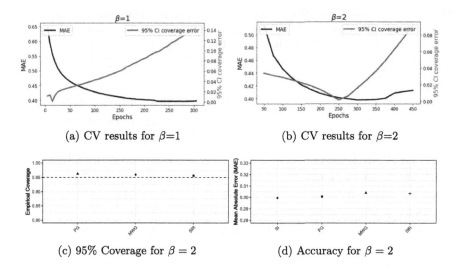

(a) CV results for $\beta=1$ (b) CV results for $\beta=2$

(c) 95% Coverage for $\beta=2$ (d) Accuracy for $\beta=2$

Fig. 2. Multiple imputation with β-VAEs provides calibrated coverage. The standard VAE ($\beta=1$) cannot achieve a balance of high accuracy and calibrated coverage **(a)**. While the β-VAE with $\beta=2$ **(b)** gets close to the error minimum while maintaining accurate uncertainty estimation (as measured by empirical coverage with a 95% CI. After imputing by SI, MWG, PG and SIR, we summarize imputation performance by **(c)** the empirical coverage at 95% CIs (dotted line represents the desired coverage at 0.95) and **(d)** the accuracy at imputed values, comparing single imputation with all three MI strategies.

discriminating genes in the true dataset (Table 1). When comparing the estimated coefficients from the ground truth data to the (averaged) estimated coefficients based on the imputed data, this results in a slightly higher MAE for multiple imputation approaches (0.066, 0.064 and 0.069 for PG, MWG and SIR, respectively) compared to single imputation (0.053), which also has a set of 31 discriminating genes, although these are not identical to the ground truth set. However, when we inspect the coverage across the multiple imputations, we find that our coverage is close to the desired 95% across PG, MWG and SIR (Table 1, Supplementary Figure A.7 [36]).

To identify discriminating gene sets across multiple imputations, we consider two approaches: selecting genes that 1) do not include a coefficient of zero in the 95% CI computed from the 100 imputed datasets, and 2) have an inclusion probability, denoted P_{incl} and defined as the fraction of imputed datasets that the gene has a non-zero LASSO coefficient, greater than a specified threshold. The first approach results in the same set of 12 genes across all three multiple imputation approaches that are all in the true set of non-zero LASSO coefficients (Table 1, Fig. 3), giving a false discovery rate (FDR) of 0%. These 12 genes are also contained within the set for single imputation; however, single imputation results in 7 false positives (Fig. 3), yielding an FDR of 22.6% (7/31). In the second approach, if we threshold at $P_{incl} > 0.5$, this results in a final set of 25

Table 1. Performance of different imputation techniques, single imputation (SI) and multiple imputation by PG, MWG and SIR for imputation at missing value indices (first two rows) and downstream impact on LASSO regression (subsequent rows). The final row reports the false discovery rate, based genes with an inclusion probability > 0.5 for multiple imputation.

Metric	SI	PG	MWG	SIR
MAE	0.302	0.301	0.304	0.303
95% CI coverage	N/A	96.2%	95.9%	95.6%
LASSO: MAE	0.053	0.066	0.064	0.069
LASSO: 95% CI coverage	N/A	97.4%	97.2%	96.6%
LASSO: total number of non-zero coefficients	31	155	143	149
LASSO: number of genes without zero in 95% CI	N/A	12	12	12
LASSO: number of genes with $P_{incl} > 0.5$	N/A	25	25	25
LASSO: False discovery rate	22.6%	8%	8%	8%

discriminating genes for each multiple imputation approach (Table 1, Supplementary Figure A.8 [36]). In this case, our gene set contains 2 false positives, yielding an FDR of 8.0% (Fig. 3). In summary, we find that multiple imputation with β-VAEs not only provides well-calibrated uncertainty but also results in much more acceptable FDRs in downstream tasks.

4.4   Multiple Imputation in New Missing Scenarios and Additional Transcriptomic Datasets

Lastly, we show that our results are consistent when applied to another transcriptomic dataset and with different missingness scenarios. As missing-not-at-random (MNAR) is common in transcriptomic data, due to either low coverage or artefacts of the sequencing protocol, we choose to explore this additional missing scenario [6]. Here we select genes with GC content at the highest 10% and randomly mask half of these values to generate our MNAR simulated dataset. We additionally explore a new pan-cancer transcriptomic dataset, which is comprised of 17,175 features and 953 samples across 2 cancer types, lung adenocarcinoma (LUAD) and lung squamous carcinoma (LUSC). This makes up four groups for which we run our imputation framework: **(1)** MCAR for LGG and GBM, **(2)** MNAR for LGG and GBM, **(3)** MCAR for LUAD and LUSC and **(4)** MNAR for LUAD and LUSC.

For all four groups, we simulate missingness as described previously. We first tune β and the number of epochs by simulating additional MCAR missingness, then train the VAE with these tuned hyper-parameters before imputing at missing values. We evaluate accuracy by MAE. Coverage is evaluated by looking at the EC and the FPR in the downstream task of identifying discriminating gene sets with LASSO regression. We find that running cross-validation to tune β on the new transcriptomic dataset (LUAD-LUSC) results in the selection of

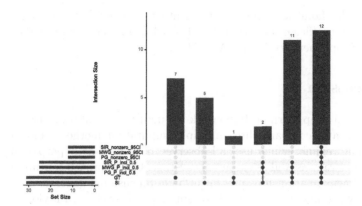

Fig. 3. Upset plot of discriminating gene sets from different imputation approaches. We report the discriminating gene sets by single imputation (SI), ground truth (GT), and all three multiple imputation approaches PG, MWG and SIR with two different inclusion criteria, zero not contained in 95% CI (nonzero_95CI) and inclusion probability, $P_{incl} > 0.5$ (P_incl_0.5).

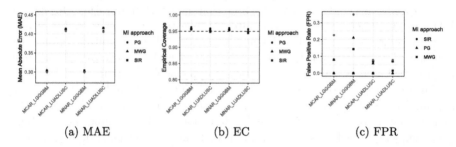

(a) MAE   (b) EC   (c) FPR

Fig. 4. Multiple imputation across new missing scenarios and new transcriptomic datasets. Across different missing scenarios (MCAR and MNAR) for both transcriptomic datasets (LGG versus GBM and LUAD versus LUSC), we report the **(a)** MAE, **(b)** EC (empirical coverage), and **(c)** false positive rate (FPR) of discriminating gene sets from LASSO regression defined by SI and $P_{incl} = 0.5$ for MI settings. In plots **(a)** and **(c)**, the red dot represents the estimate from the single imputation approach.

approximately the same optimal values for β and the number of epochs ($\beta = 2$ and *epochs* = 250). Our results show that in all four contexts, we are able to retain imputation accuracy compared to single imputation (Fig. 4a) while still estimating coverage appropriately at the 95% level (Fig. 4b). Evaluating the discriminating gene sets identified by LASSO regression in the new LUAD-LUSC dataset and MNAR missingness scenarios, we repeat our finding that the false positive rate (Fig. 4c) is reduced and precision is increased (Supplementary Figure A.9 [36]) across all MI settings compared to SI. Here we have used the gene set for $P_{incl} > 0.5$ for each MI setting to increase our true positive rate, but we see this holds for the more stringent set as well, which are genes that do not include a coefficient of zero in the 95% CI computed from the 100 imputed datasets (Supplementary Figure A.10 [36]).

5 Discussion

We describe a deep learning framework for multiple imputation using β-VAEs. We propose and compare three multiple imputation methods and develop a new training regime, which uses all observed data to tune hyperparameters by assessing accuracy as well as empirical coverage. Our approach captures the complex, non-linear relationships present in high-dimensional genomic data, imputing values with high accuracy while retaining good coverage. Previous work [34] employed standard VAEs for genomic data imputation by single imputation, resulting in inaccurate and overconfident imputations at extreme missing values. More recent work has investigated multiple imputation using VAEs, but has not leveraged the potential of tuning β for proper uncertainty calibration [27]. Here we investigate the impact of these different imputation approaches on downstream tasks, namely discriminating gene sets identified by logistic regression with the LASSO penalty. We find that multiple imputation through β-VAEs identifies genes that discriminate between the two cancer subtypes with lower false discovery rates than previous methods. All three multiple imputation approaches perform similarly in terms of accuracy and coverage though SIR may be preferred as it permits parallelization (Supplementary Figure A.11 [36]).

Future work will continue to investigate missing not at random settings [7,17] and mixed data [24]. In addition, extensions using ensembles of deep generative models may improve robustness and calibration. Such ensembles can be built from simple approaches, such as training with multiple initializations [20], composing models across different epochs [16], or Monte Carlo dropout [9], to more advanced approaches, such as Bayesian methods [8].

Acknowledgements. SW was supported by the Royal Society of Edinburgh (RSE) (grant number 69938). BRH and JW acknowledge the receipt of studentship awards from the Health Data Research UK & The Alan Turing Institute Wellcome PhD Programme in Health Data Science (Grant Ref: 218529/Z/19/Z).

Code is available at https://github.com/roskamsh/BetaVAEMultImpute along with the appendix for this paper, including supplementary figures.

References

1. Barron, A., Schervish, M.J., Wasserman, L.: The consistency of posterior distributions in nonparametric problems. Ann. Stat. **27**(2), 536–561 (1999)
2. Bissiri, P.G., Holmes, C.C., Walker, S.G.: A general framework for updating belief distributions. J. R. Stat. Soc. Ser. B (Statistical Methodology) **78**(5), 1103–1130 (2016)
3. Camino, R.D., Hammerschmidt, C.A., State, R.: Improving missing data imputation with deep generative models. arXiv preprint arXiv:1902.10666 (2019)

4. Chatterjee, S., Diaconis, P.: The sample size required in importance sampling. Ann. Appl. Probab. **28**(2), 1099–1135 (2018)
5. Chen, R.T., Li, X., Grosse, R.B., Duvenaud, D.K.: Isolating sources of disentanglement in variational autoencoders. In: Advances in Neural Information Processing. vol. 31 (2018)
6. Chen, Y.C., Liu, T., Yu, C.H., Chiang, T.Y., Hwang, C.C.: Effects of GC bias in next-generation-sequencing data on de novo genome assembly. PLoS ONE **8**(4), e62856 (2013)
7. Collier, M., Nazabal, A., Williams, C.K.: Vaes in the presence of missing data. arXiv preprint arXiv:2006.05301 (2020)
8. Daxberger, E., Hernández-Lobato, J.M.: Bayesian variational autoencoders for unsupervised out-of-distribution detection. arXiv preprint arXiv:1912.05651 (2019)
9. Gal, Y., Ghahramani, Z.: Dropout as a Bayesian approximation: representing model uncertainty in deep learning. In: International Conference on Machine Learning, pp. 1050–1059. PMLR (2016)
10. García-Laencina, P.J., Sancho-Gómez, J.L., Figueiras-Vidal, A.R.: Pattern classification with missing data: a review. Neural Comput. Appl. **19**(2), 263–282 (2010)
11. Gershman, S., Goodman, N.: Amortized inference in probabilistic reasoning. In: Proceedings of the Annual Meeting of the Cognitive Science Society. vol. 36 (2014)
12. Gondara, L., Wang, K.: MIDA: multiple imputation using denoising autoencoders. In: Phung, D., Tseng, V.S., Webb, G.I., Ho, B., Ganji, M., Rashidi, L. (eds.) PAKDD 2018. LNCS (LNAI), vol. 10939, pp. 260–272. Springer, Cham (2018). https://doi.org/10.1007/978-3-319-93040-4_21
13. Graham, J.W., Olchowski, A.E., Gilreath, T.D.: How many imputations are really needed? Some practical clarifications of multiple imputation theory. Prev. sci. **8**, 206–213 (2007)
14. Higgins, I., et al.: beta-VAE: learning basic visual concepts with a constrained variational framework. In: International Conference on Learning Representations (2017). https://openreview.net/forum?id=Sy2fzU9gl
15. Holmes, C.C., Walker, S.G.: Assigning a value to a power likelihood in a general Bayesian model. Biometrika **104**(2), 497–503 (2017)
16. Huang, G., Li, Y., Pleiss, G., Liu, Z., Hopcroft, J.E., Weinberger, K.Q.: Snapshot ensembles: Train 1, get m for free. arXiv preprint arXiv:1704.00109 (2017)
17. Ipsen, N.B., Mattei, P.A., Frellsen, J.: not-MIWAE: Deep generative modelling with missing not at random data. arXiv preprint arXiv:2006.12871 (2020)
18. Kingma, D.P., Welling, M.: Auto-encoding variational bayes. In: International Conference on Learning Representations (2013)
19. Kingma, D.P., Welling, M.: An introduction to variational autoencoders. arXiv preprint arXiv:1906.02691 (2019)
20. Lakshminarayanan, B., Pritzel, A., Blundell, C.: Simple and scalable predictive uncertainty estimation using deep ensembles. In: Advances in Neural Information Processing. vol. 30 (2017)
21. Lewis, S., et al.: Accurate imputation and efficient data acquisition with transformer-based vaes. In: NeurIPS 2021 Workshop on Deep Generative Models and Downstream Applications (2021)
22. Little, R.J., Rubin, D.B.: Statistical analysis with missing data. vol. 793. John Wiley & Sons (2019)
23. Ma, C., Gong, W., Hernández-Lobato, J.M., Koenigstein, N., Nowozin, S., Zhang, C.: Partial VAE for hybrid recommender system. In: NIPS Workshop on Bayesian Deep Learning. vol. 2018 (2018)

24. Ma, C., Tschiatschek, S., Hernández-Lobato, J.M., Turner, R., Zhang, C.: VAEM: a deep generative model for heterogeneous mixed type data. arXiv preprint arXiv:2006.11941 (2020)
25. Ma, C., Tschiatschek, S., Palla, K., Hernández-Lobato, J.M., Nowozin, S., Zhang, C.: EDDI: Efficient dynamic discovery of high-value information with partial VAE. arXiv preprint arXiv:1809.11142 (2018)
26. Ma, C., Zhang, C.: Identifiable generative models for missing not at random data imputation. In: Advances in Neural Information Processing. vol. 34 (2021)
27. Ma, Q., Li, X., Bai, M., Wang, X., Ning, B., Li, G.: MIVAE: multiple imputation based on variational auto-encoder. Eng. Appl. Artif. Intell. **123**, 106270 (2023). https://doi.org/10.1016/j.engappai.2023.106270, https://www.sciencedirect.com/science/article/pii/S0952197623004542
28. Mattei, P.A., Frellsen, J.: Leveraging the exact likelihood of deep latent variable models. In: Advances in Neural Information Processing. vol. 31 (2018)
29. Mattei, P.A., Frellsen, J.: MIWAE: deep generative modelling and imputation of incomplete data sets. In: International Conference on Machine Learning, pp. 4413–4423. PMLR (2019)
30. Murray, J.S.: Multiple imputation: a review of practical and theoretical findings. Stat. Sci. **33**(2), 142–159 (2018)
31. Nazabal, A., Olmos, P.M., Ghahramani, Z., Valera, I.: Handling incomplete heterogeneous data using VAEs. Pattern Recogn. **107**, 107501 (2020)
32. Nelwamondo, F.V., Mohamed, S., Marwala, T.: Missing data: A comparison of neural network and expectation maximization techniques. Curr. Sci. **93**(11), 1514–1521 (2007)
33. Nguyen, A., Yosinski, J., Clune, J.: Deep neural networks are easily fooled: High confidence predictions for unrecognizable images. In: Proceedings of the IEEE Conference on Computer Vision and Pattern Recognition, pp. 427–436 (2015)
34. Qiu, Y.L., Zheng, H., Gevaert, O.: Genomic data imputation with variational autoencoders. GigaScience **9**(8), giaa082 (2020)
35. Rezende, D.J., Mohamed, S., Wierstra, D.: Stochastic backpropagation and approximate inference in deep generative models. In: International Conference on Machine Learning, pp. 1278–1286. PMLR (2014)
36. Roskams-Hieter, B.: Betavaemultimpute. https://github.com/roskamsh/BetaVAEMultImpute (2023)
37. Schafer, J.L., Olsen, M.K.: Multiple imputation for multivariate missing-data problems: a data analyst's perspective. Multivar. Behav. Res. **33**(4), 545–571 (1998)
38. Sinharay, S., Stern, H.S., Russell, D.: The use of multiple imputation for the analysis of missing data. Psychol. Methods **6**(4), 317 (2001)
39. Szegedy, C., et al.: Intriguing properties of neural networks. arXiv preprint arXiv:1312.6199 (2013)
40. Walker, S., Hjort, N.L.: On Bayesian consistency. J. R. Stat. Soc. Ser. B **63**(4), 811–821 (2001)

A New Framework for Classifying Probability Density Functions

Anis Fradi[(✉)] and Chafik Samir

University of Clermont Auvergne, LIMOS CNRS(UMR 6158), 63000
Clermont-Ferrand, France
{anis.fradi,chafik.samir}@uca.fr

Abstract. This paper introduces a new framework for classifying probability density functions. The proposed method fits in the class of constrained Gaussian processes indexed by distribution functions. Firstly, instead of classifying observations directly, we consider their isometric transformations which enables us to satisfy both positiveness and unit integral hard constraints. Secondly, we introduce the theoretical proprieties and give numerical details of how to decompose each transformed observation in an appropriate orthonormal basis. As a result, we show that the coefficients are belonging to the unit sphere when equipped with the standard Euclidean metric as a natural metric. Lastly, the proposed methods are illustrated and successfully evaluated in different configurations and with various dataset.

Keywords: Classification · Constrained Gaussian Processes · Distribution Functions · Bayesian Inference

1 Introduction

Supervised learning is a powerful tool for solving many real-world problems in various fields [2]. It has a wide range of applications, including but not limited to, image recognition, natural language processing, sentiment analysis, fraud detection, and prediction in finance and health-care. For example, in image recognition [20], supervised learning algorithms can be trained on large datasets of labeled images to identify objects and classify them into specific categories. In language processing [16], supervised learning can be used for text classification, sentiment analysis, and language translation. In finance [26], supervised learning can be used to predict stock prices. Some popular supervised learning algorithms include linear regression [14], logistic regression [13], decision trees [6], random forests [9] and support vector machines [30]. These algorithms have different strengths and weaknesses and are suitable for different types of problems. The choice of an algorithm depends on the nature of the problem, the amount of labeled data available and the desired level of accuracy.

Nowadays, Gaussian processes are powerful methods for modeling complex data that does not have a simple linear relationship between the input and the

© The Author(s), under exclusive license to Springer Nature Switzerland AG 2023
D. Koutra et al. (Eds.): ECML PKDD 2023, LNAI 14169, pp. 507–522, 2023.
https://doi.org/10.1007/978-3-031-43412-9_30

output variables [28,32]. They are particularly useful when data have a high degree of noise or/and uncertainty. A Gaussian process (GP) can also be used for Bayesian optimization and for active learning. In probability and statistics a standard GP is a stochastic process (a collection of random variables indexed by time or space), such that every finite collection has a multivariate normal distribution, i.e., every finite linear combination of them is normally distributed [10]. GP regression models have been extensively developed for statistical machine learning. One of the main advantages of GP regression is that it provides a measure of uncertainty in the predictions. A Gaussian process classifier (GPc) is a machine learning method that adapts GPs for the classification task where the goal is to learn a mapping from input features to a categorical output. The first step of a GPc is to specify a covariance function that defines the covariance between the input features. The covariance function essentially captures the similarity between pairs of data points. Once the covariance function is specified the GPc can be trained on a labeled dataset using a technique called maximum likelihood estimation. This involves finding the values of the covariance hyperparameters that maximize the marginal likelihood of the observed data.

However, standard GPs were limited to data in vector spaces. In fields such as shape analysis [19,31] and diffusion tensor imaging [1] data often lie on a manifold. Therefore, the standard GP model is not straightforwardly applicable to a non-Euclidean space due to hard constraints/limitations imposed by the underlying function [24]. This usually makes the GP model nonviable since the resulting predictive distribution does not live in the correct geometric space. In this context, the linear regression was first generalized to solve the problem of manifold-valued data based on the geodesic regression before being extended for multidimensional covariates [18]. Furthermore, [22] generalized GPs to Riemannian manifolds as wrapped Gaussian processes. Recently, [4] constructed covariance functions in order to obtain GPs indexed by probability measures endowed with the Wasserstein metric. More recently, [29] provided a unified framework of GPs indexed by non-decreasing distribution functions (SNDF) endowed with the Fisher-Rao metric. The closest to our work is that of [11] for which authors have represented functional data by their corresponding probability density functions (PDFs). They also benefited from the connection between the set of PDFs endowed with the Fisher-Rao metric and the set of square-root density functions (SRDFs) endowed with the $\mathbb{L}^2$ metric resulting to be the Hilbert upper-hemisphere with many advantageous geometric tools [12].

In general, functional data analysis (FDA) is about the analysis of information on univariate functions, multidimensional curves, surfaces, etc [27]. Some of commonly used techniques in FDA include functional principal component analysis [33]. A relevant reference on this topic includes the classification of functional data with a segmentation approach [7] and FDA via neural networks [21]. In particular, a PDF is a type of functional data that describes the probability distribution of a continuous random variable. In other words, the PDF of a continuous random variable is a function that maps each realization of the random variable to the relative probability of that value occurring. The set of

PDFs is a constrained functional space that has been applied in many real-world applications [5]. Indeed, PDFs are most commonly preferred as a representation of functional data thanks to their ability to improve the local distributions and explore the skewness of original data [15]. Contrariwise, such representations even their ability to describe functional data prevent the linearity of transformed data due to both positiveness and unit integral constraints [3]. To overcome such issue one should define a metric on the set of PDFs which matches the mentioned constraints. In particular, the consistency of regression and classification with PDFs as inputs was established in [23, 25].

One of the main disadvantages of GPs indexed by Riemannian manifolds is that they can be computationally expensive especially for large datasets. In fact, the distance should be evaluated in functional spaces. However, several approximate methods can be used to make this class of GPs more computationally efficient. Keeping the same idea, in this paper, we will develops GPs indexed by PDFs as a measure of divergence between them based on the well-defined covariance function. In contrast to [11] we consider the formal expansion of a SRDF in terms of a $\mathbb{L}^2$ basis yielding from the convergent orthogonal series expansion [8]. We then exploit the fact that the set of SRDFs endowed with the $\mathbb{L}^2$ functional metric resulting to be the Hilbert hemi-sphere is isometric to the Euclidean sphere endowed with the l^2 square-summable metric generated by the set of coefficients resulting from the expansion at hand. Given a finite set of $\mathbb{L}^2$ basis assumed to maintain most information of the SRDF the restriction to the (uncountably) infinite-dimensional Hilbert sphere translates to a restriction to the (countably) finite-dimensional sphere endowed with the l^2 Euclidean metric.

The rest of the paper is organized as follows. In Sect. 2, we review the GPc model, inference, learning, and prediction. Section 3 presents how to move from a PDF to a vector of coefficients belonging to the tangent space of the Euclidean sphere when dealing with the convergent orthogonal series expansion. Section 4 introduces the GPc indexed by the set of PDFs thanks to the isometry with the tangent space of the Euclidean sphere. Empirical results are presented and discussed in Sect. 5. Finally, Sect. 6 concludes the paper.

2   Standard Gaussian Process Classifier

We are given N observations $(x_1, y_1), \ldots, (x_N, y_N)$ with $x_i \in \mathbb{R}^d$ are the d-dimensional inputs (predictors) and y_i are the associated responses ($i = 1, \ldots, N$). In this paper, we consider the binary classification where y_i takes values in $\{-1, +1\}$ for which a GP becomes a GPc. A GPc is a probabilistic model that makes predictions by learning a mapping from inputs to class probabilities. In particular, we are interested in finding the probability of the target class "+1" satisfying: $\pi(x) = \mathbb{P}(y = +1|f(x)) = \sigma(f(x))$, depending on an activation function $\sigma : \mathbb{R} \to [0, 1]$ and usually referring to the sigmoid $\sigma(t) = 1/(1+\exp(-t))$. In a Bayesian framework, we model f with a zero mean GPc of a covariance function $c(.,.)$ controlling its underlying structure, i.e., $f(x) \sim \mathcal{GP}(0, c(x, x'))$. Note that, in this context, our formulation is different from kernel-based methods [17] and all predictions are guaranteed to be PDFs. Since y_i is of binary values then $y_i|f(x_i)$ follows a Bernoulli law $\sim \mathcal{B}(\sigma(f(x_i)))$. The standard GPc model is

$$\begin{cases} f \sim \mathcal{GP}(0, c) \\ y_i|f(x_i) \sim \mathcal{B}(\sigma(f(x_i))) \end{cases}$$

In this paper, the covariance function $c(.,.)$ is supposed to be homogeneous which means that it is associated with a stationary parametrized kernel $K_\theta : \mathbb{R} \to \mathbb{R}$ such that $c(x, x') = K_\theta(||x - x'||_2)$.

Likelihood. Let $\mathbf{x} = (x_1, ..., x_N)^T$, $\mathbf{y} = (y_1, ..., y_N)^T$ and $\mathbf{f} = (f_1, ..., f_N)^T = (f(x_1), ..., f(x_N))^T$. The likelihood term is the product of individual likelihoods

$$\mathbb{P}(\mathbf{y}|\mathbf{f}) = \prod_{i=1}^{N} \mathbb{P}(y_i|f_i) = \prod_{i=1}^{N} \sigma(y_i f_i) \tag{1}$$

Prior. Since $f \sim \mathcal{GP}(0, c)$ then $\mathbf{f}|\mathbf{x}$ follows a multivariate Gaussian law

$$\mathbb{P}(\mathbf{f}|\mathbf{x}) = \mathcal{N}(\mathbf{f}|0, \mathbf{C}); \quad \mathbf{C} = c(\mathbf{x}, \mathbf{x}) \tag{2}$$

Posterior. From the Bayes' rule we write the posterior distribution as

$$\mathbb{P}(\mathbf{f}|\mathbf{x}, \mathbf{y}) = \frac{\mathbb{P}(\mathbf{f}|\mathbf{x}) \times \mathbb{P}(\mathbf{y}|\mathbf{f})}{\mathbb{P}(\mathbf{y}|\mathbf{x})} \propto \mathbb{P}(\mathbf{f}|\mathbf{x}) \times \mathbb{P}(\mathbf{y}|\mathbf{f}) \tag{3}$$

where $\mathbb{P}(\mathbf{y}|\mathbf{x})$ refers to the marginal likelihood. The posterior is analytically intractable and need to be approximated due to the likelihood term. To handle this issue one can introduce the Laplace approximation by finding the maximum a posteriori (MAP) estimator of $\mathbf{f}$ denoted $\hat{\mathbf{f}} = (\hat{f}_1, ..., \hat{f}_N)^T$ from the Newton-Raphson method, iteratively

$$\mathbf{f}^{k+1} = \left(\mathbf{C}^{-1} + \mathbf{W}^k\right)^{-1}\left(\mathbf{W}^k\mathbf{f}^k + \nabla \log \mathbb{P}(\mathbf{y}|\mathbf{f})|_{\mathbf{f}=\mathbf{f}^k}\right); \quad k = 1, 2, \cdots \tag{4}$$

$\mathbf{W}^k$ is the negative Hessian matrix of the likelihood at $\mathbf{f}^k$: $\mathbf{W}^k = -\nabla^2 \log \mathbb{P}(\mathbf{y}|\mathbf{f})|_{\mathbf{f}=\mathbf{f}^k}$. Once we estimate $\hat{\mathbf{f}}$ and $\hat{\mathbf{W}} = -\nabla^2 \log \mathbb{P}(\mathbf{y}|\mathbf{f})|_{\mathbf{f}=\hat{\mathbf{f}}}$ yields a posterior approximation from a second order Taylor expansion of $\log \mathbb{P}(\mathbf{f}|\mathbf{x}, \mathbf{y})$ around $\hat{\mathbf{f}}$ as

$$\hat{\mathbb{P}}(\mathbf{f}|\mathbf{y}, \mathbf{x}) = \mathcal{N}(\mathbf{f}|\hat{\mathbf{f}}, (\mathbf{C}^{-1} + \hat{\mathbf{W}})^{-1}) \tag{5}$$

Given a test input x^* the predictive distribution at $f^* = f(x^*)$ is then

$$\hat{\mathbb{P}}(f^*|\mathbf{x}, \mathbf{y}, x^*) = \mathcal{N}(f^*|\mu(x^*), \sigma^2(x^*)) \tag{6}$$

with

$$\begin{cases} \mu(x^*) = \mathbf{C}_*^T \mathbf{C}^{-1}\hat{\mathbf{f}} \\ \sigma^2(x^*) = \mathbf{C}_{**} - \mathbf{C}_*^T(\mathbf{C} + \hat{\mathbf{W}}^{-1})^{-1}\mathbf{C}_* \end{cases} \tag{7}$$

where $\mathbf{C}_* = c(\mathbf{x}, x^*)$ and $\mathbf{C}_{**} = c(x^*, x^*)$. Using the moments of prediction the predictor of $y^* = +1$ satisfies

$$\bar{\pi}(x^*) = \mathbb{P}(y^* = 1|x^*) \approx \int_{\mathbb{R}} \sigma(f^*)\hat{\mathbb{P}}(f^*|\mathbf{x}, \mathbf{y}, x^*)df^* \tag{8}$$

For some applications, the hyperparameter θ associated to the kernel K_θ is known a priori and is chosen according to, for example, certain physical properties. However, in many applied environments the kernel's hyperparameter is learned from data for instance when maximizing the approximate log marginal likelihood satisfying

$$\log \hat{\mathbb{P}}(\mathbf{y}|\mathbf{x}) = -\frac{1}{2}\hat{\mathbf{f}}^T\mathbf{C}^{-1}\hat{\mathbf{f}} + \log \mathbb{P}(\mathbf{y}|\hat{\mathbf{f}}) - \frac{1}{2}\log|\mathcal{I}_N + \hat{\mathbf{W}}^{\frac{1}{2}}\mathbf{C}\hat{\mathbf{W}}^{\frac{1}{2}}| \tag{9}$$

where $\mathcal{I}_N$ refers to the $N \times N$ diagonal matrix. At this stage, it becomes possible to fit the kernel hyperparameters, for instance, by a gradient-descent algorithm. Inferring the predictive distribution or learning the hyperparameters from the log approximate marginal likelihood is dominated by the inversion of the $N \times N$ covariance matrix $\mathbf{C}$, which incurs a computational cost of $O(N^3)$. Additionally, the memory requirements for GPc scale with a computational complexity of $O(N^2)$.

3   Manifold Structure

Let p be a PDF of a real-valued random variable with respect to the Lebesgue measure. The set of all PDFs defined on $I = [0, 1]$ is a simplex satisfying

$$\mathcal{P} = \left\{ p : I \to \mathbb{R} \mid p \text{ is nonnegative and } \int_I p(t)dt = 1 \right\} \tag{10}$$

$\mathcal{P}$ is a Riemannian manifold when endowed with the Fisher-Rao metric

$$\langle g_1, g_2 \rangle_p = \int_I \frac{g_1(t)g_2(t)}{p(t)} dt \tag{11}$$

where $g_1, g_2 \in \mathcal{T}_p(\mathcal{P})$ are two tangent vectors at p belonging to

$$\mathcal{T}_p(\mathcal{P}) = \left\{ g : I \to \mathbb{R} \mid \int_I g(t)dt = 0 \right\} \tag{12}$$

As a second representation we introduce the set of SRDFs satisfying

$$\mathcal{H} = \left\{ \psi : I \to \mathbb{R} \mid \psi \text{ is nonnegative, and } ||\psi||_{\mathbb{L}^2} = \left(\int_I \psi(t)^2 dt \right)^{1/2} = 1 \right\} \tag{13}$$

Endowed with the $\mathbb{L}^2$ metric $\mathcal{H}$ results to be the Hilbert upper-hemisphere (nonnegative part). In addition, the tangent space of $\mathcal{H}$ locally at ψ is

$$\mathcal{T}_\psi(\mathcal{H}) = \left\{ f : I \to \mathbb{R} \mid \langle \psi, f \rangle_{\mathbb{L}^2} = \int_I \psi(t)f(t)dt = 0 \right\} \tag{14}$$

Associated with any $p \in \mathcal{P}$ is a unique $\psi \in \mathcal{H}$ (isometrically) expressed as

$$\psi(t) = \sqrt{p(t)}; \quad t \in I \tag{15}$$

The advantage of representing a PDF $p \in \mathcal{P}$ with $\psi \equiv \sqrt{p} \in \mathcal{H}$ is that it greatly simplifies the underlying geometry of $\mathcal{P}$ with some nice tools on the Hilbert sphere. Since ψ is an element of $\mathbb{L}^2(I, \mathbb{R})$, it can be represented as a convergent orthogonal series expansion

$$\psi(t) = \sum_{l=1}^{\infty} a_l \phi_l(t) \tag{16}$$

where $(\phi_l)_l$ is a complete orthonormal basis in $\mathbb{L}^2(I, \mathbb{R})$. Note that $\psi(t)$ can be re-written as

$$\psi(t) = \Phi(t)^T A \tag{17}$$

for $A = (a_1, a_2, \dots)^T$ and $\Phi(t) = (\phi_1(t), \phi_2(t), \dots)^T$. Consequently, $\psi(t)$ is a SRDF if and only if, in addition to the non-negativity constraint, $A \in \mathcal{S}^\infty$ from the following equality

$$\|\psi\|_{\mathbb{L}^2}^2 = \int_I \psi(t)^2 dt = \sum_{l=1}^{\infty} a_l^2 \int_I \phi_l(t)^2 dt = \sum_{l=1}^{\infty} a_l^2 = \|A\|_2^2 \tag{18}$$

Here, $\mathcal{S}^\infty$ refers to the unit infinite-dimensional Euclidean (square-summable) sphere satisfying

$$\mathcal{S}^\infty = \left\{ A \in l^2 \mid \|A\|_2 = \left(\sum_{l=1}^{\infty} a_l^2 \right)^{1/2} = 1 \right\} \tag{19}$$

with the corresponding tangent space locally at A as

$$T_A(\mathcal{S}^\infty) = \left\{ B \in l^2 \mid \langle A, B \rangle_2 = \sum_{l=1}^{\infty} a_l b_l = 0 \right\} \tag{20}$$

Exponential Map. Let A be an element of $\mathcal{S}^\infty$ and $B \in T_A(\mathcal{S}^\infty)$. We define the exponential map as

$$\exp_A(B) = \cos\left(\|B\|_2\right) A + \sin\left(\|B\|_2\right) \frac{B}{\|B\|_2} \tag{21}$$

The exponential map is a diffeomorphism between the tangent space and the unit finite-dimensional sphere if we restrict B so that $\|B\|_2 \in [0, \pi[$.

Log Map. For $A_1, A_2 \in \mathcal{S}^\infty$ such that A_1 does not belong to the cut locus of A_2. We define $B \in T_{A_2}(\mathcal{S}^\infty)$ to be the inverse exponential (log) map of A_1 if $\exp_{A_2}(B) = A_1$. We then use the notation

$$B = \log_{A_2}(A_1) \tag{22}$$

where $B = \frac{\alpha}{\|\alpha\|_2} d_{\mathcal{S}^\infty}(A_1, A_2)$ and $\alpha = A_2 - \langle A_1, A_2 \rangle_2 A_1$. Here, $d_{\mathcal{S}^\infty}(.,.)$ refers to the geodesic distance on the sphere (the angle of the shortest arc), i.e., $d_{\mathcal{S}^\infty}(A_1, A_2) = \arccos(\langle A_1, A_2 \rangle_2)$.

4 Gaussian Process Classifier on PDFs

In this section, we focus on constructing a GPc on $\mathcal{P}$ based on the connection to the tangent space of the finite-dimensional sphere. A GPc Z on $\mathcal{P}$ is a random field indexed by $\mathcal{P}$ so that $(Z(p_1), \ldots, Z(p_N))^T$ is a multivariate Gaussian vector for $p_1, \ldots, p_N \in \mathcal{P}$. A zero mean GPc Z is completely specified by its covariance function $c_{\mathcal{P}} : \mathcal{P} \times \mathcal{P} \to \mathbb{R}$ defined as

$$c_{\mathcal{P}}(p_i, p_j) = cov(Z(p_i), Z(p_j)) \tag{23}$$

A covariance function $c_{\mathcal{P}}(.,.)$ on $\mathcal{P}$ should satisfy the following condition: for any $N \geq 1$ and $\mathbf{p} = (p_1, \ldots, p_N)^T$ the matrix $\mathbf{C}_{\mathcal{P}} = c_{\mathcal{P}}(\mathbf{p}, \mathbf{p})$ is symmetric nonnegative definite.

Lemma 1. *Given an orthonormal basis for $\mathbb{L}^2$, the set of PDFs equipped with the Fisher-Rao metric $(\mathcal{P}, \langle ., . \rangle_p)$ is isometric to the sphere with its natural Euclidean metric $(\mathcal{S}^\infty, \langle ., . \rangle_2)$.*

Proof. The proof yields by composing two isometric maps in (15) and (18). □

Since $A_1 \mapsto \log_{A_2}(A_1)$ is an isometry between $\mathcal{S}^\infty$ and $T_{A_2}(\mathcal{S}^\infty)$ for $A_2 \in \mathcal{S}^\infty$ then from Lemma 1 we get an isometry between $\mathcal{P}$ and $T_{A_2}(\mathcal{S}^\infty)$; $p(.) \equiv (\Phi(.)^T A_1)^2 \mapsto \log_{A_2}(A_1)$ by composition of two isometries. As a special case, let $\mathcal{E} = T_1(\mathcal{S}^\infty)$ be the tangent space of $\mathcal{S}^\infty$ at the infinite unity pole $\mathbf{1} = (0, \ldots, 0, 1)$. The strategy that we adopt to construct covariance functions is to exploit the isometric map $\log_1$ based on the linear tangent space $\mathcal{E}$. That is, we construct covariance functions with (i, j) component as

$$c_{\mathcal{P}}(p_i, p_j) = K_\theta(\| \log_1(A_i) - \log_1(A_j) \|_2) \tag{24}$$

It seems natural to consider a truncated version of ψ at order d expressed as $\psi^d(t) = \sum_{l=1}^d a_l \phi_l(t)$ and consider the rest of the sum as an error approximation: $e^d(t) = \sum_{l=d+1}^\infty a_l \phi_l(t)$. The truncation $\psi^d(t)$ is then re-written as $\psi^d(t) = \Phi^d(t)^T A^d$ for $A^d = (a_1 \ldots, a_d)^T \in \mathcal{S}^{d-1}$ and $\Phi^d(t) = (\phi_1(t), \ldots, \phi_d(t))^T$. The covariance on $\mathcal{P}$ approximately becomes

$$c_{\mathcal{P}}(p_i, p_j) \approx K_\theta(\| \log_{1^d}(A_i^d) - \log_{1^d}(A_j^d) \|_2) \tag{25}$$

where 1^d is the d-dimensional unity pole of $\mathcal{S}^{d-1}$.

Proposition 1. *Let $K_\theta : \mathbb{R} \to \mathbb{R}$ be a kernel associated to a homogeneous covariance function $c(x_i, x_j)$ defined on $\mathbb{R}^d \times \mathbb{R}^d$, i.e., $c(x_i, x_j) = K_\theta(\|x_i - x_j\|_2)$ and $c_\mathcal{P}(.,.)$ be defined like in (25). Then, $c_\mathcal{P}(.,.)$ is approximately a covariance function.*

Proof. Let p_i $(i = 1, \ldots, N)$ be a sample of i.i.d. observations on the PDF p depending on the corresponding finite-dimensional spherical coefficients $A_i^d \in \mathcal{S}^{d-1}$ and $B_i^d = \log_{\mathbf{1}^d}(A_i^d)$. Consider the matrix $\tilde{\mathbf{C}}$ with entries $\tilde{\mathbf{C}}_{ij} \approx \langle B_i^d, B_j^d \rangle_2$. Then $\tilde{\mathbf{C}}$ is approximately a Gram matrix in $\mathbb{R}^{N \times N}$. Therefore, there exists a $d \times d$ nonnegative diagonal matrix D and a $N \times d$ orthogonal matrix P such that $\tilde{\mathbf{C}} \approx PDP^T$. If $e_1, \ldots, e_N$ denote the canonical basis of $\mathbb{R}^N$ then $e_i^T \tilde{\mathbf{C}} e_j \approx x_i^T x_j$ with $x_i = D^{1/2} P^T e_i \in \mathbb{R}^d$ depending on $p_1, \ldots, p_N$. This implies that $\langle B_i^d, B_j^d \rangle_2 \approx x_i^T x_j$ and consequently $\| \log_{\mathbf{1}^d}(A_i^d) - \log_{\mathbf{1}^d}(A_j^d)\|_2 \approx \|x_i - x_j\|_2$. Finally, any matrix with entries $K_\theta(\| \log_{\mathbf{1}^d}(A_i^d) - \log_{\mathbf{1}^d}(A_j^d)\|_2)$ can be approximately seen as a covariance matrix with entries $K_\theta(\|x_i - x_j\|_2)$ and inherits its properties. □

Let p_i $(i = 1, \ldots, N)$ be a sample of i.i.d. observations on the PDF p depending on the corresponding spherical coefficients $A_i^d \in \mathcal{S}^{d-1}$, respectively.

Corollary 1. *If Z is a GPc indexed by PDFs such that*

$$\begin{cases} Z \sim \mathcal{GP}(0, c_\mathcal{P}) \\ y_i | Z(p_i) \sim \mathcal{B}(\sigma(Z(p_i))) \end{cases}$$

then there is an approximated standard GPc f on $\mathcal{E}_d = \mathcal{T}_{\mathbf{1}^d}(\mathcal{S}^{d-1})$ satisfying

$$\begin{cases} f \sim \mathcal{GP}(0, c) \\ y_i | f(B_i^d) \sim \mathcal{B}(\sigma(f(B_i^d))) \\ B_i^d = \log_{\mathbf{1}^d}(A_i^d) \end{cases}$$

5   Experimental Results

In this section, we evaluate the proposed model on various datasets and compare it to other state-of-the-art methods. We consider the squared exponential (SE) kernel satisfying

$$K(\tau) = \sigma^2 \exp(-0.5\tau^2/\gamma^2); \quad \tau = \|x - x'\|_2 \tag{26}$$

Functions drawn from a GP with this kernel are infinitely differentiable, and can display long-range trends. GPs with a SE kernel are well-suited for modeling functions that exhibit smoothness and continuity properties, such as classification problems. The covariance structures that can be learned from data are the variance σ^2 and the length-scale γ. The orthonormal basis in $\mathbb{L}^2(I, \mathbb{R})$ is set to $\phi_l(t) = \sqrt{2} \sin(l\pi t)$ and the truncation order is fixed to $d = 30$, see more details in [12]. Note that all the methods tested in this section have been carefully implemented in Python programming language on a standard desktop machine running linux.

5.1   Illustrative and Challenging Datasets

Synthetic PDFs. We consider two datasets of simulated PDFs: beta and inverse gamma distributions. They have been applied to model randomness on intervals of finite length and have been widely used in simulation studies for a variety of disciplines. We performed this experiment by simulating 1000 PDFs slightly different for two classes in each dataset. Each observation p_i represents a PDF when we add a random uniform noise to initial parameters. For beta dataset we take $\mathbb{P}(p_i|y_i = +1) = \mathcal{B}(2 + \epsilon_i; 2)$ for the first class and $\mathbb{P}(p_i|y_i = -1) = B(1.8+\epsilon_i; 2)$ for the second one where $\epsilon_i \sim \mathcal{U}([-0.2; 0.2])$ is a realization of the uniform law. For inverse gamma dataset we take $\mathbb{P}(p_i|y_i = +1) = \mathcal{IG}(3 + \epsilon_i)$ for the first class and $\mathbb{P}(p_i|y_i = -1) = \mathcal{IG}(2.8 + \epsilon_i)$ for the second one. We show some examples of p_i in Fig. 1 (top) with different colors (blue and red) for the two classes.

Real PDFs. In this part, a real study was conducted with two datasets of PDFs. The first dataset consists of 1500 observations giving the segmented and preprocessed electrocardiogram (ECG) signals for Heartbeat (500 normal and 1000 abnormal) ECG Heartbeat Categorization Dataset. This dataset contains a collection of ECG recordings with a sampling frequency: 125 Hz, where the goal is to classify each heartbeat into normal or abnormal when the human was affected by different arrhythmias and myocardial infarction. Each signal includes information about the symptoms during a short period. The information in this dataset

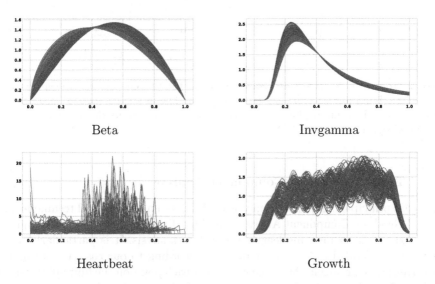

Beta

Invgamma

Heartbeat

Growth

Fig. 1. Some examples of PDFs with first class (blue) and second class (red). For Growth: boys (blue) and girls (red) and Heartbeat: normal (blue) and abnormal (red). (Color figure online)

could be used to develop strategies to control this problem. It could also be used to develop better treatments for other similar problems. We display some examples of signals represented by their PDFs registered on $I = [0, 1]$ and normalized to admit an unit integral in Fig. 1 (bottom-left). Moreover, the second dataset used in this analysis consists of monthly clinical growth charts for children from 1 to 12 years (100 girls and 100 boys) National Center for Health Statistics. It is a typical example of biological dynamics observed over months. Each growth chart represents the size (the increase in centimeters) of a child during 132 months. In this context, all growth charts were represented by PDFs of child sizes registered on $I = [0, 1]$, see some examples in Fig. 1 (bottom-right) for which we make the use of nonparametric kernel method with an automatic bandwidth.

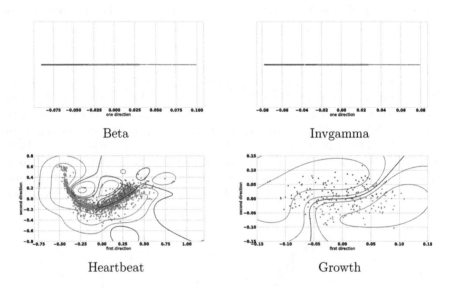

Fig. 2. Top: TPCA of projected coefficients into the tangent space of the sphere with first class (blue) and second class (red). Bottom: The predicted class "1" probabilities are shown in the contour plots. The black dashed line represents the decision boundary at $\bar{\pi}(Color figure online)(C_i^{d,k}) = \frac{1}{2}$.

5.2   Tangent Principal Component Analysis

Tangent principal component analysis (TPCA) is a mathematical technique, also called Geodesic Component Analysis, used for dimensionality reduction and feature extraction in machine learning and data analysis. It is particularly useful for data embedded on curved manifolds. According to our case, this technique involves first computing the tangent space at each point on the finite-dimensional sphere $\mathcal{S}^{d-1}$ then performs to obtain a set of orthogonal basis vectors that capture the most important variations in data. If some point movements B_i^d were to be totally correlated manifold learning methods including: t-SNE, Isomap,

LLE, and MDS are useful for nonlinear dimensionality reduction. Since our vector data B_i^d are not of high-dimension ($d = 30$) and belong to the Euclidean tangent space we establish the TPCA. The central idea of TPCA is to reduce the dimensionality of projected vectors into the tangent space of $\mathcal{S}^{d-1}$ belonging to a linear sub-space of $\mathbb{R}^d$ by keeping one ($k = 1$), two ($k = 2$) or three ($k = 3$) dimensions in $\mathbb{R}^k$. This is achieved when transforming to a new set of variables, known as principal components (PCs) so that the first directions retain most of the variation presented in the original variables. First, we find the eigenvectors of the covariance matrix of the whole dataset B_i^d. Second, we sort the eigenvectors by decreasing the corresponding eigenvalues and choose k eigenvectors of the largest eigenvalues to be the principal directions. Finally, we transform the original data B_i^d into the new sub-space of reduced dimension $\mathbb{R}^k$. Let $C_i^{d,k}$ ($i = 1, \ldots, N$) be the resulting coefficients in $\mathbb{R}^k$. Generally, the variance ratio indicates the proportion of the total variance that is accounted by each principal component. Specifically, principal components with high variance ratios are considered to be more important and should be retained, while those with low variance ratios may be discarded. In Fig. 2 (top) we show results of the coefficients projected into one principal direction for Beta and Invgamma datasets. Indeed, only one principal component ($k = 1$) accounts for the largest proportion of the variance, with a variance ratio of 0.99 for both. Figure 2 (bottom) shows a scatter plot of the data with the first two principal components ($k = 2$) for the Heartbeat and Growth datasets. The first principal component (which explains 67% of the variance for Heartbeat and 38% for Growth) separates the two classes along the x-axis, while the second principal component (which explains 19% of the variance for Heartbeat and 15% for Growth) separates the classes along the y-axis. Although the action of TPCA is not by isometry but only a dimensionality reduction technique that finds the directions of maximum variance we add the contour plot in each region associated with the predicted class "1" probability that shows how GPc can be successfully performed in low-dimensional tangent spaces mainly when real data are not linearly separable.

5.3   Results and Comparison

To evaluate the performance of the proposed method, we split the labeled dataset into two subsets: training and test. The training set (75% of the dataset: 50% for training and 25% for validation) is used to train the model, while the test set (25% of the dataset) is used to evaluate its performance. Some commonly used metrics for evaluating the performance of a classification model include:

- Accuracy: The proportion of correctly classified instances in the test set.
- AUC: The measure of the overall performance of the model based on the ROC curve.
- LOSS: The measure of the logarithmic (also known as cross-entropy loss) between the predicted probability distribution and the true label.

In order to get an accurate estimate of the model's performance, we perform multiple random splits of the dataset into training and test sets, and train and

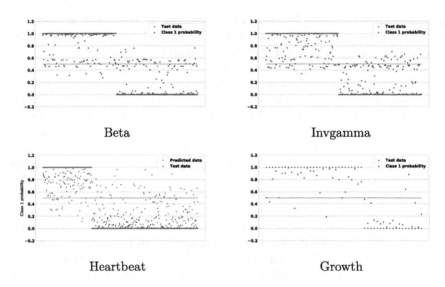

Fig. 3. The classification results with first class (label 1) and second class (label 0).

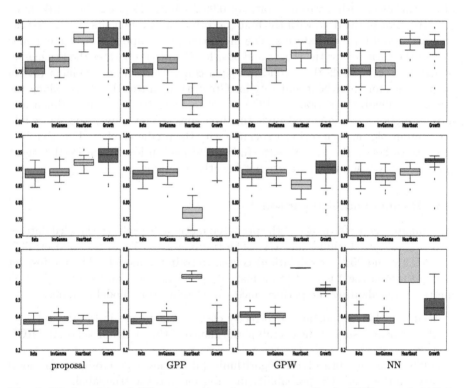

Fig. 4. The boxplots of different metrics: Accuracy score (top), AUC score (middle), and LOSS measure (bottom).

test the model on each split which could reduce the variance in the performance metrics obtained from a single split. The predicted class probabilities in our model provide a measure of uncertainty in the model's predictions and used to make informed decisions based on the level of confidence in the classification result. Now, we show results of the predicted class "1" probabilities of one among 100 runs in Fig. 3. The observed values involve computing the mean and variance of the conditional distribution of the output labels given the input data and the model parameters, and then using them to compute the predicted class probabilities. We state that most well classified test data are far from the decision boundary at $\bar{\pi}(B_i^d) = \frac{1}{2}$, which gives a good precision to our method.

At this stage, we will compare the results of our approach with some baseline methods: i) GPs indexed by PDFs (GPP), ii) GPs based on the Wasserstein distance (GPW), and iii) neural network (NN) model for classifying univariate functional data to determine whether the differences in performance are significant. We remind that standard classification models are not suitable for curved spaces and can not be applied in this context. For an attempt to show it is different, we provide some details about the NN model architecture. We first define the NN model using Keras' Sequential function in Python. The model has an input layer equal to the number of time instances of each observation. The first hidden layer a fully connected layer with 32 neurons and a ReLU activation function, followed by a dropout (regularization) layer that randomly sets 50% of the input units to 0 during training to prevent overfitting. Then, we add a second hidden layer with 16 neurons and ReLU activation, followed by another dropout layer with a dropout rate of 50%. Finally, the model has an output layer with one neuron and sigmoid activation. This produces a scalar output between 0 and 1, representing the model's prediction for the binary classification problem. We compile the model with binary cross-entropy loss and Adam optimizer.

In Fig. 4 we illustrate boxplots of the accuracy, AUC and LOSS metrics for the binary classification problem across the 100 runs of the model. The boxplots of most dataset are relatively narrow for the Accuracy and AUC scores, indicating that these metrics are consistent across different runs. However, we also see a few outliers with other datasets that are in somewhat lower/higher than the rest, which may indicate that there are some runs where the model is performing poorly or exceptionally well. Since most criteria values are sometimes very close for different methods which rends comparison nontrivial we also summarize the mean and the standard deviations (std) values in Table 1. Accordingly, our proposed method achieved a mean accuracy of 0.761, 0.779, 0.849 and 0.847 for Beta, InvGamma, Heartbeat and Growth, which is significantly better than the baseline GPP, GPW and NN. However, our proposed method outperformed the same methods in terms of AUC, achieving a score of 0.885, 0.891, 0.918 and 0.938, respectively, see Table 2. Regarding the LOSS measure in Table 3, our proposed method achieves a lower value for three among four datasets: Beta, Heartbeat and Growth. Overall, our proposed method showed promising results and outperformed the baseline methods on all datasets in terms of accuracy and AUC, while it still competitive in terms of LOSS measure. Our method, on the other hand, is designed to be computationally efficient. This is because it considers some coefficients instead of PDFs directly that are optimized for an efficient training. This allows our method to achieve comparable or better accuracy than traditional methods, while requiring less computational resources. To illustrate this, let's compare the computational time of our method against the baseline methods, particularly for the Beta dataset. We assume that all programs run on a desktop machine with 32 GB memory and CPU Xeon(R) 3.60 GHz. Note that the elapsed times for predicting all the Beta test set are 10^{-3}, 8.9×10^{-4} and 3×10^{-2} seconds using GPW, GPP, and NN respectively while it takes 5.7×10^{-4} seconds for our proposal.

Table 1. Accuracy score.

Dataset	Proposal		GPP		GPW		NN	
	mean	std	mean	std	mean	std	mean	std
Beta	**0.761**	0.027	0.757	0.025	0.757	0.026	0.755	0.025
InvGamma	**0.779**	0.023	0.773	0.024	0.77	0.024	0.757	0.025
Heartbeat	**0.849**	0.017	0.666	0.022	0.802	0.018	0.837	0.015
Growth	**0.847**	0.046	0.841	0.047	0.844	0.036	0.825	0.025

Table 2. AUC score.

Dataset	Proposal		GPP		GPW		NN	
	mean	std	mean	std	mean	std	mean	std
Beta	**0.885**	0.018	0.882	0.018	0.884	0.018	0.878	0.017
InvGamma	**0.891**	0.016	0.887	0.017	0.888	0.016	0.878	0.016
Heartbeat	**0.918**	0.004	0.768	0.024	0.853	0.018	0.89	0.014
Growth	**0.938**	0.03	0.923	0.029	0.901	0.037	0.923	0.017

Table 3. LOSS measure.

Dataset	Proposal		GPP		GPW		NN	
	mean	std	mean	std	mean	std	mean	std
Beta	**0.368**	0.021	0.371	0.021	0.41	0.024	0.393	0.035
InvGamma	0.387	0.017	0.388	0.021	0.406	0.022	**0.378**	0.038
Heartbeat	**0.367**	0.018	0.638	0.015	0.689	0.001	0.919	0.343
Growth	**0.334**	0.058	0.337	0.056	0.563	0.014	0.464	0.063

6   Conclusion

In this paper, we have introduced a novel approach for classifying probability density functions with a Gaussian process classifier model. Our methodology benefits from the use of functions decomposed with coefficients projected into the tangent space of the sphere, which can perform inference on PDFs. The theoretical foundation detailed in this paper exploits the simple geometry implied the nonparametric Fisher-Rao metric. The experimental evaluation has demonstrated that this new model is competitive on several challenging datasets. Furthermore, the problem formulation can be extended to many other supervised and unsupervised areas of statistical machine learning. Nevertheless, it would be very interesting to further investigate substantial impacts on the computational costs.

References

1. Alexander, A., Lee, J., Lazar, M., Field, A.: Diffusion tensor imaging of the brain. Neurother. J. Am. Soc. Exp. NeuroTher **4**, 316–29 (2007)
2. Alpaydin, E.: Introduction to Machine Learning, 2nd edn. MIT Press, Cambridge, MA (2010)
3. Amari, Si.: Differential geometry of statistical inference. In: Prokhorov, J.V., Itô, K. (eds.) Probability Theory and Mathematical Statistics. Lecture Notes in Mathematics. vol 1021. Springer, Berlin, Heidelberg (1983). https://doi.org/10.1007/BFb0072900
4. Bachoc, F., Gamboa, F., Loubes, J.M., Venet, N.: A gaussian process regression model for distribution inputs. IEEE Trans. Inf. Theor. **64**, 6620–6637 (2018)
5. Botev, Z.I., Grotowski, J.F., Kroese, D.P.: Kernel density estimation via diffusion. Ann. Stat. **38**, 2916–2957 (2010)
6. Breiman, L., Friedman, J.H., Olshen, R.A., Stone, C.J.: Classification and Regression Trees. Wadsworth International Group, Belmont, CA (1984)
7. Cardot, H., Ferraty, F., Sarda, P.: Classification of functional data: a segmentation approach. Comput. Stat. Data Anal. **44**, 315–337 (2003)
8. Cencov, N.N.: Evaluation of an unknown distribution density from observations. Doklady **3**, 1559–1562 (1962)
9. Chen, L., Li, J.: Fraud detection for credit cards using random forest. J. Financ. Data Science **1**, 83–94 (2018)
10. Djolonga, J., Krause, A., Cevher, V.: High-dimensional Gaussian process bandits, pp. 1025–1033. NIPS2013, Curran Associates Inc., Red Hook, NY, USA (2013)
11. Fradi, A., Feunteun, Y., Samir, C., Baklouti, M., Bachoc, F., Loubes, J.M.: Bayesian regression and classification using gaussian process priors indexed by probability density functions. Inf. Sci. **548**, 56–68 (2021)
12. Holbrook, A., Lan, S., Streets, J., Shahbaba, B.: Nonparametric fisher geometry with application to density estimation. In: Proceedings of the 36th Conference on Uncertainty in Artificial Intelligence (UAI), pp. 101–110. Proceedings of Machine Learning Research (2020)
13. Hosmer, D.W., Lemeshow, S., Sturdivant, R.X.: Applied Logistic Regression, 3rd edn. Wiley, Hoboken, NJ (2013)
14. James, G., Witten, D., Hastie, T., Tibshirani, R.: An Introduction to Statistical Learning. STS, vol. 103. Springer, New York (2013). https://doi.org/10.1007/978-1-4614-7138-7

15. Julian, P.R., Murphy, A.H.: Probability and statistics in meteorology: a review of some recent developments. Bull. Am. Meteorol. Soc. **53**, 957–965 (1972)
16. Jurafsky, D., Martin, J.H.: Speech and Language Processing: An Introduction to Natural Language Processing, Computational Linguistics, and Speech Recognition, 3rd edn. Pearson Education, Harlow, England (2020)
17. Kanagawa, M., Hennig, P., Sejdinovic, D., Sriperumbudur, B.K.: Gaussian processes and kernel methods: A review on connections and equivalences (2018)
18. Kim, H.J., et al.: Multivariate general linear models (MGLM) on Riemannian manifolds with applications to statistical analysis of diffusion weighted images. In: IEEE Conference on Computer Vision and Pattern Recognition (CVPR), pp. 2705–2712. IEEE Computer Society, Los Alamitos, CA, USA (2014)
19. Kneip, A., Ramsay, J.O.: Combining registration and fitting for functional models. J. Am. Stat. Assoc. **103**, 1155–1165 (2008)
20. Krizhevsky, A., Sutskever, I., Hinton, G.E.: ImageNet classification with deep convolutional neural networks. Adv. Neural Inf. Process. Syst. **25**, 1097–1105 (2012)
21. Lagani, V., Fotiadis, D.I., Likas, A.: Functional data analysis via neural networks: an application to speaker identification. Expert Syst. Appl. **39**, 9188–9194 (2012)
22. Mallasto, A., Feragen, A.: Wrapped Gaussian process regression on Riemannian manifolds. In: IEEE Conference on Computer Vision and Pattern Recognition (CVPR), pp. 5580–5588. IEEE Computer Society, Los Alamitos, CA, USA (2018)
23. Oliva, J.B., Neiswanger, W., Póczos, B., Schneider, J.G., Xing, E.P.: Fast distribution to real regression. In: Proceedings of the Seventeenth International Conference on Artificial Intelligence and Statistics, pp. 706–714 (2014)
24. Patrangenaru, V., Ellingson, L.: Nonparametric Statistics on Manifolds and their Applications to Object Data Analysis, 1st edn. Chapman & Hall/CRC Monographs on Statistics & Applied Probability, CRC Press Inc, USA (2015)
25. Póczos, B., Singh, A., Rinaldo, A., Wasserman, L.: Distribution-free distribution regression. In: Proceedings of the Sixteenth International Conference on Artificial Intelligence and Statistics, pp. 507–515. Proceedings of Machine Learning Research, Scottsdale, Arizona, USA (2013)
26. Lopez de Prado, M.: Advances in financial machine learning. Wiley, Hoboken, New Jersey (2018)
27. Ramsay, J.O., Silverman, B.W.: Functional Data Analysis. Springer, New York (2005). https://doi.org/10.1007/b98888
28. Rasmussen, C.E., Williams, C.: Gaussian Processes for Machine Learning. The MIT Press, Cambridge, London (2006)
29. Samir, C., Loubes, J.-M., Yao, A.-F., Bachoc, F.: Learning a gaussian process model on the Riemannian manifold of non-decreasing distribution functions. In: Nayak, A.C., Sharma, A. (eds.) PRICAI 2019. LNCS (LNAI), vol. 11671, pp. 107–120. Springer, Cham (2019). https://doi.org/10.1007/978-3-030-29911-8_9
30. Schölkopf, B., Smola, A.J.: Learning with Kernels: Support Vector Machines, Regularization, Optimization, and Beyond. MIT Press, Adaptive computation and machine learning (2002)
31. Srivastava, A., Klassen, E., Joshi, S.H., Jermyn, I.H.: Shape analysis of Elastic curves in Euclidean spaces. IEEE Trans. Pattern Anal. Mach. Intell. **33**, 1415–1428 (2011)
32. Terenin, A.: Gaussian processes and statistical decision-making in non-Euclidean spaces. arXiv (2022). https://arxiv.org/abs/2202.10613
33. Yao, F., Müller, H.G., ling Wang, J.: Functional data analysis for sparse longitudinal data. J. Am. Stat. Assoc. **100**, 577–590 (2005)

Causality

Causality

Learning Conditional Instrumental Variable Representation for Causal Effect Estimation

Debo Cheng[✉], Ziqi Xu, Jiuyong Li, Lin Liu, Thuc Duy Le, and Jixue Liu

University of South Australia, Adelaide, Australia
{Debo.Cheng,Ziqi.Xu}@mymail.unisa.edu.au,
{Jiuyong.Li,Lin.Liu,Thuc.Le,Jixue.Liu}@unisa.edu.au

Abstract. One of the fundamental challenges in causal inference is to estimate the causal effect of a treatment on its outcome of interest from observational data. However, causal effect estimation often suffers from the impacts of confounding bias caused by unmeasured confounders that affect both the treatment and the outcome. The instrumental variable (IV) approach is a powerful way to eliminate the confounding bias from latent confounders. However, the existing IV-based estimators require a nominated IV, and for a conditional IV (CIV) the corresponding conditioning set too, for causal effect estimation. This limits the application of IV-based estimators. In this paper, by leveraging the advantage of disentangled representation learning, we propose a novel method, named DVAE.CIV, for learning and disentangling the representations of CIV and the representations of its conditioning set for causal effect estimations from data with latent confounders. Extensive experimental results on both synthetic and real-world datasets demonstrate the superiority of the proposed DVAE.CIV method against the existing causal effect estimators.

Keywords: Causal Inference · Instrumental Variable · Latent Confounder

1 Introduction

It is a fundamental task to query or estimate the causal effect of a treatment (a.k.a. exposure, intervention or action) on an outcome of interest in causal inference. Causal effect estimation has wide applications across many fields, including but not limited to, economics [19], epidemiology [16,28], and computer science [30]. The gold standard method for causal effect estimation is randomised controlled trials (RCT), but they are often impractical or unethical due to cost restrictions or ethical constraints [19,30]. Instead of conducting an RCT, estimating causal effects from observational data offers an alternative to evaluate the effect of a treatment on the outcome of interest.

D. Cheng and Z. Xu—These authors contributed equally.

© The Author(s), under exclusive license to Springer Nature Switzerland AG 2023
D. Koutra et al. (Eds.): ECML PKDD 2023, LNAI 14169, pp. 525–540, 2023.
https://doi.org/10.1007/978-3-031-43412-9_31

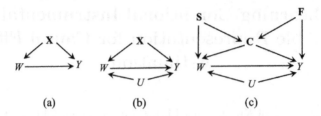

Fig. 1. Three causal DAGs are utilised to illustrate the problems of causal effect estimation from observational data. In all three DAGs, **X**, U, W and Y are the set of pre-treatment variables, latent confounder, treatment and outcome variables, respectively. (a) indicates the unconfoundedness assumption holding, and (b) shows the causal effect of W on Y is non-identification since there is a latent confounder U. (c) illustrates the problem studied in this work, in which the set **X** is represented by three sets $\{\mathbf{S}, \mathbf{C}, \mathbf{F}\}$.

Confounding bias is a major obstacle in estimating causal effects from observational data. It arises from confounders that affect both the treatment variable W and the outcome variable Y. When all confounders are measured (i.e., the unconfoundedness assumption [19,31] is satisfied), adjusting for the set of all measured confounders is sufficient to obtain an unbiased estimation of the causal effect from observational data [1,19]. For example, in the causal graph of Fig. 1(a), the unconfoundedness is satisfied when given **X**. Nevertheless, the unconfoundedness assumption is untestable, and there exists a latent (a.k.a. unobserved, unmeasured) confounder affecting both W and Y in many real-world applications, e.g. the latent confounder U affects both W and Y in the causal graph in Fig. 1(b). In such a situation, the causal effect of W on Y is non-identification [30]. Most existing data-driven methods rely on the unconfoundedness assumption and thus it becomes challenging and questionable for them to obtain unbiased causal effects from data with latent confounders.

The instrumental variable (IV) approach is a practical and powerful technique for addressing the challenging problem of causal effect estimation in the presence of latent confounders. The IV approach requires a valid IV for eliminating the confounding bias caused by latent confounders [2,18]. Valid IVs are exogenous variables that are associated with W but not directly associated with Y [16,27]. A valid IV S needs to satisfy three conditions: (1) S is correlated to W; (2) S and Y do not share confounders (i.e. *unconfounded instrument*); and (3) the effect of S on Y is entirely through W (i.e. *exogenous*) [16,27]. However, the last two conditions are too strict and not testable in real-world applications. Therefore, in many existing IV-based methods, an IV is nominated based on prior or domain knowledge. However, in many real-world applications, the nominated IVs based on domain knowledge could violate one of the three conditions, resulting in a biased estimate and potentially leading to incorrect conclusions [6,16].

It is a challenging problem to discover a valid IV directly from data. Investigators usually collect as many covariates as possible, but few of them are valid IVs that satisfy the three conditions. Instead of discovering a valid IV, Kang et al. [20] proposed a data-driven method, referred to as sisVIVE, based on the assumption of some invalid and some valid IVs (i.e. more than half of candidate IVs are valid IVs) to provide a bound of causal effect estimations. Hartford et al. [14] proposed DeepIV, a deep learning based IV approach for counterfactual predictions, but it requires a nominated IV and the corresponding conditioning set. Kuang et al. [23] developed a method to model a summary IV as a latent variable based on the statistical dependencies of the set of candidate IVs. Yuan et al. [36] proposed a data-driven method to automatically generate a synthetic IV for counterfactual predictions, but the method does not consider the confounding bias between the IV and the outcome, and the condition of *unconfounded instrument* may be violated in many cases. Therefore, it is desirable to develop an algorithm for learning a valid IV that considers the unconfounded instrument for causal effect estimations, especially conditional average causal effect estimations, from data with latent confounders.

To provide a practical solution for conditional average causal effect estimations, in this work, we focus on conditional IV (CIV), which can be considered as an IV with relaxed conditions and a CIV requires a conditioning set to instrumentalise it to function as an IV (details see Definition 1). We propose to leverage disentangled representation learning technique to learn from data the representations of a CIV and its conditioning set.

Specifically, as shown in Fig. 1(c), we assume that the observed covariates are learned through three representations, $\mathbf{S}$, $\mathbf{C}$ and $\mathbf{F}$. Here, $\mathbf{S}$ affects both treatment W and $\mathbf{C}$, $\mathbf{C}$ represents the confounding factor affecting both W and the outcome Y, and $\mathbf{F}$ represents the risk factor affecting both $\mathbf{C}$ and Y. We then establish a theorem that $\mathbf{S}$ is a valid CIV that is instrumentalised by $\{\mathbf{C}, \mathbf{F}\}$, meaning that $\{\mathbf{C}, \mathbf{F}\}$ is the conditioning set of $\mathbf{S}$. Supported by this theorem, we design and develop a novel disentangled representation learning algorithm called DVAE.CIV model, which is based on the Variational AutoEncoder (VAE) model [22]. This model allows us to obtain the representations of the CIV $\mathbf{S}$ and its conditioning set $\{\mathbf{C}, \mathbf{F}\}$, enabling us to use $\mathbf{S}$ as a valid IV conditioning on $\{\mathbf{C}, \mathbf{F}\}$ for estimating the conditional average causal effects of W on Y from data when there are latent confounders. The main contributions of the paper are summarised as follows.

- We address a challenging problem in conditional average causal effect estimations from data with latent confounders by utilising the CIV approach and VAE models.
- We propose a novel disentanglement learning model based on the conditional VAE model to learn and disentangle the representations of covariates into the representations of a CIV $\mathbf{S}$ and its conditioning set $\{\mathbf{C}, \mathbf{F}\}$ for conditional average causal effect estimations from data with latent confounders.

– We conduct extensive experiments on synthetic and real-world datasets to show the performance of the DVAE.CIV model, w.r.t. causal effect estimations from data with latent confounders.

2   Preliminaries

In this paper, uppercase and lowercase letters are utilised to represent variables and their values, respectively. Bold-faced uppercase and lowercase letters indicate a set of variables and a value assignment of the set, respectively.

A DAG (direct acyclic graph) is a graph that contains directed edges (i.e. →) without cycles. In a DAG $\mathcal{G}$, the directed edge $X_i \rightarrow X_j$ represents that X_i is a cause of X_j, and X_j is an effect of X_i. A DAG is a causal DAG when a direct edge $X_i \rightarrow X_j$ represents that X_i is a cause of X_j. In this work, we assume a causal DAG $\mathcal{G} = (\mathbf{V}, \mathbf{E})$ to represent the underlying system, where $\mathbf{V} = \mathbf{X} \cup \mathbf{U} \cup \{W, Y\}$, and $\mathbf{E} \subseteq \mathbf{V} \times \mathbf{V}$ denotes directed edges. In $\mathbf{V}$, we assume that $\mathbf{X}$ is the set of pretreatment variables, $\mathbf{U}$ is the set of latent confounders, W is a binary treatment variable ($w = 1$ and $w = 0$ denote the treated sample and control sample, respectively), and $Y(w)$ is an outcome of interest. Following the potential outcome model [19,31], we have the potential outcomes $Y(w = 1)$ and $Y(w = 0)$ relative to the treatment W. Note that we can only measure one of the two potential outcomes for a given individual x_i. Conceptually, the individual causal effect (ICE) at x_i is defined as $ICE_i = Y_i(w = 1) - Y_i(w = 0)$. The average causal effect of W on Y is defined as $\text{ACE}(W, Y) = \mathbb{E}[Y_i(w = 1) - Y_i(w = 0)]$, where $\mathbb{E}$ is the expectation function.

The conditional average causal effect (CACE) of W on Y is referred to as $\text{CACE}(W, Y)$, and defined as the form $P(Y|do(w), \mathbf{X})$, where $do(\cdot)$ is do-operation and indicates an intervention on the treatment (i.e. set the value of W as per [30]). Conceptually, $P(Y|do(w), \mathbf{X})$ can be obtained as:

$$\text{CACE}(W, Y) = \mathbb{E}[Y_i(w = 1) - Y_i(w = 0) \mid \mathbf{x}_i = x] \tag{1}$$

In this work, we would like to estimate $\text{CACE}(W, Y)$ from data that there exists at least a latent confounder U affecting both W and Y. When there is an IV S and the set of conditioning covariates $\mathbf{Z}$ available in data, $\text{CACE}(W, Y)$ can be calculated by the following formula as in [3,19]:

$$\text{CACE}(W, Y) = \frac{\mathbb{E}(Y|W = 1, S = 1, \mathbf{Z}) - \mathbb{E}(Y|W = 0, S = 1, \mathbf{Z})}{\mathbb{E}(W|S = 1, \mathbf{Z}) - \mathbb{E}(W|S = 0, \mathbf{Z})} \tag{2}$$

The approach of CIV allows a measured covariate to be a valid IV conditioning on a set of measured variables. The formal definition of the CIV in a DAG (Definition 7.4.1 on Page 248 [30]) is introduced as follows.

Definition 1 (Conditional IV). *Let $\mathcal{G} = (\mathbf{V}, \mathbf{E})$ be a DAG with $\mathbf{V} = \mathbf{X} \cup \mathbf{U} \cup \{W, Y\}$, a variable $Q \in \mathbf{X}$ is a conditional IV w.r.t. $W \rightarrow Y$ if there exists a set of measured variables $\mathbf{Z} \subseteq \mathbf{X}$ such that (i) $Q \not\perp_d W \mid \mathbf{Z}$, (ii) $Q \perp_d Y \mid \mathbf{Z}$ in $\mathcal{G}_{\underline{W}}$, and (iii) $\forall Z \in \mathbf{Z}$, Z is not a descendant of Y.*

Here, $\perp\!\!\!\perp_d$ and $\not\perp_d$ are d-separation and d-connection for reading the conditioning relationships between nodes in a DAG [30]. The manipulated DAG $\mathcal{G}_{\underline{W}}$ in Definition 1 is obtained by deleting the direct edge $W \rightarrow Y$ from the DAG $\mathcal{G}$. Note that Definition 1 is defined on a single CIV Q that can be generalised to a set of CIVs $\mathbf{Q}$ easily.

With the pretreatment variables assumption, there is not a descendant of Y in $\mathbf{X}$, i.e. the condition (iii) of Definition 1 is always held. It means that one needs to check the first two conditions for verifying whether a variable is a CIV or not. Note that discovering a conditioning set $\mathbf{Z}$ from a given DAG is NP-complete [37]. Under the pretreatment assumption, the time complexity of discovering a conditioning set is still NP-complete. Instead of discovering a conditioning set from a given causal DAG, in this work, we will utilise disentangled representation learning to learn the representations of CIVs and the representations of the conditioning set directly from data with latent confounders.

3   The Proposed DVAE.CIV Model

3.1   The Disentangled Representation Learning Scheme for Causal Effect Estimation

In this work, we would like to estimate $CACE(W, Y)$ from observational data with latent confounders. Note that the causal effect of W on Y is non-identifiable when there exists a latent confounder $U \in \mathbf{U}$ affecting both W and Y, i.e. $W \leftarrow U \rightarrow Y$ in the underlying DAG [6,30]. It is challenging to recover $CACE(W, Y)$ from data with latent confounders due to the effect of U is not computable. If there is a nominated CIV and its corresponding conditioning set, $CACE(W, Y)$ can be obtained unbiasedly from data by using an IV-based estimator. However, a CIV and its conditioning set are usually unknown in many real-world applications. Furthermore, if an invalid CIV is used, the wrong result or conclusion may be drawn [9,27].

To estimate the conditional average causal effects and average causal effects from data with latent confounders, we propose and design the DVAE.CIV model to learn three representations $\{\mathbf{S}, \mathbf{C}, \mathbf{F}\}$ as in the scheme of Fig. 1(c). Here $\mathbf{S}$ is the representation of CIVs that only affect W but not Y, $\mathbf{F}$ is the representation of the risk factors that affects Y but not W, and $\mathbf{C}$ is the confounding representation that affecting both W and Y.

Our proposed DVAE.CIV model relies on VAEs: we assume that the measured covariates factorise conditioning on the latent variables, and use an inference model [22] which follows a factorisation of the true posterior [15,26]. Based on our disentanglement setting in Fig. 1(c), we have the following theoretical result for causal effect estimation from data with latent confounders.

Theorem 1. *Let $\mathcal{G} = (\mathbf{X} \cup \mathbf{U} \cup \{W, Y\}, \mathbf{E})$ be a causal DAG, in which $\mathbf{X}$ is a set of pretreatment variables, $\mathbf{U}$ is a set of latent confounders, W and Y are treatment and outcome variables, respectively, and $W \rightarrow Y$ is in $\mathbf{E}$. If we can learn the three representations as per the scheme in Fig. 1(c), then the quantities of $CACE(W, Y)$ can be calculated by using IV-based method.*

Proof. The directed edge $W \to Y$ in $\mathcal{G}$ is to ensure that W has a causal effect on Y. In the causal DAG in Fig. 1(c), we first show that the set $\mathbf{C} \cup \mathbf{F}$ instrumentalists $\mathbf{S}$ to be a valid CIV. $\mathbf{S}$ is a common cause of W and $\mathbf{C}$, so $S \not\perp_d W$, i.e. the first condition of Definition 1 holds. In the causal DAG $\mathcal{G}$ in Fig. 1(c), $\mathbf{C}$ is a collider and is a common cause of W and Y. That is, conditioning on $\mathbf{C}$, the path $W \leftarrow \mathbf{S} \to \mathbf{C} \leftarrow \mathbf{F} \to Y$ is open, but $\mathbf{F}$ is sufficient to block this path. For the path $\mathbf{S} \to \mathbf{C} \to Y$, $\mathbf{C}$ blocks it. Furthermore, in the manipulated DAG $\mathcal{G}_{\underline{W}}$, W is a collider such that the empty set blocks the three paths between $\mathbf{S}$ and Y, i.e. $\mathbf{S} \to W \leftarrow U \to Y$, $\mathbf{S} \to W \leftarrow \mathbf{C} \leftarrow \mathbf{F} \to Y$ and $\mathbf{S} \to W \leftarrow \mathbf{C} \to Y$. Hence, the set $\mathbf{C} \cup \mathbf{F}$ blocks all paths between $\mathbf{S}$ and Y in $\mathcal{G}_{\underline{W}}$, i.e. the second condition of Definition 1 holds. Finally, $\mathbf{C} \cup \mathbf{F}$ does not contains a descendant of Y due to the pretreatment variables assumption. Thus, the set $\mathbf{C} \cup \mathbf{F}$ instrumentalists $\mathbf{S}$. As in Eq.(2), the IV-based estimators, such as DeepIV [14], can be applied to remove the effect of U by inputting the CIV representation $\mathbf{S}$ and the representations of its conditioning set $\mathbf{C} \cup \mathbf{F}$. Therefore, the quantities of CACE(W, Y) can be obtained by using the CIV $\mathbf{S}$ and its conditioning set $\mathbf{C} \cup \mathbf{F}$ in an IV-based estimator.

Theorem 1 ensures that a family of data-driven methods can be applied for causal effect estimation from data with latent confounders.

3.2   Learning the Three Representations

Based on Theorem 1, we have known that the set $\{\mathbf{C}, \mathbf{F}\}$ instrumentalists $\mathbf{S}$. In this section, we present our proposed DVAE.CIV model for obtaining the three latent representations from data by using the VAE technique [22], and the architecture of DVAE.CIV is presented in Fig. 2. As shown in Fig. 2, the DVAE.CIV model is to learn and disentangle the latent representation $\mathbf{\Phi}$ of $\mathbf{X}$ into two disjoint sets $\{\mathbf{S}, \mathbf{F}\}$ by using disentangled variational autoencoder [15,38], and generate the representation $\mathbf{C}$ conditioning on $\mathbf{X}$ by jointing the Conditional Variational AutoEncoder (CVAE) network [32].

The DVAE.CIV model is designed to learn three representations shown in Fig. 1(c) by utilising the inference model and generative model to approximate the posterior distribution $p(\mathbf{X}|\mathbf{S}, \mathbf{C}, \mathbf{F})$. The inference model comprises three independent encoders $q(\mathbf{S}|\mathbf{X})$, $q(\mathbf{C}|\mathbf{X})$, and $q(\mathbf{F}|\mathbf{X})$, which are treated as variational posteriors over the three latent representations. The generative model utilises the three latent representations with a decoder model $p(\mathbf{X}|\mathbf{S}, \mathbf{C}, \mathbf{F})$ to reconstruct the measured distribution $\mathbf{X}$.

Following the standard VAE model [22], the prior distributions $p(\mathbf{S})$ and $p(\mathbf{F})$ are drawn from the Gaussian distributions as:

$$p(\mathbf{S}) = \prod_{i=1}^{D_\mathbf{S}} \mathcal{N}(S_i|0,1); \; p(\mathbf{F}) = \prod_{i=1}^{D_\mathbf{F}} \mathcal{N}(F_i|0,1). \tag{3}$$

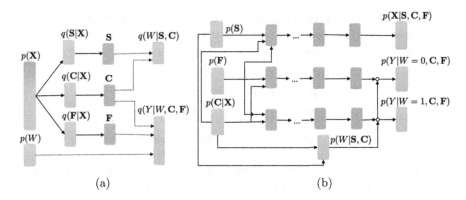

Fig. 2. The architecture of DVAE.CIV model. A yellow box indicates the drawing of samples from the respective distributions, a grey box indicates the parameterised deterministic neural network transitions, and a circle represents switching paths based on the value of W. (Color figure online)

where $D_{\mathbf{S}}$ and $D_{\mathbf{F}}$ are the dimensions of $\mathbf{S}$ and $\mathbf{F}$, respectively. In the inference model, the variational approximations of the posteriors are described as:

$$q(\mathbf{S}|\mathbf{X}) = \prod_{i=1}^{D_{\mathbf{S}}} \mathcal{N}(\mu = \hat{\mu}_{\mathbf{S}_i}, \sigma^2 = \hat{\sigma}_{\mathbf{S}_i}^2); \quad q(\mathbf{C}|\mathbf{X}) = \prod_{i=1}^{D_{\mathbf{C}}} \mathcal{N}(\mu = \hat{\mu}_{\mathbf{C}_i}, \sigma^2 = \hat{\sigma}_{\mathbf{C}_i}^2);$$

$$q(\mathbf{F}|\mathbf{X}) = \prod_{i=1}^{D_{\mathbf{F}}} \mathcal{N}(\mu = \hat{\mu}_{\mathbf{F}_i}, \sigma^2 = \hat{\sigma}_{\mathbf{F}_i}^2), \tag{4}$$

where $D_{\mathbf{C}}$ is the dimension of $\mathbf{C}$, and $\hat{\mu}_{\mathbf{S}}, \hat{\mu}_{\mathbf{C}}, \hat{\mu}_{\mathbf{F}}$ and $\hat{\sigma}_{\mathbf{S}}^2, \hat{\sigma}_{\mathbf{C}}^2, \hat{\sigma}_{\mathbf{F}}^2$ are the parameters of means and variances in the Gaussian distributions parameterised by neural networks.

In the generative model, we utilise the Monte Carlo (MC) sampling strategy to sample the distribution $\mathbf{C}$ based on the Conditional Variational AutoEncoder network (CVAE) [32] such that the latent representation of $\mathbf{C}$ is generated from the distribution $\mathbf{X}$:

$$p(\mathbf{C}) \backsim p(\mathbf{C}|\mathbf{X}). \tag{5}$$

Furthermore, the generative models for W and $\mathbf{X}$ with the three latent representations are formalised as:

$$p(W|\mathbf{S}, \mathbf{C}) = Bern(\sigma(\psi_1(\mathbf{S}, \mathbf{C}))); \quad p(\mathbf{X}|\mathbf{S}, \mathbf{F}) = \prod_{i=1}^{D_{\mathbf{X}}} p(X_i|\mathbf{S}, \mathbf{C}), \tag{6}$$

where $\psi_1(\cdot)$ is a function parameterised by neural networks, $\sigma(\cdot)$ is the logistic function and $Bern(\cdot)$ is the function of Bernoulli distribution.

In our generative model, the latent representation for the outcome Y is based on the data type of Y. For the outcome Y with continuous values, we use a

Gaussian distribution with its mean and variance parameterised by a pair of independent neural networks, i.e. $p(Y|w = 0, \mathbf{C}, \mathbf{F})$ and $p(Y|w = 1, \mathbf{C}, \mathbf{F})$. Thus, the continuous Y is modelled by:

$$
\begin{aligned}
p(Y|W, \mathbf{C}, \mathbf{F}) &= \mathcal{N}(\mu = \hat{\mu}_Y, \sigma^2 = \hat{\sigma}_Y^2), \\
\hat{\mu}_Y &= W \cdot \psi_2(\mathbf{C}, \mathbf{F}) + (1 - W) \cdot \psi_3(\mathbf{C}, \mathbf{F}); \\
\hat{\sigma}_Y^2 &= W \cdot \psi_4(\mathbf{C}, \mathbf{F}) + (1 - W) \cdot \psi_5(\mathbf{C}, \mathbf{F}),
\end{aligned}
\tag{7}
$$

where $\psi_2(\cdot), \psi_3(\cdot), \psi_4(\cdot)$ and $\psi_5(\cdot)$ are neural networks parameterised by their own parameters.

For the outcome Y with binary values, a Bernoulli distribution function based on neural networks is employed to model it and described as:

$$
p(Y|W, \mathbf{C}, \mathbf{F}) = Bern(\sigma(\psi_6(W, \mathbf{C}, \mathbf{F}))),
\tag{8}
$$

where $\psi_6(\cdot)$ is the same with the function ψ_1. These parameters of neural networks can be approximated by maximising the Evidence lower bound (ELBO) $\mathcal{L}_{ELBO}$:

$$
\begin{aligned}
\mathcal{L}_{ELBO}(\mathbf{X}, W, Y) = \ &\mathbb{E}_q[\log p(\mathbf{X}|\mathbf{S}, \mathbf{C}, \mathbf{F})] - D_{KL}[q(\mathbf{S}|\mathbf{X})||p(\mathbf{S})] \\
&- D_{KL}[q(\mathbf{C}|\mathbf{X})||p(\mathbf{C}|\mathbf{X})] - D_{KL}[q(\mathbf{F}|\mathbf{X})||p(\mathbf{F})],
\end{aligned}
\tag{9}
$$

where the decoder $p(\mathbf{C}|\mathbf{X})$ is to ensure that the latent representation $\mathbf{C}$ captures as much information of $\mathbf{X}$ as possible.

To ensure that the treatment W can be recovered from the latent representations $\mathbf{S}$ and $\mathbf{C}$, and the outcome Y can be recovered from the latent representations $\mathbf{C}$ and $\mathbf{F}$, two auxiliary predictors are added and the objective function of DVAE.CIV can be formalised as:

$$
\begin{aligned}
\mathcal{L}_{DVAE.CIV} = \ &-\mathcal{L}_{ELBO}(\mathbf{X}, W, Y) + \alpha\mathbb{E}_q[\log q(W|\mathbf{S}, \mathbf{C})] \\
&+ \beta\mathbb{E}_q[\log q(Y|W, \mathbf{C}, \mathbf{F})],
\end{aligned}
\tag{10}
$$

where α and β are the weights for the auxiliary predictors.

After training the DVAE.CIV model, we get the CIV representation $\mathbf{S}$ and the conditioning set representations $\{\mathbf{C}, \mathbf{F}\}$ based on Theorem 1. For estimating conditional causal effects, we employ an IV-based prediction, DeepIV [14], to implement this part, i.e. we feed $\mathbf{S}$ and $\{\mathbf{C}, \mathbf{F}\}$ into the DeepIV method for conditional causal effect estimation.

4   Experiments

In this section, we evaluate the performance of the proposed DVAE.IV model by applying it to a set of synthetic datasets and three real-world datasets for CACE(W, Y) and average causal effect (ACE) estimation. The three real-world datasets include SchoolingReturns [7], Cattaneo [8] and RHC [11] that are usually utilised in evaluating the methods of causal effect estimation from observational data. Details of the implementation of DVAE.CIV and the appendix are provided in the GitHub[1].

---

[1] https://github.com/IRON13/DVAE.CIV.

4.1 Experimental Setup

We compare the DVAE.CIV against the famous estimators in conditional causal effect estimation that are widely utilised in causal inference from observational data. Note that the ACE can be obtained by averaging the $CACE(W, Y)$ of all individuals. These compared causal effect estimators are introduced in the following.

Compared Causal Effect Estimators. We compare our proposed DVAE.CIV with two Variational AutoEncoder based (VAE-based) causal effect estimators, three tree-based causal effect estimators, two machine learning based (ML-based) causal effect estimators, and three IV-based causal effect estimators. The two VAE-based causal effect estimators are Causal Effect Variational AutoEncoder (CEVAE) [26] and Treatment Effect estimation by Disentangled Variational AutoEncoder (TEDVAE) [38]). The three tree-based causal effect estimators are the standard Bayesian Additive Regression Trees (BART) [17], causal random forest (CF) [35] and causal random forest for IV regression (CFIVR) [4]. Note that CFIVR also belongs to IV-based estimators. The two ML-based causal effect estimators are double machine learning (DML) [10] and doubly robust learning (DRL) [12]. The three IV-based causal effect estimators are DeepIV [14], orthogonal instrumental variable (OrthIV) [33] and double machine learning based IV (DMLIV) [10].

Remarks. The five estimators TEDVAE, BART, CF, DML and DRL rely on the assumption of unconfoundedness [19] (i.e. no latent confounders in data), so the five estimators cannot deal with the case with the data with latent confounders. CEVAE can deal with latent confounders, but it requires that all measured variables are proxy variables of the latent confounders, while our DVAE.CIV model does not have the restriction. The IV-based estimators CFIVR, DeepIV, OrthIV and DMLIV require a known IV that is nominated based on domain knowledge, but the nominated IV usually is not a valid IV and thus may result in a wrong conclusion as argued in Introduction.

Implementation Details. We use *Python* and the libraries including *pytorch* [29], *pyro* [5] and *econml* to implement DVAE.CIV. In our experiments, the dimension of latent representations is set as $|S| = 1$, $|C| = 5$ and $|F| = 5$, respectively. The implementation of CEVAE is based on the *Python* library *pyro* [5] and the code of TEDVAE is from the authors' GitHub[2]. For BART, we use the implementation in the *R* package *bartCause* [17]. For CF and CFIVR, we use the implementations in the *R* functions *causal_forest* and *instrumental_forest* in the *R* package *grf* [4], respectively. The implementations of DML, DRL, DeepIV, OrthIV and DMLIV are from the *Python* package *enconml*.

---

[2] https://github.com/WeijiaZhang24/TEDVAE.

Evaluation Metrics. For performance evaluation, two commonly used metrics are employed in our experiments. For the synthetic datasets, we use absolute error of average causal effect [17], i.e. $\varepsilon_{ACE} = |ACE - A\hat{C}E|$ where ACE is the true causal effect and $A\hat{C}E$ is the estimated causal effect, and Precision of the Estimation of Heterogeneous Effect (PEHE, it is used to evaluate the CACE estimations.) [17,26] $\sqrt{\varepsilon_{PEHE}} = \sqrt{\mathbf{E}(((y_1 - y_0) - (\hat{y}_1 - \hat{y}_0))^2)}$ where y_1, y_0 are the true outcomes and $\hat{y}_1, \hat{y}_0$ are the predicted outcomes, to assess the performance of all methods in terms of the causal effect estimation. Lower values of both metrics indicate better performance. For multiple replications, we present the mean with standard deviation. For the three real-world datasets, we use the reference causal effect in the literature as the baseline to evaluate the performance of all estimators since there is no ground truth causal effect available.

4.2   Simulation Study

It is challenging to evaluate a causal effect estimation method with real-world data since there is no ground truth in the real-world data. In this section, we design simulation studies to evaluate the performance of our proposed DVAE.CIV method in the case that there exists a latent confounder U affecting both W and Y, and there exists a CIV and its conditioning set in the synthetic datasets.

We use a causal DAG $\mathcal{G}$ provided in the appendix to generate synthetic datasets with a range of sample sizes: 2k, 6k, 10k, and 20k. In the causal DAG $\mathcal{G}$, $\mathbf{X} = \{S, X_1, X_2, X_3, X_4, X_5\}$ is the set of measured covariates and $\mathbf{U} = \{U, U_1, U_2, U_3, U_4\}$ is the set of latent confounders in which U affects both W and Y. Note that S is a CIV conditioning on the set $\{X_1, X_2\}$ for all synthetic datasets. Moreover, the data generation process allows the synthetic datasets to have the true individual causal effect. We provide the details of the synthetic data generating process in the appendix. In our experiments, the IV-based estimators OrthIV, DMLIV, DeepIV and CFIVR utilise the true CIV S and the conditioning set $\{X_1, X_2\}$ as input for causal effect estimation.

To provide a reliable assessment, we repeatedly generate 30 synthetic datasets for each sample size setting and utilize the aforementioned metrics to evaluate the performance of the DVAE.CIV against the compared estimators with respect to the task of ACE estimation and CACE estimation from data with latent confounders. For each dataset, we randomly take 70% of samples for training and 30% for testing. The results of all estimators with respect to the ACE estimations and CACE estimations measured by the metrics ε_{ACE} and $\sqrt{\varepsilon_{PEHE}}$ in the out-of-sample set are provided in Tables 1 and 2, respectively. The out-of-sample set is on testing samples, and the within-sample set is on training samples. The results of the within-sample set are provided in the appendix.

Results. By analysing the experiment results in Table 1, we have the following observations: (1) the ML-based and VAE-based estimators, DML, DRL, CEVAE and TEDVAE have the largest ε_{ACE} because the confounding bias caused by confounders and the latent confounder U is not adjusted at all. (2) the tree-based

Table 1. The out-of-sample absolute error ε_{ACE} (mean ± std) over 30 synthetic datasets. The best results are highlighted in boldface and the runner-up results are underlined. DVAE.CIV is the runner-up on all synthetic datasets, and it relies on the least domain knowledge among all estimators compared since it learns and disentangles the representations of CIV and its conditioning set from data directly.

Samples		2k	6k	10k	20k
Estimators		ε_{ACE}	ε_{ACE}	ε_{ACE}	ε_{ACE}
ML-based	DML	5.507 ± 0.387	5.624 ± 0.182	5.619 ± 0.122	5.633 ± 0.096
	DRL	5.746 ± 0.404	5.833 ± 0.186	5.825 ± 0.156	5.860 ± 0.106
tree-based	BART	3.586 ± 0.179	3.596 ± 0.090	3.613 ± 0.065	3.622 ± 0.060
	CF	3.226 ± 0.342	3.246 ± 0.141	3.274 ± 0.127	3.312 ± 0.074
VAE-based	CEVAE	5.595 ± 0.455	5.652 ± 0.183	5.631 ± 0.179	5.726 ± 0.123
	TEDVAE	5.615 ± 0.455	5.655 ± 0.181	5.634 ± 0.172	5.696 ± 0.112
IV-based	OrthIV	2.212 ± 1.260	1.952 ± 0.585	1.792 ± 0.607	1.974 ± 0.419
	DMLIV	2.170 ± 1.189	1.888 ± 0.572	1.790 ± 0.626	1.971 ± 0.432
	DeepIV	$\mathbf{0.352 \pm 0.180}$	0.632 ± 0.245	0.726 ± 0.315	0.757 ± 0.354
	CFIVR	1.228 ± 0.949	$\mathbf{0.504 \pm 0.369}$	$\mathbf{0.543 \pm 0.474}$	$\mathbf{0.415 \pm 0.307}$
DVAE.CIV		$\underline{0.577 \pm 0.117}$	$\underline{0.577 \pm 0.064}$	$\underline{0.561 \pm 0.075}$	$\underline{0.512 \pm 0.091}$

estimators, BART and CF have the second largest ε_{ACE} as they fail to deal with the confounding bias caused by the latent confounder U. (3) the IV-based estimators including DVAE.CIV significantly outperform the other estimators including DML, DRL, BART, CF, CEVAE and TEDVAE. (4) DVAE.CIV is the second best performer on all synthetic datasets and its performance is comparable with CFIVR and DeepIV. (5) as the sample size increases, the standard deviation of most estimators including DVAE.CIV decreases significantly. It's worth mentioning that DVAE.CIV requires the least domain knowledge among all estimators since it only relies on the assumption that there exists a CIV and the conditioning set (maybe an empty set). This is very important in practice, as in many real-world applications, there is rarely sufficient prior knowledge for nominating a valid IV.

From the results in Table 2, we can conclude that (1) the ML-based, tree-based, and VAE-based estimators have the worst performance with respect to conditional causal effect estimations. (2) Among the IV-based estimators, DeepIV achieves the best performance on the first two groups of synthetic datasets and the second-best performance on the other datasets, and CFIVR obtains the best performance on the last four groups of synthetic datasets and the second-best performance on the first two groups of synthetic datasets. (3) DVAE.CIV obtains the second-best performance on all synthetic datasets. (4) The standard deviation of DVAE.CIV is the smallest on all datasets, and as the sample size increases, the standard deviation of DVAE.CIV reduces significantly. These conclusions demonstrate that DVAE.CIV can learn and disentangle the

Table 2. The out-of-sample $\sqrt{\varepsilon_{PEHE}}$ (mean±std) over 30 synthetic datasets. The lowest $\sqrt{\varepsilon_{PEHE}}$ are highlighted in boldface and the runner-up results are underlined. DVAE.CIV is in the runner-up results on the first two groups of synthetic datasets and achieves the third smallest $\sqrt{\varepsilon_{PEHE}}$ on the last four groups of synthetic datasets. It's worth mentioning that DVAE.CIV obtains the lowest standard deviation on all synthetic datasets.

Samples		2k	6k	10k	20k
Estimators		$\sqrt{\varepsilon_{PEHE}}$	$\sqrt{\varepsilon_{PEHE}}$	$\sqrt{\varepsilon_{PEHE}}$	$\sqrt{\varepsilon_{PEHE}}$
ML-based	DML	5.484 ± 0.382	5.584 ± 0.167	5.580 ± 0.128	5.609 ± 0.105
	DRL	5.701 ± 0.408	5.773 ± 0.179	5.767 ± 0.156	5.815 ± 0.112
tree-based	BART	4.791 ± 0.205	4.790 ± 0.083	4.789 ± 0.072	4.790 ± 0.060
	CF	3.483 ± 0.319	3.500 ± 0.134	3.523 ± 0.120	3.554 ± 0.070
VAE-based	CEVAE	6.093 ± 0.396	6.138 ± 0.175	6.107 ± 0.160	6.192 ± 0.112
	TEDVAE	6.111 ± 0.392	6.138 ± 0.177	6.110 ± 0.158	6.167 ± 0.103
IV-based	OrthIV	3.070 ± 0.718	2.798 ± 0.299	2.734 ± 0.256	2.795 ± 0.218
	DMLIV	3.027 ± 0.682	2.767 ± 0.278	$2.736 \pm .0.268$	2.794 ± 0.221
	DeepIV	$\mathbf{2.396 \pm 0.054}$	2.412 ± 0.042	$\mathbf{2.418 \pm 0.060}$	2.425 ± 0.065
	CFIVR	3.016 ± 0.658	$\mathbf{2.421 \pm 0.235}$	2.423 ± 0.351	$\mathbf{2.203 \pm 0.145}$
DVAE.CIV		2.448 ± 0.044	2.460 ± 0.037	2.452 ± 0.024	2.442 ± 0.025

representations of the CIV and its conditioning set for CACE estimation from data with latent confounders.

In conclusion, DVAE.CIV achieves competitive performance compared to state-of-the-art causal effect estimators while requiring the least prior knowledge in ACE and CACE estimations from observational data with latent confounders.

4.3   Experiments on Three Real-World Datasets

We selected three real-world datasets with their empirical causal effect values available and commonly used in the literature to assess the performance of DVAE.CIV in ACE estimations. We did not conduct experiments on CACE estimation on the three datasets since there were no ground truth or empirical estimates of CACEs available for these datasets. The three real-world datasets are SchoolingReturns [7], Cattaneo [8], and RHC [11]. These datasets are widely utilized in the evaluation of either IV estimators or data-driven causal effect estimators [13]. Note that SchoolingReturns has a nominated CIV, and the last two datasets do not have a nominated IV for causal effect estimation. Thus, we only compared the DVAE.CIV model with all the aforementioned estimators on SchoolingReturns and the ML-based, tree-based, and VAE-based estimators on both Cattaneo and RHC datasets.

SchoolingReturns. The dataset is from the national longitudinal survey of youth (NLSY), a well-known dataset of US young employees, aged range from 24 to

Table 3. Estimated ACEs by all methods on the three real-world datasets. We highlight the estimated causal effects within the empirical interval on SchoolingReturns and Cattaneo. We use '-' to indicate that an IV-based estimator does not work on Cattaneo and RHC since there is not a nominated IV. Note that all estimators on RHC obtain a consistent result.

Samples		SchoolingReturns	Cattaneo	RHC
ML-based	DML	−0.0227	−150.21	**0.0244**
	DRL	−0.0154	−164.32	**0.0447**
tree-based	BART	−0.0384	−172.53	**0.0381**
	CF	**0.1400**	**−232.33**	**0.0278**
VAE-based	CEVAE	0.02617	**−221.23**	**0.0322**
	TEDVAE	0.0029	**−228.65**	**0.0293**
IV-based	OrthIV	1.3180	−	−
	DMLIV	1.2806	−	−
	DeepIV	0.0328	−	−
	CFIVR	1.1510	−	−
DVAE.CIV		**0.1855**	**−224.79**	**0.0414**

34 [7]. The dataset has 3,010 samples and 19 variables [7]. The variable of the education of employees is the treatment variable, and the variable of the raw wages in 1976 (in cents per hour) is the outcome variable. The dataset was collected to study the causal effect of education on earnings. Note that the variable of geographical proximity to a college, i.e. *nearcollege* is nominated to be an IV by Card [7]. The empirical estimate $ACE(W, Y) = 0.1329$ with 95% confidence interval (0.0484, 0.2175) is from [34] and used as the reference value.

Cattaneo. The dataset has the birth weights of 4,642 singleton births with 20 variables ([8]) that were collected from Pennsylvania, USA for the study of the average of maternal smoking status during pregnancy (W) on a baby's birth weight $(Y$, in grams). The dataset contains several covariates: mother's age, mother's marital status, an indicator for the previous infant where the newborn died, mother's race, mother's education, father's education, number of prenatal care visits, months since last birth, an indicator of firstborn infant and indicator of alcohol consumption during pregnancy. The authors [8] found a strong negative effect of maternal smoking on the weights of babies, i.e., about 200g to 250g lighter for a baby with a mother smoking during pregnancy.

Right Heart Catheterization (RHC). RHC is a real-world dataset obtained from an observational study regarding a diagnostic procedure for the management of critically ill patients [11]. The RHC dataset can be downloaded from the **R** package *Hmisc*[3]. The dataset contains 2,707 samples with 72 covariates [11,25].

---

[3] https://CRAN.R-project.org/package=Hmisc.

RHC was for investigating the adult patients who participated in the Study to Understand Prognoses and Preferences for Outcomes and Risks of Treatments (SUPPORT). The treatment variable W is whether a patient received an RHC within 24 h of admission, and the outcome variable Y is whether a patient died at any time up to 180 d after admission. Note that the empirical conclusion is that applying RHC leads to higher mortality within 180 d than not applying RHC [11].

Results. All results on the three real-world datasets are reported in Table 3. From Table 3, we make the following observations: (1) the estimated causal effects by DVAE.CIV and CF on SchoolingReturns and Cattaneo fall within the empirical intervals, while DML, DRL, and BART provide an opposite estimate to the empirical value on SchoolingReturns; (2) as there is no nominated IV on Cattaneo and RHC, the estimators OrthIV, DMLIV, DeepIV, and CFIVR do not work on both datasets; (3) all estimators, including DVAE.CIV, obtain a consistent estimation on the RHC data, and they reach the same conclusion as the empirical conclusion [11]. These observations further confirm that DVAE.CIV is capable of removing the bias between W and Y in real-world datasets.

In conclusion, our simulation studies show the high performance of DVAE.CIV in ACE and CACE estimations from data with latent confounders, and our experiments on three real-world datasets further confirm the capability of DVAE.CIV in ACE estimation from observational data.

Limitations. The performance of DVAE.CIV relies on the assumptions made in this work and the assumptions on the VAE model. Note that the identification of the VAE model [21] is an important issue for our proposed DVAE.CIV model. When some of the assumptions or the VAE identification do not hold, DVAE.CIV may obtain an inconsistent conclusion. To obtain a consistent conclusion, it would be better to conduct a sensitivity analysis [19,30] together with DVAE.CIV to achieve a reliable conclusion in real-world applications.

5   Conclusion

It is a crucial challenge to deal with the bias caused by latent confounders in conditional causal effect estimations from observational data. IV-based methods allow us to remove such confounding bias in an effective way, but it relies on a nominated IV/CIV based on domain knowledge. In this paper, we propose an efficient approach, DVAE.CIV for conditional causal effect estimations from observational data with latent confounders. The DVAE.CIV utilizes the advantages of deep generative models for learning the representations of a CIV and its conditioning set from data with latent confounders. We theoretically show the soundness of the DVAE.CIV model. The effectiveness and potential of the DVAE.CIV are demonstrated by extensive experiments. In simulation studies, DVAE.CIV achieves competitive performance against state-of-the-art estimators that require extra prior knowledge in ACE and CACE estimation from data with latent confounders. The experimental results on three real-world datasets show the superiority of the DVAE.CIV model on ACE estimation over the existing estimators.

Acknowledgments. This work has been supported by the Australian Research Council (grant number: DP200101210 and DP230101122).

References

1. Abadie, A., Imbens, G.W.: Large sample properties of matching estimators for average treatment effects. Econometrica **74**(1), 235–267 (2006)
2. Angrist, J.D., Imbens, G.W.: Two-stage least squares estimation of average causal effects in models with variable treatment intensity. J. Am. Stat. Assoc. **90**(430), 431–442 (1995)
3. Angrist, J.D., Imbens, G.W., Rubin, D.B.: Identification of causal effects using instrumental variables. J. Am. Stat. Assoc. **91**(434), 444–455 (1996)
4. Athey, S., Tibshirani, J., Wager, S.: Generalized random forests. Ann. Stat. **47**(2), 1148–1178 (2019)
5. Bingham, E., Chen, J.P., et al.: Pyro: deep universal probabilistic programming. J. Mach. Learn. Res. **20**(1), 973–978 (2019)
6. Brito, C., Pearl, J.: Generalized instrumental variables. In: Proceedings of the Eighteenth Conference on Uncertainty in Artificial Intelligence, pp. 85–93 (2002)
7. Card, D.: Using geographic variation in college proximity to estimate the return to schooling (1993)
8. Cattaneo, M.D.: Efficient semiparametric estimation of multi-valued treatment effects under ignorability. J. Econometrics **155**(2), 138–154 (2010)
9. Cheng, D., Li, J., Liu, L., Liu, J., Le, T.D.: Data-driven causal effect estimation based on graphical causal modelling: A survey. arXiv preprint arXiv:2208.09590 (2022)
10. Chernozhukov, V., et al.: Double/debiased machine learning for treatment and structural parameters. Econometrics J. **21**(1), C1–C68 (2018)
11. Connors, A.F., Speroff, T., et al.: The effectiveness of right heart catheterization in the initial care of critically III patients. J. Am. Med. Assoc. **276**(11), 889–897 (1996)
12. Foster, D.J., Syrgkanis, V.: Orthogonal statistical learning. arXiv preprint arXiv:1901.09036 (2019)
13. Guo, R., Cheng, L., Li, J., Hahn, P.R., Liu, H.: A survey of learning causality with data: problems and methods. ACM Comput. Surv. (CSUR) **53**(4), 1–37 (2020)
14. Hartford, J., Lewis, G., et al.: Deep IV: A flexible approach for counterfactual prediction. In: International Conference on Machine Learning, pp. 1414–1423 (2017)
15. Hassanpour, N., Greiner, R.: Learning disentangled representations for counterfactual regression. In: International Conference on Learning Representations, pp. 1–11 (2019)
16. Hernán, M.A., Robins, J.M.: Instruments for causal inference: an epidemiologist's dream? Epidemiology **17**(4), 360–372 (2006)
17. Hill, J.L.: Bayesian nonparametric modeling for causal inference. J. Comput. Graph. Stat. **20**(1), 217–240 (2011)
18. Imbens, G.W.: Instrumental variables: an econometrician's perspective. Stat. Sci. **29**(3), 323–358 (2014)

19. Imbens, G.W., Rubin, D.B.: Causal Inference in Statistics, Social, and Biomedical Sciences. Cambridge University Press, Cambridge (2015)
20. Kang, H., Zhang, A., Cai, T.T., Small, D.S.: Instrumental variables estimation with some invalid instruments and its application to mendelian randomization. J. Am. Stat. Assoc. **111**(513), 132–144 (2016)
21. Khemakhem, I., Kingma, D., Monti, R., Hyvarinen, A.: Variational autoencoders and nonlinear ICA: a unifying framework. In: International Conference on Artificial Intelligence and Statistics, pp. 2207–2217. PMLR (2020)
22. Kingma, D.P., Welling, M.: Auto-encoding variational bayes. In: International Conference on Learning Representations (2014)
23. Kuang, Z., Sala, F., et al.: Ivy: instrumental variable synthesis for causal inference. In: International Conference on Artificial Intelligence and Statistics, pp. 398–410 (2020)
24. LaLonde, R.J.: Evaluating the econometric evaluations of training programs with experimental data. Am. Econ. Rev. **76**(4), 604–620 (1986)
25. Loh, W.W., Vansteelandt, S.: Confounder selection strategies targeting stable treatment effect estimators. Stat. Med. **40**(3), 607–630 (2021)
26. Louizos, C., Shalit, U., Mooij, J.M., Sontag, D., Zemel, R., Welling, M.: Causal effect inference with deep latent-variable models. In: Advances in Neural Information Processing Systems, pp. 6446–6456 (2017)
27. Martens, E.P., Pestman, W.R., de Boer, A., Belitser, S.V., Klungel, O.H.: Instrumental variables: application and limitations. Epidemiology **17**(3), pp. 260–267 (2006)
28. Martinussen, T., Nørbo Sørensen, D., Vansteelandt, S.: Instrumental variables estimation under a structural cox model. Biostatistics **20**(1), 65–79 (2019)
29. Paszke, A., Gross, S., et al.: Pytorch: an imperative style, high-performance deep learning library. In: International Conference on Neural Information Processing Systems, pp. 8026–8037 (2019)
30. Pearl, J.: Causality. Cambridge University Press, Cambridge (2009)
31. Rosenbaum, P.R., Rubin, D.B.: The central role of the propensity score in observational studies for causal effects. Biometrika **70**(1), 41–55 (1983)
32. Sohn, K., Yan, X., Lee, H.: Learning structured output representation using deep conditional generative models. In: Proceedings of the 28th International Conference on Neural Information Processing Systems. vol. 2, pp. 3483–3491 (2015)
33. Syrgkanis, V., Lei, V., et al.: Machine learning estimation of heterogeneous treatment effects with instruments. In: International Conference on Neural Information Processing Systems, pp. 15193–15202 (2019)
34. Verbeek, M.: A Guide to Modern Econometrics. Wiley, Hoboken (2008)
35. Wager, S., Athey, S.: Estimation and inference of heterogeneous treatment effects using random forests. J. Am. Stat. Assoc. **113**(523), 1228–1242 (2018)
36. Yuan, J., Wu, A., et al.: Auto IV: counterfactual prediction via automatic instrumental variable decomposition. ACM Trans. Knowl. Discov. Data **16**(4), 1–20 (2022)
37. Van der Zander, B., Liśkiewicz, M., Textor, J.: Efficiently finding conditional instruments for causal inference, pp. 3243–3249 (2015)
38. Zhang, W., Liu, L., Li, J.: Treatment effect estimation with disentangled latent factors. In: The AAAI Conference on Artificial Intelligence, pp. 10923–10930 (2021)

A KNN-Based Non-Parametric Conditional Independence Test for Mixed Data and Application in Causal Discovery

Johannes Huegle$^{(\boxtimes)}$, Christopher Hagedorn, and Rainer Schlosser

University of Potsdam, Hasso Plattner Institute, Potsdam, Germany
{Johannes.Huegle,Christopher.Hagedorn,Rainer.Schlosser}@hpi.de

Abstract. Testing for Conditional Independence (CI) is a fundamental task for causal discovery but is particularly challenging in mixed discrete-continuous data. In this context, inadequate assumptions or discretization of continuous variables reduce the CI test's statistical power, which yields incorrect learned causal structures. In this work, we present a non-parametric CI test leveraging k-nearest neighbor (kNN) methods that are adaptive to mixed discrete-continuous data. In particular, a kNN-based conditional mutual information estimator serves as the test statistic, and the p-value is calculated using a kNN-based local permutation scheme. We prove the CI test's statistical validity and power in mixed discrete-continuous data, which yields consistency when used in constraint-based causal discovery. An extensive evaluation of synthetic and real-world data shows that the proposed CI test outperforms state-of-the-art approaches in the accuracy of CI testing and causal discovery, particularly in settings with low sample sizes.

Keywords: Non-Parametric CI Testing · Causal Discovery · Mixed Data

1 Introduction

Conditional Independence (CI) testing is at the core of causal discovery (Sect. 1.1), but particularly challenging in many real-world scenarios (Sect. 1.2). Therefore, we propose a data-adaptive CI test for mixed discrete-continuous data (Sect. 1.3).

1.1 Conditional Independence in Causal Discovery

Causal discovery has received widespread attention as the knowledge of underlying causal structures improves decision support within many real-world scenarios [17,46]. For example, in discrete manufacturing, causal discovery is the key to root cause analysis of failures and quality deviations, cf. [25].

© The Author(s), under exclusive license to Springer Nature Switzerland AG 2023
D. Koutra et al. (Eds.): ECML PKDD 2023, LNAI 14169, pp. 541–558, 2023.
https://doi.org/10.1007/978-3-031-43412-9_32

Causal structures between a finite set of random variables $\mathbf{V} = \{X, Y, \dots\}$ are encoded in a Causal Graphical Model (CGM) consisting of a Directed Acyclic Graph (DAG) $\mathcal{G}$, and the joint distribution over the variables $\mathbf{V}$, denoted by $P_\mathbf{V}$, cf. [38,46]. In $\mathcal{G}$, a directed edge $X \rightarrow Y$ depicts a direct causal mechanism between the two respective variables X and Y, for $X, Y \in \mathbf{V}$. Causal discovery aims to derive as many underlying causal structures in $\mathcal{G}$ from observational data as possible building upon the coincidence between the causal structures of $\mathcal{G}$ and the CI characteristics of $P_\mathbf{V}$ [46]. Therefore, constraint-based methods, such as the well-known PC algorithm, apply CI tests to recover the causal structures, cf. [8]. For instance, if a CI test states the conditional independence of variables X and Y given a (possibly empty) set of variables $Z \subseteq \mathbf{V} \setminus \{X, Y\}$, denoted by $X \perp\!\!\!\perp Y | Z$, then there is no edge between X and Y. Constraint-based methods are flexible and exist in various extensions, e.g., to allow for latent variables or cycles [42,46,47], or are used for causal feature selection [50]. Hence, they are popular in practice [33].

1.2   Challenges in Practice

In principle, constraint-based methods do not make any assumption on the functional form of causal mechanisms or parameters of the joint distribution. However, they require access to a CI oracle that captures all CI characteristics such that selecting an appropriate CI test is fundamental and challenging [17,33]. In practice, the true statistical properties are mostly unknown such that inadequate assumptions, e.g., of parametric CI tests, yield incorrect learned causal structures [46]. For example, the well-known partial Pearson's correlation-based CI test via Fisher's Z transformation assumes that $P_\mathbf{V}$ is multivariate Gaussian [3,27]. Hence, the underlying causal mechanisms are assumed to be linear and conditional independence cannot be detected if the mechanisms are non-linear. Further, the omnipresence of mixed discrete-continuous data, e.g., continuous quality measurements and discrete failure messages in discrete manufacturing [20], impedes the selection of appropriate CI tests in real-world scenarios [19,33]. In this case, parametric models that allow for mixed discrete-continuous data usually make further restrictions, such as conditional Gaussian models assuming that discrete variables have discrete parents only [40]. Hence, for simplification in practice, continuous variables are often discretized to use standard CI tests such as Pearson's χ^2 test for discrete data, cf. [20,23,35], to the detriment of the accuracy of the learned causal structures [12,40].

1.3   Contribution and Structure

In this work, we propose mCMIkNN[1], a data-adaptive CI test for mixed discrete-continuous data and its application to causal discovery. Our contributions are:

- We propose a kNN-based local conditional permutation scheme to derive a non-parametric CI test using a kNN-based CMI estimator as a test statistic.
- We provide theoretical results on the CI test's validity and power. In particular, we prove that mCMIkNN is able to control type I and type II errors.

---

[1] Code and Appendix can be found on https://github.com/hpi-epic/mCMIkNN.

- We show that mCMIkNN allows for consistent estimation of causal structures when used in constraint-based causal discovery.
- An extensive evaluation on synthetic and real-world data shows that mCMIkNN outperforms state-of-the-art competitors, particularly for low sample sizes.

The remainder of this paper is structured as follows. In Sect. 2, we examine the problem of CI testing and related work. In Sect. 3, we provide background on kNN-based CMI estimation. In Sect. 4, we introduce mCMIkNN and prove theoretical results. In Sect. 5, we empirically evaluate the accuracy of our CI test mCMIkNN compared to state-of-the-art approaches. In Sect. 6, we conclude our work.

2   Conditional Independence Testing Problem

In this section, we provide a formalization of the CI testing problem (Sect. 2.1) together with existing fundamental limits of CI testing (Sect. 2.2) before considering related work on CI testing for mixed discrete-continuous data (Sect. 2.3).

2.1   Problem Description

Let $(\mathcal{X} \times \mathcal{Y} \times \mathcal{Z}, \mathcal{B}, P_{XYZ})$ be a probability space defined on the metric space $\mathcal{X} \times \mathcal{Y} \times \mathcal{Z}$ with dimensionality $d_X + d_Y + d_Z$, equipped with the Borel σ-algebra $\mathcal{B}$, and a regular joint probability measure P_{XYZ}. Hence, we assume that the d_X, d_Y, and d_Z-dimensional random variables X, Y, and Z take values in $\mathcal{X}$, $\mathcal{Y}$, and $\mathcal{Z}$ according to the marginal mixed discrete-continuous probability distributions P_X, P_Y, and P_Z. I.e., single variables in X, Y, or Z may follow a discrete, a continuous, or a mixture distribution.

We consider the problem of testing the CI of two random vectors X and Y given a (possibly empty) random vector Z sampled according to the mixed discrete-continuous probability distribution P_{XYZ}, i.e., testing the null hypothesis of CI $H_0 : X \perp\!\!\!\perp Y \,|\, Z$ against the alternative hypothesis of dependence $H_1 : X \not\perp\!\!\!\perp Y \,|\, Z$. Therefore, let $(x_i, y_i, z_i)_{i=1}^n$ be n i.i.d. observations sampled from P_{XYZ} such that we aim to derive a CI test $\Phi_n : \mathcal{X}^n \times \mathcal{Y}^n \times \mathcal{Z}^n \times [0,1] \to \{0,1\}$ that rejects H_0 if $\Phi_n = 1$ given a nominal level $\alpha \in [0,1]$.

2.2   Fundamental Limits of CI Testing

The general problem of CI testing is extensively studied, as it is a fundamental concept beyond its application in constraint-based causal discovery [11]. In this context, it is necessary to note that Shah and Peters [45] provided a *no-free lunch theorem* for CI that, given a continuously distributed conditioning set Z, it is impossible to derive a CI test that is able to control the type I error, via for instance a permutation scheme, and has nontrivial power without additional restrictions. But, under the restriction that the conditional distribution $P_{X|Z}$ is known or can be approximated sufficiently, conditional permutation (CP) tests can calibrate a test statistic guaranteeing a controlled type I error [4]. Further, the recent work of Kim et al. [28] shows that the problem of CI testing is more generally determined by the probability of observing *collisions* in Z.

2.3 Related Work

We consider the problem of CI testing and its application in causal discovery. In this context, constraint-based methods require CI tests that (R1) yield accurate CI decisions, and (R2) are computationally feasible as they are applied hundreds of times. Generally, CI testing for mixed discrete-continuous data can be categorized into discretization-based, parametric, and non-parametric approaches.

Discretization-Based Approaches: As CI tests for discrete variables are well-studied, continuous variables are often discretized, cf. [23,35]. In this context, commonly used CI tests for discrete data are Pearson's $\mathcal{X}^2$ and likelihood ratio tests [13,39,46]. Although discretization simplifies the testing problem, the resulting information loss yields a decreased accuracy [12,40], cf. (R1).

Parametric CI Testing: Postulating an underlying parametric functional model allows for a regression-based characterization of CI that can be used to construct valid CI tests. Examples are well-known likelihood ratio tests, e.g., assuming conditional Gaussianity (CG) [1,44] or using multinomial logistic regression models [48]. Another stream of research focuses on Copula models to examine CI characteristics in mixed discrete-continuous data, where variables are assumed to be induced by latent Gaussian variables such that CI can be determined by examining the correlation matrix of the latent variables model [9,10]. As these approaches require that the postulated parametric models hold, they may yield invalid CI decisions if assumptions are inaccurate [46], cf. (R1).

Non-Parametric CI Testing: Non-parametric CI testing faces the twofold challenge to, first, derive a test statistic from observational data without parametric assumptions, and second, derive the p-value given that the test statistic's distribution under H_0 may be unknown. In continuous data, a wide range of methods is used for non-parametric CI testing, as reviewed by Li and Fan [32]. For example, kernel-based approaches, such as KCIT [52], test for vanishing correlations within Reproducing Kernel Hilbert Spaces (RKHS). Another example is CMIknn from Runge [43], which uses a kNN-based estimator to test for a vanishing Conditional Mutual Information (CMI) in combination with a local permutation scheme. The recent emergence of non-parametric CMI estimators for mixed discrete-continuous data provides the basis for new approaches to non-parametric CI testing. For example, the construction of adaptive histograms derived following the minimum description length (MDL) principle allows for estimating CMI from mixed discrete-continuous data [6,34,36,51]. In this case, CMI can be estimated via discrete plug-in estimators as the data is adaptively discretized according to the histogram with minimal MDL. Hence, the estimated test statistic follows the common $\mathcal{X}^2$ distribution, which allows for derivation via Pearson's $\mathcal{X}^2$ test, aHisχ^2, see [36]. However, MDL approaches suffer from their worst-case computational complexity and weaknesses regarding a low number of samples, cf. (R2). Another approach for non-parametric CMI estimation builds upon kNN methods, which are well-studied in continuous data, cf. [15,29,30], and have recently been applied to mixed discrete-continuous data [16,37]. As the asymptotic distribution of kNN-based estimators is unclear, it remains to show that they can be used as a test statistic for a valid CI. In this context, it is worth noticing that permutation tests yield more robust constraint-based causal discovery than asymptotic CI tests, particularly for small sample sizes [49], cf. (R1). Following this, we combine a kNN-based CMI estimator and a kNN based local CP scheme (similar to Runge [43], which is restricted to the continuous case), and additionally provide theoretical results on the test's validity and power.

3   Background: KNN-Based CMI Estimation

In this section, we provide information on kNN-based CMI estimation for mixed discrete-continuous data (Sect. 3.1). Further, we introduce an algorithmic description of the estimator (Sect. 3.2) and recap theoretical results (Sect. 3.3).

3.1   Introduction to CMI Estimation

A commonly used test statistic is the Conditional Mutual Information (CMI) $I(X;Y|Z)$ as it provides a general measure of variables' CI, i.e., $I(X;Y|Z) = 0$ if and only if $X \perp\!\!\!\perp Y \mid Z$, see [16,18,43]. Generally, $I(X;Y|Z)$ is defined as $I(X;Y|Z) = \int \log\left(\frac{dP_{XY|Z}}{d\left(P_{X|Z} \times P_{Y|Z}\right)}\right) dP_{XYZ}$, where $\frac{dP_{XY|Z}}{d\left(P_{X|Z} \times P_{Y|Z}\right)}$ is the Radon-Nikodym derivative of the joint conditional measure, $P_{XY|Z}$, with respect to the product of the marginal conditional measures, $P_{X|Z} \times P_{Y|Z}$. Note the non-singularity of P_{XYZ} ensures the existence of a product reference measure and that the Radon-Nikodym derivative is well-defined [37, Lem. 2.1, Thm. 2.2]. Although well-defined, estimating CMI $I(X;Y|Z)$ from mixed discrete-continuous data is a particularly hard challenge [16,36,37]. Generally, CMI estimation can be tackled by expressing $I(X;Y|Z)$ in terms of Shannon entropies, i.e., $I(X;Y|Z) = H(X,Y,Z) - H(X,Z) - H(Y,Z) + H(Z)$ with Shannon entropy $H(W)$ for all cases $W = XYZ, XZ, YZ, Z$, respectively, cf. [18,36,37]. In the continuous case, the KSG technique from Kraskov et al. [30] estimates the Shannon entropy $H(W)$ locally for every sample $(w_i)_{i=1}^n$ where $w_i \sim P_W$, i.e., estimating $H(W)$ via $\widehat{H}_n(W) = -\sum_{i=1}^n \log \widehat{f_W(w_i)}$ by considering the k-nearest neighbors within the ℓ_∞-norm for every sample $i = 1, ..., n$ to locally estimate the density f_W density of $W = XYZ, XZ, YZ, Z$, respectively, cf. [18,36,37]. For mixed discrete-continuous data, there is a non-zero probability that the kNN distance is zero for some samples. In this case, Gao et al. [16] extended the KSG technique by fixing the radius and using a plug-in estimator that differentiates between mixed, continuous, and discrete points. Recently, Mesner and Shalizi [37] extended this idea to derive a consistent CMI estimator in the mixed discrete-continuous case.

Algorithm 1. kNN-based CMI Estimator [37]

Input: Samples $(x, y, z) := (x_i, y_i, z_i)_{i=1}^n$, and kNN-parameter k_{CMI}
Output: The estimated value $\hat{I}_n(x; y|z)$ of the CMI $I(X; Y|Z)$
1: Let $d_{i,j}(w) := \|(w_i) - (w_j)\|_\infty$ for $w \subseteq (x, y, z)$, $i, j = 1, \ldots, n$
2: **for** $i = 1, \ldots, n$ **do**
3:     $\rho_i :=$ the k_{CMI}-smallest distance in $\{d_{i,j}(x, y, z), j \neq i\}$ $\triangleright$ Adapt k_{CMI} acc. ρ_i
4:     $\tilde{k}_i := |\{(x_j, y_j, z_j) : d_{i,j}(x, y, z) \leq \rho_i, j \neq i\}|$
5:     $n_{xz,i} := |\{(x_j, z_j) : d_{i,j}(x, z) \leq \rho_i, j \neq i\}|$ $\triangleright$ Local estimates
6:     $n_{yz,i} := |\{(y_j, z_j) : d_{i,j}(y, z) \leq \rho_i, j \neq i\}|$
7:     $n_{z,i} := |\{(z_j : d_{i,j}(z) \leq \rho_i, j \neq i\}|$
8:     $\xi_i := \psi(\tilde{k}_i) - \psi(n_{xz,i}) - \psi(n_{yz,i}) + \psi(n_{z,i})$
9: **end for**
10: $\hat{I}_n(x; y|z) = \frac{1}{n} \sum_{i=1}^n \xi_i$ $\triangleright$ Global CMI estimation
11: **return** $\max(\hat{I}_n(x; y|z), 0)$

3.2   Algorithm for KNN-Based CMI Estimation

Algorithm 1 provides an algorithmic description of the theoretically examined estimator $\hat{I}_n(X; Y|Z)$ developed by Mesner and Shalizi [37]. The basic idea is to take the mean of Shannon entropies estimated locally for each sample $i = 1, ..., n$ considering samples $j \neq i$, $j = 1, ..., n$, that are close to i according to the ℓ_∞-norm, i.e., under consideration of the respective sample distance $d_{i,j}(w) := \|(w_i) - (w_j)\|_\infty$, $i, j = 1, ..., n$, of $w = (w_i)_{i=1}^n$ for all cases $w = xyz, xy, yz, z$ (see Algorithm 1, line 1). In this context, fixation of a kNN radius ρ_i used for local estimation of Shannon entropies yields a consistent global estimator. Therefore, for each sample $i = 1, \ldots, n$, let ρ_i be the smallest distance between (x_i, y_i, z_i) and the k_{CMI}-nearest sample (x_j, y_j, z_j), $j \neq i, j = 1, \ldots, n$, and replace k_{CMI} with $\tilde{k}_i$, the number of samples whose distance to (x_i, y_i, z_i) is smaller or equal to ρ_i (see Algorithm 1, line 3-4). For discrete or mixed discrete-continuous samples $(x_i, y_i, z_i)_{i=1}^n$ it holds that $\rho_i = 0$, and there may be more samples than k_{CMI} samples with zero distance. In this case, adapting the number of considered samples $\tilde{k}_i$ to all samples with zero distance prevents undercounting, which, otherwise, yields a bias of the CMI estimator, see [37]. In case of continuous samples $(x_i, y_i, z_i)_{i=1}^n$, there are exactly $\tilde{k}_i = k_{CMI}$ samples within the k_{CMI}-nearest distance with probability 1. The next step estimates the Shannon entropies required by the $3H$-principle locally for each sample i, $i = 1, \ldots, n$. Therefore, let $n_{xz,i}, n_{yz,i}$, and $n_{z,i}$ be the numbers of $\tilde{k}_i$-nearest samples within the distance of ρ_i in the respective subspace XZ, YZ, and Z (see Algorithm 1, lines 5-7). Fixing the local kNN distance ρ_i, using the ℓ_∞-norm, simplifies the local estimation as most relevant terms for CMI estimation using the $3H$-principle cancel out, i.e., $\xi_i := -\widehat{f_{XYZ}(x_i, y_i, z_i)} + \widehat{f_{XZ}(x_i, z_i)} + \widehat{f_{YZ}(y_i, z_i)} - \widehat{f_Z(z_i)} = \psi(\tilde{k}_i) - \psi(n_{xz,i}) - \psi(n_{yz,i}) + \psi(n_{z,i})$, with digamma function ψ (see Algorithm 1, line 8) [16,37]. Then, the global CMI estimate $\hat{I}_n(x; y|z)$ is the average of the local CMI estimates ξ_i of each sample $(x_i, y_i, z_i)_{i=1}^n$, and the positive part is returned, as CMI or MI are non-negative (see Algorithm 1, line 10-11).

3.3   Properties of KNN-Based CMI Estimation

We recap the theoretic results of $\hat{I}_n(X,Y|Z)$ proved by Mesner and Shalizi [37]. Under mild assumptions, $\hat{I}_n(x;y|z)$ is asymptotically unbiased, see [37, Thm. 3.1].

Corollary 1 (Asymptotic-Unbiasedness of $\hat{I}_n(x;y|z)$ [37, Thm. 3.1])
Let $(x_i,y_i,z_i)_{i=1}^n$ be i.i.d. samples from P_{XYZ}. Assume

(A1) $P_{XY|Z}$ is non-singular such that $f \equiv \frac{dP_{XY|Z}}{d(P_{X|Z} \times P_{Y|Z})}$ is well-defined, and
   assume, for some $C > 0$, $f(x,y,z) < C$ for all $(x,y,z) \in \mathcal{X} \times \mathcal{Y} \times \mathcal{Z}$;

(A2) $\{(x,y,z) \in \mathcal{X} \times \mathcal{Y} \times \mathcal{Z} : P_{XYZ}((x,y,z)) > 0\}$ countable and nowhere dense
   in $\mathcal{X} \times \mathcal{Y} \times \mathcal{Z}$;

(A3) $k_{CMI} = k_{CMI,n} \to \infty$ and $\frac{k_{CMI,n}}{n} \to 0$ as $n \to \infty$;

then $\mathbb{E}_{P_{XYZ}}\left[\hat{I}_n(x;y|z)\right] \to I(X;Y|Z)$ as $n \to \infty$.

While (A1) seems rather technical, checking for non-singularity is helpful for data analysis by checking sufficient conditions. Given non-singularity, assumptions (A2) and (A3) are satisfied whenever P_{XYZ} is (i) (finitely) discrete, (ii) continuous, (iii) some dimensions are (countably) discrete and some are continuous, and (iv) a mixture of the previous cases, which covers most real-world data. For more details on the assumptions, see Appendix A.

We prove that the CMI estimator $\hat{I}_n(X;Y|Z)$ described in Algorithm 1 is consistent.

Corollary 2 (Consistency of $\hat{I}_n(x;y|z)$)
Let $(x_i,y_i,z_i)_{i=1}^n$ be i.i.d. samples from P_{XYZ} and assume (A1)-(A3) of Cor. 1 hold. Then, for all $\epsilon > 0$, $\lim_{n\to\infty} \mathbb{P}_{P_{XYZ}}\left(\left|\hat{I}_n(x;y|z) - I(X;Y|Z)\right| > \epsilon\right) = 0$.

Proof. Recap that $\hat{I}_n(x;y|z)$ has asymptotic vanishing variance [37, Thm. 3.2], i.e., $\lim_{n\to\infty} \mathrm{Var}(\hat{I}_n(x;y|z)) = 0$, and is asymptotically unbiased, see Cor. 1 or [37, Thm. 3.1]. The consistency of $\hat{I}_n(x;y|z)$ follows from Chebyshev's inequality. $\square$

Therefore, the kNN-based estimator described in Algorithm 1 serves as a valid test statistic for $H_0 : X \perp\!\!\!\perp Y \mid Z$ vs. $H_1 : X \not\!\perp\!\!\!\perp Y \mid Z$. Note that, $\hat{I}_n(x;y|z)$ is biased towards zero for high-dimensional data with fixed sample size, i.e., it suffers from the curse of dimensionality, see [37, Thm. 3.3].

Corollary 3 (Dimensionality-Biasedness of $\hat{I}_n(x;y|z)$ [37, Thm. 3.3])
Let $(x_i,y_i,z_i)_{i=1}^n$ be i.i.d. samples from P_{XYZ} and assume (A1)-(A3) of Cor. 1 hold, if the entropy rate of Z is nonzero, i.e., $\lim_{d_Z \to \infty} \frac{1}{d_Z} H(Z) \neq 0$, then, for fixed dimensions d_X and d_Y, $\mathbb{P}_{P_{XYZ}}\left(\hat{I}_n(x;y|z) = 0\right) \to 1$ as $d_Z \to \infty$.

Hence, even with asymptotic consistency, one must pay attention when estimating $\hat{I}_n(X;Y|Z)$ in high-dimensional settings, particularly for low sample sizes.

4 mCMIkNN: Our Approach on Non-Parametric CI Testing

In this section, we recap the concept of Conditional Permutation (CP) schemes for CI testing (Sect. 4.1). Then, we introduce our approach for kNN-based CI testing in mixed discrete-continuous data, called mCMIkNN (Sect. 4.2). We prove that mCMIkNN is able to control type I and type II errors (Sect. 4.3). Moreover, we examine mCMIkNN-based causal discovery and prove its consistency (Sect. 4.4).

4.1 Introduction to Conditional Permutation Schemes

Using permutation schemes for non-parametric independence testing between two variables X and Y has a long history in statistics, cf. [5,22,31]. The basic idea is to compare an appropriate test statistic for independence calculated from the original samples $(x_i, y_i)_{i=1}^n$ against the test statistics calculated M_{perm} times from samples $(x_{\pi_m(i)}, y_i)_{i=1}^n$ for a permutation π_m of $\{1, \ldots, n\}$, $m = 1, \ldots, M_{perm}$, i.e., where samples of X are randomly permuted such that $H_0 : X \perp\!\!\!\perp Y$ holds. In the discrete case, a permutation scheme to test for CI, i.e., for $H_0 : X \perp\!\!\!\perp Y \mid Z$, can be achieved by permuting X for each realization $Z = z$ to utilize the unconditional $X \perp\!\!\!\perp Y \mid Z = z$. In contrast, testing for CI in continuous or mixed discrete-continuous data is more challenging [45], as simply permuting X without considering the confounding effect of Z may yield very different marginal distributions, hence, suffers in type I error control [4,28]. Therefore, Conditional Permutation (CP) schemes aim to compare a test statistic estimated from the original data $(x_i, y_i, z_i)_{i=1}^n$, with test statistics estimated from, conditionally on Z, permuted samples $(x_{\pi_m(i)}, y_i, z_i)_{i=1}^n$, $m = 1, ..., M_{perm}$ to ensure $H_0 : X \perp\!\!\!\perp Y \mid Z$. Then, the $M_{perm} + 1$ samples $(x_i, y_i, z_i)_{i=1}^n$ and $(x_{\pi_m(i)}, y_i, z_i)_{i=1}^n$, $m = 1, ..., M_{perm}$ are exchangeable under H_0, i.e., are drawn with replacement such that the p-value can be calculated in line with common Monte Carlo simulations [4,28]. This requires either an approximation of $P_{X|Z}$ either based upon model assumptions to simulate $P_{X|Z}$ [4], or using an adaptive binning strategy of Z such that permutations can be drawn for each binned realization $Z = z$ [28] (both focusing on the continuous case). To provide a data-adaptive approach valid in mixed discrete-continuous data without too restrictive assumptions, cf. (R1), which is computationally feasible, cf. (R2), we propose a local CP scheme leveraging ideas of kNN-based methods, cf. Section 3. In particular, our local CP scheme draws samples $(x_{\pi_m(i)}, y_i, z_i)_{i=1}^n$ such that (I) the marginal distributions are preserved, and (II) x_i is replaced by $x_{\pi_m(i)}$ only locally regarding the k_{perm}-nearest distance σ_i in the space of Z. Intuitively, the idea is similar to common conditional permutation schemes in the discrete case, where entries of the variable X are permuted for each realization $Z = z$, but considering local permutations regarding the neighborhood of $Z = z$.

4.2 Algorithm for KNN-Based CI Testing

Algorithm 2 gives an algorithmic description of our kNN-based local CP scheme for non-parametric CI testing in mixed discrete-continuous data.

Algorithm 2. mCMIkNN: kNN-based non-parametric CI Test

Input: Samples $(x, y, z) := (x_i, y_i, z_i)_{i=1}^n$, and parameters k_{CMI}, k_{perm}, and M_{perm}
Output: The estimated p-value $p_{perm,n}$ for $H_0 : X \perp\!\!\!\perp Y \,|\, Z$
1: $\hat{I}_n := \hat{I}_n(x; y|z)$
2: **for** $i = 1, \dots, n$ **do**   ▷ Neighbors within k_{perm}NN-distance σ_i in Z
3:    $\sigma_i := k_{perm}$ smallest distance in $\{\|(z_i) - (z_j)\|_\infty, j \neq i,$ for $i, j = 1, ..., n\}$
4:    $\tilde{\mathbf{z}}_i := \{j : \|(z_i) - (z_j)\|_\infty \leq \sigma_i, j \neq i\}$
5: **end for**
6: **for** $m = 1, \dots, M_{perm}$ **do**   ▷ Local CP scheme
7:    $\pi_m^i :=$ permutation of $\tilde{\mathbf{z}}_i, i = 1, \dots, n$
8:    $\pi_m := \pi_m^1 \circ \cdots \circ \pi_m^n;$
9:    $\hat{I}_n^{(m)} := \hat{I}_n\left(x^{(m)}; y|z\right)$ where $x^{(m)} := (x_{\pi_m(i)})_{i=1}^n$
10: **end for**
11: $p_{perm,n} := \frac{1}{1+M_{perm}} \left(1 + \sum_{m=1}^{M_{perm}} \mathbb{1}\{\hat{I}_n^{(m)} \geq \hat{I}_n\}\right)$ ▷ Monte Carlo p-value
12: **return** $p_{perm,n}$

First, the sample CMI $\hat{I}_n := \hat{I}_n(x; y|z)$ is estimated from the original samples via Algorithm 1 with parameter k_{CMI} (see Algorithm 2, line 1). To receive local conditional permutations for each sample $(x_i, y_i, z_i)_{i=1}^n$, the k_{perm}-nearest neighbor distance σ_i w.r.t. the ℓ_∞-norm of the subspace of Z is considered. Hence, $\tilde{\mathbf{z}}_i$ is the respective set of indices $j \neq i$, $j = 1, ..., n$ of points with distance smaller or equal to σ_i in the subspace of Z (see Algorithm 2, lines 3-4). According to a Monte Carlo procedure, samples are permuted M_{perm} times (see Algorithm 2, line 6). For each $m = 1, \dots, M_{perm}$, the local conditional permutation π_m^i, $i = 1, \dots, n$, is a random permutation of the index set of $\tilde{\mathbf{z}}_i$ such that the global permutation scheme π_m of the samples' index set $\{1, \dots, n\}$ is achieved by concatenating all local permutations, i.e., $\pi_m := \pi_m^1 \circ ... \circ \pi_m^n$ (see Algorithm 2, lines 7-8). In the case of discrete data, $\tilde{\mathbf{z}}_i$ contains all indices of samples j with distance $\rho_i = 0$ to z_i, i.e., the permutation scheme coincides with discrete permutation tests where permutations are considered according to $Z = z_i$. In the continuous case, $\tilde{\mathbf{z}}_i$ contains exactly the, in space Z, k_{perm}-nearest neighbors' indices and the global permutation scheme approximates $P_{X|Z=z_i}$ locally within k_{perm}-NN distance σ_i of z_i. Therefore, local conditional permuted samples $(x_{\pi_m(i)}, y_i, z_i)$ are drawn by shuffling the values of x_i according to π_m and respective CMI values $\hat{I}_n^{(m)} := \hat{I}_n\left(x^{(m)}; y|z\right)$ are estimated using Algorithm1 (see Algorithm 2, line 9). Hence, by construction, $(x_{\pi_m(i)}, y_i, z_i)$ are drawn under $H_0 : X \perp\!\!\!\perp Y \,|\, Z$ such that the p-value $p_{perm,n}$ can be calculated according to a Monte Carlo scheme comparing the samples' CMI value $\hat{I}_n$ with the H_0 CMI values $\hat{I}_n^{(m)}$ (see Algorithm 2, line 11).

We define the CI test mCMIkNN as $\Phi_{perm,n} := \mathbb{1}\{p_{perm,n} \leq \alpha\}$ for the $p_{perm,n}$ returned by Algorithm 2 and, hence, reject $H_0 : X \perp\!\!\!\perp Y \,|\, Z$ if $\Phi_n = 1$. The computational complexity of mCMIkNN is determined by the kNN searches in Algorithms 1 and 2, which is implemented in $\mathcal{O}(n \times log(n))$ using k-d trees. For more details on assumptions, parameters, and computational complexity, see Appendix A.

4.3   Properties of mCMIkNN

The following two theorems show that mCMIkNN is valid, i.e., is able to control type I errors, and has non-trivial power, i.e., is able to control type II errors.

Theorem 1 *(Validity: Type I Error Control of* $\Phi_{perm,n}$*)*
Let $(x_i, y_i, z_i)_{i=1}^{n}$ *be i.i.d. samples from* P_{XYZ}*, and assume (A1), (A2), and*

(A4) $k_{perm} = k_{perm,n} \to \infty$ *and* $\frac{k_{perm,n}}{n} \to 0$ *as* $n \to \infty$,

hold, then $\Phi_{perm,n}$ *with p-value estimated according to Algorithm 2 is able to control type I error, i.e., for any desired nominal value* $\alpha \in [0,1]$*, when* H_0 *is true, then*

$$\lim_{n \to \infty} \mathbb{E}_{P_{XYZ}}[\Phi_{perm,n}] \leq \alpha. \tag{1}$$

Note that this holds true independent of the test statistic $T_n : \mathcal{X}^n \times \mathcal{Y}^n \times \mathcal{Z}^n \to \mathbb{R}$. The idea of the proof is to bound the type I error using the total variation distance between the samples' conditional distribution $P_{X|Z}^n$ and the conditional distribution $\tilde{P}_{X|Z}^n$, approximated by the local CP scheme to simulate H_0 and show that it vanishes for $n \to \infty$. For a detailed proof, see Appendix B.

Theorem 2 *(Power: Type II Error Control of* $\Phi_{perm,n}$*)*
Let $(x_i, y_i, z_i)_{i=1}^{n}$ *be i.i.d. samples from* P_{XYZ}*, and assume (A1) - (A4) hold. Then* $\Phi_{perm,n}$*, with p-value estimated according to Algorithm 2, is able to control type II error, i.e., for any desired nominal value* $\beta \in \left[\frac{1}{1+M_{perm}}, 1\right]$*, when* H_1 *is true, then*

$$\lim_{n \to \infty} \mathbb{E}_{P_{XYZ}}[1 - \Phi_{perm,n}] = 0. \tag{2}$$

Hence, mCMIkNN's power is naturally bounded according to M_{perm}, i.e., $1 - \beta \leq 1 - \frac{1}{1+M_{perm}}$. The proof follows from the asymptotic consistency of $\hat{I}_n(x; y|z)$ and that the local CP scheme allows asymptotic consistent approximating $P_{X|Z}$. For a detailed proof, see Appendix B. Therefore, our work is in line with the result of Shah and Peters [45] and Kim et al. [28] by demonstrating that, under the mild assumptions (A1) and (A2) which allow approximating $P_{X|Z}$, one can derive a CI test that is valid (see Thm. 1), and has non-trivial power (see Thm. 2).

4.4   mCMIkNN-based Constraint-based Causal Discovery

We examine the asymptotic consistency of mCMIkNN-based causal discovery, in particular, using the well-known PC algorithm [46]. Note that constraint-based methods for causal discovery cannot distinguish between different DAGs $\mathcal{G}$ in the same equivalence class. Hence, the PC algorithm aims to find the Completed Partially Directed Acyclic Graph (CPDAG), denoted with $\mathcal{G}_{CPDAG}$, that represents the Markov equivalence class of the true DAG $\mathcal{G}$. Constraint-based methods apply CI tests to test whether $X \perp\!\!\!\perp Y \mid Z$ for $X, Y \in \mathbf{V}$ with $d_X = d_Y = 1$, and

$Z \in \mathbf{V} \setminus \{X, Y\}$ iteratively with increasing d_Z given a nominal value α to estimate the undirected skeleton of $\mathcal{G}$ and corresponding separation sets in the first step. In a second step, orienting as many of the undirected edges through the repeated application of deterministic orientation rules yields $\hat{\mathcal{G}}_{CPDAG}(\alpha)$ [26, 46].

Theorem 3 *(Consistency of mCMIkNN-based Causal Discovery)*
*Let $\mathbf{V}$ be a finite set of variables with joint distribution $P_{\mathbf{V}}$ and assume (A1) -
(A4) hold. Further, assume the general assumptions of the PC algorithm hold,
i.e., causal faithfulness and causal Markov condition, see [46]. Let $\hat{\mathcal{G}}_{CPDAG,n}(\alpha_n)$
be the estimated CPDAG of the PC algorithm and $\mathcal{G}_{CPDAG}$ the CPDAG of the
true underlying DAG $\mathcal{G}$. Then, for $\alpha_n = \frac{1}{1+M_{perm,n}}$ with $M_{perm,n} \to \infty$ as $n \to \infty$,*

$$\lim_{n \to \infty} \mathbb{P}_{P_{\mathbf{V}}} \left(\hat{\mathcal{G}}_{CPDAG,n}(\alpha_n) = \mathcal{G}_{CPDAG} \right) = 1. \tag{3}$$

The idea of the proof is to consider wrongly detected edges due to incorrect CI decisions and show that they can be controlled asymptotically. For detailed proof and more information on causal discovery, see Appendix C. As the upper bound on the errors is general for constraint-based methods, the consistency statement of Thm. 3 holds for modified versions of the PC algorithm, e.g., its order-independent version PC-stable [8], too. Hence, mCMIkNN for constraint-based causal discovery allows consistently estimating the $\mathcal{G}_{CPDAG}$ for $n \to \infty$.

5   Empirical Evaluation

We consider the mixed additive noise model (MANM) (Sect. 5.1) to synthetically examine mCMIkNN's robustness (Sect. 5.2). Further, we compare mCMIkNN's empirical performance against state-of-the-art competitors regarding CI decisions (Sect. 5.3), causal discovery (Sect. 5.4), and in a real-world scenario (Sect. 5.5).

5.1   Synthetic Data Generating

We generate synthetic data according to the MANM [24]. Hence, for all $X \in \mathbf{V}$, let X be generated from its J discrete parents $\mathcal{P}^{dis}(X) \subseteq \mathbf{V} \setminus X$, where $J := \#\mathcal{P}^{dis}(X)$, its K continuous parents $\mathcal{P}^{con}(X) \subseteq \mathbf{V} \setminus X$, where $K := \#\mathcal{P}^{con}(X)$, and (continuous or discrete) noise term N_X according to $X = \frac{1}{J} \sum_{j=1,\dots,J} f_j(Z_j) + (\sum_{k=1,\dots,K} f_k(Z_k)) \bmod d_X + N_X$ with appropriately defined functions f_j, f_k between $\mathbb{Z}$ and $\mathbb{R}$. Hence, by construction (A1) and (A2) hold true for all combinations of $X, Y, Z \subseteq \mathbf{V}$. For experimental evaluation, we generate CGMs that either directly induce CI characteristics between variables X and Y conditioned on $Z = \{Z_1, \dots, Z_{d_Z}\}$, d_Z between 1 and 7, (see Sect. 5.2 - 5.3) or are randomly generated with between 10 to 30 variables and varying densities between 0.1 and 0.4 (see Sect. 5.4). Moreover, we consider different ratios of discrete variables between 0 and 1. We consider the cyclic model with $d_X \in \{2, 3, 4\}$ for discrete X, and continuous functions that are equally drawn from $\{id(\cdot), (\cdot)^2, cos(\cdot)\}$. Note that we scale the parents' signals to reduce the noise for subsequent variables avoiding high varsortability [41], and max-min normalize all continuous variables. For more information on the MANM and all parameters used for synthetic data generation, see Appendix D.1.

5.2   Calibration and Robustness of mCMIkNN

We provide recommendations for calibrating mCMIkNN and show its robustness, i.e., the ability to control type I and II errors in the finite case. Therefore, we restrict our attention to two simple CGMs $\mathcal{G}$ with variables $\mathbf{V} = (X, Y, Z_1, \ldots, Z_{d_Z})$, where first, X and Y have common parents $Z = \{Z_1, \ldots, Z_{d_Z}\}$ in $\mathcal{G}$, i.e., $H_0 : X \perp\!\!\!\perp Y \mid Z$, and second, there exists an additional edge connecting X and Y in $\mathcal{G}$, i.e., $H_1 : X \not\!\perp\!\!\!\perp Y \mid Z$. Accordingly, we generate the data using the MANM model with parameters described in Sect. 5.1.

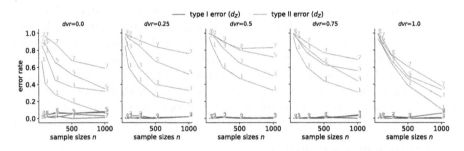

Fig. 1. Type I and II error rates of mCMIkNN for different dimensions $d_Z \in \{1,3,5,7\}$ of Z (smaller better) given varying sample sizes n for settings with different discrete variable ratios from $dvr = 0.0$, i.e., continuous (left), to $dvr = 1.0$, i.e., discrete (right).

Calibration: We evaluate the accuracy of CI decisions for different combinations of k_{CMI} and k_{perm} by comparing the area under the receiver operating curve (ROC AUC), as it provides a balanced measure of type I and type II errors. In particular, we examine different combinations of k_{CMI} and k_{perm} in settings with varying $d_Z \in \{1, 3, 5, 7\}$, discrete variable ratios $dvr \in \{0.0, 0.25, 0.5, 0.75, 1.0\}$ and sample sizes n ranging from 50 to 1 000. Note, we set $\alpha = 0.05$ and $M_{perm} = 100$, cf. [14]. We find that small values of k_{CMI} and k_{perm} are sufficient to calibrate the CI test while not affecting accuracy much for the finite case, such that we set $k_{CMI} = 25$ and $k_{perm} = 5$ in the subsequent experiments. Note that Appendix D.2 provides detailed evaluation results. Moreover, for more information on all parameters, see Appendix A.

Robustness: We evaluate mCMIkNN's robustness regarding validity and power in the finite case by examining the type I and II error rates as depicted in Fig. 1. In particular, we see that mCMIkNN is able to control type I errors for all discrete variable ratios dvr and sizes of the conditioning sets d_Z (cf. Appendix D.3). Moreover, the type II error rates decrease for an increasing number of samples

n. Hence, mCMIkNN achieves non-trivial power, particularly for small sizes of the conditioning sets d_Z. In this context, higher type II errors in the case of higher dimensions d_Z point out that mCMIkNN suffers from the curse of dimensionality, cf. Cor. 3. In summary, the empirical results are in line with the theoretical results on the asymptotic type I and II error control, cp. Thm. 1 and Thm. 2.

5.3   Conditional Independence Testing

Next, we compare mCMIkNN's empirical performance to state-of-the-art CI tests valid for mixed discrete-continuous data. We chose a likelihood ratio test assuming conditional Gaussianity (CG) [1], a discretization-based approach, where we discretize continuous variables before applying Pearson's χ^2 test (discχ^2), a non-parametric CI test based upon adaptive histograms (aHistχ^2) [36], and a non-parametric kernel-based CI test (KCIT) [52]. In this experiment, we again consider the two CGMs used for the calibration in Sect. 5.2 and examine the respective ROC AUC scores from 20 000 CI decisions ($\alpha = 0.01$) in Fig. 2.

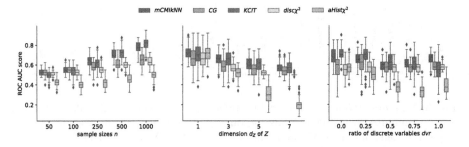

Fig. 2. ROC AUC scores (higher better) of 20 000 CI decisions of the CI tests mCMIkNN, CG, KCIT, discχ^2, and aHistχ^2 with varying sample sizes n (left), dimensions of the conditioning sets d_Z (center), and ratios of discrete variables dvr (right) (Note, we limited the execution time to 10 min per CI test (Approx. 4 900 runs of aHistχ^2 exceeded this time. Thus, aHistχ^2 is excluded for causal discovery).).

We compare the CI test's performance for various sample sizes (Fig. 2 left), sizes of conditioning sets d_Z (center), and ratios of discrete variables (right). While the ROC AUC scores of all CI tests increase as n grows (left), mCMIkNN outperforms all competitors, particularly for small sizes, e.g., $n \leq 500$. With increasing sample sizes, the performance of KCIT catches up to ROC AUC scores of mCMIkNN, cf. $n = 1\,000$. For an increasing size of the conditioning sets d_Z (center), we observe that all methods suffer from the curse of dimensionality, while mCMIkNN achieves higher ROC AUC scores than the competitors. Moreover, mCMIkNN achieves the highest ROC AUC independent of the ratio of discrete variables dvr (right), only beaten by KCIT for some dvr's. For a detailed evaluation and an examination of type I and II errors, see Appendix D.4.

5.4   Causal Discovery

We evaluate the consistency of causal discovery using the PC-stable algorithm from [8] ($\alpha = 0.05$ with $M_{perm} = 100$) to estimate $\mathcal{G}_{CPDAG}$ of the DAG $\mathcal{G}$ generated according to Sect. 5.1. We examine the F1 scores [7] of erroneously detected edges in the skeletons of $\hat{\mathcal{G}}_{CPDAG,n}(0.05)$ estimated with PC-stable using the respective CI tests in comparison to the true skeleton of $\mathcal{G}$, see Fig. 3. While F1 grows for all methods as n increases, mCMIkNN outperforms the competitors (left). Further, mCMIkNN achieves the highest F1 scores for high discrete variables ratios (center left). In this context, F1 scores are balanced towards type I errors, crucial in causal discovery. Further, constraint-based causal discovery requires higher sample sizes for consistency due to the multiple testing problem [17,46]. All methods suffer from the curse of dimensionality, i.e., a decreasing F1 score for increasing densities (center right) and numbers of variables (right) which yields larger conditioning sizes d_Z. For more information, see Appendix D.6.

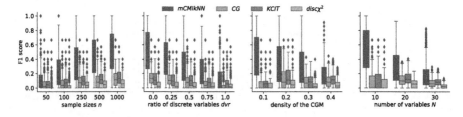

Fig. 3. F1 scores (higher better) of PC-stable with CI tests mCMIkNN, CG, KCIT, and discχ^2 computed over 3 000 CGMs for varying the sample sizes n, discrete variable ratios dvr, densities of CGMs, and numbers of variables N (left to right)[2].

5.5   Real-World Scenario: Discrete Manufacturing

Finally, we apply mCMIkNN in causal discovery on real-world manufacturing data. Therefore, we consider a simplified discrete manufacturing process whose underlying causal structures are confirmed by domain experts. In particular, we consider quality measurements Q_{con} and rejections R_{con} within a configuration phase used for adjustment of the processing speed S_{con} to reduce the number of rejected goods R_{prod} within a production phase. Besides these causal structures for configuration, rejections within the production phase R_{prod} vary given the corresponding locality within one of nine existing units U. In contrast to commonly applied discretization-based approaches, cf. [20], an experimental evaluation shows that mCMIkNN covers more of the CI characteristics present in the mixed discrete-continuous real-world data, hence, yields better estimates of causal structures when used in constraint-based causal discovery, F1 = 0.57 for mCMIkNN vs. F1 = 0.4 for discχ^2. For additional details, see Appendix E.

6   Conclusion

We addressed the problem of testing CI in mixed discrete-continuous data and its application in causal discovery. We introduced the non-parametric CI test mCMIkNN, and showed its validity and power theoretically and empirically. We demonstrated that mCMIkNN outperforms state-of-the-art approaches in the accuracy of CI decisions, particularly for low sample sizes.

While mild assumptions simplify the application of mCMIkNN in practice, we cannot derive bounds on type I and II error control for the finite case as provided in [28], but the empirical results show that mCMIkNN is robust in the finite case, too. These bounds can be achieved by considering stronger assumptions, such as lower bounds on probabilities for discrete values, cf. [2,28], or smoothness assumptions for continuous variables, cf. [4,53]. Further, the current implementation of mCMIkNN is restricted to metric spaces. To extend the implementation to categorical variables, an isometric mapping into the metric space can be examined, cf. [37]. Note that kNN methods are not invariant regarding the scaling of variables, and their computational complexity yields long runtimes, particularly for large sample sizes. For an evaluation of runtimes, see Appendix D.5. We consider parallel execution strategies to speed up the computation, e.g., parallelizing the execution of M_{perm} permutations in Algorithm 2, cf. [43], or using GPUs [21].

References

1. Andrews, B., Ramsey, J., Cooper, G.F.: Scoring bayesian networks of mixed variables. Int. J. Data Sci. Analytics **6**(1), 3–18 (2018)
2. Antos, A., Kontoyiannis, I.: Convergence properties of functional estimates for discrete distributions. Random Struct. Algorithms **19**(3–4), 163–193 (2001)
3. Baba, K., Shibata, R., Sibuya, M.: Partial correlation and conditional correlation as measures of conditional independence. Aust. N. Z. J. Stat. **46**(4), 657–664 (2004)
4. Berrett, T.B., Wang, Y., Barber, R.F., Samworth, R.J.: The conditional permutation test for independence while controlling for confounders. J. Roy. Stat. Soc. B (Statistical Methodology) **82**(1), 175–197 (2020)
5. Bradley, J.V.: Distribution-Free Statistical Tests. Prentice-Hall, Inc. XII, Englewood Cliffs, N. J. (1968)
6. Cabeli, V., Verny, L., Sella, N., Uguzzoni, G., Verny, M., Isambert, H.: Learning clinical networks from medical records based on information estimates in mixed-type data. PLoS Comput. Biol. **16**(5), 1–19 (2020)
7. Cheng, L., Guo, R., Moraffah, R., Sheth, P., Candan, K.S., Liu, H.: Evaluation methods and measures for causal learning algorithms. IEEE Trans. Artif. Intell. **3**, 924–943 (2022)
8. Colombo, D., Maathuis, M.H.: Order-independent constraint-based causal structure learning. J. Mach. Learn. Res. **15**(116), 3921–3962 (2014)
9. Cui, R., Groot, P., Heskes, T.: Copula PC algorithm for causal discovery from mixed data. In: Frasconi, P., Landwehr, N., Manco, G., Vreeken, J. (eds.) ECML PKDD 2016. LNCS (LNAI), vol. 9852, pp. 377–392. Springer, Cham (2016). https://doi.org/10.1007/978-3-319-46227-1_24

10. Cui, R., Groot, P., Schauer, M., Heskes, T.: Learning the causal structure of copula models with latent variables. In: Globerson, A., Silva, R. (eds.) Proceedings of the Thirty-Fourth Conference on Uncertainty in Artificial Intelligence, UAI, pp. 188–197 (2018)
11. Dawid, A.P.: Conditional independence. Encycl. stat. sci. update **2**, 146–153 (1998)
12. Deckert, A.C., Kummerfeld, E.: Investigating the effect of binning on causal discovery. In: Proceedings of 2019 IEEE International Conference on Bioinformatics and Biomedicine (BIBM), pp. 2574–2581 (2019)
13. Edwards, D.: Introduction to Graphical Modelling. Springer (2012)
14. Ernst, M.D.: Permutation methods: a basis for exact inference. Stat. Sci. **19**(4), 676–685 (2004)
15. Frenzel, S., Pompe, B.: Partial mutual information for coupling analysis of multivariate time series. Phys. Rev. Lett. **99**(20), 204101 (2007)
16. Gao, W., Kannan, S., Oh, S., Viswanath, P.: Estimating mutual information for discrete-continuous mixtures. In: Proceedings of the 31st International Conference on Neural Information Processing Systems, pp. 5988–5999 (2017)
17. Glymour, C., Zhang, K., Spirtes, P.: Review of causal discovery methods based on graphical models. Front. genetics **10**, 524 (2019)
18. Gray, R.M.: Entropy and Information Theory. Springer (2011)
19. Guo, R., Cheng, L., Li, J., Hahn, P.R., Liu, H.: A survey of learning causality with data: problems and methods. ACM Comput. Surv. **53**(4), 1–37 (2020)
20. Hagedorn, C., Huegle, J., Schlosser, R.: Understanding unforeseen production downtimes in manufacturing processes using log data-driven causal reasoning. J. Intell. Manuf. **33**(7), 2027–2043 (2022)
21. Hagedorn, C., Lange, C., Huegle, J., Schlosser, R.: GPU acceleration for information-theoretic constraint-based causal discovery. In: Proceedings of The KDD 2022 Workshop on Causal Discovery, pp. 30–60 (2022)
22. Higgins, J.J.: An Introduction to Modern Nonparametric Statistics. Brooks/Cole Pacific Grove, CA (2004)
23. Huang, T.M.: Testing conditional independence using maximal nonlinear conditional correlation. Ann. Stat. **38**(4), 2047–2091 (2010)
24. Huegle, J., Hagedorn, C., Boehme, L., Poerschke, M., Umland, J., Schlosser, R.: MANM-CS: data generation for benchmarking causal structure learning from mixed discrete-continuous and nonlinear data. In: WHY-21 @ NeurIPS 2021 (2021)
25. Huegle, J., Hagedorn, C., Uflacker, M.: How causal structural knowledge adds decision-support in monitoring of automotive body shop assembly lines. In: Proceedings of the Twenty-Ninth International Joint Conference on Artificial Intelligence, pp. 5246–5248 (2020)
26. Kalisch, M., Bühlmann, P.: Estimating high-dimensional directed acyclic graphs with the PC-algorithm. J. Mach. Learn. Res. **8**, 613–636 (2007)
27. Kalisch, M., Mächler, M., Colombo, D., Maathuis, M.H., Bühlmann, P.: Causal inference using graphical models with the R package pcalg. J. Stat. Softw. **47**(11), 1–26 (2012)
28. Kim, I., Neykov, M., Balakrishnan, S., Wasserman, L.: Local permutation tests for conditional independence. Ann. Stat. **50**(6), 3388–3414 (2022)
29. Kozachenko, L.F., Leonenko, N.N.: Sample estimate of the entropy of a random vector. Probl. Inf. Transm. **23**(2), 9–16 (1987)
30. Kraskov, A., Stögbauer, H., Grassberger, P.: Estimating mutual information. Phys. Rev. E **69**(6), 066138 (2004)
31. Lehmann, E.L., D'Abrera, H.J.M.: Nonparametrics: Statistical Methods Based on Ranks (1975)

32. Li, C., Fan, X.: On nonparametric conditional independence tests for continuous variables. Wiley Interdiscip. Rev. Comput. Stat. **12**(3) (2020)
33. Malinsky, D., Danks, D.: Causal discovery algorithms: a practical guide. Philos Compass **13**(1), e12470 (2018)
34. Mandros, P., Kaltenpoth, D., Boley, M., Vreeken, J.: Discovering functional dependencies from mixed-type data. In: Proceedings of the ACM SIGKDD International Conference on Knowledge Discovery and Data Mining, pp. 1404–1414 (2020)
35. Margaritis, D.: Distribution-free learning of bayesian network structure in continuous domains. In: Proceedings of the National Conference on Artificial Intelligence, pp. 825–830. AAAI (2005)
36. Marx, A., Yang, L., van Leeuwen, M.: Estimating conditional mutual information for discrete-continuous mixtures using multi-dimensional adaptive histograms. In: Proceedings of the 2021 SIAM International Conference on Data Mining (SDM), pp. 387–395 (2021)
37. Mesner, O.C., Shalizi, C.R.: Conditional mutual information estimation for mixed, discrete and continuous data. IEEE Trans. Inf. Theory **67**(1), 464–484 (2021)
38. Pearl, J.: Causality: Models, Reasoning, and Inference. Cambridge University Press, 1st edn. (2000)
39. Pearson, K.: X. on the criterion that a given system of deviations from the probable in the case of a correlated system of variables is such that it can be reasonably supposed to have arisen from random sampling. Lond. Edinb. Dublin Philos. Mag. J. Sci. **50**(302), 157–175 (1900)
40. Raghu, V.K., Poon, A., Benos, P.V.: Evaluation of causal structure learning methods on mixed data types. In: Proceedings of 2018 ACM SIGKDD Workshop on Causal Disocvery, vol. 92, pp. 48–65 (2018)
41. Reisach, A., Seiler, C., Weichwald, S.: Beware of the simulated dag! causal discovery benchmarks may be easy to game. In: Advances in Neural Information Processing Systems, vol. 34, pp. 27772–27784 (2021)
42. Rohekar, R.Y., Nisimov, S., Gurwicz, Y., Novik, G.: Iterative causal discovery in the possible presence of latent confounders and selection bias. Adv. Neural. Inf. Process. Syst. **34**, 2454–2465 (2021)
43. Runge, J.: Conditional independence testing based on a nearest-neighbor estimator of conditional mutual information. In: International Conference on Artificial Intelligence and Statistics, pp. 938–947. PMLR (2018)
44. Scutari, M.: Learning bayesian networks with the bnlearn R package. J. Stat. Softw. **35**, 1–22 (2010)
45. Shah, R.D., Peters, J.: The hardness of conditional independence testing and the generalised covariance measure. Ann. Stat. **48**(3), 1514–1538 (2020)
46. Spirtes, P., Glymour, C.N., Scheines, R.: Causation, Prediction, and Search. MIT Press, Adaptive Computation and Machine Learning (2000)
47. Strobl, E.V.: A constraint-based algorithm for causal discovery with cycles, latent variables and selection bias. Int. J. Data Sci. Analytics **8**(1), 33–56 (2019)
48. Tsagris, M., Borboudakis, G., Lagani, V., Tsamardinos, I.: Constraint-based causal discovery with mixed data. Int. J. Data Sci. Analytics **6**(1), 19–30 (2018)
49. Tsamardinos, I., Borboudakis, G.: Permutation testing improves bayesian network learning. In: Balcázar, J.L., Bonchi, F., Gionis, A., Sebag, M. (eds.) Machine Learning and Knowledge Discovery in Databases, pp. 322–337. Springer, Berlin Heidelberg, Berlin, Heidelberg (2010)
50. Yu, K., et al.: Causality-based feature selection: methods and evaluations. ACM Comput. Surv. **53**(5), 1–36 (2020)

51. Zan, L., Meynaoui, A., Assaad, C.K., Devijver, E., Gaussier, E.: A conditional mutual information estimator for mixed data and an associated conditional independence test. Entropy **24**(9), 1234 (2022)
52. Zhang, K., Peters, J., Janzing, D., Schölkopf, B.: Kernel-based conditional independence test and application in causal discovery. In: Proceedings of the Twenty-Seventh Conference on Uncertainty in Artificial Intelligence, pp. 804–813 (2011)
53. Zhao, P., Lai, L.: Analysis of KNN information estimators for smooth distributions. IEEE Trans. Inf. Theory **66**(6), 3798–3826 (2019)

PEACE: Cross-Platform Hate Speech Detection - A Causality-Guided Framework

Paaras Sheth[1]([✉])(ID), Tharindu Kumarage[1](ID), Raha Moraffah[1](ID), Aman Chadha[2,3](ID), and Huan Liu[1](ID)

[1] Arizona State University, Tempe, AZ, USA
{psheth5,kskumara,rmoraffa,huanliu}@asu.edu
[2] Stanford University, Stanford, CA, USA
hi@aman.ai
[3] Amazon Alexa AI, Sunnyvale, CA, USA

Abstract. Hate speech detection refers to the task of detecting hateful content that aims at denigrating an individual or a group based on their religion, gender, sexual orientation, or other characteristics. Due to the different policies of the platforms, different groups of people express hate in different ways. Furthermore, due to the lack of labeled data in some platforms it becomes challenging to build hate speech detection models. To this end, we revisit if we can learn a generalizable hate speech detection model for the cross platform setting, where we train the model on the data from one (source) platform and generalize the model across multiple (target) platforms. Existing generalization models rely on linguistic cues or auxiliary information, making them biased towards certain tags or certain kinds of words (e.g., abusive words) on the source platform and thus not applicable to the target platforms. Inspired by social and psychological theories, we endeavor to explore if there exist inherent causal cues that can be leveraged to learn generalizable representations for detecting hate speech across these distribution shifts. To this end, we propose a causality-guided framework, **PEACE**, that identifies and leverages two intrinsic causal cues omnipresent in hateful content: the overall sentiment and the aggression in the text. We conduct extensive experiments across multiple platforms (representing the distribution shift) showing if causal cues can help cross-platform generalization.

Keywords: Causal Inference · Generalizability · Hate-Speech Detection

1 Introduction

Warning: *this paper contains contents that may be offensive or upsetting.*

Social media sites have served as global platforms for users to express and freely share their opinions. However, some people utilize these platforms to share hateful content targeted toward other individuals or groups based on their religion, gender, or other characteristics resulting in the generation and spread of hate speech. Failing to moderate online hate speech has shown to have negative impacts in real world scenarios, ranging from mass lynchings to global increase in violence toward minorities [19].

P. Sheth and T. Kumarage—Both authors contributed equally.
A. Chadha—Work does not relate to the position at Amazon.

© The Author(s), under exclusive license to Springer Nature Switzerland AG 2023
D. Koutra et al. (Eds.): ECML PKDD 2023, LNAI 14169, pp. 559–575, 2023.
https://doi.org/10.1007/978-3-031-43412-9_33

Thus, building hate speech detection models has become a necessity to limit the spread of hatred. Recent years have witnessed the development of these models across disciplines [2, 13, 27, 39].

Hate speech varies based on the platform and the specific targets of the speech, influenced by factors such as social norms, cultural practices, and legal frameworks. Platforms with strict regulation policies may lead to users expressing hate in subtle ways (e.g., sarcasm), while platforms with lenient policies may have more explicit language. Collecting large labeled datasets for hate speech detection models is challenging due to the emotional burden of labeling and the requirement for skilled annotators [21]. One solution is to train a generalizable model under a cross-platform setting, leveraging the labeled data from other platforms.

Recent works developed to improve the cross-platform performance utilize either linguistic cues such as vocabulary [29] or Parts-Of-Speech (POS) tags [22]. Another direction leverages datasets with auxiliary information such as implications of various hate posts [17] or the groups or individuals attacked in the hate post [15]. Although effective, these methods suffer from shortcomings, such as linguistic methods form spurious correlations towards certain POS tags (e.g., adjectives and adverbs) or a particular category of words (e.g., abusive words). In addition, methods that utilize auxiliary information (e.g., implications of the post or the target(s)) are not extendable as the auxiliary information may not be available for large datasets or different platforms.

In contrast to previous approaches, we contend that identifying inherent causal cues is necessary for developing effective cross-platform hate speech detection models that can distinguish between hateful and non-hateful content. Since causal cues are immune to distribution shifts [5], leveraging them for learning the representations can aid in better generalization. Various studies in social sciences and psychology verify the existence of several cues that can aid in detecting hate [4, 9, 18, 34, 44] such as the hater's prior history, the conversational thread, overall sentiment, and aggression in the text. However, when dealing with a cross-platform setting, several cues may not be accessible. For instance, not all platforms allow access to user history or the entire conversation thread. Thus, we propose to leverage two causal cues namely, the overall sentiment and the aggression in the text. Both these cues can be measured easily with the aid of aggression detection tasks [3] and sentiment analysis task [43]. Moreover, both aggression and sentiment are tightly linked to hate speech. For instance, due to the anonymity on online platforms, users adopt more aggressive behavior when expressing hatred towards someone [31]. Thus, the aggression in the content could act as a causal cue to indicate hate. Similarly, hateful content is meant to denigrate someone. Thus, the sentiment also serves as a causal cue [30].

To this end, we propose a novel causality-guided framework, namely, Platform-indEpendent cAusal Cues for generalizable hatE speech detection **PEACE**[1], that leverages the overall sentiment and the aggression in the text, to learn generalizable representations for hate speech detection across different platforms. We summarize our main contributions as follows:

– We identify two causal cues, namely, the overall sentiment and the aggression in the text content, to learn generalizable representations for hate speech detection.

---

[1] The code for PEACE can be accessed from: https://github.com/paras2612/PEACE.

- We propose a novel framework, namely, **PEACE** consisting of multiple modules to capture the essential latent features helpful for predicting sentiment and aggression. Finally, we utilize these features and the original content to learn generalizable representations for hate speech detection.
- Experimental results on five different platforms demonstrate that **PEACE** achieves state-of-the-art performance compared with vital baselines, and further experiments highlight the importance of each causal cue and interpretability of **PEACE**.

2   Related Work

Social media provides a vast and diverse medium for users to interact with each other effectively and share their opinions. Unfortunately, however, a large share of users exploits these platforms to spread and share hateful content mainly directed toward an individual or a group of people. Considering the massive volume of online posts, it is impractical to moderate them manually. To address this shortcoming, researchers have proposed various methods ranging from lexical-based approaches [14,22,38] to deep learning-based approaches [24,32,36].

However, these models have been shown to possess poor generalization capabilities. Hate speech on social media is highly volatile and is constantly evolving. A hate speech detection model that fails to generalize well may exhibit poor detection skills when dealing with a new topic of hate [10,26] or when dealing with different styles of expressing hate [1,8], thus making it critical to develop generalizable hate speech detection models. Over recent years there has been an increase in developing generalizable models.

Generalizable hate speech detection methods can be broadly classified into two parts, namely models that leverage auxiliary information such as implications of hate posts [17], information of the dataset annotators [41], or user attributes [36]. For instance, the authors of the work [17] proposed a generalizable model for implicit hate speech detection that utilizes the implications of hateful posts and learns contrastive pairs for a more generalizable representation of the hate content. Similarly, the authors of the work [41] argue that when dealing with subjective tasks such as hate speech detection, it is hard to achieve agreement amongst annotators. To this end, they propose leveraging the annotator's characteristics and the ground truth label during the training to learn better representations and improve hate speech detection. Unlike annotators' information, the authors of [36] trained a bert model with users' profiles and related social environment and generated tweets to infer better representations for hate speech detection. Although these models have improved generalizability, the auxiliary information utilized may not be easily accessible and challenging to get when dealing with cross-platform settings.

Since language models are trained on large corpora, they exhibit some generalization prowess [35]. However, the generalization can be improved by finetuning these models on datasets related to a specific downstream task. Thus, the second category leverages language models such as BERT [11] and finetuning them on large hate speech corpora [6,23]. For instance, the authors of [6] finetuned a BERT model on approximately 1.6 million hateful data points from Reddit and generated HateBERT, a state-of-the-art model for hate speech detection. Similarly, the authors of [23] finetuned BERT for explainable hate speech detection. Aside from these works, some methods focus on leveraging lexical cues such as vocabulary used [33], emotion words, and different POS tags in the content [22], the target-specific keyphrases [12].

Although these methods have been shown to improve hate speech detection capabilities, these require large labeled corpora for finetuning language models, which may not be feasible in the real-world setting as the number of posts generated in a moment is extremely large or rely on lexical features which may not aid as a lot of the social media posts are filled with grammatical inconsistencies (such as misspelled words). In this work, inspired by works in social and psychological fields, we leverage inherent characteristics readily available in the text to learn generalizable representations, such as the aggression and the overall sentiment of the text.

3   Methodology

This section describes the methodology behind our **PEACE** framework. As shown in Fig. 1 the framework consists of two major components: (i) a cue extractor component and (ii) a hate detector component. The cue extractor component extracts the proposed innate cues, sentiment, and aggression. Moreover, this component is responsible for navigating the hate detector component toward learning a cross-platform generalized representation for hate speech detection. Consequently, the hate detector component classifies a given input to hate or non-hate classes while attending to the causal guidance of the cue extractor. In the subsequent sections, we discuss the cue extractor and hate detector components in detail.

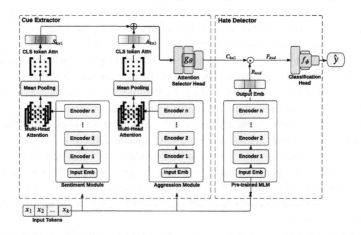

Fig. 1. Proposed framework architecture for **PEACE**. The pre-trained sentiment and aggression modules guide the representation learning process to ensure generalizability.

3.1   Causal Cue Extraction

We propose utilizing sentiment and aggression as two inherent causal cues for learning generalizable representations for better hate speech detection. Therefore, the cue extractor consists of two modules, one for extracting sentiment and one for aggression. Given an input text $X = (x_1, x_2, ..., x_k)$, the purpose of the cue extractor model is to generate an attention vector $C_{k \times 1}$ where k is the input sequence length. And here, the vector $C_{k \times 1}$ should represent an accumulation of sentiment and aggression score for each token in the sequence X, i.e., for a given token in the input X, $C_{k \times 1}$ contains how vital that token is towards the overall input's sentiment and/or aggression. We will first discuss the architecture of each cue module (sentiment and aggression) and then elaborate on how the attention vector $C_{k \times 1}$ is generated.

Sentiment Module. The sentiment module is a transformer encoder stack with n encoders that have learned a function s_γ such that given an input text $X = (x_1, x_2, ..., x_k)$, it can classify the sentiment of X, i.e., this module is a pre-trained transformer-based large language model finetuned for the sentiment detection downstream task where given an input text X, it predicts the sentiment label y (positive, neutral, negative), $y = s_\gamma(X)$.

Aggression Module. Similarly, the aggression module is also a transformer encoder stack with n encoders that have learned a function a_λ such that given an input text $X = (x_1, x_2, ..., x_k)$, it can classify whether X contains aggressive speech, i.e., this module is a pre-trained transformer-based large language model finetuned for the aggression detection downstream task where given an input text X, it predicts the aggression label y (aggressive, non-aggressive), $y = a_\lambda(X)$.

And it is essential to note here that the cue extraction module's wights are frozen when we conduct the end-to-end training of the hate detector component, i.e., we don't finetune the sentiment and aggression modules with the hate speech data.

Attention Extraction for Individual Causal Cues. As mentioned above, the cue extractor component aims to integrate the two cue modules, sentiment, and aggression, towards generating the final causal cue guidance as an attention vector $C_{k \times 1}$. The first step towards this objective is extracting each individual attention vector from the cue modules. Since both the sentiment and aggression cue modules are same-sized transformer encoder stacks (n-encoders), the attention extraction process is the same for both modules. Let's take the sentiment cue module; it contains n-encoder blocks and thus consists of n multi-head attention layers. The multi-head attention layer of a given encoder block can be defined as the Eq. 1.

$$MultiHead(Q, K, V) = head_1(Q, K, V) \oplus ...head_n(Q, K, V)$$
$$where; \quad head_i(Q, K, V) = softmax(\frac{QK^T}{\sqrt{d_i}})V \tag{1}$$

Here Q, K, V are Query, Key, and Value vectors of the transformer block i, and d_i is the hidden state size [37].

Our goal in using the sentiment cue module attention is to figure out the words/phrases in the input text that has particular importance towards the sentiment of the text. Therefore, we need to consider an encoder block that gives comprehensive attention to the whole input. Previous research shows that the attention heads in the BERT model's last encoder block have very broad attention - i.e., attending broadly to the entire input [7]. The architecture we consider for the sentiment module is similar to the BERT architecture (transformer encoder blocks); thus, we select the last (n^{th}) encoder block's multi-head attention layer as the candidate to extract the final attention from the sentiment module. We take the mean pooling output of the nth block's multi-headed attention layer as a matrix $M_{k \times k}$ where k is the input sequence length.

$$M_{k \times k} = Mean(MultiHead_n(Q, K, V))$$ (2)

Then the final attention vector $S_{k \times 1}$ for the input sequence is taken by selecting the attention at CLS token of the matrix $M_{k \times k}$. Following the same process, we extract the aggression attention vector $A_{k \times 1}$ from the aggression cue module.

Cue Integration. The final step towards creating the attention vector $C_{k \times 1}$ is to aggregate each attention vector we get from cue modules. i.e., we need to weigh and aggregate the token attentions from each cue module to get the final accumulated attention vector $C_{k \times 1}$. Once the representative attention vectors from both sentiment and aggression modules are extracted, we input the concatenated vectors through the attention selector head (g_θ). The attention selector head is a fully connected neural network that takes concatenated aggression and sentiment attention to map the final attention vector $C_{k \times 1}$.

$$C_{k \times 1} = g_\theta([S_{k \times 1} \oplus A_{k \times 1}])$$ (3)

The intuition behind the attention selector head is that we need our framework to learn how to weigh the sentiment and aggression cues relevant to the context of the given input. For example, there can be cases where aggression could be the stronger cue towards hate speech than sentiment or vice versa.

3.2 Hate Detector

The hate detector component consists of a similar transformer encoder stack to learn the semantic representation of the given input. However, the output of the cue detector component, attention vector $C_{k \times 1}$, will be provided as an auxiliary signal. We select the representation learned by the hate detector blocks as $R_{k \times d}$ where k is the sequence length, and d is the hidden state size of an encoder block. Then the extracted attention is used to navigate the hate detector to adjust the representation to incorporate the causal cues. The final representation $F_{k \times d}$ is calculated as; $F_{k \times d} = R_{k \times d} \odot C_{k \times 1}$. Then the representation corresponding to the end of the sequence token ($F_{1 \times d}^{CLS}$) is passed through the classification head (f_ϕ). The classification head (f_ϕ) is a fully connected neural network that takes the learned semantic embedding as the input and predicts the hate label $\hat{y}$ as $\hat{y} = f_\phi(F_{1 \times d}^{CLS})$. The overall framework is trained via the cross-entropy loss for the classification, where y is the ground truth.

$$L = -\sum_i y_i \log(\hat{y}_i) \qquad (4)$$

4   Experiments

This section discusses the experimental settings used to validate our framework, including the datasets and evaluation metrics used, and the baselines, followed by a detailed analysis of the experiments. We conducted a series of experiments to understand whether the identified causal cues, namely the sentiment and the aggression in the text, can aid in learning generalizable representations for hate speech detection and answer the following research questions.

- **RQ.1** Does the identified causal cues, namely, sentiment and aggression, enhance the generalization performance?
- **RQ.2** What is the importance of each causal cue in improving the generalization performance (ablation study)?
- **RQ.3** Which features does the **PEACE** utilize in input and whether these features are causal when compared to the other baselines?

Table 1. Dataset statistics of the experimental datasets with corresponding platforms and percentage of hateful comments or posts.

Datasets	Description	Number of Posts/Comments	Hateful Posts/Comments	Percent of Hateful Posts/Comments
GAB [15]	A collection of posts from the GAB social media platform	31,640	7,657	24.2
Reddit [28]	Conversation threads from the Reddit platform	13,633	4,219	31
Wikipedia [40]	A collection of comments on Wikipedia website	1,13,728	22,796	20
Twi-Red-You	Social media comments from three sites, namely, Twitter, Reddit, and YouTube	86,283	49,273	57.2
FRENK	Social media comments from Facebook targeting LGBT and Migrants	10,034	3,592	35.8

4.1   Datasets and Evaluation Metrics

We perform binary classification of detecting hate speech on various widely used benchmark hate datasets. Since we aim to verify cross-platform generalization, for cross-platform evaluation, we use four datasets from different platforms: Wikipedia, Facebook, Reddit, GAB, and Twitter-Reddit-YouTube. All datasets are in the English language. Wikipedia dataset [40] is a collection of user comments from the Wikipedia platform consisting of binary labels denoting whether a comment is hateful. Reddit [28] is a collection of conversation threads classified into hate and not hate. GAB [15] is a collection of annotated posts from the GAB website. It consists of binary labels indicating whether a post is hateful or not. Finally, Twitter-Reddit-YouTube [16] is a collection of posts and comments from three platforms: Twitter, Reddit, and YouTube. It contains ten ordinal labels (sentiment, (dis)respect, insult, humiliation, inferior status, violence, dehumanization, genocide, attack/defense, hate speech), which are debiased and aggregated into a continuous hate speech severity score (hate speech score). We binarize this data such that any data with a hate speech score less than 0.5 is considered non-hateful and vice-versa. Although Twi-Red-You and Reddit both contain data from Reddit, these data do not necessarily have the same distribution. The distribution of datasets from the same platform can still defer due to variations in the timestamps, targets, locations, and demographic attributes. The FRENK dataset [20] contains Facebook comments in English and Slovene covering LGBTQ and Migrant targets. We only consider the English dataset. The dataset was manually annotated for different types of unacceptable discourses (e.g., violence, threat). We use the binary hate speech classes hate and not-hate. A summary of the datasets can be found in Table 1. For comparison with baseline methods, macro F-measure (F1) is used as an evaluation metric for validation.

4.2   Baselines

- **ImpCon (AugCon Variant)** [17] - this baseline utilizes contrastive learning with data augmentation to map similar posts closer to each other in the representation space to enable better generalization.
- **POS+EMO** [22] - this baseline proposed to use linguistic cues such as POS tags, stylometric features, and emotional cues derived by different words and the global emotion lexicon named, NRC lexicon [25] to enhance the generalizable capabilities for multilingual cross-domain hate speech detection.
- **HateBERT** [6] - finetune the BERT-base model using approximately 1.5 million Reddit messages published by suspended communities for promoting hateful content. It results in a shifted BERT model that has learned language variety and hate polarity (e.g., hate, abuse). We report the results of fine-tuned HateBERT for all the datasets.
- **HateXplain** [23] - fine-tuned using hate speech detection datasets from Twitter and Gab for a three-class classification task (hate, offensive, or normal). It combines human-annotated rationales and BERT to improve performance by reducing unintended bias toward target communities. For each dataset, we present the results of fine-tuned HateXplain.

Both HateBERT and HateXplain are not explicitly designed for generalizability but primarily for better hate speech detection. We include these baselines as they are state-of-the-art hate speech detection methods, and due to the generalization capabilities of large language models these baselines do possess better generalization [17,42].

4.3   Implementation Details

Our framework **PEACE** is built using the Huggingface Transformers library. We utilized existing RoBERTa-base models that were finetuned on social media posts for sentiment and aggression detection tasks. Additionally, a pre-trained RoBERTa-base model with 12 encoder blocks was used for the hate detection module.

During training, we employed cross-entropy loss with class balancing and optimized the framework using the Adam optimizer. The learning rate was set to 0.00002, and a dropout rate of 0.2 was used for optimal performance. Training was conducted on a NVIDIA GeForce RTX 3090 GPU with 40 GB VRAM, and the early-stopping strategy was employed.

Table 2. Cross-platform and in-dataset evaluation results for the different baseline models compared against **PEACE**. Boldfaced values denote the best performance and the underline denotes the second-best performance among different baselines.

Platforms		HateBERT	ImpCon (AugCon variant)	HateXplain	POS+EMO	PEACE
Source	Target					
Twi-Red-You	**GAB**	0.58	0.58	<u>0.60</u>	0.54	**0.63**
	Reddit	<u>0.71</u>	0.64	**0.74**	0.54	**0.74**
	Wikipedia	<u>0.71</u>	0.70	0.70	0.60	**0.78**
	Twi-Red-You	**0.96**	0.94	0.92	0.87	<u>0.95</u>
	FRENK	0.46	0.44	<u>0.48</u>	0.45	**0.53**
GAB	**GAB**	**0.84**	0.65	**0.84**	<u>0.76</u>	<u>0.76</u>
	Reddit	0.69	0.64	<u>0.70</u>	0.56	**0.71**
	Wikipedia	<u>0.74</u>	0.64	0.70	0.49	**0.78**
	Twi-Red-You	0.61	**0.71**	0.61	0.59	<u>0.70</u>
	FRENK	**0.71**	0.57	0.60	0.59	<u>0.69</u>
Reddit	**GAB**	0.56	0.51	<u>0.59</u>	0.53	**0.61**
	Reddit	<u>0.88</u>	0.84	**0.89**	0.59	<u>0.88</u>
	Wikipedia	<u>0.66</u>	0.63	0.64	0.56	**0.74**
	Twi-Red-You	0.73	0.70	<u>0.77</u>	0.65	**0.78**
	FRENK	0.42	0.42	0.44	<u>0.49</u>	**0.54**
Wikipedia	**GAB**	<u>0.65</u>	0.63	0.64	0.56	**0.68**
	Reddit	<u>0.73</u>	0.71	**0.74**	0.58	0.72
	Wikipedia	<u>0.95</u>	0.93	0.86	0.94	**0.97**
	Twi-Red-You	0.73	0.72	<u>0.74</u>	0.69	**0.78**
	FRENK	0.60	0.51	<u>0.61</u>	0.52	**0.65**
FRENK	**GAB**	0.65	<u>0.67</u>	0.63	0.58	**0.69**
	Reddit	0.62	<u>0.66</u>	<u>0.66</u>	0.55	**0.71**
	Wikipedia	0.67	<u>0.76</u>	0.73	0.53	**0.81**
	Twi-Red-You	<u>0.65</u>	<u>0.65</u>	0.64	0.62	**0.78**
	FRENK	<u>0.78</u>	**0.79**	0.75	0.72	<u>0.78</u>

4.4   RQ.1 Performance Comparison

Cross-Platform Generalization. We compare the different baseline models with **PEACE** on five real-world datasets. To evaluate the generalization capabilities of the models for each dataset, we split the data into train and test tests. We train all the models on the training data for one platform and evaluate the test sets of all the platforms. Table 2 demonstrates the performance comparison across the different test sets for the macro-F1 metric. The column **Platforms** showcases the Source platform on which the models were trained and the Target platforms used for evaluation. For each source dataset, we show the Average Performance of each model in both in-platform and cross-platform settings. As a result, we have the following observations regarding the cross-platform performance w.r.t. RQ.1:

– Overall, **PEACE** consistently yields the best performance across cross-platform evaluation for all the datasets while maintaining good in-platform macro F1. Comparing only the cross-platform performance, **PEACE** leads to a 5% improvement when trained on the Twi-Red-You dataset, 3% improvement for the GAB dataset, 6% improvement for Reddit, 3% improvement for the Wikipedia dataset, and 4% improvement for FRENK dataset.
– Among the four baselines, HateBERT serves as the strongest baseline in most cases, followed by HateXplain. This result is justified as both HateBERT and HateXplain are fine-tuned BERT models on large corpora of hateful content. We further fine-tune both HateBERT and HateXplain for each dataset. ImpCon performs well for some of the combinations, while for others, it cannot outperform HateBERT and HateXplain. We believe this is because the AugCon variant utilizes simple data augmentation. As a result, it might not be able to learn as good representations as the ImpCon variant that leverages the implications of hate. Furthermore, the utilization of the ImpCon variant is a challenging task in real-world scenarios, as the implications are not readily available for large datasets.
– The linguistic feature-based baseline (POS + EMO) doesn't generalize well to these datasets. We argue this is because the posts in these datasets are highly unstructured and grammatically incorrect. Even after pre-processing the inferred POS tags and emotion words may not be reflective of the hate content. As a result, the reliance on these features hurts the generalization performance.
– Majority of the baselines attain improved performance when trained on the Wikipedia dataset. We argue this is because of the size of the dataset. Among the four datasets, Wikipedia is the largest dataset indicating that a model can generalize better when it's trained on large datasets.

Cross-Target Generalization. Furthermore, we also conducted another experiment for the FRENK dataset to evaluate how the different models generalize in a cross-target setting, where the datasets belong to the same platform (i.e., have similar ways of expressing hate) but discuss different targets of hate. Along with the hate labels, the FRENK dataset also provides the targets of hate in the dataset, namely, *LGBTQ* and *Migrants*. Table 3 demonstrates the performance comparison for the macro-F1 metric.

Table 3. Cross-target evaluation results for the different baseline models compared against **PEACE**. Boldfaced values denote the best performance among different baselines.

targets		HateBERT	ImpCon (AugCon variant)	HateXplain	POS+EMO	PEACE
Source	Target					
Migrants	**LGBTQ**	<u>0.74</u>	0.68	0.65	0.61	**0.78**
LGBTQ	**Migrants**	0.66	<u>0.67</u>	0.64	0.58	**0.72**

We had the following observations regarding the cross-target generalization performance w.r.t. **RQ.1**:

- Comparing the cross-target generalization, we observe that C-Hate leads to an average gain of 4% improvement over the baselines. The results indicate that utilizing causal cues such as the overall sentiment and the aggression aids in learning generalizable representations and improve cross-target generalization performance.
- Across the different baselines HateBERT and ImpCon perform the best. The overall performance of HateBERT indicate that the large language models such as BERT when fine-tuned on a particular downstream task (fine-tuning BERT on hate content resulted in generation of HateBERT) can lead to competitive generalization capabilities. Furthermore, the ImpCon model performs well as it leverages data augmentation which results in more training data leading to better generalization.

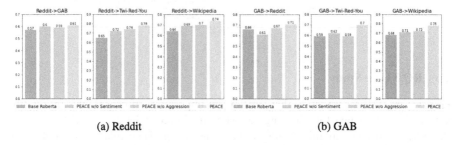

(a) Reddit   (b) GAB

Fig. 2. Comparison of cross-platform macro-F1 score to calculate the importance of each cue compared with the final model for Reddit and GAB datasets.

4.5 RQ.2 Importance of Each Cue

To assess the individual importance of the different causal cues used in **PEACE** with regard to the performance, we conduct the following experiments. We consider three variants of **PEACE**, one which utilizes only sentiment as the causal cue, namely, *Sentiment* one which utilizes only aggression as the causal cue, namely, *Aggression*, and one which utilizes a RoBERTa base classifier without any causal cues, namely, *Base Roberta*. We conduct cross-platform experiments by training these three variants on the Reddit and the GAB datasets. The results obtained can be seen in Fig. 2(a) for Reddit and Fig. 2(b) for GAB. As observed, **PEACE** performs the best when both causal cues are considered. The results can deteriorate by as little as 5% to as high as 13% without the inclusion of causal cues. Among the three variants, it is observed that **PEACE** mostly benefits from the aggression cue and for some datasets, it benefits from the sentiment cue. The main reason for aggression being a strong cue is because aggression and hate are very similar tasks and earlier works have shown that aggression leads to hatred [34]. However, the base model consistently does worst, indicating that the utilization of causal cues is important to enhance the generalizability performance for hate speech detection.

Table 4. Case study illustrating the different features/tokens chosen as important tokens to detect hateful content across different models. Darker shades of the color represents the importance level of the token.

Model	Platform	
	Gab	**Reddit**
HateXplain	the feminist liberal sheeple ; will finally get it one day very soon	you ' re subscribed to the christianity subreddit for reasons other than demanding the forced eradication of christian putridity . that in itself makes you unworthy ;
ImpCon	the feminist liberal sheeple ; will finally get it one day very soon	you ' re subscribed to the christianity subreddit for reasons other than demanding the forced eradication of christian putridity . that in itself makes you unworthy .
Sentiment	The feminist liberal sheeple will finally get it one day very soon	You're subscribed to the Christianity subreddit for reasons other than demanding the forced eradication of Christian putridity That in itself makes you unworthy
Ours + Aggression	The feminist liberal sheeple, will finally get it one day very soon	You're subscribed to the Christianity subreddit for reasons other than demanding the forced eradication of Christian putridity. That in itself makes you unworthy.
↓ Full Model	The feminist liberal sheeple will finally get it one day very soon	You're subscribed to the Christianity subreddit for reasons other than demanding the forced eradication of Christian putridity That in itself makes you unworthy.

4.6   RQ.3 Case Study

Here we provide a case study that verifies the importance of causal cues in identifying the correct context for detecting hate speech Moreover, here we visually compare **PEACE** token level attention with the baseline models HateXplain and ImpCon. In order to visualize the token importance of a given model towards its prediction, we followed a similar procedure as the cue extractor [7], where the final encoder block's attention layer was utilized to accumulate the token importance by visualizing the attention weights.

We randomly sampled hate speech text from Reddit and Gab platforms to select candidate examples for the case study. Table 4 shows a few such samples with the attention token importance visualization. In the **C-Hate's** row, we annotate the sentiment module attention in violet and aggression module attention orange . The example from the Gab platform is an instance of hate towards feminist liberals. The word *"sheeple"* and phrase *"get it one day"* can be considered as the deciding components of the text being hate speech. In contrast to the HateXplain and ImpCon, **PEACE** is attending to the word "sheeple" correctly. And we see that both the sentiment and aggression modules are giving high importance to the *"sheeple."* We have a similar observation about the phrase *"get it one day"* where **PEACE** is successful in giving more attention to that phrase towards hate speech detection. A notable observation here is that the sentiment module is attending to the above phrase well, which could be the reason behind **C-Hate's** successfully identifying the correct context towards hate.

The next example from the Reddit platform was a complex sentence for hate speech detection, given that hate is implied, not directly expressed. As we can see, both ImpCon and HateXplain models tend to the word *"putridity"* but not to the critical contextual components that signify implicit hate, such as *"forced eradication"* and *"unworthy."* This example illustrates the issue in vocabulary-based approaches to generalized hate speech detection. On the contrary, we can see that the sentiment and aggression modules accurately attend to the *"forced eradication"* and *"unworthy"* phrases navigating **PEACE** to correctly identify the hate speech context.

5   Limitations and Error Analysis

In this section, we conduct an error analysis to better understand our work's limitations and aid future work in cross-platform generalized hate speech detection. For this analysis, we select the FRENK dataset (Facebook) as the testing dataset, given it contains fine-grained information about the data, such as hate targets (LGBTQ vs. migrants) and hate types (offense vs. violence). We used the **PEACE** models trained on other platforms (Twitter, Gab, Reddit, and Wiki) to run the test on the FRENK dataset mentioned above. Finally, we analyze each model's misclassification rate/error rate under dimensions of hate target and hate type.

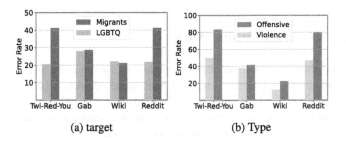

Fig. 3. Analysing error rate of **PEACE** under different Dimensions such as (a) hate targets (LGBTQ vs. migrants) and (b) hate type (offense vs. violence).

As seen in Fig. 3(a), the model tends to have a higher error rate in detecting migrants-related samples, particularly when trained on Reddit and Twi-Red-You datasets. One notable characteristic we observed in the Reddit and Twi-Red-You datasets is that the hate examples tend to include a majority of targeted hate towards particular individuals. Similarly, the LGBTQ target in FRENK dataset contains a majority of hate examples towards individuals. However, in contrast, the migrant target contains more generic hate examples towards a group of people. This mismatch in training and

Table 5. Examples representing the different kinds of hate. The violence hate type is more explicit and direct, whereas the offense hate type is more subtle and implicit.

Hate Type	Examples
Violence	shoot them all, done!!! let the communists solve the problem!!! coz i believe that these people wont stop, sooner or later, Germany will have to use guns
	Quick... Bomb it
Offensive	The annoying thing is that 75% of the migrants are Young men, why aren't they fighting for THEIR country? Or is it more a case of they can get more from European countries (money, house,education etc.)
	Are there terrorists hidden in migration groups? Likely

testing platforms might be causing the high error rate in the migrants compared to the LGBTQ.

The error analysis (Fig. 3(b)) reveals that the **PEACE** model exhibits a higher error rate in the offensive hate type compared to the violence type. To further investigate this, we examine the textual traits associated with each hate type. Representative samples from both categories are provided in Table 5. In the violence hate type, the hate aspect is explicit and easily recognizable to both readers and the model. Sentiment and aggression cues are also readily detectable in these instances. However, in the offensive hate type, hate is inherently more implicit than explicit. Consequently, learning valuable signals through causal cues becomes challenging when the expressed hatred is implicit.

6   Conclusions and Future Work

Social media platforms facilitate global opinion sharing but are often misused for spreading targeted hate speech. Automatic hate speech detection is crucial but challenging due to evolving hate and limited labeled data. To address this, we propose **PEACE**, a hate speech detection model that leverages aggression, sentiment, and causal cues to learn generalizable representations. Our extensive experiments demonstrate that **PEACE** outperforms state-of-the-art baselines on multiple platforms and targets. We also emphasize the importance of each causal cue and perform case studies to identify the features used by **PEACE** for hate speech detection. To enhance **PEACE**'s generalization, we will explore automating the identification of causal cues and develop an end-to-end system.

Acknowledgements. This material is based upon work supported by, or in part by the Office of Naval Research (ONR) under contract/grant number N00014-21-1-4002, the Army Research Office under the grant number W911NF2110030, and Defense Advanced Research Projects Agency (DARPA) under the grant number HR001120C0123. The views, opinions and/or findings expressed are those of the author and should not be interpreted as representing the official views or policies of the Department of Defense or the U.S. Government.

Ethical Statement.

Freedom of Speech and Censorship. Our research aims to develop algorithms that can effectively identify and mitigate harmful language across multiple platforms. We recognize the importance of protecting individuals from the adverse effects of hate speech and the need to balance this with upholding free speech. Content moderation is one application where our method could help censor hate speech on social media platforms such as Twitter, Facebook, Reddit, etc. However, one ethical concern is our system's false positives, i.e., if the system incorrectly flags a user's text as hate speech, it may censor legitimate free speech. Therefore, we discourage incorporating our methodology in a purely automated manner for any real-world content moderation system until and unless a human annotator works alongside the system to determine the final decision.

Use of Hate Speech Datasets. In our work, we incorporated publicly available well-established datasets. We have correctly cited the corresponding dataset papers and followed the necessary steps in utilizing those datasets in our work. We understand that the hate speech examples used in the paper are potentially harmful content that could be used for malicious activities. However, our work aims to help better investigate and help mitigate the harms of online hate. Therefore, we have assessed that the benefits of using these real-world examples to explain our work better outweigh the potential risks.

Fairness and Bias in Detection. Our work values the principles of fairness and impartiality. To reduce biases and ethical problems, we openly disclose our methodology, results, and limitations and will continue to assess and improve our system in the future.

References

1. Ali, R., Farooq, U., Arshad, U., Shahzad, W., Beg, M.O.: Hate speech detection on twitter using transfer learning. Comput. Speech Lang. **74**, 101365 (2022)
2. Alkomah, F., Ma, X.: A literature review of textual hate speech detection methods and datasets. Information **13**(6), 273 (2022)
3. Aroyehun, S.T., Gelbukh, A.: Aggression detection in social media: using deep neural networks, data augmentation, and pseudo labeling. In: Proceedings of the First Workshop on Trolling, Aggression and Cyberbullying (TRAC-2018), pp. 90–97 (2018)
4. Bauwelinck, N., Lefever, E.: Measuring the impact of sentiment for hate speech detection on Twitter. Proc. HUSO, 17–22 (2019)
5. Bühlmann, P.: Invariance, causality and robustness. Stat. Sci. (2020)
6. Caselli, T., Basile, V., Mitrović, J., Granitzer, M.: HateBERT: retraining BERT for abusive language detection in english. arXiv preprint arXiv:2010.12472 (2020)
7. Clark, K., Khandelwal, U., Levy, O., Manning, C.D.: What does BERT look at? An analysis of BERT's attention. In: Proceedings of the 2019 ACL Workshop BlackboxNLP: Analyzing and Interpreting Neural Networks for NLP, pp. 276–286 (2019)
8. Corazza, M., Menini, S., Cabrio, E., Tonelli, S., Villata, S.: Cross-platform evaluation for Italian hate speech detection. In: CLiC-it 2019–6th Annual Conference of the Italian Association for Computational Linguistics (2019)
9. Craig, K.M.: Examining hate-motivated aggression: a review of the social psychological literature on hate crimes as a distinct form of aggression. Aggress. Violent. Beh. **7**(1), 85–101 (2002)

10. Del Vigna, F., Cimino, A., Dell'Orletta, F., Petrocchi, M., Tesconi, M.: Hate me, hate me not: hate speech detection on Facebook. In: Proceedings of the first Italian conference on cybersecurity (ITASEC 2017), pp. 86–95 (2017)
11. Devlin, J., Chang, M.W., Lee, K., Toutanova, K.: BERT: pre-training of deep bidirectional transformers for language understanding. arXiv preprint arXiv:1810.04805 (2018)
12. ElSherief, M., Kulkarni, V., Nguyen, D., Wang, W.Y., Belding, E.: Hate lingo: a target-based linguistic analysis of hate speech in social media. In: Proceedings of the International AAAI Conference on Web and Social Media, vol. 12 (2018)
13. Fortuna, P., Nunes, S.: A survey on automatic detection of hate speech in text. ACM Comput. Surv. (CSUR) 51(4), 1–30 (2018)
14. Gitari, N.D., Zuping, Z., Damien, H., Long, J.: A lexicon-based approach for hate speech detection. Int. J. Multimedia Ubiquit. Eng. 10(4), 215–230 (2015)
15. Kennedy, B., et al.: The gab hate corpus: a collection of 27k posts annotated for hate speech. PsyArXiv. 18 (2018)
16. Kennedy, C.J., Bacon, G., Sahn, A., von Vacano, C.: Constructing interval variables via faceted Rasch measurement and multitask deep learning: a hate speech application. arXiv preprint arXiv:2009.10277 (2020)
17. Kim, Y., Park, S., Han, Y.S.: Generalizable implicit hate speech detection using contrastive learning. In: Proceedings of the 29th International Conference on Computational Linguistics, pp. 6667–6679 (2022)
18. Krahé, B.: The Social Psychology of Aggression. Routledge (2020)
19. Laub, Z.: Hate speech on social media: global comparisons. Counc. Foreign Relat. 7 (2019)
20. Ljubešić, N., Fišer, D., Erjavec, T.: The FRENK datasets of socially unacceptable discourse in Slovene and English. In: Ekštein, K. (ed.) TSD 2019. LNCS (LNAI), vol. 11697, pp. 103–114. Springer, Cham (2019). https://doi.org/10.1007/978-3-030-27947-9_9
21. MacAvaney, S., Yao, H.R., Yang, E., Russell, K., Goharian, N., Frieder, O.: Hate speech detection: challenges and solutions. PLoS ONE 14(8), e0221152 (2019)
22. Markov, I., Ljubešić, N., Fišer, D., Daelemans, W.: Exploring stylometric and emotion-based features for multilingual cross-domain hate speech detection. In: Proceedings of the Eleventh Workshop on Computational Approaches to Subjectivity, Sentiment and Social Media Analysis, pp. 149–159 (2021)
23. Mathew, B., Saha, P., Yimam, S.M., Biemann, C., Goyal, P., Mukherjee, A.: HateXplain: a benchmark dataset for explainable hate speech detection. In: Proceedings of the AAAI Conference on Artificial Intelligence, vol. 35, pp. 14867–14875 (2021)
24. Mazari, A.C., Boudoukhani, N., Djeffal, A.: BERT-based ensemble learning for multi-aspect hate speech detection. Cluster Comput., 1–15 (2023)
25. Mohammad, S.M., Turney, P.D.: Crowdsourcing a word-emotion association lexicon. Comput. Intell. 29(3), 436–465 (2013)
26. Pamungkas, E.W., Basile, V., Patti, V.: A joint learning approach with knowledge injection for zero-shot cross-lingual hate speech detection. Inf. Process. Manag. 58(4), 102544 (2021)
27. Paz, M.A., Montero-Díaz, J., Moreno-Delgado, A.: Hate speech: a systematized review. SAGE Open 10(4), 2158244020973022 (2020)
28. Qian, J., Bethke, A., Liu, Y., Belding, E., Wang, W.Y.: A benchmark dataset for learning to intervene in online hate speech. arXiv preprint arXiv:1909.04251 (2019)
29. Ramponi, A., Tonelli, S.: Features or spurious artifacts? Data-centric baselines for fair and robust hate speech detection. In: Proceedings of the 2022 Conference of the North American Chapter of the Association for Computational Linguistics: Human Language Technologies, pp. 3027–3040. Association for Computational Linguistics, Seattle, United States, July 2022
30. Rodriguez, A., Argueta, C., Chen, Y.L.: Automatic detection of hate speech on Facebook using sentiment and emotion analysis. In: 2019 International Conference on Artificial Intelligence in Information and Communication (ICAIIC), pp. 169–174. IEEE (2019)

31. Rösner, L., Krämer, N.C.: Verbal venting in the social web: effects of anonymity and group norms on aggressive language use in online comments. Soc. Media+ Soc. **2**, 2056305116664220 (2016)

32. Roy, S.G., Narayan, U., Raha, T., Abid, Z., Varma, V.: Leveraging multilingual transformers for hate speech detection. arXiv preprint arXiv:2101.03207 (2021)

33. Schmidt, A., Wiegand, M.: A survey on hate speech detection using natural language processing. In: Proceedings of the Fifth International Workshop on Natural Language Processing for Social Media, pp. 1–10 (2017)

34. Sengupta, A., Bhattacharjee, S.K., Akhtar, M.S., Chakraborty, T.: Does aggression lead to hate? Detecting and reasoning offensive traits in Hinglish code-mixed texts. Neurocomputing **488**, 598–617 (2022)

35. Tamkin, A., Singh, T., Giovanardi, D., Goodman, N.: Investigating transferability in pretrained language models. arXiv preprint arXiv:2004.14975 (2020)

36. del Valle-Cano, G., Quijano-Sánchez, L., Liberatore, F., Gómez, J.: SocialHaterBERT: a dichotomous approach for automatically detecting hate speech on twitter through textual analysis and user profiles. Exp. Syst. Appl. **216**, 119446 (2023)

37. Vaswani, A., et al.: Attention is all you need. In: Advances in Neural Information Processing Systems, vol. 30 (2017)

38. Wiegand, M., Ruppenhofer, J., Schmidt, A., Greenberg, C.: Inducing a lexicon of abusive words-a feature-based approach. In: Proceedings of the 2018 Conference of the North American Chapter of the Association for Computational Linguistics: Human Language Technologies, Volume 1 (Long Papers), pp. 1046–1056 (2018)

39. Williams, M.L., Burnap, P., Javed, A., Liu, H., Ozalp, S.: Hate in the machine: anti-black and anti-muslim social media posts as predictors of offline racially and religiously aggravated crime. Br. J. Criminol. **60**(1), 93–117 (2020)

40. Wulczyn, E., Thain, N., Dixon, L.: Ex machina: personal attacks seen at scale. In: Proceedings of the 26th International Conference on World Wide Web, pp. 1391–1399 (2017)

41. Yin, W., Agarwal, V., Jiang, A., Zubiaga, A., Sastry, N.: AnnoBERT: effectively representing multiple annotators' label choices to improve hate speech detection. arXiv preprint arXiv:2212.10405 (2022)

42. Yin, W., Zubiaga, A.: Towards generalisable hate speech detection: a review on obstacles and solutions. PeerJ Comput. Sci. **7**, e598 (2021)

43. Yue, L., Chen, W., Li, X., Zuo, W., Yin, M.: A survey of sentiment analysis in social media. Knowl. Inf. Syst. **60**, 617–663 (2019)

44. Zhou, X., et al.: Hate speech detection based on sentiment knowledge sharing. In: Proceedings of the 59th Annual Meeting of the Association for Computational Linguistics and the 11th International Joint Conference on Natural Language Processing (Volume 1: Long Papers), pp. 7158–7166 (2021)

Estimating Treatment Effects Under Heterogeneous Interference

Xiaofeng Lin[(✉)], Guoxi Zhang, Xiaotian Lu, Han Bao, Koh Takeuchi,
and Hisashi Kashima

Graduate School of Informatics, Kyoto University, Kyoto, Japan
{lxf,guoxi,lu}@ml.ist.i.kyoto-u.ac.jp,
{bao,takeuchi,kashima}@i.kyoto-u.ac.jp

Abstract. Treatment effect estimation can assist in effective decision-making in e-commerce, medicine, and education. One popular application of this estimation lies in the prediction of the impact of a treatment (e.g., a promotion) on an outcome (e.g., sales) of a particular unit (e.g., an item), known as the individual treatment effect (ITE). In many online applications, the outcome of a unit can be affected by the treatments of other units, as units are often associated, which is referred to as interference. For example, on an online shopping website, sales of an item will be influenced by an advertisement of its co-purchased item. Prior studies have attempted to model interference to estimate the ITE accurately, but they often assume a homogeneous interference, i.e., relationships between units only have a single view. However, in real-world applications, interference may be heterogeneous, with multi-view relationships. For instance, the sale of an item is usually affected by the treatment of its co-purchased and co-viewed items. We hypothesize that ITE estimation will be inaccurate if this heterogeneous interference is not properly modeled. Therefore, we propose a novel approach to model heterogeneous interference by developing a new architecture to aggregate information from diverse neighbors. Our proposed method contains graph neural networks that aggregate same-view information, a mechanism that aggregates information from different views, and attention mechanisms. In our experiments on multiple datasets with heterogeneous interference, the proposed method significantly outperforms existing methods for ITE estimation, confirming the importance of modeling heterogeneous interference.

Keywords: Causal Inference · Treatment Effect Estimation · Heterogeneous Graphs · Interference

1 Introduction

In recent years, treatment effect estimation has been performed to enable effective decision-making in many fields, such as medicine [25], education [22], and e-commerce [18,29,37]. For example, estimating treatment effects helps us understand whether an advertisement affects the sales of the advertised products.

D. Koutra et al. (Eds.): ECML PKDD 2023, LNAI 14169, pp. 576–592, 2023.
https://doi.org/10.1007/978-3-031-43412-9_34

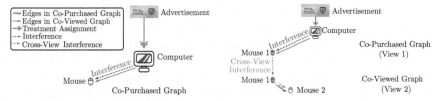

(a) Interference on a homogeneous graph   (b) Interference on heterogeneous graphs

Fig. 1. An example of the difference between interference on a homogeneous graph and heterogeneous graphs. An edge in a co-purchased graph represents the relationship that both items are bought together by many customers, while an edge in a co-viewed graph represents the relationship that both items are viewed on an e-commerce platform together by many customers. Edges in different views or graphs constitute multi-view or heterogeneous edges.

The effect of a treatment (e.g., advertisement) for a particular unit (e.g., product) is known as the individual treatment effect (ITE) [42], while that for a given group is known as the average treatment effect (ATE) [42].

This study aims to estimate treatment effects from observational graph data, which contain records of covariates of units, relationships between units (i.e., graph structure), and treatment assignments with their outcomes. For example, data from an e-commerce platform typically include the logs of information regarding assignments of advertisements, sales of items, item profiles, and relationships between items, e.g., a co-purchased relationship.

As units are associated in these graphs, the outcome for a unit will be influenced by the treatments assigned to its neighboring units. This phenomenon is referred to as *interference* [17,21], an example of which is shown in Fig. 1a. In a co-purchased graph, many customers buy the Mouse when they buy the Computer. In this case, advertising the Computer may also influence the sales of the Mouse, whose sales can no longer be independent of the advertisement, making it challenging to estimate the ITE accurately. Previous works have attempted to accurately estimate ITE given graph data by modeling interference, such as *group-level interference* [9,15,32], which is a *partial interference* and models interference within subgroups of units but ignores inter-group interference; *pairwise interference* [1,3,21,36], which considers interference from immediate neighbors only; and *networked interference* [17], which can model interference from distant neighbors. All these methods assume single-view interference, such that a graph is homogeneous and can only represent the same relationship among units, such as a co-purchased graph.

However, real-world graphs are rarely homogeneous, e.g., YouTube dataset [31], and Amazon dataset [8]. Therefore, we consider addressing interference on heterogeneous graphs that have multi-view edges, such as co-viewed and co-purchased item-to-item graphs of the Amazon dataset [8]. In this case, units are influenced by treatments of their heterogeneous neighbors via the multi-view edges, which is referred to as *heterogeneous interference* and often leads to *cross-view interference*, an example of which is shown in Fig. 1b. Although there is no direct edge between the Computer and the Mouse 2, the advertisement of the Computer still affects sales of the Mouse 2 via the edge between the Computer and the Mouse 1 in the co-purchased graph and the edge between the Mouse 1 and the Mouse 2 in the co-viewed graph. Without properly modeling the heterogeneous interference, the cross-view interference cannot be addressed, which will result in inaccurate ITE estimation.

To overcome the difficulty caused by heterogeneous interference, we propose a novel method called **I**ndividual **T**reatment **E**ffects Estimator Under **H**eterogeneous **I**nterference (HINITE; see Fig. 2). The core idea of HINITE is to model the propagation of heterogeneous interference across units and views. To this end, inspired by Wang et al. [39], we design a heterogeneous information aggregation (HIA) layer, as shown in Fig. 3. In the HIA layer, multiple single-layered graph neural networks (GNNs) [12] are used to capture information within the same views, and a view-level information aggregation mechanism is then used to combine information from different views. To properly model heterogeneous interference, the HIA layer also infers importances of different edges and views of heterogeneous graphs by applying attention mechanisms [34,35,39]. A single HIA layer can help units aggregate information from their 1-hop or direct neighbors across all views of heterogeneous graphs, enabling the HINITE to model the propagation of cross-view interference by stacking multiple HIA layers. Other components of the HINITE are explained in Sect. 3.

The contributions of this study can be summarized as follows:

- This study describes a new issue of interference on heterogeneous (multi-view) graphs. Moreover, we formalize the problem of estimating ITE under heterogeneous interference.
- This study proposes a method to address interference on heterogeneous graphs with multi-view edges.
- Results of extensive experiments reveal that the proposed method outperforms existing methods for estimating ITE under heterogeneous interference while confirming the importance of modeling heterogeneous interference.

2   Problem Setting

In this study, we aim to estimate ITE from observational heterogeneous graphs. Herein, we use $x_i \in \mathbb{R}^d$ to denote the covariates of a unit i (e.g., brand), $t_i \in \{0, 1\}$ to denote the treatment assigned to a unit i (e.g., an advertisement), $y_i \in \mathbb{R}$ to denote the observed outcome of a unit i (e.g., the observed sales of a unit i), and non-bold, italicized, and capitalized letters (e.g., X_i) to denote random variables. Moreover, a unit with $t = 1$ is treated, and $t = 0$ is controlled.

Homogeneous Graphs. Homogeneous graphs have only a single view of edges. We use an adjacency matrix $\mathbf{A} \in \{0, 1\}^{n \times n}$ to represent the structure of a homogeneous graph, where n is the number of nodes (units). If there is an edge between units j and i, $A_{ij} = 1$; otherwise, $A_{ij} = 0$. We let $A_{ii} = 0$.

Heterogeneous Graphs. This study considers heterogeneous graphs[1] that have multiple views of edges [30], which are called heterogeneous or multi-view edges. We use the $\mathbf{H} = \{\mathbf{A}^v\}_{v=1}^m$ to denote all the multi-view graph structures, where $\mathbf{A}^v \in \{0,1\}^{n \times n}$ denotes the adjacency matrix of the v-th view, and m is the number of views. We use $\mathbf{N}_i^v$ to denote the set of neighboring units of the unit i in the v-th view, $\mathbf{N}_i = \{\mathbf{N}_i^v\}_{v=1}^m$ to denote the set of neighbors of the unit i across all views. Here, the units in $\mathbf{N}_i$ are heterogeneous neighbors of the unit i.

ITE Estimation Without Interference. In traditional treatment effect estimation [24,42], non-graph data are given and it is assumed that there is no interference between units [24,42]. In this case, the potential outcomes y_i^1 and y_i^0 of a unit i are defined as the real value of outcome for a unit i with treatment value $t = 1$ and $t = 0$,[2] respectively [42]. Additionally, the ITE is defined as $\tau_i = \mathbb{E}[Y_i^1 | X_i = \boldsymbol{x}_i] - \mathbb{E}[Y_i^0 | X_i = \boldsymbol{x}_i]$ [42].

ITE Estimation Under Heterogeneous Interference. This study aims to estimate the ITE from observational heterogeneous graph data. The data can be denoted by $(\mathbf{X}, \mathbf{T}, \mathbf{Y}, \mathbf{H})$, where $\mathbf{X} = \{\boldsymbol{x}_i\}_{i=1}^n$, $\mathbf{T} = \{t_i\}_{i=1}^n$, and $\mathbf{Y} = \{y_i\}_{i=1}^n$. We assume that there exists interference between units in heterogeneous graphs. In this case, the outcome of a unit is not only influenced by its own treatments and covariates but also influenced by those of its neighbors [17,21]. In heterogeneous graphs, every unit can receive interference from its heterogeneous neighbors through multi-view edges, so the interference in heterogeneous graphs is referred to as heterogeneous interference. Such heterogeneous interference contains two types of interference: *same-view interference* and cross-view interference. The former is that interference occurs within the same views, and the latter happens when interference propagates across different views through multi-view edges. To formalize the ITE under heterogeneous interference, we use $\boldsymbol{s}_i$ to denote a summary vector of $\mathbf{X}_{-i}$ and $\mathbf{T}_{-i}$ on heterogeneous graphs $\mathbf{H}$, where the subscript $-i$ denotes all other units except i. The potential outcomes of the unit i in heterogeneous graphs, denoted by $y_i^1(\boldsymbol{s}_i)$ and $y_i^0(\boldsymbol{s}_i)$, are real outcomes for the unit i under $\boldsymbol{s}_i$ and treatment value $t = 1$ and $t = 0$, respectively. Then, we define the ITE under heterogeneous interference as follows:

$$\tau_i = \mathbb{E}[Y_i^1(S_i = \boldsymbol{s}_i) | X_i = \boldsymbol{x}_i] - \mathbb{E}[Y_i^0(S_i = \boldsymbol{s}_i) | X_i = \boldsymbol{x}_i]. \tag{1}$$

Confounder. The existence of confounders is a well-known issue when estimating the ITE from observational data [26]. Confounders are parts of covariates, which can simultaneously affect the treatment assignment and outcome [42], resulting in an imbalance in the distributions of different treatment assignments. For instance, we consider that the treatment is whether a product is advertised. Famous brands have more promotion funds to advertise their products.

---

[1] Heterogeneous graphs can be classified into two types: those with multiple types of nodes and multiple types (views) of edges [30], and those with a single type of node and multiple types of edges [30]. In this study, we focus on the latter type.

[2] Outcomes with $1 - t$ are called counterfactual outcomes [42].

Meanwhile, customers tend to buy a product (e.g., a computer) from a famous brand (e.g., Apple). In this case, the brand is a confounder. Without accurately addressing confounders, ITE estimation will be biased.

Assumption 1. Following the previous studies [16,17], we assume that there exists an aggregation function that can aggregate information of other units on heterogeneous graphs while outputting a vector s, i.e., $s_i = \text{AGG}(\mathbf{T}_{-i}, \mathbf{X}_{-i}, \mathbf{H})$. Here, we extend the neighbor interference assumption [3] to heterogeneous interference, for $\forall i$, $\forall \mathbf{T}_{-i}, \mathbf{T}'_{-i}, \forall \mathbf{X}_{-i}, \mathbf{X}'_{-i}$, and $\forall \mathbf{H}, \mathbf{H}'$: when $s_i = \text{AGG}(\mathbf{T}_{-i}, \mathbf{X}_{-i}, \mathbf{H}) = \text{AGG}(\mathbf{T}'_{-i}, \mathbf{X}'_{-i}, \mathbf{H}') = s'_i$, $Y_i^t(S_i = s_i) = Y_i^t(S_i = s'_i)$ holds.

Assumption 2. We extend consistency assumption [3] to heterogeneous interference setting. We assume $Y_i = Y_i^{t_i}(S_i = s_i)$ on the heterogeneous graphs $\mathbf{H}$ for the unit i with t_i and s_i.

Assumption 3. To address confounders, we extend the unconfoundedness assumption [3,16] to the heterogeneous interference setting. For any unit i, given the covariates, the treatment assignment and output of the aggregation function are independent of potential outcomes, i.e., $T_i, S_i \perp\!\!\!\perp Y_i^1(s_i), Y_i^0(s_i)|X_i$.

Theoretical Analysis. To model potential outcomes using observed data under heterogeneous interference, we prove the identifiability of the expected potential outcome $Y_i^t(s_i)$ ($t = 1$ or $t = 0$) based on the above assumptions as follows:

$$\mathbb{E}[Y_i|X_i = x_i, T_i = t, X_{-i} = \mathbf{X}_{-i}, T_{-i} = \mathbf{T}_{-i}, H = \mathbf{H}]$$
$$= \mathbb{E}[Y_i|X_i = x_i, T_i = t, S_i = s_i] \qquad\qquad (Assumption\ 1)$$
$$= \mathbb{E}[Y_i^t(s_i)|X_i = x_i, T_i = t, S_i = s_i] \qquad\quad (Assumptions\ 1\ and\ 2)$$
$$= \mathbb{E}[Y_i^t(s_i)|X_i = x_i] \qquad\qquad\qquad\qquad (Assumption\ 3)$$

Based on the above proof, once we aggregate $\mathbf{X}_{-i}$ and $\mathbf{T}_{-i}$ on heterogeneous graphs $\mathbf{H}$ into s_i, we can estimate the potential outcomes $Y_i^1(s_i)$ and $Y_i^0(s_i)$. This enables us to estimate the ITE using Eq. (1).

3   Proposed Method: Individual Treatment Estimator Under Heterogeneous Interference

This study proposes HINITE, a method that can estimate the ITE from observed data $(\mathbf{X}, \mathbf{T}, \mathbf{Y}, \mathbf{H})$ under heterogeneous interference. Figure 2 shows the architecture of HINITE. As can be seen, HINITE consists of three components to address confounders, model heterogeneous interference, and predict outcomes, respectively. Specifically, the first component addresses confounders by learning balanced representations of covariates with the Hilbert-Schmidt Independence Criterion (HSIC) regularization [6]. The second component aggregates interference by modeling the propagation of interference across units and views, and generates representations of units, which are referred to as interference representations. The last component consists of two outcome predictors that infer potential outcomes using the covariate and interference representations.

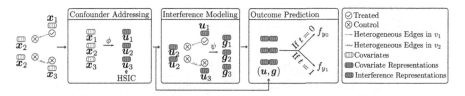

Fig. 2. An example of the model architecture of HINITE. In this case, there are two views, i.e., v_1 and v_2.

3.1 Learning Balanced Covariate Representations

To address the imbalance in distributions of different treatment groups caused by confounders, HINITE learns balanced covariate representations using an existing approach [17]. The key idea is to find a representation space in which the treatment assignments and covariate representations become approximately independent [17]. This goal can be achieved by applying the HSIC regularization [6], which is an independence test criterion of two random variables. The value of HSIC is 0 when two random variables are independent. Thus, minimizing the HSIC can achieve the abovementioned goal.

Specifically, we learn a balanced covariate representation u_i for the x_i using a map function ϕ that consists of multiple feed-forward (FF) layers, i.e., $u_i = \phi(x_i)$, resulting in covariate representations for all units, denoted as $\mathbf{U}$. We train ϕ by minimizing the HSIC between u and t, which is denoted as HSIC_ϕ and designed as follows:

$$\mathrm{HSIC}_\phi(\mathbf{U}, \mathbf{T}) = \frac{1}{N^2}\mathrm{tr}(\mathbf{KMLM}), \quad \mathbf{M} = \mathbf{I}_N - \frac{1}{N}\mathbf{1}_N\mathbf{1}_N^\top, \tag{2}$$

where N is the number of training units, $\cdot^\top$ represents the transposition operation, $\mathbf{I}_N$ is the identity matrix, and $\mathbf{1}_N$ is the vector of all ones. $\mathbf{K}$ and $\mathbf{L}$ represent the Gaussian kernel applied to $\mathbf{U}$ and $\mathbf{T}$, respectively, i.e.,

$$K_{ij} = \exp\left(-\frac{\|u_i - u_j\|_2^2}{2}\right), \quad L_{ij} = \exp\left(-\frac{(t_i - t_j)^2}{2}\right). \tag{3}$$

3.2 Learning Heterogeneous Interference Representations

To properly model heterogeneous interference, it is necessary to capture both same-view and cross-view interference. To this end, we model the propagation of the same-view and cross-view interference. Inspired by Wang et al. [39], we design an HIA layer, as shown in Fig. 3, which contains node-level and view-level aggregation mechanisms. The node-level aggregation mechanism aggregates same-view interference received by units. It utilizes m single-layered GNNs [12,35] to perform aggregations within each view. The view-level aggregation mechanism combines (i.e., sums up) the results aggregated by the node-level aggregations

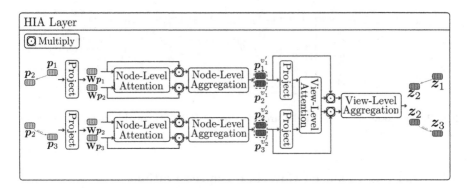

Fig. 3. The architecture of the HIA layer. This layer consists of node-level and view-level aggregation mechanisms with their attention mechanisms.

to generate new representations of units. Therefore, by employing an HIA layer, units are able to aggregate interference received from their one-hop heterogeneous neighbors. This enables capturing cross-view interference by stacking HIA layers. Similarly, same-view interference from multi-hop neighbors can also be captured by stacking HIA layers.

Consider again the co-purchased and co-viewed graphs in Fig. 1b. Suppose that we feed units and their co-purchased and co-viewed graphs to a network stacked by two HIA layers. For the Mouse 1, the first HIA layer performs two node-level aggregations. One aggregation helps the Mouse 1 aggregate interference within the co-purchased graph, while the other helps the Mouse 1 aggregate interference within the co-viewed graph, resulting in two aggregated results. Then, the view-level aggregation mechanism combines these results obtained by node-level aggregations to generate the Mouse 1's new representation, while updating the new representation in all views. This enables the Mouse 1 to aggregate interference from the Computer. Similarly, the first HIA layer also generates new representations for other units. Then, by taking these new representations of all units as inputs of the second HIA layer, the second HIA layer enables the Mouse 2 to capture interference from the Mouse 1, which contains interference from the Computer. Therefore, the cross-view interference from the Computer to the Mouse 2 can be captured by stacking two HIA layers.

Apart from cross-view interference, another challenge is that the importance of edges and views may differ in heterogeneous graphs [39]. For example, in a co-viewed graph, the importance of products in the same category tends to be higher than that of products in different categories. Here, the weights of edges in the same view can be different. Furthermore, a co-purchased graph may have more significant importance than a co-viewed graph in terms of interference, leading to different importance for each view. To overcome these difficulties and properly model the propagation of interference, we infer different weights for every edge via a graph attention mechanism [35] (called node-level attention) before node-level aggregations, and learn different importance for every view via an attention mechanism [34,39] (called view-level attention) before view-level aggregations.

More specifically, given covariate representations $\mathbf{U}$, treatment assignments $\mathbf{T}$, and structures of heterogeneous graphs $\mathbf{H}$, we aim to obtain interference representations $\mathbf{G}$ using a function ψ that consists of multiple HIA layers, i.e., $\mathbf{G} = \psi(\mathbf{U}, \mathbf{T}, \mathbf{H})$. For a unit i, its interference representation $\boldsymbol{g}_i$ is supposed to capture the interference from its heterogeneous neighbors. Let $\boldsymbol{p}$ be a representation of a unit, which is the input of the current HIA layer and the output of the previous HIA layer. For the first HIA layer, $\boldsymbol{p}$ is the concatenation of $\boldsymbol{u}$ and $\boldsymbol{t}$. Let $\boldsymbol{z}$ denote a new representation for the unit i computed by the current HIA layer, α_{ij}^v denote the inferred weight of the edge between units j and i at the v-th view, w_i^v denote the learned importance of the v-th view for the unit i, and β_i^v denote the normalized value for w_i^v.

Now, we describe the architecture of the HIA layer in detail. First, the HIA layer infers the edge weight α_{ij}^v by the node-level attention mechanism as follows:

$$\alpha_{ij}^v = \frac{\exp(\mathrm{LeakyReLU}(\boldsymbol{a}^\top[\mathbf{W}\boldsymbol{p}_i \| \mathbf{W}\boldsymbol{p}_j]))}{\sum_{k \in \mathbf{N}_i^v \bigcup \{i\}} \exp(\mathrm{LeakyReLU}(\boldsymbol{a}^\top[\mathbf{W}\boldsymbol{p}_i \| \mathbf{W}\boldsymbol{p}_k]))}, \tag{4}$$

where $\boldsymbol{a}$ and $\mathbf{W}$ represent a learnable parameter vector and matrix, respectively, and $\|$ represents the concatenation operation. Next, it performs node-level aggregations. The node-level aggregation at the v-th view is computed as follows:

$$\boldsymbol{p}_i^{v'} = \sigma \left(\sum_{j \in \mathbf{N}_i^v \bigcup \{i\}} \alpha_{ij}^v \mathbf{W}\boldsymbol{p}_j \right), \tag{5}$$

where σ is an activation function, such as ReLU. Next, the view-attention mechanism is applied to learn the importance of different views as follows:

$$w_i^v = \frac{1}{n} \sum_{i=1}^n \boldsymbol{q}^\top \mathrm{LeakyReLU}(\mathbf{W}\boldsymbol{p}_i^{v'} + \boldsymbol{b}), \quad \beta_i^v = \frac{\exp\left(w_i^v\right)}{\sum_{v=1}^m \exp\left(w_i^v\right)}, \tag{6}$$

where $\boldsymbol{b}$ is a bias vector, and $\boldsymbol{q}$ is a learnable parameter vector. Finally, the view-level aggregation is applied to aggregate the information from different views as follows:

$$\boldsymbol{z}_i = \sum_{v=1}^m \beta_i^v \boldsymbol{p}_i^{v'}. \tag{7}$$

3.3   Outcome Predictions and ITE Estimation

Given the covariate representations $\mathbf{U}$, interference representations $\mathbf{G}$, and treatment assignments $\mathbf{T}$, we train two predictors that consist of multiple FF layers to infer the outcomes with different t. Specifically, let f_{y_0} and f_{y_1} denote the predictor for $t = 0$ and $t = 1$, respectively. We optimize the two predictors by minimizing the following mean square error (MSE) between prediction outcomes and observed outcomes with the HSIC regularization:

$$\mathcal{L} = \frac{1}{N} \sum_{i=1}^{N} \left(f_{y_{t_i}}(\boldsymbol{u}_i, \boldsymbol{g}_i) - y_i \right)^2 + \gamma \text{HSIC}_\phi, \tag{8}$$

where the γ is a regularization hyperparameter.

Finally, we can estimate the ITE using $\hat{\tau}_i = f_{y_1}(\boldsymbol{u}_i, \boldsymbol{g}_i) - f_{y_0}(\boldsymbol{u}_i, \boldsymbol{g}_i)$.

4   Experiments

4.1   Datasets

We used three heterogeneous graph datasets: Amazon Software (AMZ S) [8], Youtube [31], and Flicker [40]. Following prior studies on ITE/ATE [16,17,26], we simulated outcomes[3] as the ground-truth values for counterfactual outcomes are not available.

Outcome Simulation: Similar to the outcome simulation in Ma et al. [16], we used available data and heterogeneous graph structures to simulate outcomes under heterogeneous interference of the unit i:

$$y_i = f_0(\boldsymbol{x}_i) + f_t(t_i, \boldsymbol{x}_i) + f_s(\mathbf{T}, \mathbf{X}, \mathbf{N}_i) + \epsilon_i, \tag{9}$$

where $f_0(\boldsymbol{x}_i) = \boldsymbol{w}_0^\top \boldsymbol{x}_i$ simulates the outcome of a unit i under treatment $t_i = 0$ without interference, and every element of $\boldsymbol{w}_0$ follows a Gaussian distribution or uniform distribution (i.e., $\mathcal{N}(0,1)$ or $\mathcal{U}(0,1)$). $f_t(t_i, \boldsymbol{x}_i) = t_i \times \boldsymbol{w}_1^\top \boldsymbol{x}_i$ simulates the ITE of the unit i, where $\boldsymbol{w}_1 \sim \mathcal{N}(0, \mathbf{I})$ or $\mathcal{U}(0, \mathbf{I})$. In the literature, the effect caused by interference is known as *spillover effect* [21]. We simulate it through $f_s(\mathbf{T}, \mathbf{X}, \mathbf{N}_i) = o_i^{(1)} + o_i^{(2)}$, where $o_i^{(1)} = \text{Agg}(\text{Concat}(\mathbf{X}, \mathbf{T}), \mathbf{N}_i)$ represents a spillover effect from 1-hop heterogeneous neighbors for the unit i, $o_i^{(2)} = \text{Agg}(\mathbf{O}^{(1)}, \mathbf{N}_i)$ represents the spillover effect of 2-hop heterogeneous neighbors, and $\mathbf{O}^{(1)}$ represents the spillover effects from 1-hop heterogeneous neighbors for all units. Here, the aggregation function is defined as $\text{Agg}(\mathbf{C}, \mathbf{N}_i) = \sum_{v=1}^{m} e^v \left(\frac{1}{|\mathbf{N}_i^v|} \sum_{j \in \mathbf{N}_i^v} \boldsymbol{w}_{ij}^\top \boldsymbol{c}_j \right)$, where e^v and every element of $\boldsymbol{w}_{ij}$ follow $\mathcal{N}(0,1)$ or $\mathcal{U}(0,1)$. Lastly, $\epsilon_i \sim \mathcal{N}(0,1)$ is a random noise.

Amazon Software Dataset [8]: The Amazon dataset [8] is collected from Amazon[4]. In the graphs of the Amazon dataset, each node is a product. To study causal effects, we chose the co-purchased and co-viewed graphs from the software category of the Amazon dataset. After removing nodes with missing values, there are 11,089 items with 11,813 heterogeneous edges. The covariates consist of reviews and the number of customer reviews of items. We put reviews

---

[3] The simulated outcomes and the codes of the HINITE are available at https://github.com/LINXF208/HINITE.

[4] https://www.amazon.com/.

into the SimCSE [5] model to generate 768-dimensional sentence embeddings. The review rating of items is considered as a treatment: an item is treated ($t = 1$) when the average review rating is at least 3, and an item is controlled ($t = 0$) when the average review rating is less than 3. The causal problem in this dataset is whether review rating has a role in influencing the sales of items. Due to the heterogeneous edges among items, the sales of an item might be influenced by its heterogeneous neighbors' treatments.

YouTube Dataset [31]: Tang et al. [31] used YouTube Data API[5] to crawl the information of contacts, subscriptions, and favorites of users from YouTube[6], while extending them to a contact graph, co-subscription graph, co-subscribed graph, and favorite graph. Every node in the graphs is a user of YouTube. In this case, we consider a causal problem: "how much recommendation of a video (treatment) to a user will affect the user's experience of this video (outcome)?" Moreover, users might share the recommended video with heterogeneous neighbors, which constitutes heterogeneous interference. We took 5,000 users with their heterogeneous graphs containing 3,190,622 heterogeneous edges to simulate outcomes and study heterogeneous interference. As detailed information about each user is missing, we simulated the covariates via $x_i \sim \mathcal{N}(0, \mathbf{I})$ (100-dimensional vector), and simulated treatment t_i as follows, following most existing works, such as Ma et al. [16]:

$$t_i \sim \mathrm{Ber}(\mathrm{sigmoid}(x_i^\top w_t) + \epsilon_{t_i}), \tag{10}$$

where $\mathrm{Ber}(\cdot)$ represents a Bernoulli distribution, w_t is a 100-dimensional vector in which every element follows $\mathcal{U}(-1, 1)$, and ϵ_{t_i} is random Gaussian noise.

Flicker Dataset [40]: Flicker[7] is an online social website where users can share their images. Qu et al. [19] constructed a dataset with multi-view graphs, i.e., friendship view and similarity view, from the Flicker dataset [40]. Every node in the graphs is a user of Flicker. Following Qu et al. [19], we also consider friendship-view and similarity-view graphs that have 7,575 users with approximately 1,236,976 heterogeneous edges. Here, the causal question is: "how much recommending a hot photo (treatment) to a user will affect the user's experience (outcome) of this photo?" In this case, users might share recommended photos with their heterogeneous neighbors, which constitutes heterogeneous interference. We used the 1206-dimensional embeddings that are provided by Guo et al. [7], generated using a list of users' interest tags, and simulated the treatments using Eq. (10).

4.2   Baselines

BNN [11]: Balancing Neural Network [11] (BNN) addresses confounders by minimizing the discrepancy of distributions of units belonging to different groups, without considering interference. Following Johansson et al. [11], we considered

---

[5] https://developers.google.com/youtube/?csw=1.

[6] https://www.youtube.com/.

[7] https://www.flickr.com/.

two structures: BNN-4-0 and BNN-2-2. The former has four representation layers but no prediction layers, and the latter has two representation layers and two prediction layers. Both have one linear output layer.

CFR [26]: Counterfactual Regression (CFR) [26] minimizes the maximum mean discrepancy (MMD) and Wasserstein distance between different distributions of two groups. Similar to BNN, it also ignores interference. Following Shalit et al. [26], we considered two different schemes: CFR_{MMD} and CFR_{Wass}. The former minimizes the MMD of two different distributions, while the latter minimizes the Wasserstein distance.

TARNet [26]: TARNet consists of the same model architecture as the CFR model but removes the balance term (MMD or Wasserstein distance).

GCN-Based Methods [17]: Ma et al. [17] proposed methods to address interference on a homogeneous graph using graph convolutional networks (GCNs) [41]. The GCN-based method can use only a single view rather than all views of heterogeneous graphs. To overcome it, we consider two schemes. The first scheme is to replace heterogeneous graphs with a projection graph $\mathbf{A}_{Proj}$ and apply the GCN-based method to the $\mathbf{A}_{Proj}$, denoted as GCN_{Proj}. If two units have an edge in either of the original heterogeneous graphs, there will be an edge in this projection graph. The second scheme is to augment the GCN-based method with mixing operations, which includes two variants: $MGCN_C$ and $MGCN_M$. The $MGCN_C$ concatenates interference representations from different views into a single vector, while the $MGCN_M$ computes the mean vector of these interference representations.

4.3 Experiment Settings

For all datasets, we calculated $\epsilon_{PEHE}/\epsilon_{ATE}$ to evaluate the error on ITE/ATE estimations as follows:

$$\epsilon_{PEHE} = \frac{1}{n}\sum_{i=1}^{n}(\tau_i - \hat{\tau}_i)^2, \quad \epsilon_{ATE} = \left|\frac{1}{n}\sum_{i=1}^{n}\tau_i - \frac{1}{n}\sum_{i=1}^{n}\hat{\tau}_i\right|. \quad (11)$$

Following Ma et al. [17], the entire $\mathbf{X}$, $\mathbf{T}$, and heterogeneous graph structures were given during the training, validation, and testing phases. However, only the observed outcomes of the units in the training set were provided during the training phase.

We randomly split all datasets into training/validation/test splits with a ratio of 70%/15%/15%. Results on the Youtube and Flicker datasets were averaged over ten realizations, while the results on the AMZ S dataset were averaged over three repeated executions. We trained all models with the NVIDIA RTX A5000 GPU. All methods utilized the Adam optimizer with 2,000 training iterations for all datasets. In addition, dropout and early stopping were applied for all methods to avoid overfitting.

For all datasets, we set the learning rate to 0.001 with a weight decay of 0.001, set the training batch size to 512, and searched γ in the range of $\{0.01, 0.1, 0.5, 1.0, 1.5\}$ using the validation sets. We used ReLU as activation

Table 1. Results (mean ± standard errors) of performance of ITE and ATE estimation. Results in bold indicate the lowest mean error. HINITE is our method.

Method	Youtube		Flicker		AMZ S	
	ϵ_{PEHE}	ϵ_{ATE}	ϵ_{PEHE}	ϵ_{ATE}	$\sqrt{\epsilon_{PEHE}}$	ϵ_{ATE}
TARNet	40.75 ± 7.95	0.51 ± 0.23	24.20 ± 6.79	0.30 ± 0.26	112.37 ± 11.54	103.91 ± 12.78
BNN-2-2	93.03 ± 16.02	0.26 ± 0.23	27.91 ± 7.53	$\mathbf{0.13 \pm 0.07}$	199.37 ± 0.20	196.36 ± 0.20
BNN-4-0	105.38 ± 22.50	0.26 ± 0.23	29.22 ± 7.53	$\mathbf{0.13 \pm 0.07}$	206.03 ± 0.08	203.12 ± 0.08
CFR$_{MMD}$	42.02 ± 9.96	0.43 ± 0.36	24.44 ± 7.49	0.29 ± 0.17	103.18 ± 25.02	89.76 ± 32.13
CFR$_{WASS}$	39.36 ± 8.76	0.51 ± 0.41	24.02 ± 6.71	0.35 ± 0.17	109.91 ± 24.49	99.40 ± 30.40
GCN$_{Proj}$	42.37 ± 7.45	0.61 ± 0.39	24.59 ± 5.11	0.21 ± 0.13	139.14 ± 20.63	135.57 ± 22.86
MGCN$_C$	53.10 ± 11.83	0.29 ± 0.27	26.87 ± 6.43	0.25 ± 0.20	95.14 ± 8.25	72.08 ± 13.47
MGCN$_M$	53.99 ± 13.46	0.37 ± 0.33	29.48 ± 7.17	0.29 ± 0.25	87.33 ± 3.40	60.81 ± 3.27
HINITE	$\mathbf{14.43 \pm 3.27}$	$\mathbf{0.21 \pm 0.20}$	$\mathbf{18.45 \pm 4.42}$	0.15 ± 0.11	$\mathbf{76.16 \pm 3.82}$	$\mathbf{15.21 \pm 3.89}$

function for ϕ, $f_{y_{t_i}}$, and node-level aggregations. The hidden layers of ϕ were set to $(128, 64, 64)$-dimensions, ψ are set to $(64, 64, 32)$-dimensions, $f_{y_{t_i}}$ are set to $(128, 64, 32)$-dimensions, and the dimensions of view-level attention were set to $(128, 128, 64)$-dimensions. Moreover, we searched for hyperparameters for all baseline methods from the search range suggested in the corresponding literature.

4.4   Results

Treatment Effect Estimation Performance. Table 1 lists the results of ITE and ATE estimations on test sets of all datasets. It can be seen that the HINITE outperforms all baseline methods in ITE estimation, while there are significant gaps (p-values of the t-test are far less than 0.05) in ITE estimation between the proposed and baseline methods. It can also be seen that HINITE outperforms most baseline methods in ATE estimation, at least, achieving comparative performance of ATE estimation to those of the baseline methods. These results reveal that HINITE has a powerful ability to address heterogeneous interference. Moreover, the GCN$_{Proj}$ and MGCN with some simple mixers cannot always achieve better performance than other baseline methods. This implies that modeling cross-view interference using the HIA layers is important.

Ablation Study. To further investigate the importance of each component of HINITE, we conducted ablation experiments. Let us start by introducing some variants of HINITE: (i) HINITE-PG applies the HINITE to the projection graph A_{Proj}, which was described when introduced the GCN-based method. (ii) HINITE-NHG replaces the HIA layers with GCN layers [12] while using the A_{Proj}. (iii) HINITE-NB removes the HSIC regularization by setting γ to 0.

Figure 4 presents the results of the ablation experiments. A clear performance gap can be seen in ITE and ATE estimation between the HINITE-PG/HINITE-NHG and HINITE. This implies that it is important to model the heterogeneous interference using the information of heterogeneous graphs and the proposed HIA

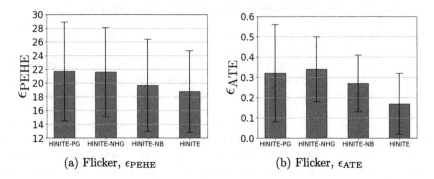

(a) Flicker, ϵ_{PEHE} (b) Flicker, ϵ_{ATE}

Fig. 4. Results (mean and standard error) of ablation experiments. We set γ to 1.5 for HINITE-PG, HINITE-NHG, and HINITE in the ablation experiments.

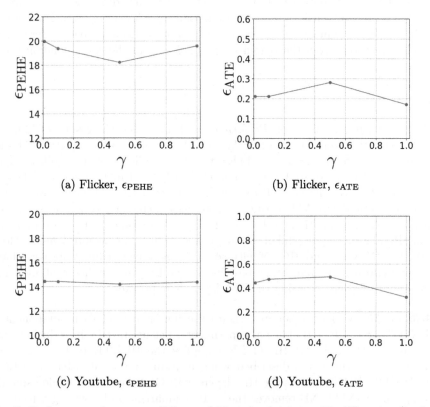

(a) Flicker, ϵ_{PEHE} (b) Flicker, ϵ_{ATE}

(c) Youtube, ϵ_{PEHE} (d) Youtube, ϵ_{ATE}

Fig. 5. Performance changes on Filker and Youtube datasets with different γ (in the range of $\{0.01, 0.1, 0.5, 1.0\}$) . Results are averaged over ten realizations with a fixed value of γ.

layer. Comparing the results of HINITE and HINITE-NB, we can also observe that removing the HSIC regularization results in performance degradation. This reveals that it is also important to balance the different distributions.

Sensitivity analysis. To investigate whether HINITE is sensitive to γ, we conducted experiments with different γ and present the results in Fig. 5. No significant change in performance was observed with different values of γ. This reveals that HINITE is not particularly sensitive to the value of γ.

5 Related Work

In the literature, efforts have been made to estimate treatment effect without interference [2,7,11,13,23,24,26,42,43] and with interference on homogeneous graphs [1,3,9,15,17,32,33,36] or hyper-graphs [16]. A few studies have considered heterogeneous graphs. For example, Qu et al. [20] assumed a partial interference and could only estimate ATE. Zhao et al. [46] proposed a method to construct a heterogeneous graph from a homogeneous graph by learning a set of weights for each edge using an attention mechanism, but their method cannot capture interference between multi-view graph structures. We offer the first approach for handling interference on multi-view graphs.

Meanwhile, heterogeneous graphs have been the subject of recent graph analysis studies, focusing on tasks such as node classification, link prediction, and graph classification [4,10,14,27,28,38,39,44,45]. The proposed HINITE shares some similarities with the heterogeneous graph attention network (HAN) [39]. However, HAN aggregates information from each view at the end of forward propagation only once, while the proposed HINITE does aggregation layer-by-layer, which is essential for capturing cross-view interference. In addition, we use LeakyReLU (for view-level attention) instead of the tanh function as an activation function to address the vanishing gradient issue, and we use single-head instead of multi-head attention for better efficiency.

6 Conclusion

In this paper, we described the problem of heterogeneous interference and the difficulty of treatment effect estimations under heterogeneous interference. This paper proposed HINITE to model the propagation of heterogeneous interference using HIA layers that contain node-level aggregation, view-level aggregation, and attention mechanisms. We conducted extensive experiments to verify the performance of the proposed HINITE, where the results validate the effectiveness of the HINITE in ITE and ATE estimation under heterogeneous interference.

Acknowledgements. This work was supported by JST, the establishment of university fellowships towards the creation of science technology innovation, Grant Number JPMJFS2123, and supported by JSPS KAKENHI Grant Number 20H04244.

Ethics. This study only involved public datasets that are freely available for academic purposes.

References

1. Aronow, P.M., Samii, C.: Estimating average causal effects under general interference, with application to a social network experiment. Ann. Appl. Stat. **11**, 1912–1947 (2017)
2. Chu, Z., Rathbun, S.L., Li, S.: Graph infomax adversarial learning for treatment effect estimation with networked observational data. In: Proceedings of the 27th ACM SIGKDD Conference on Knowledge Discovery and Data Mining, pp. 176–184 (2021)
3. Forastiere, L., Airoldi, E.M., Mealli, F.: Identification and estimation of treatment and interference effects in observational studies on networks. J. Am. Stat. Assoc. **116**(534), 901–918 (2021)
4. Fu, X., Zhang, J., Meng, Z., King, I.: MAGNN: metapath aggregated graph neural network for heterogeneous graph embedding. In: Proceedings of the Web Conference 2020, pp. 2331–2341 (2020)
5. Gao, T., Yao, X., Chen, D.: SimCSE: simple contrastive learning of sentence embeddings. In: Proceedings of the 2021 Conference on Empirical Methods in Natural Language Processing (2021)
6. Gretton, A., Bousquet, O., Smola, A., Schölkopf, B.: Measuring statistical dependence with Hilbert-Schmidt norms. In: Proceedings of the 16th International Conference on Algorithmic Learning Theory, pp. 63–77 (2005)
7. Guo, R., Li, J., Liu, H.: Learning individual causal effects from networked observational data. In: Proceedings of the 13th International Conference on Web Search and Data Mining, pp. 232–240 (2020)
8. He, R., McAuley, J.: Ups and downs: modeling the visual evolution of fashion trends with one-class collaborative filtering. In: Proceedings of the 2016 World Wide Web Conference, pp. 507–517 (2016)
9. Hudgens, M.G., Halloran, M.E.: Toward causal inference with interference. J. Am. Stat. Assoc. **103**(482), 832–842 (2008)
10. Jin, D., Huo, C., Liang, C., Yang, L.: Heterogeneous graph neural network via attribute completion. In: Proceedings of the Web Conference 2021, pp. 391–400 (2021)
11. Johansson, F., Shalit, U., Sontag, D.: Learning representations for counterfactual inference. In: Proceedings of the 33rd International Conference on Machine Learning, vol. 48, pp. 3020–3029 (2016)
12. Kipf, T.N., Welling, M.: Semi-supervised classification with graph convolutional networks. In: International Conference on Learning Representations (2017)
13. Li, Q., Wang, Z., Liu, S., Li, G., Xu, G.: Deep treatment-adaptive network for causal inference. Int. J. Very Large Data Bases **31**(5), 1127–1142 (2022)
14. Liang, X., Ma, Y., Cheng, G., Fan, C., Yang, Y., Liu, Z.: Meta-path-based heterogeneous graph neural networks in academic network. Int. J. Mach. Learn. Cybern. **13**(6), 1553–1569 (2022)
15. Liu, L., Hudgens, M.G.: Large sample randomization inference of causal effects in the presence of interference. J. Am. Stat. Assoc. **109**(505), 288–301 (2014)

16. Ma, J., Wan, M., Yang, L., Li, J., Hecht, B., Teevan, J.: Learning causal effects on hypergraphs. In: Proceedings of the 28th ACM SIGKDD Conference on Knowledge Discovery and Data Mining, pp. 1202–1212 (2022)
17. Ma, Y., Tresp, V.: Causal inference under networked interference and intervention policy enhancement. In: Proceedings of the 24th International Conference on Artificial Intelligence and Statistics, vol. 130, pp. 3700–3708 (2021)
18. Nabi, R., Pfeiffer, J., Charles, D., Kıcıman, E.: Causal inference in the presence of interference in sponsored search advertising. Front. Big Data **5**, 888592 (2022)
19. Qu, M., Tang, J., Shang, J., Ren, X., Zhang, M., Han, J.: An attention-based collaboration framework for multi-view network representation learning. In: Proceedings of the 2017 ACM on Conference on Information and Knowledge Management, pp. 1767–1776 (2017)
20. Qu, Z., Xiong, R., Liu, J., Imbens, G.: Efficient treatment effect estimation in observational studies under heterogeneous partial interference. arXiv preprint arXiv:2107.12420 (2021)
21. Rakesh, V., Guo, R., Moraffah, R., Agarwal, N., Liu, H.: Linked causal variational autoencoder for inferring paired spillover effects. In: Proceedings of the 27th ACM International Conference on Information and Knowledge Management, pp. 1679–1682 (2018)
22. Raudenbush, S.W., Schwartz, D.: Randomized experiments in education, with implications for multilevel causal inference. Annu. Rev. Stat. Appl. **7**(1), 177–208 (2020)
23. Rosenbaum, P.R., Rubin, D.B.: The central role of the propensity score in observational studies for causal effects. Biometrika **70**(1), 41–55 (1983)
24. Rubin, D.B.: Randomization analysis of experimental data: the fisher randomization test comment. J. Am. Stat. Assoc. **75**(371), 591–593 (1980)
25. Schnitzer, M.E.: Estimands and estimation of COVID-19 vaccine effectiveness under the test-negative design: connections to causal inference. Epidemiology **33**(3), 325 (2022)
26. Shalit, U., Johansson, F.D., Sontag, D.: Estimating individual treatment effect: generalization bounds and algorithms. In: Proceedings of the 34th International Conference on Machine Learning, vol. 70, pp. 3076–3085 (2017)
27. Shi, C., Ding, J., Cao, X., Hu, L., Wu, B., Li, X.: Entity set expansion in knowledge graph: a heterogeneous information network perspective. Front. Comp. Sci. **15**(1), 1–12 (2021)
28. Song, Y., Yang, X., Xu, C.: Self-supervised calorie-aware heterogeneous graph networks for food recommendation. ACM Trans. Multimedia Comput. Commun. Appl. **19**, 1–23 (2022)
29. Sun, W., Wang, P., Yin, D., Yang, J., Chang, Y.: Causal inference via sparse additive models with application to online advertising. In: Proceedings of the 29th AAAI Conference on Artificial Intelligence, pp. 297–303 (2015)
30. Tang, L., Wang, X., Liu, H.: Uncovering groups via heterogeneous interaction analysis. In: Proceedings of IEEE International Conference on Data Mining, pp. 503–512 (2009)
31. Tang, L., Wang, X., Liu, H.: Uncovernng groups via heterogeneous interaction analysis. In: 2009 Ninth IEEE International Conference on Data Mining, pp. 503–512. IEEE (2009)
32. Tchetgen, E.J.T., VanderWeele, T.J.: On causal inference in the presence of interference. Stat. Methods Med. Res. **21**(1), 55–75 (2012)
33. Tchetgen Tchetgen, E.J., Fulcher, I.R., Shpitser, I.: Auto-G-Computation of causal effects on a network. J. Am. Stat. Assoc. **116**(534), 833–844 (2021)

34. Vaswani, A., et al.: Attention is all you need. In: Advances in Neural Information Processing Systems, vol. 30 (2017)
35. Veličković, P., Cucurull, G., Casanova, A., Romero, A., Liò, P., Bengio, Y.: Graph attention networks. In: Proceedings of the 6th International Conference on Learning Representations (2018)
36. Viviano, D.: Policy targeting under network interference. arXiv preprint arXiv:1906.10258 (2019)
37. Wang, P., Sun, W., Yin, D., Yang, J., Chang, Y.: Robust tree-based causal inference for complex ad effectiveness analysis. In: Proceedings of the 8th ACM International Conference on Web Search and Data Mining, pp. 67–76 (2015)
38. Wang, X., Bo, D., Shi, C., Fan, S., Ye, Y., Philip, S.Y.: A survey on heterogeneous graph embedding: methods, techniques, applications and sources. IEEE Trans. Big Data 9(2), 415–436 (2022)
39. Wang, X., et al.: Heterogeneous graph attention network. In: Proceedings of the 2019 World Wide Web Conference, pp. 2022–2032 (2019)
40. Wang, X., Tang, L., Liu, H., Wang, L.: Learning with multi-resolution overlapping communities. Knowl. Inf. Syst. 36, 517–535 (2013)
41. Welling, M., Kipf, T.N.: Semi-supervised classification with graph convolutional networks. In: Proceedings of the 4th International Conference on Learning Representations (2016)
42. Yao, L., Chu, Z., Li, S., Li, Y., Gao, J., Zhang, A.: A survey on causal inference. ACM Trans. Knowl. Discov. Data 15(5), 1–46 (2021)
43. Yao, L., Li, S., Li, Y., Huai, M., Gao, J., Zhang, A.: Representation learning for treatment effect estimation from observational data. In: Advances in Neural Information Processing Systems, vol. 31 (2018)
44. Zhang, C., Song, D., Huang, C., Swami, A., Chawla, N.V.: Heterogeneous graph neural network. In: Proceedings of the 25th ACM SIGKDD International Conference on Knowledge Discovery & Data Mining, pp. 793–803 (2019)
45. Zhao, J., Wang, X., Shi, C., Hu, B., Song, G., Ye, Y.: Heterogeneous graph structure learning for graph neural networks. In: Proceedings of the 35th AAAI Conference on Artificial Intelligence, vol. 35, pp. 4697–4705 (2021)
46. Zhao, Z., Kuang, K., Xiong, R., Wu, F.: Learning individual treatment effects under heterogeneous interference in networks. arXiv preprint arXiv:2210.14080 (2022)

Regularization for Uplift Regression

Krzysztof Rudaś[1,2]([✉]) [iD] and Szymon Jaroszewicz[1,2] [iD]

[1] Institute of Computer Science, Polish Academy of Sciences, Warsaw, Poland
[2] Faculty of Mathematics and Information Science,
Warsaw University of Technology, Warsaw, Poland
`krzysztof.rudas@ipipan.waw.pl`

Abstract. We address the problem of regularization of linear regression models in uplift modeling and heterogeneous treatment effect estimation. We consider interaction models which are commonly used by statisticians in medicine and social sciences to estimate the causal effect of a treatment, and introduce a new type of such a model. We demonstrate the equivalence of all interaction models when no regularization is present, and that this is no longer the case when the model is regularized. Interaction terms introduce implicit correlations between treatment and control coefficients into the regularizer, a fact which has not been previously noted. The correlations depend on the type of interaction model, and by interpreting the regularizer as a prior distribution we were able to pinpoint cases when a given regularized interaction model is most appropriate. An interesting property of the proposed new interaction type is that it allows for smooth interpolation between two types of uplift regression models: the double model and the transformed target model. Our results are valid for both ridge (L_2) and Lasso (L_1) regularization. Experiments on synthetic data fully confirm our analyses. We also compare the usefulness of various regularization schemes on real data.

Keywords: uplift modeling · heterogeneous treatment effect · regularization · linear models · Lasso

1 Introduction

Uplift modeling is a method of selecting targets for an action, such as a marketing campaign or a medical treatment. To clarify the problem, consider the following example. We administer a factory which produces a certain kind of product i.e. skis. In order to increase our income we send discounts to potential customers. Consider three kinds of customers. The first kind decides to buy skis, *because* they received a discount (without the discount they wouldn't have bought). The second kind decides to not buy skis and sending the discount had no effect. Customers of the third kind bought the skis but would have bought even without the discount. For us it is profitable to send the discount only to the customers of the first kind, but not to the second (no profits) and especially not to the third (lost income due to sale at a lower price). A typical approach to solving

D. Koutra et al. (Eds.): ECML PKDD 2023, LNAI 14169, pp. 593–608, 2023.
https://doi.org/10.1007/978-3-031-43412-9_35

the problem of choosing appropriate targets for an action is to predict results after conducting a pilot campaign on a sample of the customers. If the predicted income is above a given threshold, the observation is classified as suitable for the action. However this approach in not correct because it doesn't take into consideration the counterfactual response in case the action would not have been taken. The three groups of customers cannot be distinguished.

In uplift modeling our goal is to predict, for the i-th observation, the difference of responses y_i^T when action was taken on it, and y_i^C when the action was not taken. Unfortunately we cannot directly compare those two outcomes, because we observe only one of them. This is known as the *Fundamental Problem of Causal Inference* [10].

Uplift modeling offers a solution of this problem. In this method we divide our population into two groups: treatment on which the action is taken, and control, which is not subjected to the action. Thanks to this we may decompose the effect observed in the treatment group into two parts. The first is the background (control) outcome and the second is the influence of the action which is only observed in the treatment group. Using this decomposition we may construct a model which will estimate the true effect of an action on an individual.

1.1 Related Work

Uplift modeling is a part of a broader problem of causal discovery, concentrating not on predicting future responses, but on effects of interventions, which may be dependent on the values of other variables [23]. Causal discovery has two major branches. The first uses purely observational data [23,30]. In the second, the action being analyzed has to be actively applied to a subgroup of individuals. Those methods have many applications in social science and medicine [12].

Methods presented in this paper are relevant to the second approach. Most research in this area focuses on cases when the treatment group is not selected randomly, i.e. the treatment assignment mechanism is biased [7,12]. Those methods typically come under the name of Heterogeneous Treatment Effect estimation [1,9]. Unfortunately those approaches (e.g. propensity score matching or weighting) are based on untestable assumptions like 'no unmeasured confounders'. The main focus of those methods is to correct the assignment bias not on the estimation problem itself. Uplift modeling, in contrast, concentrates on finding the best possible estimator under random assignment assumptions, which guarantee that the causal effect of the action is identified correctly.

Most of publications on uplift modeling concentrate on the classification problem. First works were based on decision trees [25,29]. They modified splitting criteria in order to maximize difference in responses between two groups. Similar methods have been invented under the name of estimating heterogeneous treatment effect [1,9]. Several publications use modified response variable [13,14,18] with linear models with such as logistic regression or Support Vector Machines [17,31,32]. Estimators for regression problem where analyzed in [27], where basic double regression approach is confronted with some new ideas. Another way of improving on double regression is using shrinkage estimators such as those proposed in [28].

Regression models with interaction terms have been used for causal prediction for decades, see [12, Chap. 7.6] or [7, Chap. 15]. The majority of works use treatment interaction models described in the next section.

There are currently few works devoted specifically to the problem of regularization in uplift modeling or heterogeneous treatment effect estimation. The main textbook on causal effect modeling [12] only discusses the Lasso method for variable selection on one page, and another [7] mentions the term 'regularization' only twice.

There are a few papers which introduce regularized uplift models but do not thoroughly analyze the problem. Imai et al. [11] proposed an SVM model for treatment effect estimation which used the Lasso penalty. This is in fact a variant of a regularized treatment interaction model, frequently used in literature. In [5] a Lasso style model for uplift regression has been introduced, inspired by multitask learning. The proposed model is similar to the models analyzed in this work but includes interaction terms for both treatment and control making it overparametrized which may lead to estimation problems. A similar approach called Shared Data Representation was presented in [3].

The problem of regularization has been addressed by several authors working on nonrandomized treatment assignment. In [22] fused lasso was applied to regularize propensity scores. Hahn et al. [6] discussed pitfalls of regularizing causal models under non-random treatment assignment. Chernozhukov [2] addressed the problem of variable selection for instrumental variables and confounding controls. The goals of those works are different from ours, since we focus on predictive accuracy in the case of randomized treatment assignment.

1.2 Notation

In the text, lowercase Latin and Greek letters denote vectors, uppercase letters: matrices. Let $'$ denote matrix transpose, I_p a $p \times p$ identity matrix, 0 the matrix of zeros of appropriate size, and $\otimes$ the Kronecker product of matrices. All vectors will be assumed to be column vectors, except the feature vectors, denoted with letter x, assumed to be row vectors.

We assume to have a training set of n samples, with i-th sample being a triple (x_i, y_i, t_i), where $x_i \in \mathbb{R}^p$ is a p-dimensional feature vector, $y_i \in \mathbb{R}$ the response, and $t_i \in \{0, 1\}$ the treatment indicator, where $t_i = 1$ means that the i-th case is in the experimental group (was subjected to the action) and $t_i = 0$ indicates a control case.

Quantities related to the treatment group will be denoted with superscript T and to the control group with superscript C. The superscript U will indicate quantities related to the estimated uplift, i.e. the effect of the action. For example, n^T (n^C) denotes the number of cases in the treatment (control) group. We will make the usual assumptions taken when working with linear models, namely, that the treatment and control responses are linear functions of the predictors [8]

$$
y_i = \begin{cases} x_i \beta^C + \varepsilon_i & \text{if } t_i = 0 \\ x_i \beta^T + \varepsilon_i = x_i \beta^C + x_i \beta^U + \varepsilon_i & \text{if } t_i = 1, \end{cases} \tag{1}
$$

where β^T and β^C are the true coefficient vectors for treatment and control cases, and ε_i are independent random error terms with equal variances and $E \varepsilon_i = 0$.

Notice that for treatment cases the response is the sum of control response $x_i \beta^C$ and the effect of the action $x_i \beta^U$. Clearly, $\beta^U = \beta^T - \beta^C$ is the parameter of interest we want to estimate. We also introduce a vector $\beta^S = \beta^T + \beta^C$ such that $\frac{1}{2} x_i \beta^S$ is the average of treatment and control responses for a case x_i.

Finally, let us introduce a matrix $X^T \in \mathbb{R}^{n^T \times p}$ whose rows are feature vectors of treatment cases, and a vector $y^T \in \mathbb{R}^{n^T}$ of corresponding responses. For the control group, X^C and y^C are defined analogously. The pairs (X^T, y^T), (X^C, y^C) can be interpreted as two separate treatment and control training sets.

2   Linear Models of Causal Influence

In this section we describe basic types of linear models used to estimate causal effects and demonstrate their equivalence. Here we assume that the models do not use regularization, which will be discussed in the next section.

2.1   The Double Model

The most common approach to uplift regression is the so called *double model* [27], denoted as D. The model is also known as the T-learner [16]. To estimate β^U, the model simply subtracts the coefficient vectors estimated separately on the treatment and control samples: $\hat{\beta}^U = \hat{\beta}^T - \hat{\beta}^C$, where both sub-estimators are obtained by minimizing some loss function ℓ, such as square loss:

$$\hat{\beta}^T = \arg \min_\beta \sum_{i=1}^{n^T} \ell(y_i^T, x_i^T \beta), \quad \hat{\beta}^C = \arg \min_\beta \sum_{i=1}^{n^C} \ell(y_i^C, x_i^C \beta). \quad (2)$$

Let us rewrite the double model as a single regression model. Define an $n \times 2p$ matrix $\tilde{X}$ and coefficient vector $\tilde{\beta} \in \mathbb{R}^{2p}$ as

$$\tilde{X} = \begin{bmatrix} X^T & 0 \\ 0 & X^C \end{bmatrix}, \qquad \tilde{\beta} = \begin{bmatrix} \beta^T \\ \beta^C \end{bmatrix}, \quad (3)$$

and let $\tilde{x}_i$ denote the i-th row of X. It is easy to see that estimating $\tilde{\beta}$ by minimizing

$$\sum_{i=1}^{n} \ell(y_i, \tilde{x}_i \tilde{\beta}) \quad (4)$$

is equivalent to Eq. 2.

2.2   Interaction Models

In medicine and social sciences casual effects are often estimated using so called *interaction models*. A single regression model is build on combined treatment and control data. The model includes a special interaction term which allows for estimating the causal effect's coefficients β^U. We now discuss several such models.

Treatment Interaction Model (TI). The most common approach [11] is to use an interaction between treatment indicator and all predictor variables, resulting in a model based on the following assumption

$$y_i = t_i x_i \beta^U + x_i \beta^C + \varepsilon_i. \tag{5}$$

The coefficient β^C describes the responses in the control group. Since $x_i \beta^C$ is also present in the treatment group, $x_i \beta^U$ has to represent the effect of the treatment. We call this model the *treatment interaction model* because the interaction involves the treatment indicator. Later in the text the model will be denoted with abbreviation TI.

It is easy to see that the model can be represented with a single regression model whose design matrix and coefficient vector are

$$\begin{bmatrix} X^T & X^T \\ 0 & X^C \end{bmatrix}, \quad \begin{bmatrix} \beta^U \\ \beta^C \end{bmatrix}, \tag{6}$$

respectively. While this is the most common interaction model, other approaches are also possible.

Symmetric Interaction Model (SI). Let us now introduce another interaction model which is one of the contributions of this paper

$$y_i = \left(t_i - \tfrac{1}{2}\right) x_i \beta^U + \tfrac{1}{2} x_i \beta^S + \varepsilon_i. \tag{7}$$

The model uses so called effect or deviation coding of the categorical treatment variable, see [8, Sect. 10.8] or [4, Sect. 2.3.2]. The interpretation is that $\tfrac{1}{2} x_i \beta^S$ is the average of treated and control outcomes for case x_i, and $\pm \tfrac{1}{2} x_i \beta^U$ is the difference from the mean for control/treatment response. The design matrix and coefficient vector for the corresponding single regression model are

$$\tfrac{1}{2} \begin{bmatrix} X^T & X^T \\ -X^C & X^C \end{bmatrix}, \quad \begin{bmatrix} \beta^U \\ \beta^S \end{bmatrix}. \tag{8}$$

Some advantages of this model, such as lack of correlations in the prior and a relationship with a model based on target variable transformation will be discussed in the following sections.

The model is called the *symmetric interaction model* since the indicators for treatment and control groups are treated in a symmetric fashion.

Table 1. Summary of linear interaction models analyzed in the paper

Model	Double (D)	Treatment Interaction (TI)	Symmetric Interaction (SI)	Control Interaction (CI)
Form	$t_i \beta^T x_i$ $+ (1-t_i)\beta^C x_i$	$t_i \beta^U x_i + \beta^C x_i$	$(t_i - \tfrac{1}{2}) x_i \beta^U$ $+ \tfrac{1}{2} x_i \beta^S$	$- (1-t_i)\beta^U x$ $+ \beta^T x$
Design matrix	$\begin{bmatrix} X^T & 0 \\ 0 & X^C \end{bmatrix}, \begin{bmatrix} \beta^T \\ \beta^C \end{bmatrix}$	$\begin{bmatrix} X^T & X^T \\ 0 & X^C \end{bmatrix}, \begin{bmatrix} \beta^U \\ \beta^C \end{bmatrix}$	$\tfrac{1}{2}\begin{bmatrix} X^T & X^T \\ -X^C & X^C \end{bmatrix}, \begin{bmatrix} \beta^U \\ \beta^S \end{bmatrix}$	$\begin{bmatrix} 0 & X^T \\ -X^C & X^C \end{bmatrix}, \begin{bmatrix} \beta^U \\ \beta^T \end{bmatrix}$
Matrix $\tilde{A}$	$\begin{bmatrix} 1 & 0 \\ 0 & 1 \end{bmatrix}$	$\begin{bmatrix} 1 & 1 \\ 0 & 1 \end{bmatrix}$	$\sqrt{2}\begin{bmatrix} \tfrac{1}{2} & \tfrac{1}{2} \\ -\tfrac{1}{2} & \tfrac{1}{2} \end{bmatrix}$	$\begin{bmatrix} 0 & 1 \\ -1 & 1 \end{bmatrix}$
Regularizer	$\lambda_1 \|\beta^T\| + \lambda_2 \|\beta^C\|$	$\lambda_1 \|\beta^U\| + \lambda_2 \|\beta^C\|$	$\lambda_1 \|\beta^U\| + \lambda_2 \|\beta^S\|$	$\lambda_1 \|\beta^U\| + \lambda_2 \|\beta^T\|$

Control Interaction Model (CI). For completeness we also introduce a model with interaction between the control group indicator and x's, although we have never seen this model used in literature:

$$y_i = \beta^T x_i - (1 - t_i)\beta^U x_i + \varepsilon_i. \tag{9}$$

Here we estimate the treatment response for all cases, and correct for the strength of causal influence in the control group.

All proposed models are summarized in Table 1. The first row displays the models' names and abbreviations. The following rows provide the models' formulas, design matrices and coefficient vectors. The remaining rows will be explained in the next section.

2.3   Unified Representation of Interaction Models

In this section we aim to unify all interaction models and demonstrate their equivalence. The theorem below shows that when no regularization is present all interaction models are in fact statistically equivalent with the double model and, as a consequence, with each other.

Theorem 1. *There is a one-to-one mapping between treatment interaction models and double models such that the corresponding models have identical values of the training set losses and provide the same estimates of β^U. An analogous result holds for symmetric and control interaction models.*

Proof. Recall that the double model (Eq. 2) can be recast as a single model (Eq. 2) trained on the matrix $\tilde{X}$ given in Eq. 3, leading to an optimization problem given in Eq. 4. For any nonsingular $2p \times 2p$ matrix A we have

$$\sum_{i=1}^{n} \ell(y_i, \tilde{x}_i \tilde{\beta}) = \sum_{i=1}^{n} \ell\left(y_i, (\tilde{x}_i A)(A^{-1}\tilde{\beta})\right). \tag{10}$$

So, for a given double model, multiplying the feature vectors and the coefficient vector respectively by A and A^{-1} does not change the predicted value and thus yields a model with the same empirical risk. This is a direct consequence of the so called affine equivariance of classic least squares linear models [26, p. 116].

Take A to be

$$\begin{bmatrix} 1 & 1 \\ 0 & 1 \end{bmatrix} \otimes I_p = \begin{bmatrix} I_p & I_p \\ 0_p & I_p \end{bmatrix},$$

and apply Eq. 10 to each row of the design matrix. We have

$$\tilde{X}A = \begin{bmatrix} X^T & 0 \\ 0 & X^C \end{bmatrix} \begin{bmatrix} I_p & I_p \\ 0_p & I_p \end{bmatrix} = \begin{bmatrix} X^T & X^T \\ 0 & X^C \end{bmatrix},$$

and after left-multiplying $\tilde{\beta}$ by A^{-1}

$$A^{-1}\tilde{\beta} = \left(\begin{bmatrix} 1 & -1 \\ 0 & 1 \end{bmatrix} \otimes I_p\right) \begin{bmatrix} \beta^T \\ \beta^C \end{bmatrix} = \begin{bmatrix} \beta^T - \beta^C \\ \beta^C \end{bmatrix} = \begin{bmatrix} \beta^U \\ \beta^C \end{bmatrix},$$

which is the design matrix and coefficient vector defining the treatment interaction model (Eq. 6). Thus, the matrix A defines a linear mapping between the double and treatment interaction models such that the corresponding models have the same empirical risk. The fact that the correspondence is one-to-one follows from nonsingularity of matrix A. As a result, both types of models lead to the same empirical risk minimizer and the same estimate of β^U.

To obtain an analogous mapping for symmetric interaction model use the matrix $A = \begin{bmatrix} \frac{1}{2} & \frac{1}{2} \\ -\frac{1}{2} & \frac{1}{2} \end{bmatrix} \otimes I_p$, and for the control interaction model, the matrix $A = \begin{bmatrix} 0 & 1 \\ -1 & 1 \end{bmatrix} \otimes I_p$.

To show the equivalence between two types of interaction models, consider mapping models of the first type to the double model and than to the interaction model of the second type. Equivalence follows from the fact that the composition of one-to-one mappings is one-to-one. □

A consequence of the theorem is that, when no regularization is used, all interaction models and the double model are essentially equivalent from the statistical perspective: they provide identical estimates and the same predictions on future data. A generic estimation procedure for interaction models can thus be implemented conceptually as follows

1. Form the matrix $\tilde{X}$
2. Compute the matrix $\tilde{X}A$
3. Obtain an estimate $\hat{\beta}$ based on $\tilde{X}A$ and y
4. Compute $\hat{\beta}^U = [I_p| - I_p]A^{-1}\hat{\beta}$

In the last step above, we first transform $\hat{\beta}$ into $(\hat{\beta}^T, \hat{\beta}^C)$ and then multiply it by $[I_p| - I_p]$ to obtain $\hat{\beta}^U = \hat{\beta}^T - \hat{\beta}^C$.

Notice that all transformation matrices used in the proof have the form

$$A = \tilde{A} \otimes I_p$$

for some 2×2 matrix $\tilde{A}$. The third row of Table 1 lists the matrices $\tilde{A}$ for all considered interaction models. The matrix for the symmetric interaction model has an additional $\sqrt{2}$ factor. This factor cancels out in Eq. 10 and in step 4 of the above procedure, so it will not affect the final estimate. The reason for its introduction is explained in the next section.

3 Regularized Interaction Models

In the previous section we showed that all unregularized interaction models are equivalent. We will now show that when regularization is present, this will no longer be the case. Our analysis will be valid for all regularizers based on L_q norms raised to the power q, but later we will focus on L_1 and L_2 norms.

The most obvious way to regularize the double model is to separately regularize the estimators for β^T and β^C thus minimizing the following cost function

$$\sum_{i=1}^{n} \ell(y, \tilde{x}_i \tilde{\beta}) + \lambda_1 \|\beta^T\|_q^q + \lambda_2 \|\beta^C\|_q^q = \sum_{i=1}^{n} \ell(y, \tilde{x}_i \tilde{\beta}) + \left\| \begin{bmatrix} \sqrt[q]{\lambda_1} & 0 \\ 0 & \sqrt[q]{\lambda_2} \end{bmatrix} \tilde{\beta} \right\|_q^q. \quad (11)$$

For the interaction models, all approaches in literature apply regularization directly to coefficient vectors present in the model. The fourth row of Table 1 lists the form of the regularizer for each type of model considered in the paper.

For example, in the treatment interaction model we separately regularize β^U and β^C. This scheme looks appealing since we directly regularize the quantity of interest, which is β^U. However, this type of regularization introduces unexpected interactions between the two regularized vectors. For example, letting $\lambda_2 \to \infty$ does not just influence the estimate of β^C. The estimate of β^U is also affected: regularization will force $\beta^C \to 0$ and, as a result, β^U will tend towards β^T.

We will now analyze those issues further and provide guidelines on the scenarios where different types of regularized interaction models are most useful.

As we have seen above in Eq. 10, every interaction model can be expressed as a linear transformation of the double model with an appropriately chosen nonsingular matrix A. Using this fact and Eq. 11, every regularized interaction model can be expressed as

$$\sum_{i=1}^{n} \ell \left(y, (\tilde{x}_i A)(A^{-1}\tilde{\beta}) \right) + \left\| \Lambda_q A^{-1} \tilde{\beta} \right\|_q^q, \quad (12)$$

where $\Lambda_q = \begin{bmatrix} \sqrt[q]{\lambda_1} & 0 \\ 0 & \sqrt[q]{\lambda_2} \end{bmatrix}$. Here the regularization is applied to the transformed coefficient vector $A^{-1}\tilde{\beta}$. Since A^{-1} does not cancel within the regularization term, the model is no longer invariant under linear transformations, and therefore different interaction models will lead to different regularization terms.

The equation demonstrates one of the main claims of the paper: regularized interaction models are equivalent to the double model regularized with a penalty based on a linear transformation of a unit sphere determined by the type of interaction model used.

Indeed, let us now analyze the generic regularizer by looking at the shape of the contours of its regularization regions. The contours are the sets of points

$$\left\{ \tilde{\beta} : \left\| \Lambda_q A^{-1} \tilde{\beta} \right\|_q = r \right\}, \quad (13)$$

where $r > 0$ is a positive constant defining the contour. Substituting $\beta = \Lambda_q A^{-1} \tilde{\beta}$ the contour equation becomes

$$\left\{ A\Lambda_q^{-1} \beta : \|\beta\|_q = r \right\}. \quad (14)$$

Therefore the contour is a linear transform of an L_q norm sphere of radius r. The shape of the contour will depend on the transformation matrix $A\Lambda_q^{-1}$.

Before providing a detailed analysis of the regularizers, let us first address the question of scaling of the regularization parameters λ_1, λ_2. It would be desirable if the same values of those parameters led to regularization regions of identical size regardless of the type of interaction model used. Here, we chose to measure the size of regularization contours by the volume they enclose. Let $V_q(r, p)$ be the volume of an L_q norm p-dimensional sphere of radius r. Since the regularization regions are linear transformations of such spheres their volume is

$$\left| \det \left(A\Lambda_q^{-1} \right) \right| V_q(r, p) = |\det(A)| \det \left(\Lambda_q^{-1} \right) V_q(r, p). \tag{15}$$

The equation follows since the Jacobian matrix of a linear transformation is constant. Notice that the type of interaction only affects the matrix A which has the form $\tilde{A} \otimes I_p$, and whose determinant is $\det^p(\tilde{A}) \det(I_p)^2 = \det^p(\tilde{A})$ [24]. Notice that $|\det(\tilde{A})| = 1$ for all matrices $\tilde{A}$ given in Table 1, so the volume of the regularization regions will not depend on the type of interaction model used, only on the values of λ_1, λ_2. To ensure this property, an additional $\sqrt{2}$ factor was added to the symmetric interaction model's design matrix.

3.1 Interpretation of Regularized Interaction Models

In order to give an intuition and visualize those contours we restrict ourselves to the one variable case $p = 1$. The two coefficient vectors now become scalars which can be visualized on a two dimensional plot. Figure 1 shows regularization regions for $r = 1$ (unit sphere being transformed) and selected values of λ_1 and λ_2 parameters for the four types of models given in Table 1. The corresponding figure for the L_2 norm is given in the supplementary materials[1]: it gives the same overall picture with polygons replaced by ellipses. Supplementary materials also include an illustrative figure with superimposed regions for different methods.

The main axes of the plots correspond to coefficients β^T and β^C. Additionally we introduce two more diagonal axes corresponding to β^U and β^S respectively, such that it is possible to see how the parameter of interest β^U is regularized. It can be seen (supplementary material) the for the L_2 norm, the regularization regions are ellipsoids whose main axes do not necessarily align with the main axes of the plot. For the L_1 norm the shapes are analogues of ellipsoids in that norm.

Equivalently, we can view the regularizers from a Bayesian perspective as prior distributions. For the L_2 norm the prior will be Gaussian but with a non-spherical covariance matrix; that is we assume a-priori, that parameter vectors are correlated. In other words we assume some combinations of values of parameters vectors to be more likely than others. For the L_1 norm the prior is a form of multivariate Laplace distribution which, to the best of our knowledge, has not been analyzed in literature.[2] Nevertheless, correlation patterns are clearly visible. Let us now discuss the priors of the four types of regularized models.

---

[1] https://github.com/RudasKAP/ECML_PKDD_2023_supplementary.

[2] The most popular definition of the multivariate Laplace distribution is based on the square root of a quadratic form, see e.g. [15].

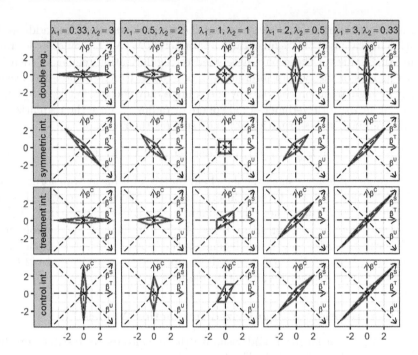

Fig. 1. Regularization regions in L_1 norm, for different types of estimators and different parameters λ_1, λ_2 for $p = 1$

Table 2. Scenarios in which different interaction models match the true coefficients

	Scenario	Condition	Estimator			
			D	SI	TI	CI
1.	$\beta^S \approx 0$; β^T, β^C large	$\beta^T \approx -\beta^C$		✓		
2.	$\beta^T \approx 0$; β^U, β^C large	$\beta^U \approx -\beta^C$	✓			✓
3.	$\beta^C \approx 0$; β^U, β^T large	$\beta^U \approx \beta^T$	✓		✓	
4.	$\beta^U \approx 0$; β^T, β^C large	$\beta^T \approx \beta^C$		✓	✓	✓

First, it can be seen that the regularized double model does not assume a-priori correlation between β^T and β^C. More interestingly the symmetric interaction model does not assume correlation between β^U and β^S. We believe this property to be important in practice, since the parameter of interest β^U is not affected by the other regularization term. In other words the average response β^S can be regularized with arbitrary strength without affecting β^U. Out of all four models, this is the *only one* possessing this property.

On the other hand the TI and CI models assume a-priori correlations between the true uplift β^U and other coefficients. For example, in the TI model β^U is assumed to be positively correlated with β^T and β^S.

3.2 Applicability Scenarios for Regularized Interaction Models

Let us now examine scenarios in which various types of regularized interaction models are likely to yield the most accurate predictive models. We confirm those arguments experimentally in the next section.

We assume that the regularization (or equivalently prior distribution) gives the best results if it corresponds to the true values of the estimated parameters. Table 2 lists several such scenarios and indicates which models are appropriate for them. The third column gives the condition describing the region to which the parameters belong.

For example, in Scenario 1, the average of treatment and control responses for a given feature vector x is close to zero, while treatment and control responses are relatively large. This implies $\beta^T \approx -\beta^C$ and the true parameters lie in the upper left and lower right corners in the plots in Fig. 1. Looking at the figure it can be seen that only the symmetric interaction model (SI) is able to provide a prior matching those areas (the first chart in the second row in the figure). Other models can only achieve this by significantly decreasing the overall regularization strength.

Similar arguments can be used to pinpoint models most suitable in other scenarios in Table 2. From the practical point of view the most important are Scenarios 3 and 4, which correspond, respectively, to low control response and small effect of the action. The treatment interaction model is able to cover both those cases which may explain its popularity in literature.

Notice also that when both $\beta^T, \beta^C \approx 0$ all models should provide effective regularization.

3.3 Relationship Between Symmetric Interaction Model and Transformed Target Variable Regression

In [27] a different estimator for treatment effect coefficients has been proposed, which works by concatenating the treatment and control training sets and building a single regression model on a transformed target variable

$$\bar{y}_i = \begin{cases} 2y_i & \text{if } t_i = 1, \\ -2y_i & \text{if } t_i = 0. \end{cases}$$

Theorem 2. *When $n^T = n^C$, the square loss is used, and $\lambda_2 \to \infty$ with λ_1 held fixed, the symmetric interaction model (SI) tends to the variable transformation model regularized with $4\lambda_1 \|\beta^U\|_q^q$.*

The proof can be found in the supplementary material.

4   Experimental Evaluation

In this section let n_{test} denote the number of test cases, x_{test_i} the feature vector of i-th test case and τ_i the true uplift for the i-th test case, i.e. the difference between potential outcome has case i been subjected to the action and the potential outcome has case i been a control. This value is available only for synthetic data since in real data only one of the outcomes is observed [10].

4.1 Evaluation of Uplift Regression Models

We first need to discuss the issue of evaluation of uplift regression models. A natural choice is the Mean Squared Error $MSE(\hat{\beta}^U) = \frac{1}{n_{test}} \sum_{i=1}^{n_{test}} (\tau_i - x_{test_i}\hat{\beta}^U)^2$. Unfortunately, τ_i is unknown for real data so there is a need for an alternative measure. We therefore propose a measure for evaluating uplift regression models which we call *by quantile MSE* or QMSE for short. This measure is similar to *expected uplift calibration error (EUCE)* proposed in [21], except that squared loss is used instead of absolute value. The measure is calculated as follows.

Let X_{test}^T and X_{test}^C be the treatment and control test sets. Compute the corresponding vectors of model predictions $X_{test}^T\hat{\beta}^U$, $X_{test}^C\hat{\beta}^U$. The vectors are sorted and split into J quantiles (10 in our case). Let Q_j^T and Q_j^C denote the indices of, respectively, treatment and control test records in the j-th treatment or, respectively, control quantile. Compute the MSE within j-th quantile as

$$MSE_j(\hat{\beta}^U) = \frac{1}{n_j^T} \sum_{i \in Q_j^T} \left(x_{test_i}\hat{\beta}^U - \left(\frac{1}{n_j^T} \sum_{i \in Q_j^T} y_i - \frac{1}{n_j^C} \sum_{i \in Q_j^C} y_i \right) \right)^2,$$

where n_j^T and n_j^C are the number of treatment and control records in the j-th quantile. The final QMSE measure is $QMSE(\hat{\beta}^U) = \frac{1}{J} \sum_{i=1}^J MSE_j(\hat{\beta}^U)$.

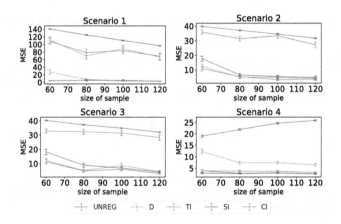

Fig. 2. MSE of estimators with L_1 penalty under different simulation scenarios

4.2 Synthetic Data

In this section we evaluate regularized uplift regression estimators on synthetic data. We begin by describing the experimental procedure.

For a given number of columns ($p = 160$) we generated random predictor matrices X with increasing number of rows. For L_1 regularization we used $n \in \{60, 80, 100, 120\}$ and for L_2 regularization $n \in \{180, 200, 250, 500\}$. The reason was that L_1 regularization is supposed to work better when $p > n$ and L_2 regularization when $n > p$. Each row x_i of X is generated from the multivariate normal distribution with zero mean and unit covariance matrix. Each sample is assigned to the treatment or control group at random but with fixed group proportions $\frac{n^T}{n} = \frac{n^C}{n} = \frac{1}{2}$. The outcome variables are then generated based on Eq. 1 with $\varepsilon_i \sim \mathcal{N}(0, 1)$. $n_{test} = 10\,000$ was used with identical data generation mechanism.

Regularized models require the choice of regularization parameter values. In our case we use 3-fold crossvalidation and select all regularization parameters from the set $\{10^{-3}, 10^{-2}, 10^{-1}, 1, 10\}$ for both λ_1 and λ_2.

Since τ_i is known for simulated data, we use the classic MSE criterion to assess model performance. Parameter selection is still performed based on $QMSE$ for consistency with experiments on real data.

In our simulations we use vectors β^C and β^U corresponding to the four scenarios presented in Table 2. The actual coefficient vectors are given in supplementary materials. We include five estimators in the comparison: the nonregularized double model (UNREG), the regularized double model (D), and three regularized interaction models: treatment interaction (TI), symmetric interaction (SI) and control interaction (CI). Note that all unregularized models are equivalent so only one of them is included.

Results for L_1 regularization are presented in Fig. 2. We observe that for the first scenario the best results are achieved by the symmetric interaction method. This is consistent with Table 2 and discussion in Sect. 3 which suggest the SI method is most suitable when values of β^S are small. Interestingly the double regularized model also performed well.

The second and third plots correspond to the situation when $\beta^T \approx 0$ and $\beta^C \approx 0$ respectively. In both cases double regularized method performs well. When $\beta^T \approx 0$ the control interaction model also attains good results, but treatment interaction model behaves badly. For $\beta^C \approx 0$ we have the opposite situation. Again, those results are in line with theoretical predictions.

The fourth plot presents the case when the action's impact (β^U) is small. All regularized methods, except the double regularized model achieve good and comparable results. This observation is again consistent with the fact that regularization regions with small values of uplift occur naturally in those methods.

Similar conclusions could be drawn from the results for L_2 regularization, which are shown in the supplementary material due to lack of space. Overall we conclude that experiments on synthetic data fully confirm theoretical analysis from Sect. 3 for both L_1 and L_2 regularized models.

4.3   Experiments on Real Data

Description of datasets. The first dataset we use is the IHDP dataset [20]. The dataset describes the results of a program whose target groups were low birth-weight infants. A randomly selected subset of them received additional support such as home visits and access to a child development center. We want to identify infants whose IQ (the target variable) increased *because* of the intervention program. There are 377 treatment and 608 control cases. We also ran experiments on the well known Lalonde dataset [19], see supplementary materials.

Results. During experiments each dataset was split into training (70%) and test parts (30%), stratified by treatment. Models are built and tuned on the training part (λ_1 and λ_2 are chosen form the same set $\{10^{-5}, 10^{-4}, 10^{-3}, 10^{-2}, 10^{-1}, 1, 10\}$) and their QMSE's are computed on the test part. To make the results easier to understand for each model we compute the difference $\delta\,\text{QMSE}$ from the best model, i.e. for a model m

$$\delta\,\text{QMSE}_m = |\,\text{QMSE}_m - \min_i \text{QMSE}_i\,|,$$

where QMSE_m is the QMSE of model m. The train/test split is repeated 100 times and box plots of $\delta\,\text{QMSE}_m$ are shown for each model. This way we can visualize in a single plot how well, each model performed relative to others.

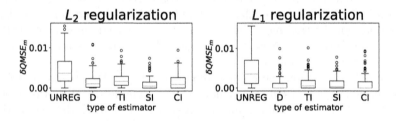

Fig. 3. Results for the IHDP dataset

Results for the IHDP dataset are presented in Fig. 3. All regularizers perform very well and beat unregularized models by a wide margin. We notice that symmetric interaction method achieves the best results out of all of L_2 regularizers. For L_1 regularization the smallest values of $\delta\,\text{QMSE}_m$ were obtained by the regularized double model. While all methods perform well in general, it is worth trying different interaction models since there is a possibility that some of them may better match true coefficient vectors.

5   Conclusions

We have analyzed the problem of regularizing uplift regression models. We have shown that the type of interaction term used has a strong influence on the corresponding prior in unexpected ways. As a result, we were able to describe scenarios where each regularized model is most useful. Experiments on simulated data fully confirm our analyses, and experiments on real data demonstrate the usefulness of regularizing interaction models.

References

1. Athey, S., Imbens, G.: Recursive partitioning for heterogeneous causal effects. Proc. Natl. Acad. Sci. **113**(27), 7353–7360 (2016)
2. Belloni, A., Chernozhukov, V., Hansen, C.: High-dimensional methods and inference on structural and treatment effects. J. Econ. Perspect. **28**(2), 1–23 (2014)
3. Betlei, A., Diemert, E., Amini, M.-R.: Uplift prediction with dependent feature representation in imbalanced treatment and control conditions. In: Cheng, L., Leung, A.C.S., Ozawa, S. (eds.) ICONIP 2018. LNCS, vol. 11305, pp. 47–57. Springer, Cham (2018). https://doi.org/10.1007/978-3-030-04221-9_5
4. Chambers, J.M., Hastie, T.J.: Statistical Models in S. Chapman & Hall, Boca Raton (1993)
5. Gross, S.M., Tibshirani, R.: Data shared Lasso: a novel tool to discover uplift. Comput. Stat. Data Anal. **101**, 226–235 (2016)
6. Hahn, P.R., Murray, J.S., Carvalho, C.M.: Bayesian regression tree models for causal inference: regularization, confounding, and heterogeneous effects (with Discussion). Bayesian Anal. **15**(3), 965–2020 (2020)
7. Hernán, M., Robins, J.: Causal Inference. Chapman & Hall/CRC, Boca Raton (2018). forthcoming
8. Heumann, C., Nittner, T., Rao, C., Scheid, S., Toutenburg, H.: Linear Models: Least Squares and Alternatives. Springer, New York (2013). https://doi.org/10.1007/978-1-4899-0024-1
9. Hill, J.L.: Bayesian nonparametric modeling for causal inference. J. Comput. Graph. Stat. **20**(1), 217–240 (2011)
10. Holland, P.: Statistics and causal inference. J. Am. Stat. Assoc. **81**(396), 945–960 (1986)
11. Imai, K., Ratkovic, M.: Estimating treatment effect heterogeneity in randomized program evaluation. Ann. Appl. Stat. **7**, 443–470 (2013)
12. Imbens, G., Rubin, D.: Causal Inference for Statistics, Social, and Biomedical Sciences: An Introduction. Cambridge University Press, New York (2015)
13. Jaśkowski, M., Jaroszewicz, S.: Uplift modeling for clinical trial data. In: ICML 2012 Workshop on Machine Learning for Clinical Data Analysis, Edinburgh, June 2012
14. Kane, K., Lo, V.S.Y., Zheng, J.: Mining for the truly responsive customers and prospects using true-lift modeling: comparison of new and existing methods. J. Mark. Analytics **2**(4), 218–238 (2014)
15. Kozubowski, T.J., Podgórski, K., Rychlik, I.: Multivariate generalized Laplace distribution and related random fields. J. Multivar. Anal. **113**, 59–72 (2013)
16. Künzel, S.R., Sekhon, J.S., Bickel, P.J., Yu, B.: Metalearners for estimating heterogeneous treatment effects using machine learning. Proc. Natl. Acad. Sci. **116**(10), 4156–4165 (2019). https://doi.org/10.1073/pnas.1804597116
17. Kuusisto, F., Costa, V.S., Nassif, H., Burnside, E., Page, D., Shavlik, J.: Support vector machines for differential prediction. In: Calders, T., Esposito, F., Hüllermeier, E., Meo, R. (eds.) ECML PKDD 2014. LNCS (LNAI), vol. 8725, pp. 50–65. Springer, Heidelberg (2014). https://doi.org/10.1007/978-3-662-44851-9_4
18. Lai, L.Y.T.: Influential marketing: a new direct marketing strategy addressing the existence of voluntary buyers. Master's thesis, Simon Fraser University (2006)
19. Lalonde, R.: Evaluating the econometric evaluations of training programs. Am. Econ. Rev. **76**, 604–620 (1986)

20. Liaw, F., Klebanov, P., Brooks-Gunn, J.: Effects of early intervention on cognitive function of low birth weight preterm infants. J. Pediatr. **120**, 350–359 (1991)
21. Nyberg, O., Kuśmierczyk, T., Klami, A.: Uplift modeling with high class imbalance. In: Proceedings of the 13th Asian Conference on Machine Learning, pp. 315–330, Bangkok, November 2021
22. Padilla, O.H.M., Chen, Y., Ruiz, G.: A causal fused Lasso for interpretable heterogeneous treatment effects estimation (2022)
23. Pearl, J.: Causality. Cambridge University Press, Cambridge (2009)
24. Petersen, K.B., Pedersen, M.S.: The Matrix Cookbook. Technical University of Denmark, November 2012. version 20121115
25. Radcliffe, N.J., Surry, P.D.: Real-world uplift modelling with significance-based uplift trees. Portrait Technical report TR-2011-1, Stochastic Solutions (2011)
26. Rousseeuw, P.J., Leroy, A.M.: Robust Regression and Outlier Detection. Wiley, New York (1987)
27. Rudaś, K., Jaroszewicz, S.: Linear regression for uplift modeling. Data Min. Knowl. Disc. **32**(5), 1275–1305 (2018)
28. Rudaś, K., Jaroszewicz, S.: Shrinkage estimators for uplift regression. In: Brefeld, U., Fromont, E., Hotho, A., Knobbe, A., Maathuis, M., Robardet, C. (eds.) ECML PKDD 2019. LNCS (LNAI), vol. 11906, pp. 607–623. Springer, Cham (2020). https://doi.org/10.1007/978-3-030-46150-8_36
29. Rzepakowski, P., Jaroszewicz, S.: Decision trees for uplift modeling with single and multiple treatments. Knowl. Inf. Syst. **32**, 303–327 (2011)
30. Spirtes, P., Glymour, C., Scheines, R.: Causation, Prediction, and Search. MIT Press, Cambridge (2001)
31. Zaniewicz, Ł., Jaroszewicz, S.: Support vector machines for uplift modeling. In: The First IEEE ICDM Workshop on Causal Discovery (CD 2013), Dallas, December 2013
32. Zaniewicz, Ł., Jaroszewicz, S.: l_p-support vector machines for uplift modeling. Knowl. Inf. Syst. **53**(1), 269–296 (2017)

Clustering

Powered Dirichlet Process - Controlling the "Rich-Get-Richer" Assumption in Bayesian Clustering

Gaël Poux-Médard[(✉)] [iD], Julien Velcin [iD], and Sabine Loudcher [iD]

Université de Lyon, Lyon 2, ERIC UR 3083, 5 avenue Pierre Mendès France,
69676 Bron Cedex, France
{gael.poux-medard,julien.velcin,sabine.loudcher}@univ-lyon2.fr

Abstract. The Dirichlet process is one of the most widely used priors in Bayesian clustering. This process allows for a nonparametric estimation of the number of clusters when partitioning datasets. The "rich-get-richer" property is a key feature of this process, and transcribes that the *a priori* probability for a cluster to get selected dependent linearly on its population.

In this paper, we show that such hypothesis is not necessarily optimal. We derive the Powered Dirichlet Process as a generalization of the Dirichlet-Multinomial distribution as an answer to this problem. We then derive some of its fundamental properties (expected number of clusters, convergence). Unlike state-of-the-art efforts in this direction, this new formulation allows for direct control of the importance of the "rich-get-richer" prior. We confront our proposition to several simulated and real-world datasets, and confirm that our formulation allows for significantly better results in both cases.

Keywords: Dirichlet processes · Rich-get-richer · Discrete mathematics · Clustering · Bayesian prior

1 Introduction

The Bayesian clustering approach received a broad attention over the last decades. A non-exhaustive list of application includes medicine, [13], natural language processing [4,33], genetics [16,20,23], recommender systems [1,10,22], sociology [6,12], etc. The key idea is to generate a set of independent observations according to a set of latent variables (clusters). Given a set of existing observations, the prior probability that the next one is generated by any cluster depends on the number of observations they already generated. A very popular prior on clusters distributions that allows this is the Dirichlet distribution. It can be expressed as a process, the Dirichlet process, which allows new observations to be generated by yet unobserved clusters (that have not generated any observations).

D. Koutra et al. (Eds.): ECML PKDD 2023, LNAI 14169, pp. 611–626, 2023.
https://doi.org/10.1007/978-3-031-43412-9_36

However, the Dirichlet process' (and the related Pitman-Yor process') underlying hypothesis is that the prior probability depends linearly on the number of existing observations from a cluster: the *rich-get-richer* property [7]. While this seems a reasonable hypothesis in the complete absence of additional information on the generative process, it fails to describe situations where data is available beforehand. Depending on the data, there might not be any reason for clusters growth to rely linearly on their population, if at all [23,30] In most cases, an ad-hoc solution is to fine-tune the Dirichlet process' concentration parameter α. However, this practice makes the resulting model unable to consider new data without fine tuning the α parameter again. This is a major problem due to most Dirichlet processes being used for online inference, where data is considered sequentially. Any new observation thus requires fitting the whole model once again. The need for alternatives to vanilla Dirichlet processes has already been pointed out in earlier works [31]. This problem is especially visible in the case of imbalanced data and scale-dependent clustering.

As an example of the imbalance problem, consider a case where data is treated sequentially –which is often the case when it comes to Dirichlet process. A new observation would have a much larger *a priori* probability to belong to a populated but irrelevant cluster, than to open a new one (this probability decreases as $\frac{1}{N_{obs}}$ in vanilla Dirichlet processes). In most situations where it is used, the "rich-get-richer" hypothesis does not transcribe the reality of a situation. For instance, when sampling topics from news streams [30,32], there is no reason for a new topic to appear in the feed at a rate $\alpha \log N$ as in Dirichlet processes.

As for scale-dependent clustering, similar problems arise. Consider clustering people pinpointed on a map. Tiny clusters (at the scale of cities, for instance) might go unnoticed if clusters are created for larger scales (countries, for instance). The problem can be avoided by fine-tuning the α parameter so that city-scale clusters are found. But then, adding new observations would break the so-found balance on the clusters' scale, because of the rich-get-richer property. In vanilla Dirichlet processes, the number of clusters grow logarithmically with the number of observations; for instance, if the number of cities grows sublogarithmically with the population instead, adding new observations would require fine-tuning α and fitting the whole model again to get relevant results. In this case, the "rich-get-richer" assumption as is may be too strong a hypothesis, but a "rich-get-no-richer" [30] might as well fail to capture any density-related effect; the optimal solution would be in-between these two priors, depending on the clustering objective. We explore such a case in Fig. 4.

We design a method to bridge the variety of possible priors between the Dirichlet process (DP) and the Uniform process (UP), in a continuous fashion. By generalizing these works, we show the existence of an unexplored class of behaviours, such as "rich-get-less-richer", "rich-get-more-richer" and "poor-get-richer". Little has been done in exploring alternative forms of priors for nonparametric Bayesian modeling. In the present work, we propose to explicitly tune the importance of the "rich-get-richer" assumption. The resulting Powered Dirichlet Process (PDP) generalizes state-of-the-art works such as UP [30] and DP. We show that controlling the "rich-get-richer" prior allows for better results on both synthetic and real-world datasets.

2   Background

2.1   Motivation

This work is motivated by the need to control the "rich-get-richer" assumption's importance in Dirichlet process priors. The "rich-get-richer" property of the DP may not always make it the suitable prior for modeling a given dataset. The usual motivation for using a DP prior is that a new observation has a prior probability of being assigned to any cluster proportional to its population. This leads to a prior probability of opening a new cluster decreasing as the inverse of the number of observations, which makes little sense in a number of real-world situations.

Most state-of-the-art works rely on tuning a parameter α (see Eq. 1) to get the "right" number of clusters. This parameter shifts the distribution of the number of clusters as $\mathbb{E}(K|N) \propto \alpha \log N$ with K the number of clusters and N the number of observations. However, we argue this is a bad practice in some cases, typically when clusters size N_c grows sublinearly with the number of observations N [3]. For instance, tackling entity resolution problems need such sublinear growth [26, 27]. When data is treated sequentially, the α parameter has to be fine-tuned after the fit has been performed; because its value depends on the number of observations, it makes the model unsuitable to train on new data without fitting and fine-tuning α again.

To alleviate this problem, we derive a more general form of the DP process that allows for natural control of the "rich-get-richer" property.

2.2   Previous Works

Dirichlet Process. A well-known metaphor for the Dirichlet process is referred to as "Chinese restaurant". The corresponding process is named "Chinese Restaurant Process" (CRP): if a nth client enters a Chinese restaurant, they will sit at one of the K already occupied table with a probability proportional to the number of persons already sat at this table. They can also go to a new table and be the first client to sit there with a probability inversely proportional to the total number of clients in the restaurant. It can be written formally as:

$$CRP(C_i = c|\alpha, C_1, C_2, ..., C_{i-1}) = \begin{cases} \frac{N_c}{\alpha+N} & \text{if } c = 1, 2, ..., K \\ \frac{\alpha}{\alpha+N} & \text{if } c = K+1 \end{cases} \quad (1)$$

where c is the cluster chosen by the ith customer, N_k is the population of cluster k, K is the number of already occupied tables and α the concentration parameter. When the number of clients goes to infinity, this process is equivalent to a draw from a Dirichlet distribution over an infinite number of clusters with a uniform concentration parameter α. It can be shown that the expected number of clusters after N observations evolves as $\log N$ [2].

The two best-known variations of the regular Dirichlet process that address the "rich-get-richer" property control are the seminal Pitman-Yor process and the Uniform process. Each of them can be expressed in a similar form as Eq. 1.

Uniform Process. The Uniform process has been used in some occasions [16, 23] without proper definition. More recently, it has been formalized and studied in comparison with the regular Dirichlet and Pitman-Yor processes [30]. It reads:

$$UP(C_i = c|\alpha, C_1, C_2, ..., C_{i-1}) = \begin{cases} \frac{1}{\alpha+K} & \text{if } c = 1, 2, ..., K \\ \frac{\alpha}{\alpha+K} & \text{if } c = K+1 \end{cases} \tag{2}$$

Its formulation completely gets rid of the "rich-get-richer" property. The probability of a new client joining an occupied table is a uniform distribution over the number of occupied tables; it does not depend on the tables' population. In [30], it has been shown that the expected number of tables evolves with N as $\sqrt{N}$. Removing the "rich-get-richer" property leads to a flat prior. As we show later, our formulation allows to retrieve such flat priors and thus generalizes the Uniform Process.

The authors also address the non-exchangeability of this process; they argue that it plays a minor role in inference tasks when using Gibbs sampling algorithms. A recent extension of the Uniform process that guarantees its exchangeability has been proposed in [18]. In this work, the *a priori* probability of opening a new cluster is a constant anymore, and the *a priori* probability to belong to either cluster is constant as in [30]. However, it does not allow for direct control of the "rich-get-richer" property, which is absent of the proposed process.

Pitman-Yor Process. Following the Chinese Restaurant process metaphor, the Pitman-Yor process [15,21] proposed to incorporate a *discount* β when a client opens a new table. Mathematically, the process can be formulated as:

$$PY(C_i = c|\alpha, \beta, C_1, C_2, ..., C_{i-1}) = \begin{cases} \frac{N_c-\beta}{\alpha+N} & \text{if } c = 1, 2, ..., K \\ \frac{\alpha+\beta K}{\alpha+N} & \text{if } c = K+1 \end{cases} \tag{3}$$

The introduction of the discount parameter increases the probability of creating new clusters. A table with fewer customers has significantly less chances to gain new ones, while the probability of opening a new table increases significantly. It can be shown that the number of tables evolves with the number of clients N as N^β [11,28]. However, this process does not control the arguable "rich-get-richer" hypothesis [31], since the relation to the population of a table remains linear; it only scales the linear dependence of a value β. The Pitman-Yor process thus comes with two limitations. First, since $\beta > 0$, it cannot be tuned to generate fewer clusters. Second, the discount parameter does not affect the linear dependence on previous observations for cluster allocations—rich still get richer.

Other Rich-Get-Richer Priors. Another similar prior, the Power-law Indian Buffet Process, has been proposed so that a realization would yield a number of clusters obeying a power-law as the number of observations increases [29]. This formulation can be seen as a generalization of the Pitman-Yor process; it adds an additional parameter that sums with the number of observations. However, the posterior probability for a new customer to belong to a cluster depends linearly on each cluster's size, and the "rich-get-richer" hypothesis is preserved.

Finally, the Generalized Gamma Process proposed a similar discount idea to increase the probability of opening new clusters in [19]. The proposed prior [19]-Eq. 4 modifies a cluster's probability to get chosen by subtracting a constant term to each cluster's population. Thus, the "rich-get-richer" property is not alleviated in their approach either, since the dependence on cluster's population is still linear. As for the PY process, this formulation only allows to increase the number of clusters and does not alleviate the "rich-get-richer" hypothesis.

2.3   Contributions

In the present work, we derive the Powered Dirichlet Process (PDP) that allows controlling the "rich-get-richer" property while generalizing state-of-the-art works. This allows to define new classes of a priori hypotheses: poor-get-richer, rich-get-no-richer (Uniform process), rich-get-less-richer, rich-get-richer (DP), and rich-get-more-richer. We detail some key-properties of the Powered Dirichlet Process (convergence, expected number of clusters). Finally, we show that controlling the "rich-get-richer" prior of simple models yields better results on synthetic and real-world datasets.

3   The Model

3.1   The Dirichlet-Multinomial Distribution

We recall:

$$
Dir(\boldsymbol{p}|\boldsymbol{\alpha}) = \frac{\prod_k p_k^{\alpha_k-1}}{B(\boldsymbol{\alpha})} \qquad Mult(\boldsymbol{N}|N,\boldsymbol{p}) = \frac{\Gamma(n+1)}{\prod_k \Gamma(N_k+1)} \prod_k p_k^{N_k} \qquad (4)
$$

With $\boldsymbol{N} = (N_1, N_2, ..., N_K)$ where N_k is the integer number of draws assigned to cluster k, $N = \sum_k N_k$ the total number of draws, $\Gamma(x) = (x-1)!$ and $B(\boldsymbol{x}) = \prod_k \Gamma(x_k)/\Gamma(\sum_k x_k)$.

The regular Dirichlet process can be derived from the Dirichlet-Multinomial distribution. The Dirichlet-Multinomial distribution is defined as follows:

$$
\begin{aligned}
DirMult(\boldsymbol{N}|\boldsymbol{\alpha}, n) &= \int_p Mult(\boldsymbol{N}|\boldsymbol{p}, n)Dir(\boldsymbol{p}|\boldsymbol{\alpha})d\boldsymbol{p} \\
&= \frac{B(\boldsymbol{\alpha}+\boldsymbol{N})\Gamma(n+1)}{B(\boldsymbol{\alpha})\prod_k \Gamma(N_k+1)} \int_p \underbrace{\frac{\prod_k p_k^{N_k+\alpha_k-1}}{B(\boldsymbol{\alpha}+\boldsymbol{N})}}_{Dir(p|\alpha+N)} d\boldsymbol{p} \\
&= \frac{\Gamma(\sum_k \alpha_k)\Gamma(n+1)}{\Gamma(\sum_k \alpha_k + N_k)} \prod_{k=1}^{K} \frac{\Gamma(N_k+\alpha_k)}{\Gamma(N_k+1)\Gamma(\alpha_k)}
\end{aligned} \qquad (5)
$$

In Eq. 5, we sample n values over a space of K distinct clusters each with probability $\boldsymbol{p} = (p_1, p_2, ..., p_K)$, using a Dirichlet prior with parameter $\boldsymbol{\alpha} = (\alpha_1, \alpha_2, ..., \alpha_K)$.

Now to express this as a Dirichlet Process, we need the probability for a new observation to belong to either cluster given the history of draws. Given Eq. 5, it is equivalent to drawing from a Categorical distribution with a Dirichlet prior with concentration parameter $\boldsymbol{\alpha} + \boldsymbol{N}$.

3.2 Powered Conditional Dirichlet Prior

In the standard Dirichlet-Multinomial posterior predictive, the categorical distribution is coupled with a Dirichlet prior $Dir(\boldsymbol{p}|\boldsymbol{\alpha}+\boldsymbol{N})$. We propose to modify this prior by defining the Powered Dirichlet prior that has a nonlinear dependence on the history of draws:

$$Dir_r(\boldsymbol{p}|\boldsymbol{\alpha}, \boldsymbol{N}) = \frac{1}{B(\boldsymbol{\alpha} + \boldsymbol{N}^r)} \prod_k p_k^{\alpha_k + N_k^r - 1} \tag{6}$$

where $\boldsymbol{N}^r = (N_1^r, ..., N_K^r)$ still represents the population of each cluster, but at the power r. The parameter $r \in \mathbb{R}$ controls the intensity of the shift on the concentration parameter. It is straightforward to demonstrate that the Powered Dirichlet distribution is a conjugate prior of the Multinomial distribution.

3.3 Posterior Predictive

We are looking for the probability of the nth draw belonging to cluster k. Let $\boldsymbol{c} = (c_1, ..., c_K)$ where $c_k = 1$ if the observation belongs to cluster k, and 0 otherwise. The probability of a draw from the Categorical distribution $Cat(\boldsymbol{c}|\boldsymbol{p}) = \prod_k p_k^{c_k}$ given a Powered Dirichlet prior as defined Eq. 6 reads:

$$DirCat_r(\boldsymbol{c}|\boldsymbol{\alpha}, \boldsymbol{N}) = \int_p Cat(\boldsymbol{c}|\boldsymbol{p}) Dir_r(\boldsymbol{p}|\boldsymbol{\alpha}, \boldsymbol{N}) d\boldsymbol{p}$$

$$= \int_p \frac{1}{B(\boldsymbol{\alpha} + \boldsymbol{N}^r)} \prod_k p_k^{c_k + \alpha_k + N_k^r - 1} d\boldsymbol{p} = \frac{B(\boldsymbol{c} + \boldsymbol{\alpha} + \boldsymbol{N}^r)}{B(\boldsymbol{\alpha} + \boldsymbol{N}^r)} \tag{7}$$

3.4 Powered Dirichlet Process

We finally derive an expression for the Powered Dirichlet Process from Eq. 7. Taking back the conditional probability for the nth observation to belong to cluster c (Eq. 7), we have:

$$
\begin{aligned}
DirCat_r(\boldsymbol{c}|\boldsymbol{N}, \boldsymbol{\alpha}) &= B(\boldsymbol{c} + \boldsymbol{\alpha} + \boldsymbol{N}^r)/B(\boldsymbol{\alpha} + \boldsymbol{N}^r) \\
&= \frac{(N_c^r + \alpha_c) \prod_k \Gamma(N_k^r + \alpha_k)}{(\sum_k N_k^r + \alpha_k) \Gamma(\sum_k N_k^r + \alpha_k)} \cdot \frac{\Gamma(\sum_k N_k^r + \alpha_k)}{\prod_k \Gamma(N_k^r + \alpha_k)} \\
&= \frac{N_c^r + \alpha_c}{\sum_k N_k^r + \alpha_k}
\end{aligned}
\tag{8}
$$

Now that we have the probability for each draw to belong to any cluster, we can iterate Eq. 8 as a process over K clusters. Finally, we assume an infinity of available clusters ($K \to \infty$). When considering a new observation, we must associate it to one of these clusters, that can be empty ($N_k = 0$) or non-empty ($N_k > 0$).

From Eq. 8, the probability of choosing a non-empty cluster c linearly depends on $N_c^r + \alpha_c$; the probability of choosing *one* empty cluster linearly depends on α_c. However, all empty clusters are rigorously interchangeable, because they are fully characterized by their (null) population. We can therefore describe the initial probability of choosing *any* cluster with a single value $\alpha := \sum_k^\infty \alpha_k$. Because the number clusters is infinite, it follows that $\sum_k^K \alpha_k \to 0$ for any finite set of K clusters. Therefore, for the finite set of non-empty clusters, $\alpha_k = 0$. On the other hand, for the infinite set of empty clusters, the sum of their α_k goes to α.

In the following, we rewrite K the number of non-empty clusters, and $K+1$ any of the empty clusters. This transition between the finite Dirichlet-Categorical distribution and the infinite Dirichlet Process is standard in the literature [8,17]. From these considerations and Eq. 8, the Powered Dirichlet Process follows:

$$PDP(C_n = c | \alpha, C_1, C_2, ..., C_{i-1}) = \begin{cases} \frac{N_c^r}{\alpha + \sum_k^K N_k^r} & \text{if } c = 1, 2, ..., K \\ \frac{\alpha}{\alpha + \sum_k^K N_k^r} & \text{if } c = K+1 \end{cases} \qquad (9)$$

This formulation generalizes the Uniform process when $r = 0$ and the Dirichlet process when $r = 1$.

We illustrate the change on prior probability for an existing cluster to get chosen due to the Powered Dirichlet Process in Fig. 1. This figure plots the

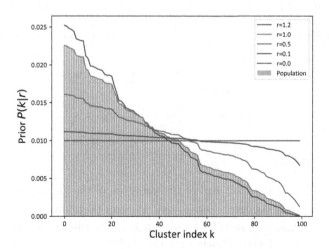

Fig. 1. Illustration of the effect of r on the Powered Dirichlet Process prior probability. Populations have been randomly sampled from a uniform distribution.

population of clusters (grey bars) and their associated prior probability of being selected. When $r > 1$, the most populated clusters are associated with a higher prior probability than in the standard CRP, whereas the less populated ones have even less chances to get chosen; rich-get-more-richer. When $r < 1$, the exact opposite is observed; rich-get-less-richer. In the limit case $r = 0$, we recover the Uniform Process; rich get-no-richer.

4   Properties of the Powered Dirichlet Process

4.1   Convergence

Proposition 1. *For $N \to \infty$, the Powered Dirichlet Process converges to a stationary distribution. When $r < 1$, it converges to a uniform distribution, and when $r > 1$, it converges to a Dirac distribution.*

Proof. We start with a simple situation where only 2 clusters are involved. The generalization to the case where $K \to \infty$ clusters are involved is straightforward. When clusters' population is large enough, we make the following Taylor approximation:

$$(N_i + 1)^r = N_i^r (1 + \frac{1}{N_i})^r = N_i^r + rN_i^{r-1} + \mathcal{O}(N^{r-2}) \tag{10}$$

Since the population of a cluster N_i is a non-decreasing function of N, we assume that first order Taylor approximation holds when $N \to \infty$. Given clusters population at the Nth observation, we perform a stability analysis of the gap between probabilities $\Delta p(N) = p_1(N) - p_2(N)$. We recall that the probability for cluster i to get selected at step N is $p_i(N) = N_i^r / (\sum_k N_k^r)$. Either cluster is selected with this probability at step $N + 1$: $\Delta p(N + 1) = p_1(N + 1) - p_2(N)$ with probability $p_1(N)$, and $\Delta p(N + 1) = p_1(N) - p_2(N + 1)$ with probability $p_2(N)$). Explicitly, the variation of the gap between probabilities when N grows is written as:

$$\frac{p_1(N)(p_1(N + 1) - p_2(N)) + p_2(N)(p_1(N) - p_2(N + 1)) - \Delta p(N)}{\Delta p(N)}$$

$$\overset{\text{Eq. 10}}{\approx} \frac{1}{p_1(N) - p_2(N)} \times \left(p_1(N) \frac{N_1^r - N_2^r + rN_1^{r-1}}{N_1^r + N_2^r + rN_1^{r-1}} + p_2(N) \frac{N_1^r - N_2^r - rN_2^{r-1}}{N_1^r + N_2^r + rN_2^{r-1}} \right) \tag{11}$$

$$= \frac{2rN_1^r N_2^r}{(N_1^r + N_2^r + rN_1^{r-1})(N_1^r + N_2^r + rN_2^{r-1})} \left(\frac{N_1^{r-1} - N_2^{r-1}}{N_1^r - N_2^r} \right)$$

We see in Eq. 11 that the sign of the variation of the gap between probabilities depend only on the term $\frac{N_1^{r-1} - N_2^{r-1}}{N_1^r - N_2^r}$. We can therefore perform a stability analysis of the Powered Dirichlet Process using only this expression.
— For $0 < r < 1$ the following relation holds: $N_1^{r-1} - N_2^{r-1} < 0 \Leftrightarrow N_1^r - N_2^r > 0 \ \forall N_1, N_2$, and conversely. That makes right hand side of Eq. 11 negative. Therefore adding a new observation statistically reduces the gap between the

probabilities of the two clusters. We could forecast this prediction from Eq. 10. We see that the more a cluster is populated, the less a new observation increases its probability at the next step – rich-get-less-richer. Moreover, we see from Eq. 10 that a crowded cluster (such as $N_1^r \gg N_2^r$) see its probability evolve as N^{r-1}. Asymptotically, the only fixed point of Eq. 11 when $N \to \infty$ is $N_1 \to N_2$, which implies a uniform distribution. We verify this result numerically in Fig. 2-left.

— For $r > 1$ the following relation holds: $N_1^{r-1} - N_2^{r-1} > 0 \Leftrightarrow N_1^r - N_2^r > 0 \; \forall N_1, N_2$; that makes right hand side of Eq. 11 positive. Adding a new observation statistically increases the gap between probabilities. From Eq. 10, we see that the more a cluster is populated, the more a new observation increases its probability at the next step – rich-get-more-richer. In this case, Eq. 11 has $K+1$ fixed points, with K the number of clusters. The uniform distribution is an unstable fixed point, while K Dirac distributions (each on one cluster) are stable fixed points of the system. It means the gap converges to 1, that is a probability of 1 for one cluster and a probability of 0 for the others.

— For $r = 1$, the right hand side of Eq. 11 is null. It means the gap remains statistically constant $\forall N_i$, which is a classical result for the regular Dirichlet process. This convergence has already been studied on many occasions [2,7].

— For $r \to 0$, Eq. 11 is not defined anymore. That is because the probability for a cluster to be chosen does not depend on its population anymore. In this case, $p_1(N) - p_2(N) \propto N_1^0 - N_2^0 = 0$: the probability for any cluster to be chosen is equal at all times, hence the Uniform process – "rich-get-no-richer".

4.2   Expected Number of Tables

Proposition 2. *When N is large, $\sum_k N_k^r$ varies with N as $N^{\frac{r^2+1}{2}}$ when $r < 1$, and with N^r when $r \geq 1$.*

Proof. Taking back Eq. 9, we are interested in the variation of $p_i = \frac{N_i^r}{\sum_k N_k^r}$ according to N when N_i^r is large. Since N_i is either way a non-decreasing function of N, we reformulate the constraint N_i^r large into N^r large:

$$p_i(N+1) - p_i(N) = \begin{cases} \frac{rN_i^{r-1} + \mathcal{O}(N^{r-2})}{\sum_k N_k^r} & \text{if } N_i \text{ grows} \\ 0 & \text{otherwise} \end{cases} \tag{12}$$

— For $r < 1$, the larger N_i the slower the variation of p_i. It means that for large N_i^r, we can write $N_i \propto N p_i$, with p_i being now independent N.

— For $r > 1$, the probability p_i varies greatly with N and quickly converges to 1 for large N (see Proposition 1), and so $N_i \approx N$ for cluster i and $N_{j \neq i} \ll N_i \; \forall j$.

Because the sum $\sum_k N_k^r$ mostly varies according to large N_k, we approximate $\sum_k N_k^r \approx N^r \sum_k p_k^r$ for large N^r.

Besides, we showed in Proposition 1 that for large N the process converges to a uniform distribution for $r < 1$ and to a Dirac distribution when $r > 1$. Therefore, we can express $\sum_k^K p_k^r$ as:

$$\sum_k^K p_k^r \overset{N \gg 1}{\approx} \begin{cases} K \cdot (\frac{1}{K})^r = K^{1-r} & \text{for } r < 1 \\ 1 & \text{for } r \geq 1 \end{cases} \tag{13}$$

Based on the demonstration of Eq. 4 in [30], we assume that K evolves with N as $N^{\frac{1-r}{2}}$ when $r < 1$. We verify that this assumption holds in the Experiment section, Fig. 2-middle.

Therefore, we can write:

$$\sum_k N_k^r \approx N^r \sum_k^K p_k^r \approx \begin{cases} N^r \left(N^{\frac{1-r}{2}} \right)^{1-r} = N^{\frac{1+r^2}{2}} & \text{for } r < 1 \\ N^r & \text{for } r \geq 1 \end{cases} \tag{14}$$

Proposition 3. *For $N \gg 1$, the expected number of tables of the Powered Dirichlet Process grows with N as $H_{\frac{r^2+1}{2}}(N)$ for $r < 1$ and as $H_r(N)$ when $r \geq 1$, where $H_m(n)$ is the generalized harmonic number.*

Proof. In general, the expected number of clusters at the Nth step can be written as:

$$\mathbb{E}(K|N,r) = \sum_1^N \frac{\alpha}{\sum_k N_k^r + \alpha} \overset{N^r \gg 1}{\propto} \sum_1^N \frac{1}{\sum_k N_k^r} \tag{15}$$

We showed in Proposition 2 that we can rewrite $\sum_k N_k^r \propto N^{\frac{r^2+1}{2}}$ when $r < 1$ and $\sum_k N_k^r \propto N^r$ when $r \geq 1$. Injecting this result in Eq. 15, we get:

$$\mathbb{E}(K|N,r) \overset{N^r \gg 1}{\propto} \begin{cases} \sum_1^N N^{-\frac{r^2+1}{2}} = H_{\frac{r^2+1}{2}}(N) & \text{for } r < 1 \\ \sum_1^N N^{-r} = H_r(N) & \text{for } r \geq 1 \end{cases} \tag{16}$$

This result is verified numerically in Fig. 2-right.

— For $r = 1$, $\mathbb{E}(K|N, r = 1) \propto H_1(N) \approx \gamma + \log(N)$ where γ is the Euler-Mascheroni constant, which is a classical result for the regular Dirichlet process.

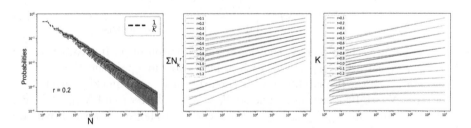

Fig. 2. Numerical validation of Propositions 1 (left), 2 (middle), 3 (right). In the first plot, K is the number of non-empty clusters. In the second and third plots, the theoretical results are the solid lines and the associated numerical results are the transparent lines of same color. Except for small N, the difference between theory and experiments is almost indistinguishable.

— For $r > 1$ and $N \to \infty$, the term $H_{\frac{r^2+1}{2}}(N)$ converges towards a finite value and the sum $\sum_k p_k^r$ goes to 1 (see Proposition 1). By definition $\mathbb{E}(K|N, r > 1) \overset{N \to \infty}{\propto} \zeta(\frac{r^2+1}{2})$, where ζ is the Riemann Zeta function.

— For $r < 1$, we need to approximate the harmonic number in a continuous setting. We rewrite Eq. 16 as:

$$\sum_{n=1}^{N} n^{-\frac{r^2+1}{2}} \overset{N^r \gg 1}{\approx} \int_1^N n^{-\frac{r^2+1}{2}} dn = \frac{2}{1-r^2}(N^{\frac{1-r^2}{2}} - 1) \qquad (17)$$

One can show that $\frac{N^{1-x}-1}{1-x} = H_x(N) + \mathcal{O}(\frac{1}{N^x})$. Therefore, the number of expected clusters in the Powered Dirichlet Process exhibits a power-law behaviour, similar to the Pitman-Yor process for $r = \sqrt{1 - 2\beta}$ for $0 < r < 1$. For values of $r > 1 \Leftrightarrow \beta < 0$, the equivalent Pitman-Yor process is not defined. Note that there is no *a priori* reason for r to be constrained in the domain of positive real number. Complex and negative analysis of the process might be an interesting lead for future works.

5   Experiments

5.1   Use Case: Infinite Gaussian Mixture Model

We consider a classical infinite Gaussian mixture model coupled with a Powered Dirichlet Process prior. We choose this application to ease visual understanding of the implications of the PDP, but the argument holds for other models using DP priors as well (text modeling, gene expression clustering, etc.). We fit the data using a standard collapsed Gibbs sampling algorithm for IGMM [24,30,33], with a Normal Inverse Wishart prior on the Gaussians' parameters. The order in which input data is processes is set at random at each iteration, so that we reduce the ordering bias from the dataset [30]. Note that we cannot completely

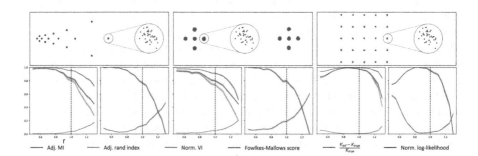

Fig. 3. Application on synthetic data. (Top) Original datasets used for the experiments (Density, Diamond and Grid). (Bottom) Results for various values of r; the x and y axes all the same. The dashed line indicates the regular DP prior as $r = 1$. The error correspond to the standard error of the mean over all runs.

get rid of it because the Powered Dirichlet Process is not exchangeable for all r. The problem has been addressed on numerous occasions (Uniform process [30], distance-dependent CRP [5,9], spectral CRP [25], balance-neutral partition [18]) and shown to induce negligible variations of results in the case of Gibbs sampling. We stop the sampler once the likelihood reaches stability; we perform 100 runs for each value of r. Finally, the parameter α is set to 1.[1]

Note that we choose not to compare to other types of clustering algorithms. This section aims to demonstrate the usefulness of a generalized form of the Dirichlet process with respect to the vanilla one. The argument on a simple model (here a regular DP combined with IGMM) extends to other priors built on Dirichlet processes (Hierarchical and Nested Dirichlet processes). Comparison of DP-based priors to other clustering methods (KNN, DBScan, Spectral clustering, etc.) has already been done numerous times and is out of our scope.

Synthetic Data. Synthetic datasets are represented in Fig. 3-top, and comprise $N = 1000$ observations each, that have been generated by sampling from 2D Gaussian distributions. We present the results on synthetic data in Fig. 3-bottom and in Table 1. We consider standard metrics in clustering evaluation with a non-fixed number of clusters: mutual information score and rand index both adjusted for chance (**Adj.MI** and **Adj.RI**, higher is better), normalized variation of information (**Norm.VI**, lower is better), Fowlkes-Mallow score (higher is better), marginal likelihood (normalized for visualization, higher is better) and absolute relative variation of the inferred number of clusters according to the number used in the generation process ($\frac{K_{inf}-K_{true}}{K_{true}}$, lower is better). The datasets are designed to investigate the effect varying r when clustering can take place on different scales.

Real-World Data. In Table 1, we report the results for the 20Newsgroup (20-NG) real-world dataset, which is a collection of 18 000 users posts published on Usenet, organized in 20 Newsgroup (which are our target thematic clusters). As a model, we consider a modified version of LDA [4] that uses a PDP prior instead of DP in the words sampling step. Note that because the number of clusters must be provided to LDA, we do not compute $\frac{K_{inf}-K_{true}}{K_{true}}$. We also run additional experiments on well known real-world datasets from sklearn: Iris (4 attributes, 3 classes), Wines (13 attributes, 3 classes), and Cancer (30 attributes, 2 classes). We see PDP allows for improved performances on every dataset.

We now illustrate the interest of using an alternate form of prior for the IGMM on real-world data. We consider a dataset of 4.300 roman sepulchral inscriptions comprising the substring "Antoni" that have been dated between 150AC and 200AC and assigned with map coordinates. The dates correspond to the reign of Antoninus Pius over the Roman empire. The dataset is available on Clauss-Slaby repository[2]. It was common to give children or slaves the name

---

[1] Codes and datasets available at https://github.com/GaelPouxMedard/PDPs.
[2] http://www.manfredclauss.de/fr/index.html.

Table 1. Numerical results of the various priors coupled to a standard IGMM. PDP allows to outperform the baselines consistently. The standard error on the last digit(s) over 100 runs is given in shorthand notation $(0.123(12) \Leftrightarrow 0.123 \pm 0.012)$.

		Adj.MI (↑)	Adj.RI (↑)	Norm.VI (↓)	$\frac{K_{inf}-K_{true}}{K_{true}}$ (↓)
Density	PDP (r=0.60)	**0.992(1)**	**0.980(2)**	**0.006(1)**	**0.045(5)**
	DP (r=1.00)	0.951(4)	0.797(17)	0.037(3)	0.128(10)
	UP (r=0.00)	0.939(2)	0.854(4)	0.050(1)	0.548(1)
Diamond	PDP (r=0.50)	**0.982(2)**	**0.956(5)**	**0.011(1)**	**0.063(7)**
	DP (r=1.00)	0.909(7)	0.731(19)	0.053(4)	0.202(12)
	UP (r=0.00)	0.927(2)	0.844(6)	0.051(2)	0.544(2)
Grid	PDP (r=0.85)	**0.997(1)**	**0.990(2)**	**0.003(1)**	**0.014(2)**
	DP (r=1.00)	0.995(1)	0.977(4)	**0.004(1)**	**0.018(3)**
	UP (r=0.00)	0.811(1)	0.517(3)	0.154(1)	2.120(1)
Iris	PDP (r=0.90)	**0.868(4)**	**0.866(7)**	**0.057(2)**	**0.000(0)**
	DP (r=1.00)	0.843(6)	0.820(12)	0.065(2)	0.030(10)
	UP (r=0.00)	0.544(2)	0.295(3)	0.303(2)	2.777(32)
Wines	PDP (r=0.10)	0.712(15)	0.637(20)	0.102(5)	**0.157(17)**
	DP (r=1.00)	0.589(19)	0.461(16)	0.128(4)	0.327(13)
	UP (r=0.00)	**0.713(17)**	**0.657(21)**	**0.103(5)**	**0.147(17)**
Cancer	PDP (r=0.10)	0.254(17)	0.278(21)	**0.118(1)**	**0.000(0)**
	DP (r=1.00)	0.085(16)	0.094(19)	0.108(2)	**0.000(0)**
	UP (r=0.00)	**0.271(17)**	**0.300(21)**	**0.118(1)**	**0.000(0)**
20-NG	PDP (r=0.80)	**0.421(4)**	**0.119(3)**	**0.477(3)**	-
	DP (r=1.00)	0.404(4)	0.105(4)	0.491(3)	-
	UP (r=0.00)	0.000(4)	0.000(0)	0.830(3)	-

of the emperor; the dataset gives a global idea of the main areas of the roman empire at that time [14]. The task is to discover spatial clusters of individuals named after the emperor. We present the results in Fig. 4.

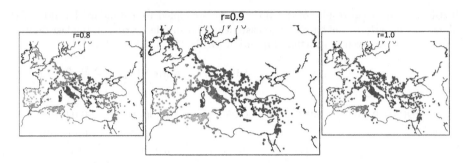

Fig. 4. Application to spatial clustering on geolocated data for $r = 0.8$ (left), $r = 1$ (right) and $r = 0.9$ (middle). We see that the model using a PDP prior for $r = 0.9$ and $r = 0.8$ describes the data better than the same model using a DP prior ($r = 1$).

We see that when $r = 1$, the classical DP prior is not fit for describing this dataset, as it misses most of the clusters. The problem could be solved by fine-tuning the α parameter, but such model would not be hold if we added new observations. On the other hand, when $r = 0.9$, the infinite Gaussian mixture model retrieves relevant clusters. It also finds some clusters that were not expected, such as the north Italian cluster or the long cluster going through Spain and France that corresponds to roman roads layout (via Augusta and via Agrippa; it was common to bury the dead on roads edges). Finally, when $r = 0.8$, some of the main clusters are broken into smaller ones (Italy breaks into Rome, North Italy, and South Italy; Britain becomes an independent cluster, etc.). In this case, tuning r controls the level of details of the clustering.

6   Conclusion

We discussed the need for controlling the "rich-get-richer" property that arises from the usual Dirichlet Process. We then derived the Powered Dirichlet Process to allow for its control. This formulation allows reducing the expected number of clusters, which is not possible with existing processes, while generalizing two of them. We derived elementary results on convergence and expected number of clusters of the PDP. Finally, we showed that it yields better results on both synthetic and real-world data. For future works, it might be interesting to investigate cases where r takes non-positive values (which might lead to a "poor-get-richer" kind of process), and to develop a procedure to infer this parameter based on data (by minimizing a dispersion criterion, for instance).

The regular Dirichlet Process has been used for decades as a powerful prior in many real-world applications. However, alternate forms for this prior have been little explored. It would be very interesting to study the changes brought to state-of-the-art models based on Dirichlet priors by varying the importance of the "rich-get-richer" assumption as proposed in this paper.

References

1. Airoldi, E., Blei, D., Fienberg, S., Xing, E.: Mixed membership stochastic block-models. J. Mach. Learn. Res. **9**, 1991–1992 (2008)
2. Arratia, R., Barbour, A.D., Tavaré, S.: Poisson process approximations for the Ewens sampling formula. Ann. Appl. Probab. **2**(3), 519–535 (1992)
3. Betancourt, B., Zanella, G., Miller, J.W., Wallach, H., Zaidi, A., Steorts, R.C.: Flexible models for microclustering with application to entity resolution, vol. 29 (2016). https://proceedings.neurips.cc/paper/2016/file/670e8a43b246801ca1eaca97b3e19189-Paper.pdf
4. Blei, D.M., Ng, A.Y., Jordan, M.I.: Latent dirichlet allocation. J. Mach. Learn. Res. **3**, 993–1022 (2003)
5. Blei, D., Frazier, P.: Distance dependent Chinese restaurant processes. J. Mach. Learn. Res. **12**, 2461–2488 (2011)
6. Cobo-López, S., Godoy-Lorite A., Duch, J.: Optimal prediction of decisions and model selection in social dilemmas using block models. EPJ Data Sci. **7**(48) (2018)
7. Ferguson, T.S.: A Bayesian analysis of some nonparametric problems. Ann. Stat. **1**(2), 209–230 (1973)
8. Frigyik, A.B., Kapila, A., Gupta, M.R.: Introduction to the Dirichlet distribution and related processes (2010)
9. Ghosh, S., Raptis, M., Sigal, L., Sudderth, E.B.: Nonparametric clustering with distance dependent hierarchies. In: UAI 2014, pp. 260–269 (2014)
10. Godoy-Lorite, A., Guimerà, R., Moore, C., Sales-Pardo, M.: Accurate and scalable social recommendation using mixed-membership stochastic block models. PNAS **113**(50), 14207–14212 (2016)
11. Goldwater, S., Griffiths, T.L., Johnson, M.: Producing power-law distributions and damping word frequencies with two-stage language models. JMLR **12**(68) (2011)
12. Guimera, R., Llorente, A., Sales-Pardo, M.: Predicting human preferences using the block structure of complex social networks. PLOS One **7**(9) (2012)
13. Guimerá, R., Sales-Pardo, M.: A network inference method for large-scale unsupervised identification of novel drug-drug interactions. PLoS Comput. Biol. (2013)
14. Hanson, J.W., Ortman, S.G., Lobo, J.: Urbanism and the division of labour in the roman empire. J. R. Soc. Interface **14**(136), 20170367 (2017)
15. Ishwaran, H., James, L.: Generalized weighted Chinese restaurant processes for species sampling mixture models. Statistica Sinica **13**, 1211–1235 (2003)
16. Jensen, S., Liu, J.: Bayesian clustering of transcription factor binding motifs. J. Am. Stat. Assoc. **103**, 188–200 (2008)
17. Jordan, M.: Dirchlet processes, Chinese restaurant processes and all that. In: ICML (2005)
18. Lee, C.J., Sang, H.: Why the rich get richer? On the balancedness of random partition models. In: Chaudhuri, K., Jegelka, S., Song, L., Szepesvari, C., Niu, G., Sabato, S. (eds.) Proceedings of the 39th International Conference on Machine Learning. Proceedings of Machine Learning Research, vol. 162, pp. 12521–12541. PMLR, 17–23 July 2022
19. Lijoi, A., Mena, R.H., Prünster, I.: Controlling the reinforcement in Bayesian non-parametric mixture models. J. Roy. Stat. Soc. Ser. B (Stat. Methodol.) **69**(4), 715–740 (2007). https://doi.org/10.1111/j.1467-9868.2007.00609.x. https://rss.onlinelibrary.wiley.com/doi/abs/10.1111/j.1467-9868.2007.00609.x
20. McDowell, I.C., Manandhar, D., Vockley, C.M., Schmid, A.K., Reddy, T.E., Engelhardt, B.E.: Clustering gene expression time series data using an infinite Gaussian process mixture model. PLoS Comput. Biol. **14**(1), e1005896 (2018)

21. Pitman, J., Yor, M.: The two-parameter Poisson-Dirichlet distribution derived from a stable subordinator. Ann. Probab. **25**(2), 855–900 (1997)
22. Poux-Médard, G., Velcin, J., Loudcher, S.: Interactions in information spread: quantification and interpretation using stochastic block models. arXiv (2020)
23. Qin, Z.S., McCue, L.A., Thompson, W., Mayerhofer, L., Lawrence, C.E., Liu, J.S.: Identification of co-regulated genes through Bayesian clustering of predicted regulatory binding sites. Nat. Biotechnol. **21**, 435–439 (2003)
24. Rasmussen, C.E.: The infinite gaussian mixture model. In: NIPS 1999, pp. 554–560. MIT Press (1999)
25. Socher, R., Maas, A., Manning, C.: Spectral Chinese restaurant processes: nonparametric clustering based on similarities. In: JMLR - Proceedings, vol. 15, pp. 698–706 (2011)
26. Steorts, R.C.: Entity resolution with empirically motivated priors **10**, 849 (2015)
27. Steorts, R.C., Hall, R., Fienberg, S.E.: SMERED: a Bayesian approach to graphical record linkage and de-duplication, vol. 33, pp. 922–930 (2014)
28. Sudderth, E., Jordan, M.: Shared segmentation of natural scenes using dependent Pitman-Yor processes. In: NIPS, vol. 21 (2009)
29. Teh, Y., Gorur, D.: Indian buffet processes with power-law behavior, vol. 22 (2009)
30. Wallach, H., Jensen, S., Dicker, L., Heller, K.: An alternative prior process for nonparametric Bayesian clustering. In: Proceedings of the Thirteenth International Conference on Artificial Intelligence and Statistics, pp. 892–899. JMLR (2010)
31. Welling, M.: Flexible priors for infinite mixture models. In: Workshop on Learning with Non-parametric Bayesian Methods (2006)
32. Xu, W., Li, Y., Qiang, J.: Dynamic clustering for short text stream based on Dirichlet process. Appl. Intell. (2021). https://doi.org/10.1007/s10489-021-02263-z
33. Yin, J., Wang, J.: A dirichlet multinomial mixture model-based approach for short text clustering. In: Proceedings of the 20th ACM SIGKDD International Conference on Knowledge Discovery and Data Mining, KDD 2014, pp. 233–242. Association for Computing Machinery, New York, NY, USA (2014)

Contrastive Hierarchical Clustering

Michał Znalezniak[1], Przemysław Rola[2,4], Patryk Kaszuba[3], Jacek Tabor[4],
and Marek Śmieja[4(✉)]

[1] Advanced Micro Devices, Inc., Santa Clara, USA
[2] Institute of Quantitative Methods in Social Sciences,
Cracow University of Economics, Krakow, Poland
[3] Faculty of Mathematics and Computer Science,
Adam Mickiewicz University, Poznan, Poland
[4] Faculty of Mathematics and Computer Science,
Jagiellonian University, Kraków, Poland
marek.smieja@uj.edu.pl

Abstract. Deep clustering has been dominated by flat models, which
split a dataset into a predefined number of groups. Although recent methods achieve an extremely high similarity with the ground truth on popular benchmarks, the information contained in the flat partition is limited.
In this paper, we introduce CoHiClust, a Contrastive Hierarchical Clustering model based on deep neural networks, which can be applied to
typical image data. By employing a self-supervised learning approach,
CoHiClust distills the base network into a binary tree without access to
any labeled data. The hierarchical clustering structure can be used to
analyze the relationship between clusters, as well as to measure the similarity between data points. Experiments demonstrate that CoHiClust
generates a reasonable structure of clusters, which is consistent with our
intuition and image semantics. Moreover, it obtains superior clustering
accuracy on most of the image datasets compared to the state-of-the-
art flat clustering models. Our implementation is available at https://
github.com/MichalZnalezniak/Contrastive-Hierarchical-Clustering.

Keywords: Hierarchical clustering · Contrastive learning · Deep
embedding clustering

1 Introduction

Clustering, a fundamental branch of unsupervised learning, is often one of the
first steps in data analysis, which finds applications in anomaly detection [2], personalized recommendations [45] or bioinformatics [22]. Since it does not use any
information about class labels, representation learning becomes an integral part
of deep clustering methods. Initial approaches use representations taken from

---

Supplementary Information The online version contains supplementary material
available at https://doi.org/10.1007/978-3-031-43412-9_37.

pre-trained models [13,30] or employ autoencoders in joint training of the representation and the clustering model [14,26]. Recent models designed to image data frequently follow the self-supervised learning principle, where the representation is trained on pairs of similar images generated automatically by data augmentations [9,23]. Since augmentations used for image data are class-invariant, the latter techniques of ten obtain a very high similarity to the ground truth classes. However, we should be careful when comparing clustering techniques only by inspecting their accuracy with ground truth classes because the primary goal of clustering is to deliver information about data and not to perform classification.

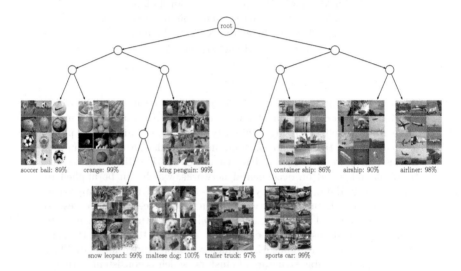

Fig. 1. A hierarchy generated by CoHiClust for ImageNet-10. As can be seen, CoHiClust reliably reflected the ground-truth classes in leaf nodes. In addition to information delivered by flat partition, in hierarchical models neighbor leaves contain images sharing similar characteristic. It is evident that images with soccer ball are similar to pictures with oranges because of their shapes. Dogs are more similar to leopards than to penguins, which is reflected in the constructed hierarchy. The same hold when analyzing the leafs representing cars, trucks and ships. Looking at the first hierarchy level, we observe a distinction on the right sub-tree representing machines and left-sub-tree dominated by animals. Moreover, balls and oranges are separated from the animal branch.

Most of the works in the area of deep clustering focus on producing flat partitions with a predefined number of groups. Although hierarchical clustering has gained considerable attention in classical machine learning and has been frequently applied in real-life problems [32,47], its role has been drastically marginalized in the era of deep learning. In the case of hierarchical clustering, the exact number of clusters does not have to be specified because we can inspect the partition at various tree levels. Moreover, we can analyze the clusters' relationships, e.g. by finding superclusters or measuring the distance between groups in the hierarchy. These advantages make hierarchical clustering an excellent tool for analyzing complex data. However, to take full advantage of hierarchical clustering, it is necessary to create an appropriate image representation, which is possible due to the use of deep neural networks. To our knowledge, DeepECT [26,27] is the only hierarchical clustering model trained jointly with the neural network. However, this method has not been examined for larger datasets of color images.

To fill this gap, we introduce CoHiClust (**Co**ntrastive **Hi**erarchical **Clust**ering), which creates a cluster hierarchy and works well on typical color image databases. CoHiClust uses a neural network to generate a high-level representation of data, which is then distilled into the tree hierarchy by applying the projection head, see Fig. 2. The whole framework is trained jointly in an end-to-end manner without labels using our novel contrastive loss and data augmentations generated automatically following the self-supervised learning principle.

The constructed hierarchy uses the structure of a binary tree, where the sequence of decisions made by the internal nodes determines the final assignment to the clusters (leaf nodes). In consequence, similar examples are processed longer by the same path than dissimilar ones. By inspecting the number of edges needed to connect two clusters (leaves), we obtain a natural similarity measure between data points. By applying a pruning strategy, which removes the least informative leaf nodes, we can restrict the hierarchy to a given number of leaves and fine-tune the whole hierarchy.

The proposed model has been examined on various image datasets and compared with hierarchical and flat clustering baselines. By analyzing the constructed hierarchies, we show that CoHiClust generates a structure of clusters that is consistent with our intuition and image semantics, see Figs. 1 and 3 for illustration and discussion. Our analysis is supported by a quantitative study, which shows that CoHiClust outperforms the current clustering models on 5 out of 7 image datasets, see Tables 1 and 6.

Our main contributions are summarized as follows:

- We introduce a hierarchical clustering model CoHiClust, which converts the base neural network into a binary tree. The model is trained effectively without supervision using our novel hierarchical contrastive loss applied to self-generated data augmentations.
- We conducted an extensive experimental study, which confirms that CoHiClust is very competitive with current state-of-the-art flat clustering models. Moreover, we show that it builds hierarchies based on well-defined and intuitive patterns retrieved from the data.
- Since CoHiClust is the first deep hierarchical clustering model applied to color image datasets, we provide a benchmark, which can be used to compare hierarchical clustering methods.

2 Related Work

In this section, we briefly introduce some recent developments on three related topics: contrastive learning, deep clustering, and hierarchical methods.

Contrastive Learning. The basic idea of contrastive learning is to learn a feature space in which similar pairs stay close to each other, while dissimilar ones are far apart [8]. In recent works, it was observed that in selected domains, such as computer vision, positive (similar) pairs can be generated automatically using adversarial perturbations [28] or data augmentation [16], giving rise to a new field called self-supervised learning [7]. Fine-tuning a simple classifier on self-supervised representation allows for obtaining the accuracy comparable to a fully supervised setting. SimCLR [16] applies NT-Xent loss to maximize the agreement between differently augmented views of the same sample. Barlow Twins [41] learns to make the cross-correlation matrix between two distorted versions of the same samples close to the identity. BYOL [12] claims to achieve new state-of-the-art results without using negative samples. Other works use memory banks to reduce the cost of computing the embeddings of negative samples in every batch [16,37].

Deep Clustering. A primary focus in deep embedded clustering has merely been on flat clustering objectives with the actual number of clusters known a priori. DEC [38] is one of the first works, which combines the auto-encoder loss with a clustering objective to jointly learn the representation and perform clustering. This idea was further explored with some improvements in IDEC [14], JULE [39] and DCEC [15]. IMSAT [17] and IIC [19] use perturbations to generate pairs of similar examples and apply information-theoretic objectives for training. PICA [18] maximizes the global partition confidence of the clustering solution to find the most semantically plausible data separation. Following progress in self-supervised learning, CC [23] and DCSC [44] perform contrastive learning by generating pairs of positive and negative instances through data augmentations.

Hierarchical Methods. Hierarchical clustering algorithms are a well-established area within classical data mining [29], but have rarely been studied in deep learning. DeepECT [26,27] is the only method that jointly learns deep representation using autoencoder architecture and performs hierarchical clustering in a top-down manner. Unfortunately, no comparative study has been conducted on large image data. The experimental study of objective-based hierarchical clustering methods performed on the embedding vectors of pre-trained deep learning models is presented in [30]. In the case of classification, there is a growing interest in deep hierarchical methods, which in our opinion should also be reflected in the area of unsupervised learning. SDT [10] is one of the first models that distills the base neural networks into a soft decision tree. More advanced methods automatically generate deep networks with a tree structure in a multistep or end-to-end manner [1,33,35].

3   CoHiClust model

The proposed CoHiClust builds a hierarchy of clusters based on the output of the base neural network. There are three key components of CoHiClust:

- The base neural network that generates the representation used by the tree.
- The tree model, which assigns data points to clusters by a sequence of decisions.
- The regularized contrastive loss, which allows for training the whole framework.

We discuss the above components in detail in the following parts.

3.1   Tree Hierarchy

We use a soft binary decision tree to create a hierarchical structure, where leaves play the role of clusters (similar to [10]). In contrast to hard decision trees, every internal node defines the probability of taking a left/right branch. The final assignment of the input examples to clusters involves partial decisions made by the internal nodes. Aggregating these decisions induces the posterior probability over leaves.

Let us consider a complete binary tree with T levels, where the root is located at the level 0 and the leaves are represented at the level T. This gives us 2^t nodes at the level t denoted by tuples (t, i), for $i = 0, 1, \ldots, 2^t - 1$, see Fig. 2. The path from root to node (t, i) is given by the sequence of binary decisions $y = (y_1, \ldots, y_t) \in \{0, 1\}^t$ made by the internal nodes, where $y_s = 0$ ($y_s = 1$) means that we take the left (right) branch that is at the node at the level s. Observe that we can retrieve the index j of the node at the level s from y by taking $j = b_s(y) = \sum_{m=1}^{s} y_m 2^{s-m}$. In other words, the first s bits of y are a binary representation of the number j.

We consider the path induced by the sequence of decisions $y = (y_1, \ldots, y_t) \in \{0, 1\}^t$, which goes from the root to the node (t, i), where $i = b_t(y)$. We want to calculate the probability $P_t^i(x)$ that the input example $x \in \mathbb{R}^D$ reaches node (t, i). If $p_s^{b_s(y)}(x)$ is the probability of going from the parent node $(s-1, b_{s-1}(y))$ to its descendant $(s, b_s(y))$, then

$$P_t^i(x) = p_1^{b_1(y)}(x) \cdot p_2^{b_2(y)}(x) \cdot \ldots p_t^{b_t(y)}(x).$$

Observe that $P_t(x) = [P_t^0(x), P_t^1(x), \ldots, P_t^{2^t-1}(x)]$ defines a proper probability distribution, i.e. $\sum_{j=0}^{2^t-1} P_t^j(x) = 1$. As a consequence, the probability distribution on the clusters (leaves) is equal to $P_T(x)$, see Fig. 2.

3.2   Tree Generation

To generate our tree model, we need to parameterize the probabilities $p_t^i(x)$ of taking the left/right branch in every internal node. To this end, we employ a neural network $g : \mathbb{R}^D \to \mathbb{R}^N$ with an additional projection head $\pi : \mathbb{R}^N \to \mathbb{R}^K$, where $K = 2^T - 1$ and T is the height of the tree. The number K of output neurons equals the number of internal tree nodes.

The neural network g is responsible for extracting high-level information from the data. It can be instantiated by a typical architecture, such as ResNet, and is used to generate embeddings $z = g(x)$ of the input data.

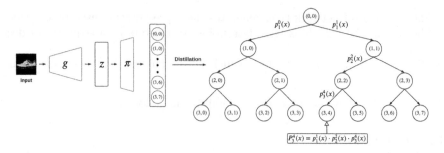

Fig. 2. Illustration of CoHiClust. The output neurons of the projection head π (appended to the base network g) model decisions made by the internal tree nodes. The final assignment of the input example to the cluster (leaf node) is performed by aggregating edge probabilities located on the path from the root to this leaf.

The projection head π operates on the embeddings z and parameterizes the decisions made by the internal tree nodes. In our case, π is a single layer network with the output dimension equal to the number of internal nodes. To model binary decisions of internal nodes, we apply the sigmoid function σ. Consequently, the projection head is given by $\pi(z) = [\sigma(w_1^T z + b_1), \ldots, \sigma(w_K^T z + b_K)]$, where $w_n \in \mathbb{R}^N$ and $b_n \in \mathbb{R}$ are trainable parameters of π. By interpreting the output neurons of π as the internal nodes of the decision tree, we obtain the probabilities of the left edges in the nodes:

$$p_{t+1}^{2i}(x) = \sigma(w_n^T z + b_n) \text{ , for } n = 2^t + i.$$

Note that $p_{t+1}^{2i-1}(x) = 1 - p_{t+1}^{2i}(x)$ always corresponds to the probability of the right edge.

3.3 Contrastive Hierarchical Loss

To train CoHiClust, we introduce the hierarchical contrastive loss function designed for trees. Our idea is based on maximizing the likelihood that similar data points will follow the same path. The more similar data points, the longer they should be routed through the same nodes. Since we work in an unsupervised setting, we use a self-supervised approach and generate similar images using data augmentations.

Let us consider two data points x_1, x_2 and their posterior probabilities $P_t(x_1), P_t(x_2)$ at the level t. The probability that x_1 and x_2 reach the same node at this level is given by the scalar product $P_t(x_1) \cdot P_t(x_2) = \sum_{i=0}^{2^t-1} P_t^i(x_1) P_t^i(x_2)$. This term is maximal if both probabilities are identical one-hot vectors. In a training phase, we do not want to force hard splits in the nodes (binary probabilities), because in this way the model quickly finds a local minimum by assigning data points to fixed leaves with high confidence. Instead of sticking to hard assignments in a few training epochs, we want to let the model explore possible solutions. To this end, we take the square root before applying the scalar product, which corresponds to the Bhattacharyya coefficient [4]:

$$s_t(x_1, x_2) = \sqrt{P_t(x_1) \cdot P_t(x_2)} = \sum_{i=0}^{2^t-1} \sqrt{P_t^i(x_1)P_t^i(x_2)}. \tag{1}$$

Observe that $s_t(x_1, x_2) = 1$, if only $P_t(x_1) = P_t(x_2)$ (probabilities do not have to binarize), which leads to the exploration of possible paths. By aggregating the similarity scores over all tree levels, we arrive at our final similarity function $s(x_1, x_2) = \sum_{t=0}^{T-1} s_t(x_1, x_2)$.

In a training phase, we take a minibatch $\{x_j\}_{j=1}^N$ of N examples and generate its augmented view $\{\tilde{x}_j\}_{j=1}^N$. Every pair $(x_j, \tilde{x}_j)$ is considered positive, which means that we will maximize their similarity score. As a consequence, we encourage the model to assign them to the same leaf node. To avoid degenerate solutions, where all points end up in the same leaf, we treat all other pairs as negative and minimize their similarity scores. Finally, the proposed hierarchical contrastive loss is given by:

$$\text{CoHiLoss} = \frac{1}{N(N-1)} \sum_{j=1}^N \sum_{i \neq j} s(x_j, \tilde{x}_i) - \frac{1}{N} \sum_{j=1}^N s(x_j, \tilde{x}_j).$$

By minimizing the above loss, we maximize the likelihood that similar data points follow the same path (second term) and minimize the likelihood that dissimilar ones are grouped together.

3.4 Regularization

The final cluster assignments are induced by aggregating several binary decisions made by the internal tree nodes. In practice, the base neural network may not train all nodes and, in consequence, use only a few leaves for clustering. While selecting the number of clusters in flat clustering is desirable, here we would like to create a hierarchy, which is not restricted to a given number of leaves. To enable end-to-end training of the base neural network with an arbitrary number of leaves, we consider two regularization strategies.

The first regularization (dubbed R_1) explicitly encourages the model to use both left and right sub-trees equally [10]. We realize this postulate by minimizing the cross-entropy between the desired distribution $[0.5, 0.5]$ and the actual distribution to choose the left or right path in a given node.

The second regularization (dubbed R_2) does not directly influence the routing in the tree, but focuses on improving the output representation of the base network g. For this purpose, we use a projection head $\phi : \mathbb{R}^N \to \mathbb{R}^M$, which transforms the embeddings $z = g(x)$ of the input data, and apply the NT-Xent loss [7] to $\tilde{z} = \phi(z)$. With the NT-Xent loss, we maximize the cosine similarity for all positive pairs and minimize the cosine similarity for all negative pairs. For simple datasets, such as MNIST or F-MNIST, ϕ is an identity function, while for more complex color images, it is a two-layer network.

Table 1. Comparison with flat clustering methods on datasets of color images.

Dataset	CIFAR-10			CIFAR-100			STL-10			ImageNet-10			ImageNet-Dogs		
Metrics	NMI	ACC	ARI	NMI	ACC	ARI	NMI	ACC	ARI	NMI	ACC	ARI	NMI	ACC	ARI
K-means [25]	0.087	0.229	0.049	0.084	0.130	0.028	0.125	0.192	0.061	0.119	0.241	0.057	0.055	0.105	0.020
SC [43]	0.103	0.247	0.085	0.090	0.136	0.022	0.098	0.159	0.048	0.151	0.274	0.076	0.038	0.111	0.013
AC [11]	0.105	0.228	0.065	0.098	0.138	0.034	0.239	0.332	0.140	0.138	0.242	0.067	0.037	0.139	0.021
NMF [5]	0.081	0.190	0.034	0.079	0.118	0.026	0.096	0.180	0.046	0.132	0.230	0.065	0.044	0.118	0.016
AE [3]	0.239	0.314	0.169	0.100	0.165	0.048	0.250	0.303	0.161	0.210	0.317	0.152	0.104	0.185	0.073
DAE [34]	0.251	0.297	0.163	0.111	0.151	0.046	0.224	0.302	0.152	0.206	0.304	0.138	0.104	0.190	0.078
DCGAN [31]	0.265	0.315	0.176	0.120	0.151	0.045	0.210	0.298	0.139	0.225	0.346	0.157	0.121	0.174	0.078
DeCNN [42]	0.240	0.282	0.174	0.092	0.133	0.038	0.227	0.299	0.162	0.186	0.313	0.142	0.098	0.175	0.073
VAE [20]	0.245	0.291	0.167	0.108	0.152	0.040	0.200	0.282	0.146	0.193	0.334	0.168	0.107	0.179	0.079
JULE [39]	0.192	0.272	0.138	0.103	0.137	0.033	0.182	0.277	0.164	0.175	0.300	0.138	0.054	0.138	0.028
DEC [38]	0.257	0.301	0.161	0.136	0.185	0.050	0.276	0.359	0.186	0.282	0.381	0.203	0.122	0.195	0.079
DAC [6]	0.396	0.522	0.306	0.185	0.238	0.088	0.366	0.470	0.257	0.394	0.527	0.302	0.219	0.275	0.111
DCCM [36]	0.496	0.623	0.408	0.285	0.327	0.173	0.376	0.482	0.262	0.608	0.710	0.555	0.321	0.383	0.182
PICA [18]	0.591	0.696	0.512	0.310	0.337	0.171	0.611	0.713	0.531	0.802	0.870	0.761	0.352	0.352	0.201
CC [24]	0.705	0.790	0.637	0.431	0.429	0.266	**0.764**	**0.850**	**0.726**	0.859	0.893	0.822	**0.445**	**0.429**	**0.274**
CoHiClust	**0.779**	**0.839**	**0.731**	**0.467**	**0.437**	**0.299**	0.584	0.613	0.474	**0.907**	**0.953**	**0.899**	0.411	0.355	0.232

Taking together the contrastive loss CoHiLoss with two regularization functions R_1 (for entropy) and R_2 (for NT-Xent), we arrive at our final loss:

$$\text{Loss} = \text{CoHiLoss} + \beta_1 R_1 + \beta_2 R_2, \tag{2}$$

where β_1, β_2 are the hyperparameters that define the importance of the regularization terms R_1 and R_2, respectively. To generate a complete hierarchy (complete tree with assumed height), we set β_1 proportional to the depth of the tree $\beta_1 = 2^{-T}$ [10] and $\beta_2 = 1$ [24].

3.5   Training

CoHiClust can be trained end-to-end by minimizing (2). We verified that training is even more effective when we introduce a pre-training phase of the base neural network. To this end, we perform self-supervised representation learning of the base network g using R_2 regularization (it corresponds to the SimCLR model [7]). In Section 4.2, we show that pre-training allows us to reduce the number of training epochs and leads to a better overall performance of CoHiClust.

The proposed model builds a complete tree with 2^T leaves. Although such a structure is useful for analyzing the hierarchy of clusters, in some cases we are interested in creating a tree with the requested number of groups. For this purpose, we apply a pruning step that reduces the least significant leaf nodes. Namely, we reduce leaves with the lowest expected fraction of data points: $P_T^i = \frac{1}{|X|} \sum_{x \in X} P_T^i(x)$. Pruning is realized after a few first training epochs of CoHiClust (after the pre-training phase). We remove one leave per epoch. Next, CoHiClust is trained with the final number of leaves.

4 Experiments

First, we evaluate our method on several datasets of color images of various resolutions and with a diverse number of classes. In addition to reporting similarity scores with ground-truth partitions, we analyze the constructed hierarchies, which in our opinion is equally important in practical use-cases. Next, we perform an ablation study and investigate the properties of CoHiClust. Finally, we compare CoHiClust with existing hierarchical methods. Details of the experimental settings and additional results are included in [46, Appendix].

4.1 Clustering Color Images

Benchmark. We perform the evaluation on typical bemchmark datasets: CIFAR-10, CIFAR-100, STL-10, ImageNet-Dogs, and ImageNet-10, see [46, Appendix] for their summary. We process each data set at its original resolution. Since none of the previous hierarchical methods have been examined on these datasets, we use the benchmark that includes the flat clustering methods reported in [24]. According to previous works in contrastive clustering, CoHiClust uses ResNet architectures as a backbone network. To measure the similarity of the constructed partition with the ground truth, we apply three widely-used clustering metrics: normalized mutual information (NMI), clustering accuracy (ACC), and adjusted rand index (ARI). In [46, Appendix], we also show the DP (dendrogram purity) of the hierarchies generated by CoHiClust.

The results presented in Table 1 show that CoHiClust outperforms the comparative methods in 3 out of 5 datasets. It gives extremely good results on CIFAR-10 and ImageNet-10, but is notably worse than CC on STL-10. We suspect that lower performance on STL-10 can be caused by inadequate choice of the backbone architecture to process images at resolution 96×96. Nevertheless, one should keep in mind that CoHiClust is the only hierarchical method in this comparison, and constructing a clustering hierarchy, which resembles ground truth classes, is more challenging than directly generating a flat partition.

Analyzing Clustering Hierarchies. To better analyze the results returned by CoHiClust, we plot the constructed hierarchies. Figures 1 and 3 present and discuss the results obtained for ImageNet-10 and CIFAR-10, respectively (we refer the reader to [46, Appendix] for more examples). In both cases, CoHiClust was able to accurately model ground-truth classes as leaf nodes. In addition to the information contained in a flat partition, CoHiClust allows us to find relations between clusters. In particular, we observe that similar classes are localized on neighboring nodes.

The hierarchy also allows us to define the distance $d(a, b)$ between two examples a, b using the number of edges that connect them. We use the average of this score to calculate the similarity between the ground truth classes A and B as $d(A, B) = \frac{1}{Z} \sum_{a \in A} \sum_{b \in B} d(a, b)$, where Z is the number of all pairs. The distance is small if examples from classes A and B are located in nearby leaf nodes (on average).

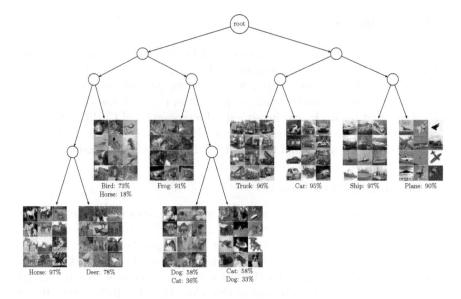

Fig. 3. A tree hierarchy generated by CoHiClust for CIFAR-10. There is an evident distinction into animals (left branch) and machines (right branch). Moreover, all neighbor leaves represent visually similar classes (horses and deers, dogs and cats, trucks and cars, ships and planes). Images with frogs seem to be visually similar to cats and dogs, which leads to their placement in the neighbor leaves (however cats and dogs are connected by a stronger relationship). Interestingly, a small portion of images with horses' heads are grouped together with birds because of their similar shapes. Although there is a slight mismatch between dogs and cats classes, the left leaf contains pets with bright fur photographed in front, while the right leaf includes animals with dark fur presented from the side, which coincides with our intuition.

Analysis of the distance matrix in Figure 4 confirms that objects representing the same class have the strongest relationship in the hierarchy (the diagonal entries contain the smallest values in the matrix). We also see high similarities between classes representing dogs and cats (1.8 jumps), cars and trucks (2 jumps), etc. In general, the distance matrix supports our previous findings quantitatively.

4.2   Analysis of the CoHiClust model

We analyze selected properties of CoHiClust including the choice of the backbone network, the influence of regularization functions, the initial depth of the tree, and the training curves. Additionally, we demonstrate that training typical hierarchical methods on top of self-supervised learning models is sub-optimal. All experiments were carried out on the CIFAR-10 dataset.

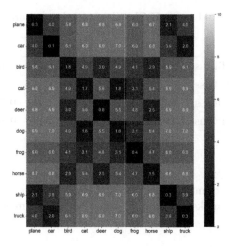

Fig. 4. Distance matrices retrieved from the constructed hierarchies for ground truth classes of CIFAR-10 dataset, see text in the paper for the interpretation.

Reliance on Backbone Network. In Table 2, we show how the selection of the architecture of the base network g influences the clustering results. As can be seen, CoHiClust gradually improves its performance with the depth of the architecture, suggesting that CoHiClust adapts well to deeper networks. In contrast, CC seems to be resistant to the selection of architecture and obtains optimal results on a medium-sized network.

Table 2. The importance of architecture choice.

Method	CoHiClust			CC [24]		
Backbone	NMI	ACC	ARI	NMI	ACC	ARI
ResNet18	0.711	0.768	0.642	0.650	0.736	0.569
ResNet34	0.730	0.788	0.667	**0.705**	**0.790**	**0.637**
ResNet50	**0.767**	**0.840**	**0.720**	0.663	0.747	0.585

Analysis of Loss Function Next, we explain the influence of particular components of the CoHiClust loss function. Additionally, we verify the role of pre-training phase. As shown in Table 3, regularization functions have a significant impact on the results of CoHiClust boosting the NMI score by 0.2. It is also evident that pre-trainig is an essential ingredient of CoHiClust, which allows selecting a better starting point for building a clustering tree.

Selecting Depth of the Tree. We investigate the choice of the initial depth of the clustering hierarchy. In Table 4, we observe a slight increase in performance by changing depth from 4 to 5. However, adding one more level does not lead

Table 3. Ablation study of CoHiClust loss function performed on CIFAR-10.

	NMI	ACC	ARI
CoHiLoss	0.567	0.569	0.457
CoHiLoss + R1	0.629	0.726	0.549
CoHiLoss + R1 + R2	**0.767**	**0.84**	**0.72**
CoHiClust w/o pre-training	0.59	0.657	0.50

to further improvement. In our opinion, using deeper trees allows for better exploration and leads to more fine-grained clusters. On the other hand, increasing the number of nodes makes optimization harder, which might explain the lower results for depth 6.

Table 4. Influence of tree depth on the clustering results.

Depth	NMI	ACC	ARI
4	0.767	**0.840**	0.720
5	**0.779**	0.839	**0.731**
6	0.689	0.713	0.581

Learning Curves. To illustrate the training phases of CoHiClust, we show the learning curves in Figure 5. Up to epoch 1000, we only trained the backbone model. Since in the pre-training phase, the clustering tree returns random decisions, we get a very low NMI value. After that, we start optimizing the CoHiLoss, and the NMI rapidly grows. In epoch 1050, we have a pruning phase, which results in further improvement of the NMI score. As can be seen, the model

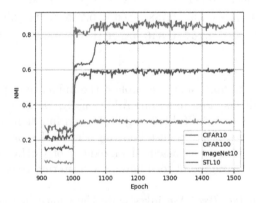

Fig. 5. Learning curves on the validation set of CIFAR-10. Pre-training is performed until epoch 1000 and pruning is applied in epoch 1050. The model stabilizes its performance quickly after pruning.

stabilizes its performance just after the pruning stage, which suggests that we can stop the training in epoch 1100. In conclusion, CoHiClust requires less than 100 epochs to obtain an optimal clustering score given a pre-trained model.

Comparison with Agglomerative Clustering. We show that our top layer responsible for constructing a decision tree is an important component of CoHiClust and cannot be replaced by alternative hierarchical clustering methods. For this purpose, we first train a backbone network with a typical self-supervised SimCLR technique. Next, we apply agglomerative clustering to the resulting representation. As can be seen in Table 5, agglomerative clustering gets very low results, which means that joint optimization of the backbone network and clustering tree using the proposed CoHiLoss is a significantly better choice. In consequence, the representation taken from a typical self-supervised learning model does not provide a representation, which can be clustered accurately using simple methods.

Table 5. Comparison with agglomerative clustering trained on the representation generated by the self-supervised learning model.

	NMI	ACC	ARI
Agglomerative clustering	0.265	0.363	0.147
CoHiClust	**0.767**	**0.84**	**0.72**

4.3 Comparison with Hierarchical Clustering Methods

To our knowledge, DeepECT [26] is the only hierarchical clustering method based on deep neural networks. Following their experimental setup, we report the results on two popular image datasets, MNIST and F-MNIST, and consider classical hierarchical algorithms evaluated on the latent representation created by the autoencoder and IDEC [14]. In addition to the previous clustering metrics, we also use dendrogram purity (DP) [21,40], which directly compares the constructed hierarchy with the ground-truth partition. It attains its maximum value of 1 if and only if all data points from the same class are assigned to some pure sub-tree.

The results summarized in Table 6 demonstrate that CoHiClust outperforms all baselines on both MNIST and F-MNIST datasets in terms of all metrics. Interestingly, DeepECT benefits from data augmentation in the case of MNIST, while on F-MNIST it deteriorates its performance. All methods except CoHiClust and DeepECT failed completely to create a hierarchy recovering true classes (see the DP measure), which confirms that there is a lack of powerful hierarchical clustering methods based on neural networks. The disproportion between the results obtained on MNIST and F-MNIST demonstrates that recovering true classes of clothes is a significantly more challenging task than recognizing handwritten digits.

Table 6. Comparison with hierarchical models in terms of DP, NMI and ACC (higher is better).

Method	MNIST			F-MNIST		
	DP	NMI	ACC	DP	NMI	ACC
DeepECT	0.82	0.83	0.85	0.47	0.60	0.52
DeepECT + Aug	0.94	0.93	0.95	0.44	0.59	0.50
IDEC (agglomerative complete*)	0.40	0.86	0.85	0.35	0.58	0.53
AE + k-means (bisecting*)	0.53	0.70	0.77	0.38	0.52	0.48
CoHiClust	**0.97**	**0.97**	**0.99**	**0.52**	**0.62**	**0.65**

* To report DP for flat clustering models, we use (optimally selected) typical hierarchical algorithms to build a hierarchy on the obtained data representation.

5 Conclusion

We proposed a contrastive hierarchical clustering model CoHiClust, which suits well to clustering of large-scale image databases. The hierarchical structure constructed by CoHiClust provides significantly more information about the data than typical flat clustering models. In particular, we can inspect the similarity between selected groups by measuring their distance in the hierarchy tree and, in consequence, find super-clusters. Experimental analysis performed on typical clustering benchmarks confirms that the produced partitions are highly similar to ground-truth classes. At the same time, CoHiClust allows us to discover important patterns that have not been encoded in the class labels.

Acknowledgments. The research of P. Rola was supported by the National Science Centre (Poland), grant no. 2021/41/B/ST6/01370. The research of J. Tabor was supported by the National Science Centre (Poland), grant no. 2022/45/B/ST6/01117. The research of M. Śmieja was supported by the Foundation for Polish Science cofinanced by the European Union under the European Regional Development Fund in the POIR.04.04.00-00-14DE/18-00 project carried out within the Team-Net program.

References

1. Alaniz, S., Marcos, D., Schiele, B., Akata, Z.: Learning decision trees recurrently through communication. In: Proceedings of the IEEE/CVF Conference on Computer Vision and Pattern Recognition, pp. 13518–13527 (2021)
2. Barai, A., Dey, L.: Outlier detection and removal algorithm in k-means and hierarchical clustering. World J. Comput. Appli. Technol. 5(2), 24–29 (2017)
3. Bengio, Y., Lamblin, P., Popovici, D., Larochelle, H.: Greedy layer-wise training of deep networks. In: Schölkopf, B., Platt, J., Hoffman, T. (eds.) Advances in Neural Information Processing Systems, vol. 19. MIT Press (2006)
4. Bhattacharyya, A.: On a measure of divergence between two multinomial populations. Sankhyā: the Indian. Stat. 401–406 (1946)

5. Cai, D., He, X., Wang, X., Bao, H., Han, J.: Locality preserving nonnegative matrix factorization **9**, 1010–1015 (2009)
6. Chang, J., Wang, L., Meng, G., Xiang, S., Pan, C.: Deep adaptive image clustering. In: Proceedings of the IEEE International Conference on Computer Vision (ICCV) (Oct 2017)
7. Chen, T., Kornblith, S., Norouzi, M., Hinton, G.: A simple framework for contrastive learning of visual representations. In: III, H.D., Singh, A. (eds.) Proceedings of the 37th International Conference on Machine Learning. Proceedings of Machine Learning Research, vol. 119, pp. 1597–1607. PMLR (13–18 Jul 2020), https://proceedings.mlr.press/v119/chen20j.html
8. Chopra, S., Hadsell, R., LeCun, Y.: Learning a similarity metric discriminatively, with application to face verification. In: 2005 IEEE Computer Society Conference on Computer Vision and Pattern Recognition (CVPR 2005), vol. 1, pp. 539–546. IEEE (2005)
9. Dang, Z., Deng, C., Yang, X., Wei, K., Huang, H.: Nearest neighbor matching for deep clustering. In: Proceedings of the IEEE/CVF Conference on Computer Vision and Pattern Recognition, pp. 13693–13702 (2021)
10. Frosst, N., Hinton, G.: Distilling a neural network into a soft decision tree. arXiv preprint arXiv:1711.09784 (2017)
11. Gowda, K.C., Krishna, G.: Agglomerative clustering using the concept of mutual nearest neighbourhood. Pattern Recogn. **10**, 105–112 (1978)
12. Grill, J.B., et al.: Bootstrap your own latent-a new approach to self-supervised learning. Adv. Neural. Inf. Process. Syst. **33**, 21271–21284 (2020)
13. Guérin, J., Gibaru, O., Thiery, S., Nyiri, E.: Cnn features are also great at unsupervised classification. arXiv preprint arXiv:1707.01700 (2017)
14. Guo, X., Gao, L., Liu, X., Yin, J.: Improved deep embedded clustering with local structure preservation. In: IJCAI, pp. 1753–1759 (2017)
15. Guo, X., Liu, X., Zhu, E., Yin, J.: Deep clustering with convolutional autoencoders. In: International Conference on Neural Information Processing, pp. 373–382. Springer (2017). https://doi.org/10.1007/978-3-319-70096-0_39
16. He, K., Fan, H., Wu, Y., Xie, S., Girshick, R.: Momentum contrast for unsupervised visual representation learning. In: 2020 IEEE/CVF Conference on Computer Vision and Pattern Recognition (CVPR), pp. 9726–9735 (2020). https://doi.org/10.1109/CVPR42600.2020.00975
17. Hu, W., Miyato, T., Tokui, S., Matsumoto, E., Sugiyama, M.: Learning discrete representations via information maximizing self-augmented training. In: International Conference on Machine Learning, pp. 1558–1567. PMLR (2017)
18. Huang, J., Gong, S., Zhu, X.: Deep semantic clustering by partition confidence maximisation. In: Proceedings of the IEEE/CVF Conference on Computer Vision and Pattern Recognition, pp. 8849–8858 (2020)
19. Ji, X., Henriques, J.F., Vedaldi, A.: Invariant information clustering for unsupervised image classification and segmentation. In: Proceedings of the IEEE International Conference on Computer Vision, pp. 9865–9874 (2019)
20. Kingma, D.P., Welling, M.: Auto-encoding variational bayes. arXiv preprint arXiv:1312.6114 (2013)
21. Kobren, A., Monath, N., Krishnamurthy, A., McCallum, A.: A hierarchical algorithm for extreme clustering. In: Proceedings of the 23rd ACM SIGKDD International Conference on Knowledge Discovery and Data Mining, pp. 255–264 (2017)
22. Lakhani, J., Chowdhary, A., Harwani, D.: Clustering techniques for biological sequence analysis: a review. J. Appli. Inform. Sci. **3**(1), 14–32 (2015)

23. Li, Y., Hu, P., Liu, Z., Peng, D., Zhou, J.T., Peng, X.: Contrastive clustering. In: Proceedings of the AAAI Conference on Artificial Intelligence, vol. 35, pp. 8547–8555 (2021)
24. Li, Y., Hu, P., Liu, Z., Peng, D., Zhou, J.T., Peng, X.: Contrastive clustering. In: Proceedings of the AAAI Conference on Artificial Intelligence, vol. 35(10), pp. 8547–8555 (May 2021), https://ojs.aaai.org/index.php/AAAI/article/view/17037
25. MacQueen, J.: Some methods for classification and analysis of multivariate observations **1**, 281–297 (1967)
26. Mautz, D., Plant, C., Böhm, C.: Deep embedded cluster tree. In: 2019 IEEE International Conference on Data Mining (ICDM), pp. 1258–1263. IEEE (2019)
27. Mautz, D., Plant, C., Böhm, C.: Deepect: the deep embedded cluster tree. Data Sci. Eng. **5**(4), 419–432 (2020)
28. Miyato, T., Maeda, S.I., Koyama, M., Ishii, S.: Virtual adversarial training: a regularization method for supervised and semi-supervised learning. IEEE Transa]. Pattern Anal. Mach. Intell. **41**(8), 1979–1993 (2018)
29. Murtagh, F., Contreras, P.: Algorithms for hierarchical clustering: an overview. Wiley Interdiscip. Rev. Data Min. Knowl. Discov. **2**(1), 86–97 (2012)
30. Naumov, S., Yaroslavtsev, G., Avdiukhin, D.: Objective-based hierarchical clustering of deep embedding vectors. In: AAAI, pp. 9055–9063 (2021)
31. Radford, A., Metz, L., Chintala, S.: Unsupervised representation learning with deep convolutional generative adversarial networks. arXiv preprint arXiv:1511.06434 (11 2015)
32. Śmieja, M., Warszycki, D., Tabor, J., Bojarski, A.J.: Asymmetric clustering index in a case study of 5-ht1a receptor ligands. PLoS ONE **9**(7), e102069 (2014)
33. Tanno, R., Arulkumaran, K., Alexander, D., Criminisi, A., Nori, A.: Adaptive neural trees. In: International Conference on Machine Learning, pp. 6166–6175. PMLR (2019)
34. Vincent, P., Larochelle, H., Lajoie, I., Bengio, Y., Manzagol, P.A.: Stacked denoising autoencoders: Learning useful representations in a deep network with a local denoising criterion. J. Mach. Learn. Res. **11**(110), 3371–3408 (2010)
35. Wan, A., et al.: Nbdt: neural-backed decision trees. arXiv preprint arXiv:2004.00221 (2020)
36. Wu, J., et al.: Deep comprehensive correlation mining for image clustering. In: Proceedings of the IEEE/CVF International Conference on Computer Vision (ICCV) (October 2019)
37. Wu, Z., Xiong, Y., Yu, S.X., Lin, D.: Unsupervised feature learning via non-parametric instance discrimination. In: Proceedings of the IEEE Conference on Computer Vision and Pattern Recognition, pp. 3733–3742 (2018)
38. Xie, J., Girshick, R., Farhadi, A.: Unsupervised deep embedding for clustering analysis. In: International Conference on Machine Learning, pp. 478–487. PMLR (2016)
39. Yang, J., Parikh, D., Batra, D.: Joint unsupervised learning of deep representations and image clusters. In: Proceedings of the IEEE Conference on Computer Vision and Pattern Recognition, pp. 5147–5156 (2016)
40. Yang, R., Qu, D., Qian, Y., Dai, Y., Zhu, S.: An online log template extraction method based on hierarchical clustering. EURASIP J. Wirel. Commun. Netw. **2019**(1), 1–12 (2019)
41. Zbontar, J., Jing, L., Misra, I., LeCun, Y., Deny, S.: Barlow twins: self-supervised learning via redundancy reduction. In: International Conference on Machine Learning, pp. 12310–12320. PMLR (2021)

42. Zeiler, M.D., Krishnan, D., Taylor, G.W., Fergus, R.: Deconvolutional networks. In: 2010 IEEE Computer Society Conference on Computer Vision and Pattern Recognition, pp. 2528–2535 (2010)
43. Zelnik-Manor, L., Perona, P.: Self-tuning spectral clustering. In: Advances in Neural Information Processing Systems, vol. 17. MIT Press (2004)
44. Zhang, F., Li, L., Hua, Q., Dong, C.R., Lim, B.H.: Improved deep clustering model based on semantic consistency for image clustering. Knowl.-Based Syst. **253**, 109507 (2022) https://doi.org/10.1016/j.knosys.2022.109507, https://www.sciencedirect.com/science/article/pii/S0950705122007560
45. Zhang, Y., Ahmed, A., Josifovski, V., Smola, A.: Taxonomy discovery for personalized recommendation. In: Proceedings of the 7th ACM International Conference on Web Search and Data Mining, pp. 243–252 (2014)
46. Znaleźniak, M., Rola, P., Kaszuba, P., Tabor, J., Śmieja, M.: Contrastive hierarchical clustering. arXiv preprint arXiv:2303.03389 (2023)
47. Zou, Q., Lin, G., Jiang, X., Liu, X., Zeng, X.: Sequence clustering in bioinformatics: an empirical study. Brief. Bioinform. **21**(1), 1–10 (2020)

Contrastive Learning
with Cluster-Preserving Augmentation
for Attributed Graph Clustering

Yimei Zheng, Caiyan Jia$^{(\boxtimes)}$, and Jian Yu

School of Computer and Information Technology, Beijing Jiaotong University,
Beijing, China
{ymmzheng,cyjia,jianyu}@bjtu.edu.cn

Abstract. Graph contrastive learning has attracted considerable attention and made remarkable progress in node representation learning and clustering for attributed graphs. However, existing contrastive-based clustering methods separate the processes of node representation learning and graph clustering into two stages, making it difficult to ensure good clustering. Therefore, it remains a challenge to design an effective contrastive learning method that jointly optimizes node representations and graph clustering. Moreover, existing random augmentation strategies to generate contrastive views may destroy the original topological structures of clusters in graphs. So it is crucial to construct an augmented graph that preserves the cluster structure of a given graph while benefitting graph clustering. To address these problems, we propose a contrastive learning method with cluster-preserving augmentation for attributed graph clustering. Specifically, we construct a contrasting view based on the generated kNN graph and edge betweenness centrality to preserve the inherent cluster structure of a graph. Then, a multilevel contrastive mechanism is proposed to maximize the agreement between node representations in multiple latent spaces. Finally, the objective of node representation learning is jointly optimized with the self-supervised clustering objective to obtain cluster distributions and discriminative node representations simultaneously. Extensive experiments on seven widely used real-world graphs demonstrate that the proposed model consistently outperforms existing state-of-the-art methods on clustering tasks.

Keywords: Augmentation · Contrastive learning · Attributed graph · Clustering

1 Introduction

Graphs or networks are widely used to model complex relationships between objects in various fields, including computer vision [26], natural language processing [20], and complex network analysis [2,33]. In many scenarios, these graphs not only contain topological relationships but also features characterizing the properties of each node, known as attributed graphs or attributed networks. One of

D. Koutra et al. (Eds.): ECML PKDD 2023, LNAI 14169, pp. 644–661, 2023.
https://doi.org/10.1007/978-3-031-43412-9_38

the fundamental yet challenging tasks in complex attributed network analysis is deep graph clustering, which involves partitioning the nodes into several disjoint clusters in an unsupervised manner with the help of deep neural network architectures to reveal the underlying structures and semantics of graphs. Moreover, identifying clusters in attributed graphs can be utilized for many tasks in reality, such as recommendation [24] and anomaly detection [10].

Graph neural networks (GNNs) [4,12,29,35,37] follow a message-passing scheme and process graphs by aggregating features from neighborhood nodes. They have been proven to be an effective way to utilize both the topology and node attribute information in attributed networks and possess powerful graph representation learning capabilities. Taking GNNs as the backbone, graph contrastive learning has attracted more and more attention from researchers and has achieved promising improvement in node representation learning and clustering [5,30,47,48]. The core idea behind existing methods is to generate two augmentations of an input graph and utilize a specific contrastive loss to make the representations of positive pairs as similar as possible, while those of negative pairs are far away from each other. With the learned powerful representations, a typical clustering method, such as K-means [17] or spectral clustering [25], can be applied to obtain node clusters.

As we know, a critical challenge in graph contrastive learning is how to design effective augmentation schemes to construct contrasting views. Existing random or specific augmentation strategies that are applied to graph topology and node attributes, such as dropping edges and masking nodes, may introduce additional noise or even destroy the intrinsic graph structure [43]. Moreover, they take less account of the cluster structure during augmentation, thereby potentially affecting the performance of downstream clustering tasks. Another main issue with existing contrastive-based graph clustering methods is that the representation learning and clustering processes are separated. We refer to these as two-stage deep graph clustering methods. They aim to learn discriminative representations under the self-supervision of contrastive mechanisms. However, the cluster distribution cannot benefit from joint optimization, which may result in the learned representations that are suboptimal for node clustering [5,19].

Recently, many methods have proposed the idea of deep embedded clustering (DEC) [1,31] to jointly learn node representations and cluster graphs in a unified model based on autoencoder frameworks. Correspondingly, we call them one-stage deep graph clustering methods. They introduce a specific clustering loss and train in conjunction with the reconstruction loss of autoencoders to optimize the cluster iteratively. Specifically, their cluster distribution can be calculated according to the encoded representations directly, avoiding the issue of two-stage clustering. Although these autoencoder-based methods are simple and easy to implement, some existing studies argue that their representational learning ability and development lag behind recent emerging contrastive learning methods [7]. Therefore, it is worth investigating whether the contrastive mechanism can be used to replace the autoencoder framework in DEC to obtain more discriminative node representations and clearer clusters during joint optimization.

To address the above challenges, we propose a $\underline{C}$ontrastive learning method with $\underline{C}$luster-preserving $\underline{A}$ugmentation for $\underline{A}$ttributed $\underline{G}$raph $\underline{C}$lustering (CCA-AGC for abbreviation). In detail, we first generate a k-nearest neighbor graph from node features and remove its edges that are more likely to connect different clusters according to the introduced edge betweenness centrality. That is, instead of perturbing the original graph, we construct another feature structural graph as a high-quality contrasting view while fully exploiting the inherent cluster structure in the original graph. We utilize a GCN encoder and a nonlinear projection layer to learn encoding and projecting representations of nodes from both topology and feature attributed graphs. A multilevel contrast mechanism is then proposed to maximize the similarity between positive pairs in these two latent spaces enabling us to capture more discriminative representations that are useful for clustering. Finally, we conduct soft clustering on encoding representations to learn cluster distributions and design a distribution consistency constraint based on KL divergence to ensure the consistency of the clusters learned from different views. Overall, CCA-AGC integrates the contrast and clustering objectives into a unified framework and obtains clusters directly by jointly optimizing node representations and cluster distributions.

In summary, we make the following contributions:

- We propose a novel generative augmentation strategy to construct a complementary contrast graph based on the kNN graph and edge betweenness centrality, which effectively captures the cluster structure hidden in node features while preserving the original graph structure.
- We integrate multilevel contrast and clustering into a unified framework to jointly optimize node representations and cluster distributions.
- Extensive experiments on real-world datasets demonstrate the superiority of the proposed model in clustering compared with state-of-the-art methods.

2   Related Work

2.1   Graph Augmentation

Graph augmentation is a crucial technique to enhance the generalization ability of graph learning and is also a vital component of graph contrastive learning [28,44,46]. For example, GAUG [45] leverages the class-homophilic structure encoded by GAE [11] predictors to remove "noisy" edges and add "missing" edges that may exist in the original graph, thus improving the performance of GNNs. Recently, various graph augmentation techniques, such as attribute masking, edge perturbation, node dropping, subgraph extracting, and graph diffusion, are commonly used in existing graph contrastive learning methods [13,40]. However, these methods are not universally applicable since graph topology and semantics vary greatly across different domains. Furthermore, some random perturbations may destroy the inherent graph structure completely, even if they are weak. To alleviate these problems, JOAO [39] and LP-Info [41] propose to select augmentation pairs automatically on specific graphs for contrastive learning.

However, they still rely on human prior knowledge to construct and configure the augmentation pool for selection. In contrast, our generative augmentation strategy combines attribute similarity and edge betweenness centrality to generate a cluster-aware augmented graph that can improve the quality of the graph while preserving its inherent graph structure and cluster information.

2.2 Graph Contrastive Learning

Graph contrastive learning has gained increasing popularity in self-supervised graph representation learning and has shown competitive performance [15,34, 47]. DGI [30] first extends the idea of DIM [6] from images to graphs by maximizing mutual information (MI) between patch representations and the corresponding graph representations. Since then, many subsequent methods [9,21,27] focus on defining MI between local-level and global-level representations of different granularities. MVGRL [5] generates a correlated view by performing diffusion on a graph and contrasts node representation from one view with graph representation from another view. Other methods aim to perform contrast at the same scale. For example, GraphCL [3] and GRACE [48] randomly drop edges and mask node features to generate different views and maximize the agreement of learned node representations. GCA [49] further introduces adaptive augmentation to obtain different views. MERIT [8] employs cross-view and cross-network contrast to maximize the agreement between node representations across different views and networks. While we perform contrast on both encoded-level and projected-level representations to capture information in multiple latent spaces of different views, improving the representation learning ability of the model.

2.3 Deep Graph Clustering

Inspired by the success of contrastive learning, several contrastive-based attributed graph clustering methods have been proposed. For example, HSAN [16] and CCGC [38] introduce high-confidence clustering pseudo labels to explicitly influence the construction of positive and negative samples during contrasting. Although these methods have achieved good performance in graph clustering, they still rely on an additional K-means algorithm to obtain final clusters. Instead, deep embedded clustering (DEC) models jointly optimize node representation and clustering, avoiding the above shortage. Wang et al. [31,32] generate a soft cluster distribution based on node representations learned by GAT and GCN encoders and achieve self-training through KL-based clustering loss. Furthermore, SDCN [1] combines a GCN encoder with a DNN autoencoder via a delivery operator and designs a dual self-supervised mechanism for clustering. AGCN [22] and DAGC [23] design the attention-driven graph clustering network that merges numerous features and enhances representation learning through an adaptive mechanism. Compared to the former two-stage clustering methods, these one-stage DEC methods are more effective due to their specific clustering loss term. However, the autoencoder frameworks may limit their discriminative representation ability when compared to the latest contrastive mechanism. Therefore, our goal is to investigate whether the contrastive mechanism can replace the autoencoder framework in DEC models to obtain clusters directly.

3 Methodology

3.1 Notations and Problem Definition

An undirected attributed network can be represented as a graph $G = (V; E; \mathbf{X})$, where $V = \{v_1, v_2, \ldots, v_n\}$ consists a set of n nodes, and $E = \{e_{ij}\}$ represents a set of edges. The topological structure of G is specified by an adjacency matrix $\mathbf{A} \in \mathbb{R}^{n \times n}$. If there is an edge between node v_i and v_j (i.e., $e_{ij} = (v_i, v_j) \in E$), then $a_{ij} = 1$, otherwise $a_{ij} = 0$. Furthermore, $\mathbf{X} \in \mathbb{R}^{n \times m}$ represents the attribute matrix, where m is the dimension of attributes. Each row $\mathbf{x}_i$ describes the attributes of node v_i.

In this study, given an attributed graph G, we aim to learn low-dimensional node representations while clustering the graph into clusters in a unified framework, where the two tasks can boost each other during training. Specifically, we will learn a map function $f : (\mathbf{A}, \mathbf{X}) \mapsto \mathbf{H} \in \mathbb{R}^{n \times d}$, where h_i is the i-th row of $\mathbf{H}$, representing the latent representation of node v_i. Meanwhile, the attributed graph is partitioned into K disjoint clusters $(C_1, C_2, \ldots, C_K)$, so that not only are the nodes in the same cluster more closely connected than nodes outside the cluster, but the attribute similarity of a pair of nodes within the same cluster is higher than that of only one in the cluster.

3.2 Overall Framework

In the following subsections, we will provide a detailed introduction to our proposed Contrastive learning method with Cluster-preserving Augmentation for Attributed Graph Clustering (CCA-AGC), as shown in Fig. 1. The entire model begins with generative augmentation, which constructs a cluster-aware contrasting view. Then, we propose a multilevel contrast mechanism that maximizes agreement between node representations in multiple latent spaces. Furthermore, the learned encoding representations are utilized to generate cluster assignments. Finally, we formulate a self-supervised clustering objective with the help of a distribution consistency constraint and integrate it with the contrastive representation learning process for joint optimization.

3.3 Generative Augmentation

In an attributed graph G, nodes with similar features are more likely to belong to the same cluster. To capture this similarity, we generate a k-nearest neighbor (kNN) graph based on the node features $\mathbf{X}$. Specifically, we use Euclidean distance to measure the similarity s_{ij} between attribute vectors $\mathbf{x}_i$ and $\mathbf{x}_j$ of two nodes v_i and v_j, obtaining the similarity matrix $\mathbf{S} \in \mathbb{R}^{n \times n}$. Then, we select

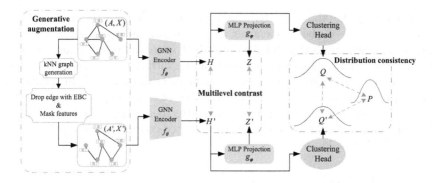

Fig. 1. The overall framework of the proposed CCA-AGC model. It contains three main strategies: generative augmentation, multi-level contrast, and distribution consistency constraint.

the top-k most similar node pairs based on $\mathbf{S}$ and connect them with edges to form an undirected kNN attributed graph $G_f = (\mathbf{A}_f, \mathbf{X})$, where $\mathbf{A}_f \in \mathbb{R}^{n \times n}$ is the corresponding adjacency matrix for the kNN graph, and the attribute matrix $\mathbf{X} \in \mathbb{R}^{n \times m}$ remains unchanged. It should be noticed that G_f captures the underlying topology structure reflected by node features, which complements the original graph G and provides additional information for clustering.

To fully exploit the inherent cluster structure present in the feature space, we introduce the concept of edge betweenness centrality (EBC) [2] to update and filter the connection relationships in the kNN graph G_f.

Definition 1. *Edge Betweenness Centrality (EBC). The number of the shortest paths that run along an edge between pairs of nodes in a graph, where the shortest path is the path with the smallest distance between any two nodes. EBC can be formalized as follows:*

$$c_B(e) = \sum_{s,t \in V} \frac{\sigma(s,t|e)}{\sigma(s,t)},$$

where V is the set of nodes in the graph, $\sigma(s,t)$ is the number of the shortest (s,t)-paths, and $\sigma(s,t|e)$ is the number of those paths passing through edge e.

In the generated kNN attributed graph G_f, we can calculate the EBC for each edge. An edge with a high score indicates that it is more likely to connect different clusters in the graph, and its removal will divide the graph into two densely connected groups. Inspired by this, we find the top-τ edges with the highest EBC and remove them, where $\tau = p_e \times |E_f|$, $|E_f|$ is the number of edges in the kNN graph, and p_e is the removal probability. Then, the filtered feature graph can be represented as $G'_f = (\mathbf{A}', \mathbf{X})$, where $\mathbf{A}'$ is the new adjacency matrix formed from the remaining edges. By reducing the number of inter-cluster edges in G'_f, the clusters are separated from each other and the underlying cluster structure is revealed more clearly.

We refer to the above strategy as a generative augmentation to generate contrasting views. Without perturbing the structure of the original graph, we generate another graph that fully utilizes the feature information and preserves the cluster structure. This approach provides us with richer information to learn more discriminative representations and achieve better clusters. In addition to graph topology, we adopt the general way [3,48] of randomly masking a fraction (p_m) of dimensions in node attributes with zeros to construct the feature matrix $\mathbf{X}'$ of the contrastive view. Finally, the constructed contrastive view is formalized as $G' = (\mathbf{A}', \mathbf{X}')$ as input.

3.4   Multilevel Contrast

With the obtained contrasting pairs $G = (\mathbf{A}, \mathbf{X})$ and $G' = (\mathbf{A}', \mathbf{X}')$, we employ a GCN as an encoder f_θ to aggregate information from neighbors in a given graph. Then the *encoding representations* $\mathbf{H} = f_\theta(\mathbf{X}, \mathbf{A})$ and $\mathbf{H}' = f_\theta(\mathbf{X}', \mathbf{A}')$ of both the original topology and the generated feature attributed graphs are obtained based on shared parameters. In addition, we also use a multilayer perceptron (MLP) as a projection head g_φ following the encoder to improve the quality of the learned representations. The *projecting representations* of nodes in graphs G and G' are represented as $\mathbf{Z} = g_\varphi(\mathbf{H})$ and $\mathbf{Z}' = g_\varphi(\mathbf{H}')$, respectively.

We argue that the *encoding representation* $\mathbf{H}$ contains more view-specific information about the input attributed graph, while the *projecting representation* $\mathbf{Z}$ contains more fine-grained information after transformation. Therefore, to capture more comprehensive information in multiple latent spaces, we propose a multilevel contrast strategy to perform contrast on both encoding and projecting representations simultaneously. Following the most popularly used InfoNCE [18] loss, we formalize the contrastive loss for *encoding representation* as follows:

$$\ell(h_i, h_i') = -\log \frac{\exp(sim(h_i, h_i'))}{\exp(sim(h_i, h_i')) + \sum_{k \neq i} \exp(sim(h_i, h_k)) + \sum_{k \neq i} \exp(sim(h_i, h_k'))},$$

(1)

where $sim(\cdot, \cdot)$ is the cosine similarity. (h_i, h_i') is a positive sample pair, h_i is the encoding representation of node v_i in the original graph G, and h_i' corresponds to that of the constructed graph G'. Naturally, we treat all other nodes different from node v_i as negative samples, which come from the same graph G and another contrastive graph G', expressed by the second and third terms in the denominator of Eq. (1). Since the two views are symmetric, the loss of another view is defined similarly by $\ell(h_i', h_i)$. Thus, we maximize the agreement of node representations in encoding space by optimizing the following contrastive loss:

$$\mathcal{L}_{enc} = \frac{1}{2n} \sum_{i=1}^{n} [\ell(h_i, h_i') + \ell(h_i', h_i)].$$

(2)

Correspondingly, the optimization objective for representation in the projecting space takes a similar form, as shown below:

$$\mathcal{L}_{pro} = \frac{1}{2n} \sum_{i=1}^{n} \left[\ell(z_i, z_i') + \ell(z_i', z_i) \right]. \tag{3}$$

Overall, combining the contrastive loss of encoding and projecting representations, we formalize the following multilevel contrast objective, where $\lambda > 0$ is a trade-off parameter to balance them.

$$\mathcal{L}_{tra} = \lambda * \mathcal{L}_{enc} + \mathcal{L}_{pro} \tag{4}$$

3.5   Attributed Graph Clustering

Once we obtain the encoding representations $\mathbf{H}, \mathbf{H}' \in \mathbb{R}^{n \times d}$, we introduce a clustering head to achieve clustering. Specifically, we use Student's t-distribution as a kernel to measure the similarity between node embeddings h_i, h_i' and cluster center, generating soft cluster assignments $\mathbf{Q}, \mathbf{Q}' \in \mathbb{R}^{n \times K}$ for the two contrastive views. The generation of $\mathbf{Q}$ for the original graph can be expressed as follows (and $\mathbf{Q}'$ of the other view is similar):

$$q_{ik} = \frac{(1 + \|h_i - \mu_k\|^2)^{-1}}{\sum_j (1 + \|h_i - \mu_j\|^2)^{-1}}, \quad p_{ik} = \frac{q_{ik}{}^2 / \sum_i q_{ik}}{\sum_j (q_{ij}{}^2 / \sum_i q_{ij})}, \tag{5}$$

where q_{ik} represents the probability that node v_i is assigned to cluster k. The cluster centers μ_k $(k = 1, 2, \cdots, K)$ are trainable parameters, which are initialized by employing K-means on the pre-trained node representations and updated throughout training. Moreover, if a node v_i is closer to a particular cluster center μ_k, then q_{ik} has a larger value, and vice versa.

As formulated in Eq. (5), we follow previous studies [31,36] and construct an auxiliary target distribution $\mathbf{P}$ by emphasizing the confident part with large values and weakening the relatively unimportant part in $\mathbf{Q}$. In this way, the obtained assignment is more reliable and can be used to refine clusters. Therefore, we achieve self-supervised clustering by forcing the current assignment $\mathbf{Q}, \mathbf{Q}'$ to approach that of target $\mathbf{P}$, i.e., by minimizing the KL divergence between them:

$$\mathcal{L}_{KL} = KL(\mathbf{P}\|\mathbf{Q}) + KL(\mathbf{P}\|\mathbf{Q}') = \sum_i \sum_k p_{ik} \log \frac{p_{ik}}{q_{ik}} + \sum_i \sum_k p_{ik} \log \frac{p_{ik}}{q_{ik}'}. \tag{6}$$

Recalling the assumption that the cluster distribution of network topology and that of node attributes should be consistent for an attributed graph, we propose a distribution consistency constraint to make the soft cluster assignments $\mathbf{Q}, \mathbf{Q}'$ learned from the original and augmented graphs as consistent as possible. This is because the two contrasting views are used to learn the information contained in the network topology and node features, respectively. Similarly, we achieve this by minimizing the KL divergence between $\mathbf{Q}$ and $\mathbf{Q}'$. Therefore, the overall clustering optimization process can be expressed as follows:

$$\mathcal{L}_{clu} = \mathcal{L}_{KL} + \mathcal{L}_{con} = KL(\mathbf{P}\|\mathbf{Q}) + KL(\mathbf{P}\|\mathbf{Q}') + KL(\mathbf{Q}\|\mathbf{Q}'). \tag{7}$$

3.6   Joint Training

In summary, our proposed CCA-AGC model aims to learn node representations and cluster assignments simultaneously by jointly optimizing the multilevel contrastive learning and deep embedded clustering objectives. The loss function for the model is given below:

$$\mathcal{L} = \mathcal{L}_{tra} + \mathcal{L}_{clu}. \tag{8}$$

The entire learning process of the CCA-AGC model is shown in Algorithm 1 of the supplementary material. Moreover, the final clustering result is directly obtained from the cluster assignment $\mathbf{Q}$ of the original attributed graph G. Namely, the cluster c_i for node v_i can be estimated as $c_i = \arg\max_k q_{ik}$.

4   Experiments

In this section, we present extensive experiments and detailed analyses that illustrate the performance of our proposed CCA-AGC model[1] and the effectiveness of each component.

4.1   Experimental Setups

Datasets. We evaluate the clustering performance of our proposed model on seven widely used real-world attributed graphs, including Cora, CiteSeer, PubMed, WikiCS, Amazon-Photo, Amazon-Computers (AmazonCom), and Coauthor-CS. Detailed descriptions and statistics of these datasets are summarized in the supplementary material.

Baselines. To verify the effectiveness of the proposed CCA-AGC model, we compare it with eleven state-of-the-art self-supervised baselines, including two-stage deep graph clustering methods and one-stage deep embedded clustering methods based on autoencoder (SDCN [1] and AGCN [22]). Furthermore, two-stage methods can be further divided into contrastive-based representation learning methods (DGI [30], MVGRL [5], GRACE [48], GCA [49], MERIT [8], CCA-SSG [42], and AFGRL [14]), cluster-guided contrastive clustering method (CCGC [38]), and autoencoder-based representation learning method (Graph-MAE [7]).

Evaluation Metrics. In our experiments, clustering performance is evaluated using four popular metrics. Accuracy (ACC), Normalized Mutual Information (NMI), Average Rand Index (ARI), and F1-score (F1). For these metrics, a larger value indicates a better clustering result.

---

[1] The code is available at https://github.com/Zhengymm/CCA-AGC.

Experimental Settings. We use a two-layer GCN and a two-layer MLP as encoder and projector. The Adam optimizer with weight decay 10^{-5} is utilized for optimization. We perform a grid search for each dataset to find the optimal hyperparameters. Due to space constraints, in the supplementary material, we specify these parameters, list the default values used in the experiments, and also perform sensitivity analyses for some important parameters. To ensure a fair comparison, we replicate all baseline methods using their published codes and default settings. With their learned node representations of the original graph, we perform K-means to get the final clusters. We report the average results of 10 runs for all methods to avoid extreme cases.

4.2   Performance Comparison

Table 1 summarizes the performance of all methods for attributed graph clustering. Generally, the proposed CCA-AGC model consistently outperforms other baseline methods on all datasets. For example, we improve NMI and ACC by 2.37% and 2.82% compared to the best CCGC model on the Amazon-Photo dataset. Specifically, existing contrastive-based two-stage clustering methods show poor clustering performance because they fail to preserve the cluster structure of the original graph during augmentation. Although the newly proposed CCGC [38] and GraphMAE [7] methods achieve good results on some datasets, they still require additional clustering with the K-means algorithm. On the contrary, our CCA-AGC model introduces a cluster-preserving contrasting view and inherits the idea of DEC, directly obtaining a clearer cluster distribution and achieving better clustering results. Moreover, compared with existing autoencoder-based one-stage clustering methods, our multilevel contrastive mechanism is more helpful for joint optimization and learning cluster-aware discriminative representations, resulting in improved clustering performance.

To further illustrate the effectiveness of our one-stage deep embedded clustering, we also perform K-means on our learned encoding representations to show the performance of two-stage clustering, denoted as "CCA-AGC+K-means" in Table 1. We can see that the results are slightly worse than directly deriving clusters from soft assignments during training. However, our CCA-AGC+K-means still shows superiority over other baselines. This indicates that representation learning and clustering can promote each other through our joint optimization, and the learned representation is more discriminative for clustering.

Table 1. Performance comparison of attributed graph clustering (mean±std in percentage), where the best results are highlighted in bold, and the sub-optimal ones are underlined. OOM means out of memory.

Method	Dataset	Cora	CiteSeer	PubMed	WikiCS	AmazonCom	Amazon-Photo	Coauthor-CS
DGI	ACC	72.03 ± 1.97	68.85 ± 0.57	52.03 ± 0.90	31.92 ± 2.95	40.79 ± 2.52	46.57 ± 2.06	71.53 ± 1.41
	NMI	56.63 ± 1.22	44.28 ± 0.66	11.06 ± 3.54	12.04 ± 1.95	32.47 ± 1.58	37.88 ± 1.80	76.84 ± 1.17
	ARI	52.14 ± 2.40	44.88 ± 0.66	9.33 ± 3.54	3.30 ± 0.83	23.37 ± 2.50	24.72 ± 1.32	63.87 ± 1.88
	F1	69.21 ± 1.58	64.60 ± 0.48	44.43 ± 0.87	15.39 ± 1.80	25.41 ± 1.02	39.98 ± 3.07	66.92 ± 4.55
MVGRL	ACC	71.85 ± 1.76	68.51 ± 0.31	64.52 ± 0.49	29.75 ± 2.15	38.28 ± 0.49	50.91 ± 0.60	67.66 ± 0.60
	NMI	57.16 ± 1.16	43.86 ± 0.29	31.17 ± 0.92	15.24 ± 2.63	30.38 ± 0.86	42.34 ± 1.79	74.34 ± 0.32
	ARI	52.47 ± 2.32	43.91 ± 0.34	27.65 ± 0.77	4.35 ± 0.90	17.72 ± 0.64	28.62 ± 1.79	60.72 ± 0.47
	F1	68.83 ± 1.20	63.49 ± 0.41	64.46 ± 0.62	17.32 ± 1.95	23.37 ± 0.33	43.71 ± 2.09	64.74 ± 1.70
GRACE	ACC	61.30 ± 3.81	65.09 ± 0.54	67.79 ± 2.83	35.71 ± 3.23	47.45 ± 1.69	57.84 ± 5.17	74.31 ± 4.35
	NMI	47.10 ± 3.06	39.59 ± 0.92	31.23 ± 5.31	27.36 ± 4.41	42.71 ± 1.07	47.30 ± 3.68	75.44 ± 1.28
	ARI	38.73 ± 4.65	39.86 ± 0.80	29.45 ± 4.97	9.27 ± 4.50	22.59 ± 1.66	29.99 ± 4.53	65.49 ± 5.61
	F1	58.06 ± 3.43	61.38 ± 0.60	67.81 ± 2.49	24.14 ± 3.18	39.15 ± 1.15	53.33 ± 5.33	74.12 ± 3.15
GCA	ACC	56.13 ± 4.69	64.36 ± 2.26	66.39 ± 6.55	29.86 ± 2.50	47.83 ± 1.19	63.17 ± 5.30	74.13 ± 3.67
	NMI	46.59 ± 3.77	39.90 ± 1.64	33.13 ± 6.98	16.13 ± 4.73	43.09 ± 1.07	54.12 ± 4.87	75.95 ± 1.21
	ARI	30.61 ± 6.97	39.56 ± 2.51	28.89 ± 8.82	2.81 ± 2.19	23.88 ± 1.17	40.21 ± 6.42	66.51 ± 4.97
	F1	51.46 ± 3.69	60.10 ± 2.07	66.32 ± 6.39	13.97 ± 4.10	38.69 ± 0.76	56.98 ± 5.49	73.17 ± 2.37
MERIT	ACC	68.03 ± 3.54	69.11 ± 0.44	63.70 ± 0.38	36.89 ± 3.16	55.16 ± 1.38	76.19 ± 1.92	72.78 ± 1.82
	NMI	54.08 ± 1.77	44.38 ± 0.66	26.68 ± 0.36	25.00 ± 1.36	52.51 ± 0.71	66.20 ± 3.07	<u>79.08 ± 0.61</u>
	ARI	46.31 ± 2.70	45.31 ± 0.71	24.26 ± 0.41	10.67 ± 2.77	36.23 ± 2.50	54.92 ± 3.84	66.30 ± 1.13
	F1	63.96 ± 4.09	**64.70 ± 0.47**	64.54 ± 0.38	23.64 ± 1.72	42.48 ± 2.13	71.33 ± 1.93	72.32 ± 3.66
CCA-SSG	ACC	58.17 ± 5.32	<u>69.36 ± 0.70</u>	59.58 ± 5.56	37.09 ± 2.35	45.41 ± 0.71	48.93 ± 1.12	37.45 ± 2.50
	NMI	48.55 ± 4.28	44.46 ± 0.85	27.43 ± 5.09	29.18 ± 2.62	41.63 ± 0.85	45.06 ± 1.18	32.20 ± 5.63
	ARI	35.07 ± 10.34	45.47 ± 1.09	23.47 ± 7.35	9.42 ± 1.88	26.42 ± 1.16	22.78 ± 0.55	8.61 ± 6.03
	F1	46.44 ± 6.83	64.19 ± 0.86	57.38 ± 8.70	27.76 ± 2.37	42.04 ± 0.78	49.58 ± 0.84	24.66 ± 1.99
AFGRL	ACC	68.67 ± 2.17	66.24 ± 1.93	63.64 ± 2.14	50.53 ± 1.55	48.05 ± 1.60	71.24 ± 2.29	74.71 ± 1.67
	NMI	52.73 ± 1.81	41.36 ± 1.36	31.74 ± 1.28	41.57 ± 0.74	<u>54.07 ± 0.89</u>	65.29 ± 2.07	78.65 ± 0.43
	ARI	45.54 ± 2.81	41.07 ± 1.96	27.75 ± 1.26	31.65 ± 1.51	31.84 ± 1.37	52.49 ± 3.41	67.07 ± 0.72
	F1	67.52 ± 2.05	61.86 ± 2.47	62.94 ± 2.46	42.62 ± 1.23	40.24 ± 1.54	67.36 ± 1.27	72.82 ± 2.91
CCGC	ACC	<u>73.73 ± 1.81</u>	<u>69.61 ± 0.67</u>	67.43 ± 0.77	37.90 ± 0.81	**61.62 ± 3.42**	77.53 ± 0.76	OOM
	NMI	55.93 ± 1.58	44.12 ± 0.70	30.98 ± 1.29	23.32 ± 1.39	52.19 ± 1.74	66.68 ± 0.89	
	ARI	51.52 ± 2.44	44.03 ± 1.39	29.56 ± 1.07	17.29 ± 1.28	<u>42.38 ± 5.57</u>	<u>58.96 ± 2.20</u>	
	F1	<u>70.83 ± 2.92</u>	62.34 ± 1.82	67.27 ± 0.75	29.41 ± 2.46	**46.42 ± 3.30**	<u>71.59 ± 1.47</u>	
GraphMAE	ACC	67.61 ± 3.69	68.47 ± 0.40	69.60 ± 0.53	42.55 ± 2.54	52.23 ± 1.39	72.25 ± 1.34	59.96 ± 6.07
	NMI	57.24 ± 1.76	43.14 ± 0.34	34.20 ± 0.53	35.86 ± 1.37	52.24 ± 0.81	64.45 ± 1.83	70.22 ± 4.17
	ARI	49.66 ± 3.87	43.99 ± 0.54	<u>32.63 ± 0.67</u>	22.88 ± 2.07	36.66 ± 1.72	55.68 ± 1.67	52.61 ± 6.12
	F1	62.67 ± 3.84	64.47 ± 0.34	69.27 ± 0.55	36.47 ± 2.22	40.84 ± 0.49	66.28 ± 2.60	50.53 ± 6.69
SDCN	ACC	54.76 ± 2.75	65.05 ± 1.19	62.57 ± 0.80	48.11 ± 0.52	50.50 ± 5.25	58.00 ± 4.27	65.80 ± 1.66
	NMI	36.52 ± 3.02	38.05 ± 0.85	22.76 ± 1.02	39.08 ± 0.75	35.79 ± 4.53	47.15 ± 3.94	66.02 ± 1.63
	ARI	28.97 ± 2.55	39.28 ± 1.36	21.16 ± 1.10	27.37 ± 0.35	30.44 ± 8.23	38.16 ± 4.36	65.04 ± 2.14
	F1	46.06 ± 3.34	59.88 ± 0.86	63.07 ± 0.72	41.90 ± 1.12	26.84 ± 3.09	47.36 ± 5.27	37.29 ± 2.89
AGCN	ACC	58.71 ± 0.36	68.65 ± 0.20	61.20 ± 0.39	**55.50 ± 1.49**	57.18 ± 1.43	61.03 ± 2.55	77.73 ± 0.99
	NMI	40.61 ± 0.27	41.52 ± 0.27	23.03 ± 0.29	<u>42.66 ± 0.04</u>	41.65 ± 1.05	54.73 ± 1.17	72.16 ± 0.78
	ARI	34.19 ± 0.28	43.67 ± 0.22	20.96 ± 0.47	<u>35.11 ± 1.36</u>	2.25 ± 1.91	44.32 ± 2.27	<u>74.64 ± 0.89</u>
	F1	50.59 ± 0.32	62.37 ± 0.15	62.12 ± 0.48	<u>43.05 ± 0.38</u>	30.77 ± 1.32	53.85 ± 1.54	53.88 ± 1.67
CCA-AGC +K-means	ACC	73.50 ± 0.26	68.77 ± 0.12	<u>70.00 ± 0.06</u>	50.04 ± 2.92	51.64 ± 0.06	<u>77.85 ± 0.06</u>	78.98 ± 3.00
	NMI	<u>57.45 ± 0.89</u>	44.81 ± 0.23	<u>35.72 ± 0.09</u>	36.53 ± 1.90	51.16 ± 0.07	<u>68.34 ± 0.10</u>	75.87 ± 1.79
	ARI	<u>54.82 ± 1.21</u>	<u>45.53 ± 0.22</u>	32.28 ± 0.11	29.77 ± 3.42	34.20 ± 0.07	**64.06 ± 0.15**	71.70 ± 7.31
	F1	70.08 ± 2.07	64.56 ± 0.11	<u>69.81 ± 0.07</u>	33.08 ± 2.70	42.14 ± 0.06	**73.94 ± 0.06**	<u>78.15 ± 1.07</u>
CCA-AGC	ACC	**74.46 ± 0.26**	69.01 ± 0.12	**70.91 ± 0.08**	<u>52.58 ± 1.05</u>	<u>60.35 ± 0.17</u>	**80.35 ± 0.07**	**83.51 ± 0.32**
	NMI	**58.50 ± 0.31**	45.06 ± 0.24	**36.57 ± 0.04**	**42.78 ± 0.45**	54.18 ± 0.06	**69.80 ± 0.10**	**79.42 ± 0.34**
	ARI	**56.13 ± 0.33**	**45.91 ± 0.20**	**34.11 ± 0.10**	**35.23 ± 0.92**	**44.31 ± 0.20**	**64.06 ± 0.15**	**79.18 ± 0.61**
	F1	**72.00 ± 0.24**	<u>64.69 ± 0.11</u>	**70.77 ± 0.08**	**45.50 ± 0.84**	<u>43.95 ± 0.31</u>	**73.94 ± 0.06**	**80.90 ± 0.20**

4.3   Ablation Study

In this section, we conduct ablation studies to verify the benefit of each component of the proposed CCA-AGC model.

Augmentation Mechanism. To examine the influence of the contrasting view construction strategy on the proposed CCA-AGC model, we substitute our generative augmentation strategies, i.e., generate a kNN graph and filter its edges according to the EBC, with commonly used augmentation strategies, including random edge dropping and diffusion graph construction. Therefore, we implement three variants of our model: (1) kNN + Random dropping, which generates a kNN graph but drops edges randomly. (2) Random dropping, which randomly drops edges in the original graph. (3) Diffusion, which employs diffusion to construct another contrasting view. The clustering results on the CiteSeer and Amazon-Photo datasets are shown in Fig. 2.

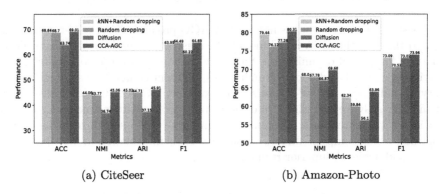

(a) CiteSeer   (b) Amazon-Photo

Fig. 2. Clustering performance of CCA-AGC model under different contrasting view augmentation strategies.

We see that the proposed generative augmentation performs the best among all variants. In detail, performing corruption on the generated kNN graph rather than on the original graph leads to better clustering results. This is because the generated kNN graph not only emphasizes feature similarity but also preserves the inherent structure of the original graph. Meanwhile, compared to randomly dropping edges, the introduction of EBC can remove edges that are more likely to exist between clusters, facilitating better identification of the cluster structure and improving the overall clustering performance. Besides, a diffusion graph is not well-suited for our model, as it yields poor results. In general, our generative augmentation strategy is effective and important for the CCA-AGC model.

Multilevel Contrast. To illustrate the effectiveness of our multilevel contrast mechanism, which performs contrast in both the encoding and the projecting representation spaces, we validate the clustering performance of the CCA-AGC model when contrasted only on one of the representations. Figure 3 presents

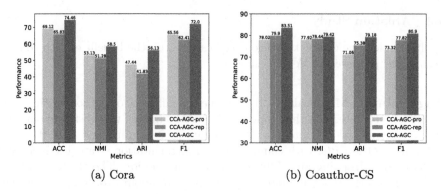

Fig. 3. Performance of CCA-AGC model with/without multilevel contrast.

the results on Cora and Coauthor-CS datasets, where "CCA-AGC-pro" and "CCA-AGC-rep" indicate that we maximize the agreement of positive sample pairs by optimizing the *projecting representation* and *encoding representation*, respectively.

As shown in Fig. 3, the results of CCA-AGC-pro and CCA-AGC-rep are inferior to those of the CCA-AGC model, demonstrating the benefits of multilevel contrast for overall optimization. Since the encoder and projector exploit information in a graph at different granularities, different contrasting strategies show varying influences across datasets. For example, CCA-AGC-pro works better than CCA-AGC-rep on the Cora dataset, but the opposite is true on Coauthor-CS in our presented case. Therefore, we mitigate this issue through multilevel contrast, which comprehensively considers various information in multiple latent spaces and achieves superior results.

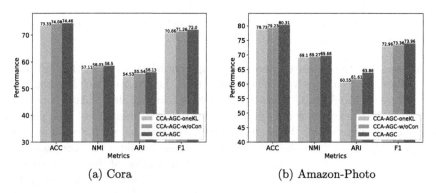

Fig. 4. Clustering performance of CCA-AGC model with different self-supervised clustering constraints.

Self-supervised Clustering. We utilize KL divergence to measure the self-supervised clustering process of the original graph and the augmented graph, as well as the distribution consistency constraint, which corresponds to the three parts represented in Eq. (7). We evaluate the influence of each part on the model in this section. The clustering performance of the CCA-AGC model on Cora and Amazon-Photo datasets is shown in Fig. 4, where "CCA-AGC-oneKL" indicates only utilizing the KL divergence constraint for the original graph, i.e., $KL(\mathbf{P}\|\mathbf{Q})$. "CCA-AGC-w/oCon" indicates ignoring the distribution consistency constraint, i.e., we use $KL(\mathbf{P}\|\mathbf{Q}) + KL(\mathbf{P}\|\mathbf{Q}')$ for clustering.

From Fig. 4, we find that CCA-AGC-w/oCon works better than CCA-AGC-oneKL, and the final CCA-AGC model outperforms CCA-AGC-w/oCon. It shows that each part of the clustering loss can affect joint training and improve the final clustering results. With the increasing constraints in self-supervised clustering, we can refine the cluster distribution from different aspects and obtain clear clusters. Specifically, with the former two constraints in Eq. (7), the target distribution can guide the refinement of soft assignments calculated from the original and augmented attributed graphs simultaneously. Meanwhile, they are forced to be consistent through the last distribution consistency constraint.

4.4   Convergence Analysis

To provide a more intuitive understanding of the training process, we present the convergence trends of the CCA-AGC model in Fig. 5, showcasing the overall loss and clustering performance on the WikiCS and AmazonCom datasets. Note that the x-axis represents the training epoch, the y-axis on the left denotes the value of the overall loss, and the one on the right represents the clustering results.

According to Fig. 5, our model can achieve convergence quickly. In the first few epochs, both the total loss of the model and the clustering performance change rapidly. However, after about 100 training epochs, the model gradually stabilizes and tends to converge, where the loss decreases steadily and the clustering results increase slightly. Importantly, our results show that optimal

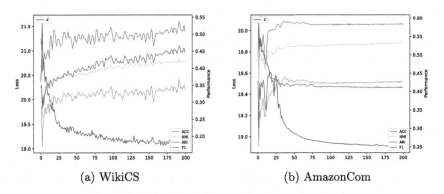

(a) WikiCS   (b) AmazonCom

Fig. 5. The convergence curves of CCA-AGC model for the overall loss and clustering performance over the training process.

performance can be achieved upon convergence, further demonstrating the feasibility of joint optimization of representation learning and clustering based on contrastive mechanisms.

5   Conclusion

Motivated by the great success of graph contrastive learning and deep embedded clustering, we propose a simple yet effective contrastive learning method with cluster-preserving augmentation for attributed graph clustering. Our CCA-AGC model differs from existing graph contrastive learning methods by constructing another cluster-aware contrasting view that considers the similarity of node features while preserving the original graph structure. Moreover, we jointly optimize the contrasting objective defined in multiple latent representation spaces with the specific clustering objective, allowing node representation learning and clustering to reinforce each other. Extensive experiments on clustering tasks demonstrate the superior performance of CCA-AGC over existing methods and validate the effectiveness of each component. Overall, our proposed model provides insight for designing attributed graph clustering models that leverage the advantages of graph contrastive learning and deep embedded clustering. In the future, we plan to utilize cluster distribution as a pseudo-label to guide the construction of positive and negative sample pairs in the contrastive objective during training.

Acknowledgments. This work was supported by the National Natural Science Foundation of China (61876016) and the National Key R&D Program of China (2018AAA0100302).

Ethical Statement. Our research aims to introduce a new algorithm for attributed graph clustering. This study does not involve human or animal participants. The data used in this research are obtained from publicly available datasets, and no data (including images) have been fabricated or manipulated to support the conclusions. The authors declare that they have no conflict of interest in this work. All co-authors have agreed to the submission of this version. We certify that this manuscript is original and has not been previously published or submitted elsewhere. The article is also not divided into several parts to increase the number of submissions. We are committed to ensuring the transparency and fairness of our research results and our research are conducted in accordance with relevant ethical standards and principles of academic integrity.

References

1. Bo, D., Wang, X., Shi, C., Zhu, M., Lu, E., Cui, P.: Structural deep clustering network. In: Proceedings of the The Web Conference 2020, pp. 1400–1410 (2020)
2. Girvan, M., Newman, M.E.: Community structure in social and biological networks. Proc. Natl. Acad. Sci. **99**(12), 7821–7826 (2002)

3. Hafidi, H., Ghogho, M., Ciblat, P., Swami, A.: Negative sampling strategies for contrastive self-supervised learning of graph representations. Signal Process. **190**, 108310 (2022)

4. Hamilton, W.L., Ying, Z., Leskovec, J.: Inductive representation learning on large graphs. In: Advances in Neural Information Processing Systems 30, pp. 1024–1034 (2017)

5. Hassani, K., Ahmadi, A.H.K.: Contrastive multi-view representation learning on graphs. In: Proceedings of the 37th International Conference on Machine Learning, vol. 119, pp. 4116–4126 (2020)

6. Hjelm, R.D., Fedorov, A., Lavoie-Marchildon, S., Grewal, K., Bachman, P., Trischler, A., Bengio, Y.: Learning deep representations by mutual information estimation and maximization. In: Proceedings of the 7th International Conference on Learning Representations (2019)

7. Hou, Z., et al.: Graphmae: Self-supervised masked graph autoencoders. In: Proceedings of the 28th ACM SIGKDD Conference on Knowledge Discovery and Data Mining, pp. 594–604 (2022)

8. Jin, M., Zheng, Y., Li, Y., Gong, C., Zhou, C., Pan, S.: Multi-scale contrastive siamese networks for self-supervised graph representation learning. In: Proceedings of the 30th International Joint Conference on Artificial Intelligence, pp. 1477–1483 (2021)

9. Jing, B., Park, C., Tong, H.: HDMI: high-order deep multiplex infomax. In: Proceedings of the The Web Conference 2021, pp. 2414–2424 (2021)

10. Keyvanpour, M.R., Shirzad, M.B., Ghaderi, M.: AD-C: a new node anomaly detection based on community detection in social networks. Int. J. Electron. Bus. **15**(3), 199–222 (2020)

11. Kingma, D.P., Welling, M.: Auto-encoding variational bayes. In: Proceedings of the 2nd International Conference on Learning Representations (2014)

12. Kipf, T.N., Welling, M.: Semi-supervised classification with graph convolutional networks. In: Proceedings of the 5th International Conference on Learning Representations (2017)

13. Klicpera, J., Weißenberger, S., Günnemann, S.: Diffusion improves graph learning. In: Advances in Neural Information Processing Systems 32, pp. 13333–13345 (2019)

14. Lee, N., Lee, J., Park, C.: Augmentation-free self-supervised learning on graphs. In: Proceedings of the 36th AAAI Conference on Artificial Intelligence, pp. 7372–7380 (2022)

15. Liu, X., Zhang, F., Hou, Z., Mian, L., Wang, Z., Zhang, J., Tang, J.: Self-supervised learning: Generative or contrastive. IEEE Trans. Knowl. Data Eng. **35**(1), 857–876 (2023)

16. Liu, Y., et al.: Hard sample aware network for contrastive deep graph clustering. In: Proceedings of the 37th AAAI Conference on Artificial Intelligence (2023)

17. MacQueen, J.B.: Some methods for classification and analysis of multivariate observations. In: Proceedings of the 5th Berkeley Symposium on Mathematical Statistics and Probability, vol. 1, pp. 281–297 (1967)

18. Oord, A.v.d., Li, Y., Vinyals, O.: Representation learning with contrastive predictive coding. arXiv preprint arXiv:1807.03748 (2018)

19. Park, J., Lee, M., Chang, H.J., Lee, K., Choi, J.Y.: Symmetric graph convolutional autoencoder for unsupervised graph representation learning. In: Proceedings of the 2019 IEEE/CVF International Conference on Computer Vision, pp. 6518–6527 (2019)

20. Peng, H., et al.: Large-scale hierarchical text classification with recursively regularized deep graph-cnn. In: Proceedings of the 2018 World Wide Web Conference, pp. 1063–1072 (2018)
21. Peng, Z., et al.: Graph representation learning via graphical mutual information maximization. In: Proceedings of the The Web Conference, pp. 259–270 (2020)
22. Peng, Z., Liu, H., Jia, Y., Hou, J.: Attention-driven graph clustering network. In: Proceedings of the ACM Multimedia Conference, pp. 935–943 (2021)
23. Peng, Z., Liu, H., Jia, Y., Hou, J.: Deep attention-guided graph clustering with dual self-supervision. IEEE Trans. Circ. Syst. Video Technol. (2022)
24. Satuluri, V., et al.: Simclusters: community-based representations for heterogeneous recommendations at twitter. In: Proceedings of the 26th ACM SIGKDD Conference on Knowledge Discovery and Data Mining, pp. 3183–3193 (2020)
25. Shi, J., Malik, J.: Normalized cuts and image segmentation. IEEE Trans. Pattern Anal. Mach. Intell. **22**(8), 888–905 (2000)
26. Shi, W., Rajkumar, R.: Point-gnn: graph neural network for 3d object detection in a point cloud. In: Proceedings of the 2020 IEEE/CVF Conference on Computer Vision and Pattern Recognition, pp. 1708–1716 (2020)
27. Sun, F., Hoffmann, J., Verma, V., Tang, J.: Infograph: unsupervised and semi-supervised graph-level representation learning via mutual information maximization. In: Proceedings of the 8th International Conference on Learning Representations (2020)
28. Trivedi, P., Lubana, E.S., Yan, Y., Yang, Y., Koutra, D.: Augmentations in graph contrastive learning: Current methodological flaws & towards better practices. In: Proceedings of the ACM Web Conference 2022, pp. 1538–1549 (2022)
29. Velickovic, P., Cucurull, G., Casanova, A., Romero, A., Liò, P., Bengio, Y.: Graph attention networks. In: Proceedings of 6th International Conference on Learning Representations (2018)
30. Velickovic, P., Fedus, W., Hamilton, W.L., Liò, P., Bengio, Y., Hjelm, R.D.: Deep graph infomax. In: Proceedings of the 7th International Conference on Learning Representations (2019)
31. Wang, C., Pan, S., Hu, R., Long, G., Jiang, J., Zhang, C.: Attributed graph clustering: a deep attentional embedding approach. In: Proceedings of the 28th International Joint Conference on Artificial Intelligence, pp. 3670–3676 (2019)
32. Wang, C., Pan, S., Yu, C.P., Hu, R., Long, G., Zhang, C.: Deep neighbor-aware embedding for node clustering in attributed graphs. Pattern Recogn. **122**, 108230 (2022)
33. Wasserman, S., Faust, K.: Social Network Analysis: Methods and Applications. Cambridge University Press (1994)
34. Wu, L., Lin, H., Tan, C., Gao, Z., Li, S.Z.: Self-supervised learning on graphs: contrastive, generative, or predictive. IEEE Trans. Knowl. Data Eng. **35**(4), 4216–4235 (2023)
35. Wu, Z., Pan, S., Chen, F., Long, G., Zhang, C., Yu, P.S.: A comprehensive survey on graph neural networks. IEEE Trans. Neural Netw. Learn. Syst. **32**(1), 4–24 (2021)
36. Xie, J., Girshick, R.B., Farhadi, A.: Unsupervised deep embedding for clustering analysis. In: Proceedings of the 33nd International Conference on Machine Learning, vol. 48, pp. 478–487 (2016)
37. Xu, K., Hu, W., Leskovec, J., Jegelka, S.: How powerful are graph neural networks? In: Proceedings of the 7th International Conference on Learning Representations (2019)

38. Yang, X., et al.: Cluster-guided contrastive graph clustering network. In: Proceedings of the 37th AAAI Conference on Artificial Intelligence (2023)
39. You, Y., Chen, T., Shen, Y., Wang, Z.: Graph contrastive learning automated. In: Proceedings of the 38th International Conference on Machine Learning, vol. 139, pp. 12121–12132 (2021)
40. You, Y., Chen, T., Sui, Y., Chen, T., Wang, Z., Shen, Y.: Graph contrastive learning with augmentations. In: Advances in Neural Information Processing Systems 33 (2020)
41. You, Y., Chen, T., Wang, Z., Shen, Y.: Bringing your own view: Graph contrastive learning without prefabricated data augmentations. In: Proceedings of the 15th ACM International Conference on Web Search and Data Mining, pp. 1300–1309 (2022)
42. Zhang, H., Wu, Q., Yan, J., Wipf, D., Yu, P.S.: From canonical correlation analysis to self-supervised graph neural networks. In: Advances in Neural Information Processing Systems 34, pp. 76–89 (2021)
43. Zhang, Y., Zhu, H., Song, Z., Koniusz, P., King, I.: COSTA: covariance-preserving feature augmentation for graph contrastive learning. In: Proceedings of the 28th ACM SIGKDD Conference on Knowledge Discovery and Data Mining, pp. 2524–2534 (2022)
44. Zhao, T., Liu, G., Günnemann, S., Jiang, M.: Graph data augmentation for graph machine learning: a survey. arXiv preprint arXiv:2202.08871 (2022)
45. Zhao, T., Liu, Y., Neves, L., Woodford, O.J., Jiang, M., Shah, N.: Data augmentation for graph neural networks. In: Proceedings of the 35th AAAI Conference on Artificial Intelligence, pp. 11015–11023 (2021)
46. Zhou, J., Xie, C., Wen, Z., Zhao, X., Xuan, Q.: Data augmentation on graphs: a survey. arXiv preprint arXiv:2212.09970 (2022)
47. Zhu, Y., Xu, Y., Liu, Q., Wu, S.: An empirical study of graph contrastive learning. In: Proceedings of the Neural Information Processing Systems Track on Datasets and Benchmarks 1 (2021)
48. Zhu, Y., Xu, Y., Yu, F., Liu, Q., Wu, S., Wang, L.: Deep graph contrastive representation learning. arXiv preprint arXiv:2006.04131 (2020)
49. Zhu, Y., Xu, Y., Yu, F., Liu, Q., Wu, S., Wang, L.: Graph contrastive learning with adaptive augmentation. In: Proceedings of the The Web Conference 2021, pp. 2069–2080 (2021)

k-SubMix: Common Subspace Clustering on Mixed-Type Data

Mauritius Klein[1,2(✉)], Collin Leiber[1,2], and Christian Böhm[3]

[1] LMU Munich, Munich, Germany
{klein,leiber}@dbs.ifi.lmu.de
[2] Munich Center for Machine Learning (MCML), Munich, Germany
[3] Faculty of Computer Science, University of Vienna, Vienna, Austria
christian.boehm@univie.ac.at

Abstract. Clustering heterogeneous data is an ongoing challenge in the data mining community. The most prevalent clustering methods are designed to process datasets with numerical features only, but often datasets consist of mixed numerical and categorical features. This requires new approaches capable of handling both kinds of data types. Further, the most relevant cluster structures are often hidden in only a few features. Thus, another key challenge is to detect those specific features automatically and abandon features not relevant for clustering. This paper proposes the subspace mixed-type clustering algorithm k-SubMix, which tackles both challenges. Its cost function can handle both numerical and categorical features while simultaneously identifying those with the biggest impact for a high-quality clustering result. Unlike other subspace mixed-type clustering methods, k-SubMix preserves inter-cluster comparability, as it is the first mixed-type approach that defines a common subspace for all clusters. Extensive experiments show that k-SubMix outperforms competitive methods and reduces the data's complexity by a simultaneous dimensionality reduction.

Keywords: Subspace Clustering · Heterogeneous Data · Dimensionality Reduction

1 Introduction

Automatically identifying meaningful structures, e.g. clusters in data, is a key challenge both in science and in economy. Applications range from medicine, over social sciences to customer segmentation. Taking a closer look at certain datasets, one will notice that some features like blood type, gender or educational background are categorical, while others like age or income are numerical. Despite this, the most widely used clustering approaches only focus on a single data type. E.g., k-Means [17] can only group data with numerical features, while k-Modes [20] can only process categorical data. To overcome this, a common way is to map one data type to another. Examples are one-hot encoding or discretization. However, these concepts imply either a dimensional extension or a loss of information. Further, A. Diop et al. [13] conclude, that mixed-type clustering methods applying data type specific metrics perform better than methods homogenizing features to a single type.

The cost function of our proposed k-SubMix algorithm, therefore consists of two terms to minimize the clustering objective with different metrics for numerical and categorical features. For numerical features, we apply the commonly used k-Means objective function. For categorical features, our proposed metric measures the heterogeneity of the feature values within a cluster. This enables us to keep clusters as pure as possible when assigning the samples to the cluster. However, identifying meaningful groups in data is not only challenging due to different data types but also because cluster structures might be hidden only within a few features. This applies especially to high-dimensional datasets. For this reason, the research area of subspace clustering has emerged, which has proposed a variety of different procedures. These proposals can essentially be divided into two groups. While in *Classical Subspace Clustering*, each cluster is assigned its own subspace, *Common Subspace Clustering* algorithms define a common subspace for all clusters. This benefits the comparability of the found structures [15], which is why we mainly focus on this group. Current procedures are, however, mainly limited to numerical data. K-SubMix extends the idea of common subspace clustering to mixed-type data and dynamically assigns features to either the clustered space (containing structures useful for clustering and used for the actual clustering) or noise subspace (containing irrelevant structures). The assignment of features to clustered or noise subspace is updated constantly after every cluster assignment step, which means both clustering and feature selection iteratively learn from each other. As informative structures can be contained both within numerical and categorical features it is crucial that the feature selection happens simultaneously and that it is based on a clustering which was defined from features of both data types. Our proposed categorical feature selection is therefore complemented very well by the SubKMeans [24] method, which is able to automatically determine the relevant numerical features of the clustered subspace. Our main contributions can be summarized as follows:

- k-SubMix is the first common subspace mixed-type clustering method
- The integrated feature reduction method automatically detects those features that are especially relevant for clustering
- Both feature selection and clustering iteratively enhance each other
- The objective function for categorical data runs independently from a cluster center and uses the entire feature distribution to measure similarity
- Our proposal can be combined with various numeric common subspace clustering algorithms and only requires the number of clusters as input parameter

2   Related Work

Mixed-Type Clustering. Ahmad et al. [4] provide a detailed overview of the state-of-the-art mixed-type clustering algorithms. Due to its simplicity, k-Prototypes [19,20] is among the most used mixed-type clustering approaches.

Like in most partional approaches, its cost function differs for numerical and for categorical attributes. For numerical attributes it works the same as k-Means with mean values as cluster centers and the Euclidean distance as distance function. For categorical attributes it works similar to k-Modes [9] with the modes as cluster centers and the Hamming distance as distance function. K-Means mixed [2] tackles the problem that due to the simple 0 or 1 matching, k-Prototypes is unable to capture the actual categorical feature distribution. Therefore, it calculates categorical costs based on the co-occurrence of attribute values and defines a frequency-based cluster center representation. Furthermore, they apply the same cost metric on both data types as they discretize numerical features and map them onto categorical values. Discretization, however, highly depends on the chosen window size and often implies a loss of information.

Generally, k-Means like partitional mixed-type clustering approaches differ in three aspects. Firstly, the definition of cluster centers. Examples of varying center definitions are frequency-based concepts like [2,32], and [26] and the Mode as categorical center [19,20]. Secondly, the definition of a distance measure. For categorical attributes, this includes e.g. Hamming distance [19,20], Cosine similarity [26], and frequency-based approaches [2]. Regarding the numerical metric, the Euclidean distance is mostly used. This leads us to our third point, the weighting of numerical and categorical costs. As different metrics are applied for different data types, balancing their influence is a key challenge. Even though some approaches, like e.g. [2] claim to be parameter-free concerning attribute weighting, a detailed view into the approach reveals the dependency of the discretization's window size. As [4] states, the scale defining the balance between numerical and categorical features is unclear and, due to different similarity measures and center definitions, even harder to obtain. INTEGRATE [7] tries to automatically balance their influence by using the Minimum Description Length Principle (MDL) [5].

Common Subspace Clustering. Other than traditional subspace clustering approaches like e.g. 4C [8], which define individual subspaces for every cluster and are only able to analyze intra-cluster relationships, common subspace clustering approaches as FOSSCLU [15] aim to both cluster in a subspace setting but additionally preserve the ability to compare clusters in terms of their inter-cluster relationship. Furthermore, one must differentiate common subspace clustering from mere dimensionality reduction methods like e.g. PCA [28] or LDA [14] for numerical features, MCA [1] for categorical features and Factor Analysis on mixed-data (FAMD) [27] for mixed-type data. Those techniques are not included in the actual clustering approach. Thus, the current state of the clustering procedure does not influence the resulting subspaces. Actual common subspace clustering approaches applicable to numeric data are LDA k-Means [12], FOSSCLU [15], SubKMeans [24] and Dip'n'Sub [6]. LDA k-Means integrates LDA into the traditional k-Means framework by utilizing the fact that both LDA and k-Means have the properties of minimizing within-class scatter and/or maximizing the between-class scatter. FOSSCLU [15] is not based on k-Means but on the EM-Algorithm [11] and combines it with rigid transformation.

SubKmeans [24] projects features to a rotated clustered and noise subspace by an eigenvalue decomposition that determines if a feature reduces the cost function. Dip'n'Sub [6] utilizes the statistical Dip-test [16] to identify relevant features.

To the best of our knowledge, so far, no common subspace clustering method for mixed-type data has been proposed. INCONCO [29] uses the MDL-principle to find attribute weights. Jia and Cheung propose a mixed-type clustering approach OCIL [10] with a unified distance metric for categorical and numerical features. Its extension, WOCIL is a soft subspace clustering approach [21], which computes attribute-cluster weights by considering both intra/- and inter-cluster impact of features. Other mixed-type feature weighting methods like EWKM [22] (entropy-based) or WKM [18] (weights depend on current assignment), can be integrated into mixed-type clustering approaches [3,21]. However, all mentioned methods cluster only within the entire feature set, and the interpretability of inter-cluster relations is lacking with different feature-cluster weights. To the best of our knowledge, k-SubMix is the first approach addressing common subspace clustering on mixed-type data.

3   k-SubMix Approach

3.1   Cost Function and Algorithmic Procedure

This section introduces the k-SubMix approach for clustering mixed-type data in common subspaces. Table 1 shows the used symbols and definitions. The k-SubMix underlying cost function is k-Means-based, and as in most k-Means-based mixed-type clustering approaches, the cost function $\mathcal{J}$ comprises two independent sub-cost functions, one for minimizing numerical costs and one for minimizing categorical costs. We apply the standard Euclidean distance for numerical features, and the cluster centers μ correspond to the average of all points assigned to a cluster. The orthogonal matrix V rotates the numerical feature space. Since the mode as a cluster center (as used by e.g. k-Prototypes for categorical features) cannot capture the full diversity of information within a cluster, we do not specify categorical cluster centers, but use the entire attribute distribution within a cluster to measure the similarity between points and clusters.

$$
\mathcal{J} = \sum_{k=1}^{K_c} \sum_{x \in C_k} \left(\overbrace{||P_c^{Num^T} V^T x - P_c^{Num^T} V^T \mu_k||^2}^{numerical} + \gamma \overbrace{\frac{\sum\limits_{y \in C_k} f(P_c^{Cat^T} x, P_c^{Cat^T} y)}{l_c |C_k|}}^{categorical} \right)
$$

$$
+ \sum_{x \in \mathcal{D}} \left(\underbrace{||P_n^{Num^T} V^T x - P_n^{Num^T} V^T \mu_{\mathcal{D}}||^2}_{numerical} + \gamma \underbrace{\frac{\sum\limits_{y \in \mathcal{D}} f(P_n^{Cat^T} x, P_n^{Cat^T} y)}{l_n |\mathcal{D}|}}_{categorical} \right)
$$

where the braces indicate *clustered space* and *noise space*.

Table 1. Symbols table

Symbol	Interpretation
D_{cat}, D_{num}	Set of categorical and numerical features in the original feature space
$d = d_{cat} + d_{num}$	Number of features in the original feature space (categorical + numerical)
$l_c \in \mathbb{N}, l_n \in \mathbb{N}$	Number of categorical features of the clustered (c) and noise space (n)
$m_c \in \mathbb{N}, m_n \in \mathbb{N}$	Number of numerical features of the clustered (c) and noise space (n)
$K_c \in \mathbb{N}, K_n = 1$	Number of clusters in the clustered (c) and noise space (n)
$\gamma \in \mathbb{R}$	Trade-off parameter to regulate numerical and categorical costs
$\mathcal{D}, N = |\mathcal{D}|$	Set of all data objects $\mathcal{D}$ and its cardinality N
$x_j \in \mathbb{R}$	Data object x with feature value j
$C_k \subseteq \mathcal{D}$	Set of all objects assigned to Cluster k in the clustered subspace
$\mu_k \in \mathbb{R}^{d_{num}}$	Mean of all data objects of a cluster k regarding the numerical features
$b \in \mathbb{N}$	Bias value of the clustered subspace ($b = K_c$)
$P_s^{Cat} \in \mathbb{R}^{d_{cat} \times l_s}$	Categorical projection onto subspace s (either clustered c or noise n)
$P_s^{Num} \in \mathbb{R}^{d_{num} \times m_s}$	Numerical projection onto subspace s (either clustered c or noise n)
$V \in \mathbb{R}^{d_{num} \times d_{num}}$	Orthogonal rotational matrix regarding numerical features
$I_w, 0_{w,r}$	$w \times w$ identity matrix and $w \times r$ zero matrix

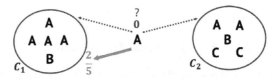

$$k-SubMix: \Delta(A, (C_1, C_2)) = |dist_{cat}(A, C_1)\text{-}dist_{cat}(A, C_2)| = |\tfrac{1}{5} - \tfrac{3}{5}| = \tfrac{2}{5}$$

$$k-Prototypes: \Delta(A, (C_1, C_2)) = |Hamming(A, C_1)\text{-} Hamming(A, C_2)| = |0\text{-}0| = 0$$

Fig. 1. Difference between the categorical costs of a sample A when assigning to clusters C_1 and C_2. K-SubMix assigns A to C_1. With the Mode A as centers for both C_1 and C_2, k-Prototypes is indifferent between both clusters.

The k-SubMix cost function $\mathcal{J}$ calculates for categorical features the deviation of a point to a cluster distribution. The functions $f(x, y)$ and respectively $g(x_j, y_j)$ (see Eq. 1) determine for a point x of dimensionality $dim(x)$ how many points y within the cluster C_k have the same attribute value for a feature j. By dividing this value by the overall number of points assigned to cluster C_k, we obtain information about how well a certain point matches a cluster. The more points within a cluster have equal attribute values as x, the lower are its categorical costs when assigned to a certain cluster. These categorical costs of a single point can range from 0 to 1.

$$f(x, y) = \sum_{1 \leq j \leq dim(x)} g(x_j, y_j), \qquad g(x_j, y_j) = \begin{cases} 1, & \text{if } x_j \neq y_j \\ 0, & \text{else} \end{cases} \qquad (1)$$

Figure 1 illustrates how the k-SubMix categorical cost function correctly assigns a sample A to the pure cluster C_1, whereas k-Prototypes is indifferent between C_1 and C_2. The fact that k-SubMix uses the entire cluster distribution

---

Algorithm 1: k-SubMix

Input : Dataset $\mathcal{D}$, number of clusters K_c, trade-off parameter γ
Output: Clusters $C_1, ... C_k$ in clustered subspace

1 $m_c, m_n, l_c, l_n \leftarrow$ initial values, e.g. $\dfrac{d_{num}}{2}, \dfrac{d_{cat}}{2}$

2 $P_c^{Num}, P_n^{Num}, P_c^{Cat}, P_n^{Cat} \leftarrow$ initialize using m_c, m_n, l_c, l_n

3 $C_k \leftarrow$ Initial assignments using the 1st iteration of k-Prototypes$(\mathcal{D}, K_c)$

4 $\mu_k = \dfrac{1}{|C_k|} \sum_{x_{num} \in C_k} x_{num}; \quad \mu_{\mathcal{D}} = \dfrac{1}{N} \sum_{x_{num} \in \mathcal{D}_{num}} x_{num}$

5 **repeat**

6   // Keep old cluster assignment for categorical cost function and initialize new empty clusters

7    $\forall k \in [1, K_c] : C_k^{old} \leftarrow C_k \wedge C_k \leftarrow \emptyset$

8   **for** $x \in \mathcal{D}$ **do**

9      $k \leftarrow \underset{i \in [1, K_c]}{argmin}(|P_c^{Num^T} V^T x - P_c^{Num^T} V^T \mu_i|^2 + \gamma \dfrac{\sum\limits_{y \in C_i^{old}} f(P_c^{Cat^T} x, P_c^{Cat^T} y)}{l_c |C_i^{old}|})$

10      $C_k \leftarrow C_k \cup \{x\}$ // Assign x to cluster k in clustered space

11   **end**

12    $P_c^{Num}, P_n^{Num}, V, \mu_k \leftarrow$ SubKMeans optimization (see [24])

13   **for** $j \in D_{cat}$ **do**

14   **if** $catCost_c(j) + b < catCost_n(j)$ **then**

15   Feature j is assigned to clustered space c by P_c^{Cat}

16   **else**

17   Feature j is assigned to noise space n by P_n^{Cat}

18   **end**

19   **end**

20 **until** *convergence*;

---

to determine point to cluster similarity is a clear advantage over the simple matching between a point and the mode of a cluster (as done in k-Prototypes).

Algorithm 1 shows the k-SubMix approach in detail. The k-SubMix approach assumes that most cluster-relevant structures can be contained in a lower dimensional subspace, named clustered space, with K_c clusters. K-SubMix aims to push features with a positive impact on discovering clustering structures into this space as the actual clustering takes place only in the clustered space. All other features are pushed into the noise space and not considered for the point-to-cluster assignment for the next iteration. The number of categorical and numerical features l_c and m_c belonging to the clustered space c are initially set such that $l_c = \dfrac{d_{cat}}{2}$ and $m_c = \dfrac{d_{num}}{2}$. Accordingly, the other half of the features belong to the noise space n. The following projections map features to clustered or noise subspaces:

$$P_c^{Num} = \begin{bmatrix} I_{m_c} \\ 0_{d_{num}-m_c, m_c} \end{bmatrix}, P_n^{Num} = \begin{bmatrix} 0_{m_n, d_{num}-m_n} \\ I_{m_n} \end{bmatrix}, P_c^{Cat} = \begin{bmatrix} I_{l_c} \\ 0_{d_{cat}-l_c, l_c} \end{bmatrix}, P_n^{Cat} = \begin{bmatrix} 0_{l_n, d_{cat}-l_n} \\ I_{l_n} \end{bmatrix}$$

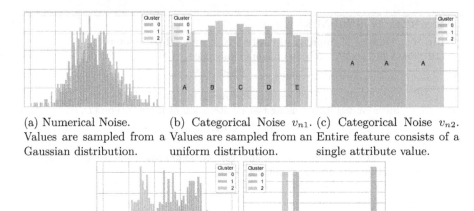

(a) Numerical Noise. Values are sampled from a Gaussian distribution.

(b) Categorical Noise v_{n1}. Values are sampled from an uniform distribution.

(c) Categorical Noise v_{n2}. Entire feature consists of a single attribute value.

(d) Numerical Clustered feature.

(e) Categorical Clustered feature v_c.

Fig. 2. Clustered and noise distributions of numerical and categorical data type.

As the k-SubMix categorical cost function depends only on the current state of cluster assignments, k-SubMix does not have a categorical cluster center update step. However, this implies that some initial clusters need to be generated in the initialisation phase. We, therefore, perform a single iteration with the Euclidean distance for numerical features and for categorical features we calculate the Hamming distance between all points and randomly set cluster centers (similarly to the k-Prototypes method) to obtain initial clusters. Following Algorithm 1 to the actual clustering phase, every point x is assigned to its closest cluster k by optimizing the clustered subspace part of the objective function $\mathcal{J}$. As clustering only takes place in the clustered space, the point vectors are reduced by P_c^{Cat} and P_c^{Num}. Features mapped to the noise subspace do not influence the point-to-cluster assignment.

3.2 Subspace Optimization

Categorical Optimization. After cluster assignment, the projection matrices mapping features to either clustered or noise subspace are updated depending on the feature's impact on the newly derived clustering result. In order to decide to which subspace a categorical feature j should be projected for the upcoming cluster iteration, we compare its overall costs in both subspaces.

Thus, given a current cluster assignment of points to clusters C_k in the clustered subspace, let $catCost_c(j)$ be the overall sum of categorical costs from all points to their current cluster for feature j. On the other hand, $catCost_n(j)$ sums up the categorical costs of all points being assigned to a single cluster.

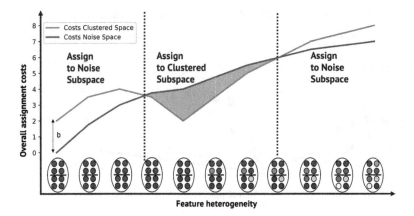

Fig. 3. Overall assignment costs in the clustered and noise subspace for features of varying heterogeneity. Cluster splits are indicated by the black separating line.

We aim to keep features that minimize the clustering cost function in the clustered space. This implies feature j is assigned to the clustered space if $catCost_c(j) < catCost_n(j)$, which means features are projected to the clustered space, if their costs are cheaper in a clustering setting than in a noise setting with a single cluster.

Figure 2 illustrates possible noise and clustered features for both data types. K-SubMix aims to detect categorical noise features v_{n1} (Fig. 2b - randomly distributed consisting in the extreme case of N unique values) and feature v_{n2} (Fig. 2c - all samples have equal feature values) and to push them into the noise subspace. Features rich in clustering structure similar to v_c (Fig. 2e) are to be kept in the clustered subspace.

For features of type v_{n1} (randomly distributed consisting of N unique values), $catCost_c(j) = N - K_c$ and $catCost_n(j) = N - 1$. To avoid a mismatch of the noise feature v_{n1} to the clustered space, we introduce the bias $b = K_c$ and add it to the clustering subspace costs. We obtain our final decision rule $catCost_c(j) + b < catCost_n(j)$, that correctly projects features of type v_{n1} and v_{n2} to the noise subspace and keeps high informative features as v_c in the clustered subspace. The projection matrices P_c^{Cat}, P_n^{Cat} and the subspace dimensionalities l_c and l_n are updated accordingly after every cluster iteration step.

Figure 3 shows how both $catCosts_c(j)$ and $catCost_n(j)$ evolve for features of varying heterogeneity. All features of the example have 8 samples and $K_c = 2$. The example clearly shows how both features of type v_{n1} and v_{n2} are correctly identified as noise and $catCost_c(j) + b > catCost_n(j)$. On the other hand features similar to v_c (see Fig. 3, features between the dotted lines) are identified as relevant for clustering, as $catCost_c(j) + b < catCost_n(j)$ and thus pushed to the clustered subspace.

Figure 4 illustrates how points-to-cluster costs are calculated within the clustered subspace. Whereas the Euclidean distance calculates $dist_{num}$, $dist_{cat}$ for

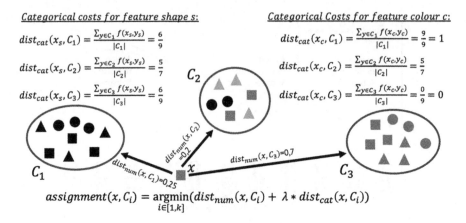

$$assignment(x, C_i) = \underset{i \in [1,k]}{\operatorname{argmin}}(dist_{num}(x, C_i) + \lambda * dist_{cat}(x, C_i))$$

Fig. 4. Example of point-to-cluster costs in the clustered subspace for numerical and categorical features.

the categorical features color and shape is obtained by our frequency-based method. Categorical costs of a single sample x range from 0 (all have equal values) to 1 (all have different values). To minimize the point-to-cluster assignment, numerical and categorical costs are added and weighted by the γ-parameter. Observing the features of the example, one can identify that the categorical feature shape is clearly a noise feature, as shapes are randomly distributed across all clusters, and k-SubMix would project it through P_n^{Cat} to the noise subspace.

The same applies to the numerical y-dimension, which is a unimodal Gaussian as in Fig. 2a. Thus, P_n^{Num} projects it to the noise subspace. The actual clustering structure is only contained within the categorical feature color and the numerical x-dimension, as both clearly separate the data into 3 clusters. Therefore, k-SubMix would project the numerical x-dimension through P_c^{Num} and the categorical color feature through P_c^{Cat} to the clustered space and clustering would only happen within this reduced feature space for the upcoming iteration.

Numerical Optimization. For numerical features we apply the SubKMeans approach [24]. Its basic idea can be summarized as follows. Firstly a random orthonormal matrix V is initialized, P_c^{Num} and P_n^{Num} are set by the initial m_c and m_n. In the assignment step, k-Means is performed on the reduced (by P_c^{Num}) and rotated (by V) data. In the update step, the full dimensionality is taken into account to update the cluster centers, the rotational matrix V and the projection matrices P_c^{Num} and P_n^{Num}. An eigenvalue decomposition is performed, and its eigenvectors form the new rotational matrix V. The size of its corresponding eigenvalue decides whether a feature should be mapped to the clustered or noise subspace. Thus, V, P_c^{Num} and P_n^{Num} are updated for the upcoming iteration. SubKMeans identifies unimodal Gaussians (Fig. 2a) as noise and only keeps features that minimize the objective goal (Fig. 2d) in the clustered space.

3.3   Complexity and Convergence

The complexity of k-SubMix consists of the complexity of the numerical and categorical parts of the cost function. The numerical complexity is equal to that of the SubKmeans approach [24] which corresponds to $\mathcal{O}(I(m_c K_c N + d_{num}^2 N + d_{num}^3))$. For the categorical part, the complexity is $\mathcal{O}(I(d_{cat} N) + d_{cat} N))$, where $\mathcal{O}(I(d_{cat} N))$ describes how for each iteration I and each feature all clusters and therefore all samples N must be looked up once to count the appearance of the distinct feature values in order to compute both clustering assignment costs and clustered subspace feature cost. As the noise subspace consists of a single cluster containing all samples and the costs for the noise space features do not change between iterations, its costs can be initially computed once and are thus $\mathcal{O}(d_{cat} N)$.

It is easy to see that k-SubMix has to converge. Its cost function decreases in each update and assignment step and has a lower bound of 0. This implies that the algorithm has to converge towards a (local) minimum.

4   Experiments

4.1   Experimental Setup and Datasets

We evaluated k-SubMix with respect to its clustering result considering the NMI (Normalized-Mutual Information) score [30], the Clustering Accuracy [31] and its ability to reduce the dimensionality of the dataset.

The evaluation is based on five real-world and three synthetically generated datasets. The real-world datasets Heart, Credit, Dermatology (Derma), Adult, and Cylinder Bands (Bands) are available at the UCI repository[1] and commonly used in mixed-type clustering. The synthetical datasets Syn1, Syn2 and Syn3, are different combinations of the features illustrated in Fig. 2. Syn1 contains all the clustering information in its categorical features, Syn2 in its numerical features and Syn3 in 3 numerical and 3 categorical features. Table 2 gives an overview of the dataset's properties. We compare k-SubMix to a variety of clustering approaches. Firstly to the well-known mixed-type methods k-Prototypes [19,20] and k-Means Mixed [2]. Secondly to mixed-type subspace (feature weighting) methods like EWKM [22], WKM [18], OCIL [10] and WOCIL [21]. Thirdly to the numerical common subspace clustering method SubKMeans [24]. Lastly to the traditional clustering approaches k-Means (for numerical data) [17] and k-Modes (for categorical data) [20]. To highlight properties of our k-SubMix method and point out the need for sophisticated common subspace mixed-type clustering methods, further variations of some methods like one-hot encoding, discretizing or preprocessing the data with FAMD, were analyzed. In all cases, we preprocess the datasets by a 0 to 1 min-max normalization on the numerical features. All algorithms were run 10 times (with the correct number of k), and average scores were taken. For k-SubMix and k-Prototypes, we evaluated

---

[1] https://archive.ics.uci.edu/ml/index.php.

Table 2. Information regarding the used datasets.

	Heart	Credit	Derma	Adult	Bands	Syn1	Syn2	Syn3
d_{num}	8	6	1	6	20	17	3	10
d_{cat}	5	9	33	8	19	3	17	10
N	303	653	366	30612	277	1500	1500	1500
K_c	2	2	2	2	2	3	3	3

runs with varying γ-parameter within $[0.1, 0.11, ..., 2]$. For k-Means Mixed, we evaluated discretization window sizes within $[2, 3, ..., 10]$ (5 are recommended and set as default). The highest average scores with equal parameter settings out of 10 runs are taken. For WOCIL, OCIL, EWKM, and WKM, we took the results from the real-world experiments of [21] (proposing WOCIL as extension of OCIL). The paper states that the feature weighting methods EWKM and WKM were integrated into a k-Prototypes kind of clustering. Furthermore we analyzed the impact of the γ-parameter on the NMI score on both a synthetical and real world dataset. The k-SubMix implementation and synthetical datasets can be downloaded from: https://doi.org/10.6084/m9.figshare.23560305.v1.

4.2 Quantitative Results

Table 3 and Table 4 present the quantitative results of our experiments. As can be deduced, regarding the NMI score and the Clustering Accuracy score, k-SubMix is highly competitive to other methods both on real-world and synthetically generated datasets. K-SubMix is the only approach that performs well consistently across all datasets. Some approaches, e.g. SubKmeans and k-Means, perform well only on numerically dominated data like Syn2 and analogously k-Modes only on categorical dominated data as, e.g. Syn1. Discretization did not have a meaningful impact on k-Modes performance. On the other hand, one-hot encoding categorical feature increased k-Means performance on most datasets and achieved a high average NMI scores, especially on the Dermatology dataset. However, one must bear in mind that, in this case, it implies an expansion from 33 to 130 features. Apart from that, the method cannot detect noise dimensions, which can be clearly observed by its low performance on Syn2, where all 17 categorical noise features are one-hot encoded. This makes it particularly hard to interpret the final clustering result. Mixed-type methods like k-Prototypes and k-Means mixed have fairly well scores on some datasets but struggle, e.g. at the Credit or Syn2 data. EWKM and WKM perform worse than pure k-Prototypes without attribute weighting regarding the NMI. However the Clustering Accuracy scores of both EWKM and WKM, such as of OCIL and its extension WOCIL are quite high. FAMD preprocessing is among the strongest competitors on many datasets.

Apart from being a highly competitive approach regarding clustering scores, the second key advantage of k-SubMix can be analyzed with Table 5, which shows

Table 3. NMI results on real-world and synthetical datasets. Average scores are taken of 10 runs. **Bold**, underlined and dotted underlined values represent the best, 2nd best and 3rd best result. Results of algorithms marked with a * are taken from [21]. As the Derma dataset only contains a single numeric feature, SubKMeans could not be executed for this dataset (†).

NMI scores	Heart	Credit	Derma	Adult	Bands	Syn1	Syn2	Syn3
k-SubMix	**0.350**	**0.372**	0.858	0.173	**0.054**	**0.793**	**0.912**	**0.955**
k-Means$_{numeric\ only}$	0.157	0.041	0.098	0.064	0.003	0.003	0.910	0.901
k-Means$_{categoric\ one\text{-}hot}$	0.328	0.022	**0.936**	0.131	0.050	0.790	0.001	0.858
FAMD + k-Means	0.274	0.249	0.695	**0.185**	0.049	0.777	**0.912**	0.931
SubKMeans$_{numeric\ only}$	0.143	0.042	†	0.063	0.003	0.002	0.910	0.902
SubKMeans$_{categoric\ one\text{-}hot}$	0.337	0.033	0.762	0.087	0.050	0.692	0.001	0.863
FAMD + SubKMeans	0.292	0.242	0.616	0.176	0.050	0.765	**0.912**	0.931
k-Modes$_{categoric\ only}$	0.283	0.278	0.588	0.087	0.046	0.770	0.000	0.404
k-Modes$_{numeric\ discretized}$	0.214	0.270	0.591	0.119	0.052	0.085	0.175	0.755
k-Prototypes	0.261	0.002	0.682	0.106	0.006	0.528	0.018	0.931
k-Means mixed	0.345	0.309	0.528	0.172	0.046	0.755	0.104	0.841
WKM*	0.184	0.287	0.096	0.091	–	–	–	–
EWKM*	0.225	0.245	0.507	0.001	–	–	–	–
OCIL*	0.233	0.182	0.796	0.004	–	–	–	–
WOCIL*	0.307	0.236	0.591	0.005	-	-	-	-

the original features of the datasets (d_{num} and d_{cat}) and the features k-SubMix selected for the clustered subspace (m_c and l_c). K-SubMix detects noise features throughout all datasets. Most categorical real-world datasets seem to have few noise features, but k-SubMix's ability to detect noise features can clearly be proven by Syn1-Syn3. For Syn1 and Syn3, k-SubMix identifies all categorical noise features correctly. Together with the numerical subspace optimization from SubKmeans, it generates a clustered subspace with less than half of the original dimensionality while still achieving the highest NMI scores. For Syn2, it detects 15 of 17 categorical noise features and reduces the total number of features from 20 to just 5. Having only 3 numerical and 2 categorical features highly increases the interpretability of the clustering outcome as one could, e.g. by using color and shape coding for categorical values, use a single 3-dimensional plot to visualize the entire remaining data. For the Adult dataset, which consists of 2 clusters (people earning more and people earning less than 50K$ a year), k-SubMix correctly identifies the categorical feature native-country as noise, as 90% of the samples are from the US. Further, the numerical features age and working hours were identified as noise features and do not influence the clustering outcome. Other features such as education and gender had a bigger impact.

Table 4. Clustering Accuracy results on real-world and synthetical datasets. Average scores are taken of 10 runs. **Bold,** <u>underlined</u> and <u>dotted underlined</u> values represent the best, 2nd best and 3rd best result. Results of algorithms marked with a * are taken from [21]. As the Derma dataset only contains a single numeric feature, SubKMeans could not be executed for this dataset (†).

Clustering Accuracy	Heart	Credit	Derma	Adult	Bands	Syn1	Syn2	Syn3
k-SubMix	**0.835**	<u>0.838</u>	<u>0.799</u>	0.707	0.574	**0.950**	**0.983**	**0.998**
k-Means$_{numeric\ only}$	0.728	0.618	0.162	0.650	0.570	0.348	<u>0.982</u>	<u>0.981</u>
k-Means$_{categoric\ one\text{-}hot}$	0.825	0.455	**0.966**	0.715	<u>0.628</u>	<u>0.947</u>	0.350	0.969
FAMD + k-Means	0.799	0.763	0.553	0.694	0.617	0.943	**0.983**	<u>0.996</u>
SubKMeans$_{numeric\ only}$	0.715	0.618	†	0.648	0.568	0.343	<u>0.982</u>	0.985
SubKMeans$_{categoric\ one\text{-}hot}$	<u>0.830</u>	0.455	0.728	0.712	<u>0.628</u>	0.943	0.351	0.972
FAMD + SubKMeans	0.815	0.755	0.490	0.681	0.617	0.936	**0.983**	<u>0.996</u>
k-Modes$_{categoric\ only}$	0.784	<u>0.799</u>	0.623	0.636	0.613	0.939	0.355	0.780
k-Modes$_{numeric\ discretized}$	0.777	<u>0.799</u>	0.667	0.654	**0.649**	0.530	0.657	0.935
k-Prototypes	0.717	0.499	0.559	0.502	0.548	0.846	0.415	<u>0.996</u>
k-Means mixed	<u>0.831</u>	0.790	0.617	0.712	0.560	0.910	0.604	0.951
WKM*	0.733	0.757	0.283	<u>0.727</u>	–	–	–	–
EWKM*	0.756	0.772	0.636	**0.751**	–	–	–	–
OCIL*	0.769	0.697	0.725	<u>0.750</u>	–	–	–	–
WOCIL*	0.815	**0.853**	0.786	<u>0.750</u>	–	–	–	–

Table 5. Original dimensionalities vs. reduced dimensionalities by k-SubMix.

	Heart	Credit	Derma	Adult	Bands	Syn1	Syn2	Syn3
d_{num}/d_{cat}	5/8	6/9	1/33	6/8	20/19	17/3	3/17	10/10
m_c/l_c	2/6	3/8	1/32	3/7	10/14	6/3	3/2	5/3

4.3 γ-Parameter Sensitivity

For mixed-type clustering algorithms, finding a good weighting of numerical and categorical features is challenging, even though data normalization helps to increase the comparability of their cost functions. We evaluated the γ-value influence on the NMI score for k-SubMix and for k-Prototypes. Both approaches handle numerical and categorical features differently and therefore need a parameter to trade-off their respective impact on the cost function.

Figure 5 shows the results of the γ-parameter sensitivity on the synthetical dataset Syn1 (Fig. 5a) and the real world dataset Heart disease (Fig. 5b). The γ-values range from $\gamma = 0$ (categorical features are ignored) over $\gamma = 1$ (numerical and categorical costs contribute equally), to $\gamma = 2$ (categorical costs weight twice as high as numerical costs). We recognize for both datasets, that for very low γ-values around 0 both algorithms have a low performance. This proves the necessity of integrating categorical features into the clustering as they have a

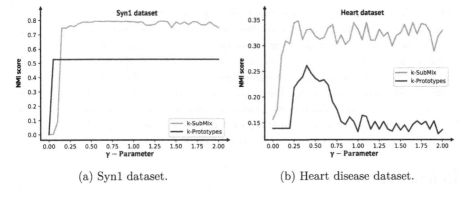

(a) Syn1 dataset.   (b) Heart disease dataset.

Fig. 5. γ-parameter sensitivity on a synthetical and real world dataset. Effect of γ on NMI scores for k-SubMix and k-Prototypes.

meaningful impact on the clustering result. One can further recognize that both algorithms perform stable on the Syn1 dataset for the remaining γ-values, but k-SubMix has a way higher overall NMI score. For the real-world Heart disease dataset γ's influence on k-Prototypes is high, as one must find the exact spot in a rather small range to obtain a good clustering result. K-SubMix's NMI scores, on the other hand, are constantly high for the Heart dataset, and the average NMI across all γ's is just 0.033 lower than the highest achieved NMI score.

For the illustrated examples k-SubMix's dependency on a good γ choice is rather low, and the results are more constant compared to k-Prototypes. However, feature weighting is an ongoing challenge, and different datasets might show different behaviours regarding the γ-parameter.

5   Conclusion

In this paper, we propose k-SubMix, which to the best of our knowledge is the first common subspace mixed-type clustering approach. It simultaneously clusters and reduces the data dimensionality by projecting features to the clustered or noise subspace. This projection is constantly improving during the clustering process, as it depends on the current state of the clustering assignment. The categorical feature reduction method of k-SubMix is complemented by the numerical method of SubKMeans, but can be easily be replaced by any other numerical common subspace method like FOSSCLU or LDA k-Means. Extensive experiments show the high value of the proposed strategy as it almost consistently surpasses the results of its competitors. Apart from that, one of k-SubMix's core strengths is to deal with datasets that have hidden cluster structures only within a few features. Its resulting lower dimensional representation increases the explainability and reduces the problem of the curse of dimensionality. Further developments could be the extension of k-SubMix to non-redundant clustering as in [25] or automatically determining the number of clusters as in [23] or [15].

Ethical Statement. Our proposed k-SubMix approach is a new clustering method in the area of unsupervised learning. We have no specific ethical concerns regarding the work of this paper, as all experiments were run on either synthetically generated data or on publicly available datasets that are commonly used in the field of mixed-type clustering. Real-world datasets containing personal data such as Heart, Derma and Adult are standard datasets for the evaluation of mixed-type clustering approaches and the resulting cluster did not reveal any new or ethically critical patterns. No data from humans has been collected for this paper. K-SubMix can be applied to any dataset and is not targeting a specific ethically critical domain.

References

1. Abdi, H., Valentin, D.: Multiple correspondence analysis. Encyclopedia Measur. Stat. **2**(4), 651–657 (2007)
2. Ahmad, A., Dey, L.: A k-mean clustering algorithm for mixed numeric and categorical data. Data Knowl. Eng. **63**(2), 503–527 (2007)
3. Ahmad, A., Dey, L.: A k-means type clustering algorithm for subspace clustering of mixed numeric and categorical datasets. Pattern Recogn. Lett. **32**(7), 1062–1069 (2011)
4. Ahmad, A., Khan, S.S.: Survey of state-of-the-art mixed data clustering algorithms. IEEE Access **7**, 31883–31902 (2019)
5. Barron, A., Rissanen, J., Yu, B.: The minimum description length principle in coding and modeling. IEEE Trans. Inf. Theory **44**(6), 2743–2760 (1998)
6. Bauer, L.G., Leiber, C., Böhm, C., Plant, C.: Extension of the dip-test repertoire-efficient and differentiable p-value calculation for clustering. In: Proceedings of the 2023 SIAM International Conference on Data Mining (SDM), pp. 109–117. SIAM (2023)
7. Böhm, C., Goebl, S., Oswald, A., Plant, C., Plavinski, M., Wackersreuther, B.: Integrative parameter-free clustering of data with mixed type attributes. In: Zaki, M.J., Yu, J.X., Ravindran, B., Pudi, V. (eds.) PAKDD 2010. LNCS (LNAI), vol. 6118, pp. 38–47. Springer, Heidelberg (2010). https://doi.org/10.1007/978-3-642-13657-3_7
8. Böhm, C., Kailing, K., Kröger, P., Zimek, A.: Computing clusters of correlation connected objects. In: ACM SIGMOD, pp. 455–466 (2004)
9. Chaturvedi, A., Green, P.E., Caroll, J.D.: K-modes clustering. J. Classif. **18**(1), 35–55 (2001)
10. Cheung, Y.M., Jia, H.: Categorical-and-numerical-attribute data clustering based on a unified similarity metric without knowing cluster number. Pattern Recogn. **46**(8), 2228–2238 (2013)
11. Dempster, A.P., Laird, N.M., Rubin, D.B.: Maximum likelihood from incomplete data via the EM algorithm. J. Roy. Stat. Soc.: Ser. B (Methodol.) **39**(1), 1–22 (1977)
12. Ding, C., Li, T.: Adaptive dimension reduction using discriminant analysis and k-means clustering. In: ICML, pp. 521–528 (2007)
13. Diop, A., El Malki, N., Chevalier, M., Peninou, A., Teste, O.: Impact of similarity measures on clustering mixed data. In: 34th International Conference on Scientific and Statistical Database Management, pp. 1–12 (2022)
14. Fisher, R.A.: The statistical utilization of multiple measurements. Ann. Eugen. **8**(4), 376–386 (1938)

15. Goebl, S., He, X., Plant, C., Böhm, C.: Finding the optimal subspace for clustering. In: ICDM, pp. 130–139. IEEE (2014)
16. Hartigan, J.A., Hartigan, P.M.: The dip test of unimodality. Ann. Stat. **13**, 70–84 (1985)
17. Hartigan, J.A., Wong, M.A.: Algorithm as 136: a k-means clustering algorithm. J. Roy. Stat. Soc.: Ser. C (Methodol.) **28**(1), 100–108 (1979)
18. Huang, J.Z., Ng, M.K., Rong, H., Li, Z.: Automated variable weighting in k-means type clustering. IEEE Trans. Pattern Anal. Mach. Intell. **27**(5), 657–668 (2005)
19. Huang, Z.: Clustering large data sets with mixed numeric and categorical values. In: PAKDD, pp. 21–34. Citeseer (1997)
20. Huang, Z.: Extensions to the k-means algorithm for clustering large data sets with categorical values. Data Min. Knowl. Disc. **2**(3), 283–304 (1998)
21. Jia, H., Cheung, Y.M.: Subspace clustering of categorical and numerical data with an unknown number of clusters. IEEE TNNLS **29**(8), 3308–3325 (2017)
22. Jing, L., Ng, M.K., Huang, J.Z.: An entropy weighting k-means algorithm for subspace clustering of high-dimensional sparse data. IEEE Trans. Knowl. Data Eng. **19**(8), 1026–1041 (2007)
23. Leiber, C., Mautz, D., Plant, C., Böhm, C.: Automatic parameter selection for non-redundant clustering. In: SIAM SDM, pp. 226–234. SIAM (2022)
24. Mautz, D., Ye, W., Plant, C., Böhm, C.: Towards an optimal subspace for k-means. In: Proceedings of the 23rd ACM SIGKDD, pp. 365–373 (2017)
25. Mautz, D., Ye, W., Plant, C., Böhm, C.: Discovering non-redundant k-means clusterings in optimal subspaces. In: Proceedings of the 24th ACM SIGKDD International Conference on Knowledge Discovery & Data Mining, pp. 1973–1982 (2018)
26. Modha, D.S., Spangler, W.S.: Feature weighting in k-means clustering. Mach. Learn. **52**(3), 217–237 (2003)
27. Pagès, J.: Multiple Factor Analysis by Example Using R. CRC Press, New York (2014)
28. Pearson, K.: LIII. On lines and planes of closest fit to systems of points in space. Lond. Edinb. Dublin Philos. Mag. J. Sci. **2**(11), 559–572 (1901)
29. Plant, C., Böhm, C.: INCONCO: interpretable clustering of numerical and categorical objects. In: Proceedings of the 17th ACM SIGKDD, pp. 1127–1135 (2011)
30. Strehl, A., Ghosh, J.: Cluster ensembles-a knowledge reuse framework for combining multiple partitions. J. Mach. Learn. Res. **3**, 583–617 (2002)
31. Yang, Y., Xu, D., Nie, F., Yan, S., Zhuang, Y.: Image clustering using local discriminant models and global integration. IEEE Trans. Image Process. **19**(10), 2761–2773 (2010)
32. Zhao, W.-D., Dai, W.-H., Tang, C.-B.: K-centers algorithm for clustering mixed type data. In: Zhou, Z.-H., Li, H., Yang, Q. (eds.) PAKDD 2007. LNCS (LNAI), vol. 4426, pp. 1140–1147. Springer, Heidelberg (2007). https://doi.org/10.1007/978-3-540-71701-0_129

Transformer-Based Contrastive Multi-view Clustering via Ensembles

Mingyu Zhao[1], Weidong Yang[1(✉)], and Feiping Nie[2]

[1] School of Computer Science, Fudan University, Shanghai, China
{myzhao19,wdyang}@fudan.edu.cn
[2] School of Artificial Intelligence, Optics and Electronics (iOPEN),
Northwestern Polytechnical University, Xi'an, Shaanxi, China

Abstract. Multi-view spectral clustering has achieved considerable performance in practice because of its ability to explore nonlinear structure information. However, most existing methods belong to shallow models and are sensitive to the original similarity graphs. In this work, we proposed a novel model of Transformer-based contrastive multi-view clustering via ensembles (TCMCE) to solve the above issues. Our model integrates the self-attention mechanism, ensemble clustering, graph reconstruction, and contrastive learning into a unified framework. From the viewpoint of orthogonal and nonnegative graph reconstruction, TCMCE aims to learn a common spectral embedding as the indicator matrix. Then the graph contrastive learning is performed on the reconstructed graph based on the fusion graph via ensembles. Extensive experiments on six real-world datasets have verified the effectiveness of our model on multi-view clustering tasks compared with the state-of-the-art models.

Keywords: Graph reconstruction · Multi-view clustering ·
Contrastive graph learning · Transformer · Ensemble clustering

1 Introduction

With the arrival of the big data era, multi-view or multi-modal data is ubiquitous [1,2]. Under such circumstances, multi-view learning has attracted more and more attention, in which multi-view clustering (MVC) is the fundamental task [3,4]. In recent years, a large number of MVC methods have been proposed, which can be roughly divided into two categories: traditional shallow models and deep models.

Traditional models utilize machine learning techniques to optimize the variables in the objective function for clustering assignment, in which graph-based ones show superior performance because of the ability to capture nonlinear structure information [5,6]. In most cases, graph-based MVC approaches are conducted via a two-stage process: 1) obtaining the common spectral embedding; 2) discretizing the embedding via the single-view clustering method, e.g., k-means, to obtain the final cluster labels. Unfortunately, the clustering performance is

D. Koutra et al. (Eds.): ECML PKDD 2023, LNAI 14169, pp. 678–694, 2023.
https://doi.org/10.1007/978-3-031-43412-9_40

limited by the post-processing, e.g., k-means is sensitive to the initialization of original data points. Strategies to implement the one-step MVC have become the research hot, in which learning a nonnegative spectral embedding [7] as the indicator matrix from the viewpoint of orthogonal and nonnegative graph reconstruction (ONGR) [8] has made great strides in improving the clustering performance. For multi-view clustering, NESE [9] was designed to integrate spectral embedding and nonnegative embedding into a joint framework. Similarly, Shi et al. proposed MCONGR [10] to fully dig out the latent structure information based on ONGR. To consider the importance of multiple views, AONGR was devised to learn a unified nonnegative spectral embedding [11]. However, these methods belong to shallow models with the limited capacity to dig out the latent information hidden in complex real-world datasets.

Deep MVC methods have gradually become a popular trend in the community due to their outstanding representation ability [12,13]. Graph convolution network (GCN) [14] is widely employed in deep MVC models because of its ability to encode the graph structure and node embedding [15,16]. However, the graphs in most GCN-based methods are fixed, making the clustering performance heavily dependent on the predefined graph. In addition, a complex loss function is often devised in this kind of model. Different modules in these models need to be trained solely without a unified optimization framework to conduct end-to-end learning.

To this end, we propose a novel model of Transformer-based contrastive multi-view clustering via ensembles (TCMCE) to obtain a nonnegative spectral embedding as the indicator matrix. In addition, an effective optimization algorithm is employed to update the variables in TCMCE with a unified framework, consisting of reconstruction loss and graph contrastive learning loss. Specifically, the reconstruction loss is devised from the viewpoint of similarity graph reconstruction and the graph contrastive learning loss is designed to draw alike nodes close and push the dissimilar ones apart in the reconstructed graph. The contributions of this work can be summarized as:

- To our best knowledge, our model is one of the first works to utilize the self-attention mechanism in the Transformer to obtain the nonnegative spectral embedding for one-step MVC.
- The co-association matrix in ensemble clustering is utilized for graph contrastive learning to make the similar nodes close and the dissimilar ones apart in the learned common graph.
- Extensive experiments on six real-world datasets are conducted to verify the effectiveness of the proposed TCMCE in comparison with the state-of-the-art (SOTA) MVC baselines.

2 Related Works

2.1 Traditional MVC Methods

With the rapid development of graph data, graph-based multi-view clustering has achieved great success. CGL [17] was proposed to learn a consensus graph in spectral embedding space and conduct k-means to get the clustering labels. To get the clustering results in a one-step process, MLAN with a rank constraint on the Laplacian matrix was proposed for multi-view clustering task [6]. In [5], GMC was proposed to fuse the similarity graphs of all views to learn a consistent graph with corresponding connected components, which could improve the graph matrix of each view in turn and give the final clustering result directly. Instead of Laplacian rank constraint, Zhang et al. proposed COMVSC to learn the common representation and label matrix simultaneously [18]. To consider the importance of multiple views, Zhan et al. proposed an unsupervised multi-view clustering method based on graph structure fusion by using the Hadamard product [19], combining similarity and graph structure learning into a unified framework. Ren et al. devised a robust auto-weighted multi-view clustering model named RAMC [20], which was robust to the outliers because of the use of l_1-norm. For the practical application of multi-view clustering, MOSTA [21] was proposed to identify groups of legal judgments. To deal with the scalability issue on large datasets, anchor-graph were applied in multi-view clustering methods. Kang et al. [22] proposed LMVSC with linear order complexity, which employed SC on a small fusion graph to obtain the clustering results. FMDC [23] was proposed to perform multi-view clustering with a small cost in terms of running time, in which the indicator matrix could be directly learned via the aggregated graph. Similarly, EOMSC [24] was proposed to integrate graph construction and anchor-graph learning into a joint framework. In most cases, however, the clustering performance of the anchor-graph-based methods is sensitive to the number of anchors.

2.2 Deep MVC Methods

To obtain the deep features from different views, the deep learning technique has been employed in many multi-view clustering methods, which can learn better feature representation than traditional shallow models. AE^2-Net [25] as an unsupervised multi-view representation learning network is effective for clustering tasks, which can flexibly balance the complementarity and consistency among multiple views due to the unified framework with the inner and outer auto-encoder networks. However, this method only learns a latent representation in multi-view data, extra post-processing is also necessary to obtain the final results. To learn the clustering labels in one stage, an end-to-end adversarial network (EAMC) [26] was devised to conduct multi-modal clustering, which contained a divergence-based clustering loss to learn the simplex embedding for cluster assignments. Owing to the success of contrastive learning, contrastive clustering [27] based methods had achieved SOTA performance in clustering tasks. Based on the loss function in EAMC, Trosten et al. proposed contrastive multi-view learning (CoMVC) [28], which fused the multiple representations of each view by a weighted linear combination and obtained the cluster results from the representation via selective alignment in the contrastive learning module. COMPLETER [29] was proposed to project the original features into a subspace with information consistency and data restorability based on contrastive learning. To consider the conflict between consensus feature learning and diversity among multiple views, MFLVC [30] was proposed to perform multi-view contrastive clustering, which obtained the common representation with multiple levels of the feature. For multi-view graph clustering tasks, O2MAC [15] employed the graph auto-encoder to obtain low-dimensional embedding. CMGEC [16] was proposed to deal with general multi-view clustering, which coupled auto-encoder, mutual information maximization, and GCN technique into a unified framework to learn a consistent representation.

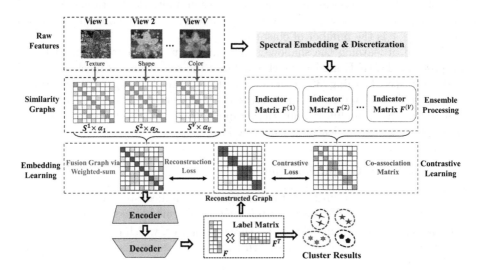

Fig. 1. The architecture of TCMCE.

3   Methodology

Given dataset $X = [x_1, x_2, ..., x_N] \in \mathbb{R}^{N \times d}$, N denotes the number of data points, d represents the feature number of each point, spectral clustering utilizes the graph form to separate the data points into corresponding clusters. Within the affinity graph, each vertex denotes a data point, and edges represent the connection between two data points. With the original graph W, the objective function of ONGR can be written as:

$$\min_{F} \left\| S - FF^T \right\|_F^2 \qquad (1)$$
$$s.t.\ F^T F = I, F \geq 0.$$

where $S = D^{-\frac{1}{2}} W D^{-\frac{1}{2}}$, D is the degree matrix of W and $L = D - W$. To extend Eq. (1) in multi-view clustering. The objective function of orthogonal and nonnegative graph reconstruction for multi-view clustering can be represented as follows:

$$\min_{\alpha_v, \boldsymbol{F}} \left\| \sum_{v=1}^{V} (\alpha_v)^r \boldsymbol{S}^v - \boldsymbol{F}\boldsymbol{F}^T \right\|_F^2 \tag{2}$$
$$s.t. \ \boldsymbol{\alpha} > 0, \boldsymbol{\alpha}^T \boldsymbol{1} = 1, \boldsymbol{F}^T \boldsymbol{F} = \boldsymbol{I}, \boldsymbol{F} \geq 0,$$

where α_v represents the weight of v-th view, r is a scalar to control the distribution of weights, V denotes the number of views in multi-view datasets. $\boldsymbol{S}^v$ is the normalization similarity graph of v-th view, and $\boldsymbol{F} \in \mathbb{R}^{N \times c}$ denotes the spectral embedding, c is the number of clusters.

Instead of learning the shallow graph embedding in traditional models, we propose the TCMCE model, which combines the self-attention mechanism [31] and contrastive learning [32] to obtain the deep nonnegative spectral embedding as the indicator matrix. Figure 1 gives the architecture of our model, which consists of three modules: similarity graph encoder, similarity graph decoder, and graph contrastive learning via ensembles.

3.1   Similarity Graph Encoder

The graph encoder is utilized to transform the unified similarity graph $\hat{\boldsymbol{S}} \in \mathbb{R}^{N \times N} = \sum_{v=1}^{V} (\alpha_v)^r \boldsymbol{S}^v$ into corresponding graph embeddings by self-attention mechanism. $\hat{\boldsymbol{S}}$ will be embedded into three subspaces, which can be represented as query, key, and value. We can learn the three features via the following formula:

$$\boldsymbol{Q} = \hat{\boldsymbol{S}}\boldsymbol{W}^Q$$
$$\boldsymbol{K} = \hat{\boldsymbol{S}}\boldsymbol{W}^K \tag{3}$$
$$\boldsymbol{V} = \hat{\boldsymbol{S}}\boldsymbol{W}^V$$

where $\boldsymbol{W}^Q \in \mathbb{R}^{N \times d}$, $\boldsymbol{W}^K \in \mathbb{R}^{N \times d}$, and $\boldsymbol{W}^V \in \mathbb{R}^{N \times d}$ denote the learned parameters. $\boldsymbol{Q} \in \mathbb{R}^{N \times d}$, $\boldsymbol{K} \in \mathbb{R}^{N \times d}$, and $\boldsymbol{V} \in \mathbb{R}^{N \times d}$ are the obtained query, key, and value features, respectively. The self-attention score among samples in the fusion graph can be learned via

$$a_{ij} = \frac{e^{\frac{1}{\sqrt{d}} \boldsymbol{K}_i \boldsymbol{Q}_j^T}}{\sum_{l=1}^{N} e^{\frac{1}{\sqrt{d}} \boldsymbol{K}_i \boldsymbol{Q}_l^T}} \tag{4}$$

We can obtain the output spectral embedding by

$$\boldsymbol{F}^a = Attention(Q, K, V) = \{F_i\}_{i=1}^{N} \tag{5}$$

where $F_i = \sum_{j=1}^{N} a_{ij} V_j$, and the final output $\boldsymbol{F}$ is the aggregation of $\boldsymbol{V}$ by the weighted attention score.

The multi-head attention module is applied in the self-attention mechanism to project the input feature into multiple sub-spaces, which makes the model own the capability to pay attention to different positions. The final output in multi-head attention is a linear projection of the concatenation of the outputs from multiple attention heads, which can be obtained by

$$F^M = Concat(F^1, ..., F^m) \cdot W^M \tag{6}$$

where $F^i = Attention(Q_i, K_i, V_i), 1 \leq i \leq m$, m denotes the number of heads. W^M is also a learnable matrix, $F^M \in \mathbb{R}^{N \times d'}$ is the output of multi-head attention module, $d' = d \times m$. In addition, Point-wise Feed Forward Network (FFN) is the last layer in the similarity graph encoder and we can get the output of it by

$$F^e = Relu(F^a \cdot W_1^e + b_1^e) \cdot W_2^e + b_2^e \tag{7}$$

In addition, the dropout layer, residual connection, and layer normalization are added to the modules in the encoder.

3.2   Similarity Graph Decoder

After obtaining the embedding F^e from the graph encoder, the low-dimension output of the graph decoder can be obtained via:

$$F = Softmax(Relu(F^e \cdot W_1^d + b_1^d) \cdot W_2^d + b_2^d) \tag{8}$$

where W_1^d, W_2^d are the learnable matrices in the decoder, and b_1^d, b_2^d denote the biases. The obtained nonnegative spectral embedding serves as the indicator matrix for the clustering assignment.

3.3   Similarity Graph Contrastive Learning

For the input normalization similarity graphs $S^1, S^2, ..., S^V$, N-cut is applied to get the original spectral embedding of each view, which can be written as:

$$\min Tr(F^{vT} L^v F^v)$$
$$s.t. \ F^{vT} D^v F^v = I, \tag{9}$$

where D^v and L^v represent the degree matrix and Laplacian matrix of S^v, respectively.

Let $F^{(v)}$ denote the basic partition for the v-th view in datasets. We fuse the basic partition in each view into the co-association matrix from ensemble clustering, which serves as the fusion similarity graph. We obtain $F^{(v)}$ by performing k-means on F^v. So the co-association matrix H can be learned by:

$$H_{ij} = \frac{1}{V} \sum_{v=1}^{V} \delta(F_i^{(v)}, F_j^{(v)}) \tag{10}$$

where H_{ij} represents the (i-th, j-th) element in $\boldsymbol{H}$, and $\delta(.)$ is the Kronecker delta function, which returns 1 with two identical input values otherwise 0. Here we regard $\boldsymbol{H}$ as the fusion similarity graph from multiple views.

In this paper, each node and its neighbours in the co-association $\boldsymbol{H}$ are regarded as positive pairs. We perform contrastive learning at the graph level by applying a contrastive regularizer on the reconstructed similarity graph $\boldsymbol{F}\boldsymbol{F}^T$. Significantly, the value of $FF^T_{\ ij}$ should be large if x_i and x_j are connected in $\boldsymbol{H}$ while small if they are disconnected in $\boldsymbol{H}$. We can get the loss of graph contrastive learning as:

$$L_{gcl} = -\frac{1}{N} \sum_i^N log \frac{\sum_{H_{ij}>0} exp(FF^T_{\ ij})}{\sum_{H_{ij}=0} exp(FF^T_{\ ij})} \tag{11}$$

3.4   Loss Function

The loss function consists of two forms: reconstruction loss and graph contrastive learning loss. From the viewpoint of the graph reconstruction, we serve $\boldsymbol{F}\boldsymbol{F}^T$ as the reconstructed similarity graph. Thus, the reconstruction loss is defined as:

$$L_{re} = \left\| \hat{\boldsymbol{S}} - \boldsymbol{F}\boldsymbol{F}^T \right\|_F^2 \tag{12}$$

The total loss function can be represented as:

$$L = L_{re} + \lambda L_{gcl} \tag{13}$$

where λ denotes the trade-off parameter to balance the two forms. We use Adam to update the loss function in TCMCE, and the learning rate is set as 10^{-3}. Optimizing the overall loss L, we can learn the final spectral embedding $\boldsymbol{F}$. We find the column index of the largest number in each row of the final graph embedding $\boldsymbol{F}$ as a label matrix. The cluster label of the i-th sample can be obtained as:

$$y_i = argmax(\boldsymbol{f}_i) \tag{14}$$

3.5   Computational Complexity

The computational cost of constructing the similarity graph for each view is $O(N^2 d_v)$, where d_v denotes the dimension of the original feature in v-th view. For the Transformer-based encoder, the main cost is the $Attention(Q, K, V)$, whose computational cost is $O(N^2 d)$. For the decoder, the most time-consuming operation is matrix multiplication, e.g., $\boldsymbol{F}^e \cdot \boldsymbol{W}_1^d \in \mathbb{R}^{N \times d_e}$, its computational complexity is $O(Nd^{'}d_e)$. For graph contrastive learning, the most cost is $\boldsymbol{F}\boldsymbol{F}^T$, whose computational complexity is $O(N^2)$. In addition, the complexity to obtain original spectral embedding on each view is $O(cN^2)$.

4 Experiments

In this section, we first give the experimental setting of this work. In addition, to illustrate the effectiveness of our model, we evaluate the clustering performance on six real-world datasets compared with the SOTA multi-view clustering methods. Finally, parameter sensitivity, convergence analysis, and ablation study are also introduced.

4.1 Experimental Setting

Table 1. Description of the benchmark multi-view dataset used in this paper.

Dataset	N	V	c	d1, d2,..., dV
MSRCV1	210	6	7	256/48/100/512/210/1302
COIL20	1440	3	20	1024/3304/6750
100leaves	1600	3	100	64/64/64
HW2sources	2000	2	10	784/256
Scene	2688	4	8	512/432/256/48
Caltech101	9144	6	102	48/40/254/1984/512/928

Datasets: Six widely used benchmark multi-view datasets are utilized in this article, including MSRCV1 [34], COIL20 [35], 100leaves [36], HW2sources [37], Scene [38] and Caltech101 [39]. The description of the above datasets is given in Table 1.

Comparison Methods: In the comparison experiment, we compare TCMCE with ten SOTA multi-view clustering methods, including Multi-view Learning with Adaptive Neighbours (MLAN) [6], Multi-view clustering via orthogonal and nonnegative graph reconstruction (MCONGR) [10], Auto-weighted Orthogonal and Nonnegative Graph Reconstruction for Multi-view Clustering (AONGR) [11], Fast Parameter-free Multi-view Subspace Clustering with Consensus Anchor Guidance (FPMVS) [40], Efficient one-pass multi-view subspace clustering with consensus anchors (EOMSC) [24], Fast Multi-view Clustering via Ensembles (FastMICE) [41], One2Multi Graph Autoencoder for Multi-view Graph Clustering (O2MAC) [15], multi-view contrastive graph clustering (MCGC) [32], Consistent Multiple Graph Embedding Clustering (CMGEC) [16], and Multi-level Feature Learning for Contrastive Multi-view Clustering (MFLVC) [30].

For the baseline methods, we follow the experimental setting reported in the papers. For our model, the original similarity graphs in different views are constructed via [33]:

$$
\boldsymbol{W}_{ij}^{(v)} = \begin{cases} \dfrac{e_{i,k+1}^{(v)} - e_{ij}^{(v)}}{k e_{i,k+1}^{(v)} - \sum_{h=1}^{k} e_{ih}^{(v)}} & j \leq k; \\ 0 & j > k, \end{cases} \tag{15}
$$

where $e_{ij}^{(v)} = \left\| x_i^{(v)} - x_j^{(v)} \right\|_2^2$ and k represents the number of neighbours, which is set as 20 in this paper. We set r equal to -1 in all the experiments. In addition, one parameter in this paper λ needs to tune and we select it from the list $[0.1, 1, 10, 100]$.

Evaluation Metrics: In this article, four measure metrics are used to evaluate the clustering performance of all the approaches, including Accuracy (ACC), Normalized Mutual Information (NMI), Purity and Adjusted Rand Index (ARI). In most cases, higher values of the above indicators mean better clustering performances. In addition, we run all the methods ten times and record the mean values and standard deviations of the clustering results.

Table 2. Clustering results (%) comparison on MSRC-V1 and 100leaves datasets.

Method	MSRC-V1				100leaves			
	ACC	NMI	Purity	ARI	ACC	NMI	Purity	ARI
MLAN	89.52 ± 0.30	83.76 ± 0.63	89.52 ± 0.30	76.57 ± 0.63	92.75 ± 0.00	95.54 ± 0.00	93.81 ± 0.00	88.70 ± 0.00
MCONGR	84.29 ± 0.00	77.18 ± 0.00	84.29 ± 0.00	70.72 ± 0.00	88.00 ± 0.00	94.16 ± 0.00	88.50 ± 0.00	82.45 ± 0.00
AONGR	93.81 ± 0.00	87.95 ± 0.00	93.81 ± 0.00	85.73 ± 0.00	92.44 ± 0.00	95.95 ± 0.00	93.13 ± 0.00	88.52 ± 0.00
FPMVS	61.43 ± 0.00	65.54 ± 0.00	82.86 ± 0.00	54.27 ± 0.00	30.81 ± 0.00	68.35 ± 0.00	44.19 ± 0.00	18.26 ± 0.00
EOMSC	87.62 ± 0.00	84.47 ± 0.00	87.62 ± 0.00	83.97 ± 0.00	42.50 ± 0.00	76.57 ± 0.00	45.06 ± 0.00	25.40 ± 0.00
FastMICE	90.81 ± 2.78	84.73 ± 2.39	90.91 ± 2.57	82.36 ± 2.92	80.30 ± 2.10	91.94 ± 1.80	82.89 ± 2.86	78.29 ± 2.38
O2MAC	45.24 ± 2.44	35.52 ± 1.82	47.05 ± 2.68	21.49 ± 1.97	52.75 ± 0.91	73.27 ± 0.76	52.99 ± 0.95	26.77 ± 0.52
MCGC	70.00 ± 1.93	61.62 ± 1.46	70.95 ± 1.69	47.87 ± 1.24	72.25 ± 0.96	83.37 ± 0.64	74.69 ± 0.87	46.35 ± 0.31
CMGEC	91.43 ± 2.48	85.39 ± 1.13	91.43 ± 2.48	83.04 ± 1.34	90.34 ± 1.32	95.32 ± 1.44	92.03 ± 1.63	85.63 ± 1.88
MFLVC	82.67 ± 1.10	80.37 ± 1.04	84.10 ± 1.65	72.55 ± 1.23	38.75 ± 2.36	70.41 ± 1.42	39.70 ± 2.20	31.32 ± 1.59
Ours	**94.10 ± 0.49**	**88.23 ± 1.13**	**94.10 ± 0.49**	**86.39 ± 0.00**	**95.60 ± 1.07**	**97.62 ± 0.43**	**96.30 ± 0.82**	**93.26 ± 1.31**

Table 3. Clustering results (%) comparison on HW2sources and COIL20 datasets.

Method	HW2sources				COIL20			
	ACC	NMI	Purity	ARI	ACC	NMI	Purity	ARI
MLAN	61.42 ± 2.26	70.53 ± 2.28	66.42 ± 2.01	49.15 ± 2.18	88.26 ± 0.00	96.93 ± 0.00	90.00 ± 0.00	88.85 ± 0.00
MCONGR	99.15 ± 0.00	97.99 ± 0.00	99.15 ± 0.00	98.12 ± 0.00	82.15 ± 0.00	92.18 ± 0.00	84.65 ± 0.00	79.52 ± 0.00
AONGR	99.00 ± 0.00	97.63 ± 0.00	99.00 ± 0.00	97.79 ± 0.00	97.99 ± 0.00	98.73 ± 0.00	97.99 ± 0.00	96.60 ± 0.00
FPMVS	69.05 ± 0.00	71.14 ± 0.00	88.40 ± 0.00	63.44 ± 0.00	47.36 ± 0.00	70.51 ± 0.00	66.38 ± 0.00	40.73 ± 0.00
EOMSC	75.55 ± 0.00	67.84 ± 0.00	75.60 ± 0.00	69.89 ± 0.00	57.50 ± 0.00	72.91 ± 0.00	59.51 ± 0.00	47.60 ± 0.00
FastMICE	96.14 ± 2.33	94.57 ± 1.27	96.15 ± 2.31	93.90 ± 2.23	79.11 ± 2.38	89.23 ± 1.47	81.24 ± 2.70	78.18 ± 1.88
O2MAC	79.11 ± 3.64	68.67 ± 2.33	88.40 ± 0.00	81.08 ± 3.05	53.61 ± 1.86	65.56 ± 2.11	57.24 ± 1.42	42.91 ± 1.64
MCGC	60.75 ± 0.73	58.29 ± 0.41	64.55 ± 0.64	45.16 ± 0.37	27.42 ± 0.76	24.76 ± 0.81	42.14 ± 0.52	10.60 ± 0.21
CMGEC	88.83 ± 1.85	90.48 ± 1.51	89.63 ± 0.99	83.21 ± 2.28	62.03 ± 1.64	82.13 ± 1.29	62.74 ± 1.53	61.31 ± 1.13
MFLVC	98.99 ± 0.30	97.53 ± 0.55	98.99 ± 0.30	97.61 ± 0.48	73.10 ± 1.29	79.81 ± 1.43	73.40 ± 1.28	65.19 ± 1.73
Ours	**99.19 ± 0.08**	**98.01 ± 0.13**	**99.19 ± 0.08**	**98.14 ± 0.11**	**99.20 ± 0.65**	**99.56 ± 0.52**	**99.20 ± 0.65**	**99.18 ± 0.58**

Table 4. Clustering results (%) comparison on Caltech101 and Scene datasets.

Method	Caltech101				Scene			
	ACC	NMI	Purity	ARI	ACC	NMI	Purity	ARI
MLAN	24.40 ± 0.94	43.23 ± 1.07	40.67 ± 1.35	10.93 ± 1.36	49.63 ± 0.00	51.05 ± 0.00	61.04 ± 0.00	28.42 ± 0.00
MCONGR	25.08 ± 0.00	46.58 ± 0.00	46.06 ± 0.00	12.90 ± 0.00	48.63 ± 0.00	42.26 ± 0.00	55.41 ± 0.00	32.52 ± 0.00
AONGR	28.00 ± 0.00	48.60 ± 0.00	46.26 ± 0.00	15.90 ± 0.00	50.04 ± 0.00	38.54 ± 0.00	53.76 ± 0.00	28.11 ± 0.00
FPMVS	**29.33 ± 0.00**	35.71 ± 0.00	33.60 ± 0.00	**17.34 ± 0.00**	27.42 ± 0.00	24.76 ± 0.00	42.14 ± 0.00	10.60 ± 0.00
EOMSC	24.70 ± 0.00	27.09 ± 0.00	27.64 ± 0.00	10.02 ± 0.00	64.16 ± 0.00	56.11 ± 0.00	62.77 ± 0.00	45.93 ± 0.00
FastMICE	22.58 ± 0.94	44.48 ± 0.71	44.52 ± 0.83	16.67 ± 0.36	70.40 ± 2.05	58.46 ± 1.50	70.68 ± 1.69	49.70 ± 1.74
O2MAC	16.08 ± 0.65	29.84 ± 1.98	27.60 ± 1.83	8.03 ± 0.78	47.07 ± 2.49	37.15 ± 1.93	49.14 ± 0.77	26.19 ± 1.09
MCGC	23.05 ± 1.22	39.23 ± 1.13	37.66 ± 1.06	13.36 ± 0.89	52.60 ± 0.56	45.74 ± 0.79	52.64 ± 0.62	30.26 ± 0.18
CMGEC	18.96 ± 0.13	42.14 ± 0.81	40.72 ± 0.21	10.44 ± 0.33	58.38 ± 1.92	53.44 ± 1.75	58.66 ± 1.31	40.11 ± 2.10
MFLVC	26.37 ± 1.86	32.53 ± 1.05	29.68 ± 1.63	7.61 ± 0.48	71.78 ± 1.27	57.48 ± 0.74	71.78 ± 1.27	49.77 ± 1.36
Ours	28.26 ± 0.86	**48.65 ± 0.63**	**47.71 ± 0.74**	17.18 ± 0.33	**75.19 ± 0.53**	**58.54 ± 0.42**	**75.19 ± 0.53**	**52.88 ± 0.31**

4.2 Clustering Results

The comparison results of multi-view clustering performances on the six real-world datasets in terms of four metrics are recorded in Tables 2, 3 and 4, in which the best performances are marked in bold and underlines mark the second-best ones. From the above results, we can draw the following conclusions: 1) Our TCMCE outperforms other baselines on all the benchmark datasets. Especially on the 100leaves dataset, the proposed TCMCE achieves 2.85%, 1.67%, 2.49% and 4.56% improvement compared with the second-best values in terms of ACC, NMI, Purity, and ARI, respectively. 2) Graph-based methods show better performance than other multi-view clustering methods on most datasets. Significantly, the proposed TCMCE outperforms other graph-based baselines because of the learned precise deep spectral embedding. 3) Although the contrastive multi-view clustering method MFLVC has achieved considerable results on the HW2sources and Scene dataset, the GCN-based baseline CMGEC shows good performance on the MSRCV1 and 100leaves datasets, our model still outperforms them on the six real-world datasets, which attributes the impact of the similarity graph reconstruction framework.

The learned common graph comparison on the COIL20 dataset between the proposed TCMCE and other graph-based baselines is exhibited in Fig. 2. Note that the reconstructed graphs exhibit clearer structures compared to the original similarity graphs. In comparison with the graph-based baselines, the unified graph obtained via our model is a typical block-diagonal matrix, which is good for clustering tasks. In addition, the reconstructed graph via TCMCE doesn't emerge the missing block reported in [8]. To make optimization easier, [8] utilizes another label matrix to be close to the graph embedding each other, which may lead to zero rows in the label matrix. In this article, we design an effective and simple loss function to update the graph embedding, making the reconstructed graph own a more stable structure.

To show the comparison of the learned spectral embedding or indicator matrix between our model and the baselines intuitively, Fig. 3 gives the t-SNE [42] visualization results on the Scene datasets. Significantly, the learned

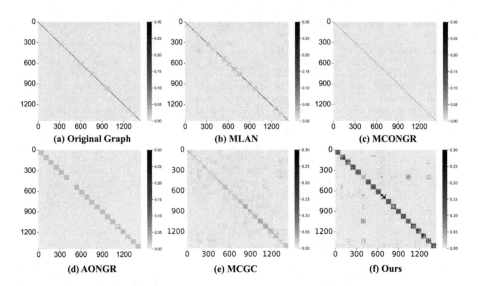

Fig. 2. The learned common similarity graphs by TCMCE and other graph-based baselines on the COIL20 dataset.

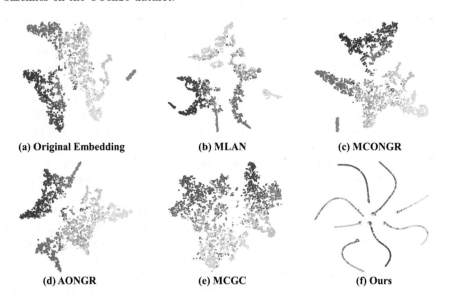

Fig. 3. The obtained spectral embedding or indicator matrices by TCMCE and other baselines on the Scene dataset.

spectral embedding via TCMCE is more cohesive compared with the ones learned by other baselines. In addition, the obtained deep spectral embedding as an indicator matrix only has one element larger than zero because of its non-negativity, which offers interpretability for clustering assignments.

4.3 Parameter Sensitivity Analysis

To investigate the robustness of our model on the predefined similarity graphs, we conduct the k-sensitivity experiments of TCMCE and other graph-based baselines, where k denotes the number of neighbours in similarity graphs construction and k is selected from the list $[5, 10, 15, 20, 25, 30]$. Figure 4 gives the clustering performance comparison between the proposed TCMCE and baselines with different k on the MSRCV1 and 100leaves datasets in terms of all metrics, from which our model is insensitive with k compared with the graph-based baselines. Thus, our model is robust to the original similarity graphs. And we set k to 20 on all the benchmark datasets in practice.

Only one parameter λ exists in our model and we tune it from the list $[0.1, 1, 10, 100]$. Figure 5 shows the clustering performance of the proposed TCMCE in terms of four metrics with different λ on six real-world datasets, from which our model performs stable clustering capability with parameter perturbations. Above all, our TCMCE model is not only effective on multi-view clustering tasks but robust to the parameter λ.

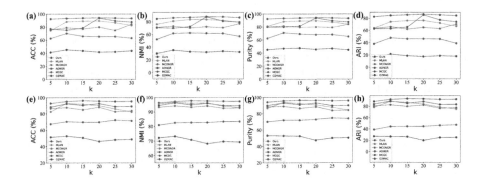

Fig. 4. The k-sensitivity comparison between TCMCE and other baselines on the MSRCV1 (a–d) and 100leaves (e–h) datasets.

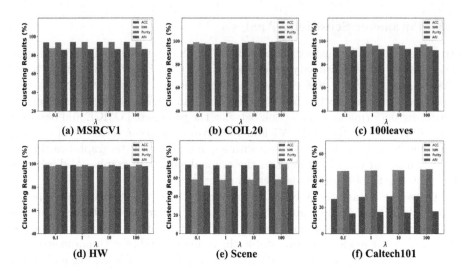

Fig. 5. The λ-sensitivity analysis of the proposed TCMCE on the six benchmark datasets.

4.4 Convergence Analysis

Figure 6 gives the convergence curves of the proposed TCMCE on six benchmark datasets. The x-axis represents the number of epochs, and the y-axis denotes the value of the loss function in TCMCE. As shown in Fig. 6, our model can realize convergence in terms of less than 30 iterations on all the benchmark datasets.

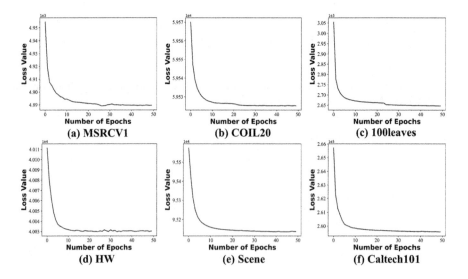

Fig. 6. The convergence curves of TCMCE model on six real-world datasets.

4.5 Ablation Study

In this sub-section, we aim to verify the effectiveness of similarity graph reconstruction, contrastive graph learning, and self-attention mechanism in our TCMCE. In TCMCE model, similarity graph reconstruction aims to learn a precise spectral embedding, contrastive learning is adopted as regularization to make the reconstructed graph clustering-friendly, and self-attention helps to capture the latent relationship among samples in the fusion similarity graph. Specifically, three variants of TCMCE are designed for the ablation study: 1) variant-1, whose loss function only contains the contrastive loss; 2) variant-2, whose loss function only contains the graph reconstruction loss; 3) variant-3, which utilizes the GCN-based encoder to learn the graph embedding instead of the Transformer-based one. The comparison of clustering results (ACC and NMI) between our model and its variants are shown in Table 5, from which the proposed TCMCE outperforms its variants on all the benchmark datasets. The above phenomena validate that the similarity graph reconstruction, contrastive graph learning, and self-attention mechanism in encoder all make positive impacts on our model.

Table 5. Comparison of the clustering results on TCMCE and its variants.

Methods		Variant-1	Variant-2	Variant-3	TCMCE
MSRCV1	ACC	$67.38_{\pm 2.62}$	$93.71_{\pm 0.47}$	$93.76_{\pm 0.31}$	$\mathbf{94.10}_{\pm \mathbf{0.49}}$
	NMI	$66.79_{\pm 0.98}$	$87.38_{\pm 0.92}$	$87.36_{\pm 0.41}$	$\mathbf{88.23}_{\pm \mathbf{1.13}}$
COIL20	ACC	$88.37_{\pm 3.23}$	$95.51_{\pm 3.66}$	$87.34_{\pm 2.72}$	$\mathbf{99.20}_{\pm \mathbf{0.65}}$
	NMI	$96.62_{\pm 0.61}$	$98.95_{\pm 0.86}$	$96.71_{\pm 0.29}$	$\mathbf{99.56}_{\pm \mathbf{0.52}}$
100leaves	ACC	$63.91_{\pm 0.22}$	$94.05_{\pm 1.59}$	$93.94_{\pm 1.05}$	$\mathbf{95.60}_{\pm \mathbf{1.07}}$
	NMI	$83.19_{\pm 0.06}$	$97.08_{\pm 0.65}$	$97.17_{\pm 0.55}$	$\mathbf{97.62}_{\pm \mathbf{0.43}}$
HW2sources	ACC	$63.65_{\pm 0.35}$	$96.01_{\pm 3.80}$	$99.05_{\pm 0.11}$	$\mathbf{99.19}_{\pm \mathbf{0.08}}$
	NMI	$64.23_{\pm 0.76}$	$95.38_{\pm 2.26}$	$97.75_{\pm 0.24}$	$\mathbf{98.01}_{\pm \mathbf{0.13}}$
Scene	ACC	$62.07_{\pm 0.47}$	$71.26_{\pm 4.27}$	$68.18_{\pm 0.52}$	$\mathbf{75.19}_{\pm \mathbf{0.53}}$
	NMI	$56.30_{\pm 0.66}$	$56.79_{\pm 2.23}$	$56.13_{\pm 0.71}$	$\mathbf{58.54}_{\pm \mathbf{0.42}}$
Caltech101	ACC	$25.43_{\pm 0.59}$	$25.17_{\pm 0.83}$	$27.43_{\pm 0.66}$	$\mathbf{28.26}_{\pm \mathbf{0.86}}$
	NMI	$44.13_{\pm 0.71}$	$47.06_{\pm 0.46}$	$47.44_{\pm 0.34}$	$\mathbf{48.65}_{\pm \mathbf{0.63}}$

5 Conclusion

In this paper, we propose a novel Transformer-based contrastive multi-view clustering via ensembles model named TCMCE, which integrates the self-attention mechanism and graph contrastive learning into a joint framework to learn the deep nonnegative spectral embedding. Due to the non-negativity, only one element in each row of the spectral embedding matrix obtained by TCMCE is non-zero, which can offer interpretability for cluster assignment. So the learned spectral embedding can be directly used as an indicator matrix without any post-processing. The common graph via learned embedding owns a clear structure, which is good for clustering tasks. In addition, a simple and powerful loss function is devised to train the proposed model, containing reconstruction loss and graph contrastive loss. Extensive experiments on six real-world datasets demonstrate that our method achieves superior multi-view clustering performance. However, the time complexity of TCMCE is still high. The researches to improve the clustering efficiency and time cost based on anchor graph or parallel computation are left in our further work. The code of TCMCE is available at Github.

Ethical Statement. The authors declare that they have no conflict of interest. This article does not contain any studies involving human participants or animals performed by any of the authors. Informed consent was obtained from all individual participants included in the study.

References

1. Zhao, J., Xie, X., Xu, X., Sun, S.: Multi-view learning overview: recent progress and new challenges. Inf. Fusion **38**, 43–54 (2017)
2. Kang, Y., Choi, S.: Restricted deep belief networks for multi-view learning. In: Gunopulos, D., Hofmann, T., Malerba, D., Vazirgiannis, M. (eds.) ECML PKDD 2011. LNCS (LNAI), vol. 6912, pp. 130–145. Springer, Heidelberg (2011). https://doi.org/10.1007/978-3-642-23783-6_9
3. Chao, G., Sun, S., Bi, J.: A survey on multiview clustering. IEEE Trans. Artif. Intell. **2**(2), 146–168 (2021)
4. Yan, X., Hu, S., Mao, Y., Ye, Y., Yu, H.: Deep multi-view learning methods: a review. Neurocomputing **448**, 106–129 (2021)
5. Wang, H., Yang, Y., Liu, B.: GMC: graph-based multi-view clustering. IEEE Trans. Knowl. Data Eng. **32**(6), 1116–1129 (2019)
6. Nie, F., Cai, G., Li, J., Li, X.: Auto-weighted multi-view learning for image clustering and semi-supervised classification. IEEE Trans. Image Process. **27**(3), 1501–1511 (2017)
7. Nie, F., Ding, C., Luo, D., Huang, H.: Improved MinMax cut graph clustering with nonnegative relaxation. In: Balcázar, J.L., Bonchi, F., Gionis, A., Sebag, M. (eds.) ECML PKDD 2010. LNCS (LNAI), vol. 6322, pp. 451–466. Springer, Heidelberg (2010). https://doi.org/10.1007/978-3-642-15883-4_29
8. Han, J., Xiong, K., Nie, F.: Orthogonal and nonnegative graph reconstruction for large scale clustering. In: IJCAI, pp. 1809–1815 (2017)
9. Hu, Z., Nie, F., Wang, R., Li, X.: Multi-view spectral clustering via integrating nonnegative embedding and spectral embedding. Inf. Fusion **55**, 251–259 (2020)
10. Shi, S., Nie, F., Wang, R., Li, X.: Multi-view clustering via nonnegative and orthogonal graph reconstruction. IEEE Trans. Neural Netw. Learn. Syst. **34**(1), 201–214 (2021)
11. Zhao, M., Yang, W., Nie, F.: Auto-weighted orthogonal and nonnegative graph reconstruction for multi-view clustering. Inf. Sci. **632**, 324–339 (2023)
12. Yang, X., Deng, C., Dang, Z., Tao, D.: Deep multiview collaborative clustering. IEEE Trans. Neural Netw. Learn. Syst. **34**(1), 516–526 (2021)

13. Huang, Z., Zhou, J.T., Peng, X., Zhang, C., Zhu, H., Lv, J.: Multi-view spectral clustering network. In: IJCAI, pp. 2563–2569 (2019)
14. Kipf, T.N., Welling, M.: Semi-supervised classification with graph convolutional networks. In: ICLR (2016)
15. Fan, S., Wang, X., Shi, C., Lu, E., Lin, K., Wang, B.: One2Multi graph autoencoder for multi-view graph clustering. In: WWW, pp. 3070–3076 (2020)
16. Wang, Y., Chang, D., Fu, Z., Zhao, Y.: Consistent multiple graph embedding for multi-view clustering. IEEE Trans. Multimedia **24**, 2461–2472 (2021)
17. Li, Z., et al.: Consensus graph learning for multi-view clustering. IEEE Trans. Multimedia **24**, 2461–2472 (2021)
18. Zhang, P., et al.: Consensus one-step multi-view subspace clustering. IEEE Trans. Knowl. Data Eng. **34**(10), 4676–4689 (2020)
19. Zhan, K., Niu, C., Chen, C., Nie, F., Zhang, C., Yang, Y.: Graph structure fusion for multiview clustering. IEEE Trans. Knowl. Data Eng. **31**(10), 1984–1993 (2018)
20. Ren, P., Xiao, Y., Xu, P.: Robust auto-weighted multi-view clustering. In: IJCAI, pp. 2644–2650 (2018)
21. De Martino, G., Pio, G., Ceci, M.: Multi-view overlapping clustering for the identification of the subject matter of legal judgments. Inf. Sci. **638**, 118956 (2023)
22. Kang, Z., Zhou, W., Zhao, Z., Shao, J., Han, M., Xu, Z.: Large-scale multi-view subspace clustering in linear time. In: AAAI, pp. 4412–4419 (2020)
23. Qiang, Q., Zhang, B., Wang, F., Nie, F.: Fast multi-view discrete clustering with anchor graphs. In: AAAI, pp. 9360–9367 (2021)
24. Liu, S., Wang, S., Zhang, P.: Efficient one-pass multi-view subspace clustering with consensus anchors. In: AAAI, vol. 36, no. 7, pp. 7576–7584 (2022)
25. Zhang, C., Liu, Y., Fu, H.: AE2-Nets: autoencoder in autoencoder networks. In: CVPR, pp. 2577–2585 (2019)
26. Zhou, R., Shen, Y.D.: End-to-end adversarial-attention network for multi-modal clustering. In: CVPR, pp. 14619–14628 (2020)
27. Li, Y., Hu, P., Liu, Z., Peng, D., Zhou, J., Peng, X.: Contrastive clustering. In: AAAI, vol. 35, no. 10, pp. 8547–8555 (2021)
28. Trosten, D.J., Lokse, S., Jenssen, R., Kampffmeyer, M.: Reconsidering representation alignment for multi-view clustering. In: CVPR, pp. 1255–1265 (2021)
29. Lin, Y., Gou, Y., Liu, Z., Li, B., Lv, J., Peng, X.: Completer: incomplete multi-view clustering via contrastive prediction. In: CVPR, pp. 11174–11183 (2021)
30. Xu, J., Tang, H., Ren, Y., Peng, L., Zhu, X., He, L.: Multi-level feature learning for contrastive multi-view clustering. In: CVPR, pp. 16051–16060 (2022)
31. Vaswani, A., et al.: Attention is all you need. In: NeurIPS, vol. 30 (2017)
32. Pan, E., Kang, Z.: Multi-view contrastive graph clustering. In: NeurIPS, vol. 34, pp. 2148–2159 (2021)
33. Nie, F., Wang, X., Jordan, M., Huang, H.: The constrained Laplacian rank algorithm for graph-based clustering. In: AAAI (2016)
34. Cai, X., Nie, F., Huang, H., Kamangar, F.: Heterogeneous image feature integration via multi-modal spectral clustering. In: CVPR, pp. 1977–1984 (2011)
35. Nene, S.A., Nayar, S.K., Murase, H.: Columbia Object Image Library (COIL-20) (1996)
36. Mallah, C., Cope, J., Orwell, J.: Plant leaf classification using probabilistic integration of shape, texture and margin features. Signal Process. Pattern Recognit. Appl. **5**(1), 45–54 (2013)
37. Wang, H., Yang, Y., Liu, B., Fujita, H.: A study of graph-based system for multi-view clustering. Knowl. Based Syst. **163**, 1009–1019 (2019)

38. Monadjemi, A., Thomas, B.T., Mirmehdi, M.: Experiments on high resolution images towards outdoor scene classification (2002)
39. Li, F., Fergus, R., Perona, P.: Learning generative visual models from few training examples: an incremental Bayesian approach tested on 101 object categories. In: CVPR Workshop, p. 178 (2004)
40. Wang, S., et al.: Fast parameter-free multi-view subspace clustering with consensus anchor guidance. IEEE Trans. Image Process. 31, 556–568 (2021)
41. Huang, D., Wang, C.D., Lai, J.H.: Fast multi-view clustering via ensembles: towards scalability, superiority, and simplicity. IEEE Trans. Knowl. Data Eng. (2023)
42. Van der Maaten, L., Hinton, G.: Visualizing data using t-SNE. J. Mach. Learn. Res. 9(11), 2579–2605 (2008)

A Deep Dynamic Latent Block Model for the Co-Clustering of Zero-Inflated Data Matrices

Giulia Marchello[1(✉)], Marco Corneli[1,2], and Charles Bouveyron[1]

[1] Université Côte d'Azur, Inria, CNRS,
Laboratoire J.A.Dieudonné, Maasai Team, Nice, France
`giulia.marchello@inria.fr`
[2] Université Côte d'Azur, Laboratoire CEPAM, Nice, France

Abstract. The simultaneous clustering of observations and features of data sets (a.k.a. *co-clustering*) has recently emerged as a central machine learning task to summarize massive data sets. However, most existing models focus on stationary scenarios, where cluster assignments do not evolve in time. This work introduces a novel latent block model for the dynamic co-clustering of data matrices with high sparsity. The data are assumed to follow dynamic mixtures of block-dependent zero-inflated distributions. Moreover, the sparsity parameter as well as the cluster proportions are assumed to be driven by dynamic systems, whose parameters must be estimated. The inference of the model parameters relies on an original variational EM algorithm whose maximization step trains fully connected neural networks that approximate the dynamic systems. Due to the model ability to work with empty clusters, the selection of the number of clusters can be done in a (computationally) parsimonious way. Numerical experiments on simulated and real world data sets demonstrate the effectiveness of the proposed methodology in the context of count data.

Keywords: Co-clustering · Latent Block Model · zero-inflated distributions · dynamic systems · VEM algorithm

1 Introduction

1.1 Context and Related Works

In a wide range of applications (e.g. signal processing, recommending systems, genetics, etc.) there is a growing need to develop machine learning models to treat time-dependent high dimensional data, in contexts of extreme data sparsity. By the simultaneous clustering of the rows (observations) and the columns (features) of a data matrix, co-clustering proved to be an useful tool for high-dimensional data analysis thanks to its ability to provide useful summaries and visualisations of the data. However, the development of *dynamic* co-clustering methods for sparse data sets still remains almost an unexplored territory.

D. Koutra et al. (Eds.): ECML PKDD 2023, LNAI 14169, pp. 695–710, 2023.
https://doi.org/10.1007/978-3-031-43412-9_41

The cornerstone of model-based co-clustering is the popular latent block model (LBM, Govaert and Nadif 2003), initially introduced for the co-clustering of binary data matrices. LBM is based on the assumption that rows and columns of a matrix are grouped in hidden clusters and that the observations within a block (intersection of a row cluster and a column cluster) are independently and identically distributed. Whereas the original formulation of the model dealt with binary data only, the model has been extended in the last two decades to count data (Govaert and Nadif 2010), continuous data (Lomet 2012), categorical data (Keribin et al. 2015), ordinal data (Corneli et al. 2020; Jacques and Biernacki 2018), functional data (Bouveyron et al. 2018) and textual data (Bergé et al. 2019). In the dynamic context, Boutalbi et al. (2020) proposed the tensor latent block model (TLBM) for the co-clustering of rows and columns of a 3D array, with covariates accounting for the third (temporal) dimension. TLBM was also implemented for different types of data: continuous, binary and counting. Recently, Marchello et al. (2022) proposed an extension of LBM allowing one to perform the simultaneous clustering of rows, columns and slices of a three dimensional counting array. Although being a first attempt to expand the LBM model to the dynamic case, this model has the limitation of not allowing cluster switches of rows/columns. In a different framework, Casa et al. (2021) prolong the latent block model to deal with longitudinal data, relying on the shape invariant model (Lindstrom 1995). Boutalbi et al. (2021) developed a model-based co-clustering method for sparse three-way data, where the third dimension can be seen as a discrete temporal one. Here, the sparsity is handled following the same assumption as in Ailem et al. (2017) that all blocks outside the main diagonal share a common parameter.

1.2 Contribution of This Work

The model that we introduce brings two major contributions in the field of dynamic co-clustering: first, observations (rows) and features (columns) are allowed to leave/join clusters over time; second, the data sparsity is explicitly taken into account by means of block dependent zero-inflated distributions. Before describing our model in more details, in the next section, we just point out the importance of the first contribution. Capturing the data dynamics is crucial in order to detect atypical phenomena that may have affected the underlying generative process. For instance, if at a given time t the value of some features suddenly increases for just one observation in a cluster, this suggests that the observation is likely to have switched to another cluster. A change point should be detected, leaving space for further analysis to inspect the causes. Thus, our aim was to develop a highly interpretable co-clustering method allowing practitioners to obtain faster visualizations of the results in order to automate the data analysis.

2 A Zero-Inflated Dynamic LBM

The observed data are assumed to be collected into time evolving matrices, over the interval $[0, T]$. We work in discrete time and assume that we have a time partition of equally spaced points

$$0 = t_0 < t_1 < t_u \leq t_U = T.$$

Now up to rescaling, we can assume without loss of generality, that $t_{u+1} - t_u = 1$. Moreover, to simplify the exposition we omit the subscript u and, with a slight abuse of notation, we denote by t the generic time point t_u and by T the number of time points U. Thus, at (discretized) time t, we introduce the incidence matrix $X(t) \in \mathbb{N}^{N \times M}$ whose entry $X_{ij}(t)$ describes the (binary, counting, real) interaction between the observation i and the feature j took place between t and $t - 1$. The rows of $X(t)$ are indexed by $i = 1, ..., N$ and the columns by $j = 1, ..., M$.

We aim at simultaneously clustering the rows and columns of the collection of the time indexed data matrices $\{X(t)\}_t$.

Cluster Modeling. The rows (i.e. observations) and columns (i.e. features) of $X(t)$ are clustered into Q and L groups, respectively. Although Q and L are assumed fixed over time, each row/column is nevertheless allowed to change its cluster membership over $[0, T]$. More formally, a latent matrix $Z(t) := \{Z_{iq}(t)\}_{i \in 1,...,N; q \in 1,...,Q}$ represents the clustering of N *rows* into Q groups at a given time point t, with $Z_{iq}(t) = 1$ if row i belongs to the q-th cluster in t, zero otherwise. We assume that the i-th row of $Z(t)$ (say $Z_i(t)$) follows an evolving multinomial distribution, parameterized by $\alpha(t)$

$$Z(t) \sim \mathcal{M}(1, \alpha(t) := (\alpha_1(t), \ldots, \alpha_Q(t))), \tag{1}$$

where $\alpha_q(t) = \mathbb{P}\{Z_{iq}(t) = 1\}$ and $\sum_{q=1}^{Q} \alpha_q(t) = 1$, for all t.

In a similar fashion, we introduce a latent matrix $W(t) \in \{0, 1\}^{M \times L}$, labelling the column clusters at time t, and whose j-th row $W_j(t)$ follows a multinomial distribution of parameter $\beta(t) := (\beta_1(t), \ldots, \beta_L(t))$.

The two random matrices Z and W are further assumed to be independent.

Sparsity Modeling. In order to model a potentially extreme data sparsity, the observed data are modeled by mixtures of block-conditional Zero-Inflated distributions, with conditionally independent entries $X_{ij}(t)$. In more detail we introduce a latent vector π of length T, whose entry $\pi(t)$ indicates the proportion of data sparsity at time t. Then we assume that, with probability $\pi(t)$, $X_{ij}(t) = 0$ a.s., whereas with probability $1 - \pi(t)$ we have[1]

$$X_{ij}(t) | Z_i(t), W_j(t) \sim \varphi(X_{ij}(t); \zeta_{Z_i(t), W_j(t)}), \tag{2}$$

---

[1] We adopt in Eq. (2) a quite common convention in the clustering literature: $Z_i(t)$ denotes both the i-th row of $Z(t)$ and a random variable whose value is q if row i is in the q-th row cluster at time t.

independently for all (i, j), where $\varphi(X_{ij}(t), \cdot)$ is some probability distribution function with parameter $\zeta \in \mathbb{R}^{Q \times L}$. In a compact notation:

$$X_{ij}(t)|Z_i(t), W_j(t) \sim ZI_\varphi(\zeta_{Z_i(t), W_j(t)}, \pi(t)) , \qquad (3)$$

where ZI stands for Zero-Inflated. Among the distributions $\varphi(\cdot)$ that could be considered, we can cite the zero-inflated versions of the log-normal and the Gamma distributions for continuous data, or the zero-inflated Poisson (ZIP) distribution (Lambert 1992) for count data.

In order to ease the illustration of the inference routine we finally provide a third, equivalent formulation of the above equations in terms of a hidden random matrix, $A \in \{0, 1\}^{N \times M}$, where independently for all i and j

$$A_{ij}(t) \sim \mathcal{B}(\pi(t)),$$

with $\mathcal{B}(p)$ denoting the Bernoulli probability mass function of parameter p and such that

$$\begin{aligned} A_{ij}(t) = 1 &\Rightarrow X_{ij}(t)|Z_i(t), W_j(t) = 0 \\ A_{ij}(t) = 0 &\Rightarrow X_{ij}(t)|Z_i(t), W_j(t) \sim \varphi(X_{ij}, (t), \zeta_{Z_i(t), W_j(t)}). \end{aligned} \qquad (4)$$

Modeling the Parameters Dynamics. The mixing parameters α and β as well as the sparsity proportions π (all vectors of length T) are assumed to be driven by systems of ordinary differential equations (ODEs). In this way, we are able to capture the temporal evolution of both the cluster proportions and the (excess of) sparsity. In continuous time, the three dynamic systems would read as:

$$\frac{d}{dt}a(t) = f_Z(a(t)), \qquad (5)$$

$$\frac{d}{dt}b(t) = f_W(b(t)), \qquad (6)$$

$$\frac{d}{dt}c(t) = f_A(c(t)), \qquad (7)$$

where $t \in [0, T]$, $f_Z : \mathbb{R}^Q \to \mathbb{R}^Q$, $f_W : \mathbb{R}^L \to \mathbb{R}^L$ and $f_A : \mathbb{R} \to \mathbb{R}$ are three unknown continuous functions and $a : [0, T] \to \mathbb{R}^Q$, $b : [0, T] \to \mathbb{R}^L$ and $c : [0, T] \to \mathbb{R}$ are three continuously differentiable functions such that

$$\alpha_q(t) := \frac{e^{a_q(t)}}{\sum_{q=1}^{Q} e_q^a(t)} \quad \beta_\ell(t) := \frac{e^{b_\ell(t)}}{\sum_{\ell=1}^{L} e_\ell^b(t)}, \qquad (8)$$

and

$$\pi(t) := \frac{e^{c(t)}}{1 + e^{c(t)}}. \qquad (9)$$

Then, since (as stated at beginning of Sect. 2) we work with discrete time points, the above dynamic systems reduce to their Euler schemes. A graphical representation of the model described so far, and named Zero-Inflated dLBM, can be seen in Fig. 1.

2.1   The Joint Distribution

The model described so far can be adapted to any zero-inflated distribution. The first formulation as well as the most well-known concerns the Zero-Inflated Poisson (Lambert 1992). However, other distributions such as Zero-Inflated Negative Binomial (Ridout et al. 2001), Zero-Inflated Beta (Ospina and Ferrari 2012), Zero-Inflated log-normal (Li et al. 2011) could be coupled with the present modeling. In the following to ease the readability of the inference procedure we make use of the Zero-Inflated Poisson ($ZI_\mathcal{P}$) formulation to illustrate our approach.

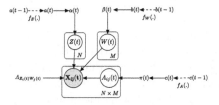

Fig. 1. Graphical representation of the Zero-Inflated dLBM model.

Hence, we can write

$$X_{ij}(t)|Z_i(t), W_j(t) \sim ZI_\mathcal{P}(\Lambda_{Z_i(t),W_j(t)}, \pi(t)),$$

where $\mathcal{P}(\cdot)$ denotes the probability mass function of a Poisson distribution and Λ is a $Q \times L$ matrix, denoting the block-dependent Poisson intensity parameter. The whole set of the model parameters is denoted by $\theta := (\Lambda, \alpha, \beta, \pi)$ and the latent variables used so far are A, Z and W. Thus, the likelihood of the complete data reads

$$p(X, A, Z, W|\theta) = p(X|A, Z, W, \Lambda, \pi) \times p(A \mid \pi)p(Z|\alpha)p(W|\beta). \tag{10}$$

The terms on the right hand side of the above equation can be further developed. Details are postponed in Appendix ?? for lack of space[2].

3   Inference

In order to infer the model parameters, two main problems occur. First, we can't adopt the EM algorithm (Bishop 2006; Dempster et al. 1977) in order to numerically compute ML estimates from the intractable quantity $p(X|\theta)$. This issue is common to all stochastic and latent block models (see for instance, Govaert and Nadif 2003) due to the intractability of the posterior distribution of the latent variables (here A, Z and W). Second, although variational strategies (Jaakkola and Jordan 1997; Jordan et al. 1998) could be employed, α, β and π cannot be updated explicitly, in the M step, due to the dynamics in Eqs. (5)–(7). This is why we combine variational inference with a Gradient Descent (GD) optimization for the ODE part.

---

[2] The supplementary materials are available at https://hal.science/hal-04150292.

3.1   Variational Decomposition

Since we cannot compute the joint posterior distribution $p(A, Z, W | X, \theta)$, we introduce a variational distribution $q(\cdot)$ over the latent variables (A, Z, W) and adopt the following standard variational decomposition of the observed log-likelihood

$$\log p(X | \theta) = \mathcal{L}(q; \theta) + KL(q(\cdot) \| p(\cdot | X, \theta)),$$

where $\mathcal{L}$ denotes a lower bound of the term on the left hand side of the equality and is defined as:

$$\mathbb{E}_{q(A,Z,W)} \left[\log \frac{p(X, A, Z, W | \theta)}{q(A, Z, W)} \right] \tag{11}$$

and KL indicates the Kullaback-Liebler divergence between the approximate and the true posterior distribution of (A, Z, W). Although the above equations hold for any distribution $q(\cdot)$, we look for one that maximizes $\mathcal{L}(\cdot; \theta)$ (or equivalently, that minimizes the KL divergence) while keeping the maximization problem tractable. Hence, we adopt the following mean-field assumption

$$q(A, Z, W) = q(A)q(Z)q(W) = \prod_{i,j,t} q(A_{ij}(t)) \prod_{i,t} q(Z_i(t)) \prod_{j,t} q(W_j(t)). \tag{12}$$

Thus, we introduce a variational expectation-maximization algorithm that alternates an expectation step (VE) maximizing the lower bound in Eq. (11) with respect to the variational distribution $q(\cdot)$, while keeping θ fixed and a maximization step (VM), maximizing the lower bound $\mathcal{L}(q, \theta)$ with respect to $\theta = (\Lambda, \alpha, \beta, \pi)$, while holding the variational distribution $q(\cdot)$ fixed. The two steps are now described in much detail.

3.2   VE-Step

The optimal variational updates of $q(\cdot)$, under the assumption in Eq. (12), can be obtained as Bishop (2006):

$$\log q(A) := \mathbb{E}_{W,Z}[\log p(X, A, Z, W \mid \theta)], \tag{13}$$

$$\log q(Z) := \mathbb{E}_{A,W}[\log p(X, A, Z, W \mid \theta)], \tag{14}$$

$$\log q(W) := \mathbb{E}_{A,Z}[\log p(X, A, Z, W \mid \theta)]. \tag{15}$$

Optimization of Q(A). The expectation in Eq. (13) can be explicitly computed leading to the following

Proposition 1. *Denoting by* $\delta_{ij}(t) := q(A_{ij}(t) = 1)$ *the variational probability of success for* $A_{ij}(t)$, *the optimal update is:*

$$\delta_{ij}(t) = \frac{\exp(R_{ij}(t))}{1 + \exp(R_{ij}(t))}, \tag{16}$$

with:

$$R_{ij}(t) := \log(\pi(t)\mathbf{1}_{\{X_{ij}(t)=0\}}) + \sum_{q,\ell} \Big[\mathbb{E}[Z_{iq}(t)]\mathbb{E}[W_{j\ell}(t)](\Lambda_{q\ell} + \tag{17}$$
$$- X_{ij}(t)\log\Lambda_{q\ell} \Big] + \log X_{ij}(t)! - \log(1 - \pi(t))$$

where $\mathbf{1}_{\{.\}}$ *denotes the indicator function.*

The proof is provided in the Appendix ??. Note that, formally, when $X_{ij}(t) \neq 0$, $R_{ij}(t) = -\infty$ and $\delta_{ij}(t) = 0$, which makes sense: non-null observations in X come from a Poisson distribution with probability one (see Eq. (4)).

Optimization of Q(Z) and Q(W). Regarding the factor $q(Z)$, the expectation in Eq. (14) can be explicitly computed leading to the following

Proposition 2. *Denoting by* $\tau_{iq}(t) := q(Z_{iq}(t) = 1)$ *the variational probability of success of* $Z_{iq}(t)$, *the optimal update is:*

$$\tau_{iq}(t) = \frac{r_{iq}(t)}{\sum_{v=1}^{Q} r_{iv}(t)}, \tag{18}$$

with

$$r_{iq}(t) \propto \exp\left(\sum_{j,\ell} F_{j\ell}^{iq} + \log(\alpha_q(t))\right) \tag{19}$$

and

$$F_{j\ell}^{iq} := (1 - \mathbb{E}[A_{ij}(t)])\Big[E[W_{j\ell}(t)](X_{ij}(t)\log(\Lambda_{q\ell}) - \Lambda_{q\ell}) \Big]. \tag{20}$$

The proof is provided in the Appendix ??. In a similar way, for the factor $q(W)$, the expectation in Eq. (15) can be explicitly computed leading to the following

Proposition 3. *Denoting by* $\eta_{j\ell}(t) := q(W_{j\ell}(t) = 1)$ *the variational probability of success of* $W_{j\ell}(t)$, *the optimal update is:*

$$\eta_{j\ell}(t) = \frac{s_{j\ell}(t)}{\sum_{v=1}^{L} s_{jv}(t)}, \tag{21}$$

with

$$s_{j\ell}(t) \propto \exp\left(\sum_{i,q} G_{iq}^{j\ell} + \log(\beta_\ell(t))\right). \tag{22}$$

$$G_{iq}^{j\ell} := (1 - \mathbb{E}[A_{ij}(t)])\Big[E[Z_{iq}(t)](X_{ij}(t)\log(\Lambda_{q\ell}) - \Lambda_{q\ell}) \Big]. \tag{23}$$

The proof is provided in the Appendix ??.

3.3 Variational M-Step

The lower bound can be explicitly computed as stated in Proposition 2 in Appendix ?? for lack of space. From that bound, we can optimize the model parameters θ, while keeping $q(\cdot)$ fixed, as stated in the reminder of this section. **Update of Λ.** We now report the update of the Zero-inflated Poisson parameter

Λ. Note that in case other zero-inflated distributions are chosen, this step must be adapted to the corresponding distributions.

Proposition 4. *The updating formula of Λ is:*

$$\Lambda_{q\ell} = \frac{\sum_{i,j,t} \tau_{iq}(t)\eta_{j\ell}(t)\Big(X_{ij}(t) - \delta_{ij}(t)X_{ij}(t)\Big)}{\sum_{i,j,t} \tau_{iq}(t)\eta_{j\ell}(t)\Big(1 - \delta_{ij}(t)\Big)}. \tag{24}$$

The proof is provided in the Appendix ??. We just wish to point out that the above update formula is indeed very intuitive: it corresponds to a sample mean accounting for both the probability that null $X_{ij}(t)$s come from a Poisson distribution (via $1 - \delta_{ij}(t)$) and the probability that non-null $X_{ij}(t)$s come from co-cluster (q, l).

Update of α, β and π Through Deep Neural Networks. The mixture proportions α and β, as well as the sparsity parameter π are driven by three systems of differential equations, in Eqs. (5), (6) and (7), respectively. As we assumed that the functions f_A, f_W and f_Z are continuous, we propose to parametrize them with three fully connected **neural networks** (Gent and Sheppard 1992), with two hidden layers of 200 neurons each, equipped with ReLu activation functions, with parameters ω_A, ω_Z and ω_W, respectively. Thus, optimizing the lower bound $\mathcal{L}(q; \theta)$ with respect to α, β and π reduces to maximize it with respect to the parameters of the neural nets as well as to the initial values $a(0), b(0)$ and $c(0)$.

For $k \in \{A, Z, W\}$, if we denote by $\omega_k(h)$ the set of weights of the corresponding neural network at iteration h of the GD algorithm, then

$$\omega_k(h) = \omega_k(h-1) - \gamma \nabla_{\omega_k} \mathcal{L}, \tag{25}$$

where γ is a user defined learning rate, $\nabla_{\omega_k}(\cdot)$ is the gradient operator, with respect to ω_k and $\omega_k(0)$ is randomly sampled. In the experiments, this update is implemented in PyTorch via automatic differentiation (Paszke et al. 2017) and relies on stochastic optimisation (ADAM, Kingma and Ba 2014). The learning rates are fixed at $\gamma = 1e^{-4}$. Once the neural nets are trained via backpropagation they provide us with the ML estimates of α, β and π. The inference procedure is summarized in Algorithm 1.

Algorithm 1 VEM-GD Algorithm (Zero-Inflated Poisson)

Require: $X, Q, L, n\_iter, nb\_epochs$ and $\alpha, \beta, \pi, \Lambda$ from Algorithm 2.
- ▸ Initialization of τ and η, sampled from $\mathcal{M}(N, \alpha)$ and $\mathcal{M}(M, \beta)$, respectively;
- ▸ Initialization of δ as ones(N, M), then setting $\delta_{ij} = 0$ when $X_{ij} > 0$;
- **while** not $\mathcal{L}$ converges **do**
    VE-Step:
    for counter $= 1$ to n_iter **do**
        alternatively update δ, τ, η % *fix point eqs*
    end for
    M-Step:
    Update Λ via Eq. (24)
    Update α, β, π via ADAM   % *over nb_epochs*
- **end while**

3.4 Initialization and Model Selection

When dealing with clustering methods based on the EM algorithm, the initialization and the selection of the appropriate numbers of clusters (for rows and columns here) are two issues which deserve an appropriate treatment. The issues related to these two points are slightly complicated here by the use of deep neural networks for modeling the dynamics of cluster and sparsity proportions. Despite this apparent difficulty due to the intrinsic complexity of these networks, they will nevertheless offer some unexpected flexibilities that we may use to lower the computational cost of the whole algorithm. Indeed, and as it is illustrated in the numerical experiments (Appendix ??), the use of deep neural networks for modeling the row and column cluster proportions will allow our algorithm to work with some empty clusters. Therefore, in the objective of avoiding the usual computationally demanding procedure of testing all pairs of row and column cluster numbers, we propose the following strategy for both initialization and model selection. First, we select a single specific slice of the data $X_{t_{init}}$ fit to it a static version of our $ZI_{\mathcal{P}}$-dLBM (technically a $ZI_{\mathcal{P}}$-LBM) for a list of pairs of cluster numbers, i.e. (q, ℓ) for $q = 2, \ldots, Q_{max}$ and $\ell = 2, \ldots, L_{max}$. We then use the ICL criterion (Integrated Classification Likelihood, Biernacki et al. 2000) to select the most appropriate row and column clusters' numbers for this specific slice of data. Let us remind that the ICL criterion aims at approximating the complete-data integrated log-likelihood and can be derived for $ZI_{\mathcal{P}}$-LBM as follows:

$$ICL(Q, L) = \log p(X, \hat{Z}, \hat{W}; \hat{\theta}) - \frac{Q-1}{2} \log N - \frac{L-1}{2} \log M - \frac{QL-1}{2} \log(NM). \quad (26)$$

The pair $(\hat{Q}, \hat{L})$ that leads to the highest value of the ICL is retained for the data $X_{t_{init}}$. Remark that, unless a further specific notice, the slice $X_{t_{init}}$ considered for this step in our experiments will be the first slice of the data, i.e. X_{t_0}. Second, in order to initialize our VEM-GD algorithm (see Algorithm 1) with useful initial values of the model parameters, we adopt a cascade process in order to propagate the parameters estimates obtained on the slice $X_{t_{init}}$ to other slices. In more detail, fixing for the moment the numbers of row and column clusters to $(\hat{Q}, \hat{L})$, we fit the static $ZI_{\mathcal{P}}$-LBM to the next slice $X_{t_{init}+1}$ with parameters $\hat{\theta}_{t_{init}}$ as initial values. Then, the estimated parameters $\hat{\theta}_{t_{init}+1}$ are used as initialization for a static $ZI_\mathcal{P}$-LBM fitted to the slice $X_{t_{init}+2}$, and so on up to X_T. This strategy allows us to obtain initial values (say $\hat{\theta}(t)$) for all the model parameters for $t = 0, ..., T$. Finally, as we expect that the choice of $\hat{Q}$ row and $\hat{L}$ column cluster components could not be the best when considering the data set as a whole, the VEM-GD algorithm (see Algorithm 1) is run with more components than considered in the initialization. Indeed, we run the VEM-GD algorithm with $Q_{max} \geq \hat{Q}$ and $L_{max} \geq \hat{L}$ cluster components. Then, part of the model parameters are initialized with $\hat{\theta}(t)$ obtained via the initialization procedure described above (see Algorithm 2) and the remaining parameters, corresponding to the additional row and column clusters are set to zero. Thus, we aim at exploiting the potential "blessing" of the use of deep neural networks allowing our VEM-GD algorithm to start with some empty clusters. These empty clusters will have the possibility to be activated later in the inference process, if needed. Therefore, we avoid the usual computationally demanding procedure of running the whole algorithm with all pairs of row and column cluster numbers for the whole data set. This strategy allows our approach to scale to massive data sets in a reasonable computational time and with satisfying results, as shown in the next section.

Algorithm 2 Initialization

Step 1: Static model selection

Require: $X, Q_{min}, Q_{max}, L_{min}, L_{max}, max\_iter, n.sim.$

  for Q $= Q_{min}$, to Q$= Q_{max}$ **do**

    for L $= L_{min}$, to L$= L_{max}$ **do**

      Initialize randomly $\alpha, \beta, \pi, \Lambda$;

      Run $ZI_\mathcal{P}$-LBM on X_1 and compute ICL;

    end for

  end for

Ensure: (Q^*, L^*) that gives the highest ICL value.

Step 2: Cascade process

Require: X , Q^*, L^*, max_iter.

  for t $= 1$ to T **do**

    if t $= 1$ **then**

      Initialize randomly $\alpha, \beta, \pi, \Lambda$;

      Run $ZI_\mathcal{P}$-LBM(Q^*, L^*) on X_1;

      Store $\hat{\alpha}(1), \hat{\beta}(1), \hat{\pi}(1), \hat{\Lambda}$.

    else

      Initialize with $\hat{\alpha}(t-1), \hat{\beta}(t-1), \hat{\pi}(t-1), \hat{\Lambda}$;

      Run $ZI_\mathcal{P}$-LBM(Q^*, L^*) on X_t;

      Store $\hat{\alpha}(t), \hat{\beta}(t), \hat{\pi}(t), \hat{\Lambda}$.

    end if

  end for

---

4   Analysis of the Adverse Drug Reaction Dataset

In Appendix ??, there are in-depth experiments to verify the performances of the model on simulated data in different scenarios. This section focuses on the application of $ZI_\mathcal{P}$-dLBM to a large-scale pharmacovigilance data set, with the aim of illustrating the potential of the tool.

4.1   Protocol and Data

This section considers a dataset consisting of an adverse drug reaction (ADR) data set, collected by the Regional Center of Pharmacovigilance (RCPV), located in the University Hospital of Nice (France). A time horizon of 7 years is considered, from January 1st, 2015 to March 3th, 2022, the unity measure for the time interval is a trimester. The overall dataset is made of 27,754 declarations, for which the market name of the drug, the notified ADR and the reception date are considered.

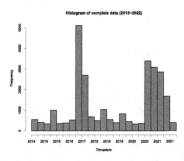

Fig. 2. Number of declarations received by the pharmacovigilance center from 2015 to 2022, sorted by trimester.

Moreover, we only considered drugs and ADRs that were notified more than 20 times over the 7 years. The resulting dataset contains 236 drugs, 324 ADRs and 29 time intervals with 12,336 non-zero entries. Looking at Fig. 2, it can be clearly noticed that there are two peaks, one in 2017 and the other in 2021. In 2017, an unexpected rise of reports for ADRs happened concerning a specific drug called Lévothyrox®. This has been marketed in France for about 40 years as a treatment for hypothyroidism and, in 2017, a new formula was introduced on the market. The Lévothyrox® case had a huge media coverage in France: Lévothyrox® spontaneous reports represent the 90% of all the spontaneous notifications that the RCPV received in 2017 (Viard et al. 2019). In addition, since the end of the year 2020, vaccinations against Covid-19 have been introduced. At that time, three vaccines are licensed in Europe, Comirnaty® was the first Covid-19 vaccine available in France in December 2020, followed by Moderna® in January 2021 and Vaxzevria® in February 2021.

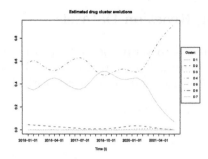
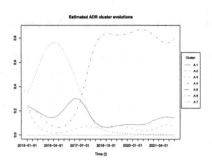

Fig. 3. Evolution of the estimates $\hat{\alpha}$.   **Fig. 4.** Evolution of the estimates $\hat{\beta}$.

From Fig. 2, one can understand the difficulty to work with such data which contain signals of very different amplitude. Indeed, behind those very visible effects, many ADR signals need to be detected for obvious public health reasons. In particular, those data also contain ADR reports regarding another health scandal happened in 2017, involving Mirena®, which is here far less visible than Lévothyrox®, but also led to many avoidable serious health issues.

4.2 Summary of the Results

To the initialize the algorithm, as explained in Sect. 3.4, we computed the ICL criterion on one data slice, corresponding to the first trimester, where the optimal numbers of clusters identified by the model selection criterion are $\hat{Q} = 4$ and $\hat{L} = 4$. Then, we initiated the model parameters through the cascade process described in Algorithm 2 and we ran $ZI_{\mathcal{P}}$-dLBM with $Q = 7$ and $L = 7$ to allow the model to fill or empty clusters as needed. Figure 5 depicts the estimated Poisson intensities Λ for $ZI_{\mathcal{P}}$-dLBM, focusing on 4 drug clusters (D) and 4 ADR clusters (A) that are activated during the inference. Each color represents a drug or ADR cluster, with higher values indicating stronger relationships (i.e., expected number of declarations received per time unit) between the respective

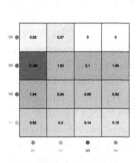
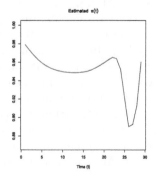

Fig. 5. Estimated Poisson intensities.   **Fig. 6.** Evolution of the estimates $\hat{\pi}$.

clusters. The figure reveals varying degrees of association, for example, cluster D3 of the drug clusters is highly related with cluster A1 of ADR clusters. Figures 3, 4 and 6 show the estimates of the model parameters $\hat{\alpha}$, $\hat{\beta}$ and $\hat{\pi}$, respectively. Figure 3 shows the estimation of the mixing parameter α. Cross-referencing the information from these results, we note that the clusters that have the highest intensity are also the less populated. For example, cluster D3 of drugs has a very high intensity of interactions with cluster A1 of adversarial effects, yet cluster D3 turns out to be very small in Fig. 3. This is due to the fact that this cluster contains drugs that are declared with an unusually high intensity. In fact, this cluster contains the drugs that are the causes of the major health crises that occurred during the reporting period: Mirena® in the first half of 2017, Lévothyrox® in the second part of 2017, and Covid-19 vaccines throughout 2021. Similarly, by analyzing the composition of cluster A1, it is possible to identify which ADRs were the most reported in each of the aforementioned crises. For instance, the most reported side effects during the Mirena® health crisis are mostly hormonal ones, such as anxiety, heat shock, and aggressive behavior. Then, looking at Fig. 4, during the Lévothyrox® health crisis we notice a peak in the A1 cluster of adversarial effects, probably because the great media coverage that the scandal had in those years made people declare the most disparate side effects. Also, we see that in 2021 there is another peak, corresponding to the period of the Covid-19 vaccination. Here, the adversarial effects found in cluster A1 are mostly linked to problems related to the vaccination site (e.g. arm pain, arm inflammation, skin reaction) and flu syndrome as a result of the vaccine. Cluster D2, on the other hand, contains a few but very common and, consequently, much-reported drugs, for example, paracetamol and some of the most popular anticoagulants. From Fig. 5 we note that this cluster has a stronger intensity of interactions with cluster A1 and A2 of undesirable effects. Looking at Fig. 4, we note that cluster A2 is thinly populated and seems to follow the trend of health crises discussed above less closely. In fact, this cluster contains less severe and more common adversarial effects, which can occur even with the more frequent medications (e.g., itching, headache, weight gain, etc.) Clusters D1 and D4, on the other hand, are characterized by very low interaction intensities and are densely populated by all other drugs. Then, looking at Figs. 5 and 4, we see that the behavior of cluster A3 of adversarial effects is very peculiar. It is characterized by almost zero interaction intensity with drug clusters D1 and D4. After the Lévothyrox® crisis, the number of reported adversarial effects significantly decreased, indicating a turning point in pharmacovigilance as people became more aware of its importance and started reporting side effects more frequently. Moreover, analysing its composition, it was noticed that at the beginning of the period it also contained all the specific side effects of Covid-19 vaccines, which were not yet known. Later, in 2021, those side effects, changed clusters moving to cluster A1 as previously described. On the other hand, Fig. 6 shows the estimated evolution of the sparsity parameter over time. We see that, at the beginning of the period, in 2015, the sparsity is at 98%, then as we approach the 2017 peak, the number of declarations increases and consequently the sparsity decreases. In 2019, it again increases slightly (97%) and then decreases as we approach the peak due to the Covid-19 vaccines. In fact, at the beginning of 2021 the sparsity level reaches its minimum at a level of 90%. Therefore, from the large initial data matrix, $ZI_\mathcal{P}$-dLBM was able to identify meaningful clusters of such data.

4.3   Benchmark on Real Data

This section focuses on comparing $ZI_\mathcal{P}$-dLBM with state of the art models on real-world data. We therefore carried out such an experiment by comparing $ZI_\mathcal{P}$-dLBM with Zip-dLBM$_\pi(\cdot) = 0$ and dLBM discussed in appendix B.3. We also included in the comparison two models that do not consider the dynamic aspect: LBM (Robert et al. 2021), baseline for model-based co-clustering methods, and k-means (MacQueen 1967), applied on rows and columns separately. As we are in an unsupervised context, the model performances are evaluated by the silhouette score using cosine distance on rows and columns. Table 1 displays the results of this comparison, in terms of average silhouette scores, reported with standard deviations. From the reported results, one sees that $ZI_\mathcal{P}$-dLBM outperforms its competitors. Also, it is worth noticing that unlike $ZI_\mathcal{P}$-dLBM, LBM and k-means, being independently applied at each time instant, suffer from label switching, which is not penalized in the silhouette score. This should make the interpretation of these results even more in favor for $ZI_\mathcal{P}$-dLBM.

Table 1. Results of $ZI_\mathcal{P}$-dLBM, Zip-dLBM$_\pi(\cdot) = 0$, dLBM, LBM and k-means on pharmacovigilance data. Average silhouette scores are reported with standard deviations.

	$ZI_\mathcal{P}$-dLBM	Zip-dLBM$_\pi(\cdot)=0$	dLBM	kmeans	LBM
Silhouette Score - Rows	**0.37 ± 0.12**	0.31 ± 0.12	−0.46 ± 0.25	0.21 ± 0.36	0.33 ± 0.12
Silhouette Score - Cols	**0.36 ± 0.23**	0.31 ± 0.25	−0.15 ± 0.06	0.31 ± 0.3	0.29 ± 0.23

5   Conclusion

We have developed a dynamic co-clustering technique for simultaneously clustering rows and columns along the time dimension of a dynamic matrix. The proposed zero-inflated dynamic latent block model can be adapted to several zero-inflated probability distributions. We use a Variational EM algorithm with GD optimization to perform inference on the model's parameters, then the model is applied to a real dataset from the Regional Center of Pharmacovigilance of Nice (France) to segment drugs and adverse drug reactions based on their dynamic interactions over time. The proposed model provided a meaningful segmentation of drugs and adverse drug reactions.

Acknowledgment. This work has been supported by the French government, through the 3IA Côte d'Azur, Investment in the Future, project managed by the National Research Agency (ANR) with the reference number ANR-19-P3IA-0002.

Ethical Statement. This paper involves the analysis of pharmacovigilance data, which are obtained in collaboration with the Regional Center of Pharmacovigilance of Nice (France). It is crucial to emphasize that before the data is shared with us, a rigorous anonymization process is employed to ensure the protection of patients privacy. These anonymized data are treated as confidential and private throughout our research. We adhere to the ethical guidelines and comply with all applicable data protection regulations to safeguard the privacy and confidentiality of the individuals involved in the pharmacovigilance reporting system.

References

Ailem, M., Role, F., Nadif, M.: Sparse poisson latent block model for document clustering. IEEE Trans. Knowl. Data Eng. **29**(7), 1563–1576 (2017)

Bergé, L.R., Bouveyron, C., Corneli, M., Latouche, P.: The latent topic block model for the co-clustering of textual interaction data. Comput. Stat. Data Anal. **137**, 247–270 (2019)

Biernacki, C., Celeux, G., Govaert, G.: Assessing a mixture model for clustering with the integrated completed likelihood. IEEE Trans. Pattern Anal. Mach. Intell. **22**(7), 719–725 (2000)

Bishop, C.M.: Approximate Inference, pp. 461–517. Springer, Heidelberg (2006)

Boutalbi, R., Labiod, L., Nadif, M.: Tensor latent block model for co-clustering. Int. J. Data Sci. Anal. **10**, 1–15 (2020)

Boutalbi, R., Labiod, L., Nadif, M.: Implicit consensus clustering from multiple graphs. Data Min. Knowl. Disc. **35**(6), 2313–2340 (2021)

Bouveyron, C., Bozzi, L., Jacques, J., Jollois, F.-X.: The functional latent block model for the co-clustering of electricity consumption curves. J. Roy. Stat. Soc. Ser. C (Appl. Stat.) **67**(4), 897–915 (2018)

Casa, A., Bouveyron, C., Erosheva, E., Menardi, G.: Co-clustering of time-dependent data via the shape invariant model. J. Classif. **38**(3), 626–649 (2021)

Corneli, M., Bouveyron, C., Latouche, P.: Co-clustering of ordinal data via latent continuous random variables and not missing at random entries. J. Comput. Graph. Stat. **29**, 1–15 (2020)

Dempster, A.P., Laird, N.M., Rubin, D.B.: Maximum likelihood from incomplete data via the EM algorithm. J. Roy. Stat. Soc. Ser. B (Methodol.) **39**(1), 1–22 (1977)

Gent, C., Sheppard, C.: Special feature. Predicting time series by a fully connected neural network trained by back propagation. Comput. Control Eng. J. **3**(3), 109–112 (1992)

Govaert, G., Nadif, M.: Clustering with block mixture models. Pattern Recogn. **36**(2), 463–473 (2003)

Govaert, G., Nadif, M.: Latent block model for contingency table. Commun. Stat. Theory Methods **39**(3), 416–425 (2010)

Jaakkola, T.S., Jordan, M.I.: A variational approach to Bayesian logistic regression models and their extensions. In: Sixth International Workshop on Artificial Intelligence and Statistics, pp. 283–294. PMLR (1997)

Jacques, J., Biernacki, C.: Model-based co-clustering for ordinal data. Comput. Stat. Data Anal. **123**, 101–115 (2018)

Jordan, M.I., Ghahramani, Z., Jaakkola, T.S., Saul, L.K.: An introduction to variational methods for graphical models. In: Jordan, M.I. (ed.) Learning in Graphical Models, vol. 89, pp. 105–161. Springer, Dordrecht (1998). https://doi.org/10.1007/978-94-011-5014-9_5

Keribin, C., Brault, V., Celeux, G., Govaert, G.: Estimation and selection for the latent block model on categorical data. Stat. Comput. **25**(6), 1201–1216 (2015)

Kingma, D.P., Ba, J.: Adam: a method for stochastic optimization. arXiv preprint arXiv:1412.6980 (2014)

Lambert, D.: Zero-inflated poisson regression, with an application to defects in manufacturing. Technometrics **34**(1), 1–14 (1992)

Li, N., Elashoff, D.A., Robbins, W.A., Xun, L.: A hierarchical zero-inflated log-normal model for skewed responses. Stat. Methods Med. Res. **20**(3), 175–189 (2011)

Lindstrom, M.J.: Self-modelling with random shift and scale parameters and a free-knot spline shape function. Stat. Med. **14**(18), 2009–2021 (1995)

Lomet, A.: Sélection de modèle pour la classification croisée de données continues. Ph.D. thesis, Compiègne (2012)

MacQueen, J.: Classification and analysis of multivariate observations. In: 5th Berkeley Symposium on Mathematical Statistics and Probability, pp. 281–297 (1967)

Marchello, G., Fresse, A., Corneli, M., Bouveyron, C.: Co-clustering of evolving count matrices with the dynamic latent block model: application to pharmacovigilance. Stat. Comput. **32**(3), 1–22 (2022)

Ospina, R., Ferrari, S.L.: A general class of zero-or-one inflated beta regression models. Comput. Stat. Data Anal. **56**(6), 1609–1623 (2012)

Paszke, A., et al.: Automatic differentiation in pyTorch (2017)

Ridout, M., Hinde, J., Demétrio, C.G.: A score test for testing a zero-inflated poisson regression model against zero-inflated negative binomial alternatives. Biometrics **57**(1), 219–223 (2001)

Robert, V., Vasseur, Y., Brault, V.: Comparing high-dimensional partitions with the co-clustering adjusted rand index. J. Classif. **38**(1), 158–186 (2021)

Viard, D., et al.: Spontaneous adverse event notifications by patients subsequent to the marketing of a new formulation of levothyrox® amidst a drug media crisis: atypical profile as compared with other drugs. Fund. Clin. Pharmacol. **33**(4), 463–470 (2019)

cuSLINK: Single-Linkage Agglomerative Clustering on the GPU

Corey J. Nolet[1,2]($\boxtimes$), Divye Gala[1], Alex Fender[1], Mahesh Doijade[1],
Joe Eaton[1], Edward Raff[2,3], John Zedlewski[1], Brad Rees[1], and Tim Oates[2]

[1] NVIDIA, Inc, Santa Clara, CA, USA
{cnolet,dgala,afender,mdoijade,featon,jzedlewski,brees}@nvidia.com
[2] University of Maryland, Baltimore County, Baltimore, MD, USA
raff_edward@bah.com, oates@umbc.edu
[3] Booz Allen Hamilton, McLean, VA, USA

Abstract. In this paper, we propose cuSLINK, a novel and state-of-the-art reformulation of the SLINK algorithm on the GPU which requires only $O(Nk)$ space and uses a parameter k to trade off space and time. We also propose a set of novel and reusable building blocks that compose cuSLINK. These building blocks include highly optimized computational patterns for k-NN graph construction, spanning trees, and dendrogram cluster extraction. We show how we used our primitives to implement cuSLINK end-to-end on the GPU, further enabling a wide range of real-world data mining and machine learning applications that were once intractable. In addition to being a primary computational bottleneck in the popular HDBSCAN algorithm, the impact of our end-to-end cuSLINK algorithm spans a large range of important applications, including cluster analysis in social and computer networks, natural language processing, and computer vision.

Keywords: KNN Graph · Neighborhood Methods · Nearest Neighbors · Spanning Tree · Single-Linkage Hierarchical Clustering · Agglomerative Clustering · Cluster Analysis · Networks · Forest · Parallel Algorithms · GPU

1 Introduction

Hierarchical agglomerative clustering (HAC) is an important and fundamental algorithm for classical machine learning and data mining. HAC variants are used in many different informatics disciplines such as micro array analysis, genome clustering, computer vision, document clustering, and social network analysis [24]. In particular, the Single-Link HAC is still critically important in bioinformatics and genomics [1,11,30], but a challenge to use due to its $\mathcal{O}(N^2)$ cost where N is the number of items to be clustered. Hierarchical agglomerative clustering builds up a hierarchy of clusters from a set of vectors bottom-up, by starting with each vector in its own cluster and merging pairs of vectors together based on predefined similarity criteria until a common root is reached, which produces this quadratic lower bound.

The seminal SLINK algorithm [27] provided the first $\mathcal{O}(N^2)$ time and $\mathcal{O}(N)$ space algorithm for the Single-link HAC problem. However, it has evaded efficient parallel implementation due to a lack of bulk work in the SLINK algorithm, causing communication overhead to dominate runtime. In this work, we will instead use a Minimum Spanning Tree (MST) based approach to the Single-link HAC that allows us to perform more parallel work, but at a potentially larger compute and memory complexity of $\mathcal{O}(N^2 + Nk \log N)$ and $\mathcal{O}(Nk)$ respectively. This required inventing a new parallel MST approach that efficiently performs the distance computations by an iterative expansion of a k-nearest neighbor graph. We find in practice, this trade-off is worth it by enabling a GPU implementation capable of 2290× faster runtime over common CPU implementations, and in all our tests is faster than alternative options today. An added benefit of this primitives-based approach is the ability to generalize cuSLINK for other distance measures, even in non-metric spaces.

We term our approach and implementation cuSLINK for its use of CUDA APIs and it produces an exact solution to the SLHC problem. The primitives we used to build cuSLINK are modular and can be reused to compose other important algorithms for graph and machine learning. For this reason, we provide separate benchmarks for these primitives, in addition to end-to-end benchmarks of our cuSLINK implementation against the currently available state-of-the-art. cuSLINK and its primitives are fully open source and have been contributed upstream to the RAFT library (https://github.com/rapidsai/raft).

In the following Sect. 2, we will outline related works and better shape the motivation for both our modular design and contributions. We present our contribution in Sect. 3, and detail our primitives, as well as our novel reformulation of single-linkage hierarchical clustering for the GPU. These primitives include constructing knn graphs by fusing the k-selection operation with the computation of distances, computing an MST using a variant of Borådvka's classic parallel algorithm, and a novel method for extracting flattened clusters from a dendrogram. Section 4 compares the performance of our single-linkage hierarchical clustering algorithm, as well as its building blocks, against previous works.

2   Related Work

Single-linkage hierarchical clustering is commonly referred to as 'nearest neighbors' clustering and as such, our implementation makes direct use of nearest neighbors computations in order to shrink the memory footprint of the naive computation of single-linkage clustering and providing a GPU-accelerated version that borrows its foundation from the original SLINK [27].

The original SLINK algorithm maintains 3 arrays, each of size n and loops over the range $[1, n]$, building up the dendrogram level by level, using two arrays of pointers to represent the dendrogram itself and a third to store distances.

Sibsen notes that $O(n^2)$ is the optimally efficient runtime upper bound because each neighbor pair will ultimately need to be compared at least once. The challenge with this algorithm, however, is in SLINK's equivalence to the inherently iterative nature of Prim's algorithm for constructing an MST. Our algorithm performs a similar iterative step to perform the agglomerative labeling, but we perform this step on the sorted edges of an MST, after all needed distances have been computed. As we describe below, we use a novel variant of Boråvka's algorithm to construct the MST in parallel. In Sect. 3, we note that our formulation increases the overall complexity to $O(N^2 + Nk \log N)$ but enables a high amount of parallelism.

Several approaches exist to perform single-linkage hierarchical clustering in parallel architectures [20]. Many are variants of Boråvka and often combine the affinities graph construction with the MST by computing distance metrics right in the solver [3,22]. Other approaches build upon Kruskal's algorithm, either by exploiting parallelism within different steps, such as the sorting step, or by building many trees independently in parallel and merging them into a single hierarchy [13,14]. The latter approach forms the basis for an end-to-end parallel algorithm for single-linkage hierarchical clustering, even up to the dendrogram construction, but at the cost of performing many redundant computations and duplicating memory. While there have been claims that only the pairwise distance computations can benefit from GPU-acceleration [7], we demonstrate in Sect. 4 that the linkage and cluster extraction steps also find performance gains.

The FAISS library is well known for containing state-of-the-art implementations of both exact and approximate nearest neighbors search on the GPU [16], though their exact implementation of nearest neighbors, known as brute-force, computes and stores an intermediate buffer of pairwise distances, performing a k-selection on each buffer. As we highlight in Sect. 3, we improve upon this design by fusing the computation of the distances with the k-selection when $k \leq 64$, allowing us to lower the memory footprint while also reducing the number of reads and writes to global memory.

Fast k-NN computations are critical for many types of algorithms in a class we refer to as 'neighborhood methods' which include information retrieval, clustering, dimensionality reduction, and classification/regression. Centroid-based clustering algorithms such as k-means and k-medioids rely on a fast computation of 1-nearest neighbors, or closest centroid, to each training data point. Manifold learning algorithms such as TSNE [6] and UMAP [19] rely on a special class of worse-case k-NN computations known as all-neighbors problems [8,23] to construct a graph of affinities. Similar to single-linkage clustering, the HDB-SCAN algorithm, which can be formulated as a special case of single-linkage clustering, these problems specifically require a fast k-NN as all n^2 point pairs (or $\frac{n}{2}$ in metric spaces [26]) might need to be computed in the worst case for exact results.

A natural optimization for k-NN-based approaches is to reduce computations by shrinking dimensionality [21], partitioning [5,10,25] and/or quantizing [15] the space. Such methods can offer further speedups, sometimes at the expense of correctness. cuSLINK demonstrates state-of-the-art performance, but the primitives-based approach also leaves room for more optimized k-NN algorithms to be used.

Implementation of the Boråvka algorithm on the GPU has been considered before by several authors [2,9,29]. Early attempts demonstrated speedups in comparison to parallel CPU solutions but focused on optimizing specific sparsity patterns [9] or data structures [12]. Those results worked for the initial goal, but tended to break down as the scope changed [2]. The breadth of MST applications kept growing meanwhile [17], and translated to many distribution patterns and use cases. Designing a fast parallel solution resilient to multiple graph types and properties remains a primary concern.

Recent shifts in human communication, such as mobile phones and the internet of things (IoT), coupled with technical progress, has triggered an extensive growth of data volume. Scalability and speed have become a major concern for MST solvers. Previous solutions tended to primarily focus on performance, often at the cost of generous memory allocations. One of the strengths of the GPU architecture is the memory bandwidth, but the memory size is limited. We designed our MST algorithm to be memory efficient by avoiding explicit graph coarsening in order to scale further than previous implementations: past a billion edges on a single GPU.

A common problem in previous variants is cycle formation. Multiple edges of equal minimum weight between two components lead to multiple equivalent solutions. This results in ties when considering parallel execution, and can be a source of non-deterministic outputs. Weight alterations have been successfully applied to algebraic multi-grid aggregation in the past as a way to extract parallelism and break ties between strongly coupled nodes [18]. Unfortunately, random weight alterations cannot be applied directly without risking a change in the global relative ordering of the weights and thus the MST solution. In this paper, we propose an alteration that guarantees that all weights are different while preserving their relative order.

Our implementation adopts the *scipy.hierarchy.linkage* format, which is also used by Scikit-learn, making it directly available on a trained *Agglomerative Clustering* estimator. In addition to enabling SLINK, our MST implementation is also capable of constructing a maximum spanning tree, which enables our hierarchical clustering algorithm to also compute a complete-linkage clustering.

3   cuSLINK

Our strategy to implement a faster SLINK is outlined in Algorithm 1, where each line denotes a sub-step with references to the section where each step is detailed further. Current SLINK methods do significant unnecessary work by computing the entire pairwise adjacency matrix at once, but maximize compute—or perform smaller work chunks but lose compute efficiency. Our strategy will instead sub-divide the work into chunks that perform some redundant work, but allow sufficient compute efficiency to result in a significant net speedup.

Algorithm 1 cuSLINK Algorithm

1: **Input:** X, n_clusters
2: **Output:** 1-d array of cluster labels
3: knn_graph = compute_connectivities(X)   ▷ §3.1.1, Alg. 3
4: mst_edges, colors = mst(knn_graph)   ▷ §3.2, Alg. 5
5: mst_edges = connect_graph(knn_graph, mst_edges, colors)   ▷ §3.1.1, Alg. 2
6: dendrogram = relabel(mst_edges)   ▷ §3.3.1
7: return extract_clusters(dendrogram, n_clusters)   ▷ §3.3.2, Alg. 8

We start by converting tabular inputs from N points in d dimensions into a sparse k-NN graph of affinities, which is then used as input to compute the MST. As mentioned, the original SLINK algorithm computes the MST sequentially by computing and maintaining the 1-NN of the data points (and clusters) while constructing each of the $O(\log N)$ levels of the resulting dendrogram. Our cuSLINK breaks the algorithm into four steps: 1) construction of affinities graph, 2) construction of MST, 3) construction of the dendrogram, and 4) extraction of flat cluster assignments from the dendrogram. This separation uses Amdahl's Law to allow parallelism of the most performance-critical pieces and isolates the sequential bits to only the third step.

In order for an MST to converge, the edges that it has available as input need to form a connected graph and it is not guaranteed that the closest k neighbors to each data point will form a connected graph. In the case where the MST construction doesn't converge, resulting in a minimum spanning forest (MSF, i.e., multiple MSTs that are not connected), we compute an additional 1-NN across the resulting super-vertexes in the MSF and perform another iteration of the MST with the new edges to connect the super vertices. It's possible there could be multiple iterations of computing 1-NNs until the MSF converges to an MST, the number of iterations bounded from above by $O(\log N)$ in the worst case when $k = 1$. The algorithm for connecting anotherwise disconnected k-NN graph is outlined in Algorithm 2

Algorithm 2 connect_graph()

1: **Input:** knn_graph, mst_edges, colors
2: **Output:** additional mst_edges to connect knn_graph
3: **while** n_unique(colors) $\neq$ 1 **do**
4:     mst_edges = mst_edges $\cup$ cross_color_1nn(knn_graph, colors)   ▷ Alg. 4
5:     mst_edges, colors = mst(mst_edges)   ▷ Alg. 5
6: return mst_edges

The $O(E \log V)$ complexity of computing the MST itself becomes $O(Nk \log N)$ in our formulation, since k-NN bounds the number of edges, E, to $N \times k$ and $V = N$. Our implementation uses brute-force k-NN, so we still perform N^2 distance computations, resulting in $O(N^2 + Nk \log N)$ overall computational complexity. While this complexity is slightly worse than the SLINK algorithm, it does so because it allows more parallel computation to occur with less overhead, resulting in a lower total runtime.

As we describe in Sect. 3.3.2, flattened cluster assignments are obtained for each point $n \in N$ by cutting the dendrogram at the level which yields the desired number of clusters and assigning a unique label to each resulting connected component. While not currently supported by cuSLINK, complete-linkage clustering can be obtained by computing the maximum spanning tree and sorting the resulting edges in descending order. With our building blocks, it's also possible to implement a variant which accepts a distance threshold for which to cut the dendrogram, however we leave this to future work.

Unlike the original SLINK formulation, cuSLINK separates the construction of the dendrogram from the k-NN graph and MST steps in order to maximize parallelism of the former steps since the order of dendrogram construction is important, making it inherently sequential. Algorithm 1 shows the cuSLINK steps and Algorithm 2 shows the steps to finding additional edges for connecting the super-vertices.

3.1   Nearest Neighbors

3.1.1 k-NN Graph Construction

The connectivities graph is constructed in parallel using a novel GPU-accelerated brute-force k-NN primitive that, as we will outline below, is able to fuse the k-selection steps with computation of the distances in order to lower the required memory footprint and remove the need for additional steps downstream.

A common approach to computing a brute-force k-NN is to first break up the computation of the full $m \times n$ pairwise distance matrix into smaller tiles, each requiring an intermediate buffer of device memory. A k-selection is performed as a follow-on computation over each tile of pairwise distances to reduce the columns down to the k smallest (or largest) distances and output them to another memory buffer. If tiling over both dimensions of the pairwise distance matrix, additional k-selection steps might be needed. These intermediate tiles and k-selection steps require additional memory accesses that can be avoided when k is small enough such that the closest neighbors can be reduced into shared memory from each warp and selected within each thread-block. We use this novel insight to develop a fast k-NN strategy outlined in Algorithm 3.

For the case where $k \leq 64$, special optimizations can be done to the k-selection in the GPU implementation of the FAISS' [16] k-selection primitive. Our improved version is detailed in the supplementary materials. This step imposes a lot of pressure on the registers as each warp maintains its own thread-level queue of new values to be merged along with a warp-wide queue of the fully sorted top-k values and a register to store the current largest value in the warp-wide queue for early filtering of candidates. When the thread-level queues reach their max for new potential top-k values, a sorting and merging step is initiated synchronously in the warp by performing a bitonic sort of the thread-level values with the warp-level queue, reducing the warp-level queue back down to size k. Our warp-level k-selection routine follows the same general design used in

Algorithm 3 Fused k-NN

1:	gridStrideY = curBlockY × batchM	▷ Determine output tile coordinates
2:	__shared__ kvp_t topKs[batchM , 64]	▷ Allocate shared mem top-k store
3:	**for** gridStrideY < m; **step** batchM * nBlocksY; **do**	
4:	gridStrideX = curBlockX × batchN	
5:	init_smem(topKs)	▷ Initialize shared mem
6:	**for** gridStrideX < n; **step** batchN × nBlocksX; **do**	
7:	prolog(gridStrideX, gridStrideY)	▷ Zero init shared mem accumulator
8:	gemm_nt_loop()	▷ Compute dot product along k
9:	epilog_op_topk(gridStrideX, gridStrideY)	▷ Norm and top-k
10:	row_epilog_op_topk(gridStrideY)	▷ Store topk in global mem

FAISS, but reduces the number of warp-selection computations, which require expensive synchronization between threads within each warp, using the stream compaction technique [4] within each block.

At the block level, each warp performs its warp-level k-selection and stores the resulting k selected distances and indices in shared memory. Next, in a grid-stride, each thread discards all distances and indices which are less than the previous warp-level k-selection, performing the stream compaction to write the new set of filtered indices and distances to shared memory. A warp-level *ballot_sync()* is performed over the filtered counts, 2×256 per warp and 2×8 per thread, resorting to a scan only if the number of filtered counts is > 0. For each set of 2×256 distances computed by a warp, the warp-select calls *any_sync()* a total of 128 times per grid-stride by whole thread block. With stream compaction, *ballot_sync()* needs to be called only 16 times in the best case.

3.1.2 k-NN Graph Connection

Unfortunately, a k-NN alone with only a naive choice of k doesn't often scale to larger datasets in practice as the size of k needed for the MST to converge to a single supervertex can grow significantly large, being bounded above by $k = N$ in the worst-case. Since our MST implementation is robust to this type of input, a minimum spanning forest (MSF) will be returned when this occurs and additional edges are added to the MSF by performing a 1-NN query that connects points only across different supervertices, or components, together before re-computing the MST.

Similar to the fused k-NN primitive outlined above, Algorithm 4 shows the general steps for our novel 1-NN primitive for Euclidean-based distances, which also fuses together the computation of the minimum neighbor with the distance computations. Since $k = 1$, we can avoid the sorting and merging of the warp-selection altogether by computing and storing a single *min* as the distances are computed. This effectively enables the use of registers alone within each thread of the GPU for fast storage, comparison, and computation of the closest neighbor.

Algorithm 4 Fused 1-NN

1: gridStrideY = curBlockY × batchM   ▷ Determine output tile coordinates
2: min_kvp = (MAX_FLOAT, MAX_INT)   ▷ Init min with max values
3: **for** gridStrideY < m; **step** batchM * nBlocksY; **do**
4:     gridStrideX = curBlockX × batchN
5:     **for** gridStrideX < n; **step** batchN × nBlocksX; **do**
6:         prolog(gridStrideX, gridStrideY)   ▷ Zero init shared mem accumulator
7:         gemm_nt_loop()   ▷ Compute dot product along k
8:         epilog(gridStrideX, gridStrideY)   ▷ L2 norm addition
9:     row_epilog_op(gridStrideY)   ▷ Global mem min reduce across all tiles for row

---

3.2   Spanning Trees

Since the graph is assumed to be undirected ($w_{i,j} = w_{j,i}$), the resulting adjacency matrix is symmetric. Our algorithm is resilient to negative weights and can solve the maximum spanning tree problem natively. The maximum spanning tree has weights greater than or equal to the weight of every other spanning tree, and is found by forming the additive inverse $G' = (V, -E)$ and solving the MST problem on G'.

Algorithm 5 provides an overview of our parallel MST implementation which relies on the property that the minimum incident edge, or closest neighbor to each vertex, has to be in the MST (e.g., same as original SLINK). The first step is to identify these edges. Then, edge contraction of the minimum incident edges is applied recursively until a steady state is reached. Instead of explicitly contracting edges through expensive graph coarsening, the MST components are represented using labels (i.e. colors). The problem is reduced to finding the minimum incident edge across color boundaries [29].

Our MST solution is artificially made unique by applying a weight alteration Sect. 3.2.1. MST and MSF are almost identical problems with the difference that MSF refers to the case where G has multiple strongly connected components. The latter is particularly relevant for k-NN applications which may consist of multiple connected components described in Sect. 3.1. The historical Borǔvka MST formula iterates until only one color, or super-vertex, remains. Instead, to find an MSF we detect a steady state and exit if no minimum incident edge to another color has been found.

We leverage the Compressed Sparse Row (CSR) format as input to our MST primitive because it enables an efficient memory access pattern.

3.2.1   Weight Alteration

Cycle detection and removal was identified as one of the main challenges in previously published GPU solutions [29]. The problem can be reduced to selecting an incident edge to every vertex in parallel without creating cycles. Multiple edges of equal minimum weight between two components result in multiple equivalent solutions for the MST problem. In parallel, each component could select a different edge which would result in adding a cycle between them and breaking the tree structure. To address this issue, we propose a simple solution to prevent

Algorithm 5 MST Algorithm

1: **Input:** G
2: **Output:** mst_edges, colors
3: G_altered = weight_alteration(G)   ▷ §3.2.1
4: **while** !exit **do**
5:     min_edges = min_edge_per_vertex(G_altered, colors)
6:     new_mst_edges = min_edge_per_supervertex(min_edges)   ▷ §3.2.2
7:     exit = len(new_mst_edges)
8:     **if** exit **then**   ▷ Return MSF by exiting
9:         break
10:    done = false   ▷ Continue iterating over label_propagation when necessary
11:    new_colors = label_propagation(new_mst_edges, done)   ▷ §3.2.3
12: return new_mst_edges, new_colors

cycle formation by generating an alteration on the edge weights that guarantees that all weights are different while preserving the relative order of all weights. For any graph that has only a distinct set of edges, this produces a deterministic result. As a result, all vertices can consistently select edges in an embarrassingly parallel fashion. Notice that this has the side effect of altering explicit zeroes, which means our solution cannot support graphs that have zeroed edge weights. The technique for altering the weights is done in 3 steps:

- Identify $\theta > 0$, where θ is the minimum edge weight difference between any two pairs of edges in the graph
- For each edge in the upper triangular side of the matrix, add noise to each edge weight by generating a random number $\epsilon \in [0, \theta)$.
- Replicate the upper triangular part into the lower triangular part so that $w_{ij} = w_{ji}$

3.2.2   Minimum Incident Edges

A common solution, as noted with [9,12], is to assign one thread per vertex to scan all edges. However, this comes with the risk that the kernel becomes bound to the slowest performing thread. With the help of Sect. 3.2.1, we overcome the issue of tie-breaking when trying to find the minimum outgoing edge per supervertex as each edge has a unique weight. Thus, overcoming the cycle-detection problem, we divide the task of finding the minimum outgoing edge in two sub-tasks:

- *Minimum Edge Per Vertex*: Using the CSR format, we assign 32 threads (one warp) to scan the edges of each vertex. These threads, using shared memory reduction, find an outgoing edge to a destination vertex that is part of a different supervertex than the source and also atomically record a minimum edge weight for that source supervertex
- *Minimum Edge Per Supervertex*: Continuing from the previous task where we found the minimum outgoing edge for each vertex, we still need to reconcile

the minimum source, destination pair for each supervertex. Whichever vertex found an edge that was the minimum for its supervertex adds it to the final solution

Note that self edges are automatically invalid because they point to the source's color.

3.2.3   Label Propagation

Label propagation in [29] is performed by ensuring all vertices explicitly try to converge to supervertex 0, while [9] uses graph contraction to form a new graph of supervertices in the current MST iteration. Instead, our label propagation improves upon the speed of the former and memory requirements of that latter by indirectly keeping track of supervertices using the *color* and *supervertex* arrays. By working only on newly added MST edges in a given iteration, we ensure that fewer iterations of label propagation are needed compared to preceding MST iterations as each iteration adds fewer edges to the solution. This was instrumental in removing the bottleneck that comes with wide graphs (such as road networks). Initially, each v_i holds the color i. Algorithm 6 shows how the minimum colors between source and destination vertices is resolved, for each newly added edge to the MST.

Algorithm 6 min_pair_colors(V)

1: **for** *vertex* $\in V$ **do**   ▷ The incident vertex
2:     edge = filtered_min_edges[vertex]
3:     **if** found_by_vertices(edge) **then**
4:         neighbor_vertex = get_neighbor_vertex[edge]   ▷ The neighbor vertex this edge connects
5:         supervertex = supervertices[vertex]
6:         color = colors[supervertex]
7:         neighbor_supervertex = supervertices[neighbor_vertex]
8:         neighbor_color = colors[neighbor_supervertex]
9:         atomicMin(next_color[supervertex], neighbor_color)
10:        atomicMin(next_color[neighbor_supervertex], color)

The color for every $v \in V$ whose supervertex changed colors in Algorithm 6 gets updated in Algorithm 7. We determine whether Algorithm 6 and Algorithm 7 need to be iterated on again, in case a supervertex has not reached its final color as defined by newly added MST edges.

Finally, we propagate and resolve colors for the entire topology by updating vertices whose supervertices changed colors.

Algorithm 7 update_colors(V)

1: **for** *vertex* $\in V$ **do**
2:     color = colors[vertex]
3:     supervertex = supervertices[vertex]
4:     new_color = next_color[supervertex]
5:     **if** color > new_color **then**
6:         colors[vertex] = new_color
7:         done = false

3.3 Dendrogram

3.3.1 Relabel into Dendrogram

After computing the minimum spanning tree on the connectivities graph, the resulting $N - 1$ edges are sorted in parallel by weight. The dendrogram is constructed on the CPU by expanding the total set of vertices from N to $(N-1)*2$ and renumbering the original vertices as they are merged together into the hierarchy. A parent vertex for any level i in the hierarchy, where $0 \leq i < \frac{N-1}{2}$, will always be $\geq N$ and can be computed with the simple formula $i+N$. A union-find structure with union-by-rank and path compression is used to achieve runtime of $O(N\alpha(N))$ [17,28].

The strict ordering of the dendrogram construction step makes it inherently sequential [7,20]. More recently, the optimization outlined by [17] produces acceptable performance on the CPU, so we exploit as much parallelism in the remaining steps as possible.

Algorithm 8 extract_flattened_clusters(dendrogram)

1: label_roots = find_label_roots()   ▷ Find the root nodes for each label
2: sort(label_roots)
3: cut_level = (n_points -1) - (n_clusters - 1)
4: labels = inherit_labels(cut_level, dendrogram)   ▷ Leaves inherit from label roots

---

3.3.2 Cut the Dendrogram

Cluster assignments (Algorithm 8) are extracted from the dendrogram by first cutting it at a particular level, yielding a desired $n\_clusters$ number of cluster tree roots. These tree roots are computed by sorting the last $n\_clusters * 2$ elements of the dendrogram and extracting the smallest $n\_clusters$ elements from the sorted array. Unique labels are given to each of these tree roots and all nodes in levels of the tree lower than the dendrogram label root nodes inherit the labels from their closest labeled ancestors in parallel (Algorithm 9).

Algorithm 9 inherit_labels(cut_level, dendrogram)

1: **for** *vertex* ∈ *dendrogram* **do**   ▷ Loop through all nodes in dendrogram
2:     cur_level = get_tree_level(vertex)
3:     **if** cur_level ≤ cut_level **then** '
4:         cur_label = get_parent_label()
5:         **while** !is_labeled(cur_label) **do**   ▷ Iterate parents until label is found
6:             cur_parent = get_parent()
7:             cur_level = get_parent_tree_level()
8:             cur_label = get_parent_label()
9:         label[vertex] = cur_label   ▷ Assign label of labeled parent

---

4 Experiments

In this section, we benchmark both cuSLINK end-to-end along with our k-NN, 1-NN and MST primitives. We show that all components of cuSLINK outperform the available state-of-the-art solutions. All benchmarks are performed w/CUDA 11.8 on Nvidia A100 GPUs. We selected our comparison implementations based on availability of packages and/or source code which was able to built and run by our best effort. We also made every effort to update existing state-of-the-art solutions to run CUDA 11.8 when needed. Note that we compare against implementations on the CPU only when corresponding GPU source code was not available.

4.1 Nearest Neighbors

We measured the performance of our fused 1-NN and k-NN implementations against FAISS on the GPU, which is the current known state-of-the-art for k-selection and brute-force nearest neighbors on the GPU.

Table 1. Performance comparison between FAISS and cuSLINK's k-NN on randomly generated data for $k = 32$. Our Fused k-NN enables consistent speedups at all sizes, particularly smaller sizes where memory transfers dominate all time spent. By fusing the operations we do not require additional allocation.

Index Rows	Query Rows	GPU-FAISS	cuSLINK
100K	100K	261 ms	**143 ms**
200K	200K	783 ms	**537 ms**
400K	400K	2706 ms	**2017 ms**
1M	1M	1.607 s	**1.218 s**

4.2 Spanning Tree

Previous work already showed that parallel MST solver on GPU outperformed CPU versions [29]. Hence we compare against previous GPU implementations

Table 2. Performance comparison between FAISS and cuSLINK's 1-NN on randomly generated data. Similar to Table 1 our performance dominates, even more dramatically for lower sizes—up to 178 × faster. Due to the iterative nature of 1 and the merging in HAC, problems of all sizes will occur during a larger clustering, so all performance levels are relevant to final speedup.

Index Rows	Query Rows	Cols	GPU-FAISS	cuSLINK
100K	100	128	98.4 ms	**0.55 ms**
100K	100	256	95.6 ms	**0.967 ms**
100K	1k	64	96.6 ms	**1.85 ms**
100K	1K	128	98.9 ms	**3.39 ms**
100K	1K	256	104 ms	**6.46 ms**
100K	10K	64	126 ms	**17 ms**
100K	10K	128	146 ms	**32 ms**
100K	10K	256	156 ms	**62.2 ms**

and consider CPU comparisons to be out of the scope of this paper. While performance of [12] is better than [29], we did not compare against it because the bitwise technique greatly limits the supported input size, as shown in [2] (Table 2).

In Table 3 we selected road networks from the 9th DIMACS challenge to compare against the experiments performed by [29].

Table 3. We selected road networks from the 9th DIMACS challenge to compare against the experiments performed by [9]. Compared to the prior state-of-the-art algorithm, our method is always faster and up to 3.5× faster as the problem size increases.

Description	no. nodes	no. edges	Sousa2015	cuSLINK
New York City	263,346	733,846	29.265ms	**20.217 ms**
SF Bay Area	321,270	800,172	32.689ms	**22.606 ms**
CO	435,666	1,057,066	38.819ms	**23.680 ms**
FL	1,070,376	2,712,7986	82.822ms	**35.552 ms**
Northwest USA	1,207,945	2,840,208	84.203ms	**36.884 ms**
Northeast USA	1,524,453	3,897,636	112.173ms	**51.879 ms**
CA & NV	1,890,815	4,657,742	132.726ms	**61.366 ms**
Great Lakes	2,758,119	6,885,658	191.827ms	**81.994 ms**
Eastern USA	3,598,623	8,778,114	265.426ms	**96.100 ms**
Western USA	6,262,104	15,248,146	450.833ms	**127.545 ms**
Central USA	14,081,816	34,292,496	1004.624ms	**278.841 ms**
Full USA	23,947,347	58,333,344	1685.172ms	**478.898 ms**

On larger road networks, our implementation scales better than [9]. Recall that the latter is explicitly forming super-vertices which becomes increasingly expensive as the size of the problem increases.

4.3   Single-Linkage Hierarchical Agglomerative Clustering

Since dendrogram construction is not often exposed as an independent step, we evaluate our end-to-end single-linkage hierarchical clustering implementation on the GPU against Scikit-learn's *AgglomerativeClustering* implementation on the CPU in Table 4. Each experiment was performed on a NVIDIA DGX1 using several real-world datasets, often encountered in clustering and nearest neighbors research. These experiments demonstrate that the performance of our SLHC implementation has the potential to lower the time spent in compute during the data analysis process, enabling near real-time speeds for data sets that take nearly 40 min to process on the CPU.

Table 4. End-to-end execution times comparing our GPU-accelerated SLHC implementation against Scikit-learn on the CPU for real-world datasets. In most cases Scikit-learn times out (after 24 h), and so no result is available.

Dataset	Shape	Clusters	Scikit-learn	cuSLINK
Deep-1B	8M × 96	100	—	**1806 s**
SIFT-128	1M × 128	100	—	**37.23 s**
NYTimes	290k × 256	100	—	**9.227 s**
MNIST	60K × 784	10	2171 s	**0.926 s**
Fashion MNIST	60K × 784	25	2169 s	**0.947 s**

5   Conclusion

In addition to a novel, modular, and state-of-the-art implementation of single-linkage hierarchical clustering, we've outlined and contributed multiple reusable, novel and state-of-the-art primitives in this paper. These primitives include k-nearest graph construction, graph-based minimum spanning tree solver, and a novel parallel dendrogram cluster extraction method.

We demonstrated that our primitives are both flexible and fast, and have a potential to impact several different industries as existing state-of-the-art methods for end-to-end single-linkage clustering are intractable on large datasets. These primitives are all fully open source and available as part of the RAFT library (https://github.com/rapidsai/raft).

References

1. Anibal, J., et al.: HAL-X: scalable hierarchical clustering for rapid and tunable single-cell analysis. PLoS Comput. Biol. **18**(10), e1010349 (2022)
2. Arefin, A.S., Riveros, C., Berretta, R., Moscato, P.: kNN-Borůvka-GPU: a fast and scalable MST construction from kNN graphs on GPU. In: Murgante, B., et al. (eds.) ICCSA 2012. LNCS, vol. 7333, pp. 71–86. Springer, Heidelberg (2012). https://doi.org/10.1007/978-3-642-31125-3_6. http://www.newcastle.edu.au/research-centre/cibm/
3. Arefin, A.S., Riveros, C., Berretta, R., Moscato, P.: KNN-MST-agglomerative: a fast and scalable graph-based data clustering approach on GPU. In: 2012 7th International Conference on Computer Science & Education (ICCSE), pp. 585–590. IEEE (2012)
4. Bakunas-Milanowski, D., Rego, V., Sang, J., Chansu, Y.: Efficient algorithms for stream compaction on GPUS. Int. J. Netw. Comput. **7**(2), 208–226 (2017)
5. Cayton, L.: Accelerating nearest neighbor search on manycore systems. In: 2012 IEEE 26th International Parallel and Distributed Processing Symposium, pp. 402–413. IEEE (2012)
6. Chan, D.M., Rao, R., Huang, F., Canny, J.F.: T-SNE-CUDA: GPU-accelerated t-SNE and its applications to modern data. In: 2018 30th International Symposium on Computer Architecture and High Performance Computing (SBAC-PAD), pp. 330–338 (2018). https://doi.org/10.1109/CAHPC.2018.8645912
7. Chang, D.J., Kantardzic, M.M., Ouyang, M.: Hierarchical clustering with CUDA/GPU. In: ISCA PDCCS, pp. 7–12. Citeseer (2009)
8. Clarkson, K.L.: Fast algorithms for the all nearest neighbors problem. In: 24th Annual Symposium on Foundations of Computer Science (SFCS 1983), pp. 226–232 (1983). https://doi.org/10.1109/SFCS.1983.16
9. Da Silva Sousa, C., Mariano, A., Proença, A.: A generic and highly efficient parallel variant of Boråvka's algorithm. In: Proceedings - 23rd Euromicro International Conference on Parallel, Distributed, and Network-Based Processing, PDP 2015, pp. 610–617 (2015). https://doi.org/10.1109/PDP.2015.72. http://cudpp.github.io/https://www.semanticscholar.org/paper/A-Generic-and-Highly-Efficient-Parallel-Variant-of-Sousa-Mariano/e9106835936711b416189cd5917dd61704510ee4
10. Dash, M., Petrutiu, S., Scheuermann, P.: pPOP: fast yet accurate parallel hierarchical clustering using partitioning. Data Knowl. Eng. **61**(3), 563–578 (2007)
11. Gasperini, M., et al.: A genome-wide framework for mapping gene regulation via cellular genetic screens. Cell **176**(1–2), 377–390 (2019)
12. Harish, P., Vineet, V., Narayanan, P.J.: Large graph algorithms for massively multithreaded architectures. Iiit/Tr(74), 1–20 (2009). 10.1.1.417.2999
13. Hendrix, W., Palsetia, D., Patwary, M.M.A., Agrawal, A., Liao, W.K., Choudhary, A.: A scalable algorithm for single-linkage hierarchical clustering on distributed-memory architectures. In: 2013 IEEE Symposium on Large-Scale Data Analysis and Visualization (LDAV), pp. 7–13. IEEE (2013)
14. Hendrix, W., Patwary, M.M.A., Agrawal, A., Liao, W.K., Choudhary, A.: Parallel hierarchical clustering on shared memory platforms. In: 2012 19th International Conference on High Performance Computing, pp. 1–9. IEEE (2012)
15. Jegou, H., Douze, M., Schmid, C.: Product quantization for nearest neighbor search. IEEE Trans. Pattern Anal. Mach. Intell. **33**(1), 117–128 (2010)
16. Johnson, J., Douze, M., Jégou, H.: Billion-scale similarity search with GPUS (2017). https://doi.org/10.48550/ARXIV.1702.08734. https://arxiv.org/abs/1702.08734

17. McInnes, L., Healy, J.: Accelerated hierarchical density based clustering. In: IEEE International Conference on Data Mining Workshops, ICDMW 2017-November, pp. 33–42 (2017). https://doi.org/10.1109/ICDMW.2017.12
18. Naumov, M., et al.: AMGX: a library for GPU accelerated algebraic multigrid and preconditioned iterative methods. SIAM J. Sci. Comput. **37**(5), S602–S626 (2015). https://doi.org/10.1137/140980260
19. Nolet, C.J., et al.: Bringing UMAP closer to the speed of light with GPU acceleration (2020). https://doi.org/10.48550/ARXIV.2008.00325. https://arxiv.org/abs/2008.00325
20. Olson, C.F.: Parallel algorithms for hierarchical clustering. Parallel Comput. **21**(8), 1313–1325 (1995)
21. Pan, J., Manocha, D.: Fast GPU-based locality sensitive hashing for K-nearest neighbor computation. In: Proceedings of the 19th ACM SIGSPATIAL International Conference on Advances in Geographic Information Systems, pp. 211–220 (2011)
22. Raff, E.: JSAT: Java statistical analysis tool, a library for machine learning. J. Mach. Learn. Res. **18**(23), 1–5 (2017)
23. Sankaranarayanan, J., Samet, H., Varshney, A.: A fast all nearest neighbor algorithm for applications involving large point-clouds. Comput. Graph. **31**(2), 157–174 (2007)
24. Shalom, S.A.A., Dash, M., Tue, M.: An approach for fast hierarchical agglomerative clustering using graphics processors with CUDA. In: Zaki, M.J., Yu, J.X., Ravindran, B., Pudi, V. (eds.) PAKDD 2010. LNCS (LNAI), vol. 6119, pp. 35–42. Springer, Heidelberg (2010). https://doi.org/10.1007/978-3-642-13672-6_4. https://link.springer.com/chapter/10.1007/978-3-642-13672-6_4
25. Shalom, S.A., Dash, M.: Efficient hierarchical agglomerative clustering algorithms on GPU using data partitioning. In: 2011 12th International Conference on Parallel and Distributed Computing, Applications and Technologies, pp. 134–139. IEEE (2011)
26. Shalom, S.A., Dash, M., Tue, M., Wilson, N.: Hierarchical agglomerative clustering using graphics processor with compute unified device architecture. In: 2009 International Conference on Signal Processing Systems, pp. 556–561. IEEE (2009)
27. Sibson, R.: SLINK: an optimally efficient algorithm for the single-link cluster method. Comput. J. **16**(1), 30–34 (1973). https://doi.org/10.1093/comjnl/16.1.30
28. Tarjan, R.E.: Efficiency of a good but not linear set union algorithm. J. ACM (JACM) **22**(2), 215–225 (1975)
29. Vineet, V., Harish, P., Patidar, S., Narayanan, P.J.: Fast minimum spanning tree for large graphs on the GPU. In: Proceedings of the SIGGRAPH/Eurographics Workshop on Graphics Hardware, pp. 167–172 (2009). https://cvit.iiit.ac.in/resources
30. Yengo, L., et al.: A saturated map of common genetic variants associated with human height. Nature **610**(7933), 704–712 (2022)

Socially Fair Center-Based and Linear Subspace Clustering

Sruthi Gorantla[1], Kishen N. Gowda[2(✉)], Amit Deshpande[3], and Anand Louis[1]

[1] Indian Institute of Science, Bengaluru, India
{gorantlas,anandl}@iisc.ac.in
[2] University of Maryland, College Park, USA
kishen19@cs.umd.edu
[3] Microsoft Research, Bengaluru, India
amitdesh@microsoft.com

Abstract. Center-based clustering (e.g., k-means, k-medians) and clustering using linear subspaces are the two most popular objectives for partitioning real-world data into smaller clusters. Both these objectives minimize the average cost of clustering over all the points. However, when the points belong to different sensitive demographic groups and the optimal clustering has a significantly different cost per point for different groups, it can cause fairness-related harms (e.g., different quality-of-service). To mitigate these harms, the socially fair clustering objective minimizes the cost of clustering per point for the worst-off group. In this work, we propose a unified framework to solve socially fair center-based and linear subspace clustering and give practical and efficient approximation algorithms for these problems. We perform extensive experiments to show that our algorithms closely match or outperform existing baselines on multiple benchmark datasets.

1 Introduction

Given a set of n data points in a d-dimensional Euclidean space, the goal of clustering is to partition these data points into k disjoint parts or clusters so that the points in the same cluster are close to each other or close to a well-defined structure. It is a challenging problem to efficiently determine the right number of clusters from the data [20,35]. As a result, in many clustering objectives, the desired number of clusters k is given as a part of the input. In *center-based clustering*, the objective is to find k points or centers that minimize the average distance of any data point to its nearest center. This definition of clustering has been widely used in applications such as computational biology [22], market segmentation [19], and many more [7,26,30].

While clustering is a widely used technique to represent the data succinctly, it is sometimes the case that clustering using subspaces gives clusters of much

---

S. Gorantla, K. N. Gowda, A. Deshpande and A. Louis—Equal contribution.

lower cost than clustering using points as centers, as has also been illustrated in [34]. Formally, *subspace clustering* asks for k subspaces of dimension at most q (where $q < d$) that minimize the average distance of any data point to its nearest subspace. Clustering using subspaces has applications in computer vision [21,40], face recognition [6,27], representation learning [32,33], and many more. We consider the *linear subspace clustering* objective that uses linear subspaces.

Previous work has observed that automated decision-making on big data can have a potentially adverse social and economic impact on individuals and sensitive demographic groups (e.g., race, gender) [5]. For example, [15] has observed highly unequal group-wise costs for different sensitive groups in several real-world datasets when clustering with the k-means objective. As a result, various fairness-constrained clustering objectives have been proposed. In this work, we study the *socially fair* clustering problem. The goal is to minimize the clustering cost per point for the worst-off group, where groups are based on socially salient features such as race, gender, etc. Here we consider the problem of clustering using the z-th power of the Euclidean distance metric. This notion generalizes the well-known clustering objectives such as socially-fair k-median ($z = 1$) [1], k-means ($z = 2$) [15], and k-center ($z = \infty$) clustering.

In the case of linear subspace clustering with $k = 1$, the optimal solution can be obtained efficiently by Principal Component Analysis (PCA). However, applying PCA to the data in a group-blind fashion might result in inequitable group-wise costs, as observed in [36]. Similarly, clustering using linear subspaces could also suffer from unequal costs for different groups. Hence, we study the socially fair variants of clustering.

In this work, we propose a framework for socially fair clustering using which we give a $(1 + \varepsilon)$ approximation algorithm for socially fair (k, z) clustering that runs in time $\tilde{\mathcal{O}}(ndk) + 2^{\mathcal{O}(\varepsilon^{-z} k^3 \ell \log L)}$, where L is the input bit complexity. We also show that the same framework also gives an algorithm to solve socially fair linear subspace clustering using k linear subspaces of dimension q each so as to minimize the clustering cost per point for the worst-off group, defined using z-th power of distances. Here the distances from a point to the linear subspaces are the lengths of orthogonal projections (in the ℓ_2 norm) of the points in linear subspace, to the power z, for $z \geqslant 1$.

Contributions. Our main contributions can be summarized as follows,

- We propose a generic framework (Algorithm 1), where we first assume that there is an oracle that, given a k-partitioning of the data, outputs k centers (or linear subspaces) such that the socially fair center-based (or linear subspace) clustering cost with respect to these centers (subspaces) is at most α times the optimal socially fair clustering cost for this k-partitioning. Then our framework gives an $\alpha(1+\varepsilon)$-approximation algorithm to the socially fair clustering problem, given access to an appropriate strong ε-coreset construction algorithm and the α approximate oracle (Theorem 2).
- If the best known strong coreset construction algorithm for an unconstrained clustering problem outputs a coreset S, we show that we can construct a

strong coreset of size $\ell \cdot |S|$ for socially fair clustering. Here ℓ is the number of groups the points belong to (Theorem 1).

- We also give constructions of efficient oracles, which, when used in our framework, give a $(1 + \varepsilon)$ approximation algorithm for socially fair center-based clustering (Theorem 3) and a $\sqrt{2}\ell^{\frac{1}{z}}\gamma_z(1 + \varepsilon)$ approximation algorithm for socially fair linear subspace clustering, for $z \geqslant 2$, where $\gamma_z \approx \sqrt{z/e}(1 + o(1))$ (Theorem 4).
- We also propose a Lloyd-like heuristic algorithm (Algorithm 2) to perform socially fair clustering efficiently on many benchmark datasets and compare the results with unconstrained as well as fair baselines wherever applicable (Sect. 6).

1.1 Related Works

Previous Results. Socially fair k-means clustering (in our case, socially fair center-based clustering with $z = 2$) has been introduced and studied in [1,15] simultaneously. [1] gave an $\mathcal{O}(\ell)$-approximation algorithm, whereas [15] gave a Lloyd-like heuristic algorithm that performs well in practice. Recently [18] came up with $(33 + \varepsilon)$ approximation algorithm which runs in time $(k/\varepsilon)^{\mathcal{O}(k)} n^{\mathcal{O}(1)}$.

For socially-fair k-medians clustering (in our case, socially fair center-based clustering with $z = 1$), a recent work [18] gave a $(5+\varepsilon)$-approximation algorithm which runs in time $(k/\varepsilon)^{\mathcal{O}(k)} n^{\mathcal{O}(1)}$.

For socially-fair center-based clustering with a general z, [29] presented a polynomial time $\left(e^{\mathcal{O}(z)} \log \ell / \log \log \ell\right)$-approximation algorithm. The work [9] generalizes the socially fair clustering objective further and asks to minimize the ℓ_p norm of the average group-wise clustering costs. When $p = \infty$, this recovers the socially fair center-based clustering. They also achieve the same approximation guarantee as [29]. In an independent and concurrent work [16] came up with a $(5 + 2\sqrt{6} + \varepsilon)$ approximation algorithm that runs in time $n^{2^{O(z) \cdot \ell^2}}$ and a $(15 + 6\sqrt{6})$ approximation algorithm that runs in time $k^\ell \cdot \mathsf{poly}(n)$. We give a $(1 + \varepsilon)$ approximation algorithm that runs in time $\widetilde{\mathcal{O}}(ndk) + 2^{\mathcal{O}(\varepsilon^{-z}k^3\ell \log L)}$, where L is the input bit complexity.

In [15], the authors study a slightly different problem, where the goal is to find optimal subspace such that among all the groups, the increase in the per-point cost of the group due to fairness constraints compared to PCA of that group is minimized. To the best of our knowledge, we are the first to study the socially fair linear subspace clustering problem and propose a unified framework for both center-based and linear subspace clustering.

Techniques. As large data sets often have a large number of points, a popular technique relevant to our paper is to construct a small *coreset* of the given data and perform clustering on the coreset. A coreset is a small weighted sample of the data such that the clustering cost for this smaller set of points gives a $(1 + \varepsilon)$ approximation to the clustering cost for the entire data. Following the unified framework for clustering using coresets proposed in [14], recent works

[10,24] have constructed coresets for k-means or k-medians clustering of size poly($k, 1/\varepsilon$), independent of n and d. Different from socially fair clustering, fair representation clustering asks for a proportional representation of all the groups in each cluster. For such a fair k-means and fair k-median objective, a coreset of size $\mathcal{O}\left(\Gamma\varepsilon^{-d}k^2\right)$ can be constructed by a deterministic algorithm [23], and a coreset of size poly($\Gamma, \log n, k, 1/\varepsilon$) can be constructed by a sampling-based algorithm [4], where Γ is the number of types of items (i.e., number of disjoint groups). It is important to keep in mind that the above fair clustering objective can be inadequate when the benefits or harms of clustering for different demographic groups are better represented by their clustering cost rather than their proportional representation, as shown in [15]. We note that we are the first to use coresets for socially fair clustering.

2   Preliminaries

2.1   Notation

Recall that we are given a set X of n points in $\mathbb{R}^d$. We assume we have the group information of the data points in X, where each point belongs to exactly one group. Henceforth we take $(X_1, X_2, \ldots, X_\ell)$ to be the input, where $X_j \subseteq X$ represents the set of points from group j. We use $C := (c_1, c_2, \ldots, c_k)$ to represent k points as centers where $c_i \in \mathbb{R}^d, \forall i \in [k]$, and $V := (V_1, V_2, \ldots, V_k)$ to represent k subspaces of dimension at most q in $\mathbb{R}^d$ as centers, where q is given as input. We use k to represent the number of clusters. We note that k is given as input to all our algorithms; however, estimating the correct value of k for the given dataset is an interesting problem and beyond the scope of this work. We use z to represent the z-th power of the cost of clustering, which is also given as input. We represent the Euclidean norm using $\|\cdot\|_2$. We use L to represent the bit complexity of the input; that is, the coordinates of each point are represented as a fraction where both the numerator and the denominator can be of at most L bits. We use S to represent a coreset, the weighted sample of the data points in X. In the rest of the paper, i represents the index of a cluster in $[k]$, and j represents the index of a group in $[\ell]$.

2.2   Problem Definition

The problem of socially fair center-based clustering can now be stated as follows.

Definition 1 (socially fair (k, z) clustering). *Given $(X_1, \ldots, X_\ell)$, $k \in \mathbb{Z}^+$ and $z \geqslant 1$, the goal of socially fair (k, z) clustering is to find k points C that minimize the clustering cost per point of the worst off group. We represent socially fair (k, z) clustering cost as,*

$$\text{fair-cost}(C, X) := \max_{j \in [\ell]} \left(\frac{1}{|X_j|} \sum_{x \in X_j} d(C, x)^z \right)^{1/z},$$

where $d(C, x) := \min_{i \in [k]} d(c_i, x)$ and $d(c_i, x) = \|c_i - x\|_2$. We call $(c_1, c_2, \ldots, c_k)$ the socially fair centers.

This definition generalizes the well-known clustering objectives such as socially-fair k-median ($z = 1$) [1], k-means ($z = 2$) [15], and k-center ($z = \infty$) clustering. Note that in Definition 1, each point is assigned to its nearest center according to the distance $\|c_i - x\|_2$, the Euclidean distance. However, the distance of a point to a subspace in the definition below is the length of the orthogonal projection of the point onto the subspace.

Definition 2 (socially fair (q, k, z) linear subspace clustering). *Given $(X_1, \ldots, X_\ell)$, $k \in \mathbb{Z}^+$, $z \geqslant 1$, and $q < d$, the goal of socially fair (q, k, z) linear subspace clustering is to find k linear subspaces V of dimension at most q in $\mathbb{R}^d$ so as to minimize the clustering cost per point of the worst off group. We represent socially fair (q, k, z) linear subspace clustering cost as*

$$\text{fair-cost}(V, X) := \max_{j \in [\ell]} \left(\frac{1}{|X_j|} \sum_{x \in X_j} d(V, x)^z \right)^{1/z},$$

where $d(V, x) := \min_{i \in [k]} d(V_i, x)$ and $d(V_i, x) = \|x^T Z_i\|_2$, where Z_i is orthogonal projection matrix corresponding to V_i, for every $i \in [k]$. We call $(V_1, V_2, \ldots, V_k)$ the socially fair linear subspaces.

We note that when all the data points are assumed to be from the same group in Definitions 1 and 2, we recover the objective functions of (k, z) clustering and (q, k, z) linear subspace clustering respectively.

3   Framework with Theoretical Guarantees

Recall that we are given a set of n points. A coreset is a small weighted sample of the data that closely approximates the clustering cost of the data. Hence, clustering algorithms run much faster on coresets. In this section, we present our theoretical results. We first show that we can construct a coreset for the socially fair clustering objective, given coresets for the unconstrained clustering objective for each of the groups. Our second result is a framework (see Algorithm 1) that can be used to solve both variants of the socially fair clustering problems described in Sect. 2.2. More formally, consider the following definition of coresets for clustering.

Definition 3 (strong coresets for (k, z) clustering). *Given a set X of n points and a constant $\varepsilon > 0$, a weighted sample S of the points with weight function $w : S \to \mathbb{R}_+$ is a strong ε-coreset of X for the (k, z) clustering problem if for every k centers $C = (c_1, \ldots, c_k)$ such that $c_i \in \mathbb{R}^d, \forall i \in [k]$,*

$$\left(\sum_{x \in S} w(x) \cdot d(C, x)^z \right)^{1/z} \in (1 \pm \varepsilon) \left(1/|X| \sum_{x \in X} d(C, x)^z \right)^{1/z}.$$

Definition 4 (strong coresets for (q, k, z) linear subspace clustering). *Given a set X of n points and a constant $\varepsilon > 0$, a weighted sample S of the points with weight function $w : S \to \mathbb{R}_+$ is a strong ε-coreset for the (q, k, z) linear subspace clustering problem if for every k linear subspaces $V = (V_1, V_2, \ldots, V_k)$, where each V_i is a linear subspace in $\mathbb{R}^d$ of dimension at most q,*

$$\left(\sum_{x \in S} w(x) \cdot d(V, x)^z \right)^{1/z} \in (1 \pm \varepsilon) \left(1/|X| \sum_{x \in X} d(V, x)^z \right)^{1/z}.$$

Henceforth, whenever we say coreset, we refer to a strong coreset. Recall that we are additionally given that the points belong to ℓ disjoint groups. Given the partition of the data based on these groups, $X_1, \ldots, X_\ell$, the key observation we first make is that a union of coresets for each of the groups for the unconstrained clustering cost is also a coreset for the entire data for the socially fair clustering cost. This applies to socially fair (k, z) clustering and socially fair (q, k, z) linear subspace clustering. Note that a union of coresets for groups has been used as a coreset for other variants of fair clustering (e.g., [23], for the problem of (α, β)-proportionally-fair clustering).

Theorem 1 (coresets for socially fair clustering) *Let S_j be a strong ε-coreset for X_j, for each $j \in [\ell]$, with respect to the clustering cost. Then, $S = \bigcup_{j=1}^{\ell} S_j$ is a strong ε-coreset for the entire data X with respect to the socially fair clustering cost.*

Proof. Let S_j be a strong ε-coreset for the points belonging to group $j \in [\ell]$ with respect to the clustering cost and w_j be the corresponding weight function. Then for any k centers $C = (c_1, \ldots, c_k)$, let $X_1, X_2, \ldots, X_k$ be clustering obtained by assigning the points in X to their closest centers in C. For any $S \subseteq X$ and a given weight function $w : S \to \mathbb{R}_+$, let $\text{cost}(C, S, w) := \left(\sum_{x \in S} \min_{i \in [k]} w(s) \cdot d(c_i, x)^z \right)^{1/z}$. When there are no weights on the points, we use $\text{cost}(C, S, 1)$ or simply $\text{cost}(C, S)$ to represent the cost function with uniform weights, i.e., $1(x) = 1/|S|$. Then we have,

$$(1 - \varepsilon) \cdot \text{cost}(C, X_j) \leqslant \text{cost}(C, S_j, w_j) \leqslant (1 + \varepsilon) \cdot \text{cost}(C, X_j).$$

Now let $S = \bigcup_{j=1}^{\ell} S_j$. For the same cluster centers and partitioning of the data, we have,

$$\text{fair-cost}(C, S) = \max_{j \in [\ell]} \text{cost}(C, S_j, w_j)$$

$$\implies \max_{j \in [\ell]} (1 - \varepsilon) \cdot \text{cost}(C, X_j) \leqslant \text{fair-cost}(C, S) \leqslant \max_{j \in [\ell]} (1 + \varepsilon) \cdot \text{cost}(C, X_j)$$

$$\implies (1 - \varepsilon) \cdot \max_{j \in [\ell]} \text{cost}(C, X_j) \leqslant \text{fair-cost}(C, S) \leqslant (1 + \varepsilon) \cdot \max_{j \in [\ell]} \text{cost}(C, X_j)$$

$$\implies (1 - \varepsilon) \cdot \text{fair-cost}(C, X) \leqslant \text{fair-cost}(C, S) \leqslant (1 + \varepsilon) \cdot \text{fair-cost}(C, X),$$

where the first implication is because S_j is an ϵ coreset of X_j. Therefore S is an ε-coreset for the whole dataset w.r.t. the socially fair clustering cost. The same arguments also work for socially fair (q, k, z) linear subspace clustering.

Algorithm 1. Socially Fair (k, z) Clustering

Input: The set of points X and their group memberships, the numbers k, z.
Output: The cluster centers C.
1: Compute S_j, a strong $\varepsilon/3$-coreset for group $j, \forall j \in [\ell]$.
2: Let $S := \bigcup_{j \in [\ell]} S_j$.
3: **for** each k partitioning of the coreset $\mathcal{P}(S, k) := (P_1(S), P_2(S), \ldots, P_k(S))$ **do**
4:    $C := \text{FAIR-CENTERS}(\mathcal{P}(S, k))$.
5:    $t := \max_{j \in [\ell]} \text{cost}(C, S_j)$.
6: **return** The centers C with minimum value of t.

As a consequence of Theorem 1, we propose an iterative framework to solve socially fair clustering (see Algorithm 1). The framework crucially depends on the existence of an efficient algorithm called FAIR-CENTERS, that, given a set of clusters, outputs α-approximate socially fair centers. Then the socially fair clustering cost output by this function is at most α times the optimal socially fair clustering cost, where $\alpha \geqslant 1$. Our socially fair (q, k, z) linear subspace clustering (see Algorithm 3 in the full version of the paper [17]) also follows the same framework. Therefore, this framework is generic in the sense that we can recover algorithms to solve both variants of the socially fair clustering problems given appropriate oracles in Step 4. We now state our theorem for socially fair center-based clustering. The same result also holds for socially fair linear subspace clustering with an appropriate oracle for finding fair linear subspaces for each partition in Step 4.

Theorem 2. *Let S_j be a strong $\varepsilon/3$-coreset for group j for some $\varepsilon \in [0, 1]$, $\forall j \in [\ell]$. Let $t(S, \alpha)$ be the time taken by FAIR-CENTERS that gives an α-approximate socially fair cluster centers, given clusters. Then there exists an $\alpha(1 + \varepsilon)$ approximation algorithm for the socially fair clustering problem that runs in time $\mathcal{O}\left(k^{|S|} \cdot t(S, \alpha)\right)$ where $S = \bigcup_{j=1}^{\ell} S_j$.*

Proof of Theorem 2 can be found in the full version of the paper [17, Theorem 8].

4 Implementation of FAIR-CENTERS

In this section, we give an exact implementation of FAIR-CENTERS for socially fair (k, z) clustering and an approximate one for socially fair (q, k, z) linear subspace clustering. We do both by formulating them as convex programs that can be solved efficiently using the well-known Ellipsoid method. Note that in Algorithm 2 we call the function FAIR-CENTERS for the ε-coreset S corresponding to the given dataset X for the socially fair clustering objective. We show the implementation of the FAIR-CENTERS for S, but it works for any subset of X.

4.1 Socially Fair (k, z) Clustering

Similar to X, S can also be partitioned into $S_1, S_2, \ldots, S_\ell$, based on groups. Let $P_i(S)$ represent the ith cluster (or partition) of the coreset S and $S_{ij} :=$

$P_i(S) \cap S_j$. Then the problem of finding k centers that minimize the socially fair (k, z) clustering cost, given the clusters, can be expressed as the following convex program,

$$\min_{\beta \in \mathbb{R}, c_1, \cdots, c_k \in \mathbb{R}^d} \quad \beta, \tag{1}$$

$$\text{such that} \quad \frac{1}{|S_j|} \sum_{i \in [k]} \sum_{x \in S_{ij}} \|x - c_i\|^z \leqslant \beta, \quad \forall j \in [\ell].$$

It is easy to see that the optimal solution to this convex program $\beta^*, c_1^*, c_2^*, \ldots, c_k^*$ gives socially fair clustering cost β^*, with the centers $(c_1^*, c_2^*, \ldots, c_k^*)$. Let L be the bit complexity of the input; that is, each point x is a vector in $\mathbb{Q}^d$, and all the rational numbers are represented as fractions where the values of numerator and denominator can be represented using at most L bits. Then our framework results in the following theorem.

Theorem 3. *Given* $(X_1, X_2, \ldots, X_\ell)$, *with bit complexity* L, *numbers* $k \in \mathbb{Z}_{\geqslant 0}$, $z \geqslant 1$, *an algorithm with running time* T_S *to compute a strong* ε-coreset S *for socially fair* (k, z) *clustering, there exists a* $(1 + \varepsilon)$-*approximation algorithm to socially fair* (k, z) *clustering that runs in time*

$$\tilde{\mathcal{O}}\left(k^{|S|} \cdot \left(k^2 d^2 + \ell k L^2 (d + z)|S| \right) \cdot k^2 d^2 \cdot (Lz + d + \log |S|)^2 + T_S \right).$$

To the best of our knowledge, the best-known coreset size for the (k, z) clustering is $|S| = \tilde{\mathcal{O}}\left(\min\{\varepsilon^{-2z-2}, 2^{2z}\varepsilon^{-4}k\}\ell k \right)$ by [24]. We note that the size of the coreset is independent of n. This makes the number of iterations in Step 3 of our algorithm the same for any size of the dataset. The algorithm to construct this coreset runs in time $\tilde{\mathcal{O}}(ndk)$. Moreover, [28] shows that the cost of any clustering is preserved up to a factor of $(1 + \varepsilon)$ under a projection onto a random $\mathcal{O}(\log(k/\varepsilon)/\varepsilon^2)$-dimensional subspace. Therefore, the running time of our algorithm is $\tilde{\mathcal{O}}(ndk) + 2^{\mathcal{O}(\varepsilon^{-z}k^3\ell \log L)}$. Note that even for unconstrained k-means clustering problem, the best known $(1 + \varepsilon)$ approximation algorithm runs in time exponential in k (see Theorem 1 in [8]). Many works have given polynomial time algorithms for k means clustering under some additional assumptions on the data [2,3]. Studying our problem with additional assumptions on the data remains an interesting open direction.

4.2   Socially Fair (q, k, z) Linear Subspace Clustering

Let $z_{i,1}, z_{i,2}, \cdots, z_{i,d-q}$ denote the orthonormal basis of the orthogonal complement of V_i and let $Z_i \in \mathbb{R}^{d \times d-q}$ denote the matrix with the hth column as $z_{i,h}$. We know that the distance of a point x to the ith subspace is its projection on the orthogonal subspace. Thus, $d(x, V_i) = \|x^T Z_i\|_2$. Here let S be an ε-coreset for

X with respect to the socially fair (q, k, z) linear subspace clustering objective. Then, the oracle can be expressed as follows,

$$\min_{\beta \in \mathbb{R}, Z_1, \cdots, Z_k \in \mathbb{R}^{d \times d-q}} \beta, \tag{2}$$

$$\text{s.t.,} \quad \frac{1}{|S_j|} \sum_{i \in [k]} \sum_{x \in S_{ij}} \|x^T Z_i\|_2^z \leqslant \beta, \quad \forall j \in [\ell],$$

$$\|Z_i^{(h)}\|_2 \geqslant 1, \quad \forall i \in [k], \forall h \in [d-q],$$

$$\langle Z_i^{(h_1)}, Z_i^{(h_2)} \rangle = 0, \quad \forall h_1 \neq h_2, i \in [k].$$

This problem can be approximated by utilizing techniques from [11]. More precisely, we have the following theorem,

Theorem 4. *Given* $(X_1, X_2, \ldots, X_\ell)$, *with bit complexity* L, *numbers* $k, q \in \mathbb{Z}_{\geqslant 0}$, $z \geqslant 1$, *and an algorithm with running time* T_S *to compute a strong* ε-*coreset* S *for socially fair* (q, k, z) *linear subspace clustering, there exists a* $\sqrt{2}\ell^{\frac{1}{z}}\gamma_z(1+\varepsilon)$ *approximation algorithm to socially fair* (q, k, z) *linear subspace clustering that runs in time*

$$\widetilde{O}\left(k^{|S|} \cdot \left(k^2 d^4 + \ell k d^2 z L |S| + \ell d^3 L\right) \cdot k^2 d^4 \cdot (Lz + d + \log|S|)^2 + T_S\right).$$

In a recent work [39] that studies the problem of constructing a strong coreset for (q, k, z)-projective clustering when the points come from a polynomial grid, the authors provide a $\mathcal{O}(1)$-approximation coreset of size $\mathcal{O}\left(\left(8q^3 \log(d\Delta)\right)^{O(qk)}\right)$ for $z = \infty$, with running time $\mathcal{O}\left(nq^4 (\log \Delta)^{q^2 k}\right)$, and an ε-coreset of size $\mathcal{O}\left(\left(8q^3 \log(d\Delta)\right)^{O(qk)} \log n\right)$ for $z = 2$ with running time $\mathcal{O}\left(n^2 q^4 (\log \Delta)^{q^2 k}\right)$, where Δ is the ratio of the largest and the smallest coordinate magnitudes. Substituting this we get that our algorithm runs in time $\mathcal{O}\left(n^2 q^4 (\log \Delta)^{q^2 k}\right) + n \cdot 2^{\mathcal{O}((q \log(d\Delta)^{O(qk)} \log L)}$ for socially fair $(q, k, 2)$ linear subspace clustering.

Due to space constraints, we omit all the proofs here. We refer the reader to the full version of the paper [17] for all the omitted proofs. In the next section, we propose a practical heuristic algorithm for solving socially fair clustering with the ideas developed in this section combined with a Lloyd-like update step.

5   A Practical Method for Socially Fair Clustering

In this section, we first describe a Lloyd-like heuristic implementation of our framework (see Algorithm 2) that is more practical in running time for experiments on real-world datasets. In Algorithm 2, rather than iterating over all possible k-clusters of the representative set, we perform a Lloyd-like iterative update. Note that unlike described in Algorithm 1, we construct a representative subset of each of the partitions in every iteration. This enables us to take

---

Algorithm 2. Socially Fair (k, z) Lloyd's Heuristic

Input: The set of points X and their group memberships, the clustering parameters k, z, and the sample size M.

Output: Cluster centers C. *(Note that we also get a similar heuristic for socially fair (q, k, z) linear subspace clustering by replacing Step 7 with an appropriate function to find linear subspaces).*

1: Initialize the clusters $\mathcal{P}(X, k) = (P_1(X), P_2(X), \ldots, P_k(X))$ uniformly at random.

2: **for** T iterations **do**

3:     $X_{ij} := P_i(X) \cap X_j, \forall i \in [k], j \in [\ell]$.

4:     Construct S_{ij} by sampling M points from X_{ij} uniformly at random and set the weight of each point to be $|X_{ij}|/M$. (Note: If $M > |X_{ij}|$, then $S_{ij} = X_{ij}$ with weights as 1).

5:     $S := \bigcup_{i \in [k]} \bigcup_{j \in [\ell]} S_{ij}$.

6:     $\widehat{\mathcal{P}} := (P_1(X) \cap S, P_2(X) \cap S, \ldots, P_k(X) \cap S)$.

7:     $C = \text{FAIR-CENTERS}\left(\widehat{\mathcal{P}}\right)$.

8:     Update the clusters $\mathcal{P}$ by assigning points in X to their nearest center in C.

9: **return** cluster centers C.

---

advantage of the partitions created in every iteration by constructing a representative subset for the 1-means (and 1-median) objective for every X_{ij} and taking a union of these representative sets.

Speedup on Real-World Data. We observe in our experimental results that our practical algorithm finds a good enough solution in a very small number of iterations – maximum 20 iterations in all our experiments – at which point we stop the algorithm and return the current centers (subspaces). This suggests that our practical algorithm runs much faster in practice rather than Algorithm 1 due to the replacement of a large number of iterations ($k^{|S|}$) with a small number of Lloyd-like update steps. We note that [15] also proposed a variant of Lloyd's heuristic called Fair-Lloyd where, starting with a uniform random set of clusters of the whole data, in each iteration, it finds a set of centers that minimize the socially-fair k-means clustering cost for the current set of clusters, and re-assigns all the points to their nearest center. For an arbitrary number of groups, [15] finds the centers via a heuristic based on the multiplicative weights update method. Different from this, we work with a representative sample of the data, and in each iteration, we find α-approximate centers for the clusters in that iteration, where α is as given in Sect. 4. Our experimental results show that [15] incurs a much higher cost compared to our algorithm when there are more than two groups (see Fig. 1).

6   Experimental Results

Utilizing Algorithm 2, we perform an experimental evaluation on multiple benchmark datasets for center-based clustering (k-means and k-medians objectives) as well as linear subspace clustering. The experiments were run on an Intel(R)

Xeon(R) Silver 4110 CPU consisting of 8 cores, with a clock speed of 2.1 GHz and DRAM of 128 GB. We refer the reader to the full version of the paper [17] for running time comparison plots for the algorithms.

We experiment over a diverse set of real-world datasets comprising various sensitive features. Table 1 summarizes the datasets. We normalize the continuous attributes to have mean 0 and variance 1 and encode the categorical attributes using one-hot encoding, similar to our baseline [15]. It is a common practice to reduce the dimension using PCA as a pre-processing step [12], also used in the baseline for socially fair k-means, Fair-Lloyd [15]. In our experiments for socially fair k-means and k-medians, we use PCA to get the best k dimensional approximation of the data. All the algorithms are initialized with the same set of centers in all experiments. All choices of hyperparameters have been made after much experimentation, and these choices appear in the caption of the Figures for specific datasets.

Table 1. Datasets

Dataset	#samples	#attr.	Sensitive feature	Groups
Credit [41]	30000	23	Education	Higher, Lower
Adult Income [13]	48842	104	Gender	Male, Female
			Race	Amer-Indian-Eskim, Asian-Pac-Islander, Black, White, Other
Bank [31]	41188	63	Age	$\leqslant 25$, 25–60, $\geqslant 60$
German Credit [13]	1000	51	Age	$\leqslant 25$, 25–60, $\geqslant 60$
Skillcraft [38]	3340	20	Age	< 21, $\geqslant 21$

6.1 Socially Fair *K-Means*

Before proceeding to the experimental observations, consider the following.

Lemma 1 (Lemma 2.1 in [25]). *Let X be a set of n points in $\mathbb{R}^d$ belonging to ℓ groups $X_1, \cdots, X_\ell \subseteq X$. Given a partition $\mathcal{P}(X, k) = (P_1(X), \cdots, P_k(X))$, let X_{ij} denote $P_i(X) \cap X_j$. Given a set of centers $C = (c_1, \cdots, c_k)$, $\forall i \in [k], j \in [\ell]$, $\sum_{x \in X_{ij}} \|x - c_i\|^2 = \sum_{x \in X_{ij}} \|x - \mu_{ij}\|^2 + |X_{ij}| \cdot \|\mu_{ij} - c_i\|^2$, where μ_{ij} is the centroid of the set X_{ij}.*

Due to Lemma 1 we get a very small "exact" representation (or, a 0-coreset) for k-means clustering to use in Algorithm 2, as follows. We add to the coreset S, the mean μ_{ij} of the points in X_{ij} with weight $|X_{ij}|$, for all $i \in [k]$ and $j \in [\ell]$. This gives us a coreset of size $k\ell$.

For the experimental analysis of socially fair k-means clustering, we run Algorithm 2 (with the coreset defined above) along with the baselines on the Adult Income, Credit and Bank datasets. We perform experiments both with and without the *PCA* pre-processing. We run the algorithms for 50 different initializations. Algorithm 2 is run for 20 iterations while the baselines are run for 100 iterations each.

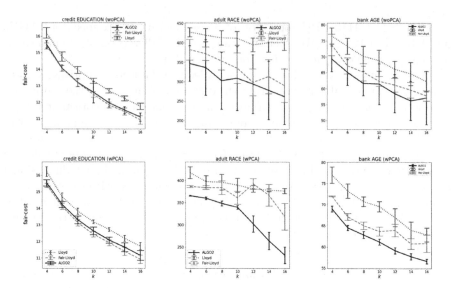

Fig. 1. All algorithms are run on 50 different initializations; ALGO2 is run for 20 iterations, and Fair-Lloyd and Lloyd are run for 100 iterations. For ALGO2, coreset construction uses 5 samples of size $M = 100$ for each P_{ij}. The plots show mean and standard deviation of the socially fair clustering cost (woPCA = without PCA, wPCA = with PCA, ALGO2 = Algorithm 2).

Baselines and Comparison. We compare our results with (i) Fair-Lloyd [15] for socially fair k means clustering. This is a Lloyd-like heuristic algorithm that performs well for practical purposes. (ii) In our results we also show the socially fair clustering cost obtained by the unconstrained Lloyd's algorithm. To the best of our knowledge, there are no implementations of the other socially fair clustering algorithms available for public use. As established in [15], different groups incur very different costs with Lloyd's algorithm (see Fig. 1). On the Credit (Education) dataset, both Fair-Lloyd and Algorithm 2 incur almost equal socially fair k means cost. In the multi-group case, such as Adult Income (Race) and Bank (Age), Algorithm 2 outperforms Fair-Lloyd. These observations are consistent with or without PCA preprocessing of the data. In all the experiments in Fig. 1 both Fair-Lloyd and Algorithm 2 incur much less fair-cost compared to Lloyd. Due to paucity of space, we refer the reader to the full version of the paper [17] for the group-wise costs plots.

6.2 Socially Fair Subspace Approximation

For experiments on the socially fair linear subspace clustering problem, we consider the socially fair variant of the well studied subspace approximation problem, which is equivalent to the socially fair $(q, 1, 2)$ linear subspace clustering problem, as defined. We run Algorithm 2 along with the baseline on the Adult (Gender) dataset for the two groups case. We also run experiments on the Adult

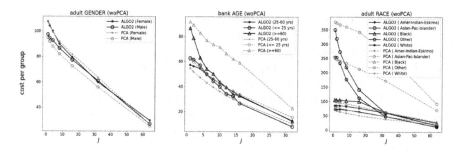

Fig. 2. For ALGO2, coreset construction uses 20 samples of size $M = 500$ for each group. Plots show the average group wise cost incurred. J on x-axis represents dimension of the linear subspace.

(Race) and Bank (Age) datasets for the multigroups case. Since there is only one subspace (one cluster), the algorithms neither have to be run for multiple iterations nor do we have to consider multiple initializations.

Baselines and Comparison. As a baseline, we run the unconstrained *PCA* algorithm. To the best of our knowledge, there is no implementation of a socially fair linear subspace clustering available. Both Algorithm 2 and PCA perform almost equally good on the Adult Income dataset (Gender) in terms of fair-cost (see Fig. 2). However, we observe that for more than two groups (Adult Income (Race) and Bank (Age)), Algorithm 2 outperforms PCA significantly in terms of fair-cost and achieves almost equal group-wise costs as the dimension of the subspace increases.

6.3 Experiments for Socially Fair *K-Medians*

For the socially fair k-medians experiments, we use the German Credit (Age) and Skillcraft (Age) datasets (Fig. 3). Both algorithms are initialized with the same set of centers and run on 10 different initializations for 20 iterations. We consider both cases of with and without PCA pre-processing.

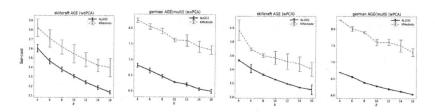

Fig. 3. Both ALGO2 and KMedoids are run on 10 different initializations for 20 iterations. For ALGO2, coreset construction uses 5 samples of size $M = 20$ for each P_{ij}. The plots show mean and standard deviation of the socially fair clustering cost (woPCA = without PCA, wPCA = with PCA, ALGO2 = Algorithm 2).

Baselines and Comparison. We compare our results with (*i*) *FasterPAM* [37], a fast and practical k-Medoids based algorithm. (*ii*) We consider the socially fair k-medians cost obtained by the unconstrained *FasterPAM* algorithm. Although *FasterPAM* is time-efficient, it is space-inefficient. Hence, we run experiments on datasets with relatively smaller number of data points. The baseline k-medoids based algorithm incurs very different costs for different groups. Further, the fair-cost obtained by the k-medoids algorithm is much higher compared to that of Algorithm 2 (see Fig. 3). Algorithm 2 achieves almost equal costs for different groups in all experiments.

7   Conclusion

Clustering using center-based objectives and subspaces on large image, text, financial and scientific data sets has a wide range of applications. In order to alleviate harms to different demographic groups arising from inequitable clustering costs across different groups, we study the objective of socially fair clustering. We develop a unified framework to solve socially fair center-based clustering and linear subspace clustering problems, and propose practical and efficient approximation algorithms for them. Our algorithms either closely match or outperform the state-of-the-art baselines on standard real-world data sets in fairness literature. When p and the number of groups l are constants, an interesting open problem is to find the optimal approximation algorithms for socially fair center-based ℓ_p-norm clustering objectives and affine subspace clustering objectives with running time polynomial in k, n, and d.

Acknowledgments. SG was supported by a Google PhD Fellowship. Kishen was supported in part by NSF Grant No. CNS-2317194. Part of this work was done while Kishen was at IISc, Bengaluru. AL was supported in part by SERB Award ECR/2017/003296 and a Pratiksha Trust Young Investigator Award. AL is also grateful to Microsoft Research for supporting this collaboration.

References

1. Abbasi, M., Bhaskara, A., Venkatasubramanian, S.: Fair clustering via equitable group representations. In: FAccT (2021)
2. Awasthi, P., Blum, A., Sheffet, O.: Clustering under natural stability assumptions (2002)
3. Awasthi, P., Blum, A., Sheffet, O.: Stability yields a PTAS for K-median and K-means clustering. In: FOCS (2010)
4. Bandyapadhyay, S., Fomin, F.V., Simonov, K.: On coresets for fair clustering in metric and Euclidean spaces and their applications (2020)
5. Barocas, S., Selbst, A.D.: Big data's disparate impact. Calif. L. Rev. (2016)
6. Batur, A.U., III, M.H.H.: Segmented linear subspaces for illumination-robust face recognition. Int. J. Comput. Vis. **57**, 49–66 (2004)
7. Bewley, A., Shekhar, R., Leonard, S., Upcroft, B., Lever, P.: Real-time volume estimation of a dragline payload. In: 2011 IEEE International Conference on Robotics and Automation (2011)

8. Bhattacharya, A., Jaiswal, R., Kumar, A.: Faster algorithms for the constrained K-means problem. Theor. Comp. Syst. **62**, 93–115 (2018)
9. Chlamtác, E., Makarychev, Y., Vakilian, A.: Approximating fair clustering with cascaded norm objectives. In: SODA (2022)
10. Cohen-Addad, V., Saulpic, D., Schwiegelshohn, C.: A new coreset framework for clustering (2021)
11. Deshpande, A., Tulsiani, M., Vishnoi, N.K.: Algorithms and hardness for subspace approximation. In: SODA (2011)
12. Ding, C., He, X.: K-means clustering via principal component analysis. In: ICML (2004)
13. Dua, D., Graff, C.: UCI machine learning repository (2017)
14. Feldman, D., Langberg, M.: A unified framework for approximating and clustering data. In: STOC (2011)
15. Ghadiri, M., Samadi, S., Vempala, S.: Socially fair k-means clustering. In: FAccT. Association for Computing Machinery (2021)
16. Ghadiri, M., Singh, M., Vempala, S.S.: Constant-factor approximation algorithms for socially fair k-clustering (2022)
17. Gorantla, S., Gowda, K.N., Deshpande, A., Louis, A.: Socially fair center-based and linear subspace clustering (2022). arxiv.org/abs/2208.10095
18. Goyal, D., Jaiswal, R.: FPT approximation for socially fair clustering. CoRR (2021)
19. Haben, S., Singleton, C., Grindrod, P.: Analysis and clustering of residential customers energy behavioral demand using smart meter data. IEEE Trans. Smart Grid (2016)
20. Hamerly, G., Elkan, C.: Learning the K in K-means. In: NeurIPS (2003)
21. Ho, J., Yang, M.H., Lim, J., Lee, K.C., Kriegman, D.: Clustering appearances of objects under varying illumination conditions. In: CVPR (2003)
22. Holzer, H.J., Neumark, D.: What does affirmative action do? ILR Rev. (2000)
23. Huang, L., Jiang, S., Vishnoi, N.K.: Coresets for clustering with fairness constraints. In: NeurIPS (2019)
24. Huang, L., Vishnoi, N.K.: Coresets for clustering in Euclidean spaces: importance sampling is nearly optimal. In: STOC (2020)
25. Kanungo, T., Mount, D.M., Netanyahu, N.S., Piatko, C.D., Silverman, R., Wu, A.Y.: A local search approximation algorithm for K-means clustering. Comput. Geometry (2004). Special Issue on the 18th Annual Symposium on Computational Geometry - SoCG2002
26. Karlgren, J.: Newsgroup clustering based on user behavior - a recommendation algebra (1994)
27. Lee, K.C., Ho, J., Kriegman, D.: Acquiring linear subspaces for face recognition under variable lighting. IEEE Trans. Pattern Anal. Mach. Intell. **27**, 684–698 (2005)
28. Makarychev, K., Makarychev, Y., Razenshteyn, I.: Performance of Johnson-lindenstrauss transform for K-means and K-medians clustering. In: STOC (2019)
29. Makarychev, Y., Vakilian, A.: Approximation algorithms for socially fair clustering. ArXiv (2021)
30. Mishra, N., Schreiber, R., Stanton, I., Tarjan, R.E.: Clustering social networks. In: Bonato, A., Chung, F.R.K. (eds.) WAW 2007. LNCS, vol. 4863, pp. 56–67. Springer, Heidelberg (2007). https://doi.org/10.1007/978-3-540-77004-6_5
31. Moro, S., Cortez, P., Rita, P.: A data-driven approach to predict the success of bank telemarketing. Decis. Support Syst. **62**, 22–31 (2014)
32. Mu, J., Bhat, S., Viswanath, P.: Geometry of polysemy. In: ICLR (2017)

33. Mu, J., Bhat, S., Viswanath, P.: Representing sentences as low-rank subspaces. In: ACL (2017)
34. Parsons, L., Haque, E., Liu, H.: Subspace clustering for high dimensional data: a review **6**(1), 90–105 (2004)
35. Pelleg, D., Moore, A.W.: X-means: extending K-means with efficient estimation of the number of clusters. In: ICML (2000)
36. Samadi, S., Tantipongpipat, U., Morgenstern, J.H., Singh, M., Vempala, S.: The price of fair PCA: one extra dimension. In: NeurIPS (2018)
37. Schubert, E., Rousseeuw, P.J.: Fast and eager K-medoids clustering: O(k) runtime improvement of the PAM, CLARA, and CLARANS algorithms. Inf. Syst. **101**, 101804 (2021)
38. Thompson, J.J., Blair, M.R., Chen, L., Henrey, A.J.: Video game telemetry as a critical tool in the study of complex skill learning. PLOS ONE **8**, e75129 (2013)
39. Tukan, M., Wu, X., Zhou, S., Braverman, V., Feldman, D.: New coresets for projective clustering and applications. In: AIStats (2022)
40. Vidal, R.: A tutorial on subspace clustering (2010)
41. Yeh, I.C., hui Lien, C.: The comparisons of data mining techniques for the predictive accuracy of probability of default of credit card clients. Exp. Syst. Appl. **36**, 2473–2480 (2009)

Visualizing Overlapping Biclusterings and Boolean Matrix Factorizations

Thibault Marette[1]([⊠]) [ID], Pauli Miettinen[2] [ID], and Stefan Neumann[1] [ID]

[1] KTH Royal Institute of Technology, Stockholm, Sweden
{marette,neum}@kth.se
[2] University of Eastern Finland, Kuopio, Finland
pauli.miettinen@uef.fi

Abstract. Finding (bi-)clusters in bipartite graphs is a popular data analysis approach. Analysts typically want to visualize the clusters, which is simple as long as the clusters are disjoint. However, many modern algorithms find overlapping clusters, making visualization more complicated. In this paper, we study the problem of visualizing *a given clustering* of overlapping clusters in bipartite graphs and the related problem of visualizing Boolean Matrix Factorizations. We conceptualize three different objectives that any good visualization should satisfy: (1) proximity of cluster elements, (2) large consecutive areas of elements from the same cluster, and (3) large uninterrupted areas in the visualization, regardless of the cluster membership. We provide objective functions that capture these goals and algorithms that optimize these objective functions. Interestingly, in experiments on real-world datasets, we find that the best trade-off between these competing goals is achieved by a novel heuristic, which locally aims to place rows and columns with similar cluster membership next to each other.

Keywords: Visualization · Biclustering · Boolean Matrix Factorization

1 Introduction

Finding biclusters in bipartite graphs has been studied for several decades [10, 30] and it is closely related to other problems, such as co-clustering [5] and Boolean Matrix Factorization [16]. While the goal of classic methods is to find mutually disjoint biclusters, i.e., each vertex appears in at most one bicluster, modern methods allow for *overlap*: vertices can appear in multiple clusters [12, 15–17, 20].

To assess the outputs of biclustering algorithms, it can be helpful to visualize their outputs. If all clusters are *disjoint,* one can plot the biclusters one after another in an arbitrary order. If clusters *overlap,* the visualization task becomes more difficult [28]: it might not be possible to draw all biclusters as consecutive rectangles, as is the case in Fig. 2c, forcing the visualization to choose which clusters to split up.

D. Koutra et al. (Eds.): ECML PKDD 2023, LNAI 14169, pp. 743–758, 2023.
https://doi.org/10.1007/978-3-031-43412-9_44

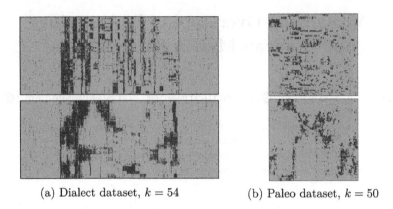

(a) Dialect dataset, $k = 54$ (b) Paleo dataset, $k = 50$

Fig. 1. Visualization of the same biclustering using ADVISER [4] (top) and our TSP-based heuristic (bottom). The pictures at the bottom contain larger uninterrupted areas, which makes it easier to assess the structure in the data. (Color figure online)

This problem was studied in earlier work [4,13], with the main goal of optimizing the proximity of elements that belong to the same bicluster. However, this notion has drawbacks as biclusters which are similar in one dimension but non-overlapping in another are not incentivized to be visualized close to another. This leads to suboptimal visualizations for some biclusterings, as shown in Fig. 1.

In this paper, we revisit the problem of visualizing given biclusterings. Rather than just looking at the proximity of elements from the same bicluster, we identify three different aspects of good visualizations: (1) Proximity of elements from the same bicluster. (2) Large consecutive areas of elements from the same bicluster. (3) Large uninterrupted areas in the visualization, regardless of the bicluster membership. For each of these three different aspects, we provide novel objective functions that allow us to formally capture these intuitions. Especially Aspect (3) will help us to bypass the limitations from the approaches in [4,13].

We also present several algorithms to optimize our objective functions. As optimizing them directly is expensive in terms of time and difficult in terms of quality, we present a novel heuristic which is based on the concept of *demerit*, which penalizes visualizations that place rows and columns close to each other when they belong to different biclusters. We present experiments on real-world datasets which show that this heuristic can be computed efficiently and that it provides a very good tradeoff between the three objective functions, outperforming the method from Colantonio et al. [4]. In our experiments we focus on medium-sized datasets, since visualizing large bipartite graphs requires different methods [23].

Additionally, we introduce a novel post-processing step, which automatically finds unclustered rows and columns that have high similarity with the provided biclusters. We believe that this will enable domain experts to efficiently find structures that might have been missed by the original biclustering algorithm.

We make our code[1] and plots[2] for all datasets available on GitHub. We note that, even though previous works studied the question of visualizing overlapping biclusterings, none of these works has its code available online. Due to lack of space, we present pseudocode and additional experiments in the full version of our paper, which is available on arxiv.

Related Work. Computing biclusterings of bipartite graphs is a classic problem that has been studied at least since the 1970s [10] and it is related to several other problems, such as bipartite graph partitioning [30], hypergraph partitioning [1], bipartite stochastic block models [20] and co-clustering [5]. It is also known that Boolean Matrix Factorization, which has been a popular problem in the data mining community [11,14,16], is closely related [17].

Colantonio et al. [4] studied the visualization of a given set of overlapping biclusters as a biadjacency matrix. They introduced an objective function, which optimizes the proximity of the rows and columns that are contained in biclusters and which simultaneously tries to minimize gaps in the visualization of each bicluster. They also proposed a greedy heuristic called ADVISER for optimizing this objective function. They experimentally showed that their approach is superior to the approach by Jin et al. [13], which only considers the perimeter of the visualized biclusters. The main drawback of the approach in [4] is that biclusters which are highly similar in one dimension but are non-overlapping in another (e.g., they have overlapping column clusters but non-overlapping row clusters) are not incentivized to be visualized close to another.

Classic seriation methods [2,29] that visualize biadjacency matrices are related to our work, but they do not support visualizing a given input biclustering. Leaf-ordering methods that visualize dendrograms, e.g., [25], can visualize a given hierarchical clustering, but biclustering algorithms do not report a hierarchy of the biclusters and thus these methods are not applicable. The BiVoC algorithm [9] is also related, but its visualization repeats rows and columns, which we do not permit here because visualizations with many repetitions quickly become unclear.

We use biadjacency matrices to visualize biclusterings. Alternatives include edge bundlings [26,27] or anchored-maps [18]. Our algorithms are completely unsupervised, but semi-supervised methods [29] exist.

2   Preliminaries

Let $G = (R \cup C, E)$ be an unweighted, undirected bipartite graph and set $m = |R|$ and $n = |C|$. We assume that $R = [m]$ and $C = [n]$, where $[k] := \{1, \ldots, k\}$. A *biclustering* $((R_1, C_1), \ldots, (R_k, C_k))$ of G is a set of *biclusters* (R_i, C_i), where $R_i \subseteq R$ and $C_i \subseteq C$ for all i. Note that this is a very general definition of biclustering: we do not assume that the clusters R_i are mutually disjoint or that $\bigcup_i R_i = R$, and neither do we make these assumptions for the C_i. Two biclusters (R_i, C_i) and (R_j, C_j) *overlap* if $R_i \cap R_j \neq \emptyset$ and $C_i \cap C_j \neq \emptyset$.

---

[1]   https://github.com/tmarette/biclusterVisualization.

[2]   https://github.com/tmarette/VisualizingOverlappingBiclusteringsAndBMF-plots.

Visualization. We visualize G using its $m \times n$ biadjacency matrix $A \in \{0,1\}^{m \times n}$. Note that the vertices in R correspond to the rows of A and the vertices in C correspond to the columns of A. Thus, we will often refer to the clusters R_i as the *row clusters* and to the clusters C_i as the *column clusters*. When plotting A, we use bright tiles for 1-entries and dark tiles for 0-entries.

To visualize A, our goal is to find permutations $\pi_R : [m] \to [m]$ and $\pi_C : [n] \to [n]$ of the rows and columns of the biadjacency matrix, respectively. Each element $r \in R$ ($c \in C$) is visualized in the $\pi_R(r)$'th row ($\pi_C(c)$'th column) of the biadjacency matrix, i.e., we set $A_{\pi_R(r), \pi_C(c)} = 1$ iff $(r, c) \in E$.

Throughout the paper we study the following problem. Given a bipartite graph $G = (R \cup C, E)$ and a biclustering $((R_1, C_1), \dots, (R_k, C_k))$, find permutations $\pi_R : [m] \to [m]$ and $\pi_C : [n] \to [n]$ of the rows and columns that optimize an objective function, which encodes how well the biclustering is visualized.

Notation. Let X be a set of integers and π a permutation. We write $\pi(X) = \{\pi(x) : x \in X\}$ to denote X under the permutation π. We write $cons(X)$ to denote the partition of X into maximal disjoint sets of consecutive integers. For instance, if $X = \{1, 2, 5\}$ then $cons(X) = \{\{1, 2\}, \{5\}\}$. Note that if R_i is a set of rows and π_R is the row permutation, then $\pi_R(R_i)$ is the set of rows in which the elements of R_i are visualized; the sets of consecutive rows (columns) in which elements from R_i (C_i) are visualized is given by $cons(\pi_R(R_i))$ ($cons(\pi_C(C_i))$).

Finally, for our algorithms it will be convenient to operate on *row and column blocks*. For brevity, we only give the definition for row blocks. The row blocks partition the sets of rows, and they are defined such that each cluster can be expressed as the union of a set of blocks. More formally, for $r \in [m]$ we let $clusters_R(r) = \{i : r \in R_i\}$ denote the set of indices of all row clusters that contain row r. Now, the *row block of r* is given by $block_R(r) = \{r' : clusters_R(r) = clusters_R(r')\}$, i.e., it is the set of all rows r' that are contained in exactly the same row clusters as r. Next, the set of row blocks is given by $\mathcal{B}^R = \{block_R(r) : r \in R\}$; see Fig. 3 for an example. Given a row block $b \in \mathcal{B}^R$ it will be convenient for us to write $clusters_R(b)$ to denote the row clusters in which b is contained, i.e., $clusters_R(b) = clusters_R(r)$ for all $r \in b$. For column blocks, we define $clusters_C(c)$, $block_C(c)$ and $\mathcal{B}^C$ in the same way.

Visualizing Weighted and Directed Graphs. The algorithm we propose in this paper is tailored to visualize unweighted bipartite graphs, through their Boolean biadjacency matrix A. We note that since in general A is asymmetric, our algorithms can also be used to visualize the adjacency matrix of directed graphs (note that in this case the set of row and column clusters will be the identical). It is also possible to use our algorithm to visualize weighted graphs; however, in this case one has to make adjustments to the coloring scheme to visualize the different weights (here, we focus on the Boolean case in which we never need more than six colors).

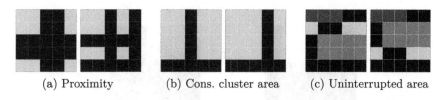

(a) Proximity   (b) Cons. cluster area   (c) Uninterrupted area

Fig. 2. Visualizations of biclusters for each of our objective functions. For each of them, the right visualization is preferable. Every color represents a different bicluster, except for purple which represents 0-elements. Observe that in Fig. c, no matter how we arrange the columns, one of the three biclusters must always be visualized with non-consecutive columns. (Color figure online)

3 Visualization Objectives

In this section, we introduce our objective functions that measure different aspects of how well a biclustering is visualized.

Recall that biclusters represent pairs of elements that relate to each other. An ideal depiction of a single bicluster (R_i, C_i) consists of a single large consecutive rectangle in the visualized matrix. More formally, we would like to have that $|cons(\pi_R(R_i))| = 1$ and $|cons(\pi_C(C_i))| = 1$. However, when the row or column clusters of a biclustering overlap, obtaining a visualization which simultaneously presents all biclusters ideally is not possible (see, e.g., Fig. 2c). Thus, we have to define criteria that enable us to compare non-ideal depictions of biclusters.

Informally, the three criteria that we study are as follows:

1. **Proximity:** All rows and columns of each bicluster should be close to each other, as shown in Fig. 2a.
2. **Size of the consecutive cluster areas:** The rows and columns of each bicluster should form large consecutive areas, as shown in Fig. 2b.
3. **Size of uninterrupted areas:** Areas that belong to (possibly different) biclusters should form large uninterrupted areas, as shown in Fig. 2c. Unlike the previous objectives, this objective is global, i.e., it is not limited to individual biclusters.

The formal definitions follow below. Note that even though the first and second criteria look similar at first, they are different: even when a bicluster is visualized with low proximity, it may still consist of several non-consecutive areas. Furthermore, the third criterion is particularly important when dealing with non-overlapping biclusterings; it will be useful, for instance, when visualizing biclusterings that have non-overlapping row clusters but overlapping column clusters, which is not captured by the previous two definitions. Previous work focused on proximity [4,13] and also implicitly the consecutive area [4].

Next, we formally present three different objective functions, one for each criterion. Having different objective functions, instead of a single combined one, allows a more fine-grained evaluation of the visualizations.

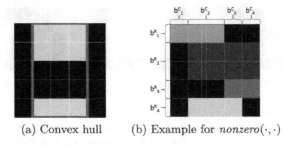

(a) Convex hull   (b) Example for $nonzero(\cdot, \cdot)$

Fig. 3. Examples of how the concepts translate to the visualization. We assume $\pi_R = id_R$ and $\pi_C = id_C$. Purple colored tiles are 0-elements, and identically colored tiles belong to the same bicluster. On the left, $cons(\pi_R(R_1)) = \{\{1,2\},\{5\}\}$ and $cons(\pi_C(C_1)) = \{\{2,3,4\}\}$. The convex hull of the cluster is shown in red and $S_{\text{prox}}(\pi_R, \pi_C) = 15$. On the right, four biclusters are visualized with different color and $nonzero(b_2^C, \pi_R) = \{1,2,3,5\}$ and $nonzero(b_3^C, \pi_R) = \{2,3,4,5\}$. (Color figure online)

Proximity. Our first objective function measures proximity. As stated above, our intuition is that for each bicluster, all of its rows and columns should be close to each other. To capture this intuition, we want to visualize the biclusters so that the *convex hull* of rows and columns that belong to the bicluster is small.

Consider permutations π_R and π_C and a bicluster (R_i, C_i). The size of the convex hull of (R_i, C_i) in the biadjacency matrix A is given by

$$S_{\text{prox}}((R_i, C_i), (\pi_R, \pi_C))$$
$$= [\max\{\pi_R(R_i)\} - \min\{\pi_R(R_i)\} + 1] \cdot [\max\{\pi_C(C_i)\} - \min\{\pi_C(C_i)\} + 1]. \tag{1}$$

Observe that for a single bicluster (R_i, C_i) this quantity is minimized when it is visualized as a single consecutive rectangle, i.e., $|cons(\pi_R(R_i))| = 1$ and $|cons(\pi_C(C_i))| = 1$. See also Fig. 3.

For all k biclusters, our objective function for minimizing the proximity is

$$f_{\text{prox}}(\pi_R, \pi_C) = \sum_{i=1}^{k} S_{\text{prox}}((R_i, C_i), (\pi_R, \pi_C)). \tag{2}$$

Size of the Consecutive Cluster Areas. Next, we consider the aspect that the rows and columns of the same bicluster should form large consecutive areas.

First observe that when we visualize a bicluster (R_i, C_i) under permutations π_R and π_C, then the consecutive areas are given by $cons(\pi_R(R_i)) \times cons(\pi_C(C_i))$. For instance, if $cons(\pi_R(R_i)) = \{\{1,2\},\{5\}\}$ and $cons(\pi_C(C_i)) = \{\{3\},\{7\}\}$, then the consecutive areas are $\{\{(1,3),(2,3)\},\{(5,3)\},\{(1,7),(2,7)\},\{(5,7)\}\}$.

Given this observation, we define the score $S_{\text{clArea}}((R_i, C_i), (\pi_R, \pi_C))$ for a single bicluster (R_i, C_i) under the permutations π_R and π_C as follows:

$$S_{\text{clArea}}((R_i, C_i), (\pi_R, \pi_C)) = \sum_{(X,Y) \in cons(\pi_R(R_i)) \times cons(\pi_C(C_i))} |X \times Y|^2. \tag{3}$$

In this score, we sum over the *squared* areas of the induced submatrices. Note that maximizing this score incentivizes layouts with larger consecutive areas. In particular, $S_{\text{clArea}}((R_i, C_i), (\pi_R, \pi_C))$ is maximized iff the bicluster (R_i, C_i) is visualized as a single connected component, i.e., when the rows and columns in $\pi_R(R_i)$ and $\pi_C(C_i)$ are consecutive. Also observe that if in the score we summed over $|X \times Y|$ instead of $|X \times Y|^2$, the sum would be independent of the permutations and always equal to $|R_i \times C_i|$; this is why we sum over $|X \times Y|^2$.

The corresponding global objective function is:

$$f_{\text{clArea}}(\pi_R, \pi_C) = \sum_{i=1}^{k} S_{\text{clArea}}((R_i, C_i), (\pi_R, \pi_C)). \qquad (4)$$

Size of Uninterrupted Areas. Lastly, we introduce an objective function which incentivizes that areas that belong to (possibly different) biclusters should form large uninterrupted areas. This is for useful for visualizing biclusters that are similar but non-overlapping, e.g., because they have disjoint row clusters but highly similar column clusters.

Recall that $\mathcal{B}^R = \{b_1^R, \ldots, b_s^R\}$ and $\mathcal{B}^C = \{b_1^C, \ldots, b_t^C\}$ are the row and column blocks, respectively. Since splitting up elements of blocks would only be detrimental to our visualizations, we henceforth assume that the elements from all row and column blocks are consecutive in our permutations, i.e., $|cons(\pi_R(b_i^R))| = 1$ and $|cons(\pi_C(b_j^C))| = 1$ for all i and j.

Now consider a row block b_i^R and the submatrix $A[\pi_R(b_i^R), :]$ which it induces. Observe that in this submatrix, column $\pi_C(c)$ is contained in a bicluster if $c \in b_j^C$ and $clusters_R(b_i^R) \cap clusters_C(b_j^C) \neq \emptyset$, i.e., if c is from a column block b_j^C which co-occurs in a bicluster together with a row block b_i^R. Similarly, if $c \in b_j^R$ for j with $clusters_R(b_i^R) \cap clusters_C(b_j^C) = \emptyset$ then column $\pi_C(c)$ is not contained in a bicluster. Thus, the set of all columns in $A[\pi_R(b_i^R), :]$ which are contained a bicluster after applying the permutation π_C is $nonzero(b_i^R, \pi_C) := \bigcup_{j:\ clusters_R(b_i^R) \cap clusters_C(b_j^C) \neq \emptyset} \pi_C(b_j^C)$. See Fig. 3 for an example. Thus, the size of the uninterrupted area of columns in biclusters in $A[\pi_R(b_i^R), :]$ is given by

$$S_{\text{uninter}}^R(b_i^R, \pi_C) = \sum_{Y \in cons(nonzero(b_i^R, \pi_C))} |b_i^R \times Y|^2. \qquad (5)$$

Notice the similarity of (5) and (3) above. The main difference is that in (3) we sum over the areas induced by the biclusters, whereas here we sum over the area induced by columns inside biclusters, regardless of bicluster membership. This is beneficial since when row block b_i^R co-occurs with column block $b_{j_1}^C$ and with column block $b_{j_2}^C$, then this definition incentivizes to place the column blocks $b_{j_1}^C$ and $b_{j_2}^C$ next to each other, even though they might not share a bicluster (i.e., even when $clusters_C(b_{j_1}^C) \cap clusters_C(b_{j_2}^C) = \emptyset$), which is not covered by (3).

Similar to above, we also want to measure the area of consecutive rows that appear in a bicluster in a submatrix $A[:, \pi_C(b_j^C)]$ that is induced by a fixed column cluster b_j^C. We thus define $nonzero(b_j^C, \pi_R)$ $=$ $\bigcup_{i:\ clusters_R(b_i^R) \cap clusters_C(b_j^C) \neq \emptyset} \pi_R(b_i^R)$ and set $S_{uninter}^C(b_j^C, \pi_R)$ $=$ $\sum_{X \in cons(nonzero(b_j^R, \pi_R))} |X \times b_j^C|^2$.

Now our overall objective function becomes:

$$f_{uninter}(\pi_R, \pi_C) = \sum_{i=1}^{s} S_{uninter}^R(b_i^R, \pi_C) + \sum_{j=1}^{t} S_{uninter}^C(b_j^C, \pi_R). \tag{6}$$

4   Algorithms

In this section, we describe our algorithms to obtain the permutations $\pi_R: [m] \to [m]$ and $\pi_C: [n] \to [n]$ that optimize our objective functions.

For better efficiency, we focus on finding permutations in which the rows of row blocks are always consecutive (and the same holds for the columns of column blocks). Observe that this assumption is without loss of generality, i.e., splitting the elements of a row or column block into multiple consecutive parts will never improve the objective functions we study.

Thus, suppose that we have row blocks $b_1^R, \ldots, b_s^R \subseteq [m]$. Then our new goal is to find a row block permutation $\sigma: [s] \to [s]$ that optimizes our objective functions.[3] This will be more efficient since in practice $s \ll m$. The same can be done for finding a column block permutation.

We present the pseudocode of our algorithms in the full paper.

4.1   Greedy Algorithms

We start by considering a simple greedy algorithm for optimizing the three objective functions from Sect. 3. Our algorithm starts by sorting the row and column blocks based on their importance. Here, the *importance score* of a block b is the sum of the area of the biclusters b belongs to, i.e., $\sum_{i \in clusters(b)} |R_i \times C_i|$. The idea is that blocks which are involved in large clusters are treated first and thus have priority when picking their position.

The greedy algorithm computes the row and column block permutations σ_R and σ_C simultaneously. Initially, they are set to the empty permutations $\sigma_R \leftarrow \emptyset$ and $\sigma_C \leftarrow \emptyset$ without any elements. Now the greedy algorithm proceeds in iterations until all row and column blocks have been assigned to the permutations. In iteration j, we add the row (column) block b with j'th highest importance to σ_R (σ_C). To pick the position of b, we iterate over $i = 1, \ldots, j$ and consider the permutation σ_R with b added in the i'th position. Then we insert b in the position i^* that achieved the best objective function value.

---

[3] Note that we can turn the row block permutation σ into a row permutation $\pi_R: [m] \to [m]$ as follows: For each $i \in [s]$, we fix an arbitrary order of the elements in b_i^R. Now we create a list L by iterating over $i \in [s]$ and adding the elements in $b_{\sigma(i)}^R$ one after another to L. If element r is at the p'th position in L, then we set $\pi_R(r) = p$.

We note that while building the permutations above, they only map to the subset of the rows and columns that are contained in the row and column blocks that were assigned to the permutations. Therefore, to compute the objective function values, we only consider rows and columns that are contained in blocks that were already added to the permutations.

4.2   Demerit-Based Algorithms

In practice, the greedy algorithm can be inefficient as it recomputes the objective functions several times during each iteration and each such recomputation requires a global pass over all clusters and blocks.

To remedy this problem, next we introduce the notion of *demerit*, which can be optimized locally and which acts as a penalty function for placing dissimilar blocks next to each other. Formally, the *demerit for row block b^R and column blocks b_i^C and b_j^C* is given by:

$$demerit(b^R; b_i^C, b_j^C) = \begin{cases} |b^R| \cdot (|c_1 \cup c_2| + 1) & \text{if } c_1 = \emptyset \text{ or } c_2 = \emptyset, \\ |b^R| \cdot (|c_1 \cup c_2| - |c_1 \cap c_2|) & \text{otherwise,} \end{cases}$$

where $c_1 = clusters_R(b^R) \cap clusters_C(b_i^C)$ and $c_2 = clusters_R(b^R) \cap clusters_C(b_j^C)$. Observe that the demerit is a penalty term that measures the size of the row block b^R and how dissimilar the blocks b_i^C and b_j^C are in terms of their cluster membership, i.e., it counts the number of clusters which contain row block b^R but only exactly one of b_i^C and b_j^C.

To measure the *demerit of the column block permutation σ_C*, we set

$$demerit(\sigma_C) = \sum_{b^R \in \mathcal{B}^R} \sum_{i=1}^{t-1} demerit(b^R; b_{\sigma_C(i)}^C, b_{\sigma_C(i+1)}^C),$$

where t is the number of column blocks. This is the overall penalty incurred across all row blocks for column blocks that are placed next to each other. Optimizing this objective function should be somewhat simpler than the previous ones, because we only have to consider consecutive pairs of column blocks $b_{\sigma_C(i)}^C$ and $b_{\sigma_C(i+1)}^C$, which can be checked locally. This is in contrast to our previous objective functions, which have to globally take into account all blocks that belong to a single bicluster (proximity and consecutive cluster area) or all blocks that appear consecutively (uninterrupted area).

Next, we introduce algorithms for minimizing the demerit, where we assume that we have a fixed row block permutation σ_R and we wish to compute an improved ordering of the column blocks σ_C. The same procedure can be used for fixed σ_C and for finding σ_R with small demerit.

TSP Heuristic. We first consider a TSP (traveling salesperson) heuristic to find a permutation σ_C that minimizes the demerit. First, we construct a complete graph containing all column blocks $b^C \in \mathcal{B}^C$ as nodes. For two column blocks b_i^C and b_j^C, we set the weight of the corresponding edge to

$w_{i,j} = \sum_{b^R \in \mathcal{B}^R} demerit(b^R; b_i^C, b_j^C)$ which corresponds to the demerit of placing b_i^C and b_j^C next to each other. This is a complete graph, i.e., there are edges for all pairs of column blocks. Then we use a TSP solver to find a TSP tour in the corresponding graph, which is given by a cycle $(b_{i_1}^C, \ldots, b_{i_t}^C)$ that visits every vertex exactly once. This corresponds to a column block permutation σ_C. Since the objective of TSP is to minimize the cost of the cycle, this corresponds to minimizing the demerit. Note that for defining σ_C, we can start with any of the blocks from the cycle, i.e., we can set $\sigma_C(1) = b_{i_j}^C$ for any j and then proceed in the order of the cycle. To obtain the best results in practice, we pick the value j which maximizes the cluster area (4).

Greedy Demerit Algorithm. We also consider a greedy algorithm which orders the blocks by their importance score and inserts them one by one. When inserting a block, it tries out all possible positions and picks the one which minimizes the total demerit. See the full version of the paper for details.

4.3   Post-processing: Suggesting Unclustered Rows and Columns

Finally, we present a post-processing scheme that finds unclustered rows and columns that have high similarity with existing biclusters. This will enable domain experts to easily identify structures which might have been missed by the biclustering algorithm. We describe our post-processing scheme for finding unclustered rows whose 1-entries have high similarity to existing column clusters; it can also be used for finding columns that are similar to existing row clusters.

We say that a row r is *unclustered* if it is not contained in any row cluster, i.e., if $r \notin \bigcup_i R_i$, and we write $\bar{R}$ to denote the set of unclustered rows. For $r \in \bar{R}$, we write $nonzero(r) = \{c \in C : A_{rc} = 1\}$ to denote the columns of all 1-entries in r. Now the *similarity* of r and a column cluster C_i is given by $similarity(r, C_i) = |C_i|^{-1}|nonzero(r) \cap C_i|$, i.e., it measures the fraction of elements from C_i that also appear in $nonzero(r)$. Furthermore, the *density of a bicluster* (R_i, C_i) is $density(R_i, C_i) = (|R_i| \cdot |C_i|)^{-1} \sum_{r \in R_i, c \in C_i} A_{r,c}$, i.e., it is the average number of non-zero entries in the submatrix induced by $R_i \times C_i$.

Now our idea is to create biclusters $(\bar{R}_i, C_i)$, which consist of unclustered rows $\bar{R}_i$ and "original" column clusters C_i. Here, we assign a row $r \in \bar{R}$ to $\bar{R}_i$ if $similarity(r, C_i) \geq density(R_i, C_i)/2$. This encodes the intuition that the rows in $\bar{R}_i$ are allowed to be slightly sparser than those in the original bicluster (R_i, C_i); for a domain expert it might be interesting to inspect them because the original biclustering algorithm might have "missed" them.

In the visualization, these new biclusters have a special place. The original biclusters (R_i, C_i) are situated in the middle of the figure. Then, adjacent to that central part, the new biclusters $(\bar{R}_i, C_i)$ and $(R_i, \bar{C}_i)$ are added, and then the remaining unclustered rows and columns follow.

5   Experiments

We implemented our algorithms in Python and we practically evaluate them on real-world datasets. The source code (see Footnote 1) and the plots (see Footnote

2) of all biclusterings are available on GitHub. The experiments were performed on a 40-core Intel(R) Xeon(R) CPU E5-2630 v4 @ 2.20 GHz.

The datasets we used are listed in Table 1, where we focused on small- to medium-sized datasets since visualizing very large datasets requires other techniques [23]. We note that for 20news and movieLens we only considered the top-500 densest rows and columns to reduce the size of the datasets.

To obtain our biclusterings, we used the PCV algorithm [20], which returns non-overlapping row clusters but overlapping column clusters, and the basso algorithm [16], which returns overlapping row and column clusters. Both algorithms have a parameter k that determines the number of clusters and we report the choice of k for each experiment.

In some of our visualizations, we use a 6-color system to convey more information (e.g., Fig. 1, 5a and 5c). Each of the colors is associated with a distinct category of data in the visualization: clustered elements appear in green, unclus-

Table 1. Datasets used in the experiments

dataset	rows	columns	density	ref.
20news	500	500	0.221	[24]
americas_large	3485	10127	0.005	[19]
americas_small	3477	1687	0.018	[19]
apj	2044	1164	0.003	[19]
dialect	1334	506	0.161	[6,7]
domino	79	231	0.040	[19]
fire1	365	709	0.123	[19]
fire2	325	709	0.158	[19]
healthcare	46	46	0.702	[19]
movieLens	500	500	0.550	[21]
Mushroom (sample)	250	117	0.368	[13]
paleo	124	139	0.115	[8]

tered elements that were picked in our post-processing step (Sect. 4.3) are red, and all remaining unclustered elements are blue. The dark tones of each color correspond to 1-entries in the original matrix.[4] This allows us to assert whether or not an element belongs to the biclustering and/or to the original data, and it further allows to assess the density of the clustered (and non-clustered) areas.

In our experiments, we consider four greedy algorithms for optimizing the objective functions, denoting them greedyProximity, greedyConsecutiveCluster-sArea, greedyUninterruptedArea, greedyDemerit. Our TSP-based algorithm is denoted TSPheuristic and to solve TSP we use a solver from Google OR tools [22]. We compare them against the state-of-the-art method ADVISER [4]. Since there was no code available for ADVISER, we implemented our own version of it, available with our software.

Qualitative Evaluation. We start with the qualitative evaluation of the algorithms. Our findings in this section are twofold: our TSPheuristic provides better visualizations than ADVISER [4] and our objective functions indeed measure the aspects of the visualizations which they are supposed to measure.

---

[4] We picked the colors using color brewer [3], so that the core set of colors (excluding the post-processing step) is colorblind safe and print friendly. As there is no 6-colors set that is colorblind safe, the final set of colors only retains the print friendly property.

First, let us briefly argue about the merit of visualizing biclusterings. In Fig. 4a, we present visualizations of Fire1 without any ordering and the visualization created using TSPheuristic. The unordered dataset hints that some rows and columns seem related. After using basso for biclustering with $k = 5$ and reordering the data with TSPheuristic, we can easily see the relation between rows and columns, as well as notice sparser areas inside the biclusters.

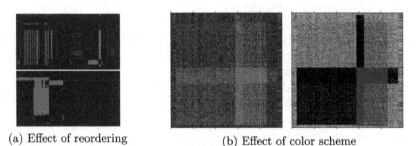

(a) Effect of reordering   (b) Effect of color scheme

Fig. 4. (a): Visualization of Fire1 without any reordering (top) and after reordering using TSPheuristic (bottom). (b): Visualization of movieLens using ADVISER. The result is colored using plain 0/1 entries (left) and our color scheme (right). (Color figure online)

Next, we consider biclusterings obtained from PCV, which returns non-overlapping row clusters but overlapping column clusters. Figures 1a and 1b depict visualizations of dialect and paleo using ADVISER and TSPheuristic. Since ADVISER's objective function does not take into account uninterrupted areas, its visualization is much less coherent than the one by TSPheuristic. The uninterrupted areas objective function captures this aspect well, where TSPheuristic obtains an 18.9 % higher score on dialect and a 7 % higher score on paleo.

Now we consider basso's more complex biclusterings for 20news with $k = 11$, which contains overlapping row and column clusters. In this case, TSPheuristic is more resilient than ADVISER w.r.t. the proximity of the bicluster elements. In Figs. 5a and 5c, we show the convex hulls of the same bicluster in red. One can see that the representation of the cluster is more compact in the visualization generated from TSPheuristic, compared to ADVISER. This also translates to the proximity objective function, where TSPheuristic achieves a proximity score that is 30.8 % lower than that of ADVISER (note that optimizing the proximity is a minimization problem).

Next, let us consider the uninterrupted areas that are generated by the algorithms. In Figs. 5b and 5d, the respective biclusters have a similar proximity score (269 125 and 253 400), but the visualization proposed by greedyDemerit is nicer, as all the clusters are drawn as one consecutive block. This is also highlighted by the objective function value for uninterrupted bicluster area, which is 26.4 % higher for greedyDemerit.

Finally, we highlight the usefulness of our coloring scheme and our post-processing step from Sect. 4.3 in Fig. 4b. The coloring scheme highlights the very dense areas that basso selected as biclusters in green. Then our post-processing scheme clearly indicates that the remaining unclustered rows and columns contain areas similar to the original clusters, but of slightly lower density, which could be worth considering when manually inspecting the clusters. We note that the dense area in the bottom right of the plot is not marked in red, since the corresponding submatrix was not considered as part of the bicluster by basso; we decided not to consider such areas in our post-processing step.

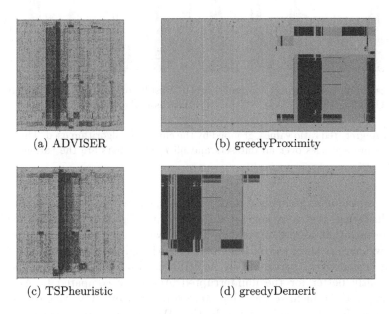

(a) ADVISER   (b) greedyProximity

(c) TSPheuristic   (d) greedyDemerit

Fig. 5. Visualizations (a) and (c) represent 20news. The red boxes denote the convex hull of the same cluster in both visualizations. The biclustering was obtained using basso with $k = 11$. Visualizations (b) and (d) represent Fire1. The biclustering was obtained using basso with $k = 10$. (Color figure online)

Quantitative Evaluation. For the quantitative validation, we run basso and PCV on all datasets from Table 1 with $k = 6, 10, 14, \ldots, 54$ to obtain biclusterings. We run all visualization algorithms for each of these biclusterings and compute our objective function values from Sects. 3 and 4.2. We also compute the objective function *visualisationCost* from ADVISER [4]. All plots are available online (see Footnote 2).

To obtain comparability across different datasets and different biclusterings, we use normalization: For each dataset and a fixed biclustering, we report the ratio $r_A^f = \frac{f(A) - averageRandomScore}{\max_{A' \in \mathcal{A}}(f(A')) - averageRandomScore}$, where A is the visualization algorithm we consider, $f(A)$ is the objective function value obtained by A and $\mathcal{A}$

is the set of all visualization algorithms. We subtract the *averageRandomScore* which denotes the average objective function of five random permutations; this is motivated by the fact that even the worst possible visualization will achieve non-negligible scores in our objective functions since typically their values are lower bounded by the squares of the block sizes. Note that if $r_A^f = 1$, A achieved the best objective function value among all algorithms we compare.

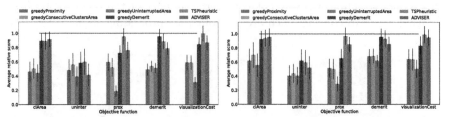

(a) Results on biclusterings computed by the PCV algorithm

(b) Results on biclusterings computed by the basso algorithm

Fig. 6. Aggregated ratio values, grouped by the clustering algorithm used. The reported numbers are averages over all datasets and all k, error bars are the variances of the ratio values.

We report our experimental results in Fig. 6, where Fig. 6a presents the results on biclusterings that were generated by PCV and Fig. 6b presents the results on biclusterings that were generated by basso. We observe that TSPheuristic performs well across all objective functions, even though on the consecutiveCluster-Area it is slightly outperformed by ADVISER. Notably, TSPheuristic performs significantly better for the uninterrupted area score compared to ADVISER, especially for the biclusterings that were computed by PCV; this corroborates our findings from the qualitative evaluation. We note that among the greedy algorithms, greedyDemerit is the best, which further underscores that using demerit to guide visualizations is a good idea. Furthermore, on both sets of experiments, TSPheuristic outperforms ADVISER on the *visualisationCost* objective function which is being optimized by ADVISER. We conclude that TSPheuristic provides the best tradeoff across the different datasets and objective functions.

We present the running times of the algorithms in the full paper.

6   Conclusion

We studied the visualization of overlapping biclusterings and identified three different aspects that good visualizations should satisfy: proximity of cluster elements, large consecutive areas consisting of cluster elements, and large uninterrupted areas of clusters. We provided objective functions that capture these goals and showed experimentally that the best trade-off between these competing aspects is achieved by optimizing the demerit, which aims to place rows and columns with similar cluster membership next to each other.

Acknowledgements. This research is supported by the EC H2020 RIA project SoBig-Data++ (871042) and the Wallenberg AI, Autonomous Systems and Software Program (WASP) funded by the Knut and Alice Wallenberg Foundation. Some of the computations were enabled by the National Academic Infrastructure for Supercomputing in Sweden (NAISS) and Swedish National Infrastructure for Computing (SNIC) partially funded by the Swedish Research Council through grant agreements no. 2022-06725 and 2018-05973.

Ethical Statement. Boolean matrix factorization and similar pattern mining techniques can be used to identify tightly-knit communities (biclusters) from bipartite networks, which can help authorities to identify terrorist networks or dissidents from inter-communication networks. They can also be used to identify people's political opinions (e.g., by studying their social network behavior). The visualization methods discussed in this paper cannot be used for these actions directly, as they require the underlying mining algorithm, but they do facilitate the use of the mining algorithms in benign as well as nefarious purposes. We do consider that the overall positive effects of these methods greatly outweigh the problems caused by the as-such unavoidable negative use cases.

References

1. Alistarh, D., Iglesias, J., Vojnovic, M.: Streaming min-max hypergraph partitioning. In: NeurIPS, pp. 1900–1908 (2015)
2. Behrisch, M., Bach, B., Henry Riche, N., Schreck, T., Fekete, J.D.: Matrix reordering methods for table and network visualization. Comput. Graph. Forum. **35**, 693–716 (2016)
3. Brewer, C.A., Harrower, M., Sheesley, B., Woodruff, A., Heyman, D.: Color-Brewer 2.0: color advice for cartography. The Pennsylvania State University (2009). http://colorbrewer2.org/. Accessed 6 Feb 2010
4. Colantonio, A., Di Pietro, R., Ocello, A., Verde, N.V.: Visual role mining: a picture is worth a thousand roles. IEEE Trans. Knowl. Data Eng. **24**(6), 1120–1133 (2011)
5. Dhillon, I.S.: Co-clustering documents and words using bipartite spectral graph partitioning. Data Min. Knowl. Discov., 269–274 (2001)
6. Embleton, S., Wheeler, E.S.: Finnish dialect atlas for quantitative studies. J. Quant. Linguist. **4**(1–3), 99–102 (1997)
7. Embleton, S.M., Wheeler, E.S.: Computerized dialect atlas of Finnish: dealing with ambiguity. J. Quant. Linguist. **7**(3), 227–231 (2000)
8. Fortelius, M.: New and old worlds database of fossil mammals (NOW) (2003). www.helsinki.fi/science/now/
9. Grothaus, G.A., Mufti, A., Murali, T.: Automatic layout and visualization of biclusters. Algorithms Mol. Biol. **1**(1), 1–11 (2006)
10. Hartigan, J.A.: Direct clustering of a data matrix. J. Am. Stat. Assoc. **67**(337), 123–129 (1972)
11. Hess, S., Morik, K., Piatkowski, N.: The PRIMPING routine - tiling through proximal alternating linearized minimization. Data Min. Knowl. Discov. **31**(4), 1090–1131 (2017)
12. Hess, S., Pio, G., Hochstenbach, M., Ceci, M.: BROCCOLI: overlapping and outlier-robust biclustering through proximal stochastic gradient descent. Data Min. Knowl. Discov., 1–35 (2021)

13. Jin, R., Xiang, Y., Fuhry, D., Dragan, F.F.: Overlapping matrix pattern visualization: a hypergraph approach. In: IEEE International Conference on Data Mining, pp. 313–322 (2008)
14. Lucchese, C., Orlando, S., Perego, R.: Mining top-k patterns from binary datasets in presence of noise. In: SIAM International Conference on Data Mining, pp. 165–176 (2010)
15. Madeira, S., Oliveira, A.: Biclustering algorithms for biological data analysis: a survey. IEEE/ACM Trans. Comput. Biol. Bioinform. 1(1), 24–45 (2004)
16. Miettinen, P., Mielikäinen, T., Gionis, A., Das, G., Mannila, H.: The discrete basis problem. IEEE Trans. Knowl. Data Eng. 20(10), 1348–1362 (2008)
17. Miettinen, P., Neumann, S.: Recent developments in Boolean matrix factorization. In: International Joint Conference on Artificial Intelligence (2020)
18. Misue, K.: Drawing bipartite graphs as anchored maps. In: IEEE Pacific Visualisation, CRPIT, vol. 60, pp. 169–177 (2006)
19. Molloy, I., Li, N., Li, T., Mao, Z., Wang, Q., Lobo, J.: Evaluating role mining algorithms. In: Proceedings ACM Symposium Access Control Models and Technologies, pp. 95–104 (2009)
20. Neumann, S.: Bipartite stochastic block models with tiny clusters. In: Neural Information Processing Systems, pp. 3871–3881 (2018)
21. Pedregosa, F., et al.: Scikit-learn: machine learning in Python. J. Mach. Learn. Res. 12, 2825–2830 (2011)
22. Perron, L., Furnon, V.: Or-tools. https://developers.google.com/optimization/
23. Pezzotti, N., Fekete, J., Höllt, T., Lelieveldt, B.P.F., Eisemann, E., Vilanova, A.: Multiscale visualization and exploration of large bipartite graphs. Comput. Graph. Forum 37(3), 549–560 (2018)
24. Rennie, J.: 20 newsgroups. http://qwone.com/~jason/20Newsgroups/
25. Sakai, R., Winand, R., Verbeiren, T., Vande Moere, A., Aerts, J.: Dendsort: modular leaf ordering methods for dendrogram representations in R. F1000Research 3, 177 (2014)
26. Sun, M., Zhao, J., Wu, H., Luther, K., North, C., Ramakrishnan, N.: The effect of edge bundling and seriation on sensemaking of biclusters in bipartite graphs. IEEE Trans. Vis. Comput. Graph. 25(10), 2983–2998 (2019)
27. Tatti, N., Miettinen, P.: Boolean matrix factorization meets consecutive ones property. In: SIAM International Conference on Data Mining, pp. 729–737 (2019)
28. Vehlow, C., Beck, F., Weiskopf, D.: Visualizing group structures in graphs: a survey. Comput. Graph Forum 36 (2017)
29. Xu, P., Cao, N., Qu, H., Stasko, J.: Interactive visual co-cluster analysis of bipartite graphs. IEEE Pac. Vis., 32–39 (2016)
30. Zha, H., He, X., Ding, C.H.Q., Gu, M., Simon, H.D.: Bipartite graph partitioning and data clustering. In: ACM International Conference on Information and Knowledge Management, pp. 25–32 (2001)

Author Index